Butterworths Scottish Housing Law Handbook

Butterworths Scottish Housing Law Handbook

Editor:

Tom Mullen LLB, LLM
Senior Lecturer in Law at the University of Glasgow,
Convener of the Legal Services Agency

BUTTERWORTHS
LEGAL SERVICES AGENCY

EDINBURGH
1992

United Kingdom	Butterworth & Co (Publishers) Ltd, 4 Hill Street, EDINBURGH EH2 3JZ, 88 Kingsway, LONDON WC2B 6AB
Australia	Butterworths Pty Ltd, SYDNEY, MELBOURNE, BRISBANE, ADELAIDE, PERTH, CANBERRA and HOBART
Belgium	Butterworth & Co (Publishers) Ltd, BRUSSELS
Canada	Butterworths Canada Ltd, TORONTO and VANCOUVER
Ireland	Butterworth (Ireland) Ltd, DUBLIN
Malaysia	Malayan Law Journal Sdn Bhd, KUALA LUMPUR
New Zealand	Butterworths of New Zealand Ltd, WELLINGTON and AUCKLAND
Puerto Rico	Equity de Puerto Rico, Inc, HATO REY
Singapore	Butterworth & Co (Asia) Pte Ltd, SINGAPORE
USA	Butterworth Legal Publishers, ST PAUL, Minnesota; SEATTLE, Washington; BOSTON, Massachusetts; AUSTIN, Texas and D & S Publishers, CLEARWATER, Florida

All rights reserved. No part of this publication may be reproduced in any material form (including photocopying or storing it in any medium by electronic means and whether or not transiently or incidentally to some other use of this publication) without the written permission of the copyright owner except in accordance with the provisions of the Copyright, Designs and Patents Act 1988 or under the terms of a licence issued by the Copyright Licensing Agency Ltd, 90 Tottenham Court Road, London, England W1P 9HE. Applications for the copyright owner's written permission to reproduce any part of this publication should be addressed to the publisher.

Warning: The doing of an unauthorised act in relation to a copyright work may result in both a civil claim for damages and criminal prosecution.

© Butterworth & Co (Publishers) Ltd 1992

A CIP Catalogue record for this book is available from the British Library.

ISBN 0 406 11551 6

Typeset by Phoenix Photosetting, Chatham, Kent
Printed and bound in Great Britain by Mackays of Chatham PLC, Chatham, Kent

Preface

This collection of enactments relating to housing law in Scotland is designed for all who have to deal with housing matters, whether solicitors in private practice, local government solicitors, or housing professionals. Many aspects of housing law were the subject of consolidating enactments in the 1980s, but each of the consolidating measures has itself since been amended, and many important matters are covered in other legislation. This volume brings together the texts of the relevant acts, and statutory instruments in updated form. Subject to what is said in the next paragraph, the material in general is up to date **as at 1 May 1991**.

The selection of enactments is comprehensive without being absolutely exhaustive. In deciding what counts as housing legislation rather than legislation on other topics there is considerable room for judgment. The introduction to this book explains in more detail what has been included and why.

The notes appended to sections of the Acts and to statutory instruments are annotations only, and are not intended to be any form of commentary: the aim is merely to provide the legal practitioner or housing professional with the source material on which he can work. The notes identify amendments, give cross-references, and provide any background information essential for an understanding of the text.

In the text, words which have been added, substituted or amended are enclosed within square brackets, and three dots (. . .) indicate where the words have been repealed. Three asterisks (★ ★ ★) show where we have omitted material which is either repealed or which, although still live law, is not relevant to this book. Bold paragraph numbers in brackets at the end of sections etc are used for the purposes of cross-references and the index.

It has been necessary in a few instances to upset the normal order paragraph numbering; for example, paragraphs [1487A] to [1487R] have been inserted after paragraph [1487].

Finally in this preface, I would like to thank Simon Collins and Suzanne Fitzpatrick for their invaluable help in preparing the materials for editing, and in the final collation of the manuscript.

Tom Mullen
Glasgow
June 1992

Contents

	PAGE
Preface	v
Alphabetical List of Statutes	ix
Alphabetical List of Statutory Instruments	xi
Chronological List of Statutes	xiii
Chronological List of Statutory Instruments	xv
Introduction	1
1. Statutes	21
2. Statutory Instruments	622
Index	817

Alphabetical List of Statutes

	PARA
Bankruptcy (Scotland) Act 1985 (c 66)	[454]
Civic Government (Scotland) Act 1982 (c 45)	[204]
Cost of Leases Act 1958 (c 52)	[76]
Ejection Caution Act 1594 (c 27)	[2]
Housing Associations Act 1985 (c 69)	[457]
Housing (Scotland) Act 1987 (c 26)	[568]
Housing (Scotland) Act 1988 (c 43)	[1092]
Industrial and Provident Societies Act 1965 (c 12)	[77]
Land Compensation (Scotland) Act 1973 (c 56)	[161]
Land Tenure Reform (Scotland) Act 1974 (c 38)	[175]
Leases Act 1449 (c 6)	[1]
Local Government and Housing Act 1989 (c 42)	[1221]
Long Leases (Scotland) Act 1954 (c 49)	[68]
Matrimonial Homes (Family Protection) (Scotland) Act 1981 (c 59)	[183]
Race Relations Act 1976 (c 74)	[182]
Registration of Leases (Scotland) Act 1857 (c 26)	[3]
Removal Terms (Scotland) Act 1886 (c 50)	[32]
Rent (Scotland) Act 1984 (c 58)	[248]
Sheriff Courts (Scotland) Act 1907 (c 51)	[37]
Sheriff Courts (Scotland) Act 1971 (c 58)	[160A]
Social Security Act 1990 (c 27)	[1223A]
Tenancy of Shops Act 1949 (c 25)	[65]

Alphabetical List of Statutory Instruments

	PARA
Assured Tenancies (Exceptions) (Scotland) Regulations 1988, SI 1988/2068	[1433]
Assured Tenancies (Forms) (Scotland) Regulations 1988, SI 1988/2109	[1440]
Assured Tenancies (Notices to Quit) (Prescribed Information) (Scotland) Regulations 1988, SI 1988/2067	[1428]
Assured Tenancies (Rent Book) (Scotland) Regulations 1988, SI 1988/2085	[1437]
Assured Tenancies (Rent Information) (Scotland) Order 1989, SI 1989/685	[1467]
Assured Tenancies (Tenancies at a Low Rent) (Scotland) Regulations 1988, SI 1988/2069	[1435]
Cancellation of Registration (Procedure) (Scotland) Regulations 1980, SI 1980/670	[1308]
Civic Government (Scotland) Act 1982 (Licensing of Houses in Multiple Occupation) Order 1991, SI 1991/1253	[1507]
Home Energy Efficiency Grants Regulations 1990, SI 1990/1791	[1487R]
Homes Insulation Grants Order 1987, SI 1987/2185	[1382]
Homes Insulation Grants Order 1988, SI 1988/1239	[1426]
Home Purchase Assistance (Price Limits) Order 1991, SI 1991/819	[1506C]
Home Purchase Assistance (Recognised Lending Institutions) Order 1982, SI 1982/976	[1324]
Home Purchase Assistance (Recognised Savings Institutions) Order 1978, SI 1978/1785	[1261]
Home Purchase Assistance (Winding Up of Scheme) Order 1990, SI 1990/374	[1485]
Housing (Computation of Floor Area) Regulations (Scotland) 1935, SI 1935/912	[1224A]
Housing Corporation (Recognised Bodies for Heritable Securities Indemnities) (Scotland) Order 1987, SI 1987/1389	[1377]
Housing Defects (Application to Lenders) (Scotland) Regulations 1986, SI 1986/843	[1351]
Housing (Disapplication of Financial Hardship Provision for Repairs Grant) (Scotland) Order 1982, SI 1982/1154	[1334]
Housing (Forms) (Scotland) Regulations 1980, SI 1980/1647	[1286]
Housing (Grants for Fire Escapes in Houses in Multiple Occupation) (Prescribed Percentage) (Scotland) Order 1990, SI 1990/2242	[1504]
Housing (Homeless Persons) (Appropriate Arrangements) (No 2) Order 1978, SI 1978/661	[1247]
Housing (Improvement and Repairs Grants) (Approved Expenses Maxima) (Scotland) Order 1987, SI 1987/2269	[1385]
Housing (Limits of Rateable Value for Improvement Grants and Repairs Grants) (Scotland) Order 1985, SI 1985/297	[1343]
Housing (Management of Houses and Buildings in Multiple Occupation) (Scotland) Regulations 1964, SI 1964/1371	[1226]
Housing (Percentage of Approved Expense for Improvement Grants) (Scotland) Order 1980, SI 1980/2029	[1316]
Housing (Percentage of Approved Expense for Improvement Grants) (Disabled Occupants) (Scotland) Order 1982, SI 1982/1809	[1337]
Housing (Percentage of Approved Expense for Repairs Grant) (Lead Plumbing Works) (Scotland) Order 1984, SI 1984/514	[1340]
Housing (Preservation of Right to Buy) (Scotland) Regulations 1992, SI 1992/325	[1530]
Limits on Rent Increases (Scotland) Order 1989, SI 1989/2469	[1472]

Alphabetical List of Statutory Instruments

PARA

Local Authorities (Recognised Bodies for Heritable Securities Indemnities) (Scotland) Order 1987, SI 1987/1388 . . . . [1372]
Matrimonial Homes (Forms of Consent) (Scotland) Regulations 1982, SI 1982/971 . . . . [1323A]
Protected Tenancies (Exceptions) (Scotland) Regulations 1974, SI 1974/1374 [1244]
Protected Tenancies (Further Exception) (Scotland) Regulations 1982, SI 1982/702 . . . . [1322]
Protected Tenancies and Part VII Contracts (Rateable Value Limits) (Scotland) Order 1985, SI 1985/314 . . . . [1347]
Race Relations Code of Practice (Non-Rented Housing) Order 1992, SI 1992/619 . . . . [1579]
Race Relations Code of Practice (Rented Housing) Order 1991, SI 1991/227 [1506A]
Registered Housing Associations (Accounting Requirements) Order 1988, SI 1988/395 . . . . [1395]
Rent Assessment Committees (Scotland) Regulations 1980, SI 1980/1665 [1296]
Rent Assessment Committee (Assured Tenancies) (Scotland) Regulations 1989, SI 1989/81 . . . . [1454]
Rent Officers (Additional Functions) (Scotland) Order 1990, SI 1990/396 [1487A]
Rent Regulation (Forms and Information etc) (Scotland) Regulations 1991, SI 1991/1521 . . . . [1510]
Right to Purchase (Application Form) (Scotland) Order 1986, SI 1986/2138 [1365]
Right to Purchase From A Public Sector Landlord (Application Form) (Scotland) Order 1989, SI 1989/423 . . . . [1463]
Right to Purchase (Loans) (Scotland) Regulations 1980, SI 1980/1430 . . [1268]
Right to Purchase (Loan Application) (Scotland) Order 1980, SI 1980/1492 [1282]
Right to Purchase (Prescribed Persons) (Scotland) Order 1986, SI 1986/2140 [1369]
Secure Tenancies (Abandoned Property) (Scotland) Order 1982, SI 1982/981 [1326]
Secure Tenancies (Proceedings for Possession) Order 1980, SI 1980/1389 [1265]
Short Tenancies (Prescribed Information) (Scotland) Order 1980, SI 1980/1666 [1305]

Chronological List of Statutes

	PARA
Leases Act 1449 (c 6)	[1]
Ejection Caution Act 1594 (c 27)	[2]
Registration of Leases (Scotland) Act 1857 (c 26)	[3]
Removal Terms (Scotland) Act 1886 (c 50)	[32]
Sheriff Courts (Scotland) Act 1907 (c 51)	[37]
Tenancy of Shops Act 1949 (c 25)	[65]
Long Leases (Scotland) Act 1954 (c 49)	[68]
Cost of Leases Act 1958 (c 52)	[76]
Industrial and Provident Societies Act 1965 (c 12)	[77]
Sheriff Courts (Scotland) Act 1971 (c 58)	[160A]
Land Compensation (Scotland) Act 1973 (c 56)	[161]
Land Tenure Reform (Scotland) Act 1974 (c 38)	[175]
Race Relations Act 1976 (c 74)	[182]
Matrimonial Homes (Family Protection) (Scotland) Act 1981 (c 59)	[183]
Civic Government (Scotland) Act 1982 (c 45)	[204]
Rent (Scotland) Act 1984 (c 58)	[248]
Bankruptcy (Scotland) Act 1985 (c 66)	[454]
Housing Associations Act 1985 (c 69)	[457]
Housing (Scotland) Act 1987 (c 26)	[568]
Housing (Scotland) Act 1988 (c 43)	[1092]
Local Government and Housing Act 1989 (c 42)	[1221]
Social Security Act 1990 (c 27)	[1223A]

Chronological List of Statutory Instruments

		PARA
1935/912	The Housing (Computation of Floor Area) Regulations (Scotland) 1935	[1224A]
1964/1371	The Housing (Management of Houses and Buildings in Multiple Occupation) (Scotland) Regulations 1964	[1226]
1974/1374	The Protected Tenancies (Exceptions) (Scotland) Regulations 1974	[1244]
1978/661	The Housing (Homeless Persons) (Appropriate Arrangements) (No 2) Order 1978	[1247]
1978/1785	The Home Purchase Assistance (Recognised Savings Institutions) Order 1978	[1261]
1980/1389	The Secure Tenancies (Proceedings for Possession) Order 1980	[1265]
1980/1430	The Right to Purchase (Loans) (Scotland) Regulations 1980	[1268]
1980/1492	The Right to Purchase (Loan Application) (Scotland) Order 1980	[1282]
1980/1647	The Housing (Forms) (Scotland) Regulations 1980	[1286]
1980/1665	The Rent Assessment Committees (Scotland) Regulations 1980	[1296]
1980/1666	The Short Tenancies (Prescribed Information) (Scotland) Order 1980	[1305]
1980/1670	The Cancellation of Registration (Procedure) (Scotland) Regulations 1980	[1308]
1980/2029	The Housing (Percentage of Approved Expense for Improvement Grants) (Scotland) Order 1980	[1316]
1982/702	The Protected Tenancies (Further Exception) (Scotland) Regulations 1982	[1322]
1982/971	The Matrimonial Homes (Forms of Consent) (Scotland) Regulations 1982	[1323A]
1982/976	The Home Purchase Assistance (Recognised Lending Institutions) Order 1982	[1324]
1982/981	The Secure Tenancies (Abandoned Property) (Scotland) Order 1982	[1326]
1982/1154	The Housing (Disapplication of Financial Hardship Provision for Repairs Grant) (Scotland) Order 1982	[1334]
1982/1809	The Housing (Percentage of Approved Expense for Improvement Grants) (Disabled Occupants) (Scotland) Order 1982	[1337]
1984/514	The Housing (Percentage of Approved Expense for Repairs Grant) (Lead Plumbing Works) (Scotland) Order 1984	[1340]
1985/297	The Housing (Limits of Rateable Value for Improvement Grants and Repairs Grants) (Scotland) Order 1985	[1343]
1985/314	The Protected Tenancies and Part VII Contracts (Rateable Value Limits) (Scotland) Order 1985	[1347]
1986/843	The Housing Defects (Application to Lenders) (Scotland) Regulations 1986	[1351]
1986/2138	The Right to Purchase (Application Form) (Scotland) Order 1986	[1365]
1986/2140	The Right to Purchase (Prescribed Persons) (Scotland) Order 1986	[1369]
1987/1388	The Local Authorities (Recognised Bodies for Heritable Securities Indemnities) (Scotland) Order 1987	[1372]
1987/1389	The Housing Corporation (Recognised Bodies for Heritable Securities Indemnities) (Scotland) Order 1987	[1377]

		PARA
1987/2185	The Homes Insulation Grants Order 1987	[1382]
1987/2269	The Housing (Improvement and Repairs Grants) (Approved Expenses Maxima) (Scotland) Order 1987	[1385]
1988/395	The Registered Housing Associations (Accounting Requirements) Order 1988	[1395]
1988/1239	The Homes Insulation Grants Order 1988	[1426]
1988/2067	The Assured Tenancies (Notices to Quit) (Prescribed Information) (Scotland) Regulations 1988	[1428]
1988/2068	The Assured Tenancies (Exceptions) (Scotland) Regulations 1988	[1433]
1988/2069	The Assured Tenancies (Tenancies at a Low Rent) (Scotland) Order 1988	[1435]
1988/2085	The Assured Tenancies (Rent Book) (Scotland) Regulations 1988	[1437]
1988/2109	The Assured Tenancies (Forms) (Scotland) Regulations 1988	[1440]
1989/81	The Rent Assessment Committee (Assured Tenancies) (Scotland) Regulations 1989	[1454]
1989/423	The Right to Purchase From A Public Sector Landlord (Application Form) (Scotland) Regulations 1989	[1463]
1989/685	The Assured Tenancies (Rent Information) (Scotland) Order 1989	[1467]
1989/2469	The Limits on Rent Increases (Scotland) Order 1989	[1472]
1990/374	The Home Purchase Assistance (Winding Up of Scheme) Order 1990	[1485]
1990/396	The Rent Officers (Additional Functions) (Scotland) Order 1990	[1487A]
1990/1791	The Home Energy Efficiency Grants Regulations 1990	[1487R]
1990/2242	The Housing (Grants for Fire Escapes in Houses in Multiple Occupation) (Prescribed Percentage) (Scotland) Order 1990	[1504]
1991/227	The Race Relations Code of Practice (Rented Housing) Order 1991	[1506A]
1991/819	The Home Purchase Assistance (Price-Limits) Order 1991	[1506C]
1991/1253	The Civic Government (Scotland) Act 1982 (Licensing of Houses in Multiple Occupation) Order 1991	[1507]
1991/1521	The Rent Regulation (Forms and Information etc) (Scotland) Regulations 1991	[1510]
1992/325	The Housing (Preservation of Right to Buy) (Scotland) Regulations 1992	[1530]
1992/619	The Race Relations Code of Practice (Non-Rented Housing) Order 1992	[1579]

Introduction

The preface to this volume explains how it should be used and the conventions which have been followed in presenting the material. The purpose of this introduction is to make it easier for those without a comprehensive knowledge of the subject to find their way about the legislation, describing briefly the matters which have been made the subject of legislation, and relating those matters to the particular provisions which govern them. It is not intended to be a detailed exposition of the relevant law.

The phrase 'housing law' is inherently ambiguous, but in this volume it is used to refer to two main areas of legislative activity. The first is the legislation which regulates the relationship of landlord and tenant in residential, as opposed to commercial, leases. The second is the legislation introduced to improve the housing circumstances of Scottish people as a matter of social policy. This second area includes legislation governing the functions of local authorities and other public bodies such as housing authorities, and the regulatory structure for housing associations. The justification for excluding legislation dealing with land-ownership and conveyancing is that lawyers are already well served by published collections of legislation in that area.

The selection of material reflects those aims and is intended to meet the needs of lawyers and housing professionals both in the public sector and in the private sector. Some material which falls within the selection criteria has, however, been omitted in order to keep the volume of a manageable size.

The most obvious omissions are the Reserve and Auxiliary Forces (Prevention of Civil Interest) Act 1951, the Housing Forms (Scotland) Regulations 1974, SI 1974/1982 and the Housing (Forms) (Scotland) Amendment Regulations 1975, SI 1975/1644, of which the latter two contain many of the forms relating to local authority regulatory and grant awarding functions.

A. LANDLORD AND TENANT LEGISLATION

Landlord and tenant legislation includes provisions which (a) give tenants security of tenure and various ancillary rights; (b) regulate court procedure; (c) protect occupiers from unlawful eviction and harassment; (d) impose obligations regarding habitability and state of repair in leases, and (e) confer special rights on public sector tenants.

It is convenient also in this section to include description of certain legislation which is not strictly landlord and tenant legislation but deals with matters which are certainly of interest to persons in both categories. These are (f) the rights of spouses in the matrimonial home, and (g) rights of compensation for home loss, disturbance, and other matters.

(a) Legislation giving tenants security of tenure

Numerous enactments give tenants of residential property a higher degree of security of tenure than they would have enjoyed at common law.

The Leases Act 1449. Whereas a contract usually creates only personal rights, the Act of 1449 gave tenants a real right in the property which was the subject of the lease enforceable against the landlord's singular successors, ie persons who become owners of the property other than through inheritance. Provided the lease satisfies the requirements of the Act, a tenant in possession is entitled to keep the benefit of a lease until it reaches its term regardless of changes of ownership.

The Registration of Leases Act 1857. This Act gave tenants protection against singular successors of the landlord if the lease was registered in the Register of Sasines or the Land Register of Scotland and satisfied the conditions laid down in the Act. The Act originally applied only to leases for thirty-one years or longer, but this period was reduced to twenty years by the Land Tenure Reform (Scotland) Act 1974. The 1974 Act also prevents property which is subject to a long lease (exceeding twenty years) being used as a private dwellinghouse, and regulates the consequences of breach of the prohibition. The maximum length of lease of a dwellinghouse which can be granted today is, therefore, twenty years, but some long leases of dwellinghouses may still be extant and the 1857 Act is, accordingly, included in this volume.

Both the Act of 1449 and the Long Leases Act of 1857 limited protection of the tenant's enjoyment of the property to the duration of the leases, and were largely concerned with protecting the tenant's enjoyment in questions between the tenant and the landlord's successors in title. In the twentieth century, legislation has been primarily concerned with extending security of tenure beyond the contractual period, and protecting the tenant's enjoyment of the property as against the landlord.

The Rent (Scotland) Act 1984. The Rent (Scotland) Act 1984 is the last of a series of Acts which provided for rent control and security of tenure in lets of private sector dwellinghouses. It has been replaced by a different form of regulation under the Housing (Scotland) Act 1988, but the transitional arrangements have the result that a significant number of tenancies in existence are still governed by the 1984 Act.

Rent regulation was first introduced, as a temporary measure, in 1915, but continued until 1989 with the exception of a brief period of de-control between 1957 and 1965. Until 1965, tenancies protected by the rent legislation were referred to as controlled tenancies. This system of regulation was felt to be unsatisfactory and a new system—'regulated tenancies' was introduced by the Rent Act 1965, but without changing the status of existing controlled tenancies. The two systems ran in tandem for a number of years until all remaining controlled tenanices were converted into regulated tenancies by the Tenants' Rights etc (Scotland) Act 1980, section 46. Controlled tenancies can, therefore, be ignored by the practitioner.

Originally only unfurnished tenancies enjoyed the full measure of protection, but full protection was extended to furnished tenancies in 1974. A new form of protected tenancy known as a short tenancy was introduced by the Tenants' Rights etc (Scotland) Act 1980. A short tenancy would have a duration of between one and five years with the landlord being entitled to recover possession at the end of the let. All the relevant legislation was consolidated in the Rent (Scotland) Act 1984 which (as amended) continues to govern such regulated tenancies as still exist.

(i) Regulated tenancies. The expression 'regulated tenancy' covers both

'protected tenancies' and 'statutory tenancies'. A protected tenancy is a contractual tenancy of a dwellinghouse. A statutory tenancy arises when the contractual tenancy is validly terminated by either party. The former protected tenant continues to have a statutory tenancy so long as he retains possession of the dwellinghouse. Security of tenure is guaranteed because a protected or statutory tenant cannot be evicted without a court order which can be made only in the cases specified in section 11 of and Schedule 2 to the 1984 Act.

The other main benefit enjoyed by tenants under the 1984 Act is rent control. A protected or statutory tenant may at any time apply to the rent officer for a fair rent to be registered. If a rent is registered it is the maximum which the landlord can charge. If either party is dissatisfied with this figure he can appeal to a rent assessment committee. The statutory formula to be applied both by the rent officer and the rent assessment committee will almost invariably have the effect that the fair rent determined is below the market level.

In addition to security of tenure and rent control, the 1984 Act also confers on certain relatives of protected and statutory tenants the right to succeed to the tenancy on the death of the tenant.

(ii) Transitional provisions. New forms of tenancy were introduced by the Housing (Scotland) Act 1988, but without prejudice to the rights of existing tenants, so it is important to be able to identify those tenancies which continue to be governed by the Rent (Scotland) Act 1984. By virtue of section 42 of the Housing (Scotland) Act 1988, no new protected tenancies could be created on or after 2 January 1989 unless (a) the tenancy was entered into pursuant to a contract made before that date; or (b) (except where the tenant was a protected or statutory tenant under a short tenancy) the tenant was, immediately before the tenancy was granted, a protected tenant or a statutory tenant of the same landlord; or (c) certain other circumstances apply.

For tenancies created before 2 January 1989 (or after that date, in the limited circumstances described above), the tenancy is a protected tenancy if (a) under it a dwellinghouse is let as a separate dwelling; (b) the rateable value of the house falls within certain limits; (c) none of the statutory exceptions applies. The exceptions include public sector tenancies, tenancies of agricultural land, and tenancies where there is a resident landlord. Tenants of resident landlords, and certain others who were not protected tenants enjoyed a more limited form of protection under Part VII of the Rent (Scotland) Act 1984. In Part VII contracts the rent assessment committee has a discretion to fix the rent payable. The committee also had the power to grant security of tenure by postponing the effect of a notice to quit for a six month period. Where the Part VII contract was entered into on or after 1 December 1980 the power to grant security of tenure is transferred to the sheriff and the maximum period is three months. No new Part VII contracts could be created after 2 January 1989, by virtue of section 44 of the Housing (Scotland) Act 1988 unless entered into in pursuance of a contract made before that date. Given that, and the limited degree of security of tenure conferred by Part VII, it can be assumed that very few Part VII contracts remain in existence.

(iii) Housing association tenants. Tenancies in which the landlord is a housing association are also affected by the 1984 Act even although they are not protected tenancies. Before 2 January 1989 housing association tenants had secure tenancies in terms of the Housing (Scotland) Act 1987 (see below). However, the maximum rent for such tenancies was determined by the rent officer under Part VI of the 1984 Act in a manner similar to that for the determination of fair

rents in protected tenancies. Housing association landlords, therefore, had little discretion in the settling of rent levels. Such a tenancy is referred to in section 43 of the Housing (Scotland) Act 1988 as as 'housing association tenancy', and that section provides that no new housing association tenancies could be created on or after 2 January 1989 unless (a) entered into in pursuance of a contract made before that date; or (b) granted to a person who was an existing tenant under a housing association tenancy of the same landlord; or (c) the tenant is being provided with suitable alternative accommodation following an order of possession and the court directs that the new accommodation should be a housing association tenancy. The effect of the transitional provision is that those who were tenants of housing associations before 2 January 1989 continue to enjoy the benefits of the special rent regime for housing association tenants so long as they remain with the same landlord. For the determination of rent in post-1989 housing association lets different legislation applies (see below).

The Housing (Scotland) Act 1987. Before 1980 tenants of local authorities and other public sector landlords did not have substantial security of tenure in law, although it was assumed that, as a matter of policy, public sector landlords would provide housing to people as a public service. However, the Tenants' Rights etc (Scotland) Act 1980 gave public sector tenants a form of security of tenure similar to that enjoyed by private sector tenants, together with other rights, collectively referred to as 'The Tenants Charter'. These provisions are now to be found consolidated with other housing enactments in the Housing (Scotland) Act 1987, Part III.

Security of tenure is provided through the concept of the secure tenancy. A secure tenancy cannot be brought to an end except in one of the following six ways: (a) the death of the tenant where there is no person qualified to succeed to it; (b) where a person who is qualified to succeed declines to do so; (c) by written agreement; (d) through the abandonment procedure; (e) where the tenant gives four weeks written notice to the landlord; (f) by an order for recovery of possession granted by the court under section 48(2) of the 1987 Act. An order for recovery of possession can be granted only on the grounds specified in Schedule 3 to the Act.

A secure tenant also has a number of other rights in relation to the tenancy, which include the right to a written lease, and the right of certain family members to succeed to the tenancy on the death of the tenant. In addition, under certain conditions, a secure tenant has the right to buy the house he lives in (see below).

A tenancy is a secure tenancy if the house is let as a separate dwelling, the tenant is an individual, and the house is his only or principal home, provided the landlord is a public sector landlord as defined in section 44 of the 1987 Act. The original definition includes amongst others, local authorities, new town development corporations, and Scottish Homes. As regards housing associations, whether or not their tenants have secure tenancies is governed by the Housing (Scotland) Act 1988, section 43(3). Tenancies entered into on or after 2 January 1989 cannot be secure tenancies unless the landlord is one of the bodies specified in that subsection which does not include housing associations. However, where the landlord is a housing association, a tenancy will be a secure tenancy (a) if it was entered into in pursuance of a contract made before 2 January 1989, or (b) if it is granted to a person who, immediately before it was entered into was a secure tenant of the same landlord, or (c) the tenant is being provided with suitable alternative accommodation following an order for recovery of possession and the court directs that the new accommodation should be a secure tenancy.

The consequence of these transitional provisions is that those who were tenants of housing associations before 2 January 1989 continue to have the status of secure tenants and corresponding rights so long as they remain with the same landlord. Those who become tenants of housing association landlords for the first time on or after 2 January 1989 will have assured tenancies under the Housing (Scotland) Act 1988.

The Housing (Scotland) Act 1988. Part II of the 1988 Act introduced two new forms of tenancy in the private sector from 2 January 1989—the assured tenancy and the short assured tenancy—under which landlords can charge market rents rather than the fair rents which could be determined under the Rent (Scotland) Act 1984. Tenants under assured tenancies enjoy substantial security of tenure, although the grounds for recovery of possession are not identical to the cases in which possession might be recovered under the Rent (Scotland) Act 1984. However, in a short assured tenancy, the landlord is entitled to recover possession at the end of the contractual period.

(i) Assured tenancies. Security of tenure for assured tenants is achieved by a similar mechanism to that employed in the 1984 Act. When a contractual assured tenancy is terminated the person who immediately before termination of the tenancy was the assured tenant of the house continues to have the benefit of a statutory assured tenancy so long as he retains possession of the house. A statutory assured tenancy cannot be brought to an end without an order of the sheriff and proceedings for eviction of a tenant with a contractual or statutory assured tenancy can be brought only on one or more of the grounds set out in Schedule 5 to the Act.

Although assured tenants do not have the benefit of the system of rent control which operates under the 1984 Act, there is a limited role for the rent assessment committee preventing profiteering. Except in tenancies where the contract provides a mechanism for increases in rent, the rent assessment committee can limit the rent to the market rate for the property if a notice of a proposed increase is referred to them. Assured tenants also have a right to a written lease and spouses and cohabitees can succeed to the tenancy on the death of the tenant.

A tenancy under which (a) the house is let as a separate dwelling; (b) the tenant is an individual; and (c) the tenant occupies his house as his only or principal home is an assured tenancy unless one of the statutory exceptions in Schedule 4 applies. The exceptions include tenancies entered into before 2 January 1989, tenancies at a low rent, tenancies of shops, licensed premises, agricultural land and buildings, student lettings by educational institutions, holiday lettings, where there is a resident landlord, and public sector tenancies. It is expressly provided that a tenancy is not an assured tenancy if it is either (a) a protected tenancy under the Rent (Scotland) Act 1984; (b) a housing association tenancy under Part III of the Act; and (c) a secure tenancy under Part III of the Housing (Scotland) Act 1987. A consequence of the redefinition of secure tenancy by the Housing (Scotland) Act 1988 is that new housing association lettings since 2 January 1989 have not been secure tenancies. The assured tenancy is therefore being used both by those letting for profit and by 'social landlords'. Housing associations which have been letting since before that date are likely to have two kinds of tenants—secure and assured—subject to different statutory regulation.

(ii) Short assured tenancies. A short assured tenancy is a variant on the assured tenancy, and is an assured tenancy which is for a term of not less than six months. In order to create a short assured tenancy the landlord must serve on the

prospective tenant before the creation of the tenancy a notice in the prescribed form stating that it is to be a short assured tenancy. The tenant has no security of tenure because the landlord is entitled to recover possession at the end of the contractual period provided he gives the tenant notice of the appropriate length that he requires possession of the house. In contrast to the ordinary assured tenancy, the tenant may at any time apply to the rent assessment committee, but their power to limit the rent of the property to the market rate is more restricted than in the case of ordinary assured tenancies.

(b) Procedures in actions for recovery of possession

In addition to the substantive restrictions on the ability of landlords to recover possession of houses which have been let, there are important procedural provisions which regulate the manner in which the right to recover possession can be exercised. Proceedings in court are always necessary to evict a tenant who refuses to remove. For court action to be successful certain preliminaries are necessary. In many cases, a notice to quit is necessary. Minimum lengths of notice to quit are specified in the Removal Terms (Scotland) Act 1886, the Sheriff Courts (Scotland) Act 1907, sections 34–38, and the Rent (Scotland) Act 1984, section 112. In the case of protected and assured tenancies notices to quit must be in writing and contain prescribed information (Rent (Scotland) Act 1984). In a secure tenancy, the landlord must always serve a notice of intention to take proceedings for recovery of possession on the tenant (1987 Act, section 47). In an assured tenancy, the landlord must always serve a notice of intention to raise proceedings for possession on the tenant (1988 Act, section 19).

Assuming all necessary preliminary notices have been served, the action will normally be raised as a summary cause. The summary cause rules are not reproduced in this volume. However, relevant rules relating to ordinary actions (some of which apply equally to summary causes) are reproduced (Sheriff Courts (Scotland) Act 1907).

(c) Protection from unlawful eviction and harassment

The 1984, 1987, and 1988 Acts protect the interests of protected, secure and assured tenants by placing both substantive and procedural constraints on the landlord's right to recover possession. In the case of each of the three statutory forms of security of tenure, court proceedings are required for eviction. However, tenants in general, including those not protected under the three statutory regimes, are protected by both criminal and civil sanctions under other legislation.

The Rent (Scotland) Act 1984. Section 23 of the 1984 Act defines three separate offences—one of unlawful eviction and two of harassment. The offences protect not only tenants, but also other residential occupiers against unlawful eviction and harassment. Harassment is action short of eviction intended or likely to cause the occupier to give up occupation of the premises. Section 23 of the 1984 Act defines a prohibition on eviction without due process of law ie court proceedings, which will be of relevance in establishing criminal and civil liability. Section 24 makes special provision for agricultural employees, and section 23A provides for exceptions to the general prohibition in sections 23 and 24.

The Housing (Scotland) Act 1988. Sections 36 and 37 of the 1988 Act provide a new civil remedy of damages for unlawful eviction, or harassment which results in the residential occupier of premises giving up occupation. Special provision is made for the measure of damages. This remedy is available as an alternative to any claim that might be made at common law.

(d) Landlord's repairing obligation

Section 113 of and Schedule 10 to the Housing (Scotland) Act 1987 imply into most leases of houses onerous conditions regarding the fitness for human habitation and state of repair of the house. The provisions apply to both public and private sector leases, and the scope for contracting out of or varying the obligations is very limited.

Whilst these provisions are very important, landlords' and tenants' advisers will also wish to consider the legislation conferring regulatory powers on housing authorities in relation to repairs, and the legislation authorising housing authorities to make grants for the repair and improvement of housing (see below).

(e) Rights of public sector tenants

The Housing (Scotland) Act 1987 confers a number of rights specific to public sector tenants. These include a right of succession for family members when a secure tenant dies (1987 Act, section 52), a right to have a written lease (1987 Act, section 53), and a right to buy the house the tenant lives in (1987 Act, sections 61–81B). The Housing (Scotland) Act 1988 introduced a further right—the right to choose a different landlord. The two last-mentioned rights deserve fuller treatment.

Tenants right to buy. Sections 61–81B govern the exercise by public sector tenants of their right to purchase the houses they live in. The right is enjoyed by all secure tenants (with limited exceptions) who have occupied relevant accommodation for the minimum period of two years. The purchase price is based on the market value of the house less a discount based on the length of occupation of relevant accommodation, but all or part of the discount is repayable if the house is resold within three years of the exercise of the right to purchase. The legislation provides for a detailed procedure for exercise of the right to purchase and procedures for the resolution of disputes about the exercising of the right to purchase.

Change of landlord. Part III (sections 56–64) of the Housing (Scotland) Act 1988 gives secure tenants of public sector landlords the ability to require the landlord to transfer ownership of the tenant's house to a new landlord. This takes the form of conferring on persons approved by Scottish Homes or on Scottish Homes the right to buy houses from the existing public sector landlords. Apart from Scottish Homes, public sector landlords may not be approved persons. Housing associations may be approved persons, but houses let by housing associations are not themselves subject to compulsory sale to approved persons. The legislation lays down a procedure for the exercise of this right which includes a number of features to protect the interests of individual tenants, including a requirement that a tenant consent in writing to the transfer of his house to a new landlord.

In practice, it appears that this procedure—colloquially referred to as 'tenants' choice'—is not being used. However, the policy of encouraging transfer of public authority rented housing to other landlords (mostly housing associations or other 'social landlords') is being effected by other legal means. Local authorities have powers to sell land (including houses) under sections 12–13 of the Housing (Scotland) Act 1987. This procedure differs in a number of respects from the tenants' choice procedure under the 1988 Act outlined above. The sale is a voluntary act of the local authority. The Secretary of State's consent is required and the individual tenant is not entitled to veto the sale of his house. Sections 81A and 81B and Schedule 6A preserve the right to buy for tenants affected by voluntary transfers, impose requirements of consultation on local authorities, and limit the Secretary of State's discretion in consenting to a sale.

(f) The rights of spouses in the matrimonial home

Formerly, the law of property gave a spouse no automatic right to occupy the matrimonial home. Whether a spouse was entitled to occupy the matrimonial home depended on whether that spouse had a legal right to occupy as owner, or tenant, or in some other way. In the absence of such a right, the spouse who was entitled to occupy could exclude the other spouse. The Matrimonial Homes (Family Protection) (Scotland) Act 1981 gives a 'non-entitled spouse' a statutory right to occupy the matrimonial home and a number of important ancillary rights including the right to make payments due in respect of the house, and to make essential repairs. The Act also protects the non-entitled spouse against dealings in respect of the matrimonial home by the entitled spouse. It gives the court power to regulate the occupancy rights of the parties and, in some cases, to exclude either spouse from the matrimonial home. Many of the provisions of the Act apply as equally to matrimonial homes which are leased as to those which are owned. In addition, the court has the power to transfer a tenancy from the spouse who is the tenant to the non-entitled spouse.

(g) Rights of compensation for home loss and disturbance etc

Occupiers and those possessing certain other interests in housing who are displaced or disturbed by development enjoy rights to compensation in certain circumstances under the Land Compensation (Scotland) Act 1973. Specified categories of person are entitled to home loss payments on the compulsory acquisition of the dwelling in which they have an interest, on the making of certain orders affecting the dwelling, on the carrying out of improvements, and in certain other circumstances. The payment is made by the housing authority or landlord according to the circumstances. The right to claim a home loss payment is extended to those whose interest in the dwelling is derived solely from the Matrimonial Homes (Family Protection) (Scotland) Act 1981. Home loss payments are not made unless certain conditions relating to occupation can be satisfied throughout the year leading up to displacement, but there is a power to make a 'discretionary payment' when the conditions can only be satisfied on the date of displacement. Home loss payments may also be made to certain caravan dwellers.

The Land Compensation (Scotland) Act 1973 also imposes on relevant authorities a duty to rehouse residential occupiers and caravan dwellers displaced in specified circumstances.

Separately from these obligations Part XV of the Housing (Scotland) Act 1987 imposes additional obligations to make additional compensation payments for well maintained houses subject to compulsory purchase or closure or demolition orders.

B. FUNCTIONS OF LOCAL AUTHORITIES AND OTHER HOUSING BODIES

For convenience, the functions of local authorities under housing legislation can be divided into three types—(a) provision of housing services; (b) regulatory functions; and (c) providing financial assistance. Included under service provision are the powers and duties relating to the provision of council housing, the management of council housing, and duties to house homeless persons.

Regulatory functions include ensuring improvement of houses which are below the tolerable standard, compulsory powers to order repair, closure and demolition of houses, supervision of overcrowding, and supervision of houses in multiple occupation.

The function of providing financial assistance for housing includes making loans to persons to assist them to buy houses, making grants for improvement, repair and conversion of housing, and giving financial assistance to owners of defective housing.

The enactments conferring powers and imposing duties on local authorities in housing matters have been consolidated in the Housing (Scotland) Act 1987 (hereinafter 'the 1987 Act'). Other legislation which may be used to achieve housing purposes has also been included.

It is convenient also in this section to deal with (d) the structure of public sector housing finance; (e) the functions of Scottish Homes; and (f) the regulatory structure for housing associations.

(a) Provision of housing

There are two general functions of this sort: firstly, providing and managing local authority housing; and, secondly, duties to rehouse homeless persons.

Providing local authority housing. (1987 Act, Part I) Local authorities which are island councils or district councils are obliged to consider the housing conditions in their area and the needs of the area for further housing accommodation. They also have broad powers to provide housing accommodation, and to provide various facilities in connection with their provision of housing accommodation, to acquire land for the provision of housing, and to sell it or lease it. Sale of land bought for housing purposes, or of council housing requires the consent of the Secretary of State unless it is a sale to a sitting tenant under the right to buy legislation. There are further provisions permitting local authorities to make byelaws for the management and regulation of their housing stock, and restricting their discretion in the admission of persons to the housing waiting list, and in the allocation of houses. Management functions may be delegated to housing cooperatives.

Homeless persons. (1987 Act, Part II) Local authorities which are housing authorities are under a duty to ensure that certain categories of homeless person are rehoused, and a duty to furnish advice and assistance to those categories of homeless person who are not owed a duty to be rehoused. Part II of the 1987 Act defines the circumstances in which a person is to be considered homeless, classifies homeless persons according to whether they have a priority need for accommodation, imposes various duties in relation to the rehousing of homeless persons, and determines when an application for assistance by a homeless person may be referred by one local authority to another.

(b) Local authority regulatory functions

Local authorities have a wide range of statutory powers and duties whose aim is the maintenance and/or improvement of the standard of housing in their areas, both in the public and private sectors. Most of the relevant powers and duties are to be found in the 1987 Act, but other legislation also confers powers in specific areas.

Sub-standard housing: area procedures. (1987 Act, Part IV) Section 85 of the 1987 Act imposes on local authorities a duty to secure that all houses in their district which do not meet the tolerable standard (as defined in section 86) are either closed, demolished or brought up to the tolerable standard within such period as is reasonable in the circumstances. In order to implement this duty local authorities may attempt improvement of individual houses or whole areas of housing. As regards the latter, a local authority may declare a housing action area for the purpose of demolition, for the purpose of improvement, or for both purposes together. Part IV governs the procedure for, and the consequences of declaring a housing action area. As regards the former, local authorities may compel owners of houses which are below the tolerable standard, but outside a housing action area, to bring them up to the tolerable standard, and put them in a good state of repair.

Compulsory powers exercisable against individual houses. Local authorities can make orders affecting individual houses or buildings under several statutory provisions. The exercise of these powers does not depend on the house being in a housing action area. A compulsory repairs notice may be made and enforced against any house in a state of serious disrepair under sections 108–112 of the 1987 Act. A house which is below the tolerable standard may be made subject to a closing order, a building consisting of houses below the tolerable standard may be made the subject of a demolition order, and an obstructive building may be demolished (1987 Act, sections 114–132). In addition to these powers, a local authority has power to require repairs to houses under section 87 of the Civic Government (Scotland) Act 1982. Other provisions of the 1982 Act give local authorities various powers in relation to common stairs and other common property to ensure lighting, cleaning, painting and safety. Local authorities also have powers in relation to dangerous buildings under the Building (Scotland) Act 1959 (not included in this volume).

Overcrowding. (1987 Act, Part VII) Part VII of the 1987 Act defines overcrowding in terms of a room standard and a space standard, and an occupier who causes or permits overcrowding commits an offence. Part VII also provides for exceptions to the criminal offence, and imposes duties of inspection and enforcement on the local authority. However, a number of the overcrowding provisions are not fully in force (see notes to 1987 Act, section 151).

Houses in multiple occupation. (1987 Act, Part VIII) Part VIII of the 1987 Act permits a local authority to make a registration scheme for houses in multiple occupation in their area, subject to confirmation by the Secretary of State. Under section 157 of the 1987 Act the local authority may apply to a particular house the management code provided by regulations made under section 156. A local authority has extensive powers in relation to houses in multiple occupation which have been made subject to the management code, including the making of a control order in an appropriate case, which gives the local authority possession of the house and the right to manage it.

In addition to the powers contained in the 1987 Act, a local authority may regulate certain houses in multiple occupation under Part I of the Civic Government (Scotland) Act 1982. Regulations have been made under section 44 of that Act designating the management of a house in multiple occupation as an activity requiring a licence.

(c) Provision of grants and other financial assistance

Local authority powers and duties to provide financial assistance to persons come in three main forms: powers to make loans for obtaining housing; grants for improvement, repair and conversion of housing; and assistance for owners of defective housing.

Housing loans etc. (1987 Act, Part XII) Local authorities have general powers to make loans to persons for the purposes of obtaining housing accommodation, acquiring, constructing, altering, improving, repairing or enlarging a house, or converting another building into a house, or repaying an earlier loan. In addition, tenants exercising the right to buy are entitled to a loan from their local authority or landlord if they cannot obtain one from commercial lenders. Part XII also deals with other local authority powers and duties, to make loans and other forms of financial assistance, rates of interest on loans, a scheme of assistance for first time buyers (sections 222–228), local authority indemnities for building societies, and financial assistance towards tenants' removal expenses, and the expenses of housing pensioners and disabled persons.

Grants for improvement, repair and conversion. (1987 Act, Part XIII) Several kinds of grants are made by local authorities under the authority of Part XIII and subordinate legislation.

1. Improvement grants. Grants for the improvement of housing are of two types: 'discretionary' and 'mandatory' improvement grants. Section 244 specifies the circumstances in which a local authority has a duty to make an improvement grant if an application is duly made. In other circumstances, the making of a grant is at the discretion of the local authority.

2. Repair grants. By virtue of section 248 of the 1987 Act, where a repairs notice has been served under section 108 of the 1987 Act, the local authority has a duty to approve an application for a repairs grant for the works required by the notice. In other cases the granting of an application is at the discretion of the local authority.

3. Grants for fire escapes. (1987 Act, section 249) A local authority must approve an application for a grant for a fire escape in a house in multiple occupation

(HMO), where it has served a notice under section 162 requiring the provision of a means of escape from fire in that house. In other circumstances, the local authority has a discretion to approve an application for a grant for a fire escape in a HMO.

4. *Improvement of amenity grants.* (1987 Act, section 251) A local authority may, for the purpose of improving the amenities of a predominantly residential area, carry out works on land or make grants and loans to assist the carrying out of works or acquire land.

5. *Thermal insulation grants.* (1987 Act, sections 252–253) Grants to improve the thermal insulation of dwellings must be made by local authorities in accordance with schemes prepared by the Secretary of State. Sections 252 and 253 are prospectively repealed by the Social Security Act 1990, and the current scheme—The Homes Insulation Scheme 1987—will be replaced by regulations made under that Act when the repeal becomes effective.

Assistance for owners of defective housing. (1987 Act, Part XIV) Under Part XIV of the 1987 Act the Secretary of State may designate classes of buildings as defective if they have design or construction defects which have caused a substantial reduction in their value. Owners of defective houses are eligible for assistance which may take the form of reinstatement grant or repurchase of the defective dwelling. Local authorities have powers under sections 287–289 to designate as defective additional classes of buildings in their area, in order to supplement the national scheme.

(d) Public housing finance

There are three main aspects to the legal structure of public housing finance: the provisions relating to central government grants, local authority housing revenue accounts, and local authority rent and service charges.

Part IX of the 1987 Act governs the making of housing support grants to local authorities, grants to development corporations and Scottish Homes, and financial assistance to voluntary organisations concerned with housing.

Part X of the 1987 Act requires local authorities to keep a housing revenue account which separates housing-related expenditure from other expenditure, empowers the Secretary of State to limit the amount of subsidy which a local authority can give to housing expenditure out of its general fund, and also requires a local authority to keep a rent rebate account and a rent allowance account.

Part XI of the 1987 Act regulates rent, service charges and rent increases in local authority houses.

(e) Scottish Homes

Part I of the Housing (Scotland) Act 1988 creates a new Scottish Housing Agency which took over the property, rights, liabilities, and obligations of the former Scottish Special Housing Association, and of the Housing Corporation in Scotland. Part I provides for the constitution and proceedings of Scottish Homes; its general and particular functions and powers; the transfer of property etc from the Scottish Special Housing Association, and from the Housing Corporation in Scotland; and regulates its financial arrangements.

Scottish Homes has three main functions. First, it has taken over from the Housing Corporation the function of maintaining a register of housing associations under the Housing Associations Act 1985, and exercising supervision and control over housing associations. Second, as a result of taking over the property of the Scottish Special Housing Association it has also become a major public sector landlord. Third, it provides funding for housing development to housing associations and other bodies.

(f) Housing associations

Housing associations are significant social landlords who provide housing for rent in a different manner from both local authorities and profit-orientated landlords. Their tenants usually have either secure or assured tenancies (although there are exceptions) depending on the date when they became tenants of the association. The rights of tenants under secured and assured tenancies have already been discussed. There are two Acts of Parliament which provide for the regulation of housing associations. In Scotland, housing associations may be registered in the register maintained by the Registrar of Friendly Societies under the Industrial and Provident Societies Act 1965. Scottish Homes may also register those, but only those, societies already registered under the 1965 Act provided they satisfy certain conditions, in the register maintained by it under the Housing Associations Act 1985.

Both Acts make extensive provision with regard to the constitution, rules, membership, property, accounts and audit of registered housing associations. In the case of the 1965 Act regulatory powers are vested in the Assistant Registrar of Friendly Societies for Scotland. In the case of the 1985 Act more extensive regulatory powers are vested in Scottish Homes.

1. STATUTES

Leases Act 1449
(c 6)

Of takis of landis for termes

Item it is ordanit for the sauftie and fauour of the pure pepil that labouris the grunde that thai and al vthiris that has takyn or sal tak landis in tym to cum fra lordis and has termes and yeris thereof that suppose the lordis sel or analy thai landis that the takaris sall remayn with thare takis on to the ische of thare termes quhais handis at euir thai landis cum to for sic lik male as thai tuk thaim of befoir . . .

[1]

NOTES

The words of the statute may be expressed in modern usage, thus:
> 'that they [the poor people], and all others that have taken or shall take lands in time to come from lords, and have terms and years thereof, that suppose the lords sell or annaly those land or lands, the takers shall remain with their tacks, until the issue of their terms, whose hands so ever those lands come to, for suchlike maill as they took them of before.'

See, W M Gordon *Scottish Land Law* (W Green & Son, 1989), p 568
Words repealed by Statute Law Revision (Scotland) Act 1906 (c 38)
Short title 'The Leases Act 1449' given by Statute Law Revision (Scotland) Act 1964 (c 80), Sch 2.

Ejection Caution Act 1594
(c 27)

That cautioun be found in actionis of eiectioun

Oure Souerane Lord with auise of the estaitis of this present parliament Vnderstanding the greit disordour quhilk hes arysen and daly dois aryse among his hienes leigis quhar as personis wrangouslie intrusing thame selffis in the rowmes and possessionis of vtheris be bangstre and force being altogither vnresponsall thame selffis mantenis thair possessioun thairof And quhen thai ar challengit befoir the lordis of the sessioun or vther Jugeis ordiner be the pairtie grevit The personis intrusaris of thame selffis in sic possessioun delayis the mater be proponing of peremptour exceptionis quhilkis ar nocht of veritie and delayis vpoun the probatioun thairof And efter lang pley quhen as the pairtie grevit hes gottin decreit Ordaning him to be repossessit to his rowme and proffittis thairof his pairtie being vnresponsall altogider gettis na commoditie thairof for remeid of the quhilk It is statute and Ordanit that in all tyme cuming the pairtie persewit be ane vther for eiectioun sall find cautioun for the violent proffittis as in causes of removing the first dyet of the litiscontestatioun or vtherwyis decreit to be gevin ordinand the pairtie to be repossessit. [2–5]

NOTES
Short title 'The Ejection Caution Act 1594' given by Statute Law Revision (Scotland) Act 1964 (c 80), Sch 2

Registration of Leases (Scotland) Act 1857
(c 26)

ARRANGEMENT OF SECTIONS

1	Long leases, and assignations thereof, registerable in Register of Sasines .	[6]
2	Recorded leases effectual against singular successors in the lands let .	[7]
3	Assignations of recorded leases .	[8]
4	Assignations in security .	[9]
5	Where Party presenting for Registration not original Lessee or Assignee .	[10]
6	Translation of assignations in security. Creditor's entry to possession in default of payment .	[11]

* * *

8	Heir or disponee may complete title by recording notarial instrument	[12]
9	Where assignee has died without recording assignation, mode of making up title	[13]
10	Adjudgers to complete right by recording abbreviate	[14]
11	Trustees on sequestrated estate may be entered on register	[15]
12	Preferences regulated by date of recording transfer	[16]
13	Renunciations and discharges to be recorded	[17]
14	Entry of Decree of Reduction	[18]
15	Mode of registering. Extracts to make faith as writs registered	[19]
16	Registration equivalent to possession	[20]
17	Leases, with obligation to renew, registerable	[21]

* * *

19	Extracts registerable where leases recorded in Court of Session or Sheriff Court Books prior to Act	[22]
20	Clauses in Schedules to be held to import and to have effect as declared by 10 & 11 Vict c 50.	[23]
21	Short title	[24]

SCHEDULES:

Schedule (A)—Form of assignation of lease	[25]
Schedule (B)—Form of bond and assignation in security	[26]
Schedule (C)—Forms of notarial instruments in favour of a party not the original grantee	[27]
Schedule (D)—Form of translation of assignation in security	[28]

* * *

Schedule (F)—Form of notarial instrument in favour of heir in recorded lease or assignation in security, or of trustee on sequestrated estate	[29]
Schedule (G)—Renunciation of lease	[30]
Schedule (H)—Form of discharge of bond and assignation in security	[31]

An Act to provide for the Registration of Long Leases in Scotland, and Assignations thereof [10th August 1857]

1. Long leases, and assignations thereof, registerable in Register of Sasines.

It shall be lawful to record in the general register of sasines in Scotland, . . . probative leases, whether executed before or after the passing of this Act, for a period [exceeding twenty years], of lands and heritages in Scotland . . . and to record respectively in the register in which any such lease as aforesaid shall have been registered the assignations, and assignations in security of such lease, and translations thereof, all herein-after mentioned. [6]

NOTES to section 1

Amendments: Words repealed by Statute Law Revision Act 1892 (c 19); words substituted retrospectively by Land Tenure Reform (Scotland) Act 1974 (c 38) Sch 6, para 1; words repealed by Burgh Registers (Scotland) Act 1926 (c 50), s 4, Sch 2.

General: By virtue of s 29(2) of the Land Registration (Scotland) Act 1979 (c 33), in relation to any operational area, the reference to the Register of Sasines should be construed as a reference to the Land Register of Scotland, and the references to recording should be construed as references to registration therein.

2. Recorded leases effectual against singular successors in the lands let.

Leases registerable under this Act, and valid and binding as in a question with the granters thereof, which shall have been duly recorded, as herein provided, . . . shall, by virtue of such registration, be effectual against any singular successor in the lands and heritages thereby let, whose infeftment is posterior in date to the date of such registration: Provided always, that, except for the purposes of this Act, it shall not be necessary to record any such lease as aforesaid, but that all such leases which would, under the existing law prior to the passing of this Act, have been valid and effectual against any such singular successor as aforesaid, shall, though not recorded, be valid and effectual against such singular successor, as well as against the granters of the said leases. [7]

3. Assignations of recorded leases.

(1) When any such lease as aforesaid shall have been recorded as herein provided, it shall be lawful for the party in right of such lease, and whose right is recorded in terms of this Act, but in accordance always with the conditions and stipulations of such lease, and not otherwise, to assign the same, in whole or in part, by assignation, in the form as nearly as may be of the Schedule (A) to this Act annexed; and the recording of such assignation shall fully and effectually vest the assignee with the right of the granter thereof in and to such lease to the extent assigned: Provided always, that such assignation shall be without prejudice to the right of hypothec, or other rights of the landlord.

(2) Notwithstanding—
(a) any restriction imposed by subsection (1) above on the power under that subsection to assign such a lease; or
(b) any rule of law to the contrary,
it shall be, and shall be deemed always to have been, competent in an assignation under this section to impose conditions and make stipulations which, upon the recording of such assignation or the registration under the Land Registration (Scotland) Act 1979 of the assignee's interest, shall be as effectual against any singular successor of the assignee in the subjects assigned as if such assignee had been a grantee of the lease and it had been duly recorded or, as the case may be, the grantee's interest had been so registered.

(3) Nothing in subsection (2) above makes effectual against any successor of the assignee any obligation of periodical payment other than a payment—
(a) of rent or of an apportionment of rent;
(b) in defrayal of a contribution towards some continuing cost related to the lands and heritages subject to the lease assigned; or
(c) under a heritable security.

(4) A provision in an assignation which purports to make effectual against any successor of the assignee any obligation of periodic payment other than one specified in paragraphs (a) to (c) of subsection (3) above shall not render the deed void or unenforceable, but the assignation shall have, and shall be deemed always to have had, effect only to the extent (if any) that it would have had effect if it had not imposed such obligation.

(5) Section 32 of the Conveyancing (Scotland) Act 1874 (which enables reservations, conditions, covenants etc. affecting lands to be effectually imported into one deed by reference to another) and section 17 of the Land Registration (Scotland) Act 1979 (which provides that certain obligations in deeds of conditions shall become real obligations upon the recording of the deed or registration of the obligation) shall, with the necessary modifications, respectively apply for the purposes of enabling conditions and stipulations to be effectually imported into any assignation under this section and enabling land obligations in a deed of conditions relating to the land subject to the assignation to become real obligations affecting the land.

In this subsection "land obligation" has the meaning assigned to it by section 1(2) of the Conveyancing and Feudal Reform (Scotland) Act 1970. [8]

NOTES to section 3

Amendments: Section 3 renumbered as sub-s 1 of that section by Law Reform (Miscellaneous Provisions) (Scotland) Act 1985 (c 73), s 3; sub-ss (2) to (5): added by *Ibid.*

4. Assignations in security.

It shall be lawful for the party in right of any such lease recorded as aforesaid, and whose right thereto is recorded in terms of this Act, but in accordance always with the conditions and stipulations of such lease, and not otherwise, to assign the same, in whole or in part, in security for the payment of borrowed money, or of annuities, or of provisions to wives or children, or in security of cash credits or other legal debt or obligation, in the form as near as may be of the Schedule (B) to this Act annexed; and the recording of such assignation in security shall complete the right thereunder; and such assignation in security so recorded shall constitute a real security over such lease to the extent assigned. [9]

NOTES to section 4

Section 4 excluded by Conveyancing and Feudal Reform (Scotland) Act 1970 (c 35), s 32, Sch 8, para 2.

5. Where party presenting for registration not original lessee or assignee.

Where the party in right of any such lease or assignation in security as aforesaid is not the original lessee in such lease, or the original assignee in such assignation in security, he shall, before presenting such lease or assignation in security for registration, expede an instrument, under the hand of a notary public, in the form as nearly as may be of the Schedule (C) to this Act annexed; and the keeper of the register, on such notarial instrument being produced to him, but not otherwise, shall thereupon record such lease or assignation in security, together with the said instrument. [10]

NOTES to section 5

Section 5 excluded by Conveyancing and Feudal Reform (Scotland) Act 1970 (c 35), s 2, Sch 8, para 3.

6. Translation of assignations in security. Creditor's entry to possession in default of payment.

All such assignations in security as aforesaid shall, when recorded, be transferable, in whole or in part, by translation, in the form as nearly as may be of the Schedule (D) to this Act annexed; and the recording of such translation shall fully and effectually vest the party in whose favour it was granted with the right of the granter thereof in such assignation in security to the extent assigned; and the creditor or party in right of such assignation in security, without prejudice to the exercise of any power of sale therein contained, shall be entitled, in default of payment of the capital sum for which such assignation in security has been granted, or of a term's interest thereof, or of a term's annuity, for six months after such capital sum or term's interest or annuity shall have fallen due, to apply to the sheriff for a warrant to enter on possession of the lands and heritages leased; and the sheriff, after intimation to the lessee for the time being, to the landlord, shall, if he see cause, grant such warrant, which shall be a sufficient title for such creditor or party to enter into possession of such lands and heritages, and to uplift the rents from any sub-tenants therein, and to sub-let the same, as freely and to the like effect as the lessee might have done: Provided always, that no such creditor or party, unless and until he enter into possession as aforesaid, shall be personally liable to the landlord in any of the obligations and prestations of the lease. [11]

NOTES to section 6

Section 6 excluded by Conveyancing and Feudal Reform (Scotland) Act 1970 (c 35), s 32, Sch 8, para 4. Section 6 (in part) is not affected by s 29(2) of the Land Registration (Scotland) Act 1979 (c 33), by virtue of s 29(3) of that Act.

7. ...

NOTES to section 7
Repealed with Saving by Succession (Scotland) Act 1964 (c 41), s 34(2), Sch 3.

8. Heir or disponee may complete title by recording notarial instrument.

It shall be competent to the heir . . ., or to the general disponee of any party who shall have died fully vested in right of any such lease or assignation in security, recorded as aforesaid, to expede a notarial instrument in the form as nearly as may be of the Schedule (F) to this Act annexed; and the recording of such instrument in the register in which such lease is recorded shall complete the title of such heir or disponee to such lease or assignation in security. [12]

NOTES to section 8
Words repealed with Saving by Statute Law Revision Act 1892 (c 19) and Succession (Scotland) Act 1964 (c 41), s 34(2), Sch 3.

9. Where assignee has died without recording assignation, mode of making up title.

Where any assignation, assignation in security, or translation granted in pursuance of this Act shall not have been registered as aforesaid in the lifetime of the grantee in such writ respectively, it shall be competent to the heir or general disponee of such grantee to make up his title by expeding an instrument under the hand of a notary public in the form, as nearly as may be, of the Schedule (F) to this Act annexed; and the keeper of the register, on such notarial instrument being presented to him, but not otherwise, shall thereupon record such assignation, assignation in security, or translation, together with the said instrument. [13]

NOTES to section 9
Amendment: Amended by Succession (Scotland) Act 1964 (c 41), s 34(1), Sch 2, para 5.

10. Adjudgers to complete right by recording abbreviate.

When an adjudication of any such lease of assignation in security recorded as aforesaid shall have been obtained against the party vested in the right thereof respectively, or against the heir of such party, the recording of the abbreviate of adjudication in the register in which the lease is recorded shall complete the right of the adjudger to such lease or assignation in security. [14]

11. Trustees on sequestrated estate may be entered on register.

It shall be lawful for the trustee on the sequestrated estate of any party in right of any such lease or assignation in security as aforesaid to expede a notarial instrument in the form as nearly as may be of the Schedule (F) to this Act annexed; and the recording of such instrument in the register in which such lease is recorded shall complete the right of such trustee to such lease or assignation in security. [15]

12. Preferences regulated by date of recording transfer.

All such leases executed after the passing of this Act, and all assignations, assignations in security of any such lease recorded as aforesaid, and translations thereof, and all adjudications of such leases recorded as aforesaid, or assignations in security, shall in competition be preferable according to their dates of recording. [16]

NOTES to section 12
Section 12 is not affected by s 29(2) of the Land Registration (Scotland) Act 1979 (c 33), by virtue of s 29(3) of that Act.

13. Renunciations and discharges to be recorded.

On the production to the keeper of the register of a renunciation of any such lease as aforesaid recorded therein, or of a discharge of any such assignation in security as aforesaid therein recorded, by or on behalf of the party appearing on the register as in right of such lease or assignation in security, which renunciation or discharge may be in the form of the Schedules (G) and (H) respectively to this Act annexed, and may be endorsed on such lease or assignation in security, he shall forthwith duly record the same.
[17]

NOTES to section 13

Amendments: Amended by Conveyancing (Scotland) Act 1924 (c 27), s 24(5); excluded by Conveyancing and Feudal Reform (Scotland) Act 1970 (c 35), s 32, Sch 8, para 5.

---

14. Entry of decree of reduction.

On the production to any such keeper of an extract of a decree of reduction of any such lease, assignation, assignation in security, translation, adjudication, instrument, discharge, or renunciation recorded in the register of which he is the keeper, he shall forthwith duly record the same. [18]

15. Mode of registering
Extracts to make faith as writs registered.

Leases, assignations, assignations in security, translations, adjudications, instruments, discharges, renunciations, and other writs, duly presented for registration in pursuance of this Act, shall be forthwith shortly entered in the minute book of the register in common form, and shall, with all due despatch, be fully registered in the register book, and thereafter re-delivered to the parties, with certificates of due registration thereon, which shall be probative of such registration, such certificates specifying the date of presentation, and the book and folio in which the engrossment has been made, . . . and the date of entry in the minute book shall be held to be the date of registration; . . .
[19]

NOTES to section 15

Amendments: Words repealed by Conveyancing and Feudal Reform (Scotland) Act 1970, Sch 11, Pt III; words repealed by Statute Law (Repeals) Act 1976, s 1, Sch 1.
General: Section 15 is not affected by s 29(2) of the Land Registration (Scotland) Act 1979 (c 33), by virtue of s 29(3) of that Act.

[16. Registration equivalent to possession.

(1) The registration of all such leases, assignations, assignations in security, translations, adjudications, writs of acknowledgment, and notarial instruments as aforesaid, in manner herein provided, shall complete the right under the same respectively, to the effect of establishing a preference in virtue thereof, as effectually as if the grantee, or party in his right, had entered into the actual possession of the subjects leased under such writs respectively at the date of registration thereof.]

[(2) The registration of any such lease or other writ as aforesaid, in manner herein provided, on or after 1st September 1974, shall, without prejudice to the foregoing provisions of this section and to the provisions of section 2 of the Prescription and Limitation (Scotland) Act 1973, complete the right under the same to the effect of establishing in virtue thereof such a preference as aforesaid over the right of any part to any such lease or writ, or of any party in his right, granted after that date and not registered in manner herein provided at the time of the registration of the lease or writ first mentioned.] [20]

NOTES to section 16

Amendments: Section 16 renumbered as sub-s (1) of that section by Land Tenure Reform (Scotland) Act 1974 (c 38), Sch 6, para 3; s 16(2) added by *Ibid*.

General: Section 16 is not affected by s 29(2) of the Land Registration (Scotland) Act 1979, by virtue of s 29(3) of that Act.

17. Leases, with obligation to renew, registerable.

Leases containing an obligation upon the granter to renew the same from time to time at fixed periods, or upon the termination of a life or lives, or otherwise, shall be deemed leases within the meaning of this Act, and registerable as such, provided such leases shall by the terms of such obligation be renewable from time to time so as to endure for a period [exceeding twenty years] **[21]**

NOTES to section 17

Amendment: Words substituted retrospectively by Land Tenure Reform (Scotland) Act 1974 (c 38), Sch 6, para 4.

18. ...

NOTE to section 18

Repealed by Land Tenure Reform (Scotland) Act 1974 (c 38), Sch 6, para 5, Sch 7.

19. Extracts registerable where leases recorded in Court of Session or Sheriff Court Books prior to Act.

Where any such lease as aforesaid registerable under this Act shall, . . ., have been recorded in the books of council and session, or in the books of any sheriff [commissary] or burgh court, the production to the keeper of the register of an extract of such lease shall be a sufficient warrant for him to record the same, and he shall thereupon duly record it, and the recording thereof shall be as valid and effectual as if the original lease had been presented to him. **[22]**

NOTES to section 19

Amendments: Words repealed retrospectively by Land Tenure Reform (Scotland) Act 1974, para 6, Sch 7; word inserted by Registration of Leases (Scotland) Act 1877 (c 36), s 1.

20. Clauses in schedules to be held to import and to have effect as declared by 10 & 11 Vict c 50.

1. The several clauses in the schedules to this Act annexed shall be held to import such and the like meaning and to have such and the like effect as is declared by the Act of the tenth and eleventh of Queen Victoria, chapter fifty, sections second and third, to belong to the corresponding clauses in the Schedule to the said recited Act annexed, and the procedure thereby prescribed for a sale under a bond and disposition in security shall be applicable to a sale of any such lease as aforesaid under any such assignation in security as is herein-before mentioned.

2. The clause of assignation of rents to become due or payable shall be held to import an assignation to rents from and after the term from which interest on the sum in the bond commences to run in the fuller form now generally in use, including therein a power to the creditor, on default in payment, to enter into possession of the lands disponed in security and uplift the rents thereof, subject to accounting to the debtor for any balance of rents actually recovered beyond what is necessary for payment of the creditor; and the clause of assignation of writs shall be held to import an assignation to writs and evidents to the same effect as in the fuller form now in use in a bond and disposition in security with power of sale; and the clause of warrandice shall be held to import absolute warrandice as regards the lands and the title deeds thereof, and warrandice from fact and deed as regards the rents; and the clause consenting to registration for preservation and execution shall import a consent to registration and a procuratory for registration in the books of council and session, or other judge's books competent for preservation, and that letters of horning or six days charge, and all other necessary execution, may pass on a decree to be interponed thereto; and the clause consenting to registration in the general or particular or burgh register of sasines shall entitle the creditor to register the said bond accordingly, either in the general register of sasines, or particular register of sasines, or burgh register of sasines, as the tenure of the lands embraced in the security may require.

3. The clauses reserving right of redemption, and obliging the granter to pay the expences of assigning or discharging the security, and, on default in payment, granting power of sale, shall be in all respects as valid, effectual, and operative as if it had been in such bond and disposition in security specially provided and declared that the lands and others thereby disponed should be redeemable by the granter, his heirs and successors, from the grantee and his heirs and successors, at the term and place of payment, or at any term of Whitsunday or Martinmas thereafter, upon premonition of three months, to be made by the granter or his foresaids to the grantee or his foresaids, personally or at their dwelling places, if within Scotland, and if furth thereof at the time then at the office of the keeper of the record of edictal citations within the general register house, Edinburgh, in presence of a notary public and witnesses, and that by payment to them of the whole principal sum payable under the bond and disposition in security, interest due thereon, and liquidated expences and termly failures corresponding thereto, if incurred, and in case of their absence or refusal to receive the same, by consignation thereof, in one or other of the banks in Scotland, incorporated by Act of Parliament or Royal Charter, having an office or branch at the place of payment, to be made furthcoming on the peril of the consigner, the place of redemption to be within the office of such bank or branch thereof; and as if it had been thereby further provided and declared, that any discharge and renunciation, disposition and assignation, or other deed necessary, to be granted by the grantee and his foresaids, upon the granter or his foresaids making payment and redeeming as aforesaid, and also the recording thereof, should always be at the expence of the granter and his foresaids; and as if it had been thereby further provided and declared that if the granter or his foresaids should fail to make payment of the sums that should be due by the personal obligation contained in the said bond and disposition in security within three months after a demand of payment intimated to the granter or his foresaids, whether of full age or in pupillarity or minority, or although subject to any legal incapacity, personally, or at their dwelling places if within Scotland, or if furth thereof at the office of the keeper of the record of edictal citations above mentioned, by a notary public and witnesses, then and in that case it should be lawful to and in the power of the grantee or his foresaids, immediately after the expiration of the said three months, and without any other intimation or process at law, to sell and dispose, in whole or in lots, of the said lands and others by public roup, at Edinburgh or Glasgow, or at the head burgh of the county within which the said lands and others, or the chief part thereof, are situated, or at the burgh or town sending or contributing to send a member to Parliament, which, whether within or without the county, shall be nearest to such lands, or the chief part thereof, on previous advertisement stating the time and place of sale, and published once weekly for at least six weeks subsequent to the expiry of the said three months, in any newspaper published in Edinburgh, and also in any newspaper published in such county, or if there be no newspaper published in such county, then in any newspaper published in the next or a neighbouring county, the grantee being always bound, upon payment of the price, to hold count and reckoning with the granter or his foresaids for the same, after deduction of the principal sum secured, interest due thereon, and liquidated penalties corresponding to both which may be incurred, and all expences attending the sale, and for that end to enter into articles of roup, grant dispositions, containing all usual and necessary clauses, and in particular a clause binding the granter of the said bond and disposition in security, and his heirs, in absolute warrandice of such dispositions, and obliging him and them to corroborate and confirm the same, and to grant all other deeds and securities requisite and necessary by the laws of Scotland for rendering such sale or

sales effectual, in the same manner and as amply in every respect as the granter could do himself: and as if it had been thereby further provided and declared that the said proceedings should all be valid and effectual whether the debtor in the said bond and disposition in security for the time should be of full age, or in pupillarity or minority, or although subject to any legal incapacity, and that such sale or sales should be equally good to the purchaser or purchasers as if the granter himself had made them, and also that in carrying such sale or sales into execution, it should be lawful to the grantee and his foresaids to prorogate and adjourn the day of sale from time to time as they should think proper, previous advertisement of such adjournment being given in the newspapers above mentioned once weekly for at least three weeks: and as if the granter had bound and obliged himself and his foresaids to ratify, approve of, and confirm any sale or sales that should be made in consequence thereof and to grant absolute and irredeemable dispositions of the lands and others so to be sold to the purchaser or purchasers, their heirs and assignees, and to execute and deliver all others deeds and writings necessary for rendering their rights complete.

★   ★   ★

7. Any sale duly carried through in terms of this Act shall be as valid and effectual to the purchaser as if made by the granter of the security himself, and that whether the granter shall have died before or after such sale, and without the necessity of confirmation by him or his heirs, and notwithstanding that the party debtor in the security and in right of the lands at the time shall be in pupillarity or minority or subject to any legal incapacity: Provided always, that nothing herein contained shall be held to affect or prejudice the obligation of the granter and his heirs to execute, or the right of the creditor or purchaser to require the granter and his heirs to execute, any deed or deeds which, independently of this enactment, would at common law be necessary for rendering the sale effectual, or otherwise completing in due form the titles of such purchaser.

8. The creditor, upon receipt of the price, shall be bound to hold count and reckoning therefor with the debtor and postponed creditor, if any such there be, and their heirs and assignees, or with any other party having interest, and to consign the surplus which may remain after deducting the debt secured, with the interest due thereon and penalties incurred, and whole expences attending such sale, and after paying all previous incumbrances and the expence of discharging the same, in one or other of the said banks, or in a branch of any such bank, in the joint names of the seller and purchaser, for behoof of the party or parties having best right thereto; and the particular bank in which such consignation is to be made shall be specified in the articles of roup.

9. Upon a sale being carried through in terms of this Act, and upon consignation of the surplus of the price, if any be, as aforesaid, the disposition by the creditor to the purchaser shall have the effect of completely disencumbering the lands and others sold of all securities and diligences posterior to the security of such creditor, as well as of the security and diligence of such creditor himself. [23]

NOTES to section 20

The Act 10 & 11 Vict c 50 was repealed by the Titles to Land Consolidation (Scotland) Act 1868 (c 101), s 4. Sections 2, 3 and 7–9 are reproduced here.

21.   Short title.

This Act may be cited for all purposes as 'The Registration of Leases (Scotland) Act 1857.' [24]

SCHEDULES

SCHEDULE (A)

Form of Assignation of Lease

I, *A B*, [*designation*] in consideration of the sum of   now paid to me, [*or otherwise, as the case may be,*] assign to *C D* [*designation*] a lease, dated   , and recorded in the   Register of Sasines at   , of date   , granted by *E F* [*designation*] in my favour [*or if not in assigner's favour, name and design grantee*], of [*shortly mention subjects*] in the parish of   and county of   . . . [but (*where the lease is assigned in part only*) in so far only as regards the following portion of the subjects leased; viz. (*specify particularly the portion*),] with entry as at (*term of entry*). And [*where sub-lease*] I assign the rents from [*term*]; and I grant warrandice; and I bind myself to free and relieve the said *C D* of all rents and burdens due to the landlord or others at and prior to the term of entry in respect of said lease; and I consent to registration for preservation and execution.

[*Testing clause in common form*]

[25]

SCHEDULE (B)

Form of Bond and Assignation in Security

I, *A B*, [*designation*] bind myself, my heirs and executors, without the necessity of discussing them in their order, to make payment, at the term of [*date and place of payment*], to *C D* [*designations*] or his heirs, executors, or assignees, of the sum of   , being money borrowed by me from him, [*or as a provision to the said C D, or of the yearly annuity of   during his lifetime, as the case may be,*] with the interest of the said capital sum at the rate of   per cent. per annum, payable by equal portions half-yearly at Whitsunday and Martinmas, beginning the first payment at   . And, in security of the personal obligation before written, I assign to the said *C D* and his foresaids, heritably but redeemably, as after mentioned, yet irredeemably in the event of a sale by virtue hereof, a lease of [*shortly mention subjects leased*] in the parish of   and county of   , which lease was granted by *E F*, [*designation,*] of date   , and recorded [*insert register, with date of recording*], . . .; [but (*where only a portion of the subjects are assigned*) in so far only as regards the following portion of the subjects leased; viz (*specify particularly the portion*)]. And I assign the rents; and I assign the writs; and I grant warrandice; and I reserve power of redemption; and I oblige myself and my foresaids for the expenses of assigning and discharging this security; and, on default of payment, I grant power of sale; and I consent to registration for preservation and execution. [26]

NOTE to Schedule B

Words repealed by Conveyancing and Feudal Reform (Scotland) Act 1970 (c 35), s 47, Sch 11, Pt I.

SCHEDULE (C)

Forms of Notarial Instruments in favour of a Party not the original Grantee.

No 1. *Case of Lease*

Be it known, that by lease, dated   , *A B* [*designation*] let to *C D* [*designation*] that piece of ground [*or as the case may be, shortly describing the property leased*] in the parish of   and county of   , to which lease *E F* [*designation*] has made up title by service as eldest son [*or as the case may be*] and heir of the said *C D*, dated [*insert date of service*] before the [*specify the*] *court by which confirmation has been granted*], [*or, as the case may be*, as general disponee or assignee of the said *C D* in virtue of (*here mention the writs or decreets instructing the right, with the dates thereof, and, if recorded the register and date of recording*)★]: Wherefore this instrument is taken by the said *E F* in the hands of *G H* [*designation of notary public*], in terms of the Registration of Leases (Scotland) Act 1857.

[*Testing clause*]

No 2. *Case of Assignation in Security*

Be it known, that by bond and assignation in security of date   , *C D* [*designation*] assigned to *J K* [*designation*], in security of a sum of   [*or as the case may be*], a lease granted by *A B* [*designation*] of [*shortly describe the subjects leased*], in the parish of   , and county of   , which lease is dated   , and recorded [*register, and date of recording*], to which assignation in security *E F* [*designation*] has acquired right as eldest son [*or as the case may be*] and heir of the said *J K*, &c [*as in Form No 1*].

★*Note*—If the person in whose favour the instrument is taken is not the heir or disponee of the original grantee, but of one who has acquired right to the lease or assignation in security, here specify shortly the series of titles by which the predecessor acquired the right.

NOTE to Schedule C

Amended by Succession (Scotland) Act 1964 (c 41), s 34(1), Sch 2, paras 5 and 6.

SCHEDULE (D)

Form of Translation of Assignation in Security

I, *A B*, [*designation*] in consideration of the sum of   now paid to me [*or as the case may be,*] assign and transfer to *C D* [*designation*] a bond and assignation in security for the principal sum of   [*or as the case my be*], granted by *E F* [*designation*] in my favour, [*or, if not in granter's favour, name and design the party in whose favour granted,*] dated   and recorded [*register and date of recording*] of and over a lease granted by *G H* [*designation*] of [*shortly describe subjects leased*], in the parish of   , and county of   , which lease is dated   , and is recorded in the said register of date   ..., [but (*where the translation is partial*) only to the extent of (*insert sum*), and to the effect of giving pari passu preference to the said *C D* over the said lease with me, my heirs and assigns, as regards the remainder of the said principal sum and corresponding interest], with the interest from [*date*].

[*Testing clause*]

NOTE to Schedule D

Words repealed by Conveyancing and Feudal Reform (Scotland) Act 1970 (c 35), s 47, Sch 11, Pt I. Schedule D is not affected by s 29(2) of the Land Registration (Scotland) Act 1979, by virtue of s 29(3) of that Act.

SCHEDULE (E)

* * *

NOTES to Schedule E
Repealed with Saving by Succession (Scotland) Act 1964 (c 41), s 34(2), Sch 3.

SCHEDULE (F)
Sch (F) amended by Succession (Scotland) Act 1964 (c 41), s 34(1), Sch 2 para 5

FORM OF NOTARIAL INSTRUMENT IN FAVOUR OF HEIR IN RECORDED LEASE OR ASSIGNATION IN SECURITY, OR OF TRUSTEE ON SEQUESTRATED ESTATE.

No 1. *Case of Lease*

Be it known, that by lease dated   , A B [*designation*] let to C D [*designation*] that piece of ground [*or as the case may be, shortly describing the property leased,*] in the parish of   and county of   , which lease is recorded [*register, and date of recording*], and to which E F [*designation*] has made up title by service as [*specify relationship*], and heir of the said C D, dated the [*insert date of service*], before the [*specify the [court by which confirmation has been granted]*] . . ., [*or, as the case may be,* as general disponee of the said C D, *or* as heir (*or* general disponee) of L M in an assignation by the said C D of date   , *or* as trustee confirmed on the sequestrated estate of the said C D, in virtue of (*here mention the writs or decreets, instructing the rights, with the dates thereof, and, if recorded, the register, and date of recording.*)] Whereupon this instrument is taken by the said E F, in the hands of G H [*designation of notary public*], in terms of the Registration of Leases (Scotland) Act, 1857.

[*Testing clause*]

No 2. *Case of Assignation in Security*

Be it known, that by bond and assignation in security, of date C D [*designation*] assigned to I K [*designation*] in security of a sum of   [*or as the case may be,*] a lease granted by A B [*designation*] of [*shortly describe the subjects leased*] in the parish of   and county of   , dated   , and recorded [*register and date of recording*], to which bond and assignation in security E F [*designation*] has acquired right as [*specify relationship*], and heir of the said I K, &c [*as in Form* No 1]. [29]

NOTES to Schedule F
Amendments: Amended by Succession (Scotland) Act 1964 (c 41), s 34(1), Sch 2, paras 5 and 7; words repealed by Statute Law Revision Act 1892 (c 19).

SCHEDULE (G)

RENUNICATION OF LEASE

I, A B [*designation,*] renounce as from the term of   in favour of C D [*designation*] a lease granted by the said C D [*or as the case may be*] of [*shortly set forth subjects*] in the parish of   and county of   , which lease is dated   and recorded [*register, and date of recording,*] . . ..

[*Testing clause*] [30]

NOTES to Schedule G
Amendments: Amended by Conveyancing (Scotland) Act 1924 (c 27), s 24(5); Words repealed by Conveyancing and Feudal Reform (Scotland) Act 1970 (c 35), s 47, Sch 11, Pt I.

SCHEDULE (H)

FORM OF DISCHARGE OF BOND AND ASSIGNATION IN SECURITY

I, *A B* [*designation,*] in consideration of the sum of   now paid to me by *C D* [*designation,*] discharge a bond and assignation in security for the sum of   , granted by the said *C D* in my favour [*or as the case may be*], and which is dated   and recorded in the [*register, and date of recording*]; and I declare to be disburdened thereof a lease granted by *E F* [*designation*] of [*shortly mention subjects leased*] in the parish of   and county of   which lease is dated   and recorded [*register, and date of recording*].

[*Testing clause*]   [31]

NOTES to Schedule H

Words substituted by Conveyancing and Feudal Reform (Scotland) Act 1970 (c 35), s 47, Sch 10, para 1.

Removal Terms (Scotland) Act 1886

(c 50)

ARRANGEMENT OF SECTIONS

1	Short title and extent	[32]

★ ★ ★

3	Definitions	[33]
4	Terms of entry and removal from houses	[34]
5	Period of notice of removal in certain cases	[35]
6	Notice of removal by registered letter	[36]

An Act to amend the Law relating to the Terms of Removal from Houses in Scotland. [25th June 1886]

Whereas in many counties and burghs in Scotland a custom exists whereby for the purpose of a tenant's entry to or removal from a house a period beyond the date of the legal term of entry or removal is allowed within which such entry or removal may take place:

And whereas the period so allowed is not uniform but varies according to local usage:

And whereas such want of uniformity is productive of great inconvenience, and it is expedient that the terms for such entry and removal should be uniform:

1. Short title and extent.

This Act may be cited as the Removal Terms (Scotland) Act, 1886, and shall extend to Scotland only.   [32]

2. . . .

NOTE to section 2

Repealed by Statute Law Revision Act 1898 (c 22).

3. Definitions

In this Act the following expressions shall have the following meanings:

'House' shall mean a dwelling-house, shop, or other building and their appurtenances, and shall include a dwelling-house or building let along with land for agricultural or other purposes:

'Burgh' shall mean royal burgh, parliamentary burgh, or any populous place, the boundaries whereof have been fixed and ascertained under the General Police and Improvement (Scotland) Act, 1862, and subsequent Acts:

'Lease' shall include tack and set, and shall apply to any lease, tack, or set, whether constituted by writing or verbally, or by tacit relocation, and of whatever duration:

'Tenant' shall mean a tenant under any lease as defined by this Act: and

'Person' shall mean any person or individual, and shall apply to and include companies and corporations. [33]

4. Terms of entry and removal from houses.

Where under any lease entered into after the passing of this Act, the terms for a tenant's entry to, or removal from, a house shall be one or other of the terms of Whit Sunday or Martinmas, the tenant shall, in the absence of express stipulation to the contrary, enter to, or remove from, the said house (any custom or usage to the contrary notwithstanding) at noon on the twenty-eighth day of May, if the term be Whit Sunday, or at noon on the twenty-eighth day of November, if the term be Martinmas, or on the following day at the same hour, where the said terms fall on a Sunday.

Notwithstanding anything in this Act contained, in all cases in which warning is required forty days before a Whit Sunday or Martinmas term of removal, such warning shall be given forty days before the fifteenth day of May and the eleventh day of November respectively. [34]

NOTES to section 4

Amendment: Amended by House Letting and Rating (Scotland) Act 1911 (c 53), ss 1, 3, 11, 12.

5. Period of notice of removal in certain cases.

Where a house, other than a dwelling-house or building let along with land for agricultural purposes, is let for any period not exceeding four calendar months, notice of removal therefrom shall, in the absence of express stipulation, be given as many days before the date of ish as shall be equivalent to at least one-third of the full period of duration of the lease.

[Provided that in no case shall notice of removal be given less than 28 days before the date on which it is to take effect.] [35]

NOTES to section 5

Amendment: Words added by Rent (Scotland) Act 1971 (c 28), s 135(2), Sch 18, Pt II.

6. Notice of removal by registered letter.

Notice of removal from a house, other than a dwelling-house or building let along with land for agricultural purposes, may hereafter be given by registered letter, signed by the person entitled to give such notice, or by the law agent or factor of such person, posted at any post office within the United Kingdom, in time to admit of its being delivered at the address thereon, on or prior to the last date upon which by law such notice of removal must be given, addressed to the person entitled to receive such notice, and bearing the particular address of such person at the time, if the same be known, or, if the same be not known, then the last known address of such person. [36]

NOTES to section 6

Applied by Agricultural Holdings (Scotland) Act 1949 (c 75), s 24(4).

…

Sheriff Courts (Scotland) Act 1907

(c 51)

ARRANGEMENT OF SECTIONS

* * *

Removings

34	Removings	[37]
35	Letter of removal	[38]
36	Notice to remove	[39]
37	Notice of termination of tenancy	[40]

Summary Removings

38	Summary removing	[41]
38A	Notice of termination in respect of dwelling-houses	[42]

Procedure Rules

39	Procedure rules	[43]
40	Court of Session to regulate fees, &c	[44]

* * *

Schedule

Rules for regulating Procedure in the Ordinary Court . . . . [45–64]

Removings

34. Removings.

Where lands exceeding two acres in extent are held under a probative lease specifying a term of endurance, and whether such lease contains an obligation upon the tenant to remove without warning or not, such lease, or an extract thereof from the books of any court of record, shall have the same force and effect as an extract decree of removing obtained in an ordinary action at the instance of the lessor, or any one in his right, against the lessee or any party in possession, and such lease or extract shall, along with authority in writing signed by the lessor or any one in his right or by his factor or law agent, be sufficient warrant to any sheriff officer or messenger-at-arms of the sheriffdom within which such lands or heritages are situated to eject such party in possession, his family, sub-tenants, cottars, and dependants, with their goods, gear and effects, at the expiry of the term or terms of endurance of the lease: Provided that previous notice in writing to remove shall have been given—
  (a) When the lease is for three years and upwards not less than one year and not more than two years before the termination of the lease; and
  (b) In the case of leases from year to year (including lands occupied by tacit relocation) or for any other period less than three years, not less than six months before the termination of the lease (or where there is a separate ish as regards land and houses or otherwise before that ish which is first in date):
    Provided that if such written notice as aforesaid shall not be given the lease shall

be held to be renewed by tacit relocation for another year, and thereafter from year to year: Provided further that nothing contained in this section shall affect the right of the landlord to remove a tenant who has been sequestrated under the Bankruptcy (Scotland) Act 1913, or against whom a decree of cessio has been pronounced under the Debtors (Scotland) Act 1880, or who by failure to pay rent has incurred any irritancy of his lease or other liability to removal: Provided further that removal or ejectment in virtue of this section shall not be competent after six weeks from the date of the ish last in date: Provided further that nothing herein contained shall be construed to prevent proceedings under any lease in common form; and that the foregoing provisions as to notice shall not apply to any stipulations in a lease entitling the landlord to resume land for building, planting, feuing, or other purposes or to subjects let for any period less than a year. [37]

NOTES to section 34

The reference to the Bankruptcy (Scotland) Act 1913 (c 20) should be construed as a reference to the Bankruptcy (Scotland) Act 1985 (c 66); Interpretation Act 1889 (c 63), s 38(1) and Bankruptcy (Scotland) Act 1985, s 75(10).

35. Letter of removal.

Where any tenant in possession of any lands exceeding two acres in extent (whether with or without a written lease) shall, either at the date of entering upon the lease or at any other time, have granted a letter of removal, either holograph or attested by one witness, such letter of removal shall have the same force and effect as an extract decree of removing, and shall be a sufficient warrant for ejection to the like effect as is provided in regard to a lease or extract thereof, and shall be operative against the granter of such letter of removal or any party in his right within the same time and in the same manner after the like previous notice to remove: Provided always that where such letter is dated and signed within twelve months before the date of removal or before the first ish, if there be more than one ish, it shall not be necessary that any notice of any kind shall be given by either party to the other. [38]

36. Notice to remove.

Where lands exceeding two acres in extent are occupied by a tenant without any written lease, and the tenant has given to the proprietor or his agent no letter of removal, the lease shall terminate on written notice being given to the tenant by or on behalf of the proprietor, or to the proprietor by or on behalf of the tenant not less than six months before the determination of the tenancy, and such notice shall entitle the proprietor, in the event of the tenant failing to remove, to apply for and obtain a summary warrant of ejection against the tenant and everyone deriving right from him. [39]

37. Notice of termination of tenancy.

In all cases where houses, with or without land attached, not exceeding two acres in extent, lands not exceeding two acres in extent let without houses, mills, fishings, shootings, and all other heritable subjects (excepting land exceeding two acres in extent) are let for a year or more, notice of termination of tenancy shall be given in writing to the tenant by or on behalf of the proprietor or to the proprietor by or on behalf of the tenant: Provided always that notice under this section shall not warrant summary ejection from the subjects let to a tenant, but such notice, whether given to or by or on behalf of the tenant, shall entitle the proprietor to apply to the sheriff for a warrant for summary ejection in common form against the tenant and every one deriving right from him: Provided further that the notice provided for by this section shall be given at least forty days before the fifteenth day of May when the termination of the tenancy is the term of Whitsunday, and at least forty days before the eleventh day of November when the termination of the tenancy is the term of Martinmas. [40]

SUMMARY REMOVINGS

38. Summary Removing.

Where houses or other heritable subjects are let for a shorter period than a year, any person by law authorised may present to the sheriff a summary application for removing, and a decree pronounced in such summary cause shall have the full force and effect of a decree of removing and warrant of ejection. Where such a let is for a period not exceeding four months, notice of removal therefrom shall, in the absence of express stipulation, be given as many days before the ish as shall be equivalent to at least one-third of the full period of the duration of the let; and where the let exceeds four months, notice of removal shall, in the absence of express stipulation be given at least forty days before the expiry of the said period.

[Provided that in no case shall notice of removal be given less than 28 days before the date on which it is to take effect.] [41]

NOTES to section 38

Words added by Rent (Scotland) Act 1971 (c 28), s 135(3), Sch 18, Pt II.

[38A. Notice of termination in respect of dwelling-houses.

Any notice of termination of tenancy or notice of removal given under section 37 or 38 above in respect of a dwelling-house, on or after 2nd December 1974, shall be in writing and shall contain such information as may be prescribed by virtue of section 112 of the Rent (Scotland) Act 1984, and Rule 112 of Schedule 1 to this Act shall no longer apply to any such notice under section 37 above.] [42]

NOTES to section 38A

Section originally added by Housing Act 1974 (c 44), Sch 13, para 1. New s 38A substituted by Housing (Scotland) Act 1987 (c 26), s 339, Sch 23, para 4.

PROCEDURE RULES

39. Procedure rules.

Subject to the provisions of any Act of Parliament in force after the passing of this Act, the procedure in all civil causes shall be conform to the rules of procedure set forth in the First Schedule hereto annexed. Such rules shall be construed and have effect as part of this Act. [43]

40. Court of Session to regulate fees, &c.

The Court of Session may from time to time, by Act of Sederunt, make such regulations, . . . for regulating the fees of . . . officers, shorthand writers, and others, and, with the concurrence of the Treasury, for regulating the fees of courts; . . . Provided . . . that every such Act of Sederunt shall, within one week from the date thereof, be transmitted by the Lord President of the Court of Session to the [Secretary of State], in order that it may be laid before the Houses of Parliament; and, if either of the Houses of Parliament shall within thirty-six days after it has been laid before them resolve that the whole or any part of such Act of Sederunt ought not to continue in force, the whole or such part thereof as shall be included in such resolution shall from and after the date of the passing of such resolution cease to be binding. [44]

41–49. . . .

NOTES to section 40

Section 40 was amended by the Divorce, Jurisdiction, Court Fees and Legal Aid (Scotland) Act 1983 (c 12), s 6(1), Sch 1, para 7, s 6(2), Sch 2, and by the Law Reform (Miscellaneous Provisions) (Scotland) Act 1990 (c 40), s 74, Sch 9.

FIRST SCHEDULE

ARRANGEMENT OF ORDINARY CAUSE RULES

* * *

Particular Procedures

Sequestration for Rent

Rule
99	Actions craving payment of rent	[45]
100	Warrant to inventory and secure	[46]
101	Sale of effects	[47]
102	Care of effects	[48]

Removing

103	Action of removing where fixed term of removal	[49]
104	Form of notice of removal	[50]
105	Form of notice under section 37	[51]
106	Removal notices	[52]
107	Evidence of notice to remove	[53]

* * *

Particular Procedures

SEQUESTRATION FOR RENT

Actions craving payment of rent

99.—(1) In actions for sequestration and sale in respect of non-payment of rent, for recovery, or in security of rent, whether brought before or after the term of payment, payment of rent may be craved and decree for payment of such rent or part thereof when due and payable, may be pronounced and extracted in common form.

[(2) There shall be served on the defender in such actions, along with the initial writ, warrant and citation, a notice in accordance with form H8 as set out in the Appendix to the Schedule.] [45]

Warrant to inventory and secure

100.—(1) In the first deliverance on an initial writ for sequestration for rent the sheriff may sequestrate the effects of the tenant, and grant warrant to inventory and secure them.

(2) All warrants to sequestrate, inventory, sell, eject or relet shall include authority to open shut and lockfast places for the purpose of carrying such warrant into execution. [46]

Sale of effects

101.—(1) The sheriff may order the sequestrated effects to be sold at the sight of an officer of court or other named person.

(2) When a sale follows it shall be reported within 14 days and the pursuer shall lodge with the sheriff clerk the roup rolls or certified copies thereof and a state of debt.

(3) In the interlocutor approving the report of sale, or by separate interlocutor, the sheriff may grant decree against the defender for any balance remaining due. [47]

Care of effects

102. The sheriff may at any stage appoint a fit person to take charge of the sequestrated effects, or may require the tenant to find caution that they shall be made available. **[48]**

REMOVING

Action of removing where fixed term of removal

103.—(1) Subject to section 24 of the Agricultural Holdings (Scotland) Act 1949, (a) an action of removing may be raised at any time, provided the tenant has bound himself to remove by writing, dated and signed within 12 months of the term of removal, or, where there is more than one ish, of the ish first in date to remove.

(2) Subject to the said section 24, when the tenant has not so bound himself an action or removing may be raised at any time, but—
   (a) in the case of a lease of lands exceeding 2 acres in extent for 3 years and upwards, an interval of not less than one year nor more than 2 years shall elapse between the date of notice of removal and the term of removal first in date;
   (b) in the case of a lease of lands exceeding 2 acres in extent, whether written or verbal, held from year to year [or] under tacit relocation, or for any other period less than 3 years, an interval of not less than 6 months shall elapse between the date of notice of removal and the term of removal first in date; and
   (c) in the case of houses let with or without land attached not exceeding 2 acres in extent, as also of land not exceeding 2 acres in extent without houses, as also of mills, fishings, shootings, and all other heritable subjects excepting land exceeding 2 acres in extent, and let for a year or more, 40 days at least shall elapse between the date of notice of removal and the term of removal first in date.

(3) In any defended action of removing the sheriff may order the defender to find caution for violent profits.

(4) In actions of declarator of irritancy and removing by a superior against a vassal, the pursuer shall call as parties the last entered vassal and such heritable creditors and holders of postponed ground burdens as are disclosed by a search for 20 years prior to the raising of the action and the expense of the search shall form part of the pursuer's expenses of process. **[49]**

Form of notice of removal

104. Notices under sections 34, 35 and 36 of the [Act of 1907] shall be as nearly as may be in terms of Form L as set out in the Appendix to this Schedule, and a letter of removal may be in terms of Form M as set out in the Appendix to this Schedule. **[50]**

Form of notice under section 37

105. Notices under section 37 of the [Act of 1907] shall be as nearly as may be in terms of Form N as set out in the Appendix to this Schedule, and such form may be used also for notices to the proprietor by or on behalf of the tenant. **[51]**

Removal notices

106. Removal notices under sections 34, 35, 36, 37 and 38 of the [Act of 1907] may be given by a messenger-at-arms or sheriff officer, or by registered letter signed by the person entitled to give such notice, or by the law agent or factor of such person, posted at any post office within the United Kingdom in time to admit of its being delivered at the address thereon on or prior to the last date upon which by law such notice must be given, addressed to the person entitled to receive such notice, and bearing the particular address of such person at the time if the same be known, or, if the same be not known, then to the last known address of such person. **[52]**

Evidence of notice to remove

107.—(1) A certificate of notice under rule 104 dated and endorsed upon the lease or extract, or upon the letter of removal, and signed by the sheriff officer, messenger-at-arms, or by the person giving the notice, or his law agent, or factor, or an acknowledgement of notice endorsed on the lease or extract of letter of removal by the party in possession or his agent shall be sufficient evidence that notice has been given.

(2) Where there is no lease, a certificate endorsed upon a copy of the notice or letter, certified to be correct, by the person, sheriff officer, messenger-at-arms, law agent, or factor sending the same, which certificate shall be signed by such party sending the notice or letter, shall also be sufficient evidence that notice has been given.

(3) A certificate of notice under rule 105 dated and endorsed upon a copy of the notice or letter signed by the party sending the notice, shall be sufficient evidence that such notice has been given. [53]

Rule 99(2) FORM H8

SEQUESTRATION FOR RENT—NOTICE INFORMING DEFENDER OF RIGHT TO APPLY FOR CERTAIN ORDERS UNDER THE DEBTORS (SCOTLAND) ACT 1987

Where articles are sequestrated for rent you have the right to apply to the sheriff for certain orders under the Debtors (Scotland) Act 1987.

1. You may apply to the sheriff within 14 days from the date articles are sequestrated for an order releasing any article on the ground that—
   (a) it is exempt from sequestration for rent. (Articles which are exempt are listed in section 16 of the Debtors (Scotland) Act 1987); or
   (b) Its inclusion in the sequestration for rent or its subsequent sale is unduly harsh.

2. Where a mobile home, such as a caravan, is your only or principal residence and it has been sequestrated for rent you may apply to the sheriff before a warrant to sell is granted for an order that for a specified period no further steps shall be taken in the sequestration.
Any enquiry relating to the above rights should be made to a solicitor, Citizens Advice Bureau or other local advice centre or to the sheriff clerk at (*address*). [54]

Rule 104 FORM L

NOTICE OF REMOVAL

To (*name, designation, and address of party in possession*).

You are required to remove from (*describe subjects*) at the term of (*or if different terms, state them and the subjects to which they apply*), in terms of lease (*describe it*) or (*in terms of your letter of removal of date*   ) or (*otherwise as case may be*). [55]

Rule 104 FORM M

LETTER OF REMOVAL

To (*name and designation of addressee*).
              (*Place and date*) I am to remove from (*state subjects by usual name of short description sufficient for identification*) at the term of
                               KL (*add designation and address*).

Sheriff Courts (Scotland) Act 1907 (c 51), s 107

If not holograph to be attested thus—

MN (*add designation and address*), witness.

Rule 105   FORM N

NOTICE OF REMOVAL UNDER S 37 of [1907] ACT

To KL (*designation and address*).

You are required to remove from (   ) that portion of ground (*describe it*); or the mill of (*describe it*); or the shootings of the lands and estate of (*describe them*); or (*other subjects to which this notice is applicable*), at the term of Whitsunday (*insert year*) (*or Martinmas, as the case may be, inserting after the year the words, being the 15th day of May, or the 11th day of November, or the 28th day of May, or the 28th day of November, as the case may be*).

NOTES to Schedule

The first Schedule was substituted by the Act of Sederunt (Ordinary Cause Rules, Sheriff Court) 1983, SI 1983/747. Rule 99 was subsequently amended by the Act of Sederunt (Amendment of Sheriff Court Ordinary Causes, and Summary Cause Rules) 1988, SI 1988/1978. Form H8 was added by *Ibid*. Rules 103–106 were subsequently amended by the Act of Sederunt (Ordinary Cause Rules Amendment) 1983, SI 1983/1546. Rules 103–107 apply to Summary Causes by virtue of the Act of Sederunt (Summary Cause Rules, Sheriff Court) 1976, para 3.

★ ★ ★

Tenancy of Shops Act 1949

(c 25)

An Act to make provision with regard to tenancies of shops in Scotland.

[29th March 1949]

1. Provision for renewal of tenancies of shops.

(1) If the landlord of any premises consisting of a shop and occupied by a tenant gives or has given to the tenant notice of termination of tenancy taking effect after the passing of this Act, and the tenant is unable to obtain a renewal of his tenancy on terms that are satisfactory to him, he may, at any time before the notice takes effect and not later than the expiry of twenty-one days after the service of the notice or after the passing of this Act, whichever is the later, apply to the sheriff for a renewal of his tenancy.

(2) On any application under the foregoing subsection the sheriff may, subject as hereinafter provided, determine that the tenancy shall be renewed for such period, not exceeding one year, at such rent, and on such terms and conditions as he shall, in all the circumstances, think reasonable, and thereafter the parties shall be deemed to have entered into a new lease of the premises for that period, at that rent and on those terms and conditions.

(3) Notwithstanding anything in the last foregoing subsection, the sheriff may, if in all the circumstances he thinks it reasonable to do so, dismiss any application under this section, and shall not determine that a tenancy shall be renewed, if he is satisfied—

    (a) that the tenant is in breach of any condition of his tenancy which in the opinion of the sheriff is material; or

    (b) that the tenant is notour bankrupt or is divested of his estate by virtue of a trust deed for behoof of creditors, or, being a company, is unable to pay its debts; or

    (c) that the landlord has offered to sell the premises to the tenant at such price as may, failing agreement, be fixed by a single arbiter agreed on by the parties or appointed, failing such agreement, by the sheriff; or

(d) that the landlord has offered to afford to the tenant, on terms and conditions which in the opinion of the sheriff are reasonable, alternative accommodation which, in the opinion of the sheriff, is suitable for the purposes of the business carried on by the tenant in the premises; or

(e) that the tenant has given notice of termination of tenancy and in consequence of that notice the landlord has contracted to sell or let the premises or has taken any other steps as a result of which he would in the opinion of the sheriff be seriously prejudiced if he could not obtain possession of the premises; or

(f) that, having regard to all the circumstances of the case, greater hardship would be caused by determining that the tenancy shall be renewed than by refusing so to do.

(4) Where a tenancy has been renewed under subsection (2) of this section, the tenant shall have the like right to apply for further renewals as if the tenancy has been renewed by agreement between the landlord and the tenant, and accordingly the foregoing provisions of this section shall, with any necessary modifications, apply to a tenancy which has been renewed under the said subsection (2) or under this subsection.

(5) If on any application under this section the sheriff is satisfied that it will not be possible to dispose finally of the application before the notice of termination of tenancy takes effect, he may make an interim order authorising the tenant to continue in occupation of the premises at such rent, for such period (which shall not exceed three months) and on such terms and conditions as the sheriff may think fit.

★ ★ ★

[(7) An application under this section shall be made by way of a summary cause within the meaning of the Sheriff Courts (Scotland) Act 1971]. [65]

NOTES to section 1

Section 1(b) repealed by Tenancy of Shops (Scotland) Act 1964 (c 50), s 1(2).
Section 1(7) substituted by Sheriff Courts (Scotland) Act 1971 (c 58), s 47(2), Sch 1, para 3.

2. Application to Crown property.

The foregoing section shall apply to any such premises as are mentioned therein in which the interest of the landlord or tenant belongs to His Majesty in right of the Crown or to a government department or is held on behalf of His Majesty for the purposes of a government department, in like manner as the said section applies to any other such premises. [66]

3. Citations, extent, interpretation and duration.

(1) This Act may be cited as the Tenancy of Shops (Scotland) Act, 1949, and shall extend to Scotland only.

(2) In this Act the expression 'shop' includes any shop within the meaning of the Shops Acts, 1912 to 1936, or any of those Acts.

(3) . . . [67]

NOTES to section 3

Section 3(3) repealed by Tenancy of Shops (Scotland) Act 1964 (c 50), s 1(1).

Long Leases (Scotland) Act 1954
(c 49)

ARRANGEMENT OF SECTIONS

* * *

PART II
EXTENSION AND AMENDMENT OF REGISTRATION OF LEASES (SCOTLAND) ACT 1857

26	Extension of 20 & 21 Vict c 26	[68]
27	Amendment of s 18 of 20 & 21 Vict c 26	[69]

PART III
GENERAL

28	Applications to sheriff	[70]
29	Application to Crown	[71]
30	Construction of references to enactments	[72]
31	Citation, commencement and extent	[73]

* * *

PART II
EXTENSION AND AMENDMENT OF REGISTRATION OF LEASES (SCOTLAND) ACT, 1857

26. Extension of 20 & 21 Vict c 26.

(1) Where a lease registrable under the Registration of Leases (Scotland) Act, 1857, has not been recorded in the Register of Sasines and cannot be found, it shall be lawful to record a copy of such lease in the Register of Sasines under the said Act as if it were the lease if there is endorsed on such copy and recorded therewith a probative declaration signed by the landlord and lessee for the time being and containing—
  (a) a statement that the lease cannot be found and that the copy is a true copy of the lease; and
  (b) the names and designations of the said landlord and lessee (unless such names and designations are set forth in the copy).

(2) Where the landlord fails to sign a declaration as provided in the foregoing subsection within two months after he has been called upon to do so, the lessee may present an application to the sheriff craving him to ordain the landlord to sign the declaration within such period as to the sheriff shall seem reasonable; and, if the landlord fails to sign the declaration as so ordained, the sheriff may make an order dispensing with the signature to the declaration of the landlord and directing the sheriff clerk to sign the declaration on behalf of the landlord.

(3) Where in pursuance of an order made by the sheriff under this section a declaration is signed by the sheriff clerk on behalf of a landlord, such declaration shall have the like force and effect as if it had been signed by such landlord.

(4) Where in pursuance of this section a copy of any lease has been recorded in the Register of Sasines, such lease shall be deemed to have been so recorded on the date of the recording of the said copy. **[68]**

NOTE to section 26

By virtue of the Land Registration (Scotland) Act 1979 (c 33), s 29(2), in relation to any operational area, the reference to the Register of Sasines should be construed as a reference to the Land Register of Scotland, and the references to recording should be construed as references to registration therein.

27. Amendment of s 18 of 20 & 21 Vict c 26.

(1) . . .

(2) A lease recorded in the Register of Sasines under the said Act of 1857 before the commencement of this Act shall not be held to have been invalidly recorded by reason only that the name of the lands of which the subjects let consist or form a part is not set forth in such lease or by reason only that the extent of the land let is not set forth in such lease, if there is set forth in such lease a particular description of the subjects let under the lease or a description by reference of the said subjects in accordance with the provisions of the Conveyancing (Scotland) Act, 1874, and the Conveyancing (Scotland) Act, 1924, . . . [69]

NOTES to section 27
Subsection repealed by Land Tenure Reform (Scotland) Act 1974, (c 38), Sch 6, para 7, Sch 7.
Words repealed by Land Tenure Reform (Scotland) Act 1974, (c 38), Sch 6, para 7, Sch 7.
'The said Act of 1857' means the Registration of Leases (Scotland) Act 1857 (c 26).

PART III
GENERAL

28. Applications to sheriff.

(1) Any dispute arising out of the provisions of this Act shall be referred to the sheriff and determined by him.

(2) The decision of the sheriff in any application made to him under this or any other section of this Act shall be final and not subject to review.

(3) The sheriff may in any such application make such award of expenses as he thinks proper, or may make no award of expenses.

(4) Any such application shall be conducted and disposed of in a summary manner.

(5) In this Act any reference to the sheriff shall, in relation to any lease or sub-lease, be construed as a reference to the sheriff within whose jurisdiction the property let under such lease or sub-lease, or any part of such property, is situated. [70]

29. Application to Crown.

This Act shall, subject to the provisions of section four thereof, apply where there is an interest belonging to Her Majesty in right of the Crown or to a Government department or held on behalf of Her Majesty for the purposes of a Government department in like manner as where no such interest subsists. [71]

30. Construction of references to enactments.

Any reference in this Act to any previous enactment shall, except in so far as the contrary intention appears, be construed as a reference to that enactment as amended, extended or applied by any subsequent enactment, including this Act. [72]

31. Citation, commencement and extent.

(1) This Act may be cited as the Long Leases (Scotland) Act, 1954.

(2) This Act shall come into operation on the first day of September, nineteen hundred and fifty-four.

(3) This Act shall apply to Scotland only. [73]

Cost of Leases Act 1958

(c 52)

An Act to make provision for the incidence of the costs of leases. [23rd July 1958]

1. Costs of leases.

Notwithstanding any custom to the contrary, a party to a lease shall, unless the parties thereto agree otherwise in writing, be under no obligation to pay the whole or any part of any other party's solicitor's costs of the lease. [74]

2. Interpretation.

In this Act—
(a) 'lease' includes an underlease and an agreement for a lease or underlease or for a tenancy or sub-tenancy;
(b) 'costs' includes fees, charges, disbursements (including stamp duty), expenses and remuneration. [75]

3. Short Title.

This Act may be cited as the Cost of Leases Act 1958. [76]

Industrial and Provident Societies Act 1965

(c 12)

ARRANGEMENT OF SECTIONS

Registered societies

1	Societies which may be registered	[77]
2	Registration of society	[78]
3	Registration to effect incorporation of society with limited liability	[79]
4	Existing societies deemed to be registered	[80]

Name and maximum shareholding

5	Name of society	[81]
6	Maximum shareholding in society	[82]

Operations of registered society

7	Carrying on of banking by societies	[83]
8	Society registered in one area carrying on business in another	[84]

Provisions as to rules

9	Acknowledgment of registration of rules	[85]
10	Amendment of registered rules	[86]
11	Rules as to fund for purchase of government securities	[87]
12	Rules of agricultural, horticultural or forestry society	[88]

Industrial and Provident Societies Act 1965 (c 12) [76]

13	Supplementary provisions as to rules	[89]
14	Rules to bind members	[90]
15	Provision of copies of rules	[91]

Cancellation, suspension or refusal of registration of society or rules

16	Cancellation of registration of society	[92]
17	Suspension of registration of society	[93]
18	Appeal from refusal, cancellation or suspension of registration of society or rules	[94]

Membership and special provisions affecting members

19	Bodies corporate as members of society	[95]
20	Members under 21	[96]
21	Advances to members	[97]
22	Remedy for debts from members	[98]
23	Nomination to property in society	[99]
24	Proceedings on death of nominator	[100]
25	Provision for intestacy	[101]
26	Payments in respect of mentally incapable persons	[102]
27	Validity of payment to persons apparently entitled	[103]

Contracts, property, etc, of society

28	Promissory notes and bills of exchange	[104]
29	Contracts	[105]
30	Holding of land	[106]
31	Investments	[107]
32	Proxy voting by societies	[108]
33	Discharge of mortgages in England and Wales	[109]
34	Discharge of securities in Scotland	[110]
35	Receipt on payment of moneys secured to a society	[111]
36	Execution of deeds in Scotland	[112]

Accounts, etc

★ ★ ★

39	Annual returns	[113]
40	Display of latest balance sheet	[114]

Officers, receivers, etc

41	Security by officers	[115]
42	Duty of officers of society to account	[116]
43	Duties of receiver or manager of society's property	[117]

Registers, books, etc

44	Register of members and officers	[118]
45	Restriction on inspection of books	[119]
46	Inspection of books by members, etc	[120]
47	Inspection of books by order of registrar	[121]
48	Production of documents and provision of information for certain purposes	[122]
49	Appointment of inspectors and calling of special meetings	[123]

Amalgamations, transfers of engagements and conversions

50	Amalgamation of socieities .	[124]
51	Transfer of engagements between societies .	[125]
52	Conversion into, amalgamation with, or transfer of engagements to company	[126]
53	Conversion of company into registered society	[127]
54	Saving for rights of creditors	[128]

Dissolution of society

55	Dissolution of registered society .	[129]
56	Power of registrar to petition for winding up	[130]
57	Liability of members in winding up	[131]
58	Instrument of dissolution	[132]

Special restriction on dissolution, etc

59	Restriction on dissolution or cancellation of registration of society .	[133]

Disputes, offences and legal proceedings

60	Decision of disputes	[134]
61	General offences by societies, etc	[135]
62	Offences by societies to be also offences by officers, etc .	[136]
63	Continuing offences .	[137]
64	Punishment of fraud or misappropriation	[138]
65	Penalty for falsification	[139]
66	Institution of proceedings	[140]
67	Recovery of costs, etc .	[141]
68	Service of process	[142]

Miscellaneous and general

69	Remuneration of county court registrars	[143]
70	Fees .	[144]
71	Regulations	[145]
72	Form, deposit and evidence of documents	[146]
73	Registrars, central office, etc	[147]
74	Interpretation—general	[148]
75	Channel Islands .	[149]
76	Northern Ireland societies	[150]
77	Repeals and savings	[151]
78	Short title, extent and commencement .	[152]

SCHEDULES:

Schedule 1—Matters to be provided for in society's rules	[153]
Schedule 2—Form of statement by society carrying on banking	[154]
Schedule 3—Form of receipt on mortgage, heritable security, etc	[157]
Schedule 4—Forms of Bond for Officers of Society	[159]

★ ★ ★

An Act to consolidate certain enactments relating to industrial and provident societies, being those enactments as they apply in Great Britain and the Channel Islands with corrections and improvements made under the Consolidation of Enactments (Procedure) Act 1949. [2nd June 1965]

Registered societies

1. Societies which may be registered.

(1) Subject to sections 2(1) and 7(1) of this Act, a society for carrying on any industry, business or trade (including dealings of any description with land), whether wholesale or retail, may be registered under this Act if—
   (a) it is shown to the satisfaction of the appropriate registrar that one of the conditions specified in subsection (2) of this section is fulfilled; and
   (b) the society's rules contain provision in respect of the matters mentioned in Schedule 1 to this Act; and
   (c) the place which under those rules is to be the society's registered office is situated in Great Britain or the Channel Islands.

(2) The conditions referred to in subsection (1)(a) of this section are—
   (a) that the society is a bona fide co-operative society; or
   (b) that, in view of the fact that the business of the society is being, or is intended to be, conducted for the benefit of the community, there are special reasons why the society should be registered under this Act rather than as a company under the Companies Act [1985].

(3) In this section, the expression 'co-operative society' does not include a society which carries on, or intends to carry on, business with the object of making profits mainly for the payment of interest, dividends or bonuses on money invested or deposited with, or lent to, the society or any other person. [77]

NOTES to section 1

Amendment: Sub-s (2) amended by the Companies Act 1985 (c 9), s 30, Sch 2.
Definition: 'appropriate registrar': see s 73 below:

2. Registration of society.

(1) Subject to subsection (2) of this section—
   (a) no society shall be registered under this Act if the number of the members thereof is less than seven; and
   (b) an application for the registration of a society under this Act shall be signed by seven members and the secretary of the society and shall be sent with two printed copies of the society's rules to the appropriate registrar.

(2) A society whose members consist solely of two or more registered societies may be registered under this Act if the application for registration is signed by two members of the committee and the secretary of each (or, if more than three, of each of any three) of the constituent societies and is accompanied by two printed copies of the registered rules of each of the constituent societies as well as of the rules of the society sought to be registered.

(3) On being satisfied that a society has complied with the provisions of this Act as to registration thereunder, the appropriate registrar shall issue to the society an acknowledgment of registration in the prescribed form which shall be conclusive evidence that the society is duly registered under this Act unless it is proved that the registration of the society has been cancelled or is for the time being suspended. [78]

NOTES to section 2

Amendments: Sub-s (1) was modified in relation to credit unions by the Credit Unions Act 1979 (c 34), s 6; sub-s (3) was modified in relation to credit unions by the Credit Unions Act 1979 (c 34), s 2. The text printed here is the unmodified form.
Definitions: 'appropriate registrar': see s 73 below; 'committee': see s 74 below; 'registered rules': Ibid.

3. Registration to effect incorporation of society with limited liability.

A registered society shall by virtue of its registration be a body corporate by its registered name, by which it may sue and be sued, with perpetual succession and a common seal and with limited liability; and that registration shall vest in the society all property for the time being vested in any person in trust for the society, and all legal proceedings pending by or against the trustees of the society may be brought or continued by or against the society in its registered name. **[79]**

NOTE to section 3
Definitions: 'registered society': see s 74 below; 'property': *Ibid*.

4. Existing societies deemed to be registered.

Any society which at the date immediately before the commencement of this Act was registered or deemed to be registered under the Industrial and Provident Societies Act 1893 (hereafter in this Act referred to as 'the Act of 1893'), being a society whose registered office was at that date in Great Britain or the Channel Islands, shall be deemed to be registered under this Act; and—
   (a)   any acknowledgment of registry of that society issued by virtue of section 5(4), 6 or 7(2) of the Act of 1893 shall be deemed to be an acknowledgment of the registration under this Act of that society and, by virtue of section 9 of this Act, of the rules of the society in force at the date of the acknowledgment;
   (b)   any acknowledgment of registry of an amendment of the society's rules issued by virtue of section 7(2) or 10(3) of the Act of 1893 shall be deemed to be an acknowledgment of the registration of that amendment under this Act;
   (c)   any change of the society's name duly made before the date of commencement of this Act in accordance with section 52 of the Act of 1893 as in force at the time of the change, and any change in the situation of the society's registered office of which notice was duly given before that date under section 11 of that Act, shall be deemed for the purposes of this Act to be a duly registered amendment of the society's rules;
   (d)   any rules of that society which, having been made before 1st January 1894, continued in force immediately before the commencement of this Act by virtue of section 3 of the Act of 1893 shall be deemed to be registered under this Act. **[80]**

Name and maximum shareholding

5. Name of society.

(1) No society shall be registered under this Act under a name which in the opinion of the appropriate registrar is undesirable.

(2) Subject to subsection (5) of this section, the word 'limited' shall be the last word in the name of every society registered under this Act.

(3) A registered society may change its name in the following manner and in that manner only, that is to say—
   (a)   by a resolution for the purpose passed at a general meeting of the society after the giving of such notice as is required by the rules of the society of such a resolution or, if the rules do not make special provision as to notice of such a resolution, after the giving of such notice as is required by the rules of a resolution to amend the rules; and
   (b)   with the approval in writing—
      (i)   in the case of a society registered, and doing business exclusively, in Scotland, of the assistant registrar for Scotland; or
      (ii) in any other case, of the chief registrar.

(4) No change in the name of a registered society shall affect any right or obligation of the society, or of any member thereof, and any pending legal proceedings may be continued by or against the society notwithstanding its new name.

(5) If the appropriate registrar is satisfied that the objects of a society applying for registration under this act or of a registered society are wholly charitable or benevolent, he may register the society by a name which does not contain the word 'limited' or, as the

case may be, permit the society to change its name to one which does not contain that word; but if it subsequently appears to that registrar that the society, whether in consequence of a change in its rules or otherwise, is not being conducted wholly for charitable or benevolent objects, he may direct that the word 'limited' be added as the last word in the name of the society and shall notify the society accordingly.

(6) Every registered society shall cause its registered name to be painted or affixed, and to be kept painted or affixed, in a conspicuous position and in letters easily legible, on the outside of its registered office and every other office or place in which the business of the society is carried on, and shall have that name engraven in legible characters on its seal and mentioned in legible characters—
(a) in all notices, advertisements and other official publications of the society;
(b) in all business letters of the society;
(c) in all bills of exchange, promissory notes, endorsements, cheques, and orders for money or goods, purporting to be signed by or on behalf of the society;
(d) in all bills, invoices, receipts, and letters of credit of the society.

(7) Any officer of a registered society, or any other person acting on such a society's behalf, who—
(a) uses any seal purporting to be a seal of the society which does not have the society's registered name engraven on it in legible characters; or
(b) issues or authorises the issue of any document such as is mentioned in subsection (6)(a) or (d) of this section in which that name is not mentioned in legible characters; or
(c) signs or authorises to be signed on behalf of the society any document such as is mentioned in subsection (6)(c) of this section in which that name is not so mentioned.
shall be liable on summary conviction to a fine not exceeding fifty pounds and, in the case of a conviction by virtue of paragraph (c) of this subsection, shall further be personally liable to the holder of any such document as is referred to in that paragraph for the amount specified in the document unless that amount is duly paid by the society. [81]

NOTES to section 5

Definitions: 'appropriate registrar': see s 73 below; 'assistant registrar': *Ibid*; 'Chief registrar': *Ibid*; 'officer': see s 74 below; 'registered name': *Ibid*; 'registered society': *Ibid*.

6. Maximum shareholding in society

(1) Where a society is, or is to be, registered under this Act, no member thereof other than—
(a) a registered society; or
(b) an authority who acquired the holding by virtue of section [58(2) or 59(2) of the Housing Associations Act 1985]; or
(c) a member who acquired the holding by virtue of paragraph 2 of Part I of the Schedule to the Agricultural Credits Act 1923 at a time when section 2 of that Act applied to the society,
shall have or claim any interest in the shares of the society exceeding [five thousand pounds.]

(2) Where in the case of a society to which section 4 of this Act applies—
(a) immediately before 27th April 1952 the rules of the society provided for the maximum amount of the interest in the shares of the society permitted to be held by a member (other than a registered society) to be two hundred pounds; and
(b) no amendment of the rules of the society has been registered since that date; and
(c) on or after that date and before 22nd July 1961 the society's committee has by a resolution recorded in writing resolved that the said maximum amount shall be a specified amount greater than two hundred pounds but not greater than five hundred pounds,
then, subject to subsection (4) of this section, the registered rules of the society shall have effect subject to that resolution.

(3) Where in the case of a society to which section 4 of this Act applies—
  (a) immediately before 22nd July 1961 the rules of the society provided for the maximum amount aforesaid to be five hundred pounds; and
  (b) no amendment of the society's rules has been registered since that date; and
  (c) on or after that date and before 22nd January 1963 the society's committee has by a resolution recorded in writing resolved that the said maximum amount shall be a specified amount greater than five hundred pounds but not greater than one thousand pounds,
then, subject to subsection (4) of this section, the registered rules of the society shall have effect subject to that resolution.

(4) Where subsection (2) or (3) of this section applies to any society, the society's committee shall not have power to vary or revoke the resolution referred to in that subsection; but upon the registration after the commencement of this Act under section 10 thereof of any amendment of the society's rules the registered rules of the society shall have effect as if the resolution had not been passed, so, however, that this subsection shall not affect any interest in the shares of the society held by a member immediately before the date of that registration. **[82]**

NOTES to section 6
Amendments: In sub-s (1) words substituted by the Industrial and Provident Societies Act 1975 (c 41), s 1(1), and by the Housing (Consequential Provisions) Act 1985, Sch 2.
Definitions: 'registered society': see s 74 below; 'registered rules': *Ibid*; 'committee': *Ibid*.

Operations of registered society

7. Carrying on of banking by societies.

(1) A society which has any withdrawable share capital—
  (a) shall not be registered with the object of carrying on, and
  (b) if a registered society shall not carry on,
the business of banking.

(2) Every registered society which carries on the business of banking shall on the first Monday in February and August in each year make out, and until the next such Monday keep hung up in a conspicuous position in its registered office and in every other office or place of business belonging to the society where the business of banking is carried on, a statement in the form set out in Schedule 2 to this Act or as near thereto as the circumstances admit.

(3) The taking of deposits of not more than [ten pounds] in any one payment and not more than [two hundred and fifty pounds] for any one depositor, payable on not less than two clear days' notice, shall not be treated for the purposes of subsections (1) and (2) of this section as carrying on the business of banking; but no society which takes such deposits shall make any payment of withdrawable capital while any payment due on account of any such deposit is unsatisfied.

(4) Where, in the case of a society to which section 4 of this Act applies, being a society registered under the Act of 1893 before 27th April 1952—
  (a) no amendment of the society's registered rules has been registered since that date; and
  (b) those rules permit the taking of deposits up to, but not in excess of, ten shillings in any one payment and twenty pounds for any one depositor; and
  (c) the society's committee has since that date by a resolution recorded in writing, whether passed before or after the commencement of this Act, resolved that there shall be substituted for the said limits of ten shillings and twenty pounds specified higher limits not exceeding two pounds and fifty pounds respectively,
then, subject to subsection (5) of this section, the society's registered rules shall have effect subject to that resolution.

(5) Where subsection (4) of this section applies to any society, the society's committee shall not have power to vary or revoke any resolution such as is mentioned in paragraph (c) of that subsection; but upon the registration after the commencement of this Act under section 10 thereof of any amendment of the rules of the society—
  (a) the registered rules of the society shall have effect as if any such resolution had not been passed; and
  (b) if not already exercised, the power of the society's committee to pass such a resolution shall determine,
so, however, that paragraph (a) of this subsection shall not affect any sums standing deposited with the society immediately before the date of registration of the amendment.

(6) Any registered society which—
  (a) carries on the business of banking in contravention of subsection (1) of this section; or
  (b) fails to comply with subsection (2) of this section; or
  (c) makes any payment of withdrawable capital in contravention of subsection (3) of this section,
shall be liable on summary conviction to a fine not exceeding five pounds. **[83]**

NOTES to section 7
Amendment: In sub-s (3), words substituted by the Industrial and Provident Societies Act 1978 (c 34) s 1.
Definitions: 'registered society': see s 74 below; 'registered rules': *Ibid*; 'committee': *Ibid*.

8. Society registered in one area carrying on business in another.

(1) Subsection (2) of this section shall have effect where a registered society whose registered office is situated in one of the registration areas for the purposes of this Act, that is to say—
  (a) England, Wales and the Channel Islands; or
  (b) Scotland,
carries on business in the other of those areas.

(2) The society shall not be entitled in that other area to any of the privileges of this Act as a registered society until a copy of the registered rules of the society has been sent by the society to, and those rules have been recorded by, the appropriate registrar for that other area; and any registered amendment of the rules so recorded shall not have effect in that other area until a copy of that amendment has been so sent and the amendment so recorded. **[84]**

NOTES to section 8
Definitions: 'registered society': see s 74 below; 'registered office': *Ibid*; 'registered rules': *Ibid*; 'appropriate registrar': see s 73 below.

Provisions as to rules

9. Acknowledgment of registration of rules.

Without prejudice to section 53(3) of this Act, an acknowledgment of the registration of a society issued under section 2(3) of this Act shall also constitute an acknowledgment, and be conclusive evidence, of the registration under this Act of the rules of that society in force at the date of the society's registration. **[85]**

10. Amendment of registered rules.

(1) Subject to subsection (2) of this section, any amendment of a society's rules as for the time being registered under this Act shall not be valid until the amendment has been so registered, for which purpose there shall be sent to the appropriate registrar two copies of the amendment signed—

(a) in the case of a society for the time being consisting solely of registered societies, by the secretary of the society and by two members of the committee and the secretary of each (or, if more than three, of each of any three) of the constituent societies;

(b) in any other case, by three members and the secretary of the society.

(2) The foregoing subsection shall not apply to a change in the situation of a society's registered office or in the name of a society; but—

(a) notice of any change in the situation of a society's registered office shall be sent to the appropriate registrar; and

(b) where such a notice is duly sent, or where a change in the name of a registered society is made in accordance with section 5(3) of this Act, the change in the situation of the society's registered office or, as the case may be, the change in the society's name shall be registered by the appropriate registrar as an amendment of the society's rules.

(3) The appropriate registrar, on being satisfied that any amendment of a society's rules is not contrary to the provisions of this Act, shall issue to the society in respect of that amendment an acknowledgment of registration in the prescribed form which shall be conclusive evidence that it is duly registered. **[86]**

NOTES to section 10

Amendment: Sub-s (3) was modified in relation to credit unions by the Credit Unions Act 1979 (c 34), s 4. The text printed here is the unmodified form. Section 10 is excluded by the Friendly and Industrial and Provident Societies Act 1968 (c 55), s 12(3).

Definitions: 'the appropriate registrar': see s 74 below; 'registered society': *Ibid*; 'committee': *Ibid*; 'registered office': *Ibid*.

11. Rules as to fund for purchase of government securities.

(1) The rules of a society registered or to be registered under this Act may make provision for the setting up and administration by the society of a fund for the purchase on behalf of members contributing to the fund of defence bonds or national saving certificates or such other securities of Her Majesty's Government in the United Kingdom as may for the time being be prescribed under [section 47(1) of the Friendly Societies Act 1974] by the chief registrar or some other person appointed by him for the purpose; and any such rules may make provision for enabling persons to become members of the society for the purpose only of contributing to that fund and without being entitled to any rights as members other than rights as contributors to that fund.

(2) Any rule which, immediately before the commencement of this Act, was included among the registered rules of a registered society by virtue of section 8(3) of the [Societies (Miscellaneous Provisions) Act 1940] shall have effect as if it had been duly passed by the society. **[87]**

NOTES to section 11

Amendments: In sub-s (1) and (2), words substituted by the Friendly Societies Act 1974 (c 46), s 116, Sch 9, para 18.

Definitions: 'Chief registrar': see s 73 below; 'registered rules': see s 74 below; 'registered society': *Ibid*; 'amendment': *Ibid*.

12. Rules of agricultural, horticultural or forestry society.

Where a society registered or to be registered under this Act consists mainly of members who are producers of agricultural or horticultural produce or persons engaged in forestry, or organisations of such producers or persons so engaged, and the object or principal object of the society is the making to its members of advances of money for agricultural, horticultural or forestry purposes, registration under this Act of the rules of the society or any amendment thereof shall not be refused on the ground that the rules provide, or would as amended provide, for the making of such advances without security. **[88]**

Industrial and Provident Societies Act 1965 (c 12), s 15 [91]

NOTE to section 12
Definition: 'amendment': see s 74 below.

13. Supplementary provisions as to rules.

(1) The rules of a registered society or any schedule thereto may specify the form of any instrument necessary for carrying the purposes of the society into effect.

(2) The rules of a registered society may impose reasonable fines on persons who contravene or fail to comply with any of those rules.

(3) Any fine imposed by the rules of a registered society shall be recoverable on the summary conviction of the offender.

(4) Any provision of, or of any instrument made under, this or any other Act requiring or authorising the rules of a registered society to deal with particular matters shall be without prejudice to the power of such a society to make rules with respect to any other matter which are not inconsistent with any such provision or with any other provision of this or any other Act and which are not otherwise unlawful. [89]

NOTES to section 13
Definition: 'registered society': see s 74 below.

14. Rules to bind members.

(1) Subject to subsections (2) and (3) of this section, the registered rules of a registered society shall bind the society and all members thereof and all persons claiming through them respectively to the same extent as if each member had subscribed his name and affixed his seal thereto and there were contained in those rules a covenant on the part of each member and any person claiming through him to conform thereto subject to the provisions of this Act.

(2) A member of a registered society shall not, without his consent in writing having been first obtained, be bound by any amendment of the society's rules registered after he became a member, being an amendment registered after 27th March 1928, if and so far as that amendment requires him to take or subscribe for more shares than the number held by him at the date of registration of the amendment, or to pay upon the shares so held any sum exceeding the amount unapid upon them at that date, or in any other way increases the liability of that member to contribute to the share or loan capital of the society.

(3) In the case of a society to which section 4 of this Act applies which was a registered society under the Act of 1893 on 1st January 1894, the society or the members thereof may respectively exercise any power given by this Act and not made to depend on the provisions of the society's rules notwithstanding anything in any of those rules registered before 12th September 1893.

(4) In its application to Scotland, subsection (1) of this section shall have effect as if the words 'and affixed his seal' were omitted. [90]

NOTE to section 14
Definitions: 'registered rules': see s 74 below; 'registered society':' Ibid; 'amendment': Ibid.

15. Provision of copies of rules

(1) A copy of the registered rules of any registered society shall be delivered by the society to any person who demands it, subject to payment by that person of such sum not exceeding two shillings as the society may see fit to charge.

(2) If any person, with intent to midlead or defraud, gives to any other person—
(a) a copy of any rules other than rules for the time being registered under this Act on the pretence that they are the existing rules, or that there are no other rules, of a registered society; or

(b) a copy of the rules of a society which is not registered under this Act on the pretence that they are the rules of a registered society,

he shall be liable on summary conviction to a fine not exceeding five pounds. [91]

NOTES to section 15

Definitions: 'registered rules': see s 74 below; 'registered society': *Ibid*.

Cancellation, suspension or refusal of registration of society or rules

16. Cancellation of registration of society.

(1) Subject to the provisions of this section and sections 18(1)(c) and 59 of this Act, and without prejudice to section 52(4) thereof, the appropriate registrar may, by writing under his hand or seal or, in Scotland, in writing, cancel the registration of any registered society—
  (a) if at any time it is proved to his satisfaction—
    (i) that the number of members of the society has been reduced, in the case of a society for the time being consisting solely of registered societies, to less than two or, in any other case, to less than seven; or
    (ii) that an acknowledgment of registration has been obtained by fraud or mistake; or
    (iii) that the society has ceased to exist;
  (b) if he thinks fit, at the request of the society, to be evidenced in such manner as he shall from time to time direct;
  (c) with the approval of the Treasury—
    (i) on proof to his satisfaction that the society exists for an illegal purpose, or has wilfully and after notice from a registrar violated any of the provisions of this Act or any enactment repealed thereby; or
    (ii) if at any time it appears to him that neither of the conditions specified in section 1(2) of this Act is fulfilled in the case of that society; or
    (iii) in the case of a society whose registered rules contain such a provision as is authorised by section 12 of this Act, if it appears to him that the society no longer consists mainly of such members as are mentioned in that section or that the activities carried on by it do not mainly consist in making advances to its members for such purposes as are so mentioned.

(2) Subsection (1)(c)(ii) of this sectioon shall not authorise the cancellation of the registration of any society to which section 4 of this Act applies which was registered or deemed to be registered under the Act of 1893 before 26th July 1938 if no invitation to subscribe for or to acquire or offer to acquire securities, or to lend or deposit money, has been made on or after that date by or on behalf of the society.

(3) Not less than two months previous notice in writing specifying briefly the ground of the proposed cancellation shall be given by the appropriate registrar to a society before its registration is cancelled otherwise than—
  (a) at its own request; or
  (b) by virtue of section 52(4) of this Act; or
  (c) after the lodging with the appropriate registrar of such a certificate as is referred to in section 59 of this Act;

and if before the expiration of the period of that notice the society duly lodges an appeal under section 18(1)(c) of this Act, then, without prejudice to section 17(2) of this Act, the society's registration shall not be cancelled before the date of the determination or abandonment of the appeal.

(4) Where the ground specified in any notice under subsection (3) of this section is that referred to in subsection (1)(c)(ii) thereof—
  (a) the appropriate registrar shall consider any representations with respect to the proposed cancellation made to him by the society within the period of duration of

the notice and, if the society so requests, afford it an opportunity of being heard by him before its registration is cancelled;
   (b) if it appears to the appropriate registrar at any time after the expiration of one month from the date of the giving of the notice that there have not been taken the steps which by that time could reasonably have been taken for the purpose—
      (i) of converting the society into, or amalgamating it with, or transferring its engagements to, a company in accordance with section 52 of this Act; or
      (ii) of dissolving the society under section 55 of this Act,
   he may give such directions as he thinks fit for securing that the affairs of the society are wound up before cancellation of the registration takes effect.

(5) Any person who contravenes or fails to comply with any directions given by the appropriate registrar under subsection (4)(b) of this section shall be liable on summary conviction to a fine not exceeding fifty pounds or to imprisonment for a term not exceeding three months or to both.

(6) Notice of every cancellation under this section of a society's registration shall, as soon as practicable after it takes place, be published in the Gazette and in some local newspaper circulating in or about the locality in which the society's registered office is situated.

(7) As from the date of the publication in the Gazette under subsection (6) of this section of notice of the cancellation of a society's registration, the society shall absolutely cease to be entitled to any of the privileges of this Act as a registered society, but without prejudice to any liability actually incurred by the society which may be enforced against it as if the cancellation had not taken place. [92]

NOTES to section 16
Amendment: Sub-s (1) was modified in relation to credit unions by the Credit Unions Act 1979 (c 34), s 6.
Definitions: 'appropriate registrar': see s 73 below; 'registered society': see s 74 below; 'the Gazette': *Ibid*.

17. Suspension of registration of society.

(1) Where under section 16(1)(c) of this Act the appropriate registrar might with the approval of the Treasury cancel the registration of a registered society, that registrar may, by writing under his hand or seal—
   (a) subject to subsection (3) of this section, suspend the registration of that society for any term not exceeding three months; and
   (b) with the approval of the Treasury, but subject to section 18(1)(d) of this Act, from time to time renew any such suspension for the like period.

(2) Where before the expiration of the period of a notice under section 16(3) of this Act of the proposed cancellation of a society's registration, that society duly lodges an appeal from the proposed cancellation under section 18(1)(c) of this Act, the appropriate registrar may by writing under his hand or seal suspend the society's registration from the expiration of that period until the date of the determination or abandonment of the appeal.

(3) Not less than two months previous notice in writing specifying briefly the ground of the proposed suspension shall be given by the appropriate registrar to a society before its registration is suspended under subsection (1)(a) of this section.

(4) Notice of every suspension of a society's registration under subsection (1)(a) or (2) of this section and of any renewal of a suspension under subsection (1)(b) thereof shall, as soon as practicable after it takes place, be published in the Gazette and in some local newspaper circulating in or about the locality in which the society's registered office is situated.

(5) From the date of publication in the Gazette of a notice under subsection (4) of this section of the suspension of any society's registration under subsection (1)(a) or (2) of this

section until the period of that suspension and any renewal thereof under subsection (1)(b) of this section ends (whether on the expiration of that period or on a successful appeal under section 18(1)(d) of this Act from such a renewal) the society shall not be entitled to any of the privileges of this Act as a registered society, but without prejudice to any liability actually incurred by the society which may be enforced against it as if the suspension had not taken place.

(6) In the application of this section to Scotland, subsections (1) and (2) thereof shall have effect as if for the words 'by writing under his hand or seal' there were substituted the words 'in writing'. **[93]**

NOTES to section 17

Definitions: 'appropriate registrar': see s 73 below; 'registered society': see s 74 below; 'registered rules': *Ibid*; 'the Gazette': *Ibid*.

18. Appeal from refusal, cancellation or suspension of registration of society or rules.

(1) A society may appeal from any decision of the appropriate registrar—
(a) to refuse registration of the society (including a refusal by reason only of anything contained in or omitted from the society's rules) on any ground other than that he is not satisfied that either of the conditions specified in section 1(2) of this Act is fulfilled; or
(b) to refuse registration of any amendment of the society's rules; or
(c) to cancel the society's registration (being a cancellation of which notice is required under section 16(3), and not being a cancellation by virtue of section 16(1)(c)(ii), of this Act) if the appeal is lodged before the expiration of the period of notice of the proposed cancellation given under the said section 16(3); or
(d) to renew under section 17(1)(b) of this Act a suspension of the society's registration so far as that renewal provides for the suspension to continue more than three months from the original date of suspension.

(2) An appeal under the foregoing subsection shall lie—
(a) from a decision of the central office, to the High Court,
(b) from a decision of the assistant registrar for Scotland, to the chief registrar and, if the chief registrar confirms the decision, to the Court of Session.

(3) If any decision such as is mentioned in subsection (1)(a) or (b) of this section is overruled on appeal, the appropriate registrar shall thereupon issue to the society an acknowledgment of registration of the society under section 2(3), or, as the case may be, of the amendment under section 10(3), of this Act. **[94]**

NOTES to section 18

Definitions: 'appropriate registrar': see s 73 below; 'amendment': see s 74 below.

Membership and special provisions affecting members

19. Bodies corporate as members of society.

(1) Shares in a registered society may be held by any other body corporate (if that body's regulations so permit) by its corporate name.

(2) Where a registered society is a member of another registered society, then, for the purposes of any enactment with respect to the making or signing of any application, instrument or document by members of a registered society, any reference therein to such a member shall, in relation to the first-mentioned society as a member of the second-mentioned society, be construed as a reference to two members of the committee and the secretary of the society. **[95]**

NOTES to section 19
Definitions: 'registered society': see s 74 below; 'committee': *Ibid.*

20. Members under 21.

A person under the age of [¹eighteen] but above the age of sixteen may be a member of a registered society unless provision to the contrary is made by the society's registered rules and may, subject to those rules and to the provisions of this Act, enjoy all the rights of a member and execute all instruments and give all receipts necessary to be executed or given under those rules, but shall not be a member of the committee, trustee, manager or treasurer of the society. **[96]**

NOTES to section 20
Amendment: word substituted by the Age of Majority (Scotland) Act 1969 (c 39), s 1, Sch 1, Pt 1.
Definitions: 'registered society': see s 73 below; 'registered rules': see s 74 below; 'committee': *Ibid.*

21. Advances to members.

Without prejudice to any provision included by virtue of section 12 of this Act, the rules of a registered society may provide for advances of money to members—
  (a) on the security of real or personal property or, in Scotland, of heritable or moveable estate; or
  (b) if the society is registered to carry on banking business, in any manner customary in the conduct of such business. **[97]**

NOTE to section 21
Definition: 'registered society': see s 74 below.

22. Remedy for debts from members.

(1) All moneys payable to a registered society by a member thereof shall be a debt due from that member to the society and shall be recoverable as such in the county court, or, in Scotland, before the sheriff, within whose jurisdiction the society's registered office is situate or within whose jurisdiction the member resides, at the option of the society.

(2) A registered society shall have a lien on the shares of any member for any debt due to the society by that member, and may set off any sum credited to the member on those shares in or towards the payment of that debt. **[98]**

NOTES to section 22
Definition: 'registered society': see s 74 below.

23. Nomination to property in society.

(1) Subject to subsections (2) and (3) of this section, a member of a registered society may, by a written statement signed by him and delivered at or sent to the society's registered office during his lifetime or made in any book kept at that office, nominate a person or persons to become entitled at his death to the whole, or to such part or respective parts as may be specified in the nomination, of any property in the society (whether in shares, loans or deposits or otherwise) which he may have—
  (a) in the case of a nomination made before 1st January 1914, at the date of the nomination; or
  (b) in any other case, at the time of his death.

(2) The nomination by a member of a society under the foregoing subsection of a person who is at the date of the nomination an officer or servant of the society shall not be valid unless that person is the husband, wife, father, mother, child, brother, sister, nephew or niece of the nominator.

(3) For the purposes of the disposal of any property which is the subject of a nomination under subsection (1) of this section—
 (a) if the nomination was made before 1st January 1914 and at the date of the nomination the amount credited to the nominator in the society's books exceeded one hundred pounds, the nomination shall not be valid;
 (b) if the nomination was made after 21st December 1913 and before 5th August 1954 and at the date of the nominator's death the amount of his property in the society comprised in the nomination exceeds one hundred pounds, the nomination shall be valid to the extent of one hundred pounds but not further or otherwise;
 (c) if the nomination was made after 4th August 1954 and at the date of the nominator's death the amount of his property in the society comprised in the nomination exceeds [£1,500], the nomination shall be valid to the extent of [£1,500], but not further or otherwise.

(4) A nomination by a member of a society under subsection (1) of this section may be varied or revoked by a subsequent nomination by him thereunder or by any similar document in the nature of a revocation or variation signed by the nominator and delivered at or sent to the society's registered office during his lifetime, but shall not be revocable or variable by the will of the nominator or by any codicil thereto.

(5) Every registered society shall keep a book in which the names of all persons nominated under subsection (1) of this section and any revocation or variation of any nomination under that subsection shall be recorded.

(6) The marriage of a member of a society shall operate as a revocation of any nomination made by him before the marriage and after 31st December 1913; but if any property of that member has been transferred by an officer of the society in pursuance of that nomination in ignorance of a marriage contracted by the nominator subsequent to the date of the nomination, the receipt of the nominee shall be a valid discharge to the society and the society shall be under no liability to any other person claiming the property. **[99]**

NOTES to section 23

Amendment: In sub-s (3), words substituted by the Administration of Estates (Small Payments) (Increase of Limits) Order 1975, SI 1975/1137.

Definitions: 'registered society': see s 74 below; 'registered office': *Ibid*; 'property': *Ibid*; 'officer': *Ibid*.

24. Proceedings on death of nominator.

(1) Subject to subsections (2) and (4) of this section, where any member of a registered society has made a nomination under section 23 of this Act, the committee of the society, on receiving satisfactory proof of the death of that member, and if and to the extent that the nomination is valid under subsections (2) and (3) of that section, shall in the case of each person entitled under the nomination either transfer to him, or pay him the full value of, any property to which he is so entitled.

(2) Where any of the property comprised in such a nomination as aforesaid consists of shares in the society, the foregoing subsection shall have effect notwithstanding that the rules of the society declare the shares therein not to be transferable; but if the transfer of any shares comprised in the nomination in the manner directed by the nominator would raise the share capital of any nominee beyond the maximum for the time being permitted in the case of that society, the committee of the society shall not transfer to that nominee more of those shares than will raise his share capital to that maximum and shall pay him the value of any of those shares not transferred.

(3) Where any sum falls to be paid under the foregoing provisions of this section to a nominee who is under sixteen years of age, the society may pay that sum to either parent, or to a guardian, of the nominee or to any other person of full age who will undertake to hold it on trust for the nominee or to apply it for his benefit and whom the society may

Industrial and Provident Societies Act 1965 (c 12), s 27 [103]

think a fit and proper person for the purpose, and the receipt of that parent, guardian or other person shall be a sufficient discharge to the society for all moneys so paid.

(4) . . . [100]

NOTES to section 24

Amendment: Sub-s (4) was repealed by the Administration of Estates (Small Payments) Act 1965 (c 32) s 7, Sch 4.
Definitions: 'registered society': see s 74 below; 'committee': *Ibid*; 'property': *Ibid*.

25. Provision for intestacy.

(1) If any member of a registered society dies . . . and at his death his property in the society in respect of shares, loans or deposits does not exceed in the whole [£1,500] and is not the subject of any nomination under section 23 of this Act, then, subject to subsection (2) of this section, the committee of the society may, without letters of administration [or probate of any will] or, in Scotland, without confirmation having been obtained, distribute that property among such persons as appear to the committee on such evidence as they deem satisfactory to be entitled by law to receive it.

(2) If the member aforesaid was illegitimate [and leaves no widow, widower or issue, (including any illegitimate child of the member) and mother of his parents survive him], the committee shall deal with his property in the society as the Treasury shall direct.
[101]

NOTES to section 25

Amendments: Sub-s (1) was amended by the Administration of Estates (Small Payments) Act 1965, s 3, Sch 3, and by the Administration of Estates (Small Payments) (Increase of Limits) Order 1975, SI 1975/1137; in sub-s (2), words substituted by the Family Law Reform Act 1969 (c 46) s 19(2).
Definitions: 'registered society': see s 74 below; 'property': *Ibid*; 'committee': *Ibid*.

26. Payments in respect of mentally incapable persons.

(1) Subject to subsection (2) of this section, where in the case of a member of a registered society or a person claiming through such a member the society's committee are satisfied after considering medical evidence that the member or person is incapable through disorder or disability of mind of managing his own affairs and are also satisfied that no person has been duly appointed to administer his property on his behalf, and it is proved to the satisfaction of the committee that it is just and expedient so to do, the society may pay the amount of any shares, loans, and deposits belonging to that member or person to any person whom they judge proper to receive it on his behalf, whose receipt shall be a good discharge to the society for any sum so paid.

(2) The foregoing subsection shall not apply when the member or person in question is—
 (a) a patient with the meaning of Part VIII of the Mental Health Act 1959; or
 (b) a person as to whom powers are exercisable and have been exercised under section 104 of that Act. [102]

NOTES to section 26
Definitions: 'registered society': see s 74 below; 'committee': *Ibid*; 'property': *Ibid*.

27. Validity of payment to persons apparently entitled.

All payments or transfers made by the committee of a registered society under section 25 or 26(1) of this Act or any corresponding provision of any Act repealed by this Act to any person appearing to the committee at the time of the payment or transfer to be entitled thereunder shall be valid and effectual against any demand made upon the committee or society by any other person. [103]

NOTES to section 27
Definitions: 'committee': see s 74 below; 'registered society': *Ibid.*

Contracts, property, etc, of society

28. Promissory notes and bills of exchange.

A promissory note or bill of exchange shall be deemed to have been made, accepted or endorsed on behalf of any registered society if made, accepted or endorsed in the name of the society, or by or on behalf or account of the society, by any person acting under the authority of the society. [104]

NOTES to section 28
Definition: 'registered society': see s 74 below.

29. Contracts

(1) Any contract which, if made between private persons, would be by law required to be in writing and, if made according to English law, to be under seal may be made, varied or discharged on behalf of a registered society in writing under the common seal of the society; and any contract which may be or have been made, varied or discharged in accordance with this subsection shall, so far as concerns its form, be effectual in law and binding on all parties thereto, their heirs, executors or administrators, as the case may be.

(2) A signature purporting to be made by a person holding any office in a registered society attached to a writing whereby any contract purports to be made, varied or discharged by or on behalf of the society shall, until the contrary is proved, be taken to be the signature of a person holding that office at the time when the signature was made.

(3) Subsection (1) of this section shall not apply to Scotland; and nothing in that subsection shall prejudice the operation in England and Wales of the Corporate Bodies' Contracts Act 1960. [105]

NOTE to section 29
Definition: 'registered society': see s 74 below.

30. Holding of land.

(1) A registered society may, unless its registered rules direct otherwise, hold, purchase or take on lease in its own name any land and may sell, exchange, mortgage or lease any such land and erect, alter or pull down buildings on it; and—
(a) no purchaser, assignee, mortgagee or tenant shall be bound to inquire as to the authority for any such dealing with the land by the society; and
(b) the receipt of the society shall be a discharge for all moneys arising from or in connection with any such dealing.

(2) In the application of the foregoing subsection to Scotland—
(a) for the word 'exchange' there shall be substituted the word 'excamb';
(b) for the word 'mortgage' there shall be substituted the words 'grant a heritable security over';
(c) for the word 'mortgagee' there shall be substituted the words 'creditor in a heritable security'. [106]

NOTES to section 30
Definitions: 'registered society': see s 74 below; 'registered rules': *Ibid*; 'land': *Ibid*; 'heritable security': *Ibid.*

31. Investments.

A registered society may invest any part of its funds in or upon any security authorised by its registered rules, and also, unless those rules direct otherwise—
- (a) in or upon any mortgage, bond, debenture, debenture stock, corporation stock, annuity, rent charge, rent or other security (not being securities payable to bearer) authorised by or under any Act of any local authority within the meaning of the Local Loans Act 1875;
- (b) in the shares or on the security of any other registered society, of any [building society within the meaning of the Building Societies Act 1986], or of any company registered under the Companies Acts or incorporated by act of Parliament or by charter, being a society or company with limited liability;
- (c) in or upon any other security, being a security in which trustees are for the time being authorised by law to invest, for which purposes sections 1 to 6 of the Trustee Investments Acts 1961 shall apply as if the society were a trustee and its funds were trust property. **[107]**

NOTES to section 31
Amendment: Section 31 was amended by the Building Societies Act 1986 (c 53) s 120, Sch 18, para 6.
Definitions: 'registered societies': see s 74 below; 'Companies Acts': *Ibid.*

32. Proxy voting by societies.

(1) A registered society which has invested any part of its funds in the shares or on the security of any other body corporate may appoint as proxy any one of its members notwithstanding that he is not personally a shareholder of that other body corporate.

(2) Any member of the society so appointed shall during the continuance of his appointment be taken by virtue thereof as holding the number of shares held by the society for all purposes other than the transfer of any such share or the giving of a receipt for any dividend thereon. **[108]**

NOTE to section 32
Definition: 'registered society': see s 74 below;

33. Discharge of mortgages in England and Wales.

(1) Where, in the case of any mortgage or other assurance to a registered society of any property in England or Wales, a receipt in full for all moneys secured thereby on that property is endorsed on or annexed to the mortgage or other assurance, being a receipt—
- (a) signed by two members of the committee and counter-signed by the secretary of the society or, if the society is in liquidation, signed by the liquidator or liquidators for the time being, described as such; and
- (b) in one of the forms set out in Part I of Schedule 3 to this Act, or in any other form specified in the rules of the society or any schedule thereto,

then, for the purposes of the provisions of section 115 of the Law of Property Act 1925 specified in subsection (2) of this section, that receipt shall be deemed to be a receipt which fulfils the requirements of subsection (1) of that section.

(2) The provisions of the said section 115 referred to in the foregoing subsection are—
- (a) subsection (1) so far as it relates to the operation of such a receipt as is mentioned in that subsection;
- (b) if, but only if, the receipt under this section states the name of the person who pays the money, subsection (2);
- (c) subsections (3), (6), (8), (10) and (11);
- (d) where consistent with the terms of the form authorised by subsection (1)(b) of this section which is used for the receipt, subsection (7). **[109]**

[109] *Industrial and Provident Societies Act 1965 (c 12), s 33*

NOTES to section 33
Definitions: 'registered society': see s 74 below; 'committee': *Ibid*.

34. Discharge of securities in Scotland.

(1) Where land in Scotland is held in security by a registered society by virtue of a heritable security constituted by an *ex facie* absolute conveyance, whether qualified by a back letter or not, a receipt in or as nearly as may be in form C in Part II of Schedule 3 to this Act endorsed on or annexed to the conveyance shall, on the registration thereof in the General Register of Sasines, effectually discharge that heritable security and disburden the land comprised therein, and vest that land in the person or persons entitled thereto at the date of the granting of the receipt in the like manner and to the like effect as if a conveyance containing all usual and necessary clauses had been granted by the society to that person or persons and duly registered as aforesaid.

(2) Where land in Scotland is held in security by a registered society by virtue of a heritable security other than the one constituted by an *ex facie* absolute conveyance, a receipt in or as nearly as may be in form D in the said Part II endorsed on or annexed to the deed constituting that heritable security shall, on the registration thereof in the General Register of Sasines, effectually discharge that heritable security and disburden the land comprised therein in the like manner and to the like effect as if a discharge containing all usual and necessary clauses had been granted by the society and duly registered as aforesaid.

(3) Where property other than land is held in security by a registered society in Scotland, a receipt in or as nearly as may be in form E in the said Part II shall discharge the security, and vest the property comprised therein in the person or persons entitled thereto at the date of the granting of the receipt without the necessity of any further deed:

Provided that where the original security was intimated to any person that security shall not be discharged nor the property vested as aforesaid until the receipt has been duly intimated to that person.

(4) The fees payable in respect of the registration of receipts mentioned in this section shall in no case exceed [25p] . . .

(5) In this section—
(a) the expression 'a receipt', in relation to any security, means a receipt, signed by two members of the committee and countersigned by the secretary of the society or, if the society is in liquidation, signed by the liquidator or liquidators for the time being, described as such, for all moneys advanced by the society on the security of the property comprised in that security;
(b) the expressions 'conveyance' and 'deed' have the meanings respectively assigned to them by the Conveyancing (Scotland) Act 1924. **[110]**

NOTES to section 34
Amendments: In sub-s (4), words substituted by the Decimal Currency Act 1969 (c 19), s 10(1), words repealed by the Finance Act 1974 (c 58), s 64, Sch 14, Pt VI.
Definitions: 'land': see s 74 below; 'registered society': *Ibid*; 'heritable security': *Ibid*.

35. Receipt on payment of moneys secured to a society.

On payment of all moneys intended to be secured to a registered society on the security of any property, the debtor or his successor or representatives shall be entitled to a receipt in the appropriate form specified in Schedule 3 to this Act. **[111]**

NOTES to section 35
Definitions: 'registered society': see s 74 below; 'property': *Ibid*.

36. Execution of deeds in Scotland.

In Scotland, any deed or writ to which any registered society is a party shall be held to be duly executed on behalf of that society if it is sealed with the common seal of the society subscribed on behalf of the society by two members of the committee and the secretary thereof, whether that subscription is attested by witnesses or not. **[112]**

NOTES to section 36
Definitions: 'registered society': see s 74 below; 'committee': *Ibid.*

Accounts, etc

37, 38. . . .

NOTES to sections 37 and 38
Sections 37 and 38 were repealed by the Friendly and Industrial and Provident Societies Act 1968 (c 55), s 20, Sch 2.

39. Annual returns.

(1) Every registered society shall, not later than 31st March in each year, send to the appropriate registrar a return [relating to its affairs for the period required by this section to be included in the return], together with—
- (a) a copy of the report of the auditor or auditors on the society's accounts for the period included in the return; and
- (b) a copy of each balance sheet made during that period and of any report of the auditor or auditors on that balance sheet.

(2) The said return shall—
(a), (b) . . .
(c) subject to subsections (3) and (4) of this section, be made up for the period beginning with the date of the society's registration under this Act or [with the date to which the society's last annual return was made up, whichever is the later, and ending—
- (i) with the date of the last balance sheet published by the society before the appropriate date; or
- (ii) if the date of that balance sheet is earlier than 31st August immediately preceding the appropriate date or later than 31st January of the year in which the appropriate date falls, with 31st December immediately preceding the appropriate date,]

[(2A) For the purposes of paragraph (c) of subsection (2) of this section 'the appropriate date', in relation to an annual return of a society, is 31st March of the year in which that return is required by subsection (1) of this section to be sent to the appropriate registrar or the date on which that return is so sent, whichever is the earlier.]

(3) If the appropriate registrar is of opinion that special circumstances exist he may allow a society to make a return under this section up to a date other than that specified in subsection (2)(c)(i) or (ii) of this section, and in that case the return shall be sent to the registrar not later than three months after the date to which it is to be made up.

(4) The last return under this section by a registered society which is being terminated by an instrument of dissolution under section 55(b) of this Act shall be made up to the date of the instrument of dissolution.

(5) Every registered society shall supply free of charge to every member or person interested in the funds of the society who applies for it a copy of the latest return of the society under this section. **[113]**

NOTES to section 39

Amendments: In sub-s (1), words substituted by the Friendly and Industrial and Provident Societies Act 1968 (c 55), s 11; sub-s (2) amended by Friendly and Industrial and Provident Societies Act 1968 (c 55), s 20, Sch 2, and by *Ibid*, s 20, Sch 1, para 10; sub-s (2A) added by *Ibid*, s 20, Sch 1, para 10.

Definitions: 'registered society': see s 74 below; 'appropriate registrar': see s 73 below.

40. Display of latest balance sheet.

Every registered society shall keep a copy of the latest balance sheet of the society, together with the report thereon of the auditor or auditors, hung up at all times in a conspicuous position at the registered office of the society. **[114]**

NOTES to section 40

Definitions: 'registered society': see s 74 below; 'registered office': *Ibid*.

Officers, receivers, etc

41. Security by officers.

(1) Every officer of a registered society having receipt or charge of money shall, if the rules of the society so require, before entering upon the execution of his office give security in such sum as the society's committee may direct conditioned for his rendering a just and true account of all moneys received and paid by him on account of the society at such times as its rules appoint or as the society or its committee require him so to do and for the payment by him of all sums due from him to the society.

(2) An officer of a registered society shall give security in accordance with the foregoing subsection either—
   (a)   by becoming bound, either with or without a surety as the society's committee may require, in a bond in one of the forms set out in Schedule 4 to this Act or such other form as the society's committee may approve; or
   (b)   by giving the security of a guarantee society.

(3) In the application of this section to Scotland, for the reference in subsection (2)(a) thereof to a surety there shall be substituted a reference to a cautioner. **[115]**

NOTES to section 41

Definitions: 'officer': see s 74 below; 'registered society': *Ibid*; 'committee': *Ibid*.

42. Duty of officers of society to account.

(1) Every officer of a registered society having receipt or charge of money, and every servant of such a society in receipt or charge of money who is not engaged under a special agreement to account, shall—
   (a)   at such times as he is required so to do by the rules of the society; or
   (b)   on demand; or
   (c)   on notice in writing requiring him so to do given or left at his last or usual place of residence,

render an account as may be required by the society or its committee to be examined and allowed or disallowed by them, and shall, on demand or on such notice as aforesaid, pay over all moneys and deliver all property for the time being in his hands or custody to such person as the society or committee may appoint.

(2) Any duty imposed by the foregoing subsection on an officer or servant of a society shall, after his death, be taken to be imposed on his personal representatives.

(3) In case of any neglect or refusal to comply with the foregoing provisions of this section, the society—
   (a)   may sue on any bond or security given under section 41 of this Act; or

Industrial and Provident Societies Act 1965 (c 12), s 44 [118]

(b) may apply to the county court (which may proceed in a summary way) or to a magistrates' court and, notwithstanding anything in section [77 of the County Courts Act 1984], the order of that county court or magistrates' court shall be final and conclusive.

(4) In its application to Scotland, this section shall have effect as if for subsection (3)(b) thereof there were substituted the following:—
'(b) may apply to the sheriff, and, notwithstanding anything in section 62 of the Summary Jurisdiction (Scotland) Act 1954, the order of the sheriff shall be final and conclusive.'. [116]

NOTES to section 42
Amendment: Sub-s (3) amended by the County Courts Act 1984, (c 28), s 148, Sch 2, para 29.
Definitions: 'officer': see s 74 below; 'registered society': *Ibid*; 'committee': *Ibid*.

43. Duties of receiver or manager of society's property.

Every receiver or manager of the property of a registered society who has been appointed under the powers contained in any instrument shall—
(a) within one month from the date of his appointment notify the appropriate registrar of his appointment; and
(b) within one month (or such longer period as that registrar may allow) after the expiration of the period of six months from that date, and of every subsequent period of six months, deliver to that registrar a return showing his receipts and his payments during that period of six months; and
(c) within one month after he ceases to act as receiver or manager deliver to that registrar a return showing his receipts and his payments during the final period and the aggregate amount of his receipts and of his payments during all preceding periods since his appointment. [117]

NOTES to section 43
Definitions: 'property': see s 74 below; 'registered society': *Ibid*; 'appropriate registrar': see s 73 below.

Registers, books, etc

44. Register of members and officers.

(1) Every registered society shall keep at its registered office a register and enter therein the following particulars:—
(a) the names and addresses of the members;
(b) a statement of the number of shares held by each member and of the amount paid or agreed to be considered as paid on the shares of each member;
(c) a statement of other property in the society, whether in loans, deposits or otherwise, held by each member;
(d) the date at which each person was entered in the register as a member, and the date at which any person ceased to be a member;
(e) the names and addresses of the officers of the society, with the offices held by them respectively, and the dates on which they assumed office.

(2) The said register may be kept either by making entries in bound books or by recording the matters in question in any other manner; but, where it is not kept by making entries in a bound book but by some other means, adequate precautions shall be taken for guarding against falsification and facilitating its discovery.

(3) Every registered society shall either—
(a) keep at its registered office a duplicate register containing the particulars in the register kept under subsection (1) of this section other than those entered under paragraph (b) or (c) of that subsection; or

[118]

(b) so construct the register kept under the said subsection (1) that it is possible to open to inspection the particulars therein other than the particulars entered under the said paragraph (b) or (c) without exposing those last-mentioned particulars.

(4) The appropriate registrar or a person acting on his behalf may at all reasonable hours inspect any particulars in any register or duplicate register kept under this section.

(5) A registered society's register or duplicate register kept under this section, or any other register or list of members or shares kept by the society, shall be prima facie evidence of any of the following particulars entered therein, that is to say—
- (a) the names, addresses and occupations of the members;
- (b) the number of shares respectively held by the members, the distinguishing numbers of those shares, if they are distinguished by numbers, and the amount paid or agreed to be considered as paid on any of those shares;
- (c) the date at which the name of any person, company or society was entered in that register or list as a member;
- (d) the date at which any such person, company or society ceased to be a member.

[118]

NOTES to section 44

Definitions: 'registered society': see s 74 below; 'registered office': *Ibid*; 'property': *Ibid*; 'officer': *Ibid*; 'appropriate registrar': see s 73 below.

45. Restriction on inspection of books.

(1) Save as provided by this Act, no member or other person shall have any right to inspect the books of a registered society.

(2) In the case of a society to which section 4 of this Act applies, the foregoing subsection shall have effect notwithstanding anything relating to such inspection in any rules of the society made before 12th September 1893. [119]

NOTE to section 45

Definition: 'registered society': see s 74 below.

46. Inspection of books by members, etc.

(1) Subject to any regulations as to the time and manner of inspection which may be made from time to time by the general meetings of a registered society, any member, and any person having an interest in the funds, of the society shall be allowed to inspect at all reasonable hours—
- (a) his own account; and
- (b) all the particulars contained in the duplicate register kept under section 44(3)(a) of this Act or, if no duplicate register is so kept, all the particulars in the register kept under section 44(1) of this Act other than those entered under paragraph (b) or (c) thereof.

(2) A registered society may by its rules (not being rules made earlier than 12th September 1893) authorise, in addition to any inspection in pursuance of the foregoing subsection, the inspection of such of the society's books upon such conditions as may be specified in the rules, but no person who is not an officer of the society or specially authorised by a resolution of the society shall be authorised by the rules to inspect the loan or deposit account of any other person without that other person's written consent.

[120]

NOTES to section 46

Definitions: 'meeting': see s 74 below; 'registered society': *Ibid*; 'officer': *Ibid*.

47. Inspection of books by order of registrar.

(1) Subject to subsection (2) of this section, the appropriate registrar may, if he thinks fit, on the application of ten members of a registered society each of whom has been a

member of the society for not less than twelve months immediately preceding the date of the application, appoint an accountant or actuary to inspect the books of the society and to report thereon.

(2) The members making an application under the foregoing subsection shall deposit with the appropriate registrar as security for the costs of the proposed inspection such sum as he may require; and all expenses of and incidental to the inspection shall be defrayed by the applicants, or out of the funds of the society, or by the members or officers, or former members or officers, of the society, in such proportions as that registrar may direct.

(3) A person appointed under this section shall have power to make copies of any books of the society, and to take extracts therefrom, at all reasonable hours at the society's registered office or at any other place where those books are kept.

(4) The appropriate registrar shall communicate the results of any inspection under this section to the applicants and to the society. [121]

NOTES to section 47

Definitions: 'the appropriate registrar': see s 73 below; 'registered society': see s 74 below; 'officer': *Ibid*.

48. Production of documents and provision of information for certain purposes.

(1) The appropriate registrar may at any time, by notice in writing served on a registered society or on any person who is or has been an officer of such a society, require that society or person to produce to that registrar such books, accounts and other documents relating to the business of the society, and to furnish to him such other information relating to that business, as that registrar considers necessary for the exercise of any of the powers which he has by virtue of section 16(1)(c)(ii), 16(4) or 56 of this Act; and any such notice may contain a requirement that any information to be furnished in accordance with the notice shall be verified by a statutory declaration.

(2) Any society or other person failing to comply with the requirements of a notice under the foregoing subsection shall be liable on summary conviction to a fine not exceeding fifty pounds or to imprisonment for a term not exceeding three months or to both.

(3) The appropriate registrar may, if he considers it just, direct that all or any of the expenses incurred by him in exercising his powers under subsection (1) of this section in relation to any society shall, either wholly or to such extent as he may determine, be defrayed out of the funds of the society or by the officers or former officers thereof or any of them; and any sum which any society or other person is required by such a direction to pay shall be a debt due to the appropriate registrar from that society or person. [122]

NOTES to section 48

Definitions: 'the appropriate registrar': see s 73 below; 'registered society': see s 74 below; 'officer': *Ibid*.

49. Appointment of inspectors and calling of special meetings.

(1) Upon the application of one-tenth of the whole number of members of a registered society or, in the case of a society with more than one thousand members, of one hundred of those members, the chief registrar may, with the consent of the Treasury—
- (a) appoint an inspector or inspectors to examine into and report on the affairs of the society; or
- (b) call a special meeting of the society.

(2) An application under this section shall be supported by such evidence for the purpose of showing that the applicants have good reason for requiring the examination

or meeting and are not actuated by malicious motives, and such notice of the application shall be given to the society, as the chief registrar shall direct.

(3) The chief registrar may, if he thinks fit, require the applicants to give security for the costs of the proposed examination or meeting before appointing any inspector or calling the meeting.

(4) All expenses of and incidental or preliminary to any such examination or meeting shall be defrayed by the members applying for it, or out of the funds of the society, or by the members or officers, or former members or officers, of the society, in such proportions as the chief registrar shall direct.

(5) An inspector appointed under this section may require the production of all or any of the books, accounts, securities, and documents of the society, and may examine on oath its officers, members, agents and servants in relation to its business, and may for that purpose administer oaths.

(6) The chief registrar may direct at what time and place a special meeting under this section is to be held, and what matters are to be discussed and determined at the meeting; and the meeting shall have all the powers of a meeting called according to the rules of the society, and shall have power to appoint its own chairman notwithstanding any rule of the society to the contrary.

(7) In the case of a society registered, and doing business exclusively, in Scotland, references in this section to the chief registrar shall be construed as references to the assistant registrar for Scotland. [123]

NOTES to section 49
Definitions: 'registered society': see s 74 below; 'Chief Registrar': see s 73 below; 'meeting': see s 74 below; 'officer': *Ibid.*

Amalgamations, transfers of engagements and conversions

50. Amalgamation of societies.

(1) Any two or more registered societies may by special resolution of each of those societies become amalgamated together as one society, with or without any dissolution or division of the funds of those societies or any of them; and the property of each of those societies shall become vested in the amalgamated society without the necessity of any form of conveyance other than that contained in the special resolution.

(2) In this section the expression 'special resolution' means a resolution which is—
(a) passed by not less than two-thirds of such members of the society for the time being entitled under the society's rules to vote as may have voted in person, or by proxy where the rules allow proxies, at any general meeting of which notice, specifying the intention to propose the resolution, has been duly given according to those rules; and
(b) confirmed by a majority of such members of the society for the time being entitled as aforesaid as may have voted as aforesaid at a subsequent general meeting of which notice has been duly given held not less than fourteen days nor more than one month from the day of the meeting at which the resolution was passed in accordance with paragraph (a) of this subsection.

(3) At any such meeting as aforesaid, a declaration by the chairman that the resolution has been carried shall be deemed conclusive evidence of that fact.

(4) A copy of every special resolution for the purposes of this section signed by the chairman of the meeting at which the resolution was confirmed and countersigned by the secretary of the society shall be sent to the appropriate registrar and registered by him; and until that copy is so registered the special resolution shall not take effect.

(5) It shall be the duty of a registered society to send any special resolution for registration in accordance with the last foregoing subsection within fourteen days from the day on which the resolution is confirmed under subsection (2)(b) of this section, but this subsection shall not invalidate registration of the resolution after that time. [124]

NOTE to section 50
Amendment: Section 50 was restricted by the Housing Associations Act 1985 (c 69), s 21(2).

51. Transfer of engagements between societies.

(1) Any registered society may by special resolution transfer its engagements to any other registered society which may undertake to fulfil those engagements; and if that resolution approves the transfer of the whole or any part of the society's property to that other society, the whole or, as the case may be, that part of the society's property shall vest in that other society without any conveyance or assignment.

(2) Subsections (2) to (5) of section 50 of this Act shall have effect for the purposes of this section as they have effect for the purposes of that section.

(3) In its application to Scotland, subsection (1) of this section shall have effect as if for the word 'assignment' there were substituted the word 'assignation'. [125]

NOTES to section 51
Amendment: Section 51 was restricted by the Housing Associations Act 1985 (c 69), s 21(2).
Definitions: 'registered society': see s 74 below; 'property': *Ibid*.

52. Conversion into, amalgamation with, or transfer of engagements to company.

(1) A registered society may by special resolution determine to convert itself into, or to amalagamate with or transfer its engagements to, a company under the Companies Acts.

(2) If a special resolution for converting a registered society into a company contains the particulars required by the [Companies Act 1985] to be contained in the memorandum of association of a company and a copy thereof has been registered by the appropriate registrar, a copy of that resolution under the seal and stamp of the central office or bearing the signature of the assistant registrar for Scotland, as the case may require, shall have the same effect as a memorandum of association duly signed and attested under the said [Act of 1985].

(3) Subsections (2) and (5) of section 50 of this Act shall have effect for the purposes of this section as they have effect for the purposes of that section but as if in paragraph (a) of the said subsection (2) for the words 'two-thirds' there were substituted the words 'three-fourths'.

(4) Subject to subsection (5) of this section, if a registered society is registered as, or amalgamates with, or transfers all its engagements to, a company under the Companies Acts, the registration of that society under this Act shall thereupon become void and, subject to section 59 of this Act, shall be cancelled by the chief registrar or, under the direction of the chief registrar, by the assistant registrar for Scotland.

(5) Registration of a registered society as a company shall not affect any right or claim for the time being subsisting against the society or any penalty for the time being incurred by the society; and—
  (a) for the purpose of enforcing any such right, claim or penalty, the society may be sued and proceeded against in the same manner as if it had not become registered as a company; and
  (b) every such right or claim, or the liability to any such penalty, shall have priority as against the property of the company over all other rights or claims against or liabilities of the company. [126]

NOTES to section 52

Amendments: Sub-s (2) was amended by the Companies Consolidation (Consequential Provisions) Act 1985 (c 9), s 30, Sch 2; s 52 was restricted by the Housing Associations Act 1985 (c 69), s 21(3).

Definitions: 'registered society': see s 74 below; 'Companies Acts': *Ibid*; 'assistant registrar': see s 73 below; 'Chief registrar': *Ibid*; 'property': see s 74 below.

53. Conversion of company into registered society.

(1) A company registered under the Companies Acts may, by a special resolution as defined by section [738 of the Companies Act 1985], determine to convert itself into a registered society; and for this purpose, in any case where the nominal value of the company's shares held by any member other than a registered society exceeds [the maximum for the time being permitted by section 6(1) of this Act in the case of a member of a registered society], the resolution may provide for the conversion of the shares representing that excess into a transferable loan stock bearing such rate of interest as may be fixed, and repayable on such conditions only as are determined by the resolution.

(2) Any such resolution as aforesaid shall be accompanied by a copy of the rules of the society therein referred to and shall appoint seven persons, being members of the company, who, together with the secretary, shall sign the rules and who may either—
   (a) be authorised to accept any alterations made by the appropriate registrar therein without further consulting the company; or
   (b) be required to lay any such alterations before the company in general meeting for acceptance as the resolution may direct.

(3) A copy of the resolution aforesaid shall be sent with a copy of the rule aforesaid to the appropriate registrar who, upon the registration of the society under this Act, shall give to it, in addition to an acknowledgment of registration under section 2(3) of this Act, a certificate similarly sealed or signed that the rules of the society referred to in the resolution have been registered.

(4) A copy of any such resolution as aforesaid under the seal of the company together with the certificate issued as aforesaid by the appropriate registrar shall be sent for registration to the office of the registrar of companies within the meaning of the Companies Act 1948 and, upon his registering that resolution and certificate, the conversion shall take effect.

(5) The name under which any company is registered under this section as a registered society shall not include the word 'company'.

(6) Subject to the next following subsection, upon the conversion of a company into a registered society under this section, the registration of the company under the Companies Acts shall become void and shall be cancelled by the registrar of companies aforesaid.

(7) The registration of a company as a registered society shall not affect any right or claim for the time being subsisting against the company or any penalty for the time being incurred by the company; and—
   (a) for the purpose of enforcing any such right, penalty or claim the company may be sued and proceeded against in the same manner as if it had not been registered as a society;
   (b) any such right or claim and the liability to any such penalty shall have priority as against the property of the registered society over all other rights or claims against or liabilities of the society.

NOTES to section 53

Amendments: Sub-s (1) was amended by the Companies Consolidation (Consequential Provisions) Act 1985 (c 9), s 30, Sch 2, and by the Industrial and Provident Societies Act 1975 (c 41), s 3(3); s 53 was modified in relation to credit unions by the Credit Unions Act 1979 (c 34), ss 6, 23.

Industrial and Provident Societies Act 1965 (c 12), s 57 [131]

Definitions: 'registered society': see s 74 below; 'appropriate registrar': see s 73 below; 'property': see s 74 below.

54. Saving for rights of creditors.

An amalgamation or transfer of engagements in pursuance of section 50, 51 or 52 of this Act shall not prejudice any right of a creditor of any registered society which is a party thereto. [128]

NOTE to section 54
Definition: 'registered society': see s 74 below.

Dissolution of society

55. Dissolution of registered society.

Subject to section 59 of this Act, a registered society may be dissolved—
(a) on its being wound up in pursuance of an order or resolution made as is directed in regard to companies by the [Insolvency Act 1986], the provisions whereof shall apply to that order or resolution as if the society were a company, but subject to the following modifications, that is to say—
  (i) any reference in those provisions to the registrar within the meaning of that Act shall for the purposes of the society's winding up be construed as a reference to the appropriate registrar within the meaning of this Act; and
  (ii) if the society is wound up in Scotland, the court having jurisdiction shall be the sheriff court within whose jurisdiction the society's registered office is situated; or
(b) in accordance with section 58 of this Act, by an instrument of dissolution to which not less than three-fourths of the members of the society have given their consent testified by their signatures to the instrument. [129]

NOTES to section 55
Amendments: Words substituted by the Insolvency Act 1986 (c 45), s 439, Sch 14; section 55 was restricted by the Housing Associations Act 1985 (c 69), s 21(4).
Definitions: 'registered society': see s 74 below; 'the appropriate registrar': see s 73 below.

56. Power of registrar to petition for winding up.

In the case of a society to which section 4 of this Act applies which was registered or deemed to be registered under the Act of 1893 before 26th July 1938, a petition for the winding up of the society may be presented to the court by the appropriate registrar if it appears to that registrar—
(a) that neither of the conditions specified in section 1(2) of this Act is fulfilled in the case of that society; and
(b) that it would be in the interests of persons who have invested or deposited money with the society or of any other person that the society should be wound up. [130]

NOTES to section 56
Definition: 'appropriate registrar': see s 74 below.

57. Liability of members in winding up.

Where a registered society is wound up by virtue of section 55(a) of this Act, the liability of a present or past member of the society to contribute for payment of the debts and liabilities of the society, the expenses of winding up, and the adjustment of the rights of contributories amongst themselves, shall be qualified as follows, that is to say—
(a) no person who ceased to be a member not less than one year before the beginning of the winding up shall be liable to contribute;

(b) no person shall be liable to contribute in respect of any debt or liability contracted after he ceased to be a member;
(c) no person who is not a member shall be liable to contribute unless it appears to the court that the contributions of the existing members are insufficient to satisfy the just demands on the society;
(d) no contribution shall be required from any person exceeding the amount, if any, unpaid on the shares in respect of which he is liable as a past or present member;
(e) in the case of a withdrawable share which has been withdrawn, a person shall be taken to have ceased to be a member in respect of that share as from the date of the notice or application for withdrawal. [131]

NOTES to section 57
Definition: 'registered society': see s 74 below.

58. Instrument of dissolution.

(1) The following provisions of this section shall have effect where a society is to be dissolved by an instrument of dissolution under section 55(b) of this Act.

(2) The instrument of dissolution shall set forth—
(a) the liabilities and assets of the society in detail;
(b) the number of the members and the nature of their respective interests in the society;
(c) the claims of creditors, if any, and the provision to be made for their payment; and
(d) unless stated in the instrument of dissolution to be left to the award of the chief registrar, the intended appropriation or division of the funds and property of the society.

(3) Alterations in the instrument of dissolution may be made by the consent of not less than three-fourths of the members of the society testified by their signatures to the alteration.

(4) The instrument of dissolution shall be sent to the appropriate registrar accompanied by a statutory declaration made by three members and the secretary of the society that all relevant provisions of this Act have been complied with; and any person knowingly making a false or fraudulent declaration in the matter shall be guilty of a misdemeanour or, in Scotland, an offence.

(5) The instrument of dissolution and any alterations thereto shall be registered in like manner as an amendment of the rules of the society and shall be binding upon all the members of the society, but shall not be so registered until the appropriate registrar has received such a final return from the society as is referred to in section 39(4) of this Act.

(6) The appropriate registrar shall cause notice of the dissolution to be advertised at the expense of the society in the Gazette and in some newspaper circulating in or about the locality in which the society's registered office is situated; and unless—
(a) within three months from the date of the Gazette in which that advertisement appears a member or other person interested in or having any claim on the funds of the society commences in the county court, or in Scotland before the sheriff, having jurisdiction in that locality proceedings to set aside the dissolution of the society; and
(b) that dissolution is set aside accordingly,
then, subject to subsection (7) of this section, the society shall be legally dissolved from the date of the advertisement and the requisite consents to the instrument of dissolution shall be deemed to have been duly obtained without proof of the signatures thereto.

(7) If the certificate referred to in section 59 of this Act has not been lodged with the appropriate registrar by the date of the advertisement referred to in subsection (6) of this section, the society shall be legally dissolved only from the date when that certificate is so lodged.

(8) Notice of any proceedings to set aside the dissolution of a society shall be sent to the appropriate registrar by the person taking those proceedings not later than seven days after they are commenced or not later than the expiration of the period of three months referred to subsection (6) of this section, whichever is the earlier; and notice of any order setting the dissolution aside shall be sent by the society to the appropriate registrar within seven days after the making of the order.

(9) In the application of the section to a society which for the time being consists solely of two registered societies, the reference in subsection (4) thereof to three members shall be construed as a reference to both members. [132]

NOTES to section 58
Amendment: Section 58 was restricted by the Housing Associations Act 1985 (c 69), s 21(5).
Definitions: 'Chief Registrar': see s 73 below; 'property': see s 74 below; 'appropriate registrar': see s 73 below; 'the Gazette': see s 74 below.

Special restriction on dissolution, etc

59. Restriction on dissolution or cancellation of registration of society.

Where a registered society is to be dissolved in accordance with section 55 of this Act, or where a registered society's engagements are transferred under section 51 or 52 of this Act, the society shall not be dissolved, and the registration of the society shall not be cancelled, until there has been lodged with the appropriate registrar a certificate signed by the liquidator or by the secretary or some other officer of the society approved by that registrar that all property vested in the society has been duly conveyed or transferred by the society to the persons entitled. [133]

NOTES to section 59
Definitions: 'registered society': see s 74 below; 'appropriate registrar': see s 73 below; 'officer': see s 74 below; 'property': *Ibid.*

Disputes, offences and legal proceedings

60. Decision of disputes.

(1) Subject to subsections (2), (4) and (5) of this section, every dispute between a registered society or an officer thereof and—
 (a) a member of the society; or
 (b) any person aggrieved who has ceased to be a member of the society not more than six months previously; or
 (c) any person claiming through a member of the society or any such person aggrieved; or
 (d) any person claiming under the rules of the society,
shall, if the society's rules give directions as to the manner in which such disputes are to be decided, be decided in that manner.

(2) Unless the rules of the society expressly forbid it, the parties to a dispute in a registered society may by consent refer the dispute to the chief registrar or to the assistant registrar for Scotland who shall either by himself or by some other registrar hear and determine the dispute.

(3) A decision made under subsection (1) or (2) of this section on any dispute shall be binding and conclusive on all parties without appeal; and—
 (a) the decision shall not be removable into any court of law or restrainable by injunction; and
 (b) application for the enforcement of the decision may be made to the county court.

(4) Subject to subsection (5) of this section, any dispute directed by the rules of a registered society to be referred to justices shall be determined by a magistrates' court.

(5) Where, whether by virtue of subsection (4) of this section or otherwise, a dispute is congnisable under the rules of a registered society by a magistrates' court, the parties to the dispute may by agreement refer the dispute to the county court, who may hear and determine it.

(6) Where the rules of a registered society contain no direction as to disputes, or where no decision is made on a dispute within forty days after application to the society for a reference under its rules, any person such as is mentioned in subsection (1)(a) to (d) of this section who is a party to the dispute may apply either to the county court or to a magistrates' court, who may hear and determine the matter in dispute.

(7) In the application of the foregoing provisions of this section to Scotland—
 (a) in subsection (3), paragraph (a) shall be omitted and in paragraph (b) for the words 'county court' there shall be substituted the word 'sheriff';
 (b) subsections (4) to (6) shall not apply, but in Scotland—
  (i) any dispute directed by the rules of a registered society to be referred to justices, a justice of the peace court, or a court of summary jurisdiction, shall be determined by the sheriff;
  (iii) where the rules of a registered society contain no direction as to disputes, or where no decision is made on a dispute within forty days after application to the society for a reference under its rules, any person such as is mentioned in subsection (1)(a) to (d) of this section who is a party to the dispute may apply to the sheriff, who may hear and determine the matter in dispute.

(8) For the purposes of the hearing or determination of a dispute under this section—
 (a) without prejudice to any powers exercisable in England or Wales by virtue of the Arbitration Act 1950, a registrar may administer oaths and require the attendance of all parties concerned and of witnesses and the production of all books and documents relating to the matter in question, and shall have power to order the expenses of determining the dispute to be paid either out of the fund of the society or by such parties to the dispute as he shall think fit; and any person refusing to attend, or to produce any documents, or to give evidence, before the registrar shall be liable on summary conviction to a fine not exceeding five pounds;
 (b) in England and Wales, a magistrates' court may grant to either party such discovery as to documents and otherwise, or such inspection of documents, being, in the case of discovery to be made on behalf of the society, discovery by such officer of the society as the court may determine, as might have been granted by virtue of section 12 of the said Act of 1950 by a registrar to whom the dispute had been referred;
 (c) in Scotland, a registrar may grant such warrant for the recovery of documents and examination of havers as might be granted by the sheriff.

(9) Section 21 of the Arbitration Act 1950 shall not apply to any dispute referred under subsections (2) to (7) of this section and, notwithstanding anything in any other Act, the court or registrar to whom any dispute is so referred shall not be compelled to state a case on any question of law arising in the dispute but may at the request of either party state such a case for the opinion of the High Court or, as the case may be, the Court of Session.

[134]

NOTES to section 60

Definitions: 'registered society': see s 74 below; 'Chief registrar': see s 73 below; 'person claiming through a member': see s 74 below; 'assistant registrar': see s 73 below.

61. General offences by societies, etc.

If any registered society, or any officer or member thereof, or any other person—
 (a) fails to give any notice, send any return or other document, do anything or allow anything to be done which that society, officer, member or other person is by this Act required to give, send, do or allow to be done, as the case may be; or
 (b) wilfully neglects or refuses to do any act, or to furnish any information, required for the purposes of this Act by the chief registrar or any assistant registrar or by

Industrial and Provident Societies Act 1965 (c 12), s 65 [139]

      any other person authorised under this Act, or does anything forbidden by this Act; or

(c)   makes a return required by this Act, or wilfully furnishes information so required, which is in any respect false or insufficient,

that society, officer, member or other person, as the case may be, shall be liable on summary conviction to a fine not exceeding [Level 3 on the Standard Scale].   [135]

NOTES to section 61

Amendment: Section 61 was amended by the Criminal Justice Act 1982 (c 48), s 56, Sch 6; s 61 was applied to credit unions by the Credit Unions Act 1979 (c 34), s 28.

Definitions: 'registered society': see s 74 below; 'officer': *Ibid*; 'Chief registrar': see s 73 below; 'assistant registrar': *Ibid*; 'level 3 on the Standard Scale': level 3 is currently £400. See the Increase of Criminal Penalties Etc. (Scotland) Order 1984, SI 1984/526.

62. Offences by societies to be also offences by officers, etc.

Every offence committed by a registered society under this Act shall be deemed to have been also committed by every officer of that society bound by the society's rules to fulfil the duty of which that offence is a breach or, if there is no such officer, by every member of the society's committee who is not proved to have been ignorant of, or to have attempted to prevent, the commission of that offence.   [136]

NOTES to section 62

Amendment: Section 62 was applied to credit unions by the Credit Unions Act 1979 (c 34), s 28.

Definitions: 'registered society': see s 74 below; 'officer': *Ibid*; 'committee': *Ibid*.

63. Continuing offences.

Every act or default under this Act constituting an offence shall constitute a new offence in every week during which it continues.   [137]

NOTE to section 63

Amendment: Section 63 was applied to credit unions by the Credit Unions Act 1979 (c 34), s 28.

64. Punishment of fraud or misappropriation.

(1) Subject to subsection (2) of this section, any person who obtains possession by false representation or imposition of any property of a registered society, or having any such property in his possession withholds or misapplies it or wilfully applies any part of it to purposes which are not authorised by the rules of the society or which are not in accordance with this Act, shall be liable on summary conviction to a fine not exceeding twenty pounds with costs or expenses and to be ordered to deliver up that property or to repay all moneys improperly applied and, in default of such delivery or repayment or of the payment of any such fine, to be imprisoned for a term not exceeding three months; but nothing in this subsection shall prevent any such person from being proceeded against by way of indictment for any offence if he has not previously been convicted in respect of the same matters under this subsection.

(2) If on proceedings under the foregoing subsection it is not proved that the person charged acted with any fraudulent intent, he may be ordered to deliver up any property belonging to the society or to repay any money improperly applied, with costs or expenses, but shall not be liable to conviction under that subsection.   [138]

NOTES to section 64

Amendment: Section 42 was applied to credit unions by the Credit Unions Act 1979 (c 34), s 28.

Definitions: 'property': see s 74 below; 'registered society': *Ibid*.

65. Penalty for falsification.

If any person, with intent to falsify it or to evade any of the provisions of this Act, wilfully makes, or orders or allows to be made, any entry or erasure in, or omission from, any balance-sheet of a registered society, or any contribution or collecting book, or any return or document required to be sent, produced or delivered for the purposes of this Act, he shall be liable on summary conviction to a fine not exceeding fifty pounds.

[139]

NOTES to section 65

Amendment: Section 65 was applied to credit unions by the Credit Unions Act 1979 (c 34), s 28.
Definition: 'registered society': see s 74 below.

---

66. Institution of proceedings.

(1) Proceedings for the recovery of a fine which under this Act is recoverable on the summary conviction of the offender may be instituted by, and in England and Wales only by, the following persons, that is to say—
  (a) in the case of proceedings by virtue of section 64(1) of this Act—
    (i) the registered society concerned; or
    (ii) any member of that society authorised by the society or its committee or by the central office; or
    (iii) the chief registrar or, with the authority of the chief registrar, an assistant registrar;
  (b) in the case of proceedings by virtue of section 13(3) of this Act, the registered society concerned;
  (c) in any other case, the chief registrar, any assistant registrar or any person aggrieved.

(2) Notwithstanding any limitation on the time for the taking of proceedings contained in any Act, any proceedings such as are mentioned in subsection (1) of this section which are instituted by a registrar or procurator-fiscal may be brought at any time within one year of the first discovery of the offence by the appropriate registrar, but not in any case more than three years after the commission of the offence. **[140]**

NOTES to section 66

Amendment: Section 66 was applied to credit unions by the Credit Unions Act 1979 (c 34), s 28.
Definitions: 'registered society': see s 74 below; 'Chief registrar': see s 73 below; 'assistant registrar': *Ibid*; 'the appropriate registrar': *Ibid*.

---

67. Recovery of costs, etc.

(1) Any costs or expenses ordered or directed by the chief registrar or any other registrar to be paid by any person under this Act shall be recoverable summarily as a civil debt.

(2) In the application of the foregoing subsection to Scotland, the word 'summarily' shall be omitted. **[141]**

NOTE to section 67

Definition: 'Chief registrar': see s 73 below.

---

68. Service of process.

Where proceedings are taken against a registered society for the recovery of any fine under this Act, the summons or other process shall be sufficiently served by leaving a true copy thereof at the registered office of the society or, if that office is closed, by posting that copy on the outer door of that office. **[142]**

NOTES to section 68

Amendment: Section 68 was applied to credit unions by the Credit Unions Act 1979 (c 34), s 28.
Definitions: 'registered society': see s 74 below; 'registered office': *Ibid*.

Industrial and Provident Societies Act 1965 (c 12), s 73 [147]

Miscellaneous and general

69. Remuneration of county court registrars.

Registrars of county courts shall be remunerated for any duties to be performed by them under this Act in such manner as the Treasury may with the consent of the Lord Chancellor from time to time direct. [143]

70. Fees.

(1) The Treasury may determine a scale of fees to be paid for matters to be transacted or for the inspection of documents under this Act.

(2) All fees received by any registrar under or by virtue of this Act shall be paid into the Exchequer. [144]

71. Regulations.

(1) The Treasury may make regulations respecting registration and procedure under this Act, the forms to be used for such registration, and the duties and other functions of, and the inspection of documents kept by, the appropriate registrar under this Act, and generally for carrying this Act into effect.

(2) Any such regulations may impose reasonable fines on persons who contravene or fail to comply with any of those regulations; and any such fine shall be recoverable on the summary conviction of the offender.

(3) Any regulations made under this section shall be made by statutory instrument and shall be laid before Parliament after they are made. [145]

72. Form, deposit and evidence of documents.

(1) Subject to any regulations under section 71 of this Act, every return and other document required for the purposes of this Act shall be made in such form and shall contain such particulars, and shall be deposited and registered or recorded, with or without observations thereon, in such manner, as the chief registrar may direct.

(2) Every document bearing the seal or stamp of the central office, including in particular any document purporting to be a copy or extract of a registered society's rules or of any other instrument or document whatsoever, shall be received in evidence without further proof; and every document purporting to be signed by the chief registrar or any assistant registrar or by any inspector . . . under this Act shall, in the absence of any evidence to the contrary, be received in evidence without proof of the signature.
[146]

NOTES to section 72

Amendment: In sub-s (2), words repealed by the Friendly and Industrial and Provident Societies Act 1968 (c 55), s 20, Sch 2.
Definitions: 'chief registrar': see s 73 below; 'assistant registrar': *Ibid.*

73. Registrars, central office, etc.

(1) In this Act—
(a) the expressions 'chief registrar' and 'assistant registrar' mean respectively the chief registrar of friendly societies appointed under the Friendly Societies Act 1896 and an assistant registrar of friendly societies so appointed;
(b) the expression 'central office' means the central office established under the said Act of 1896;
(c) the expression 'appropriate registrar' in relation to any society registered, to be registered or deemed to be registered, under this Act means—
  (i) if the society's registered office is for the time being, or, as the case may be, is to be, in England, Wales or the Channel Islands, the central office;

(ii) if the society's registered office is for the time being, or, as the case may be, is to be, in Scotland, the assistant registrar for Scotland;

and, except where the context otherwise requires, any reference in this Act to a registrar shall be construed as including the chief and any assistant registrar.

(2) Sections 3, 4(2) and (3), and 6 of the said Act of 1896 (which relate to the duties of the chief and assistant registrars under that Act) shall apply for the purposes of this Act as they apply for the purposes of that Act. **[147]**

74. Interpretation—general.

In this Act, except where the context otherwise requires, the following expressions have the following meanings respectively, that is to say—

'Act of 1893', means the Industrial and Provident Societies Act 1893;

'amendment', in relation to the rules of a registered society, includes a new rule, and a resolution rescinding a rule, of the society;

'committee', in relation to a society, means the committee of management or other directing body of the society;

'Companies Acts' includes the [Companies Act 1985], any earlier enactment for the like purposes which has been repealed, and any law for the like purposes which is or has been in force in Northern Ireland or any of the Channel Islands;

'Gazette', in relation to a registered society, means such one or more of the following as may be appropriate in the circumstances of the case, that is to say—
  (a) the London Gazette if the society's registered office is situated, or its rules are recorded, in England, Wales or the Channel Islands;
  (b) the Edinburgh Gazette if the society's registered office is situated, or its rules are recorded, in Scotland;
  (c) the Belfast Gazette if the society's rules are recorded in Northern Ireland;

'heritable security' has the same meaning as in the Conveyancing (Scotland) Act 1924 except that it includes a security constituted by *ex facie* absolute disposition or assignation;

'land' includes hereditaments and chattels real, and in Scotland, heritable subjects of whatever description;

'meeting', in relation to a society, includes, where the rules of that society so allow, a meeting of delegates appointed by members;

'officer', in relation to a registered society, includes any treasurer, secretary, member of the committee, manager or servant of the society other than a servant appointed by the society's committee, but does not include an [auditor appointed by the society in accordance with the requirements of the Friendly and Industrial and Provident Societies Act 1968];

'persons claiming through a member', in relation to a registered society, includes the heirs, executors or administrators and assignees of a member and, where nomination is allowed, his nominee;

'prescribed' means prescribed by regulations under section 71 of this Act;

'property' includes all real, personal or heritable and moveable estate, including books and papers;

'registered' in relation to the name or an office of a society means for the time being registered under this Act;

'registered rules', in relation to a registered society, means the rules of the society registered or deemed to be registered under this Act as for the time being in force after any amendment thereof so registered;

'registered society' means, subject to section 76 of this Act, a society registered or deemed to be registered under this Act. **[148]**

NOTES to section 74

Amendment: Definition of 'Companies Acts' amended by the Companies Consolidation (Consequential Provisions) Act 1985 (c 9), s 30, Sch 2.

Industrial and Provident Societies Act 1965 (c 12), s 77 **[151]**

75. Channel Islands.

(1) Subject to any express provision of this Act with respect to the Channel Islands, this Act in its application to those Islands shall have effect subject to such adaptations and modifications as Her Majesty may by Order in Council specify.

(2) Any Order in Council under the foregoing subsection may be varied or revoked by a subsequent Order in Council so made. **[149]**

76. Northern Ireland societies.

(1) Where in the case of any society for the time being registered under the law for the time being in force in Northern Ireland for purposes corresponding to those of this Act, copies of that society's rules so registered have been sent to the central office or to the assistant registrar for Scotland to be recorded by that office or registrar and have been so recorded, then, for the purposes of the operation of this Act in the area for which that office or registrar is the appropriate registrar, references to a registered society in such, but such only, of the provisions of this Act as are specified in subsection (2) of this section shall, subject to subsection (3) of this section include a reference to that society, and for the purposes of those provisions that society, those rules and any amendment of those rules registered and recorded as aforesaid shall in that area be deemed to be a society, rules or an amendment duly registered under this Act by the appropriate registrar for that area.

(2) The provisions of this Act referred to in the foregoing subsection are sections 2(2), 3, 5(4), (6) and (7), 6(1)(a), 7(1)(b), (2) (3) and (6), 10(1)(a), 13(3), 14, 15, 16(1)(a)(i), 19(2), 22, 26 to 30, 31(b), 32 to 36, 41, 42, 44(5), 45(1), 50, 51, 52(5), 54, 60 to 62, 64 to 66 and 72.

(3) Nothing in this section shall confer any power or impose any obligation or liability with respect to the taking or refraining from taking of, or a failure to take, any action outside Great Britain and the Channel Islands; and in the application of section 45(1) of this Act by virtue of this section the reference therein to this Act shall be construed as a reference to the law for the time being in force in Northern Ireland for purposes corresponding to those of this Act.

(4) In relation to any society for the time being registered as mentioned in subsection (1) of this section, Article 22 of the Government of Ireland (Companies, Societies, &c) Order 1922 shall have effect as if the words from 'a society registered in Northern Ireland' to 'United Kingdom, and' and the words 'both in their application to the United Kingdom exclusive of Northern Ireland and' were omitted. **[150]**

77. Repeals and savings.

(1) . . .

(2) Without prejudice to section 4 of this Act, any regulations, application or notice made or given and any other thing whatsoever done under or in pursuance of any of the enactments repealed by this Act shall be deemed for the purposes of this Act to have been made, given or done, as the case may be, under or in pursuance of the corresponding provision of this Act; and anything begun under any of the said enactments may be continued under this Act as if begun under this Act.

(3) So much of any document as refers expressly or by implication to any enactment repealed by this Act shall, if and so far as the context permits, be construed as referring to this Act or the corresponding enactment therein.

(4) Nothing in section 4 of this Act or in this section shall be taken as affecting the general application of section 38 of the Interpretation Act 1889 with regard to the effect of repeals. **[151]**

NOTE to section 77

Amendment: Sub-s (1) was repealed by the Statute Law Repeals Act 1974 (c 22), s 1, Sch 1, Pt XI.

78. Short title, extent and commencement.

(1) This Act may be cited as the Industrial and Provident Societies Act 1965.

(2) This Act extends to the Channel Islands but does not extend to Northern Ireland.

(3) This Act shall come into operation on such day as Her Majesty may by Order in Council appoint. [152]

SCHEDULES

SCHEDULE 1

MATTERS TO BE PROVIDED FOR IN SOCIETY'S RULES

1 The name of the society, which shall comply with the requirements of section 5 of this Act.

2 The objects of the society.

3 The place which is to be the registered office of the society to which all communications and notices to the society may be addressed.

4 The terms of admission of the members, including any society or company investing funds in the society under the provisions of this Act.

5 The mode of holding meetings, the scale and right of voting, and the mode of making, altering or rescinding rules.

6 The appointment and removal of a committee, by whatever name, and of managers or other officers and their respective powers and remuneration.

7 Determination in accordance with section 6 of this Act of the maximum amount of the interest in the shares of the society which may be held by any member otherwise than by virtue of section 6(1)(a), (b) or (c) of this Act.

8 Determination whether the society may contract loans or receive moneys on deposit subject to the provisions of this Act from members or others; and, if so, under what conditions, under what security, and to what limits of amount.

9 Determination whether the shares or any of them shall be transferable, and provision for the form of transfer and registration of the shares, and for the consent of the committee thereto; determination whether the shares of any of them shall be withdrawable, and provision for the mode of withdrawal and for payment of the balance due thereon on withdrawing from the society.

10 Provision for the audit of accounts by one or more [auditor appointed by the society in accordance with the requirements of the Friendly and Industrial and Provident Societies Act 1968].

11 Determination whether and, if so, how members may withdraw from the society, and provision for the claims of the representatives of deceased members, or the trustees of the property of bankrupt members or, in Scotland, members whose estate has been sequestrated, and for the payment of nominees.

12 The mode of application of profits of the society.

13 Provision for the custody and use of the society's seal.

14 Determination whether and, if so, by what authority, and in what manner, any part of the society's funds may be invested. [153]

NOTES to Schedule 1

Amendment: Words substituted by the Friendly and Industrial and Provident Societies Act 1968 (c 55), s 20, Sch 1, para 12.

Industrial and Provident Societies Act 1965 (c 12), Sch 2 [157]

Definitions: 'registered office': see s 74 above; 'meeting': *Ibid*; 'committee': *Ibid*.

SCHEDULE 2

Form of Statement by Society Carrying on Banking

1. Capital of the society:—
   (a) nominal amount of each share;
   (b) number of shares issued;
   (c) amount paid up on shares. [154]

2. Liabilities of the society on 1st January or 1st July last previous:—
   (a) on judgments;
   (b) on specialty;
   (c) on notes or bills;
   (d) on simple contract;
   (e) on estimated liabilities. [155]

3. Assets of the society on the same date:—
   (a) government securities (stating them);
   (b) bills of exchange and promissory notes;
   (c) cash at the bankers;
   (d) other securities. [156]

SCHEDULE 3

Form of Receipt on Mortgage, Heritable Security, Etc

Part I

Forms applicable in England and Wales

Form A

The   Limited hereby acknowledges to have received all moneys intended to be secured by the [within (or above) written] [annexed] deed [and by a further charge dated, etc, *or otherwise as required*].

Dated this   day of

} *Members of the Committee.*
} *Secretary.*

Form B

The   Limited hereby acknowledges that it has this day of   received the sum of   pounds representing all moneys intended to be secured by the [within (or above) written] [annexed] deed [and by a further charge dated, etc *or otherwise as required*], the payment having been made by CD of   and EF of

} *Members of the Committee.*
} *Secretary.*

Note. If the persons paying are not entitled to the equity of redemption but are paying the money out of a fund applicable to the discharge of the mortgage or other assurance, insert a statement to that effect.

A statement may also be inserted as to whether the recept is or is not to operate as a transfer of the benefit of the mortgage or other assurance. **[157]**

Part II

Forms applicable in Scotland

Form C

The   Limited acknowledges that (1) the foregoing disposition granted by A (with consent) in favour of the said society dated
and recorded in the Division of the General Register of Sasines for   on   was granted in security only of a loan of   pounds made by the said society to the said   , and (2) the said society have received repayment of all moneys secured by the said disposition.

Signed at   on the   day of

} Members of the Committee.

} Secretary.

Form D

The   Limited acknowledges to have received repayment of all moneys secured by the foregoing bond and disposition in security [bond and assignation in security] [bond and such other deed of heritable security as may have been agreed] granted by A in the said society's favour dated   and recorded in the Division of the General Register of Sasines for   on

Signed at   this   day of

} Members of the Committee.

} Secretary.

Form E

The   Limited hereby acknowledges to have received repayment of all moneys secured by the foregoing [*describe deed*] by A in the said society's favour.

Signed at   on the   day of

} Members of the Committee.

} Secretary.   **[158]**

SCHEDULE 4

Forms of Bond for Officers of Society

Part I

Forms applicable in England, Wales and the Channel Islands

Form A

Know all men by these presents, that we, *AB*, of   , one of the officers of the   Limited, herein-after referred to as 'the Society,'

Industrial and Provident Societies Act 1965 (c 12), Sch 4 [159]

whose registered office is at   in the country of
                    , and *CD*, of   (as surety on behalf of the said *AB*), are jointly and severally held and firmly bound to the said society in the sum of   , to be paid to the said society, or its certain attorney, for which payment well and truly to be made we jointly and severally bind ourselves, and each of us by himself, our and each of our heirs, executors, and administrators, firmly by these presents. Sealed with our seals. Dated the   day of
Whereas the above-bounden *AB* has been duly appointed to the office of   of the   Society, and he, together with the above-bounden *CD* as his surety, have entered into the above-written bond, subject to the condition herein-after contained: Now therefore the condition of the above-written bond is such, that if the said *AB* do render a just and true account of all moneys received and paid by him on account of the society, at such times as the rules thereof appoint, and do pay over all the moneys remaining in his hands, and assign and transfer or deliver all property (including books and papers) belonging to the society in his hands or custody to such person or persons as the society or the committee thereof appoint, according to the rules of the society, together with the proper and legal receipts or vouchers for such payments, then the above-written bond shall be void, but otherwise shall remain in full force. **[159]**

Sealed and delivered in the presence of

FORM B

Know all men by these presents that I   , of
                    , in the county of   , am firmly bound to   Limited, herein-after referred to as 'the Society,' whose registered office is at   , in the county of   , in the sum of   pounds sterling to be paid to the said society or its assigns, for which payment to be truly made to the said society or its certain attorney or assigns I bind myself, my heirs, executors, and administrators, by these presents sealed with my seal.

[And know further that I [we]
as surety [sureties] for the above-named principal obligor and such obligor are jointly and severally bound to the society in the sum aforesaid to be paid to the society or its assigns, for which payment to be truly made to the society or its certain attorney or assigns we firmly bind ourselves and each of us and each of our heirs, executors, and administrators by these presents sealed with our seals.]

Dated the   day of

The condition of the above-contained bond is that if the said
faithfully execute the office of   to the society during such time as he continues to hold the same in virtue either of his present appointment, or of any renewal thereof if such office is of a renewable character [without washing, embezzling, losing, misspending, misapplying, or unlawfully making away with any of the moneys, goods, chattels, wares, merchandise or effects whatsoever of the said society at any time committed to his charge, custody, or keeping by reason or means of his said office], and render a true and full account of all moneys received or paid by him on its behalf as and when he is required by the committee of the society for the time being, and pay over all the moneys remaining in his hands from time to time, and assign, transfer, and deliver up all securities, books, papers, property, and effects whatsoever of or belonging to the society in his charge, custody, or keeping, to such person or persons as the said committee may appoint, according to the rules or regulations of the society for the time being, together with the proper or legal receipts or vouchers for such payments; and in all other respects well and faithfully perform and fulfil the said office of   to the society according to the rules thereof, then the above-contained bond shall be void and of no effect; but otherwise shall remain in full force.

Sealed and delivered by the above-named

[The words between brackets against which we have set out initials being first struck out*] in the presence of us

and

PART II

Form applicable in Scotland

FORM C

I, *A B*, of , hereby bind and oblige myself to the extent of £ as cautioner for *C D*, a person employed by the society, that he, the said *C D*, shall on demand faithfully and truly account for all moneys received and paid to him for behoof of the said society, and also assign and transfer or deliver all property (including books and papers) belonging to the said society in his hands or custody, and that to such person or persons as the said society or the committee thereof appoint, according to the rules of the said society.

Signed at this day of

Signature of cautioner.

E F, witness.

G H, witness.

*If no words are struck out in the bond or condition, strike out these words and let the witnesses set their initials in the margin.

SCHEDULE 5

NOTE to Schedule 5
Schedule 5 was repealed by the Statute Law Repeals Act 1974 (c 22), s 1, Sch 1, Part XI.

Sheriff Courts (Scotland) Act 1971
(c 58)

★ ★ ★

Summary causes

35.—(1) The definition of 'summary cause' contained in paragraph (*i*) of section 3 of the Sheriff Courts (Scotland) Act 1907 shall cease to have effect, and for the purposes of the procedure and practice in civil proceedings in the sheriff court there shall be a form of process, to be known as a 'summary cause', which shall be used for the purposes of all civil proceedings brought in that court, being proceedings of one or other of the following descriptions, namely—
 (a) actions for payment of money not exceeding £1,500 in amount (exclusive of interest and expenses);
 (b) actions of multiplepoinding, actions of furthcoming and actions of sequestration for rent, where the value of the fund *in medio*, or the value of the arrested fund or subject, or the rent in respect of which sequestration is asked, as the case may be, does not exceed £1,500 (exclusive of interest and expenses);

(c) actions *ad factum praestandum* and actions for the recovery of possession of heritable or moveable property, other than actions in which there is claimed in addition, or as an alternative, to a decree *ad factum praestandum* or for such recovery, as the case may be, a decree for payment of money exceeding £1,500 in amount (exclusive of interest and expenses);

(d) proceedings which, according to the law and practice existing immediately before the commencement of this Act, might competently be brought in the sheriff's small debt court or where required to be conducted and disposed of in the summary manner in which proceedings were conducted and disposed of under the Small Debt Acts;

and any reference in the following provisions of this Act, or in any other enactment (whether passed or made before or after the commencement of this Act) relating to civil procedure in the sheriff court, to a summary cause shall be construed as a reference to a summary cause within the meaning of this subsection.

(1A) For the avoidance of doubt it is hereby declared that nothing in subsection (1) above shall prevent the Court of Session from making different rules of procedure and practice in relation to different descriptions of summary cause proceedings.

(2) There shall be a form of summary cause process, to be known as a 'small claim', which shall be used for the purposes of such descriptions of summary cause proceedings as are prescribed by the Lord Advocate by order.

(3) No enactment or rule of law relating to admissibility or corroboration of evidence before a court of law shall be binding in a small claim.

(4) An order under subsection (2) above shall be by statutory instrument but shall not be made unless a draft of it has been approved by a resolution of each House of Parliament. **[160A]**

NOTES to section 35

Amendments: Sub-s (1) was amended by the Sheriff Courts (Scotland) Act 1971 (Privative Jurisdiction etc) Order 1976, SI 1976/900, and by the Sheriff Courts (Scotland) Act 1971 (Summary Cause) Order 1981, SI 1981/842, and by the Sheriff Courts (Scotland) Act 1971 (Privative Jurisdiction and Summary Cause) Order 1988, SI 1988/1993; sub-s (1A) was inserted by the Law Reform (Miscellaneous Provisions) (Scotland) Act 1985 (c 73), s 59, Sch 2, Para 14; new sub-ss (2)–(4) substituted and added by the Law Reform (Miscellaneous Provisions) (Scotland) Act 1985 (c 73), s 18(1).

Land Compensation (Scotland) Act 1973

(c 56)

ARRANGEMENT OF SECTIONS

* * *

Part III
Provisions for Benefit of Persons Displaced from Land

27	Right to home loss payment where person displaced from dwelling	**[161]**
27A	Spouses having statutory occupancy rights	**[162]**
28	Amount of home loss payment	**[163]**
29	Supplementary provisions about home loss payments	**[164]**
30	Home loss payments for certain caravan dwellers	**[165]**

* * *

[TEXT CONTINUES ON PAGE 87]

Rehousing

36	Duty to rehouse residential occupiers	**[166]**
37	Duty to rehouse certain caravan dwellers	**[167]**
38	Power of relevant authority to make advances repayable on maturity to displaced residential owner-occupiers	**[168]**
39	Duty of displacing authority to indemnify rehousing or lending authority for net losses	**[169]**
40	Power of relevant authority to defray expenses in connection with acquisition of new dwellings	**[170]**

★ ★ ★

PART VI
SUPPLEMENTARY PROVISIONS

80	General interpretation	**[171]**
81	Repeal of Land Compensation Act 1973 in relation to Scotland and reprinting of Act as it applies to England and Wales	**[172]**
82	Savings and transitional	**[173]**
83	Short title and extent	**[174]**

★ ★ ★

PART III
PROVISIONS FOR BENEFIT OF PERSONS DISPLACED FROM LAND

27. Right to home loss payment where person displaced from dwelling.

(1) Where a person is displaced from a dwelling on any land in consequence of—
(a) the compulsory acquisition of an interest in the dwelling;
(b) the making, passing or acceptance of a housing order, resolution or undertaking in respect of the dwelling;
(c) where the land has been previously acquired by an authority possessing compulsory purchase powers or appropriated by a local authority and is for the time being held by the authority for the purposes for which it was acquired or appropriated, the carrying out of [any improvement to the dwelling or of] redevelopment on the land,
[(d) the carrying out of any improvement to the dwelling or of redevelopment on the land by a housing association which has previously acquired the land and at the date of the displacement is registered,]
[(e) a requirement to remove from the building containing the dwelling in pursuance of section 13 of the Building (Scotland) Act 1959 (dangerous buildings) or any other enactment which requires the demolition of the building on account of its condition]
[(f) an order for recovery of possession of the dwelling under section 48(2) of the Housing (Scotland) Act 1987, on the ground set out in paragraph 10 of Part I of Schedule 3 to that Act]
he shall, subject to the provisions of this section and section 29 below, be entitled to receive a payment (hereafter referred to as a 'home loss payment') from
[(i) where paragraph (a) above applies, the acquiring authority;
(ii) where paragraph (b) above applies, the authority who made the order, . . . or accepted the undertaking;
(iii) where paragraph (c) above applies, the authority carrying out the improvement or redevelopment; . . .
(iv) where paragraph (d) above applies, the housing association carrying out the improvement or redevelopment.] [and]

[(v) where paragraph (e) above applies the authority requiring the removal.]
[(vi) where paragraph (f) above applies, the landlord]

[(2) A person shall not be entitled to a home less payment unless the following conditions have been satisfied throughout the period of one year ending with the date of displacement—
(a) he has been in occupation of the dwelling, or a substantial part of it, as his only or main residence; and
(b) he has been in occupation by virtue of an interest or right to which this section applies.

but, if those conditions are satisfied on the date of displacement, a payment (referred to in this section and sections 29 and 30 below as a 'discretionary payment') may be made to him of an amount not exceeding the amount to which he would have been entitled if he had satisfied those conditions throughout that period.]

(3) For the purposes of this section a person shall not be treated as displaced from a dwelling in consequence of the compulsory acquisition of an interest therein if he gives up his occupation thereof before the date on which the acquiring authority were authorised to acquire that interest, but, subject to that, it shall not be necessary for the acquiring authority to have required him to give up his occupation of the dwelling.

[(3A) For the purposes of this section a person shall not be treated as displaced from a dwelling in consequence of [(a)] the carrying out of any improvement to the dwelling [or; (b) a requirement to remove as mentioned in subsection (1)(e) above] unless he is permanently displaced from it in consequence of the carrying out of the improvement in question [or removal] as the case may be.]]

(4) This section applied to the following interests and rights—
(a) any interest in the dwelling;
[(b) a right to occupy the dwelling
  (i) as a statutory tenant within the meaning of the Rent (Scotland) Act 1984 or
  (ii) under a contract to which Part VII of that Act (furnished lettings) applies or would apply if the contract or dwelling-house were not excluded by section 63(3) to (5) or under section 64(3) respectively of that Act; and]
[(bb) a right to occupy the dwelling as a statutory assured tenant within the meaning of the Housing (Scotland) Act 1988]
(c) a right to occupy the dwelling under a contract of employment.

(6) Where an authority possessing compulsory purchase powers acquire the interest of any person in a dwelling by agreement, then, in consequence of the acquisition, subsection (1) to (4) above shall have effect as if the acquisition were compulsory and the authority (if not authorised to acquire the interest compulsorily) had been so authorised on the date of the agreement.

(7) In this section 'a housing order, resolution or undertaking' means—
(a) a demolition or closing order under Part [VI] of the Housing (Scotland) Act [1987] [or an order under section [88] of that Act];
(b) a resolution under section [125] of the said Act . . .;
(c) an undertaking accepted under section [117(2)(a)] of the said Act . . .; [or
(d) a final resolution under Part I of Schedule 8 to that Act]

[(7A) In this section
'improvement' includes alteration and enlargement; and 'redevelopment' includes a change of use]

(8) Where an interest in a dwelling is vested in trustees and a person beneficially entitled (whether directly or derivatively) under the trust is entitled or permitted by reason of his interest to occupy the dwelling, he shall be treated for the purposes of this section as occupying it by virtue of an interest in the dwelling.

(9) [Subject to subsection (2) above] this section applies if the date of displacement is on or after 17th October 1972 [except that, where the displacement is in consequence of the circumstances referred to in subsection (1)(e) above, it applies if the date of

displacement is on or after the coming into force of paragraph 12 of Schedule 2 to the Housing (Financial Provisions) (Scotland) Act 1978]. [161]

NOTES to section 27

Amendments: Sub-s (1)(c)—words inserted by Housing Act 1974 (c 44), s 130, Sch 13, para 42(1)(a); sub-s (1)(d) substituted by Housing Rents and Subsidies (Scotland) Act 1975 (c 28), Sch 3, para 9(1); sub-s (1)(e) inserted by Housing (Financial Provisions) (Scotland) Act 1978 (c 14), Sch 2, para 12(a)(i); sub-s (1)(f) inserted by Housing (Scotland) Act 1986, (c 65), s 20(2)(a); in sub-s (1), paras (i) to (iv) substituted for original wording by Housing Act 1974 (c 44), s 130, Sch 13, para 42(1)(b) and words repealed by the Planning and Compensation Act 1991 (c 34), s 79, Sch 17, para 20; para (v) added by Housing (Financial Provisions) (Scotland) Act 1978 (c 14), (Sch 2, para 12(a)(ii); para (vi) added by Housing (Scotland) Act 1986 (c 65), s 20(2)(b); sub-s (2) substituted by the Planning and Compensation Act 1991 (c 34), s 71(1); sub-s (3A) inserted by Housing Act 1974 (c 44), s 130, Sch 13, para 42(2)—words inserted by Housing (Financial Provisions) (Scotland) Act 1978 (c 14), Sch 12, para 12(b)(i)–(iii); sub-s (4)(b) substituted by the Planning and Compensation Act 1991 (c 34), s 79, Sch 17, para 20; sub-s (4)(bb) inserted by Housing (Scotland) Act 1988 (c 43), s 72, Sch 9, para 1; sub-s (5) repealed by the Planning and Compensation Act 1991 (c 34), s 71(2); sub-s (7)(a) amended by Housing (Financial Provisions) (Scotland) Act 1974 (c 14), Sch 2, para 39 and by Housing (Scotland) Act 1987, s 339, Sch 23, para 19(2); sub-s (7)(b)—word repealed by Housing (Scotland) Act 1974, amended by Housing (Scotland) Act 1987, s 339, Sch 23, para 19(2); sub-s (7)(c) amended by Housing (Scotland) Act 1987 (c 26), s 339, Sch 23, para 19(2); sub-s 7(d) amended by Housing (Scotland) Act 1987 (c 26), s 339, Sch 23, para 19(2); sub-s (7)—words at end repealed by Housing Act 1974 (c 44), s 130, Sch 15; sub-s (7A) inserted by Housing Act 1974 (c 44), s 130, Sch 13, para 42(3); sub-s (9)—words inserted by Housing Rents and Subsidies (Scotland) Act 1975 (c 28), Sch 3, para 9(3).

The amendments effected by the Planning and Compensation Act 1991 (c 34) have effect in relation to displacements occurring on or after 16th November 1990: see the 1991 Act, s 71(9).

Definitions: 'acquiring authority', 'authority possessing compulsory purchase powers', 'dwelling': see s 80 below.

[27A. Spouses having statutory occupancy rights.

(1) This section applies where, by reason of the entitlement of one spouse ('A') to occupy a dwelling by virtue of an interest or right to which section 27 above applies, the other spouse ('B') acquires occupancy rights (within the meaning of the Matrimonial Homes (Family Protection) (Scotland) Act 1981).

(2) So long as—
(a) those occupancy rights continue;
(b) B is in occupation of the dwelling and A is not; and
(c) B is not, apart from this section, treated as occupying the dwelling by virtue of an interest or right to which that section applies,

B shall be treated for the purposes of that section as occupying the dwelling by virtue of such an interest (but not an owner's interest within the meaning of section 28 below).

(3) References in this section to a dwelling include a reference to a substantial part of it.] [162]

NOTES to section 27A

Amendment: Section 27A was added by the Planning and Compensation Act 1991 (c 34), s 72 and has effect in relation to displacements occurring on or after 16th November 1990: see the 1991 Act, s 71(9).

Definitions: 'dwelling': see also s 80 below; 'occupancy rights': see the 1981 Act, ss 1 and 18, paras [183, 199] below.

[28. Amount of home loss payment.

(1) In the case of a person who on the date of displacement is occupying, or is treated for the purposes of section 27 above as occupying, the dwelling by virtue of an interest in it which is an owner's interest, the amount of the home loss payment shall be 10 per cent. of the market value of his interest in the dwelling or, as the case may be, the interest in the

dwelling vested in trustees, subject to a maximum of £15,000 and a minimum of £1,500.

(2) In any other case, the amount of the home loss payment shall be £1,500.

(3) For the purposes of this section and section 29 below the market value of an interest in a dwelling—
  (a) in a case where the interest is compulsorily acquired, is the amount assessed for the purposes of the acquisition as the value of the interest; and
  (b) in any other case, is the amount which, if the interest were being compulsorily acquired in pursuance of a notice to treat served on the date of displacement, would be assessed for the purposes of the acquisition as the value of the interest,

and any dispute as to the amount referred to in paragraph (b) above shall be determined by the Lands Tribunal.

(4) In determining for the purposes of this section and section 29 below the market value of an interest in a dwelling, the dwelling shall be taken to include any garden, yard, outhouses and appurtenances belonging to or usually enjoyed with that dwelling.

(5) The Secretary of State may from time to time by regulations prescribe a different maximum or minimum for the purposes of subsection (1) above and a different amount for the purposes of subsection (2) above.

(6) The power to make regulations under subsection (5) above shall be exercisable by statutory instrument which shall be subject to annulment in pursuance of a resolution of either House of Parliament.

(7) In this section "owner's interest" means the interest of a person who is an owner as defined in section 45(1) of the Land Compensation (Scotland) Act 1963.]   **[163]**

NOTES to section 28

Amendment: Section 28 was substituted by the Planning and Compensation Act 1991 (c 34) and has effect in relation to displacements occurring on or after 16th November 1990: see the 1991 Act, s 71(9).

Definitions: 'dwelling': see s 80 below; 'home loss payment': see s 27 above.

29. Supplementary provision about home loss payments.

[(1) No home loss payment or discretionary payment shall be made except on a claim in writing made by the person entitled thereto ("the claimant") giving such particulars as the authority responsible for making the payment may reasonably require for the purpose of determining whether the payment should be made and, if so, its amount.

(2) Where a person is entitled to a home loss payment, the payment shall be made on or before the latest of the following dates—
  (a) the date of displacement;
  (b) the last day of the period of three months beginning with the making of the claim; and
  (c) where the amount of the payment is to be determined in accordance with section 28(1) above, the day on which the market value of the interest in question is agreed or finally determined.

(2A) Where the amount of the payment is to be determined in accordance with section 28(1) above—
  (a) the acquiring authority may at any time make a payment in advance; and
  (b) if, on the later of the dates referred to in subsection (2)(a) and (b) above, the market value of the interest in question has not been agreed or finally determined, the acquiring authority shall make a payment in advance (where they have not already done so).

(2B) The amount of the payment in advance shall be the lesser of—
  (a) the maximum amount for the purposes of section 28(1) above,
  (b) 10 per cent of the amount agreed to be the market value of the interest in question or, if there is no such agreement, 10 per cent of the acquiring authority's estimate of that amount.

(2C) Where the amount of a payment in advance differs from the amount of the home loss payment, the shortfall or excess shall be paid by or, as the case may be, repaid to the acquiring authority when the market value of the interest in question is agreed or finally determined.

(3) Where the claimant has satisfied, throughout any period, the conditions mentioned in section 27(2) above, that period shall be treated for the purposes of that subsection as including any immediately preceding period throughout which—
  (a) he has resided in the dwelling as his only or main residence but without satisfying those conditions, and
  (b) another person or other persons have satisfied those conditions,
and references in this subsection and subsection (3A) below to a dwelling include a reference to a substantial part of it.

(3A) Where the claimant has satisfied, throughout any period, the conditions mentioned in section 27(2) above, that period (or that period as extended under subsection (3) above) shall be treated for the purposes of section 27(2) above as including any immediately preceding period, or successive periods, throughout which he satisfied the conditions mentioned in section 27(2) above in relation to another dwelling or, as the case may be, other dwellings (applying subsection (3) above to determine the length of any period or periods).]

(4) [Where a person ('the deceased') entitled to a home loss payment dies without having claimed it, a claim to the payment may be made] by any person, not being a person under the age of eighteen, who—
  (a) throughout a period of not less than [one year] ending with the date of displacement of the deceased, has resided in the dwelling, or a substantial part of it, as his only or main residence; and
  (b) is entitled to benefit by virtue of—
    (i) a testamentary disposition or any other deed with testamentary effect taking effect on, or the law of intestate succession as applied to, the death of the deceased; or
    (ii) a right to jus relicti, jus relictae or legitim out of the deceased's estate

(5) Where the claimant has successively been in occupation of or resided in different dwellings in the same building, being dwellings consisting of a room or rooms not constructed or structurally adapted for use as a separate dwelling, section 27(2) above and subsections [(3) to (4)] above shall have effect as if those dwellings were the same dwelling.

(6) Where there are two or more persons entitled to make a claim to a home loss payment in respect of the same dwelling (whether by virtue of joint occupation or of subsection (4) above) the payment to be made on each claim shall be equal to the whole amount of the home loss payment divided by the number of such persons.

(7) Where an interest in a dwelling is acquired by agreement by an authority possessing compulsory purchase powers, the authority may, in connection with the acquisition, make to the person from whom the interest is acquired a payment corresponding to any home loss payment [or discretionary payment] which they would be required [or authorised] to make to him if the acquisition were compulsory and the authority had been authorised to acquire that interest before he gave up occupation of the dwelling.

[(7A) Section 6 of the Prescription and Limitation (Scotland) Act 1973 (extinction of obligations by prescriptive period of five years) shall apply to an obligation to make a home loss payment, and in relation to such obligation the appropriate date for the purposes of subsection (1) of the said section 6 shall be the date of displacement.]

[(7AA) If a landlord recovers possession of a dwelling by agreement—
  (a) after serving notice under section 47 and 48(2) of the Housing (Scotland) Act 1987 on the tenant specifying the ground set out in paragraph 10 of Part I of Schedule 3 to that Act; or
  (b) where, but for that agreement, it would have served such notice on him specifying that ground,

It may, in connection with the recovery, make to him a payment corresponding to any home loss payment [or discretionary payment] which it would be required [or authorised] to make to him if the recovery were by order under section 145(2) of that Act.] [164]

NOTES to section 29

Amendments: Sub-s (1) to (3A)—substituted by the Planning and Compensation Act 1991 (c 34), s 71(4); sub-s (4)—words substituted by Local Government, Planning and Land Act 1980 (c 65), s 114(2), (6) and by the Planning and Compensation Act 1991 (c 34), s 71(5); sub-s (5)—words substituted by the Planning and Compensation Act 1991 (c 34), s 71(6); sub-s (7A) inserted by Local Government, Planning and Land Act 1980 (c 65), s 114(5), (6); sub-s (7)—words substituted by the Planning and Compensation Act 1991 (c 34), s 71(7); sub-s (7AA) inserted by Housing (Scotland) Act 1986 (c 65), s 20(3)—amended by Housing (Scotland) Act 1987, s 339, Sch 23, para 19(3) and by the Planning and Compensation Act 1991 (c 34), s 71(7); sub-s (8) repealed by Local Government, Planning and Land Act 1980 (c 65), Sch 34, Pt XII.
The amendments effected by the Planning and Compensation Act 1991 (c 34) have effect in relation to displacements occurring on or after 16th November 1990: See the 1991 Act, s 71(9).

Definitions: 'home loss payment', 'discretionary payment': see s 27 above; 'acquiring authority': see s 80 below.

30. Home loss payments for certain caravan dwellers.

(1) Sections 27 to 29 above shall, so far as applicable, have effect in relation to a person residing in a caravan on a caravan site who is displaced from that site as they have effect in relation to a person displaced from a dwelling on any land but shall so have effect subject to the following modifications.

(2) No home loss payment [or discretionary payment] shall be made to any person by virtue of this section except where no suitable alternative site for stationing a caravan is available to him on reasonable terms.

(3) Subsection (1) of section 27 above shall have effect as if for the words preceding paragraph (a) there were substituted the words 'Where a person residing in a caravan on a caravan site is displaced from that site in consequence of' and subsection (2) of that section shall have effect as if for paragraphs (a) and (b) there were substituted—
[(a) he has been in occupation of caravan site by using a caravan stationed on it as his only or main residence; and
(b) he has been in such occupation of the site by virtue of an interest or right to which this section applies,]

[(4) Section 28 above shall have effect as if the references to a person occupying a dwelling by virtue of an interest in it and to his interest in the dwelling were to a person occupying a caravan site by virtue of an interest in it and to that interest.,]

(5) Section 29 above shall have effect—
[(a) as if in subsections (3) and (3A) the references to a dwelling were to a caravan site;]
(b) as if in subsection (4) for the words 'resided in the dwelling, or a substantial part of it' there were substituted the words 'resided in a caravan on the caravan site'; and
(c) as if for subsection (5) there were substituted—
'(5) Where any land comprises two or more caravan sites and the claimant has successively been in occupation of or resided in a caravan on different caravan sites on that land, section 27(2) above and subsections [(3) to (4)] above shall have effect as if those sites were the same site'.

(6) Sections 27 to 29 above shall have effect as if in any provision not modified as aforesaid for any reference to a dwelling or land there were substituted a reference to a caravan site.

(7) In this section 'caravan site' means land on which a caravan is stationed for the purpose of human habitation and land which is used in conjunction with land on which a caravan is so stationed. [165]

Land Compensation (Scotland) Act 1973 (c 56), s 36 [166]

NOTES to section 30

Amendments: In sub-s (2), words inserted by the Planning and Compensation Act 1991 (c 34), s 71(8); in sub-s (3), paras substituted by *Ibid*; sub-s (4) substituted by *ibid*; in sub-s (5), para (a) substituted by, and words in para (c) substituted by *Ibid*.

These amendments have effect in relation to displacements occurring on or after 16 November 1990: see the Planning and Compensation Act 1991 (c 34), s 71(9).

Definitions: 'home loss payment', 'discretionary payment': see s 27 above; 'dwelling': see s 80 below.

* * *

Rehousing

36. Duty to rehouse residential occupiers.

(1) Where a person is displaced from residential accommodation on any land in consequence of—
- (a) the acquisition of the land by an authority possessing compulsory purchase powers;
- (b) the making, passing or acceptance of a housing order, resolution or undertaking in respect of a house or building on the land;
- (c) where the land has been previously acquired by an authority possessing compulsory purchase powers or appropriated by a local authority and is for the time being held by the authority for the purposes for which it was acquired or appropriated, the carrying out of [any improvement to a house or building on the land or of] redevelopment on the land,
- [(d) a requirement to remove the building containing the residential accommodation in pursuance of section 13 of the Building (Scotland) Act 1959 (dangerous buildings), or any other enactment which requires the demolition of the building on account of its condition,]

and suitable alternative residential accommodation on reasonable terms is not otherwise available to that person, then subject to the provisions of this section, it shall be the duty of the relevant authority to secure that he will be provided with such other accommodation.

(2) Subsection (1) above shall not by virtue of paragraph (a) thereof apply to a person if the acquisition is in pursuance of the service by him of a blight notice within the meaning of section 181 of the Town and Country Planning (Scotland) Act 1972.

(3) Subsection (1) above shall not apply to any person who is a trespasser on the land or who has been permitted to reside in any house or building on the land pending its demolition [or improvement].

(4) Subsection (1) above shall not apply to any person to whom money has been advanced—
- (a) under section 38 below;
- (b) under the Small Dwellings Acquisition (Scotland) Acts 1899 to 1923 or section 49 of the Housing (Financial Provisions) (Scotland) Act 1968 [or section 214 of the Housing (Scotland) Act 1987]; or
- (c) by a development coporation otherwise then under section 38 below,

for the purpose of enabling him to obtain accommodation in substitution for that from which he is displaced as mentioned in that subsection.

(5) Subsection (1)(a) above shall not apply to any acquisition of land in relation to which the Secretary of State has before 23rd May 1973 decided under paragraph 1 of Schedule 8 to the Housing (Scotland) Act 1966 that a housing scheme is not necessary.

(6) For the purposes of subsection (1) above a person shall not be treated as displaced in consequence of any such acquisition [improvement] or redevelopment as is mentioned in paragraph (a) or (c) of that subsection unless he was residing in the accommodation in question—
- (a) in the case of land acquired under a compulsory purchase order, at the time when notice was first published of the making of the order prior to its subsection for

confirmation or, where the order did not require confirmation, of the preparation of the order in draft;
(b) in the case of land acquired under an Act specifying the land as subject to compulsory acquisition, at the time when the provisions of the Bill for the Act specifying the land were first published;
(c) in the case of land acquired by agreement, at the time when the agreement was made;

and a person shall not be treated as displaced in consequence of any such order, resolution [undertaking or requirement as is mentioned in paragraph (b) or (d)] of that subsection unless he was residing in the accommodation in question at the time when the order was made, the resolution was passed [the undertaking was accepted or he was required to remove.]

(7) Subject to subsection (8) below, 'the relevant authority' for the purposes of this section is the local authority having functions in relation to the district where the land is situated under Part [I] of the Housing (Scotland) Act [1987].

(8) Where the land is in an area designated as the site of a new town—
(a) paragraph (c) of subsection (1) above shall apply if the land on which the redevelopment is carried out has been previously acquired by the development corporation and is for the time being held by that corporation;
(b) the development corporation shall, in a case falling within paragraph (a) or (c) of that subsection, be the relevant authority for the purposes of this section.

(9) In this section 'a housing order, resolution or undertaking' ['improvement'] and 'redevelopment' have the same meaning as in section 27 above. **[166]**

NOTES to section 36
Amendments: Sub-s (1)(c)—words inserted by the Housing Act 1974 (c 44), s 130, Sch 13, para 44(1); sub-s (1)(d) inserted by the Housing (Financial Provisions) (Scotland) Act 1978 (c 14), Sch 2, para 14(a); sub-s (3)—words added by the Housing Act 1974 (c 44), s 130, Sch 13, para 44(2); sub-s (4)(b) amended by Housing (Scotland) Act 1987 (c 26), s 339, Sch 23, para 19(5); sub-s (6)—words inserted by *Ibid*, para 44(3); words substituted by Housing (Financial Provisions) (Scotland) Act 1978 (c 14), Sch 2, para 14(b); sub-s 7—amended by Housing (Scotland) Act 1987 (c 26), s 339, Sch 23, para 19(5); sub-s (9)—word inserted by the Housing Act 1974 (c 44), s 130, Sch 13, para 44(4).

37. Duty to rehouse certain caravan dwellers

(1) Section 36 above shall, so far as applicable, have effect in relation to a person residing in a caravan on a caravan site who is displaced from that site as it has effect in relation to a person displaced from residential accommodation on any land but shall so have effect subject to the following modifications.

(2) Subsection (1) of the said section 36 shall have effect—
(a) as if for the words preceding paragraph (a) there were substituted the words 'Where a person residing in a caravan on a caravan site is displaced from that site in consequence of'; and
(b) as if for the words following paragraph (c) there were substituted the words 'and neither suitable residential accommodation nor a suitable alternative site for stationing a caravan is available to that person on reasonable terms, then, subject to the provisions of this section, it shall be the duty of the relevant authority to secure that he will be provided with suitable residential accommodation.'.

(3) Subsection (6) of the said section 36 shall have effect as if in the words preceding paragraph (a) for the words 'unless he was residing in the accommodation in question' there were substituted the words 'unless he was residing in a caravan on the caravan site in question'.

(4) The said section 36 shall have effect as if in any provision not modified as aforesaid for any reference to land there were substituted a reference to a caravan site.

(5) In this section 'caravan site' has the same meaning as in section 30 above. **[167]**

38. Power of relevant authority to make advances repayable on maturity to displaced residential owner-occupiers.

(1) Where a person displaced from a dwelling in consequence of any of the matters mentioned in subsection (1)(a), (b) or (c) of section 36 above—
  (a) is an owner-occupier of the dwelling; and
  (b) wishes to acquire or construct another dwelling in substitution for that from which he is displaced,
the relevant authority for the purposes of that section may advance money to him for the purpose of enabling him to acquire or construct the other dwelling.

(2) The power conferred by this section shall be exercisable subject to such conditions as may be approved by the Secretary of State and the following provisions shall apply with respect to any advance made in the exercise of that power.

(3) The advance shall be made—
  (a) on terms providing for the payment of the principal—
    (i) at the end of a fixed period, with or without a provision allowing the authority to extend that period; or
    (ii) upon notice given by the authority,
    subject, in either case, to a provision for earlier repayment on the happening of a specified event;
  (b) on such other terms as the authority may think fit having regard to all the circumstances.

(4) An advance for the construction of a dwelling may be made by instalments from time to time as the works of construction progress.

(5) The principal of the advance, together with interest thereon, shall be secured by a heritable security of the borrower's interest in the dwelling, and the amount of the principal shall not exceed the value which, in accordance with a valuation duly made on behalf of the relevant authority, it is estimated that the borrower's interest will bear or, as the case may be, will bear when the dwelling has been constructed.

(6) Before advancing money under this section the relevant authority shall satisfy themselves that the dwelling to be acquired meets or will meet the tolerable standard as determined for the purposes of the [Housing (Scotland) Act 1987 by section 86] of that Act.

(7) While the payment of the principal of an advance made by a local authority under this section is not required in accordance with the terms of the advance, the local authority may suspend, with respect to so much of any sum borrowed by them as is referable to the advance, any periodical provision for repayment that may be required by any enactment.

(8) The power conferred by this section on a relevant authority is without prejudice to any power to advance money exercisable by the authority under any other enactment.

(9) In this section 'owner-occupier' in relation to any dwelling, means a person who occupies it on the date of displacement and either—
  (a) occupies it on that date in right of an owner's interest of a lease of which not less than three years remain unexpired or by virtue of a tenancy or other interest to which the Crofters (Scotland) Acts 1955 and 1961 or the Small Landholders (Scotland) Acts 1886 to 1931 apply; or
  (b) if the displacement is in consequence of the matters mentioned in paragraph (c) of section 36(1) above, occupied it in right of such an interest or lease or by virtue of such a tenancy or interest on the date on which the land was acquired or appropriated as mentioned in that paragraph.

(10) In this section references to the construction of a dwelling include references to the acquisition of a building and its conversion into a dwelling and to the conversion into a dwelling of a building previously acquired. **[168]**

NOTES to section 38

Amendments: Sub-s (6)—words substituted by Housing (Scotland) Act 1974 (c 45), s 50, Sch 3, para 50 as amended by Housing (Scotland) Act 1987 (c 26), s 339, Sch 23, para 19(5).

39. Duty of displacing authority to indemnify rehousing or lending authority for net losses.

(1) Where a relevant authority within the meaning of section 36 above provide or secure the provision of accommodation for any person in pursuance of subsection (1)(a) or (c) of that section, then, if—
  (a) the authority providing the accommodation ('the rehousing authority') are not the same as the authority by whom the land in question is acquired or redeveloped ('the displacing authority'); and
  (b) the displacing authority are not an authority having functions under Part [I] of the Housing (Scotland) Act [1987]
the displacing authority shall make to the rehousing authority periodical payments, or if the rehousing authority so require a lump sum payment, by way of indemnity against any net loss in respect of the rehousing authority's provision of that accommodation which may be incurred by that authority in any year during the period of ten years commencing with the year in which the accommodation is first provided.

(2) For the purposes of subsection (1) above a local authority incur a net loss in respect of their provision of accommodation for a person whom they are rehousing—
  (a) if they rehouse him in a house provided by them under Part [I] of the said Act of [1987] for the purpose of rehousing him; or
  (b) if—
    (i) they rehouse him in a house to which the housing revenue account relates not so provided, and
    (ii) provide under the said Part [I] in the year immediately preceding that in which he first occupies it, or in the period of three years commencing with the year in which he first occupies it, a house of a similar type or size.

(3) Where money has been advanced to a person as mentioned in section 36(4) above, then if—
  (a) the authority making the advance ('the lending authority') are not the same as the displacing authority; and
  (b) the lending authority incur a net loss in respect of the making of the advance,
the displacing authority shall make to the lending authority a lump sum payment by way of indemnity against that loss.

(4) For the purposes of subsection (3) above, a lending authority incur a net loss in respect of the making of an advance to any person if—
  (a) he does not fully discharge his liability to the authority in respect of principal, interest and expenses in accordance with the terms on which the advance is made; and
  (b) the deficiency exceeds the net proceeds arising to the authority on a sale of the interest on which the principal and interest is secured.

(5) The Secretary of State may—
  (a) for the purposes of subsection (1) above from time to time determine a method to be used generally in calculating net losses incurred by rehousing authorities;
  (b) for the purposes of that subsection or subsection (3) above, determine the net loss incurred by a rehousing authority or lending authority in any particular case;
  (c) give directions as to the manner in which any payment under this section is to be made.

(6) Subsection (2) above shall be construed as one with the Housing [(Scotland) Act 1987].

Land Compensation (Scotland) Act 1973 (c 56), s 80 [171]

NOTES to section 39

Amendments: Sub-s (1) amended by Housing (Scotland) Act 1987 (c 26), s 339, Sch 23, para 19(7)(a); sub-s (2) amended by *Ibid*; sub-s (6) amended by *Ibid*, para 19(7)(b).

40. Power of relevant authority to defray expenses in connection with acquisition of new dwellings.

(1) Where a person displaced from a dwelling in consequence of [any of the events specified in paragraphs (a) to (c) of section 36(1) above]
 (a) has no interest in the dwelling or no greater interest therein than as tenant for a year or from year to year; and
 (b) wishes to acquire another dwelling in substitution for that from which he is displaced,
[then, according to the nature of the event in consequence of which he was displaced, the acquiring authority, the authority who made the order, passed the resolution or accepted the undertaking or the authority carrying out the improvement or redevelopment] may pay any reasonable expenses incurred by him in connection with the acquisition, other than the purchase price.

(2) No payment shall be made under this section in respect of expenses incurred by any person in connection with the acquisition of a dwelling unless the dwelling is acquired not later than one year after the displacement and is reasonably comparable with that from which he is displaced.

(3) For the purposes of subsection (2) above a dwelling acquired pursuant to a contract shall be treated as acquired when the contract is made.

(4) Subsections (3) and (6) of section 36 above shall have effect in relation to subsection (1) above and to [any provision of subsection (1)] of that section as applied thereby.
[170]

NOTES to section 40

Amendments: Sub-s (1)—words substituted by Housing Act 1974, s 130, Sch 13, para 45(1); sub-s (4)—words substituted by *Ibid*.

* * *

PART VI
SUPPLEMENTARY PROVISIONS

80. General interpretation.

(1) In this Act—
'agriculture', 'agricultural' and 'agricultural land' have the meaning given in section 86 of the Agriculture (Scotland) Act 1948, and references to the farming of land include references to the carrying on in relation to the land of any agricultural activities;
'agricultural holding' has the meaning given in section 1 of the Agricultural Holdings (Scotland) Act 1949 and 'landlord', 'tenant' and 'notice to quit', in relation to an agricultural holding, have the same meaning as in that Act;
'agricultural unit' has the meaning given in section 196(1) of the Town and Country Planning (Scotland) Act 1972;
'acquiring authority', and 'authority possessing compulsory purchase powers' have the same meaning as in the Land Compensation (Scotland) Act 1963;
'aerodrome' has the meaning given in section 63(1) of the Civil Aviation Act 1949;
'cottar' has the same meaning as in section 28(4) of the Crofters (Scotland) Act 1955;
'croft', 'crofter' and 'landlord', in relation to a croft, have the same meanings respectively as in the Crofters (Scotland) Act 1955;
'disabled person' means a person in need under section 12 of the Social Work (Scotland) Act 1968 as read with section 1 of the Chronically Sick and Disabled Persons (Scotland) Act 1972;

'dwelling' means a building or part of a building occupied or (if not occupied) last occupied or intended to be occupied as a private house, and (except in section 27) includes any garden, yard, outhouses and appurtenances belonging to or usually enjoyed with that building or part;

'heritable security' means any security capable of being constituted over any interest in land by a disposition or assignation of that interest in security of any debt and of being recorded in the Register of Sasines;

'holding, in relation to a landholder and a statutory small tenant, has the same meaning as in section 2(1) of the Small Landholders (Scotland) Act 1911 and 'landlord', in relation to such a holding, has the same meaning as in the Agricultural Holdings (Scotland) Act 1949;

['housing association' has the meaning assigned to it by the Housing Association Act 1985;]

'landholder' has the same meaning as in section 2(2) of the Small Landholders (Scotland) Act 1911;

'Lands Tribunal' means the Lands Tribunal for Scotland;

'owner' has the same meaning as in section 45(1) of the Land Compensation (Scotland) Act 1963;

['registered', in relation to a housing association, means registered under the Housing Associations Act 1985;]

'road' has the meaning assigned to it in the Roads (Scotland) Act 1970;

'statutory small tenant' has the same meaning as in section 32(1) of the Small Landholders (Scotland) Act 1911.

(2) . . .

(3) Except where the context otherwise requires, references in this Act to any enactment are references to that enactment as amended, and include references to that enactment as extended or applied, by any other enactment, including this Act. **[171]**

NOTES to section 80

Amendments: Sub-s (1)—Definitions of 'housing association' and 'registered' inserted by Housing Rents and Subsidies (Scotland) Act 1975 (c 28), Sch 3 para 11, amended by Housing (Scotland) Act 1987 (c 26), s 339, Sch 23, para 19(11); sub-s (2) repealed by the Roads (Scotland) Act 1984, s 156, Sch 11.

81. Repeal of Land Compensation Act 1973 in relation to Scotland and reprinting of Act as it applies to England and Wales.

(1) The Land Compensation Act 1973 (except section 86 and Schedule 3) shall cease to apply to Scotland . . .

(2) . . . **[172]**

NOTES to section 81

The words omitted repeal certain provisions of the Land Compensation Act 1973 (c 26).
Sub-s (2) repealed by Statute Law (Repeals) Act 1978, Sch 1, Pt XXI.

82. Savings and transitional.

(1) Notwithstanding the repeal of the Land Compensation Act 1973, in so far as anything done under that Act could have been done under a corresponding provision in this Act, it shall have effect as if done under that provision.

(2) Notwithstanding the repeal of the said Act, section 3 of that Act (claims) shall have effect in relation to offences committed thereunder before the passing of this Act.

(3) The inclusion in this section of any express savings shall not be taken as prejudicing the operation of [sections 16(1) and 17(2)(a) of the Interpretation Act 1978] (which relates to the effect of repeals).

(4) Section 44 above does not affect any compensation which fell or falls to be assessed by reference to prices current on a date before 23rd May 1973, and the other provisions of

Part IV of this Act relating to the assessment of compensation do not affect any compensation which fell or falls to be assessed by reference to prices current on a date before 17th October 1972. [173]

NOTE to section 82
Sub-s (3)—words substituted by virtue of Interpretation Act 1978, s 25(2).

83. Short title and extent.

(1) This Act may be cited as the Land Compensation (Scotland) Act 1973.

(2) This Act, except section 81 and Schedule 2, extends to Scotland only. [174]

Land Tenure Reform (Scotland) Act 1974
(c 38)

ARRANGEMENT OF SECTIONS

★ ★ ★

PART II
LIMITATIONS ON RESIDENTIAL USE OF PROPERTY LET UNDER FUTURE LONG LEASES

8	Property let under future long lease, etc not to be used as private dwelling-house	[175]
9	Consequences of use as dwelling-house of property subject to long lease	[176]
10	Modification of s 9 where lease subject to sub-lease or heritable security	[177]

★ ★ ★

PART IV
GENERAL

21	Provisions for contracting out to be void	[178]
22	Application to Crown	[179]
23	Interpretation and repeals	[180]
24	Short title, commencement and extent	[181]

★ ★ ★

PART II
LIMITATIONS ON RESIDENTIAL USE OF PROPERTY LET UNDER FUTURE LONG LEASES

8. Property let under future long lease, etc not to be used as private dwelling-house.

(1) It shall be a condition of every long lease executed after the commencement of this Act that, subject to the provisions of this Part of this Act, no part of the property which is subject to the lease shall be used as or as part of a private dwelling-house.

(2) For the purposes of this Part of this Act, any garden, yard, garage, outhouse or

pertinent used along with any dwelling-house shall be deemed to form part of a dwelling-house, and use as a dwelling-house shall not include use as the site of a caravan.

(3) The use as or as part of a private dwelling-house of part of a property which is subject to a long lease shall not constitute a breach of the condition contained in subsection (1) above if such use if ancillary to the use of the remainder of the property otherwise than as or as part of a private dwelling-house and it would be detrimental to the efficient exercise of the use last-mentioned if the said ancillary use did not occur on that property.

(4) For the purposes of this Part of this Act—
'lessor' and 'lessee' mean any person holding for the time being the interest of lessor or lessee (as the case may be); and
'long lease' means any grant of—
  (a) a lease, or
  (b) a liferent or other right of occupancy granted for payment (other than payment in defrayal of or contribution towards some continuing cost related to such liferent use or such occupancy, as the case may be),
which is either—
  (i) subject to a duration, whether definite or indefinite, which could (in terms of the grant and without any subsequent agreement, express or implied, between the persons holding the interests of the grantor and the grantee) extend for more than 20 years, or
  (ii) subject to any provision whereby any person holding the interest of the grantor or the grantee is under a future obligation, if so requested by the other, to renew the grant so that the total duration could so extend for more than 20 years, or whereby, if he does not so renew it, he will be liable to make some payment or to perform some other obligation;
[but in relation to a lease granted before 1st September 1974, does not include its renewal (whether before or after the commencement of section 1 of the Law Reform (Miscellaneous Provisions) Scotland Act 1985) in implement of an obligation in or under it.]

(5) This Part of the Act shall not apply in relation to the use of property for the time being forming part or deemed to form part of—
  (a) an agricultural holding, within the meaning of the Agricultural Holdings (Scotland) Act 1949;
  (b) a holding, within the meaning of the Small Landholders (Scotland) Acts 1886 to 1931;
  (c) A croft, within the meaning of the Crofters (Scotland) Acts 1955 and 1961.

(6) Nothing in this Part of the Act shall effect the right of the lessor to terminate the lease and recover possession of the property subject thereto on the ground of breach of a conventional condition of the lease which has the effect of prohibiting such use of the property as constitutes a breach of the condition contained in subsection (1) above.

(7) Nothing in this Part of the Act shall prevent a tenancy from being or becoming a protected or statutory tenancy within the meaning of the Rent (Scotland) Act [1984 or a secure tenancy within the meaning of the Housing (Scotland) Act 1987] but nothing in [either of those Acts] restricting the power of a court to make an order for possession of a dwelling-house shall prevent the granting of a decree of removing under section 9(1) of this Act.

NOTES to section 8
Amendments: Sub-s (4)—words added by Law Reform (Miscellaneous Provisions) (Scotland) Act 1985 (c 73), s 1; sub-s (7)—amended by Housing (Scotland) Act 1986 (c 65) and Housing (Scotland) Act 1987 (c 26).

9. Consequences of use as dwelling-house of property subject to long lease.

(1) A breach of the condition of a long lease executed after the commencement of this

Act, contained in section 8(1) of this Act, shall not render the lease void or unenforceable, but, subject to the provisions of this section and of section 10 of this Act, where such a breach occurs, the lessor shall be entitled to give to the lessee notice to terminate the use constituting the breach within 28 days from the date of the notice; and, if the lessee shall fail to terminate that use within that period, the lessor shall be entitled to raise an action of removing against the lessee concluding for his removal from such part of the property as is subject to the use at the expiry of 28 days after the decree of removing is extracted, and the court may decern for the termination of the lease in respect of such part and the removal of the lessee therefrom and, failing such removal, for his ejection therefrom on expiry of the 28 days last mentioned.

(2) A notice under subsection (1) above shall be in or as nearly as may be in the form contained in Schedule 5 to this Act.

(3) It shall be a defence to an action under subsection (1) above that the breach of condition constituting the ground of action has ceased.

(4) Subject to section 10(3) of this Act, in an action under subsection (1) above, if it is proved that the use of the property constituting the ground of action has at any time been approved by the person holding at that time the interest of the lessor in the lease, either expressly or by his actings, and the said use has not subsequently been discontinued, the court shall not decern in terms of that subsection, but—
   (a) where the lease is subject to a duration expiring in a year more than 20 years after the year in which the notice under subsection (1) above relative to the breach was given, the court shall decern that the lease shall, in respect of such part of the property as is subject to the use, have effect as if for the year of expiry there were substituted the year 20 years after the year in which the said notice was given;
   (b) where the lease is subject to a duration expiring in a year less than 20 years after that year, the lease shall continue in force according to its terms;
and the said part of the property subject to the lease (and, during the remaining period of the lease as determined by reference to this subsection, any over-lease, insofar as it relates to that part) shall cease to be subject to the condition contained in section 8(1) of this Act.

(5) Where the breach of condition constituting the ground of action under subsection (1) above relates to part only of the property subject to the lease, any decree granted to the pursuer in the action under subsection (1) or (4)(a) above shall contain a particular description or a description by reference (in accordance with the provisions of the Conveyancing (Scotland) Act 1874 and the Conveyancing (Scotland) Act 1924) of such part; and in such a case the court shall decern for such adjustment (if any) as it thinks fit (to take effect on the termination of the lease of such part in terms of the decree) in the rent of the remaining part of the property and in the conditions of the lease, including the addition of new conditions, but not including any provision for the payment of money.

(6) Subject to the provisions of this Part of this Act and of section 37(1) of the Sheriff Courts (Scotland) Act 1971, and notwithstanding section 35(1)(c) of that Act, the procedure in an action of removing under this section shall be that in an ordinary cause; and on the granting of a decree to the pursuer in such an action, or at any time before the decree is extracted, the court may sist extract of the decree for such period or periods as it thinks fit to enable any facts to be established which (if the action were still pending) would constitute a defence thereto, and if the court is satisfied that any such facts are established it may vary or rescind the decree, subject to such conditions (if any) with regard to payment of arrears of rent and otherwise as the court thinks fit.

(7) Notwithstanding the provisions of section 24 of the Court of Session Act 1868, Rule 63(b) of the Rules of Court 1965 or Rule 25 of Schedule 1 to the Sheriff Courts (Scotland) Act 1907, a decree granted in an action under this section shall, as in a question with third parties who have acted onerously and in good faith in reliance on the records, be final and not subject to challenge when an extract thereof shall have been recorded in the Register of Sasines.

(8) The provisions of this section and of section 10 of this Act shall apply in relation to

a grant (not being a lease) mentioned in section 8(4) of this Act as they apply in relation to a lease, and any reference to a lease, over-lease or sub-lease, to the parties thereto, or to rent, shall be construed accordingly. **[176]**

10. Modification of s 9 where lease subject to sub-lease or heritable security.

(1) For the avoidance of doubt, it is hereby declared that (subject to the provisions of this section) sections 8 and 9 of this Act shall apply, as between the parties to any over-lease or sub-lease executed after the commencement of this Act, as they apply as between the parties to any other lease so executed.

(2) The pursuer in an action under section 9 of this Act shall give such intimation thereof as the court may direct—
  (a) to every person appearing, from a search in the Register of Sasines for a period of 20 years immediately prior to the raising of the action, to hold for the time being the interest of creditor in a heritable security over the lease which is the subject of the action; and
  (b) where the said lease is, in relation to any part of the property which is subject to the use constituting the ground of action, subject to any sub-lease, to every person appearing from such a search and from examination of the valuation roll or otherwise to be the lessee in any such sub-lease (of whatever duration) or the creditor in a heritable security over any such sub-lease;

and any such creditor or lessee as aforesaid shall, subject to the provisions of this section, be entitled to plead in the action any defence which could be pleaded by the defender in the action.

(3) The defence provided under section 9(4) of this Act shall not be available to the lessee in a lease in respect of the use of property subject to a sub-lease derived from that lease.

(4) A sub-lessee, provided that he could have pleaded the defence provided by section 9(4) of this Act in any action by the lessor in the sub-lease, may, on being sisted to an action under the said section 9 by the lessor in any over-lease, plead that defence in relation to the approval by the lessor in that over-lease or in any sub-lease under that over-lease of property which is subject to the use constituting the ground of action; and the court, on being satisfied that the defence is established to that effect, shall be entitled to decern in terms of the said section 9(4) as if the action had been brought by the lessor in the sub-lease first mentioned.

(5) The right provided by subsection (4) above shall be available to a sub-lessee whose lease is not a long lease to the same extent as if it had been a long lease. **[177]**

* * *

Part IV
General

21. Provisions for contracting out to be void.

Subject to the provisions of sections 8(6) and 11(3) of this Act, any agreement or other provision, however constituted, which is made after the commencement of this Act, shall be void in so far as it purports to exclude or limit the operation of any enactment contained in this Act. **[178]**

22. Application to Crown.

This Act shall apply to land held of the Crown and of the Prince and Steward of Scotland, and to land in which there is any other interest belonging to Her Majesty in right of the Crown or to a Government department, or held on behalf of Her Majesty for the purposes of a Government department, in like manner as it applies to other land.
[179]

23. Interpretation and repeals.

(1) In this Act, unless the context otherwise requires—
'deed' has the meaning assigned to it in section 3 of the Titles to Land Consolidation (Scotland) Act 1868, section 3 of the Conveyancing (Scotland) Act 1874 and section 2 of the Conveyancing (Scotland) Act 1924;
'heritable security' (except in relation to sections 4(5), 5(10) and 10(2)) does not include any security for the purpose of securing the payment of a ground annual or other periodical sum payable in respect of land, and 'heritable creditors' shall be construed accordingly;
'land' has the meaning assigned to it in section 2 of the said Act of 1924.

(2) Unless the context otherwise requires, any reference in this Act to any other enactment is a reference thereto as amended, and includes a reference thereto as extended or applied, by or under any other enactment, including this Act.

(3) . . .   [180]

NOTE to section 23
Sub-s (3) repeals various enactments.

24. Short title, commencement and extent.

(1) This Act may be cited as the Land Tenure Reform (Scotland) Act 1974.

(2) This Act shall come into operation on 1st September 1974.

(3) This Act shall extend to Scotland only.   [181]

Race Relations Act 1976
(c 74)

★ ★ ★

47. Codes of Practice.

(1) The Commission may issue codes of practice containing such practical guidance as the Commission think fit for [all or any] of the following purposes, namely—
 (a) the elimination of discrimination in the field of employment;
 (b) the promotion of equality of opportunity in that field between persons of different racial groups;
 [(c) the elimination of discrimination in the field of housing;
 (d) the promotion of equality of opportunity in the field of housing between persons of different racial groups.]

(2) When the Commission propose to issue a code of practice, they shall prepare and publish a draft of that code, shall consider any representations made about the draft and may modify the draft accordingly.

(3) In the course of preparing any draft code of practice [relating to the field of employment] for eventual publication under subsection (2) the Commission shall consult with—
 (a) such organisations or associations of organisations representative of employers or of workers; and
 (b) such other organisations, or bodies,
as appear to the Commission to be appropriate.

[(3A) In the course of preparing any draft code of practice relating to the field of housing for eventual publication under subsection (2) the Commission shall consult with such organisations or bodies as appear to the Commission to be appropriate having regard to the content of the draft code.]

(4) If the Commission determine to proceed with [a draft code of practice], they shall transmit the draft to the Secretary of State who shall—
(a) if he approves of it, lay it before both Houses of Parliament; and
(b) if he does not approve of it, publish details of his reasons for withholding approval.

(5) If, within the period of forty days beginning with the day on which a copy of a draft code of practice is laid before each House of Parliament, or, if such copies are laid on different days, with the later of the two days, either House so resolves, no further proceedings shall be taken thereon, but without prejudice to the laying before Parliament of a new draft.

(6) In reckoning the period of forty days referred to in subsection (5), no account shall be taken of any period during which Parliament is dissolved or prorogued or during which both Houses are adjourned for more than four days.

(7) If no such resolution is passed as is referred to in subsection (5), the Commission shall issue the code in the form of the draft and the code shall come into effect on such day as the Secretary of State may by order appoint.

(8) Without prejudice to section 74(3), an order under subsection (7) may contain such transitional provisions or savings as appear to the Secretary of State to be necessary or expedient in connection with the code of practice thereby brought into operation.

(9) The Commission may from time to time revise the whole or any part of a code of practice issued under this section and issue that revised code, and subsections (2) to (8) shall apply (with appropriate modifications) to such a revised code as they apply to the first issue of a code.

(10) A failure on the part of any person to observe any provision of a code of practice shall not of itself render him liable to any proceedings; but in any proceedings under this Act before an industrial tribunal [a county court or, in Scotland, a sheriff court] any code of practice issued under this section shall be admissible in evidence, and if any provision of such a code appears to the tribunal [or the court] to be relevant to any question arising in the proceedings it shall be taken into account in determining that question.

(11) Without prejudice to subsection (1), a code of practice issued under this section may include such practical guidance as the Commission think fit as to what steps it is reasonably practical for employers to take for the purpose of preventing their employees from doing in the course of their employment acts made unlawful by this Act.

NOTES to section 47

Amendments: Sub-s (1) was amended by the Housing Act 1988 (c 50), s 137, which amendments were varied by the Local Government and Housing Act 1989 (c 42), s 180; sub-s (3), (4) and (10) were amended by the Housing Act 1988 (c 50), s 137; sub-s (3A) was added by the Housing Act 1988 (c 50), s 137 and amended by the Local Government and Housing Act 1989 (c 42), s 180.

Definitions: 'Commission': see s 78(1); 'discrimination': see s 3(3); 'employment': see s 78(1); 'racial groups': see s 3(1); 'industrial tribunal': see s 78(1).

Sub-ss (1)–(11): See the Race Relations Code of Practice (Rented Housing) Order 1991, SI 1991/227 and paras [1506A] ff below, and the Race Relations Code of Practice (Non-Rented Housing Order) 1992, SI 1992/619 and paras [1579] ff below.

★ ★ ★

Matrimonial Homes (Family Protection) (Scotland) Act 1981
(c 59)

ARRANGEMENT OF SECTIONS

Protection of occupancy rights of one spouse against the other

1	Right of spouse without title to occupy matrimonial home	[183]
2	Subsidiary and consequential rights	[184]
3	Regulation by court of rights of occupancy of matrimonial home	[185]
4	Exclusion orders	[186]
5	Duration of orders under ss 3 and 4	[187]

Occupancy rights in relation to dealings with third parties

6	Continued exercise of occupancy rights after dealing	[188]
7	Dispensation by court with spouse's consent to dealing	[189]
8	Interests of heritable creditors	[190]
9	Provisions where both spouses have title	[191]

Protection of rights of spouse against arrangements intended to defeat them

★ ★ ★

11	Poinding	[192]
12	Adjudication	[193]

Transfer of tenancy

13	Transfer of tenancy	[194]

Matrimonial interdicts

14	Interdict competent where spouses live together	[195]
15	Attachment of powers of arrest to matrimonial interdicts	[196]
16	Police powers after arrest	[197]
17	Procedure after arrest	[198]

Cohabiting couples

18	Occupancy rights of cohabiting couples	[199]

Miscellaneous and General

19	Rights of occupancy in relation to division and sale	[200]

★ ★ ★

21	Procedural provision	[201]
22	Interpretation	[202]
23	Short title, commencement and extent	[203]

An Act to make new provision for Scotland as to the rights of occupancy of spouses in a matrimonial home and of cohabiting couples in the house where they cohabit; to provide for the transfer of the tenancy of a matrimonial home between the spouses in certain circumstances during marriage and on granting decree of divorce or nullity of

Matrimonial Homes (Family Protection) (Scotland) Act 1981 (c 59), s 1

marriage, and for the transfer of the tenancy of a house occupied by a cohabiting couple between the partners in certain circumstances; to strengthen the law relating to matrimonial interdicts; and for connected purposes. [30th October 1981]

Protection of occupancy rights of one spouse against the other

1. Right of spouse without title to occupy matrimonial home.

(1) Where, apart from the provisions of this Act, one spouse is entitled, or permitted by a third party, to occupy a matrimonial home (an 'entitled spouse') and the other spouse is not so entitled or permitted (a 'non-entitled spouse'), the non-entitled spouse shall, subject to the provisions of this Act, have the following rights—
 (a) if in occupation, a right [to continue to occupy the matrimonial home;]
 (b) if not in occupation, a right to enter into and occupy the matrimonial home.

(1A) The rights conferred by subsection (1) above to continue to occupy or, as the case may be, to enter and occupy the matrimonial home include, without prejudice to their generality, the right to do so together with any child of the family.

(2) In subsection (1) above, an 'entitled spouse' includes a spouse who is entitled, or permitted by a third party, to occupy a matrimonial home along with an individual who is not the other spouse only if that individual has waived his or her right of occupation in favour of the spouse so entitled or permitted.

(3) If the entitled spouse refuses to allow the non-entitled spouse to exercise the right conferred by subsection (1)(b) above, the non-entitled spouse may exercise that right only with the leave of the court under section 3(3) or (4) of this Act.

(4) In this Act, the rights mentioned in paragraphs (a) and (b) of subsection (1) above are referred to as occupancy rights.

(5) A non-entitled spouse may renounce in writing his or her occupancy rights only—
 (a) in a particular matrimonial home; or
 (b) in a particular property which it is intended by the spouses will become a matrimonial home.

(6) A renunciation under subsection (5) above shall have effect only if at the time of making the renunciation, the non-entitled spouse has sworn or affirmed before a notary public that it was made freely and without coercion of any kind. [In this subsection, 'notary public' includes any person duly authorised by the law of the country (other than Scotland) in which the swearing or affirmation takes place to administer oaths or receive affirmations in that other country.] **[183]**

NOTES to section 1

Amendments: Sub-s (1) amended by Law Reform (Miscellaneous Provisions) (Scotland) Act 1985 (c 73), s 13(2); sub-s (1A), inserted by *Ibid*, s 13(3); sub-s (6)—words added by *Ibid*, s 13(4).

2. Subsidiary and consequential rights.

(1) For the purpose of securing the occupancy rights of a non-entitled spouse, that spouse shall, in relation to a matrimonial home, be entitled without the consent of the entitled spouse—
 (a) to make any payment due by the entitled spouse in respect of rent, rates, secured loan instalments, interest or other outgoings (not being outgoings on repairs or improvements);
 (b) to perform any other obligation incumbent on the entitled spouse (not being an obligation in respect of non-essential repairs or improvements);
 (c) to enforce performance of an obligation by a third party which that third party has undertaken to the entitled spouse to the extent that the entitled spouse may enforce such performance;
 (d) to carry out such essential repairs as the entitled spouse may carry out;
 (e) to carry out such non-essential repairs or improvements as may be authorised by an order of the court, being such repairs or improvements as the entitled spouse

may carry out and which the court considers to be appropriate for the reasonable enjoyment of the occupancy rights;
- (f) to take such other steps, for the purpose of protecting the occupancy rights of the non-entitled spouse, as the entitled spouse may take to protect the occupancy rights of the entitled spouse.

(2) Any payment made under subsection (1)(a) above or any obligation performed under subsection (1)(b) above shall have effect in relation to the rights of a third party as if the payment were made or the obligation were performed by the entitled spouse; and the performance of an obligation which has been enforced under subsection (1)(c) above shall have effect as if it had been enforced by the entitled spouse.

(3) Where there is an entitled and a non-entitled spouse, the court, on the application of either of them, may, having regard in particular to the respective financial circumstances of the spouses, make an order apportioning expenditure incurred or to be incurred by either spouse—
- (a) without the consent of the other spouse, on any of the items mentioned in paragraphs (a) and (d) of subsection (1) above;
- (b) with the consent of the other spouse, on anything relating to a matrimonial home.

(4) Where both spouses are entitled, or permitted by a third party, to occupy a matrimonial home—
- (a) either spouse shall be entitled, without the consent of the other spouse, to carry out such non-essential repairs or improvements as may be authorised by an order of the court, being such repairs or improvements as the court considers to be appropriate for the reasonable enjoyment of the occupancy rights;
- (b) the court, on the application of either spouse, may, having regard in particular to the respective financial circumstances of the spouses, make an order apportioning expenditure incurred or to be incurred by either spouse, with or without the consent of the other spouse, on anything relating to the matrimonial home.

(5) Where one spouse owns or hires, or is acquiring under a hire-purchase or conditional sale agreement, furniture and plenishings in a matrimonial home—
- (a) the other spouse may, without the consent of the first mentioned spouse—
    - (i) make any payment due by the first mentioned spouse which is necessary, or take any other step which the first mentioned spouse is entitled to take, to secure the possession or use of any such furniture and plenishings (and any such payment shall have effect in relation to the rights of a third party as if it were made by the first mentioned spouse); or
    - (ii) carry out such essential repairs to the furniture and plenishings as the first mentioned spouse is entitled to carry out;
- (b) the court, on the application of either spouse, may, having regard in particular to the respective financial circumstances of the spouses, make an order apportioning expenditure incurred or to be incurred by either spouse—
    - (i) without the consent of the other spouse, in making payments under a hire, hire-purchase or conditional sale agreement, or in paying interest charges in respect of the furniture and plenishings, or in carrying out essential repairs to the furniture and plenishings; or
    - (ii) with the consent of the other spouse, on anything relating to the furniture and plenishings.

(6) An order under subsection (3), (4)(b) or (5)(b) above may require one spouse to make a payment to the other spouse in implementation of the apportionment.

(7) Any application under subsection (3), (4)(b) or 5(b) above shall be made within five years of the date on which any payment in respect of such incurred expenditure was made.

(8) Where—
- (a) the entitled spouse is a tenant of a matrimonial home; and

(b) possession thereof is necessary in order to continue the tenancy; and
(c) the entitled spouse abandons such possession,
the tenancy shall be continued by such possession by the non-entitled spouse.

(9) In this section 'improvements' includes alterations and enlargement.

3. **Regulation by court of rights of occupancy of matrimonial home.**

(1) Where there is an entitled and a non-entitled spouse, or where both spouses are entitled, or permitted by a third party, to occupy a matrimonial home, either spouse may apply to the court for an order—
   (a) declaring the occupancy rights of the applicant spouse;
   (b) enforcing the occupancy rights of the applicant spouse;
   (c) restricting the occupancy rights of the non-applicant spouse;
   (d) regulating the exercise by either spouse of his or her occupancy rights;
   (e) protecting the occupancy rights of the applicant spouse in relation to the other spouse.

(2) Where one spouse owns or hires, or is acquiring under a home purchase or conditional sale agreement, furniture and plenishings in a matrimonial home, the other spouse, if he or she has occupancy rights in that home, may apply to the court for an order granting to the applicant the possession or use in the matrimonial home of any such furniture and plenishings; but, subject to section 2 of this Act, an order under this subsection shall not prejudice the rights of any third party in relation to the non-performance of any obligation under such hire-purchase or conditional sale agreement.

(3) The court shall grant an application under subsection (1)(a) above if it appears to the court that the application relates to a matrimonial home, and, on an application under any of paragraphs (b) to (e) of subsection (1) or under subsection (2) above, the court may make such order relating to the application as appears to it to be just and reasonable having regard to all the circumstances of the case including—
   (a) the conduct of the spouses in relation to each other and otherwise;
   (b) the respective needs and financial resources of the spouses;
   (c) the needs of any child of the family;
   (d) the extent (if any) to which—
      (i) the matrimonial home; and
      (ii) in relation only to an order under subsection (2) above, any item of furniture and plenishings referred to in that subsection,
      is used in connection with a trade, business or profession of either spouse; and
   (e) whether the entitled spouse offers or has offered to make available to the non-entitled spouse any suitable alternative accommodation.

(4) Pending the making of an order under subsection (3) above, the court, on the application of either spouse, may make such interim order as it may consider necessary or expedient in relation to—
   (a) the residence of either spouse in the home to which the application relates;
   (b) the personal effects of either spouse or of any child of the family; or
   (c) the furniture and plenishings:
Provided that an interim order may be made only if the non-applicant spouse has been afforded an opportunity of being heard by or represented before the court.

(5) The court shall not make an order under subsection (3) or (4) above if it appears that the effect of the order would be to exclude the non-applicant spouse from the matrimonial home.

(6) If the court makes an order under subsection (3) or (4) above which requires the delivery to one spouse of anything which has been left in or removed from the matrimonial home, it may also grant a warrant authorising a messenger-at-arms or sheriff officer to enter the matrimonial home or other premises occupied by the other spouse and to search for and take possession of the thing required to be delivered, if need be by opening shut and lockfast places, and to deliver the thing in accordance with the said order:

Provided that a warrant granted under this subsection shall be executed only after expiry of the period of a charge, being such period as the court shall specify in the order for delivery.

(7) Where it appears to the court—
(a) on the application of a non-entitled spouse, that that spouse has suffered a loss of occupancy rights or that the quality of the non-entitled spouse's occupation of a matrimonial home has been impaired; or
(b) on the application of a spouse who has been given the possession or use of furniture and plenishings by virtue of an order under subsection (3) above, that the applicant has suffered a loss of such possession or use or that the quality of the applicant's possession or use of the furniture and plenishings has been impaired,
in consequence of any act or default on the part of the other spouse which was intended to result in such loss or impairment, it may order that other spouse to pay to the applicant such compensation as the court in the circumstances considers just and reasonable in respect of that loss or impairment.

(8) A spouse may renounce in writing the right to apply under subsection (2) above for the possession or use of any item of furniture and plenishings. [185]

4. Exclusion orders.

(1) Where there is an entitled and a non-entitled spouse, or where both spouses are entitled, or permitted by a third party, to occupy a matrimonial home, either spouse, [whether or not that spouse is in occupation at the time of the application] may apply to the court for an order (in this Act referred to as 'an exclusion order') suspending the occupancy rights of the other spouse ('the non-applicant spouse') in a matrimonial home.

(2) Subject to subsection (3) below, the court shall make an exclusion order if it appears to the court that the making of the order is necessary for the protection of the applicant or any child of the family from any conduct or threatened or reasonably apprehended conduct of the non-applicant spouse which is or would be injurious to the physical or mental health of the applicant or child. [186]

NOTE to section 4
Amendment: Sub-s (1)—words inserted by Law Reform (Miscellaneous Provisions) (Scotland) Act 1985 (c 73), s 13(5).

5. Duration of orders under sections 3 and 4.

(1) The court may, in the application of either spouse, vary or recall any order made by it under section 3 or 4 of this Act, but, subject to subsection (2) below, any such order shall, unless previously so varied or recalled, cease to have effect—
(a) on the termination of the marriage; or
(b) subject to section 6(1) of this Act, where there is an entitled and a non-entitled spouse, on the entitled spouse ceasing to be an entitled spouse in respect of the matrimonial home to which the order relates; or
(c) where both spouses are entitled, or permitted by a third party, to occupy the matrimonial home, on both spouses ceasing to be so entitled or permitted.

(2) Without prejudice to the generality of subsection (1) above, an order under section 3(3) or (4) of this Act which grants the possession or use of furniture and plenishings shall cease to have effect if the furniture and plenishings cease to be permitted by a third party to be retained in the matrimonial home.

(3) The court shall not make an exclusion order if it appears to the court that the making of the order would be unjustified or unreasonable—
(a) having regard to all the circumstances of the case including the matters specified in paragraphs (a) to (e) of section 3(3) of this Act; and

(b) where the matrimonial home—
  (i) is or is part of an agricultural holding within the meaning of section 1 of the Agricultural Holdings (Scotland) Act 1949; or
  (ii) is let, or is a home in respect of which possession is given, to the non-applicant spouse or to both spouses by an employer as an incident of employment,
  subject to a requirement that the non-applicant spouse or, as the case may be, both spouses must reside in the matrimonial home, having regard to that requirement and the likely consequences of the exclusion of the non-applicant spouse from the matrimonial home.

(4) In making an exclusion order the court shall, on the application of the applicant spouse,—
  (a) grant a warrant for the summary ejection of the non-applicant spouse from the matrimonial home;
  (b) grant an interdict prohibiting the non-applicant spouse from entering the matrimonial home without the express permission of the applicant;
  (c) grant an interdict prohibiting the removal by the non-applicant spouse, except with the written consent of the applicant or by a further order of the court, of any furniture and plenishings in the matrimonial home;
unless, in relation to paragraph (a) or (c) above, the non-applicant spouse satisfied the court that it is unnecessary for it to grant such a remedy.

(5) In making an exclusion order the court may—
  (a) grant an interdict prohibiting the non-applicant spouse from entering or remaining in a specified area in the vicinity of the matrimonial home;
  (b) where the warrant for the summary ejection of the non-applicant spouse has been granted in his or her absence, give directions as to the preservation of the non-applicant spouse's goods and effects which remain in the matrimonial home;
  (c) on the application of either spouse, make the exclusion order or the warrant or interdict mentioned in paragraph (a), (b) or (c) of subsection (4) above or paragraph (a) of this subsection subject to such terms and conditions as the court may prescribe;
  (d) on application as aforesaid, make such other order as it may consider necessary for the proper enforcement of an order made under subsection (4) above or paragraph (a), (b) or (c) of this subsection.

(6) Pending the making of an exclusion order, the court may, on the application of the applicant spouse, make an interim order suspending the occupancy rights of the non-applicant spouse in the matrimonial home to which the application for the exclusion order relates; and subsections (4) and (5) above shall apply to such interim order as they apply to an exclusion order:
Provided that an interim order may be made only if the non-applicant spouse has been afforded an opportunity of being heard by or represented before the court.

(7) Without prejudice to subsections (1) and (6) above, where both spouses are entitled, or permitted by a third party, to occupy a matrimonial home, it shall be incompetent for one spouse to bring an action of ejection from the matrimonial home against the other spouse.

Occupancy rights in relation to dealings with third parties

6. Continued exercise of occupancy rights after dealing.

(1) Subject to subsection (3) below—
  (a) the continued exercise of the rights conferred on a non-entitled spouse by the provisions of this Act in respect of a matrimonial home shall not be prejudiced by reason only of any dealing of the entitled spouse relating to that home; and
  (b) a third party shall not by reason only of such a dealing be entitled to occupy that matrimonial home or any part of it.

(2) In this section and section 7 of this Act—
'dealing' includes the grant of a heritable security and the creation of a trust but does not include a conveyance under section 80 of the Lands Clauses Consolidation (Scotland) Act 1845;
'entitled spouse' does not include a spouse who, apart from the provisions of this Act,—
  (a) is permitted by a third party to occupy a matrimonial home; or
  (b) is entitled to occupy a matrimonial home along with an individual who is not the other spouse, whether or not that individual has waived his or her right of occupation in favour of the spouse so entitled;
and 'non-entitled spouse' shall be construed accordingly.

(3) This section shall not apply in any case where—
  (a) the non-entitled spouse in writing either—
    (i) consents or has consented to the dealing, and any consent shall be in such form as the Secretary of State may, by regulations made by statutory instrument, prescribe; or
    (ii) renounces or has renounced his or her occupancy rights in relation to the matrimonial home or property to which the dealing relates;
  (b) the court has made an order under section 7 of this Act dispensing with the consent of the non-entitled spouse to the dealing;
  (c) the dealing occurred, or implements, a binding obligation entered into by the entitled spouse before his or her marriage to the non-entitled spouse;
  (d) the dealing occurred, or implements, a binding obligation entered into before the commencement of this Act;
  (e) the dealing comprises [a sale to] a third party who has acted in good faith, if there is produced to the third party by the [seller—
    (i) an affidavit sworn or affirmed by the seller declaring that the subjects of sale are not [or were not at the time of dealing] a matrimonial home in relation to which a spouse of the seller has [or had] occupancy rights;] or
    (ii) a renunciation of occupancy rights or consent to the dealing which bears to have been properly made or given by the non-entitled spouse.
[For the purposes of this paragraph, the time of the dealing, in the case of the sale of an interest in heritable property, is the date of delivery to the purchaser of the deed transferring title to that interest; or
  (f) the entitled spouse has permanently ceased to be entitled to occupy the matrimonial home, and at any time thereafter a continuous period of 5 years has elapsed during which the non-entitled spouse has not occupied the matrimonial home.]

(4) . . .   [188]

NOTES to section 6

Amendments: Sub-s (3)(e) amended by Law Reform (Miscellaneous Provisions) (Scotland) Act 1985 (c 73), s 13(6) with effect from 30 December 1985, and by the Law Reform (Miscellaneous Provisions) (Scotland) Act 1990 (c 40), s 74, Sch 8, para 31 with effect from 11 January 1991; sub-s (3)(f) added by the 1985 Act, s 13(6); s 13(11) of the 1985 Act provides:
  Any—
  (a) affidavit lawfully sworn or affirmed before the commencement of this section in pursuance of paragraph (e) of subsection (3) of section 6 or subsection (2) of section 8 of that Act;
  (b) consent lawfully given before such commencement in pursuance of the said subsection (2),
  shall have effect for the purpose of the said subsection (3) as amended by this section or, as the case may be, section 8(2A) of that Act as if it had been duly sworn, affirmed, or, as the case may be, given in pursuance of the said paragraph (e) as so amended or, as the case may be, the said section 8(2A).
Sub-s (3)(a): See the Matrimonial Homes (Forms of Consent) (Scotland) Regulations 1982, SI 1982/971, paras [1323A] ff below.
Sub-s (4): amends Land Registration (Scotland) Act 1979 (c 33).

7. Dispensation by court with spouse's consent to dealing.

(1) The court may, on the application of an entitled spouse or any other person having an interest, make an order dispensing with the consent of a non-entitled spouse to a dealing which has taken place or a proposed dealing, if—
  (a) such consent is unreasonably withheld;
  (b) such consent cannot be given by reason of physical or mental disability;
  (c) the non-entitled spouse cannot be found after reasonable steps have been taken to trace him or her; or
  (d) the non-entitled spouse is a minor.

(2) For the purposes of subsection (1)(a) above, a non-entitled spouse shall have unreasonably withheld consent to a dealing which has taken place or a proposed dealing, where it appears to the court—
  (a) that the non-entitled spouse has led the entitled spouse to believe that he or she would consent to the dealing and that the non-entitled spouse would not be prejudiced by any change in the circumstances of the case since such apparent consent was given; or
  (b) that the entitled spouse has, having taken all reasonable steps to do so, been unable to obtain an answer to a request for consent.

(3) The court, in considering whether to make an order under subsection (1) above, shall have regard to all the circumstances of the case including the matters specified in paragraphs (a) to (e) of section 3(3) of this Act.

(4) Where—
  (a) an application is made for an order under this section; and
  (b) an action is or has been raised by a non-entitled spouse to enforce occupancy rights,
the action shall be sisted until the conclusion of the proceedings on the application.

(5) . . .   [189]

NOTES to section 7
Amendment: Sub-s (5) repealed by Family Law (Scotland) Act 1985 (c 37), s 28(2), Sch 2.

8. Interests of heritable creditors.

(1) The rights of a third party with an interest in the matrimonial home as a creditor under a secured loan in relation to the non-performance of any obligation under the loan shall not be prejudiced by reason only of the occupancy rights of the non-entitled spouse; but where a non-entitled spouse has or obtains occupation of a matrimonial home and—
  (a) the entitled spouse is not in occupation; and
  (b) there is a third party with such an interest in the matrimonial home,
the court may, on the application of the third party, make an order requiring the non-entitled spouse to make any payment due by the entitled spouse in respect of the loan.

(2) This section shall not apply [to secured loans in respect of which the security was granted prior to the commencement of section 13 of the Law Reform (Miscellaneous Provisions) (Scotland) Act 1985] unless the third party in granting the secured loan acted in good faith and . . . there was produced to the third party by the entitled spouse—
  (a) an affidavit sworn or affirmed by the entitled spouse declaring that there is no non-entitled spouse; or
  (b) a renunciation of occupancy rights or consent to the taking of the loan which bears to have been properly made or given by the non-entitled spouse.

(2A) This section shall not apply to secured loans in respect of which the security was granted after the commencement of section 13 of the Law Reform (Miscellaneous Provisions) (Scotland) Act 1985 unless the third party in granting the secured loan acted in good faith and . . . there was produced to the third party by the grantor—

(a) an affidavit sworn or affirmed by the grantor declaring that the security subjects are not [or were not at the time of granting of the security] a matrimonial home in relation to which a spouse of the grantor has [or had] occupancy rights; or
(b) a renunciation of occupancy rights or consent to the granting of the security which bears to have been properly made or given by the non-entitled spouse.

(2B) For the purposes of subsections (2) and (2A) above, the time of granting a security, in the case of a heritable security, is the date of delivery of the deed creating the security. [190]

NOTES to section 8
Amendments: Sub-s (2)—words inserted with effect from 30 December 1985 by Law Reform (Miscellaneous Provisions) (Scotland) Act 1985 (c 73), s 13(7); sub-s (2A) and (2B) inserted by *Ibid*, s 13(8); sub-s 2A amended with effect from 1st January 1991 by the Law Reform (Miscellaneous Provisions) (Scotland) Act 1990 (c 41), s 74, Sch 8, para 31; s 13(11) of the 1985 Act provides:
Any—
(a) affidavit lawfully sworn or affirmed before the commencement of this section in pursuance of paragraph (e) of subsection (3) of section 6 or subsection (2) of section 8 of that Act;
(b) consent lawfully given before such commencement in pursuance of the said subsection (2),
shall have effect for the purpose of the said subsection (3) as amended by this section or, as the case may be, section 8(2A) of that Act as if it had been duly sworn, affirmed, or, as the case may be, given in pursuance of the said paragraph (e) as so amended or, as the case may be, the said section 8(2A).

9. Provisions where both spouses have title.

(1) Subject to subsection (2) below, where, apart from the provisions of this Act, both spouses are entitled to occupy a matrimonial home—
(a) the rights in that home of one spouse shall not be prejudiced by reason only of any dealing of the other spouse; and
(b) a third party shall not be reason only of such a dealing be entitled to occupy that matrimonial home or any part of it.

(2) The definition of 'dealing' in section 6(2) of this Act and sections 6(3) and 7 of this Act shall apply for the purposes of subsection (1) above as they apply for the purposes of section 6(1) of this Act subject to the following modifications—
(a) any reference to the entitled spouse and to the non-entitled spouse shall be construed as a reference to a spouse who has entered into or as the case may be, proposes to enter into a dealing and to the other spouse respectively; and
(b) in paragraph (b) of section 7(4) the reference to occupancy rights shall be construed as a reference to any rights in the matrimonial home. [191]

Protection of rights of spouse against arrangements intended to defeat them

10. ...

NOTE to section 10
Repealed by Bankruptcy (Scotland) Act 1985 (c 66), s 75(2), Sch 8.

11. Poinding.

Where a poinding has been executed of furniture and plenishings of which the debtor's spouse has the possession or use by virtue of an order under section 3(3) or (4) of this Act, the sheriff, on the application of that spouse within 40 days of the date of execution of the poinding, may—
(a) declare that the poinding is null; or
(b) make such order as he thinks appropriate to protect such possession or use by that spouse,

if he is satisfied that the purpose of the diligence was wholly or mainly to prevent such possession or use.

12. Adjudication.

(1) Where a matrimonial home of which there is an entitled spouse and a non-entitled spouse is adjudged, the Court of Session, on the application of the non-entitled spouse within 40 days of the date of the decree of adjudication, may—
(a) order the reduction of the decree; or
(b) make such order as it thinks appropriate to protect the occupancy rights of the non-entitled spouse,
if it is satisfied that the purpose of the diligence was wholly or mainly to defeat the occupancy rights of the non-entitled spouse.

(2) In this section, 'entitled spouse' and 'non-entitled spouse' have the same meanings respectively as in section 6(2) of this Act.

Transfer of tenancy

13. Transfer of tenancy.

(1) The court may, on the application of a non-entitled spouse make an order transferring the tenancy of a matrimonial home to that spouse and providing, subject to subsection (11) below, for the payment by the non-entitled spouse to the entitled spouse of such compensation as seems just and reasonable in all the circumstances of the case.

[(2) In an action—
(a) for divorce, the Court of Session or a sheriff;
(b) for nullity of marriage, the Court of Session,
may, on granting decree or within such period as the court may specify on granting decree, make an order granting an application under subsection (1) above.]

(3) In determining whether to grant an application under subsection (1) above, the court shall have regard to all the circumstances of the case including the matters specified in paragraphs (a) to (e) of section 3(3) of this Act and the suitability of the applicant to become the tenant and the applicant's capacity to perform the obligations under the lease of the matrimonial home.

(4) The non-entitled spouse shall serve a copy of an application under subsection (1) above on the landlord making an order under subsection (1) above, the court shall give the landlord an opportunity of being heard by it.

(5) On the making of an order granting an application under subsection (1) above, the tenancy shall vest in the non-entitled spouse without intimation to the landlord, subject to all the liabilities under the lease (other than any arrears of rent for the period before the making of the order, which shall remain the liability of the original entitled spouse).

(6) The clerk of court shall notify the landlord of the making of an order granting an application under subsection (1) above.

(7) It shall not be competent for a non-entitled spouse to apply for an order under subsection (1) above where the matrimonial home—
(a) is let to the entitled spouse by his or her employer as an incident of employment, and the lease is subject to a requirement that the entitled spouse must reside therein;
(b) is or is part of an agricultural holding;
(c) is on or pertains to a croft or the subject of a cottar or the holding of a landholder or a statutory small tenant;
(d) is let on a long lease;
(e) is part of the tenancy land of a tenant-at-will.

(8) In subsection (6) above—
'agricultural holding' has the same meaning as in section 1 of the [Agricultural Holdings (Scotland) Act 1991;]
'cottar' has the same meaning as in section 28(4) of the Crofters (Scotland) Act 1955;
'croft' has the same meaning as in the Crofters (Scotland) Act 1955;
'holding', in relation to a landholder and a statutory small tenant, 'landholder' and 'statutory small tenant' have the same meaning respectively as in sections 2(1), 2(2) and 32(1) of the Small Landholders (Scotland) Act 1911;
'long lease' has the same meaning as in section 28(1) of the Land Registration (Scotland) Act 1979;
'tenant-at-will' has the same meaning as in section 20(8) of the Land Registration (Scotland) Act 1979.

(9) Where both spouses are joint or common tenants of a matrimonial home, the court may, on the application of one of the spouses, make an order vesting the tenancy in that spouse solely and providing, subject to subsection (11) below, for the payment by the applicant to the other spouse of such compensation as seems just and reasonable in the circumstances of the case.

(10) Subsections (2) to (8) above shall apply for the purposes of an order under subsection (9) above as they apply for the purposes of an order under subsection (1) above subject to the following modifications—
(a) in subsection (3) for the word 'tenant' there shall be substituted the words 'sole tenant';
(b) in subsection (4) for the words 'non-entitled' there should be substituted the word 'applicant';
(c) in subsection (5) for the words 'non-entitled' and 'liability of the original entitled spouse' there shall be substituted respectively the words 'applicant' and 'joint and several liability of both spouses';
(d) in subsection (7)—
  (i) for the words 'a non-entitled' there shall be substituted the words 'an applicant';
  (ii) for paragraph (a) there shall be substituted the following paragraph—
    '(a) is let to both spouses by their employer as an incident of employment, and the lease is subject to a requirement that both spouses must reside there;';
  (iii) paragraphs (c) and (e) shall be omitted.

(11) Where the matrimonial home is a secure tenancy within the meaning of [Part III of the Housing (Scotland) Act 1987], no account shall be taken, in assessing the amount of any compensation to be awarded under subsection (1) or (9) above, of the loss, by virtue of the transfer of the tenancy of the home, of a right to purchase the home under Part I of that Act.

(12) . . . [194]

NOTES to section 13
Amendments: Sub-s (2) substituted by Family Law (Scotland) Act 1985 (c 37), s 28(1), Sch 1, para 11; sub-s (11)—words substituted by Housing (Scotland) Act 1987 (c 26), s 339, Sch 23; sub-s (12). The repeal originally effected by sub-s (12)(a) has been superseded—see now Housing (Scotland) Act 1987 (c 26), Sch 3, Pt I; sub-s (12)(b) repealed and deemed never to have had effect by Tenants' Rights Etc (Scotland) Amendment Act 1984 (c 18), s 8(2), Schedule.

Matrimonial interdicts

14. Interdict competent where spouses live together

(1) It shall not be incompetent for the court to entertain an application by a spouse for a matrimonial interdict by reason only that the spouses are living together as man and wife.

(2) In this section and section 15 of this Act—
'matrimonial interdict' means an interdict including an interim interdict which—

(a) restrains or prohibits any conduct of one spouse towards the other spouse or a child of the family, or
(b) prohibits a spouse from entering or remaining in a matrimonial home or in a specified area in the vicinity of the matrimonial home. **[195]**

15. Attachment of powers of arrest to matrimonial interdicts.

(1) The court shall, on the application of the applicant spouse, attach a power of arrest—
(a) to any matrimonial interdict which is ancillary to an exclusion order, including an interim order under section 4(6) of this Act;
(b) to any other matrimonial interdict where the non-applicant spouse has had the opportunity of being heard by or represented before the court, unless it appears to the court that in all the circumstances of the case such a power is unnecessary.

(2) A power of arrest attached to an interdict by virtue of subsection (1) above shall not have effect until such interdict [together with the attached power of arrest] is served on the non-applicant spouse, and such a power of arrest shall, unless previously recalled, cease to have effect upon the termination of the marriage.

(3) If, by virtue of subsection (1) above, a power of arrest is attached to an interdict, a constable may arrest without warrant the non-applicant spouse if he has reasonable cause for suspecting that spouse of being in breach of the interdict.

(4) If, by virtue of subsection (1) above, a power of arrest is attached to an interdict, the applicant spouse shall, as soon as possible after service of the interdict [together with the attached power of arrest] on the non-applicant spouse, ensure that there is delivered—
(a) to the chief constable of the police area in which the matrimonial home is situated; and
(b) if the applicant spouse resides in another police area, to the chief constable of that other police area,
a copy of the application for the interdict and of the interlocutor granting the interdict together with a certificate of service of the interdict [and, where the application to attach the power of arrest to the interdict was made after the interdict was granted, a copy of that application and of the interdict granting it and a certificate of service of the interdict together with the attached power of arrest.]

(5) Where any matrimonial interdict to which, by virtue of subsection (1) above there is attached a power of arrest, is varied or recalled, the spouse who applied for the variation or recall shall ensure that there is delivered—
(a) to the chief constable of the police area in which the matrimonial home is situated; and
(b) if the applicant spouse (within the meaning of subsection (6) below) resides in another police area, to the chief constable of that other police area,
a copy of the application for variation or recall and of the interlocutor granting the variation or recall.

(6) In this section and in sections 16 and 17 of this Act—
'applicant spouse' means the spouse who has applied for the interdict; and
'non-applicant spouse' shall be construed accordingly. **[196]**

NOTES to section 15

Amendment: In sub-s (2) and (4), words added with effect from 1 January 1991 by the Law Reform (Miscellaneous Provisions) (Scotland) Act 1990 (c 40), s 64.

16. Police powers after arrest.

(1) Where a person has been arrested under section 15(3) of this Act, the officer in charge of a police station may—
(a) if satisfied that there is no likelihood of violence to the applicant spouse or any child of the family, liberate that person unconditionally; or

(b) refuse to liberate that person;
and such refusal and the detention of that person until his or her appearance in court by virtue of—
  (i) section 17(2) of this Act; or
  (ii) any provision of the Criminal Procedure (Scotland) Act 1975,
shall not subject the officer to any claim whatsoever.

(2) Where a person arrested under section 15(3) of this Act is liberated under subsection (1) above, the facts and circumstances which gave rise to the arrest shall be reported forthwith to the procurator fiscal who, if he decides to take no criminal proceedings in respect of those facts and circumstances, shall at the earliest opportunity take all reasonable steps to intimate his decision to the persons mentioned in paragraphs (a) and (b) of section 17(4) of this Act. [197]

17. Procedure after arrest.

(1) The provisions of this section shall apply only where—
(a) the non-applicant spouse has not been liberated under section 16(1) of this Act; and
(b) the procurator fiscal decides that no criminal proceedings are to be taken in respect of the facts and circumstances which gave rise to the arrest.

(2) The non-applicant spouse who has been arrested under section 15(3) of this Act shall wherever practicable be brought before the sheriff sitting as a court of summary criminal jurisdiction for the district in which he or she was arrested not later than in the course of the first day after the arrest, such day not being a Saturday, a Sunday or a court holiday prescribed for that court under section 10 of the Bail etc (Scotland) Act 1980:

Provided that nothing in this subsection shall prevent the non-applicant spouse from being brought before the sheriff on a Saturday, a Sunday or such a court holiday where the sheriff is in pursuance of the said section 10 sitting on such a day for the disposal of criminal business.

(3) Subsections (1) and (2) of section 3 of the Criminal Justice (Scotland) Act 1980 (intimation to a named person) shall apply to a non-applicant spouse who has been arrested under section 15(3) of this Act as they apply to a person who has been arrested in respect of any offence.

(4) The procurator fiscal shall at the earliest opportunity, and in any event prior to the non-applicant spouse being brought before the sheriff under subsection (2) above, take all reasonable steps to intimate—
(a) to the applicant spouse; and
(b) to the solicitor who acted for that spouse when the interdict was granted or to any other solicitor who the procurator fiscal has reason to believe acts for the time being for that spouse,
that the criminal proceedings referred to in subsection (1) above will not be taken.

(5) On the non-applicant spouse being brought before the sheriff under subsection (2) above, the following procedure shall apply—
(a) the procurator fiscal shall present to the court a petition containing—
  (i) a statement of the particulars of the non-applicant spouse;
  (ii) a statement of the facts and circumstances which gave rise to the arrest; and
  (iii) a request that the non-applicant spouse be detained for a further period not exceeding 2 days;
(b) if it appears to the sheriff that—
  (i) the statement referred to in paragraph (a)(ii) above discloses a *prima facie* breach of interdict by the non-applicant spouse;
  (ii) proceedings for breach of interdict will be taken; and
  (iii) there is a substantial risk of violence by the non-applicant spouse against the applicant spouse or any child of the family,
  he may order the non-applicant spouse to be detained for a further period not exceeding 2 days;

(c) in any case to which paragraph (b) above does not apply, the non-applicant spouse shall, unless in custody in respect of any other matter, be released from custody;

and in computing the period of two days referred to in paragraphs (a) and (b) above, no account shall be taken of a Saturday or Sunday or of any holiday in the court in which the proceedings for breach of interdict will require to be raised. **[198]**

Cohabiting couples

18. Occupancy rights of cohabiting couples.

(1) If a man and a woman are living with each other as if they were man and wife ('a cohabiting couple') in a house which, apart from the provisions of this section—
 (a) one of them (an 'entitled partner') is entitled, or permitted by a third party, to occupy; and
 (b) the other (a 'non-entitled partner') is not so entitled or permitted to occupy,
the court may, on the application of a non-entitled partner, if it appears that the man and the woman are a cohabiting couple in that house, grant occupancy rights therein to the applicant for such period, not exceeding six months, as the court may specify:

Provided that the court may extend the said period for a further period or periods, no such period exceeding [6] months.

(2) In determining whether for the purpose of subsection (1) above a man and woman are a cohabiting couple the court shall have regard to all the circumstances of the case including—
 (a) the time for which it appears they have been living together; and
 (b) whether there are any children of the relationship.

(3) While an order granting an application under subsection (1) above or an extension of such an order is in force, or where both partners of a cohabiting couple are entitled, or permitted by a third party, to occupy the house where they are cohabiting, the following provisions of this Act shall subject to any necessary modifications—
 (a) apply to the cohabiting couple as they apply to parties to a marriage, and
 (b) have effect in relation to any child residing with the cohabiting couple as they have effect in relation to a child of the family,
section 2;
section 3, except subsection (1)(a);
section 4;
in section 5(1), the words from the beginning to 'Act' where it first occurs;
sections 13 and 14;
section 15, except the words in subsection (2) from 'and such a power of arrest' to the end;
sections 16 and 17;
and
section 22,
and any reference in these provisions to a matrimonial home shall be construed as a reference to a house.

(4) Any order under section 3 or 4 of this Act as applied to a cohabiting couple by subsection (3) above shall have effect—
 (a) if one of them is a non-entitled partner, for such a period, not exceeding the period or periods which from time to time may be specified in any order under subsection (1) above for which occupancy rights have been granted under that subsection, as may be specified in the order;
 (b) if they are both entitled, or permitted by a third party, to occupy the house, until a further order of the court.

(5) Nothing in this section shall prejudice the rights of any third party having an interest in the house referred to in subsection (1) above.

(6) In this section—
'house' includes a caravan, houseboat or other structure in which the couple are cohabiting and any garden or other ground or building attached to, and usually occupied with, or otherwise required for the amenity or convenience of, the house, caravan, houseboat or other structure;
'occupancy rights' means the following rights of a non-entitled partner—
  (a) if in occupation, a right [to continue to occupy the house;]
  (b) if not in occupation, a right to enter into and occupy the house;
  [and, without prejudice to the generality of these rights, includes the right to continue to occupy or, as the case may be, to enter and occupy the house together with any child residing with the cohabiting couple;]
'entitled partner' includes a partner who is entitled, or permitted by a third party, to occupy the house along with an individual who is not the other partner only if that individual has waived his or her right of occupation in favour of the partner so entitled or permitted. [199]

NOTES to section 18
Amendments: Sub-s (1)—word substituted by Law Reform (Miscellaneous Provisions) (Scotland) Act 1985 (c 73), s 13(9); sub-s (6) amended by *Ibid.*

Miscellaneous and General

19. Rights of occupancy in relation to division and sale.

Where a spouse brings an action for the division and sale of a matrimonial home which the spouses own in common, the court, after having regard to all the circumstances of the case including—
  (a) the matters specified in paragraphs (a) to (d) of section 3(3) of this Act; and
  (b) whether the spouse bringing the action offers or has offered to make available to the other spouse any suitable alternative accommodation,
may refuse to grant decree in that action or may postpone the granting of decree for such period as it may consider reasonable in the circumstances or may grant decree subject to such conditions as it may prescribe. [200]

20. Spouse's consent in relation to calling up of standard securities over matrimonial homes.

. . .

NOTES to section 20
Amendment of Conveyancing and Feudal Reform (Scotland) Act 1970 (c 35).

21. Procedural provision.

Section 2(2) of the Law Reform (Husband and Wife) Act 1962 (dismissal by court of delictual proceedings between spouses) shall not apply to any proceedings brought before the court in pursuance of any provision of this Act. [201]

22. Interpretation.

In this Act—
'caravan' means a caravan which is mobile or affixed to the land;
'child of the family' includes any child or grandchild of either spouse, and any person who has been brought up or accepted by either spouse as if he or she were a child of that spouse, whatever the age of such a child, grandchild or person may be;
'the court' means the Court of Session or the sheriff;
'furniture and plenishings' means any article situated in a matrimonial home which—
  (a) is owned or hired by either spouse or is being acquired by either spouse under a hire-purchase agreement or conditional sale agreement; and

(b) is reasonably necessary to enable the home to be used as a family residence, but does not include any vehicle, caravan or houseboat, or such other structure as is mentioned in the definition of 'matrimonial home';

'matrimonial home' means any house, caravan, houseboat or other structure which has been provided or has been made available by one or both of the spouses as, or has become, a family residence and includes any garden or other ground or building attached to, and usually occupied with, or otherwise required for the amenity or convenience of, the house, caravan, houseboat or other structure [but does not include a residence provided or made available by one spouse for that spouse to reside in, whether with any child of the family or not, separately from the other spouse;]

'occupancy rights' has, subject to section 18(6) of this Act, the meaning assigned by section 1(4) of this Act;

'the sheriff' includes the sheriff having jurisdiction in the district where the matrimonial home is situated;

'tenant' includes sub-tenant and a statutory tenant as defined in section 3 of the Rent (Scotland) Act 1984 and a statutory assured tenant as defined in section 16(1) of the Housing (Scotland) Act 1988 and 'tenancy' shall be construed accordingly;

'entitled spouse' and 'non-entitled spouse', subject to sections 6(2) and 12(2) of this Act, have the meanings respectively assigned to them by section 1 of this Act.

[202]

NOTE to section 22

Amendment: Words in definition of 'matrimonial home' inserted by Law Reform (Miscellaneous Provisions) (Scotland) Act 1985 (c 73), s 13(10).

23. Short title, commencement and extent.

(1) This Act may be cited as the Matrimonial Homes (Family Protection) (Scotland) Act 1981.

(2) This Act (except this section) shall come into operation on such day as the Secretary of State may by order made by statutory instrument appoint, and different days may be so appointed for different provisions and for different purposes.

(3) This Act extends to Scotland only. [203]

NOTE to section 23

The whole Act as originally enacted came into force on 1st September 1982—SI 1982/972.

Civic Government (Scotland) Act 1982

(c 45)

ARRANGEMENT OF SECTIONS

Part I
Licensing—General Provisions

1	Application of Parts I and II of this Act	[204]
2	Licensing authorities	[205]
3	Discharge of functions of licensing authorities	[206]
4	Further provisions as to licensing	[207]
5	Rights of entry and inspection	[208]
6	Powers of entry to and search of unlicensed premises	[209]
7	Offences, etc	[210]
8	Interpretation of Parts I and II	[211]

Part II
Licensing and Regulation—Particular Activities

9	Application of sections 10 to 27 and 38 to 44	[211A]

* * *

44	Additional activities	[211B]

Part VIII
Buildings, Etc

Miscellaneous works etc

87	Local authorities' powers in relation to buildings in need of repair	[212]
88	Installation of pipes through neighbouring property	[213]

* * *

90	Lighting of common stairs etc	[214]
91	Installation of lights in private property	[215]
92	Cleaning and painting of common stairs, etc	[216]
93	Fire precautions in common stairs etc	[217]

* * *

Powers of entry, execution of works, etc

99	Power to enter, execute works and recover expense	[218]
100	Interest on expenses	[219]
101	Offences relating to powers of entry and carrying out of works	[220]
102	Entry warrants	[221]
103	Execution of owner's works by occupier	[222]
104	Powers of entry: occupier and owner	[223]
105	Contents of notices	[224]
106	Appeals	[225]
107	Time for enforcing certain notices	[226]

108	Recovery of expense incurred under section 87 by charging order	[227]
109	Replacement of provisions of this Part by Health and Safety Regulations	[228]

* * *

133	Interpretation	[228A]

* * *

137	Citation, commencement, repeals and extent	[228B]

* * *

Schedule 1—Licensing—Further provisions as to the general system . [229–247]

* * *

An Act to make provision as regards Scotland for the licensing and regulation of certain activities; for the preservation of public order and safety and the prevention of crime; . . . as to the rights and duties of the owners and users of certain land, buildings and other structures; . . . and to enable [local authorities] to make management rules applying to land or premises under their control; as to certain other functions of local authorities and their officers; as to the time when the Burgh Police (Scotland) Acts 1892 to 1911 and certain local statutory provisions cease to have effect; and for connected purposes. [28th October 1982]

PART I
LICENSING—GENERAL PROVISIONS

1. Application of Parts I and II of this Act.

This Part of this Act shall have effect with respect to the licensing of the activities for which licences are required under Part II of this Act. **[204]**

NOTES to section 1
'This Part': Part I comprises ss 1–8.
'activities for which licences are required under Part II': Part II comprises ss 9–44. For the activities concerned, see the note following the notes to s 9 below. Part I thus forms a licensing code for those activities.
Definition: 'licence': see s 8 below.

2. Licensing authorities.

(1) For the administration of licensing in relation to the activities in connection with which licences are required under Part II of this Act there shall be a licensing authority for each district and islands area.

(2) The licensing authority shall be the district or islands council within whose area the activity is, or is to be, carried on.

(3) Notwithstanding subsection (2) above, a district or islands council shall not be exempt from any requirement to have a licence or any other obligation under this Part or Part II of this Act and a licensing authority shall have power to entertain and dispose of an application by a district or islands council for a licence or in respect of a licence held by them. **[205]**

NOTES to section 2
Sub-s (1): Part II comprises ss 9–44.
Sub-s (3): 'this Part': Part I comprises ss 1–8.
Definition: 'licence': see s 8 below.

3. Discharge of functions of licensing authorities.

(1) For the purpose of the discharge of their functions under this Part of this Act, every licensing authority shall consider, within 3 months of its having been made to them

under paragraph 1 of Schedule 1 to this Act, each application so made and, subject to the following provisions of this section, reach a final decision on it within 6 months.

(2) On summary application by the licensing authority within the 6 month period referred to in subsection (1) above, the sheriff may, if it appears to him that there is good reason to do so, extend that period as he thinks fit.

(3) The applicant shall be entitled to be a party to a summary application under subsection (2) above.

(4) Where the licensing authority have failed to reach a final decision on the application before the expiry of—
- (a) the 6 month period referred to in subsection (1) above, or
- (b) such further period as the sheriff may have specified on application under subsection (2) above,

the licence applied for shall be deemed to have been granted or, as the case may be, renewed unconditionally on the date of such expiry and shall remain in force for one year, but this subsection is without prejudice to the powers of revocation under section 7(6)(a) of this Act, of variation under paragraph 10 of Schedule 1 to this Act and of suspension under paragraphs 11 and 12 of that Schedule and to the provisions of paragraph 8(5) of that Schedule.

(5) The licensing authority shall make out and deliver the licence to the applicant to whom it has been deemed to have been granted under subsection (4) above. [206]

NOTES to section 3
Sub-s (1): 'this Part': Part I comprises ss 1–8.
Definitions: 'licensing authority': see s 2 above; 'licence': see s 8 below.

4. Further provisions as to licensing.

Schedule 1 to this Act (which contains further provisions as to licensing and regulation in relation to the activities in connection with which licences are required under Part II of this Act) shall have effect. [207]

NOTES to section 4
Part II comprises ss 9–44.
Definition: 'licence': see s 8 below.

5. Rights of entry and inspection.

(1) Without prejudice to any other provision of this Act, an authorised officer of the licensing authority or the fire authority or a constable may, for the purposes specified in subsection (2) below, at any reasonable time—
- (a) enter and inspect any premises, vehicle or vessel used or to be used for an activity in relation to which a licence is in force or has been applied for under this Act;
- (b) require production of and inspect any equipment, plant, apparatus or stock-in-trade which is or is to be kept or used in connection with any such activity;
- (c) require production of and inspect any records or other documents required by or under this Part or Part II of this Act to be kept by the holder of the licence and take copies of or extracts from any such record or document.

(2) The purposes referred to in subsection (1) above are—
- (a) where a licence is in force—
  - (i) seeing whether the terms of the licence are being complied with and, if they are not, obtaining information in respect of such non-compliance;
  - (ii) obtaining information relevant to the question whether the terms of the licence should be varied under paragraph 10 of Schedule 1 to this Act or whether the licence should be renewed or, under paragraph 11 or 12 of that Schedule, suspended; or
- (b) where the grant of a licence has been applied for, obtaining information relevant to the question whether the application should be granted.

[208]

(3) Any person who—
(a) being a person for the time being in charge of any premises, vehicle or vessel, fails without reasonable excuse to permit a constable or an authorised officer of a licensing authority or a fire authority who, in pursuance of subsection (1) above, demands to do so to enter or inspect the premises, vehicle or vessel or obstructs the entry thereto of a constable or such an officer, in pursuance of that subsection;
(b) being a person in respect of whom powers are exercised under subsection (1) above, on being required under that subsection to do so by a constable or an authorised officer of the licensing authority or the fire authority, fails without reasonable excuse to produce any equipment, plant, apparatus or stock-in-trade or to permit a constable or such an officer, in pursuance of that subsection, to inspect any equipment, plant, apparatus or stock-in-trade;
(c) being a holder of a licence, on being required by a constable or an authorised officer of the licensing authority or the fire authority, in pursuance of subsection (1) above, to produce any records or other document required by or under this Part or Part II of this Act to be kept by the holder of a licence, fails without reasonable excuse to produce them;
shall be guilty of an offence and liable, on summary conviction, to a fine not exceeding [level 3 on the standard scale].

(4) An authorised officer of a licensing authority or a constable may require any person who the officer or constable has reasonable ground to believe is carrying on an activity which requires to be licensed to produce his licence within 5 days of being required to do so.

(5) Any person who, having been required under subsection (4) above to produce a licence, fails without reasonable excuse to do so within the period of 5 days specified in that subsection shall be guilty of an offence and liable, on summary conviction, to a fine not exceeding [level 1 on the standard scale].

(6) An authorised officer of a licensing authority or the fire authority shall not be entitled to exercise the powers which he may exercise under subsection (1) or (4) above until he has produced his authorisation—
(a) in relation to the exercise of powers under subsection (1)(a) above, to the person for the time being in charge of the premises, vehicle or vessel; and
(b) in any other case, to the person in respect of whom the powers are to be exercised.

(7) A constable who is not in uniform shall not be entitled to exercise the powers which he may exercise under subsection (1) or (4) above until he has produced his identification—
(a) in relation to the exercise of powers under subsection (1)(a) above, to the person for the time being in charge of the premises, vehicle or vessel; and
(b) in any other case, to the person in respect of whom the powers are to be exercised. [208]

NOTES to section 5
Sub-s (1): 'this Part or Part II': Part I comprises ss 1–8, and Part II comprises ss 9–44.
Sub-s (3) is amended by virtue of the Criminal Procedure (Scotland) Act 1975 (c 21), s 289F (added by the Criminal Justice Act 1982 (c 48), s 54). Level 3 is £400: Increase of Criminal Penalties etc (Scotland) Order 1984, SI 1984/526, art 4.
Sub-s (5) is similarly amended. Level 1 is £50.
Definitions: 'fire authority'; 'licence' and 'premises': see s 8 below; 'vessel': see s 133 below.

6. Powers of entry to and search of unlicensed premises.

(1) If a justice of the peace or sheriff is satisfied by evidence on oath that there is reasonable ground for suspecting that—
(a) an activity in respect of which a licence under this Act is required is being carried on in any premises, vehicle, or vessel; and
(b) no such licence is in force,
he may grant a warrant authorising any constable to enter and search the premises, vehicle or vessel specified in the warrant.

(2) A constable may use reasonable force in executing a warrant granted under subsection (1) above.

(3) A constable who is not in uniform shall produce his identification if required to do so by any person in or upon any premises, vehicle or vessel which the constable is about to enter, is entering or has entered under the powers conferred under subsection (1) above, and if he has been so required to produce his identification, he shall not be entitled to enter or search the premises, vehicle or vessel or, as the case may be, remain there or continue to search the premises, vehicle or vessel until he has produced it.

(4) Any person who fails without reasonable excuse to permit a constable in pursuance of a warrant granted under this section to enter and search any premises, vehicle or vessel or who obstructs the entry thereto or search thereof by a constable shall be guilty of an offence and liable, on summary conviction, to a fine not exceeding [level 3 on the standard scale]. [209]

NOTES to section 6

Sub-s (4) is amended by virtue of the Criminal Procedure (Scotland) Act 1975 (c 21), s 289F (added by the Criminal Justice Act 1982 (c 48), s 54). Level 3 is £400: Increase of Criminal Penalties etc (Scotland) Order 1984, SI 1984/526, art 4.
Definitions: 'licence' and 'premises': see s 8 below; 'vessel': see s 133 below.

7. Offences, etc.

(1) Any person who without reasonable excuse does anything for which a licence is required under Part II of this Act without having such a licence shall be guilty of an offence and liable, on summary conviction, to a fine not exceeding [level 4 on the standard scale].

(2) If a condition attached to a licence is not complied with, the holder of the licence shall, subject to subsection (3) below, be guilty of an offence and liable, on summary conviction, to a fine not exceeding [level 3 on the standard scale].

(3) It shall be a defence for a person charged with an offence under subsection (2) above to prove that he used all due diligence to prevent the commission of the offence.

(4) Any person who, in making an application under this Part of this Act to the licensing authority, makes any statement which he knows to be false or recklessly makes any statement which is false in a material particular shall be guilty of an offence and liable, on summary conviction, to a fine not exceeding [level 4 on the standard scale].

(5) Any person who, being the holder of a licence—
(a) fails without reasonable excuse to notify the licensing authority of a material change of circumstances in accordance with paragraph 9(1) of Schedule 1 to this Act;
(b) without reasonable excuse makes or causes or permits to be made any material change in any premises, vehicle or vessel in contravention of paragraph 9(2) of Schedule 1 to this Act;
(c) fails without reasonable excuse to deliver his licence to the licensing authority in accordance with paragraph 13(2) of Schedule 1 to this Act,
shall be guilty of an offence and liable, on summary conviction, to a fine not exceeding, in the case of an offence under paragraph (a) or (b) above, [level 3 on the standard scale], and in the case of an offence under paragraph (c) above, [level 1 on the standard scale].

(6) Where a holder of a licence is convicted of an offence under section 5 (other than subsection (5) thereof), 6 or this section, the court by which he is convicted may, in addition to any other penalty which the court may impose, make an order in accordance with one or both of the following paragraphs—
(a) that the licence shall be revoked;
(b) that the holder of the licence shall be disqualifed from holding a licence for a period not exceeding 5 years.

[210]

(7) Where the holder of a licence is convicted of an offence under this section, an extract of such conviction and sentence (if any) shall, within 6 days after the date of the conviction, be transmitted by the clerk of the court to the licensing authority which granted the licence.

(8) A person may appeal against an order under subsection (6) above in the same manner as against sentence and the court which made the order may, pending the appeal, suspend the effect of the order.

(9) A person may, at any time after the expiry of the first year of his disqualification under subsection (6) above, apply to the court which ordered the disqualification to remove it, and, on such application, the court may by order remove the disqualification as from such date as may be specified in the order or refuse the application, and, in either case, may order the applicant to pay the whole or any part of the expenses of such application.

(10) Where an offence is alleged to have been committed under subsection (2) above by an employee or agent named in a licence, proceedings in respect of that offence may be instituted against the joint licence holder who is the employer of the employee or principal of the agent, whether or not proceedings have been instituted against the employee or agent. **[210]**

NOTES to section 7

Sub-s (1), (2), (4), (5) are amended by virtue of the Criminal Procedure (Scotland) Act 1975 (c 21), s 289F (added by the Criminal Justice Act 1982 (c 48), s 54). Level 1 is £50, level 3 is £400 and level 4 is £1,000: Increase of Criminal Penalties etc (Scotland) Order 1984, SI 1984/526, art 4.

Sub-s (4): 'this Part': Part I comprises ss 1–8.
Definition: 'licence': see s 8 below.

8. Interpretation of Parts I and II.

In this Part and in Part II of this Act except where the context otherwise requires—
'chief constable' means, in relation to a licensing authority's area, the chief constable for the area which includes the area of the licensing authority;
'fire authority' means, in relation to a licensing authority's area, the authority discharging in that area the functions of fire authority under the Fire Services Acts 1947 to 1959;
'licence' means a licence granted under this Part and Part II of this Act, and cognate expressions shall be construed accordingly;
'premises' includes land. **[211]**

NOTES to section 8
'this Part and in Part II': Part I comprises ss 1–8, and Part II comprises ss 9–44.
'licensing authority': see s 2 above.

PART II
LICENSING AND REGULATION—PARTICULAR ACTIVITIES

9. Application of sections 10 to 27 and 38 to 44.

(1) Sections 10 to 27 (except section 20), any regulations made under the said section 20, and sections 38 to 43 [(except section 41A)] of this Act and any order made under section 44(1)(a) of this Act (which sections regulations and order are in this section called the 'optional provisions') shall have effect in the area of a licensing authority only if and insofar as the authority have so resolved in accordance with subsections (2) to (8) below.

(2) A licensing authority may, in accordance with this section, resolve that, as from a day specified in the resolution (which must not be before the expiration of the period of nine months beginning with the day on which the resolution was made) any activity

provision for the licensing and regulation of which is made by the optional provisions shall require to be licensed in accordance with the provisions of this Act relating to that activity and shall be regulated by those provisions.

(3) Subject to subsections (4) and (5) below, a resolution under this section may be made—
(a) in relation to all or any of the activities referred to in subsection (2) above;
(b) in relation to the whole or any part of the area of the licensing authority;
(c) in relation to—
   (i) all classes of an activity referred to in any of the optional provisions; or
   (ii) all such classes subject to exceptions; or
   (iii) any particular such class or classes.

(4) A licensing authority may not make a resolution under this section relating to any of the activities provision for the licensing and regulation of which is made in sections 10 to 23 of this Act (that is to say the operation of a vehicle as a taxi, the operation of a vehicle as a hire car, the driving of a taxi and the driving of a hire car) unless it relates to all these activities.

(5) A resolution made under this section by the licensing authority relating to—
(a) the activity provision for the licensing and regulation of which is made in sections 24 to 27 of this Act (that is to say the carrying on of business as a second-hand dealer) shall specify the particular class or classes of that activity which shall thereby fall to be licensed and regulated;
(b) the activity provision for the licensing of which is made in section 41 of this Act (that is to say the use of premises as a place of public entertainment) shall specify the place or places, or class or classes thereof, which shall thereby fall to be licensed.

(6) A licensing authority shall not make a resolution under this section unless they have—
(a) published in a newspaper or newspapers circulating in their area the terms of the proposed resolution together with a notice stating—
   (i) that they intend to make the resolution; and
   (ii) that representations about the resolution may be made in writing to the authority within 28 days of the first publication of the notice; and
(b) considered any representations so made.

(7) A licensing authority, before proceeding to make a resolution under this section, may make such modifications to the proposed resolution as they think fit in the light of representations made to them about it provided such modifications do not extend its scope.

(8) The licensing authority shall, as soon as they have made a resolution under subsection (2) above, publish in a newspaper or newspapers circulating in their area—
(a) the terms of the resolution so made; together with
(b) a notice stating—
   (i) that with effect from the date specified as that on which the resolution comes into effect it will be an offence under section 7(1) of this Act to do without a licence whatever the resolution specifies as being an activity requiring to be licensed; and
   (ii) that applications for licences in respect of the activity will be considered by the authority after the expiry of one month after the date of the making of the resolution.

(9) A resolution under this section may be varied or rescinded by a subsequent resolution made in like manner except that, in relation to the time when it takes effect, a resolution under this subsection—
(a) varying a resolution under this section so as to reduce its scope; or
(b) rescinding a resolution under this section shall take effect on such date as may be specified in it being any date subsequent to the making of the resolution.

(10) Anything which must or may be done under or by virtue of Part I or this Part of this Act may, at any time after the making by the licensing authority of the resolution, be done so far as may be necessary or expedient for the purpose of giving full effect to the resolution at or after the time it takes effect but no application for a licence in respect of an activity requiring to be licensed in consequence of the resolution shall be considered by the authority until the expiry of one month after the making of the resolution.   **[211A]**

NOTES to section 9

Amendment: Sub-s (1) was amended by the Fire Safety and Safety of Places of Sport Act 1987 (c 27), s 44(4).

Sub-s (10): 'Part I or this Part': Part I comprises ss 1–8, and this Part (Part II) comprises ss 9–44.

Definitions: 'optional provisions': see sub-s (1); 'licensing authority': see s 2 above; 'licence': see s 8 below.

44. Additional activities.

(1) The Secretary of State may, by order made by statutory instrument, designate any activity other than one of those specified in this Part of this Act—
(a) as an activity for which, subject to a resolution of the licensing authority in relation to it under section 9 of this Act, a licence shall be required and which, subject to such a resolution, shall be regulated in accordance with the provisions specified in the order; or
(b) as an activity for which a licence shall be required and which shall be regulated in accordance with the provisions specified in the order.

(2) An order made under this section may provide—
(a) that Part I of this Act, with such modifications if any as may be specified in the order, shall have effect for the purposes of the licensing of the activity designated by the order;
(b) for the regulation of the activity designated by the order;
(c) for the repeal or modification of any enactment which provides (whether consistently or not) for the same matter as the order;
(d) without prejudice to any provision of Part I of this Act which has effect, with or without modification, by virtue of paragraph (a) above, for the creation of offences and for making offenders liable, on summary conviction, to imprisonment for a period not exceeding 60 days or such lesser maximum period as may be specified in the order or to a fine not exceeding £200 or such lesser maximum fine as may be so specified or to both such fine and such imprisonment.

(3) No order shall be made under this section unless a draft of it has been laid before and approved by a resolution of each House of Parliament.   **[211B]**

NOTE to section 44

Sub-ss (1), (2): See the Civic Government (Scotland) Act 1982 (Licensing of Houses in Multiple Occupation) Order 1991 SI 1991/1253. See paras [1507] to [1509].

★ ★ ★

Part VIII
Buildings, Etc

87. Local authorities' powers in relation to buildings in need of repair.

(1) A local authority may, by notice in writing, require the owner of any building in their area to rectify such defects in the building as are specified in the notice being defects which require rectification in order to bring the building into a reasonable state of repair, regard being had to its age, type and location.

(2) For the purposes of this section, any object or structure fixed to a building or forming part of the land and comprised within the curtilage of a building shall be treated as part of the building.

(3) Where it appears to a local authority to be necessary in the interests of health or safety or to prevent damage to any property that they should repair immediately a building in their area, they may without prior notice rectify such defects in the building as could have been specified in a notice under subsection (1) above had such a notice been served and any person authorised by them may, on their behalf, for these purposes, enter the building and the land pertaining thereto.

(4) The local authority may recover from the owner of the building the expense of anything done by them under subsection (3) above or, where there is more than one owner, apportion such expense among them and recover from each the appropriate sum, but may remit any sum or any part of any sum due to them under this subsection as they think fit.

(5) A person who, in compliance with a notice served under subsection (1) above or under section 20 of the Public Health (Scotland) Act 1897, carries out work on a building which is, for the purposes of [Part V of the Housing (Scotland) Act 1987], a house shall have the same entitlement to loans and grants as he would have had if the notice had been served and to the extent that it could have been served under section [108 of that Act].

(6) In this section, 'local authority' means the district or island council except that in the case of districts situated within the Highland, Borders or Dumfries and Galloway region it means the council of that region. [212]

NOTES to section 87
Amendment: Sub-s (5) was amended by the Housing (Scotland) Act 1987 (c 26), s 339(2), Sch 23, para 28(1).
Sub-s (5): Part V of the Housing (Scotland) Act 1987 (ss 108–113) relates to the repair of houses.
Definition: 'local authority': see sub-s (6).

88. Installation of pipes through neighbouring property.

(1) The sheriff may, on summary application by an owner of a part of a building who requires, but has been refused or otherwise has been unable to obtain, the consent of any other person for—
  (a) the installation—
    (i) on the outside surface of any external wall or roof of the building;
    (ii) in, through or under any part of the building which is held in common by the owner and the other person or any land pertaining to the building which is so held;
    (iii) in, through or under any part of the building owned by the other person or any land pertaining to the building which is so owned
    of such pipes or drains as are necessary for the purpose of water supply to, or the soil, waste or rainwater drainage or the ventilation in connection with such drainage of, the owner's part of the building;
  (b) the making of connections with common water supply pipes, or soil, waste or rainwater drains or drain ventilating pipes; or
  (c) access to the pipes or drains referred to in paragraph (a) above for the purpose of their maintenance and repair,
subject to subsection (2) below, grant warrant authorising such installation, making of connections or access.

(2) The sheriff shall not grant warrant under—
  (a) subsection (1) above unless it appears to him that it is reasonable that the installation be carried out, the connections be made or, as the case may be, the maintenance or repair for which access is applied for under that subsection, be done;
  (b) under paragraph (a) or (b) of that subsection or, except for repair in an emergency, paragraph (c) of that subsection to an owner who has been otherwise unable to obtain consent unless it appears to him that the owner's request for consent was made in writing to the other person at least 28 days before the application under that subsection.

(3) The sheriff may—
(a) make a warrant granted by him under this section subject to such conditions as he thinks fit;
(b) make such award of expenses as he sees fit in relation to an application under this section.

(4) An appeal shall lie to the Court of Session from the decision of the sheriff under this section.

(5) This section is without prejudice to any requirement to obtain approval under or any other obligation imposed by or by virtue of the Building (Scotland) Acts 1959 and 1970, the Sewerage (Scotland) Act 1968, the Town and Country Planning (Scotland) Acts 1972 to 1974, the Water (Scotland) Act 1980 or any other enactment relating to building, the provision of public sewerage services, planning or the public supply of water. [213]

* * *

90. Lighting of common stairs etc.

(1) In this section—
'common property' means common stairs or passages or private courts;
'owner', in relation to common property, means the owner or owners of lands or premises having a right of access by the common property;
'private court' means any area which—
(a) is maintained or liable to be maintained by a person other than a local authority; and
(b) forms a common access to lands or premises separately occupied.

(2) A district or islands council may—
(a) provide and maintain lighting in common property; and
(b) light and extinguish the lights in the common property or arrange for that to be done.

(3) A district or islands council may continue to provide and maintain lighting in any place where they provided and maintained it immediately before the commencement of subsection (2) above notwithstanding that the place is not common property.

(4) Where, and to the extent that, the district or islands council for the area in which any common property is situated has not exercised the powers conferred upon them by subsection (2) above, it shall be the duty of the owner—
(a) to provide and maintain lighting in the common property to the satisfaction of the district or islands council; and
(b) to light and extinguish the lights in the common property at such times as the district or islands council may require by order published in accordance with subsection (6) below.

(5) A district or islands council may by notice in writing require the owner to comply with subsection (4)(a) above within 14 days of the date of service of the notice on the owner.

(6) An order made under subsection (4)(b) above shall be published once weekly for at least two weeks in a newspaper circulating in the area of the district or islands council.

(7) In the event of the owner's failing to comply with subsection (4) above, the district or islands council may provide and maintain lighting or, as the case may be, light and extinguish the lights in the common property.

(8) An authorised officer of the district or islands council shall be entitled at any reasonable time to enter common property for the purpose of determining whether subsection (4) above is being complied with and a person authorised to do so by such a council shall be entitled at any reasonable time to enter such property and to do there anything which the district or islands council are entitled to do under subsection (2), (3) or (7) above.

[(9) A district or islands council who have, under subsection (2), (3) or (7) above, provided or maintained lighting or lit or extinguished lights shall be entitled to recover—
(a) from the owner of the lands or premises the expense incurred by the council; or
(b) where there is more than one owner of the lands or premises, that is, where the lands or premises are common property, from each owner such proportion of the expense thereby incurred by the council as the council may determine,
but the council may remit any sum or part of any sum due to them under this subsection.] [214]

NOTES to section 90
Amendment: Sub-s (9) was substituted by the Abolition of Domestic Rates Etc (Scotland) Act 1987 (c 47), s 6, Sch 1, para 39.
Definitions: 'common property'; 'owner' and 'private court': see sub-s (1).

91. Installation of lights in private property.

(1) A district or islands council or an owner of common property may, where it is necessary to do so for the purpose of performing their or, as the case may be, his functions under section 90 of this Act, provide and maintain lights in or on any land or building in or on which they have no right (apart from this section) to do so, and any person authorised by such council or by such owner may, at any reasonable time, enter that land or building in order to do so on their behalf.

(2) A district or islands council who provide and maintain or an owner of common property who provides and maintains lights under this section shall, in doing so, cause as little inconvenience and damage as possible and pay compensation for any damage done; and, in case of dispute, the amount of such compensation shall be determined summarily by the sheriff, whose decision in the matter shall be final.

(3) The person having right to any land or building in or on which lights have been provided and maintained under subsection (1) above may, on giving 14 days written notice to that effect, require the district or islands council or, as the case may be, the owner of the common property to remove them temporarily during any reconstruction, repair or similar works relating to the land or building, and if the council or, as the case may be, the owner fails to do so, the person having right as aforesaid may do so and recover the expense thereof from the council or, as the case may be, the owner, with interest thereon at such reasonable rate as that person may determine from the date on which a demand for the expenses is served until payment. [215]

92. Cleaning and painting of common stairs, etc.

(1) In this section—
'common property' means common stairs, passages, water-closets, backgreens or basements or other similar areas or private courts;
'occupier', in relation to common property, means the occupier or occupiers of lands or premises having a right of access by, or a right in common to, the common property.

(2) It shall be the duty of the occupier to keep the common property clean to the satisfaction of the district or islands council within whose area the common property is situated.

(3) A district or islands council may make byelaws for the regulation of the cleaning of common property by the occupier in accordance with this section and such byelaws may provide that persons contravening such provisions of the byelaws as may be specified as provisions contravention of which is an offence shall be liable, on summary conviction, to a fine not exceeding [level 1 on the standard scale] or such lesser sum as the byelaws may specify.

(4) A district or islands council may by notice in writing require the occupier to comply with subsection (2) above or with byelaws made under subsection (3) above within such reasonable time as may be specified in the notice.

(5) Sections 99(4) and 106 of this Act shall not apply to a notice served under subsection (4) above.

(6) A district or islands council may by notice in writing require the owner or owners of lands or premises having a right of access by common stairs or passages to paint or otherwise suitably decorate the common stairs or passages within such reasonable time as may be specified in the notice.

(7) A district or islands council may remove litter from a backgreen or private court.

(8) An authorised officer of a district or islands council shall be entitled at any reasonable time to enter common property for the purpose of—
(a) determining whether subsection (2) above and any byelaws made under subsection (3) above are being complied with;
(b) determining whether any common stairs or passages referred to in subsection (6) above require to be painted or otherwise suitably decorated,
and a person authorised to do so by such a council shall be entitled at any reasonable time to enter such property and to do there anything which the council may do under subsection (7) above.

(9) A person who throws down, drops or otherwise deposits, and leaves, litter in any common property shall be guilty of an offence and liable, on summary conviction, to a fine not exceeding [level 3 on the standard scale]. **[216]**

NOTES to section 92
Sub-s (3) and (9) are amended by virtue of the Criminal Procedure (Scotland) Act 1975 (c 21), s 289F (added by the Criminal Justice Act 1982 (c 48), s 54). Level 1 is £50 and level 3 is £400: Increase of Criminal Penalties etc (Scotland) Order 1984, SI 1984/526, art 4.
Definitions: 'common property' and 'occupier': see sub-s (1).

93. Fire precautions in common stairs etc.

(1) In this section—
'common property' and 'occupier' have respectively the same meanings as in section 92 of this Act;
'combustible substance' means anything which is dangerously combustible in normal conditions and includes any container holding the combustible substance including any such container forming part of a motor vehicle but does not include anything forming part of any common property.

(2) It shall be the duty of the occupier to keep the common property free of—
(a) any combustible substances;
(b) anything which might obstruct egress from and access to the property in the event of fire.

(3) An authorised officer of the fire authority shall be entitled—
(a) to enter common property for the purpose of determining whether subsection (2) above is being complied with; and
(b) if it is not, and there is thereby an immediate risk of fire likely to endanger life, to enter the property and to do there anything he may consider necessary to remove that risk including seizing and arranging as he sees fit for the retention of any substance or other thing until claimed by a person having a right of possession to it.

(4) The fire authority may by notice in writing require the occupier to comply with subsection (2) above within such reasonable time as may be specified in the notice by removing or rendering safe the substance or other thing (if any) there specified.

(5) Any person who fails without reasonable excuse to comply with a notice served under subsection (4) above shall be guilty of an offence and liable, on summary conviction, to a fine not exceeding [level 3 on the standard scale].

(6) Section 105 of this Act shall apply to a notice served by a fire authority under subsection (4) above, as it applies to notices served by local authorities.

(7) The fire authority shall be entitled to recover the expense of doing anything under subsection (3)(b) above from the occupier or person having a right of possession to such substances or articles as are referred to in the said subsection (3)(b) but may remit any sum or any part of any sum due to them under this subsection as they think fit.

(8) This section is without prejudice to any other enactment relating to fire precautions.

(9) In this section, 'fire authority' means the authority discharging in the area in which the common property is situated the functions of fire authority under the Fire Services Acts 1947 to 1959. [217]

NOTES to section 93
Sub-s (5) is amended by virtue of the Criminal Procedure (Scotland) Act 1975 (c 21), s 289F (added by the Criminal Justice Act 1982 (c 48), s 54). Level 3 is £400: Increase of Criminal Penalties etc (Scotland) Order 1984, SI 1984/526, art 4.
Sub-s (9): As to Fire authorities, see the Fire Services Act 1947 (c 41), s 4, and para [10] above.
Definitions: 'combustible substance'; 'common property' and 'occupier': see sub-s (1); 'fire authority': see sub-s (9).

* * *

Powers of entry, execution of works, etc

99. Power to enter, execute works and recover expense.

(1) Where, under any notice served by a local authority under this Part of this Act, anything is required to be done by the owner or occupier of land or premises in relation to the land or premises an authorised officer of the local authority may, on the expiration of any period of time specified in the notice as that in which the thing has to be done, enter the land or premises to see if whatever is required to be done under the notice has been done.

(2) Where—
(a) under any notice served by a local authority under this Part of this Act, anything is required to be done by the owner or occupier of land or premises in relation to the land or premises and the owner, or as the case may be, the occupier fails to do it in accordance with the notice; and
(b) there is no express provision in this Act, apart from this section, authorising the local authority to do whatever is required by the notice to be done,
any person authorised by the local authority may enter the land or premises and do or cause to be done whatever is required by the notice to be done.

(3) A person shall not be entitled to exercise the powers which he may exercise under subsections (1) or (2) above until he has produced his authorisation to do so to the person for the time being in charge of the land or premises.

(4) Subject to subsection (7) below, a local authority shall be entitled to recover the expense of doing anything in relation to any land or premises under subsection (2) above from the owner or, as the case may be, the occupier of the land or premises but may remit any sum or any part of any sum due to them under this subsection as they think fit.

(5) Where such expense as is mentioned in subsection (4) above is recoverable under that subsection from more than one person, the local authority may apportion such expense among them.

(6) Where a local authority claim to recover any expense as is mentioned in subsection (4) above from a person and he proves that he—
(a) is receiving the rent of the land or premises merely as trustee, tutor, curator, factor or agent for some other person; and

(b) has not, and since the date of service on him of the demand for payment has not had, in his hands on behalf of that other person sufficient money to discharge the whole demand of the authority,

his liability shall be limited to the total amount of money which he has or has had in his hands as aforesaid.

(7) Subsection (4) above does not apply in relation to any cleaning of common property done under subsection (2) above.

(8) In this section and in sections 100 to 109 of this Act references to the occupier of land or premises include references to the occupier of common property within the meaning given to those expressions by section 92 of this Act. [218]

NOTES to section 99
Sub-s (1): 'this Part': Part VIII comprises ss 87–109.
Definitions: 'occupier': see sub-s (8); 'local authority': see s 133 below.

100. Interest on expenses.

Where under any provision of this Part of this Act a local authority is entitled to recover expenses, they shall also be entitled to interest thereon at such reasonable rate as they may determine from the date on which a demand for the expenses is served until payment but they may remit any sum or any part of any sum due to them as interest as they think fit. [219]

NOTES to section 100
'this Part': Part VIII comprises ss 87–109.
Definition: 'local authority': see s 133 below.

101. Offences relating to powers of entry and carrying out of works.

Any person who—
(a) fails without reasonable excuse to permit—
  (i) an authorised officer of a local authority who, in pursuance of sections 90(8), 91(1), 92(8) or 99(1) of this Act, demands to do so, to enter any land or premises; or
  (ii) a person authorised by a local authority under section 87(3), 90(8), 91(1), 92(8) or 99(2) of this Act to enter any land or premises and do or cause anything to be done there who demands to do so or an owner of land, building or other premises or his contractors or workmen who having been authorised under section 88 or 104 or being entitiled under section 91(1) of this Act to enter the land, building or other premises and execute work there demands or demand to do so, to enter the land, building or other premises and do there whatever is to be done; or
(b) obstructs the entry in pursuance of this Act to any land or premises of, or the doing there in accordance with this Act of anything by, any such authorised officer or other person who has demanded so to enter or so to do that thing,

shall be guilty of an offence and liable, on summary conviction, to a fine not exceeding [level 3 on the standard scale]. [220]

NOTES to section 101
Section 101 is amended by virtue of the Criminal Procedure (Scotland) Act 1975 (c 21), s 289F (added by the Criminal Justice Act 1982 (c 48), s 54). Level 3 is £400: Increase of Criminal Penalties etc (Scotland) Order 1984, SI 1984/526, art 4.
Definition: 'local authority': see s 133 below.

102. Entry warrants.

(1) If a justice of the peace or sheriff is satisfied by evidence on oath that—
(a) entry to any land or premises which a person is entitled to enter in pursuance of

this Part of this Act has been refused to that person or he has been prevented from doing there anything which he is entitled to do in pursuance of this Part of this Act or such refusal or prevention is apprehended or that the land or premises are unoccupied or that the occupier is temporarily absent or that the case is one of emergency; and

(b) there is reasonable ground for entry to the land or premises for the purposes for which entry is required

he may grant a warrant to the person to enter the land or premises specified in the warrant if need be by force and to do whatever is to be done.

(2) A warrant issued in pursuance of this section shall continue in force for a period of one month beginning with the day on which it was granted or until the purpose for which entry is required has been satisfied, whichever is the shorter.

(3) A person who has been granted a warrant under this section to enter any unoccupied land or premises or land or premises the occupier of which is temporarily absent shall leave the land or premises as effectively secured against trespassers as he found it or them. [221]

NOTES to section 102

Sub-s (1): 'this Part': Part VIII comprises ss 87–109.
Definition: 'occupier': see s 99(8) above.

103. Execution of owner's works by occupier.

(1) If, in relation to any land or premises, the owner of the land or premises fails to do anything which he is required to do by notice served under this Part of this Act, the tenant or other occupier of the land or premises may, with the consent of the local authority which served the notice, do whatever the notice requires to be done, and may, subject to subsection (2) below, deduct the expense of doing so (with interest thereon from the date on which the expense was incurred at such reasonable rate as the local authority may determine) from any rent due or to be due by the tenant or occupier to the owner in respect of the land or premises.

(2) Nothing in subsection (1) above authorises the deduction of any expenses from any rent where the deduction would be at variance with any right or obligation arising apart from that subsection between the owner of the land or premises and the tenant or occupier thereof. [222]

NOTES to section 103

Sub-s (1): 'this Part': Part VIII comprises ss 87–109.
Definitions: 'occupier': see s 99(8) above; 'local authority': see s 133 below.

104. Powers of entry: occupier and owner.

If the tenant or other occupier of any land or premises prevents the owner of them from executing any work which he is required to execute in pursuance of any notice served by a local authority under this Part of this Act, the sheriff may, on the application of the owner, authorise the owner and his contractors and workmen to enter the land or premises for the purpose of executing such work. [223]

NOTES to section 104

'this Part': Part VIII comprises ss 87–109.
Definition: 'occupier': see s 99(8) above.

105. Contents of notices.

Except where otherwise expressly provided under this Part of this Act, any notice issued or served by a local authority under this said Part regarding the doing of any thing in relation to land or premises shall, so far as necessary and reasonably practicable, specify—

(a) details, including the location, of the land or premises;
(b) the nature of any works which have to be carried out and of any requirements which have to be met; and
(c) the period within which the notice has to be complied with. **[224]**

NOTES to section 105
'this Part': Part VIII comprises ss 87–109.
Definition: 'local authority': see s 133 below.

106. Appeals.

(1) A person may, in accordance with subsection (3) below, appeal to the sheriff—
(a) against any requirement in any notice served on him under this part of this Act by a local authority; or
(b) in respect of the amount of any expenses or interest claimed from him or the rate at which interest is charged against him under this Part of this Act.

(2) The owner of any land or premises may, in accordance with subsection (3) below, appeal to the sheriff in respect of any expenses or interest (including the rate at which interest is charged) claimed or deducted under section 103 of this Act.

(3) An appeal under subsection (1) or (2) above shall be made by way of summary application and shall be lodged within 14 days of—
(a) in the case of an appeal under paragraph (a) of subsection (1) above, the date of service of the notice; and
(b) in other cases, the date of service of the claim for payment or, in the case of an appeal under subsection (2) above where the expense or interest has been deducted from rent, the date of that deduction.

(4) The sheriff may, on an appeal under this section—
(a) order that the requirement appealed against shall be of no effect or that it shall have effect subject to such modifications as he may specify in his order or confirm it;
(b) make such order as to the expenses which are or interest which is the subject of the appeal as appears to him appropriate.

(5) Any party to an appeal under subsection (1) or (2) above may appeal on a point of law from the sheriff's decision to the Court of Session within 14 days from the date of that decision.

(6) No appeal shall lie from the opinion of the Court of Session given in pursuance of subsection (5) above. **[225]**

NOTES to section 106
Sub-s (1): 'this Part': Part VIII comprises ss 87–109.
Definition: 'local authority': see s 133 below.

107. Time for enforcing certain notices.

A notice containing a requirement which may be appealed against under paragaph (a) of section 106(1) of this Act shall not be acted upon by a local authority or any person authorised by a local authority to do anything until the time for appealing under that paragraph has expired or, if an appeal thereunder has been lodged, until it is disposed of or abandoned. **[226]**

NOTE to section 107
Definition: 'local authority': see s 133 below.

108. Recovery of expenses incurred under section 87 by charging order.

(1) Where, under—
(a) section 87(3) of this Act; or

(b) section 99(4) thereof (to the extent that it relates to failure to rectify a defect specified in a notice served under section 87(1) thereof)
a local authority are entitled to recover any expenses, they may make in favour of themselves an order providing and declaring that the land, building or premises is thereby charged and burdened with an annuity to pay the amount of the expenses.

(2) Paragraphs 2 to 8 of Schedule [9 to the Housing (Scotland) Act 1987] shall apply to an order under subsection (1) above as they apply to a charging order under paragraph 1 of that Schedule but with the following modifications, that is to say, in sub-paragraph (b)(i) of paragraph 4 of that Schedule at the end there shall be inserted the words 'or any sum secured by virtue of section 5(5) to (8) of the Land Tenure Reform (Scotland) Act 1974' and in sub-paragraph (b)(ii) of that paragraph, after the word 'Act', where thirdly occurring, there shall be inserted the words 'or under the Building (Scotland) Act 1959.' [227]

NOTES to section 108
Amendment: Sub-s (2) was amended by the Housing (Scotland) Act 1987 (c 26), s 339(2), Sch 23, para 28(2).
Definition: 'local authority': see s 133 below.

109. Replacement of provisions of this Part by Health and Safety Regulations.

Subsection (1) of section 80 of the Health and Safety at Work etc Act 1974 (repeal or modification of certain provisions by regulations) shall apply to any provision of this Part of this Act and to any byelaws made under any such provision as it applies to any provision mentioned in subsection (2) of that section. [228]

NOTE to section 109
'this Part': Part VIII comprises ss 87–109.

* * *

133. Interpretation.

In this Act, except where the context otherwise requires—
'local authority' means a regional, islands or district council;
'proper officer' shall be construed in accordance with section 235(3) of the Local Government (Scotland) Act 1973;
'public place' means any place (whether a thoroughfare or not) to which the public have unrestricted access and includes—
  (a) the doorways or entrances of premises abutting on any such place; and
  (b) any common passage, close, court, stair, garden or yard pertinent to any tenement or group of separately owned houses; and
['public road', 'roads authority' and 'road' have the same meanings as in the Roads (Scotland) Act 1984;]
'vessel' means any kind of water-craft including a hovercraft within the meaning of the Hovercraft Act 1968 but not including a vessel in Her Majesty's service. [228A]

NOTES to section 133
Amendment: Section 133 was amended by the Roads (Scotland) Act 1984 (c 54), s 156(1), Sch 9, para 87.
'public road' etc: See the Roads (Scotland) Act 1984, s 151(1), and para [793] below.
'vessel': For the meaning of 'hovercraft', see the Hovercraft Act 1968 (c 59), s 4(1).

* * *

[228B]   *Civic Government (Scotland) Act 1982 (c 45), s 137*

137. Citation, commencement, repeals and extent.

(1) This Act may be cited as the Civic Government (Scotland) Act 1982.

(2) This Act, other than sections 134 to 136 and subsections (1) above, (3) to (6) and (9) below and this subsection, shall come into force on such date or dates as the Secretary of State may by order made by statutory instrument appoint and different dates may be appointed under this section for different provisions of this Act or for different purposes of the same provision.

(3) An order under subsection (2) above shall of itself have the effect of repealing—
(a) any provision of the Burgh Police (Scotland) Acts 1892 to 1911;
(b) any local statutory provision (whether or not subject to an order under section 225(6) of the Local Government (Scotland) Act 1973 (exemption from and postponement of repeal of local statutory provision))

to the extent that the provision provides for any matter which is also provided for (whether consistently or not) by or under any provision of this Act commenced by that order.

(4) A repeal under subsection (3) above shall take effect on the date of commencement of the provision of this Act the commencement of which gives rise, under that subsection, to that repeal.

(5) In this section 'local statutory provision' means—
(a) a provision of a local Act, the Bill for which was promoted by a local authority;
(b) a provision of an Act confirming a provisional order made on the application of a local authority;
(c) a provision of an order made on such an application which was subject to special parliamentary procedure,

not being a provision relating to a statutory undertaking or a protective provision for the benefit of any person.

(6) In subsection (5) above, 'statutory undertaking' means any railway, light railway, tramway, road transport, water transport, canal, inland navigation, ferry, dock, harbour, pier or lighthouse undertaking, any market undertaking, or any undertaking for the supply of electricity, gas, hydraulic power, water or district heating.

(7) *(with Schedule 3 amends certain enactments)*

(8) *(with Schedule 4 repeals certain enactments)*

(9) This Act (except section 16, which applies to England and Wales) applies to Scotland only.   **[228B]**

NOTES to section 137

Subs-s (2):   The Civic Government (Scotland) Act 1982 Commencement Order 1983, SI 1983/201 (amended by SI 1984/573 and SI 1984/774) brought into force on 1 April 1983 ss 45–61, 67–109, 111–133, Sch 2, and Sch 3, paras 1–4, and, for certain purposes, ss 1–44, 62–66, 110(1), (2), 137(7), (8), and Schs 1, 3, 4. It brought the Act fully into force on 1 July 1984.

Definitions: 'local statutory provision': see sub-s (5); 'statutory undertaking': see subs-s (6).

★ ★ ★

SCHEDULES

Section 4

SCHEDULE 1

Licensing—Further Provisions as to the General System

Applications for the grant and renewal of licences

1.—(1) An application to a licensing authority for the grant or renewal of a licence shall be—
- (a) made in writing in such form as may be determined by the licensing authority;
- (b) signed by the applicant or his agent; and
- (c) accompanied by such fee as the authority may charge under paragraph 15 below.

(2) An application under sub-paragraph (1) above shall specify—
- (a) the kind of licence in respect of which the application is made;
- (b) where the applicant is a natural person, his full name and address and, where the applicant himself is not to be carrying on the day-to-day management of the activity in relation to which the application is made, the full name and address of any employee or agent who is;
- (c) where the application is made by or on behalf of a person other than a natural person,
  - (i) the full name of the person;
  - (ii) the address of its registered or principal office;

[TEXT CONTINUES ON PAGE 138]

(iii) the names and private addresses of its directors, partners or other persons responsible for its management; and
(iv) the full name and address of any employee or agent who is to carry on the day-to-day management of the activity in relation to which the application is made;
(d) the address of the premises, if any, in or from which and the area in which the activity is to be carried on; and
(e) such other information as the authority may reasonably require.

(3) Where the application relates to a licence for an activity which is wholly or mainly to be carried on in premises, it shall contain one or other of the following declarations by the applicant, that is to say, a declaration that he is complying with paragraph 2(2) below or a declaration by him that he is unable to do so because he has no such rights of access or other rights in respect of the premises as would enable him to do so, but that he has taken such reasonable steps as are open to him (specifying them) to acquire those rights and has been unable to acquire them. **[229]**

NOTES to Schedule 1, para 1
Definitions: 'licensing authority': see s 2 above; 'licence' and 'premises': see s 8 above.

2.—(1) A licensing authority shall, as soon as an application for the grant or renewal of a licence is made to them, send a copy of the application to the chief constable and, where the activity is wholly or mainly to be carried on in premises, the fire authority.

(2) Where an application is for the grant or renewal of a licence in relation to an activity wholly or mainly to be carried on in premises, the applicant shall, for a period of 21 days beginning with the date on which the application was submitted to the licensing authority, display a notice complying with sub-paragraph (3) below at or near the premises so that it can conveniently be read by the public.

(3) The notice shall state—
(a) that application has been made for a licence;
(b) the particulars required under paragraph 1(2) above to be specified in the application;
(c) that objections and representations in relation to the application may be made to the licensing authority in accordance with paragraph 3 below;
(d) the effect of paragraph 3(1) to (3) below.

(4) Where an application contains a declaration that the applicant is complying with sub-paragraph (2) above, the applicant shall, as soon as possible after the expiry of the period of 21 days referred to in that sub-paragraph, submit to the licensing authority a certificate stating that he has so complied.

(5) An applicant shall not be treated as having failed to comply with sub-paragraph (2) above if the notice was, without any fault or intention of his, removed, obscured or defaced before the 21 days referred to in that sub-paragraph have elapsed, so long as he has taken reasonable steps for its protection and, if need be, replacement; and if he has cause to rely on this sub-paragraph, his certificate under sub-paragraph (4) above shall state the relevant circumstances.

(6) Where an application contains a declaration that the applicant is complying with sub-paragraph (2) above, and—
(a) he fails to submit the certificate required by sub-paragraph (4) above;
(b) in the circumstances referred to in sub-paragraph (5) above, he has not, in the opinion of the licensing authority, taken reasonable steps for the protection or, as the case may require, replacement of the notice; or
(c) the licensing authority is, at any time before they reach a final decision on the application, satisfied that the notice, was not displayed in accordance with this paragraph,
they may require the applicant to display the notice again for a period of 21 days

beginning with such date as they may specify and the provisions of this paragraph shall apply in respect of such display as they apply in respect of display under sub-paragraph (2) above.

(7) The licensing authority—
(a) shall, in accordance with sub-paragraph (8) below, cause public notice to be given of every application made to them for the grant or renewal of a licence falling within a prescribed class;
(b) shall, in accordance with sub-paragraph (8) below, cause public notice to be given of an application made to them for the grant or renewal of a licence in relation to an activity wholly or mainly to be carried on in premises if the application contains a declaration that the applicant has been unable to comply with the requirements of sub-paragraph (2) above;
(c) may, if they think fit, cause public notice to be given, in accordance with sub-paragraph (8) below, of any application for the grant or renewal of a licence which is made to them and notice of which they are not obliged to give under this sub-paragraph.

(8) Public notice of an application shall be given for the purposes of sub-paragraph (7) above by publication of a notice in a newspaper or newspapers circulating in the area of the authority stating—
(a) the particulars required under paragraph 1(2) above to be specified in the application;
(b) that objections or representations in relation to the application may be made to the licensing authority in accordance with paragraph 3 below; and
(c) the effect of paragraph 3(1) to (3) below.

(9) The Secretary of State may, by order made by statutory instrument subject to annulment in pursuance of a resolution of either House of Parliament, prescribe a class or classes of licences for the purposes of sub-paragraph (7) above. [230]

NOTES to Schedule 1, para 2
Definitions: 'licensing authority': see s 2 above; 'chief constable', 'fire authority', 'licence' and 'premises': see s 8 above.

Objections and representations

3.—(1) Any objection or representation relating to an application for the grant or renewal of a licence shall, subject to sub-paragraph (2) below, be entertained by the licensing authority if, but only if, the objection or representation—
(a) is in writing;
(b) specifies the grounds of the objection or, as the case may be, the nature of the representation;
(c) specifies the name and address of the person making it;
(d) is signed by him or on his behalf;
(e) was made to them within 21 days of whichever is the later or, as the case may be, latest of the following dates—
  (i) where public notice of the application was given under paragraph 2(7) above, the date when it was first so given;
  (ii) where the application relates to a licence for an activity which is wholly or mainly to be carried out in premises and the authority have specified a date under paragraph 2(6) above, that date;
  (iii) in any other case, the date when the application was made to them.

(2) Notwithstanding sub-paragraph (1)(e) above, it shall be competent for a licensing authority to entertain an objection or representation received by them before they take a final decision upon the application to which it relates if they are satisfied that there is sufficient reason why it was not made in the time required under that sub-paragraph.

(3) An objection or representation shall be made for the purposes of sub-paragraph (1)

above if it is delivered by hand within the time there specified to the licensing authority or posted (by registered or recorded delivery post) so that in the normal course of post it might be expected to be delivered to them within that time.

(4) The licensing authority shall send a copy of any relevant objection or representation (within the meaning of paragraph 19 below) to the applicant to whose application it relates. [231]

NOTES to Schedule 1, para 3

Para 3(2): See *Grampian Chief Constable v City of Aberdeen District Licensing Board* 1979 SLT (Sh Ct) 2.
Definitions: 'licensing authority': see s 2 above; 'licence' and 'premises': see s 8 above.

Disposal of applications for the grant and renewal of licences

4.—(1) In considering an application for the grant or renewal of a licence, a licensing authority may make such reasonable inquiries as they think fit and include the results of these inquiries in matters they take into account, but where they intend so to include any of these results they shall notify the applicant of that intention.

(2) A licensing authority may, before reaching a final decision upon such an application, give the applicant and any person who has made a relevant objection or representation (within the meaning of paragraph 19 below) in relation to the application an opportunity to be heard by the authority and, where they propose to do so, shall, within such reasonable period (not being less than 7 days) of the date of the hearing, notify the applicant and each such person of that date.

(3) A licensing authority shall not reach a final decision upon such an application—
(a) in relation to which a relevant objection or representation (within the meaning of paragraph 19 below) has been made to them or in relation to which they intend to take into account any result of their inquiries under sub-paragraph (1) above; and
(b) in respect of which they have not, under this paragraph, given the applicant and any person who has made any such objection or representation an opportunity to be heard,
unless they have given the applicant an opportunity to notify them in writing of his views on such objection or representation or, as the case may be, result within such reasonable period (not being less than 7 days) as they may specify.

(4) The period referred to in sub-paragraphs (2) and (3) above shall begin with the date when the notification given by the licensing authority for the purpose of sub-paragraph (2) or, as the case may be, (3) is delivered to the person concerned and, when it is sent by post, it shall be treated as being delivered at the time when it might be expected to be delivered in the normal course of post. [232]

NOTES to Schedule 1, para 4

Definitions: 'relevant objection or representation': see para 19 below; 'licensing authority': see s 2 above; and 'licence': see s 8 above.

5.—(1) Where an application for the grant or renewal of a licence has been made to a licensing authority they shall, in accordance with this paragraph—
(a) grant or renew the licence unconditionally;
(b) grant or renew the licence subject to conditions; or
(c) refuse to grant or renew the licence.

(2) The conditions referred to in sub-paragraph (1)(b) above shall be such reasonable conditions as the licensing authority think fit and, without prejudice to that generality, may include—
(a) conditions restricting the validity of a licence to an area or areas specified in the licence; and
(b) in relation to the grant of a licence, where that licence is intended to replace an

existing licence, a condition requiring the holder of the existing licence to surrender it in accordance with paragraph 13 below.

(3) A licensing authority shall refuse an application to grant or renew a licence if, in their opinion—
  (a) the applicant or, where the applicant is not a natural person, any director of it or partner in it or any other person responsible for its management, is either—
    (i) for the time being disqualified under section 7(6) of this Act, or
    (ii) not a fit and proper person to be the holder of the licence;
  (b) the activity to which it relates would be managed by or carried on for the benefit of a person, other than the applicant, who would be refused the grant or renewal of such a licence if he made the application himself;
  (c) where the licence applied for relates to an activity consisting of or including the use of premises or a vehicle or vessel, those premises are not or, as the case may be, that vehicle or vessel is not suitable or convenient for the conduct of the activity having regard to—
    (i) the location, character or condition of the premises or the character or condition of the vehicle or vessel;
    (ii) the nature and extent of the proposed activity;
    (iii) the kind of persons likely to be in the premises, vehicle or vessel;
    (iv) the possibility of undue public nuisance; or
    (v) public order or public safety; or
  (d) there is other good reason for refusing the application;
and otherwise shall grant the application.

(4) A licensing authority shall not, in a case where a certificate falls to be submitted to them under paragraph 2(4) above, reach a final decision under this paragraph in respect of the application to which the certificate relates until it has been so submitted.

(5) A licensing authority shall in accordance with sub-paragraph (6) below, notify their decision under sub-paragraph (1) above to—
  (a) the applicant;
  (b) the chief constable;
  (c) any person who made a relevant objection or representation (within the meaning of paragraph 19 below) in relation to the application; and
  (d) where the application was for a licence for an activity wholly or mainly to be carried on in premises, the fire authority.

(6) Notification shall be made under sub-paragraph (5)(a), (b) or (d) above within 7 day of the decision to be notified by sending to the person concerned written notice of the decision and under sub-paragraph (5)(c) above either by so doing or by publishing, within that time, in a newspaper circulating in the area of the licensing authority, notice of the decision.

(7) A licensing authority shall make out and deliver a licence to every person to whom a licence is granted or whose licence is renewed by the authority, and shall when requested by any such person and on payment of such fee as they may charge under paragraph 15 below, make out a duplicate of any licence issued under this sub-paragraph and certify such duplicate to be a true copy of that original licence; and any document purporting to be so certified by the proper officer of the authority shall be sufficient evidence of the terms of that licence.

(8) Where a licensing authority grant a licence in respect of which an employee or agent has been named under paragraph 1(2)(b) or (c)(iv) above, the licence shall be granted jointly in the names of the applicant and of the employee or agent, and in such a case any reference in this Schedule or in Part I or II of this Act to the holder of a licence includes a reference to one or both of those persons, as the case may require. [233]

NOTES to Schedule 1, para 5

Para 5(3): See *Francey v Cunninghame District Council* 1987 SCLR 6, Sh Ct, *McDowall v Cunninghame District Council* 1987 SCLR 587, 1987 SLT 662, and *Noble Organisation Ltd v City of Glasgow District Council* 1990 SCLR 64, Sh Ct.

[233] Civic Government (Scotland) Act 1982 (c 45), Sch 1

Para 5(8): Parts I and II comprise ss 1–8 and ss 9–44.
Definitions: 'licensing authority': see s 2 above; 'chief constable', 'fire authority', 'licence' and 'premises': see s 8 above; and 'proper officer' and 'vessel': see s 133 above.

Restriction on successive applications

6. Where a licensing authority have refused an application for the grant or renewal of a licence they shall not, within one year of their refusal, entertain a subsequent application from the same applicant for the grant of the same kind of licence in respect of the same activity in the same area or, where the activity consists of or includes the use of premises or a vehicle or vessel, in respect of an activity consisting of or including the same use of the same premises, vehicle or vessel unless in their opinion there has been, since their refusal, a material change of circumstances. [234]

NOTES to Schedule 1, para 6
Definitions: 'licensing authority': see s 2 above; 'licence' and 'premises': see s 8 above; and 'vessel': see s 133 above.

Temporary licences

7.—(1) A licensing authority may grant a licence to have effect for such period not exceeding 6 weeks from its being granted as they may determine, and such a licence shall be known as a 'temporary licence'.

(2) This Schedule shall apply with the modifications specified in sub-paragraphs (3) to (5) below in relation to applications for temporary licences.

(3) Paragraphs 1(3), 2 to 4, and 5(1), (2) and (4) to (6) shall not apply, but in relation to each application for a temporary licence the licensing authority—
  (a) shall consult the chief constable and, where the application relates to an activity wholly or mainly to be carried on in premises, the fire authority; and
  (b) may grant it subject to such conditions as they think fit.

(4) Paragraph 6 shall not apply so as to prevent a licensing authority from entertaining an application for the grant of a licence where they have, within one year, refused an application from the same applicant for a temporary licence for the same activity.

(5) Paragraphs 8, 9, 10 and 18 shall not apply.

(6) A temporary licence shall not be capable of being renewed but, where the holder of or the applicant for a temporary licence has also made an application for a licence under paragraph 1 above in respect of the same activity, the temporary licence, if granted, shall continue to have effect until—
  (a) the licence applied for under paragraph 1 has been granted, whether as a result of an appeal under paragraph 18 below or not, or has been deemed to have been granted; or
  (b) where the licensing authority have refused that application, the time within which an appeal under paragraph 18 below against that decision may be made has elapsed; or
  (c) when such an appeal has been lodged, it has been abandoned or determined. [235]

NOTES to Schedule 1, para 7
Definitions: 'licensing authority': see s 2 above; 'chief constable', 'fire authority', 'licence' and 'premises': see s 8 above.

Duration of licences

8.—(1) Subject to and in accordance with the provisions of this paragraph, a licence shall come into force on being granted by a licensing authority or on such later date as

Civic Government (Scotland) Act 1982 (c 45), Sch 1 [237]

they may specify as a condition of the licence and shall continue in force on being renewed by them.

(2) Subject to the provisions of this paragraph, a licence shall have effect—
(a) for a period of three years from the date when it comes into force; or
(b) for such shorter period as the licensing authority may decide at the time when they grant or renew the licence.

(3) In the event of the death of a holder of a licence (except in the case of a licence referred to in section 13 of this Act) that licence shall be deemed to have been granted to his executor and shall, unless previously revoked, suspended or surrendered, remain in force until the end of the period of 3 months beginning with the death and shall then expire; but the licensing authority may from time to time, on the application of the executor, extend or further extend that period if they are satisfied that the extension is necessary for the purpose of winding up the deceased's estate and that no other circumstances make it undesirable.

(4) Where one of the joint holders of a licence ceases to be such, the licence shall continue in force as if held by its remaining holder for a period of six weeks from the date of such cessation but, where the remaining holder has made an application under paragraph 1 above for a licence in respect of the same activity within that period of six weeks, that period shall be extended until the time specified in sub-paragraph (6) below.

(5) If an application for the renewal of a licence is made before its expiry, the existing licence shall continue to have effect until the time specified in sub-paragraph (6) below.

(6) The time referred to in sub-paragraphs (4) and (5) above is—
(a) the time when the licence applied for under paragraph 1 above is granted or renewed, whether as a result of an appeal under paragraph 18 below or not, or has been deemed to have been granted or renewed; or
(b) where the licensing authority have refused that application, the time within which an appeal under paragraph 18 below against that decision may be made has elapsed; or
(c) where such an appeal has been lodged, the time when it has been abandoned or determined.

(7) Where a relevant objection or representation (within the meaning of paragraph 19 below) has been made in relation to an application for the grant of a licence, that licence shall not, unless it has been deemed to have been granted under section 3(4) of this Act, come into force until—
(a) the time within which an appeal under paragraph 18 below against the grant of the licence may be made has elapsed; or
(b) where such an appeal has been lodged, it has been abandoned or determined in favour of the applicant.

(8) This paragraph is subject to paragraphs 11 to 14 below. [236]

NOTES to Schedule 1, para 8
Definitions: 'relevant objection or representation': see para 19 below; 'licensing authority': see s 2 above; and 'licence': see s 8 above.

Notification of changes and alterations

9.—(1) Where there is a material change of circumstances affecting a holder of a licence, or the activity to which the licence relates, the holder of the licence shall, in accordance with this paragraph, notify the licensing authority of the change as soon as reasonably practicable after it has taken place.

(2) The holder of a licence which relates to an activity consisting of or including the use of premises, a vehicle or a vessel shall not, unless in accordance with a requirement imposed by or in pursuance of any enactment other than Parts I or II of this Act, make or

143

cause to be made or permit there to be made any material change in the premises or, as the case may be, the vehicle or vessel without the prior consent of the licensing authority.

(3) A notification under sub-paragraph (1) above or application for consent under sub-paragraph (2) above shall be accompanied by such fee as the licensing authority may charge under paragraph 15 below.

(4) A licensing authority, before considering whether or not to give their consent under sub-paragraph (2) above, shall be entitled to require the holder of the licence to furnish them with specifications, including plans, of the proposed changes.

(5) A licensing authority, before deciding whether or not to give their consent under sub-paragraph (2) above, shall consult with the chief constable and, in the case of a change in premises, with the fire authority.

(6) Where the licensing authority have given their consent under sub-paragraph (2) above to a change in premises or a vehicle or vessel, it shall not be necessary for the holder or the licence relating to those premises or that vehicle or vessel to notify the licensing authority of that change under sub-paragraph (1) above.

(7) A licensing authority shall, within 7 days of their decision under sub-paragraph (2) above, send written notice of their decision to the holder of the licence and the chief constable and, where the change is to premises, to the fire authority.

(8) In this paragaph, a 'material change' includes any material change in the particulars given or referred to in the application for the grant, or, where the licence has been renewed, the most recent application for the renewal, of the licence. **[237]**

NOTES to Schedule 1, para 9

Definitions: 'material change': see para 9(8) below; 'licensing authority': see s 2 above; 'chief constable', 'fire authority', 'licence' and 'premises': see s 8 above; and 'vessel': see s 133 above.

Variation and suspension of licences

10.—(1) A licensing authority may, at any time, whether or not upon an application made to them by the holder of the licence, vary the terms of a licence on any grounds they think fit.

(2) A licensing authority, before proceeding to vary the terms of a licence under sub-paragraph (1) above—
(a) shall, not later than 7 days before the day on which the proposed variation is to be considered, notify the holder of the licence, the chief constable and, where the licence relates to an activity wholly or mainly carried on in premises, the fire authority of the proposed variation; and
(b) shall give each of the persons mentioned in sub-sub-paragraph (a) above an opportunity to be heard by the authority on that day.

(3) A licensing authority shall have complied with sub-paragraph (2)(b) above if they have invited each of the persons whom they must notify under that sub-paragraph to attend and to be heard by the authority when the variation of the licence is to be considered.

(4) A licensing authority shall, within 7 days of their decision under sub-paragraph (1) above, send written notice of their decision to the holder of the licence and the chief constable and, where the licence relates to an activity wholly or mainly carried on in premises, to the fire authority.

(5) A variation in the terms of a licence shall come into force—
(a) when the time within which an appeal under paragraph 18 below may be made has elapsed; or
(b) where such an appeal has been lodged, when the appeal has been abandoned or determined in favour of the variation. **[238]**

NOTES to Schedule 1, para 10

Definitions: 'licensing authority': see s 2 above; 'chief constable', 'fire authority', 'licence' and 'premises': see s 8 above.

11.—(1) A licensing authority may, whether upon a complaint made to them or not, suspend a licence in accordance with the provisions of this paragraph.

(2) A licensing authority may order the suspension of a licence if in their opinion—
 (a) the holder of the licence or, where the holder is not a natural person, any director of it or partner in it or any other person responsible for its management, is not or is no longer a fit and proper person to hold the licence;
 (b) the activity to which the licence relates is being managed by or carried on for the benefit of a person, other than the licence holder, who would have been refused the grant or renewal of the licence under paragraph 5(3) above;
 (c) the carrying on of the activity to which the licence relates has caused, is causing or is likely to cause undue public nuisance or a threat to public order or public safety;
 (d) a condition of the licence has been contravened.

(3) A licensing authority may make an order under sub-paragraph (2)(d) above in respect of a contravention of a condition of a licence notwithstanding that there has been no conviction in that respect.

(4) In considering whether to suspend a licence the licensing authority may—
 (a) have regard to—
  (i) any misconduct on the part of the holder of the licence, whether or not constituting a breach of any provision of Part I or II of this Act or this Schedule, which in the opinion of the authority has a bearing on his fitness to hold a licence;
  (ii) where the licence relates to an activity consisting of or including the use of premises or a vehicle or vessel, any misconduct on the part of persons frequenting or using the premises, vehicle or vessel occurring there or any misconduct in the immediate vicinity of the premises, vehicle or vessel which is attributable to those persons;
 (b) make such reasonable inquiries as they think fit and, subject to sub-paragraph (5) below, include the results of their inquiries in the matters to which they have regard in such consideration.

(5) Where a licensing authority intend to include any of the results of their inquiries under sub-paragraph (4)(b) above in the matters to which they have regard for the purposes of sub-paragraph (4) above, they shall notify the holder of the licence of that intention.

(6) A licensing authority may, whether upon an application made to them or not, recall an order made under this paragraph.

(7) A licensing authority in considering whether or not to suspend a licence may, but before deciding to do so shall, give—
 (a) the holder of the licence;
 (b) any person who has made a complaint relevant to the matters to be considered at the hearing;
 (c) the chief constable; and
 (d) where the licence relates to an activity wholly or mainly carried on in premises, the fire authority,
an opportunity to be heard by the licensing authority.

(8) The licensing authority shall have complied with their duty under sub-paragraph (7) above if they have caused to be sent to the persons entitled under that sub-paragraph to an opportunity to be heard, not later than 21 days before the hearing, notice in writing that the authority proposes to hold a hearing, together with a copy of any complaints relevant to the matters to be considered at the hearing and a note of the grounds upon

which the suspension of the licence is to be considered and, where they decide to exercise their power under that sub-paragraph, they shall cause such notice, copy and note to be sent to those persons not later than that time.

(9) Where a licensing authority decide to order the suspension of a licence, the suspension shall not, subject to sub-paragraph (10) below, take effect until the expiry of the time within which the holder of the licence may appeal under paragraph 18 below against the suspension or, if such an appeal has been lodged, until it has been abandoned or determined in favour of the suspension.

(10) If, in deciding to order the suspension of a licence, a licensing authority determine that the circumstances of the case justify immediate suspension they may, without prejudice to their other powers under this paragraph, order that the licence shall be suspended immediately.

(11) The period of suspension of a licence under this paragraph shall be the unexpired portion of the duration of the licence, or such shorter period as the licensing authority may fix; and the effect of suspension shall be that the licence shall cease to have effect during the period of the suspension.

(12) A licensing authority shall, within 7 days of their decision under sub-paragraph (1) above, send written notice of their decision to the persons referred to in sub-paragraph (7)(a), (c) and (d) above in relation to the licence and to any person who, in pursuance of sub-paragraph (7)(b) above, was heard by the authority before they reached that decision.

NOTES to Schedule 1, para 11
Para 11(4): Parts I and II comprise ss 1–8 and 9–44.
Definitions: 'licensing authority': see s 2 above; 'chief constable', 'fire authority', 'licence' and 'premises': see s 8 above; and 'vessel': see s 133 above.

12.—(1) A licensing authority shall, whether upon a complaint made to them or not, order the suspension under this paragraph of a licence if they are of the opinion that the carrying on of the activity to which the licence relates is causing or is likely to cause a serious threat to public order or public safety.

(2) In considering whether to suspend a licence under this paragraph, a licensing authority may make such reasonable inquiries as they think fit and include the results of their inquiries in the matters to which they have regard in such consideration.

(3) Where a licensing authority intend to include any of the results of their inquiries under sub-paragraph (2) above in the matters to which they have regard for the purposes of this paragraph they shall notify the holder of the licence of that intention.

(4) A licensing authority shall, before reaching a decision on the question whether or not to suspend a licence under this paragraph, consult the chief constable and, where the licence relates to an activity wholly or mainly carried on in premises, the fire authority.

(5) An order under this paragraph suspending a licence shall have effect from the date on which it is made until whichever is the earlier of the following two dates—
(a) a date six weeks after the order was made;
(b) the date of any decision of the licensing authority whether or not to suspend the licence under paragraph 11 above.

(6) A licensing authority may, whether upon an application made to them or not, recall an order made under this paragraph.

(7) A licensing authority shall, within 7 days of their decision under sub-paragraph (1) or (6) above, send written notice of their decision to the holder of the licence, the chief constable and, where the licence relates to an activity wholly or mainly carried on in premises, to the fire authority.

NOTES to Schedule 1, para 12

Definitions: 'licensing authority': see s 2 above; 'chief constable', 'fire authority', 'licence' and 'premises': see s 8 above.

Supplementary

13.—(1) A holder of a licence may at any time surrender the licence to the licensing authority and it shall thereupon cease to have effect.

(2) A holder of a licence shall deliver the licence to the licensing authority—
  (a) within 7 days after the coming into effect of a decision of a licensing authority to suspend or vary the terms of the licence or of a court, under section 7(6)(a) of this Act, to revoke it;
  (b) where the licence relates to an activity which he has given up.

(3) A licensing authority shall, on making an order suspending a licence or on deciding to vary the terms of a licence, cause notice in writing to be given to the holder of the licence of his duty to deliver it under sub-paragraph (2) above.

(4) Where a licence has been surrendered under this paragraph on its revocation under section 7(6)(a) of this Act or its suspension under this Schedule and the revocation or suspension is quashed or recalled the licensing authority shall re-issue the licence. **[241]**

NOTES to Schedule 1, para 13

Definitions: 'licensing authority': see s 2 above; and 'licence'': see s 8 above.

14.—(1) A licensing authority shall cause to be kept a register of applications under this Schedule (in this paragraph referred to as 'the register') and shall, as soon as reasonably practicable after—
  (a) the receipt of each application, cause details of such receipt; and
  (b) their final decision on each application, cause details of that decision
to be entered in the register.

(2) The register shall include—
  (a) a note of the kind and terms of each licence granted by the licensing authority;
  (b) a note of any suspension, variation of the terms, or surrender, of a licence.

(3) The register shall be open to the inspection of any member of the public at such reasonable times and places as may be determined by the licensing authority and any member of the public may make a copy thereof or an extract therefrom.

(4) A licensing authority may, on payment of such fee as they may charge under paragraph 15 below, issue a certified true copy of any entry in the register; and any document purporting to be certified by the proper officer of the licensing authority as a true copy of an entry shall be sufficient evidence of the terms of the original entry. **[242]**

NOTES to Schedule 1, para 14

Definitions: 'licensing authority': see s 2 above; 'licence': see s 8 above; and 'proper officer': see s 133 above.

Fees

15.—(1) A licensing authority shall, subject to sub-paragraph (2) below—
  (a) in respect of applications made to them under this Schedule;
  (b) in respect of the issue of certified duplicate licences under paragraph 5(7) above;
  (c) in respect of their consideration of a material change of circumstances or in premises or a vehicle or vessel under paragraph 9 above and their diposal of the matter;
  (d) in respect of the issue under paragraph 14 above of certified true copies
charge such reasonable fees as they may, in accordance with sub-paragraph (2) below, determine; and the authority may under this sub-paragraph detemine different fees for

different classes of business, and items of business may be classed for that purpose by reference to any factor or factors whatsoever.

(2) Subject to sub-paragraph (3) below, in determining the amount of the different fees under sub-paragraph (1) above, the licensing authority shall seek to ensure that from time to time the total amount of fees receivable by the authority is sufficient to meet the expenses of the authority in exercising their functions under Parts I and II of this Act and this Schedule.

(3) Sub-paragraph (2) above does not apply in respect of the fees and expenses in respect of which provision is made by section 12 of this Act. **[243]**

NOTES to Schedule 1, para 15
Para 15(2): Parts I and II comprise ss 1–8 and ss 9–44.
Definitions: 'licensing authority': see s 2 above; 'licence' and 'premises': see s 8 above; and 'vessel': see s 133 above.

Sending of notice by post

16. When a licensing authority sends by post, for the purposes of paragraphs 5(6), 9(7), 10(4), 11(12), or 12(7), written notice of its decision, it shall be treated as having been sent within the time required if it was posted so that in the normal course of post it might be expected to be delivered to the person concerned within that time. **[244]**

NOTE to Schedule 1, para 16
Definition: 'licensing authority': see s 2 above.

Notification of decisions and giving of reasons

17.—(1) A licensing authority shall, within 10 days of being required to do so under sub-paragraph (2) below, give reasons in writing for arriving at any decision of theirs under this Schedule—
(a) to grant or renew a licence or to refuse to do so;
(b) to consent or to refuse to consent to a material change in any premises, vehicle or vessel;
(c) to vary or refuse to vary the terms of a licence;
(d) in relation to paragraph 11 above—
   (i) to suspend a licence or to refuse to do so;
   (ii) as to the period of suspension;
   (iii) ordering immediate suspension;
(e) to suspend a licence under paragraph 12 above or to refuse to do so.

(2) Reasons for a decision referred to in sub-paragraph (1) above shall be given by the licensing authority on a request being made to the authority by a relevant person within 28 days of the date of the decision.

(3) Nothing in this paragraph affects the power of the sheriff under paragraph 18 below to require a licensing authority to give reasons for a decision of the authority—
(a) which is being appealed to the sheriff under that paragraph; and
(b) for which reasons have not been given under this paragraph.

(4) In this paragraph, 'relevant person' means—
(a) in respect of a decision specified in sub-paragraph (1)(a) above, the applicant or any person who made a relevant objection or representation (within the meaning of paragraph 19 below) in relation to the application to which the decision relates;
(b) in respect of a decision specified in sub-paragraph (1)(b) to (e) above, the holder of the licence or the chief constable;
(c) in respect of a decision specified in sub-paragraph (1)(b) to (e) above which relates to an activity wholly or mainly carried on in premises, the fire authority;

Civic Government (Scotland) Act 1982 (c 45), Sch 1 [246]

(d) in respect of a decision to consent or to refuse to consent to a material change in premises, the fire authority; and
(e) in respect of a decision specified in sub-paragraph (1)(d) above, any person who, in pursuance of paragraph 11(7)(b) above, was heard by the licensing authority. [245]

NOTES to Schedule 1, para 17
Para 17(1): See *Troc Sales Ltd v Kirkcaldy District Licensing Board* 1982 SLT (Sh Ct) 77.
Definitions: 'relevant person': see para 17(4); 'licensing authority': see s 2 above; 'chief constable', 'fire authority', 'licence' and 'premises': see s 8 above.

Appeals

18.—(1) Subject to sub-paragraph (2) below, a person who may, under this Schedule, require a licensing authority to give him reasons for their decision may appeal to the sheriff against that decision.

(2) A person shall be entitled to appeal under this paragraph only if he has followed all such procedures under this Schedule for stating his case to the licensing authority as have been made available to him.

(3) A licensing authority may be a party to an appeal under this paragraph.

(4) An appeal under this paragraph shall be made by way of summary application and shall be lodged with the sheriff clerk within 28 days from the date of the decision appealed against.

(5) On good cause being shown, the sheriff may hear an appeal under this paragraph notwithstanding that it was not lodged within the time mentioned in sub-paragraph (4) above.

(6) For the purpose of an appeal under this paragraph, the sheriff may, in the case of a decision of a licensing authority for which reasons have not been given by the authority under paragraph 17 above, require the authority to give reasons for that decision, and the authority shall comply with such a requirement.

(7) The sheriff may uphold an appeal under this paragraph only if he considers that the licensing authority, in arriving at their decision—
(a) erred in law;
(b) based their decision on any incorrect material fact;
(c) acted contrary to natural justice; or
(d) exercised their discretion in an unreasonable manner.

(8) In considering an appeal under this paragraph, the sheriff may hear evidence by or on behalf of any party to the appeal.

(9) On upholding an appeal under this paragraph, the sheriff may—
(a) remit the case with the reasons for this decision to the licensing authority for reconsideration of their decision; or
(b) reverse or modify the decision of the authority,
and on remitting a case under sub-sub-paragraph (a) above, the sheriff may—
 (i) specify a date by which the reconsideration by the authority must take place;
 (ii) modify any procedural steps which otherwise would be required in relation to the matter by or under any enactment (including this Act).

(10) In considering an appeal under this paragraph against suspension of a licence the sheriff may, pending his decision on the appeal, order the recall of any order by the licensing authority under paragraph 11(10) above that the suspension be immediate or of any order made by the authority under paragraph 12 above but he shall not do so unless he is satisfied that all steps which in the circumstances were reasonable have been taken with a view to securing that notice of the appeal and an opportunity of being heard with respect to it have been given to the authority.

[246]

(11) The sheriff may include in his decision on an appeal under this paragraph such order as to the expenses of the appeal as he thinks proper.

(12) Any party to an appeal to the sheriff under this paragraph may appeal on a point of law from the sheriff's decision to the Court of Session within 28 days from the date of that decision. **[246]**

NOTES to Schedule 1, para 18

Para 18(7): See *Robertson v Inverclyde Licensing Board* 1979 SLT (Sh Ct) 16; *Johnston v City of Edinburgh District Licensing Board* 1981 SLT 257; *Sutherland v City of Edinburgh Distrist Licensing Board* 1984 SLT 241; *Holmes v Hamilton District Council* 1987 SCLR 407, Sh Ct; *McGinley v Cumberneuld and Kilsyth District Council* 1988 GWD 12–528, Sh Ct; and *Thomson v Motherwell District Council* 1988 GWD 38–1575.
Definitions: 'licensing authority': see s 2 above; 'licence': see s 8 above.

Interpretation

19. In this Schedule, 'relevant objection or representation' means—
(a) in paragraphs 1 to 4, objection or representation which, under paragraph 3 above, the licensing authority are obliged to or intend to entertain; and
(b) in the other paragraphs, an objection or representation which, under the said paragraph 3, they were obliged to or intended to entertain. **[247]**

NOTE to Schedule 1, para 19
Definition: 'licensing authority': see s 2 above.

★ ★ ★

Rent (Scotland) Act 1984

(c 58)

A Table showing the derivation of the provisions of this consolidation Act will be found at the end of the Act. The Table has no official status.

ARRANGEMENT OF SECTIONS

PART I
PRELIMINARY

1	Protected tenancies	**[248]**
2	Tenancies excepted from definition of 'protected tenancy'	**[249]**
3	Statutory tenants and tenancies	**[250]**
3A	Statutory tenants and tenancies: further provision as to succession	**[251]**
4	No protected or statutory tenancy where landlord's interest belongs to Crown	**[252]**
5	No protected or statutory tenancy where landlord's interest belongs to local authority, etc	**[253]**
6	No protected tenancy where landlord's interest belongs to resident landlord	**[254]**
7	Rateable value and the appropriate day	**[255]**
8	Regulated tenancies	**[256]**
9	Short tenancies	**[257]**
10	Premises with business use	**[258]**

Rent (Scotland) Act 1984 (c 58) [248]

PART II
SECURITY OF TENURE

11	Grounds for possession of certain dwelling-houses	[259]
12	Extended discretion of court in claims for possession of certain dwelling-houses	[260]
13	Effect of tenancy being short tenancy	[261]
14	Conditions applying to landlord's right to recovery of possession	[262]
15	Terms and conditions of statutory tenancies	[263]
16	Payments demanded by statutory tenants as a condition of giving up possession	[264]
17	Change of statutory tenant by agreement	[265]
18	No pecuniary consideration to be required on change of tenant under s 17	[266]
19	Effect on sub-tenancies of determination of tenancy	[267]
20	Effect on furnished sub-tenancy of determination of superior unfurnished tenancy	[268]
21	Compensation for misrepresentation or concealment in Cases 7 and 8	[269]

PART III
PROTECTION AGAINST HARASSMENT AND EVICTION WITHOUT DUE PROCESS OF LAW

22	Unlawful eviction and harassment of occupier	[270]
23	Prohibition of eviction without due process of law	[271]
23A	Excluded tenancies and occupancy rights	[272]
24	Special provisions with respect to agricultural employees	[273]
25	Interpretation	[274]
26	Application to Crown	[275]
27	Application to sheriff	[276]

PART IV
RENTS UNDER REGULATED TENANCIES

28	Limit of rent during contractual periods	[277]
29	Limit of rent during statutory periods	[278]

* * *

31	Adjustment, with respect to services and furniture, of recoverable rent for statutory periods before registration	[279]
32	Notices of increase	[280]
33	Limits on rent increases	[281]
34	Rent agreements	[282]
35	Rent agreements: special provisions following conversion	[283]
36	Failure to comply with provisions of rent agreements	[284]
37	Recovery from landlord of sums paid in excess of recoverable rent, etc	[285]
38	Onus on landlord	[286]
39	Rectification of rent books in light of determination of recoverable rent	[287]
40	Adjustment for differences in lengths of rental periods	[288]
41	Regulations	[289]
42	Interpretation of Part IV	[290]

PART V
REGISTRATION OF RENTS UNDER REGULATED TENANCIES

43	Registration areas and rent officers	[291]
44	Rent assessment committees	[292]

45	Register of rents	[293]
46	Applications for registration of rents	[294]
47	Certificates of fair rent	[295]
48	Determination of fair rent	[296]
49	Amount to be registered as rent	[297]
50	Effect of registration of rent	[298]
51	Cancellation of registration of rent	[299]
52	Cancellation at instance of landlord	[300]
53	Regulations	[301]
54	Interpretation of Part V	[302]

Part VI
Rent Limit for Dwelling-houses let by Housing Associations and the Housing Corporation

55	Tenancies to which sections 55 to 59 apply	[303]
56	Rents to be registrable under Part V	[304]
57	The rent limit	[305]
58	Phasing of progression to registered rent	[306]
59	Increase of rent without notice to quit	[307]
60	Supplemental to sections 55 to 59	[308]
61	Interpretation of Part VI	[309]

Part VII
Part VII Contracts

62	Registration areas for purposes of Part VII	[310]
63	Part VII contracts	[311]
64	Dwelling-houses to which Part VII applies	[312]
65	Reference of contracts to rent assessment committees and obtaining by them of information	[313]
66	Powers of rent assessment committees on reference of contracts	[314]
67	Register of rents under Part VII contracts	[315]
68	Reconsideration of rent after registration	[316]
69	Effect of registration of rent	[317]
70	Cancellation of entries in register at instance of landlord	[318]
71	Notice to quit served after reference of contract to rent assessment committee	[319]
72	Application to rent assessment committe for security of tenure where notice to quit is served	[320]
73	Notices to quit served by owner-occupiers	[321]
74	Reduction of period of notice on account of lessee's default	[322]
75	Power of sheriff, in action for possession, to reduce period of notice to quit	[323]
76	Notice to quit relating to later Part VII contracts	[324]
77	Jurisdiction of rent assessment committees	[325]
78	Publication of information	[326]
79	Rent book to be provided	[327]
80	Regulations	[328]
81	Interpretation of Part VII	[329]

Part VIII
Premiums, Etc

82	Prohibition of premiums and loans on grant of protected tenancies	[330]

83	Prohibition of premiums and loans on assignation of protected tenancies	[331]
84	Power to charge premium on assignation of tenancy where premium lawfully charged on earlier assignation	[332]
85	Prohibition of premiums on grant, etc of Part VII contracts	[333]
86	Excessive price for furniture to be treated as premium	[334]
87	Punishment of attempts to obtain from prospective tenants excessive prices for furniture	[335]
88	Recovery of premiums and loans unlawfully required or received	[336]
89	Avoidance of requirements for advance payment of rent in certain cases	[337]
90	Interpretation of Part VIII	[338]

PART IX
HERITABLE SECURITIES

91	Heritable securities to which Part IX applies	[339]
92	Regulated heritable securities	[340]
93	Powers of court to mitigate hardship	[341]
94	Miscellaneous	[342]

PART X
MISCELLANEOUS AND GENERAL

95	Release from rent regulation	[343]
96	Provisions where tenant shares accommodation with landlord	[344]
97	Provisions where tenant shares accommodation with persons other than landlord	[345]
98	Application of Part VII to tenancies falling within section 6	[346]
99	Certain sublettings not to exclude any part of sublessor's premises from protection under the Act	[347]
100	Obligation to notify sublettings of dwelling-houses let on or subject to protected or statutory tenancies	[348]
101	Landlord's consent to work	[349]
102	Jurisdiction	[350]
103	Application to sheriff	[351]
104	Rules as to procedure	[352]
105	Powers of local authorities for the purposes of giving information	[353]
106	Consent of tenant	[354]
107	Prosecution of offences	[355]
108	Service of notices on landlord's agents	[356]
109	Rents of subsidised private houses	[357]
110	Restriction on diligence and expenses	[358]
111	Implied condition in all protected tenancies	[359]
112	Minimum length of notice to quit	[360]
113	Rent book to be provided	[361]
114	Service of notices	[362]
115	Interpretation	[363]
116	Application to Crown property	[364]
117	Amendments, transitional provisions, repeals, etc	[365]
118	Short title, commencement and extent	[366]

Schedules:

Schedule 1—Statutory tenants by succession . . . . . [367–375]

Schedule 1A—Statutory or statutory assured tenants by succession in a case to which s 3A(1) applies . . . . . . [376–383]

Schedule 1B—Statutory assured tenants by succession in a case to which s 3A(2) applies . . . . [384–390]

Schedule 2—Grounds for possession of dwelling-houses let on or subject to
        protected or statutory tenancies . . . . . . **[391–400]**

* * *

Schedule 4—Rent assessment committees . . . . . . **[401–412]**
Schedule 5—Applications for registration of rents . . . . **[413–428]**
Schedule 6—Certificates of fair rent . . . . **[429–438]**
Schedule 7—Premium allowed on assignation of tenancy where premium
        lawfully paid on grant. . . . . . . **[439–443]**
Schedule 8—Enactments amended . . . . **[444–445]**
Schedule 9—Savings and transitional provisions . . . . **[446–453]**

* * *

An Act to consolidate in relation to Scotland certain enactments relating to rents and tenants' rights and connected matters. [31st October 1984]

Be it enacted by the Queen's most Excellent Majesty, by and with the advice and consent of the Lords Spiritual and Temporal, and Commons, in this present Parliament assembled, and by the authority of the same, as follows:—

PART I
PRELIMINARY

1. Protected tenancies.

(1) A tenancy under which a dwelling-house (which may be a house or part of a house) is let as a separate dwelling is a protected tenancy for the purposes of this Act unless—
  (a) the rateable value of the dwelling-house on the appropriate day exceeded or, as the case may be, exceeds £200, or in the case of a dwelling-house comprising or forming part of lands and heritages for which a rateable value is or was first shown on the valuation roll on or after 1st April 1978, £600; or
  (b) the tenancy is one with respect to which section 2 below otherwise provides; or
  (c) by virtue of section 4 or 5 below, the tenancy is for the time being precluded from being a protected tenancy by reason of the body or entity in whom the landlord's interest is vested; or
  (d) by virtue of section 6 below, the tenancy has at all times since it was granted been precluded from being a protected tenancy;
and any reference to a protected tenant shall be construed accordingly.

(2) In relation to dwelling-houses comprising or forming part of lands and heritages for which a rateable value is or was first shown on the valuation roll on or after 1st April 1978, the Secretary of State may by order made by statutory instrument subject to annulment in pursuance of a resolution of either House of Parliament increase the said sum of £600 in subsection (1) above, and he may make different provision for different classes of case.

(3) For the purposes of this Act, any land or premises let together with a dwelling-house shall, unless it consists of agricultural land exceeding two acres in extent, be treated as part of the dwelling-house.

(4) If any question arises in any proceedings whether a dwelling-house is within the limits of rateable value in subsection (1)(a) above, it shall be deemed to be within that limit unless the contrary is shown. **[248]**

NOTES to section 1

Sub-s (1): If a dwelling-house first appeared on the valuation roll between 1 April 1978 and 1 April 1985, the rateable value limit is £600. If it first appeared on the valuation roll after 1 April 1975, the rateable value limit is £1600. See the Protected Tenancies and Part VII Contracts (Rateable Value Limits) (Scotland) Order 1985, SI 1985/314 and paras [1347] ff below.

Sub-s (2): The rateable value limit was increased by SI 1985/314 (see above).
Definitions: 'agricultural land': see s 115(1) below; 'the appropriate day': see s 115(1) and s 7(3) below; 'landord': see s 115(1) below; 'let' includes 'sub-let': see s 115(1) below; 'rateable value': see s 115(1) and s 7 below: 'tenancy' includes 'sub-tenancy': see s 115(1) below.

2. Tenancies excepted from definition of 'protected tenancy'.

(1) A tenancy is not a protected tenancy if—
(a) under the tenancy either no rent is payable or the rent payable is less than two-thirds of the rateable value which is or was the rateable value of the dwelling-house on the appropriate day; or
(b) under the tenancy the dwelling-house is bona fide let at a rent which includes payments in respect of board or attendance; or
(c) the tenancy is granted to a person who is pursuing or intends to pursue a course of study provided by a specified educational institution and is so granted either by that institution or by another specified institution or body of persons; or
(d) the purpose of the tenancy is to confer on the tenant the right to occupy the dwelling-house for a holiday; or
(e) subject to section 1(3) above, the dwelling-house which is subject to the tenancy is let together with land other than the site of the dwelling-house.

(2) Paragraph (a) of subsection (1) above shall not apply to be a converted tenancy after the conversion.

(3) In the following provisions of this Act, a tenancy falling within paragraph (a) of subsection (1) above is referred to as a 'tenancy at a low rent'.

(4) For the purposes of paragraph (b) of subsection (1) above, a dwelling-house shall not be taken to be bona fide let at a rent which includes payments in respect of attendance unless the amount of rent which is fairly attributable to attendance, having regard to the value of the attendance to the tenant, forms a substantial part of the whole rent.

(5) In paragraph (c) of subsection (1) above 'specified' means specified, or of a class specified, for the purposes of that paragraph by regulations made by the Secretary of State by statutory instrument; and a statutory instrument containing any such regulations shall be subject to annulment in pursuance of a resolution of either House of Parliament. [249]

NOTES to section 2
Sub-s (5): see the Protected Tenancies (Exceptions) (Scotland) Regulations 1974, SI 1974/1374 and the Protected Tenancies (Further Exceptions) (Scotland) Regulations 1982, SI 1982/702, paras [1244] ff and [1322] ff respectively.
Definitions: 'tenancy' includes 'sub-tenancy': see s 115(1) below; 'protected tenancy': see s 115(1) below and s 1 above; 'rateable value': see s 115(1) and s 7 below; 'dwelling-house': see s 1 above; 'the appropriate day': see s 115(1) and s 7(3) below; 'converted tenancy': see s 115(1) below; 'conversion': *Ibid*.

3. Statutory tenants and tenancies.

(1) Subject to sections [3A], 4 and 5 below—
(a) after the termination of a protected tenancy of a dwelling-house the person who, immediately before that termination, was the protected tenant of the dwelling-house shall, so long as he retains possession of the dwelling-house without being entitled to do so under a contractual tenancy, be the statutory tenant of it; and
(b) the provisions of Schedule 1 to this Act shall have effect for determining what person (if any) is the statutory tenant of a dwelling-house at any time after the death of a person who, immediately before his death, was either a protected tenant of the dwelling-house or the statutory tenant of it by virtue of paragraph (a) above;

and a dwelling-house is referred to as subject to a statutory tenancy when there is a statutory tenant of it.

(2) A person who becomes a statutory tenant of a dwelling-house as mentioned in paragraph (a) of subsection (1) above is, in this Act, referred to as a statutory tenant by virtue of his previous protected tenancy, and a person who becomes a statutory tenant as mentioned in paragraph (b) of that subsection is, in this Act, referred to as a statutory tenant by succession. **[250]**

NOTES to section 3

Amendment: Reference to s 3A added as from 2 January 1989 by the Housing (Scotland) Act 1988 (c 43), s 46(1).

Definitions: 'protected tenancy': see s 115(1) below and s 1 above; 'dwelling-house': see s 1 above; 'protected tenant': see s 115(1) below and s 1 above; 'tenant' includes 'sub-tenancy': see s 115(1) below.

[3A. Statutory tenants and tenancies: further provision as to succession.

(1) Where the person who is the original tenant, within the meaning of Schedule 1 to this Act, dies after the commencement of section 46 of the Housing (Scotland) Act 1988, the provisions of Schedule 1A to this Act shall have effect for determining what person (if any) is entitled to a statutory or statutory assured tenancy of the dwelling-house.

(2) Where subsection (1) above does not apply but the person who is the first successor, within the meaning of the said Schedule 1, dies after the commencement of the said section 46, the provisions of Schedule 1B to this Act shall have effect for determining what person (if any) is entitled to a statutory assured tenancy of the dwelling-house by succession.

(3) In any case where, by virtue of any provision of the said Schedules 1A or 1B to this Act, a person becomes entitled to an assured tenancy of a dwelling-house by succession, that tenancy shall be a statutory assured tenancy arising by virtue of the said section 46.] **[251]**

NOTES to section 3A

Amendments: Section 23 was added as from 2 January 1989 by the Housing (Scotland) Act 1988 (c 43), s 46(2).

Definitions: 'tenant': see s 115(1) below; 'statutory tenancy': see s 115(1) below and s 3 above; 'statutory assured tenancy': see Housing (Scotland) Act 1988 (c 43), s 55(1) and s 16(1); 'dwelling-house': see s 1 above; 'assured tenancy': see Housing (Scotland) Act 1988, s 12.

4. No protected or statutory tenancy where landlord's interest belongs to Crown.

(1) Subject to subsection (3) below, a tenancy shall not be a protected tenancy at any time when the interest of the landlord under that tenancy belongs to Her Majesty in right of the Crown or to a Government department, or is held in trust for Her Majesty for the purposes of a Government department.

(2) A person shall not at any time be a statutory tenant of a dwelling-house if the interest of his immediate landlord, at that time, belongs or is held as mentioned in subsection (1) above.

(3) An interest belonging to Her Majesty in right of the Crown shall not prevent a tenancy from being a protected tenancy or a person from being a statutory tenant if the interest is under the management of the Crown Estate Commissioners. **[252]**

NOTES to section 4

Definitions: 'tenancy' includes 'sub-tenancy': see s 115(1) below; 'protected tenancy': see s 115(1) below and s 1 above; 'landlord': see s 115(1) below; 'statutory tenant': see s 115(1) below and s 3 above.

5. No protected tenancy where landlord's interest belongs to local authority etc.

(1) A tenancy shall not be a protected tenancy at any time when the interest of the landlord under that tenancy belongs to any of the bodies or entities specified in subsection (2) below, nor shall a person at any time be a statutory tenant of a dwelling-house if the interest of his immediate landlord belongs at that time to any of those bodies or entities.

(2) The bodies and entities referred to in subsection (1) above are—
(a) a regional, islands or district council, or a joint board or joint committee as respectively defined by the Local Government (Scotland) Act 1973, or the common good of an islands or district council or any trust under the control of a regional, islands or district council;
(b) a development corporation established by an order made, or having effect as if made, under the New Towns (Scotland) Act 1968;
(c) the Housing Corporation;
(d) the Scottish Special Housing Association, or any housing trust which was in existence on 13th November 1953 . . .;
(e) an urban development corporation within the meaning of Part XVI of the Local Government, Planning and Land Act 1980.

(3) In subsection (2)(d) above, 'housing trust' means a corporation or body of persons which is required by the terms of its constituent instrument to devote the whole of its funds, including any surplus which may arise from its operations, to the provision of houses and to other purposes incidental thereto.

(4) A tenancy shall not be a protected tenancy at any time when the interest of the landlord under that tenancy [belongs to a housing association which—
(a) is registered under the Housing Associations Act 1985, or
(b) is a co-operative housing association within the meaning of that Act; nor shall a person at any time be a statutory tenant of a dwelling-house if the interest of his immediate landlord belongs at that time to such a housing association.]

(5) A tenancy shall not be a protected tenancy at any time when the interest of the landlord under the tenancy belongs to a housing co-operative, as defined in section [22 of the Housing (Scotland) Act 1987] (agreements for exercise by housing co-operatives of local authority housing functions) and the dwelling-house is comprised in an agreement to which that section applies or in a similar agreement between the co-operative and the Scottish Special Housing Association.

[(5A) A tenancy which is a lease under a shared ownership agreement within the meaning of section 106(2) of the Housing Associations Act 1985 shall not be a protected tenancy.]

(6) Where—
(a) a tenancy is not a protected tenancy or a statutory tenancy by virtue only of this section, and
(b) a sub-tenancy of the dwelling-house or any part thereof is created,
then in ascertaining, in relation to the sub-tenancy, what rent is recoverable from the sub-tenant, the provisions of this Act shall apply as if the tenancy were a protected tenancy or a statutory tenancy, as the case may be, and neither the dwelling-house nor any part thereof had ever been let before the beginning of the tenancy. **[253]**

NOTES to section 5

Amendments: Sub-s (2)(d) was amended by the Housing (Scotland) Act 1987, (c 26), s 339, Sch 24; sub-s (4) was amended by the Housing (Consequential Provisions) (Scotland) Act 1985 (c 71), s 4, Sch 2, para 59; sub-s (5) was amended by the Housing (Scotland) Act 1987, (c 26), s 339, Sch 23, para 29; sub-s (5A) was added as from 2 January 1989 by the Housing (Scotland) Act 1988, (c 43), s 47.

Definitions: 'tenancy' includes 'sub-tenancy': see s 115(1) below; 'protected tenancy': see s 115(1) below and s 1 above; 'statutory tenancy': see s 115(1) below and s 3 above; 'dwelling-house': see s 1 above.

Sub-ss (2), (5): The references to the 'Scottish Special Housing Association' can now be read as references to 'Scottish Homes'. See the Housing (Scotland) Act 1988 (c 43), s 3, Sch 2, para 1.

6. No protected tenancy where landlord's interest belongs to resident landlord.

(1) Subject to subsection (6) below, a tenancy of a dwelling-house which is granted on or after 1st December 1980 shall not be a protected tenancy at any time if—
- (a) the dwelling-house (not being a whole flat in a purpose-built block of flats) forms part only of a building; and
- (b) subject to subsection (2) below, the tenancy was granted by a person who, at the time when he granted it, occupied as his residence another dwelling-house which also forms part of the building; and
- (c) subject to subsection (3) below, at all times since the tenancy was granted the interest of the landlord under the tenancy has belonged to a person who, at the time he owned that interest, occupied as his residence another dwelling-house which also formed part of the building.

(2) The condition in paragraph (b) of subsection (1) above shall be deemed to be fulfilled if the tenancy was granted by trustees and, at the time when the tenancy was granted, the interest of the landlord under the tenancy thereby created was held on trust for a person who was entitled to the liferent or to the fee or a share of the fee of that interest and who occupied as his residence a dwelling-house which forms part of the building referred to in paragraph (a) of that subsection.

(3) In determining whether the condition in paragraph (c) of subsection (1) above is at any time fulfilled with respect to a tenancy, there shall be disregarded—
- (a) any period of not more than 28 days beginning with the date of the conveyance of the interest of the landlord under the tenancy to an individual who, during that period, does not occupy as his residence another dwelling-house which forms part of the building concerned;
- (b) if, within a period falling within paragraph (a) above, the individual concerned notifies the tenant in writing of his intention to occupy as his residence another such dwelling-house as is referred to in that paragraph, the period beginning with the date of the conveyance mentioned in that paragraph and ending—
  - (i) at the expiry of the period 6 months beginning on that date, or
  - (ii) on the date on which the interest of the landlord under the tenancy ceases to be held by that individual, or
  - (iii) on the date on which the condition in subsection (1)(c) above again applies,

  whichever is the earlier; and
- (c) any period of not more than 24 months beginning with the date of death of the landlord under the tenancy during which the interest of the landlord under the tenancy is vested in his executor.

(4) Throughout any period which, by virtue of subsection (3)(a) or (b) above, falls to be disregarded for the purpose of determining whether the condition in subsection (1)(c) above is fulfilled with respect to a tenancy, no order for possession of the dwelling-house subject to that tenancy shall be made, other than an order which might be made if that tenancy were or, as the case may be, had been a regulated tenancy.

(5) During any period when—
- (a) the interest of the landlord under the tenancy referred to in subsection (1) above is vested in trustees, and
- (b) that interest in held on trust for a person who is entitled to the liferent or to the fee or a share of the fee of that interest and who occupies as his residence a dwelling-house which forms part of the building referred to in paragraph (a) of that subsection,

the condition in paragraph (c) of that subsection shall be deemed to be fulfilled and, accordingly, no part of that period shall be disregarded by virtue of subsection (3) above.

(6) This section does not apply to a tenancy of a dwelling-house which forms part of a building if the tenancy is granted to a person who, immediately before it was granted, was a protected or statutory tenant of that dwelling-house or of any other dwelling-house in that building.

(7) For the purposes of this section, a person shall be treated as occupying a dwelling-house as his residence if, so far as the nature of the case allows, he would be regarded as retaining possession of the dwelling-house for the purposes of paragraph (a) of section 3(1) above if he were such a person as is referred to in that paragraph.

(8) For the purposes of this section—
(a) a building is a purpose-built block of flats if as constructed it contained, and it contains, two or more flats, and for this purpose 'flat' has the same meaning as in section [338 of the Housing (Scotland) Act 1987];
(b) 'conveyance' includes the grant of a tenancy and any other conveyance or transfer other than upon death;
(c) 'the date of the conveyance' means the date on which the conveyance was granted, delivered or otherwise made effective.

(9) This section shall apply to a tenancy of a dwelling-house granted on or after 14th August 1974 but before 1st December 1980 as it applies to such a tenancy granted on or after 1st December 1980, but with the substitution for paragraph (a) of subsection (1) above of the following paragraph—
'(a) the dwelling-house forms part only of a building which is not a purpose-built block of flats; and'. [254]

NOTES to section 6
Amendment: Sub-s (8) was amended by the Housing (Scotland) Act 1987, (c 26), s 339, Sch 23; para 29;
Definitions: 'tenancy' includes 'sub-tenancy': see s 115(1); 'dwelling-house': see s 1 above; 'protected tenancy': see s 115(1) below and s 1 above; 'landlord': see s 115(1) below; 'regulated tenancy': see s 115(1) and s 8 below; 'statutory tenant': see s 115(1) below and s 3 above.

7. Rateable value and the appropriate day.

(1) Except where this Act otherwise provides, the rateable value on any day of a dwelling-house shall be ascertained for the purposes of this Act as follows:—
(a) if the dwelling-house comprises lands and heritages for which a rateable value is then shown on the valuation roll, it shall be that rateable value;
(b) if the dwelling-house forms part only of such lands and heritages, its rateable value shall be taken to be such value as is found by a proper apportionment of the rateable value so shown.

(2) Any question arising under this section as to the proper apportionment of any value shall be determined by the sheriff, and the decision of the sheriff shall be final.

(3) In this Act 'the appropriate day',—
(a) in relation to any dwelling-house which, on 23rd March 1965, comprised or formed part of land and heritages for which a rateable value was shown on the valuation roll then in force, means that date;
(b) in relation to any dwelling-house of which a tenancy granted before 1st December 1980 becomes, or would but for its low rent become, a protected tenancy by virtue of section 4(3) above, means 1st December 1980; and
(c) in relation to any other dwelling-house means the date on which a rateable value is or was first shown on the valuation roll.

(4) Where, after the date which is the appropriate day in relation to any dwelling-house, the valuation roll is altered so as to vary the rateable value of the lands and heritages of which the dwelling-house consists or forms part and the alteration has effect from a date not later than the appropriate day, the rateable value of the dwelling-house on the appropriate day shall be ascertained as if the value shown on the valuation roll on the appropriate day had been the value shown on the roll as altered.

(5) The preceding provisions of this section apply in relation to any other land as they apply in relation to a dwelling-house. [255]

[255] Rent (Scotland) Act 1984 (c 58), s 7

NOTES to section 7
Definition: 'dwelling-house': see s 1 above.

8. Regulated tenancies.

(1) For the purposes of this Act, a 'regulated tenancy' is a protected or statutory tenancy.

(2) Where a regulated tenancy is followed by a statutory tenancy of the same dwelling-house, the two shall be treated for the purposes of this Act as together constituting one regulated tenancy. [256]

NOTES to section 8
Definitions: 'protected tenancy': see s 115(1) below and s 1 above; 'statutory tenancy': see s 115(1) below and s 3 above; 'dwelling-house': see s 1 above.

9. Short tenancies.

(1) A protected tenancy created on or after 1st December 1980 is a short tenancy for the purposes of this Act where—
  (a) immediately before the creation of the tenancy the tenant was not a protected or statutory tenant of the dwelling-house, except where he was then a tenant under a short tenancy or a statutory tenant following on the expiry of a short tenancy;
  (b) the tenancy is for a period specified in the tenancy agreement of not less than one year nor more than five years;
  (c) the tenancy agreement does not contain any provision whereby the landlord may terminate the tenancy before the expiry of the said specified period other than for non-payment of rent or for breach of any other obligation of the tenancy;
  (d) before the creation of the tenancy the landlord has served on the tenant notice in writing informing him that the tenancy will be a short tenancy for the purposes of this Act; and
  (e) either—
    (i) there is, at the commencement of the tenancy, a rent registered for the dwelling-house which is the subject of the tenancy in the register of rents kept for the purposes of Part V of this Act, or
    (ii) the landlord has applied for and been granted a certificate of fair rent under section 47 below, and has, within 14 days after the commencement of the tenancy, made an application for that fair rent to be registered under subsection (4) of that section.

(2) Where a short tenancy has been created in a case to which sub-paragraph (e)(ii) of subsection (1) above applies, the application referred to in that sub-paragraph may not be withdrawn and, notwithstanding the provisions of section 50(1) and (4) below, the rent registered for the dwelling-house shall take effect from the commencement of the tenancy.

(3) The Secretary of State may by order made by statutory instrument subject to annulment in pursuance of a resolution of either House of Parliament dispense with the requirements of subsection (1)(e) above in relation to any registration area within the meaning of section 43 below.

(4) The Secretary of State may by order made by statutory instrument prescribe the form of notice required under subsection (1)(d) above. [257]

NOTES to section 9
Sub-s (3): The power to make an order has not yet been exercised.
Sub-s (4): The form of notice is prescribed by the Short Tenancies (Prescribed Information) (Scotland) Order 1980, SI 1980/1666. See paras [1305] ff below.
Definitions: 'protected tenancy and protected tenant': see s 115(1) below and s 1 above; 'tenancy'

includes 'sub-tenancy': see s 115(1) below; 'statutory tenant': see s 115(1) below and s 3 above; 'dwelling-house': see s 1 above.

10. Premises with business use.

(1) A tenancy of a dwelling-house which consists of or comprises premises licensed for the sale of exciseable liquor for consumption on the premises shall not be a protected tenancy, nor shall such a dwelling-house be the subject of a statutory tenancy.

(2) A tenancy shall not be a regulated tenancy if it is a tenancy to which the Tenancy of Shops (Scotland) Act 1949 applies (but this provision is without prejudice to the application of any other provision of this Act to a sub-tenancy of any part of the premises comprised in such a tenancy). [258]

NOTES to section 10

Definitions: 'tenancy' includes 'sub-tenancy': see s 115(1) below; 'dwelling-house': see s 1 above; 'protected tenancy': see s 115(1) below and s 1 above; 'statutory tenancy': see s 115(1) below and s 3 above; 'regulated tenancy': see s 115(1) below and s 8 above.

PART II
SECURITY OF TENURE

11. Grounds for possession of certain dwelling-houses.

(1) Subject to the following provisions of this Part of this Act, a court shall not make an order for possession of a dwelling-house which is for the time being let on a protected tenancy or subject to a statutory tenancy unless the court considers it reasonable to make such an order and either—
  (a) the court is satisfied that suitable alternative accommodation is available for the tenant or will be available for him when the order in question takes effect, or
  (b) the circumstances are as specified in any of the Cases in Part I of Schedule 2 to this Act.

(2) If, apart from the provisions of subsection (1) above, the landlord would be entitled to recover possession of a dwelling-house which is for the time being let on or subject to a regulated tenancy, the court shall make an order for possession if the circumstances of the case are as specified in any of the Cases in Part II of Schedule 2 to this Act.

(3) The provisions of Part III of Schedule 2 to this Act shall have effect in relation to Case 8 in that Schedule and for determining the relevant date for the purposes of the Cases in Part II of that Schedule.

(4) The provisions of Part IV of Schedule 2 to this Act shall have effect for determining whether, for the purposes of subsection (1)(a) above, suitable alternative accommodation is or will be available for a tenant. [259]

NOTES to section 11

Definitions: 'order for possession': see s 115(1) below; 'dwelling-house': see s 1 above; 'protected tenancy': see s 115(1) below and s 1 above; 'statutory tenancy': see s 115(1) below and s 3 above; 'tenant': see s 115(1) below; 'landlord': see s 115(1) below; 'regulated tenancy': see s 115(1) below and s 8 above.

12. Extended discretion of court in claims for possession of certain dwelling-houses.

(1) Subject to subsection (5) below, a court may adjourn, for such period or periods as it thinks fit, proceedings for possession of a dwelling-house which is let on a protected tenancy or subject to a statutory tenancy.

(2) On the making of an order for possession of such a dwelling-house, or at any time before the execution of such an order (whether made before or after the commencement of this Act), the court, subject to subsection (5) below, may—
(a) sist or suspend execution of the order, or
(b) postpone the date of possession,
for such period or periods as the court thinks fit.

(3) Any such adjournment as is referred to in subsection (1) above and any such sist, suspension or postponement as is referred to in subsection (2) above may be made subject to such conditions with regard to payment by the tenant of arrears of rent, rent or compensation to the owner for loss of possession and otherwise as the court thinks fit.

(4) If any such conditions as are referred to in subsection (3) above are complied with, the court may, if it thinks fit, discharge or rescind any such order as is referred to in subsection (2) above.

(5) The preceding provisions of this section shall not apply if the circumstances are as specified in any of the Cases in Part II of Schedule 2 to this Act. [260]

NOTES to section 12
Definitions: 'dwelling-house': see s 1 above; 'protected tenancy': see s 115(1) below and s 1 above; 'statutory tenancy': see s 115(1) below and s 3 above; 'tenant': see s 115(1) below.

13. Effect of tenancy being short tenancy.

(1) At the expiry of the period of a short tenancy as specified in the tenancy agreement, the landlord shall, subject to section 14 below, be entitled to recover posession of the dwelling-house.

(2) The tenant under a short tenancy may terminate it by giving to the landlord—
(a) where the period of the tenancy specified in the tenancy agreement is two years or less, one month's notice;
(b) in any other case, three months' notice.

(3) Notwithstanding anything contained in any enactment or rule of law, but subject to subsection (5) below, a landlord under a short tenancy who becomes entitled to recover possession of the dwelling-house which is the subject of the short tenancy shall be entitled to enforce his right to recover possession against any assignee or sub-tenant or against any statutory tenant who has succeeded to the tenancy.

(4) Notwithstanding anything contained in the tenancy agreement, a tenant under a short tenancy shall not be liable to pay to the landlord on termination of the tenancy any sum greater than the outstanding rent (if any) together with any sum due by the tenant to the landlord in respect of damage to the dwelling-house or its contents or in respect of any household accounts incurred by the tenant for which the landlord is or has become responsible.

(5)(a) Where a short tenancy is terminated by the death of the tenant before the expiry of the period specified in the tenancy agreement any statutory tenant by succession within the meaning of Schedule 1 to this Act shall be entitled to retain possession of the premises until the expiry of that period only.
(b) Where a short tenancy is terminated for any reason before the expiry of the period specified in the tenancy agreement, any subtenant of the dwelling-house shall be entitled to retain possession of the premises until the expiry of that period only.

(6) For the purposes of subsection (5) above 'subtenant' means any person deriving title from the original tenant or from a subtenant, provided that his title has not been granted in contravention of the tenancy agreement. [261]

NOTES to section 13
Definitions: 'short tenancy': see s 9 above; 'landlord': see s 115(1) below; 'tenant': see s 115(1) below; 'dwelling-house': see s 1 above; 'statutory tenant': see s 115(1) below and s 3 above.

14. Conditions applying to landlord's right to recovery of possession.

(1) A landlord under a short tenancy who seeks recovery of possession of the dwelling-house on or after termination of the tenancy, subject to subsection (2) below, may recover possession of the dwelling-house in accordance with Case 15 of Schedule 2 to this Act.

(2) A landlord who at any time seeks an order under the said Case 15 shall, either before or not later than three months after the expiry of the period specified in the tenancy agreement, or, in a case to which subsection (3) below applies, not later than three months after the expiry of any period of 12 months for which the tenancy is continued under that subsection, serve on the tenant a notice in writing of his intention to apply for the order, and the relative application shall be made not less than three nor more than six months after service of the said notice.

(3) Where a landlord fails timeously to serve a notice in compliance with subsection (2) above, the tenancy shall be continued as a short tenancy for a period of 12 months beginning with the expiry of the period specified in the tenancy agreement or with the expiry of any period of 12 months for which the tenancy is continued under this subsection. [262]

NOTES to section 14

Definitions: 'landlord': see s 115(1) below; 'short tenancy': see s 9 above; 'dwelling-house': see s 1 above; 'tenancy' includes 'sub-tenancy': see s 115(1) below.

15. Terms and conditions of statutory tenancies.

(1) So long as he retains possession, a statutory tenant of a dwelling-house shall observe and be entitled to the benefit of all the terms and conditions of the original contract of tenancy, so far as they are consistent with the provisions of this Act.

(2) It shall be a condition of a statutory tenancy of a dwelling-house that the statutory tenant shall afford to the landlord access to the dwelling-house and all reasonable facilities for executing therein any repairs which the landlord is entitled to execute.

(3) A statutory tenant of a dwelling-house shall be entitled to give up possession of the dwelling-house if, and only if, he gives such notice as would have been required under the provisions of the original contract of tenancy, or, if no notice would have been so required, on giving not less than three months' notice.

(4) Nothing in subsection (3) above shall be construed as affecting section 112 below (under which at least four weeks' notice to quit is required in respect of premises used as a dwelling-house).

(5) Notwithstanding anything in the contract of tenancy, a landlord who obtains an order for possession of a dwelling-house as against a statutory tenant shall not be required to give to the statutory tenant any notice to quit. [263]

NOTES to section 15

Definitions: 'statutory tenant' and 'statutory tenancy': see s 115(1) below and s 3 above; 'tenancy' includes 'sub-tenancy': see s 115(1) below; 'landlord': see s 115(1) below; 'dwelling-house': see s 1 above; 'order for possession': see s 115(1) below.

16. Payments demanded by statutory tenants as a condition of giving up possession.

(1) A statutory tenant of a dwelling-house who, as a condition of giving up possession of the dwelling-house, asks or receives the payment of any sum, or the giving of any other consideration, by any person other than the landlord, shall be guilty of an offence.

(2) Where a statutory tenant of a dwelling-house requires that furniture or other articles shall be purchased as a condition of his giving up possession of the dwelling-

house, the price demanded shall, at the request of the person on whom the demand is made, be stated in writing, and if the price exceeds the reasonable price of the articles the excess shall be treated, for the purposes of subsection (1) above, as a sum asked to be paid as a condition of giving up possession.

(3) A person guilty of an offence under this section shall be liable to a fine not exceeding level 3 on the standard scale.

(4) The court by which a person is convicted of an offence under this section may order the payment—
(a) to the person who made any such payment, or gave any such consideration, as is referred to in subsection (1) above, of the amount of that payment or the value of that consideration, or
(b) to the person who paid any such price as is referred to in subsection (2) above, of the amount by which the price paid exceeds the reasonable price. **[264]**

NOTES to section 16
Definitions: 'statutory tenant' and 'statutory tenancy': see s 115(1) below and s 3 above; 'tenancy' includes 'sub-tenancy': see s 115(1) below; 'landlord': see s 115(1) below; 'level 3 on the standard scale': level 3 is £400: see Increase of Criminal Penalties Etc (Scotland) Order 1984, SI 1984/526.

17. Change of statutory tenant by agreement.

(1) Where it is so agreed in writing between a statutory tenant (in this section referred to as 'the outgoing tenant') and a person proposing to occupy the dwelling-house (in this section referred to as 'the incoming tenant'), the incoming tenant shall, subject to the following provisions of this section, be deemed to be the statutory tenant of the dwelling-house as from such date as may be specified in the agreement (in this section referred to as 'the transfer date').

(2) Such an agreement as is referred to in subsection (1) above shall not have effect unless the landlord is a party thereto, and, if the consent of any superior landlord would have been required to an assignation of the previous contractual tenancy, the agreement shall not have effect unless the superior landlord is a party thereto.

(3) If the outgoing tenant is the statutory tenant by virtue of his previous protected tenancy, then, subject to subsection (6) below, the provisions of this Act shall have effect, on and after the transfer date, as if the incoming tenant had been a protected tenant and had become the statutory tenant by virtue of his previous protected tenancy.

(4) Subject to subsections (5) and (6) below, if the outgoing tenant is a statutory tenant by succession, then, on and after the transfer date,—
(a) the provisions of this Act shall have effect as if the incoming tenant were a statutory tenant by succession, and
(b) the incoming tenant shall be deemed to have become a statutory tenant by virtue of that paragraph of Schedule 1 to this Act by virtue of which the outgoing tenant became (or is deemed to have become) a statutory tenant.

(5) If the outgoing tenant is a statutory tenant by succession, the agreement referred to in subsection (1) above may provide that, notwithstanding anything in subsection (4) above, on and after the transfer date, the provisions of this Act shall have effect, subject to subsection (6) below, as if the incoming tenant had been a protected tenant and had become the statutory tenant by virtue of his previous protected tenancy.

(6) Unless the incoming tenant is deemed, by virtue of subsection (4)(b) above, to have become a statutory tenant by virtue of paragraph 6 or 7 of Schedule 1 to this Act, paragraphs 5 to 7 of that Schedule shall not apply where a person has become a statutory tenant by virtue of this section.

(7) In this section 'the dwelling-house' means the aggregate of the premises comprised in the statutory tenancy of the outgoing tenant. **[265]**

NOTES to section 17

Definitions: 'statutory tenant and statutory tenancy': see s 115(1) below and s 3 above; 'tenant and tenancy': see s 115(1) below; 'landlord': *Ibid*; 'protected tenancy': see s 115(1) below and s 1 above; 'statutory tenant by succession': see s 3(2) above.

18. No pecuniary consideration to be required on change of tenant under s 17.

(1) Any person who requires the payment of any pecuniary consideration for entering into such an agreement as is referred to in section 17(1) above shall be liable to a fine not exceeding level 3 on the standard scale.

(2) The court by which a person is convicted of an offence under subsection (1) above may order the amount of the payment to be repaid by the person to whom it was paid.

(3) Without prejudice to subsection (2) above, the amount of any such payment as is referred to in subsection (1) above shall be recoverable by the person by whom it was made either by proceedings for its recovery or, if it was made to the landlord by a person liable to pay rent to the landlord, by deduction from any rent so payable.

(4) Notwithstanding anything in subsection (1) above, if apart from this section he would be entitled to do so, the outgoing tenant may require the payment by the incoming tenant—
 (a) of so much of any outgoings discharged by the outgoing tenant as is referable to any period after the transfer date;
 (b) of a sum not exceeding the amount of any expenditure reasonably incurred by the outgoing tenant in carrying out any structural alteration of the dwelling-house or in providing or improving fixtures therein, being fixtures which, as against the landlord, the outgoing tenant is not entitled to remove;
 (c) where the outgoing tenant became a tenant of the dwelling-house by virtue of an assignation of the previous protected tenancy, of a sum not exceeding any reasonable amount paid by him to his assignor in respect of expenditure incurred by the assignor, or by any previous assignor of the tenancy, in carrying out any such alteration or in providing or improving any such fixtures as are mentioned in paragraph (b) above; or
 (d) where part of the dwelling-house is used as a shop or office, or for business, trade or professional purposes, of a reasonable amount in respect of any goodwill of the business, trade or profession, being goodwill transferred to the incoming tenant in connection with his becoming a statutory tenant of the dwelling-house or accruing to him in consequence thereof.

(5) In this section 'outgoing tenant', 'incoming tenant', 'the transfer date' and 'the dwelling-house' have the same meanings as in section 17 above. [266]

NOTES to section 18

Definitions: 'Level 3 on the standard scale': Level 3 is £400: see Increase of Criminal Penalties Etc (Scotland) Order 1984, SI 1984/526; 'landlord' see s 115(1) below; 'tenant': *Ibid*; 'dwelling-house': see s 1 above; 'protected tenancy': see s 115(1) below and s 1 above; 'tenancy' includes 'sub-tenancy': see s 115(1) below; 'statutory tenant': see s 115(1) below and s 3 above.

19. Effect on sub-tenancies of determination of tenancy.

(1) If a court makes an order for possession of a dwelling-house from a tenant and the order is made by virtue of paragraph (a) or paragraph (b) of section 11(1) above, nothing in the order shall affect the right of any sub-tenant to whom the dwelling-house or any part of it has been lawfully sublet before the commencement of the proceedings to retain possession by virtue of this Part of this Act, nor shall the order operate to give a right to possession as against any such sub-tenant.

(2) Where a protected or statutory tenancy of a dwelling-house is determined, either as a result of an order for possession or for any other reason (apart from a determination by virtue of section 5 above), any sub-tenant to whom the dwelling-house or any part of it

has been lawfully sublet shall, subject to the provisions of this Act, be deemed to become the tenant of the landlord on the same terms as he would have held from the tenant if the tenant's protected or statutory tenancy had continued.

(3) A tenancy at a low rent which, had it not been a tenancy at a low rent, would have been a protected tenancy of a dwelling-house shall be treated for the purposes of subsection (2) above as a protected tenancy. **[267]**

NOTES to section 19

Definitions: 'order for possession': see s 115(1) below; 'tenant': *Ibid*; 'protected tenancy': see s 115(1) below and s 1 above; 'statutory tenancy': see s 115(1) below and s 3 above; 'landlord': see s 115(1) below and s 2(3) above; 'tenancy at a low rent': see s 115(1) below and s 2(3) above.

20. Effect on furnished sub-tenancy of determination of superior unfurnished tenancy.

(1) If, in a case where section 19(2) above applies, the relevant conditions are fulfilled, the terms on which the sub-tenant is, by virtue of that subsection, deemed to become the tenant of the landlord shall not include any terms as to the provision by the landlord of furniture or services.

(2) The relevant conditions referred to in subsection (1) above are—
  (a) that the tenancy or statutory tenancy which is determined as mentioned in the said section 19(2) was neither a protected furnished tenancy nor a statutory furnished tenancy;
  (b) that, immediately before the determination of that tenancy or statutory tenancy, the sub-tenant referred to in that section was the tenant under a protected furnished tenancy or a statutory furnished tenancy; and
  (c) that the landlord, within the period of six weeks beginning with the day on which the tenancy or statutory tenancy referred to in that section is determined, serves notice on the sub-tenant that this section is to apply to his tenancy or statutory tenancy.

(3) In this section, 'services' has the same meaning as in section 81(1) below. **[268]**

NOTES to section 20

Definitions: 'tenant': see s 115(1) below; 'landlord': *Ibid*; 'statutory tenancy': see s 115(1) below and s 3 above;'protected furnished tenancy': see s 115(1) below; 'statutory furnished tenancy': *Ibid*.

21. Compensation for misrepresentation or concealment in Cases 7 and 8.

Where, in such circumstances as are specified in Case 7 or Case 8 in Schedule 2 to this Act, a landlord obtains an order for possession of a dwelling-house let on a protected tenancy or subject to a statutory tenancy and it is subsequently made to appear to the court that the order was obtained by misrepresentation or concealment of material facts, the court may order the landlord to pay to the former tenant such sum as appears sufficient as compensation for damage or loss sustained by that tenant as a result of the order. **[269]**

NOTES to section 21

Definitions: 'landlord': see s 115(1) below; 'order for possession': *Ibid*; 'protected tenancy': see s 115(1) below and s 1 above; 'statutory tenancy': see s 115(1) below and s 3 above; 'tenant': see s 115(1) below.

PART III
PROTECTION AGAINST HARASSMENT AND EVICTION WITHOUT DUE PROCESS OF LAW

22. Unlawful eviction and harassment of occupier.

(1) If any person unlawfully deprives the residential occupier of any premises of his

occupation of the premises or any part thereof or attempts to do so he shall be guilty of an offence unless he proves that he believed, and had reasonable cause to believe, that the residential occupier had ceased to reside in the premises.

(2) If any person with intent to cause the residential occupier of any premises—
  (a) to give up the occupation of the premises or any part thereof; or
  (b) to refrain from exercising any right or pursuing any remedy in respect of the premises or part thereof;
does acts [likely] to interfere with the peace or comfort of the residential occupier or members of his household, or persistently withdraws or withholds services reasonably required for the occupation of the premises as a residence, he shall be guilty of an offence.

[(2A) Subject to Subsection (2B) below, the landlord of any premises or an agent of the landlord shall be guilty of an offence if—
  (a) he does acts likely to interfere with the peace or comfort of the residential occupier or members of his household; or
  (b) he persistently withdraws or withholds services reasonably required for the occupation of the premises in question as a residence.
and (in either case) he knows, or has reasonable cause to believe, that that conduct is likely to cause the residential occupier to give up the occupation of the whole or part of the premises or to refrain from exercising any right or pursuing any remedy in respect of the whole or part of the premises.

(2B) A person shall not be guilty of an offence under subsection (2A) above if he proves that he had reasonable grounds for doing the acts or withdrawing or withholding the services in question.]

(3) A person guilty of an offence under this section shall be liable—
  (a) on summary conviction, to a fine not exceeding the statutory maximum or to imprisonment for a term not exceeding six months or to both; and
  (b) on conviction on indictment, to a fine or to imprisonment for a term not exceeding two years or to both.

(4) Nothing in this section shall be taken to prejudice any liability or remedy to which a person guilty of an offence thereunder may be subject in civil proceedings.

(5) In this section 'residential occupier', in relation to any premises, means a person occupying the premises as a residence, whether under a contract or by virtue of any enactment or rule of law giving him the right to remain in occupation or restricting the right of any other person to recover possession of the premises. [270]

NOTES to section 22
Amendments: The words 'likely' has been substituted for the word 'calculated' as from 2 January 1989 by the Housing (Scotland) Act 1988 (c 43), s 38, as amended by the Housing Act 1988 (c 50), s 140, Sch 17, para 87; sub-s (2A) was added with effect from 2 January 1989 by the Housing (Scotland) Act 1988, (c 43), s 38, as amended by the Housing Act 1988 (c 50), s 140, Sch 17, para 87; sub-s (2B) was added with effect from 2 January 1989 by the Housing (Scotland) Act 1988 (c 43), s 38.
Definitions: 'landlord': see s 115(1) below; 'the statutory maximum': currently £2,000: see the Increase of Criminal Penalties Etc (Scotland) Order 1984, SI 1984/526.

23. Prohibition of eviction without due process of law.

(1) Where any premises have been let as a dwelling under a tenancy which is not a statutorily protected tenancy within the meaning of this Part of this Act or a right of a kind to which Part VII of this Act applies to use a dwelling-house has been granted before or after the commencement of this Act and—
  (a) the tenancy or, as the case may be, the right to use (in this Part of this Act referred to as the former tenancy) has come to an end; but
  (b) the occupier continues to reside in the premises or part of them;
[subject to section 23A] it shall not be lawful for the owner to enforce against the occupier,

otherwise than by proceedings in the court, his right to recover possession of the premises.

(2) For the purposes of this Part of this Act a person who, under the terms of his employment, had exclusive possession of any premises otherwise than as a tenant shall be deemed to have been a tenant and the expressions "let" and "tenancy" shall be construed accordingly.

[(2A) Subsections (1) and (2) above apply in relation to any premises occupied (whether exclusively or not) as a dwelling other than under a tenancy as they apply in relation to premises let as a dwelling under a tenancy, and in those subsections the expressions "let" and "tenancy" shall be construed accordingly.]

(3) In this Part of this Act "the owner", in relation to any premises, means the person who, as against the occupier, is entitled to possession thereof; and in this section "the occupier", in relation to any premises, means any person lawfully residing in the premises or part of them at the termination of the former tenancy.

(4) The preceding provisions of this section shall, with the necessary modifications, apply where the owner's right to recover possession arises on the death of the tenant under a statutory tenancy.

(5) Nothing in this section shall be taken to affect any rule of law prohibiting the securing of possession otherwise than by due process of law. **[271]**

NOTES to section 23

Amendments: In sub-s (1), the words 'subject to section 23A' were added with effect from 2 January 1989 by the Housing (Scotland) Act 1988, (c 43), s 39; sub-s (2A) was added with effect from 2 January 1989 by the Housing (Scotland) Act 1988, (c 43), s 39.

Definitions: 'tenancy' includes 'sub-tenancy': see s 115(1) below; 'Statutorily protected tenancy': see s 25(1) below; 'dwelling-house': see s 1 above; 'the court': see s 25(1) below; 'statutory tenancy': see s 115(1) below and s 3 above.

[23A. Excluded tenancies and occupancy rights.

(1) Nothing in section 23 or 24 of this Act applies to a tenancy or right of occupancy if—
  (a) under its terms the occupier has the use of any accommodation in common with the owner or a member of his family (whether or not in common with other persons); and
  (b) immediately before the tenancy or right was granted and at all times since then the owner occupied as his only or principal home premises of which the whole or part of the accommodation referred to in paragraph (a) above formed part.

(2) In subsection (1) above—
  (a) 'accommodation' includes neither an area used for storage nor a staircase, passage, corridor or other means of access;
  (b) 'owner' means, in relation to a tenancy, the landlord and, in relation to a right to occupy, the person granting it, and in any case where there are joint landlords or grantors any one of them shall be regarded as the 'owner'; and
  (c) 'occupier' means, in relation to a tenancy, the tenant and, in relation to a right to occupy, its grantee;
and section 83 of the Housing (Scotland) Act 1987 shall apply to determine whether a person is for the purposes of subsection (1) above a member of another's family as it applies for the purposes of that Act.

(3) Nothing in section 23 or 24 of this Act applies to a tenancy or right of occupancy if it was granted as a temporary expedient to a person who entered the premises in question or any other premises without right or title (whether or not before the beginning of that tenancy or grant of that right another tenancy or right to occupy the premises or any other premises had been granted to him.)

(4) Nothing in section 23 or 24 of this Act applies to a tenancy or right of occupancy if it confers on the tenant or occupier the right to occupy the premises for a holiday only.

(5) Nothing in section 23 or 24 of this Act applies to a right of occupancy which confers rights of occupation in a hostel, within the meaning of the Housing (Scotland) Act 1987, which is provided by—
- (a) a local authority within the meaning of the Local Government (Scotland) Act 1973 or a joint board or joint committee within the meaning of that Act;
- (b) a development corporation within the meaning of the New Towns (Scotland) Act 1968;
- (c) an urban development corporation within the meaning of Part XVI of the Local Government, Planning and Land Act 1980;
- (d) the Scottish Special Housing Association;
- (e) Scottish Homes;
- (f) a registered housing association, within the meaning of the Housing Associations Act 1985; or
- (g) any other person who is, or who belongs to a class of person which is, specified in an order made by the Secretary of State.

(6) The power to make an order under subsection (5)(g) above shall be exercisable by statutory instrument which shall be subject to annulment in pursuance of a resolution of either House of Parliament.] [272]

NOTES to section 23A

Amendments: Section 23A was added with effect from 2 January 1989 by the Housing (Scotland) Act 1988, (c 43), s 40.
Definition: 'tenancy' includes 'sub-tenancy': see s 115(1) below.

24. Special provisions with respect to agricultural employees.

(1) The following provisions of this section shall apply where the tenant under the former tenancy occupied the premises under the terms of his employment as a person employed in agriculture (as defined in section 17 of the Agricultural Wages (Scotland) Act 1949).

(2) In this section 'the occupier', in relation to any premises, means—
- (a) the tenant under the former tenancy; or
- (b) the widow or widower of the tenant under the former tenancy residing with him at his death or, if the former tenant leaves no such widow or widower, any member of his family residing with him at his death.

[(2A) In accordance with section 23(2A) above, any reference in subsections (1) and (2) above to the tenant under the former tenancy includes a reference to the person having a right to occupy premises as a dwelling otherwise than under a tenancy, being a right which has come to an end; and in the following provisions of this section the expressions 'tenancy' and 'rent' and any other expressions referable to a tenancy shall be construed accordingly.]

(3) Without prejudice to any power of the court apart from this section to postpone the operation or suspend the execution of a decree of removing or warrant of ejection or other like order (in this section referred to as an 'order for possession'), if in proceedings by the owner against the occupier the court makes an order for the possession of the premises the court may suspend the execution of the order on such terms and conditions, including conditions as to the payment by the occupier of arrears of rent, compensation to the owner for loss of possession and otherwise as the court thinks reasonable.

(4) Where the order for possession is made within the period of six months beginning with the date when the former tenancy came to an end, then, without prejudice to any powers of the court under the preceding provisions of this section or apart from this section to postpone the operation or suspend the execution of the order for a longer period, the court shall suspend the execution of the order (on such terms and conditions, including conditions as to the payment by the occupier of arrears of rent, compensation

to the owner for loss of possession and otherwise as the court thinks reasonable) for the remainder of the period of six months aforesaid unless the court—
- (a) is satisfied either—
  - (i) that other suitable accommodation is, or will within that period be made, available to the occupier; or
  - (ii) that the efficient management of any agricultural land or the efficient carrying on of any agricultural operations would be seriously prejudiced unless the premises are available for occupation by a person employed or to be employed by the owner; or
  - (iii) that greater hardship (being hardship in respect of matters other than the carrying on of such a business as aforesaid) would be caused by the suspension of the order until the end of that period than by its execution within that period; or
  - (iv) that the occupier, or any person residing or lodging with the occupier, has been causing damage to the premises or has been guilty of conduct which is a nuisance or annoyance to persons occupying other premises; and
- (b) considers that it would be reasonable not to suspend the execution of the order for the remainder of that period;

but a decision of the court not to suspend the execution of the order under this subsection shall not prejudice any other power of the court to postpone the operation or suspend the execution of the order for the whole or part of the period of six months aforesaid.

(5) Where the court has under the preceding provisions of this section suspended the execution of an order for possession it may from time to time vary the period of suspension or terminate it and may vary any terms or conditions imposed by virtue of this section.

(6) In considering whether or how to exercise its powers under subsection (3) of this section the court shall have regard to all the circumstances and, in particular, to the following, that is to say—
- (a) whether other suitable accommodation is or can be made available to the occupier;
- (b) whether the efficient management of any agricultural land or the efficient carrying on of any agricultural operations would be seriously prejudiced unless the premises were available for occupation by a person employed or to be employed by the owner; and
- (c) whether greater hardship would be caused by the suspension of the execution of the order than by its execution without suspension or further suspension.

(7) Where in proceedings for the recovery of possession of the premises the court makes an order for possession but suspends the execution of the order by virtue of this section, it shall make no order for expenses, unless it appears to the court, having regard to the conduct of the owner or of the occupier, that there are special reasons for making such an order.

(8) Where, in the case of an order for possession of the premises to which subsection (4) of this section applies, the execution of the order is not suspended under that subsection or, the execution of the order having been so suspended, the suspension is terminated, then, if it is subsequently made to appear to the court that the failure to suspend the execution of the order or, as the case may be, the termination of the suspension was—
- (a) attributable to the provisions of paragraph (a)(ii) of that subsection, and
- (b) due to misrepresentation or concealment of material facts by the owner of the premises,

the court may order the owner to pay the occupier such sum as appears sufficient as compensation for damage or loss sustained by the occupier as a result of that failure or termination. [273]

NOTES to section 24

Amendment: Sub-s (2A) was added with effect from 2 January 1989 by the Housing (Scotland) Act 1988, (c 43), s 39.

Definitions: 'the court': see s 25(1) below; 'owner': see s 23(3).

25. Interpretation.

(1) In this Part of this Act—
'the court', subject to the provisions of this section, means the sheriff;
'statutorily protected tenancy' means a protected tenancy or a tenancy to which any of the following Acts apply—
- (i) the Small Landholders (Scotland) Acts 1886 to 1931;
- (ii) the Tenancy of Shops (Scotland) Act 1949;
- [(iii) the Agricultural Holdings (Scotland) Act 1991;]
- (iv) the Crofters (Scotland) Acts 1955 and 1961.

(2) Nothing in this Part of this Act shall affect any jurisdiction of the Court of Session in relation to actions of removing.

(3) Nothing in this Part of this Act shall affect the operation of—
- (a) section 19 of the Defence Act 1842;
- (b) section 89 of the Lands Clauses Consolidation (Scotland) Act 1845;
- (c) section 403 of the Burgh Police (Scotland) Act 1892. [274]

26. Application to Crown.

In so far as this Part of this Act requires the taking of proceedings in the court for the recovery of possession or confers any powers on the court, it shall be binding on the Crown. [275]

NOTES to section 26
Definition: 'the court': see s 25(1).

27. Application to sheriff.

Where an application is made to the sheriff for an order under this Part of this Act, it shall be made by way of summary cause within the meaning of the Sheriff Courts (Scotland) Act 1971. [276]

PART IV
RENTS UNDER REGULATED TENANCIES

28. Limit of rent during contractual periods.

(1) Where the rent payable for any contractual period of a regulated tenancy of a dwelling-house would exceed the limit specified in the following provisions of this section (in this Part of this Act referred to as 'the contractual rent limit'), the amount of the excess shall, notwithstanding anything in any agreement, be irrecoverable from the tenant.

(2) Where a rent for the dwelling-house is registered under Part V of this Act then, subject to section 33 . . . below, the contractual rent limit is the rent so registered. [277]

NOTES to section 28
Amendment: In sub-s (2) words repealed by Housing (Scotland) Act 1988, (c 43), s 71, Sch 10.
Definitions: 'contractual period': see s 42(1) below; 'regulated tenancy': see s 115(1) below and s 8 above; 'dwelling-house': see s 1 above; 'tenancy' includes 'sub-tenancy': see s 115(1) below; 'tenant': *Ibid.*

29. Limit of rent during statutory periods.

(1) Except as otherwise provided by the following provisions of this Part of this Act, where the rent payable for any statutory period of a regulated tenancy of a dwelling-house

would exceed the rent recoverable for the last contractual period thereof, the amount of the excess shall, notwithstanding anything in any agreement, be irrecoverable from the tenant.

(2) . . . where a rent for the dwelling-house is registered under Part V of this Act the following provision shall apply with respect to the rent for any statutory period of a regulated tenancy of the dwelling-house, that is to say—
   (a) if the rent payable for any statutory period would exceed the rent so registered, the amount of the excess shall, notwithstanding anything in any agreement, be irrecoverable from the tenant; and
   (b) if the rent payable for any statutory period would be less than the rent so registered, it may, subject to section 33 below, be increased up to the amount of that rent by a notice of increase served by the landlord on the tenant and specifying the date (which may be any date during a rental period) from which the increase is to take effect.

(3) The date specified in a notice of increase under subsection (2)(b) above shall not be earlier than the date from which the registration of the rent took effect nor earlier than four weeks before the service of the notice.

(4) Where no rent for the dwelling-house is registered under Part V of this Act the provisions of sections 30 and 31 below shall have effect with respect to the rent recoverable for any statutory period under a regulated tenancy of the dwelling-house.

(5) In relation to any rental period beginning after a tenancy has become a converted tenancy, this and the two next following sections shall have effect as if references therein to the last contractual period were references to the last rental period beginning before the conversion. [278]

NOTES to section 29

Amendment: In sub-s (2) words repealed by Housing (Scotland) Act 1988, (c 43), s 72, Sch 10.
Definitions: 'statutory period': see s 42(1) below; 'regulated tenancy': see s 115(1) below and s 8 above; 'dwelling-house': see s 1 above; 'contractual period': see s 42(1) below; 'tenant': see s 115(1) below; 'landlord': *Ibid*; 'converted tenancy': *Ibid*.

30. . . .

NOTES to section 30

Section 30 was repealed by the Housing (Scotland) Act 1988, (c 43), s 72, Sch 10.

31. Adjustment, with respect to services and furniture, of recoverable rent for statutory periods before registration.

(1) Where section 29(4) above applies and for any statutory period there is with respect to—
   (a) the provision of services for the tenant by the landlord or a superior landlord, or
   (b) the use of furniture by the tenant,
or any circumstances relating thereto any difference, in comparison with the last contractual period, such as to affect the amount of the rent which it is reasonable to charge, the recoverable rent for the statutory period shall be increased or decreased by an appropriate amount.

(2) Any question whether, or by what amount, the recoverable rent for any period is increased or decreased by virtue of this section shall be determined by agreement in writing between the landlord and the tenant or by the sheriff; and any such determination—
   (a) may be made so as to relate to past statutory periods; and
   (b) shall have effect with respect to statutory periods subsequent to the periods to which it relates until revoked or varied by any such agreement as is referred to in this subsection or by the sheriff. [279]

NOTES to section 31

Definitions: 'statutory period': see s 42(1) below; 'tenant': see s 115(1) below; 'landlord': *Ibid*; 'contractual period': see s 42(1) below; 'recoverable rent': *Ibid*.

32. Notices of increase.

(1) Any reference in the following provisions of this section to a notice of increase is a reference to a notice of increase under section 29(2) . . . above.

(2) A notice of increase must be in the prescribed form.

(3) Notwithstanding that a notice of increase relates to statutory periods, it may be served during a contractual period; and where such a notice is served during a contractual period and the protected tenancy could, by a notice to quit served by the landlord at the same time, be brought to an end before the date specified in the notice of increase, the notice of increase shall operate to convert the protected tenancy into a statutory tenancy as from that date.

(4) If the sheriff is satisfied that any error or omission in a notice of increase is due to a bona fide mistake on the part of the landlord, the sheriff may order the amendment of the notice by correcting any error or supplying any omission therein which, if not corrected or supplied, would render the notice invalid and, if the sheriff so directs, the notice as so amended shall have effect and be deemed to have had effect as a valid notice.

(5) Any amendment of a notice of increase under subsection (4) above may be made on such terms and conditions with respect to arrears of rent or otherwise as appear to the sheriff to be just and reasonable.

(6) No increase of rent which becomes payable by reason of an amendment of a notice of increase under subsection (4) above shall be recoverable in respect of any statutory period which ended more than six months before the date of the order making the amendment. [280]

NOTES to section 32

Amendments: In sub-s (1) words repealed by Housing (Scotland) Act 1988, (c 43), s 72, Sch 10.
Sub-s (2): For the prescribed form, see the Rent Regulation (Forms, and Information etc) (Scotland) Regulations 1991, SI 1991/1521 and para [1510] ff below.
Definitions: 'prescribed': see s 42(1) below; 'statutory period': *Ibid*; 'contractual period': *Ibid*; 'protected tenancy': see s 115(1) below and s 1 above; 'landlord': see s 115(1) below; 'statutory tenancy': see s 115(1) below and s 3 above; 'tenancy' includes 'sub-tenancy': see s 115(1) below.

33. Limits on rent increases.

(1) The Secretary of State shall by order make the following provisions in relation to regulated tenancies in respect of which there are registered rents which are registered on or after 1st December 1980 under Part V of this Act, that is to say he shall—
  (a) specify the maximum amount by which the total of the rent payable under a tenancy to which this subsection applies in any period [specified in the order] beginning with the relevant date for the purposes of sections 46 and 47 below or with any subsequent anniversary of that date may be increased;
  (b) restrict the total additional rental income which may be recovered by a landlord under such a tenancy in any period [specified in the order] beginning with the relevant date for the purposes of sections 46 and 47 below or with any subsequent anniversary of that date of such amount as is specified in the order.

(2) An order made under subsection (1) above shall be made by statutory instrument subject to annulment in pursuance of a resolution by either House of Parliament, and may contain such supplementary and incidental provisions as the Secretary of State thinks fit.

(3) For the purposes of subsection (1) above 'rent' and 'rental income' do not include sums paid to the landlord in respect of the provision of any services. [281]

NOTES to section 33

The Secretary of State has power to repeal s 33 by order: see Housing (Scotland) Act 1988 (c 43), s 41. The power has not yet been exercised.
Amendments: Sub-s (1) was amended by the Housing (Scotland) Act 1988, (c 43), s 41.
Sub-s 1: See the Limit on Rent Increases (Scotland) Order 1989, SI 1989/2469 and paras [1472] ff below.
Definitions: 'regulated tenancy': see s 115(1) below and s 8 above; 'tenancy' includes 'sub-tenancy': see s 115(1) below.

34. Rent agreements.

(1) In this Part of this Act 'a rent agreement with a tenant having security of tenure' means—
   (a) an agreement increasing the rent payable under a protected tenancy which is a regulated tenancy, or
   (b) the grant to the tenant under a regulated tenancy, or to any person who might succeed him as a statutory tenant, of another regulated tenancy of the dwelling-house at a rent exceeding the rent under the previous tenancy:

. . .

(2) If a rent agreement with a tenant having security of tenure takes effect on or after 1st January 1973, and at a time when no rent is registered for the dwelling-house under Part V of this Act, the requirements of subsection (3) below shall be observed as respects the agreement.

(3) The said requirements are that—
   (a) the agreement is in writing signed by the landlord and the tenant,
   (b) the agreement contains a statement, in characters not less conspicuous than those used in any other part of the agreement, that the tenant's security of tenure under this Act will not be affected if he refuses to enter into the agreement, and that entry into the agreement will not deprive the tenant or the landlord of the right to apply at any time to the rent officer for the registration of a fair rent under Part V of this Act, or words to that effect,
   (c) the agreement contains a statement that, if a rent is registered under Part V of this Act in respect of the dwelling-house, any increase in the rent may be limited under section 33 above, and
   (d) the statements mentioned in paragraphs (b) and (c) above are set out at the head of the agreement.

NOTES to section 34

Amendments: In sub-s (1) words repealed by the Housing (Scotland) Act 1988, (c 43), s 72, Sch 10.
Definitions: 'protected tenancy': see s 115(1) below and s 1 above; 'regulated tenancy': see s 115(1) below and s 8 above; 'tenant': see s 115(1) below; 'tenancy': includes sub-tenancy: *Ibid*; 'landlord': *Ibid*; 'dwelling-house': see s 1 above.

35. Rent agreements: special provisions following conversion.

(1) Subject to subsections (2) and (3) below, this section applies where a rent agreement with a tenant having security of tenure of a dwelling-house is entered into, whether before or after a tenancy becomes a converted tenancy, which is expressed to take effect—
   (a) on or after 1st January 1973 and after the conversion, and
   (b) at a time when no rent is registered for the dwelling-house under Part V of this Act.

(2) This section shall not apply to any agreement where the tenant is neither the person who, at the time of the conversion, was the tenant, nor a person who might succeed the tenant at that time as a statutory tenant, and where this section has applied to any agreement, it shall not apply to any subsequent agreement relating to the dwelling-house which takes effect more than three years after the first such agreement took effect.

(3) Where a rent is registered for the dwelling-house and the registration is subsequently cancelled, this section shall not apply to the agreement submitted to the rent officer in connection with the cancellation nor to any agreement which takes effect after the cancellation.

(4) The provisions of this section are without prejudice to the requirements imposed by section 34 above.

(5) The following requirements shall be observed with respect to any such agreement as is mentioned in subsection (1) above—
  (a) the agreement shall contain the prescribed particulars,
  (b) the agreement, when duly completed, shall be lodged by the landlord with the rent officer, and
  (c) the landlord shall, not later than the date when the agreement is lodged with the rent officer, serve a copy of the agreement on the tenant.

(6) No such agreement shall take effect earlier than 28 days after it is lodged with the rent officer under subsection (5)(b) above, and it may only take effect on or after that date if the rent officer has not before that date notified both the landlord and the tenant in writing that he proposes to treat the agreement as an application for the registration of a rent for the dwelling-house under Part V of this Act made jointly by the landlord and the tenant.

(7) The rent officer may treat an agreement as such a joint application as is referred to in subsection (6) above before the conversion if an application for the registration of a rent could have been made by virtue of section 38 of the Housing (Financial Provisions) (Scotland) Act 1972.

(8) A rent officer may treat an agreement as such a joint application only if he is satisfied that the rent payable under the agreement exceeds a fair rent for the dwelling-house.

(9) Where an agreement is treated by the rent officer as such a joint application then, subject to subsection (10) below, Schedule 5 to this Act shall apply as if the application had been made to him and as if any reference in that Schedule to the rent specified in the application included a reference to the rent expressed to be payable under the agreement.

(10) For the purposes of subsection (9) above, paragraph 3(1) of the said Schedule 5 shall have effect as if for the words 'he may register that rent without further proceedings' there were substituted the words 'he shall notify both the landlord and the tenant in writing that he is no longer treating the agreement as a joint application for the registration of a rent and that the agreement may take effect on or after the date of such notification if that date is later than 28 days after the agreement was lodged with him.'

(11) The rent officer shall make available for public inspection, without charge, any agreement which has been lodged with him under this section unless the agreement is treated by him as a joint application for the registration of a rent and a rent is subsequently registered in pursuance of such application; and any agreement which is made available for public inspection under this subsection shall be so available for a period of three years from the date which is 28 days after it has been lodged with the rent officer.

(12) A copy of such an agreement certified by the rent officer or any person duly authorised by him shall be receivable in evidence, and shall be sufficient evidence of the agreement in any court and in any proceedings.

(13) A person requiring such a certified copy shall be entitled to obtain it on payment of the prescribed fee.

(14) No stamp duty shall be chargeable on any agreement to which this section applies which contains—
  (a) the statement required by section 34(3)(b) above as read with subsection (4) above, and
  (b) the particulars prescribed pursuant to this section.

NOTES to section 35

Definitions: 'rent agreement with a tenant having security of tenure': see s 42(1) below and s 34(1) above; 'tenant': see s 115(1) below; 'dwelling-house': see s 1 above; 'tenancy' includes 'sub-tenancy': see s 115(1) below; 'statutory tenant': *Ibid*; 'conversion' and 'converted tenancy': *Ibid*; 'prescribed': see s 42(1) below; 'landlord': see s 115(1) below.

36. Failure to comply with provisions of rent agreements.

(1) If, in the case of a variation of the terms of a regulated tenancy, there is a failure on the part of the landlord to observe any of the requirements of section 34 or 35 above, any excess of the rent payable under the terms as varied over the terms without the variation shall be irrecoverable from the tenant.

(2) If, in the case of the grant of a tenancy, there is a failure on the part of the landlord to observe any of the requirements of section 34 or 35 above, any excess of the rent payable under the tenancy so granted (for any contractual or any statutory period of the tenancy) over the previous limit shall be irrecoverable from the tenant.

(3) In subsection (2) above the 'previous limit' shall be taken to be the amount which (taking account of any previous operation of this section) was recoverable by way of rent for the last rental period of the previous tenancy of the dwelling-house, or which would have been so recoverable if all notices of increase authorised by section 36(2) of the Housing (Financial Provisions) (Scotland) Act 1972 or by this Act had been served.

(4) A default in complying with subsection (5)(c) of section 35 above shall not apply to rent for any rental period after the default is made good, and, if a rent agreement with a tenant having security of tenure is put into effect earlier than the date when it is provided under section 35 above that it may take effect, such a default shall not affect the rent for any rental period beginning after that date.

NOTES to section 36

Definitions: 'regulated tenancy': see s 115(1) below and s 8 above; 'tenancy' includes 'sub-tenancy': see s 115(1) below; 'landlord': *Ibid*; 'tenant': *Ibid*; 'contractual period': see s 42(1) below; 'statutory period': *Ibid*; 'rental period': *Ibid*; 'rent agreement with a tenant having security of tenure': see s 42(1) below and s 34 above.

37. Recovery from landlord of sums paid in excess of recoverable rent, etc.

(1) Where a tenant has paid on account of rent any amount which, by virtue of this Part of this Act, is irrecoverable by the landlord, then, subject to subsection (3) below, the tenant who paid it shall be entitled to recover that amount from the landlord who received it or his personal representatives.

(2) Subject to subsection (3) below, any amount which a tenant is entitled to recover under subsection (1) above may, without prejudice to any other method of recovery, be deducted by the tenant from any rent payable by him to the landlord.

(3) No amount which a tenant is entitled to recover under subsection (1) above shall be recoverable at any time after the expiry of two years from the date of payment.

NOTES to section 37

Definitions: 'tenant': see s 115(1) below; 'landlord': *Ibid*.

38. Onus on landlord.

(1) Any person who, in any rent book or similar document, makes an entry showing or purporting to show any tenant as being in arrears in respect of any sum on account of rent which is irrecoverable by virtue of this Part of this Act shall be liable to a fine not exceeding level 3 on the standard scale, unless he proves that, at the time of the making of the entry, the landlord had a bona fide claim that the sum was recoverable.

(2) If, where any such entry has been made by or on behalf of any landlord, the landlord on being requested by or on behalf of the tenant to do so, refuses or neglects to cause the entry to be deleted within seven days, the landlord shall be liable to a fine not exceeding level 3 on the standard scale, unless he proves that, at the time of the neglect or refusal to cause the entry to be deleted, he had a bona fide claim that the sum was recoverable. [286]

NOTES to section 38
Definitions: 'tenant': see s 115(1) below; 'the standard scale': see s 115(1) below; level 3 on the standard scale is £400. See the Increase of Criminal Penalties Etc (Scotland) Order; 1984, SI 1984/526 'landlord': see s 115(1) below.

39. Rectification of rent books in light of determination of recoverable rent.

Where, in any proceedings, the recoverable rent of a dwelling-house subject to a regulated tenancy is determined by a court, then, on the application of the tenant (whether in those or in any subsequent proceedings) the court may call for the production of the rent book or any similar document relating to the dwelling-house and may direct the clerk of court to correct any entries showing, or purporting to show, the tenant as being in arrears in respect of any sum which the court has determined to be irrecoverable. [287]

NOTES to section 39
Definitions: 'recoverable rent': see s 42(1) below; 'dwelling-house': see s 1 above; 'regulated tenancy': see s 115(1) below and s 8 above; 'tenancy' includes 'sub-tenancy': see s 115(1) below; 'tenant': *Ibid.*

40. Adjustment for differences in lengths of rental periods.

In ascertaining for the purposes of this Part of this Act whether there is any difference with respect to rents between one rental period and another (whether of the same tenancy or not) or the amount of any such difference, any necessary adjustment shall be made to take account of periods of different lengths; and for the purposes of such an adjustment a period of one month shall be treated as equivalent to one-twelfth of a year and a period of a week as equivalent to one-fifty-second of a year. [288]

NOTES to section 40
Amendment: Words repealed by Housing (Scotland) Act 1988, (c 43), s 72, Sch 10.
Definitions: 'rental period': see s 42(1) below; 'tenancy' includes 'sub-tenancy': see s 115(1) below.

41. Regulations.

(1) The Secretary of State may make regulations—
(a) prescribing the form of any notice or other document to be given or used in pursuance of this Part of this Act;
(b) prescribing anything required or authorised to be prescribed by this Part of this Act; and
(c) prescribing matters as to which notice is to be given to a tenant of a dwelling-house let on or subject to a regulated tenancy by means of notices inserted in rent books and similar documents and the forms of such notices.

(2) Any such regulations shall be made by statutory instrument which shall be subject to annulment in pursuance of a resolution of either House of Parliament.

(3) If any rent book or similar document which does not conform to the prescribed requirements is used by or on behalf of any landlord, the landlord shall be liable to a fine not exceeding level 3 on the standard scale. [289]

[289]   *Rent (Scotland) Act 1984 (c 58), s 41*

NOTES to section 41

Sub-s (1): See the Rent Regulation (Forms and Information Etc) (Scotland) Regulations 1991, SI 1991/1521, paras [1510] ff below.

Definitions: 'tenant': see s 115(1) below; 'landlord': *Ibid*; 'prescribed': see s 42(1) below; 'the standard scale': see s 115(1) below; level 3 on the standard scale is currently £400. See the Increase of Criminal Penalties Etc (Scotland) Order; 1984, SI 1984/526.

42. Interpretation of Part IV.

(1) In this Part of this Act—

'contractual period' means a rental period of a regulated tenancy which is a period beginning before the expiry or termination of the protected tenancy;

'contractual rent limit' has the meaning assigned to it by section 28(1) above;

'notice of increase' means a notice of increase under section 29(2) or 30(2) above, as the case may require;

'prescribed' means prescribed by regulations under section 41 above, and references to a prescribed form include references to a form substantially to the same effect as the prescribed form;

'recoverable rent' means rent which, under a regulated tenancy, is or was for the time being recoverable, having regard to the provisions of this Part of this Act;

'a rent agreement with a tenant having security of tenure' has the meaning assigned to it by section 34 above;

'rental period' means a period in respect of which a payment of rent falls to be made;

'statutory period' means any rental period of a regulated tenancy which is not a contractual period.

(2) . . .   [290]

NOTES to section 42

Amendment: Sub-s (2) was repealed by the Housing (Scotland) Act 1988, (c 43), s 72, Sch 10.

Definitions: 'regulated tenancy': see s 115(1) below and s 8 above; 'protected tenancy': see s 115(1) below and s 1 above; 'tenancy' includes 'sub-tenancy': see s 115(1) below.

PART V
REGISTRATION OF RENTS UNDER REGULATED TENANCIES

43. Registration areas and rent officers.

(1) The registration areas for the purposes of this Part of this Act shall be the districts and islands areas.

(2) The Secretary of State may, after consultation with the local authority or local authorities concerned, make directions—

(a) as to the groupings of registration areas or parts thereof, or

(b) deeming any part of a registration area to be a separate registration area,

and any reference in this Part of this Act to a registration area shall include a reference to a grouping of registration areas or parts thereof and any area deemed to be a separate registration area by virtue of this subsection.

(3) The Secretary of State shall for every registration area, after consultation with the local authority or local authorities for that area, appoint such number of rent officers for the area as he may think fit.

(4) Where the Secretary of State made a direction under subsection (2) above, or an appointment under subsection (3) above, which came into force on 16th May 1975, he shall be deemed to have consulted the local authority or local authorities concerned for the purposes of the said subsection (2) or (3) if he consulted either the existing or the new local authority or local authorities before that date.

(5) The Secretary of State may pay to rent officers such remuneration and allowances as he may, with the approval of the Treasury, determine, defray their expenses to such amount as he may with the like approval determine, and may provide them with such accommodation and services as they may require.

(6) The Secretary of State may, with the approval of the Treasury, make such arrangements to provide for the superannuation of rent officers as he may consider appropriate; and where such arrangements in respect of a rent officer are made with a local authority the rent officer shall for the purposes of regulations under section 7 of the Superannuation Act 1972 and of any local Act scheme within the meaning of section 8 of that Act be deemed to be an officer of that local authority.

(7) References in this Act to the rent officer are references to any rent officer appointed for any area under this section. [291]

NOTES to section 43
Definition 'local authority': see s 115(1) below.

44. Rent assessment committees.

Rent assessment committees shall be constituted in accordance with the provisions of Schedule 4 to this Act. [292]

45. Register of rents.

(1) The rent officer for any area shall prepare and keep up to date a register for the purposes of this Part of this Act and shall make the register available for inspection in such place or places and in such manner as the Secretary of State may direct.

(2) The register shall contain, in addition to the rent payable under a regulated tenancy of a dwelling-house—
(a) the prescribed particulars with regard to the tenancy; and
(b) a specification of the dwelling-house.

(3) A copy of an entry in the register certified under the hand of the rent officer or any person duly authorised by him shall be receivable in evidence, and shall be sufficient evidence of that entry, in any court and in any proceedings.

(4) A person requiring such a certified copy shall be entitled to obtain it on payment of the prescribed fee.

(5) Any entry—
(a) in a register (hereinafter referred to as 'the old register')
 (i) which was kept under section 39 of the Rent (Scotland) Act 1971 before 16th May 1975, or
 (ii) which is kept for any area which ceases to be a registration area as a result of the establishment of a new registration area, or
(b) in a separate part of an old register in which rents are registered for dwelling-houses in respect of tenancies to which sections 55 to 59 below apply,
which relates to a dwelling-house which is situated in a new registration area shall be deemed for the purposes of this Part of this Act to be an entry in the register or, as the case may be, in such a separate part of the register kept under this section for that new registration area.

(6) The old register shall be kept by such rent officer, and made available for inspection in such place or places and in such manner as the Secretary of State may direct; and subsection (3) and (4) above shall apply to any entry in the old register which is deemed to be an entry in the register kept for a new registration area.

(7) In this section 'new registration area' means a registration area established under section 37 of the Rent (Scotland) Act 1971 or section 43 above on or after 16th May 1975. [293]

NOTES to section 45

Sub-s (4): The prescribed fee is £1.50: see the Rent Regulation (Forms and Information Etc) (Scotland) Regulations 1991, SI 1991/1521, paras [1510] ff below.

Definitions: 'regulated tenancy': see s 115(1) below and s 8 above; 'dwelling-house': see s 1 above; 'prescribed': see s 42(1) above; 'tenancy' includes 'sub-tenancy': see s 115(1) below.

46. Applications for registration of rents.

(1) An application for the registration of a rent for a dwelling-house may be made to the rent officer by the landlord or the tenant, or jointly by the landlord and the tenant, under a regulated tenancy of the dwelling-house.

(2) Any such application must be in the prescribed form and contain the prescribed particulars in addition to the rent which it is sought to register.

(3) Subject to subsection (4) below, where a rent for a dwelling-house has been registered under this Act no application by the tenant alone or by the landlord alone for the registration of a different rent for that dwelling-house shall be entertained before the expiry of three years from the relevant date (as defined in subsection (5) below) except on the ground that, since that date, there has been such a change in the condition of the dwelling-house (including the making of any improvement therein), the terms of the tenancy, the quantity, quality or condition of any furniture provided for use under the tenancy (excluding any deterioration in that furniture due to fair wear and tear) or any other circumstances taken into consideration when the rent was registered or confirmed as to make the registered rent no longer a fair rent.

(4) An application such as is mentioned in subsection (3) above which is made by the landlord alone and is so made within the last three months of the period of three years referred to in that subsection may be entertained before the expiry of that period, notwithstanding that the application is not made upon any of the grounds mentioned in that subsection.

(5) In this section and section 47 below, 'relevant date', in relation to a rent which has been registered under this Part of this Act, means the date from which the registration took effect or, in the case of a registered rent which has been confirmed by the rent officer, the date from which the confirmation (or, where there have been two or more confirmations, the last of them) took effect.

(6) For the purposes of subsection (5) above, where a rent is registered as a result of a decision of a rent assessment committee the date from which that registration took effect shall be taken to be the date on which the rent determined by the rent officer was registered or, as the case may be, the confirmation of the registered rent by the rent officer was noted.

(7) No application for the registration of a rent for a dwelling-house shall be entertained at a time when there is in operation, with respect to that dwelling-house, a condition relating to rent imposed under any of the following enactments, that is to say,—
    (a) section 3 of the Housing (Rural Workers) Act 1926;
    (b) section 101 of the Housing (Scotland) Act 1950; and
    (c) Schedule 4 to the Housing (Financial Provisions) (Scotland) Act 1968.

(8) Subject to section 47(4) below, the provisions of Part I of Schedule 5 to this Act shall have effect with respect to the procedure to be followed on applications for the registration of rents.

NOTES to section 46

Definitions: 'dwelling-house': see s 1 above; 'landlord': see s 115(1) below; 'tenant': *Ibid*; 'regulated tenancy': see s 115(1) below and s 8 above; 'prescribed': see s 42(1) above; 'improvement': *Ibid*; 'tenancy' includes 'sub-tenancy': see s 115(1) below.

47. Certificates of fair rent.

(1) A person intending—
(a) to provide a dwelling-house by the erection or conversion of any premises or to make any improvements in a dwelling-house, or
(b) to let on a regulated tenancy a dwelling-house which is not for the time being subject to such a tenancy and which satisfies the condition either that no rent for it is registered under this Part of this Act or that a rent is so registered but not less than three years have elapsed since the relevant date (as defined in section 46(5) above),
may apply to the rent officer for a certificate, to be known as a certificate of fair rent, specifying a rent which, in the opinion of the rent officer, would be a fair rent under a regulated tenancy of the dwelling-house or, as the case may be, of the dwelling-house after the erection or conversion or after the completion of the improvements.

(2) The regulated tenancy to which the application for the certificate of fair rent relates shall be assumed to be a tenancy on such terms as may be specified in the application and, except in so far as other terms are so specified, on the terms that the tenant would be liable for internal decorative repairs, but no others, and that no services or furniture would be provided for him.

(3) The provisions of Schedule 6 to this Act shall have effect with respect to applications for certificates of fair rent.

(4) Subject to section 46(7) above, where a certificate of fair rent has been issued in respect of a dwelling-house, an application for the registration of a rent for the dwelling-house in accordance with the certificate may be made within three years of the date of the certificate either,—
(a) by the landlord under such a regulated tenancy of the dwelling-house as is specified in the certificate; or
(b) by a person intending to grant such a regulated tenancy of the dwelling-house; and, in lieu of the provisions of Part I of Schedule 5 to this Act, the provisions of Part II of that Schedule shall have effect with respect to an application so made. [295]

NOTES to section 47
Definitions: 'dwelling-house': see s 1 above; 'improvement': see s 4(1) below; 'regulated tenancy': see s 115(1) below and s 8 above; 'tenancy' includes 'sub-tenancy': see s 115(1) below; 'landlord': *Ibid*.

48. Determination of fair rent.

(1) In determining for the purposes of this Part of this Act what rent is or would be a fair rent under a regulated tenancy of a dwelling-house, it shall be the duty of the rent officer or, as the case may be, of the rent assessment committee, subject to the provisions of this section, to have regard to all the circumstances (other than personal circumstances), and in particular to apply their knowledge and experience of current rents of comparable property in the area, as well as having regard to the age, character and locality of the dwelling-house in question and to its state of repair and, if any furniture is provided for use under the tenancy, to the quantity, quality and condition of the furniture.

(2) For the purposes of the determination it shall be assumed that the number of persons seeking to become tenants of similar dwelling-houses in the locality on the terms (other than those relating to rent) of the regulated tenancy is not substantially greater than the number of such dwelling-houses in the locality which are available for letting on such terms.

(3) There shall be disregarded—
(a) any disrepair or other defect attributable to a failure by the tenant under the regulated tenancy or any predecessor in title of his to comply with any terms thereof, and
(b) any improvement (including any improvement to the furniture provided for use

under the tenancy), or the replacement of any fixture or fitting carried out, otherwise than in pursuance of the terms of the tenancy, by the tenant under the regulated tenancy or any predecessor in title of his, and

(c) if any furniture is provided for use under the regulated tenancy, any deterioration in the condition of the furniture due to any ill-treatment by the tenant, any person residing or lodging with him, or any subtenant of his.

(4) In the application of this section to a converted tenancy, the references in subsection (3) above to the tenant under the regulated tenancy shall include references to the tenant under the tenancy before the conversion. **[296]**

NOTES to section 48

Definitions: 'regulated tenancy': see s 115(1) below and s 8 above; 'tenancy': see s 115(1) below; 'dwelling-house': see s 1 above; 'tenant': see s 115(1) below; 'improvement': see s 54(1) below; 'converted tenancy': see s 115(1) below.

49. Amount to be registered as rent.

(1) The amount to be registered as the rent of any dwelling-house shall include any sums payable by the tenant to the landlord for the use of furniture or for services, whether or not those sums are separate from the sums payable for the occupation of the dwelling-house or are payable under separate agreements.

(2) Subject to subsection (3) below, there shall be noted separately on the register the amount, if any, of the registered rent which, in the opinion of the rent officer or rent assessment committee, is fairly attributable to each of the following—
 (a) the use of furniture;
 (b) the provision of services;
 (c) the use of part of the premises comprised in a dwelling-house as a shop or office or for business, trade or professional purposes.

(3) There shall not be noted on the register under subsection (2) above any amount which in the opinion of the rent officer or rent assessment committee is less than 5 per cent of the registered rent.

. . .

(6) Where, under a regulated tenancy, the sums payable by the tenant to the landlord include any sums varying according to the cost from time to time of any services provided by the landlord or a superior landlord or of any works of maintenance or repair carried out by the landlord or a superior landlord, the amount to be registered under this Part of this Act as rent may, if the rent officer is satisfied or, as the case may be, the rent assessment committee are satisfied, that the terms as to the variation are reasonable, be entered as an amount variable in accordance with those terms. **[297]**

NOTES to section 49

Amendment: Sub-ss (4), (5), were repealed by the Housing (Scotland) Act 1988, (c 43), s 72, Sch 10.

Definitions: 'dwelling-house': see s 1 above; 'tenant': see s 115(1) below; 'landlord': *Ibid*; 'rent assessment committee': see s 44 above; 'regulated tenancy': see s 115(1) below and s 8 above.

50. Effect of registration of rent.

(1) Subject to subsection (2) below, the registration of a rent for a dwelling-house takes effect if the rent was determined by the rent officer, from the date when it was registered.

(2) If (by virtue of section 46(4) above) an application for registration of rent is made before the expiry of the period of three years referred to in subsection (3) of that section, the registration of a rent for the dwelling-house does not take effect before the end of that period.

(3) If, on application for the registration of a different rent, the rent officer confirms the rent for the time being registered, the confirmation of that rent takes effect from the date when it is noted in the register.

(4) If the rent for a dwelling-house is determined by a rent assessment committee, the registration of that rent takes effect from the date when the committee make their decision.

(5) The date from which the registration or confirmation of a rent takes effect shall be entered in the register.

(6) As from the date on which the registration of a rent takes effect any previous registration of a rent for a dwelling-house ceases to have effect.

(7) Where a valid notice of increase under any provision of Part IV of this Act has been served on a tenant and, in consequence of the registration of a rent, part but not the whole of the increase specified in the notice becomes irrecoverable from the tenant, the registration shall not invalidate the note, but the notice shall, as from the date from which the registration takes effect, have effect as if it specified such part only of the increase as has not become irrecoverable. [298]

NOTES to section 50

Definitions: 'dwelling-house': see s 1 above; 'rent assessment committee': see s 44 above; 'notice of increase': see s 32 above; 'register': see s 45 above.

51. Cancellation of registration of rent.

(1) Where a rent agreement is made in writing as respects a dwelling-house for which a rent is registered, an application may be made in accordance with this section for the cancellation of the registration.

(2) The application shall be made jointly by the landlord and the tenant under the agreement to the rent officer, and the application shall not be entertained before the expiry of three years from the relevant date as defined in section 46(5) above.

(3) An application under this section must be in the prescribed form and contain the prescribed particulars, and must be accompanied by a copy of the rent agreement.

(4) The Secretary of State may make regulations under section 53 below prescribing the procedure on an application under this section.

(5) If the rent officer is satisfied that the rent payable under the rent agreement does not exceed a fair rent for the dwelling-house, he shall, subject to subsection (6) below, cancel the registration, and he shall make an entry in the register of that fact and of the date from which the cancellation takes effect.

(6) Where under the terms of the rent agreement the sums payable by the tenant to the landlord include any sums varying according to the cost from time to time of any services provided by the landlord, the rent officer shall not cancel the registration unless he is satisfied that those terms are reasonable.

(7) The cancellation of the registration shall be without prejudice to a further registration of a rent at any time after cancellation.

(8) The rent officer shall notify the applicants of his decision to grant, or to refuse, any application under this section and, where he grants the application, of the date from which the cancellation takes effect.

(9) In this section 'rent agreement' means—
(a) an agreement increasing the rent payable under a protected tenancy which is a regulated tenancy, or
(b) where a regulated tenancy is terminated, and a new regulated tenancy is granted at a rent exceeding the rent under the previous tenancy, the grant of the new tenancy. [299]

NOTES to section 51

Sub-ss (3), (4): See the Cancellation of Registrations (Procedure) (Scotland) Regulations 1980, SI 1980/1670, paras [1308] ff below.

Definitions: 'dwelling-house': see s 1 above; 'landlord': see s 115(1) below; 'tenant': *Ibid*; 'prescribed': see s 54 below; 'register': see s 45 above; 'protected tenancy': see s 115(1) below and s 8 above; 'regulated tenancy': *Ibid*; 'tenancy' includes 'sub-tenancy': see s 115(1) below.

52. Cancellation at instance of landlord.

Where the rent for a dwelling-house has been registered but the dwelling-house has ceased to be let under a regulated tenancy, an application to the rent officer may be made by the landlord in accordance with this section for the cancellation of the registration, and the provisions of section 51(2) to (4), (7) and (8) above shall apply, with any necessary modifications, to an application made under this section as they apply to an application made under the said section 51. **[300]**

NOTES to section 52

Definitions: 'dwelling-house': see s 1 above; 'regulated tenancy': see s 115(1) below and s 8 above; 'tenancy': see s 115(1) below; 'landlord': *Ibid*.

53. Regulations

(1) The Secretary of State may make regulations—
  (a) prescribing the form of any notice, application, register or other document to be given, made or used in pursuance of this Part of this Act;
  (b) regulating the procedure to be followed by rent officers and rent assessment committees [whether under this Act or the Housing (Scotland) Act 1988]; and
  (c) prescribing anything required or authorised to be prescribed by this Part of this Act.

(2) Regulations under subsection 1(b) above may contain provisions modifying section 46, 47 or 50 above or Schedule 5 or 6 to this Act; but no regulations containing such provisions shall have effect unless approved by a resolution of each house of Parliament.

(3) Regulations made under this section shall be made by statutory instrument which, except in a case falling within subsection (2) above, shall be subject to annulment in pursuance of a resolution of either House of Parliament. **[301]**

NOTES to section 53

Amendment: Sub-s (1) was amended by the Housing (Scotland) Act (c 43), s 48.

Sub-s (1): See the Rent Regulation (Forms and Information Etc) (Scotland) Regulations 1991, SI 1991/1521, paras [1510] ff below.

54. Interpretation of Part V.

(1) In this Part of this Act—

'improvement' includes structural alteration, extension or addition and the provision of additional fixtures or fittings, but does not include anything done by way of decoration or repair;

'prescribed' means prescribed by regulations under section 53 above, and references to a prescribed form include references to a form substantially to the same effect as the prescribed form;

'rental period' means a period in respect of which a payment of rent falls to be made.

(2) . . . **[302]**

NOTES to section 54

Amendment: Sub-s (2) was repealed by the Housing (Scotland) Act 1988, (c 43), s 72, Sch 10.

Part VI
Rent Limit for Dwelling-houses Let by Housing Associations and the Housing Corporation

55. Tenancies to which sections 55 to 59 apply.

This section and sections 56 to 59 below apply to a tenancy where—
(a) the interest of the landlord under that tenancy belongs to a housing association or to the Housing Corporation, and
(b) the tenancy would be a protected tenancy but for section 1(1)(a) or 5 above,
[but do not apply and shall be deemed never to have applied, to a tenancy which is a lease under a shared ownership agreement within the meaning of section 106(2) of the Housing Associations Act 1985], and in this section and the said sections 56 to 59 'tenancy' means, unless the context otherwise requires, a tenancy to which those sections apply. [303]

NOTES to section 55

Amendment: Section 55 was amended by the Housing (Scotland) Act 1988, (c 43), s 47.
Definitions: 'tenancy': see s 115(1) below; 'landlord': *Ibid*; 'housing association': see s 61(1) below; 'protected tenancy': see s 115(1) below and s 1 above.

56. Rents to be registrable under Part V.

(1) There shall be a separate part of the register under Part V of this Act in which rents may be registered for dwelling-houses which are let, or are, or are to be, available for letting, under a tenancy to which sections 55 to 59 of this Act apply.

(2) Sections [22 to 27], 45 to 49, section 50(2) and section 53 above and Schedules 5 and 6 to this Act (and no other provisions of this Act) shall apply to a tenancy to which the said sections 55 to 59 apply and, in their application to such tenancies, shall, in relation to that part of the register, have effect as if for any reference in those provisions to a regulated tenancy there were substituted a reference to a tenancy to which the said sections 55 to 59 apply.

(3) Registration in the said part of the register shall take effect on the date of registration:
Provided that registration before 1st January 1973 shall be provisional only until that date, and the date of registration shall be 1st January 1973.

(4) From the date of registration any previous registration of a rent for the dwelling-house shall cease to have effect.

(5) A rent registered in any part of the register for a dwelling-house, which becomes or ceases to be a dwelling-house under a tenancy to which the said sections 55 to 59 apply, shall be as effective as if it were registered in any other part of the register.

(6) Subject to subsection (5) above, references in the said sections 55 to 59 to registration are, unless the context otherwise requires, references to registration pursuant to this section. [304]

NOTES to section 56

Amendments: Sub-s (2) was amended by the Law Reform (Miscellaneous Provisions) (Scotland) Act 1985 (c 73), s 59, Sch 2, para 28, and by the Housing (Scotland) Act 1988 (c 43), s 72, Sch 10.
Definitions: 'dwelling-house': see s 1 above; 'let': see s 115(1) below; 'tenancy': *Ibid*; 'regulated tenancy': see s 115(1) below and s 8 above.

57. The rent limit.

(1) Where the rent payable under a tenancy would exceed the rent limit determined in accordance with sections 55 to 59 of this Act, the amount of the excess shall be irrecoverable from the tenant.

(2) Where a rent for the dwelling-house is registered, then, subject to section 58 below, the rent limit is the rent so registered:

. . .

(3) Where no rent for the dwelling-house is registered, then, subject to subsection (5) below, the rent limit shall be determined as follows—
  (a) if the lease or agreement creating the tenancy was made before 1st January 1973, the rent limit is the rent recoverable under the tenancy, as varied by any agreement made before that date (but not as varied by any later agreement),
  (b) if paragraph (a) above does not apply, and, not more than three years before the tenancy began, the dwelling-house was subject to another tenancy (whether before 1973 or later) the rent limit is the rent recoverable under that other tenancy (or, if there was more than one, the last of them) for the last rental period thereof,
  (c) if paragraph (a) and paragraph (b) above do not apply, the rent limit shall be the rent payable under the terms of the lease or agreement creating the tenancy (and not by the rent so payable under those terms as varied by any subsequent agreement).

(4) The reference in paragraph (b) of subsection (3) above to another tenancy includes, in addition to a tenancy to which sections 57 to 59 of this Act apply, a regulated tenancy within the meaning of this Act—
  (a) which subsisted at any time after the operative date, within the meaning of the Housing Act 1974; and
  (b) under which, immediately before it came to an end, the interest of the landlord belonged to a housing association.

. . .

(6) Section 37 above shall apply as if any amount made irrecoverable by virtue of this section were irrecoverable by virtue of Part IV of this Act.

(7) A tenancy commencing (whether before or after the commencement of this Act) while there is in operation a condition relating to rent imposed under any of the enactments mentioned in section 46(7) above shall be disregarded for the purposes of subsection (3)(b) above in determining the rent limit under any subsequent tenancy of the dwelling-house.

(8) Where the rent is subject to the rent limit under subsection (3)(b) above, the landlord shall, on being so requested in writing by the tenant, supply him with a statement in writing of the rent which was recoverable for the last rental period of the other tenancy referred to in that paragraph.

(9) If, without reasonable excuse, a landlord who has received such a request as is referred to in subsection (8) above—
  (a) fails to supply the statement referred to in that subsection within 21 days of receiving the request, or
  (b) supplies a statement which is false in any material particular,
he shall be liable to a fine not exceeding level 3 on the standard scale.

(10) This section shall not apply to rent for any rental period beginning before 1st January 1973.

NOTES to section 57

Amendments: Sub-s (2) was amended by and sub-s (5) was repealed by the Housing (Scotland) Act 1988, (c 43), s 7, Sch 10.

Definitions: 'tenancy, tenant': see s 115(1) below; 'dwelling-house': see s 1 above; 'rental period': see s 61(1) below; 'regulated tenancy': see s 115(1) below and s 8 above; 'housing association': see s 61(1) below; 'landlord': see s 115(1) below.

58. Phasing of progression to registered rent.

(1) This section applies where a rent is registered for a dwelling-house (whether it is

the first or any subsequent registration) which exceeds the rent limit for the dwellinghouse immediately before the date of registration, unless at the date of registration there is no tenant and no person to whom the tenancy has been granted.

(2) Subject to subsection (9) below, the rent limit shall progress from the rent limit immediately before the date of registration to the registered rent in stages, and . . .
[(a) for any rental period beginning in the first stage, the rent limit shall be the rent limit immediately before the date of registration plus the greatest of—
 (i) £104; or
 (ii) one quarter of the previous rent limit; or
 (iii) one-half of the difference between the previous rent limit and the amount of the registered rent:
Provided that nothing in this paragraph shall enable the rent to be increased above the amount of the registered rent;
(b) for any rental period beginning in the second stage the rent limit shall be the rent payable for the first stage plus any amount required to increase the rent payable to the registered rent.]

(3) The first stage shall last for 52 weeks from the date of registration, or from the beginning of the first rental period for which the rent is first increased (by any amount) on or after that date, whichever is the later, [or for such other period as the Secretary of State may by order specify.]

(4) Any subsequent stage shall last for 52 weeks from the end of the last previous stage, or from the beginning of the first rental period for which the rent is first increased (by any amount) after the end of the last previous stage, whichever is the later, [or for such other period as the Secretary of State may by order specify.]

(5) If a tenancy of the dwelling-house is granted at any time when the rent limit is less than the registered rent, and the tenant is neither the person who, at the time when the previous tenancy (or the last previous tenancy) ended, was the tenant under that tenancy nor a member of that tenant's family who resided with him, the registered rent shall become the rent limit from the beginning of the new tenancy, and the stages by which the rent limit was to progress up to the registered rent shall terminate.

(6) The registration of a lower or higher rent during the progression from the rent limit in force before the prior registration shall not alter the stages by which the rent limit is to progress, and if a higher rent is registered in the 52 weeks beginning with the first rental period for which the rent is increased up to the rent registered on the prior registration, the first stage in the progression from that rent up to the later registered rent shall not begin until the end of that period of 52 weeks.

(7) The Secretary of State may by order amend subsection (2) above by varying [or repealing any of the provisions of] paragraphs (a) and (b) thereof, and the order may contain such supplementary or incidental provisions as he thinks fit.

[(7A) An order under subsection (3) or (4) above shall be made by statutory instrument subject to annulment in pursuance of a resolution of either House of Parliament and may contain such supplementary or incidental material as the Secretary of State thinks fit.]

(8) An order under subsection (7) above shall be made by statutory instrument subject to annulment in pursuance of a resolution of either House of Parliament and may be varied or revoked by a subsequent order made under that subsection.

(9) In subsection (2)(a) and (b) above, in relation to a rent registered before 1st December 1980, for the words from 'the greater' to 'limit' there shall be substituted the words '£78 per year'.

(10) In this section—
'noted amount' means the amount of the registered rent noted as fairly attributable to the provision of services under section 49(2) above;
'previous rent limit' means—

(a) where the increase is the first to be made since the date of registration of the rent, the amount payable by way of rent on the relevant anniversary of that date, or
(b) in all other cases, the amount payable by way of rent on the relevant anniversary of that date,

the rent in either case not including a noted amount as defined above.   **[306]**

NOTES to section 58

Amendments: Sub-s (2) was amended by the Housing (Scotland) Act 1988, (c 43), s 72, Sch 10 then substituted with effect from 5 February 1990 by the Limits on Rent Increases (Housing Associations) (Scotland) Order 1989, SI 1989/2468; sub-ss (4) and (5) were amended by *Ibid*, s 41(5); sub-s (7) was amended by the Local Government and Housing Act 1989 (c 42), s 195, Sch 11; and sub-s 7A was added by the Housing (Scotland) Act 1988 (c 43), s 41(5).

Sub-s (2):   The Secretary of State may by order repeal or amend this section by statutory instrument. The version of sub-s (2) substituted by SI 1989/2468 applies to a rent registered before 5 February 1990 at the date of the next subsequent stage as though it were the first stage and the rent limit the rent payable before that date.

Sub-ss (3) and (4):   The power to make an order has not yet been exercised.

Definitions: 'dwelling-house': see s 1 above; 'tenant': see s 115(1) below; 'tenancy': *Ibid*; 'rental period': see s 61(1) below.

---

59. Increase of rent without notice to quit.

[Sections 212 and 213 of the Housing (Scotland) Act 1987] (increase of rents of houses belonging to certain authorities without notice of removal) shall apply to a housing association such as is referred to in section 5(4) above or the Housing Corporation as they apply to any authority to which that section applies . . .   **[307]**

NOTES to section 59

Amendments: Section 59 was amended by the Housing (Scotland) Act 1987 (c 28), s 339, Sch 23 and Sch 24.

---

60. Supplemental to sections 55 to 59.

(1) Section 40 above shall apply for the purposes of sections 55 to 59 above as it applies for the purposes of Part IV of this Act.

(2) Where a rent determined by a rent assessment committee is registered in substitution for a rent determined by the rent officer, the date of registration shall be deemed for the purposes of sections 55 to 59 above to be the date on which the rent determined by thr rent officer was registered:

Provided that a landlord shall not, by virtue of this subsection, be entitled to recover any rent for a rental period beginning before the date when the rent determined by the rent assessment committee was registered.

(3) The sheriff shall have jurisdiction, either in the course of any proceedings relating to a dwelling-house or on an application made for the purpose by the landlord or the tenant, to determine any question as to the rent limit under the said sections 55 to 59, or as to any matter which is or may become material for determining any such question; and section 103(1) below shall apply to any application to the sheriff under this subsection as it applies to any application under any of the provisions mentioned in section 103(2) below.

(4) Nothing in sections 55 to 59 above shall prevent or limit an increase in any amounts payable to the landlord for the provision of services which are variable by virtue of section 49(6) above.   **[308]**

NOTES to section 60

Definitions: 'rent assessment committee': see s 44 above; 'landlord': see s 115(1) below; 'rental period': see s 61(1) below; 'dwelling-house': see s 1 above; 'tenant': see s 115(1) below.

61. Interpretation of Part VI

(1) In this Part of this Act, unless the context otherwise requires—
'housing association' has the same meaning as in the Housing Associations Act 1985, except that it does not include—

[(a) . . .
(b) a development corporation (within the meaning of the New Towns (Scotland) Act 1968; or
(c) a co-operative housing association within the meaning of the Housing Associations Act 1985]

'rental period' means a period in respect of which a payment of rent falls to be made.

(2) Expressions used in this Part of this Act which are also used in Part IV or V of this Act shall, unless the context otherwise requires, have the same meaning in this Part as in those Parts. [309]

NOTES to section 61

Amendments: In sub-s (1), the definition of 'housing association' was amended by the Housing (Consequential Provisions) Act 1985, (c 71), s 4, Sch 2, and the Housing (Scotland) Act 1988 (c 43), s 69; the words repealed were repealed by *Ibid*, ss 1 and 3, Sch 2, s 72, Sch 10. The definition of housing association is deemed always to have had effect as amended.

PART VII
PART VII CONTRACTS

62. Registration areas for purposes of Part VII.

(1) The registration areas for the purposes of this Part of this Act shall be the districts and islands areas.

(2) The Secretary of State may after consultation with the local authority or local authorities concerned, make directions—
(a) as to the groupings of registration areas, or parts thereof, or
(b) deeming any part of a registration area to be a separate registration area.

(3) Where the Secretary of State made a direction under subsection (2) above which came into force on 16th May 1975, he shall be deemed to have consulted the local authority or local authorities concerned for the purposes of that subsection if he has consulted either the existing or the new local authority or local authorities before that date.

(4) Any reference in this Part of this Act to a registration area shall include a reference to a grouping of registration areas or parts thereof and any area deemed to be a separate registration area by virtue of a direction under subsection (2)(b) above. [310]

NOTE to section 62

Definition: 'local authority': see s 115(1) below.

63. Part VII contracts.

(1) Subject to the following provisions of this section, this Part of this Act applies to a contract, whether entered into before or after the commencement of this Act, whereby one person grants to another person, in consideration of a rent which includes payment for the use of furniture or for services, the right to occupy as a residence a dwelling-house to which this Part of this Act applies.

(2) Subject to subsection (3) below, a contract falling within subsection (1) above and relating to a dwelling-house which consists of only part of a house is a contract to which

this Part of this Act applies whether or not the lessee is entitled, in addition to exclusive occupation of that part, to the use in common with any other person of other rooms or accommodation in the house.

(3) Subject to subsection (5) below, this Part of this Act does not apply—
   (a) to a contract under which the interest of the lessor belongs to Her Majesty in right of the Crown, or to a government department, or is held in trust for Her Majesty for the purposes of a government department; nor
   (b) to a contract entered into on or after 3rd October 1980, where the interest of the lessor belongs to one of the bodies mentioned in subsection (4) below; nor
   (c) to a contract for the letting of any dwelling-house at a rent which includes payment in respect of board if the value of the board to the lessee forms a substantial proportion of the whole rent; nor
   (d) to a contract which creates a regulated tenancy; nor
   (e) to a contract which created a controlled tenancy if that tenancy subsequently becomes a converted tenancy within the meaning of section 115(1) below.

(4) The bodies referred to in subsection (3)(b) above are—
   (a) an islands or district council, or a joint board or joint committee of an islands or district council or the common good of an islands or district council, or any trust under the control of an islands or district council;
   (b) a development corporation established by an order made, or having effect as if made, under the New Towns (Scotland) Act 1968;
   (c) the Scottish Special Housing Association;
   (d) the Housing Corporation;
   (e) a registered housing association within the meaning of the Housing Act 1974;
   (f) a housing co-operative within the meaning of section [22 of the Housing (Scotland) Act 1987]; and
   (g) any housing trust which was in existence on 13th November 1953 . . .

(5) An interest belonging to Her Majesty in right of the Crown shall not prevent this Part of this Act from applying to a contract if the interest is under the management of the Crown Estate Commissioners.

(6) No right to occupy a dwelling-house for a holiday shall be treated for the purposes of this Part of this Act as a right to occupy it as a residence.

(7) A contract to which this Part of this Act applies is, in the following provisions of this Part of this Act, referred to as a 'Part VII contract'. [311]

NOTES to section 63
Amendments: Sub-s (4) was amended by the Housing (Scotland) Act 1987, (c 26), s 339, Sch 23, 24.
Definitions: 'dwelling-house': see s 1, above; 'lessee': see s 81(1) below; 'regulated tenancy': see s 115(1) below and s 8 above; 'services': see s 81(1) below; 'rent': see s 81(3) below; 'lessor': see s 81(1) below.

64. Dwelling-houses to which Part VII applies.

(1) Subject to the following provisions of this section this Part of this Act applies to any dwelling-house the rateable value of which on the appropriate day did not or, as the case may be, does not exceed £200, or in the case of a dwelling-house comprising or forming part of lands and heritages for which a rateable value is or was first shown on the valuation roll on or after 1st April 1978, £600.

(2) In relation to dwelling-houses comprising or forming part of lands and heritages for which a rateable value is or was first shown on the valuation roll on or after 1st April 1978, the Secretary of State may by order made by statutory instrument subject to annulment in pursuance of a resolution of either House of Parliament increase the said sum of £600 in subsection (1) above, and he may make different provision for different classes of case.

(3) The Secretary of State may by order under this section provide that, as from such date as may be specified in the order, this Part of this Act shall not apply to a dwelling-house the rateable value of which on such day as may be specified in the order exceeds such amount as may be so specified.

(4) An order under subsection (3) above—
(a) may be made so as to relate to the whole of Scotland or to such area in Scotland as may be specified in the order, and so as to apply generally or only to, or except to, such classes or descriptions of dwelling-houses as may be specified in the order; and
(b) may contain such transitional provisions as appear to the Secretary of State to be desirable.

(5) The power to make an order under subsection (3) above shall be exercisable by statutory instrument and no such order shall have effect unless it is approved by a resolution of each House of Parliament.

(6) For the purposes of this section, in relation to a dwelling-house which is not separately rated, 'rateable value' means such proportion of the rateable value of the premises of which the dwelling-house forms part as may be detemined to reflect the relationship between the value of the dwelling-house and the value of the said premises—
(a) by agreement in writing between the lessor and lessee; or
(b) failing such agreement, by the sheriff, on a summary application by either party.

NOTES to section 64

Sub-s (2): If a dwelling-house first appeared on the valuation roll between 1 April 1978 and 1 April 1985, the rateable value limit is £600. If it first appeared on the valuation roll after 1 April 1985, the rateable value limit is £1600. See the Protected Tenancies and Part VII Contracts (Rateable Value Limits) (Scotland) Order 1985, SI 1985/314 and paras [1347] ff below.

Sub-s (3): The rateable value limit was increased by SI 1985/314 (see above).

Definitions: 'dwelling-house': see s 7 above; 'the appropriate day': see s 115(1) below and s 7(3) above; 'rateable value': see s 115(1) below and s 7 above.

65. Reference of contracts to rent assessment committees and obtaining by them of information.

(1) Either the lessor or the lessee under a Part VII contract . . . may refer the contract to the rent assessment committee for the area in question.

(2) Where a Part VII contract is referred to a rent assessment committee under subsection (1) above they may, by notice in writing served on the lessor, require him to give to them, within such period (which shall not be less than seven days from the date of the service of the notice) as may be specified in the notice, such information as they may reasonably require regarding such of the prescribed particulars relating to the contract as are specified in the notice.

(3) If, within the period specified in a notice under subsection (2) above, the lessor fails without reasonable cause to comply with the provisions of the notice he shall be liable to a fine not exceeding level 3 on the standard scale.

NOTES to section 65

Amendments: In sub-s (1), words repealed by the Housing (Scotland) Act 1988, (c 43), s 68, Sch 10.

Definitions: 'lessor': see s 81(1) below; 'lessee': *Ibid*; 'rent assessment committee': see s 44 above; 'Part VII contract': see s 63(7) above; 'prescribed': see s 115(1) below; 'the standard scale': see s 115(1) below; level 3 is currently at £400. See the Increase of Criminal Penalties Etc (Scotland) Order; 1984, SI 1984/526.

66. Powers of rent assessment committees on reference of contracts.

(1) Where a Part VII contract is referred to a rent assessment committee and the reference is not, before the committee have entered upon consideration of it, withdrawn by the party . . . who made it, the committee shall consider it and then, after making such inquiry as they think fit and giving to each party to the contract and, if the dwelling-house is or forms part of a dwelling-house to which section [203 of the Housing (Scotland) Act 1987] applies, to the local authority, an opportunity of being heard or, at his or their option, of submitting representations in writing, the committee, subject to subsection (2) below,—
  (a) may approve the rent payable under the contract, or
  (b) may reduce or increase the rent to such sum as they may, in all the circumstances, think reasonable, or
  (c) may, if they think fit in all the circumstances, dismiss the reference,
and shall notify the parties and the local authority of their decision.

(2) On the reference of a Part VII contract relating to a dwelling-house for which a rent is registered under Part V of this Act, the committee may not reduce the rent payable under the contract below the amount which would be recoverable from the tenant under a regulated tenancy of the dwelling-house.

(3) An approval, reduction or increase under this section may be limited to rent payable in respect of a particular period.

(4) Where the rent under a Part VII contract has been registered under section 67 below, a rent assessment committee shall not be required to entertain a reference, made otherwise than by the lessor and the lessee jointly, for the registration of a different rent for the dwelling-house concerned before the expiry of the period of three years beginning on the date on which the rent was last considered by the committee, except on the ground that, since that date, there has been such a change in the condition of the dwelling-house, the furniture or services provided, the terms of the contract or any other circumstances taken into consideration when the rent was last considered as to make the registered rent no longer a reasonable rent.

NOTES to section 66
Amendments: Sub-s (1) was amended by the Housing (Scotland) Act 1987, (c 26), s 339, Sch 23, para 29, and repealed in part by the Housing (Scotland) Act 1988, (c 43), s 72, Sch 10.
Definitions: 'rent assessment committee': see s 44 above; 'Part VII contract': see s 115(1) below and s 63(7) above; 'party': see s 81(2) below; 'dwelling-house': see s 81(1) below; 'local authority': see s 115(1) below; 'rent': see s 81(3) below; 'regulated tenancy': see s 115(1) below and s 8 above; 'lessor': see s 81(1) below; 'lessee': *Ibid*; 'services': *Ibid*.

67. Register of rents under Part VII contracts.

(1) The rent assessment committee shall keep a register and shall make the register available for inspection in such place or places and in such manner as the Secretary of State may direct.

(2) The committee shall cause to be entered in the register, with regard to any contract under which a rent is payable which has been approved, reduced or increased under section 66 above—
  (a) the prescribed particulars with regard to the contract;
  (b) a specification of the dwelling-house to which the contract relates; and
  (c) the rent as approved, reduced or increased by the committee, and, in a case in which the approval, reduction or increase is limited to rent payable in respect of a particular period, a specification of that period.

(3) . . .

(4) A document purporting to be a certificate signed by the clerk or other authorised officer of the committee relating to any entry in the register under subsection (2) above

shall, until the contrary is shown, be deemed to have been signed by such clerk or other officer, and shall be sufficient evidence of the matters contained in the entry in the register.

(5) Any entry in a register (hereinafter referred to as 'the old register')
(a) which was kept under section 89 of the Rent (Scotland) Act 1971 before 16th May 1975, or
(b) which is kept for any area which ceases to be a registration area as a result of the establishment of a new registration area,

which relates to a dwelling-house which is situated in a new registration area shall be deemed for the purposes of this Part of this Act to be an entry in the register kept under this section for that new registration area.

(6) The old register shall be kept by such committee and made available for inspection in such place or places and in such manner as the Secretary of State may direct; and subsection (4) above shall apply to any entry in the old register which is deemed to be an entry in the register kept for a new registration area.

(7) In this section 'new registration area' means a registration area established under Part VII of the Rent (Scotland) Act 1971 or this Part of this Act on or after 16th May 1975. [315]

NOTES to section 67
Amendments: Sub-s (3), was repealed by the Housing (Scotland) Act 1988, (c 43), s 72, Sch 10.
Definitions: 'rent assessment committee': see s 44 above; 'prescribed': see s 115(1) below; 'rent': see s 81(3) below; 'dwelling-house': see s 81(1) below.

68. Reconsideration of rent after registration.

Where the rent payable for any dwelling-house has been entered in the register under section 67 above then, subject to section 66(4) above, the lessor or the lessee . . . may refer the case to the rent assessment committee for reconsideration of the rent so entered. [316]

NOTES to section 68
Amendment: Section 68 was repealed in part by the Housing (Scotland) Act 1988, (c 43), s 72, Sch 10.
Definitions: 'rent': see s 81(3) below; 'dwelling-house': see s 81(1) below; 'lessor': *Ibid*; 'lessee': *Ibid*; 'rent assessment committee': see s 44 above.

69. Effect of registration of rent.

(1) Where the rent payable for any dwelling-house is entered in the register under section 67 above, it shall not be lawful to require or receive on account of rent for that dwelling-house under a Part VII contract payment of any amount in excess of the rent so registered in respect of any period subsequent to the date of the entry or, where a particular period is specified in the register, in respect of that period.

(2) . . .

(3) Where any payment has been made or received in contravention of this section, the amount of the excess shall be recoverable by the person by whom it was paid.

(4) Any person who requires or receives any payment in contravention of this section shall be liable—
(a) on summary conviction, to a fine not exceeding the statutory maximum or to imprisonment for a term not exceeding three months or to both; and
(b) on conviction on indictment, to a fine or to imprisonment for a term not exceeding six months or to both;

and, without prejudice to any other method of recovery, the court by which a person is found guilty of an offence under this subsection may order the amount paid in excess to be repaid to the person by whom the payment was made. **[317]**

NOTES to section 69

Amendment: Sub-s (2), was repealed by the Housing (Scotland) Act 1988, (c 43), s 72, Sch 10.
Definitions: 'rent': see s 81(3) below; 'dwelling-house': see s 81(1) below; 'register': see s 81(1) below and s 67 above; 'Part VII contract': see s 115(1) below and s 67(3) above; 'the statutory maximum': see s 115(1) below; the maximum is currently £2000. See the Increase of Criminal Penalties Etc (Scotland) Order; 1984, SI 1984/526.

70. Cancellation of entries in register at instance of landlord.

(1) Where a rent has been registered under section 67 above but the dwelling-house has ceased to be subject to a Part VII contract, an application to a rent assessment committee may be made by the landlord in accordance with this section for the cancellation of the registration.

(2) . . .

(3) On an application under subsection (1) above the committee shall, where subsections (1) and (2) above are complied with, cancel the registration, and shall make an entry in the register noting the cancellation and the date from which the cancellation takes effect.

(4) The president of the panel set up under Schedule 4 to this Act may, if he thinks fit, direct that in considering applications made under subsection (1) above, the chairman sitting alone may exercise the functions of a rent assessment committee.

(5) An application under this section shall be in the prescribed form and contain the prescribed particulars.

(6) The committee shall notify the applicant of its decision to grant or to refuse any application under this section and, where it grants the application, of the date from which the cancellation takes effects. **[318]**

NOTES to section 70

Amendment: Sub-s (2), was repealed by the Housing (Scotland) Act 1988, (c 43), s 44, Sch 10.
Definitions: 'rent': see s 81(3) below; 'dwelling-house': see s 81(1) below; 'Part VII contract': see s 115(1) below and s 6(7) above; 'rent assessment committee': see s 44 above; 'landlord': see s 115(1) below; 'register': see s 81(1) below and s 67 above.

71. Notice to quit served after reference of contract to rent assessment committee.

(1) If, after a Part VII contract has been referred to a rent assessment committee by the lessee . . . under section 65 or 68 above, a notice to quit the dwelling-house to which the contract relates is served by the lessor on the lessee at any time before the decision of the committee is given or within the period of six months thereafter, then, subject to subsection (2) and sections 73 and 74 below, the notice shall not take effect before the expiry of that period.

(2) In a case falling within subsection (1) above,—
(a) the committee may, if they think fit, direct that a shorter period shall be substituted for the period of six months specified in that subsection; and
(b) if the reference to the committee is withdrawn, the period during which the notice to quite is not to take effect shall end on the expiry of seven days from the withdrawal of the reference. **[319]**

NOTES to section 71

Amendment: Sub-s (1), was repealed in part by the Housing (Scotland) Act 1988, (c 43), s 72, Sch 10.
Definitions: 'Part VII contract': see s 115(1) below and s 63(7) above; 'rent assessment committee': see s 44 above; 'lessee': see s 81(1) below; 'lessor': *Ibid*; 'dwelling-house': *Ibid*.

72. Application to rent assessment committee for security of tenure where notice to quit is served.

(1) Subject to sections 73 and 74(3) below, where—
(a) a notice to quit a dwelling-house which is the subject of a Part VII contract has been served, and
(b) the Part VII contract has been referred to a rent assessment committee under section 65 or 68 above (whether before or after the service of the notice to quit) and the reference has not been withdrawn, and
(c) the period at the end of which the notice to quit takes effect (whether by virtue of the contract, of section 71 above or of this section) has not expired,

the lessee may apply to the committee for the extension of the period referred to in paragraph (c) above.

(2) Where an application is made under this section, the notice to quit to which the application relates shall not have effect before the determination of the application unless the application is withdrawn.

(3) On an application under this section, the committee, after making such inquiry as they think fit and giving to each party an opportunity of being heard or at his option, of submitting representations in writing, may direct that the notice to quit shall not have effect until the end of such period, not exceeding six months from the date on which the notice to quit would have effect apart from the direction, as may be specified in the direction.

(4) If the committee refuse to give a direction under this section,—
(a) the notice to quit shall not have effect before the expiry of seven days from the determination of the application; and
(b) no subsequent application under this section shall be made in relation to the same notice to quit.

(5) On coming to a determination on an application under this section, the committee shall notify the parties of their determination. [320]

NOTES to section 72

Definitions: 'dwelling-house': see s 81(1) below; 'Part VII contract': see s 115(1) below and s 63(7) above; 'rent assessment committee': see s 44 above; 'lessee': see s 81(1) below.

73. Notices to quit served by owner-occupiers.

Where a person who has occupied a dwelling-house as a residence (in this section referred to as 'the owner-occupier') has, by virtue of a Part VII contract, granted the right to occupy the dwelling-house to another person and—
(a) at or before the time when the right was granted or, if it was granted before 8th December 1965, not later than 7th June 1966, the owner-occupier has given notice in writing to that other person that he is the owner-occupier within the meaning of this section, and
(b) if the dwelling-house is part of a house, the owner-occupier does not occupy any other part of the house as his residence,

neither section 71 nor section 72 above shall apply where a notice to quit the dwelling-house is served if, at the time the notice is to take effect, the dwelling-house is required as a residence for the owner-occupier or any member of his family who resided with him when he last occupied the dwelling-house as a residence. [321]

NOTES to section 73

Definitions: 'dwelling-house': see s 81(1) below; 'Part VII contract': see s 115(1) below and s 63(7) above.

74. Reduction of period of notice on account of lessee's default.

(1) The provisions of this section apply where a Part VII contract has been referred to a

rent assessment committee and the period at the end of which a notice to quit will take effect has been determined by section 71 above or extended under section 72 above.

(2) If, in a case where this section applies, it appears to the committee, on an application made by the lessor for a direction under this section,—
(a) that the lessee has not complied with the terms of the contract, or
(b) that the lessee or any person residing or lodging with him has been guilty of conduct which is a nuisance or annoyance to adjoining occupiers or has been convicted of using the dwelling-house, or allowing the dwelling-house to be used, for an immoral or illegal purpose, or
(c) that the condition of the dwelling-house has deteriorated owing to any act or neglect of the lessee or any person residing or lodging with him, or
(d) that the condition of any furniture provided for the use of the lessee under the contract had deteriorated owing to any ill-treatment by the lessee or any person residing or lodging with him,

the committee may direct that the period referred to in subsection (1) above shall be reduced so as to end at a date specified in the direction.

(3) No application may be made under section 72 above with respect to a notice to quit if a direction has been given under this section reducing the period at the end of which the notice is to take effect. **[322]**

NOTES to section 74

Definitions: 'Part VII contract': see s 115(1) below and s 63(7) above; 'rent assessment committee': see s 44 above; 'lessor': see s 81(1) below; 'lessee': *Ibid*; 'dwelling-house': *Ibid*.

75. Power of sheriff, in action for possession, to reduce period of notice to quit.

In any case where—
(a) a notice to quite a dwelling-house which is the subject of a Part VII contract has been served, and
(b) the period at the end of which the notice to quit takes effect is for the time being extended by virtue of section 71 or section 72 above, and
(c) at some time during that period the lessor institutes proceedings before the sheriff for possession of the dwelling-house, and
(d) in those proceedings the sheriff is satisfied that any of paragraphs (a) to (d) of section 74(2) above applies,

the sheriff may direct that the period referred to in paragraph (b) above shall be reduced so as to end at a date specified in the direction. **[323]**

NOTES to section 75

Definitions: 'dwelling-house': see s 81(1) below; 'Part VII contract': see s 115(1) below and s 63(7) above; 'lessor': see s 81(1) below.

76. Notice to quit relating to later Part VII contracts.

(1) This section applies to Part VII contracts entered into on or after 1st December 1980.

(2) Where this section applies, sections 71 to 75 above shall not apply, but in any proceedings for possession the sheriff may, if he thinks fit, postpone the date of possession for a period, which shall not exceed three months.

(3) A postponement under subsection (2) above may be made subject to such conditions regarding payment of outstanding rent or other conditions as the sheriff thinks fit. **[324]**

NOTES to section 76

Definitions: 'Part VII contracts': see s 115(1) below and s 63(7) above; 'rent': see s 81(3) below.

77. Jurisdiction of rent assessment committees.

Where a Part VII contract is referred to a rent assessment committee under this Part of this Act and—
- (a) the contract relates to a dwelling-house consisting of or comprising part only of lands and heritages, and
- (b) no apportionment of the rateable value of the lands and heritages has been made under section 7 above,

then, unless the lessor in the course of the proceedings requires that such an apportionment shall be made and, within two weeks of making the requirement, brings proceedings in the sheriff court for the making of the apportionment, the committee shall have jurisdiction to deal with the reference if it appears to them that, had the apportionment been made, they would have had jurisdiction. [325]

NOTE to section 77

Definitions: 'Part VII contract': see s 115(1) below and s 63(7) above; 'rent assessment committee': see s 44 above; 'dwelling-house': see s 81(1) below; 'lessor': *Ibid*.

78. Publication of information.

The local authority shall have power to publish information regarding the provisions of this Part of this Act. [326]

NOTE to section 78

Definition: 'the local authority': see s 115(1) below.

79. Rent book to be provided.

(1) Where rent is payable weekly under a Part VII contract, it shall be the duty of the lessor to provide a rent book or other similar document for use in respect of the dwelling-house, containing particulars of the rent and of the other terms and conditions of the contract.

(2) If at any time the lessor fails to comply with the requirements of this section he, and any person who on his behalf demands or receives rent under the contract, shall be liable to a fine not exceeding level 4 on the standard scale. [327]

NOTES to section 79

Definitions: 'rent': see s 81(3) below; 'Part VII contract': see s 115(1) below and s 63(7) above; 'dwelling-house': see s 81(1) below; 'lessor': *Ibid*; 'the standard scale': see s 115(1) below; level 4 is currently £1000. See the Increase of Criminal Penalties Etc (Scotland) Order; 1984, SI 1984/526.

80. Regulations.

(1) The Secretary of State may by statutory instrument make regulations—
- (a) with regard to the tenure of office of chairmen and other members of rent assessment committees;
- (b) with regard to proceedings before rent assessment committees under this Part of this Act;
- (c) prescribing anything which is required by this Part of this Act to be prescribed;
- (d) prescribing the form of, and the information to be contained in, any rent book or other similar document required by section 79(1) above to be provided; and
- (e) generally for carrying into effect the provisions of this Part of this Act.

(2) Any statutory instrument making regulations under subsection (1)(d) above shall be subject to annulment in pursuance of a resolution of either House of Parliament. [328]

NOTES to section 80

Sub-s (1): The Regulations currently in force issued under sub-s (1) are the Rent Assessment Committee (Scotland) Regulations 1980, SI 1980/1665, paras [1296] ff below; the Cancellation of Registration (Procedure) (Scotland) Regulations 1980, SI 1980/1670, paras [1308] below; and the Rent Regulation (Forms and Information) (Scotland) Regulations 1991, SI 1991/1521, paras [1510] ff below.

Definitions: 'rent assessment committee': see s 81(1) below.

81. Interpretation of Part VII.

(1) In this Part of this Act, unless the context otherwise requires,—

'dwelling-house' means a house or part of a house;

'lessee' means the person to whom is granted, under a Part VII contract, the right to occupy the dwelling in question as a residence and includes any person directly or indirectly deriving title from the grantee;

'lessor' means the person who, under a Part VII contract, grants to another the right to occupy the dwelling in question as a residence and includes any person directly or indirectly deriving title from the grantor;

'register' means the register kept by a rent assessment committee in pursurance of section 67 above;

'rental period' means a period in respect of which a payment of rent falls to be made;

'services' includes attendance, the provision of heating or lighting, the supply of hot water and any other privilege or facility connected with the occupancy of a dwelling-house.

(2) References in this Part of this Act to a party to a contract include references to any person directly or indirectly deriving title from such a party.

(3) Where separate sums are payable by the lessee of any dwelling-house to the lessor for any two or more of the following, namely—

(a) occupation of the dwelling-house,
(b) use of furniture, and
(c) services,

any reference in this Part of this Act to 'rent' in relation to that dwelling-house is a reference to the aggregate of those sums and, where those sums are payable under separate contracts, those contracts shall be deemed to be one contract. **[329]**

PART VIII
PREMIUMS, ETC

82. Prohibition of premiums and loans on grant of protected tenancies.

(1) Any person who, as a condition of the grant, renewal or continuance of a protected tenancy, requires, in addition to the rent, the payment of any premium or the making of any loan (whether secured or unsecured) shall be guilty of an offence under this section.

(2) Any person who, in connection with the grant, renewal or continuance of a protected tenancy, receives any premium in addition to the rent shall be guilty of an offence under this section.

(3) A person guilty of an offence under this section shall be liable to a fine not exceeding level 3 on the standard scale.

(4) The court by which a person is convicted of an offence under this section relating to requiring or receiving any premium may order the amount of the premium to be repaid to the person by whom it was paid. **[330]**

NOTES to section 82

Definitions: 'protected tenancy': see s 115(1) below and s 1 above; 'tenancy': see s 115(1) below; 'premium': see s 90(1) below; 'the standard scale': see s 115(1) below; level 3 is currently £400. See the Increase of Criminal Penalties Etc (Scotland) Order 1984, SI 1984/526.

83. Prohibition of premiums and loans on assignation of protected tenancies.

(1) Subject to the following provisions of this section and to section 84 below, any person who, as a condition of the assignation of a protected tenancy, requires the payment of any premium or the making of any loan (whether secured or unsecured) shall be guilty of an offence under this section.

(2) Subject to the following provisions of this section and to section 84 below, any person who, in connection with the assignation of a protected tenancy, receives any premium shall be guilty of an offence under this section.

(3) Notwithstanding anything in subsections (1) and (2) above, an assignor of a protected tenancy of a dwelling-house may, if apart from this section he would be entitled to do so, require the payment by the assignee or receive from the assignee a payment—
  (a) of so much of any outgoings discharged by the assignor as is referable to any period after the assignation takes effect;
  (b) of a sum not exceeding the amount of any expenditure reasonably incurred by the assignor in carrying out any structural alteration of the dwelling-house or in providing or improving fixtures therein, being fixtures which, as against the landlord, he is not entitled to remove;
  (c) where the assignor became a tenant of the dwelling-house by virtue of an assignation of the protected tenancy, of a sum not exceeding any reasonable amount paid by him to his assignor in respect of expenditure incurred by that assignor, or by any previous assignor of the tenancy, in carrying out any such alteration or in providing or improving any such fixtures as are mentioned in paragraph (b) above; or
  (d) where part of the dwelling-house is used as a shop or office, or for business, trade or professional purposes, of a reasonable amount in respect of any goodwill of the business, trade or profession, being goodwill transferred to the assignee in connection with the assignation or accruing to him in consequence thereof.

(4) Without prejudice to subsection (3) above, the assignor shall not be guilty of an offence under this section by reason only that—
  (a) any payment of outgoings required or received by him on the assignation was a payment of outgoings referable to a period before the assignation took effect; or
  (b) any expenditure which he incurred in carrying out structural alterations of the dwelling-house or in providing or improving fixtures therein and in respect of which he required or received the payment of any sum on the assignation was not reasonably incurred; or
  (c) any amount paid by him as mentioned in subsection (3)(c) above was not a reasonable amount; or
  (d) any amount which he required to be paid, or which he received, on the assignation in respect of goodwill was not a reasonable amount;
but nothing in this subsection shall prejudice any right of recovery under section 88(1) below.

(5) Notwithstanding anything in subsections (1) and (2) above, the provisions of Schedule 7 to this Act shall have effect in relation to the assignation of protected tenancies which are regulated tenancies in cases where a premium was lawfully required or received at the commencement of the tenancy.

(6) A person guilty of an offence under this section shall be liable to a fine not exceeding level 3 on the standard scale.

(7) The court by which a person is convicted of any offence under this section relating to requiring or receiving any premium may order the amount of the premium, or so much of it as cannot lawfully be required or received under this section (including any amount which, by virtue of subsection (4) above, does not give rise to an offence) to be repaid to the person by whom it was paid.

NOTES to section 83

Definitions: 'protected tenancy': see s 115(1) below and s 1 above; 'premium': see s 90(1) below; 'dwelling-house': see s 1 above; 'regulated tenancy': see s 115(1) below and s 8 above; 'tenant,' 'tenancy': see s 115(1) below; 'the standard scale': see s 115(1) below; level 3 is currently £400. See the Increase of Criminal Penalties Etc (Scotland) Order 1984, SI 1984/526.

84. Power to charge premium on assignation of tenancy where premium lawfully charged on earlier assignation.

(1) Where before 2nd June 1949 a premium has been paid on the assignation of a protected tenancy, then subject as hereinafter provided section 83 above shall not prevent the requiring or receiving on an assignation of that tenancy after 29th August 1954 of a premium not exceeding the amount hereinafter specified.

(2) The said amount is an amount which bears to the premium paid on the earlier assignation the same proportion as the period of the tenancy still to run at the time of the later assignation bears to the period of the tenancy still to run at the time of the earlier assignation, it being assumed that no power to determine the tenancy not yet exercised will be exercised either by the landlord or the tenant.

(3) Where before 2nd June 1949 a premium has been paid on more than one occasion on the assignation of the same tenancy, any of those assignations except the last shall be disregarded for the purposes of this section.

(4) In so far as any premium paid on the assignation of a protected tenancy before 2nd June 1949 has been recovered under the provisions of section 88(1) below, the premium shall be treated for the purposes of the foregoing provisions of this section as not having been paid.

(5) Where apart from this subsection the requirement or receiving of a premium would be allowable both under the foregoing provisions of this section and under Schedule 7 to this Act, the foregoing provisions of this section shall have effect to the exclusion of the said Schedule 7.

(6) Any reference in this section to a premium does not include a premium which consisted only of any such outgoings, sum or amount as fall within section 83(3) above and, in the case of a premium which included any such outgoings, sum or amount, so much only of the premium as does not consist of those outgoings, sum or amount shall be treated as the premium for the purposes of this section.

NOTES to section 84

Definitions: 'premium': see s 90(1) below; 'protected tenancy': see s 115(1) below and s 1 above; 'tenant,' 'tenancy': see s 115(1) below; 'landlord': *Ibid*.

85. Prohibition of premiums on grant, etc of Part VII contracts.

(1) The provisions of this section apply in relation to any dwelling-house if
  (a) under Part VII of this Act, a rent is registered for that dwelling-house in the register kept in pursuance of section 67 above; and
  (b) in a case where the approval, reduction or increase of the rent by the rent assessment committee is limited to rent payable in respect of a particular period, that period has not expired.

(2) Subject to subsection (3) below, any person who, as a condition of the grant, renewal, continuance of assignation of rights under a Part VII contract, requires the payment of any premium shall be guilty of an offence under this section.

(3) Nothing in subsection (2) above shall prevent a person from requiring—
  (a) that there shall be paid so much of any outgoings discharged by a grantor or assignor as is referable to any period after the grant or assignation takes effect; or
  (b) that there shall be paid a reasonable amount in respect of goodwill of a business,

trade, or profession, where the goodwill is transferred to a grantee or assignee in connection with the grant or assignation or accrues to him in consequence thereof.

(4) A person guilty of an offence under this section shall be liable to a fine not exceeding level 3 on the standard scale.

(5) The court by which a person is convicted of an offence under this section may order the amount of the premium, or so much of it as cannot lawfully be required under this section, to be repaid to the person by whom it was paid. [333]

NOTES to section 85

Definitions: 'dwelling-house': see s 115(1) below; 'rent assessment committee': see s 44 above; 'Part VII contract': see s 115(1) below and s 63(7) above; 'premium': see s 90(1) below; 'the standard scale': see s 115(1) below; level 3 is currently £400. See the Increase of Criminal Penalties Etc (Scotland) Order 1984, SI 1984/526.

86. Excessive price for furniture to be treated as premium.

Where the purchase of any furniture has been required as a condition of the grant, renewal, continuance or assignation—
(a) of a protected tenancy, or
(b) of rights under a Part VII contract which relates to a dwelling-house falling within section 85(1) above,

then, if the price exceeds the reasonable price of the furniture, the excess shall be treated, for the purposes of this Part of this Act, as if it were a premium required to be paid as a condition of the grant, renewal, continuance or assignation of the protected tenancy or, as the case may be, the rights under the Part VII contract. [334]

NOTES to section 86

Definitions: 'furniture': see s 90(1) below; 'protected tenancy': see s 115(1) below and s 1 above; 'Part VII contract': see s 115(1) below and s 63(7) above; 'dwelling-house': see s 1 above; 'premium': see s 90(1) below.

87. Punishment of attempts to obtain from prospective tenants excessive prices for furniture.

(1) Any person who, in connection with the proposed grant, renewal, continuance or assignation of a protected tenancy on terms which require the purchase of furniture,—
(a) offers the furniture at a price which he knows or ought to know is unreasonably high, or otherwise seeks to obtain such a price for the furniture, or
(b) fails to furnish, to any person seeking to obtain or retain accommodation whom he provides with particulars of the tenancy, a written inventory of the furniture, specifying the price sought for each item,

shall be liable to a fine not exceeding level 3 on the standard scale.

(2) Where a local authority have reasonable grounds for suspecting that an offence under subsection (1)(a) above has been committed with respect to a protected tenancy or proposed protected tenancy of a dwelling-house, they may give notice to the person entitled to possession of the dwelling-house or his agent that, on such date as may be specified in the notice, which shall not be earlier than 24 hours after the giving of the notice or, if the dwelling-house is unoccupied, than the expiry of such period after the giving of the notice as may be reasonable in the circumstances, facilities will be required for entry to the dwelling-house and inspection of the furniture therein.

(3) A notice under this section may be given by post.

(4) Where a notice is given under this section any person authorised by the local authority may avail himself of any facilities for such entry and inspection as are referred to in subsection (2) above which are provided on the specified date but shall, if so required,

produce some duly authenticated document showing that he is authorised by the local authority.

(5) If it is shown to the satisfaction of the sheriff or to a justice having jurisdiction in the place where the dwelling-house is situated, on a sworn statement in writing, that a person required to give facilities under this section has failed to give them, the sheriff or justice may, by warrant under his hand, empower the local authority, by any person authorised by them, to enter the dwelling-house in question, if need be by force, and inspect the furniture therein.

(6) A person empowered by or under the foregoing provisions of this section to enter a dwelling-house may take with him such other persons as may be necessary and, if the dwelling-house is unoccupied, shall leave it as effectively secured against trespassers as he found it.

(7) Any person who wilfully obstructs a person acting in pursuance of a warrant issued under subsection (5) above shall be liable to a fine not exceeding level 3 on the standard scale. **[335]**

NOTE to section 87

Definitions: 'protected tenancy': see s 115(1) below and s 1 above; 'furniture': see s 90(1) below; 'the standard scale': see s 115(1) below; level 3 is currently £400. See the Increase of Criminal Penalties Etc (Scotland) Order 1984, SI 1984/526; 'local authority': see s 115(1) below; 'dwelling-house': see s 1 above.

88. Recovery of premiums and loans unlawfully required or received.

(1) Where under any agreement (whether made before or after 12th August 1971) any premium is paid after 12th August 1971 and the whole or any part of that premium could not lawfully be required or received under the preceding provisions of this Part of this Act, the amount of the premium or, as the case may be, so much of it as could not lawfully be required or received, shall be recoverable by the person by whom it was paid.

(2) Nothing in section 82 or 83 above shall invalidate any agreement for the making of a loan or any security issued in pursuance of such an agreement but, notwithstanding anything in the agreement for the loan, any sum lent in circumstances involving a contravention of either of those sections shall be repayable to the lender on demand. **[336]**

NOTE to section 88

Definition: 'premium': see s 90(1) below.

89. Avoidance of requirements for advance payment of rent in certain cases.

(1) Where a protected tenancy which is a regulated tenancy is granted, continued or renewed, any requirement that rent shall be payable—
  (a) before the beginning of the rental period in respect of which it is payable, or
  (b) earlier than six months before the end of the rental period in respect of which it is payable (if that period is more than six months),
shall be void, whether the requirement is imposed as a condition of the grant, renewal or continuance of the tenancy or under the terms thereof; and any requirement avoided by this section is, in the following provisions of this section, referred to as a 'prohibited requirement'.

(2) Rent for any rental period to which a prohibited requirement relates shall be irrecoverable from the tenant.

(3) Any person who purports to impose any prohibited requirement shall be liable to a fine not exceeding level 3 on the standard scale, and the court by which he is convicted may order any amount of rent paid in compliance with the prohibited requirement to be repaid to the person by whom it was paid.

(4) Where a tenant has paid on account of rent any amount which, by virtue of this section is irrecoverable by the landlord, then, subjet to subsection (6) below, the tenant who paid it shall be entitled to recover that amount from the landlord who received it or his personal representatives.

(5) Subject to subsection (6) below, any amount which a tenant is entitled to recover under subsection (4) above may, without prejudice to any other method of recovery, be deducted by the tenant from any rent payable by him to the landlord.

(6) No amount which a tenant is entitled to recover under subsection (4) above shall be recoverable at any time after the expiry of two years from the date of payment.

(7) Any person who, in any rent book or similar document, makes any entry showing or purporting to show any tenant as being in arrears in respect of any sum on account of rent which is irrecoverable by virtue of this section shall be liable to a fine not exceeding level 3 on the standard scale, unless he proves that, at the time of the making of the entry, the landlord had a bona fide claim that the sum was recoverable.

(8) If, where any such entry has been made by or on behalf of any landlord, the landlord, on being requested by or on behalf of the tenant to do so, refuses or neglects to cause the entry to be deleted within seven days, the landlord shall be liable to a fine not exceding level 3 on the standard scale, unless he proves that, at the time of the neglect or refusal to cause the entry to be deleted, he had a bona fide claim that the sum was recoverable. [337]

NOTES to section 89

Definitions: 'protected tenancy': see s 115(1) below and s 1 above; 'regulated tenancy': see s 115(1) below and s 8 above; 'tenant,' 'tenancy': see s 115(1) below; 'rental period': see s 90(1) below; 'the standard scale': see s 115(1) below; level 3 is currently £400. See the Increase of Criminal Penalties Etc (Scotland) Order 1984, SI 1984/526; 'landlord': see s 115(1) below.

90. Interpretation of Part VIII.

(1) In this Part of this Act, unless the context otherwise requires—
'furniture' includes fittings and other articles;
'premium' includes any fine or other like sum and any other pecuniary consideration in addition to rent;
'registered rent' means the rent registered under Part V of this Act; and
'rental period' means a period in respect of which a payment of rent falls to be made.

(2) For the avoidance of doubt it is hereby declared that nothing in this Part of this Act shall render any amount recoverable more than once.

(3) For the avoidance of doubt, it is hereby declared that a deposit returnable at the termination of a tenancy or of a Part VII contract given as security for the tenant's obligations for accounts for supplies of gas, electricity, telephone or other domestic supplies and for damage to the dwelling-house or contents is not a premium for the purposes of this Part of this Act provided that it does not exceed the amount of two months' rent payable under the tenancy or under the Part VII contract, as the case may be. [338]

NOTES to section 90

Definitions: 'tenant,' 'tenancy': see s 115(1) below; 'Part VII contract': see s 115(1) below and s 63(7) above.

PART IX
HERITABLE SECURITIES

91. Heritable securities to which Part IX applies.

(1) The heritable securities with which this Part of this Act is concerned are heritable securities which—

(a) were created before 8th December 1965; and
(b) are regulated heritable securities as hereinafter defined.

(2) Any reference in this Part of this Act to a regulated heritable security shall be construed in accordance with section 92 below. **[339]**

NOTES to section 91

Definitions: 'heritable security': see s 115(1) below; '8th December 1965': see s 94(2) below.

92. Regulated heritable securities.

(1) Subject to subsection (2) below, a heritable security which falls within section 91(1)(a) is a regulated heritable security if—
(a) it is a heritable security over land consisting of or including a dwelling-house which is let on or subject to a regulated tenancy; and
(b) the regulated tenancy is binding on the creditor in the heritable security.

(2) Notwithstanding that a heritable security falls within subsection (1) above, it is not a regulated heritable security if—
(a) the rateable value on the appropriate day of the dwelling-house which falls within subsection (1)(a) above, or if there is more than one such dwelling-house comprised in the heritable security, the aggregate of the rateable values of those dwelling-houses on the appropriate day, is less than one-tenth of the rateable value on the appropriate day of the whole of the land comprised in the heritable security; or
(b) the debtor in the heritable security is in breach of agreement, but for this purpose a breach of the agreement for the repayment of the principal money shall be disregarded unless it provides for repayment by instalments. **[340]**

NOTES to section 92

Definitions: 'dwelling-house': see s 1 above; 'regulated tenancy': see s 115(1) below and s 8 above; 'creditor in the heritable security': see s 94(1) below; 'rateable value': see s 115(1) below and s 7 above; 'the appropriate day': see s 115(1) below and s 7(3) above; 'debtor in the heritable security': see s 94(1) below.

93. Powers of court to mitigate hardship.

(1) The powers of the court under this section relate only to regulated heritable securities, and those powers become exercisable in relation to such a heritable security only on an application made by the debtor in the security within 21 days, or such longer time as the court may allow, after the occurrence of one of the following events, that is to say,—
(a) the rate of interest payable in respect of the heritable security is increased; or
(b) a rent for a dwelling-house comprised in the heritable security is registered under Part V of this Act and the rent so registered is lower than the rent which was payable immediately before the registration; or
(c) the creditor in the security, not being a creditor who was in possession on 8th December 1965, demands payment of the principal money secured by the heritable security or takes any steps for exercising any right of foreclosure or sale or for otherwise enforcing his security.

(2) If the court is satisfied on any such application as is referred to in subsection (1) above that, by reason of the event in question and of the operation of this Act the debtor in the security would suffer severe financial hardship unless relief were given under this section, the court may by order make such provision limiting the rate of interest, extending the time for the repayment of the principal money or otherwise varying the terms of the heritable security or imposing any limitation or condition on the exercise of any right or remedy in respect thereof, as the court thinks appropriate.

(3) Where the court makes an order under subsection (2) above in relation to a heritable

security which comprises other land as well as a dwelling-house or dwelling-houses let on or subject to a regulated tenancy the order may, if the creditor in the security so requests, make provision for apportioning the money secured by the heritable security between that other land and the dwelling-house or dwelling-houses.

(4) Where such an apportionment is made as is referred to in subsection (3) above, the other provisions of the order made by the court shall not apply in relation to the other land referred to in that subsection and the money secured by the other land, and the heritable security shall have effect for all purposes as two separate heritable securities of the apportioned parts.

(5) Where the court has made an order under this section it may vary or revoke it by a subsequent order.

(6) The court for the purposes of this section is the sheriff, except that where an application under subsection (1) above is made in pursuance of any step taken by the creditor in the heritable security in the Court of Session, it is that court. [341]

NOTES to section 93

Definitions: 'regulated heritable security': see s 92 above; 'heritable security': see s 115(1) below; 'debtor in the security': see s 94(1) below; 'dwelling-house': *Ibid*; 'creditor in the security': *Ibid*; 'regulated tenancy': see s 115(1) below and s 8(1) above; '8th December 1965': see s 94(2) below.

94. Miscellaneous.

(1) In this Part of this Act the expressions 'creditor in a heritable security' and 'debtor in a heritable security', however expressed, include any person from time to time deriving title under the original creditor or debtor.

(2) In the application of this Part of this Act to a dwelling-house subject to a regulated furnished tenancy, for any reference to 8th December 1965 there shall be substituted a reference to 14th August 1974. [342]

NOTE to section 94

Definition: 'heritable security': see s 115(1) below.

Part X
Miscellaneous and General

95. Release from rent regulation.

(1) Where the Secretary of State is satisfied with respect to every part of any area that the number of persons seeking to become tenants there—

. . .

(b) of any class or description of dwelling-house . . .
is not substantially greater than the number of such dwelling-houses in that part, he may by order provide that no such dwelling-house in the area shall be the subject of a regulated tenancy.

(2) An order under this section may contain such transitional provisions, including provisions to avoid or mitigate hardship, as appear to the Secretary of State to be desirable.

(3) The power to make an order under this section shall be exercisable to statutory instrument and no such order shall have effect unless is it approved by a resolution of each House of Parliament. [343]

NOTES to section 95

Amendment: In sub-s (1) words repealed by the Housing (Scotland) Act 1988, (c 43), s 72, Sch 10.
Sub-ss (1), (2), (3): The power to make an order has not been exercised.

Definitions: 'tenant': see s 115(1) below; 'dwelling-house': see s 1 above; 'rateable value': see s 115(1) below and s 7 above; 'regulated tenancy': see s 115(1) below and s 8 above.

96. Provisions where tenant shares accommodation with landlord.

Where under any contract—
(a) a tenant has the exclusive occupation of any accommodation, and
(b) the terms on which he holds the accommodation include the use of other accommodation in common with his landlord or in common with his landlord and other persons, and
(c) by reason only of the circumstances mentioned in paragraph (b) above or by reason of those circumstances and the operation of section 6 above, the accommodation referred to in paragraph (a) above is not a dwelling-house let on a protected tenancy,

Part VII of this Act shall apply to the contract notwithstanding that the rent does not include payment for the use of furniture or for services.

NOTES to section 96

Definitions: 'tenant': see s 115(1) below; 'landlord': *Ibid*; 'protected tenancy': see s 115(1) below and s 1 above.

97. Provisions where tenant shares accommodation with persons other than landlord.

(1) Where a tenant has the exclusive occupation of any accommodation (in this section referred to as 'the separate accommodation') and
(a) the terms as between the tenant and his landlord on which he holds the separate accommodation include the use of other accommodation (in this section referred to as 'the shared accommodation') in common with another person or other persons, not being or including the landlord, and
(b) by reason only of the circumstances mentioned in paragraph (a) above, the separate accommodation would not, apart from this section, be a dwelling-house let on or subject to a protected or statutory tenancy,

the separate accommodation shall be deemed to be a dwelling-house let on a protected tenancy or, as the case may be, subject to a statutory tenancy and the following provisions of this section shall have effect.

(2) For the avoidance of doubt it is hereby declared that where, for the purpose of determining the rateable value of the separate accommodation, it is necessary to make an apportionment under this Act, regard is to be had to the circumstances mentioned in subsection (1)(a) above.

(3) For the purposes of any provisions of this Act relating to increases of rent, or to the transfer to tenants of burdens or liabilities previously borne by landlords—
(a) any such change of circumstances as is mentioned in subsection (4) below, being a change affecting so much of the shared accommodation as is living accommodation, shall be deemed to be an alteration of rent;
(b) where, as the result of any such change as is mentioned in paragraph (a) above, the terms on which the separate accommodation is held are on the whole less favourable to the tenant than the previous terms, the rent shall be deemed to be increased, whether or not the sum periodically payable by way of rent is increased;
(c) any increase of rent in respect of any such change as is mentioned in paragraph (a) above where, as a result of the change and of the increase of rent, the terms on which the separate accommodation is held are on the whole not less favourable to the tenant than the previous terms, shall be deemed not to be an increase of rent.

(4) The change of circumstances referred to in subsection (3) above is any increase or diminution of the rights of the tenant to use accommodation in common with others, or any improvement or worsening of accommodation so used by the tenant.

(5) Subject to subsection (6) below, while the tenant is in possession of the separate accommodation (whether as a protected or statutory tenant) any term or condition of the contract of tenancy terminating or modifying, or providing for the termination or modification of, his right to the use of any of the shared accommodation which is living accommodation shall be of no effect.

(6) Where the terms and conditions of the contract of tenancy are such that at any time during the tenancy the persons in common with whom the tenant is entitled to the use of the shared accommodation could be varied, or their number could be increased, nothing in subsection (5) above shall prevent those terms and conditions from having effect so far as they relate to any such variation or increase.

(7) Subject to subsection (8) below and without prejudice to the enforcement of any order made thereunder, while the tenant is in possession of the separate accommodation, no order shall be made for possession of any of the shared accommodation, whether on the application of the immediate landlord of the tenant or on the application of any person under whom that landlord derives title, unless a like order has been made, or is made at the same time, in respect of the separate accommodation; and the provisions of section 11(1) above shall apply accordingly.

(8) Without prejudice to subsection (3) abvove, the sheriff, on the application of the landlord, may make such order, either terminating the right of the tenant to use the whole or any part of the shared accommodation other than living accommodation, or modifying his right to use the whole or any part of the shared accommodation, whether by varying the persons or increasing the number of persons entitled to the use of that accommodation, or otherwise, as the sheriff thinks just:
Provided that no order shall be made under this subsection so as to effect any termination or modification of the rights of the tenant which, apart from subsection (5) above, could not be effected by or under the terms of the contract of tenancy.

(9) Any question arising under subsection (3) above shall be determined on the application either of the landlord or of the tenant by the sheriff whose decision shall be final and conclusive.

(10) In this section, 'living accommodation' means accommodation of such a nature that the fact that it constitutes or is included in the shared accommodation is sufficient to prevent the tenancy from constituting a protected or statutory tenancy of a dwelling-house. [345]

NOTES to section 97
Definitions: 'tenant,' 'tenancy': see s 115(1) below; 'landlord': *Ibid*; 'dwelling-house': see s 1 above; 'protected tenancy': see s 115(1) below and s 1 above; 'statutory tenancy': see s 115(1) below and s 3 above; 'rateable value': see s 115(1) below and s 7 above.

98. Application of Part VII to tenancies falling within section 6.

(1) If and so long as a tenancy is, by virtue only of section 6 above, precluded from being a protected tenancy, it shall be treated for all purposes as a contract to which Part VII of this Act applies, notwithstanding that the rent may not include payment for the use of furniture or for services.

(2) In any case where—
(a) a tenancy which, by virtue only of section 6 above, was precluded from being a protected tenancy ceases to be so precluded and accordingly becomes a protected tenancy, and
(b) before it became a protected tenancy a rent was registered for the dwelling-house concerned under Part VII of this Act,
the amount which is so registered shall be deemed to be registered under Part V of this Act as the rent for the dwelling-house which is let on that tenancy, and that registration shall be deemed to take effect on the day the tenancy becomes a protected tenancy.

(3) Section 46(3) above shall not apply to an application for the registration under Part

V of this Act of a rent different from that which is deemed to be registered as mentioned in subsection (2) above.

(4) The reference in section 47(1)(b) above to a rent being registered for a dwelling-house does not include a rent which is deemed to be registered as mentioned in subsection (2) above.

(5) . . .

(6) If, in a case where a tenancy becomes a protected tenancy as mentioned in subsection (2)(a) above,—
  (a) a notice to quit had been served in respect of the dwelling-house concerned before the date on which the tenancy became a protected tenancy, and
  (b) the period at the end of which that notice to quit takes effect had, before that date, been extended under Part VII of this Act, and
  (c) that period has not expired before that date,
the notice to quit shall take effect on the day following that date (whenever it would otherwise take effect) and, accordingly, on that day the protected tenancy shall become a statutory tenancy. [346]

NOTES to section 98
Amendment: Sub-s (5) was repealed by the Housing (Scotland) Act 1988, (c 43), s 72, Sch 10.
Definitions: 'tenancy': see s 115(1) below; 'protected tenancy': see s 115(1) below and s 1 above; 'dwelling-house': see s 1 above; 'statutory tenancy': see s 115(1) below and s 3 above.

99. Certain sublettings not to exclude any part of sublessor's premises from protection under the Act.

(1) Where the tenant of any premises, consisting of a house or part of a house, has sublet a part, but not the whole, of the premises, then, as against his landlord or any superior landlord, no part of the premises shall be treated as not being a dwelling-house let on or subject to a protected or statutory tenancy by reason only that—
  (a) the terms on which any person claiming under the tenant holds any part of the premises include the use of accommodation in common with other persons; or
  (b) part of the premises is let to any such person at a rent which includes payments in respect of board or attendance.

(2) Nothing in this section affects the rights against, and liabilities to, each other of the tenant and any person claiming under him, or of any two such persons. [347]

NOTES to section 99
Definitions: 'tenant,' 'tenancy': see s 115(1) below; 'landlord': *Ibid*; 'protected tenancy': see s 115(1) below and s 1 above; 'statutory tenancy': see s 115(1) below and s 3 above.

100. Obligation to notify sublettings of dwelling-houses let on or subject to protected or statutory tenancies.

(1) If the tenant of a dwelling-house let on or subject to a protected or statutory tenancy sublets any part of the dwelling-house on a protected tenancy, then, subject to subsection (2) below, he shall within 14 days after the subletting supply the landlord with a statement in writing of he subletting giving particulars of occupancy, including the rent charged.

(2) Subsection (1) above shall not require the supply of a statement in relation to a subletting of any part of a dwelling-house if the particulars which would be required to be included in the statement as to the rent and other conditions of the subtenancy would be the same as in the last statement supplied in accordance with that subsection with respect to a previous subletting of that part.

(3) A tenant who is required to supply a statement in accordance with subsection (1) above and who, without reasonable excuse,—

(a) fails to supply a statement, or
(b) supplies a statement which is false in any material particular,
shall be liable to a fine not exceeding level 1 on the standard scale. **[348]**

NOTES to section 100

Definitions: 'tenant,' 'tenancy': see s 115(1) below; 'dwelling-house': see s 1 above; 'protected tenancy': see s 115(1) below and s 1 above; 'statutory tenancy': see s 115(1) below and s 3 above; 'landlord': see s 115(1) below; 'the standard scale': see s 115(1) below: level 1 is currently £50. See the Increase of Criminal Penalties Etc (Scotland) Order 1984, SI 1984/526.

101. Landlord's consent to work.

(1) It shall be a term of every protected or statutory tenancy (unless express provision is made to the contrary in the tenancy agreement) that the tenant shall not carry out work, other than interior decoration, in relation to the dwelling-house without the consent in writing of the landlord, which shall not be unreasonably withheld.

(2) In this section, and in Schedule 4 to the Tenants' Rights, Etc (Scotland) Act 1980 as it applies to a protected or statutory tenancy, 'work' means—
(a) alteration, improvement or enlargement of the dwelling-house or of any fittings or fixtures;
(b) addition of new fittings or fixtures (including wireless or television aerials);
(c) erection of a garage, shed or other structure,
but does not include repairs or maintenance of any of these.

(3) The provisions of Schedule 4 to the Tenants' Rights, Etc (Scotland) Act 1980 shall have effect as terms of every protected or statutory tenancy as they have effect as terms of secure tenancies. **[349]**

NOTES to section 101

Sub-ss (2) and (3): Schedule 4 of the Tenants' Rights, Etc (Scotland) Act 1980 (c 52) is no longer in force. As a result of Consolidation, those provisions are now to be found in the Housing (Scotland) Act 1987 (c 26), Sch 5.
Definitions: 'protected tenancy': see s 115(1) below and s 1 above; 'statutory tenancy': *Ibid*; 'tenant,' 'tenancy': see s 115(1) below; 'landlord': *Ibid*.

102. Jurisdiction.

(1) The sheriff shall have jurisdiction, either in the course of any proceedings relating to a dwelling-house or on an application made for the purpose by the landlord or the tenant, to determine any question as to the application of this Act or as to any matter which is or may become material for determining any such question.

(2) The sheriff shall have jurisdiction to deal with any claim or other proceeding arising out of any provision of this Act which falls to be dealt with by a court unless that provision stipulates that the Court of Session shall have jurisdiction.

(3) If under any provision of this Act a person takes proceedings in the Court of Session which he could have taken before the sheriff, he shall not be entitled to recover any expenses. **[350]**

NOTES to section 102

Definitions: 'dwelling-house': see s 1 above; 'landlord': see s 115(1) below; 'tenant': *Ibid*.

103. Application to sheriff.

(1) Any application to the sheriff under any of the provisions referred to in subsection (2) below shall be . . . [by way of summary application.]

(2) The provisions of this Act referred to in this subsection are sections 7(2), 31(2), 32(4), . . . and 93(1) and paragraphs [2 and] 7 of Schedule 1. **[351]**

[351]   *Rent (Scotland) Act 1984 (c 58), s 103*

NOTES to section 103

Amendments: Sub-s (1) was amended by the Housing (Scotland) Act 1988, (c 43), s 72, Sch 9, Para 4. Sub-s (2) was amended by *Ibid*, s 72, Sch 9, Sch 10.

104. Rules as to procedure.

The Court of Session may make such act of sederunt and give such directions as they think fit for the purpose of giving effect to the provisions of this Act and may, by such act of sederunt or directions, provide—
(a) for the conduct so far as desirable in private of any proceedings for the purposes of those provisions and for the remission of any fees; and
(b) for any question arising under or in connection with those provisions being referred by consent of the parties interested for final determination by the sheriff sitting as an arbiter or by an arbiter appointed by the sheriff.   [352]

105. Powers of local authorities for the purposes of giving information.

(1) Any local authority shall have power—
(a) to publish information, for the assistance of landlords and tenants, as to their rights and duties under the provisions of this Act and as to the procedure for enforcing those rights or securing the performance of those duties; and
(b) to furnish particulars as to the availability, extent and character of alternative accommodation.

(2) . . .   [353]

NOTES to section 105

Amendment: Sub-s (2) was repealed by the Housing (Scotland) Act 1988, s 72, Sch 10.
Definitions: 'local authority': see s 115(1) below; 'landlord': see s 115(1) below; 'tenant': *Ibid*.

106. Consent of tenant.

(1) Where a dwelling-house which does not satisfy the qualifying conditions is subject to a statutory tenancy and the tenant is unwilling to give his consent to the carrying out of the works required for those conditions to be satisfied, then, if those works were specified in an application for a grant under Part II of the Housing (Financial Provisions) (Scotland) Act 1968 or Part I of the Housing (Scotland) Act 1974 and the application has been approved, the sheriff may, on the application of the landlord, make an order empowering him to enter to carry out the works.

(2) An order under subsection (1) above may be made subject to such conditions as to the time at which the works are to be carried out and as to any provision to be made for the accommodation of the tenant and his household while they are carried out as the sheriff may think fit; and where such an order is made subject to any condition as to time, compliance with that condition shall be deemed to be also compliance with any condition imposed by the local authority under section 27(6A) or section 41(6) of the said Act of 1968 or section 4(2) of the said Act of 1974.

(3) In determining whether to make such an order and, if it is made, subject to what, if any, conditions, the sheriff shall have regard to all the circumstances (other than the means of the tenant) and, in particular, to any disadvantage to the tenant that might be expected to result from the works and the accommodation that might be available for him while the works are carried out.

(4) For the purpose of this section, a dwelling-house satisfies the qualifying conditions if it is provided with all the standard amenities, it is in good repair having regard to its age, character and locality and disregarding internal decorative repair, and it meets the tolerable standard.

(5) In this section 'standard amenities' [and 'tolerable standard' have the meaning respectively assigned to them by section 49(3) of the said Act of 1974.] **[354]**

NOTES to section 106

Amendment: Sub-s (5) was amended by the Law Reform (Miscellaneous Provisions) (Scotland) Act 1985 (c 73), s 59, Sch 2, para 29.

Sub-s (1): Neither the Housing (Financial Provisions) (Scotland) Act 1968 (c 31), nor the Housing (Scotland) Act 1974 (c 45) are still in force. The provisions contained in Part I of the 1974 Act are now to be found in Part XIII of the Housing (Scotland) Act 1987 (c 26).

Sub-s (2): Section 27(6A) of the 1968 Act was repealed by the Housing (Scotland) Act 1974 (c 45), s 50, Sch 5; s 41(6) was repealed by the Housing (Scotland) Act 1974 (c 45), s 50, Sch 5; s 4(2) of the 1974 Act is now s 241 of the Housing (Scotland) Act 1987 (c 26).

Sub-s (5): The Housing (Scotland) Act 1974 is no longer in force. The 'tolerable standard' and 'standard amenities' are now defined in the Housing (Scotland) Act 1987 (c 26), ss 86 and 244(6) respectively.

107. Prosecution of offences.

(1) Offences under this Act are punishable summarily unless the context otherwise requires.

(2) For the avoidance of doubt it is declared that conduct in respect of which a person is made liable to a fine by this Act is an offence.

(3) Where an offence under this Act committed by a body corporate is proved to have been committed with the consent or connivance of, or to be attributable to any neglect on the part of, any director, manager or secretary or other similar officer of the body corporate or any person who was purporting to act in any such capacity, he as well as the body corporate shall be guilty of that offence and shall be liable to be proceeded against and punished accordingly. **[355]**

108. Service of notices on landlord's agents.

(1) Subject to subsection (5) and section 114 below, any document required or authorised by this Act to be served by the tenant of a dwelling-house on the landlord thereof shall be deemed to be duly served on him if it is served—
(a) on any agent of the landlord named as such in the rent book or other similar document; or
(b) on the person who receives the rent of the dwelling-house.

(2) Where a dwelling-house is subject to a regulated tenancy, subsection (1) above shall apply also in relation to any document required or authorised by this Act to be served on the landlord by a person other than the tenant.

(3) Subject to subsection (5) below, if for the purpose of any proceedings (whether civil or criminal) brought or intended to be brought under this Act, any person serves upon any such agent or other person as is referred to in paragraph (a) or paragraph (b) of subsection (1) above a notice in writing requiring the agent or other person to disclose to him the full name and place of abode or place of business of the landlord, that agent or other person shall forthwith comply with the notice.

(4) If any such agent or other persons as is referred to in subsection (3) above fails or refuses forthwith to comply with a notice served on him under that subsection, he shall be liable to a fine not exceeding level 4 on the standard scale, unless he shows to the satisfaction of the court that he did not know, and could not with reasonable diligence have ascertained, such of the facts required by the notice to be disclosed as were not disclosed by him.

(5) Subsections (1) to (4) above shall not apply to any document required or authorised to be served by, or to any proceedings brought or intended to be brought under, Part VII or Part VIII of this Act, other than proceedings under section 89 above. **[356]**

[356]

NOTES to section 108

Definitions: 'tenant,' 'tenancy': see s 115(1) below; 'dwelling-house': see s 1 above; 'landlord': see s 115(1) below; 'regulated tenancy': see s 115(1) below and s 8(1) above; 'the standard scale': see s 115(1) below; level 4 is currently £400. See the Increase of Criminal Penalties Etc (Scotland) Order 1984, SI 1984/526.

109. Rents of subsidised private houses.

(1) Any condition which—
(a) is mentioned in any of the enactments specified in subsection (2) below, or
(b) has effect by virtue of any undertaking or agreement entered into in pursuance of any such enactment,
shall, in so far as it relates to the rent to be charged in respect of any dwelling-house, limit that rent, and if such condition was imposed before 6th July 1957, shall have effect as if it limited that rent, to the amount specified in subsection (3) below.

(2) The enactments referred to in subsection (1) above are—
(a) section 2 of the Housing (Financial Provisions) Act 1924;
(b) section 3 of the Housing (Rural Workers) Act 1926;
(c) section 101 of the Housing (Scotland) Act 1950;
(d) Schedule 4 to the Housing (Financial Provisions) (Scotland) Act 1968.

(3) The amount of rent specified in this subsection shall be an amount equal to the rent which might be properly charged in respect of the dwelling-house by virtue of any such condition as is mentioned in subsection (1) above together with any sum recoverable in respect thereof by way of repairs increase or section 50 increase within the meanings assigned to those expressions in section 133(1) of the Rent (Scotland) Act 1971. **[357]**

110. Restriction on diligence and expenses.

No diligence shall be done in respect of the rent of any dwelling-house let on a protected tenancy or subject to a statutory tenancy except with the leave of the sheriff; and the sheriff shall, with respect to any application for such leave, have the same or similar powers with respect to adjournment, sist, suspension, postponement and otherwise as are conferred by section 12 above in relation to proceedings for possession of such a dwelling-house. **[358]**

NOTES to section 110

Definitions: 'dwelling-house': see s 1 above; 'protected tenancy': see s 115(1) below and s 1 above; 'statutory tenancy': see s 115(1) below and s 3 above; 'tenancy': see s 115(1) below.

111. Implied condition in all protected tenancies.

It shall be a condition of a protected tenancy of a dwelling-house that the tenant shall afford to the landlord access to the dwelling-house and all reasonable facilities for executing therein any repairs which the landlord is entitled to execute. **[359]**

NOTES to section 111

Definitions: 'protected tenancy': see s 115(1) below and s 1 above; 'dwelling-house': see s 1 above; 'tenant,' 'tenancy': see s 115(1) below; 'landlord': *Ibid*.

112. Minimum length of notice to quit.

(1) No notice by a landlord or a tenant to quit any premises let (whether before or after the commencement of this Act) as a dwelling-house shall be valid unless it is in writing and contains such information as may be prescribed and is given not less than four weeks before the date on which it is to take effect.

(2) In this section 'prescribed' means prescribed by regulations made by the Secretary of State by statutory instrument, and a statutory instrument containing any such

Rent (Scotland) Act 1984 (c 58), s 115 [363]

regulations shall be subject to annulment in pursuance of a resolution of either House of Parliament.

(3) Regulations under this section may make different provision in relation to different descriptions of lettings and different circumstances. [360]

NOTES to section 112
Sub-s (2): The Regulations made under this section are the Rent Regulation (Forms and Information Etc) (Scotland) Regulations 1991, SI 1991/1521, and the Assured Tenancies (Notices to Quit Prescribed Information) (Scotland) Regulations 1988, SI 1988/2067. See paras [1510] ff and [1428] ff below respectively.
Definitions: 'landlord': see s 115(1) below; 'tenant': *Ibid*; 'dwelling-house': see s 1 above.

113. Rent book to be provided.

(1) Where under a protected or statutory tenancy rent is payable weekly, it shall be the duty of the landlord to provide a rent book or other similar document for use in respect of the dwelling-house.

(2) If at any time the landlord fails to comply with the requirements of this section he, and any person who on his behalf demands or receives rent in respect of the tenancy, shall be liable to a fine not exceeding level 4 on the standard scale. [361]

NOTES to section 113
Definitions: 'protected tenancy': see s 115(1) below and s 1 above; 'statutory tenancy': see s 115(1) below and s 3 above; 'tenancy': see s 115(1) below; 'landlord':*Ibid*; 'dwelling-house': see s 1 above; 'the standard scale': see s 115(1) below; level 4 is currently £1000. See the Increase of Criminal Penalties Etc (Scotland) Order 1984, SI 1984/526.
Regulations: See the Rent Regulation (Forms and Information Etc) (Scotland) Regulations 1991, SI 1991/1521, paras [1510] below.

114. Service of notices.

(1) A notice or other document which requires to be served on a person under any provision of this Act may be given to him—
 (a) by delivering it to him;
 (b) by leaving it at his proper address; or
 (c) by sending it by recorded delivery post to him at that address.

(2) For the purposes of this section and of section 7 of the Interpretation Act 1978 (references to service by post) in its application to this section, a person's proper address shall be his last known address. [362]

115. Interpretation.

(1) In this Act, except where the context otherwise requires,—
'agricultural land' means land used only for agricultural or pastoral purposes or used as woodlands, market gardens, orchards, allotments or allotment gardens and any lands exceeding one-quarter of an acre used for the purpose of poultry farming, but does not include any lands occupied together with a house as a park, garden or pleasure ground or any land kept or preserved mainly or exclusively for sporting purposes;
the appropriate day' has the meaning assigned to it by section 7(3) above;
'converted tenancy' means a tenancy which became a regulated tenancy by virtue of Part VI of, or paragraph 5 of Schedule 2 to, the Rent (Scotland) Act 1971, section 34 of the Housing (Financial Provisions) (Scotland) Act 1972 or section 46(1) of the Tenants' Rights, Etc (Scotland) Act 1980; and 'the conversion' means the time when the tenancy became a regulated tenancy;
'heritable security' has the same meaning as in the Conveyancing (Scotland) Act 1924 except that it includes a security constituted by ex facie absolute disposition or

assignation and a standard security within the meaning of Part II of the Conveyancing and Feudal Reform (Scotland) Act 1970;

'landlord' includes any person from time to time deriving title under the original landlord and also includes, in relation to any dwelling-house, any person other than the tenant who is, or but for Part II of this Act would be, entitled to possession of the dwelling-house;

'let' includes 'sub-let';

'local authority' means an islands council or district council;

'order for possession' means decree of removing or warrant of ejection or other like order; and 'action for possession' and 'proceedimgs for possession' shall be construed accordingly;

'Part VII contract' has the meaning assigned to it in section 63(7) above;

'premium' includes any fine or other like sum and any other pecuniary consideration in addition to rent;

'prescribed' means prescribed by regulations made by the Secretary of State by statutory instrument;

'protected furnished tenancy', 'regulated furnished tenancy' and 'statutory furnished tenancy' mean a protected or, as the case may be, regulated or statutory tenancy—

(a) under which the dwelling-house concerned is bona fide let at a rent which includes payments in respect of the use of furniture, and

(b) in respect of which the amount of rent which is fairly attributable to such use, having regard to the value of that use to the tenant, forms a substantial part of the whole rent;

'protected tenant' and 'protected tenancy' shall be construed in accordance with section 1 above;

'rateable value' shall be construed in accordance with section 7 above;

'rates' means any charges payable in respect of a rate as defined in the Local Government (Scotland) Act 1947;

'regulated tenancy' shall be construed in accordance with section 8 above;

'rent assessment committee' has the meaning assigned to it by section 44 above;

'the standard scale' means the standard scale of fines set out in section 298G of the Criminal Procedure (Scotland) Act 1975;

'the statutory maximum' means the prescribed sum as defined in section 289B(6) of the Criminal Procedure (Scotland) Act 1975;

'statutory tenant' and 'statutory tenancy' shall be construed in accordance with section 3 above;

'tenancy' includes 'sub-tenancy';

'tenancy at a low rent' has the meaning assigned to it by section 2(3) above;

'tenant' includes statutory tenant and also includes a sub-tenant and any person deriving title under the original tenant or sub-tenant.

(2) Any reference in any enactment to a rent tribunal shall have effect as if it were a reference to a rent assessment committee within the meaning of section 44 above.

(3) Except in so far as the context otherwise requires, any reference in this Act to, or to anything done or omitted under, any provision of this Act shall be construed as including a reference to, or to anything done or omitted under, any enactment which (being repealed) is substantially re-enacted in the said provision.

116. Application to Crown property.

(1) Subject to sections 4 and 63(3)(a) above, this Act shall apply in relation to premises in which there subsists, or at any material time subsisted, a Crown interest as it applies in relation to premises in which no such interest subsists or ever subsisted.

(2) In this section 'Crown interest' means an interest which belongs to Her Majesty in right of the Crown or of the Duchy of Lancaster or to the Duchy of Cornwall, or to a government department, or which is held in trust for Her Majesty for the purposes of a government department.

(3) Where an interest belongs to Her Majesty in right of the Duchy of Lancaster, for the purposes of this Act the Chancellor of the Duchy of Lancaster shall be deemed to be the owner of the interest.

(4) Where an interest belongs to the Duchy of Cornwall, for the purposes of this Act the Secretary of the Duchy of Cornwall shall be deemed to be the owner of the interest. [364]

117. Amendments, transitional provisions, repeals, etc.

(1) Subject to subsection (2) below, the enactments specified in Schedule 8 to this Act shall have effect subject to the amendments specifed in that Schedule.

(2) The savings and transitional provisions in Schedule 9 to this Act shall have effect.

(3) Subject to subsection (2) above, the enactments specified in Schedule 10 to this Act are hereby repealed to the extent specified in the third column of that Schedule. [365]

118. Short title, commencement and extent.

(1) This Act may be cited as the Rent (Scotland) Act 1984.

(2) This Act shall come into force at the end of the period of three months beginning with the date on which it is passed.

(3) This Act shall extend to Scotland only. [366]

NOTES to section 118

Sub-s (2): The Act was passed on 31 October 1984 and came into force on 1 February 1985.

SCHEDULES

SCHEDULE 1

Statutory Tenants by Succession

1. The provisions of paragraph 2 or, as the case may be, paragraph 3 of this Schedule shall have effect for the purpose of determining who is the statutory tenant of a dwelling-house by succession after the death of the person (in this Schedule referred to as 'the original tenant') who, immediately before his death, was a protected tenant of the dwelling-house of the statutory tenant of it by virtue of his previous protected tenancy. [367]

2. The original tenant's spouse where the dwelling-house was [that spouse's] only or principal home at the time of the tenant's death shall be the statutory tenant so long as the said spouse retains possession of the dwelling-house without being entitled to do so under a contractual tenancy. [368]

3. Where paragraph 2 above does not apply, but a person who was a member of the original tenant's family was residing with him at the time of and for the period of six months immediately before his death then, after his death, that person or if there is more than one such person such one of them as may be decided by agreement, or in default of agreement by the sheriff, shall be the statutory tenant so long as he retains possession of the dwelling-house without being entitled to do so under a contractual tenancy. [369]

4. A person who becomes the statutory tenant of a dwelling-house by virtue of paragraph 2 or paragraph 3 above is in this Schedule referred to as 'the first successor'. [370]

5. If, immediately before his death, the first sucessor was still a statutory tenant, the provisions of paragraph 6 or, as the case may be, paragraph 7 below shall have effect for the purpose of determining who is the statutory tenant after the death of the first successor. **[371]**

6. The first successor's spouse, where the dwelling-house was his only or principal home at the time of the tenant's death, shall be the statutory tenant so long as the said spouse retains possession of the dwelling-house without being entitled to do so under a contractual tenancy. **[372]**

7. Where paragraph 6 above does not apply but a person who was a member of the first successor's family was residing with him at the time of and for the period of six months immediately before his death then, after his death, that person or if there is more than one such person such one of them as may be decided by agreement, or in default of agreement by the sheriff, shall be the statutory tenant so long as he retains possession of the dwelling-house without being entitled to do so under a contractual tenancy. **[373]**

8.—(1) Where after a succession the successor becomes the tenant of the dwelling-house by the grant to him of another tenancy, 'the original tenant' and 'the first successor' in this Schedule shall, in relation to that other tenancy, mean the persons who were respectively the original tenant and the first successor at the time of the succession, and accordingly—
  (a) if the successor was the first successor, and immediately before his death he was still the tenant (whether protected or statutory), paragraphs 6 and 7 above shall apply on his death,
  (b) if the successor was not the first successor, no person shall become a statutory tenant on his death by virtue of this Schedule.

(2) Sub-paragraph (1) above applies even if—
  (a) a successor enters into more than one other tenancy of the dwelling-house, and
  (b) both the first successor, and the successor on his death, enter into other tenancies of the dwelling-house.

(3) This paragraph shall apply—
  (a) as respects any succession which take place on or after 27th August 1972; and
  (b) as respects a succession which took place before that date if the tenancy granted after the succession, or the first of those tenancies, was granted on or after that date.

(4) In this paragraph—
'succession' means the occasion on which a person becomes the statutory tenant of a dwelling-house by virtue of this Schedule and 'successor' shall be construed accordingly.
'tenancy' means 'regulated tenancy' and 'tenancies' shall be construed accordingly. **[374]**

9. Paragraphs 5 to 7 above do not apply where the statutory tenancy of the original tenant arose by virtue of section 20 of the Rent Act 1965. **[375]**

NOTES to Schedule 1
Amendment: Para 2 was amended by the Housing (Scotland) Act 1988, (c 43), s 72, Sch 9, para 5.
Definitions: 'statutory tenant': see s 115(1) and s 3 above; 'dwelling-house': see s 1 above; 'protected tenant': see s 115(1) and s 1 above; 'tenant,' 'tenancy': see s 115(1) above.

[SCHEDULE 1A

Statutory or Statutory Assured Tenants by Succession in a case to which section 3A(1) applies

1. The provisions of paragraph 2 of this Schedule shall have effect tor the purpose of determining who is the statutory tenant of a dwelling-house by succession after the death of the person (in this Schedule referred to as 'the original tenant') who, immediately before his death, was a protected tenant of the dwelling-house or the statutory tenant of it by virtue of his previous protected tenancy. [376]

2.—(1) The original tenant's spouse where the dwelling-house was that spouse's only or principal home at the time of the tenant's death shall be the statutory tenant so long as the said spouse retains possession of the dwelling-house without being entitled to do so under a contractual tenancy. [377]

(2) For the purposes of the paragraph, a person who was living with the original tenant as his or her wife or husband shall be treated as the spouse of the original tenant.

(3) If, immediately after the death of the original tenant, there is, by virtue of sub-paragraph (2) above, more than one person who fulfils the conditions in sub-paragraph (1) above, such one of them as then has occupancy rights under section 18 of the Matrimonial Homes (Family Protection) (Scotland) Act 1981 (rights of cohabiting couples) or, if neither or none of them has such rights, such one of them as may be decided by the sheriff, shall be treated as the surviving spouse for the purposes of this paragraph.

3. Where paragraph 2 above does not apply but a person who was a member of the original tenant's family was residing with him in the dwelling-house—
   (a) continuously for the period commencing six months before the date of coming into force of section 46 of the Housing (Scotland) Act 1988 and ending on the tenant's death (where the person was so residing on the said date); or
   (b) at the time of and for the period of two years immediately before the tenant's death,
then, after the tenant's death, that person or if there is more than one such person such one of them as may be decided by agreement, or in default of agreement by the sheriff, shall be entitled to a statutory assured tenancy of the dwelling-house by succession. [378]

4. A person who becomes the statutory tenant of a dwelling-house by virtue of paragraph 2 above is in this Schedule referred to as 'the first successor'. [379]

5. If, immediately before his death, the first successor was still a statutory tenant, the provisions of paragraph 6 below shall have effect for the purpose of determining who is entitled to a statutory assured tenancy of the dwelling-house by succession after the death of the first successor. [380]

6. Where a person who—
   (a) was a member of the original tenant's family immediately before that tenant's death; and
   (b) was a member of the first successor's family immediately before the first successor's death,
was residing with the first successor in the dwelling-house at the time of, and for the period of two years immediately before, the first successor's death, that person, or if there is more than one such person, such one of them as may be decided by agreement or, in default of agreement, by the sheriff, shall be entitled to a statutory assured tenancy of the dwelling-house by succession. [381]

7.—(1) Where after a succession the successor becomes the tenant of the dwelling-house by the grant to him of another tenancy, 'the original tenant' and 'the first successor'

in this Schedule shall, in relation to that other tenancy, mean the persons who were respectively the original tenant and the first successor at the time of the succession, and accordingly—
- (a) if the successor was the first successor, and immediately before his death he was still the tenant (whether protected or statutory), paragraph 6 above shall apply on his death;
- (b) if the successor was not the first successor, no person shall become a statutory tenant on his death by virtue of this Schedule.

(2) Sub-paragraph (1) above applies even if—
- (a) a successor enters into more than one other tenancy of the dwelling-house; and
- (b) both the first successor, and the successor on this death, enter into other tenancies of the dwelling-house.

(3) In this paragraph 'succession' means the occasion on which a person becomes the statutory or statutory assured tenant of a dwelling-house by virtue of this Schedule and 'successor' shall be construed accordingly. [382]

8. Paragraphs 5 and 6 above do not apply where the statutory tenancy of the original tenant arose by virtue of section 20 of the Rent Act 1965.] [383]

NOTES to Schedule 1A
Amendments: Schedule 1A was added by the Housing (Scotland) Act 1988, (c 43), s 46, Sch 6.
Definitions: 'statutory tenant': see s 115(1) and s 3 above; 'dwelling-house': see s 1 above; 'protected tenancy': see s 115(1) and s 1 above; 'tenant,' 'tenancy': see s 115(1) above; 'statutory assured tenancy': see Housing (Scotland) Act 1988, (c 43), s 16(1) and s 55(1).

[SCHEDULE 1B]

STATUTORY ASSURED TENANTS BY SUCCESSION IN A CASE TO WHICH SECTION 3A(2) APPLIES

1. The provisions of this Schedule shall have effect for the purpose of determining who is the statutory assured tenant of a dwelling-house by succession after the death of the person (in this Schedule referred to as 'the first successor') who, immediately before his death, was the statutory tenant of the dwelling-house by virtue of paragraph 2 or paragraph 3 of Schedule 1 above. [384]

2. If, immediately before his death, the first successor was still a statutory tenant, the provisions of paragraph 3 below shall have effect for the purpose of determining who is entitled to a statutory assured tenancy of the dwelling-house by succession after the death of the first successor. [385]

3. Where a person who—
- (a) was a member of the original tenant's family immediately before that tenant's death; and
- (b) was a member of the first successor's family immediately before the first successor's death,

was residing with the first successor in the dwelling-house—
- (i) continuously for the period commencing six months before the date of coming into force of section 46 of the Housing (Scotland) Act 1988 and ending on the tenant's death (where the person was so residing on the said date); or
- (ii) at the time of and for the period of two years immediately before the tenant's death,

that person, or if there is more than one such person, such one of them as may be decided by agreement or, in default of agreement, by the sheriff, shall be entitled to a statutory assured tenancy of the dwelling-house by succession. [386]

4.—(1) Where after a succession the successor becomes the tenant of the dwelling-house by the grant to him of another tenancy, 'the original tenant' and 'the first successor' in this Schedule shall, in relation to that other tenancy, mean the persons who were respectively the original tenant and the first successor at the time of the succession, and accordingly—
  (a) if the successor was the first successor, and immediately before his death he was still the tenant (whether protected or statutory), paragraph 3 above shall apply on his death;
  (b) if the successor was not the first successor, no person shall become a statutory tenant on his death by virtue of this Schedule.

(2) Sub-paragraph (1) above applies even if—
  (a) a successor enters into more than one other tenancy of the dwelling-house; and
  (b) both the first successor, and the successor on his death, enter into other tenancies of the dwelling-house.

(3) In this paragraph 'succession' means the occasion on which a person becomes the statutory assured tenant of a dwelling-house by virtue of this Schedule and 'successor' shall be construed accordingly. **[387]**

5. Paragraphs 2 and 3 above do not apply where the statutory tenancy of the original tenant arose by virtue of section 20 of the Rent Act 1965. **[388]**

Part II
Statutory Assured Tenants by Succession—Modification of Enactments

2. In relation to the assured tenancy to which the person becomes entitled by succession, section 18 of this Act shall have effect as if in subsection (3) after the word 'established' there were inserted the words 'or that the circumstances are as specified in any of Cases 11, 12, 17, 18, 19, and 21 in Schedule 2 to the Rent (Scotland) Act 1984'. **[389]**

3.—(1) In relation to the assured tenancy to which the person becomes entitled by succession, any notice given for the purpose of Case 13, Case 14 or Case 16 of Schedule 2 to the Rent (Scotland) Act 1984 to the original tenant (within the meaning of Schedule I to the Rent (Scotland) Act 1984) shall be treated as having been given for the purposes of whichever of Grounds 4 to 6 in Schedule 5 to this Act corresponds to the Case in question.

(2) Where sub-paragraph (1) above applies, the regulated tenancy of the said original tenant shall be treated, in relation to the assured tenancy of the person so entitled, as 'the earlier tenancy' for the purposes of Part IV of Schedule 5 to this Act.] **[390]**

NOTES to Schedule 1B
Amendment: Schedule 1B was added by the Housing (Scotland) Act 1988, (c 43), s 46, Sch 6.
Definitions: 'statutory assured tenancy': see Housing (Scotland) Act 1988, (c 43), s 16(1) and s 55(1); 'statutory tenant': see s 115(1) and s 3 above; 'tenant,' 'tenancy': see s 115(1) above.

SCHEDULE 2

GROUNDS FOR POSSESSION OF DWELLING-HOUSES LET ON OR SUBJECT TO PROTECTED OR STATUTORY TENANCIES

PART I
CASES IN WHICH COURT MAY ORDER POSSESSION

Case 1

Where any rent lawfully due from the tenant has not been paid, or any obligation of the protected or statutory tenancy which arises under this Act, or—
  (a) in the case of a protected tenancy, any other obligation of the tenancy, in so far as it is consistent with the provisions of Part II of this Act, or
  (b) in the case of a statutory tenancy, any other obligation of the previous protected tenancy which is appliable to the statutory tenancy,
has been broken or not performed.

In determining whether any rent lawfully due from a tenant has been paid in any case where the rent is payable in advance, any sums paid by the tenant in satisfaction of a decree or decrees for rent and expenses shall, if the action in which any such decree was obtained was raised before the expiry of the period in respect of which the rent sued for was due, be imputed wholly to rent and not to expenses.

Case 2

Where the tenant or any person residing or lodging with him or any sub-tenant of his has been guilty of conduct which is a nuisance or annoyance to adjoining occupiers, or has been convicted of using the dwelling-house or allowing the dwelling-house to be used for immoral or illegal purposes.

Case 3

Where the condition of the dwelling-house has, in the opinion of the court, deteriorated owing to acts of waste by, or the neglect or default of, the tenant or any person residing or lodging with him or any sub-tenant of his and, in the case of any act of waste by, or the neglect or default of, a person lodging with the tenant or a sub-tenant of his, where the court is satisfied that the tenant has not, before the making of the order in question, taken such steps as he ought reasonably to have taken for the removal of the lodger or sub-tenant, as the case may be.

Case 4

Where the condition of any furniture provided for use under the tenancy has, in the opinion of the court, deteriorated owing to ill-treatment by the tenant or any person residing or lodging with him or any sub-tenant of his and, in the case of any ill-treatment by a person lodging with the tenant or a sub-tenant or his, where the court is satisfied that the tenant has not, before the making of the order in question, taken such steps as he ought reasonably to have taken for the removal or the lodger or sub-tenant, as the case may be.

Case 5

Where the tenant has given notice to quit and, in consequence of that notice, the landlord has contracted to sell or let the dwelling-house or has taken any other steps as the result of which he would, in the opinion of the court, be seriously prejudiced if he could not obtain possession.

Case 6

Where, without the consent of the landlord, the tenant has, at any time after 8th December 1965 or, in the case of a regulated furnished tenancy, after 14th August 1974 or, in the case of a tenancy which became a regulated tenancy by virtue of section 4(3) above, after 30th November 1980, assigned or sub-let the whole of the dwelling-house or sub-let part of the dwelling-house the remainder already being sub-let.

Case 7

Where the dwelling-house is reasonably required by the landlord for occupation as a residence for some person engaged in his whole-time employment, or in the whole-time employment of some tenant from him or with whom, conditional on housing accommodation being provided, a contract for such employment has been entered into, and either
- (a) the tenant was in the employment of the landlord or a former landlord, and the dwelling-house was let to him in consequence of that employment and he has ceased to be in that employment; or
- (b) the court is satisfied by a certificate of the Secretary of State that the person for whose occupation the dwelling-house is required by the landlord is, or is to be, employed on work necessary for the proper working of an agricultural holding or as an estate workman on the maintenance and repair of the buildings, plant or equipment of agricultural holdings comprised in the estate.

Case 8

Where the dwelling-house is reasonably required by the landlord for occupation as a residence for—
- (a) himself, or
- (b) any son or daughter of his over 18 years of age, or
- (c) his father or mother, or
- (d) if the dwelling-house is let on or subject to a regulated tenancy, the father or mother of his wife or husband,

and the landlord did not become landlord by purchasing the dwelling-house or any interest therein after 23rd March 1965 or, in the case of a dwelling-house subject to a regulated furnished tenancy, after 24th May 1974 or, if the dwelling-house was on 7th November 1956 let on or subject to a controlled tenancy, after 7th November 1956.

Case 9

Where the court is satisifed that the rent charged by the tenant—
- (a) for any sub-let part of the dwelling-house which is a dwelling-house let on a protected tenancy or subject to a statutory tenancy is or was in excess of the maximum rent for the time being recoverable for that part, having regard to the provisions of Part IV of this Act, or
- (b) for any sub-let part of the dwelling-house which is subject to a contract to which Part VII of this act applies is or was in excess of the maximum (if any) which it is lawful for the lessor, within the meaning of that Part, to require or receive having regard to the provisions of that Part.

Case 10

Where the dwelling-house is so overcrowded as to be dangerous or injurious to the health of the inmates, and the court is satisfied that the overcrowding could have been abated by the removal of any lodger or sub-tenant (not being a parent or child of the tenant) whom it would, having regard to all the circumstances of the case, including the question whether other accommodation is available for him, have been reasonable to remove, and that the tenant has not taken such steps as he ought reasonably to have taken for his removal.

Part II
Cases in which Court must Order Possession where Dwelling-House Subject to Regulated Tenancy

Case 11

[Where a person (in this case referred to as 'the owner-occupier') who let the dwelling-house on a regulated tenancy had, at any time before the letting, occupied it as his residence] and—
  (a) not later than the relevant date the landlord gave notice in writing to the tenant that possession might be recovered under this Case (notwithstanding, in the case of a notice given under this paragraph before 1st December 1980, that the notice may not have referred to any of sub-paragraphs (ii) to (vi) of paragraph (c)); and
  (b) the dwelling-house has not, since 8th December 1965 or, in the case of a dwelling-house subject to a regulated furnished tenancy, 14th August 1974, been let by the owner-occupier on a regulated tenancy with respect to which the condition mentioned in paragraph (a) above was not satisfied; and
  (c) the court is satisfied that—
      (i) the dwelling-house is required as a residence for the owner-occupier or any member of his family who resided with the owner-occupier when he last occupied the dwelling-house as a residence; or
      (ii) the owner-occupier has died, and the dwelling-house is required as a residence for a member of his family who was residing with him at the time of his death; or
      (iii) the owner-occupier has died, and the dwelling-house is required as a residence by a person inheriting the dwelling-house under the will of the owner-occupier or on his intestacy; or
      (iv) the owner-occupier has died and his personal representatives wish to dispose of the dwelling-house with vacant possession; or
      (v) the dwelling-house is not reasonably suitable to the needs of the owner-occupier, having regard to his place of work, and he requires it for the purpose of disposing of it with vacant possession and of using the proceeds of that disposal in acquiring as his residence a dwelling-house which is more suitable to those needs; or
      (vi) the dwelling-house is subject to a heritable security, granted before the creation of the tenancy, and as the result of a default by the debtor the creditor is entitled to sell the dwelling-house and requires it for the purpose of disposing of it with vacant possession in exercise of that entitlement:

Provided that if the court is of the opinion that, notwithstanding that the condition in paragraph (a) or paragraph (b) above is not complied with, it is just and equitable to make an order for possession of the dwelling-house, the court may dispense with the requirements of either or both of those paragraphs, as the case may require.

For the purposes of this Case, the giving of a notice before 14th August 1974 under section 73 above shall be treated in the case of a regulated furnished tenancy as compliance with paragraph (a) above.

['Where the dwelling-house has been let by the owner-occupier on a protected tenancy (in this paragraph referred to as 'the earlier tenancy') granted on or after 16th November 1984 but not later than the end of the period of two months beginning with the commencement of the Rent (Amendment) Act 1985 and either—
  (i) the earlier tenancy was a short tenancy (within the meaning of section 9 above), or
  (ii) the conditions mentioned in paragraphs (a) to (c) of Case 21 were satisfied with respect to the dwelling-house and the earlier tenancy,
then for the purposes of paragraph (b) above the condition in paragraph (a) above is to be treated as having been satisfied with respect to the earlier tenancy.]

Case 12

Where a person (in this Case referred to as 'the owner') who acquired the dwelling-house or any interest therein with a view to occupying it as his residence at such time as he might retire from regular employment let it on a regulated tenancy before he has so retired and—
(a) not later than the relevant date the landlord gave notice in writing to the tenant that possession might be recovered under this Case (notwithstanding, in the case of a notice given under this paragraph before 1st December 1980, that the notice may not have referred to any of sub-paragraphs (iii) to (v) of paragraph (c)); and
(b) the dwelling-house has not since 14th August 1974 been let by the owner on a protected tenancy with respect to which the condition mentioned in paragraph (a) above was not satisfied; and
(c) the court is satisfied—
  (i) that the owner has retired from regular employment and requires the dwelling-house as a residence; or
  (ii) that the owner has died and the dwelling-house is required as a residence for a member of his family who was residing with him at the time of his death or for a person inheriting the dwelling-house under the will of the owner or on his intestacy; or
  (iii) that the owner has died and his personal representatives wish to dispose of the dwelling-house with vacant possession; or
  (iv) that the dwelling-house is subject to a heritable security, granted before the creation of the tenancy, and as the result of a default by the debtor the creditor is entitled to sell the dwelling-house and requires it for the purpose of disposing of it with vacant possession in exercise of that entitlement; or
  (v) that the dwelling-house is no longer reasonably suitable to the needs of the owner on his retirement, and he requires it for the purpose of disposing of it with vacant possession and of using the proceeds of that disposal in acquiring for his retirement a dwelling-house which is more suitable to those needs:

Provided that if the court is of the opinion that, notwithstanding that the condition in paragraph (a) or paragraph (b) above is not complied with, it is just and equitable to make an order for possession of the dwelling-house, the court may dispense with the requirements of either or both of those paragraphs, as the case may require.

Case 13

Where the dwelling-house is let under a tenancy for a specified period not exceeding eight months and—
(a) not later than the relevant date the landlord gave notice in writing to the tenant that possession might be recovered under this Case; and
(b) the dwelling-house was, at some time within the period of 12 months ending on the relevant date occupied under a right to occupy it for a holiday;

and for the purposes of this Case a tenancy shall be treated as being for a specified period—
  (i) of less than eight months, if it is determinable at the option of the landlord (other than in the event of an irritancy being incurred) before the expiration of eight months from the commencement of the period of the tenancy, and
  (ii) of eight months or more, if it confers on the tenant an option for renewal of the tenancy for a period which, together with the original period, amounts to eight months or more, and it is not determinable as mentioned in paragraph (i) above.

Case 14

Where the dwelling-house is let under a tenancy for a specified period not exceeding 12 months and—
(a) not later than the relevant date the landlord gave notice in writing to the tenant that possession might be recovered under this Case; and

(b) at some time within the period of 12 months ending on the relevant date the dwelling-house was subject to such a tenancy as is referred to in section 2(1)(c) above;

and for the purposes of this Case a tenancy shall be treated as being for a specified period—

(i) of less than 12 months, if it is determinable at the option of the landlord (other than in the event of an irritancy being incurred) before the expiration of 12 months from the commencement of the period of the tenancy, and

(ii) of 12 months or more, if it confers on the tenant an option for renewal of the tenancy for a period which, together with the original period, amounts to 12 months or more, and it is not determinable as mentioned in paragraph (i) above.

Case 15

Where—

(a) the dwelling-house was let on a short tenancy within the meaning of section 9 above; or

(b) in the opinion of the Court it is just and equitable that the tenancy should be treated as a short tenancy within the meaning of the said section 9, notwithstanding that a requirement of subsection (1)(d) or (e) of that section has not been complied with,

and the short tenancy has terminated:

Provided that, where a further tenancy has been created by agreement between the landlord and the tenant no application for an order for possession under this Case shall be made before the end of the period of that tenancy.

Case 16

Where the dwelling-house is held for the purpose of being available for occupation by a minister or a full-time lay missionary of any religious denomination as a residence from which to perform the duties of his office and the dwelling-house has been let on a regulated tenancy, and—

(a) not later than the relevant date, the tenant was given notice in writing that possession might be recovered under this Case, and

(b) the court is satisfied that the dwelling-house is required for occupation by such a minister or missionary as such a residence.

Case 17

Where the dwelling-house was at any time occupied by a person under the terms of his employment as a person employed in agriculture and the dwelling-house has been let on a regulated tenancy, and—

(a) the tenant neither is nor at any time was so employed by the landlord and is not the widow of a person who was so employed, and

(b) not later than the relevant date, the tenant was given notice in writing that possession might be recovered under this Case, and

(c) the court is satisfied that the dwelling-house is required for occupation by a person employed or to be employed by the landlord in agriculture;

and for the purposes of this Case 'employed', 'employment' and 'agriculture' have the same meanings as in the Agricultural Wages (Scotland) Act 1949.

Case 18

Where proposals for amalgamation, approved for the purposes of a scheme under section 26 of the Agriculture Act 1967, have been carried out and, at the time when the proposals were submitted, the dwelling-house was occupied by a person responsible

(whether as owner, tenant, or servant or agent of another) for the control of the farming of any part of the land comprised in the amalgamation and
  (a) after the carrying out of the proposals, the dwelling-house was let on a regulated tenancy otherwise than to, or to the widow of, either a person ceasing to be so responsible as part of the amalgamation or a person who is, or at any time was, employed by the landlord in agriculture, and
  (b) not later than the relevant date, the tenant was given notice in writing that possession might be recovered under this Case, and
  (c) the court is satisfied that the dwelling-house is required for occupation by a person employed or to be employed by the landlord in agriculture, and
  (d) the proceedings for possession are commenced by the landlord at any time during the period of five years beginning with the date on which the proposals for the amalgamation were approved or, if occupation of the dwelling-house after the amalgamation continued in, or was first taken by, a person ceasing to be responsible as mentioned in paragraph (a) above or his widow, during a period expiring three years after the date on which the dwelling-house next became unoccupied;
and for purposes of this Case 'employed' and 'agriculture' have the same meanings as in the Agricultural Wages (Scotland) Act 1949 and 'amalgamation' has the same meaning as in Part II of the Agriculture Act 1967.

Case 19

Where a dwelling-house has been let on a regulated tenancy and—
  (a) the last occupier of the dwelling-house before the relevant date was a person, or the widow of a person, who was at some time during his occupation responsible (whether as owner, tenant, or servant or agent of another) for the control of the farming of land which formed, together with the dwelling-house, an agricultural unit within the meaning of the Agriculture (Scotland) Act 1948, and
  (b) the tenant is neither—
    (i) a person, or the widow of a person, who is or has at any time been responsible for the control of the farming of any part of the said land, nor
    (ii) a person, or the widow of a person, who is or at any time was employed by the landlord in agriculture, and
  (c) the creation of the tenancy was not preceded by the carrying out in connection with any of the said land of an amalgamation approved for the purposes of a scheme under section 26 of the Agriculture Act 1967, and
  (d) not later than the relevant date, the tenant was given notice in writing that possession might be recovered under this Case, and
  (e) the court is satisifed that the dwelling-house is required for occupation either by a person responsible or to be responsible (whether as owner, tenant, or servant or agent of another) for the control of the farming of any part of the said land or by a person employed or to be employed by the landlord in agriculture;
and for the purposes of this Case 'employed' and 'agriculture' have the same meanings as in the Agricultural Wages (Scotland) Act 1949 and 'amalgamation' has the same meaning as in Part II of the Agriculture Act 1967.

Case 20

Where a dwelling-house has been designed or adapted for occupation by a person whose special needs require accommodation of the kind provided by the dwelling-house and—
  (a) there is no longer a person with such special needs occupying the dwelling-house; and
  (b) the court is satisfied that the landlord requires it for occupation (whether alone or with other members of his family) by a person who has such special needs.

Case 21

Where the dwelling-house is let by a person (in this Case referred to as 'the owner') at any time after 30th November 1980 and—
- (a) at the time when the owner acquired the dwelling-house he was a member of the regular armed forces of the Crown;
- (b) at the relevant date the owner was a member of the regular armed forces of the Crown;
- (c) not later than the relevant date the owner gave notice in writing to the tenant that possession might be recovered under this Case;
- (d) the dwelling-house has not, since 1st December 1980, been let by the owner on a protected tenancy with respect to which the condition mentioned in paragraph (c) above was not satisfied; and
- (e) the court is of the opinion that—
  - (i) the dwelling-house is required as a residence for the owner; or
  - (ii) of the conditions set out in paragraph (c) of Case 11 of this Schedule one of those in subparagraphs (ii) to (vi) would be satisfied if the owner of the dwelling-house concerned was the owner occupier:

Provided that if the court is of the opinion that, notwithstanding that the condition in paragraph (c) or paragraph (d) above is not complied with, it is just and equitable to make an order for possession of the dwelling-house, the court may dispense with the requirements of either or both of these paragraphs, as the case may require.

In this Case 'regular armed forces of the Crown' has the same meaning as in section 1 of the House of Commons Disqualification Act 1975.

PART III
PROVISIONS APPLICABLE TO CASE 8 AND PART II ABOVE

1. A court shall not make an order for possession of a dwelling-house by reason only that the circumstances of the case fall within Case 8 in Part I of this Schedule if the court is satisfied that, having regard to all the circumstances of the case, including the question whether other accommodation is available for the landlord or the tenant, greater hardship would be caused by granting the order than by refusing to grant it.

2. Any reference in Part II of this Schedule to the relevant date shall be construed as follows:—
- (a) except in the case of a regulated furnished tenancy, if the protected tenancy, or in the case of a statutory tenancy the previous contractual tenancy, was created before 8th December 1965, the relevant date means 7th June 1966;
- (b) in the case of a regulated furnished tenancy, if the tenancy or, in the case of a statutory furnished tenancy, the previous contractual tenancy was created before 14th August 1974, the relevant date means 14th February 1975;
- (c) in the case of a tenancy which became a regulated tenancy by virtue of section 4(3) above, the relevant date means 8th February 1981; and
- (d) in any other case, the relevant date means the date of the commencement of the regulated tenancy in question.

PART IV
SUITABLE ALTERNATIVE ACCOMMODATION

1. For the purposes of section 11(1)(a) above, a certificate of the housing authority for the district in which the dwelling-house in question is situated, certifying that the authority will provide suitable alternative accommodation for the tenant by a date specified in the certificate, shall be conclusive evidence that suitable alternative accommodation will be available for him by that date.

2. Where no such certificate as is mentioned in paragraph 1 above is produced to the court, accommodation shall be deemed to be suitable for the purposes of section 11(1)(a) above if it consists of either—
  (a) premises which are to be let as a separate dwelling such that they will then be let on a protected tenancy, or
  (b) premises to be let as a separate dwelling on terms which will, in the opinion of the court, afford to the tenant security of tenure reasonably equivalent to the security afforded by Part II of this Act in the case of a protected tenancy,
and, in the opinion of the court, the accommodation fulfils the relevant conditions as defined in paragraph 3 below. [396]

3.—(1) For the purposes of paragraph 2 above, the relevant conditions are that the accommodation is reasonably suitable to the needs of the tenant and his family as regards proximity to place of work, and either—
  (a) similar as regards rental and extent to the accommodation afforded by dwelling-houses provided in the neighbourhood by any housing authority for persons whose needs as regards extent are, in the opinion of the court, similar to those of the tenant and his family; or
  (b) reasonably suitable to the means of the tenant and to the needs of the tenant and his family as regards extent and character;
and that if any furniture was provided for use under the protected or statutory tenancy in question, furniture is provided for use in the accommodation which is either similar to that so provided or is reasonably suitable to the needs of the tenant and his family.

(2) For the purposes of sub-paragraph (1)(a) above, a certificate of a housing authority stating—
  (a) the extent of the accommodation afforded by dwelling-houses provided by the authority to meet the needs of tenants with families of such number as may be specified in the certificate, and
  (b) the amount of the rent charged by the authority for dwelling-houses affording accommodation of that extent,
shall be conclusive evidence of the facts so stated. [397]

4. Accommodation shall not be deemed to be suitable to the needs of the tenant and his family if the result of their occupation of the accommodation would be that it would be an overcrowded dwelling-house for the purposes of section [135 of the Housing (Scotland) Act 1987.] [398]

5. Any document purporting to be a certificate of a housing authority named therein issued for the purposes of this Schedule and to be signed by the clerk to that authority shall be received in evidence and, unless the contrary is shown, shall be deemed to be such a certificate without further proof. [399]

6. In this Schedule 'housing authority' means a local authority for the purposes of Part [I of the Housing (Scotland) Act 1987,] and 'district', in relation to such an authority, means the district for supplying the needs of which the authority has power under that Part of that Act. [400]

NOTES to Schedule 2
Amendments: In Part II, Case 11 amended by the Rent (Amendment) Act 1985 (c 24), s 1—The date of commencement of the Rent (Amendment) Act 1985 was 23 May 1985; in Part IV, para 4 amended by Housing (Scotland) Act 1987, s 339, Sch 23, para 29; in Part IV, para 6 amended by Housing (Scotland) Act 1987, s 339, Sch 23, para 29.
Definitions: 'tenant,' 'tenancy': see s 115(1) above; 'protected tenancy': see s 115(1) and s 1 above; 'statutory tenancy': see s 115(1) and s 3 above; 'dwelling-house': see s 1 above; 'landlord': see s 115(1) above; 'regulated tenancy': see s 115(1) and s 8 above.

SCHEDULE 3

* * *

NOTES to Schedule 3
Schedule 3 was repealed by the Housing (Scotland) Act 1988, (c 43), s 72, Sch 3.

SCHEDULE 4

Rent Assessment Committees

1. The Secretary of State shall draw up and from time to time revise a panel of persons to act as chairmen and other members of rent assessment committees. [401]

2. There shall be one panel for the registration areas in Scotland. [402]

3. The panel shall consist of a number of persons appointed by the Secretary of State, and, if the Secretary of State thinks fit, a number of persons appointed to act only in case of absence or incapacity of other members of the panel. [403]

4. The Secretary of State shall nominate two of the persons on the panel to act as president and vice-president of the panel. [404]

5. Subject to the following provisions of this Schedule, the number of rent assessment committees to act for any registration area and the constitution of those committees shall be determined by the president of the panel or, in the case of the president's absence or incapacity, by the vice-president. [405]

6. Subject to paragraph 7 below, each rent assessment committee shall consist of a chairman and one or two other members. [406]

7. The president of the panel may, if he thinks fit, direct that when dealing with such cases or dealing with a case in such circumstances as may be specified in the direction, the chairman sitting alone may, with the consent of the parties, exercise the functions or a rent assessment committee. [407]

8. There shall be paid to members of a panel such remuneration and allowances as the Secretary of State, with the consent of the Treasury, may determine. [408]

9. There shall be paid to or in respect of members of a panel, such sums by way of pensions, superannuation allowances and gratuities as the Secretary of State may, with the approval of the Treasury, determine. [409]

10. There shall be paid to any member of a panel who ceases to be a member otherwise than on the expiry of his term of office, where it appears to the Secretary of State that there are special circumstances, such sum as the Secretary of State may, with the approval of the Treasury, determine. [410]

11. The president of the panel may appoint, with the approval of the Secretary of State as to numbers, such clerks and other officers and servants of rent assessment committees as he thinks fit, and there shall be paid to the clerks and other officers and servants such salaries and allowances as the Secretary of State, with the consent of the Treasury, may determine. [411]

12. There shall be paid out of moneys provided by Parliament—
(a) the remuneration and allowances of members of a panel; the pensions, superannuation allowances and gratuities payable to or in respect of members of a panel; any compensation payable to a member of a panel;

(b) the salaries and allowances of clerks and other officers and servants appointed under this Schedule; and
(c) such other expenses of a panel as the Treasury may determine. [412]

SCHEDULE 5

Applications for Registration of Rents

Part I
Applications Unsupported by Certificate of Fair Rent

Procedure on applications to rent officer

1. On receiving any application for the registration of a rent, the rent officer may, by notice in writing served on the landlord or the tenant (whether or not the applicant or one of the applicants), require him to give to the rent officer, within such period of not less than 14 days from the service of the notice as may be specified in the notice, such information as he may reasonably require regarding such of the particulars contained in the application as may be specified in the notice. [413]

2. Where the application is made by the landlord alone the rent officer shall serve on the tenant, and where it is made by the tenant alone he shall serve on the landlord, a notice informing him of the application and specifying a period of not less than 14 days from the service of the notice during which representation in writing may be made to the rent officer against the registration of the rent specified in the application. [414]

3.—(1) Where—
(a) the application is made jointly by the landlord and the tenant, or
(b) no representations are made as mentioned in paragraph 2 above,
and it appears to the rent officer, after making such inquiry, if any, as he thinks fit and considering any information supplied to him in pursuance of paragraph 1 above, that the rent specified in the application is a fair rent, he may register that rent without further proceedings.

(2) Where the rent officer registers a rent under this paragraph he shall notify the landlord and tenant accordingly. [415]

4. Where the rent officer, in carrying out his functions under this Part of this Schedule, inspects a dwelling-house, he shall explain to the tenant or to his spouse, if either is present at the inspection, the procedure upon an application for the registration of a rent under this Part of this Schedule. [416]

5.—(1) Where representations are made as mentioned in paragraph 2 above or the rent officer is not satisfied that the rent specified in the application is a fair rent or, as the case may be, that the rent for the time being registered is any longer a fair rent, he shall serve a notice under this paragraph.

(2) A notice under this paragraph shall be served on the landlord and on the tenant informing them that the rent officer proposes, at a time (which shall not be earlier than seven days after the service of the notice) and place specified in the notice to consider in consultation with landlord and the tenant, or such of them as may appear at that time and place, what rent ought to be registered for the dwelling-house or, as the case may be, whether a different rent ought to be so registered.

(3) At any such consultation the landlord and the tenant may each be represented by a person authorised by him in that behalf, whether or not that person is an advocate or a solicitor. [417]

[418]

6. After considering, in accordance with paragraph 5 above, what rent ought to be registered or, as the case may be, whether a different rent ought to be registered, the rent officer shall, as the case may require,—
  (a) determine a fair rent and register it as the rent for the dwelling-house; or
  (b) confirm the rent for the time being registered and note the confirmation in the register;
and shall notify the landlord and the tenant accordingly by a notice stating that if, within 28 days of the service of the notice or such longer period as he or a rent assessment committee may allow, an objection in writing is received by the rent officer from the landlord or the tenant the matter will be referred to a rent assessment committee. [418]

7.—(1) If such an objection as is mentioned in paragraph 6 above is received, then—
  (a) if it is received within the period of 28 days specified in that paragraph or a rent assessment committee so direct, the rent officer shall refer the matter to a rent assessment committee;
  (b) if it is received after the expiry of that period the rent officer may either refer the matter to a rent assessment committee or seek the directions of a rent assessment committee whether so to refer it.

(2) The rent officer shall indicate in the register whether the matter has been referred to a rent assessment committee in pursuance of this paragraph. [419]

Determination of fair rent by rent assessment committee

8.—(1) The rent assessment committee to whom a matter is referred under paragraph 7 above—
  (a) may by notice in the prescribed form served on the landlord or the tenant require him to give to the committee, within such period of not less than 14 days from the service of the notice as may be specified in the notice, such further information, in addition to any given to the rent officer in pursuance of paragraph 1 above, as they may reasonably require; and
  (b) shall serve on the landlord and on the tenant a notice specifying a period of not less than 14 days from the service of the notice during which either representations in writing or a request to make oral representations may be made by him to the committee.

(2) If any person fails without reasonable cause to comply with any notice served on him under sub-paragraph (1)(a) above, he shall be liable to a fine not exceeding level 3 on the standard scale.

(3) Where an offence under sub-paragraph (2) above committed by a body corporate is proved to have been committed with the consent or connivance of, or to be attributable to any neglect on the part of, any director, manager or secretary or other similar officer of the body corporate or any person who was purporting to act in any such capacity, he as well as the body corporate shall be guilty of that offence and shall be liable to be proceeded against and punished accordingly. [420]

9. Where, within the period specified in paragraph 8(1)(b) above, or such further period as the committee may allow, the landlord or the tenant requests to make oral representations the committee shall give him an opportunity to be heard either in person or by a person authorised by him in that behalf, whether or not that person is an advocate or a solicitor. [421]

10.—(1) The committee shall make such inquiry, if any, as they think fit and consider any information supplied or representation made to them in pursuance of paragraph 8 or 9 above and—
  (a) if it appears to them that the rent registered or confirmed by the rent officer is a fair rent, they shall confirm that rent;
  (b) if it does not appear to them that that rent is a fair rent, they shall determine a fair rent for the dwelling-house.

(2) Where the committee confirm or determine a rent under this paragraph they shall notify the landlord, the tenant and the rent officer of their decision and, in the case of the determination of a rent, of the date on which their decision was made.

(3) On receiving the notification, the rent officer shall, as the case may require, either indicate in the register that the rent has been confirmed or register the rent determined by the committee as the rent for the dwelling-house. [422]

Part II
Applications Supported by Certificate of Fair Rent

Procedure on applications to rent officer

11.—(1) On receiving an application for the registration of a rent which is made as mentioned in section 47(4) above, the rent officer shall ascertain whether the works specified in the certificate of fair rent have been carried out in accordance with the plans and specifications which accompanied the application for the certificate or, as the case may be, whether—
(a) the condition of the dwelling-house is the same as at the date of the certificate, and
(b) if any furniture is or is to be provided for use under a regulated tenancy of the dwelling-house, the quantity, quality and condition of the furniture in the dwelling-house accord with the prescribed particulars contained in the application for the certificate. [423]

(2) If the rent officer is satisfied that the works have been so carried out or, as the case may be, that—
(a) the dwelling-house is in the same condition as at the date of the certificate, and
(b) if any furniture is or is to be provided for use under a regulated tenancy of the dwelling-house, the quantity, quality and condition of the furniture in the dwelling-house accord with the prescribed particulars contained in the application for the certificate,
he shall register the rent in accordance with the certificate.

(3) If the rent officer is not satisfied as mentioned in sub-paragraph (2) above, he shall serve on the applicant a notice stating the matters with respect to which he is not so satisfied and informing him that if, within 14 days from the service of the notice or such longer period as the rent officer or a rent assessment committee may allow, the applicant makes a request in writing to that effect, the rent officer will refer the matter to a rent assessment committee.

12. If such a request as is mentioned in paragraph 11(3) above is made, then—
(a) if it is made within the period of 14 days specified in that paragraph or a rent assessment committee so direct, the rent officer shall refer the matter to a rent assessment committee;
(b) if it is made after the expiry of that period, the rent officer may either refer the matter to a rent assessment committee or seek the directions of a rent assessment committee whether so to refer it. [424]

Procedure on references to rent assessment committee

13.—(1) The rent assessment committee to whom a matter is referred under paragraph 12 above shall give the applicant an opportunity to make representations in writing or to be heard either in person or by a person authorised by him in that behalf, whether or not that person is an advocate or a solicitor.

(2) After considering any representations made under sub-paragraph (1) above, the rent assessment committee shall notify the rent officer and the applicant whether they are satisfied as mentioned in paragraph (2) above and—
(a) if they are so satisfied they shall direct the rent officer to register the rent in accordance with the certificate;

[425]

(b) if they are not so satisfied they shall direct the rent officer to refuse the application for registration. **[425]**

Provisional registration

14. Where a rent is registered in pursuance of such an application as is mentioned in paragraph 11(1) above by a person who intends to grant a regulated tenancy, the registration shall be provisional only until the regulated tenancy is granted and shall be of no effect unless the rent officer is notified in the prescribed manner, within one month from the date of the registration or such longer time as the rent officer may allow, that the regulated tenancy has been granted. **[426]**

15. Where a registration is made as mentioned in paragraph 14 above, the rent officer shall indicate in the register that it is so made and—
(a) if he is notified as mentioned in that paragraph that the regulated tenancy has been granted he shall indicate that fact in the register;
(b) if he is not so notified he shall delete the registration. **[427]**

PART III
SUPPLEMENTAL

16. There shall be included, among the matters with respect to which representations may be made or consultations are to be held or notices to be given under Parts I and II of this Schedule, any amount to be noted in the register in pursuance of section 49(2) above and any amount to be recorded in the register in pursuance of an order made under section 33 above. **[428]**

NOTES to Schedule 5

Para 1: The prescribed form is in the Rent Regulation (Forms and Information Etc) (Scotland) Regulations 1991, SI 1991/1521, paras [1510] ff below.

Definitions: 'rent officer': see s 43 above; 'landlord': see s 115(1) above; 'tenant': see s 115(1) above; 'fair rent': see s 48 above; 'dwelling-house': see s 1 above; 'rent assessment committee': see s 115(1) and s 44 above.

SCHEDULE 6

CERTIFICATES OF FAIR RENT

1. An application for a certificate of fair rent—
(a) must be in the prescribed form;
(b) must state the rent to be specified in the certificate;
(c) in the case mentioned in paragraph (a) of section 47(1) above, must be accompanied by plans and specifications of the works to be carried out and, if the works to be carried out are works of improvement, must state whether the dwelling-house is for the time being subject to a regulated tenancy; and
(d) if any furniture is to be provided for use under a regulated tenancy of the dwelling-house, must contain the prescribed particulars with regard to any such furniture. **[429]**

2.—(1) If it appears to the rent officer that the information supplied to him is insufficient to enable him to issue a certificate of fair rent he shall serve on the applicant a notice stating that he will not entertain the application and that, if a request in writing to that effect is made by the applicant within 14 days from the service of the notice or such longer period as a rent officer or a rent assessment committee may allow, the rent officer will refer the application to a rent assessment committee.

(2) If such a request is made, then—
(a) if it is made within the period of 14 days referred to in sub-paragraph (1) above or a rent assessment committee so direct, the rent officer shall refer the application to a rent assessment committee;
(b) if it is made after the expiry of that period, the rent officer may either refer the application to a rent assessment committee or seek the directions of a rent assessment committee whether so to refer it. [430]

3. If it appears to the rent officer that the information supplied to him is sufficient and that the rent stated in the application would be a fair rent he may, unless the dwelling-house is subject to a regulated tenancy, issue a certificate specifying that rent and the other terms referred to in section 47(2) above. [431]

4.—(1) If it appears to the rent officer that the information is sufficient but either—
(a) he is not satisfied that the rent stated in the application would be a fair rent, or
(b) the dwelling-house is subject to a regulated tenancy,
he shall serve on the applicant a notice stating that he proposes, at a time (which shall not be earlier than seven days after the service of the notice) and place specified in the notice, to consider in consultation with the applicant, if present at that time and place, what rent ought to be specified in the certificate.

(2) At any such consultation the applicant may be represented by a person authorised by him in that behalf, whether or not that person is an advocate or a solicitor. [432]

5. After considering in accordance with paragraph 4 above what rent ought to be specified in the certificate, the rent officer shall determine a fair rent and shall serve on the applicant a notice stating that he proposes to issue a certificate specifying that rent, unless within 14 days from the service of the notice, or such longer period as the rent officer or a rent assessment committee may allow, the applicant requests in writing that the application should be referred to a rent assessment committee. [433]

6.—(1) If such a request as is referred to in paragraph 5 above is made, then—
(a) if it is made within the period of 14 days referred to in that paragraph or a rent assessment committee so direct, the rent officer shall refer the application to a rent assessment committee;
(b) if it is made after the expiry of that period, the rent officer may either refer the application to a rent assessment committee or seek the directions of a rent assessment committee whether so to refer it.

(2) If no such request is made or if such a request is made but the application is not referred to a rent assessment committee, the rent officer shall issue the certificate. [434]

7.—(1) Where an application is referred to a rent assessment committee, then if the reference is under paragraph 2 above and it appears to the committee that the information supplied by the applicant to the rent officer is insufficient to enable a certificate of fair rent to be issued they shall notify the applicant accordingly.

(2) In any other case where an application is referred to a rent assessment committee, they shall serve on the applicant a notice specifying a period of not less than 14 days from the service of the notice during which either representations in writing or a request to make oral representations may be made by him to the committee.

(3) Where, within the period specified under sub-paragraph (2) above or such further period as the committee may allow, the applicant requests to make oral representations, the committee shall give him an opportunity to be heard either in person or by a person authorised by him in that behalf, whether or not that person is an advocate or a solicitor. [435]

8.—(1) After considering any representation made to them in pursuance of paragraph 7 above, the committee shall determine a fair rent for the dwelling-house and shall notify the applicant and the rent officer accordingly.

(2) On receiving the notification the rent officer shall issue to the applicant a certificate of fair rent specifying the rent determined by the committee. **[436]**

9. Where an application under this Schedule is made with respect to a dwelling-house which it is intended to improve and the dwelling-house is subject to a regulated tenancy—
   (a) a notice under paragraph 4, 5, 7(2) or 8 above shall be served on the tenant as well as on the applicant and any notice served under paragraph 4, 5 or 7(2) above shall refer to consultation with, or, as the case may be, a request or representations by, the tenant as well as the applicant;
   (b) the tenant may make representations, request reference to a rent assessment committee and be present or represented in like manner as the applicant, and references in this Schedule to the applicant shall be construed accordingly; and
   (c) a copy of any certificate of fair rent issued in pursuance of the application shall be sent to the tenant. **[437]**

10. Where the rent specified in a certificate of fair rent includes any amount which, if the rent specified in the certificate had been registered, would require to be noted on the register in pursuance of section 49(2) above, that amount shall be noted on the certificate; and there shall be included among the matters with respect to which representations may be made or consultations are to be held or notices to be given under this Schedule, any amount to be noted on the certificate in pursuance of this paragraph. **[438]**

NOTES to Schedule 6

Definitions: 'fair rent': see s 48 above; 'prescribed': see s 54(1) above; 'improvement': *Ibid*; 'dwelling-house': see s 1 above; 'regulated tenancy': see s 115(1) and s 8 above; 'rent officer': see s 53 above; 'rent assessment committee': see s 115(1) and s 44 above; 'tenant,' 'tenancy': see s 115(1) above; 'landlord': see s 115(1) above.

SCHEDULE 7

PREMIUM ALLOWED ON ASSIGNATION OF TENANCY WHERE PREMIUM LAWFULLY PAID ON GRANT

1.—(1) The provisions of this Schedule apply where—
(a) a premium was lawfully required and paid, or lawfully received, in respect of the grant, continuance or renewal of a protected tenancy of a dwelling-house which is a regulated tenancy; and
(b) since that grant, continuance or renewal, the landlord has not granted a tenancy of the dwelling-house under which, as against the landlord, a person became entitled to possession, other than the person who was so entitled to possession of the dwelling-house immediately before that tenancy began; and
(c) a rent for the dwelling-house is registered under Part V of this Act and the rent so registered is higher than the rent payable under the tenancy.

(2) Any reference in this Schedule to a premium does not include a premium which consisted only of any such outgoings, sum or amount as fall within section 83(3) above and, in the case of a premium which included any such outgoings, sum or amount, so much only of the premium as does not consist of those outgoings, sum or amount shall be treated as the premium for the purposes of this Schedule. **[439]**

2. In a case where this Schedule applies, nothing in section 83 above shall prevent any person from requiring or receiving on an assignation of the protected tenancy referred to

in paragraph 1(1)(a) above or any subsequent protected tenancy of the same dwelling-house, a premium which does not exceed an amount calculated (subject to paragraph 4 below) in accordance with the formula in paragraph 3 below. **[440]**

3. The formula mentioned in paragraph 2 above is—

$$\frac{P \times A}{G}$$

where
- P is the premium referred to in paragraph 1(1)(a) above;
- A is the length of the period beginning on the date on which the assignation in question takes effect and ending on the relevant date; and
- G is the length of the period beginning on the date of the grant, continuance or renewal in respect of which the premium was paid and ending on the relevant date. **[441]**

4.—(1) If, although the registered rent is higher than the rent payable under the tenancy, the lump sum equivalent of the difference is less than the premium, paragraph 3 above shall have effect as if P were the lump sum equivalent.

(2) For the purposes of this Schedule, the lump sum equivalent of the difference between the two rents referred to in sub-paragraph (1) above shall be taken to be that difference multiplied by the number of complete rental periods falling within the period beginning with the grant, continuance or renewal in respect of which the premium was paid and ending on the relevant date. **[442]**

5. . . .

6.—(1) Any reference in this Schedule to the relevant date shall be construed in accordance with this paragraph.

(2) Where at the date the assignation takes effect the tenancy referred to in paragraph 1(1)(a) above was granted, continued or renewed for a specified period exceeding seven years and that period has not terminated, the relevant date is the termination of that period.

(3) In any other case the relevant date is the date of the expiration of seven years from the commencement of the tenancy, or, as the case may be, from the continuance or renewal of the tenancy, in respect of which the premium was paid.

(4) The provisions of this paragraph shall apply to a tenancy for a specified period exceeding seven years notwithstanding that it is liable to be terminated by re-entry or on the happening of any event other than the giving of notice by the landlord to terminate the tenancy; and where a tenancy may be terminated by the giving of such notice by the landlord it shall be deemed to be a tenancy for a specified period expiring on the earliest date on which such a notice given after the date of the assignation would be capable of taking effect. **[443]**

NOTES to Schedule 7

Amendment: Para 5 was repealed by the Housing (Scotland) Act 1988 (c 43), s 72, Sch 10.
Definitions: 'premium': see s 115(1) above; 'protected tenancy': see s 115(1) and s 1 above; 'dwelling-house': see s 1 above; 'regulated tenancy': see s 115(1) above; 'tenant,' 'tenancy': *Ibid*; 'registered rent' see s 90(1) above.

SCHEDULE 8

ENACTMENTS AMENDED

PART I

General provisions

1. Any reference in any enactment (other than this Act) to any provision in any enactment repealed by this Act shall, unless the context otherwise requires, be construed as a reference to the corresponding provision in this Act, and the following amendments of other enactments shall have effect without prejudice to the generality of this provision. **[444]**

2. Any reference, however expressed, in any enactment (other than this Act) to the Rent Acts or the Rent Restrictions Acts or the Rent (Scotland) Act 1971 shall, unless the context otherwise requires, be construed as a reference to the corresponding provisions of this Act. **[445]**

PART II

Specific amendments

NOTE to Schedule 8
Part II of Schedule 8 amends various other enactments.

SCHEDULE 9

SAVINGS AND TRANSITIONAL PROVISIONS

1. In so far as any regulation, order, scheme, agreement, dissent, election, reference, representation, appointment or apportionment made, notice served, certificate issued, statement supplied, undertaking or direction given, rent registered or other thing done, under or by virtue of an enactment repealed by this Act could have been made, served, issued, supplied, given, registered or done under or by virtue of the corresponding provision of this Act, it shall have effect as if made, served, issued, supplied, given, registered or done under or by virtue of that corresponding provision. **[446]**

2. Any document made, served or issued before the passing of this Act or at any time thereafter (whether before or after the commencement of this Act) and containing a reference to an enactment repealed by this Act shall, except in so far as a contrary intention appears, be construed as referring, or, as the context requires, as including a reference, to the corresponding provision of this Act. **[447]**

3. Where a period of time specified in an enactment repealed by this Act is current at the commencement of this Act, this Act shall have effect as if the corresponding provision thereof had been in force when that period began to run. **[448]**

4. Nothing in this Act shall prevent an offence against an enactment repealed by this Act from being prosecuted under the corresponding provision of this Act but, on conviction of such an offence, the fine or other penalty imposed shall be that laid down in such enactment as if it had not been repealed. **[449]**

5. A conviction of an offence under an enactment repealed by this Act shall be treated

for the purposes of this Act as a conviction of an offence under the corresponding provision of this Act. **[450]**

6. Nothing in this Act shall affect the continued operation after the commencement of this Act of any saving or transitional provision contained in an enactment repealed by this Act insofar as it was operating immediately before the commencement of this Act. **[451]**

[7. The amendments to this Act made by Schedule 2 to the Law Reform (Miscellaneous Provisions) (Scotland) Act 1985 shall be deemed to have had effect from the commencement of this Act.] **[452]**

NOTES to Schedule 9

Amendment: Para 7 was added by the Law Reform (Miscellaneous Provisions) (Scotland) Act 1985 (c 73), ss 23 and 59, Sch 2, para 30.

TABLE OF DERIVATIONS

NOTE: The following abbreviations are used in this Table:

1965	=	The Rent Act 1965 (1965 c 75).
1970	=	The Agriculture Act 1970 (1970 c 40).
1971	=	The Rent (Scotland) Act 1971 (1971 c 28).
1972	=	The Housing (Financial Provisions) (Scotland) Act 1972 (1972 c 46).
1972 (c 71)	=	The Criminal Justice Act 1972 (1972 c 71).
1973	=	The Local Government (Scotland) Act 1973 (1973 c 65).
1974 (c 44)	=	The Housing Act 1974 (1974 c 44).
1974 (c 45)	=	The Housing (Scotland) Act 1974 (1974 c 45).
1974	=	The Rent Act 1974 (1974 c 51).
1975	=	The Criminal Procedure (Scotland) Act 1975 (1975 c 21).
1975 (c 28)	=	The Housing Rents and Subsidies (Scotland) Act 1975 (1975 c 28).
1978	=	The Housing (Financial Provisions) (Scotland) Act 1978 (1978 c 14).
1980	=	The Tenants' Rights, Etc (Scotland) Act 1980 (1980 c 52).
1980 (c 61)	=	The Tenants' Rights, Etc (Scotland) Amendment Act 1980 (1980 c 61).
1980 (c 65)	=	The Local Government, Planning and Land Act 1980 (1980 c 65).
1982	=	The Criminal Justice Act 1982 (1982 c 48).
SI 1980H	=	The Increase of Rent Restriction (Housing Association) (Scotland) Order 1980 (SI 1980 No 1668).
SI 1980P	=	The Protected Tenancies and Part VII Contracts (Rateable Value Limits) (Scotland) Order 1980 (SI 1980 No 1669).
SI 1981	=	The Transfer of Functions (Minister for the Civil Service and Treasury) Order 1981 (SI 1981 No 1670).

Provision	Derivation
1	1971 s 1; 1972 s 77(1); 1974 s 2(3); 1980 s 43(a); SI 1980P.
2	1971 s 2; 1972 s 36(4); 1974 ss 1(4)(a), 2.
3	1971 s 3.
4	1971 s 4; 1980 ss 40(b), 43(a).
5	1971 s 5; 1973 Sch 13 para 1; 1974 (c 44) s 18(1), Sch 13 para 22; 1975 (c 28) Sch 3 para 4; 1980 (c 65) s 155(2).
6	1971 s 5A; 1974 Sch 2 para 2; 1980 ss 44, 45.
7	1971 s 6; 1980 s 40(2).

Provision	Derivation
8	1971 s 7.
9	1980 s 34.
10	1971 s 9.
11	1971 s 10.
12	1971 s 11.
13	1980 s 35.
14	1980 s 36(1), (2), (4).
15	1971 s 12.
16	1971 s 13; 1975 ss 289F(8), 289G(4).
17	1971 s 14.
18	1971 s 15; 1975 ss 289F(8), 289G(4).
19	1971 s 17.
20	1974 s 13.
21	1971 s 18.
22	1965 s 30; 1972 (c 71) s 30; 1975 s 289B(1)(6); 1982 s 55(2).
23	1965 s 32; 1971 Sch 18 Pt II; 1980 s 42.
24	1965 s 33; 1970 s 99.
25	1965 s 34, 35; 1971 Sch 18 Pt II.
26	1965 s 36.
27	1965 s 45.
28	1971 s 19; 1975 (c 28) Sch 2 para 11; 1980 s 37(6).
29	1971 s 21; 1972 s 36(3), Sch 9 para 23; 1975 (c 28) Sch 2 para 12; 1980 ss 37(6), 48(2), 49(3), 61.
30	1971 s 22.
31	1971 s 23.
32	1971 s 25.
33	1980 s 37(2)–(4).
34	1972 s 42; 1975 (c 28) Sch 2 para 18; 1980 s 38(1).
35	1972 s 43.
36	1972 s 45; 1975 (c 28) Sch 2 para 19.
37	1971 s 31(1)–(3); 1975 (c 28) Sch 2 para 13; 1980 s 37(6).
38	1971 s 31(4), (5); 1975 (c 28) Sch 2 para 13; 1980 s 37(6); 1975 ss 289F(8), 289G(4).
39	1971 s 32.
40	1971 s 34.
41	1971 s 35; 1972 s 47; 1975 ss 289F(8), 289G(4).
42	1971 s 36; 1972 s 36(1).
43	1971 s 37; 1973 Sch 13 para 2; SI 1981.
44	1971 s 38.
45	1971 s 39; 1973 Sch 13 para 3.
46	1971 s 40; 1974 s 4(3), Sch 1 para 17; 1980 s 48(3).
47	1971 s 41.
48	1971 s 42; 1972 s 36(5); 1974 Sch 1 para 18; 1980 s 47.
49	1971 s 43; 1972 s 40; 1975 (c 28) Sch 2 paras 14, 15; 1980 s 37(6).
50	1971 s 44; 1974 s 4(4); 1980 s 48(1).
51	1971 s 44A; 1972 s 39.
52	1971 s 44B; 1980 s 50.
53	1971 s 46; 1972 Sch 9 para 24.
54	1971 s 47.
55	1972 s 60; 1980 s 38(2).

Provision	Derivation
56	1972 s 61; 1974 (c 44) Sch 13 para 23(5); 1980 s 38(3).
57	1972 s 62; 1971 s 33; 1974 (c 44) Sch 13 para 23(6); 1975 ss 289F(6), (8), 289G(4).
58	1972 s 63; 1978 s 14; SI 1980H, Arts 2, 3; SI 1984 No 501.
59	1972 s 66; 1974 (c 44) Sch 13 para 23(7); 1980 s 41(3).
60	1972 s 67; SI 1980H, Art 3, proviso.
61	1972 s 68(2), 78(1).
62	1971 s 83; 1973 Sch 13 para 6.
63	1971 s 85; 1972 Sch 9 para 25; 1980 ss 10(2), 40(3), 53(1).
64	1971 s 86; 1972 s 77(2); 1980 ss 43, 54; SI 1980P.
65	1971 s 87; 1975 ss 289F(6), (8), 289G(4).
66	1971 s 88; 1972 Sch 9 para 26; 1974 s 9(1)(2).
67	1971 s 89; 1973 Sch 13 para 9; 1974 s 9(3).
68	1971 s 90(1); 1974 s 9(4).
69	1971 s 91; 1974 s 9(5); 1975 ss 457A(3)(b), 289B(1), (6); 1982 s 55(1), (2).
70	1971 s 91A; 1980 s 51.
71	1971 s 92.
72	1971 s 93.
73	1971 s 94.
74	1971 s 95; 1974 s 10(2).
75	1971 s 95A; 1974 s 14(3).
76	1971 s 95B; 1980 s 55.
77	1971 s 96.
78	1971 s 97(3).
79	1971 s 98; 1975 s 289H.
80	1971 s 99.
81	1971 s 100; 1974 s 9(6).
82	1971 s 101; 1975 ss 289F(8), 289G(4).
83	1971 s 102; 1975 ss 289F(8), 289G(4).
84	1971 s 103.
85	1971 s 104; 1975 ss 289F(8), 289G(4).
86	1971 s 105.
87	1971 s 106; 1975 ss 289E(5), 289F(6), (8), 289G(4).
88	1971 s 107.
89	1971 s 108; 1975 ss 289F(8), 289G(4).
90	1971 s 109; 1980 s 57.
91	1971 s 110(1), (3).
92	1971 s 111.
93	1971 s 112.
94	1971 s 116; 1974 Sch 1 para 19.
95	1971 s 117.
96	1971 s 118.
97	1971 s 119.
98	1971 s 119A; 1974 Sch 1 para 20, Sch 2 para 6; 1980 s 58.
99	1971 s 120.
100	1971 s 121; 1975 ss 289F(8), 289G(4).
101	1971 s 121A; 1980 s 60.
102	1971 s 122; 1974 Sch 1 para 21.
103	1971 s 123(1), (3); 1972 Sch 9 para 32.
104	1971 s 124; 1974 Sch 1 para 22.
105	1971 s 125(1), (3); 1972 Sch 9 para 27; 1974 Sch 1 para 23; 1980 s 62.

[453]   Rent (Scotland) Act 1984 (c 58), Sch 9

Provision	Derivation
106	1971 ss 80, 82; 1972 Sch 7 para 8; 1974 (c 45) Sch 3 para 39; 1980 s 59.
107	1971 s 126; 1982 Sch 15 para 14; 1965 s 44.
108	1971 s 127; 1975 s 289H.
109	1971 s 128.
110	1971 s 129(1).
111	1971 s 130.
112	1971 s 131; 1974 (c 44) s 123.
113	1971 s 132; 1975 s 289H.
114	1980 s 83.
115	1971 ss 2, 133; 1972 ss 36(1), 78(1); 1973 Sch 13 para 11; 1974 ss 1(1), (2), 15(1); 1980 s 52(2); 1982 ss 54, 74, 75.
116	1971 s 134; 1980 s 40(5).
117	1971 s 135(2), (3), (5).
118	1971 s 136.
Sch 1	1971 Sch 1; 1972 s 46; 1980 s 56(1).
Sch 2,	
Part I	1971 Sch 3; 1974 Sch 1 paras 1, 4(1); 1980 ss 40(4), 46(4).
Part II	1971 Sch 3; 1974 s 3, Sch 1 para 5; 1980 ss 36, 63; 1980 (c 61) s 2.
Part III	1971 Sch 3; 1974 Sch 1 para 6; 1980 s 40(4).
Part IV	1971 Sch 3; 1974 Sch 1 para 7.
Sch 3	1971 Sch 4.
Sch 4	1971 Sch 5; 1980 s 64(1), (2); SI 1981.
Sch 5,	
Part I	1971 Sch 6; 1972 s 49(1); 1975 ss 289E(5), 289F(6), (8), 289G(4); 1980 s 48(4).
Part II	1971 Sch 6; 1974 Sch 1 para 24.
Part III	1971 Sch 6; 1972 Sch 9 para 29; 1975 (c 28) Sch 2 para 16; 1980 s 37(7).
Sch 6	1971 Sch 7; 1972 Sch 9 para 28; 1974 Sch 1 para 25.
Sch 7	1971 Sch 15.
Sch 8	[Amendment of enactments].
Sch 9	[Savings and transitory provisions].
Sch 10	[Enactments repealed].

[453]

Bankruptcy (Scotland) Act 1985

(c 66)

* * *

40. Power of permanent trustee in relation to the debtor's family home.

(1) Before the permanent trustee sells or disposes of any right or interest in the debtor's family home he shall—
    (a) obtain the relevant consent; or
    (b) where he is unable to do so, obtain the authority of the court in accordance with subsection (2) below.

(2) Where the permanent trustee requires to obtain the authority of the court in terms of subsection (1)(b) above, the court, after having regard to all the circumstances of the case, including—
    (a) the needs and financial resources of the debtor's spouse or former spouse;
    (b) the needs and financial resources of any child of the family;

Bankruptcy (Scotland) Act 1985 (c 66), s 41   [455]

   (c) the interests of the creditors;
   (d) the length of the period during which (whether before or after the relevant date) the family home was used as a residence by any of the persons referred to in paragraph (a) or (b) above,
may refuse to grant the application or may postpone the granting of the application for such period (not exceeding twelve months) as it may consider reasonable in the circumstances or may grant the application subject to such conditions as it may prescribe.

   (3) Subsection (2) above shall apply—
   (a) to an action for division and sale of the debtor's family home; or
   (b) to an action for the purpose of obtaining vacant possession of the debtor's family home,
brought by the permanent trustee as it applies to an application under subsection (1)(b) above and, for the purposes of this subsection, any reference in the said subsection (2) to that granting of the application shall be construed as a reference to the granting of decree in the action.

   (4) In this section—
   (a) 'family home' means any property in which, at the relevant date, the debtor had (whether alone or in common with any other person) a right or interest, being property which was occupied at that date as a residence by the debtor and his spouse or by the debtor's spouse or former spouse (in any case with or without a child of the family) or by the debtor with a child of the family;
   (b) 'child of the family' includes any child or grandchild of either the debtor or his spouse or former spouse, and any person who has been brought up or accepted by either the debtor or his spouse or former spouse as if he or she were a child of the debtor, spouse or former spouse whatever the age of such a child, grandchild or person may be;
   (c) 'relevant consent' means in relation to the sale or disposal of any right or interest in a family home—
      (i) in a case where the family home is occupied by the debtor's spouse or former spouse, the consent of the spouse, or, as the case may be, the former spouse, whether or not the family home is also occupied by the debtor;
      (ii) where sub-paragraph (i) above does not apply, in a case where the family home is occupied by the debtor with a child of the family, the consent of the debtor; and
   (d) 'relevant date' means the day immediately preceding the date of sequestration.   [454]

NOTES to section 40

Definitions: 'permanent trustee', 'debtor', 'court', 'date of sequestration': see s 73.

---

41. Protection of rights of spouse against arrangements intended to defeat them.

(1) If a debtor's sequestrated estate includes a matrimonial home of which the debtor, immediately before the date of issue of the act and warrant of the permanent trustee (or, if more than one such act and warrant is issued in the sequestration, of the first such issue) was an entitled spouse and the other spouse is a non-entitled spouse—
   (a) the permanent trustee shall, where he—
      (i) is aware that the entitled spouse is married to the non-entitled spouse; and
      (ii) knows where the non-entitled spouse is residing,
      inform the non-entitled spouse, within the period of 14 days beginning with that date, of the fact that sequestration of the entitled spouse's estate has been awarded, of the right of petition which exists under section 16 of this Act and of the effect of paragraph (b) below; and
   (b) the Court of Session, on the petition under section 16 of this Act of the non-entitled spouse presented either within the period of 40 days beginning with that date or within the period of 10 weeks beginning with the date of sequestration may—

(i) under section 17 of this Act recall the sequestration; or
(ii) make such order as it thinks appropriate to protect the occupancy rights of the non-entitled spouse;
   if it is satisfied that the purpose of the petition for sequestration was wholly or mainly to defeat the occupancy rights of the non-entitled spouse.

(2) In subsection (1) above—
'entitled spouse' and 'non-entitled spouse' have the same meanings as in section 6 of the Matrimonial Homes (Family Protection) (Scotland) Act 1981;
'matrimonial home' has the meaning assigned by section 22 of that Act as amended by the Law Reform (Miscellaneous Provisions) (Scotland) Act 1985; and
'occupancy rights' has the meaning assigned by section 1(4) of the said Act of 1981. **[455]**

NOTES to section 41
Definitions: 'debtor', 'act and warrant', 'permanent trustee', 'date of sequestration': see s 73.

* * *

73. Interpretation

(1) In this Act, unless the context otherwise requires—
'act and warrant' means an act and warrant issued under section 25(2) of, or paragraph 2(2) of Schedule 2 to this Act;
'court' means Court of Session or sheriff;
'date of sequestration' has the meaning assigned by section 12(4) of this Act;
'debtor' includes without prejudice to the expression's generality an entity whose estate may be sequestrated by virtue of section 6 of this Act, a deceased debtor or his executor or a person entitled to be appointed as executor to a deceased debtor;
'permanent trustee' shall be construed in accordance with section 3 of this Act. **[456]**

Housing Associations Act 1985
(c 69)

A Table showing the derivations of the provisions of this consolidation Act will be found at the end of the Act. The Table has no official status.

ARRANGEMENT OF SECTIONS

PART I
REGULATION OF HOUSING ASSOCIATIONS

Introductory

1　Meaning of 'housing association' and related expressions . . . **[457]**

* * *

2A　The Corporation . . . . **[458]**

Registration

3　The register . . . . **[459]**
4　Eligibility for registration . . . . **[460]**
5　Registration . . . . **[461]**

Housing Associations Act 1985 (c 69) [457]

6	Removal from the register	[462]
7	Appeal against removal	[463]

Disposal of land

8	Power of registered housing associations to dispose of land	[464]
9	Control by Housing Corporation of dispositions of land by housing associations	[465]
10	Dispositions excepted from s 9	[466]

★ ★ ★

Control of payments to members etc

13	Payments by way of gift, dividend or bonus	[467]
14	Maximum amounts payable by way of fees, expenses, etc	[468]
15	Payments and benefits to committee members, etc	[469]
15A	Payments etc in community-based housing associations in Scotland	[470]

Constitution, change of rules, amalgamation and dissolution

16	General power to remove committee member	[471]
17	Power to appoint new committee member	[472]

★ ★ ★

19	Change of rules under the 1965 Act	[473]

★ ★ ★

21	Amalgamation and dissolution under the 1965 Act	[474]
22	Housing Corporation's power to petition for winding up	[475]
23	Transfer of net assets on dissolution	[476]

Accounts and audit

24	General requirements as to accounts and audit	[477]
25	Appointment of auditors by associations registered under the 1965 Act	[478]
26	Accounting requirements for registered housing associations not within the 1965 Act	[479]
27	Responsibility for securing compliance with accounting requirements	[480]
27A	Power of corporation to monitor associations	[481]

Inquiries into affairs of housing associations

28	Inquiry	[482]
29	Extraordinary audit for the purposes of inquiry	[483]
30	General powers exercisable as a result of inquiry or audit	[484]

★ ★ ★

32	Power to direct transfer of land to another housing association or the Housing Corporation	[485]

Miscellaneous

33	Recognition of central association	[486]
33A	Provision of services between the Corporations	[487]

★ ★ ★

36A	Issue of guidance by the Corporation	[488]

Supplementary

37	Definitions relating to the 1965 Act and societies registered under it	**[489]**

* * *

39	Minor definitions	**[490]**
40	Index of defined expressions: Part I	**[491]**

Part II
Housing Association Finance

* * *

Arrangements with local authorities

* * *

59	Powers of local authorities to promote and assist housing assocations: Scotland	**[492]**
60	Certain assistance restricted to registered housing associations	**[493]**
61	Power of local housing authority to supply furniture to housing association tenants	**[494]**

* * *

Loans by Public Works Loan Commissioners

* * *

68	Loans by Public Works Loan Commissioners: Scotland	**[495]**

Miscellaneous

69	Power to vary or terminate certain agreements with housing associations	**[496]**
69A	Land subject to housing management agreement	**[497]**
70	Continuation of arrangements under repealed enactments	**[498]**
71	Superseded contributions, subsidies and grants	**[499]**

Supplementary provisions

72	Minor definitions	**[500]**
73	Index of defined expressions: Part II	**[501]**

Part III
The Housing Corporation

Constitution and other general matters

74	The Housing Corporation	**[502]**
75	General functions of the Corporation	**[503]**
76	Directions by the Secretary of State	**[504]**
77	Advisory service	**[505]**
78	Annual report	**[506]**

Corporation's powers with respect to loans and grants

79	Lending powers	**[507]**
80	Security for loans to unregistered self-build societies	**[508]**

* * *

82	Loans made under s 2 of the Housing Act 1964	[509]
83	Power to guarantee loans	[510]

★ ★ ★

86	Agreements to indemnify building societies: Scotland	[511]
87	Financial assistance with respect to formation, management, etc of certain housing associations	[512]

Corporation's powers with respect to land and works

88	Acquisition of land	[513]
89	Provision of dwellings or hostels and clearance, management and development of land	[514]
90	Disposal of land	[515]
91	Protection of persons deriving title under transactions requiring consent	[516]

The Corporation's finances

92	Borrowing powers	[517]
93	Limit on borrowing	[518]
94	Treasury guarantees of borrowing	[519]
95	Grants to Corporation	[520]
96	General financial provisions	[521]
97	Accounts and audit	[522]

Acquisition of securities and control of subsidiaries

98	Acquisition of securities and promotion of body corporate	[523]
99	Control of subsidiaries	[524]

Supplementary provisions

★ ★ ★

101	Minor definitions	[525]
102	Index of defined expressions: Part III	[526]

PART IV
GENERAL PROVISIONS

General provisions

★ ★ ★

104	Local housing authorities	[527]
105	Members of a person's family	[528]
106	Minor definitions—general	[529]

Final provisions

107	Short title, commencement and extent	[530]

SCHEDULES:
Schedule 1—Grant-aided land . . . . [531–533]

★ ★ ★

Schedule 4—Housing associations: continuation of arrangements under repealed enactments . . . . [534–536]

★ ★ ★

Part II—Subsidy agreements with local authorities . . . **[534–535]**
Part III—Special arrangements with the Secretary of State in Scotland . **[536]**
Schedule 5—Housing association finance: superseded subsidies,
              contributions and grants . . . . . . **[537–552]**

★ ★ ★

Part II—Residual subsidies: Scotland . . . . . . **[537–543]**
Part III—Contributions and grants under arrangements with local
           authorities . . . . **[544–545]**
Part IV—Contributions under arrangements with the Secretary of State
           in Scotland . . . . **[546]**
Part V—Schemes for the unification of grant conditions . . . **[547]**
Part VI—New building subsidy and improvement subsidy . . . **[548–551]**
Part VII—Payments in respect of hostels under pre-1974 enactments . **[552]**
Schedule 6—Constitution etc of Housing Corporation . . . . **[553–561]**
Schedule 7—Powers exercisable where loan outstanding under section 2 of
              the Housing Act 1964 . . . . **[562–566]**

An Act to consolidate certain provisions of the Housing Acts relating to housing associations, with amendments to give effect to recommendations of the Law Commission and of the Scottish Law Commission. [30th October 1985]

Be it enacted by the Queen's most Excellent Majesty, by and with the advice and consent of the Lords Spiritual and Temporal, and Commons, in this present Parliament assembled, and by the authority of the same, as follows:—

PART I
REGULATION OF HOUSING ASSOCIATIONS

Introductory

1. Meaning of 'housing association' and related expressions.

(1) In this Act 'housing association' means a society, body of trustees or company—
(a) which is established for the purpose of, or amongst whose objects or powers are included those of, providing, constructing, improving or managing, or facilitating or encouraging the construction or improvement of, housing accommodation, and
(b) which does not trade for profit or whose constitution or rules prohibit the issue of capital with interest or dividend exceeding such rate as may be prescribed by the Treasury, whether with or without differentiation as between share and loan capital; [but does not include Scottish Homes.]

(2) In this Act 'fully mutual', in relation to a housing association, means that the rules of the association—
(a) restrict membership to persons who are tenants or prospective tenants of the association, and
(b) preclude the granting or assignment of tenancies to persons other than members;
and 'co-operative housing association' means a fully mutual housing association which is a society registered under the Industrial and Provident Societies Act 1965 (in this Part referred to as 'the 1965 Act').

(3) In this Act 'self-build society' means a housing association whose object is to provide, for sale to, or occupation by, its members, dwellings built or improved principally with the use of its members' own labour. **[457]**

NOTES to section 1
Amendment: Words added by Housing (Scotland) Act 1988 (c 43), Sch 2, para 6.

Housing Associations Act 1985 (c 69), s 3 [459]

2. (Applies to England and Wales.)

[2A. The Corporation.

(1) In relation to a housing association which has its registered office for the purposes of the 1965 Act in Scotland, 'the Corporation' means Scottish Homes.

(2) In relation to a housing association—
(a) which is a society registered under the 1965 Act and has its registered office for the purposes of that Act in Wales, or
(b) which is a registered charity and has its address for the purposes of registration by the Charity Commissioners in Wales,
'the Corporation' means Housing for Wales.

(3) In relation to any other housing association which is a society registered under the 1965 Act or a registered charity, 'the Corporation' means the Housing Corporation.

(4) Subject to subsections (1) to (3), in this Act, except where the context otherwise requires, 'the Corporation' means the Housing Corporation, Scottish Homes or Housing for Wales and 'the Corporations' means those three bodies.] [458]

NOTES to section 2A
Amendment: Section 2A was added by the Housing Act 1988, (c 50), s 59, Sch 6, para 1.

Registration

3. The register.

(1) A register of housing associations shall be maintained by [each of the Corporations] and shall be open to inspection at the head office of the Corporation [by which it is maintained] at all reasonable times.

(1A) In this Act, 'register' in relation to the Corporation, means the register maintained by the Corporation under this section.

(2) In this Act 'registered' and 'unregistered', and other references to registration, in relation to a housing association, refer to registration in the register . . . [459]

NOTES to section 3
Amendments: Sub-ss (1) and (3) were amended by the Housing Act 1988 (c 50), s 59, Sch 6, para 3; sub-s (2) was amended by the Housing Act 1988 (c 50), s 59, Sch 6, para 3.
Definition: 'housing association': see s 1 above.

4. Eligibility for registration.

(1) A housing association is eligible for registration if it is—
(a) a registered charity, or
(b) a society registered under the 1965 Act which fulfils the following conditions.

(2) The conditions are that the association does not trade for profit and is established for the purpose of, or has among its objects or powers, the provision, construction, improvement or management of—
(a) houses to be kept available for letting, or
(b) houses for occupation by members of the association, where the rules of the association restrict membership to persons entitled or prospectively entitled (as tenants or otherwise) to occupy a house provided or managed by the association, or
(c) hostels,
and that any additional purposes or objects are among the following.

[(3) The permissible additional purposes or objects are—

(a) providing land, amenities or services, or providing, constructing, repairing or improving buildings, for the benefit of the association's residents, either exclusively or together with other persons;
(b) acquiring, or repairing and improving, or creating by the conversion of houses or other property, houses to be disposed of on sale, on lease or on shared ownership terms;
(c) constructing houses to be disposed of on shared ownership terms;
(d) managing houses which are held on leases or other lettings (not being houses falling within subsection (2)(a) or (b)) or blocks of flats;
(e) providing services of any description for owners or occupiers of houses in arranging or carrying out works of maintenance, repair or improvement, or encouraging or facilitating the carrying out of such works;
(f) encouraging and giving advice on the formation of other housing associations or providing services or, and giving advice on the running of, such associations and other voluntary organisations concerned with housing, or matters connected with housing.

(4) A housing association shall not be ineligible for registration by reason only that its powers include power—
(a) to acquire commercial premises or businesses as an incidental part of a project or series of projects undertaken for purposes or objects falling within subsection (2) or (3);
(b) to repair, improve or convert any commerical premises acquired as mentioned in paragraph (a) or to carry on, for a limited period, any business so acquired;
(c) to repair or improve houses, or buildings in which houses are situated, after the tenants have exercised, or claimed to exercise acquisition rights;
(d) to acquire houses to be disposed of at a discount to tenants to whom section 58 of the Housing Act 1988 applies (tenants of charitable housing associations etc).

(5) In this section—
'acquisition right' means—
(a) in England and Wales, the right to buy or the right to be granted a shared ownership lease under Part V of the Housing Act 1985;
(b) in Scotland, a right to purchase under section 61 of the Housing (Scotland) Act 1987;
'block of flats' means a building—
(a) containing two or more flats which are held on leases or other lettings; and
(b) occupied or intended to be occupied wholly or mainly for residential purposes;
'disposed of on shared ownership terms' means—
(a) in England and Wales, disposed of on a shared ownership lease;
(b) in Scotland, disposed of under a shared ownership agreement;
'letting' includes the grant—
(a) in England and Wales, of a licence to occupy;
(b) in Scotland, of a right or permission to occupy;
'residents', in relation to a housing association, means the persons occupying the houses or hostels provided or managed by the association;
'voluntary organisation' means an organisation whose activities are not carried on for profit.] **[460]**

NOTES to section 4

Amendments: Sub-ss (3), (4) and (5) were substituted by the Housing Act 1988 (c 50), s 48. The said s 48 allows the Secretary of State to amend sub-ss (3) and (4), but the power has not been exercised.

Definitions: 'housing associations': see s 1 above; 'the 1965 Act' means the Industrial and Provident Societies Act 1965 (c 12): see ss 1, 37; 'house': see s 106(2) below; 'hostel': *Ibid*; 'registered': see s 3 above; 'shared ownership lease': see s 106(2) below.

---

5. Registration.

(1) The [Corporation] may register any housing association which is eligible for registration in the register but—

Housing Associations Act 1985 (c 69), s 6

(a) the Corporation shall establish criteria which should be satisfied by a housing association seeking registration, and
(b) in deciding whether to register an association the Corporation shall have regard to whether it satisfies those criteria.

[(2) Nothing in subsection (1) shall require the Corporations to establish the same criteria; and each of them may vary any criteria established by it under that subsection.]

(3) As soon as may be after registering a housing association the Corporation shall give notice of the registration—
(a) if the association is a registered charity,to the Charity Commissioners, or
(b) if the association is a society registered under the 1965 Act, to the appropriate registrar,
who shall record the registration.

[(4) Where at any time a body is, or was, on a register maintained under section 3, then, for all purposes other than rectification of that register, the body shall be conclusively presumed to be, or to have been, at that time a housing association eligible for registration in that register.] [461]

NOTES to section 5

Amendments: Sub-ss (2) and (4) were substituted by the Housing Act 1988 (c 50), s 59, Sch 6, para 4.
Definitions: 'housing association': see s 1 above; 'the Corporation': see s 2A above; 'the 1965 Act' means the Industrial and Provident Societies Act 1965 (c 12): see s 1 above and s 37 below; 'register,' 'registration': see s 3 above; 'appropriate registrar': see s 37 below.

6. Removal from the register.

(1) A body which has been registered shall not be removed from the register except in accordance with this section.

(2) If it appears to the [Corporation] that a body which is on the register—
(a) is no longer a housing association eligible for registration, or
(b) has ceased to exist or does not operate,
the Corporation shall, after giving the body at least 14 days' notice, remove it from the register.

(3) In the case of a body which appears to the Corporation to have ceased to exist or not to operate, notice under subsection (2) shall be deemed to be given to the body if it is served at the address last known to the Corporation to be the principal place of business of the body.

(4) A body which is registered may request the Corporation to remove it from the register if it has not at any time received—
[(a) a grant under section 41 (housing association grants),
(b) a grant under section 54 (revenue deficit grants),
(c) any such payment or loan as is mentioned in paragraph 2 or paragraph 3 of Schedule 1 (grant-aided land),
(d) a grant or a loan under section 2(2) of the Housing (Scotland) Act 1988,
(e) a grant under section 50 of the Housing Act 1988 (housing association grants) or
(f) a grant under section 51 of that Act (revenue deficit grants).]
and the Corporation may, if it thinks fit, do so.

(5) As soon as may be after removing a body from the register the Corporation shall give notice of the removal—
(a) if the body is a registered charity, to the Charity Commissioners,
(b) if the body is a society registered under the 1965 Act, to the appropriate registrar,
who shall record the removal. [462]

NOTES to section 6

Amendment: Words in sub-s (4) substituted by the Housing Act 1988 (c 50), s 59, Sch 6, para 5.

Definitions: 'register,' 'registered': see s 3 above; 'the Corporation': see s 2A above; 'housing association': see s 1 above; 'eligible for registration': see s 4 above; 'the 1965 Act' means the Industrial and Provident Societies Act 1965 (c 12): see s 1 above and s 37 below; 'the appropriate registrar': see s 37 below.

7. Appeal against removal.

(1) A body which is aggrieved by a decision of the Corporation to remove it from the register may appeal against the decision
[(a) where it is a decision of Scottish Homes to the Court of Session; and
(b) in any other case to the High Court.]

(2) If an appeal is brought the Corporation shall not remove the body concerned from the register until the appeal has been finally determined or is withdrawn.

(3) As soon as may be after an appeal is brought the Corporation shall give notice of the appeal—
(a) if the body concerned is a registered charity, to the Charity Commissioners, or
(b) if the body concerned is a society registered under the 1965 Act, to the appropriate registrar. [463]

NOTES to section 7
Amendment: Sub-s (1) amended by the Housing Act 1988 (c 50), s 59, Sch 6, para 6.
Definitions: 'the Corporation': see s 2A above; 'the register': see s 3 above; 'the 1965 Act' means the Industrial and Provident Societies Act 1965 (c 12): see s 1 above and s 37 below; 'the appropriate registrar': see s 37 below.

Disposal of land

8. Power of registered housing associations to dispose of land.

(1) Without prejudice to the provisions of Part V of the Housing Act 1985 (the right to buy) [and Part III of the Housing (Scotland) Act 1987 (analagous Scottish Provision)] every registered housing association has power, subject to section 9 (control by Corporation of land transactions), by virtue of this section but not otherwise, to dispose, in such manner as it thinks fit, of land held by it.

(2), (3) (Apply in England and Wales.) [464]

NOTES to section 8
Amendments: Sub-s (1) was amended by the Housing (Scotland) Act 1986 (c 65), s 25(1), Sch 2, para 4 and by the Housing (Scotland) Act 1987 (c 26), s 339, Sch 23, para 31.
Definitions: 'registered': see s 3 above; 'housing association': see s 1 above; 'the Corporation': see s 2A above.

9. Control by Housing Corporation of dispositions of land by housing associations.

[(1) Subject to section 10 and sections 81(6), 105(6), and 133(6) of the Housing Act 1988, the consent of the Corporation is required for any disposition of land by a registered housing association.

(1A) Subject to section 10, the consent of the relevant Corporation is required for any disposition of grant-aided land (as defined in Schedule 1) by an unregistered housing association; and for this purpose 'the relevant Corporation' means—
(a) if the land is in England, the Housing Corporation;
(b) if the land is in Scotland, Scottish Homes, and
(c) if the land is in Wales, Housing for Wales.]

(2) The consent of the Corporation may be so given—
(a) generally to all housing associations or to a particular housing association or description of association;

Housing Associations Act 1985 (c 69), s 10 [465]

(b) in relation to particular land or in relation to a particular description of land; and may be given subject to conditions.

(3) A disposition by a housing association which requires . . . [consent] under this section is valid in favour of a person claiming under the association notwithstanding that . . . [that consent] has not been given; and a person dealing with the association, or with a person claiming under the association, shall not be concerned to see or inquire whether any such consent has been given.

This subsection has effect subject to section 12 (avoidance of certain dispositions of houses without consent).

(4) Where at the time of its removal from the register under section 6(2) (removal of bodies no longer eligible for registration or defunct) a body owns land, this section continues to apply to that land after the removal as if the body concerned continued to be a registered housing association.

(5) For the purposes of this section 'disposition' means sale, lease, mortgage, charge or any other disposal.

[(6) References in this section to consent are references—
(a) in the case of the Housing Corporation or Housing for Wales, to consent given by order under the seal of the Corporation; and
(b) in the case of Scottish Homes, to consent in writing.] [465]

NOTES to section 9

Amendments: Sub-ss (1), (1A) substituted by the Housing Act 1988 (c 50), s 59, Sch 6, para 7; sub-ss (2), (3) amended by the Housing Act 1988 (c 50), s 59, Sch 6, para 7; sub-s (6) added by the Housing Act 1988 (c 50), s 59, Sch 6, para 7.
Definitions: 'the Corporation': see s 2A above; 'housing association': see s 1 above; 'register,' 'registered': see s 3 above; 'eligible for registration': see s 4 above.

10. Dispositions excepted from s 9.

(1) A disposition by an unregistered housing association which is a charity is not within section 9 if by virtue of section 29 of the Charities Act 1960 it cannot be made without an order of the court or the Charity Commissioners; but [before making an order in such a case the Charity Commissioners shall consult—
(a) in the case of dispositions of land in England, the Housing Corporation;
(b) in the case of dispositions of land in Scotland, Scottish Homes; and
(c) in the case of dispositions of land in Wales, Housing for Wales.]

(2) A letting by a registered housing association, or by an unregistered housing association which is a housing trust, is not within section 9 if it is—
(a) a letting of land under a secure tenancy, or
(b) a letting of land under what would be a secure tenancy but for any of paragraphs 2 to 12 of Schedule 1 to the Housing Act 1985 or paragraphs [1 to 8 of Schedule 2 to the Housing (Scotland) Act 1987] (tenancies excepted from being secure tenancies for reasons other than that they are long leases).
(c) a letting of land under an assured tenancy or an assured agricultural occupancy, or
(d) a letting of land in England or Wales under what would be an assured tenancy or an assured agricultural occupancy but for any of paragraphs 4 to 8 of Schedule 1 to the Housing Act 1988, [or
(e) a letting of land in Scotland under what would be an assured tenancy but for any of paragraphs 3 to 8 of Schedule 4 to the Housing (Scotland) Act 1988.]

(3) The grant by an unregistered housing association which does not satisfy the landlord condition in section 80 of the Housing Act 1985 (bodies which are capable of granting secure tenancies) of a lease for a term ending within the period of seven years and three months beginning on the date of the grant is not within section 9 unless—
(a) there is conferred on the lessee (by the lease or otherwise) an option for renewal for a term which, together with the original term, would expire outside that period, or

(b) the lease is granted wholly or partly in consideration of a fine.

(4) In subsection (3) the expression 'lease' includes an agreement for a lease and a licence to occupy, and the expressions 'grant' and 'term' shall be construed accordingly. **[466]**

NOTES to section 10

Amendments: Sub-s (1) amended by the Housing Act 1988 (c 50), s 59, Sch 6, para 8, sub-s (2) amended by the Housing and Planning Act 1986 (c 63), s 24, Sch 5, para 10, and by the Housing (Scotland) Act 1987 (c 26), s 339, Sch 23, para 31 and by the Housing Act 1988 (c 50), s 59, Sch 6, para 8.

Definitions: 'housing association': see s 1 above; 'registered': see s 3 above; 'housing trust': see s 2 above [does not apply in Scotland]; 'secure tenancy': see s 39 below; 'assured tenancy': see s 39 below; 'assured agricultural occupancy': see s 39 below.

---

11. (Applies in England and Wales.)

12. (Applies in England and Wales.)

Control of payments to members, etc

13. Payments by way of gift, dividend or bonus.

(1) A registered housing association shall not make a gift or pay a sum by way of dividend or bonus to—
 (a) a person who is or has been a member of the association, or
 (b) a person who is a member of the family of a person within paragraph (a), or
 (c) a company of which a person within paragraph (a) or (b) is a director, or
 (d) a Scottish firm of which a person within paragraph (a) or (b) is a member,
except as permitted by this section.

(2) The following are permitted—
 (a) the payment of a sum which, in accordance with the rules of the association concerned, is paid as interest on capital lent to the association or subscribed by way of shares in the association;
 (b) the payment by a full mutual housing association to a person who has ceased to be a member of the association, of a sum which is due to him either under his tenancy agreement with the association or under the terms of the agreement under which he became a member of the association.

(3) Where an association which is a society registered under the 1965 Act pays a sum or makes a gift in contravention of this section the association may recover the sum or the value of the gift, the proceedings for its recovery shall be taken by the association if the [Corporation] so directs. **[467]**

NOTES to section 13

Definitions: 'housing association': see s 1 above; 'registered': see s 3 above; 'member of the family': see s 105 below [does not apply in Scotland] 'fully mutual': see s 1 above; 'the 1965 Act' means the Industrial and Provident Societies Act 1965 (c 12): see s 1 above and s 37 below; 'the Corporation': see s 2A above.

---

14. Maximum amounts payable by way of fees, expenses, etc.

(1) The [Corporation] may from time to time specify the maximum amounts which may be paid by a registered housing association which is a society registered under the 1965 Act—
 (a) by way of fees or other remuneration, or by way of expenses, to a member of the association who is not a member of its committee or an officer or employee of the association,
 (b) by way of expenses to a member of its committee (including a co-opted member) who is not an officer or employee of the association, or

Housing Associations Act 1985 (c 69), s 15 [469]

(c) by way of expenses to an officer of the association who does not have a contract of employment with the association;

and different amounts may be so specified for different purposes.

(2) Where such an association makes a payment in excess of the specified maximum, the association may recover the excess and proceedings for its recovery shall be taken by the association if the Corporation so directs. **[468]**

NOTES to section 14

Definitions: 'the Corporation': see s 2A above; 'housing association': see s 1 above; 'registered': see s 3 above; 'the 1965 Act' means the Industrial and Provident Societies Act 1965 (c 12): see s 1 above and s 37 below; 'Committee': see s 37 below.

15. Payments and benefits to committee members, etc.

(1) A registered housing association which is a society registered under the 1965 Act shall not make a payment or grant a benefit to—
- (a) a committee member (including a co-opted member) officer or employee of the association, or
- (b) a person who at any time within the preceding twelve months has been a person within paragraph (a) or
- (c) a close relative of a person within paragraph (a) or (b), or
- (d) a business trading for profit of which a person falling within paragraph (a), (b) or (c) is a principal proprietor or in the management of which such a person is directly concerned,

except as permitted by this section [or by section 15A of this Act].

(2) The following are permitted—
- (a) payments made or benefits granted to an officer or employee under his contract of employment with the association;
- (b) the payment of expenses to a committee member (including a co-opted member) or to an officer of the association who does not have a contract of employment with the association;
- (c) any such payment as made in accordance with section 13(2) (interest payable in accordance with the rules and certain sums payable by a fully mutual housing association to a person who has ceased to be a member);
- (d) the grant or renewal of a tenancy by a co-operative housing association;
- (e) where a tenancy of a house has been granted to, or to a close relative of, a person who later became a committee member (including a co-opted member), officer or employee, the grant to that tenant of a new tenancy, whether of the same house or another house.
- [(f) except in the case of housing associations registered in the register maintained by Scottish Homes, payments made or benefits granted by an association in such class or classes of case as may be specified in a determination made by the Corporation with the approval of the Secretary of State;
- (g) in the case of housing associations registered in the register maintained by Scottish Homes, payments made or benefits granted by such an association with the approval of Scottish Homes (which approval may be given only in relation to a class or classes of cases).]

[(3) The Housing Corporation and Housing for Wales may make different determinations for the purposes of subsection 2(f) above and, before making such a determination, the Corporation shall consult such bodies appearing to it to be representative of housing associations as it considers appropriate; and after making such a determination the Corporation shall publish the determination in such manner as it considers appropriate for bringing it to the notice of the associations concerned.]

(4) Where an association pays a sum or grants a benefit in contravention of this section, the association may recover the sum or the value of the benefit, and proceedings for its recovery shall be taken by the association if the Housing Corporation so directs. **[469]**

[469] Housing Associations Act 1985 (c 69), s 15

NOTES to section 15

Amendments: In sub-s (1), words added by the Housing (Scotland) Act 1986 (c 65), s 25(1), Sch 2, para 4; sub-s (2) amended by the Housing Act 1988 (c 50), s 59, Sch 6, para 9; sub-s (3) added by *Ibid*.

Definitions: 'housing association': see s 1 above; 'registered': see s 3 above; 'the 1965 Act' means the Industrial and Provident Societies Act 1965 (c 12): see s 1 above and s 37 below; 'committee': see s 37 below; 'co-opted member': *Ibid*; 'fully mutual': see s 1 above; 'co-operative housing association': see s 1 above; 'house': see s 106(2) below.

[15A. Payments etc in community-based housing associations in Scotland.

(1) In relation to a community-based housing association in Scotland the following are also permitted, notwithstanding section 15(1)—
- (a) payments made by the association in respect of the purchase of a dwelling, or part of a dwelling, owned and occupied by a person described in subsection (2) who is not an employee of the association; but only if—
  - (i) such payments constitute expenditure in connection with housing projects undertaken for the purpose of improving or repairing dwellings; and
  - (ii) the purchase price does not exceed such value as may be placed on the dwelling, or as the case may be part, by the district valuer;
- (b) the granting of the tenancy of a dwelling, or part of a dwelling, to such a person but only if the person—
  - (i) lives in the dwelling or in another dwelling owned by the association; or
  - (ii) has at any time within the period of twelve months immediately preceding the granting of the tenancy lived in the dwelling (or such other dwelling) whether or not it belonged to the housing association when he lived there.

(2) The persons mentioned in subsection (1) are—
- (a) a committee member or voluntary officer of the association; or
- (b) a person who at any time in the twelve months preceding the payment (or as the case may be the granting of the tenancy) has been such a member or officer; or
- (c) a close relative of a person described in paragraph (a), or (b).

(3) For the purposes of subsection (1), a housing association is "community based" if—
- (a) prior to the specified date, it was designated as such by the Housing Corporation, or
- (b) on or after that date, it is designated as such by Scottish Homes;

and, in this subsection, "specified date" has the same meaning as in section 3 of the Housing (Scotland) Act 1988.

(4) Scottish Homes—
- (a) shall make a designation under subsection (3) only if it considers that the activities of the housing association relate wholly or mainly to the improvement of dwellings, or the management of improved dwellings within a particular community (whether or not identified by reference to a geographical area entirely within any one administrative area); and
- (b) may revoke such a designation (including a designation made by the Housing Corporation under subsection (3) above as originally enacted) if it considers, after giving the association an opportunity to make representations to it as regards such revocation, that the association's activities have ceased so to relate.] [470]

NOTES to section 15A

Amendments: Section 15A was originally inserted by s 14 of the Housing (Scotland) Act 1986 (c 65). The current version was substituted by the Housing Act 1988 (c 50), s 59, Sch 6, para 10.

Definitions: 'housing association': see s 1 above; 'dwelling': see s 106(2) below; 'committee': see s 37 below.

Constitution, change of rules, amalgamation and dissolution

16. General power to remove committee member.

(1) The [Corporation] may by order remove a committee member of a registered housing association if—
(a) in England and Wales, he has been adjudged bankrupt or he has made an arrangement with his creditors,
(b) in Scotland, he has become notour bankrupt or he has executed a trust feed for behoof of, or has made a composition contract or arrangement with, his creditors,
(c) he is incapable of acting by reason of mental disorder,
(d) he has not acted, or
(e) he cannot be found or does not act and his absence or failure to act is impeding the proper management of the association's affairs.

(2) Before making an order the Corporation shall give at least 14 days' notice of its intention to do so to the person whom it intends to remove, and to the association concerned.

(3) Notice under subsection (2) may be given by post, and if so given to the person whom the Corporation intend to remove may be addressed to his last known address in the United Kingdom.

(4) A person who is ordered to be removed under this section may appeal against the order—
[(a) if it is an order of the Housing Corporation or Housing for Wales, to the High Court, and
(b) if it is an order of Scottish Homes, to the Court of Session.] [471]

NOTES to section 16
Amendment: Sub-s (4) amended by the Housing Act 1988 (c 50), s 59, Sch 6, para 11.
Definitions: 'the Corporation': see s 2A above; 'committee': see s 37 below; 'housing association': see s 1 above; 'registered': see s 3 above; 'mental disorder': see s 39 below.

17. Power to appoint new committee member.

(1) The [Corporation] may by order appoint a person to be a committee member of a registered housing association—
(a) in place of a person removed by the Corporation,
(b) where there are no members of the committee, or
(c) where the Corporation is of opinion that it is necessary for the proper management of the association's affairs to have an additional committee member
[and the power conferred by paragraph (c) may be exercised notwithstanding that it will cause the maximum number of committee members permissible under the association's constitution to be exceeded.]

(2) A person may be so appointed whether or not he is a member of the association and, if he is not, notwithstanding that the rules of the association restrict appointment to members.

(3) A person appointed under this section shall hold office for such period and on such terms as the Corporation may specify and on the expiry of the appointment the Corporation may renew the appointment for such period as it may specify; but this does not prevent a person appointed under this section from retiring in accordance with the rules of the association.

(4) (Applies in England and Wales.) [472]

NOTES to section 17
Amendment: In sub-s (1) words added by the Housing Act 1988 (c 50), s 59, Sch 6, para 12.
Definitions: 'the Corporation': see s 2A above; 'committee': see s 37 below; 'registered': see s 3 above; 'housing association': see s 1 above.

18. (Applies in England and Wales.)

19. Change of rules under the 1965 Act.

(1) This section applies to a registered housing association—
(a) which is a society registered under the 1965 Act, and
(b) whose registration under this Part has been recorded by the appropriate registrar in accordance with section 5(3).

(2) Notice shall be sent to [the Corporation] of a change of the association's name or of the situation of its registered office.

(3) Any other amendment of the association's rules is not valid without the Corporation's consent, [given
(a) in the case of the Housing Corporation or Housing for Wales, by order under the seal of the Corporation; and
(b) in the case of Scottish Homes, by notice in writing;]
and a copy of such consent shall be sent with the copies of the amendment required by section 10(1) of the 1965 Act to be sent to the appropriate registrar.

(4) The 1965 Act applies in relation to the provisions of this section as if they were contained in section 10 of that Act (amendment of registered rules). [473]

NOTES to section 19

Amendment: Sub-s 3 amended by the Housing Act 1988 (c 50), s 59, Sch 6, para 14.
Definitions: 'registered': see s 3 above; 'housing association': see s 1 above; 'the 1965 Act' means the Industrial and Provident Societies Act 1965 (c 12): see s 1 above and s 37 below; 'the appropriate registrar': see s 37 above; 'the Corporation': see s 2A above.

20. (Applies in England and Wales.)

21. Amalgamation and dissolution under the 1965 Act.

(1) This section applies to a registered housing association—
(a) which is a society registered under the 1965 Act, and
(b) whose registration under this Part has been recorded by the appropriate registrar in accordance with section 5(3).

(2) The appropriate registrar shall not register a special resolution which is passed for the purposes of—
(a) section 50 of the 1965 Act (amalgamation of societies), or
(b) section 51 of that Act (transfer of engagements between societies),
unless, together with the copy of the resolution, there is sent to him a copy of the [Corporation's] consent to the amalgamation or transfer concerned.

(3) Section 52 of the 1965 Act (power of society to convert itself into, amalgamate with or transfer its engagements to a company registered under the Companies Act) does not apply.

(4) If the association resolves by special resolution that it be wound up voluntarily under the Companies Act, the resolution has no effect unless—
(a) before the resolution was passed the Corporation gave its consent to its passing, and
(b) a copy of the consent is forwarded to the appropriate registrar together with the copy of the resolution required to be so forwarded in accordance with the Companies Act.

(5) If the association is to be dissolved by instrument of dissolution, the appropriate registrar shall not—
(a) register the instrument in accordance with section 58(5) of the 1965 Act, or
(b) cause notice of the dissolution to be advertised in accordance with section 58(6) of that Act,
unless together with the instrument there is sent to him a copy of the Corporation's consent to its making.

(6) The references in this section to the Corporation's consent are—

[(a) in the case of the Housing Corporation or Housing for Wales, to consent given by order under the seal of the Corporation; and
(b) in the case of Scottish Homes, to consent given in writing.]

NOTES to section 21
Amendment: Sub-s (6) amended by the Housing Act 1988 (c 50), s 59, Sch 6, para 15.
Definitions: 'registered': see s 3 above; 'housing association': see s 1 above; 'the 1965 Act' means the Industrial and Provident Societies Act 1965 (c 12): see ss 1, 37; 'the appropriate registrar': see s 37 below; 'the Corporation': see s 2A above; 'the Companies Act': see s 106(2) below.

22. Housing Corporation's power to petition for winding up.

(1) The [Corporation] may present a petition for the winding up under the Companies Act of a registered housing association to which this section applies
 [(a)] on the ground that the association is failing properly to carry out its purposes or objects, [or
 (b) on the ground that the association is unable to pay its debts within the meaning of section 518 of the Companies Act 1985.]

(2) This section applies to a registered housing association which is—
(a) a company incorporated under the Companies Act, or
(b) a society registered under the 1965 Act (to which the winding up provisions of the Companies Act apply in accordance with section 55(a) of the 1965 Act).

NOTES to section 22
Amendment: Sub-s (1) amended by the Housing Act 1988 (c 50), s 59, Sch 6, para 16.
Definitions: 'the Corporation': see s 2A above; 'Companies Act': see s 106(2) below; 'registered': see s 3 above; 'housing association': see s 1 above; 'the 1965 Act' means the Industrial and Provident Societies Act 1965 (c 12): see s 1 above and s 37 below.

23. Transfer of net assets on dissolution.

(1) Where a registered housing association which is a society registered under the 1965 Act is dissolved under that Act, so much of the property of the association as remains after meeting the claims of its creditors and any other liabilities arising on or before the dissolution shall be transferred—
(a) to the [Corporation,] or
(b) if the Corporation so directs, to such registered housing association as may be specified in the direction,
notwithstanding anything in the 1965 Act or in the rules of the association.

(2) In order to avoid the necessity for the sale of land belonging to the association, and thereby secure the transfer of the land under this section, the Corporation may, if it appears to it appropriate to do so, make payments to discharge such claims or liabilities as are referred to in subsection (1).

(3) Where the association which is dissolved is a charity, the Corporation may dispose of property transferred to it by virtue of this section only to another registered housing association—
(a) which is also a charity, and
(b) the objects of which appear to the Corporation to be, as nearly as practicable, akin to those of the dissolved association.

(4) In any other case the Corporation may dispose of property transferred to it by virtue of this section to a registered housing association or to a subsidiary of the Corporation.

(5) Where property transferred to the Corporation by virtue of this section includes land subject to an existing mortgage or charge (whether in favour of the Corporation or not), the Corporation may, in exercise of its powers under Part III, dispose of the land either—

(a) subject to that mortgage or charge, or
(b) subject to a new mortgage or charge in favour of the Corporation securing such amount as appears to the Corporation to be appropriate in the circumstances. **[476]**

NOTES to section 23

Definitions: 'registered': see s 3 above; 'housing association': see s 1 above; 'the 1965 Act' means the Industrial and Provident Societies Act 1965 (c 12): see ss 1, 37; 'mortgage': see s 106(2) below.

Accounts and audit

24. General requirements as to accounts and audit.

(1) The Secretary of State may by order lay down accounting requirements for registered housing associations with a view to ensuring that the accounts of every registered housing association—
(a) are prepared in the requisite form, and
(b) give a true and fair view of the state of affairs of the association, so far as its housing activities are concerned, and of the disposition of its funds and assets which are, or at any time have been, in its hands in connection with those activities.

(2) The method by which an association [which is a registered charity] shall distinguish in its accounts between its housing activities and other activities shall be laid down by orders under subsection (1).

(3) The accounts of every registered housing association shall comply with the requirements laid down under this section; and the auditor's report shall state, in addition to any other matters which it is required to state, whether in the auditor's opinion the accounts do so comply.

(4) Every registered housing association shall furnish to [the Corporation] a copy of its accounts and auditor's report within six months of the end of the period to which they relate.

(5) An order under this section—
(a) may make different provision with respect to different cases or descriptions of case, including different provision for different areas, [or for different descriptions of housing associations or housing activities], and
(b) shall be made by statutory instrument which shall be subject to annulment in pursuance of a resolution of either House of Parliament;
and the provisions of such an order shall not apply in relation to a period beginning before the day on which the order comes into force.

[(6) For the purposes of subsection (5), descriptions may be framed by reference to any matters whatever, including in particular, in the case of housing activities, the manner in which they are financed.] **[477]**

NOTES to section 24

Amendments: Sub-s (2) was amended by the Housing Act 1988 (c 50), s 59, Sch 6, para 17; sub-s (5) was amended by the Housing Act 1988 (c 50), s 59, Sch 6, para 17; sub-s (6) was added by the Housing Act 1988 (c 50), s 59, Sch 6, para 17.

Definitions: 'registered': see s 3 above; 'housing association': see s 1 above; 'housing activities': see s 106(2) below.

Sub-ss (1), (2), (5): See the Registered Housing Associations (Accounting Requirements) Order 1988, SI 1988/395, paras [1395] ff below.

25. Appointment of auditors by associations registered under the 1965 Act.

Section 4(1) of the Friendly and Industrial and Provident Societies Act 1968 (obligation to appoint qualified auditors to audit accounts and balance sheet for each year of account) applies to every registered housing association which is a society registered under the 1965 Act, without regard to the volume of its receipts and payments, the number of its members or the value of its assets. [478]

NOTES to section 25

Definitions: 'registered': see s 3 above; 'housing association': see s 1 above; 'the 1965 Act' means the Industrial and Provident Societies Act 1965 (c 12): see s 1 above and s 37 below.

26. Accounting requirements for registered housing associations not within the 1965 Act.

(1) A registered housing association which is a registered charity shall, in respect of its housing activities (and separately from its other activities, if any) be subject to the provisions of Schedule 3 (which impose accounting and audit requirements corresponding to those imposed by the Friendly and Industrial and Provident Societies Act 1968).

(2) But this does not affect any obligation of the charity under section 8 of the Charities Act 1960 (statement of accounts to be transmitted to Charity Commissioners). [479]

NOTES to section 26

Definitions: 'registered' see s 3 above; 'housing association': see s 1 above.

27. Responsibility for securing compliance with accounting requirements.

(1) Every responsible person, that is to say, every person who—
(a) is directly concerned with the conduct and management of the affairs of a registered housing association, and
(b) is in that capacity responsible for the preparation and audit of accounts,
shall ensure that section 24 (general requirements as to accounts and audit) and, where applicable, Schedule 3 (accounting requirements for associations not within 1965 Act) are complied with by the association.

(2) If—
(a) section 24(4) (furnishing of accounts and auditor's report) is not complied with, or
(b) the accounts furnished to the [Corporation] under that provision do not comply with the accounting requirements laid down under section 24(1), or
(c) Schedule 3, where applicable, is not complied with, [or
(d) section 55(9) of the Housing Act 1988 is not complied with]
every responsible person, and the association itself, commits a summary offence and is liable on conviction to a fine not exceeding level 3 on the standard scale.

(3) It is a defence—
(a) for a responsible person to prove that he did everything that could reasonably have been expected of him by way of discharging the duty imposed by subsection (1);
(b) for an association to prove that every responsible person did everything that could reasonably have been expected of him by way of discharging the duty imposed by subsection (1) in relation to the association.

(4) Proceedings for an offence under this section may in England and Wales be brought only by or with the consent of the Corporation or the Director of Public Prosecutions. [480]

NOTES to section 27

Amendment: Sub-s (2) amended by the Housing Act 1988 (c 50), s 59, Sch 6, para 18.
Definitions: 'registered': see s 3 above; 'housing association': see s 1 above; 'the 1965 Act' means the Industrial and Provident Societies Act 1965 (c 12): see s 1 above and s 37 below; 'the Corporation': see s 2A above; 'Level 3 on the standard scale is currently £400: see the Increase of Criminal Penalties Etc (Scotland) Order 1984, SI 1984/526.

[481] *Housing Associations Act 1985 (c 69), s 27A*

'27A. **Power of Corporation to monitor associations.**

(1) If at any time required to do so by the Corporation,—
(a) a registered housing association shall produce to a person authorised in that behalf by the Corporation such books, accounts and other documents relating to the association's business as may be specified by the Corporation; and
(b) any officer, employee or member of the committee or the registered housing association shall provide an explanation of any such books, accounts and other documents.

(2) Where, by virtue of subsection (1), any books, accounts or other documents are produced to a person authorised in that behalf by the Corporation, he may take copies of or make extracts from them.

(3) In the application of this section to a registered housing association which is a charity,—
(a) the reference in subsection (1)(a) to the association's business shall be construed as a reference to its housing activities; and
(b) the reference to a member of the committee includes a reference to a trustee of the association.' [481]

NOTES to section 27A

Amendment: Section 27A was inserted by the Local Government and Housing Act 1989 (c 42), s 182.
Definitions: 'the Corporation': see s 2A above; 'registered': see s 3 above; 'housing association': see s 1 above; 'committee': see s 37 below; 'housing activities': see s 106(2) below.

Inquiries into affairs of housing associations

28. Inquiry.

(1) The [Corporation] may appoint a person (not a person who is, or at any time has been a member of the [staff of any of the Corporations]) to conduct an inquiry into the affairs of a registered housing association, [and, if the appointed person considers it necessary for the purposes of the inquiry, he may also inquire into the business of any other body which, at a time which the appointed person considers material, is or was a subsidiary or associate of the association concerned].

(2) The appointed person may by notice in writing served on
(a) the association concerned, or
(b) any person who is, or has been, an officer, agent or member of the association, or
[(c) any person who is, or has been an officer, agent or member of a subsidiary or associate of the association; or
(d) any other person whom the appointed person has reason to believe is or may be in possession of information of relevance to the inquiry;]
require the association or person to produce to him such books, accounts and other documents relating to [the business of the association or any other such body as is referred to in subsection (1)] and to give him such other information so relating, as he considers necessary for the purposes of the inquiry.

(3) An association or other person who fails without reasonable excuse to comply with the requirements of a notice under subsection (2) commits a summary offence and is liable on conviction to a fine not exceeding level 5 on the standard scale.

[(3A) Where, by virtue of subsection (2), any books, accounts or other documents are produced to the appointed person, he may take copies of or make extracts from them.

(3B) The appointed person may, if he thinks fit during the course of the inquiry, make one or more interim reports to the Corporation on such matters as appear to him to be appropriate.]

(4) On completion of the inquiry the appointed person shall make a report to the Corporation on such matters and in such form as the Corporation may specify.

(5) In this section 'agent' includes banker, solicitor and auditor; but nothing in this section requires the disclosure—
  (a) by a solicitor, of a privileged communication made to him in his capacity as solicitor, or
  (b) by a housing association's banker, of information as to the affairs of any of their other customers.

[(6) In this section, in relation to a housing association, 'subsidiary' means a company with respect to which one of the following conditions is fulfilled—
  (a) the association is a member of the company and controls the composition of the board of directors; or
  (b) the association holds more than half in nominal value of the company's equity share capital; or
  (c) the company is a subsidiary, within the meaning of the Companies Act 1985 or the Friendly and Industrial and Provident Societies Act of 1968, of another company which, by virtue of paragraph (a) or paragraph (b), is itself a subsidiary of the housing association;
and, in the case of a housing association which is a body of trustees, the reference in paragraph (a) or paragraph (b) to the association is a reference to the trustees acting as such and any reference in subsection (7) to the association shall be construed accordingly.

(7) For the purposes of subsection (6)(a) the composition of a company's board of directors shall be deemed to be controlled by a housing association if, but only if, the association, by the exercise of some power exercisable by the association without the consent or concurrence of any other person, can appoint or remove the holders of all or a majority of the directorships.

(8) In this section, in relation to a housing association, 'associate' means—
  (a) any body of which the association is a subsidiary, and
  (b) any other subsidiary of such a body,
and in this subsection 'subsidiary' has the same meaning as in the Companies Act 1985 or the Friendly and Industrial and Provident Societies Act of 1968 or, in the case of a body which is itself a housing association, has the meaning assigned by subsection (6).

(9) In relation to a company which is an industrial and provident society—
  (a) any reference in subsection (6)(a) or subsection (7) to the board of directors is a reference to the committee of management of the society; and
  (b) the reference in subsection (7) to the holders of all or a majority of the directorships is a reference to all or a majority of the members of the committee or, if the housing association is itself a member of the committee, such number as together with the association would constitute a majority.]

NOTES to section 28
Amendments: Sub-ss (1), (2), amended by the Housing Act 1988 (c 50), s 59, Sch 6, para 19; sub-ss (3A), (3B) and (6) to (9) added by the Housing Act 1988 (c 50), s 59, Sch 6, para 19.
Definitions: 'the Corporation': see s 2A above; 'registered': see s 3 above; 'housing association': see s 1 above; 'Level 5 on the standard scale' is currently £2000: see the Increase of Criminal Penalties Etc (Scotland) Order 1984, SI 1984/526.

29. Extraordinary audit for the purposes of inquiry.

(1) For the purposes of an inquiry under section 2৪ [into the affairs of a registered housing association,] the [Corporation] may require the accounts and balance sheet of the association concerned, or such of them as the Corporation may specify, to be audited by a qualified auditor appointed by the Corporation.

(2) A person is a qualified auditor for this purpose if he is under section 7(1) of the Friendly and Industrial and Provident Societies Act of 1968 a qualified auditor for the purposes of that Act, or is under section 7(2) of that Act a qualified auditor in relation to the association concerned.

(3) On completion of the audit the appointed auditor shall make a report to the Corporation on such matters and in such form as the Corporation may specify.

(4) The expenses of the audit, including the remuneration of the auditor, shall be paid by the Corporation.

(5) An audit under this section is additional to, and does not affect, any audit made or to be made under any other enactment. **[483]**

NOTES to section 29
Amendment: Sub-s (1) amended by the Housing Act 1988 (c 50), s 59, Sch 6, para 20.
Definitions: 'the Corporation': see s 2A above; 'registered': see s 3 above; 'housing association': see s 1 above.

30. General powers exercisable as a result of inquiry or audit.

(1) Where the [Corporation] is satisfied, as the result of any inquiry under section 28 or an audit under section 29, that there has been misconduct or mismanagement in the affairs of a registered housing association, it may—
   (a) by order remove any member of the committee of the association, or any officer, agent or employee of the association, who has been responsible for or privy to the misconduct or mismanagement or has by his conduct contributed to it or facilitated it;
   (b) by order suspend such a person for up to six months, pending determination whether he should be removed;
   (c) order any bank or other person who holds money or securities on behalf of the association not to part with the money or securities without the approval of the Corporation;
   (d) by order restrict the transactions which may be entered into, or the nature or amount of the payments which may be made, in the administration of the association without the approval of the Corporation.

[(1A) If at any time the appointed person makes an interim report under section 28(3B) and, as a result of that interim report, the Corporation is satisfied that there has been misconduct or mismanagement as mentioned in subsection (1)—
   (a) the Corporation may at that time exercise any of the powers conferred by paragraphs (b) to (d) of that subsection; and
   (b) in relation to the exercise at that time of the power conferred by subsection (1)(b), the reference therein to a period of six months shall be construed as a reference to a period beginning at that time and ending six months after the date of the report under section 28(4).]

(2) Before making an order under subsection (1)(a) the Corporation shall give at least 14 days' notice of its intention to do so—
   (a) to the person it intends to remove, and
   (b) to the association concerned.

(3) Notice under subsection (2) may be given by post, and if so given to the person whom the Corporation intends to remove may be addressed to his last known address in the United Kingdom.

(4) A person who is ordered to be removed under subsection (1)(a) or suspended under subsection (1)(b) may appeal against the [order
   (a) if it is an order of the Housing Corporation or Housing for Wales, to the High Court and
   (b) if it is an order of Scottish Homes, to the Court of Session.]

(5) Where a person is suspended under subsection (1)(b), the Corporation may give directions with respect to the performance of his functions and otherwise as to matters arising from the suspension.

(6) A person who contravenes an order under subsection (1)(c) commits a summary

offence and is liable on conviction to a fine not exceeding level 5 on the standard scale or imprisonment for a term not exceeding three months or both; but proceedings for such an offence may be brought in England and Wales only by or with the consent of the Corporation or the Director of Public Prosecutions. [484]

NOTES to section 30
Amendments: Sub-s (1A) was added by the Housing Act 1988 (c 50), s 59, Sch 6, para 21; sub-s (4) was amended by the Housing Act 1988 (c 50), s 59, Sch 6, para 21.

Definitions: 'the Corporation': see s 2A above; 'registered': see s 3 above; 'housing association': see s 1 above; 'committee': see s 37 below; 'bank': see s 106(2) below; 'Level 5 on the standard scale' is currently £2000: see the Increase of Criminal Penalties Etc (Scotland) Order 1984, SI 1984/526.

31. (Applies in England and Wales.)

32. Power to direct transfer of land to another housing association or the Housing Corporation.

(1) Where, as the result of an inquiry under section 28 or an audit under section 29, the [Corporation] is satisfied as regards a registered housing association which is a society registered under the 1965 Act—
  (a) that there has been misconduct or mismanagement in the administration of the association, or
  (b) that the management of the land belonging to the association would be improved if the land belonging to the association were transferred in accordance with the provisions of this section,
the Corporation may, with the consent of the Secretary of State, direct the association to make such a transfer.

(2) Where the association concerned is a charity, the Housing Corporation may only direct a transfer to be made to another registered housing association—
  (a) which is also a charity, and
  (b) the objects of which appear to the Corporation to be, as nearly as practicable, akin to those of the association concerned.

(3) In any other case the Corporation may direct a transfer to be made to the Corporation or to another registered housing association.

(4) A transfer in pursuance of a direction under this section shall be made on the terms that the transferee will pay or undertake to pay to the association concerned such sum (if any) as will be necessary to defray all its proper debts and liabilities (including debts and liabilities secured on the land) after taking into account any money or other assets belonging to the association.

(5) If it appears to the Corporation likely that the association concerned will as a result of the transfer be dissolved under the 1965 Act, the Corporation shall secure that the cost of the dissolution are taken into account in determining the sum payable to the association under subsection (4). [485]

NOTES to section 32
Definitions: 'the Corporation': see s 2A above; 'registered': see s 3 above; 'housing association': see s 1 above; 'the 1965 Act' means the Industrial and Provident Societies Act 1965 (c 12): see s 1 above and s 37 below; 'dissolved under the 1965 Act': see s 37 below.

Miscellaneous

33. Recognition of central association.

(1) The Secretary of State may, if he thinks fit, recognise for the purposes of this section a central association or other body established for the purposes of promoting the

formation and extension of housing associations [in Great Britain or in any part of Great Britain] and of giving them advice and assistance.

(2) The Secretary of State may make a grant in aid of the expenses of the association or body of such amount as he may, with the approval of the Treasury, determine. **[486]**

NOTES to section 33
Amendment: Sub-s (1) was amended by the Housing Act 1988 (c 50), s 59, Sch 6, para 23.
Definition: 'housing association': see s 1 above.

[33A. Provision of services between the Corporations.

Any of the Corporations may enter into an agreement with the others or either of them for the provision of services of any description by the one to the other or others on such terms, as to payment or otherwise, as the parties to the agreement consider appropriate.] **[487]**

NOTES to section 33A
Amendment: Section 33A was added by the Housing Act 1985 (c 50), s 59, Sch 6, para 24.
Definition: 'the Corporations': see s 2A above.

34–36. (Sections 34 to 36 apply in England and Wales.)

[36A. Issue of guidance by the Corporation.

(1) In accordance with the provisions of this section, the Corporation may issue guidance with respect to the management of housing accommodation by registered housing associations and, in considering under the preceding provisions of this Part whether action needs to be taken to secure the proper management of an association's affairs or whether there has been mismanagement, the Corporation may have regard (among other matters) to the extent to which any such guidance is being or has been followed.

(2) Guidance issued under this section may make different provision in relation to different cases and, in particular, in relation to different areas, different descriptions of housing accommodation and different descriptions of registered housing associations.

(3) Without prejudice to the generality of subsections (1) and (2), guidance issued under this section may relate to—
(a) the housing demands for which provision should be made and the means of meeting those demands;
(b) the allocation of housing accommodation between individuals;
(c) the terms of tenancies and the principles upon which the levels of rent should be determined;
(d) standards of maintenance and repair and the means of achieving these standards; and
(e) consultation and communication with tenants.

(4) Guidance issued under this section may be revised or withdrawn but, before issuing or revising any guidance under this section, the Corporation—
(a) shall consult such bodies appearing to it to be representative of housing associations as it considers appropriate; and
(b) shall submit a draft of the proposed guidance or, as the case may be, the proposed revision to the Secretary of State for his approval.

(5) If the Secretary of State gives his approval to a draft submitted to him under subsection (4)(b), the Corporation shall issue the guidance or, as the case may be, the revision concerned in such manner as the Corporation considers appropriate for bringing it to the notice of the housing associations concerned.] **[488]**

NOTES to section 36A
Amendment: Section 36A was added by the Housing Act 1988 (c 50), s 49.

Housing Associations Act 1985 (c 69), s 40 [491]

Definitions: 'the Corporation': see s 2A above; 'registered': see s 3 above; 'housing association': see s 1 above.

Supplementary

37. Definitions relating to the 1965 Act and societies registered under it.

In this Part 'the 1965 Act' means the Industrial and Provident Societies Act 1965, and in relation to a society registered under that Act—
'appropriate registrar' has the same meaning as in that Act (where it is defined in section 73(1)(c) by reference to the situation of the society's registered office);
'committee' means the committee of management or other directing body of the society;
'co-opted member', in relation to the committee, includes any person co-opted to serve on the committee, whether he is a member of the society or not;
'dissolved under the 1965 Act' means dissolved either as mentioned in section 55(a) of that Act (winding up under the Companies Act) or as mentioned in section 55(b) of that Act (instrument of dissolution). [489]

38. (Applies in England and Wales.)

39. Minor definitions.

In this Part—
['assured tenancy' has, in England and Wales, the same meaning as in Part I of the Housing Act 1988 and, in Scotland, the same meaning as in Part II of the Housing (Scotland) Act 1988;
'assured agricultural occupancy' has the same meaning as in Part I of the Housing Act 1988.]
'mental disorder' has the same meaning as in the Mental Health Act 1983 or the Mental Health (Scotland) Act 1984;
'secure tenancy' has the same meaning as in section 79 of the Housing Act 1985 [or section 445 of the Housing (Scotland) Act 1987;]
'standard scale' has the meaning given by section 75 of the Criminal Justice Act 1982. [490]

NOTES to section 39

Amendments: New definitions inserted by the Housing Act 1988 (c 50), s 59, Sch 6, para 25; definition of 'secure tenancy' amended by the Housing (Scotland) Act 1987 (c 26), s 339, Sch 23, para 31.

40. Index of defined expressions: Part I.

The following Table shows provisions defining or explaining expressions used in this Part (other than provisions defining or explaining an expression used only in the same section or paragraph)—

appropriate registrar (in relation to a society registered under the 1965 Act)	section 37
[assured agricultural occupancy	section 39
assured tenancy	section 39]
bank	section 106
charge (in relation to Scotland)	section 106
charity	section 38(a)
committee (in relation to a society registered under the 1985 Act)	section 37
compulsory disposal (in Schedule 2)	paragraph 6 of that Schedule
co-operative housing association	section 1(2)

[491]

co-opted member (in relation to the committee of a society registered under the 1965 Act)	section 37
the Companies Act	section 106
[the Corporation	section 2A]
dissolved under the 1965 Act (in relation to a society registered under that Act)	section 37
district (of a local housing authority)	section 104(2)
dwelling	section 106
eligible for registration (in relation to a housing association)	section 4
exempted disposal (in Schedule 2)	paragraph 5 of that Schedule
friendly society	section 106
fully mutual (in relation to a housing association	section 1(2)
hostel	section 106
house	section 106
housing activities	section 106
housing association	section 1(1)

. . .

housing trust	section 2
insurance company	section 106
local housing authority	section 104
member of family	section 105
mental disorder	section 39
mortgage (in relation to Scotland)	section 106
the 1965 Act	section 37
register, registered, registration and unregistered (in relation to a housing association)	section [3]
registered charity	section 38(b)
relevant disposal (in Schedule 2)	paragraph 4 of that Schedule

. . .

secure tenancy	section 39
shared ownership lease	section 106
[shared ownership agreement (in relation to Scotland)]	section 106
standard scale	section 39
trustee savings bank	section 106

[491]

NOTES to section 40

Amendments: Reference to 'shared ownership agreement' inserted by the Housing (Scotland) Act 1986 (c 65) s 25(1), Sch 2, para 4; other references inserted by the Housing Act 1988 (c 50), s 59, Sch 6, para 26; reference beginning 'register' amended by *Ibid*; references deleted by *Ibid*, Sch 18.

* * *

NOTES to sections 41–57

Sections 41 to 57 were repealed by the Housing Act 1980 (c 50), s 140, Sch 18.

58. (Applies in England and Wales.)

* * *

Housing Associations Act 1985 (c 69), s 60 [493]

PART II
HOUSING ASSOCIATION FINANCE

* * *

Arrangements with local authorities

* * *

59. Powers of local authorities to promote and assist housing associations: Scotland.

(1) A local authority or regional council may promote the formation or extension of or, subject to section 60 (assistance restricted to registered housing associations), assist a housing association whose objects include the erection, improvement or management of housing accommodation.

(2) A local authority or regional council may, with the consent of and subject to any regulations or conditions made or imposed by the Secretary of State, for the assistance of such an association—
(a) make grants or loans to the association,
(b) subscribe for share or loan capital of the association, or
(c) guarantee or join in guaranteeing the payment or the principal of, and interest on, money borrowed by the association (including money borrowed by the issue of loan capital) or of interest on share capital issued by the association,
on such terms and conditions as to rate of interest and repayment or otherwise and on such security as the local authority or regional council think fit.

(3) A term of an agreement for such a grant or loan is void if it purports to relate to the rent payable in respect of a house to which the agreement relates or the contributions payable towards the cost of maintaining such a house.

(4) Regulations under this section shall be made by statutory instrument which shall be subject to annulment in pursuance of a resolution of either House of Parliament.

[(5) Sections 6, 15, 320 and 329 of the Housing (Scotland) Act 1987 (general provisions with respect to housing functions of local authorities etc) apply in relation to this section and section 61, as they apply in relation to the provisions of that Act.] [492]

NOTES to section 59
Amendment: Sub-s (5) was added by the Housing (Scotland) Act 1987 (c 26) s 339, Sch 23, para 31.
Definitions: 'local authority': see s 106(2) below; 'registered': see s 3 above; 'housing association': see s 1 above; 'house': see s 106(2) below.
Sub-ss (2), (4): No regulations have yet been made under this power.

60. Certain assistance restricted to registered housing associations.

(1) Subject to the following provisions of this section, grants, loans and guarantees may be made or given under sections 58(2)(a) and (c) and 59(2)(a) and (c) only if the association is at the time the grant or loan is made, or the guarantee is given, a registered housing association.

(2) Subsection (1) does not apply in relation to the making of a loan to an unregistered self-build society for the purpose of enabling it to meet the whole or part of the expenditure incurred, or to be incurred, by it in carrying out its objects.

(3) Nothing in subsection (1) prevents the making of a loan to an unregistered association for the assistance of the association—
(a) in connection with works required to be carried out in pursuance of, or the acquisition of an estate or interest in a dwelling or other building for the purposes of, arrangements under section 121 of the Housing Act 1957 or section 155 of the Housing (Scotland) Act 1966 (arrangements with local authorities for the

267

improvement of housing) which were approved by the Secretary of State before 1st April 1975;
- (b) in connection with dwellings which were relevant dwellings for the purposes of section 73 of the Housing Finance Act 1972 (certain dwellings approved for purposes of subsidy before 10th August 1972);
- (c) in connection with the provision of works which are relevant works, approved for subsidy, within the meaning of section 53 of the Housing (Financial Provisions) (Scotland) Act 1972;
- (d) in connection with a building scheme within the meaning of section 75 of the Housing Finance Act 1972 (new building subsidy) which was approved by the Secretary of State for the purposes of that section before 1st April 1975;
- (e) in connection with a building scheme or improvement scheme, within the meaning of sections 55 and 57 of the Housing (Financial Provisions) (Scotland) Act 1972 which was approved by the Secretary of State for the purposes of those sections before 1st April 1975. **[493]**

NOTES to section 60

Definitions: 'registered': see s 3 above; 'housing association': see s 1 above; 'self-build society': see s 1 above; 'dwelling': see s 106(2) below; 'local authority': see s 106(2) below.

61. Power of local housing authority to supply furniture to housing association tenants.

(1) A local housing authority may sell, or supply under a hire-purchase agreement, furniture to the occupants of houses provided by a housing association under arrangements made with the authority, and may buy furniture for the purpose.

(2) In this section 'hire-purchase agreement' means a hire-purchase agreement or conditional sale agreement within the meaning of the Consumer Credit Act 1974. **[494]**

NOTES to section 61

Definitions: 'local housing authority': see s 104 below; 'house': see s 106(2) below; 'housing association' see s 1 above.

* * *

NOTES to section 62

Section 62 was repealed by the Housing Act 1980 (c 50), s 140, Sch 18.

NOTES to sections 63–66

Sections 63–66 were repealed by the Building Societies Act 1986 (c 53), s 120, Sch 18, para 19.

67. (Applies in England and Wales.)

Loans by Public Works Loan Commissioners

* * *

68. Loans by Public Works Loan Commissioners: Scotland.

(1) The Public Works Loan Commissioners may lend money to a [registered] housing association—
- (a) for the purpose of constructing or improving, or facilitating or encouraging the construction or improvement of, houses,
- (b) for the purchase of houses, and
- (c) for the purchase and development of land.

(2) A loan for any of those purposes shall be secured with interest by a heritable security over—
- (a) the land in respect of which that purpose is to be carried out, and

(b) such other land, if any, as may be offered as security for the loan;
and the money lent shall not exceed three-quarters (or, if the payment of the principal of and interest on the loan is guaranteed by the local authority, nine-tenths) of the value, to be ascertained to the satisfaction of the Public Works Loan Commissioners, of the estate or interest in the land proposed to be burdened.

(3) Loans may be made by instalments as the building of houses or other work on the land burdened under subsection (2) progresses (so, however, that the total loans do not at any time exceed the amount specified in that subsection); and the heritable security may be granted accordingly to secure such loans so to be made.

(4) If the loan exceeds two-thirds of the value referred to in subsection (2), and is not guaranteed as to principal and interest by a local authority, the Public Works Loan Commissioners shall require, in addition to such a heritable security as is mentioned in that subsection, such further security as they may think fit.

(5) Subject to subsection (6), the period for repayment of a loan under this section shall not exceed 40 years, and no money shall be lent on the security of any land unless the estate or interest proposed to be burdened is either ownership or a lease of which a period of not less than 50 years remains unexpired at the date of the loan.

(6) Where a loan under this section is made for the purposes of carrying out a scheme for the provision of houses approved by the Secretary of State, the maximum period for the repayment of the loan is 50 instead of 40 years, and money may be lent on heritable security over a lease recorded under the Registration of Leases (Scotland) Act 1857 of which a period of not less than ten years in excess of the period fixed for the repayment of the loan remains unexpired at the date of the loan. [495]

NOTES to section 68
Amendment: Sub-s (1) was amended by the Housing and Planning Act 1986 (c 63), s 24, Sch 5, para 13.
Definitions: 'register': see s 3 above; 'housing association': see s 1 above; 'house': see s 106(2) below.

Miscellaneous

69. Power to vary or terminate certain agreements with housing associations.

(1) This section applies to agreements of the following descriptions—
(a) an agreement for a loan to a housing association by the Housing Corporation under section 2 of the Housing Act 1964 [(including such an agreement under which rights and obligations have been transferred to housing for Wales)];
(b) an agreement which continues in force under Part I of Schedule 4 (arrangements with local authority for the provision or improvement of housing);
(c) an agreement to which Part II of Schedule 4 applies (subsidy agreements with local authorities);
(d) an agreement which continues in force under Part III of Schedule 4 (special arrangements with the Secretary of State);
(e) an agreement for a loan or grant to a housing association under section 58(2) or 59(2) (financial assistance by local authorities);
(f) a scheme which continues in force under Part V of Schedule 5 (schemes for unification of grant conditions).
[(g) An agreement for a loan or grant to a registered housing association under section 24 of the Local Government Act 1988 (power to provide financial assistance for privately let housing accommodation).]

(2) On the application of a party to an agreement to which this section applies, the Secretary of State may, if he thinks fit, direct—
(a) that the agreement shall have effect with such variations, determined by him or agreed by the parties, as may be specified in the direction, or
(b) that the agreement shall be terminated.

[(2A) In the case of an agreement under which rights and obligations have been transferred to housing for Wales, the reference to a party to the agreement includes a reference to Housing for Wales.]

(3) (Applies in England and Wales.)

(4) No variation shall be directed under subsection (2) which would have the effect of including in an agreement a term relating to the rent payable in respect of a house to which the agreement relates or contributions towards the cost of maintaining such a house.
This subsection extends to Scotland only. [496]

NOTES to section 69

Amendments: Sub-s (1)(a) was amended by the Housing Act 1988 (c 50), s 59, Sch 6, para 28; sub-s (1)(g) was added by the Local Government Act 1988 (c 9), s 24; sub-s (2A) was added by *Ibid*.

Definitions: 'housing association': see s 1 above; 'the Corporation': see s 2A above; 'Local authority': see s 106(2) below; 'house': *Ibid*.

[69A. Land subject to housing management agreement.

A housing association is not entitled a grant under section 50 (housing association grant) or section 51 (revenue deficit grant) of the Housing Act 1988 in respect of land comprised in—
- (a) a management agreement within the meaning of the Housing Act 1985 (see sections 27(2) and 27B(4) of that Act: delegation of housing management functions by certain authorities), or
- (b) an agreement to which section 22 of the Housing (Scotland) Act 1987 applies (agreements for exercise by housing co-operatives of certain local authority housing functions).] [497]

NOTES to section 69A

Amendments: Section 69A was added by the Housing and Planning Act 1986 (c 63), s 24, Sch 5 and amended by the Housing (Scotland) Act 1987 (c 26), s 339, Sch 23, para 31, and by the Housing Act 1988 (c 50), s 59, Sch 6, para 29.

Definition: 'housing association': see s 1 above.

70. Continuation of arrangements under repealed enactments.

The provisions of Schedule 4 have effect in relation to certain arrangements affecting housing associations which continue in force despite the repeal of the enactments under or by reference to which they were made, as follows—
    Part I —Arrangements with local authorities for the provision or improvement of housing.
    Part II —Subsidy agreements with local authorities.
    Part III—Special arrangements with the Secretary of State in Scotland. [498]

NOTES to section 70

Definitions: 'housing association': see s 1 above; 'local authorities': see s 106(2) below.

71. Superseded contributions, subsidies and grants.

The provisions of Schedule 5 have effect with respect to superseded subsidies, contributions and grants, as follows—
    Part I —Residual subsidies: England and Wales.
    Part II —Residual subsidies: Scotland.
    Part III —Contributions and grants under arrangements with local authorities.
    Part IV —Contributions under arrangements with the Secretary of State in Scotland.
    Part V —Schemes for the unification of grant conditions.

Housing Associations Act 1985 (c 69), s 74 [502]

Part VI —New building subsidy and improvement subsidy.
Part VII—Payments in respect of hostels under pre-1974 enactments. [499]

NOTE to section 71
Definition: 'hostel': see s 106(2) below.

Supplementary provisions

72. Minor definitions.

In this Part—

. . .

'registered charity' has the same meaning as in Part I. [500]

NOTES to section 72
Amendment: Definitions repealed by the Building Societies Act 1986 (c 53), s 120, Sch 18.

73. Index of defined expressions: Part II.

The following Table shows provisions defining or explaining expressions used in this Part (other than provisions defining or explaining an expression in the same section):—

. . .

co-operative housing association	section 1(2)
dwelling	section 106
fully mutual (in relation to a housing association)	section 1(2)
heritable security	section 106
hostel	section 106
. . .	
house	section 106
housing actitivies	section 106
housing association	section 1(1)
. . .	
local authority	section 106
local housing authority	section 104
. . .	
registered and related expressions (in relation to a housing association)	section 3(2)
registered charity	section 72
. . .	
self-build society	section 1(3)
. . .	

[501]

NOTES to section 73
Amendments: Definitions repealed by the Building Societies Act 1986 (c 53), s 120, Sch 18 and by the Housing Act 1988 (c 50), s 140, Sch 18.

PART III
THE HOUSING CORPORATION

Constitution and other general matters

74. The Housing Corporation.

(1) This Part has effect with respect to the Housing Corporation [and Housing for Wales, each of] which is referred to in this Part as 'the Corporation'.

[502]

(2) The provisions of Schedule 6 have effect with respect to the constitution and proceedings of, and other matters relating to, the Corporation.

[(3) In this Part 'registered housing association' in relation to the Corporation, means a housing association registered in the register maintained by the Corporation.

(4) In this Part—
(a) in relation to land in Wales held by the unregistered housing association, 'the Corporation' means Housing for Wales; and
(b) in relation to land outside Wales held by such an association, 'the Corporation' means the Housing Corporation.] [502]

NOTES to section 74

Amendments: Sub-ss (1) and (2) amended by the Housing Act 1988 (c 50), s 59, Sch 6, para 31; sub-ss (3), (4) added by *Ibid.*

75. General functions of the Corporation.

(1) The Corporation has the following general functions—
(a) to promote and assist the development of registered housing associations and unregistered self-build societies;
(b) to facilitate the proper performance of the functions, and to publicise the aims and principles of registered housing associations and unregistered self-build societies;
(c) to maintain the register of housing associations [referred to in section 3] and to exercise supervision and control over registered housing associations;

. . .

(e) to undertake, to such extent as the Corporation considers necessary, the provision (by construction, acquisition, conversion, improvement or otherwise) of dwellings for letting or for sale and of hostels, and the management of dwellings or hostels so provided.

(2) The Corporation shall exercise its general functions subject to and in accordance with the provisions of this Act.

(3) Subsection (1) is without prejudice to specific functions conferred on the Corporation by or under this Act.

(4) The Corporation may do such things and enter into such transactions as are incidental to or conducive to the exercise of any of its functions, general or specific, under this Act.

[(5) Section 71 of the Race Relations Act 1976 (local authorities general statutory duty) shall apply to the Corporation as it applies to a local authority.] [503]

NOTES to section 75

Amendments: Sub-s (1)(c) was amended by the Housing Act 1988 (c 50), s 59, Sch 6, para 32; sub-s (1)(d) was repealed by *Ibid*, s 140, Sch 18; sub-s (5) was added by *Ibid*, s 56.

Definitions: 'the Corporation': see s 74 above; 'registered', 'unregistered': see s 3 above; 'housing association': see s 1 above; 'self-build society': see s 1 above; 'dwelling': see s 106(2) below; 'hostel': see s 106(2) below.

76. Directions by the Secretary of State.

(1) The Secretary of State may give directions to the Corporation as to the exercise of its functions.

(2) A direction as to the terms of loans made under section 79 (lending powers of Corporation) requires the consent of the Treasury.

(3) Directions may be of a general or particular character and may be varied or revoked by subsequent directions.

(4) Non-compliance with a direction does not invalidate a transaction between a person and the Corporation unless the person had actual notice of the direction. **[504]**

NOTES to section 76
Definition: 'the Corporation': see s 74 above.

77. Advisory service.

(1) The Corporation may provide an advisory service for the purpose of giving advice on legal, architectural and other technical matters to housing associations (whether registered or unregistered) and to persons who are forming a housing association or are interested in the possibility of doing so.

(2) The Corporation may make charges for the service.

[(3) The powers conferred on the Corporation by subsection (1) and (2) may be exercised by the Housing Corporation and Housing for Wales acting jointly.] **[505]**

NOTES to section 77
Amendment: Sub-s (3) was added by the Housing Act 1988 (c 50), s 59, Sch 6, para 33.
Definitions: 'the Corporation': see s 74 above; 'housing association': see s 1 above; 'registered', 'unregistered': see s 3 above.

78. Annual report.

(1) The Corporation shall, as soon as possible after the end of each financial year, make a report to the Secretary of State on the exercise of its functions during the year.

(2) It shall include in the report a copy of its audited accounts and shall set out in the report any directions given to it by the Secretary of State during the year.

(3) The Secretary of State shall lay a copy of the report before each House of Parliament. **[506]**

NOTES to section 78
Definition: 'the Housing Corporation': see s 74 above.

Corporation's powers with respect to loans and grants

79. Lending powers.

(1) The Corporation may lend to—
a registered housing association,
an unregistered self-build society,
a subsidiary of the Corporation, or
any other body in which the Corporation holds an interest,
for the purpose of enabling the body to meet the whole or part of expenditure incurred or to be incurred by it in carrying out its objects.

(2) The Corporation may lend to an individual for the purpose of assisting him to acquire from the Corporation, or from any such body as is mentioned in subsection (1), a legal estate or interest in a dwelling which he intends to occupy.

(3) A loan under this section may be by way of temporary loan or otherwise, and the terms of a loan made under subsection (1) may include (though the terms of a loan made under subsection (2) may not) terms for preventing repayment of the loan or part of it before a specified date without the consent of the Corporation.

(4) The terms of a loan under this section shall, subject to subsection (3) and to any direction under section 76 (general power of Secretary of State to give directions), be such as the Corporation may determine, either generally or in a particular case. **[507]**

NOTES to section 79

Definitions: 'the Corporation': see s 74 above; 'registered', 'unregistered': see s 3 above; 'housing association': see s 1 above; 'self-build society': see s 1 above; 'subsidiary': see s 101 below; 'dwelling': see s 106(2) below.

80. Security for loans to unregistered self-build societies.

(1) Where the Corporation—
(a) makes a loan to an unregistered self-build society under section 79(1); and
(b) under a mortgage or heritable security entered into by the society to secure the loan has an interest as mortgagee or creditor in land belonging to the society,

it may, with the written consent of the Secretary of State, give the society directions with respect to the disposal of the land.

(2) The society shall comply with directions so given so long as the Corporation continues to have such an interest in the land.

(3) Directions so given may be varied or revoked by subsequent directions given with the like consent.

(4) The Secretary of State shall not consent to the Corporation's giving directions under this section requiring a society to transfer its interest in land to the Corporation, or to any other person, unless he is satisfied that arrangements have been made which will secure that the members of the society receive fair treatment in connection with the transfer. **[508]**

NOTES to section 80

Definitions: 'the Corporation': see s 74 above; 'unregistered': see s 3 above; 'self-build society': see s 1 above; 'heritable security': see s 106(2) below.

81. (Applies in England and Wales.)

82. Loans made under s 2 of the Housing Act 1964.

Schedule 7 (further powers of Corporation with respect to land of certain housing associations) applies where a loan has been made to a housing association under section 2 of the Housing Act 1964 and the loan has not been repaid. **[509]**

NOTES to section 82

Definitions: 'the Corporation': see s 74 above; 'housing association': see s 1 above.

83. Power to guarantee loans.

(1) The Corporation may, with the consent of the Secretary of State given with the approval of the Treasury, guarantee the repayment of the principal of, and the payment of interest on, sums borrowed by—
registered housing associations
unregistered self-build societies, or
other bodies in which the Corporation holds an interest.

(2) Where the Corporation gives such a guarantee, it may impose such terms and conditions as it thinks fit.

(3) The aggregate amount outstanding in respect of—
(a) loans for which the Corporation has given a guarantee under this section, and
(b) payments made by the [Housing] Corporation in meeting an obligation arising by virtue of such a guarantee and not repaid to the [Housing] Corporation,

shall not exceed £300 million or such greater sum not exceeding £500 million as the Secretary of State may specify by order, made with the approval of the Treasury.

[(3A) The aggregate amount outstanding in respect of—

(a) loans for which Housing for Wales has given a guarantee under this section, and
(b) payments made by the Housing for Wales in meeting an obligation arising by virtue of such a guarantee and not repaid to the Housing for Wales,

shall not exceed £30 million or such greater sum not exceeding £50 million as the Secretary of State may specify by order, made with the approval of the Treasury.]

(4) An order under subsection (3) [or subsection (3A)] shall be made by statutory instrument and no such order shall be made unless a draft of it has been laid before and approved by the House of Commons. **[510]**

NOTES to section 83

Amendments: Sub-ss (3), (4) were amended by the Housing Act 1988 (c 50), s 59, Sch 6, para 34; sub-s (3A) was added by *Ibid*.
Sub-ss (3), (4): The power to make an order has not been exercised.
Definitions: 'the Corporation': see s 74 above; 'registered', 'unregistered': see s 3 above; 'housing association': see s 1 above; 'self-build society': see s 1 above.

84. (Applies in England and Wales.)

85. (Applies in England and Wales.)

86. Agreements to indemnify building societies: Scotland.

(1) The Corporation may, with the approval of the Secretary of State, enter into an agreement with a building society [or recognised body] under which the Corporation binds itself to indemnify the building society [or recognised body] in respect of
(a) the whole or part of any outstanding indebtedness of a borrower; and
(b) loss or expense to the building society [or recognised body] resulting from the failure of the borrower duly to perform any obligation imposed on him by a heritable security.

(2) The agreement may also, where the borrower is made party to it, enable or require the Corporation in specified circumstances to take an assignation of the rights and liabilities of the building society [or recognised body] under the heritable security.

(3) Approval of the Secretary of State under subsection (1) may be given generally in relation to agreements which satisfy specified requirements, or in relation to individual agreements, and with or without conditions as he thinks fit, and such approval may be withdrawn at any time on one month's notice.

(4) Before issuing any general approval under subsection (1) the Secretary of State shall consult with such bodies as appear to him to be representative of islands and district councils, and of building societies, and also with the Corporation and with the Chief Registrar of Friendly Societies.

(5) Section 16(3) and (5) of the Restrictive Trade Practices Act 1976 (recommendations by services supply associations to members) does not apply to recommendations made by building societies [or recognised bodies] about the making of agreements under this section provided that the recommendations are made with the approval of the Secretary of State.

[(6) In this section 'recognised body' means a body designated, or a class or description designated in an order made under this subsection by statutory instrument by the Secretary of State with the consent of the Treasury.

(7) Before making an order under subsection (6) above varying or revoking an order previously so made, the Secretary of State shall give an opportunity for representations to be made on behalf of a recognised body which, if the orders were made would cease to be such a body.] **[511]**

NOTES to section 86

Amendments: Sub-ss (1), (2), and (5) were amended by the Housing (Scotland) Act 1986 (c 65), s 25, Sch 2, para 4; sub-ss (6) and (7) were added by *Ibid*.

Definitions: 'the Corporation': see s 74 above; 'building society': see s 72 above; 'heritable security': see s 106(2) below.
Sub-s (6): See the Housing Corporation (Recognised Bodies for Heritable Securities Indemnities) (Scotland) Order 1987, SI 1987/1389, paras [1377] ff below.

[87. Grants towards expenses in promoting or assisting registered housing associations.

(1) The Corporation may give financial assistance to any person in respect of the following activities—
  (a) promoting and giving advice on the formation of registered housing associations and co-operative housing associations (in this section referred to collectively as 'relevant associations');
  (b) managing, providing services for, and giving advice on the running of, relevant associations; and
  (c) assisting tenants and licensees of a relevant association to take part in the management of the association or of some or all of the dwellings provided by the association.

(2) Assistance under this section may be in the form of grants, loans, guarantees or incurring expenditure for the benefit of the person assisted or in such other way as the Corporation considers appropriate, except that the Corporation may not, in giving any form of financial assistance, purchase loan or share capital in a company.

(3) With respect to financial assistance under this section, the following—
  (a) the procedure to be followed in relation to applications for assistance,
  (b) the circumstances in which assistance is or is not to be given,
  (c) the method for calculating, and any limitations on, the amount of assistance, and
  (d) the manner in which, and the time or times at which, assistance is to be given,
shall be such as may be specified by the Corporation, acting in accordance with such principles as it may from time to time determine.

(4) In giving assistance under this section, the Corporation may provide that the assistance is conditional upon compliance by the person to whom the assistance is given with such conditions as it may specify.

(5) Where assistance under this section is given in the form of a grant, subsections (1), (2) and (7) to (9) of section 52 of the Housing Act 1988 (recovery, etc of grants) shall apply as they apply in relation to a grant to which that section applies, but with the substitution, for any reference in those subsections to the registered housing association to which the grant has been given, of a reference to the person to whom assistance is given under this section.

(6) Section 53 of the Housing Act 1988 (determinations under Part II) shall apply in relation to a determination under this section as it applies to a determination under sections 50 to 52 of that Act.] **[512]**

NOTES to section 87

Amendment: Section 87 was substituted by the Local Government and Housing Act 1989 (c 42), s 183 with effect from 1 April 1990.

Corporation's powers with respect to land and works

88. Acquisition of land.

(1) The Corporation may acquire land by agreement for the purpose of—
  (a) selling or leasing it to a registered housing association or an unregistered self-build society, or
  (b) providing dwellings (for letting or for sale) or hostels,
and may be authorised by the Secretary of State to acquire land compulsorily for any such purpose.

(2) Land may be so acquired by the Corporation notwithstanding that it is not immediately required for any such purpose.

(3) In relation to a compulsory purchase of land by the Corporation under this section—
(a) in England and Wales, the Acquisition of Land Act 1981 applies;
(b) in Scotland, the Acquisition of Land (Authorisation Procedure) (Scotland) Act 1947 applies as if the Corporation were a local authority and as if this section were contained in an Act in force immediately before the commencement of that Act.

(4) For the purposes of the purchase of land in Scotland by agreement by the Corporation—
(a) the Lands Clauses Acts (except so much of them as relates to the acquisition of land otherwise than by agreement, the provisions relating to access to the special Act and sections 120 to 125 of the Lands Clauses Consolidation (Scotland) Act 1845), and
(b) sections 6 and 70 to 78 of the Railways Clauses Consolidation (Scotland) Act 1845 (as originally enacted and not as amended by section 15 of the Mines (Working Facilities and Support) Act 1923),
are hereby incorporated with this section, and in construing those Acts for the purposes of this section this section shall be deemed to be the special Act and the Corporation shall be deemed to be the promotors of the undertaking or company, as the case may require.

(5) In Scotland the Corporation may (without prejudice to their own power to acquire land compulsorily) request [Scottish Homes] to acquire land compulsorily on its behalf (as provided in section [23] of the Housing (Scotland) Act 1987] for any purpose for which the Corporation may purchase land compulsorily. [513]

NOTES to section 88
Amendments: Sub-s (5) was amended by the Housing (Scotland) Act 1987 (c 26), s 339, Sch 23, para 31, and by the Housing (Scotland) Act 1988 (c 43), s 3, Sch 2, para 1.
Definitions: 'the Corporation': see s 74 above; 'registered', 'unregistered': see s 3 above; 'housing association': see s 1 above; 'self-build society': see s 1 above; 'dwelling': see s 106(2) below; 'hostel': see s 106(2) below.

89. Provision of dwellings or hostels and clearance, management and development of land.

(1) The Corporation may provide or improve dwellings or hostels on land belonging to it.

(2) The Corporation may clear land belonging to it and carry out other work on the land to prepare it as a building site or estate, including—
(a) the laying out and construction of streets or roads and open spaces, and
(b) the provision of sewerage facilities and supplies of gas, electricity and water.

(3) The Corporation may repair, maintain and insure buildings or works on land belonging to it, may generally deal in the proper course of management with such land and buildings or works on it, and may charge for the tenancy or occupation of such land, buildings or works.

(4) The Corporation may carry out such operations on, and do such other things in relation to, land belonging to it as appears to it to be conducive to facilitating the provision or improvement of dwellings or hostels on the land—
(a) by the Corporation itself, or
(b) by a registered housing association or unregistered self-build society.

(5) In the exercise of its powers under subsection (4) the Corporation may carry out any development ancillary to or in connection with the provision of dwellings or hostels, including development which makes provision for buildings or land to be used for commercial, recreational or other non-domestic purposes. [514]

NOTES to section 89

Definitions: 'the Corporation': see s 74 above; 'dwelling': see s 106(2) below; 'hostel': see s 106(2) below; 'registered', 'unregistered': see s 3 above; 'housing association': see s 1 above; 'self-build society': see s 1 above.

90. Disposal of land.

(1) The Corporation may dispose of land in respect of which it has not exercised its powers under section 89(1) (provision or improvement of dwellings or hostels) and on which it has not carried out any such development as is mentioned in section 89(5) (ancillary development) to—
   a registered housing association,
   an unregistered self-build society,
   a subsidiary of the Corporation, or
   any other body in which the Corporation holds an interest.

(2) The Corporation may dispose of land on which dwellings or hostels have been provided or improved in exercise of its powers under section 89 to—
   a registered housing association,
   a local authority,
   a new town corporation,
   [Scottish Homes],
   the Development Board for Rural Wales, or
   a subsidiary of the Corporation.

(3) The Corporation may sell or lease individual dwellings to persons for their own occupation; but where the dwelling concerned was acquired by compulsory purchase under section 88(1), it shall not be disposed of under this subsection without the written consent of the Secretary of State.

(4) The Corporation may dispose of a building or land intended for use for commercial, recreational or other non-domestic purposes in respect of which development has been carried out by virtue of section 89; but no such building or land shall be disposed of for less than the best consideration it commands except with the written consent of the Secretary of State.

(5) The Corporation may dispose of land which is not required for the purposes for which it was acquired; but where the land—
   (a) was acquired compulsorily by, or on behalf of, the Corporation or by a local housing authority who transferred it to the Corporation, or
   (b) is disposed of (otherwise than for use as, or in connection with, a highway or street) for less then the best consideration it commands,
the Corporation shall not dispose of the land except with the written consent of the Secretary of State.

(6) The Corporation may not dispose of land except in accordance with the provisions of this section. **[515]**

NOTES to section 90

Amendment: In sub-s (1), the reference to Scottish homes was substituted by the Housing (Scotland) Act 1988 (c 43), s 3, Sch 2, para 1.

Definitions: 'the Corporation': see s 74 above; 'dwelling': see s 106(2) below; 'hostel': see s 106(2) below; 'registered', 'unregistered': see s 3 above; 'housing association': see s 1 above; 'self-build society': see s 1 above; 'subsidiary': see s 101 below; 'local authority': see s 106(2) below; 'new town corporation': *Ibid*; 'local housing authority': see s 104 below.

91. Protection of persons deriving title under transactions requiring consent.

Where the Corporation purports to acquire or dispose of land—
   (a) in favour of a person claiming under the Corporation the transaction is not invalid

by reason that any consent of the Secretary of State which is required has not been given, and
(b) a person dealing with the Corporation, or with a person claiming under the Corporation, shall not be concerned to see or inquire whether any such consent has been given. [516]

NOTE to section 91
Definition: 'the Corporation': see s 74 above.

The Corporation's finances

92. Borrowing powers.

(1) The Corporation may borrow from the Secretary of State, and the Secretary of State may lend to the Corporation, by way of temporary loan or otherwise, such sums in sterling as the Corporation may require.

(2) The Corporation may, with the consent of the Secretary of State or in accordance with a general authorisation given by him, borrow temporarily by overdraft or otherwise such sums in sterling as the Corporation may require.

(3) The Corporation may, with the consent of the Secretary of State, borrow—
(a) from the European Investment Bank or the Commission of the European Communities, sums in any currency, and
(b) from any other person, sums in a currency other than sterling.

(4) A loan made to the Corporation by the Secretary of State shall be repaid to him at such times and by such methods, and interest on the loan shall be paid to him at such rates and at such times, as he may from time to time determine.

(5) The Treasury may issue to the Secretary of State out of the National Loans Fund such sums as are necessary to enable him to make loans to the Corporation in pursuance of this section; and sums received by the Secretary of State in pursuance of subsection (4) shall be paid into that Fund.

(6) The Secretary of State may act under this section only with the approval of the Treasury. [517]

NOTE to section 92
Definition: 'the Corporation': see s 74 above.

93. Limit on borrowing.

(1) The Corporation has only the borrowing powers conferred and those powers are exercisable subject to the following limit.

(2) The aggregate amount outstanding by way of principal of—
(a) advances made to the Corporation under section 9 of the Housing Act 1964 before 18th September 1974 (when that section was repealed),
(b) advances made to housing associations before 1st April 1975 in respect of which the rights and obligations of the Secretary of State were then transferred to the Corporation by section 34 of the Housing Act 1974,
(c) money borrowed by the Corporation under section 92, and
(d) money borrowed by a subsidiary of the Corporation otherwise than from the Corporation,
shall not exceed [the limit appropriate to the Corporation under subsection (2A)].

[(2A) The limit referred to in subsection (2) is,—
(a) in the case of the Housing Corporation £2000 million or such greater sum not exceeding £3000 million as the Secretary of State may specify by order made with the consent of the Treasury; and

(b) in the case of Housing for Wales, £250 million or such greater sum not exceeding £300 million as the Secretary of State may specify by order made with the consent of the Treasury.]

(3) An order under subsection [(2A)] shall be made by statutory instrument and no such order shall be made unless a draft of it has been laid before and approved by the House of Commons.

(4) In ascertaining the limit imposed by subsection [(2A)], interest payable on a loan made by the Secretary of State to the Corporation which, with the approval of the Treasury, is deferred and treated as part of the loan, shall, so far as outstanding, be treated as outstanding by way of principal.

(5) The power of the Corporation to borrow from a subsidiary of the Corporation is not affected by subsection (1) and borrowing from such a subsidiary shall be left out of account for the purposes of subsection [(2A)]. [518]

NOTES to section 93
Amendments: Sub-ss (2)–(5) were amended by the Housing Act 1988 (c 50), s 59, Sch 6, para 35; sub-s (2A) was added by *Ibid*.
Definitions: 'the Corporation': see s 74 above; 'housing association': see s 1 above; 'subsidiary': see s 101 below.

94. Treasury guarantees of borrowing.

(1) The Treasury may guarantee, in such manner and on such conditions as they think fit, the repayment of the principal of and the payment of interest on and the discharge of any other financial obligation in connection with sums which the Corporation borrows from a person other than the Secretary of State.

(2) Immediately after a guarantee is given the Treasury shall lay a statement of the guarantee before each House of Parliament.

(3) Any sums required by the Treasury for fulfilling the guarantee shall be charged on and issued out of the Consolidated Fund.

(4) If any sums are so issued, the Corporation shall make to the Treasury, at such times and in such manner as the Treasury may from time to time direct—
  (a) payments of such amounts as the Treasury so direct in or towards repayment of the sums so issued, and
  (b) payments of interest, at such rate as the Treasury so direct, on what is outstanding for the time being in respect of sums so issued.

(5) Sums received by the Treasury in pursuance of subsection (4) shall be paid into the Consolidated Fund.

(6) Where a sum is issued for fulfilling a guarantee given under this section, the Treasury shall, as soon as possible after the end of each financial year, beginning with that in which the sum is issued and ending with that in which all liability in respect of the principal of the sum and in respect of interest on it is finally discharged, lay before each House of Parliament a statement relating to the sum. [519]

NOTE to section 94
Definition: 'the Corporation': see s 74 above.

95. Grants to the Corporation.

(1) The Secretary of State may make such grants to the Corporation as appear to him to be required to enable the Corporation to meet the expenses incurred by it in the exercise of its functions.

(2) A grant may be made subject to such conditions as the Secretary of State may determine.

(3) The Secretary of State may act under this section only with the consent of the Treasury. [520]

NOTE to section 95
Definition: 'the Corporation': see s 74 above.

96. General financial provisions.

(1) The Corporation may turn its resources to account so far as they are not required for the exercise of its functions.

(2) If for an accounting year the revenues of the Corporation exceed the total sums properly chargeable to revenue account, the Corporation shall apply the excess in such manner as the Secretary of State may, after consultation with the Corporation, direct; and the Secretary of State may direct that the whole or part of the excess be paid to him.

(3) The Secretary of State may give directions to the Corporation as to matters relating to—
 (a) the establishment or management of reserves,
 (b) the carrying of sums to the credit of reserves, or
 (c) the application of reserves for the purposes of the Corporation's functions.

(4) The Secretary of State may, after consultation with the Corporation, direct the Corporation to pay to him the whole or part of any sums for the time being standing to the credit of reserves of the Corporation or being of a capital nature and not required for the exercise of the Corporation's functions.

(5) The Secretary of State may act under this section only with the approval of the Treasury. [521]

NOTE to section 96
Definition: 'the Corporation': see s 74 above.

97. Accounts and audit.

(1) The Corporation shall keep proper accounts and proper records in relation to the accounts and shall prepare in respect of each financial year annual accounts in such form as the Secretary of State may, with the approval of the Treasury, direct.

(2) The accounts of the Corporation for each financial year shall be audited by a qualified accountant appointed for the purpose by the Secretary of State.

(3) As soon as the annual accounts of the Corporation for a financial year have been audited, the Corporation shall send to the Secretary of State a copy of the accounts prepared by it for the year in accordance with this section, together with a copy of any report made on them by the auditor.

(4) The Secretary of State shall prepare in respect of each financial year, in such form and manner as the Treasury may direct, an account of—
 (a) the sums issued to him and lent to the Corporation, and
 (b) sums received by him from the Corporation and paid into the National Loans Fund in respect of the principal and interest on sums so lent, or on sums advanced to the Corporation under section 9 of the Housing Act 1964,
and shall transmit the accounts so prepared by him to the Comptroller and Auditor General on or before 30th November in the following financial year.

(5) The Comptroller and Auditor General shall examine and certify the accounts prepared by the Secretary of State and lay before each House of Parliament copies of the accounts together with his report on them.

(6) In this section 'qualified accountant' means a person who is a member, or a firm all the partners in which are members, of one or more of the following bodies—

(a) the Institute of Chartered Accountants in England and Wales;
(b) the Institute of Chartered Accountants in Scotland;
(c) the Association of Certified Accountants;
(d) the Institute of Chartered Accountants in Ireland;
(e) any other body of accountants established in the United Kingdom and recognised for the purposes of section 389(1)(a) of the Companies Act 1985. **[522]**

NOTES to section 97

Definitions: 'the Corporation': see s 74 above; 'financial year': see s 101 below.

Acquisition of securities and control of subsidiaries

98. Acquisition of securities and promotion of body corporate.

(1) The Corporation may with the consent of the Secretary of State—
(a) subscribe for or acquire securities of a body corporate, and
(b) promote or participate in the promotion of a body corporate.

(2) In this section 'securities' means shares, stock, debenture stock and other securities of a like nature. **[523]**

NOTE to section 98

Definition: 'the Corporation': see s 74 above.

99. Control of subsidiaries.

(1) The Corporation shall exercise its control over its subsidiaries so as to secure that no subsidiary—
(a) engages in an activity which the Corporation is not empowered to carry on, or
(b) engages in an activity in a manner in which the Corporation itself could not engage by reason of a direction given to it under section 76 (directions by Secretary of State).

(2) The Corporation shall also exercise its control over its subsidiaries so as to secure that no subsidiary of it—
(a) borrows money from a person other than the Corporation, or
(b) raises money by the issue of shares or stock to a person other than the Corporation,
without the consent of the Secretary of State. **[524]**

NOTES to section 99

Definitions: 'the Corporation': see s 74 above; 'subsidiary': see s 101 below.

Supplementary provisions

100. . . .

NOTES to section 100

Section 100 was repealed by the Housing (Scotland) Act 1986, s 25, Sch 3.

101. Minor definitions.

In this Part—
['building society' means a building society within the meaning of the Building Societies Act 1986];
'financial year' means the period of 12 months ending with the 31st March;
'highway', in relation to Scotland, includes a public right of way;
'subsidiary' has [the meaning given by section 736 of] the Companies Act. **[525]**

NOTES to section 101

Amendments: Section 101 was amended by the Building Societies Act 1986 (c 53), s 120, Sch 18, para 19, and by the Companies Act 1989 (c 40), s 133, Sch 18, para 41.

102. Index of defined expressions: Part III.

The following Table shows provisions defining or explaining expressions used in this Part (other than provisions defining or explaining an expression in the same section or paragraph):—

building society	section 101
the Companies Act	section 106
dwelling	section 106
financial year	section 101
heritable security	section 106
highway (in relation to Scotland)	section 101
hostel	section 106
housing association	section 1(1)
local authority	section 106
local housing authority	section 104
new town corporation	section 106
recognised body	section 85(2)
registered (in relation to a housing association)	section 3(2)
relevant advance	section 85(4)
self-build society	section 1(3)
subsidiary	section 101
unregistered (in relation to a housing association)	section 3(2)
urban development corporation	section 106

[526]

PART IV
GENERAL PROVISIONS

General provisions

103. (Applies in England and Wales.)

104. Local housing authorities.

(1) In this Act 'local housing authority'—
(a) in relation to England and Wales, has the meaning given by section 1 of the Housing Act 1985, and
(b) in relation to Scotland, means an islands or district council.

(2) References in this Act to the district of a local housing authority—
(a) in England and Wales shall be construed in accordance with section 2 of the Housing Act 1985, and
(b) in Scotland are to the island area or the district, as the case may be. [527]

105. Members of a person's family.

(1) A person is a member of another's family if—
(a) he is the spouse of that person, or he and that person live together as husband and wife, or
(b) he is that person's parent, grandparent, child, grandchild, brother, sister, uncle, aunt, nephew or niece.

(2) For the purposes of subsection (1)(b)—
(a) a relationship by marriage shall be treated as a relationship by blood,
(b) a relationship of the half-blood shall be treated as a relationship of the whole blood,
(c) the stepchild of a person shall be treated as his child, and

(d) an illegitimate child shall be treated as the legitimate child of his mother and reputed father. **[528]**

106. Minor definitions—general.

(1) In the application of this Act in England and Wales—

'bank' means—
   (a) [an institution authorised under the Banking Act 1987], or
   (b) a company as to which the Secretary of State was satisfied immediately before the repeal of the Protection of Depositors Act 1963 that it ought to be treated as a banking company or discount company for the purposes of that Act;

'the Companies Act' means the Companies Act 1985;

'dwelling' means a building or part of a building occupied or intended to be occupied as a separate dwelling, together with any yard, garden, outhouses and appurtenances belonging to it or usually enjoyed with it;

'friendly society' means a friendly society of branch of a friendly society registered under the Friendly Societies Act 1974 or earlier legislation;

'hostel' means a building in which is provided for persons generally or for a class or classes of persons—
   (a) residential accommodation otherwise than in separate and self-contained sets of premises, and
   (b) either board or facilities for the preparation of food adequate to the needs of those persons, or both;

'house' includes—
   (a) any part of a building which is occupied or intended to be occupied as a separate dwelling;
   (b) any yard, garden, outhouses and appurtenances belonging to the house or usually enjoyed with it

'housing activities' in relation to a registered association, means all its activities in pursuance of [such of its purposes, objects, or powers as are of a description mentioned in section 1(1)(a) or subsections (2) to (4) of section 4;]

'insurance company' means an insurance company to which Part II of the Insurance Companies Act 1982 applies;

'local authority' means a county, district, or London borough council, the Common Council of the City of London or the Council of the Isles of Scilly and in section 84(5) and 85(4) includes . . . a joint authority established by Part IV of the Local Government Act 1985;

'new town corporation' means the Commission for the new towns or a development corporation within the meaning of the New Towns Act 1981;

'shared ownership lease' mean a lease—
   (a) granted on payment of a premium calculated by reference to a percentage of the value of the house or dwelling or of the cost of providing it, or
   (b) under which the tenant (or his personal representatives) will or may be entitled to a sum calculated by reference directly or indirectly to the value of the house or dwelling;

'trustee savings bank' means a trustee savings bank registered under the Trustee Savings Bank Act 1981 or earlier legislation;

'urban development corporation' means an urban development corporation established under Part XVI of the Local Government, Planning and Land Act 1980.

(2) In the application of this Act in Scotland—

'bank' has the same meaning as in subsection (1);

'charge' includes a heritable security;

'the Companies Act' has the same meaning as in subsection (1);

'dwelling' means a house;

'friendly society' has the same meaning as in subsection (1);

. . .

'hostel' means—
(a) in relation to a building provided or converted before 3rd January 1962, a

building in which is provided, for persons generally or for any class or classes of persons, residential accommodation (otherwise than in separate and self-contained dwellings) and board, and
(b) in relation to a building provided or converted on or after that date, a building in which is provided for persons generally or for any class or classes of persons, residential accommodation (otherwise than in houses) and either board or common facilities for the preparation of adequate food to the needs of those persons, or both;

'house' includes—
(a) any part of a building, being a part which is occupied or intended to be occupied as a separate dwelling, and in particular includes a flat, and
(b) includes also any yard, garden, outhouses and pertinents belonging to the house or usually enjoyed with it;

'housing activities' has the same meaning as in subsection (1);
'insurance company' has the same meaning as in subsection (1);
'local authority' means an islands council or district council;
'mortgage' means a heritable security and 'mortgagee' means a creditor in such a security;
'new town corporation' means a development corporation within the meaning of the New Towns (Scotland) Act 1968;
'[shared ownership agreement' means an agreement whereby—
(a) a pro indiviso right in a dwelling is sold to a person and the remaining pro indiviso rights therein are leased to him subject to his being entitled, from time to time, to purchase those remaining rights until he has purchased the entire dwelling; or
(b) pro indiviso rights in dwellings are conveyed to trustees to hold on behalf of persons each of whom, by purchasing a share in those dwellings, becomes entitled to exclusive occupancy of one of the dwellings but with any such person who wishes to sell or otherwise dispose of his share being required to do so through the agency of the trustees,

or such other agreement as may be approved whereby a person acquires a pro indiviso right in a dwelling or dwellings and thereby becomes entitled to exclusive occupancy of the dwelling or, as the case may be, one of the dwellings;].
'shared ownership lease' has the same meaning as in subsection (1);
'trustee savings bank' has the same meaning as in subsection (1).

[(3) In the definition of 'shared ownership agreement' in subsection (2) above, 'approved' means approved by the Secretary of State after consultation with the Housing Corporation.]. [529]

NOTES to section 106

Amendments: Sub-s (1) amended by the Banking Act 1987 (c 22), s 108, para 22, and by the Housing Act 1988, (c 50), s 59, Sch 6, para 36, and by the Education Reform Act 1988, (c 40), s 237, Sch 13; sub-s (2) amended by the Housing (Scotland) Act 1986 (c 65), s 25, Sch 3; new definition of 'shared ownership agreement' substituted by the Housing (Scotland) Act 1988, (c 43), s 72, Sch 9, para 9; sub-s (3) added by the Housing (Scotland) Act 1986, (c 65), s 25, Sch 2, para 4.

Final provisions

107. Short title, commencement and extent.

(1) This Act may be cited as the Housing Associations Act 1985.

(2) This Act comes into force on 1 April 1986.

(3) The following provisions of this Act apply to England and Wales only—
section 2,
sections 8(2) and (3),
sections 11 and 12,

section 18,
section 20,
section 31,
sections 34 to 36,
section 38,
section 58,
section 67,
section 69(3),
section 81,
sections 84 and 85,
section 103,
Schedules 2 and 3,
In Schedule 4, Part I,
In Schedule 5, Part I, paragraphs 1 and 2 of Part III and paragraph 1 of Part V.

(4) The following provisions of this Act apply to Scotland only—
section 15A,
section 59,
section 66,
section 68,
section 69(4),
section 86,
In Schedule 4, Part III,
In Schedule 5, Part II, paragraphs 3 and 4 of Part III, Part IV and Part VII.

(5) This Act does not extend to Northern Ireland. **[530]**

NOTES to section 107
Amendments: Sub-s (3) amended by the Housing (Scotland) Act 1986 (c 65), s 25, Sch 2, para 4, Sch 3, by the Landlord and Tenant Act 1987 (c 31), s 61, Sch 4, para 7, and by the Housing Act 1988 (c 50), s 140, Sch 18.

SCHEDULES

Sections 6, 9.   SCHEDULE 1

Grant-Aided Land

Definition of 'grant-aided land'

1. For the purposes of section 9(1)(b) (control by Corporation of dispositions of land by unregistered housing associations) 'grant-aided land' means land—
   (a) in respect of which a payment of a description specified in paragraph 2 falls or fell to be made in respect of a period ending after 24th January 1974, or
   (b) on which is, or has been, secured a loan of a description specified in paragraph 3 in respect of which a repayment (by way of principal or interest or both) falls or fell to be made after 24th January 1974. **[531]**

Payments

2. The payments referred to in paragraph 1(a) are—
   (a) payments by way of annual grants or exchequer contributions under—
       section 31(3) of the Housing Act 1949,
       section 19(3) of the Housing (Scotland) Act 1949, or
       section 121(3) of the Housing (Scotland) Act 1950
   (arrangements by local authorities for improvement of housing accommodation);

(b) payments by way of annual grants or exchequer contributions under—
    section 12(1) or 15 of the Housing (Financial Provisions) Act 1958,
    section 89(1) of the Housing (Scotland) Act 1950,
    section 12 of the Housing (Scotland) Act 1962, or
    section 21 of the Housing (Financial Provisions) (Scotland) Act 1968
(contributions for dwellings improved under arrangements with local authorities or grants for hostels);

(c) payments by way of annual grant or exchequer contributions under—
    section 12(6) of the Housing Subsidies Act 1967,
    section 121 of the Housing (Scotland) Act 1950,
    section 62 of the Housing Act 1964, or
    section 17 of the Housing (Financial Provisions) (Scotland) Act 1968
(subsidies for conversions or improvements by housing associations);

(d) payments by way of annual grant under—
    section 21(8) of the Housing Act 1969 (contributions for dwellings provided or improved by housing associations under arrangements with local authorities);

(e) payments by way of subsidy under—
    section 72, 73, 75 or 92 or the Housing Finance Act 1972,
    section 52, 53, 55 or 57 of the Housing (Financial Provisions) (Scotland) Act 1972, or
    Parts I, II, VI and VII of Schedule 5 to this Act (basic or special residual subsidy, new building or improvement subsidy, hostel subsidy). **[532]**

Loans

3. The loans referred to in paragraph 1(b) are—
(a) loans under—
    section 119 of the Housing Act 1957,
    section 152 of the Housing (Scotland) Act 1966,
    section 58 of this Act, or
    section 59 of this Act
(powers of certain local authorities to promote and assist housing associations);

(b) loans to housing associations under—
    section 47 of the Housing (Financial Provisions) Act 1958,
    section 78 of the Housing (Scotland) Act 1950,
    section 24 of the Housing (Financial Provisions) (Scotland) Act 1968,
    section 67 of this Act, or
    section 68 of this Act
(loans by Public Works Loan Commissioners to certain bodies);

(c) advances made under —
    section 7 of the Housing Act 1961,
    section 11 of the Housing (Scotland) Act 1962, or
    section 23 of the Housing (Financial Provisions) (Scotland) Act 1968
(advances to housing associations providing housing accommodation for letting);

(d) loans under—
    section 2 of the Housing Act 1964
(loans by Housing Corporation to housing associations). **[533]**

NOTES to Schedule 1

Definitions: 'corporation': see s 2A above; 'unregistered': see s 3 above; 'housing association': see s 1 above.

SCHEDULE 2
(Applies in England and Wales.)

SCHEDULE 3
(Applies in England and Wales.)

Sections 69, 70. SCHEDULE 4

HOUSING ASSOCIATIONS: CONTINUATION OF ARRANGEMENTS UNDER
REPEALED ENACTMENTS

(Pt I applies in England and Wales.)

PART II
SUBSIDY AGREEMENTS WITH LOCAL AUTHORITIES

(s 79 of the Housing Finance Act 1972 and s 59 of the Housing (Financial Provisions) (Scotland) Act 1972)

1. In this Part 'subsidy agreement' means an agreement made between a local authority and a housing association which provides for payments to be made under or by reference to any of the following enactments—
   section 2 of the Housing (Financial Provisions) Act 1924,
   section 29(1) of the Housing Act 1930,
   section 27(3) of the Housing Act 1935,
   section 26 of the Housing (Scotland) Act 1935,
   section 94(3) of the Housing Act 1936,
   section 87(1) of the Housing (Scotland) Act 1950,
   section 1(2)(b) of the Housing Subsidies Act 1956,
   section 2, 3 or 4 of the Housing and Town Development (Scotland) Act 1957,
   section 1(2)(b) of the Housing (Financial Provisions) Act 1958,
   section 1(2) of the Housing Act 1961,
   section 2, 4, 5, 6 or 7 of the Housing (Scotland) Act 1962,
   section 1(5) or 9(4) of the Housing Subsidies Act 1967,
   section 2, 4, 6, 7, 9 or 10 of the Housing (Financial Provisions) (Scotland) Act 1968,
(being enactments with respect to which it was provided by the Housing Finance Act 1972 or the Housing (Financial Provisions) (Scotland) Act 1972 that no further payments were to be made for 1972–73 or any subsequent year). **[534]**

2. Where a subsidy agreement provides for the payment of greater amounts than those which the authority would have been obliged to pay under the relevant enactment, the authority shall continue to pay to the housing association sums equal to the difference between the amounts for the payment of which the agreement provides and the amounts which they would have been obliged to pay by that enactment. **[535]**

PART III
SPECIAL ARRANGEMENTS WITH THE SECRETARY OF STATE IN SCOTLAND

(s 1(1)(d) of the Housing (Scotland) Act 1962;
s 1(2)(d) of the Housing (Financial Provisions) (Scotland) Act 1968)

Arrangements made between the Secretary of State and a housing association under section 1(1)(d) of the Housing (Scotland) Act 1962 or section 1(2)(d) of the Housing (Financial Provisions) (Scotland) Act 1968 (special arrangements for provision of housing) which were made before 3rd August 1972 and are in force immediately before the commencement of this Act remain in force under this paragraph. **[536]**

NOTES to Schedule 4
Definitions: 'local authority': see s 106(2) above; 'housing association': see s 1 above.

Sections 69, 71. SCHEDULE 5

HOUSING ASSOCIATION FINANCE: SUPERSEDED SUBSIDIES, CONTRIBUTIONS AND GRANTS

(Pt I applies in England and Wales.)

PART II
RESIDUAL SUBSIDIES: SCOTLAND
(ss 52 and 53 of the Housing (Financial Provisions) (Scotland) Act 1972)

Entitlement to residual subsidies

1.—(1) Basic residual subsidy is payable to a housing association in accordance with the following provisions where the association received payments from the Secretary of State for the financial year 1971–72 under certain enactments under which, in accordance with the Housing (Financial Provisions) (Scotland) Act 1972, no payments were to be made for 1972–73 or any subsequent year.

(2) A housing association is entitled to basic residual subsidy for a financial year if—
(a) it was entitled to basic residual subsidy under section 52 of the Housing (Financial Provisions) (Scotland) Act 1972 for the financial year 1972–73, and
(b) it has continued to be entitled to basic residual subsidy, under that section or this Schedule, for each succeeding financial year up to and including that immediately before the year in question.

(3) The amount of basic residual subsidy payable to an association for any year is the amount (if any) by which the basic residual subsidy payable for the previous year exceeds the withdrawal factor.

(4) Subject to any direction of the Secretary of State under paragraph 4(2), the withdrawal factor is the sum produced by multiplying £20 by the number of houses as at 31st March 1972 in respect of which the association's subsidies for 1971–72 (as defined in section 52(4) of the Housing (Financial Provisions) (Scotland) Act 1972) were payable. [537]

2.—(1) Special residual subsidy is payable to a housing association in accordance with the following provisions in respect of houses—
(a) the erection of which was approved by the Secretary of State for the purposes of sections 1 to 12 of the Housing (Financial Provisions) (Scotland) Act 1968 before 3rd August 1972, and
(b) which were completed by the association during the year 1972–73, 1973–74 or 1974–75.

(2) A housing association is entitled to special residual subsidy for a financial year if—
(a) it was entitled by virtue of section 53 of the Housing (Financial Provisions) (Scotland) Act 1972 to special residual subsidy for any of the years 1972–73, 1973–74 or 1974–75, and
(b) it has continued to be entitled to special residual subsidy, under that section or this Schedule, for each succeeding financial year up to and including that immediately before the year in question.

(3) The amount of special residual subsidy payable to an association for any year is the amount (if any) by which the special residual subsidy payable for the previous year exceeds the reduction factor.

(4) Subject to any direction of the Secretary of State under paragraph 4(2), the reduction factor is the sum produced by multiplying £20 by the number of houses satisfying the description in sub-paragraph (1). [538]

3. No basic or special residual subsidy is payable to a co-operative housing association. [539]

Power to vary withdrawal factor or reduction factor

4.—(1) This paragraph applies where a housing association, by furnishing to the Secretary of State such information as to its financial position as he may require, satisfied him as regards any financial year that its income from its houses will be, or was, inadequate having regard to its normal sources of income to meet such expenditure (including loan charges) as in his opinion it would be, or was, reasonable for the association to incur for that financial year in the exercise of its housing functions.

(2) Where this paragraph applies, the Secretary of State may direct that the amount of basic residual subsidy or special residual subsidy payable to the association for the financial year in question shall be determined—
(a) by reference to a withdrawal factor or reduction factor calculated by reference to a smaller sum of money per house than that mentioned in paragraph 1(4) or 2(4), or
(b) by reference to a withdrawal factor or reduction factor of zero.

(3) A direction under this paragraph may be varied or revoked by the Secretary of State by a further direction.

(4) In sub-paragraph (1) 'housing functions' means—
(a) constructing or improving, or facilitating the construction or improvement, of houses,
(b) managing houses,
(c) the provision of houses by conversion, and
(d) the acquisition of houses;
and includes functions which are supplementary or incidental to any of those functions.

(5) For the purposes of this paragraph 'loan charges', in relation to money borrowed by an association includes loan charges made by the association itself (including charges for debt management), whether in respect of borrowing from a capital fund kept by the association or in respect of borrowing between accounts kept by the association for different functions, or otherwise. **[540]**

Administrative provisions

5.—(1) Payment of basic or special residual subsidy is subject to the making of a claim for the payment in such form, and containing such particulars, as the Secretary of State may from time to time determine.

(2) The amount of basic or special residual subsidy payable to a housing association for a financial year shall be calculated to the nearest pound by rounding up any odd amount of 50p or more and rounding down any lesser amount.

(3) Basic or special residual subsidy is payable . . . subject to such conditions as to records, certificates, audit or otherwise as the Secretary of State may, . . . impose. **[541]**

Powers exercisable in case of disposal of houses by association

6.—(1) The Secretary of State may reduce, suspend or discontinue the payment of basic or special residual subsidy to a housing association if the association leases for a term exceeding seven years or otherwise disposes of any of the houses in respect of which the association is entitled to the payment.

(2) If any houses of an association are leased for a term exceeding seven years to, or become vested in—
(a) another housing association, or trustees for another housing association, or
(b) the Housing Corporation,
the Secretary of State may pay to that association or to the Corporation any basic or special residual subsidy which he would otherwise have paid to the former association for any financial year, beginning with that in which the houses are so leased or become so vested.

(3) For the purposes of this paragraph a lease shall be treated as being for a term exceeding seven years where the original term is for a lesser period but the lease confers on the lessee an option for renewal for a term which, together with the original term, exceeds seven years. **[542]**

Saving for financial years beginning before the commencement of this Act

7.—(1) The preceding provisions apply in relation to the financial year 1986–87 and subsequent financial years.

(2) The repeal by the Housing (Consequential Provisions) Act 1985 of the provisions of the Housing (Financial Provisions) (Scotland) Act 1972 relating to basic and special residual subsidies does not affect the operation of those provisions in relation to previous financial years. **[543]**

PART III
CONTRIBUTIONS AND GRANTS UNDER ARRANGEMENTS WITH LOCAL AUTHORITIES

(Paras 1 and 2 apply in England and Wales.)

(s 17 of the Housing (Financial Provisions) (Scotland) Act 1968)

3.—(1) Contributions by the Secretary of State under section 17 of the Housing (Financial Provisions) (Scotland) Act 1968 remain payable in connection with arrangements made under section 121 of the Housing (Scotland) Act 1950 or section 155 of the Housing (Scotland) Act 1966 (arrangements between housing associations and local authorities for improvement of housing) and approved on or after 16th August 1964 and before 1st April 1975.

(2) The contributions are payable at such times and in such manner as the Treasury may direct, and subject to such conditions as to records, certificates, audit or otherwise as the Secretary of State may, with the approval of the Treasury, impose.

(3) Where such a contribution is paid to a local authority, the authority shall pay to the housing association by way of annual grant an amount not less than the contribution. **[544]**

4.—(1) The Secretary of State may, in any of the circumstances mentioned in sub-paragraph (2), reduce the amount of the contributions in respect of a particular subsidised unit, or suspend or discontinue the payment of the contributions, or part of them, as he thinks just in the circumstances.

(2) The circumstances referred to in sub-paragraph (1) are—
(a) that the housing association has made default in giving effect to the terms of the arrangments with the local authority, or
(b) that the subsidised unit has been converted, demolished or destroyed, is not fit to be used or has ceased to be used for the purpose for which it was intended, has been sold or leased for a stipulated duration exceeding twelve months or has been transferred, whether by sale or otherwise.

(3) The local authority may reduce to a corresponding or less extent the annual grant payable by them to the association, or, as the case may be, suspend payment of the whole or a corresponding part of the payment for a corresponding period, or discontinue the payment or a corresponding part. **[545]**

[546] *Housing Associations Act 1985 (c 69), Sch 5*

PART IV
CONTRIBUTIONS UNDER ARRANGEMENTS WITH THE SECRETARY OF STATE IN SCOTLAND

(s 16 of the Housing (Financial Provisions) (Scotland) Act 1968)

1.—(1) Contributions by the Secretary of State under section 16 of the Housing (Financial Provisions) (Scotland) Act 1968 remain payable in connection with arrangements made under—
   section 14 of the Housing (Scotland) Act 1962, or
   section 154 of the Housing (Scotland) Act 1966,
(arrangements between Secretary of State and housing associations) and approved before 1st April 1975.

(2) The Secretary of State may in any of the circumstances mentioned in sub-paragraph (3), reduce the amount of the contributions in respect of a particular subsidised unit, or suspend or discontinue the payment of the contributions, or part of them, as he thinks just in the circumstances.

(3) The circumstances referred to in sub-paragraph (2) are—
(a) that the housing association has made default in giving effect to the terms of the arrangements, or
(b) the subsidised unit has been converted, demolished or destroyed, is not fit to be used or has ceased to be used for the purpose for which it was intended, has been sold or leased for a stipulated duration exceeding twelve months or has been transferred, whether by sale or otherwise. **[546]**

PART V
SCHEMES FOR THE UNIFICATION OF GRANT CONDITIONS

(s 123 of the Housing Act 1957; s 157 of the Housing (Scotland) Act 1966)

(Para 1 applies in England and Wales.)

2. A scheme under section 157 of the Housing (Scotland) Act 1966 (schemes for the unification of divergent grant conditions affecting the management of a housing association's houses) which was made before 3rd August 1972 and is in force immediately before the commencement of this Act remains in force under this paragraph. **[547]**

PART VI
NEW BUILDING SUBSIDY AND IMPROVEMENT SUBSIDY

(s 75 of the Housing Finance Act 1972; ss 55 and 57 of the Housing (Financial Provisions) (Scotland) Act 1972)

1.—(1) The following subsidies remain payable in respect of building schemes or improvement schemes approved by the Secretary of State before 1st April 1975—
(a) new building subsidy under section 75 of the Housing Finance Act 1972 or section 55 of the Housing (Financial Provisions) (Scotland) Act 1972, and
(b) improvement subsidy under section 57 of the Housing (Financial Provisions) (Scotland) Act 1972.

(2) Payment of the subsidy is subject to the making of a claim for the payment in such form and containing such particulars as the Secretary of State may from time to time determine.

(3) The amount of the subsidy payable for a financial year shall be calculated to the nearest pound by rounding up any odd amount of 50p or more and rounding down any lesser amount.

Housing Associations Act 1985 (c 69), Sch 5 [551]

(4) The subsidy is payable at such times and in such manner as the Treasury may direct, and subject to such conditions as to records, certificates, audit or otherwise as the Secretary of State may, with the approval of the Treasury, impose. [548]

2.—(1) The Secretary of State may make reduced payments of subsidy, or suspend or discontinue such payments, if—
  (a) he made his approval of the scheme subject to conditions and is satisifed that any of the conditions have not been complied with, or
  (b) he is satisfied that a dwelling comprised in the scheme has been converted, demolished or destroyed, is not fit to be used or is not being used for the purpose for which it was intended, has been sold or leased for a term exceeding seven years or has ceased for any reason whatsoever to be vested in the association or trustees for the association.

(2) If any of the dwellings comprised in the scheme become vested in, or are leased for a term exceeding seven years to—
  (a) a housing association, or trustees for a housing association other than the association which received approval for the scheme, or
  (b) the Housing Corporation,
the Secretary of State may, for any year beginning with that in which they come to be so vested or are so leased, pay them the whole or any part of the subsidy which he would otherwise have paid to the association which received approval for the scheme.

(3) For the purposes of this paragraph a dwelling shall be treated as leased for a term exceeding seven years if it is leased for a lesser term by a lease which confers on the lessee an option for renewal for a term which, together with the original term, exceeds seven years. [549]

3.—(1) Where a housing association satisfies the Secretary of State, by furnishing him with such information as to its financial position as he may require, that the amount of new building subsidy for a year will be, or was, inadequate having regard to its normal sources of income to enable it to meet such expenditure (including loan charges) as in his opinion it would be, or was, reasonable for it to incur for that year in the exercise of its housing functions, he may direct that for that year the percentage of the initial deficit to be met by subsidy shall be greater than that otherwise applicable.

(2) The percentage shall not, however, be greater than 90 per cent or the percentage met by subsidy for the immediately preceding year, whichever is less.

(3) This paragraph does not apply in relation to the year of completion or the second or third year for which new building subsidy is payable.

(4) In this paragraph—
'housing functions' means constructing, improving or managing, or facilitating or encouraging the construction or improvemnt of dwellings, the provision of dwellings by conversion and the acquisition of dwellings, and includes functions which are supplementary or incidental to any of those functions;
'loan charges' includes any loan charges made by a housing association (including charges for debt management) whether in respect of borrowing from a capital fund kept by the association or in respect of borrowing between accounts kept by the association for different functions or otherwise. [550]

4.—(1) Where before 1st April 1976 a registered housing association made an application for housing association grant in respect of a housing project which was or included a building scheme or improvement scheme which had been previously approved for the purposes of any of the provisions mentioned in paragraph 1 and the Secretary of State gave his approval to that project for the purposes of housing association grant, no further payments of new building subsidy or improvement subsidy shall be made in respect of that approved scheme.

(2) A condition imposed by the Secretary of State in such a case by virtue of section

35(2)(b) of the Housing Act 1974, requiring the repayment of all or any of the payments of new building subsidy or improvement subsidy already paid, if in force immediately before the commencement of this Act, remains in force under this sub-paragraph.

(3) No account shall be taken under section 47(2)(b) (estimation of net cost of project for purposes of housing association; income to include subsidies) of payments of subsidy received which are required to be repaid in pursuance of such a condition. [551]

Part VII
Payments in Respect of Hostels Under Pre-1974 Enactments

(s 21 of the Housing (Financial Provisions) (Scotland) Act 1968)

1.—(1) Section 21 of the Housing (Financial Provisions) (Scotland) Act 1968 (exchequer contributions for hostels) continues to have effect in relation to buildings provided or converted by a housing association which were approved by the Secretary of State for the purposes of subsection (1) of that section before 1st April 1975.

(2) A registered housing association may not make an application for housing association grant in respect of a housing project which consists of or includes the carrying out of works for the provision of hostels if before 1st April 1975 any contribution has been made under section 21 of the Housing (Financial Provisions) (Scotland) Act 1968.

(3) If in a case where sub-paragraph (2) does not prevent the making of such an application a registered housing association makes an application for housing association grant in respect of a housing project falling within that sub-paragraph and the Secretary of State gives his approval to the project for the purposes of housing association grant, section 21 of the Housing (Financial Provisions) (Scotland) Act 1968 shall cease to have effect with respect to the provision of hostels referred to in that sub-paragraph. [552]

NOTES to Schedule 5
Amendment: In Part II, para 5(3) was amended by the Housing Act 1988 (c 50), s 140, Sch 18.
Definitions: 'housing association': see s 1 above; 'local authority': see s 106(2) above; 'hostels': see s 106(2) above.

Section 74.   SCHEDULE 6

Constitution of Housing Corporation

Status of Corporation

1.—(1) The Housing Corporation is a body corporate.

(2) It is a public body for the purposes of the Prevention of Corruption Acts 1889 to 1916.

(3) It shall not be regarded—
(a) as the servant or agent of the Crown, or
(b) as enjoying any status, immunity or privilege of the Crown, or
(c) as exempt from any tax, duty, rate, levy or other charge whatsoever, whether general or local;
and its property shall not be regarded as property of, or held on behalf of, the Crown. [553]

Membership of Corporation

2.—(1) The members of the Housing Corporation, of whom there shall be not more than fifteen, shall be appointed by the Secretary of State.

(2) Before appointing a person to be a member of the Corporation the Secretary of State shall satisfy himself that he will have no financial or other interest likely to affect prejudicially the exercise of his functions as member; and the Secretary of State may require a person whom he proposes to appoint to give him such information as he considers necessary for that purpose. **[554]**

3.—(1) The members of the Housing Corporation shall hold and vacate office in accordance with the terms of their appointment, subject to the following provisions.

(2) A member may resign his membership by notice in writing addressed to the Secretary of State.

(3) The Secretary of State may remove a member from office if he is satisfied that—
(a) he has been adjudged bankrupt or made an arrangement with his creditors or (in Scotland) has had his estate sequestrated or has made a trust deed for behoof of his creditors or a composition contract,
. . .
(c) he has been absent from meetings of the Corporation for a period longer than three consecutive months without the permission of the Corporation, or
(d) he is otherwise unable or unfit to discharge the functions of a member, or is unsuitable to continue as a member.

(4) The Secretary of State shall satisfy himself from time to time with respect to every member that he has no financial or other interest likely to affect prejudicially the exercise of his functions as a member; and he may require a member to give him such information as he considers necessary for that purpose. **[555]**

Chairman and Deputy Chairman

4.—(1) The Secretary of State shall appoint one of the members to be Chairman and one to be Deputy Chairman; and the members so appointed shall hold and vacate those offices in accordance with the terms of their appointment, subject to the following provisions.

(2) The Chairman or Deputy Chairman may resign his office by notice in writing addressed to the Secretary of State.

(3) If the Chairman or Deputy Chairman ceased to be a member of the Corporation, he also ceases to be Chairman or Deputy Chairman. **[556]**

Remuneration and allowances

5.—(1) The Secretary of State may pay the Chairman, Deputy Chairman and members such remuneration as he may, with the consent of the Treasury, determine.

(2) The Housing Corporation may pay them such reasonable allowances as may be so determined in respect of expenses properly incurred by them in the performance of their duties. **[557]**

Pensions

6.—(1) The Secretary of State may, with the consent of the Treasury, determine to pay in respect of a person's office as Chairman, Deputy Chairman or member—
(a) such pension, allowance or gratuity to or in respect of that person on his retirement or death as may be so determined, or
(b) such contributions or other payments towards provision for such pension, allowance or gratuity as may be so determined.

(2) As soon as may be after the making of such a determination the Secretary of State shall lay before each House of Parliament a statement of the amount payable in pursuance of the determination.

(3) Sub-paragraph (1) does not apply in the case of a member who has been admitted in pursuance of regulations under section 7 of the Superannuation Act 1972 to participate in the benefits of a superannuation fund maintained by a local authority.

(4) In such a case the Secretary of State shall make any payments required to be made to the fund in respect of the member by the employing authority and may make such deductions from his remuneration as the employing authority might make in respect of his contributions to the fund. **[558]**

Proceedings of the Corporation

7.—(1) The quorum of the Housing Corporation and the arrangements relating to its meetings shall, subject to any directions given by the Secretary of State, be such as the Corporation may determine.

(2) The validity of proceedings of the Corporation is not affected by any defect in the appointment of any of its members. **[559]**

8.—(1) Where a member of the Housing Corporation is in any way directly or indirectly interested in a contract made or proposed to be made by the Corporation—
(a) he shall disclose the nature of his interest at a meeting of the Corporation, and the disclosure shall be recorded in the minutes of the Corporation, and
(b) he shall not take any part in any decision of the Corporation with respect to the contract.

(2) A general notice given by a member at a meeting of the Corporation to the effect that he is a member of a specified company or firm and is to be regarded as interested in any contract which may be made with the company or firm is a sufficient disclosure of his interest for the purposes of this paragraph in relation to a contract made after the date of the notice.

(3) A member need not attend in person at a meeting of the Corporation in order to make any disclosure which he is required to make under this paragraph provided he takes reasonable steps to secure that the disclosure is brought up and read at the meeting. **[560]**

9.—(1) The fixing of the Housing Corporation's seal may be authenticated by the signature of the Chairman or of any other person authorised for the purpose.

(2) A document purporting to be duly executed under the seal of the Corporation shall be received in evidence and be deemed to be so executed unless the contrary is proved. **[561]**

NOTES to Schedule 6
Amendment: Para 3(3)(b) was repealed by the Housing Act 1988 (c 50), s 59, Sch 6, s 140, Sch 18.
Definition: 'local authority': see s 106(2) above.

Section 82.   SCHEDULE 7

POWERS EXERCISABLE WHERE LOAN OUTSTANDING UNDER SECTION 2 OF THE HOUSING ACT 1964

Introductory

1. This Schedule applies where the Housing Corporation has made a loan to a housing association under section 2 of the Housing Act 1964 before the repeal of that section by the Housing (Consequential Provisions) Act 1985 and the loan has not been repaid. **[562]**

Housing Associations Act 1985 (c 69), Sch 7 [566]

Directions as to disposal of land securing loan

2.—(1) The Corporation may, with the consent in writing of the Secretary of State, give the association directions with respect to the disposal of land belonging to the association in which the Corporation has an interest as mortgagee under a mortgage, or as creditor in a heritable security, entered into by the association to secure the loan.

(2) Directions so given may be varied or revoked by subsequent directions given with the like consent. [563]

3. Where the Corporation proposes to give a housing association directions under paragraph 2 requiring the association to transfer to the Corporation the association's interest in any land, the Secretary of State shall not consent to the giving of the directions unless he at the same time approves, or has previously approved, a scheme under paragraph 5 with respect to that land. [564]

4. Where the Corporation proposes to give directions under paragraph 2 to an association whose rules restrict membership to persons entitled or prospectively entitled (whether as tenants or otherwise) to occupy a dwelling provided or managed by the association requiring the association to transfer its interest in any such land to the Corporation, or to any other person, the Secretary of State shall not consent to the giving of the directions unless he is satisfied that arrangements have been made which, if the directions are given, will secure that the members of the association receive fair treatment in connection with the transfer. [565]

Schemes for Corporation to provide housing accommodation in place of association

5.—(1) If it appears to the Corporation—
(a) that the association is experiencing difficulty in providing housing accommodation on any land which it has acquired or in managing housing accommodation provided by it on any land, or is in any way failing to perform its functions as a housing association in relation to any land, and that accordingly it is undesirable for the land in question to remain in the hands of the association,
(b) that there is no other housing association, whether in existence or about to be formed, to which the association's interest in the land in question can suitably be transferred, and
(c) that the land is capable of being, or continuing to be, used to provide housing accommodation for letting,
the Corporation may prepare and submit to the Secretary of State a scheme.

(2) The scheme shall be for the Corporation—
(a) to acquire the association's interest in the land,
(b) to undertake all such operations as may be required for the provision or continued provision on the land of housing accommodation for letting (including any operation which might have been carried out by a housing association in connection with the provision of housing accommodation), and
(c) to retain the accommodation and keep it available for letting so long as the scheme has not been terminated in any manner provided for in the scheme.

(3) Where such a scheme is submitted to the Secretary of State by the Corporation, the Secretary of State, on being satisfied of—
(a) the undesirability of the land remaining in the hands of the association, and
(b) the lack of any housing association to which it can suitably be transferred,
may, if he thinks fit, approve the scheme.

(4) If he does so the Corporation shall have power to acquire for the purposes of the scheme the association's interest in the land and to carry through the provisions of the scheme.

(5) A scheme approved by the Secretary of State under this paragraph may be varied

[566] *Housing Associations Act 1985 (c 69), Sch 7*

from time to time in accordance with proposals in that behalf made by the Corporation and approved by the Secretary of State. **[566]**

NOTES to Schedule 7
Definition: 'housing association': see s 1 above.

TABLE OF DERIVATIONS

1. The following abbreviations are used in this Table:—

Acts of Parliament

1957	=	The Housing Act 1957 (c 56).
1958 (c 42)	=	The Housing (Financial Provisions) Act 1958.
1959 (c 53)	=	The Town and Country Planning Act 1959.
1959 (c 70)	=	The Town and Country Planning (Scotland) Act 1959.
1960 (c 58)	=	The Charities Act 1960.
1961	=	The Housing Act 1961 (c 65).
1963 (c 33)	=	The London Government Act 1963.
1964	=	The Housing Act 1964 (c 56).
1965 (c 12)	=	The Industrial and Provident Societies Act 1965.
1965 (c 25)	=	The Finance Act 1965.
1966 (S)	=	The Housing (Scotland) Act 1966 (c 49).
1968 (c 13)	=	The National Loans Act 1968.
1968 (S)	=	The Housing (Financial Provisions) (Scotland) Act 1968 (c 31).
1969	=	The Housing Act 1969 (c 33).
1970 (c 10)	=	The Income and Corporation Taxes Act 1970.
1970 (c 35)	=	The Conveyancing and Feudal Reform (Scotland) Act 1970.
1972 (S)	=	The Housing (Financial Provisions) (Scotland) Act 1972 (c 46).
1972	=	The Housing Finance Act 1972 (c 47).
1972 (c 70)	=	The Local Government Act 1972.
1973 (c 65)	=	The Local Government (Scotland) Act 1973.
1974	=	The Housing Act 1974 (c 44).
1975	=	The Housing Rents and Subsidies Act 1975 (c 6).
1975 (c 28)	=	The Housing Rents and Subsidies (Scotland) Act 1975.
1975 (c 55)	=	The Statutory Corporations (Financial Provisions) Act 1975.
1976 (c 75)	=	The Development of Rural Wales Act 1976.
1977 (c 42)	=	The Rent Act 1977.
1978	=	The Home Purchase Assistance and Housing Guarantee Act 1978 (c 27).
1980 (c 43)	=	The Magistrates' Courts Act 1980.
1980	=	The Housing Act 1980 (c 51).
1980 (S)	=	The Tenants Rights etc (Scotland) Act 1980 (c 52).
1981 (c 64)	=	The New Towns Act 1981.
1981 (c 67)	=	The Acquisition of Land Act 1981.
1982 (c 48)	=	The Criminal Justice Act 1982.
1983 (c 29)	=	The Miscellaneous Financial Provisions Act 1983.
1984	=	The Housing and Building Control Act 1984 (c 29).
1985 (c 9)	=	The Companies Consolidation (Consequential Provisions) Act 1985.
1985 (c 51)	=	The Local Government Act 1985.

Subordinate legislation

SI 1972/1204	=	The Isles of Scilly (Housing) Order 1972.
SI 1973/886	=	The Isles of Scilly (Housing) (No 2) Order 1973.
SI 1975/374	=	The Housing Act 1974 (Commencement No 4) Order 1975.
SI 1975/512	=	The Isles of Scilly (Housing) Order 1975.
SI 1983/664	=	The Housing Corporation Advances (Increase of Limit) Order 1983.
SI 1984/1803	=	The Housing Association Grant (Disposal of Dwellings) Order 1984.

2. The Table does not show the effect of Transfer of Functions Orders.

3. The letter R followed by a number indicates that the provision gives effect to the

Housing Associations Act 1985 (c 69) [567]

Recommendation bearing that number in the Law Commission's Report on the Consolidation of the Housing Acts (Cmnd 9515).

4. A reference followed by '*passim*' indicates that the provision of the consolidation derives from passages within those referred to which it is not convenient, and does not appear necessary, to itemise.

5. The entry 'drafting' indicates a provision of a mechanical or editorial nature affecting the arrangement of the consolidation; for instance, a provision introducing a Schedule or introducing a definition to avoid undue repetition of the defining words.

Provision	Derivation
1(1)	1957 s 189(1); 1964 s 12(1); 1966 (S) s 208(1); 1974 s 129(1), (2), Sch 13 para 6.
(2)	drafting.
(3)	1974 s 12.
2	1977 s 2(6A); 1977 (c 42) s 15(5); 1980 ss 74(2), 123(7).
3	1974 s 13(1), (7).
4(1)	1974 s 13(1).
(2)	1974 s 13(2).
(3)	1974 s 13(3); 1980 s 127(1)–(3); 1984 s 35(4); Sch 11 para 27.
5(1)	1974 s 13(1), (4), (5).
(2)	1974 s 13(4).
(3)	1974 s 16(1), (2).
(4)	1974 s 13(6).
6(1)	1974 s 15(1).
(2), (3)	1974 s 15(2).
(4)	1974 s 15(2A); 1980 s 128(1)(a), (2).
(5)	1974 s 16(1), (2).
7(1)	1974 s 15(3).
(2)	1974 s 15(4).
(3)	1974 s 16(3).
8(1)–(3)	1980 s 122(1)–(3).
9(1)	1974 s 2(1), (6).
(2)	1974 s 2(1A), (1B); 1980 s 123(2).
(3)	1974 s 2(5A); 1980 ss 123(6), 137(1).
(4)	1974 s 15(6); 1980 s 128.
(5)	1974 s 2(1).
10(1)	1974 s 2(2), (3); 1980 s 123(3).
(2)	1974 s 2(3A); 1980 s 123(4).
(3)	1974 s 2(4); 1980 s 123(5).
(4)	1974 s 2(3).
11	drafting.
12	1980 s 137(1), (2); 1984 Sch 11 para 28.
13(1)	1974 s 26(1).
(2)	1974 s 26(2); 1980 Sch 25 para 25.
(3)	1974 s 26(5); 1980 Sch 11 Part II.
14(1)	1974 s 26(3), (4), (6); 1980 Sch 16 Part II.
(2)	1974 s 26(5); 1980 Sch 16 Part II.
15(1)	1974 s 27(1)–(3); 1980 Sch 16 Part II.
(2)	1974 s 27(5)–(7); 1980 Sch 16 Part II.
(3)	1974 s 27(4); 1980 Sch 16 Part II.
16(1)	1974 s 20(2); 1970 (c 35) Sch 3 para 9(2); R 32.
(2), (3)	1974 s 20(6).
(4)	1974 s 20(6).
17(1), (2)	1974 s 20(3).
(3)	1974 s 20(4).
(4)	1980 Sch 17 para 8.

Housing Associations Act 1985 (c 69)

Provision	Derivation
18(1)	1980 Sch 17 paras 4, 5.
(2)	1980 Sch 17 para 6(b).
(3)	1980 Sch 17 para 7.
19(1)	1974 s 24(1).
(2)–(4)	1965 (c 12) s 10; 1974 s 24(5A); 1980 s 132.
20(1)	1974 s 25(1).
(2)	1960 (c 58) s 46; 1974 s 25(1)–(3).
21(1)–(6)	1974 s 24(1)–(5), (6).
22(1), (2)	1974 s 22(1), (2).
23(1)	1974 s 23(1).
(2)	1974 s 23(2).
(2)	1974 s 23(3).
(4)	1974 s 23(4).
(5)	1974 s 23(3).
24(1)	1980 s 124(1).
(2)	1980 s 124(6).
(3)	1980 s 124(2).
(4)	1980 s 124(3).
(5)	1980 ss 124(7), 151(1), (3).
25	1980 s 124(4).
26	1980 s 124(5).
27(1)	1980 s 125(1).
(2)	1980 s 125(2); 1982 (c 48) ss 37(1), 46(2).
(3)	1980 s 125(3).
(4)	1980 s 125(4).
28(1)	1974 s 19(1), (1A); 1980 Sch 17 para 1.
(2)	1974 s 19(2); 1980 Sch 17 paras 2, 6(b).
(3)	1974 s 19(3); 1975 (c 21) ss 289F, 289G; 1982 (c 48) ss 37, 46(1), 54.
(4)	1974 s 19(5).
(5)	1974 s 19(8); 1980 Sch 17 para 2.
(6)	1980 s 155(2).
29(1)	1974 s 19(4).
(2)	1974 s 19(4); 1980 Sch 17 para 6(e).
(3)	1974 s 19(5).
(4)	1974 s 19(6).
(5)	1974 s 19(7).
30(1)	1974 s 20(1); 1980 Sch 17 paras 3(a), 6(b).
(2), (3)	1974 s 20(6).
(4)	1974 s 20(5); 1980 Sch 17 para 3(c).
(5)	1974 s 20(1A); 1980 Sch 17 para 3(b).
(6)	1974 s 20(7); 1975 (c 21) ss 289F, 289G; 1980 Sch 17 para 9; 1982 (c 48) ss 37, 46(1), 54.
31(1)	1974 ss 19, 20 *passim*; 1980 Sch 17 paras 4, 5, 6(a).
(2)	1980 Sch 17 para 7.
(3)	1980 Sch 17 para 6(c)(d).
32(1)	1974 s 21(1).
(2)	1974 s 21(2)(a).
(3)	1974 s 21(2)(b).
(4)	1974 s 21(3).
(5)	1974 s 21(4).
33(1)	1957 s 124; 1966 (S) s 158(1).
(2)	1957 s 124; 1966 (S) s 158(2).
34(1), (2)	1957 s 119(2).
35(1)	1957 s 128(1); R 4(ii).
(2)	drafting.
36(1)	1957 s 128(2); R 4(ii).
(2)	1957 s 128(3); R 4(ii).

Provision	Derivation
37	'appropriate registrar' 1974 s 28; 'committee' 1965 s 74, 1974 s 28; 'co-opted member' 1974 s 26(6), 1980 Sch 16 Part II; drafting.
38	1974 ss 28, 129(1); 1980 s 133(1).
39	'mental disorder' 1974 s 20(2)(a); 'secure tenancy' 1974 s 2(6A), 1980 s 123(7).
40	drafting.
41(1)	1974 ss 29(1), 29A(2); 1975 s 6; 1975 (S) s 12; 1980 Sch 18 para 3.
(2)	1974 s 29A(1); 1980 Sch 18 para 3.
42(1)	1974 s 29(2).
(2), (3)	1974 s 29(2), (2A); 1980 Sch 18 para 1.
43	1980 s 130(1).
44(1)	1984 s 33(1).
(2)	1984 s 33(2).
(3)	drafting.
45(1), (2)	1984 s 35(1).
(3)	1984 s 35(2).
(4)	1984 s 35(3).
46	1974 s 29(3).
47(1)	1974 s 29(4).
(2), (3)	1974 s 29(6).
(4)	1974 s 29(8).
(5)	1974 s 29(6A); 1980 Sch 18 para 2.
(6)	1974 s 29(7).
48(1)	1974 s 29(5).
(2)	1974 s 29(8).
(3)	1980 s 130(2); SI 1984/1803.
(4)	1980 s 151(1), (3).
49(1)–(4)	1974 s 30(1); 1980 Sch 18 para 4.
(5)	1974 s 30(8).
(6)	1974 s 15(5).
50(1), (2)	1974 s 30(2), (2A); 1980 Sch 18 para 5.
51(1), (2)	1974 s 30(4), (6).
52(1)	1974 s 30(3); 1980 Sch 18 para 6; 1984 s 34(1).
(2)	1974 s 30(3); 1980 Sch 18 para 6.
(3)	1980 s 34(2).
(4)	1980 s 34(3).
53(1)	1980 s 131(1).
(2)	1980 s 131(2).
(3)	1980 s 131(3).
(4)	1980 s 131(3), (4).
(5)	1980 s 131(4).
(6)	1980 s 131(5).
(7)	1980 s 131(6).
54(1)	1974 s 32(1); 1975 s 6; 1975 (S) s 12; 1980 Sch 18 para 9(a).
(2), (3)	1974 s 32(3); 1980 Sch 18 para 9(c).
(4)	1976 s 32(5); 1980 Sch 18 para 9(e).
(5)	1974 s 32(3); 1980 s 133(2), Sch 18 para 9(c).
55(1)	1974 s 33(1); 1980 Sch 18 para 10(a).
(2)–(4)	1974 s 33(3); 1980 Sch 18 para 10(c).
(5)	1974 s 33(4); 1980 Sch 18 para 10(d).
(6)	1974 s 33(5); 1980 Sch 18 para 10(e).
56(1)	1974 ss 32(2), 33(2); 1980 Sch 18 paras 9(b)(i), 10(b).
(2)	1974 ss 32(2)(a), (b), 33(2), (7); 1980 Sch 18 paras 9(b)(ii), 10(b).
(3)	1974 s 32(2)(c); 1980 Sch 18 para 9(b)(iii).
57(1)–(3)	1974 ss 32(6), 33(6); 1980 Sch 18 paras 9(f), 10(f).
(4)	1974 s 15(5).
58(1)	1957 s 119(1).

[567]   *Housing Associations Act 1985 (c 69)*

Provision	Derivation
58(2)	1957 s 119(3).
(3)	1972 s 78(1), (2)(a), (4).
59(1)	1966 (S) s 152(1), (3); 1973 (c 65) Sch 12 para 10.
(2)	1966 (S) s 152(2), (3); 1973 (c 65) Sch 12 para 10.
(3)	1972 (S) s 58(1), (2)(b), (3).
(4)	1966 (S) ss 152(2), 198.
60(1)	1974 s 17(1)(b).
(2)	1974 s 17(3), (5); 1975 Sch 5 para 13; 1975 (S) Sch 3 para 13.
(3)	1974 s 17(4).
61(1)	1957 s 122; 1966 (S) s 156(1).
(2)	1957 s 122; 1966 (S) s 156(2); R 33.
62(1)	1965 (c 25) s 93(1).
(2)	1965 (c 25) s 93(6); 1970 (c 10) Sch 15 para 11 Table Pt II; 1974 s 17(2), (3).
(3)	1965 (c 25) s 93(4).
(4)	1965 (c 25) s 93(1), (2).
(5)	1965 (c 25) s 93(2).
(6), (7)	1965 (c 25) s 93(3).
63(1)	1964 s 8(1); 1974 Sch 13 para 10(2).
(2)	1964 s 8(2); 1974 Sch 13 para 10(2).
(3)	1964 s 8(10); 1974 Sch 13 para 10(2).
(4)	1964 s 8(3).
(5)	1964 s 8(4).
(6)	1964 s 8(3), (10).
64	1964 s 8(8); 1975 (c 21) s 298(1); 1977 (c 42) Sch 11; 1980 (c 44) s 32(2); 1982 (c 48) s 74(1).
65	1964 s 8(5); 1974 Sch 13 para 10(2).
66(1)(a), (b)	1964 s 8(12).
(c)	1964 s 107.
(d)	drafting.
(2)	1964 s 107.
67(1)	1958 (c 42) s 47(1), (2)(b).
(2)	1958 (c 42) s 47(3), (5)(c), (6).
(3)	1958 (c 42) s 47(5)(c).
(4)	1958 (c 42) s 47(6) proviso (b).
(5)	1958 (c 42) s 47(5)(a), (b) proviso.
68(1)	1968 (S) s 24(1).
(2)	1968 (S) s 24(2), (4)(c), (5).
(3)	1968 (S) s 24(4)(c).
(4)	1968 (S) s 24(5) proviso (b).
(5), (6)	1968 (S) s 24(4)(a), (b) proviso.
69(1)	1972 (S) ss 58(2), 59(1); 1972 ss 78(2), 79(1).
(2)	1972 (S) ss 58(5), 59(2); 1972 ss 78(6), 79(2).
(3)	1972 ss 78(1), 79(2).
(4)	1972 (S) ss 58(1), (5), 59(2).
70	drafting.
71	drafting.
72	'building society' 1964 s 8(11); 'Chief Registrar' 1964 s 8(11); 'officer' 1964 s 8(11); 'registered charity' drafting see 1974 s 32(3)(1).
73	drafting.
74(1), (2)	drafting.
75(1)	1974 s 1(2).
(2)	1974 s 1(3).
(3)	1974 s 1(2).
(4)	1964 Sch 1 para 5; 1974 Sch 1 para 3.
76(1)	1964 s 1(2); R 34(i).
(2)	1974 s 9(3).
(3)	1964 s 1(2).

Housing Associations Act 1985 (c 69) [567]

Provision	Derivation
76(4)	1959 (c 53) s 29; 1959 (c 70) s 29; 1964 s 1(4), (9).
77	1964 s 7; R 35.
78	1964 s 10(6).
79(1)	1974 s 9(1).
(2)	1974 s 9(2).
(3)	1974 s 9(1), (2), (4).
(4)	1974 s 9(3).
80(1)–(3)	1974 s 9(5).
(4)	1974 s 9(6).
81	1984 s 24(1).
82	drafting.
83(1), (2)	1974 s 10(1).
(3), (4)	1974 s 10(2); 1978 s 5(1), (2).
84(1)	1980 s 111(1); 1984 s 20(1).
(2)	1980 s 111(3); 1984 s 20(2).
(3)	1980 s 111(4); 1984 s 20(3).
(4)	1980 s 111(1), (5); 1984 s 20(4)(a).
(5)	1980 s 111(5), (6); 1984 s 20(4)(b).
(6)	1980 s 111(8); 1984 s 20(7).
85(1)	drafting.
(2)	1984 s 20(5); 'recognised body'.
(3)	1984 s 20(6).
(4)	1984 ss 18(3), (4), 20(5) 'relevant advance'.
(5)	1984 s 18(4) 'long lease'.
86	1980 (S) s 31.
87(1)–(3)	1980 s 121(2).
(4)	1980 s 121(3).
88(1)	1974 ss 1(2)(d), 3(1), (3).
(2)	1974 s 3(6).
(3)	1974 s 3(4); 1981 Sch 4 para 1.
(4)	1974 s 3(2).
(5)	1974 s 3(5).
89	1974 s 4.
90(1)	1974 s 5(2).
(2)	1974 s 5(3); 1976 (c 75) Sch 7 para 12; 1981 (c 64) Sch 12 para 13(a).
(3)	1974 s 5(3A); 1980 Sch 25 para 24.
(4)	1974 s 5(4).
(5)	1974 s 5(5)–(7).
(6)	1974 s 5(1).
91	1959 (c 53) s 29(1); 1959 (c 70) s 29(1); 1964 s 1(4), (9).
92(1)	1974 s 7(2).
(2)	1974 s 7(3).
(3)	1974 s 7(4); 1975 (c 55) Sch 4 para 8.
(4)	1974 s 7(6).
(5)	1974 s 7(8).
(6)	1974 s 7(7).
93(1)	1974 s 7(1).
(2)	1974 s 7(5); 1975 Sch 5 para 12; SI 1975/374; 1980 s 120(1); SI 1983/664.
(3)	1974 ss 7(5), 128(1).
(4)	1980 s 120(2).
(5)	1974 s 7(9).
94(1)	1974 s 8(1); 1983 (c 29) s 4.
(2)	1974 s 8(2).
(3)	1974 s 8(3).
(4)	1974 s 8(4).
(5)	1974 s 8(5).
(6)	1974 s 8(2).

Provision	Derivation
95	1980 s 121(1).
96(1)	1974 s 10(3).
(2)	1974 s 1)(4).
(3)	1974 s 10(5).
(4)	1974 s 10(6).
(5)	1974 s 10(4), (5), (6).
97(1)	1964 s 10(1).
(2)	1964 s 10(2).
(3)	1964 s 10(3).
(4)	1964 s 10(4), (5); 1968 (c 13) Sch 1; 1974 Sch 13 para 10(3).
(5)	1964 s 10(5); 1985 (c 9) Sch 2.
(6)	1964 s 10(7).
98(1)	1974 s 6(1).
(2)	1974 s 6(3).
99	1974 s 6(2).
100	1964 s 11; 1974 Sch 13 para 10(4).
101	'building society' 1980 s 111(7); 'financial year' 1964 s 10(7); 1978 (c 30) Sch 1; 'highway' 1974 s 12; 'subsidiary' 1974 s 12; 1985 (c 9) Sch 2.
102	drafting.
103	1972 s 103; 1975 Sch 5 para 7(1); SI 1972/1204; SI 1975/512; R 29.
104(1)	1963 (c 33) s 21(1), (2); 1972 (c 70) s 193(1); 1966 (S) s 1; 1973 (c 65) s 130(3), Sch 12 para 6; SI 1972/1204; SI 1973/886; SI 1975/512.
(2)	drafting.
105	1957 s 104B(4B)(c); 1984 Sch 6 para 1(2).
106(1), (2)	'bank' 1957 s 104B(6), 1978 Sch para 7, 1984 Sch 6 para 1(5); 'building society' *passim*; 'dwelling' 1966 (S) s 206(1), 1972 s 104(1), 1974 s 129(1)(2); 'friendly society' *passim*; 'hostel' 1974 s 129(1)(2), 1966 (S) s 208(1); 'house' 1957 s 189(1), (S) s 208(1), 1980 s 130(3); 'housing activities' 1980 s 133(2), Sch 18 para 9, 1984 Sch 6 para 1(5); 'insurance company' 1957 s 104B(6), 1978 Sch para 8, 1984 Sch 6 para 1(5); 'local authority' 1957 s 1, 1974 ss 5, 129, 1980 s 111, 1980 (c 52) s 31, 1984 ss 18(3), 20(5); 1985 (c 51) Sch 14 para 64(a), (b); 'new town corporation' 1972 (S) s 78(1), 1974 s 5(3)(c)(d), 1981 (c 64) Sch 12 para 13(a); 'shared ownership lease' drafting; 'trustee savings bank' 1957 s 104B(6), 1978 Sch para 6, 1984 Sch 6 para 1(5); 'urban development corporation' 1984 s 18(3).
107	drafting.
Schedules	
Sch 1	
para 1	1974 Sch 2 para 1.
para 2	1974 Sch 2 para 2.
para 3	1974 Sch 2 para 3.
Sch 2	1980 s 122(4), (5), (6).
para 1(1)	1957 s 104B(1); 1980 s 92.
(2)	1957 s 104B(2), (3); 1980 s 92; 1984 Sch 6 para 1(1).
para 2(1)	1957 s 104B(5); 1980 s 92; 1984 Sch 6 para 1(3).
(2)	1957 s 104B(5A); 1984 Sch 6 para 1(4).
(3)	1957 s 104B(7); 1980 s 92.
(4)	1957 s 104B(6); 1978 Sch paras 6–9; 1984 Sch 6 para 1(5).
para 3(1)	1957 s 104C(1), (9); 1980 s 92; 1984 Sch 6 para 2(1), (5).
(2)	1957 s 104C(2); 1980 s 92; 1984 Sch 6 para 2(2).
(3)	1957 s 104C(3); 1980 s 92.
(4)	1957 s 104C(5); 1980 s 92.
(5)	1957 s 104C(6); 1980 s 92.
(6)	1957 s 104C(8); 1980 s 92.
para 4	1957 s 104B(4), 104C(7A); 1984 Sch 6 paras 1(2), 2(4).
para 5(1)	1957 s 104B(4A); 1984 Sch 6 para 1(2).
(2)	1957 s 104B(4B), (8); 1984 Sch 6 para 1(2).
para 6	1957 s 104B(4A)(d); 1984 Sch 6 para 1(2); drafting.

Housing Associations Act 1985 (c 69) [567]

Provision	Derivation
para 7	1957 ss 104B(4C), 104C(7); 1984 Sch 6 paras 1(2), 2(4).
para 8(1)	1957 ss 104B(9), 105C(10); 1980 s 92; 1984 Sch 6 para 1(6), 2(6).
(2)	1957 s 104C(10); 1980 s 92.
Sch 3	
para 1(1), (2)	1980 Sch 16 Part I para 1(1), (2).
para 2(1), (2)	1980 Sch 16 Part I para 2(1), (2).
para 3(1)–(4)	1980 Sch 16 Part I para 3(1)–(4).
para 4(1), (2)	1980 Sch 16 Part I para 4(1), (2).
para 5	1980 Sch 16 Part I para 5(1), (2).
para 6	1980 Sch 16 Part I para 5(3), (4).
para 7	1980 Sch 16 Part I para 6.
Sch 4	
Pt I	
para 1	1972 s 78(2), (3), (5).
para 2	1974 Sch 13 para 5.
Pt II	
para 1	1972 Sch 7 Pt III; 1972 (S) Sch 1 Pts IV, VI.
para 2	1972 s 79(1); 1972 (S) s 59(1).
Pt III	1972 (S) s 58(2)(a), (g), (4).
Sch 5	
Pt I	
para 1	1972 s 72(1)–(7), (9).
para 2	1972 s 73(1)–(7).
para 3	1972 s 104(1) 'housing association'.
para 4	1972 ss 74(1), (5), 104(4).
para 5	1972 ss 15(1), (2), (5), 71(4).
para 6	1972 s 74(2)–(4).
para 7	drafting.
Pt II	
para 1	1972 (S) s 52(1)–(6), (8).
para 2	1972 (S) s 53(1)–(3), (8), (9).
para 3	1972 (S) s 78(1) 'housing association'.
para 4	1972 (S) ss 54(1), 68(1).
para 5	1972 (S) ss 13, 51(4).
para 6	1972 (S) s 54(2)–(4).
para 7	drafting.
Pt III	
para 1(1)	1969 Sch 9 para 1; 1974 Sch 14 para 6.
(2)	1958 (c 42) s 28; 1967 Sch 3 para 6; 1969 Sch 8 para 17.
(3)	1958 (c 42) s 12(1); 1967 s 12(6); 1969 s 21(8); Sch 9 para 1; 1974 Sch 14 para 6.
para 2	1958 (c 42) s 12(2); 1969 Sch 9 para 1.
para 3(1)	1968 (S) s 17(3); 1974 Sch 14 para 6.
(2)	1968 (S) s 57(1).
(3)	1968 (S) s 17(2); 1974 Sch 14 para 6.
para 4(1)	1968 (S) s 58(1).
(2)	1968 (S) s 58(3).
(3)	1968 (S) s 58(2).
Pt IV	
para 1(1)	1968 (S) s 16(2); 1974 Sch 14 para 6.
(2)	1968 (S) s 58(1).
(3)	1968 (S) s 58(3).
Pt V	
para 1	1972 s 78(2)(d), (5).
para 2	1972 (S) s 58(2)(f), (4).
Pt VI	
para 1(1)	1974 s 35(1).
(2)–(4)	1972 ss 15(1), (2), (5), 71(4); 1972 (S) ss 13(1)–(3), 51(4).
para 2(1)	1972 (S) ss 56(2), 57(4); 1972 s 76(2).
(2)	1972 (S) ss 56(3), 57(4); 1972 s 76(3).
(3)	1972 (S) ss 56(4), 57(4); 1972 s 76(4).
para 3(1)–(3)	1972 (S) s 55(12); 1972 s 75(12); 1974 Sch 13 paras 23(4), 32.

Provision	Derivation
(4)	1972 (S) s 57(4); 1972 s 74(5).
para 4	1972 s 35(2).
Pt VII	
para 1(1)	1974 s 35(1).
(2)	1974 s 35(4).
(3)	1974 s 35(5).
Sch 6	
para 1(1)	1964 Sch 1 para 1.
(2)	1964 Sch 1 para 6; 1975 Sch 1 para 4.
(3)	1964 s 1(3).
para 2(1)	1964 Sch 1 para 2(1); 1974 Sch 1 para 1.
(2)	1964 Sch 1 para 2A(1); 1974 Sch 1 para 2.
para 3(1)	1964 Sch 1 para 2(2).
(2)	1964 Sch 1 para 2(4).
(3)	1964 Sch 1 para 2(5).
(4)	1964 Sch 1 para 2A(1); 1974 Sch 1 para 2.
para 4(1)	1964 Sch 1 para 2(1), (2).
(2)	1964 Sch 1 para 2(4).
(3)	1964 Sch 1 para 2(3).
para 5(1), (2)	1964 Sch 1 para 2(7).
para 6(1), (2)	1964 Sch 1 para 2(8).
(3), (4)	1964 Sch 1 para 2(9); 1972 (c 11) Sch 6 para 47.
para 7(1)	1964 Sch 1 para 3(1).
(2)	1964 Sch 1 para 3(2).
para 8(1)	1964 Sch 1 para 2A(2); 1974 Sch 1 para 2.
(2)	1964 Sch 1 para 2A(3); 1974 Sch 1 para 2.
(3)	1964 Sch 1 para 2A(4); 1974 Sch 1 para 2.
para 9(1)	1964 Sch 1 para 4(1); 1980 Sch 25 para 13.
(2)	1964 Sch 1 para 4(2).
Sch 7	
para 1	R 36.
para 2(1)	1964 s 2(3); 1972 s 77(2); 1974 Sch 14 para 1; R 36.
(2)	1964 s 2(3).
para 3	1964 s 5(3); R 36.
para 4	1964 s 2(4); R 36.
para 5(1), (2)	1964 s 5(1); R 36.
(3), (4)	1964 s 5(2); R 36.
(5)	1964 s 5(4); R 36.

Housing (Scotland) Act 1987
(c 26)

A table showing the derivation of the provisions of this consolidation Bill will be found at the end of the Bill. The Table has no official status.

ARRANGEMENT OF SECTIONS

PART I
PROVISION OF HOUSING

Duties and powers of local authorities

1	Duty of local authority to consider needs of their area for further housing accommodation	[568]
2	Powers of local authority to provide housing accommodation	[569]
3	Power of local authority to provide shops, etc, in connection with housing accommodation	[570]
4	Power of local authority to provide furniture, etc .	[571]
5	Power of local authority to provide board and laundry facilities	[572]
6	Duty of local authority to have regard to amenities of locality, etc .	[573]
7	Execution of works by local authority in connection with housing operations outside their area	[574]
8	Adjustment of differences between local authorities as to carrying out of proposals for provision of housing accommodation .	[575]

Acquisition and disposal of land

9	Power of local authority to acquire land for, or in connection with, provision of housing accommodation	[576]
10	Procedure for acquiring land	[577]
11	Local authority may take possession of land to be acquired by agreement or appropriated for purposes of this Part	[578]
12	Powers of dealing with land acquired or appropriated for purposes of this Part	[579]
12A	Consent of Secretary of State required for certain subsequent disposals	[580]
13	Power of Secretary of State in certain cases to impose conditions on sale of local authority's houses, etc.	[581]
14	Powers of local authorities to sell certain houses without consent of Secretary of State	[582]
15	Power of local authority to enforce obligations against owner for time being of land	[583]
16	Disposal of land for erection of churches, etc	[584]

Management and allocation of local authority's houses

17	General management and inspection of local authority's houses	[585]
18	Byelaws for regulation of local authority's houses .	[586]
19	Admission to housing list	[587]
20	Persons to have priority on housing list and allocation of housing	[588]
21	Publication of rules relating to the housing list and to transfer of tenants .	[589]

Housing co-operatives

22	Agreements for exercise by housing co-operatives of local authority housing functions	[590]
23	Improvement of amenities of residential area by development corporations	[591]

PART II
HOMELESS PERSONS

Main definitions

24	Homeless persons and persons threatened with homelessness . .	[592]
25	Priority need for accommodation	[593]
26	Becoming homeless intentionally	[594]
27	Meaning of 'local connection'	[595]

Duties of local authorities with respect to homelessness and threatened homelessness

28	Inquiry into cases of possible homelessness or threatened homelessness . .	[596]
29	Interim duty to accommodate in case of apparent priority need . .	[597]
30	Notification of decision and reasons	[598]
31	Duties to persons found to be homeless	[599]
32	Duties to persons found to be threatened with homelessness . . .	[600]
33	Referral of application to another local authority	[601]
34	Duties to persons whose applications are referred	[602]
35	Supplementary provisions	[603]
36	Protection of property of homeless persons and persons threatened with homelessness	[604]

Administrative provisions

37	Guidance to authorities by the Secretary of State	[605]
38	Co-operation between authorities	[606]

Assistance for voluntary organisations

39	Financial and other assistance for voluntary organisations concerned with homelessness	[607]

Supplementary provisions

40	False statements, withholding information and failure to disclose change of circumstances	[608]
41	Meaning of accommodation available for occupation . . .	[609]
42	Application of this Part to cases arising in England or Wales . .	[610]
43	Minor definitions	[611]

PART III
RIGHTS OF PUBLIC SECTOR TENANTS

Security of tenure

44	Secure tenancies	[612]

45	Special provision for housing associations	**[613]**
46	Restriction on termination of secure tenancy	**[614]**
47	Proceedings for possession	**[615]**
48	Powers of sheriff in proceedings	**[616]**
49	Rights of landlord where a secure tenancy appears to have been abandoned	**[617]**
50	Repossession	**[618]**
51	Tenant's right of recourse to sheriff	**[619]**

Succession

52	Succession to secure tenancy	**[620]**

Leases

53	Tenant's right to written lease	**[621]**
54	Restriction on variation of terms of secure tenancies	**[622]**

Subletting

55	No subletting by secure tenant without landlord's consent	**[623]**
56	Rent payable by subtenants	**[624]**

Repairs and improvements

57	Landlord's consent to work	**[625]**
58	Reimbursement of cost of work	**[626]**
59	Effect of works on rent	**[627]**
60	Scheme giving tenant a right to carry out repairs	**[628]**

Right to buy

61	Secure tenant's right to purchase	**[629]**
62	The price	**[630]**

Procedure

63	Application to purchase and offer to sell	**[631]**
64	Conditions of sale	**[632]**
65	Variation of conditions	**[633]**
66	Notice of acceptance	**[634]**
67	Fixed price option	**[635]**
68	Refusal of applications	**[636]**

Houses provided for special purposes

69	Secretary of State's power to authorise refusal to sell certain houses provided for persons of pensionable age	**[637]**
70	Power to refuse to sell certain houses required for educational purposes	**[638]**

Lands Tribunal

71	Reference to Lands Tribunal	**[639]**

Recovery of discount

72	Recovery of discount on early resale	**[640]**
73	Cases where discount etc is not recoverable	**[641]**

Duties of landlords

74 Duties of landlords . . . . **[642]**
75 Agreements affecting right to purchase . . . . . **[643]**
76 Duty of landlords to provide information to secure tenants . . . **[644]**

Powers of Secretary of State

77 Secretary of State may make provision for vesting in landlord to bring into being tenant's right to purchase house . . . . . **[645]**
78 Secretary of State may give directions to modify conditions of sale . . **[646]**
79 Secretary of State may give financial and other assistance for tenants involved in proceedings . . . . **[647]**

★ ★ ★

81 Information from landlords in relation to Secretary of State's powers . **[648]**

Preservation of right to buy on disposal to private sector landlord

81A Preservation of right to buy on disposal to private sector landlord . . **[649]**
81B Consultation before disposal to private sector landlord . . . . **[650]**

General

82 Interpretation of this Part . . . . **[651]**
83 Members of a person's family . . . . **[652]**
84 Service of notices . . . . **[653]**
84A Application of right to buy in cases where landlord is lessee . . **[654]**

PART IV
SUB-STANDARD HOUSES

The tolerable standard

85 General duty of local authority in respect of houses not meeting tolerable standard . . . . **[655]**
86 Definition of house meeting tolerable standard . . . . . **[656]**
87 Official representation that house does not meet tolerable standard . . **[657]**

Improvement order

88 Improvement of houses below tolerable standard outside housing action areas . . . . **[658]**

Housing action areas

89 Declaration of housing action areas for demolition . . . . **[659]**
90 Declaration of housing action areas for improvement . . . . **[660]**
91 Declaration of housing action areas for demolition and improvement . **[661]**
92 Provisions supplementary to sections 89 to 91 . . . . . **[662]**
93 Consent to demolition of listed buildings, rehabilitation orders and compensation . . . . **[663]**

Powers of Secretary of State

94 Functions of Secretary of State, and duty of local authority to publish information . . . . **[664]**

Powers of local authority

95	Further procedure, powers of local authority on acquisition of land, compensation and agricultural holdings	[665]
96	Power of local authority to retain houses subject to demolition for temporary occupation	[666]
97	Local authority may control occupation of houses in housing action areas	[667]
98	Obligation of local authorities in relation to rehousing in housing action areas	[668]

Landlords and tenants in housing action areas

99	Application to sheriff for possession where house is identified in accordance with paragraph 1(1) of Schedule 8 as read with section 92(4)(a)	[669]
100	Application to sheriff for possession where house is identified in accordance with paragraph 1(1) of Schedule 8 as read with section 92(4)(c)	[670]
101	Application to sheriff for possession where house is identified in acccordance with paragraph 1 of Schedule 8 as read with section 92(4)(b)	[671]
102	Procedure; and application of s 103(1) of Rent (Scotland) Act 1984	[672]
103	Certain provisions of Rent (Scotland) Act 1984 not to apply	[673]
104	Effect of refusal to make order on validity of resolution	[674]

Miscellaneous

105	Exclusion of houses controlled by Crown	[675]
106	Power of local authority to arrange for the execution of works of improvement by agreement with the owner	[676]
107	Conditions may be attached to sale of below-standard local authority houses	[677]

Part V
Repair of Houses

Repair notices

108	Power of local authority to secure repair of house in state of serious disrepair	[678]
109	Recovery by local authority of expenses under s 108	[679]
110	Recovery by lessee of proportion of expenses incurred in repairing house	[680]

Appeals etc

111	Appeals under Part V	[681]
112	Date of operation of notices, demands and orders subject to appeal	[682]

Landlord and tenant

113	Obligations to repair	[683]

Part VI
Closing and Demolition Orders

Powers of local authority

114	Closing order	[684]
115	Demolition order	[685]

116	Revocation of closing and demolition order	[686]
117	Undertakings to bring up to tolerable standard and suspension order	[687]
118	Service	[688]
119	Listed buildings and houses subject to building preservation orders	[689]
120	Powers of local authority in relation to building consisting wholly of closed houses	[690]
121	Local authority may acquire and repair house or building liable to closing or demolition order	[691]

Offences

122	Penalty for use of premises in contravention of closing order or of undertaking	[692]

Powers of local authority following demolition order

123	Procedure where demolition order made	[693]
124	Power of local authority to purchase site of demolished building where expense of demolition cannot be recovered	[694]

Demolition of obstructive buildings

125	Local authority may by resolution require demolition of obstructive building	[695]
126	Effect of resolution for demolition of obstructive building	[696]

Possession

127	Recovery of possession of building or house subject to closing order, etc	[697]
128	Recovery of possession of house to which Rent Act applies	[698]

Appeals and date of operation of certain notices, etc

129	Appeals	[699]
130	Date of operation of notices, orders or resolutions subject to appeal	[700]

Charging orders

131	Power of local authority to make charging order in favour of themselves	[701]

Supplementary

132	Protection of superiors and owners	[702]
133	Interpretation	[703]

Saving

134	Saving for telecommunication and gas apparatus	[704]

PART VII
OVERCROWDING

Definition of overcrowding

135	Definition of overcrowding	[705]
136	The room standard	[706]
137	The space standard	[707]

Housing (Scotland) Act 1987 (c 26) [568]

Powers of Secretary of State

138	Secretary of State may increase permitted number of persons temporarily	[708]

Responsibility of occupier

139	Penalty for occupier causing or permitting overcrowding	[709]
140	Exception: children attaining age of 1 or 10	[710]
141	Exception: temporary visitor	[711]
142	Licence of local authority	[712]
143	Exception: holiday visitors	[713]

Powers and duties of landlord

144	Offence by landlord not to inform prospective tenant of permitted number of occupants	[714]
145	Recovery of possession of overcrowded house that is let	[715]

Powers and duties of local authority

146	Duty of local authority to inspect district and to make reports and proposals as to overcrowding	[716]
147	Power to require information about persons sleeping in house	[717]
148	Duty to give information to landlords and occupiers	[718]
149	Power to publish information	[719]
150	Duty to enforce this Part	[720]
151	Interpretation and application	[721]

PART VIII
HOUSES IN MULTIPLE OCCUPATION

Registration schemes

152	Registration schemes	[722]
153	Steps to inform the public about scheme	[723]
154	Proof of scheme and contents of register	[724]
155	Power to require information for purposes of scheme	[725]

Management code

156	Power of Secretary of State to make management code	[726]
157	Power of local authority to apply management code to particular house	[727]
158	Appeal against making of, or failure to revoke, order under s 157	[728]
159	Registration of order and of revocation	[729]

Powers of local authority to require works to be done

160	Notice requiring compliance with management code	[730]
161	Notice requiring compliance with standards	[731]
162	Notice requiring provision of means of escape from fire	[732]
163	Appeal against notice requiring execution of works	[733]
164	Carrying out of works by local authority	[734]
165	Penalty for failure to execute works	[735]

Overcrowding

166 Local authority may give directions to prevent or reduce overcrowding in house in multiple occupation . . . . . [736]
167 Notice of direction . . . . [737]
168 Power to require information where notice is in force . . . [738]
169 Revocation and variation . . . . [739]
170 Appeal against refusal . . . . [740]

Supplementary

171 Application of sections 156 to 161 to certain buildings comprising separate dwellings . . . . [741]
172 Management code to be available for dwellings in certain tenements . [742]
173 Warrant to authorise entry . . . . [743]
174 Application to sheriff where consent unreasonably withheld . . [744]
175 Protection of superiors and owners . . . . . . [745]
176 Identity and notice under Part VIII . . . . . . [746]
177 Statutory tenant to be regarded as lessee, etc . . . . . [747]

Control orders

178 Making of control order . . . . [748]
179 General effect of control order . . . . [749]
180 Effect of control order on persons occupying house . . . [750]
181 Effect of control order in relation to furniture in furnished lettings . [751]
182 General duties of local authority when control order in force . . [752]
183 Compensation payable to dispossessed proprietor . . . [753]
184 Duty to prepare management scheme . . . . . . [754]
185 Power of sheriff to modify or determine lease . . . . [755]

Appeals

186 Appeal against control order . . . . [756]
187 Control order revoked on appeal . . . . [757]

Expiration and revocation of control order, etc

188 Expiration of control order, and earlier revocation by local authority or sheriff . . . . [758]
189 Effect of cessation of control order . . . . . . [759]
190 Interpretation of Part VIII . . . . [760]

PART IX
GOVERNMENT GRANTS AND SUBSIDIES

Housing support grants to local authorities

191 Housing support grants: fixing of aggregate amount . . . [761]
192 Apportionment of housing support grants . . . . . [762]
193 Variation of orders . . . . [763]

Grants to the Scottish Special Housing Association and other bodies

194 Grants payable to the Scottish Housing Association and development corporations . . . . [764]

Housing (Scotland) Act 1987 (c 26) [568]

195 Grants for affording tax relief to Scottish Special Housing Association . [765]

★ ★ ★

197 Financial assistance to voluntary organisations concerned with housing . [766]

Payment of grants

198 Payment of grants and accounting provisions . . . . . [767]
199 Termination of certain exchequer payments to housing authorities. . [768]

Slum clearance subsidy

★ ★ ★

Payment of subsidies

201 Payment of subsidies and accounting provisions . . . . . [769]

Secretary of State's power to vary Exchequer contributions

202 Power of Secretary of State to reduce, suspend, discontinue or transfer particular Exchequer contributions . . . . [770]

PART X
HOUSING ACCOUNTS OF LOCAL AUTHORITIES

203 The housing revenue account . . . . [771]
204 Power of Secretary of State to limit estimated rate fund contributions to housing revenue account. . . . . [772]
205 The rent rebate account . . . . [773]
206 The rent allowance account . . . . [774]
207 The slum clearance revenue account . . . . [775]
208 Application of recipts from disposal of certain land . . . . [776]
209 Adjustment of accounts on appropriation of land . . . . . [777]

PART XI
RENTS AND SERVICE CHARGES

210 Rents for public sector housing . . . . [778]
211 Service charges . . . . [779]
212 Rent increase notice . . . . [780]
213 Removal notice . . . . [781]

PART XII
HOUSE LOANS AND OTHER FINANCIAL ASSISTANCE

House loans: general

214 Power of local authority to make advances for the purpose of increasing housing accommodation . . . . [782]
215 Requirements as to meeting tolerable standard . . . . . [783]

House loans: special cases

216 House loans to tenants exercising right to purchase . . . . [784]

315

217	Duty of local authorities to offer loans to meet expenses of improvement of houses in housing action areas	[785]
218	Duty of local authority to offer loans to meet expenses of repairs . .	[786]

Rates of interest on home loans

219	Local authority home loan interest rates	[787]
220	Variation of rate by local authority	[788]
221	Variation of rate by Secretary of State	[789]

Assistance for first-time buyers

222	Advances to recognised lending institutions to assist first-time buyers .	[790]
223	Forms of assistance and qualifying conditions	[791]
224	Recognised lending institutions	[792]
225	Recognised savings institutions	[793]
226	Terms of advances and administration	[794]
227	Modifications of building society law and disapplication of provisions of the Restrictive Trade Practices Act 1976 in relation to assistance for first-time buyers	[795]
228	Exclusion of Restrictive Trade Practices Act: agreements as to loans on security of new houses	[796]

Other assistance

229	Local authority indemnities for building societies, etc	[797]
230	Assistance by local authority for acquiring houses in need of repair and improvement	[798]
231	Loans by Public Works Loan Commissioners for provision or improvement of housing accommodation	[799]
232	Power of court in cases relating to instalment purchase agreements .	[800]
233	Power of local authority to assist in provision of separate service water pipes for houses	[801]
234	Financial assistance towards tenants' removal expenses	[802]

Contributions to assistance for elderly, etc

235	Contributions by other local authorities towards expenses of housing pensioners and disabled persons	[803]

PART XIII
LOCAL AUTHORITY GRANTS FOR IMPROVEMENT, REPAIR AND CONVERSION

Improvement grants

236	Power of local authorities to make improvement grants . . .	[804]
237	Form of application	[805]
238	Power of local authority	[806]
239	Consent of Secretary of State	[807]
239A	Power of Secretary of State to give direction to prevent duplications of grant	[808]
240	Conditions for approval of applications for improvement grant other than applications relating exclusively to the provision of standard amenities	[809]
241	Approval of application for improvement grant	[810]
242	Amount of improvement grant	[811]
243	Payment of improvement grant	[812]

244	Duty of local authorities to make improvement grants where an application relates exclusively to the provision of standard amenities or to disabled occupant; and amount thereof	[813]
245	Grants restricted to applicant and his personal representatives	[814]
246	Conditions to be observed with respect to houses in respect of which an improvement grant has been made, and registration thereof	[815]
247	Voluntary repayment of improvement grants	[816]

Repairs grants

248	Repairs grants	[817]

Grants for fire escapes

249	Grants for fire escapes for houses in multiple occupation	[818]

Grants for houses in housing action areas

250	Application of this Part to houses situated in a housing action area and power of local authority to give repair grants in such areas and amount thereof	[819]

Improvement of amenity grants

251	Powers of local authority for improvement of amenities	[820]

Grants for thermal insulation

252	Schemes for grants for thermal insulation	[821]
253	Finance and administration of schemes under s 252	[822]

Exchequer contributions

★ ★ ★

Agricultural tenants, etc

256	Application of this Part to agricultural tenants, etc	[823]
256A	Application of this Part to Scottish Homes	[824]

PART XIV
ASSISTANCE FOR OWNERS OF DEFECTIVE HOUSING

Eligibility for assistance

257	Designation of defective dwellings by Secretary of State	[825]
258	Variation or revocation of designation	[826]
259	Conditions of eligibility	[827]
260	Exceptions to eligibility	[828]
261	Construction of references to disposal, etc	[829]

Determination of entitlement

262	Application for assistance	[830]
263	Application not to be entertained where grant application pending or approved	[831]
264	Determination of eligibility	[832]
265	Determination of form of assistance to which applicant is entitled	[833]
266	Conditions for assistance by way of reinstatement grant	[834]

267	Meaning of 'work required for reinstatement' and 'associated arrangement'	[835]
268	Notice of determination	[836]

Assistance by way of reinstatement grant

269	Reinstatement grant	[837]
270	Conditions of payment of reinstatement grant	[838]
271	Amount of reinstatement grant	[839]
272	Changes in work or expenditure	[840]
273	Payment of reinstatement grant	[841]
274	Repayment of grant for breach of condition	[842]

Assistance by way of repurchase

275	Repurchase	[843]
276	Repurchase by authority other than local authority	[844]
277	Interest subject to right of pre-emption, etc	[845]
278	Compulsory purchase compensation to be made up to 95 per cent of defect-free value	[846]
279	Supplementary provisions as to payments under s 277 or 278	[847]
280	Reimbursement of expenses incidental to repurchase	[848]

Effect of repurchase on occupier

281	Effect of repurchase on certain existing tenancies	[849]
282	Grant of tenancy to former owner-occupier	[850]
283	Grant of tenancy to former statutory tenant	[851]
284	Alternative accommodation under s 282 or 283	[852]
285	Request for tenancy under s 282 or 283	[853]
286	Interpretation of ss 281 to 285	[854]

Local schemes

287	Designation of defective dwellings under local schemes	[855]
288	Variation or revocation of designation under local schemes	[856]
289	Secretary of State's control over designation, variation or revocation	[857]

Miscellaneous

290	Duty of local housing authority to publicise availability of assistance	[858]
291	Duties of public sector authority disposing of defective dwelling	[859]
292	Reinstatement of defective dwelling by local authority	[860]
293	Death of person eligible for assistance, etc	[861]
294	Dwellings included in more than one designation	[862]
295	Application of Act in relation to lenders on security of defective dwelling	[863]

★ ★ ★

Supplementary provisions

298	Service of notices	[864]
299	Jurisdiction of sheriff in Scotland	[865]
300	Meaning of 'public sector authority'	[866]
301	Disposal of certain Crown interests in land treated as disposal by public sector authority	[867]
302	Meaning of 'dwelling' and 'house'	[868]
303	Interpretation	[869]

Part XV
Compensation Payments

Payments for well-maintained houses

304 Payments in respect of well-maintained houses subject to closing orders, etc . . . . **[870]**
305 Payments in respect of well-maintained houses subject to compulsory purchase as not meeting the tolerable standard . . . . . **[871]**
306 Calculation of amount payable for well-maintained houses . . . **[872]**

Repayment of certain payments

307 Repayment of payments made in connection with closing or demolition order when revoked . . . . **[873]**

Payments for houses not meeting tolerable standard

308 Right to and amount of payments for house not meeting tolerable standard . . . . **[874]**
309 Right of parties to certain agreements secured on, or related to, houses not meeting the tolerable standard to apply to sheriff for adjustment of the agreements . . . . **[875]**
310 Provisions as to house subject to heritable security or purchased by instalments . . . . **[876]**
311 Interpretation of sections 308 to 310 . . . . **[877]**

Payments to other local authorities

312 Payment of purchase money or compensation by one local authority to another . . . . **[878]**

Part XVI
General and Miscellaneous

Byelaws

313 Byelaws with respect to houses in multiple occupation . . . . **[879]**
314 Byelaws with respect to accommodation for agricultural workers . . **[880]**
315 Byelaws with respect to accommodation for seasonal workers . . **[881]**
316 Confirmation of byelaws . . . . **[882]**

Entry

317 Power of entry for survey, etc . . . . **[883]**

Offences

318 Penalty for obstructing execution of Act . . . . . . **[884]**
319 Penalty for preventing execution of works, etc . . . . . **[885]**
320 Penalty for damage to houses, etc . . . . **[886]**
321 Liability of directors, etc in case of offence by body corporate . . . **[887]**

Powers of sheriff for housing purposes

322 Sheriff may determine lease in certain cases . . . . . . **[888]**
323 Sheriff may authorise superior to execute works, etc . . . . **[889]**

| 324 | Procedure on applications and appeals to sheriff | [890] |

Service

| 325 | Occupier or tenant may be required to state interest | [891] |
| 326 | Service by description on certain persons whose identity is unknown and on a number of persons of one description | [892] |

Landlord's identity

| 327 | Disclosure of landlord's identity | [893] |
| 328 | Duty to inform tenant of assignation of landlord's interest | [894] |

Powers of Secretary of State

329	Power of Secretary of State in event of failure of local authority to exercise powers	[895]
330	Power of Secretary of State to prescribe forms, etc	[896]
331	Regulations: procedure	[897]
332	Secretary of State's power to dispense with advertisements and notices	[898]
333	Local inquiries	[899]

Miscellaneous

334	Power of heir of entail to sell land for housing purposes	[900]
335	Crown rights	[901]
336	Limitation on liability of trustee, etc for expenses incurred by local authority	[902]

* * *

338	Interpretation	[903]
339	Minor and consequential amendments, transitional provisions and repeals	[904]
340	Citation, commencement and extent	[905]

SCHEDULES:

Schedule 1—Rules as to assessment of compensation where land purchased compulsorily in certain circumstances	[906–910]
Schedule 2—Tenancies which are not secure tenancies	[911–918]
Schedule 3—Grounds for recovery of possession of houses let under secure tenancies	[919–937]
Part I—Grounds on which court may order recovery of possession	[919–934]
Part II—Suitability of accommodation	[935–937]
Schedule 4—Terms of secure tenancy relating to subletting, etc	[938–943]
Schedule 5—Terms of secure tenancy relating to alterations, etc to house	[944–950]
Schedule 6—Vesting order under section 77: modification of enactments	[951–960]
Schedule 6A—Consultation before disposal to private sector landlord	[961–966]
Schedule 7	
Part I—Consent to demolition of listed buildings in housing action areas, etc	[967–968]
Part II—Rehabilitation orders	[969–978]
Part III—Application of enactments relating to compensation on compulsory purchase, etc, to cases under Part I or Part II of this Schedule	[979–980]
Schedule 8	
Part I—Housing action areas	[981–982]
Part II—Powers of local authority in relation to acquisition of land for housing action areas	[983–991]
Part III—Compensation in respect of land acquired compulsorily	[992]

Part IV—Adjustment of relations between lessors and lessees of agricultural holdings, etc	[993–1016]
Schedule 9—Recovery of expenses by charging order	[994–1001]
Schedule 10—Landlord's repairing obligations	[1002–1006]
Schedule 11—Houses in multiple occupation: control orders	[1007–1016]
Part I—Management schemes	[1007–1008]
Part II—Appeal and review	[1009–1012]
Part III—Consequences of cessation of control order	[1013–1015]
Part IV—Recovery of expenses by local authority executing works under section 164	[1016]
Schedule 12—Termination of Exchequer payments to local authorities and certain periodical payments to other persons	[1017–1018]
Schedule 13—Enactments specifying Exchequer contributions	[1019]
Schedule 14—Enactments specifying Exchequer contributions that may be reduced, suspended or discontinued	[1020]
Schedule 15—The housing revenue account	[1021–1029]
Part I—Application of account	[1021]
Part II—Operation of account	[1022–1029]
Schedule 16—The slum clearance revenue account	[1030–1035]
Schedule 17—Conditions relating to house loans	[1036–1045]
Schedule 18—Standard amenities	[1045A–1049]
Part I—List of amenities and maximum eligible amounts	[1045A]
Part II—Limit on amount of approved expenses for standard amenities	[1046–1049]
Schedule 19—Consequences of breach of conditions of improvement grant	[1050–1057]
Schedule 20—Assistance by way of repurchase	[1058–1069]
Part I—The agreement to repurchase	[1058–1065]
Part II—Price payable and valuation	[1066–1069]
Schedule 21—Dwellings included in more than one designation	[1070–1076]
Schedule 22—Transitional provisions and savings	[1077–1090]
Part I—Transitional provisions	[1077–1084]
Part II—Savings	[1085–1090]

★ ★ ★

An Act to consolidate with amendments to give effect to recommendations of the Scottish Law Commission, certain enactments relating to housing in Scotland.

[15th May 1987]

Be it enacted by the Queen's most Excellent Majesty, by and with the advice and consent of the Lords Spiritual and Temporal, and Commons, in this present Parliament assembled, and by the authority of the same, as follows:—

PART I
PROVISION OF HOUSING

Duties and powers of local authorities

1. Duty of local authority to consider needs of their area for further housing accommodation.

(1) Every local authority shall consider the housing conditions in their area and the needs of the area for further housing accommodation.

(2) For that purpose they shall review any information which has been brought to their notice, including in particular information brought to their notice as a result of a survey or inspections made under section 85(3).

(3) If the Secretary of State gives them notice to do so, they shall, within 3 months

after such notice, prepare and submit to him proposals for the provision of housing accommodation.

(4) In considering the needs of their area for further housing accommodation under subsection (1), every local authority shall have regard to the special needs of chronically sick or disabled persons; and any proposals prepared and submitted to the Secretary of State under subsection (3) shall distinguish any houses which they propose to provide which make special provision for the needs of such persons. [568]

NOTES to section 1
Definitions: 'local authority', 'house': see s 338 below.

2. Power of local authority to provide housing accommodation.

(1) A local authority may provide housing accommodation—
(a) by the erection of houses on any land acquired or appropriated by them;
(b) by the conversion of any buildings into houses;
(c) by acquiring houses;
(d) by altering, enlarging, repairing or improving any houses or other buildings which have, or a right or interest in which has, been acquired by the local authority.

(2) For the purpose of supplying the needs for housing accommodation in its area, a local authority may exercise any of its powers under subsection (1) outside that area.

(3) A local authority may alter, enlarge, repair or improve any house provided by them under subsection (1).

(4) For the purposes of this Part the provision of housing accommodation includes the provision of—
(a) a cottage with a garden of not more than one acre;
(b) a hostel.

(5) In this section 'hostel' means—
(a) in relation to a building provided or converted before 3 July 1962, a building in which is provided, for persons generally or for any class or classes of persons, residential accommodation (otherwise than in separate and self-contained dwellings) and board;
(b) in relation to a building provided or converted on or after 3 July 1962, a building in which is provided, for persons generally or for any class or classes of persons, residential accommodation (otherwise than in houses) and either board or common facilities for the preparation of food adequate to the needs of those persons or both.

[(6) Nothing in this Act shall be taken to require (or to have at any time required) a local authority itself to acquire or hold any houses or other land for the purposes of this Part.] [569]

NOTES to section 2
Amendment: Sub-s (6) was added by the Local Government and Housing Act 1989 (c 42), s 161.
Definitions: 'local authority', 'house', 'land': see s 338 below.

3. Power of local authority to provide shops, etc, in connection with housing accommodation.

(1) Subject to the provisions of this section, a local authority may provide and maintain—
(a) any building adapted for use as a shop;
(b) any recreation grounds;
(c) such other buildings or land as are referred to in subsection (2),
in connection with housing accommodation provided by them under this Part.

(2) The buildings or land referred to in subsection (1)(c) are buildings or land which in the opinion of the Secretary of State will serve a beneficial purpose in connection with the requirements of the persons for whom the housing accommodation is provided.

(3) The provision and maintenance of any building or land under this section—
(a) requires the consent of the Secretary of State;
(b) may be undertaken jointly with any other person.

(4) The Secretary of State may, in giving his consent to the provision of any building or land under this section, by order apply, with any necessary modifications, to that building or land any statutory provisions which would have been applicable to it if the building or land had been provided under any enactment giving any local authority powers for that purpose. [570]

NOTES to section 3
Definitions: 'local authority', 'land': see s 338 below.

4. Power of local authority to provide furniture, etc.

(1) A local authority—
(a) may fit out, furnish and supply any house erected, converted or acquired by them under section 2 with all requisite furniture, fittings and conveniences;
(b) shall have power to sell, or to supply under a hire-purchase agreement, furniture to the occupants of houses provided by the local authority and, for that purpose, to buy furniture.

(2) In this section 'hire-purchase agreement' means a hire-purchase or conditional sale agreement within the meaning of the Consumer Credit Act 1974. [571]

NOTES to section 4
Definitions: 'local authority', 'house': see s 338 below.

5. Power of local authority to provide board and laundry facilities.

(1) The power of a local authority under this Part to provide housing accommodation shall include power to provide, in connection with the provision of such accommodation for any persons, such facilities for obtaining meals and such laundry facilities and services as accord with the needs of those persons.

(2) A local authority may make such reasonable charges for meals provided by them by virtue of this section, and such reasonable charges to persons availing themselves of laundry facilities or services so provided, as the authority may determine.

(3) This section shall not authorise the grant of a licence under the Licensing (Scotland) Act 1976 for the sale of alcoholic liquor in connection with the provision under this section of facilities for obtaining meals. [572]

NOTES to section 5
Definition: 'local authority': see s 338 below.

6. Duty of local authority to have regard to amenities of locality, etc.

(1) A local authority, in preparing any proposals for the provision of houses or in taking any action under this Act, shall have regard to artistic quality in the lay-out, planning and treatment of the houses to be provided, the beauty of the landscape or countryside and the other amenities of the locality, and the desirability of preserving existing works of architectural, historic or artistic interest.

(2) For their better advice in carrying out the requirements of subsection (1), a local authority may appoint a local advisory committee including representatives of architectural and other artistic interests. [573]

[574]

NOTES to section 6
Definitions: 'local authority', 'house': see s 338 below.

7. Execution of works by local authority in connection with housing operations outside their area.

Where any housing operations under this Part are being carried out by a local authority outside their own area, that authority shall have power to execute any works which are necessary for the purposes, or are incidental to the carrying out, of the operations, subject to entering into an agreement with the local authority of the area in which the operations are being carried out as to the terms and conditions on which any such works are to be executed. [574]

NOTES to section 7
Definition: 'local authority': see s 338 below.

8. Adjustment of differences between local authorities as to carrying out of proposals for provision of housing accommodation.

Where a local authority are providing houses in the area of another local authority, any difference arising between those authorities with respect to the carrying out of the proposals may be referred by either authority to the Secretary of State, and the Secretary of State's decision shall be final and binding on the authorities. [575]

NOTES to section 8
Definitions: 'local authority', 'house': see s 338 below.

Acquisition and disposal of land

9. Power of local authority to acquire land for, or in connection with, provision of housing accommodation.

(1) A local authority may acquire—
(a) any land as a site for the erection of houses;
(b) land proposed to be used for any purpose authorised by section 3 or section 5;
(c) subject to subsection (2),
   (i) houses, and
   (ii) buildings other than houses, being buildings which may be made suitable as houses,
together with any lands occupied with the houses or buildings, or any right or interest in the houses or buildings;
(d) land for the purposes of—
   (i) selling or leasing the land under the powers conferred by this Act, with a view to the erection on the land of houses by persons other than the local authority;
   (ii) selling or leasing, under the powers conferred by this Act, any part of the land acquired, with a view to the use of that land for purposes which in the opinion of the local authority are necessary or desirable for, or incidental to, the development of the land as a building estate;
   (iii) carrying out on the land works for the purpose of, or connected with, the alteration, enlargement, repair or improvement of an adjoining house;
   (iv) selling or leasing the land under the powers conferred by this Act, with a view to the carrying out on the land by a person other than the local authority of such works as are mentioned in sub-paragraph (iii).

(2) Nothing in subsection (1)(c) shall authorise a local authority to acquire otherwise than by agreement any house or other building which is situated on land used for agriculture, and which is required in connection with that use of that land. [576]

NOTES to section 9

Definitions: 'local authority', 'land', 'houses', 'sell', 'agriculture': see s 338 below.

10. Procedure for acquiring land.

(1) Land for the purposes of this Part may be acquired by a local authority by agreement under section 70 of the Local Government (Scotland) Act 1973.

(2) A local authority may be authorised by the Secretary of State to purchase land compulsorily for the purposes of this Part, and the Acquisition of Land (Authorisation Procedure) (Scotland) Act 1947 shall apply in relation to any such compulsory purchase as if this Act had been in force immediately before the commencement of that Act.

(3) A local authority may acquire land by agreement, or may be authorised by the Secretary of State to purchase land compulsorily, for the purposes of this Part, notwithstanding that the land is not immediately required for those purposes.

(4) Where land is purchased compulsorily by a local authority for the purposes of this Part, the compensation payable in respect thereof shall be assessed by the Lands Tribunal in accordance with the Land Compensation (Scotland) Act 1963, subject to the rules set out in Schedule 1. [577]

NOTES to section 10

Definitions: 'land', 'local authority', 'Lands Tribunal': see s 338 below.

11. Local authority may take possession of land to be acquired by agreement or appropriated for purposes of this Part.

(1) Where a local authority have agreed to purchase, or have determined to appropriate, land for the purposes of this Part, subject to the interest of the person in possession of the land, and that interest is not greater than that of a tenant for a year or from year to year, then, at any time after such agreement has been made, or such appropriation takes effect, the authority may, after giving to the person in possession not less than 14 days' notice and subject to subsection (2), enter on and take possession of the land or such part of it as is specified in the notice without previous consent.

(2) The powers conferred by subsection (1) are exercisable subject to payment to the person in possession of the like compensation and interest on the compensation awarded, as if the authority had been authorised to purchase the land compulsorily and that person had in pursuance of such power been required to give up possession before the expiration of his term or interest in the land, but without the necessity of compliance with sections 83 to 88 of the Lands Clauses Consolidation (Scotland) Act 1845. [578]

NOTES to section 11

Definitions: 'local authority', 'land': see s 338 below.

12. Powers of dealing with land acquired or appropriated for purposes of this Part.

(1) Where a local authority have acquired or appropriated any land for the purposes of this Part, then, without prejudice to any of their other powers under this Act, the authority may—
  (a) lay out and construct roads and open spaces on the land;
  (b) subject to subsection (5), sell or lease the land or part of the land to any person under the condition that that person will erect on it in accordance with plans approved by the local authority, and maintain, such number of houses of such types as may be specified by the authority, and when necessary will lay out and construct public streets or roads and open spaces on the land, or will use the land for purposes which, in the opinion of the authority, are necessary or desirable for,

or incidental to, the development of the land as a building estate in accordance with plans approved by the authority;
(c) subject to [subsections (5), and (7)], sell or lease the land or excamb it for land better adapted for those purposes, either with or without paying or receiving any money for equality of exchange;
(d) subject to subsections (5) and (7), sell or lease any houses or any part share thereof on the land or erected by them on the land, subject to such conditions, restrictions and stipulations as they may think fit to impose in regard to the use of the houses or any part share thereof, and on any such sale they may agree to the price being secured by standard security over the subjects sold.

(2) Where a local authority sell or lease land under subsection (1), they may contribute or agree to contribute towards the expenses of the development of the land and the laying out and construction of roads on the land, subject to the condition that the roads are dedicated to the public use.

(3) Where a local authority have acquired a building which may be made suitable as a house, or a right or interest in such a building, they shall forthwith proceed to secure that it is so made suitable either by themselves executing any necessary work or by selling or leasing it to some person subject to conditions for securing that he will so make it suitable.

(4) Where a local authority acquire any land for the purposes of section 9(1)(d)(iv), they may, subject to subsection (5), sell or lease the land to any person for the purpose and under the condition that that person will carry out on the land, in accordance with plans approved by the authority, the works with a view to the carrying out of which the land was acquired.

(5) A local authority shall not, in the exercise of their powers under subsection (1)(b), (c) or (d), or subsection (4), dispose of land which consists or forms part of a common or open space or is held for use as allotments, except with the consent of the Secretary of State.

(6) For the purposes of subsection (5), the consent of the Secretary of State may be given either generally to all local authorities, or to any class of local authorities, or may be given specifically in any particular case, and (whether given generally or otherwise) may be given either unconditionally or subject to such conditions as the Secretary of State may consider appropriate.

(7) Notwithstanding anything in section 27(1) of the Town and Country Planning (Scotland) Act 1959 (power of local and other public authority to dispose of land without consent of a Minister), a local authority shall not, in the exercise of their powers under subsection (1)(c) or (d), sell or lease any land, house or part share thereof to which the housing revenue account kept under section 203 relates except with the consent of the Secretary of State unless in the case of a house, it is one to which section 14 applies; and, in giving his consent to such transactions as are referred to in this subsection, the Secretary of State may make general directions or a direction related to a specific transaction.

(8) Subsection (7) shall not apply in the case of a house where—
(a) the house is being sold to a tenant or to a member of his family who normally resides with him (or to a tenant together with members of his family, as joint purchasers); or
(b) the requirements of section 14(2)(b) are satisfied.

(9) Subject to the provisions of the Town and Country Planning (Scotland) Act 1959, section 74 of the Local Government (Scotland) Act 1973 (which makes provision as to price and other matters relating to the disposal of land by local authorities) shall subject to subsection (10), apply to any disposal of land by a local authority in the exercise of their powers under subsection (4), as it applies to the like disposal of land by a local authority within the meaning of the said Act of 1973 in the exercise of any power under Part VI of that Act.

(10) The said section 74 shall not apply to the disposal of a house by a local authority, being a disposal in relation to which subsection (7) has effect.

(11) For the purposes of this section land shall be taken to have been acquired by a local authority in the exercise (directly or indirectly) of compulsory powers if it was acquired by them compulsorily or was acquired by them by agreement at a time when they were authorised by or under any enactment to acquire the land compulsorily; but the land shall not be taken to have been so acquired, if the local authority acquired it (whether compulsorily or by agreement) in consequence of the service in pursuance of any enactment (including any enactment contained in this Act) of a notice requiring the authority to purchase the land. [579]

NOTES to section 12

Amendments: Sub-s (1)(c) was amended with effect from 2 January 1989 by the Housing Act 1988 (c 50), s 140, Sch 17, para 77; sub-ss (7) and (8) were amended with effect from 2 January 1989 by the Housing Act 1988 (c 50), s 140, Sch 17, para 77.
Definitions: 'local authority', 'land', 'road', 'open space', 'sell', and 'house': see s 338 below.

[12A. Consent of Secretary of State required for certain subsequent disposals.

(1) Where a person acquires any land or house from a local authority under section 12(1)(c) or (d) above and the consent of the Secretary of State is required under section 12(7) above to the local authority's disposal of the land or house to that person, that person shall not dispose of the land or house without the consent in writing of the Secretary of State.

(2) Any consent for the purposes of subsection (1) above may be given either in respect of a particular disposal or in respect of disposals of any class or description (including disposals in particular areas) and either unconditionally or subject to conditions.

(3) Before giving any consent for the purposes of subsection (1) above, the Secretary of State—
(a) shall satisfy himself that the person who is seeking the consent has taken appropriate steps to consult every tenant of any land or house proposed to be disposed of; and
(b) shall have regard to the responses of any such tenants to that consultation.

(4) The consent of Scottish Homes under section 9 of the Housing Associations Act 1985 (control of dispositions) is not required for any disposal, or disposals of any class or description, in respect of which consent is given under subsection (1) above.

(5) In this section references to disposing of property include references to—
(a) granting or disposing of any interest in property;
(b) entering into a contract to dispose of property or to grant or dispose of any such interest; and
(c) granting an option to acquire property or any such interest.] [580]

NOTE to section 12A

Amendment: Section 12A was added with effect from 15 November 1988 by the Housing Act 1988 (c 50), s 134.

13. Power of Secretary of State in certain cases to impose conditions on sale of local authority's houses, etc.

(1) If any house, building, [or land] in respect of which a local authority are required by section 203 to keep a housing revenue account is sold by the authority with the consent of the Secretary of State, the Secretary of State may in giving consent impose such conditions as he thinks just.

[(2) The matters to which the Secretary of State may have regard in determining whether to give consent and, if so, to what conditions consent should be subject shall include—
(a) the extent (if any) to which the person to whom the proposed disposal is to be made (in this subsection referred to as 'the intending purchaser') is, or is likely to be, dependent upon, controlled by or subject to influence from the local authority making the disposal or any members or officers of that authority;

(b) the extent (if any) to which the proposed disposal would result in the intending purchaser becoming the predominant or a substantial owner in any area of housing accommodation let on tenancies or subject to licences;
(c) the terms of the proposed disposal; and
(d) any other matters whatsoever which he considers relevant.

(3) Where the Secretary of State gives consent to a disposal by a local authority, he may give directions as to the purpose for which any capital money received by the authority in respect of the disposal is to be applied and, where any such directions are given, nothing in any enactment shall require his consent to be given for the application of the capital money concerned in accordance with the directions.] [581]

NOTES to section 13
Amendments: Sub-s (1) was renumbered as such by the Housing Act 1988 (c 50), s 132, and amended by the Housing Act 1988 (c 50), s 140, Sch 17, para 78; sub-ss (2) and (3) were added by the Housing Act 1988 (c 50), s 132. The amendments are retrospective and take effect from 9 June 1988.
Definitions: 'house', 'land', 'local authority': see s 338 below.

14. Powers of local authorities to sell certain houses without consent of the Secretary of State.

(1) Subject to section 74(2) of the Local Government (Scotland) Act 1973 (restriction on disposal of land) but notwithstanding anything contained in section 12(6) or in any other enactment, a local authority may sell any house to which this section applies without the consent of the Secretary of State.

(2) This section applies to a house provided for the purposes of this Part, where—
(a) the house is being sold to a tenant or to members of his family who normally reside with him (or to a tenant together with such members of his family, as joint purchasers) [or, in pursuance of Part III of the Housing (Scotland) Act 1988 (change of landlord)]; or
(b) the house is unoccupied and—
   (i) it is not held on the housing revenue account maintained in terms of section 203; or
   (ii) it is held on the housing revenue account and it is, in the opinion of the local authority, either surplus to its requirements or difficult to let, because it has been continuously vacant for a period of not less than three months immediately prior to the date of sale and during that period it has been on unrestricted offer to any applicant on the local authority's housing list (within the meaning of section 19 (admission to housing list)). [582]

NOTES to section 14
Amendment: Sub-s (2)(a) was amended by the Housing (Scotland) Act 1988 (c 43), s 56(11).
Definitions: 'land', 'local authority', 'house': see s 338 below; 'tenant': see s 82 below; 'family': see s 338 and s 83 below; 'landlord': see s 82 below.

15. Power of local authority to enforce obligations against owner for time being of land.

(1) Where—
(a) a local authority have sold or excambed land acquired by them under this Act, and the purchaser of the land or the person taking the land in exchange has entered into an agreement with the authority concerning the land; or
(b) an owner of any land has entered into an agreement with the local authority concerning the land for the purposes of any of the provisions of this Act;
then, if the agreement has been recorded in the General Register of Sasines, or, as the case may be, registered in the Land Register for Scotland, it shall, subject to subsection (2), be enforceable at the instance of the local authority against persons deriving title from the person who entered into the agreement.

(2) No such agreement shall at any time be enforceable against any party who has in good faith onerously acquired right (whether completed by infeftment or not) to the land prior to the recording of the agreement or against any person deriving title from such party. **[583]**

NOTES to section 15
Definitions: 'local authority', 'land': see s 338 below.

16. Disposal of land for erection of churches, etc.

Where a local authority, in the exercise of any power conferred on them by this Act, dispose of land to any person for the erection of a church or other building for religious worship or buildings ancillary thereto, then, unless the parties otherwise agree, such disposal shall be by way of feu. **[584]**

NOTES to section 16
Definitions: 'local authority', 'land': see s 338 below.

Management and allocation of local authority's houses

17. General management and inspection of local authority's houses.

(1) The general management, regulation and control of houses held for housing purposes by a local authority shall be vested in and exercised by the authority.

(2) A house held for housing purposes by a local authority shall be at all times open to inspection by the local authority for the area in which it is situated or by any officer duly authorised by them. **[585]**

NOTES to section 17
Definitions: 'house', 'local authority': see s 338 below.

18. Byelaws for regulation of local authority's houses.

A local authority may make byelaws for the management, use and regulation of houses held by them for housing purposes. **[586]**

NOTES to section 18
Definitions: 'local authority', 'house': see s 338 below.

19. Admission to housing list.

(1) In considering whether an applicant for local authority housing is entitled to be admitted to a housing list, a local authority shall take no account of—
 (a) the age of the applicant provided that he has attained the age of 16 years; or
 (b) the income of the applicant and his family; or
 (c) whether, or to what value, the applicant or any of his family owns or has owned (or any of them own or have owned) heritable or moveable property; or
 (d) any outstanding liability (for payment of rent or otherwise) attributable to the tenancy of any house of which the applicant is not, and was not when the liability accrued, a tenant; or
 (e) whether the applicant is living with, or in the same house as—
  (i) his spouse; or
  (ii) a person with whom he has been living as husband and wife.

(2) Where an applicant—
 (a) is employed in the area of the local authority; or
 (b) has been offered employment in the area of the local authority; or
 (c) wishes to move into the area of the local authority and the local authority is satisfied that his purpose in doing so is to seek employment; or

(d) has attained the age of 60 years and wishes to move into the area of the local authority to be near a younger relative; or
(e) has special social or medical reasons for requiring to be housed within the area of the local authority,

admission to a housing list shall not depend on the applicant being resident in the area.

(3) Where a local authority has rules which give priority to applicants on its housing list it shall apply those rules to an applicant to whom subsection (2) above applies no less favourably than it applies them to a tenant of the local authority whose housing needs are similar to those of the applicant and who is seeking a transfer to another house belonging to the local authority.

(4) In this section and in section 21 of this Act, 'housing list' means a list of applicants for local authority housing which is kept by a local authority in connection with the allocation of housing. **[587]**

NOTES to section 19
Definitions: 'local authority', 'family': see s 338 below; 'tenant', 'tenancy': see s 82 below.

20. Persons to have priority on housing list and allocation of housing.

(1) A local authority shall, in relation to all houses held by them for housing purposes, secure that in the selection of their tenants a reasonable preference is given—
 (a) to persons who—
  (i) are occupying houses which do not meet the tolerable standard; or
  (ii) are occupying overcrowded houses; or
  (iii) have large families; or
  (iv) are living under unsatisfactory housing conditions; and
 (b) to persons to whom they have a duty under sections 31 to 34 (homeless persons).

(2) In the allocation of local authority housing a local authority—
 (a) shall take no account of—
  (i) the length of time for which an applicant has resided in its area; or
  (ii) any outstanding liability (for payment of rent or otherwise) attributable to the tenancy of any house of which the applicant is not, and was not when the liability accrued, a tenant; or
  (iii) any of the matters mentioned in paragraphs (a) to (c) of section 19(1); and
 (b) shall not impose a requirement—
  (i) that an application must have remained in force for a minimum period; or
  (ii) that a divorce or judicial separation be obtained; or
  (iii) that the applicant no longer be living with, or in the same house as, some other person,
 before the applicant is eligible for the allocation of housing. **[588]**

NOTES to section 20
Definitions: 'local authority': see s 338 below; 'tenant': see s 82 below; 'tolerable standard': see s 338, and s 86 below; 'overcrowded': see Part VII, ss 135–151 below.

21. Publication of rules relating to the housing list and to transfer of tenants.

(1) It shall be the duty of every local authority, [Scottish Homes] and development corporations (including urban development corporations) to publish in accordance with subsection (2), and within 6 months of any alteration of the rules, any rules which it may have governing—
 (a) admission of applicants to any housing list;
 (b) priority of allocation of houses;
 (c) transfer of tenants from houses owned by it to houses owned by other bodies;
 (d) exchanges of houses.

(2) It shall be the duty of every registered housing association—

(a) within the period of 6 months commencing on 7th January 1987 to make rules governing the matters mentioned in paragraphs (a) to (d) of subsection (1) (unless it has, in accordance with subsections (4) to (5), published such rules before that date and those rules remain current);
(b) within 6 months of the making of any rules under paragraph (a), and within 6 months of any alteration of such rules (whether or not made under that paragraph)—
  (i) to send a copy of them to each of the bodies mentioned in subsection (3); and
  (ii) to publish them in accordance with subsections (4) and (5).

(3) The bodies referred to in subsection (2)(b)(i) are—
  (i) the Housing Corporation [(in a case where the housing association is registered in the register maintained by it);
  (ia) Scottish Homes (in a case where the housing association is registered in the register maintained by it);] and
  (ii) every local authority within whose area there is a house let, or to be let, by the association under a secure tenancy.

(4) The rules to be published by a body in accordance with subsection (1) or (2) shall be—
  (a) available for perusal; and
  (b) on sale at a reasonable price;
  (c) available in summary form on request to members of the public,
at all reasonable times—
  (i) in a case where the body is a local authority or a development corporation, at its principal offices and its housing department offices; and
  (ii) in any other case, at its principal and other offices.

(5) Rules sent to a local authority in accordance with subsection 2(b) shall be available for perusal at all reasonable times at its principal offices.

(6) An applicant for housing provided by a body mentioned in subsection (1) or (2) shall be entitled on request to inspect any record kept by that body of information furnished by him to it in connection with his application. **[589]**

NOTES to section 21

Amendment: Sub-s (3) was amended by the Housing (Scotland) Act 1988 (c 43), s 3, Sch 2, para 7.
Definitions: 'local authority', 'development corporation', 'house': see s 338 below.

Housing co-operatives

22. Agreements for exercise by housing co-operatives of local authority housing functions.

(1) A local authority may make an agreement with a society, company or body of trustees for the time being approved by the Secretary of State for the purposes of this section (in this section called a 'housing co-operative')—
  (a) for the exercise by the co-operative, on such terms as may be provided in the agreement, of any of the local authority's powers relating to land or any interest in land held by them for the purposes of this Part, and the performance by the co-operative of any of the local authority's duties relating to such land or interest; or
  (b) for the exercise by the co-operative, in connection with any such land or interest, of any of the local authority's powers under section 4 or 5 (powers to provide furniture, board and laundry facilities).

(2) An agreement to which this section applies may only be made with the approval of the Secretary of State.

(3) The Secretary of State's approval to the making of such an agreement may be given

either generally or to any local authority or description of local authority or in any particular case, and may be given unconditionally or subject to any conditions.

[(4) Without prejudice to any power to let land conferred on a local authority by any enactment, the terms of an agreement to which this section applies may include terms providing for the letting of land to the housing co-operative by the local authority for a period not exceeding 20 years.]

(5) Houses on land included in an agreement to which this section applies shall continue to be included in the local authority's housing revenue account; and neither the fact that the authority have made the agreement nor any letting of land in pursuance of it shall be treated as a ground for the reduction, suspension or discontinuance of any Exchequer contribution or subsidy under section 202.

NOTES to section 22
Amendment: Sub-s (4) was substituted by the Housing (Scotland) Act 1988 (c 43), s 72, Sch 7, para 1.
Definitions: 'local authority', 'land', 'house': see s 338 below.

[23. Improvement of amenities of residential area by development corporations.

A development corporation may for the purpose of securing the improvement of the amenities of a predominantly residential area within its designated area—
(a) carry out any works on land owned by it;
(b) with the agreement of the owner of any land, carry out or arrange for the carrying out of works on that land at his or its expense or in part at the expense of both;
(c) assist (whether by grants or loans or otherwise) in the carrying out of works on land not owned by it;
(d) acquire any land by agreement.]

NOTES to section 23
Amendment: Section 23 was substituted by the Housing (Scotland) Act 1988 (c 43), s 3, Sch 2, para 8.
Definitions: 'development corporation', 'land': see s 338 below.

PART II
HOMELESS PERSONS

Main definitions

24. Homeless persons and persons threatened with homelessness.

(1) A person is homeless if he has no accommodation in Scotland, or England or Wales.

(2) A person is to be treated as having no accommodation if there is no accommodation which he, together with any other person who normally resides with him as a member of his family or in circumstances in which the housing authority consider it reasonable for that person to reside with him—
(a) is entitled to occupy by virtue of an interest in it or by virtue of an order of court, or
(b) has a right or permission, or an implied right or permission to occupy, or in England and Wales, an express or implied licence to occupy, or
(c) occupies as a residence by virtue or any enactment or rule of law giving him the right to remain in occupation or restricting the right of any other person to recover possession.

[(2A) A person shall not be treated as having accommodation unless it is accommodation which it would be reasonable for him to continue to occupy.

(2B) Regard may be had in determining whether it would be reasonable for a person to continue to occupy accommodation, to the general circumstances prevailing in relation to housing in the area of the local authority to whom he has applied for accommodation or for assistance in obtaining accommodation.]

(3) A person is also homeless for the purposes of this Act if he has accommodation but—
- (a) he cannot secure entry to it, or
- (b) it is probable that occupation of it will lead to violence from some other person residing in it or to threats of violence from some other person residing in it and likely to carry out the threats, or
- [(bb) it is probable that occupation of it will lead to—
  - (i) violence; or
  - (ii) threats of violence which are likely to be carried out,

  from some other person who previously resided with that person, whether in that accommodation or elsewhere, or]
- (c) it consists of a moveable structure, vehicle or vessel designed or adapted for human habitation and there is no place where he is entitled or permitted both to place it and to reside in it; or
- (d) it is overcrowded within the meaning of section 135 and may endanger the health of the occupants.

(4) A person is threatened with homelessness if it is likely that he will become homeless within 28 days.' [592]

NOTES to section 24

Amendments: Sub-s (2A) and (2B) were added by the Law Reform (Miscellaneous Provisions) (Scotland) Act 1990 (c 40), s 65; para (bb) added to sub-s (3) by the Law Reform (Miscellaneous Provisions) (Scotland) Act 1990 (c 40), s 65.

Definitions: 'accommodation available for occupation': see ss 43 and 41 below; 'family': see ss 338 and 83 below; 'local authority': see s 338 below.

25. Priority need for accommodation.

(1) The following have a priority need for accommodation—
- (a) a pregnant woman or a person with whom a pregnant woman resides or might reasonably be expected to reside;
- (b) a person with whom dependent children reside or might reasonably be expected to reside;
- (c) a person who is vulnerable as a result of old age, mental illness or handicap or physical disability or other special reason, or with whom such a person resides or might reasonably be expected to reside;
- (d) a person who is homeless or threatened with homelessness as a result of an emergency such as flood, fire or any other disaster.

(2) The Secretary of State may by order made by statutory instrument—
- (a) specify further descriptions of persons as having a priority need for accommodation, and
- (b) amend or repeal any part of subsection (1).

(3) Before making such an order the Secretary of State shall consult such associations representing relevant authorities, and such other persons, as he considers appropriate.

(4) No such order shall be made unless a draft of the order has been laid before and approved by resolution of each House of Parliament. [593]

NOTES to section 25

Definitions: 'homeless': see s 43 below and s 24 above; 'threatened with homelessness': see s 43 below and s 24 above; 'relevant authority': see s 43 below.
Sub-s (2): The power to make an order has not been exercised.

26. Becoming homeless intentionally.

(1) A person becomes homeless intentionally if he deliberately does or fails to do anything in consequence of which he ceases to occupy accommodation which is available for his occupation and which it would have been reasonable for him to continue to occupy.

(2) A person becomes threatened with homelessness intentionally if he deliberately does or fails to do anything the likely result of which is that he will be forced to leave accommodation which is available for his occupation and which it would have been reasonable for him to continue to occupy.

(3) For the purposes of subsection (1) or (2) an act or omission in good faith on the part of a person who was unaware of any relevant fact shall not be treated as deliberate.

(4) Regard may be had, in determining for the purpose of subsections (1) and (2) whether it would have been reasonable for a person to continue to occupy accommodation, to the general circumstances prevailing in relation to housing in the district of the local authority to whom he applied for accommodation or for assistance in obtaining accommodation. **[594]**

NOTES to section 26

Definitions: 'homeless': see s 43 below and s 24 above; 'threatened with homelessness': see s 43 below and s 24 above; 'accommodation available for occupation': see ss 43 and 41 below; 'local authority': see s 338 below.

27. Meaning of 'local connection'.

(1) Any reference in this Part to a person having a local connection with a district is a reference to his having a connection with that district—
 (a) because he is, or in the past was, normally resident in it and his residence in it is or was of his own choice; or
 (b) because he is employed in it, or
 (c) because of family associations, or
 (d) because of any special circumstances.

(2) Residence in a district is not of a person's own choice for the purposes of subsection (1) if he became resident in it—
 (a) because he or any person who might reasonably be expected to reside with him—
  (i) was serving in the regular armed forces of the Crown, or
  (ii) was detained under the authority of any Act of Parliament, or
 (b) in such other circumstances as the Secretary of State may by order specify.

(3) A person is not employed in a district for the purposes of subsection (1)—
 (a) if he is serving in the regular armed forces of the Crown, or
 (b) in such other circumstances as the Secretary of State may by order specify.

(4) An order under subsections (2) or (3) shall be made by statutory instrument which shall be subject to annulment in pursuance of a resolution of either House of Parliament. **[595]**

NOTES to section 27

Definition: 'family': see ss 338 and s 83 below.
Sub-ss (2), (3): The powers to make orders have not been exercised.

Duties of local authorities with respect to homelessness and threatened homelessness

28. Inquiry into cases of possible homelessness or threatened homelessness.

(1) If a person ('an applicant') applies to a local authority for accommodation, or for assistance in obtaining accommodation, and the authority have reason to believe that he may be homeless or threatened with homelessness, they shall make such inquiries as are

necessary to satisfy themselves as to whether he is homeless or threatened with homelessness.

(2) If the authority are so satisfied, they shall make any further inquiries necessary to satisfy themselves as to—
  (a) whether he has a priority need, and
  (b) whether he became homeless or threatened with homelessness intentionally;
and if the authority think fit, they may also make inquiries as to whether he has a local connection with the district of another local authority in Scotland, England or Wales. [596]

NOTES to section 28

Definitions: 'local authority': see s 338 below; 'homeless': see s 43 below and s 24 above; 'threatened with homelessness': see s 43 below and s 24 above; 'priority need': see s 43 below and s 25 above; 'local connection': see s 43 below and s 27 above.

29. Interim duty to accommodate in case of apparent priority need.

(1) If the local authority have reason to believe that an applicant may be homeless and have a priority need, they shall secure that accommodation is made available for his occupation pending any decision which they may make as a result of their inquiries under section 28.

(2) This duty arises irrespective of any local connection which an applicant may have with the district of another local authority. [597]

NOTES to section 29

Definitions: 'local authority': see s 338 below; 'applicant': see s 43 below and s 28 above; 'homeless': see s 43 below and s 24 above; 'securing accommodation for a person's occupation': see ss 43 and 41 below; 'local connection': see s 43 below and s 27 above.

30. Notification of decision and reasons.

(1) On completing their inquiries under section 28, the local authority shall notify the applicant of their decision on the question whether he is homeless or threatened with homelessness.

(2) If they notify him that their decision is that he is homeless or threatened with homelessness, they shall at the same time notify him of their decision on the question whether he has a priority need.

(3) If they notify him that their decision is that he has a priority need, they shall at the same time notify him—
  (a) of their decision on the question whether he became homeless or threatened with homelessness intentionally, and
  (b) whether they have notified or propose to notify any other local authority under section 33 that his application has been made.

(4) If they notify him—
  (a) that they are not satisfied—
    (i) that he is homeless or threatened with homelessness, or
    (ii) that he has a priority need, or
  (b) that they are satisfied that he became homeless or threatened with homelessness intentionally, or
  (c) that they have notified or propose to notify another local authority under section 33 that his application has been made,
they shall at the same time notify him of their reasons.

(5) The notice required to be given to a person under this section shall be given in writing and shall, if not received by him, be treated as having been given to him only if it is made available at the authority's office for a reasonable period for collection by him or on his behalf. [598]

NOTES to section 30

Definitions: 'local authority': see s 338 below; 'applicant': see s 43 below and s 28 above; 'threatened with homelessness': see s 43 below and s 24 above; 'priority need': see s 43 below and s 25 above.

31. Duties to persons found to be homeless.

(1) This section applies where a local authority are satisfied that an applicant is homeless.

(2) Where they are satisfied that he has a priority need and are not satisfied that he became homeless intentionally, they shall, unless they notify another local authority in accordance with section 33 (referral of application on ground of local connection) secure that accommodation becomes available for his occupation.

(3) Where they are satisfied that he has a priority need but are also satisfied that he became homeless intentionally, they shall—
   (a) secure that accommodation is made available for his occupation for such period as they consider will give him a reasonable opportunity of himself securing accommodation for his occupation; and
   (b) furnish him with advice and such assistance as they consider appropriate in the circumstances, in any attempts he may make to secure that accommodation becomes available for his occupation.

(4) Where they are not satisfied that he has a priority need they shall furnish him with advice and such assistance as they consider appropriate in the circumstances, in any attempts he may make to secure that accommodation becomes available for his occupation. **[599]**

NOTES to section 31

Definitions: 'local authority': see s 338 below; 'homeless': see s 43 below and s 24 above; 'priority need': see s 43 below and s 25 above; 'local connection': see s 43 below and s 27 above; 'accommodation available for occupation': see ss 43 and 41 below.

32. Duties to persons found to be threatened with homelessness.

(1) This section applies where a local authority are satisfied that an applicant is threatened with homelessness.

(2) Where they are satisfied that he has a priority need and are not satisfied that he became threatened with homelessness intentionally they shall take reasonable steps to secure that accommodation does not cease to be available for his occupation.

(3) Where—
   (a) they are not satisfied that he has a priority need, or
   (b) they are satisfied that he has a priority need, but are also satisfied that he became threatened with homelessness intentionally,
they shall furnish him with advice and such assistance as they consider appropriate in the circumstances, in any attempts he may make to secure that accommodation does not cease to be available for his occupation.

(4) Nothing in subsection (2) shall affect any right of a local authority to secure vacant possession of accommodation, whether by virtue of a contract or of any enactment or rule of law.

(5) In section 31 and in this section, 'accommodation' does not include accommodation that is overcrowded within the meaning of section 135 or which may endanger the health of the occupants. **[600]**

NOTES to section 32

Definitions: 'local authority': see s 338 below; 'threatened with homelessness': see s 43 below and s 24 above; 'priority need': see s 43 below and s 25 above; 'accommodation available for occupation': see ss 43 and 41 below.

33. Referral of application to another local authority.

(1) If a local authority—
(a) are satisfied that an applicant is homeless and has a priority need, and are not satisfied that he became homeless intentionally, but
(b) are of opinion that the conditions are satisfied for referral of his application to another local authority,
they may notify that other local authority in Scotland, England or Wales of the fact that his application has been made and that they are of that opinion.

(2) The conditions of referral of an application to another local authority are—
(a) that neither the applicant nor any person who might reasonably be expected to reside with him has a local connection with the district of the authority to whom his application was made,
(b) that the applicant or a person who might reasonably be expected to reside with him has a local connection with that other local authority's district, and
(c) that neither that applicant nor any person who might reasonably be expected to reside with him will run the risk of domestic violence in that other local authority's district.

(3) For the purposes of this section a person runs the risk of domestic violence—
(a) if he runs the risk of violence from a person with whom, but for the risk of violence, he might reasonably be expected to reside, or from a person with whom he formerly resided, or
(b) if he runs the risk of threats of violence from such a person which are likely to be carried out.

(4) The question whether the conditions for referral of an application are satisfied shall be determined by agreement between the notifying authority and the notified authority, or in default of agreement, in accordance with such arrangements as the Secretary of State may direct by order made by statutory instrument.

(5) An order may direct that the arrangements shall be—
(a) those agreed by any relevant authorities or association of relevant authorities, or
(b) in default of such agreement, such arrangements as appear to the Secretary of State to be suitable, after consultation with such associations representing relevant authorities, and such other persons, as he thinks appropriate.

(6) No order shall be made unless a draft of the order has been laid before and approved by resolution of each House of Parliament. [601]

NOTES to section 33

Definitions: 'local authority': see s 338 below; 'applicant': see s 43 below and s 28 above; 'homeless': see s 43 below and s 24 above; 'local connection': see s 43 below and s 27 above.
Sub-s 4: See the Housing (Homeless Persons) (Appropriate Arrangements) (No 2) Order 1978, SI 1978/661, paras [1247] ff below.

34. Duties to persons whose applications are referred.

(1) Where, in accordance with section 33(1), a local authority notify another authority of an application, the notifying authority shall secure that accommodation is available for occupation by the applicant until it is determined whether the conditions for referral of his application to the other authority are satisfied.

(2) If it is determined that the conditions for referral are satisfied, the notified authority shall secure that accommodation becomes available for occupation by the applicant; if it is determined that the conditions are not satisfied, the notifying authority shall secure that accommodation becomes available for occupation by him.

(3) When the matter has been determined, the notifying authority shall notify the applicant—
(a) whether they or the notified authority and the authority whose duty it is to secure that accommodation becomes available for his occupation, and
(b) of the reasons why the authority subject to that duty are subject to it.

(4) The notice required to be given to a person under subsection (3) shall be given in writing and shall, if not received by him, be treated as having been given to him only if it is made available at the authority's office for a reasonable period for collection by him or on his behalf. **[602]**

NOTES to section 34

Definitions: 'local authority': see s 338 below; 'securing accommodation for a person's occupation': see ss 43 and 41 below; 'accommodation available for occupation': see ss 43 and 41 below.

35. Supplementary provisions.

(1) A local authority may perform any duty under section 31 or 34 (duties to persons found to be homeless to secure that accommodation becomes available for the occupation of a person)—
(a) by making available accommodation held by them under Part I (provision of housing) or under any other enactment,
(b) by securing that he obtains accommodation from some other person, or
(c) by giving him such advice and assistance as will secure that he obtains accommodation from some other person.

(2) Without prejudice to section 210(1), a local authority may require a person to whom they were subject to a duty under section 29, 31 or 34 (interim duty to accommodate pending inquiries and duties to persons found to be homeless)—
(a) to pay such reasonable charges as they may determine in respect of accommodation which they secure for his occupation (either by making it available themselves or otherwise), or
(b) to pay such reasonable amount as they may determine in respect of sums payable by them for accommodation made available by another person. **[603]**

NOTES to section 35

Definitions: 'local authority': see s 338 below; 'homeless': see s 43 below and s 24 above; 'securing accommodation for a person's occupation': see ss 43 and 41 below; 'accommodation available for occupation': see ss 43 and 41 below.

36. Protection of property of homeless persons and persons threatened with homelessness.

(1) This section applies where a local authority have reason to believe that an applicant is homeless or threatened with homelessness (or, in the case of an applicant to whom they owe a duty under section 29 (interim duty to accommodate pending inquiries), that he may be homeless) and that—
(a) there is a danger of loss of, or damage to, any moveable property of his by reason of his inability to protect it or deal with it, and
(b) no other suitable arrangements have been or are being made.

(2) If the authority have become subject to a duty towards the applicant under section 29, 31(2) or (3)(a), 32(2) or 34 (duty to accommodate during inquiries and duties to persons found to be homeless or threatened with homelessness), then, whether or not they are still subject to such a duty, they shall take reasonable steps to prevent the loss of the moveable property or prevent or mitigate damage to it; and if they have not become subject to such a duty, they may take any steps they consider reasonable for that purpose.

(3) The authority may for the purposes of this section—
(a) enter, at all reasonable times, any premises which are the usual place of residence of the applicant or which were his last usual place of residence, and

(b) deal with any moveable property of his in any way which is reasonably necessary, in particular by storing it or arranging for its storage.

(4) The authority may decline to take action under this section except upon such conditions as they consider appropriate in the particular case, which may include conditions as to—
(a) the making and recovery by the authority of reasonable charges for the action taken, or
(b) the disposal by the authority, in such circumstances as may be specified, of moveable property in relation to which they have taken action.

(5) When in the authority's opinion there is no longer any reason to believe that there is a danger of loss of or damage to a person's moveable property by reason of his inability to protect it or deal with it, the authority shall cease to have any duty or power to take action under this section; but property stored by virtue of their having taken such action may be kept in store and any conditions upon which it was taken into store shall continue to have effect, with any necessary modifications.

(6) Where the authority—
(a) cease to be subject to a duty to take action under this section in respect of an applicant's moveable property, or
(b) cease to have power to take such action, having previously taken such action,
they shall notify the applicant of that fact and of the reason why they are of opinion that there is no longer any reason to believe that there is a danger of loss of or damage to his moveable property by reason of his inability to protect it or deal with it.

(7) The notification shall be given to the applicant—
(a) by delivering it to him, or
(b) by leaving it, or sending it to him, at his last known address.

(8) References in this section to moveable property of the applicant include moveable property of any person who might reasonably be expected to reside with him. [604]

NOTES to section 36

Definitions: 'local authority': see s 338 below; 'applicant': see s 43 below and s 28 above; 'homeless': see s 43 below and s 24 above; 'threatened with homelessness': see s 43 below and s 24 above.

Administrative provisions

37. Guidance to authorities by the Secretary of State.

(1) In relation to homeless persons and persons threatened with homelessness, a relevant authority shall have regard in the exercise of their functions to such guidance as may from time to time be given by the Secretary of State.

(2) The Secretary of State may give guidance either generally or to specified descriptions of authorities. [605]

NOTES to section 37

Definitions: 'homeless': see s 43 below and s 24 above; 'threatened with homelessness': see s 43 below and s 24 above; 'relevant authority': see s 43 below.
Sub-s (2): See the Housing (Homeless Persons) Act 1977 Code of Guidance—Scotland (Scottish Office: 1991).

38. Co-operation between authorities.

Where a local authority—
(a) request another local authority in Scotland or England or Wales, a development corporation, a registered housing association or [Scottish Homes] to assist them in the discharge of their functions under sections 28, 29, 31 to 33 and 34(1) and (2)

(which relate to the duties of local authorities with respect to homelessness and threatened homelessness as such),
- (b) request a social work authority in Scotland or a social services authority in England or Wales to exercise any of their functions in relation to a case which the local authority are dealing with under those provisions, or
- (c) request another local authority in Scotland or England or Wales to assist them in the discharge of their functions under section 36 (protection of property of homeless persons and persons threatened with homelessness),

the authority to whom the request is made shall co-operate in rendering such assistance in the discharge of the functions to which the request relates as is reasonable in the circumstances. **[606]**

NOTES to section 38

Definitions: 'local authority', 'development corporation': see s 338 below; 'homeless': see s 43 below and s 24 above; 'threatened with homelessness': see s 43 below and s 24 above.

Assistance for voluntary organisations

39. Financial and other assistance for voluntary organisations concerned with homelessness.

(1) The Secretary of State, with the consent of the Treasury, may, upon such terms and subject to such conditions as he may determine, give to a voluntary organisation concerned with homelessness, or with matters relating to homelessness, assistance by way of grant or loan or partly in the one way and partly in the other.

(2) A local authority may, upon such terms and subject to such conditions as they may determine, give to such a voluntary organisation such assistance as is mentioned in subsection (1), and may also assist such an organisation by—
- (a) permitting them to use premises belonging to the authority upon such terms and subject to such conditions as may be agreed,
- (b) making available furniture or other goods, whether by way of gift, loan or otherwise, and
- (c) making available the services of staff employed by the authority.

(3) No assistance shall be given under subsection (1) or (2) unless the voluntary organisation first give an undertaking—
- (a) that they will use the money, furniture or other goods or premises made available to them for a specified purpose, and
- (b) that they will, if the person giving the assistance serves notice on them requiring them to do so, furnish, within the period of 21 days beginning with the date on which the notice is served, a certificate giving such information as may reasonably be required by the notice with respect to the manner in which the assistance given to them is being used.

(4) The conditions subject to which assistance is given under this section shall in all cases include, in addition to any conditions determined or agreed under subsection (1) or (2), conditions requiring the voluntary organisation to—
- (a) keep proper books of account and have them audited in such manner as may be specified,
- (b) keep records indicating how they have used the money, furniture or other goods or premises made available to them, and
- (c) submit the books of account and records for inspection by the person giving the assistance.

(5) If it appears to the person giving the assistance that the voluntary organisation have failed to carry out their undertaking as to the purpose for which the assistance was to be used, he shall take all reasonable steps to recover from the organisation an amount equal to the amount of the assistance; but no sum is so recoverable unless he has first served on

the voluntary organisation a notice specifying the amount which in his opinion is recoverable and the basis on which that amount has been calculated. **[607]**

NOTES to section 39
Definitions: 'local authority': see s 338 below; 'voluntary organisation': see s 43 below.

Supplementary provisions

40. False statements, withholding information and failure to disclose change of circumstances.

(1) If a person, with intent to induce a local authority to believe, in connection with the exercise of their functions under this Part, that he or another person—
   (a)   is homeless or threatened with homelessness, or
   (b)   has a priority need, or
   (c)   did not become homeless or threatened with homelessness intentionally,
knowingly or recklessly makes a statement which is false in a material particular, or knowingly withholds information which the authority have reasonably required him to give in connection with the exercise of those functions, he shall be guilty of an offence.

(2) If before an applicant receives notification of the local authority's decision on his application there is any change of facts material to his case, he shall notify the authority as soon as possible; and the authority shall explain to every applicant, in ordinary language, the duty imposed on him by this subsection and the effect of subsection (3).

(3) A person who fails to comply with subsection (2) commits an offence unless he shows that he was not given the explanation required by that subsection or that he had some other reasonable excuse for non-compliance.

(4) A person guilty of an offence under this section shall be liable on summary conviction to a fine not exceeding level 5 on the standard scale. **[608]**

NOTES to section 40
Definitions: 'local authority': see s 338 below; 'homeless': see s 43 below and s 24 above; 'threatened with homelessness': see s 43 below and s 24 above; 'priority need': see s 43 below and s 25 above; 'the standard scale': see the Criminal Procedure (Scotland) Act 1975, s 289G and the Increase of Criminal Penalties Etc (Scotland) Order, SI 1984/526; level 5 is currently £2000.

41. Meaning of accommodation available for occupation.

For the purposes of this Part accommodation shall be regarded as available for a person's occupation only if it is available for occupation both by him and by any other person who might reasonably be expected to reside with him; and references to securing accommodation for a person's occupation shall be construed accordingly. **[609]**

42. Application of this Part to cases arising in England or Wales.

(1) Sections 33 and 34 (referral of application to another local authority and duties to persons whose applications are referred) apply—
   (a)   to applications referred by a local authority in England or Wales in pursuance of section 67(1) of the Housing Act 1985, and
   (b)   to persons whose applications are so transferred,
as they apply to cases arising under this Part.

(2) Section 38 (duty of other authorities to co-operate with local authority) applies to a request by a local authority in England or Wales under section 72 of the Housing Act 1985 as it applies to a request by a local authority in Scotland.

(3) In this Part, in relation to Engand and Wales—
   (a)   'local authority' means a local housing authority within the meaning of section 1(1) of the said Act of 1985 and references to the district of such an authority are to the area of the council concerned,

(b) 'social work authority' means a social services authority for the purposes of the Local Authority Social Services Act 1970, as defined in section 1 of that Act;

and in section 38(a) (requests for co-operation) 'development corporation' means a development corporation established by an order made or having effect as if made under the New Towns Act 1981 or the Commission for the New Towns.

NOTE to section 42

Definition: 'local authority': see s 338 below.

43. Minor definitions.

In this Part—

'accommodation available for occupation' has the meaning assigned to it by section 41;

'applicant (for housing accommodation)' has the meaning assigned to it by section 28(1);

'homeless' has the meaning assigned to it by section 24(1) to (3);

'homeless intentionally or threatened with homelessness intentionally' has the meaning assigned to it by section 26;

'local connection (in relation to the district of a local authority)' has the meaning assigned to it by section 27;

'priority need (for accommodation)' has the meaning assigned to it by section 25;

'relevant authority' means a local authority or social work authority;

'securing accommodation for a person's occupation' has the meaning assigned to it by section 41;

'social work authority' means a local authority for the purposes of the Social Work (Scotland) Act 1968, that is to say, a regional or islands council;

'threatened with homelessness' has the meaning assigned to it by section 24(4);

'voluntary organisation' means a body, not being a public or local authority, whose activities are carried on otherwise than for profit.

PART III
RIGHTS OF PUBLIC SECTOR TENANTS

Security of tenure

44. Secure tenancies.

(1) Subject to subsection (4) and to section 45 and section 52(6), a tenancy (whenever created) of a house shall be a secure tenancy if—

(a) the house is let as a separate dwelling;
(b) the tenant is an individual and the house is his only or principal home; and
(c) the landlord is one of the bodies mentioned in subsection (2).

(2) The bodies referred to in subsections (1)(c) and (7) are the bodies mentioned in section 61(2)(a) and any housing trust which was in existence on 13th November 1953.

(3) Where a tenancy of a house is held jointly by two or more individuals, the requirements of subsection (1)(b) shall be deemed to be satisfied if all the joint tenants are individuals and at least one of the joint tenants occupies the house as his only or principal residence.

(4) A tenancy shall not be a secure tenancy if it is a tenancy of a kind mentioned in Schedule 2.

(5) Where the tenancy of a house is excluded from being a secure tenancy by reason only of the operation of paragraph 1 or 8 or Schedule 2, sections 53 to 60 shall nevertheless apply to that tenancy as if it were a secure tenancy.

(6) A tenancy which has become a secure tenancy shall continue to be a secure tenancy notwithstanding that the requirements of subsection (1)(b) may have ceased to be fulfilled.

Housing (Scotland) Act 1987 (c 26), s 46 [614]

(7) Where a tenant under a secure tenancy is accommodated temporarily in another house of which the landlord is a body mentioned in subsection (2), while the house which he normally occupies is not available for occupation, the other house shall be deemed for the purposes of this Part, except sections 46 and 47, to be the house which he normally occupies. [612]

NOTES to section 44

Definitions: 'house': see s 338 below; 'tenant', 'tenancy', 'landlord': see s 82 below.

45. Special provision for housing associations.

(1) A tenancy shall not be a secure tenancy at any time when the interest of the landlord belongs to a registered housing association which is a co-operative housing association.

(2) Sections 44, 46 to 50, 51, 52, and 82 to 84 shall apply to a tenancy at any time when the interest of the landlord belongs to a housing association which is a co-operative housing association and is not registered.

(3) If a registered housing association which is a registered co-operative housing association ceases to be registered, it shall notify those of its tenants who thereby become secure tenants.

(4) Notice under subsection (3) shall be given in writing to each tenant concerned, within the period of 21 days beginning with the date on which the association ceases to be registered.

(5) In this section—
(a) references to registration in relation to a housing association are to registration under the Housing Associations Act 1985;
(b) 'co-operative housing association' has the same meaning as in section 300(1)(b). [613]

NOTES to section 45

Definitions: 'tenant', 'tenancy', 'landlord': see s 82 below; 'secure tenancy': see s 82 below and s 44 above; 'registered housing association': see s 338 below.

46. Restriction on termination of secure tenancy.

(1) Notwithstanding any provision contained in the tenancy agreement, a secure tenancy may not be brought to an end except—
(a) by the death of the tenant (or, where there is more than one, of any of them), where there is no qualified person within the meaning of section 52;
(b) by operation of section 52(4) or (5);
(c) by written agreement between the landlord and the tenant;
(d) by operation of section 50(2);
(e) by an order for recovery of possession under section 48(2); or
(f) by 4 weeks' notice given by the tenant to the landlord.

(2) If, while the house which the tenant under a secure tenancy normally occupies is not available for occupation, the tenant is accommodated temporarily in another house of which the landlord is a body mentioned in section 44(2), either—
(a) by agreement; or
(b) following an order under section 48(2) (in a case where an order has also been made under subsection (5) of that section),
the landlord shall not be entitled to bring the tenant's occupation of the other house to an end before the house which he normally occupies is available for occupation unless the secure tenancy has been brought to an end. [614]

NOTES to section 46

Definitions: 'tenant', 'tenancy', 'landlord': see s 82 below; 'secure tenancy': see s 82 below and s 44 above; 'house': see s 338 below.

47. Proceedings for possession.

(1) The landlord under a secure tenancy may raise proceedings for recovery of possession of the house by way of summary cause in the sheriff court of the district in which it is situated.

(2) Proceedings for recovery of possession of a house subject to a secure tenancy may not be raised unless—
   (a) the landlord has served on the tenant a notice complying with subsection (3);
   (b) the proceedings are raised on or after the date specified in the said notice; and
   (c) the notice is in force at the time when the proceedings are raised.

(3) A notice under this section shall be in a form prescribed by the Secretary of State by statutory instrument, and shall specify—
   (a) the ground, being a ground set out in Part I of Schedule 3, on which proceedings for recovery of possession are to be raised; and
   (b) a date, not earlier than 4 weeks from the date of service of the notice or the date on which the tenancy could have been brought to an end by a notice to quit had it not been a secure tenancy, whichever is later, on or after which the landlord may raise proceedings for recovery of possession.

(4) A notice under this section shall cease to be in force 6 months after the date specified in it in accordance with subsection (3)(b), or when it is withdrawn by the landlord, whichever is earlier. **[615]**

NOTES to section 47

Definitions: 'landlord', 'tenant', 'tenancy': see s 82 below; 'prescribed': see s 338 below; 'secure tenancy': see s 82 below and s 44 above.

Sub-s (3): See the Secure Tenancies (Proceedings for Possession) (Scotland) Order 1980, SI 1980/1389, paras [1265] ff below.

48. Powers of sheriff in proceedings.

(1) The court may, as it thinks fit, adjourn proceedings under section 47 on a ground set out in any of paragraphs 1 to 7 and 16 of Part I of Schedule 3 for a period or periods, with or without imposing conditions as to payment of outstanding rent or other conditions.

(2) Subject to subsection (1), in proceedings under section 47 the court shall make an order for recovery of possession if it appears to the court that the landlord has a ground for recovery of possession, being—
   (a) a ground set out in any of paragraphs 1 to 7 of that Part and specified in the notice required by section 47 and that it is reasonable to make the order; or
   (b) a ground set out in any of paragraphs 8 to 15 of that Part and so specified and that other suitable accommodation will be available for the tenant when the order takes effect; or
   (c) the ground set out in paragraph 16 of that Part and so specified and both that it is reasonable to make the order and that other suitable accommodation will be available as aforesaid.

(3) Part II of Schedule 3 shall have effect to determine whether accommodation is suitable for the purposes of subsection (2)(b) or (c).

(4) An order under subsection (2) shall appoint a date for recovery of possession and shall have the effect of—
   (a) terminating the tenancy; and
   (b) giving the landlord the right to recover possession of the house,
at that date.

(5) Where, in proceedings under section 47 on the ground set out in paragraph 10 of Part I of Schedule 3, it appears to the court that it is the intention of the landlord—

(a) that substantial work will be carried out on the building (or a part of the building) which comprises or includes the house; and
(b) that the tenant should return to the house after the work is completed,

the court shall make an order that the tenant shall be entitled to return to the house after the work is completed; and subsection (4)(a) shall not apply in such a case. **[616]**

NOTES to section 48

Definitions: 'the court' means the sheriff court: see s 47 above; 'landlord', 'tenant', 'tenancy': see s 82 below; 'house': see s 338 below.

49. Rights of landlord where a secure tenancy appears to have been abandoned.

(1) This section shall have effect where a landlord who has let a house under a secure tenancy has reasonable grounds for believing that—
(a) the house is unoccupied; and
(b) the tenant does not intend to occupy it as his home.

(2) The landlord shall be entitled to enter the house at any time for the purpose of securing the house and any fittings, fixtures or furniture against vandalism.

(3) For the purposes of subsection (2), the landlord and its servants or agents may open, by force if necessary, doors and lockfast places.

(4) The landlord may take possession of the house in accordance with section 50. **[617]**

NOTES to section 49

Definitions: 'landlord', 'tenant', 'tenancy': see s 82 below; 'house': see s 338 below; 'secure tenancy': see s 82 below and s 44 above.

50. Repossession.

(1) A landlord wishing to take possession of a house under section 49(4) shall serve on the tenant a notice—
(a) stating that the landlord has reason to believe that the house is unoccupied and that the tenant does not intend to occupy it as his home;
(b) requiring the tenant to inform the landlord in writing within 4 weeks of service of the notice if he intends to occupy the house as his home; and
(c) informing the tenant that, if it appears to the landlord at the end of the said period of 4 weeks that the tenant does not intend so to occupy the house, the secure tenancy will be terminated forthwith.

(2) Where the landlord has—
(a) served on the tenant a notice which complies with subsection (1); and
(b) made such inquiries as may be necessary to satisfy the landlord that the house is unoccupied and that the tenant does not intend to occupy it as his home,

and at the end of the period of 4 weeks mentioned in subsection (1)(c) is so satisfied, it may serve a further notice on the tenant bringing the tenancy to an end forthwith.

(3) Where a tenancy has been terminated in accordance with this section the landlord shall be entitled to take possession of the house forthwith without any further proceedings.

(4) The Secretary of State may by order made by statutory instrument make provision for the landlord to secure the safe custody and delivery to the tenant of any property which is found in a house to which this section applies, and in particular—
(a) for requiring charges to be paid in respect of such property before it is delivered to the tenant; and
(b) for authorising the disposal of such property, if the tenant has not arranged for its delivery to him before the expiry of such period as the order may specify, and the application of any proceeds towards any costs incurred by the landlord and any rent due but unpaid by the tenant to the landlord. **[618]**

NOTES to section 50

Definitions: 'landlord': see s 82 below; 'tenant', 'tenancy': see s 82 below; 'house': see s 338 below.
Sub-s (4): See the Secure Tenancies (Abandoned Property) (Scotland) Order 1982, SI 1982/981, paras [1326] ff below.

51. Tenant's right of recourse to sheriff.

(1) A tenant under a secure tenancy who is aggrieved by termination of the tenancy by the landlord under section 50(2) may raise proceedings by summary application within 6 months after the date of the termination in the sheriff court of the district in which the house is situated.

(2) Where in the proceedings under this section it appears to the sheriff that—
 (a) the landlord has failed to comply with any provision of section 50; or
 (b) the landlord did not have reasonable grounds for finding that the house was unoccupied, or did not have reasonable grounds for finding that the tenant did not intend to occupy it as his home; or
 (c) the landlord was in error in finding that the tenant did not intend to occupy the house as his home, and the tenant had reasonable cause, by reason of illness or otherwise, for failing to notify the landlord of his intention so to occupy it,
he shall—
 (i) where the house has not been let to a new tenant, make an order that the secure tenancy shall continue; or
 (ii) in any other case, direct the landlord to make other suitable accommodation available to the tenant.

(3) Part II of Schedule 3 to this Act shal have effect to determine whether accommodation is suitable for the purposes of subsection (2)(ii).

NOTES to section 51

Definitions: 'tenant', 'tenancy', 'landlord': see s 82 below; 'secure tenancy': see s 82 below and s 44 above.

Succession

52. Succession to secure tenancy.

(1) On the death of a tenant under a secure tenancy, the tenancy shall pass by operation of law to a qualified person, unless—
 (a) there is no qualified person, or the qualified person declines the tenancy under subsection (4); or
 (b) the tenancy is terminated by operation of subsection (5).

(2) For the purposes of this section, a qualified person is—
 (a) a person whose only or principal home at the time of the tenant's death was the house and who was at that time either—
  (i) the tenant's spouse; or
  (ii) living with the tenant as husband and wife; and
 (b) where the tenancy was held jointly by two or more individuals, a surviving tenant where the house was his only or principal home at the time of the tenant's death;
 (c) where there is no person falling within paragraph (a) or (b), a member of the tenant's family who has attained the age of 16 years where the house was his only or principal home throughout the period of 12 months immediately preceding the tenant's death.

(3) Where there is more than one qualified person, the benefit of the provisions of subsection (1) or, as the case may be, of subsection (6) shall accrue—
 (a) to such qualified person; or
 (b) to such two or more qualified persons as joint tenants,

as may be decided by agreement between all the qualified persons or, failing agreement within 4 weeks of the death of the tenant, as the landlord shall decide.

(4) A qualified person who is entitled to the benefit of subsection (1) may decline the tenancy by giving the landlord notice in writing within 4 weeks of the tenant's death, and—
(a) he shall vacate the house within 3 months thereafter;
(b) he shall be liable to pay rent which becomes due after the said death only in respect of any rental period (that is to say, a period in respect of which an instalment of rent falls to be paid) during any part of which he has occupied the house after the said death.

(5) A secure tenancy which has passed under subsection (1) to a qualified person shall not, on the death of a tenant (or one of joint tenants) so pass on a second occasion, and accordingly the secure tenancy shall be terminated when such a death occurs; but the provisions of this subsection shall not operate so as to terminate the secure tenancy of any tenant under a joint tenancy where such a joint tenant continues to use the house as his only or principal home.

(6) Where a secure tenancy is terminated by operation of subsection (5) and there is a qualified person, he shall be entitled to continue as tenant for a period not exceeding 6 months, but the tenancy shall cease to be a secure tenancy.

(7) Where a tenant gives up a secure tenancy in order to occupy another house which is subject to a secure tenancy, whether by agreement or following termination of the first tenancy by an order under section 48(2)(b), for the purposes of subsections (2) and (5) those tenancies shall be treated as being a single secure tenancy. [620]

NOTES to section 52

Definitions: 'tenant', 'tenancy', 'landlord': see s 82 below; 'secure tenancy': see s 82 below and s 44 above; 'family': see ss 82 and 83 below.

Leases

53. Tenant's right to written lease.

(1) Every secure tenancy shall be constituted by writing which shall be probative or holograph of the parties.

(2) It shall be the duty of the landlord under a secure tenancy to draw up the documents required to comply with subsection (1), to ensure that they are duly executed before the commencement of the tenancy and to supply a copy of the documents to the tenant.

(3) A tenant shall not be required to pay any fees in respect of anything done under subsection (2). [621]

NOTES to section 53

Definitions: 'secure tenancy': see s 82 below and s 44 above; 'tenant', 'tenancy', 'landlord': see s 82 below.

54. Restriction on variation of terms of secure tenancies.

(1) Notwithstanding anything contained in the tenancy agreement, the terms of a secure tenancy may not be varied except—
(a) by agreement between the landlord and the tenant; or
(b) under subsection (2) or (4).

(2) The rent or any other charge payable under a secure tenancy may, without the tenancy being terminated, and subject to section 58 of the Rent (Scotland) Act 1984, be increased with effect from the beginning of any rental period (that is to say, a period in respect of which an instalment of rent falls to be paid) by a written notice of increase given by the landlord to the tenant not less than 4 weeks before the beginning of the rental

period (or any earlier day on which the payment of rent in respect of that period falls to be made).

(3) Where—
(a) a landlord wishes to vary the terms or conditions of a secure tenancy, but the tenant refuses or fails to agree the variation; or
(b) a tenant wishes to vary any term of a secure tenancy which restricts his use or enjoyment of the house, on the ground that—
  (i) by reason of changes in the character of the house or of the neighbourhood or other circumstances which the sheriff may deem material, the term is or has become unreasonable or inappropriate; or
  (ii) the term is unduly burdensome compared with any benefit which would result from its performance; or
  (iii) the existence of the term impedes some reasonable use of the house,
  but the landlord refuses or fails to agree the variation,
the landlord or, as the case may be, the tenant may raise proceedings by way of summary application in the sheriff court of the district in which the house is situated.

(4) In proceedings under subsection (3), the sheriff may make such order varying any term of the tenancy (other than a term relating to the amount of rent or of any other charge payable by the tenant) as he thinks it reasonable to make in all the circumstances, having particular regard to the safety of any person and to any likelihood of damage to the house or to any premises of which it forms part, including if the sheriff thinks fit an order that the tenant shall pay to the landlord such sum as the sheriff thinks just to compensate him for any patrimonial loss occasioned by the variation; and such an order shall not have the effect of terminating the tenancy.

(5) At any time before he grants an order in proceedings under subsection (3)(b), the sheriff may order the tenant to serve a copy of his application on any person who, in the capacity of owner or tenant of any land—
(a) appears to the sheriff to benefit from the term of which variation is sought; or
(b) appears to him to be adversely affected by the proposed variation.

(6) An agreement under subsection (1)(a) shall be in writing which is probative or holograph of the parties, and it shall be the duty of the landlord to draw up the said writing and to ensure that it is duly executed. **[622]**

NOTES to section 54
Definitions: 'tenant', 'tenancy', 'landlord': see s 82 below; 'secure tenancy': see s 82 below and s 44 above; 'house': see s 338 below.

Subletting

55. No subletting by secure tenant without landlord's consent.

(1) It shall be a term of every secure tenancy that the tenant shall not assign, sublet or otherwise give up to another person possession of the house or any part thereof or take in a lodger except with the consent in writing of the landlord, which shall not be unreasonably withheld.

(2) The landlord may refuse consent under this section if it appears to it that a payment other than—
(a) a rent which is in its opinion a reasonable rent; or
(b) a deposit returnable at the termination of the assignation, subletting or other transaction given as security for the subtenant's obligations for accounts for supplies of gas, electricity, telephone or other domestic supplies and for damage to the house or contents, which in its opinion is reasonable,
has been or is to be received by the tenant in consideration of the assignation, subletting or other transaction.

(3) This section shall not apply to any assignation, subletting or other transaction

entered into before 3rd October 1980 provided that the consent of the landlord to the transaction and to the rent which is being charged has been obtained.

(4) An assignation, subletting or other transaction to which this section applies shall not be a protected tenancy or a statutory tenancy within the meaning of the Rent (Scotland) Act 1984, [or an assured tenancy within the meaning of the Housing (Scotland) Act 1988, nor shall Part VII of the said Act of 1984] apply to such as assignation, sublet or other transaction.

(5) In this section and in section 56, 'subtenant' means a person entitled to possession of a house or any part thereof under an assignation, subletting or other transaction to which this section applies, and includes a lodger.

(6) The provisions of Schedule 4 shall have effect as terms of every secure tenancy. [623]

NOTES to section 55

Amendment: Sub-s (4) was amended by the Housing (Scotland) Act 1988 (c 43), s 72, Sch 9, para 10.
Definitions: 'secure tenancy': see s 82 below and s 44 above; 'tenant', 'tenancy': see s 82 below; 'landlord': see s 82 below.

56. Rent payable by subtenants.

(1) It shall be a term of every secure tenancy—
(a) that the tenant shall notify the landlord of any proposed increase in a rent to which this section applies; and
(b) that no increase shall be made in a rent to which this section applies if the landlord objects.

(2) Where a landlord under a secure tenancy has given consent to an assignation, subletting or other transaction under section 55, subsection (1) shall apply to the rent payable by the subtenant at the commencement of the assignation, subletting or other transaction. [624]

NOTES to section 56

Definitions: 'secure tenancy': see s 82 below and s 44 above; 'tenant', 'tenancy', 'landlord': see s 82 below.

Repairs and improvements

57. Landlord's consent to work.

(1) It shall be a term of every secure tenancy that the tenant shall not carry out work, other than interior docoration, in relation to the house without the consent in writing of the landlord, which shall not be unreasonably withheld.

(2) In this section and in Schedule 5, 'work' means—
(a) alteration, improvement or enlargement of the house or of any fittings or fixtures;
(b) addition of new fittings or fixtures;
(c) erection of a garage, shed or other structure,
but does not include repairs or maintenance of any of these.

(3) The provisions of Schedule 5 shall have effect as terms of every secure tenancy. [625]

NOTES to section 57

Definitions: 'secure tenancy': see s 82 below and s 44 above; 'tenant', 'tenancy', 'landlord': see s 82 below; 'house': see s 338 below.

58. Reimbursement of cost of work.

(1) On the termination of a secure tenancy, the landlord shall have the power (in addition to any other power which it has to make such payments) to the tenant which it considers to be appropriate in respect of any work carried out by him (or by any predecessor of his as tenant under the same secure tenancy) with the consent of the landlord under section 57, which has materially added to the price which the house might be expected to fetch if sold on the open market.

(2) The amount of any payment under subsection (1) shall not exceed the cost of the work in respect of which it is made, after deduction of the amount of any grant paid or payable under Part I of the Act of 1974 or under Part XIII.

(3) Where a secure tenancy has been terminated (under section 46(1)(a)) by the death of the tenant, a payment under subsection (1) may be made to the tenant's personal representatives. **[626]**

NOTES to section 58

Definitions: 'secure tenancy': see s 82 below and s 44 above; 'tenant', 'tenancy', 'landlord': see s 82 below; 'house': see s 338 below.

59. Effect of works on rent.

No account shall be taken at any time in the assessment of rent to be payable under a secure tenancy by a tenant who has carried out work on the house or by a person who has succeeded him in the tenancy or by the spouse of such a person of any improvement in the value or amenities of the house resulting from the work carried out by the tenant. **[627]**

NOTES to section 59

Definitions: 'secure tenancy': see s 82 below and s 44 above; 'tenant', 'tenancy', 'landlord': see s 82 below.

60. Scheme giving tenant a right to carry out repairs.

(1) The Secretary of State may by regulations make a scheme entitling a tenant under a secure tenancy, subject to and in accordance with the provisions of the scheme—
  (a) to carry out to the house which is the subject of the secure tenancy repairs which the landlord is under an obligation to carry out; and
  (b) after carrying out the repairs, to recover from the landlord such sums (not exceeding the costs that would have been incurred by the landlord in carrying out the repairs) as may be determined by or under the scheme.

(2) Regulations under this section may make different provision with respect to different cases or descriptions of case and may make such procedural, incidental, supplementary or transitional provision as may appear to the Secretary of State to be necessary or expedient.

(3) Without prejudice to the generality of subsection (2) regulations under this section—
  (a) may provide for any question arising under the scheme to be determined in such manner as the regulations may specify; and
  (b) may provide that where a tenant under a secure tenancy makes application under the scheme, the obligations of the landlord in respect of repairs to the house shall cease to apply for such period and to such extent as may be determined by or under the scheme.

(4) Regulations under this section shall be made by statutory instruments subject to annulment in pursuance of a resolution of either House of Parliament. **[628]**

NOTES to section 60

Definitions: 'tenant', 'tenancy', 'landlord': see s 82 below; 'secure tenancy': see s 82 below and s 44 above; 'house': see s 338 below.

Sub-ss (1)–(3): The power to make regulations has not been exercised.

Right to buy

61. Secure tenant's right to purchase.

(1) Notwithstanding anything contained in any agreement, a tenant of a house to which this section applies (or such one or more of joint tenants as may be agreed between them) shall, subject to this Part, have the right to purchase the house at a price fixed under section 62.

(2) This section applies to every house let under a secure tenancy where—
(a) the landlord is either—
   (i) an islands or district council, or a joint board or joint committee of an islands or district council or the common good of an islands or district council, or any trust under the control of an islands or district council; or
   (ii) a regional council, or a joint board or joint committee of 2 or more regional councils, or any trust under the control of a regional council; or
   (iii) a development corporation (including an urban development corporation); or
   (iv) [Scottish Homes;] or
   (v) The Housing Corporation; or
   (vi) a registered housing association; or
   (vii) a housing co-operative; or
   (viii) a police authority in Scotland; or
   (ix) a fire authority in Scotland; and
(b) the landlord is the heritable proprietor of the house or, in the case of a landlord who is a housing co-operative, a body mentioned in paragraph (a)(i) is the heritable proprietor; and
(c) immediately prior to the date of service of an application to purchase, the tenant has been for not less than 2 years in occupation of a house (including accommodation provided as mentioned in subsection (11)(n)) or of a succession of houses provided by any persons mentioned in subsection (11).

[(2A) For the purposes of subsection (2)(c), where the house was provided by a housing association which, at any time while the house was so provided, was not a registered housing association, the association shall, if it became a registered housing association at any later time, be deemed to have been a registered housing association.]

(3) This section also applies to a house let under a secure tenancy granted in pursuance of section [282(2) or (3)] (grant of secure tenancy on acquisition of defective dwelling), if the tenant would not otherwise have the right to purchase under this Part; and where it so applies—
(a) paragraph (c) of subsection (2) shall not have effect;
(b) the words 'beyond 2' in section 62(3)(b) shall not have effect.

(4) This section does not apply—
(a) to a house that is one of a group which has been provided with facilities (including a call system and the services of a warden) specially designed or adapted for the needs of persons of pensionable age or disabled persons; or
(b) where a landlord which is a registered housing association has at no time received a grant under—
   (i) any enactment mentioned in paragraph 2 of Schedule 1 to the Housing Associations Act 1985 (grants under enactments superseded by the Housing Act 1974);
   (ii) section 31 of the Housing Act 1974 (management grants);
   (iii) section 41 of the Housing Associations Act 1985 (housing association grants);
   (iv) section 54 of that Act (revenue deficit grants);
   (v) section 55 of that Act (hostel deficit grants);
   (vi) section 59(2) of that Act (grants by local authorities);

[(vii) section 50 of the Housing Act 1988 (housing association grants); or
(viii) section 51 of that Act (revenue deficit grants); or]
(c) where such a landlord has at no time let (or had available for letting) more than 100 dwellings; or
(d) where such a landlord is a charity—
  (i) entered in the register of charities maintained under the Charities Act 1960 by the Charity Commissioners for England and Wales; or
  (ii) which but for section 4(4) of, and paragraph (g) of the Second Schedule to, that Act (exempt charities) would require to be so entered; or
(e) where by virtue of section 49(2) of the said Act of 1960 (extent) such a landlord is not one to which Part II of that Act (registration of charities, etc) applies, but—
  (i) the landlord has, in respect of all periods from 14th November 1985 or from the date of first being registered by the Housing Corporation [or by Scottish Homes] (whichever is the later) claimed and been granted (whether or not retrospectively), under section 360(1) of the Income and Corporation Taxes Act 1970 (special exemptions for charities), exemption from tax; and
  (ii) where such exemption has not been claimed and granted in respect of all periods from the said date of registration, the rules of the landlord, registered under the Industrial and Provident Societies Act 1965 and in force at that date, were such as would have admitted of such exemption had it been claimed as at that date; or
(f) where, within a neighbourhood, the house is one of a number (not exceeding 14) of houses with a common landlord, being a landlord [which is a registered housing association], and it is the practice of that landlord to let at least one half of those houses for occupation by any or all of the following—
  (i) persons who have suffered from, or are suffering from, mental disorder (as defined in the Mental Health (Scotland) Act 1984), physical handicap, or addiction to alcohol or other drugs;
  (ii) persons who have been released from prison or other institutions;
  (iii) young persons who have left the care of a local authority,
  and a social service is, or special facilities are, provided wholly or partly for the purpose of assisting those persons.

(5) Where the spouse of a tenant or, where there is a joint tenancy, the spouse of a joint tenant, occupies the house as his only or principal home but is not himself a joint tenant, the right to purchase the house under subsection (1) shall not be exercised without the consent of such spouse.

(6) A tenant may exercise his right to purchase, if he so wishes together with one or more members of his family acting as joint purchasers, provided—
(a) that such members are at least 18 years of age, that they have, during the period of 6 months ending with the date of service of the application to purchase, had their only or principal home with the tenant and that their residence in the house is not a breach of any obligation of the tenancy; or
(b) where the requirements of paragraph (a) are not satisfied, the landlord has consented.

(7) The Secretary of State may by order made by statutory instrument amend, or add to, the description of persons set out in sub-paragraphs (i) to (ii) of paragraph (f) of subsection (4).

(8) The Commissioners of Inland Revenue shall, as regards any registered housing association, at the request of the Secretary of State provide him, the Housing Corporation [and Scottish Homes] with such information as will enable them to determine whether that association is a landlord in respect of which this section will not, by virtue of subsection (4)(d), apply; and where a registered housing association is refused exemption on a claim under section 360(1) of the Income and Corporation Taxes Act 1970 the Commissioners shall forthwith inform the Secretary of State, the Housing Corporation [and Scottish Homes] of that fact.

(9) Where information has been received by the Housing Corporation [or by Scottish Homes] under subsection (8) and having regard to that information the Corporation, [or as the case may be, Scottish Homes,] is satisfied that the housing association to which it relates is not a landlord in respect of which this section applies, they shall make an entry to that effect in the register of housing associations maintained by them under section 3(1), [or, as the case may be, 3(1A),] of the Housing Associations Act 1985; and they shall cancel that entry where subsequent information so received in relation to that housing association is inconsistent with their being so satisfied.

(10) In this section and the following section—
(a) references to occupation of a house include occupation—
   (i) in the case of joint tenants, by any one of them;
   (ii) by any person occupying the house rent-free;
   (iii) as the spouse of the tenant, joint tenant or of any such person;
   (iv) as the child, or the spouse of a child, of a tenant or a person occupying the house rent free who has succeeded, directly or indirectly, to the rights of that person in a house occupation of which would be reckonable for the purposes of this section; but only in relation to any period when the child, or as the case may be, spouse of the child, is at least 16 years of age; or
   (v) as a member of the family of a tenant or a person occupying the house rent free who, not being that person's spouse or child (or child's spouse), has succeeded, directly or indirectly, to such rights as are mentioned in paragraph (iv); but only in relation to any period when the member of the family is at least 16 years of age.
(b) for the purposes of determining the period of occupation—
   (i) any interruption in occupation of 12 months or less shall be registered as not affecting continuity; and
   (ii) any interruption in occupation of more than 12 months and less than 24 months may at the discretion of the landlord be regarded as not affecting continuity.
   [(iii) there shall be added to the period of occupation of a house by a joint tenant any earlier period during which he was at least 16 years of age and occupied the house as a member of the family of the tenant or of one or more of the joint tenants of the house.]

(11) The persons providing houses referred to in subsection (2)(c) (occupation requirement for exercise of right to purchase) and in section 62(3)(b) (calculation of discount from the market value) are—
(a) a regional, islands or district council in Scotland; any local authority in England and Wales or in Northern Ireland; and the statutory predecessors of any such council or authority, or the common good of any such council, or any trust under the control of any such council;
(b) the Commission for New Towns;
(c) a development corporation, an urban development corporation; and any development corporation established corresponding legislation in England and Wales or in Northern Ireland; and the statutory predecessors of any such authority;
(d) [Scottish Homes and] the Scottish Special Housing Association;
(e) a registered housing association;
(f) the Housing Corporation;
(g) a housing co-operative within the meaning of section 22 or a housing co-operative within the meaning of section 27B of the Housing Act 1985;
(h) the Development Board for Rural Wales;
(i) the Northern Ireland Housing Executive or any statutory predecessor;
(j) a police authority or the statutory predecessors of any such authority;
(k) a fire authority or the statutory predecessors of any such authority;
(l) a water authority in Scotland; and water authority constituted under corresponding legislation in England and Wales or in Northern Ireland; and the statutory predecessors of any such authority;

(m) the Secretary of State, where the house was at the material time used for the purposes of the Scottish Prison Service or of a prison service for which the Home Office or the Northern Ireland Office have responsibility;
(n) the Crown, in relation to accommodation provided in connection with service whether by the tenant or his spouse as a member of the regular armed forces of the Crown;
(o) the Secretary of State, where the house was at the material time used for the purposes of a health board constituted under section 2 of the National Health Services (Scotland) Act 1978 or for the purposes of a corresponding board in England and Wales, or for the purposes of the statutory predecessors of any such board; or the Department of Health and Social Services for Northern Ireland, where the house was at the material time used for the purposes of a Health and Personal Services Board in Northern Ireland, or for the purposes of the statutory predecessors of any such board;
(p) the Secretary of State, or the Minister of Agriculture, Fisheries and Food, where the house was at the material time used for the purposes of the Forestry Commission;
(q) the Secretary of State, where the house was at the material time used for the purposes of a State Hospital provided by him under section 90 of the Mental Health (Scotland) Act 1984 or for the purposes of any hospital provided under corresponding legislation in England and Wales;
(r) the Commissioners of Northern Lighthouses;
(s) the Trinity House;
(t) the Secretary of State, where the house was at the material time used for the purposes of Her Majesty's Coastguard;
(u) the United Kingdom Atomic Energy Authority;
(v) the Secretary of State, where the house was at the material time used for the purposes of any function transferred to him under section 1(2) of the Defence (Transfer of Functions) Act 1964 or any function relating to defence conferred on him by or under any subsequent enactment;
(w) such other persons as the Secretary of State may by order made by statutory instrument subject to annulment in pursuance of a resolution of either House of Parliament prescribe. **[629]**

NOTES to section 61
Amendments: Sub-s (2) was amended by the Housing (Scotland) Act 1988 (c 43), s 3.
Sub-s (2A) was added by the Housing (Scotland) Act 1988 (c 43), s 72, Sch 8, para 1.
Sub-s (3) was amended by the Local Government and Housing Act 1989 (c 42), s 195, Sch 11, para 93.
Sub-s (4) was amended by the Housing (Scotland) Act 1988 (c 43), s 3, Sch 2, para 9, s 72, Sch 7, para 2, and by the Housing Act 1988 (c 50), s 140, Sch 17, para 79.
Sub-s (8) was amended by the Housing (Scotland) Act 1988 (c 43), s 3, Sch 2, para 9.
Sub-s (9) was amended by the Housing (Scotland) Act 1988 (c 43), s 3, Sch 2, para 9.
Sub-s (10) was amended by the Local Government and Housing Act 1989 (c 42), s 176, Sch 12.
Sub-s (11) was amended by the Housing (Scotland) Act 1988 (c 43), s 3, Sch 2, para 9.
Definitions: 'tenant', 'tenancy', 'landlord', 'police authority', 'fire authority': see s 82 below; 'house': see s 338 below; 'development corporation', 'registered housing association', 'water authority': see s 338 below; 'secure tenancy': see s 82 below and s 44 above; 'housing co-operative': see s 82 below and s 22 above; 'disabled person': see ss 338 and 235 below; 'family': see ss 82 and 83 below.
Sub-s (7): The power to make regulations has not been exercised.
Sub-s (11): See the Right to Purchase (Prescribed Persons) (Scotland) Order 1986, SI 1986/2140, para [1369] ff below.

62. The price.

(1) Subject to subsection [(6A),] the price at which a tenant shall be entitled to purchase a house under this Part shall be fixed [as at the date of service of the application to purchase] by subtracting a discount from the market value of the house.

(2) The market value for the purposes of this section shall be determined by [either]—
(a) a qualified valuer nominated by the landlord and accepted by the tenant; or
(b) the district valuer,
[as the landlord thinks fit] as if the house were available for sale on the open market with vacant possession at the date of service of the application to purchase.

For the purposes of this subsection, no account shall be taken of any element in the market value of the house which reflects an increase in value as a result of work the cost of which would qualify for a reimbursement under section 58.

(3) Subject to subsection (5), the discount for the purposes of subsection (1) shall be—
(a) 32 per cent of the market value of the house except—
   (i) where the house is a flat, it shall be 44 per cent of the market value;
   (ii) where the house is one to which section 61(3) applies, it shall be 30 per cent or, where it is a flat, 40 per cent of the market value;
   together with
(b) an additional one per cent or, where the house is a flat, two per cent, of the market value for every year beyond 2 of continuous occupation by the appropriate person preceding the date of service of the application to purchase, of a house (including accommodation as provided in section 61(11)(n)) or of a succession of houses provided by any persons mentioned in section 61(11),
up to a maximum discount of 60 per cent, or where the house is a flat, 70 per cent of the market value.

(4) For the purposes of subsection (3)
(a) the 'appropriate person' is the tenant, or if it would result in a higher discount and if she is cohabiting with him at the date of service of the application to purchase, his spouse; and where joint tenants are joint purchasers the 'appropriate person' shall be whichever tenant (or, as the case may be, spouse) has the longer or longest such occupation; [and
(b) where the house was provided by a housing association which, at any time while the house was so provided was not a registered housing association, the association shall, if it became a registered housing association at any later time, be deemed to have been a registered housing association at all times since it first provided the house.]

(5) The Secretary of State may by order made with the consent of the Treasury provide that, in such cases as may be specified in the order—
(a) the minimum percentage discount,
(b) the percentage increase for each complete year of the qualifying period after two, or
(c) the maximum percentage discount,
shall be such percentage, higher than that specified in subsection (3), as may be specified in the order.

(6) An order under subsection (5)—
(a) may make different provision with respect to different cases or descriptions of case,
(b) may contain such incidental, supplementary or transitional provisions as appear to the Secretary of State to be necessary or expedient, and
(c) shall be made by statutory instrument and shall not be made unless a draft of it has been laid before and approved by resolution of each House of Parliament.

[(6A) Except where the Secretary of State so determines, the discount for the purposes of subsection (1) shall not reduce the price below the amount which, in accordance with a determination made by him, is to be taken as representing so much of the costs incurred in respect of the house as, in accordance with the determination, is to be treated as—
(a) incurred in the period commencing with the beginning of the financial year of the landlord which was current five years prior to the date of service of the application to purchase the house or such other period as the Secretary of State may by order provide; and

[630]

(b) relevant for the purposes of this subsection,

and, if the price before discount is below that amount, there shall be no discount.

(6B) An order under subsection (6A) by statutory instrument subject to anulment in pursuance of a resolution of either House of Parliament and may make different provision in relation to different cases or circumstances or different areas.]

. . .

(10) Where at the date of service of an offer to sell under section 63 any of the costs referred to in subsection [(6A)] are not known, the landlord shall make an estimate of such unknown costs for the purposes of that subsection. **[630]**

NOTES to section 62

Amendments: Sub-s (1) was amended by the Housing and Local Government Act 1989 (c 42), s 195, Sch 11, para 94.
Sub-s (2) was amended by the Housing (Scotland) Act 1988 (c 43), s 72, Sch 8, para 2.
Sub-s (4) was amended by the Housing (Scotland) Act 1988 (c 43), s 72, Sch 8, para 2.
Sub-ss (5), (6) the power to make an order has not been exercised.
Sub-ss (6A), (6B) were inserted by the Housing (Scotland) Act 1988 (c 43), s 65.
Sub-ss (7)–(9) and (11)–(13) were repealed by the Housing (Scotland) Act 1988 (c 43), s 65.
Sub-s (1) was amended by the Housing (Scotland) Act 1988 (c 43), s 65.
Definitions: 'tenant', 'landlord': see s 82 below; 'house': see s 338 below; 'application to purchase': see ss 82 and 83 below; 'registered housing association': see s 338 below.

Procedure

63. Application to purchase and offer to sell.

(1) A tenant who seeks to exercise a right to purchase a house under section 61 shall serve on the landlord a notice (referred to in this Part as an 'application to purchase') which shall be in such form as the Secretary of State shall by order made by statutory instrument prescribe, and shall contain—
  (a) notice that the tenant seeks to exercise the right to purchase;
  (b) a statement of any period of occupancy of a house on which the tenant intends to rely for the purposes of sections 61 and 62; and
  (c) the name of any joint purchaser within the meaning of section 61(6).

(2) Where an application to purchase is served on a landlord, and the landlord does not serve a notice of refusal under sections 68 to 70 it shall, within 2 months after service of the application to purchase, serve on the tenant a notice (referred to in this Part as an 'offer to sell') containing—
  (a) the market value of the house determined under section 62(2);
  (b) the discount calculated under section 62(3);
  (c) the price fixed under section 62(1);
  (d) any conditions which the landlord intends to impose under section 64; and
  (e) an offer to sell the house to the tenant and any joint purchaser named in the application to purchase at the price referred to in paragraph (c) and under the conditions referred to in paragraph (d). **[631]**

NOTES to section 63

Definitions: 'tenant', 'landlord': see s 82 below.
Sub-s (1): See the Right to Purchase (Application Form) (Scotland) Order 1986, SI 1986/2138, paras [1365] ff below.

64. Conditions of sale.

(1) Subject to section 75, an offer to sell under section 63(2) shall contain such conditions as are reasonable, provided that—
  (a) the conditions shall have the effect of ensuring that the tenant has as full enjoyment and use of the house as owner as he has had as tenant;
  (b) the conditions shall secure to the tenant such additional rights as are necessary for

Housing (Scotland) Act 1987 (c 26), s 64 [632]

his reasonable enjoyment and use of the house as owner (including, without prejudice to the foregoing generality, common rights in any part of the building of which the house forms part) and shall impose on the tenant any necessary duties relative to rights so secured; and
(c) the conditions shall include such terms as are necessary to entitle the tenant to receive a good and marketable title to the house.

(2) A condition which imposes a new charge or an increase of an existing charge for the provision of a service in relation to the house shall provide for the charge to be in reasonable proportion to the cost to the landlord of providing the service.

(3) No condition shall be imposed under this section which has the effect of requiring the tenant to pay any expenses of the landlord.

(4) Subject to subsection (6), no condition shall be imposed under this section which has the effect of requiring the tenant or any of his successors in title to offer to the landlord, or to any other person, an option to purchase the house in advance of its sale to a third party, except in the case of a house which has facilities which are substantially different from those of any ordinary house and which has been designed or adapted for occupation by a person of pensionable age or disabled person whose special needs require accommodation of the kind provided by the house.

(5) Where an option to purchase permitted under subsection (4) is exercised, the price to be paid for the house shall be determined by the district valuer who shall have regard to the market value of the house at the time of the purchase and to any amount due to the landlord under section 72 (recovery of discount on early resale).

(6) Subsection (4) shall not apply to houses in an area which is designated a rural area by the islands or district council within whose area it is situated where the Secretary of State, on the application of the islands or district council concerned, makes an order, which shall be made by statutory instrument subject to annulment in pursuance of a resolution of either House of Parliament, to that effect.

(7) An order under subsection (6) may be made where—
(a) within the said rural area more than one-third of all relevant houses have been sold [whether under this Part or otherwise]; and
[(b) the Secretary of State is satisfied that an unreasonable proportion of the houses sold consists of houses which have been resold and are not—
  (i) being used as the only or principal homes of the owners; or
  (ii) subject to regulated tenancies within the meaning of section 8 of the Rent (Scotland) Act 1984 or assured tenancies for the purposes of Part II of the Housing (Scotland) Act 1988.]

(8) For the purposes of subsection (7)(a), a 'relevant house' is one of which—
(a) at 3rd October 1980, the council concerned, or
(b) at 7th January 1987, a registered housing association,
is landlord.

(9) A condition imposed by virtue of subsection (6) shall not have effect in relation to any house for more than 10 years from the date of its conveyance to a tenant in pursuance of his right to purchase under this Part and subsection (5) shall apply to any option to purchase exercised under such a condition. [632]

NOTES to section 64
Amendment: Sub-s (7) was amended by the Housing (Scotland) Act 1988 (c 43), s 72, Sch 9, para 11.
Definitions: 'tenant', 'landlord': see s 82 below; 'house', 'registered housing association': see s 338 below; 'disabled person': see ss 338 and 236 below.
Sub-s (6): The power to make an order has not been exercised.

65. Variation of conditions.

(1) Where an offer to sell is served on a tenant and he wishes to exercise his right to purchase, but—
- (a) he considers that a condition contained in the offer to sell is unreasonable; or
- (b) he wishes to have a new condition included in it; or
- (c) he has not previously notified the landlord of his intention to exercise that right together with a joint purchaser, but now wishes to do so; or
- (d) he has previously notified the landlord of his intention to exercise that right together with any joint purchaser but now wishes to exercise the right without that joint purchaser,

he may request the landlord to strike out or vary the condition, or to include the new condition, or to make the offer to sell to the tenant and the joint purchaser, or to withdraw the offer to sell in respect of the joint purchaser, as the case may be, by serving on the landlord within one month after service of the offer to sell a notice in writing setting out his request; and if the landlord agrees, it shall accordingly serve an amended offer to sell on the tenant within one month of service of the notice setting out the request.

(2) A tenant who is aggrieved by the refusal of the landlord to agree to strike out or vary a condition, or to include a new condition, or to make the offer to sell to the tenant and the joint purchaser, or to withdraw the offer to sell in respect of any joint purchaser under subsection (1), or by his failure timeously to serve an amended offer to sell under the said subsection, may, within one month or, with the consent of the landlord given in writing before the expiry of the said period of one month, within two months of the refusal or failure, refer the matter to the Lands Tribunal for determination.

(3) In proceedings under subsection (2), the Land Tribunal may, as it thinks fit, uphold the condition or strike it out or vary it, or insert the new condition or order that the offer to sell be made to the tenant and the joint purchaser, or order that the offer to sell be withdrawn in respect of any joint purchaser, and where its determination results in a variation of the terms of the offer to sell, it shall order the landlord to serve on the tenant an amended offer to sell accordingly within 2 months thereafter. **[633]**

NOTES to section 65
Definitions: 'offer to sell': see s 82 below and s 63 above; 'tenant', 'landlord': see s 82 below; 'Lands Tribunal': see s 338 below.

66. Notice of acceptance.

(1) Where an offer to sell is served on a tenant and he wishes to exercise his right to purchase and—
- (a) he does not dispute the terms of the offer to sell by timeously serving a notice setting out a request under section 65(1) or by referring the matter to the Lands Tribunal under subsection (1)(d) of section 71; or
- (b) any such dispute has been resolved;

the tenant shall, subject to section 67(1), serve a notice of acceptance on the landlord within 2 months of whichever is the latest of—
- (i) the service on him of the offer to sell;
- (ii) the service on him of an amended offer to sell (or if there is more than one, of the latest amended offer to sell);
- (iii) a determination by the Lands Tribunal under section 65(3) which does not require service of an amended offer to sell;
- (iv) a finding or determination of the Lands Tribunal in a matter referred to it under section 71(1)(d) where no order is made under section 71(2)(b);
- (v) the service of an offer to sell on him by virtue of subsection (2)(b) of section 71;
- (vi) where a loan application under subsection (2)(a)(i) of section 216 (loans) has been served on the landlord, the service of a relative offer or refusal of loan; or
- (vii) where section 216(7) (loans) is invoked, the decision of the court.

(2) Where an offer to sell (or an amended offer to sell) has been served on the tenant and a relative notice of acceptance has been duly served on the landlord, a contract of sale of the house shall be constituted between the landlord and the tenant on the terms contained in the offer (or amended offer) to sell. [634]

NOTES to section 66

Definitions: 'offer to sell': see s 82 below and s 63 above; 'tenant' see s 82 below; 'Lands Tribunal', 'house': see s 338 below.

67. Fixed price option.

(1) Where an offer to sell (or an amended offer to sell) is served on a tenant, but he is unable by reason of the application of regulations made under section 216(3) (loans) to obtain a loan of the amount for which he has applied, he may, within 2 months of service on him of an offer of loan, or (as the case may be) of the date of a declarator by the sheriff under section 216(6) (loans), whichever is the later, serve on the landlord a notice to the effect that he wishes to have a fixed price option, which notice shall be accompanied by a payment to the landlord of £100, and in that event he shall be entitled to serve a notice of acceptance on the landlord at any time within 2 years of the service of the application to purchase.

Provided that where, as regards the house, the tenant has served a loan application in accordance with subsection (2)(a)(ii) of section 216 (loans), he shall be entitled (even if the said period of 2 years has expired) to serve a notice of acceptance on the landlord within 2 months of whichever is the later of—
(a) the service of a relative offer, or refusal, of loan; or
(b) where section 216(7) is invoked, the decision of the court.

(2) The payment of £100 mentioned in subsection (1) shall be recoverable—
(a) by the tenant, when he purchases the house in accordance with that subsection or, if he does not, at the expiry of the period of 2 years mentioned therein;
(b) by the tenant, when the landlord recovers possession of the house under subsection (3); or
(c) by his personal representatives, if he dies without purchasing the house in accordance with that subsection.

(3) The existence of a fixed price option under subsection (1) shall not prevent the landlord from recovering possession of the property in any manner which may be lawful, and in that event the option shall be terminated. [635]

NOTES to section 67

Definitions: 'offer to sell': see s 82 below and s 63 above; 'tenant', 'landlord': see s 82 below; 'house': see s 338 below.

68. Refusal of applications.

(1) Where a landlord on which an application to purchase has been served disputes the tenant's right to purchase a house under section 61, it shall by notice (referred to in this Part as a 'notice of refusal') served within one month after service of the application to purchase—
(a) refuse the application; or
(b) offer to sell the house to the tenant under section 14, or under any other power which the landlord has to sell the house.

(2) Where a landlord on which an application to purchase has been served, after reasonable inquiry (which shall include reasonable opportunity for the tenant to amend his application), is of the opinion that information contained in the application is incorrect in a material respect it shall issue a notice of refusal within 2 months of the application to purchase.

(3) A notice of refusal shall specify the grounds on which the landlord disputes the tenant's right to purchase or, as the case may be, the accuracy of the information.

(4) Where a landlord serves a notice of refusal on a tenant under this section, the tenant may within one month thereafter apply to the Lands Tribunal for a finding that he has a right to purchase the house under section 61 on such terms as it may determine. **[636]**

NOTES to section 68

Definitions: 'landlord', 'tenant': see s 82 below; 'application to purchase': see s 82 below and s 63 above; 'house', 'Lands Tribunal': see s 338 below.

Houses provided for special purposes

69. Secretary of State's power to authorise refusal to sell certain houses provided for persons of pensionable age.

(1) This section applies to a house which has facilities which are substantially different from those of an ordinary house and which has been designed or adapted for occupation by a person of pensionable age whose special needs require accommodation of the kind provided by the house.

[(1A) This section applies only to houses first let on a secure tenancy before 1st January 1990.]

(2) Where an application to purchase a house is served on a landlord and it appears to the landlord that—
 (a) the house is one to which this section applies; and
 (b) the tenant would, apart from this section, have a right under section 61 to purchase the house,
the landlord may, within one month after service of the application to purchase, instead of serving an offer to sell on the tenant, make an application to the Secretary of State under this section.

(3) An application under subsection (2) shall specify the facilities and features of design or adaptation which in the view of the landlord cause the house to be a house to which this section applies.

(4) Where the Secretary of State has received an application under this section and it appears to him that the house concerned is one to which this section applies, he shall authorise the landlord to serve on the tenant a notice of refusal under this section, which shall be served as soon as is practicable after the authority is given and in any event within one month thereafter.

(5) A notice of refusal served under subsection (4) shall specify the facilities and features specified for the purposes of subsection (3) and that the Secretary of State's authority for service of the said notice has been given.

(6) Where the Secretary of State refuses an application made under subsection (2), the landlord shall serve on the tenant an offer to sell under section 63(2)—
 (a) within the period mentioned in that section; or
 (b) where the unexpired portion of that period is less than one month or there is not an unexpired portion of that period, within one month of the Secretary of State's refusal. **[637]**

NOTES to section 69

Amendment: Sub-s (1A) was added by the Local Government and Housing Act 1989 (c 42), s 177.

Definitions: 'house': see s 338 below; 'landlord', 'tenant': see s 82 below.

70. Power to refuse to sell certain houses required for educational purposes.

(1) Where an application to purchase a house is served on an islands council as landlord and—

(a) the house is—
  (i) held by the council for the purposes of its functions as education authority; and
  (ii) required for the accommodation of a person who is or will be employed by the council for those purposes;
(b) the council is not likely to be able reasonably to provide other suitable accommodation for the person mentioned in paragraph (a)(ii); and
(c) the tenant would, apart from this section, have a right under section 61 to purchase the house,

the landlord may, within one month of service of the application to purchase, serve a notice of refusal on the tenant.

(2) A refusal by the landlord under subsection (1) shall contain sufficient information to demonstrate that the conditions mentioned in paragraphs (a) and (b) of that subsection are fulfilled in relation to the house. **[638]**

NOTES to section 70

Definitions: 'application to purchase': see s 82 below and s 63 above; 'landlord', 'tenant': see s 82 below; 'house': see s 338 below.

Lands Tribunal

71. Reference to Lands Tribunal.

(1) Where—
(a) a landlord who has been duly served with an application to purchase fails to issue timeously either an offer to sell (even if only such offer to sell as is mentioned in paragraph (d)) or a notice of refusal; or
(b) the Lands Tribunal has made a determination under section 65(3) (variation of terms of offer to sell) and the landlord has failed to issue an amended offer to sell within 2 months thereafter; or
(c) the Lands Tribunal has made a finding under section 68(4) (refusal of right to purchase) or has made an order under subsection (2)(b) of this section and the landlord has not duly progressed the application to purchase in accordance with that finding or, as the case may be, order, within 2 months thereafter; or
(d) a landlord has served an offer to sell whose contents do not conform with the requirements of paragraphs (a) to (e) of section 63(2) (or where such contents were not obtained in accordance with the provisions specified in those paragraphs),

the tenant (together with any joint purchaser) may refer the matter to the Lands Tribunal by serving on the clerk to that body a copy of any notice served and of any finding or determination made under this Part, together with a statement of his grievance.

(2) Where a matter has been referred to the Lands Tribunal under subsection (1), the Tribunal shall consider whether in its opinion—
(a) any of paragraphs (a) to (c) of that subsection apply, and if it so finds it may—
  (i) give any consent, exercise any discretion, or do anything which the landlord may give, exercise or do under or for the purposes of sections 61 to 84; and
  (ii) issue such notices and undertake such other steps as may be required to complete the procedure provided for in sections 63 and 65 to 67;
  any any consent given, any discretion exercised, or anything done, under the foregoing provisions of this subsection shall have effect as if it has been duly given, exercised or done by the landlord; or
(b) paragraph (d) of that subsection applies, and if it so finds it may order the landlord to serve on the tenant an offer to sell, in proper form, under section 63(2) within such time (not exceeding 2 months) as it may specify.

(3) Nothing in this section shall affect the operation of the provisions of any other enactment relating to the enforcement of a statutory duty whether under that enactment or otherwise. **[639]**

NOTES to section 71

Definitions: 'landlord', 'tenant': see s 82 below; 'application to purchase', 'offer to sell': see s 82 below and s 63 above; 'lands tribunal': see s 338 below.

Recovery of discount

72. Recovery of discount on early resale.

(1) A person who has purchased a house in exercise of a right to purchase under section 61, or any of his successors in title, who sells or otherwise disposes of the house (except as provided for in section 73) before the expiry of 3 years from the date of service of a notice of acceptance by the tenant under section 66, shall be liable to repay to the landlord, in accordance with subsection (3), a proportion of the difference between the market value determined, in respect of the house, under section 62(2) and the price at which the house was so purchased.

(2) Subsection (1) applies to the disposal of part of a house except in a case where—
(a) it is a disposal by one of the parties to the original sale to one of the other parties; or
(b) the remainder of the house continues to be the only or principal home of the person disposing of the part.

(3) The proportion of the difference which shall be paid to the landlord shall be—
(a) 100 per cent where the disposal occurs within the first year after the date of service of notice,
(b) 66 per cent where it occurs in the second such year, and
(c) 33 per cent where it occurs in the third such year.

(4) Where as regards a house or part of a house there is, within the period mentioned in subsection (1), more than one disposal to which that subsection would (apart from the provisions of this subsection) apply, that subsection shall apply only in relation to the first such disposal of the house, or part of the house.

(5) Where a landlord secures the liability to make a repayment under subsection (1) the security shall, notwithstanding section 13 of the Conveyancing and Feudal Reform (Scotland) Act 1970, have priority immediately after—
(a) any standard security granted in security of a loan either—
  (i) for the purchase of the house, or
  (ii) for the improvement of the house,
  and any interest present or future due thereon (including any such interest which has accrued or may accrue) and any expenses or outlays (including interest thereon) which may be, or may have been, reasonably incurred in the exercise of any power conferred on the lender by the deed expressing the said standard security; and
(b) if the landlord consents, a standard security over the house granted in security of any other loan, and in relation thereto any such interest, expenses or outlays as aforesaid.

(6) For the avoidance of doubt, paragraph (a) of subsection (5) applies to a standard security granted in security both for the purpose mentioned in sub-paragraph (i) and for that mentioned in sub-paragraph (ii) as it applies to a standard security so granted for only one of those purposes.

(7) The liability to make a repayment under subsection (1) shall not be imposed as a real burden in a disposition of any interest in the house.

NOTES to section 72
Definitions: 'house': see s 338 below; 'tenant', 'landlord': see s 82 below.

73. Cases where discount etc is not recoverable.

(1) There shall be no liability to make a repayment under section 72(1) where the disposal is made—
(a) by the executor of the deceased owner acting in that capacity; or
(b) as a result of a compulsory purchase order; or
(c) in the circumstances specified in subsection (2).

(2) The circumstances mentioned in subsection (1)(c) are that the disposal—
(a) is to a member of the owner's family who has lived with him for a period of 12 months before the disposal; and
(b) is for no consideration:
Provided that, if the disponee disposes of the house before the expiry of the 3 year period mentioned in section 72(1), the provisions of that section will apply to him as if this was the first disposal and he was the original purchaser. [641]

NOTE to section 73
Definition: 'family': see ss 82 and 83 below.

Duties of landlords

74. Duties of landlords.

It shall be the duty of every landlord of a house to which sections 61 to 84 and section 216 apply to make provision for the progression of applications under those sections in such manner as may be necessary to enable any tenant who wishes to exercise his rights under this Part to do so, and to comply with any regulations which may be made by statutory instrument by the Secretary of State in that regard. [642]

NOTES to section 74
Definitions: 'landlord', 'tenant': see s 82 below.

75. Agreements affecting right to purchase.

(1) Subject to sections 61(1), 67(1) and 72(1)—
(a) no person exercising or seeking to exercise a right to purchase under section 61(1) shall be obliged, notwithstanding any agreement to the contrary, to make any payment to or lodge any deposit with the landlord which he would not have been obliged to make, or as the case may be lodge, had he not exercised (or sought to exercise) the right to purchase;
(b) a landlord mentioned in section 61(2)(a)(i) or (ii) is required neither to enter into, nor to induce (or seek to induce) any person to enter into, such agreement as is mentioned in paragraph (a), or into any agreement which purports to restrict that person's rights under this Part.

(2) Paragraph (a) of subsection (1) does not apply to the expenses in any court proceedings. [643]

NOTE to section 75
Definition: 'landlord': see s 82 below.

76. Duty of landlords to provide information to secure tenants.

(1) Whenever a new secure tenancy is to be created, if—
(a) the landlord is [neither] the heritable proprietor of the house, [nor holds the interest of the landlord under a registered lease of the house or of land which includes it;] or
(b) by virtue of section 61(4), the house is not one to which that section applies; or
(c) [section 62(6A) may affect any price fixed as regards the house under section 62(1)]
the landlord shall so inform the prospective tenant by written notice.

(2) Where in the course of a secure tenancy the landlord ceases to be [either] the heritable proprietor of the house [or the holder of the interest of the landlord under a registered lease of the house or of land which includes it,] or the house, by virtue of section 61(4), ceases to be one to which that section applies, the landlord shall forthwith so inform the tenant by written notice.

(3) Subsection (1) and (2) do not apply if—
(a) the landlord is a housing co-operative within the meaning of section 22 and
(b) the heritable proprietor is a local authority, [or a local authority is the holder of the interest of the landlord under a registered lease of the house or of land which includes it.]

[(4) Where—
(a) by way of any enactment (including an enactment made under this Act), any change is to be made in the law relating to the calculation of the price at which the tenant of a house is entitled under this Act to purchase it, being a change which does not come into force upon the passing or making of that enactment but which, when it does come into force will affect the price of the house, and
(b) the house is one in respect of which an application to purchase has, in the period ending with the coming into force of the change, been served under section 63(1) and not withdrawn but no contract of sale of the house has been constituted under section 66(2),

the landlord shall, upon the passing or making of that enactment or, if later, upon the service of the application to purchase, forthwith given written notice to the tenant stating the nature of the change and how it will affect the price and suggesting that the tenant should seek appropriate advice.

(5) For the purposes of subsection (4), a change in the law will affect the price of a house if, on the day it falls to be calculated under the law as changed, the price will be different from what it would have been that day had there been no such change.]   **[644]**

NOTES to section 76

Amendments: Sub-s (1) was amended by the Housing (Scotland) Act 1988 (c 43), s 65 and by the Local Government and Housing Act 1989 (c 42), s 178; sub-s (2) was amended by the Local Government and Housing Act 1989 (c 42), s 178; sub-ss (4) and (5) were added by the Local Government and Housing Act 1989 (c 42), s 178.

Definitions: 'secure tenancy': see s 82 below and s 44 above; 'tenant', 'tenancy', 'landlord': see s 82 below; 'house': see s 338 below.

Powers of Secretary of State

77. Secretary of State may make provision for vesting in landlord to bring into being tenant's right to purchase house.

(1) Subject to subsection (2), where, but for the fact that a landlord is not the heritable proprietor of land on which houses have been let (or made available for letting) by it, one or more of its tenants would have a right to purchase under section 61, the Secretary of State may by order made by statutory instrument provide that the whole of the heritable proprietor's interest in the land shall vest in the landlord.

(2) An order under this section shall only be made where—
(a) the heritable proprietor is a body mentioned in paragraph (a) of section 61(2); and
(b) the Secretary of State is of the opinion, after consultation with the heritable proprietor and with the landlord, that the order is necessary if the right to purchase is to come into being.

(3) An order under this section shall have the same effect as a declaration under section 278 of the Town and Country Planning (Scotland) Act 1972 (general vesting declarations), except that, in relation to such an order, the enactments mentioned in Schedule 6 shall have effect subject to the modifications specified in that Schedule.

(4) Compensation under the Land Compensation (Scotland) Act 1963, as applied by subsection (3) and Schedule 6 shall be assessed by reference to values current on the date the order under this section comes into force.

(5) An order under this section shall have no effect until approved by resolution of each House of Parliament.

(6) An order under this section which would, apart from the provisions of this subsection, be treated for the purposes of the Standing Orders of either House of Parliament as a hybrid instrument shall proceed in that House as if it were not such an instrument.

(7) An order under this section may include such incidental, consequential or supplementary provisions as may appear to the Secretary of State to be necessary or expedient for the purposes of this Act. [645]

NOTES to section 77
Definitions: 'landlord', 'tenant': see s 82 below; 'house': see s 338 below.
Sub-s (1): The power to make an order has been exercised in the Scottish Special Housing Association (Vesting of Glasgow District Council Land) (Scotland) Order 1981, SI 1981/1860.

78. Secretary of State may give directions to modify conditions of sale.

(1) Where it appears to the Secretary of State that the inclusion of conditions of a particular kind in offers to sell would be unreasonable he may by direction require landlords generally, landlords of a particular description, or particular landlords not to include conditions of that kind (or not to include conditions of that kind unless modified in such manner as may be specified in the direction) in offers to sell served on or after a date so specified.

(2) Where a condition's inclusion in an offer to sell—
(a) is in contravention of a direction under subsection (1) or
(b) in a case where the tenant has not by the date specified in such a direction served a relative notice of acceptance on the landlord, would have been in such contravention had the offer to sell been served on or after that date,
the condition shall have no effect as regards the offer to sell.

(3) A direction under subsection (1) may—
(a) make different provision in relation to different areas, cases or classes of case and may exclude certain areas, cases or classes of case; and
(b) be varied or withdrawn by a subsequent direction so given.

(4) Section 211 of the Local Government (Scotland) Act 1973 (provision for default of local authority) shall apply as regards a failure to comply with a requirement in a direction under subsection (1) as that section applies as regards such failure as is mentioned in subsection (1) thereof. [646]

NOTES to section 78
Definitions: 'landlord', 'tenant': see s 82 below; 'offer to sell': see s 82 below and s 63 above.

79. Secretary of State may give financial and other assistance for tenants involved in proceedings.

(1) Where, in relation to any proceedings, or prospective proceedings, to which this section applies, a tenant or purchaser is an actual or prospective party, the Secretary of State may on written application to him by the tenant or purchaser give financial or other assistance to the applicant, if the Secretary of State thinks fit to do so:
Provided that assistance under this section shall be given only where the Secretary of State considers—
(a) that the case raises a question of principle and that it is in the public interest to give the applicant such assistance; or
(b) that there is some other special consideration.

(2) This section applies to—
(a) any proceedings under sections 61 to 84 and section 216; and
(b) any proceedings to determine any question arising under or in connection with those sections other than a question as to market value for the purposes of section 62.

(3) Assistance by the Secretary of State under this section may include—
(a) giving advice;
(b) procuring or attempting to procure the settlement of the matter in dispute;
(c) arranging for the giving of advice or assistance by a solicitor or counsel;
(d) arranging for representation by a solicitor or counsel;
(e) any other form of assistance which the Secretary of State may consider appropriate.

(4) In so far as expenses are incurred by the Secretary of State in providing the applicant with assistance under this section, any sums recovered by virtue of an award of expenses, or of an agreement as to expenses, in the applicant's favour with respect to the matter in connection with which the assistance is given shall, subject to any charge or obligation for payment in priority to other debts under the Legal Aid (Scotland) Act 1986 and to any provision of that Act for payment of any sum into the Scottish Legal Aid Fund, be paid to the Secretary of State in priority to any other debts.

(5) Any expenses incurred by the Secretary of State in providing assistance under this section shall be paid out of money provided by Parliament; and any sums received by the Secretary of State under subsection (4) shall be paid into the Consolidated Fund. **[647]**

NOTE to section 79
Definition: 'tenant': see s 82 below.

80. . . .

NOTE to section 80
Section 80 was repealed by the Local Government and Housing Act 1989 (c 42), s 168, Sch 12.

81. Information from landlords in relation to Secretary of State's powers.

(1) Without prejudice to section 199 of the Local Government (Scotland) Act 1973 (reports and returns by local authorities etc), where it appears to the Secretary of State necessary or expedient, in relation to the exercise of his powers under sections 61 to 84 and section 216, he may by notice in writing to a landlord require it—
(a) at such time and at such place as may be specified in the notice, to produce any document; or
(b) within such period as may be so specified or such longer period as the Secretary of State may allow, to furnish a copy of any document or supply any information.

(2) Any officer of the landlord designated in the notice for that purpose or having custody or control of the document or in a position to give that information shall, without instructions from the landlord, take all reasonable steps to ensure that the notice is complied with. **[648]**

NOTE to section 81
Definition: 'landlord': see s 82 below.

['Preservation of right to buy on disposal to private sector landlord

81A. Preservation of right to buy on disposal to private sector landlord.

(1) The right to buy provisions shall continue to apply where a person ceases to be a secure tenant of a house by reason of the disposal by the landlord of an interest in the house to a private sector landlord.

(2) The right to buy provisions shall not, however, continue to apply under subsection (1) in such circumstances as may be prescribed.

(3) The continued application under subsection (1) of the right to buy provisions shall be in accordance with and subject to such provision as is prescribed which may—
- (a) include—
  - (i) such additions and exceptions to, and adaptations and modifications of, the right to buy provisions in their continued application by virtue of this section; and
  - (ii) such incidental, supplementary and transitional provisions;
  as the Secretary of State considers appropriate;
- (b) differ as between different cases or descriptions of case and as between different areas;
- (c) relate to a particular disposal.

(4) Without prejudice to the generality of subsection (3), provision may be made by virtue of it—
- (a) specifying the persons entitled to the benefit of the right to buy provisions in their continued application by virtue of this section;
- (b) preventing, except with the consent of the Secretary of State, the disposal by the private sector landlord of less than his whole interest in a house in relation to which the right to buy provisions continue to apply by virtue of this section;
- (c) ensuring that where, under Ground 9 of Schedule 5 to the Housing (Scotland) Act 1988 (availability of suitable alternative accommodation), the sheriff makes an order for possession of a house in relation to which the right to buy provisions continue to apply by virtue of this section and the tenant would not have the right under this Part (other than this section) to buy the house which is or will be available by way of alternative accommodation, these provisions as so continued will apply in relation to the house which is or will be so available.

(5) In this section—
- (a) 'secure tenant' means a tenant under a secure tenancy;
- (b) 'private sector landlord' means a landlord other than one of those set out in sub-paragraphs (i) to (iv) and (viii) and (ix) of paragraph (a) of subsection (2) of section 61;
- (c) the 'right to buy provisions' means the provisions of this Act relating to the right of a tenant of a house to purchase it under this Part and to his rights in respect of a loan.] [649]

NOTES to section 81A

Section 81A was added by the Housing Act 1988 (c 50), s 128 with effect from 21 February 1992.
Definitions: 'secure tenant': see s 82 below and s 44 above; 'tenant': see s 82 below; 'house': see s 338 below.

[81B. Consultation before disposal to private sector landlord

The provisions of Schedule 6A have effect with respect to the duties of—
- (a) a local authority proposing to dispose of houses let on secure tenancies;
- (b) the Secretary of State in considering whether to give his consent under section 12(7) to such a disposal,

to have regard to the views of tenants liable as a result of the disposal to cease to be secure tenants (that is to say, tenants under secure tenancies).]

. . . [650]

NOTES to section 81B

Section 81B was added by the Housing Act 1988 (c 50), s 135 with effect from 21 February 1992.
Definitions: 'local authority', 'house': see s 338 below; 'secure tenancy': see s 82 below and s 44 above; 'tenant', 'tenancy': see s 82 below.

General

82. Interpretation of this Part.

In this Part and in sections 14, 19, 20 and 216, except where provision is made to the contrary,

'application to purchase' has the meaning assigned to it by section 63;

'family' and any reference to membership thereof shall be construed in accordance with section 83;

'fire authority' means a fire authority for the purposes of the Fire Services Acts 1947 to 1959 or a joint committee constituted by virtue of section 36(4)(b) of the Fire Services Act 1947;

'heritable proprietor', in relation to a house, includes any landlord entitled under section 3 of the Conveyancing (Scotland) Act 1924 (disposition of the dwelling-house etc by persons uninfeft) to grant a disposition of the house;

'housing co-operative' has the meaning assigned to it by section 22;

'landlord' means a person who lets a house to a tenant for human habitation, and includes his successors in title;

'offer to sell' has the meaning assigned to it by section 63(2) and includes such offer to sell as is mentioned in section 71(1)(d);

'police authority' means a police authority in Scotland within the meaning of section 2(1) or 19(9)(b) of the Police (Scotland) Act 1967 or a joint police committee constituted by virtue of subsection (2)(b) of the said section 19 and any police authority constituted in England and Wales or Northern Ireland under corresponding legislation;

'secure tenancy' means a secure tenancy within the meaning of section 44;

'tenancy' means any agreement under which a house is made available for occupation for human habitation, and 'leases', 'let' and 'lets' shall be construed accordingly;

'tenant' means a person who leases a house from a landlord and who derives his right therein directly from the landlord, and in the case of joint tenancies means all the tenants. **[651]**

83. Members of a person's family.

(1) A person is a member of another's family for the purposes of this Act if—
(a) he is the spouse of that person or he and that person live together as husband and wife; or
(b) he is that person's parent, grandparent, child, grandchild, brother, sister, uncle, aunt, nephew or niece.

(2) For the purposes of subsection (1)(b)—
(a) a relationship by marriage shall be treated as a relationship by blood;
(b) a relationship of the half-blood shall be treated as a relationship of the whole blood;
(c) the stepchild of a person shall be treated as his child; and
(d) a child shall be treated as such whether or not his parents are married. **[652]**

84. Service of notices.

(1) A notice or other document which requires to be served on a person under any provision of this Part or of section 216 may be given to him—
(a) by delivering it to him;
(b) by leaving it at his proper address; or
(c) by sending it by recorded delivery post to him at that address.

(2) For the purposes of this section and of section 7 of the Interpretation Act 1978 (references to service by post) in its application to this section, a person's proper address shall be his last known address. **[653]**

[84A. Application of right to buy in cases where landlord is lessee.

(1) Sections 61 to 84 (but not 76 or 77) and 216 (the 'right to buy' provisions) shall, with the modifications set out in this section, apply so as to provide for—
- (a) the acquisition by the tenant of a house let on a secure tenancy of the landlord's interest in the house as lessee under a registered lease of the house or of land which include it or as assignee of that interest; and
- (b) the obtaining of a loan by the tenant in that connection,

as these sections apply for the purposes of the purchase of a house by the tenant from the landlord as heritable proprietor of it and the obtaining by the tenant of a loan in that connection.

(2) References in the right to buy provisions to the purchase or sale of a house shall be construed respectively as references to the acquisition or disposal of the landlord's interest in the house by way of a registered assignation of that interest and cognate expressions shall be construed accordingly.

(3) The reference in section 61(2)(b) to the landlord's being the heritable proprietor of the house shall be construed as a reference to the landlord's being the holder of the interest of the lessee under a registered lease of the house or of land which includes it.

(4) References in the right to buy provisions to the market value of or price to be paid for a house shall be construed respectively as references to the market value of the landlord's interest in the house and to the price to be paid for acquiring that interest.

(5) References in section 64(1) to the tenant's enjoyment and use of a house as owner shall be construed as references to his enjoyment and use of it as assignee of the landlord's interest in the house.

(6) The reference in subsection (4) of section 64 to an option being offered to the landlord or to any other person to purchase the house in advance of its sale to a third party shall be construed as a reference to an option being offered to have the interest acquired by the tenant re-assigned to the landlord or assigned to the other person in advance of its being disposed of to a third party; and the references in subsection (5) and (9) of that section to an option to purchase shall be construed accordingly.

(7) In this section and section 76—
'registered lease' means a lease—
- (a) which is recorded in the general register of sasines; or
- (b) in respect of which the interest of the lessee is registered in the Land Register of Scotland

under the Registration of Leases (Scotland) Act 1857; and
'registered assignation' means, in relation to such a lease, an assignation thereof which is so recorded or in respect of which the interest of the assignee has been so registered.] **[654]**

NOTES to section 84A

Section 84A was added by the Local Government and Housing Act 1989 (c 42), s 178.
Definitions: 'tenant', 'tenancy': see s 338 below; 'secure tenancy': see s 82 below and s 44 above; 'landlord': see s 82 above.

PART IV
SUB-STANDARD HOUSES

The tolerable standard

85. General duty of local authority in respect of houses not meeting tolerable standard.

(1) It shall be the duty of every local authority to secure that all houses in their district

which do not meet the tolerable standard are closed, demolished or brought up to the tolerable standard within such period as is reasonable in all the circumstances.

(2) In determining what period is reasonable for the purposes of subsection (1), regard shall be had to alternative housing accommodation likely to be available for any persons who may be displaced from houses as a result of any action proposed by the local authority in pursuance of that subsection.

(3) Every local authority shall from time to time cause to be made such a survey or inspection of their district as may be necessary for the performance of the duty imposed on them by subsection (1) or for the purpose of ascertaining the availability of alternative housing accommodation. [655]

NOTES to section 85

Definitions: 'local authority', 'house': see s 338 below; 'the tolerable standard': see ss 338 and 86 below.

86. Definition of house meeting tolerable standard.

(1) Subject to subsection (2), a house meets the tolerable standard for the purposes of this Act if the house—
 (a) is structurally stable;
 (b) is substantially free from rising or penetrating damp;
 (c) has satisfactory provision for natural and artificial lighting, for ventilation and for heating;
 (d) has an adequate piped supply of wholesome water available within the house;
 (e) has a sink provided with a satisfactory supply of both hot and cold water within the house;
 (f) has a water closet available to the exclusive use of the occupants of the house and suitably located within the house;
 (g) has an effective system for the drainage and disposal of foul and surface water;
 (h) has satisfactory facilities for the cooking of food within the house;
 (i) has satisfactory access to all external doors and outbuildings;
and any reference to a house not meeting the tolerable standard or being brought up to the tolerable standard shall be construed accordingly.

(2) The Secretary of State may by order vary or extend or amplify the criteria set out in the foregoing subsection either generally or, after consultation with a particular local authority, in relation to the district, or any part of the district, of that authority.

(3) This section shall be without prejudice to section 114 (certain underground rooms to be treated as houses not meeting the tolerable standard). [656]

NOTES to section 86

Definitions: 'house', local authority': see s 338 below.

87. Official representation that house does not meet tolerable standard.

(1) The proper officer of the local authority may make an official representation to the authority whenever he is of opinion that any house in their district does not meet the tolerable standard.

(2) A local authority shall as soon as may be taken into consideration any official representation which has been made to them.

(3) Every representation made in pursuance of this section by the proper officer of the local authority shall be in writing. [657]

NOTES to section 87

Definitions: 'proper officer', 'local authority': see s 338 below; 'the tolerable standard': see ss 338 below and s 86 above.

Improvement order

88. Improvement of houses below tolerable standard outside housing action areas.

(1) Subject to subsections (2) and (3), where a local authority are satisfied that a house which is not situated in a housing action area does not meet the tolerable standard, they may by order require the owner of the house within a period of 180 days of the making of the order to improve the house by executing works—
   (a) to bring it up to the tolerable standard; and
   (b) to put it into a good state of repair;
and where the local authority are satisfied that the house has a future life of not less than 10 years, they may in addition require the execution of such further works of improvement as to ensure that the house will be provided with all of the standard amenities within that period.

(2) In subsection (1), reference to a house which does not meet the tolerable standard includes a reference to a house which does not have a fixed bath or shower and reference to executing works to bring it up to the tolerable standard includes reference to installing a fixed bath or shower.

(3) If the works of improvement required by an order under subsection (1) have not been completed within the said period of 180 days, the local authority may if—
   (a) they consider that satisfactory progress has been made on the works, or
   (b) they are given an undertaking in writing that the works will be completed by a date which they consider satisfactory,
amend the order to require the works to be completed within such further period as they may determine.

(4) If the works of improvement have not been completed within the period of 180 days or, as the case may be, the further period determined under subsection (3), the local authority, in order that they themselves may carry out the works required by the order under subsection (1), may acquire the house by agreement or may be authorised by the Secretary of State to acquire the house compulsorily; and the Acquisition of Land (Authorisation Procedure) (Scotland) Act 1947 shall apply in relation to any such compulsory purchase as if this Act had been in force immediately before the commencement of that Act.

(5) Paragraphs (a) to (c) of section 118(1) (persons upon whom closing and demolition orders are to be served) shall apply to orders under this section as they apply to orders under that section.

(6) Section 129 (appeals) shall apply to enable an aggrieved person to appeal against an order under this section as it applies to enable an aggrieved person to appeal against a closing order.

(7) A local authority shall make an improvement grant in accordance with Part XIII towards meeting the cost of the works which are required in pursuance of this section.

(8) The owner of the house in respect of which improvement works are required under this section may apply to the local authority for a loan to meet the cost of the works in so far as they are not met by a grant made under subsection (7); and subsections (2) to (9) of section 217 shall apply for the purposes of this subsection as they apply for the purposes of subsection (1) of that section. **[658]**

NOTES to section 88

Definitions: 'local authority', 'house', 'owner': see s 338 below; 'housing action area': see s 338 and ss 89–91 below; 'tolerable standard': see s 338 and s 86 above; 'standard amenities': see ss 338 and 244 below; 'closing order': see ss 338, 114 and 119 below; 'demolition order': see ss 338 and 115 below; 'improvement grant': see ss 338 and 236 below.

Housing action areas

89. Declaration of housing action areas for demolition.

(1) Where a local authority are satisfied—
   (a) that the houses, or the greater part of the houses, in any area in their district do not meet the tolerable standard, and
   (b) that the most effective way of dealing with the area is to apply to the area the provisions of subsection (2),

they may cause the area to be defined on a map and pass a draft resolution declaring the area so defined to be a housing action area for demolition, that is to say, an area which is to be dealt with in accordance with the provisions of subsection (2).

(2) A resolution passed under this section shall provide that a housing action area for demolition shall be dealt with by securing the demolition of all the buildings in the area but—
   (a) such an area shall not include the site of a building unless at least part of the building consists of a house which does not meet the tolerable standard;
   (b) there may be excluded from demolition any part of a building which is used for commercial purposes.

(3) For the purposes of this section and the following two sections, a house in respect of which a closing order has been made and not determined shall be deemed to be a house which does not meet the tolerable standard. **[659]**

NOTES to section 89

Definitions: 'local authority', 'the house': see s 338 below; 'the tolerable standard': see s 338 below and s 86 above; 'closing order': see ss 338, 114 and 119 below.

90. Declaration of housing action areas for improvement.

(1) Where a local authority are satisfied—
   (a) that the houses, or the greater part of the houses, in any area in their district lack one or more of the standard amenities or do not meet the tolerable standard, and
   (b) that the most effective way of dealing with the area is to apply to the area the provisions of subsection (2),

they may cause the area to be defined on a map and pass a draft resolution declaring the area so defined to be a housing action area for improvement, that is to say, an area which is to be dealt with in accordance with the provisions of that subsection.

(2) A resolution passed under this section shall provide that a housing action area for improvement shall be dealt with by securing the carrying out of such works on the houses in the area which do not meet the standard specified by the local authority under subsection (3) in respect of the area that on the completion of the works all the houses in the area will meet that standard.

(3) The standard specified by the local authority for the purpose of this section shall be that all the houses in the area—
   (a) shall meet the tolerable standard; and
   (b) shall be in a good state of repair (disregarding the state of internal decorative repair) having regard to the age, character and locality of the houses,

and, where the local authority are satisfied that the houses in the area have a future life of not less than 10 years, they may in addition specify that all the houses in the area shall be provided with all of the standard amenities.

(4) A housing action area for improvement shall not include the site of a building unless at least part of the building consists of a house which—
   (a) lacks one or more of the standard amenities, or
   (b) does not meet the tolerable standard, or
   (c) is not in a good state of repair (disregarding the state of internal decorative repair) having regard to the age, character and locality of the house. **[660]**

NOTES to section 90

Definitions: 'local authority', 'house': see s 338 below; 'standard amenities': see ss 338 and 244 below; 'the tolerable standard': see s 338 below and s 86 above.

91. Declaration of housing action areas for demolition and improvement.

(1) Where a local authority are satisfied—
- (a) that the houses, or the greater part of the houses, in any area in their district lack one or more of the standard amenities or do not meet the tolerable standard, and
- (b) that the most effective way of dealing with the area is to apply to the area the provisions of subsection (2),

they may cause the area to be defined on a map and pass a draft resolution declaring the area so defined to be a housing action area for demolition and improvement, that is to say, an area which is to be dealt with in accordance with the provisions of that subsection.

(2) Subject to subsection (4), a resolution passed under this section shall provide that a housing action area for demolition and improvement shall be dealt with by securing the demolition of some of the buildings in the area and by securing the carrying out of such works on those houses in the area which do not meet the standard specified by the local authority by virtue of subsection (3) in respect of the area, other than the houses in those buildings, that on the completion of the works all the houses then in the area will meet that standard.

(3) For the purposes of specifying the standard mentioned in subsection (2), the provisions of subsection (3) of section 90 shall apply as they apply for the purposes of specifying the standard mentioned in subsection (2) of that section.

(4) A local authority—
- (a) shall not secure the demolition of a building in a housing action area for demolition and improvement unless the greater part of the houses in the building are below the tolerable standard, and
- (b) may exclude from demolition any part of such a building which is used for commercial purposes.

(5) A housing action area for demolition and improvement shall not include the site of a building unless at least part of the building consists of a house which—
- (a) lacks one or more of the standard amenities, or
- (b) does not meet the tolerable standard, or
- (c) is not in a good state of repair (disregarding the state of internal decorative repair) having regard to the age, character and locality of the house. **[661]**

NOTES to section 91

Definitions: 'local authority', 'house': see s 338 below; 'standard amenities': see ss 338 below and 244 below; 'the tolerable standard': see s 338 below and s 86 above.

92. Provisions supplementary to sections 89 to 91.

(1) In considering whether to take action under sections 89 to 91 with respect to an area, a local authority shall have regard to any directions given by the Secretary of State, either generally or in respect of any particular authority or authorities, with regard to the identification of areas suitable to be declared to be housing action areas.

(2) If, on the application of a local authority, the Secretary of State is satisifed that in all the circumstances it is reasonable to do so, he may give directions as respects the waiving of the requirements in the said section 90(1)(a) or 91(1)(a) that the greater part of the houses in any area of that local authority's district lack one or more of the standard amenities or do not meet the tolerable standard.

(3) A draft resolution passed under the provisions of the said section 89, 90 or 91 shall specify the section under which it was made, be in such form and contain such

information about such matters as the Secretary of State may prescribe, and the Secretary of State may prescribe different requirements for the different resolutions.

(4) A draft resolution passed under the said section 90 or 91 shall, without prejudice to the generality of the foregoing provisions of this section, contain a statement as to the standard specified by the local authority under the said section 90 or by virtue of the said section 91 and a draft resolution shall identify—
   (a) where it is passed under section 89 or 91, those buildings in the area which consist of a house or houses which, in the opinion of the local authority, should be demolished;
   (b) where it is passed under section 90 or 91, those houses in the area which are below the standard specified as aforesaid and which, in the opinion of the local authority, should be brought up to that standard and do not fall within paragraph (c);
   (c) where it is passed under section 90 or 91, those houses in the area which form part of a building comprising two or more flats and which, in the opinion of the local authority—
      (i) are below the standard specified for the area as aforesaid, and
      (ii) require to be integrated with some other part or parts of that building;
   and that other part or parts of the building shall also be identified. **[662]**

NOTES to section 92

Definitions: 'local authority', 'house', 'flat': see s 338 below; 'housing action area': see s 338 below and ss 89–91 above; 'standard amenities': see ss 338 and 244 below; 'the tolerable standard': see s 338 below and s 86 above.

93. Consent to demolition of listed buildings, rehabilitation orders and compensation.

Schedule 7 (consent to demolition of listed buildings in housing action areas, rehabilitation orders and compensation) shall have effect for the purpose of making provision in relation to houses acquired in housing action areas and subject to rehabilitation orders. **[663]**

NOTES to section 93

Definitions: 'house': see s 338 below; 'housing action area': see ss 89–91 above.

Powers of Secretary of State

94. Functions of Secretary of State and duty of local authority to publish information.

(1) A local authority shall, as soon as may be after passing a draft resolution under section 89, 90 or 91, submit the draft resolution and a copy of the map to the Secretary of State.

(2) On receiving the draft resolution and a copy of the map, the Secretary of State shall send to the local authority a written acknowledgement of the receipt of the resolution and of the map.

(3) If it appears to the Secretary of State to be appropriate to do so he may, at any time within the period of 28 days beginning with the day on which he sent an acknowledgement under subsection (2)—
   (a) direct the local authority to rescind the resolution; or
   (b) notify the local authority that he does not propose to direct them to rescind the resolution; or
   (c) notify the local authority that he requires a further period for consideration of the resolution and as soon as practicable thereafter direct the local authority as mentioned in paragraph (a) or, as the case may be, notify them as mentioned in paragraph (b).

(4) As soon as may be after the date on which a local authority are notified as mentioned in subsection (3)(a), the local authority shall rescind the draft resolution.

(5) Where the local authority are notified as mentioned in subsection (3)(b) or, if after the expiry of the period of 28 days mentioned in subsection (3), the local authority have received no notification from the Secretary of State, the local authority shall as soon as may be—
 (a) publish in two or more newspapers circulating in the locality (of which one shall, if practicable, be a local newspaper) a notice that a draft resolution has been made and naming a place or places and times at which a copy of the resolution and a copy of the map may be inspected; and
 (b) serve on every owner, lessee and occupier of any premises to which the draft resolution related a notice stating the effect of the resolution.

(6) Any notice for the purposes of subsection (5) shall be in such form, contain such information and be served in such manner as the Secretary of State may prescribe; and the Secretary of State may prescribe different requirements for the different resolutions.

(7) Without prejudice to the generality of the provisions of subsection (6), a notice served under subsection (5)(b) shall state that such owner, lessee and occupier may, within two months from the date of service of the notice, make representations to the local authority concerning the draft resolution or any matter contained therein. [664]

NOTES to section 94

Definitions: 'local authority', 'owner': see s 338 below.
Sub-s (61): See the Housing (Forms) (Scotland) Regulations 1974, SI 1974/1982.

Powers of local authority

95. Further procedure, powers of local authority on acquisition of land, compensation and agricultural holdings.

(1) Part I of Schedule 8 shall have effect in relation to the procedure to be followed after publication and service of a draft resolution.

(2) Part II of Schedule 8 shall have effect in relation to the powers of a local authority acquiring land for the purposes of this Part.

(3) Part III of Schedule 8 shall have effect in relation to compensation in respect of land acquired compulsorily.

(4) Part IV of Schedule 8 shall have effect in relation to the adjustment of relations between lessors and lessees where improvements have been carried out on agricultural holdings under this Part. [665]

NOTES to section 95

Definitions: 'local authority', 'agricultural holding': see s 338 below.

96. Power of local authority to retain houses subject to demolition for temporary occupation.

(1) A local authority, who in a resolution passed under section 89 or 91 have provided that some or all of the buildings in a housing action area should be demolished, may postpone the demolition of any such building on land purchased by or belonging to the authority within that area, being a building which is, or which contains, a house which in the opinion of the authority must be continued in use as housing accommodation for the time being.

(2) Where the demolition of a building is postponed under subsection (1), the authority shall carry out such works as may in their opinion from time to time be required for rendering or keeping such house capable of being continued in use as housing accommodation pending its demolition.

(3) In respect of any house retained by a local authority under this section for use for housing purposes, the authority shall have the same powers and duties as they have in respect of houses provided under Part I. **[666]**

NOTES to section 96

Definitions: 'local authority', 'house': see s 338 below; 'housing action area': see s 338 below and ss 89–91 above.

97. Local authority may control occupation of houses in housing action area.

(1) Subject to subsection (3) of this section, a local authority may—
   (a) as soon as practicable after they receive notification under section 94(3)(b), or
   (b) if after the expiry of the period of 28 days mentioned in section 94(3) they have received no notification from the Secretary of State;

make an order in the prescribed form prohibiting the occupation of the houses in the area which have been identified in accordance with section 92(4)(a) and (c) except with the consent of the authority.

(2) Within 28 days of making an order under this section, the local authority shall serve a notice in the prescribed form in respect of every such house in the housing action area—
   (a) upon the person having control of the house, and
   (b) upon any other person who is an owner or occupier of the house,
stating that the order has been made and indicating the effect of the order.

(3) An order made under this section shall not prohibit the occupation of a house in the area by a person occupying it on the date of the service of the notice in respect of the house under subsection (2).

(4) If any person, knowing that an order has been made under this section, occupies or permits to be occupied a house after the date of the service of the notice in respect of the house under subsection (2) in contravention of the order, he shall be guilty of an offence and shall be liable on summary conviction—
   (a) to a fine not exceeding level 5 on the standard scale or to imprisonment for a term not exceeding 3 months or to both such fine and such imprisonment; and
   (b) in the case of a continuing offence to a further fine of £5 for every day or part of a day which he occupies the house, or permits it to be occupied, after conviction.

(5) Where an owner or a person having control of a house in respect of which an order under this section is served considers that it is unreasonable in all the circumstances of the case that the order should continue to apply to the house, he may apply to the local authority to revoke the order in respect of the house.

(6) Where an applicant for a revocation under subsection (5) is aggrieved by the refusal of the local authority to revoke the order, he may appeal to the sheriff by giving notice of appeal within 21 days of the date of the refusal.

(7) An order made under this section shall cease to have effect in relation to any house affected by any of the following events, that is to say—
   (a) on the date on which the local authority revoke an order under subsection (5);
   (b) on the date of the passing of a final resolution under paragraph 1 of Schedule 8 identifying a house in accordance with that paragraph as read with section 92(4)(b);
   (c) on the date of the rescinding of a draft resolution under paragraph 1 of Schedule 8;
   (d) in the case where the Secretary of State, in refusing to confirm an order for compulsory purchase submitted to him under paragraph 5 of Schedule 8, directs that any order made under this section shall cease to apply either generally or in respect of individual houses, on the date of that direction;
   (e) in the case where the Secretary of State, in modifying in accordance with the provisions of paragraph 5(3)(e) of Schedule 8 an order for compulsory purchase submitted to him under that paragraph, directs that any order made under this section shall cease to apply either generally or in respect of individual houses, on the date of that direction. **[667]**

NOTES to section 97

Definitions: 'local authority', 'prescribed', 'house', 'owner': see s 338 below; 'the standard scale': see the Criminal Procedure (Scotland) Act 1975 (c 21), s 289G and the Increase of Criminal Penalties (Scotland) Order 1984, SI 1984/526. Level 5 is currently £2000.

98. Obligation of local authorities in relation to rehousing in housing action areas.

Where a person is to be displaced as a result of implementation of the provisions of this Part, and where a local authority are under a duty by virtue of section 36 of the Land Compensation (Scotland) Act 1973 to rehouse him, the authority shall, if so requested by that person and in so far as practicable, secure that he will be provided with suitable alternative accommodation within a reasonable distance from the locality of the house from which he is to be displaced. [668]

NOTES to section 98

Definition: 'local authority': see s 338 below.

Landlords and tenants in housing action areas

99. Application to sheriff for possession where house is identified in accordance with paragraph 1(1) of Schedule 8 as read with section 92(4)(a).

(1) Where—
(a) an owner of a house has received a notice stating the effect of a final resolution passed under paragraph 1(1) of Schedule 8, which identifies the building of which the house consists or forms part in accordance with that paragraph as read with section 92 (4)(a);
(b) the owner of the house is willing to secure the demolition of the building of which the house consists or forms part; and
(c) the owner cannot obtain vacant possession of the house by agreement with the tenant thereof,
then, whether or not the tenancy of that house has been terminated, the owner may apply to the sheriff for an order for possession of that house.

(2) Any such order shall require the tenant to vacate the house within such period, not being less than 4 weeks nor more than 6 weeks from the date of the order, as the sheriff may determine and, where any tenancy of that house has not previously been terminated, such order shall have the effect of terminating that tenancy as from the date of the order.

(3) Any order made under this section may be made subject to such conditions (including conditions with respect to the payment of money by any party to the proceedings to any other party thereto by way of adjustment of rent or compensation for any improvements carried out by the tenant) as the sheriff may think just and equitable, having regard to the respective rights, obligations and liabilities of the parties and to all the cicumstances of the case, but no such order shall be made unless the sheriff is satisfied that suitable alternative accommodation on reasonable terms will be available to the tenant. [669]

NOTES to section 99

Definitions: 'owner', 'house', 'tenant': see s 338 below.

100. Application to sheriff for possession where house is identified in accordance with paragraph 1(1) of Schedule 8 as read with section 92(4)(c).

(1) Where—
(a) an owner of a house has received a notice stating the effect of a final resolution passed under paragraph 1(1) of Schedule 8 which identifies the house in accordance with that paragraph as read with section 92(4)(c);

(b) the owner of the house is also the owner of the other part or parts of the building of which the house forms part which have been identified as aforesaid as requiring to be integrated with that house, in whole or in part;
(c) the owner of the house is willing to carry out the necessary works of integration as aforesaid; and
(d) the owner cannot obtain vacant possession of the house or of the said other part or part of the building by agreement with any tenant thereof,

then, whether or not the tenancy of that house or of the said other part or parts of the building has been terminated, the owner may apply to the sheriff for an order for posession of that house or of the said other part or parts of the building.

(2) The provisions of section 99(2) and (3) shall apply to an order made under this section as they apply to an order made under that section but, without prejudice to the generality of the provisions of those subsections, the sheriff shall, before imposing any such conditions as are referred to in section 99(3), have regard as to whether the owner has offered to any tenant, who will be required to vacate the house by an order under this section, a tenancy of a house which will include in whole or in part that house. [670]

NOTES to section 100
Definitions: 'owner', 'house', 'tenant': see s 338 below.

101. Application to sheriff for possession where house is identified in accordance with paragraph 1 of Schedule 8 as read with section 92(4)(b).

(1) Where—
(a) an owner of a house has received a notice stating the effect of a final resolution passed under paragraph 1(1) of Schedule 8, which identifies the house in accordance with that paragraph as read with section 92(4)(b);
(b) the owner of the house is willing to carry out the necessary works to bring the house up to the standard specified for the area by the local authority under section 90(3) or, as the case may be, by virtue of section 91(3);
(c) those works cannot be carried out without the consent of the tenant of that house or without the house being vacated temporarily; and
(d) the tenant refuses to consent to the carrying out of those works or to vacate the house,

then the owner may apply to the sheriff for an order authorising the owner to enter the house and carry out those works, and, on any such application, the sheriff may, if he considers that it is necessary for the house to be vacated to enable the works to be carried out, order the tenant to vacate the house for such period, beginning not less than 4 weeks from the date of the order, as the sheriff may determine.

(2) Any order made under this section may be made subject to such conditions (including conditions with respect to the payment of rent payable under the tenancy during the carrying out of the works and as to the period during which the house is to be vacated) as the sheriff may think just and equitable, having regard to all the circumstances of the case, but no such order shall be made unless the sheriff is satisfied that suitable alternative accommodation on reasonable terms will be available to the tenant. [671]

NOTES to section 101
Definitions: 'owner', 'house', 'tenant': see s 338 below.

102. Procedure; and application of s 103(1) of Rent (Scotland) Act 1984.

Any application made to the sheriff under this Part shall be made by way of summary application and the provisions of section 103(1) of the Rent (Scotland) Act 1984 shall apply to any such application as they apply to an application made under any of the provisions referred to in subsection (2) of that section. [672]

103. Certain provisions of Rent (Scotland) Act 1984 not to apply.

Nothing in the Rent (Scotland) Act 1984 [or in Part II of the Housing (Scotland) Act 1988] restricting the power of a court to make an order for possession of a dwelling-house shall apply to any application made to the sheriff or to any order made by the sheriff under this part. [673]

NOTE to section 103
Amendment: Section 103 was amended by the Housing (Scotland) Act 1988 (c 43), s 72, Sch 9, para 12.

104. Effect of refusal to make order on validity of resolution.

Where, in relation to any application under this Part, the sheriff refuses to make the order sought, that refusal shall not affect the validity of any resolution passed by the local authority under this Part or any rights or obligations of the local authority under this Part or under any other enactment relating to housing. [674]

NOTES to section 104
Definition: 'local authority': see s 338 below.

Miscellaneous

105. Exclusion of houses controlled by Crown.

(1) No order under section 88 nor any notice of a final resolution under Part I of Schedule 8 may be served in respect of a house in which there is a Crown interest except with the consent of the appropriate authority and, where a notice of a final resolution is served with the consent of the appropriate authority, this Part shall apply in relation to the house as it applies in relation to a house in which there is no such interest.

(2) If, after a notice of a final resolution as aforesaid has been served in respect of any house in which there is a Crown interest, the appropriate authority becomes the person having control of the house, any such notice shall cease to have effect.

(3) In this section, 'Crown interest' means an interest belonging to Her Majesty in right of the Crown or belonging to a government department, or held in trust for Her Majesty for the purposes of a government department, and 'the appropriate authority'—
  (a) in relation to land belonging to Her Majesty in right of the Crown and forming part of the Crown Estate, means the Crown Estate Commissioners, and, in relation to any other land belonging to Her Majesty in right of the Crown, means the government department having the management of that land;
  (b) in relation to land belonging to a government department or held in trust for Her Majesty for the purposes of a government department, means that department,
and if any question arises as to what authority is the appropriate authority in relation to any land, that question shall be referred to the Treasury, whose decision shall be final. [675]

NOTES to section 105
Definitions: 'house', 'land': see s 338 below.

106. Power of local authority to arrange for the execution of works of improvement by agreement with the owner.

A local authority may by agreement with an owner of a house at his expense execute, or arrange for the execution of, any works of improvement or of repair to which this Part or Part V or Part XIII applies which the local authority and the owner agree are necessary or desirable. [676]

NOTES to section 106

Definitions: 'local authority', 'owner', 'house': see s 338 below.

107. Conditions may be attached to sale of below-standard local authority houses.

Where a house on land acquired or appropriated by a local authority for the purposes of Part I lacks one or more of the standard amenities or does not meet the tolerable standard, the local authority may make the sale by them of that house conditional on the purchaser providing the house with the standard amenities which it lacks or bringing the house up to the tolerable standard. [677]

NOTES to section 107

Definitions: 'house': see s 338 below; 'land', 'local authority', 'standard amenities': see ss 338 and 244 below; 'the tolerable standard': see s 338 below and s 86 above.

PART V
REPAIR OF HOUSES

Repair notices

108. Power of local authority to secure repair of house in state of serious disrepair.

(1) Where a local authority are satisfied that any house in their district is in a state of serious disrepair, they may serve upon the person having control of the house a repair notice.

(2) A repair notice shall—
(a) require that person to execute the works necessary to rectify such defects as are specified in the notice within such reasonable time, being not less than 21 days, as may be specified in the notice, and
(b) state that, in the opinion of the local authority, the rectification of those defects will bring the house up to such a standard of repair as is reasonable having regard to the age, character and location, and disregarding the internal decorative repair, of the house.

(3) Subject to subsection (5), if a notice under subsection (1) is not complied with, the local authority—
(a) may themselves execute the works necessary to rectify the defects specified in the notice or in the notice as varied by the sheriff, as the case may be, and
(b) may in addition execute any further works which are found to be necessary for the purpose of bringing the house up to the standard of repair referred to in subsection (2)(b), but which could not reasonably have been ascertained to be required prior to the service of the notice.

(4) Any question as to whether further works are necessary or could not have been reasonably ascertained under subsection (3)(b) shall be determined by the sheriff, whose decision shall be final.

(5) The local authority shall not execute any work under subsection (3) until—
(a) the expiration of the time specified in the repair notice; or
(b) if an appeal against the notice has been made and the notice confirmed with or without variation by the sheriff, the expiration of 21 days from the date of the determination of the appeal or such longer period as the sheriff may order.

(6) Any action taken under this section or under section 109 shall be without prejudice to any other powers of the local authority or any remedy available to the tenant of a house against his landlord under any enactment or rule of law.

(7) Where a local authority are of the opinion that a house in their district is in need of repair although not in a state of serious disrepair and that it is likely to deteriorate rapidly, or to cause material damage to another house, if nothing is done to repair it, they may treat it as being in a state of serious disrepair for the purposes of this Part.

(8) In this Part, 'house' includes a building which comprises or includes—
(a) a house or houses; or
(b) a house or houses and other premises. [678]

NOTES to section 108
Definitions: 'local authority', 'house': see s 338 below.

109. Recovery by local authority of expenses under s 108.

(1) Subject to the provisions of this section, any expenses incurred by a local authority under section 108(3), together with interest from the date when a demand for the expenses is served until payment, may be recovered by the authority from—
(a) the person having control of the house, or
(b) if he receives the rent of the house as trustee, tutor, curator, factor or agent or of some other person, from him or from that other person, or in part from him and in part from that other person.

(2) A local authority may apportion any such expenses among the persons having control of the houses and other premises comprised in the building.

(3) The local authority may by order declare any such expenses to be payable by weekly, monthly, half-yearly or annual instalments within a period not exceeding 30 years with interest from the date of the service of the demand until the whole amount is paid, and any such instalments and interest, or any part thereof, may be recovered from any owner or occupier of the house, and, if recovered from an occupier, may be deducted by him from the rent of the house.

(4) Any interest payable under subsection (1) or subsection (3) of this section shall be at such reasonable rate as the local authority may determine.

(5) The provisions of Schedule 9 shall have effect for the purpose of enabling a local authority to make a charging order in respect of any expenses incurred by them under section 108(3) in relation to a house or building. [679]

NOTES to section 109
Definitions: 'local authority', 'house': see s 338 below.

110. Recovery by lessee of proportion of expenses incurred in repairing house.

(1) Where the tenant of a house or his agent has—
(a) incurred expenditure in complying with a repair notice, or in paying the expenses of a local authority who have carried out the works specified in such a notice, and
(b) intimated service of the notice and its purport to the landlord under the lease in writing within 14 days after such service,
the tenant or the landlord may, in the absence of any agreement between them, apply to the sheriff to determine what part, if any, of the expenditure is payable by the landlord to the tenant.

(2) In determining an application under subsection (1), the sheriff shall make such determination as he thinks fit having regard to—
(a) the obligations of the landlord and the tenant under the lease with respect to the repair of the house;
(b) the length of the unexpired term of the lease;
(c) the rent payable under the lease; and
(d) all other relevant circumstances.

(3) Where the sheriff makes an order for payment by the landlord to the tenant, and the landlord in question is himself a tenant of the house under another lease, he shall be treated for the purposes of this section as being a tenant who has incurred expenditure under subsection (1)(a).

(4) In this section 'lease' includes a sublease and any tenancy, and the expressions 'landlord' and 'tenant' shall be construed accordingly. **[680]**

NOTES to section 110
Definitions: 'house,' 'local authority': see s 338 below.

Appeals etc

111. Appeals under Part V.

(1) Any person aggrieved by—
  (a) a repair notice,
  (b) a demand for the recovery of expenses incurred by a local authority in executing works, specified in such a notice,
  (c) an order made by a local authority with respect to any such expenses,
  (d) a charging order made under Schedule 9,
may appeal to the sheriff by giving notice of appeal within 21 days after the date of the service of the notice, demand or order, as the case may be; and no proceedings shall be taken by the local authority to enforce any notice, demand or order while an appeal against it is pending.

(2) On an appeal under paragraph (b), (c) or (d) of subsection (1), no question shall be raised which might have been raised on an appeal against the original notice requiring the execution of the works. **[681]**

NOTE to section 111
Definition: 'local authority': see s 338 below.

112. Date of operation of notices, demands and orders subject to appeal.

Any notice, demand or order against which an appeal might be brought to the sheriff under section 111 shall—
  (a) if no such appeal is brought, become operative on the expiration of 21 days after the date of the service of the notice, demand or order, as the case may be, and shall be final and conclusive as to any matters which could have been raised on such an appeal, and
  (b) if such an appeal is brought shall, if and so far as it is confirmed by the sheriff, become operative as from the date of the determination of the appeal. **[682]**

Landlord and tenant

113. Obligations to repair.

Schedule 10 shall have effect in relation to the landlord's obligation under certain leases to repair the subjects let. **[683]**

PART VI
CLOSING AND DEMOLITION ORDERS

Powers of local authority

114. Closing order.

(1) Where a local authority, on consideration of an official representation or a report by the proper officer or other information in their possession, are satisfied that

any house does not meet the tolerable standard and that it ought to be demolished and—
(a) the house forms only part of a building, and
(b) the building does not comprise only houses which do not meet the tolerable standard,
the local authority may make a closing order prohibiting the use of the house for human habitation.

(2) A closing order shall have effect from such date as may be specified in the order, not being less than 28 days from the date on which it comes into operation.

(3) In this section, 'house' includes any room habitually used as a sleeping place, the surface of the floor of which is more than 3 feet below the surface of the part of the street adjoining or nearest to the room (an 'underground room').

(4) An underground room does not meet the tolerable standard for the purpose of this section if—
(a) it is not an average of 7 feet in height from floor to ceiling, or
(b) it does not comply with such regulations as the local authority may make for securing the proper ventilation and lighting of such rooms and the protection thereof against dampness, effluvia or exhalation.

(5) If a local authority, after being required to do so by the Secretary of State, fail to make regulations under subsection (4)(b), the Secretary of State may himself make regulations which shall [have] effect as if they had been made by the authority under that subsection. [684]

NOTES to section 114

Amendment: Sub-s (5) was amended by the Housing (Scotland) Act 1988 (c 43), s 72, Sch 7, para 3.
Definitions: 'local authority', 'proper officer': see s 338 below; 'house': *Ibid*, and s 133 below; 'building': see s 133 below; 'tolerable standard': see s 338 below and s 86 above.

115. Demolition order.

Where a local authority, on consideration of an official representation or a report by the proper officer or other information in their possession, are satisfied that any building comprises only a house which does not meet, or houses which do not meet, the tolerable standard and that the house or, as the case may be, houses, ought to be demolished, they may, subject to section 119, make a demolition order requiring—
(a) that the building shall be vacated within such period as may be specified in the order, not being less than 28 days from the date on which the order comes into operation, and
(b) that the building shall be demolished within 6 weeks after the expiration of that period or, if the building is not vacated before the expiration of the period, within 6 weeks after the date on which it is vacated. [685]

NOTES to section 115

Definitions: 'local authority', 'proper officer': see s 338 below; 'house': *Ibid*, and s 133 below; 'building': see s 133 below; 'tolerable standard': see s 338 below and s 86 above.

116. Revocation of closing and demolition order.

If in the case of a house in respect of which a closing order has been made or a building in respect of which a demolition order has been made the local authority are satisfied, on an application made by any owner of the house or building, or any person appearing to the authority to have reasonable cause for making the application, that the house has, or, as the case may be, the house or houses comprised in the building have, been brought up to the tolerable standard, they shall make an order revoking the closing order or, as the case may be, the demolition order. [686]

NOTES to section 116

Definitions: 'house': see ss 338 and 133 below; 'closing order': see ss 338 and 119 below and s 114 above; 'building': see s 133 below; 'demolition order': see s 338 below and s 115 above; 'local authority', 'owner': see s 338 below; 'the tolerable standard': see s 338 below and s 86 above.

117. Undertakings to bring up to tolerable standard and suspension order.

(1) Where a closing order or a demolition order has been made in respect of a house or building and not revoked, any owner of the house or building, or any person holding a heritable security over it, may give to the local authority, within a period of 21 days from the date of service of the order or such longer period therefrom as the authority may, either during or after the expiry of the 21 days, determine to be appropriate, an undertaking in writing—
  (a) that he will within a specified period carry out such works as will, in the opinion of the local authority, bring the house or, as the case may be, all the houses in the building, up to the tolerable standard; or
  (b) in the case of a building in respect of which a demolition order has been made, that no house in the building will be used for human habitation (unless at any time all the houses therein are brought up to the tolerable standard and the local authority agree that they have been so brought).

(2) If an undertaking is so given the local authority shall as soon as may be either—
  (a) accept the undertaking and make in respect of it a suspension order suspending the closing order or, as the case may be, the demolition order, or
  (b) reject the undertaking and serve on the person who gave the undertaking notice that they have done so.

(3) A suspension order shall cease to have effect on the expiry of one year from the date of its making unless renewed, at the discretion of the local authority, at the expiry of that year; and this subsection shall apply to any suspension order so renewed as it applies to the original order.

(4) A suspension order made or renewed by a local authority may be revoked by them at any time by order if they have reasonable cause to believe that there had been a breach of the undertaking in respect of which it was made or renewed.

(5) Any period—
  (a) between the service of the closing order or demolition order and the service of a suspension order or a notice of rejection under subsection (2), and
  (b) while a suspension order is in force,
shall be left out of account in reckoning in relation to the closing order or demolition order in question the period of 21 days referred to in sections 129(1) and 130. **[687]**

NOTES to section 117

Definitions: 'closing order': see ss 338 and 119 below and s 114 above; 'demolition order': see s 338 below and s 115 above; 'house': see ss 338 and 133 below; 'building': see s 133 below; 'owner', 'local authority': see s 338 below; 'the tolerable standard': see s 338 below and s 86 above.

118. Service.

(1) Any order made or notice issued under sections 114 to 117 in respect of a house or building shall be served—
  (a) upon the person having control of the house or, as the case may be, the house or houses comprised in the building;
  (b) upon any other person who is an owner of the house or, as the case may be, any of those houses;
  (c) upon any person holding a heritable security over the house or, as the case may be, any of those houses, unless it appears to the local authority, after exercising their powers under section 325, that there is no such person; and

(d) where an application has been made in relation to the house, or, as the case may be, those houses, under section 116, by a person upon whom the order or notice is not required to be served apart from this paragraph, upon that person.

(2) In subsection (1), references to an owner of, and to any person holding a heritable security over, a building shall be construed as including respectively references to an owner of, and to any person holding a heritable security over, any part of the building. [688]

NOTES to section 118

Definitions: 'house': see ss 338 and 133 below; 'building': see s 133 below; 'owner', 'local authority': see s 338 below.

119. Listed buildings and houses subject to building preservation orders.

(1) Where apart from this section a local authority would be empowered to make a demolition order under this Part with respect to a building—
(a) in relation to which a building preservation notice served under section 56 of the Town and Country Planning (Scotland) Act 1972 is in force, or
(b) which is a listed building within the meaning of section 52(7) of that Act,
they shall not make a demolition order but instead may make a closing order or closing orders under this section in respect of the house or houses comprised in the building.

(2) Where a building to which a demolition order made under this Part by a local authority applies (whether or not that order has become operative) becomes—
(a) subject to a building preservation notice served under the said section 56, or
(b) a listed building within the meaning of the said section 52(7),
the local authority shall revoke the demolition order and may make a closing order or closing orders in respect of the house or houses comprised in the building.

(3) The provisions of sections 114(1), 116, 117 and 118 shall, subject to any necessary modifications, have effect in relation to a closing order made under this section as they have effect in relation to a closing order made under those sections. [689]

NOTES to section 119

Definitions: 'local authority': see s 338 below; 'building': see s 133 below; 'demolition order': see s 338 below and s 115 above; 'closing order': see s 338 below and s 114 above.

120. Powers of local authority in relation to building consisting wholly of closed houses.

(1) Where a building consists wholly of houses with respect to which closing orders have become operative and none of those orders has been revoked or is subject to a suspension order, then—
(a) the local authority may revoke the closing orders and make a demolition order under section 115 in respect of the whole building, but section 117 shall not apply to the order; or
(b) the local authority may purchase the land by agreement or may, subject to the provisions of this section, be authorised by the Secretary of State to purchase it compulsorily.

(2) The provisions of the Acquisition of Land (Authorisation Procedure) (Scotland) Act 1947 shall apply in relation to the compulsory purchase of land under subsection (1)(b) as if that subsection had been in force immediately before the commencement of that Act.

(3) The compensation to be paid for land purchased compulsorily under this section shall be assessed by the Lands Tribunal in accordance with the Land Compensation (Scotland) Act 1963 subject, however, to the provisions of subsections (4) and (5).

(4) The compensation payable under this section shall not (except by virtue of paragraph 3 of Schedule 2 to the said Act of 1963) exceed the value, at the time when the

valuation is made, of the site as a cleared site available for development in accordance with the requirements of the building regulations for the time being in force in the district.

(5) The references in subsections (3) and (4) to compensation are references to the compensation payable in respect of the purchase exclusive of any compensation for disturbance or for severance or for injurious affection.

(6) Where a local authority acquire land by virtue of this section, the provisions of paragraph 8(b) of Schedule 8 shall apply as if the land were in a housing action area and had been purchased for the purpose of demolishing the buildings thereon.   **[690]**

NOTES to section 120

Definitions: 'building': see s 133 below; 'house': see ss 338 below and 133 below; 'closing order': see ss 338 below and ss 114 and 119 above; 'suspension order': see s 117 above; 'local authority', 'land', 'Lands Tribunal', 'building regulations': see s 338 below; 'housing action area': see s 338 below and ss 89–91 above.

---

121. Local authority may acquire and repair house or building liable to closing or demolition order.

(1) If, in relation to any house or building to which this section applies, it appears to a local authority that having regard to—
(a) its existing condition;
(b) the needs of the area for the provision of further housing accommodation;
the house or building must remain in use as housing accommodation, they may purchase it.

(2) This section applies to any house or building in respect of which the local authority may make—
(a) a closing order under section 114; or
(b) a demolition order under section 115 or 120(1).

(3) Where a local authority determine to purchase a house or building under subsection (1), they shall serve notice of the determination on every person on whom they would be required under section 118(1) to serve a closing order or a demolition order made in respect of the house or building, and at any time after that notice comes into operation the local authority may purchase the house or building by agreement or may be authorised by the Secretary of State to purchase it compulsorily.

(4) The provisions of the Acquisition of Land (Authorisation Procedure) (Scotland) Act 1947 shall apply in relation to the compulsory purchase of a house or building under this section as if this section had been in force immediately before the commencement of that Act.

(5) The compensation to be paid for any house or building purchased compulsorily under this section shall be assessed by the Lands Tribunal in accordance with the Land Compensation (Scotland) Act 1963 subject, however, to the provisions of subsections (6) and (7).

(6) The compensation payable under this section shall not (except by virtue of paragraph 3 of Schedule 2 to the said Act of 1963) exceed the value, at the time when the valuation is made, of the site as a cleared site available for development in accordance with the requirements of the building regulations for the time being in force in the area.

(7) The references in subsections (5) and (6) to compensation are references to the compensation payable in respect of the purchase exclusive of any compensation for disturbance or for severance or for injurious affection.

(8) A local authority by whom a house or building is purchased under this section shall carry out such works as may in the opinion of the authority from time to time be required for rendering or keeping it capable of being continued in use as housing accommodation.

(9) In respect of any house purchased by a local authority under this section, the authority shall have the like powers and duties as they have in respect of houses provided under Part I. [691]

NOTES to section 121

Definitions: 'house': see ss 338 and 133 below; 'building': see s 133 below; 'local authority', 'Lands Tribunal', 'building regulations': see s 338 below; 'closing order': see s 338 below and ss 114 and 119 above; 'demolition order': see s 338 below and s 115 above.

Offences

122. Penalty for use of premises in contravention of closing order or of undertaking.

(1) If any person—
(a) knowing that a closing order made under section 114 or section 119 has become operative and applies to any premises, uses those premises or permits those premises to be used for human habitation without having obtained the consent of the local authority to the use of the premises for that purpose; or
(b) knowing that an undertaking that any premises shall not be used for human habitation has been accepted by the local authority under this Part, uses those premises for human habitation or permits them to be so used,
he shall be guilty of an offence.

(2) Any person guilty of an offence under subsection (1) shall be liable on summary conviction—
(a) to a fine not exceeding level 5 on the standard scale, or to imprisonment for a term not exceeding 3 months or to both such fine and such imprisonment; and
(b) in the case of a continuing offence, to a further fine of £5 for every day or part of a day on which he so used those premises, or permits them to be so used, after conviction. [692]

NOTES to section 122

Definitions: 'closing order': see s 338 below and s 119 above; 'local authority': see s 338 below; 'the Standard Scale': see the Criminal Procedure (Scotland) Act 1975 (c 21), s 289G (2), and the Increase of Criminal Penalties Etc (Scotland) Order 1984, SI 1984/526. Level 5 is currently £2000.

Powers of local authority following demolition order

123. Procedure where demolition order made.

(1) When a demolition order has become operative, the owner of the building to which it applies shall demolish the building within the time limited in that behalf by the order; and, if the building is not demolished within that time, the local authority may enter and demolish the building and sell the material thereof.

(2) Any expenses incurred by a local authority under subsection (1), after giving credit for any amount realised by the sale of materials, may be recovered by them from the owner of the building, and any surplus in the hands of the authority shall be paid by them to the owner of the building.

(3) In the application of this section to a demolition order made in respect of a building comprising two or more parts separately owned—
(a) any reference to the owner of the building shall be construed as a reference to the owners of the several parts comprised in the building;
(b) without prejudice to the powers of the local authority under subsection (1), the duty imposed by that subsection on the owners of the several parts comprised in the building to demolish the building shall be regarded as a duty to arrange jointly for the demolition of the building; and

(c) subsection (2) shall have effect subject to the proviso that any sum recoverable or payable by the local authority under that subsection shall be recoverable from or payable to the several owners in such proportions as the owners may agree or, failing agreement, as shall be determined by an arbiter, nominated by the owners or, failing such nomination, nominated on the application of the authority or any of the owners, by the sheriff. **[693]**

NOTES to section 123

Definitions: 'demolition order': see s 338 below and s 115 above; 'owner', 'local authority': see s 338 below; 'building': see s 133 below.

124. Power of local authority to purchase site of demolished building where expenses of demolition cannot be recovered.

(1) Where a local authority have demolished a building in exercise of the powers conferred on them by section 123 and the expenses thereby incurred by them cannot be recovered by reason of the fact that the owner of the building cannot be found, the authority may be authorised by the Secretary of State to purchase compulsorily the site of the building, including the area of any yard, garden or pertinent belonging to the building or usually enjoyed therewith.

(2) The provisions of the Acquisition of Land (Authorisation Procedure) (Scotland) Act 1947 shall apply in relation to a compulsory purchase of land under subsection (1) as if that subsection had been in force immediately before the commencement of that Act.

(3) A local authority shall be entitled to deduct from the compensation payable on the compulsory purchase of the site of a building under this section the amount of the expenses referred to in subsection (1) so far as not otherwise recovered.

(4) A local authority shall deal with any land purchased by them under this section by sale, letting or appropriation in accordance with the provisions of paragraph 8 of Schedule 8. **[694]**

NOTES to section 124

Definitions: 'local authority', 'owner', 'land': see s 338 below; 'building': see s 133 below.

Demolition of obstructive buildings

125. Local authority may by resolution require demolition of obstructive building.

(1) A local authority may serve upon the owner or owners of a building which appears to the authority to be an obstructive building notice of the time (being some time not less than one month after the service of the notice) and place at which the question of demolishing the building will be considered by the authority.

(2) Where a local authority serve a notice under subsection (1) on an owner of a building, they shall at the same time require him to furnish within two weeks thereafter a written statement specifying the name and address of the superior of whom such owner holds, and of any person holding a heritable security over the owner's interest in the building, and the authority shall as soon as may be after receipt of such statement serve on any person whose name is included therein, notice of the time and place at which the question of domolishing the building will be considered.

(3) Any person on whom a notice is served under subsection (1) or (2) shall be entitled to be heard when the question of demolishing the building to which the notice relates is taken into consideration.

(4) If after so taking the matter into consideration the local authority are satisfied that the building is an obstructive building and that the building or any part thereof ought to be demolished, they may pass a resolution that the building or that part thereof shall be

demolished and may, by such resolution, require that the building, or such part thereof as is required to be vacated for the purposes of the demolition, shall be vacated within two months from the date on which the resolution becomes operative, and, if they do so, shall serve a copy of the resolution upon the owner or owners of the building.

(5) If any person fails to give to the local authority any information required by them under subsection (2) or knowingly makes any mis-statement with reference thereto, he shall be guilty of an offence and shall be liable on summary conviction to a fine not exceeding level 1 on the standard scale.

(6) In this section, the expression 'obstructive building' means a building which, by reason only of its contact with, or proximity to, other buildings, is injurious or dangerous to health.

(7) This section shall not apply to a building which is the property of public undertakers, unless it is used for the purposes of a dwelling, showroom or office, or which is the property of a local authority. [695]

NOTES to section 125

Definitions: 'local authority', 'owner', 'public undertaker': see s 338 below; 'building': see s 133 below; 'the Standard Scale': see the Criminal Procedure (Scotland) Act 1975 (c 21), s 289G and the Increase of Criminal Penalties Etc (Scotland) Order 1984, SI 1984/526. Level 1 is currently £50.

126. Effect of resolution for demolition of obstructive building.

(1) Subject to the provisions of this section, where a local authority have made a resolution and required a building to be vacated under section 125(4), they shall be bound to purchase the building if the owner offers to sell it to them.

(2) On purchasing a building under this section, the local authority shall demolish it as soon as possible after they obtain possession of it.

(3) A local authority shall only be bound to purchase the building if—
(a) the offer is made before the expiry of the period within which the resolution requires it to be vacated; and
(b) the acquisition of the owner's interest would, apart from section 125, enable them to demolish the building.

(4) The offer to sell shall be at a price to be assessed by the Lands Tribunal in accordance with the Land Compensation (Scotland) Act 1963, as modified by Schedule 1, as if it were compensation for compulsory purchase.

(5) If no such offer as is mentioned in subsection (1) is made before the expiry of the said period, the local authority shall, as soon as may be thereafter, carry out the demolition and shall have the like right to sell the materials rendered available thereby as if they had purchased the building.

(6) Where the demolition of a building is carried out under subsection (5), compensation shall be paid by the local authority to the owner in respect of loss arising from the demolition, and that compensation shall, notwithstanding that no land is acquired compulsorily by the authority, be assessed by the Lands Tribunal in accordance with the said Act of 1963, as modified by Schedule 1, except that paragraphs (2) to (6) of section 12 of the said Act of 1963 shall not apply and that paragraph (1) of the said section 12 shall have effect with the substitution, for the reference to acquisition, of a reference to demolition. [696]

NOTES to section 126

Definitions: 'local authority', 'owner', 'Lands Tribunal': see s 338 below; 'building': see s 133 below.

Possession

127. Recovery of possession of building or house subject to closing order, etc.

(1) Where a closing order, a demolition order, or a resolution passed under section 125 has become operative, the local authority shall serve on the occupier of any building or house or any part thereof to which the order or resolution relates a notice—
   (a) stating the effect of the order or resolution, and
   (b) specifying the date by which the order or resolution requires the building or house to be vacated, and
   (c) requiring the occupier to remove from the building or house before the said date or before the expiration of 28 days from the service of the notice, whichever may be the later.

(2) If at any time after the date on which a notice under subsection (1) requires a building or house to be vacated, any person is in occupation of the building or house or of any part of it, the local authority or any owner of the building or house may make a summary application for removal and ejection to the sheriff.

(3) The sheriff may, after requiring service of such additional notice (if any) as he thinks fit, grant warrant for ejection giving vacant possession of the building or house or of the part of it in question to the authority or owner, as the case may be, within such period, not being less than 2 weeks nor more than 4 weeks, as the sheriff may determine.

(4) Subject to subsection (5), any expenses incurred by a local authority under this section in obtaining possession of any building or house or part thereof may be recovered by them from the owner of the building or house.

(5) Subsection (4) does not apply to expenses incurred in obtaining possession of—
   (a) premises to which a resolution passed under section 125 applies; or
   (b) any other premises unless the owner has failed to make within a reasonable time a summary application for removal and ejection to the sheriff or, having made such an application, has failed to take all steps necessary to have the application disposed of within a reasonable time.

(6) Any person who, knowing that a demolition order or a resolution passed under section 125 has become operative and applies to any building or house, enters into occupation of that building or house or any part of it after the date by which the order or resolution requires that building or house to be vacated, or permits any other person to enter into such occupation after that date, shall be guilty of an offence and shall be liable on summary conviction—
   (a) to a fine not exceeding level 5 on the standard scale, or to imprisonment for a term not exceeding 3 months or to both such fine and such imprisonment; and
   (b) in the case of a continuing offence to a further fine of £5 for every day, or part of a day, on which the occupation continues after conviction.

NOTES to section 127

Definitions: 'closing order': see s 338 below and ss 114 and 119 above; 'demolition order': see s 338 below and s 115 above; 'local authority': see s 338 below; 'building': see s 133 below; 'house': see ss 338 and 133 below; 'the standard scale': see the Criminal Procedure (Scotland) Act 1975 (c 21), s 289G and the Increase of Criminal Penalties Etc (Scotland) Order 1984, SI 1984/526. Level 5 is currently £2000.

128. Recovery of possession of house to which Rent Act applies.

Nothing in the Rent (Scotland) Act 1984 [or in Part II of the Housing (Scotland) Act 1988] shall be deemed to affect the provisions of this Act relating to obtaining possession of a house with respect to which a closing order, or a demolition order has been made or to which a resolution passed under section 125 applies, or to prevent possession being obtained—
   (a) of any house possession of which is required for the purpose of enabling a local authority to exercise their powers under any enactment relating to housing;

(b) of any house possession of which is required for the purpose of securing compliance with any byelaws made for the prevention of overcrowding;
(c) of any premises by any owner in a case where an undertaking has been given under this Part that those premises shall not be used for human habitation. [698]

NOTES to section 128
Amendment: Section 128 was amended by the Housing (Scotland) Act 1988 (c 43), s 72, Sch 9, para 13.
Definitions: 'house': see ss 338 and 133 below; 'closing order': see s 338 below and ss 114 and 119 above; 'demolition order': see s 338 below and s 115 above; 'local authority': see s 338 below.

Appeals and date of operation of certain notices, etc

129. Appeals.

(1) Subject to the provisions of this section and subsections (2), [to (7)] of section 324 any person aggrieved by—
(a) a closing order made under section 114 or section 119 or a refusal to determine such a closing order;
(b) a demolition order or a refusal to determine a demolition order or a resolution under section 125;
(c) a notice of determination to purchase served under section 121(3);
(d) a notice that no payment falls to be made under section 304(1) served under subsection (2) of that section;
may appear to the sheriff by giving notice of appeal within 21 days after the date of the service of the notice, or order or resolution, or after the refusal, as the case may be; and no proceedings shall be taken by the local authority to enforce any notice, or order while an appeal against it is pending.

(2) No appeal shall lie under paragraphs (a), (b) or (c) of subsection (1) at the instance of a person who is in occupation of the premises to which the order or resolution or notice relates under a lease or agreement the unexpired term of which does not exceed 6 months.

(3) On an appeal under paragraph (a) or paragraph (b) of subsection (1), the sheriff may consider any undertaking such as is specified in relation to a closing order or a demolition order, as the case may be, in section 117 and, if he thinks it proper to do so having regard to the undertaking, may direct the local authority to make a suspension order under that section. [699]

NOTES to section 129
Amendment: Sub-s (1) was amended by the Housing (Scotland) Act 1988 (c 43), s 72, Sch 7, para 4.
Definitions: 'demolition order': see s 338 below and s 115 above; 'local authority': see s 338 below.

130. Date of operation of notices, orders or resolutions subject to appeal.

(1) Any notice, or order or resolution against which an appeal might be brought to the sheriff under section 129 shall, if no such appeal is brought, become operative on the expiration of 21 days after the date of the service of the notice, or order or resolution, as the case may be, and shall be final and conclusive as to any matters which could have been raised on such an appeal.

(2) Any such notice or order or resolution against which an appeal is brought shall, if and so far as it is confirmed by the sheriff, become operative as from the date of the determination of the appeal. [700]

Charging orders

131. Power of local authority to make charging order in favour of themselves.

(1) Where a local authority have themselves incurred expenses under section 123 in the demolition of a building, they may make a charging order in favour of themselves in respect of such expenses.

(2) The provisions of Schedule 9 shall, subject to any necessary modifications and to the provisions of subsection (3), apply to a charging order so made.

(3) A charging order so made shall be made in relation to the site of the building demolished, including the area of any yard, garden or pertinent belonging to the building or usually enjoyed therewith. **[701]**

NOTE to section 131

Definition: 'local authority': see s 338 below.

Supplementary

132. Protection of superiors and owners.

(1) If the superior of any lands and heritages gives notice to the local authority of his right of superiority, the authority shall give to him notice of any proceedings taken by them in pursuance of this Part in relation to the lands and heritages.

(2) Nothing in this Part shall prejudice or interfere with the rights or remedies of any owner for the breach, non-observance or non-performance of any contract or obligation entered into by a tenant or lessee with reference to any house in respect of which an order or resolution is made by a local authority under this Part; and if any owner is obliged to take possession of any house in order to comply with any such order or resolution the taking possession shall not affect his right to avail himself of any such breach, non-observance or non-performance which may have occurred before he so took possession. **[702]**

NOTES to section 132

Definitions: 'superior', 'local authority', 'land', 'owner': see s 338 below; 'house'; *Ibid* and s 133 below.

133. Interpretation.

(1) In this Part (except sections 125, 126 and 132) any reference to a house, or to a building, includes a reference to premises occupied by agricultural workers although such premises are used for sleeping purposes only.

(2) For the purposes of this Part a crofter or a landholder shall be deemed to be the owner of any house on his croft or holding in respect of which he would, on the termination of his tenancy, be entitled to compensation under the Crofters (Scotland) Acts 1955 and 1961 or, as the case may be, the Small Landholders (Scotland) Acts 1886 to 1931, as for an improvement. **[703]**

NOTES to section 133

Definitions: 'house', 'agricultural worker', 'owner', 'landholder', 'croft', 'crofter': see s 338 below.

Saving

134. Saving for telecommunication and gas apparatus.

Paragraph 23 of Schedule 2 to the Telecommunications Act 1984 (code for cases where works involve the alteration of apparatus), as applied by paragraph 2(7) of Schedule 7 to the Gas Act 1986 to gas apparatus, shall apply to a local authority for the purposes of any works which they are authorised to execute under this Part. **[704]**

NOTES to section 134
Definitions: 'apparatus', 'local authority': see s 338 below.

PART VII
OVERCROWDING

Definition of overcrowding

135. Definition of overcrowding.

A house is overcrowded for the purposes of this Part when the number of persons sleeping in the house is such as to contravene—
  (a) the standard specified in section 136 (the room standard), or
  (b) the standard specified in section 137 (the space standard). [705]

NOTES to section 135
Definition: 'house': see s 151 below.

136. The room standard.

(1) The room standard is contravened when the number of persons sleeping in a house and the number of rooms available as sleeping accommodation is such that two persons of opposite sexes who are not living together as husband and wife must sleep in the same room.

(2) For this purpose—
  (a) children under the age of 10 shall be left out of account, and
  (b) a room is available as sleeping accommodation if it is of a type normally used in the locality either as a bedroom or as a living room. [706]

NOTE to section 136
Definition: 'house': see s 151 below.

137. The space standard.

(1) The space standard is contravened when the number of persons sleeping in a house is in excess of the permitted number, having regard to the number and floor area of the rooms of the house available as sleeping accommodation.

(2) For this purpose—
  (a) no account shall be taken of a child under the age of one and a child aged one or over but under 10 shall be reckoned as one-half of a unit, and
  (b) a room is available as sleeping accommodation if it is of a type normally used in the locality either as a living room or as a bedroom.

(3) The permitted number of persons in relation to a house is whichever is the less of—
  (a) the number specified in Table 1 in relation to the number of rooms in the house available as sleeping accommodation, and
  (b) the aggregate for all such rooms in the house of the numbers specified in column 2 of Table II in relation to each room of the floor area specified in column 1.

No account shall be taken for the purposes of either Table of a room having a floor area of less than 50 square feet.

Table I

Number of rooms	Number of persons
1	2
2	3
3	5
4	7½
5 or more	2 for each room

Table II

Floor area of room	Number of persons
110 sq ft or more	2
90 sq ft or more but less than 110 sq ft	1½
70 sq ft or more but less than 90 sq ft	1
50 sq ft or more but less than 70 sq ft	½

(4) The Secretary of State may prescribe the manner in which the floor area of a room is to be ascertained for the purposes of this section; and the regulations may provide for the exclusion from computation, or the bringing into computation at a reduced figure, of floor space in a part of the room which is of less than a specified height.

(5) Regulations under subsection (4) shall be made by statutory instrument which shall be subject to annulment in pursuance of a resolution of either House of Parliament.

(6) A certificate of the local authority stating the number and floor areas of the rooms in the house, and that the floor areas have been ascertained in the prescribed manner, is evidence for the purposes of legal proceedings of the facts stated in it. **[707]**

NOTES to section 137

Definitions: 'house': see s 151 below; 'local authority': see s 338 below.
Sub-ss (4), (5): See the Housing (Computation of Floor Area) Regulations (Scotland) 1935, SI 1935/912, paras [1224] ff below.

Powers of Secretary of State

138. Secretary of State may increase permitted number of persons temporarily.

(1) The Secretary of State may, subject to the provisions of this section, increase by order the number of permitted persons in relation to houses to which this section applies or a specified class of those houses.

(2) This section applies to houses consisting of a few rooms, or comprising rooms of exceptional floor area.

(3) The Secretary of State may make an order under this section if he is satisfied on the representation of the local authority that such houses constitute so large a proportion of the housing accommodation in their district, or in any part of it, that it would be impracticable to assess the permitted number of persons in accordance with the provisions of section 137(3).

(4) An order under this section may—
(a) direct that the provisions of section 137(3) are to have effect subject to such modifications for increasing the permitted number of persons as may be specified in the order;
(b) specify the period not exceeding 3 years during which such modifications are to apply;
(c) specify different modifications in relation to different classes of houses.

(5) Any period specified in the order may be extended by the Secretary of State on the application of the local authority.

(6) The Secretary of State shall consult the local authority before varying or revoking an order made under this section, and may vary it in respect of the modifications or of the houses to which the modifications apply or to both.

(7) An order made under this section shall be made by statutory instrument. **[708]**

NOTES to section 138

Definitions: 'house': see s 151 below; 'local authority': see s 338 below.
Sub-s (1): The power to make an order has not been exercised.

Responsibility of occupier

139. Penalty for occupier causing or permitting overcrowding.

(1) The occupier of a house who causes or permits it to be overcrowded is guilty of an offence, subject to subsection (2).

(2) The occupier is not guilty of an offence—
(a) if the overcrowding is within the exceptions specified in sections 140 or 141 (children attaining age of [one or] 10 or temporary visitor), or
(b) by reason of anything done under the authority of, and in accordance with any conditions specified in, a licence granted by the local authority under section 142 or a resolution passed under section 143.

(3) A person committing an offence under this section is liable on summary conviction to a fine not exceeding level 1 on the standard scale. [709]

NOTES to section 139

Amendment: Sub-s (2) was amended by the Housing (Scotland) Act 1988 (c 43), s 72, Sch 7, para 5.
Definitions: 'house': see s 151 below; 'the Standard Scale': see the Criminal Procedure (Scotland) Act 1975 (c 21), s 289G and the Increase of Criminal Penalties Etc (Scotland) Order 1984, SI 1984/526. Level 1 is currently £50.

140. Exception: children attaining age of 1 or 10.

(1) Where a house which would not otherwise be overcrowded becomes overcrowded by reason of a child attaining the age of one or 10, the occupier does not commit an offence under section 139(1) (occupier causing or permitting overcrowding), so long as the condition in subsection (2) is met and the occupier does not fail to accept an offer of suitable alternative accommodation or to secure the removal of any person living in the house who is not a member of his family and whose removal is reasonably practicable.

(2) The condition is that all the persons sleeping in the house are persons who were living there when the child attained that age and thereafter continuously live there, or children born after that date of any of those persons. [710]

NOTES to section 140
Definitions: 'house', 'suitable alternative accommodation': see s 151 below.

141. Exception: temporary visitor.

The occupier of a house shall not be guilty of an offence under section 139(1) in respect of overcrowding if the overcrowding is caused by a temporary resident whose stay does not exceed 16 days and to whom lodging is given by the occupier otherwise than for gain. [711]

NOTE to section 141
Definition: 'house': see s 151 below.

142. Licence of local authority.

(1) The occupier or intending occupier of a house may apply to the local authority for a licence authorising him to permit a number of persons in excess of the permitted number to sleep in the house.

(2) The authority may grant such a licence if it appears to them that there are exceptional circumstances and that it is expedient to do so; and they shall specify in the licence the number of persons authorised in excess of the permitted number.

(3) The licence shall be in the prescribed form and may be granted either unconditionally or subject to conditions specified in it.

(4) The local authority may revoke the licence at their discretion by notice in writing served on the occupier and specifying a period (at least one month from the date of service) at the end of which the licence will cease to be in force.

(5) Unless previously revoked, the licence continues in force for such period not exceeding twelve months as may be specified in it.

(6) A copy of the licence and of any notice of revocation shall, within seven days of the issue of the licence or the service of the notice on the occupier, be served by the local authority on the landlord (if any) of the house. **[712]**

NOTES to section 142
Definitions: 'house', 'landlord': see s 151 below; 'local authority': see s 338 below.

143. Exception: holiday visitors.

(1) A local authority may, for the purpose of providing for a seasonal increase of holiday visitors in their area, pass a resolution authorising—
  (a) the occupiers of houses generally;
  (b) the occupiers of houses of a specified class,
in their area or any specified part of it to permit such number of persons in excess of the permitted number as may be specified to sleep in those houses during any period it is in force.

(2) Such a resolution—
  (a) requires the approval of the Secretary of State;
  (b) is subject to such conditions as may be specified in it; and
  (c) remains in force during the year in which it is passed for such period or periods not exceeding 16 weeks in the aggregate as it may specify. **[713]**

NOTES to section 143
Definitions: 'local authority': see s 338 below; 'house': see s 151 below.

Powers and duties of landlord

144. Offence by landlord not to inform prospective tenant of permitted number of occupants.

(1) The landlord of a house is guilty of an offence if he lets or agrees to let it to any person without—
  (a) giving that person a written statement in the prescribed form of the permitted number of persons in relation to the house, and
  (b) obtaining from that person a written acknowledgement in the prescribed form, and
  (c) exhibiting the acknowledgement to the local authority on demand by them.

(2) A person guilty of an offence under subsection (1) shall be liable on summary conviction to a fine not exceeding level 1 on the standard scale.

(3) A written statement given under subsection (1)(a) shall be treated as being sufficient and correct if it agrees with information given by the local authority under section 148. **[714]**

NOTES to section 144
Definitions: 'landlord', 'house': see s 151 below; 'local authority': see s 338 below; 'the standard scale': see the Criminal Procedure (Scotland) Act 1975 (c 21), s 289G and the Increase of Criminal Penalties Etc (Scotland) Order 1984, SI 1984/526. Level 1 is currently £50.

145. Recovery of possession of overcrowded house that is let.

If the occupier of a house is guilty of an offence by reason of it being overcrowded—

(a) nothing in the Rent (Scotland) Act 1984 [or in Part II of the Housing (Scotland) Act 1988] shall prevent the landlord from obtaining possession of the house;
(b) the local authority after giving to the landlord written notice of their intention to do so may take any such steps for the termination of the occupier's tenancy or for his removal or ejection from the house as the landlord could take. **[715]**

NOTES to section 145
Amendment: Section 145 was amended by the Housing (Scotland) Act 1988, s 72, Sch 9, para 14.
Definitions: 'house', 'landlord': see s 151 below; 'local authority': see s 338 below.

Powers and duties of local authority

146. Duty of local authority to inspect district and to make reports and proposals as to overcrowding.

(1) A local authority shall, subject to the provisions of this section, carry out an inspection of their district or any part of it for the purpose of identifying houses that are overcrowded.

(2) An inspection under subsection (1) shall be carried out at such times as—
(a) it appears to the local authority that there is occasion to do so, or
(b) the Secretary of State so directs.

(3) On carrying out such an inspection the local authority shall prepare and submit to the Secretary of State a report indicating—
(a) the result of the inspection, and
(b) the additional housing accommodation required to put an end to overcrowding in the area to which the report relates, and
(c) subject to subsection (5), proposals for its provision, and
(d) in relation to such proposals, a statement of the steps the local authority propose to take to secure that priority is given to rehousing families living under the worst conditions of overcrowding or otherwise living under unsatisfactory housing conditions.

(4) The report shall give such details as the Secretary of State may direct.

(5) The report shall not require to make proposals for the additional housing accommodation required, if the local authority satisfy the Secretary of State that it will be otherwise provided.

(6) Where the Secretary of State gives a direction under subsection (2), he may fix dates before which the performance of their duties under this section is to be completed. **[716]**

NOTES to section 146
Definitions: 'local authority': see s 338 below; 'house': see s 151 below.

147. Power to require information about persons sleeping in house.

(1) The local authority may, for the purpose of enabling them to discharge their duties under this Part, serve notice on the occupier of a house requiring him to give them within 14 days a written statement of the number, ages and sexes of the persons sleeping in the house.

(2) The occupier shall be guilty of an offence if—
(a) he makes default in complying with the requirement, or
(b) he gives a statement which to his knowledge is false in a material particular,
and shall be liable on summary conviction to a fine not exceeding level 1 on the standard scale. **[717]**

NOTES to section 147
Definitions: 'local authority': see s 338 below; 'house': see s 151 below; 'the standard scale': see the

Criminal Procedure (Scotland) Act 1975 (c 21), s 289G and the Increase of Criminal Penalties Etc (Scotland) Order 1984, SI 1984/526. Level 1 is currently £50.

148. Duty to give information to landlords and occupiers.

(1) A local authority shall inform the landlord and the occupier of a house in writing of the permitted number of persons in relation to the house as soon as they have ascertained the floor area of the rooms.

(2) They shall also so inform the landlord or the occupiers if they apply for the information.

NOTES to section 148
Definitions: 'local authority': see s 338 below; 'landlord': see s 151 below; 'house': *Ibid*.

149. Power to publish information.

A local authority may publish information for the assistance of landlords and occupiers of houses as to their rights and duties under this Part.

NOTES to section 149
Definitions: 'local authority': see s 338 below; 'landlord', 'house': see s 151 below.

150. Duty to enforce this Part.

A local authority shall enforce the provisions of this Part.

NOTES to section 150
Definition: 'local authority': see s 338 below.

151. Interpretation and application.

(1) In this Part, except where the context otherwise requires—
'house' means any premises used or intended to be used as a separate dwelling . . .
'landlord' means, in relation to any house, the person from whom the occupier derives his right to occupy it;
'suitable alternative accommodation' means, in relation to the occupier of a house, a house in which the occupier and his family can live without causing it to be overcrowded, being a house which the local authority certify to be suitable to the needs of the occupier and his family as respects security of tenure and proximity to place of work and to be suitable in relation to his means.

(2) The provisions of sections 138(1) to (5), 139 . . . , 140 . . . and 144 . . . apply only to a locality in respect of which a day has been appointed under section 99 of the Housing (Scotland) Act 1966 or under any enactment referred to in that section.

NOTES to section 151
Amendments: Sub-s (1) was amended by the Housing (Scotland) Act 1988 (c 43), s 72, Sch 8, para 2, Sch 10; sub-s (2) was amended by *Ibid*, s 72, Sch 7, para 6.
Sub-s (2): Days have been appointed in respect of only two localities—the Dysart Ward of the Burgh of Kirkcaldy, and the Burgh of Queensferry.

PART VIII
HOUSES IN MULTIPLE OCCUPATION

Registration schemes

152. Registration schemes.

(1) A local authority may make and submit to the Secretary of State for confirmation by him a registration scheme authorising the authority to compile and maintain a register for their district of—

(a) houses which, or a part of which, are let in lodgings, or which are occupied by members of more than one family; and
(b) buildings which comprise separate dwellings, two or more of which lack either or both of the following—
  (i) a sanitary convenience accessible only to those living in the dwelling, and
  (ii) personal washing facilities so accessible,

and the Secretary of State may, if he thinks fit, confirm the scheme, with or without modification.

(2) A registration scheme need not be for the whole of a local authority's district and need not be for every description of house or building falling within paragraphs (a) and (b) of subsection (1).

(3) A registration scheme may—
(a) specify the particulars to be inserted in the register;
(b) make it the duty of such persons as may be specified by the scheme to notify the local authority of the fact that a house or building appears to be registrable, and to give to the authority as regards the house or building all or any of the particulars specified in the scheme;
(c) make it the duty of such persons to notify the authority of any change which makes it necessary to alter the particulars inserted in the register as regards any house or building; and
(d) make a contravention of, or failure to comply with, any provision in the scheme an offence under the scheme, and a person guilty of an offence under the scheme shall be liable on summary conviction to a fine not exceeding level 2 on the standard scale.

(4) A registration scheme may vary or revoke a previous registration scheme and a local authority may at any time, with the consent of the Secretary of State, by order revoke a registration scheme.

(5) A registration scheme shall not come into force until it has been confirmed but, subject to that, comes into force on such date as may be fixed by the scheme or, if no date is so fixed, at the expiration of one month after it is confirmed. [722]

NOTES to section 152

Definitions: 'local authority', 'house': see s 338 below; 'family': *Ibid* and s 83 above; 'the standard scale': see the Criminal Procedure (Scotland) Act 1975 (c 21), s 289G and the Increase of Criminal Penalties Etc (Scotland) Order 1984, SI 1984/526. Level 2 is currently £100.

153. Steps to inform the public about scheme.

(1) The local authority shall publish notice of their intention to submit a registration scheme to the Secretary of State for confirmation in one or more newspapers circulating in their district at least one month before the scheme is submitted to the Secretary of State for confirmation by him.

(2) As soon as any such scheme is confirmed by the Secretary of State, the local authority shall publish in one or more newspapers circulating in their district a notice—
(a) stating the fact that a registration scheme has been confirmed, and
(b) describing any steps which will have to be taken under the scheme by those concerned with registrable houses and buildings (other than steps which have only to be taken after a notice from the local authority), and
(c) naming a place where a copy of the scheme may be seen at all reasonable hours.

(3) A copy of a registration scheme confirmed by the Secretary of State—
(a) shall be printed and deposited at the offices of the local authority by whom it was made, and
(b) shall at all reasonable hours be open to public inspection without payment, and
(c) a copy thereof shall on application be furnished to any person on payment of such sum, not exceeding 5p for every copy, as the authority may determine.

(4) If a local authority revoke a registration scheme by order they shall publish notice of the order in one or more newspapers circulating in their district. **[723]**

NOTES to section 153

Definitions: 'local authority', 'house': see s 338 below.

154. Proof of scheme and contents of register.

The production of a printed copy of a registration scheme purporting to be made by a local authority upon which is endorsed a certificate purporting to be signed by the proper officer of the authority stating—
(a) that the scheme was made by the authority,
(b) that the copy is a true copy of the scheme, and
(c) that on a specified date the scheme was confirmed by the Secretary of State,
shall be prima facie evidence of the facts stated in the certificate, and without proof of the handwriting or official position of the person by whom the certificate purports to be signed. **[724]**

NOTES to section 154

Definitions: 'local authority', 'proper officer': see s 338 below.

155. Power to require information for purposes of scheme.

(1) Without prejudice to the provisions of section 325 (power of local authority to require occupier to state interest), a local authority may—
(a) for the purpose of ascertaining whether a house or building is registrable, and
(b) for the purpose of ascertaining the particulars to be entered in the register as regards the house or building,
require any person who has an estate or interest in, or who lives in, the house or building to state in writing any information in his possession which the authority may reasonably require for that purpose. **[725]**

NOTES to section 155

Definitions: 'local authority', 'house': see s 338 below.

Management code

156. Power of Secretary of State to make management code.

(1) The Secretary of State may by regulations contained in a statutory instrument with a view to providing a code for the management of houses which may be applied under section 157, make provision for the purpose of ensuring that the person managing a house which, or a part of which, is let in lodgings, or which is occupied by members of more than one family observes proper standards of management.

(2) Without prejudice to the generality of subsection (1), the regulations may, in particular, require the person managing a house to which the regulations apply to ensure the repair, maintenance, cleansing and good order of—
(a) all means of water supply and drainage in the house;
(b) kitchens, bathrooms and water closets used in common by persons living in the house;
(c) sinks and wash-basins used in common by persons living in the house;
(d) the roof and windows forming part of the house;
(e) common staircases, corridors, and passage ways;
(f) outbuildings, yards and gardens used in common by persons living in the house;
and to make satisfactory arrangements for the disposal of refuse and litter from the house.

(3) The regulations may—
(a) make different provision for different types of houses;

Housing (Scotland) Act 1987 (c 26), s 157 [727]

- (b) provide for keeping a register of the names and addresses of those who are managers of houses;
- (c) impose duties on persons who have an estate or interest in a house or any part of a house to which the regulations apply as to the giving of information to the local authority, and in particular may make it the duty of any person who acquires or ceases to hold an estate or interest in such a house to notify the authority;
- (d) impose duties on persons who live in a house to which the regulations apply for the purpose of ensuring that the person managing the house can effectively carry out the duties imposed on him by the regulations;
- (e) authorise the local authority to obtain information as to the number of individuals or households accommodated in the house;
- (f) make it the duty of the person managing the house to cause a copy of the order under section 157 and of the regulations, to be displayed in a suitable position in the house;
- (g) contain such other incidental and supplementary provisions as may appear to the Secretary of State to be expedient.

(4) If any person knowingly contravenes or without reasonable excuse fails to comply with any regulation under this section as applied under this Act in relation to any house he shall be guilty of an offence and shall be liable on summary conviction to a fine not exceeding level 3 on the standard scale.

(5) In this section, 'person managing a house' means—
- (a) the person who is an owner or lessee of the house and who, directly or through a trustee, tutor, curator, factor or agent, receives rents or other payments from persons who are tenants of parts of the house, or who are lodgers; and
- (b) where those rents or other payments are received through another person as his trustee, tutor, curator, factor or agent, that other person.

(6) Regulations under this section may vary or replace for the purposes of this section and of the regulations made under it the definition of the 'person managing a house' in subsection (5). [726]

NOTES to section 156

Definitions: 'family': see s 338 below and s 83 above; 'house', 'local authority', 'owner': see s 338 below; 'lessee': see ss 177 and 190 (1) below; 'the standard scale': see the Criminal Procedure (Scotland) Act 1975 (c 21), s 289G. Level 3 is currently £400.

Sub-ss (1), (3), (6): See the Housing (Management of Houses in Multiple Occupation) (Scotland) Regulations 1964, SI 1964/1371, paras [1226] ff below.

157. Power of local authority to apply management code to particular house.

(1) If it appears to a local authority that a house which, or a part of which, is let in lodgings, or which is occupied by members of more than one family is in an unsatisfactory state in consequence of failure to maintain proper standards of management and, accordingly, that it is necessary that the regulations made under section 156 should apply to the house, the authority may by order direct that those regulations shall so apply; and so long as the order is in force the regulations shall apply in relation to the house accordingly.

(2) Not less than 21 days before making an order under this section, the local authority shall—
- (a) serve on an owner of the house, and on every person who is to their knowledge a lessee on the house, notice of their intention to make the order, and
- (b) post such a notice in some position in the house where it is accessible to those living in the house,

and shall afford to any person on whom a notice is served an opportunity of making representations regarding their proposal to make the order.

(3) The order comes into force on the date on which it is made.

(4) The local authority shall within 7 days from the making of the order—
- (a) serve a copy of the order on an owner of the house and on every person who is to their knowledge a lessee of the house, and

(b) post a copy of the order in some position in the house where it is accessible to those living in the house.

(5) The local authority may at any time revoke the order on the application of a person having an estate or interest in the house. **[727]**

NOTES to section 157

Definitions: 'local authority', 'house', 'owner': see s 338 below; 'family': see s 338 below and s 83 above; 'lessee': see ss 177 and 190(1) below.

158. Appeal against making of, or failure to revoke, order under s 157.

(1) A person on whom a copy of an order is served under section 157(4), and any other person who is a lessee of the house, may, within 14 days from the latest date by which copies of the order are required to be served, appeal to the sheriff on the ground that the making of the order was unnecessary.

(2) On an appeal under subsection (1) the sheriff shall take into account the state of the house at the time when the local authority under section 157 served notice of their intention to make the order, as well as at the time of the making of the order, and shall disregard any improvement in the state of the house between those times unless the sheriff is satisfied that effective steps have been taken to ensure that the house will in future be kept in a satisfactory state.

(3) If the sheriff allows the appeal, he shall revoke the order, but without prejudice to its operation prior to the revocation and without prejudice to the making of a further order.

(4) If a local authority—
(a) refuse an application for the revocation of an order under section 157(5), or
(b) do not within 42 days from the making of the application, or within such further period as the applicant may in writing allow, notify the applicant of their decision on the application,
the applicant may appeal to the sheriff and the sheriff, if of the opinion that there has been a substantial change in the circumstances since the making of the order, and that it is in other respects just to do so, may revoke the order. **[728]**

NOTES to section 158

Definitions: 'lessee': see s 177 and 190(1) below; 'house': see s 338 below; 'improvement': see ss 338 and 236 below.

159. Registration of order and of revocation.

(1) The local authority shall as soon as practicable after an order under section 157 has come into force cause the order to be recorded in the General Register of Sasines or registered in the Land Register, as the case may be.

(2) If any such order is revoked the authority shall as soon as practicable cause to be recorded in the General Register of Sasines or registered in the Land Register, as the case may be, a notice stating that the order has been revoked. **[729]**

NOTES to section 159

Definition: 'local authority': see s 338 below.

Powers of local authority to require works to be done

160. Notice requiring compliance with management code.

(1) If in the opinion of the local authority the condition of a house is defective in consequence of—

(a) neglect to comply with the requirements imposed by regulations under section 156 (regulations prescribing management code), or
(b) in respect of a period falling wholly or partly before the regulations applied to the house, neglect to comply with standards corresponding to the requirements imposed by the regulations,

the authority may serve on the person managing the house a notice specifying the works which in the opinion of the authority are required to make good the neglect, and requiring the person on whom the notice is served to execute those works.

(2) If it is not practicable after reasonable inquiry to ascertain the name or address of the person managing the house, the notice under this section may be served by addressing it to him by the description of 'manager of the house' (naming the house to which it relates) and by delivering it to some person on the premises.

(3) The notice shall require the execution of the works specified in the notice within such period, being not less than 21 days from the service of the notice, as may be so specified.

(4) That period may from time to time be extended by written permission of the local authority.

(5) Where the local authority serve a notice on any person under this section they shall inform any other person who is to their knowledge an owner or lessee of the house or a person holding a heritable security over the house of the fact that such a notice has been served. [730]

NOTES to section 160

Definitions: 'local authority', 'house', 'owner': see s 338 below; 'person managing the house': see s 190 below; 'person to whom the house is let': see s 190(1) below; 'lessee': see ss 177 and 190(1) below.

161. Notice requiring compliance with standards.

(1) The local authority may serve a notice under this section where the condition of a house which, or a part of which, is let in lodgings, or which is occupied by members of more than one family is, in the opinion of the authority, so far defective with respect to any of the matters mentioned in subsection (2), having regard to the number of individuals or households, or both, accommodated for the time being on the premises, as not to be reasonably suitable for occupation by those individuals or households.

(2) The matters referred to in subsection (1) are—
natural and artificial lighting,
ventilation,
water supply,
personal washing facilities,
drainage and sanitary conveniences,
facilities for the storage, preparation and cooking of food, and for the disposal of waste water,
installations for space heating or for the use of space heating appliances.

(3) The notice shall specify the works which in the opinion of the authority are required for rendering the premises reasonably suitable—
(a) for occupation by the individuals and households for the time being accommodated there, or
(b) for a smaller number of individuals or households and the number of individuals or households, or both, which, in the opinion of the authority, the premises could reasonably accommodate if the works were carried out.

(4) The notice shall be served either—
(a) on the person having control of the house, or
(b) on any person to whom the house is let, or on any person who, as the trustee, tutor, curator, factor or agent for or of a person to whom the house is let, receives

[731] *Housing (Scotland) Act 1987 (c 26), s 161*

rents or other payments from tenants of parts of the house or lodgers in the house.

(5) The notice shall require the person on whom it is served to execute the works specified in the notice within such period (or at least 21 days from the service of the notice) as may be so specified.

(6) That period may from time to time be extended by written permission of the authority.

(7) If the local authority are satisfied that—
(a) after the service of a notice under this section in respect of any premises the number of individuals living on those premises has been reduced to a level which will make the work specified in the notice unnecessary, and
(b) that number will be maintained at or below that level whether in consequence of exercise of the authority's powers under section 166 (powers to limit number of occupants of houses) or otherwise,

they may notify in writing the person on whom the notice was served of the withdrawal of the notice, but the withdrawal of the notice shall be without prejudice to the issue of a further notice.

(8) Where the local authority serve a notice on any person under this section they shall inform any other person who is to their knowledge an owner or lessee of the house or a person holding a heritable security over the house of the fact that such a notice has been served. [731]

NOTES to section 161

Definitions: 'local authority', 'house', 'owner': see s 338 below; 'family': see s 338 below and s 83 above; 'lessee': see ss 177 and 190(1) below.

162. Notice requiring provision of means of escape from fire.

(1) If it appears to a local authority that a house which, or a part of which, is let in lodgings, or which is occupied by members of more than one family is not provided with such means of escape from fire as the authority consider necessary, the authority may, subject to this section, serve on any person on whom a notice may be served under section 161 a notice specifying the works which in the opinion of the authority are required to provide such means of escape, and requiring the person on whom the notice is served to execute those works.

(2) A local authority shall serve such a notice if such house is of such description or occupied in such manner as the Secretary of State may, with the consent of the Treasury, specify by order a draft of which has been approved by the House of Commons.

(3) A local authority shall, before serving a notice under this section, consult with the fire authority concerned.

(4) A notice under this section shall require the execution of the works within such period, being not less than 21 days from the service of the notice, as may be specified in the notice, but that period may from time to time be extended by written permission of the local authority.

(5) Where the local authority serve a notice on any person under this section they shall inform any other person who is to their knowledge an owner or lessee of the house or a person holding a heritable security over the house of the fact that such a notice has been served.

(6) In this section 'fire authority' has the same meaning as in section 82. [732]

NOTES to section 162

Definitions: 'local authority', 'house': see s 338 below; 'let': see ss 177 and 190 below.

163. Appeal against notice requiring execution of works.

(1) A person on whom a notice is served under section 160, 161 or 162 or any other person who is an owner or lessee of the house, or a person holding a heritable security over the house, to which the notice relates, may, within 21 days from the service of the notice, or within such longer period as the local authority may in writing allow, appeal to the sheriff on any of the grounds specified in subsection (2).

(2) Those grounds are—
- (a) that there has been some informality, defect or error in, or in connection with, the notice;
- (b) that the local authority have refused unreasonably to approve the execution of alternative works, or that the works required by the notice to be executed are otherwise unreasonable in character or extent, or are unnecessary;
- (c) that the time within which the works are to be executed is not reasonably sufficient for the purpose;
- (d) that some person other than the appellant is wholly or in part responsible for the state of affairs calling for the execution of the works, or will as the holder of an estate or interest in the premises derive a benefit from the execution of the works, and that that other person ought to pay the whole or any part of the expenses of executing the works;
- (e) in the case of a notice under section 160, that the condition of the house did not justify the local authority in requiring the execution of the works specified in the notice;
- (f) in the case of a notice under section 161, that—
  - (i) having regard to the matters mentioned in subsections (1) and (2) of that section, the condition of the house did not justify the local authority in requiring the execution of the works specified in the notice;
  - (ii) the number of individuals or households, or both, specified in the notice is unreasonably low;
- (g) in the case of a notice under section 162, that the notice is not justified by the terms of that section.

(3) In an appeal on ground (a), the sheriff shall dismiss the appeal if he is satisfied that the informality, defect or error was not a material one.

(4) In an appeal on ground (d)—
- (a) the appellant shall serve a copy of his notice of appeal on each other person referred to in that notice, and
- (b) on the hearing of the appeal the sheriff may, if satisfied that any other person referred to in the notice of appeal has had proper notice of the appeal, make such order as he thinks fit with respect to the payment to be made by that other person to the appellant or, where the work is executed by the local authority, to the authority. [733]

NOTES to section 163

Definitions: 'owner', 'house', 'local authority': see s 338 below; 'lessee': see ss 177 and 190(1) below.

164. Carrying out of works by local authority.

(1) If a notice under section 160, 161, or 162 (notice requiring the execution of works) is not complied with, the local authority may themselves do the works required by the notice, with any variation made by the sheriff.

(2) Compliance with a notice means the completion of the works specified in the notice within the period for compliance, which is—
- (a) if no appeal is brought against the notice, the period specified in the notice with any extension duly permitted by the local authority;
- (b) if an appeal is so brought, and the notice is confirmed in whole or in part on the

appeal, the period of 28 days from the final determination of the appeal, or such longer period as the sheriff in determining the appeal may fix.

(3) If, before the expiration of the period for compliance with the notice, the person on whom the notice was served notified the local authority in writing that he is not able to do the work in question, the authority may, if they think fit, themselves do the work forthwith.

(4) Part VI of Schedule 11 shall have effect in relation to the recovery by the local authority of expenses reasonably incurred by them under this section.

(5) If on an appeal under this section against a notice under section 161, the sheriff is satisfied that the number of persons living in the house has been reduced, and that adequate steps (whether by the exercise by the local authority of the power conferred by section 166 to limit the number of persons living in the house or otherwise) have been taken to prevent that number being again increased, the sheriff may, if he thinks fit, revoke the notice or vary the list of works specified in the notice. [734]

NOTES to section 164
Definitions: 'local authority', 'house': see s 338 below.

165. Penalty for failure to execute works.

(1) A person on whom a notice has been served under section 160, 161 or 162 who wilfully fails to comply with the notice, shall be guilty of an offence and shall be liable on summary conviction to a fine not exceeding—
  (a) in the case of a notice under section 160 or 161, level 3 on the standard scale;
  (b) in the case of a notice under section 162, level 4 on the standard scale.

(2) The obligation to execute the works specified in the notice continues notwithstanding that the period for compliance has expired; and a person who wilfully fails to comply with that obligation, after being convicted of an offence in relation to the notice under subsection (1) or this subsection, commits a further summary offence and is liable on conviction to a fine not exceeding level 43 on the standard scale.

(3) References in this section to compliance with a notice and to the period for compliance shall be construed in accordance with section 164(2).

(4) No liability arises under subsection (1) if the local authority, on being notified under section 164(3) by the person on whom any such notice requiring the execution of works was served that he is not able to do the work in question, serve notice that they propose to do the work and relieve the person served with the notice from liability under subsection (1).

(5) Subsection (1) shall be without prejudice to the exercise by the local authority of their powers of carrying out works under section 164. [735]

NOTES to section 165
Definitions: 'the standard scale': see the Criminal Procedure (Scotland) Act 1975 (c 21), s 289G and the Increase of Criminal Penalties Etc (Scotland) Order 1984, SI 1984/526 and the Increase of Criminal Penalties Etc (Scotland) Order 1984, SI 1984/526. Level 3 is currently £400. Level 4 is currently £1000; 'local authority': see s 338 below.

Overcrowding

166. Local authority may give directions to prevent or reduce overcrowding in house in multiple occupation.

(1) A local authority may, for the purpose of preventing the occurrence of, or remedying, a state of affairs calling for the service of a notice or further notice under section 161, fix as a limit for any house what is in their opinion the highest number of individuals who should, having regard to the considerations set out in subsections (1) and

(2) of that section, live in the house in its existing condition, and give a direction applying that limit to the house.

References in this section to a house include references to part of a house, and the local authority shall have regard to the desirability of applying separate limits where different parts of a house are, or are likely to be, occupied by different persons.

(2) The powers conferred by this section shall be exercisable whether or not a notice has been given under section 161 and where a local authority have served a notice under subsection (3) of that section specifying the number of individuals or households, or both, which in the opinion of the authority any premises could reasonably accommodate if the works specified in the notice were carried out, the authority may adopt that number of individuals, or a number of individuals determined by reference to that number of households, in fixing a limit under subsection (1) as respects those premises.

(3) The powers conferred by subsection (1) may be exercised as regards any premises notwithstanding the existence of any previous direction under the subsection laying down a higher maximum.

(4) A direction under subsection (1) shall have effect so as to make it the duty of the occupier for the time being of the house—
(a) not to permit any individual to take up residence in the house so as to increase the number of individuals living in the house to a number above the limit specified in the direction, and
(b) where the number of individuals living in the house is for the time being above the limit so specified and any individual ceases to reside in the house, not to permit any other individual to take up residence in the house.
In this subsection the reference to the occupier for the time being of a house shall include a reference to any person who is for the time being entitled or authorised to permit individuals to take up residence in the house or any part of it.

(5) If any person knowingly fails to comply with the requirements imposed on him by subsection (4) he shall be guilty of an offence and shall be liable on summary conviction to a fine not exceeding level 3 on the standard scale. [736]

NOTES to section 166

Definitions: 'local authority', 'house': see s 338 below; 'the standard scale': see the Criminal Procedure (Scotland) Act 1975 (c 21), s 289G. Level 3 is currently £400.

167. Notice of direction.

(1) A local authority shall, not less than 7 days before giving a direction under section 166—
(a) serve on an owner of the house, and on every person who is to their knowledge a lessee of the house, notice of their intention to give the direction, and
(b) post such a notice in some position in the house where it is accessible to those living in the house,
and shall afford to any person on whom a notice is so served an opportunity of making representations regarding their proposal to give the direction.

(2) The local authority shall within 7 days from the giving of any such direction—
(a) serve a copy of the direction on an owner of the house and on every person who is to their knowledge a lessee of the house, and
(b) post a copy of the direction in some position in the house where it is accessible to those living in the house. [737]

NOTES to section 167

Definitions: 'local authority', 'owner', 'house': see s 338 below; 'lessee': see ss 177 and 190(1) below.

168. Power to require information where notice is in force.

(1) The local authority may from time to time serve on the occupier of a house or part of a house in respect of which a direction under section 166 is in force a notice requiring

[738]

him to furnish them within 7 days with a statement in writing giving all or any of the following particulars—
 (a) the number of individuals who are, on a date specified in the notice, living in the house or part of the house, as the case may be;
 (b) the number of families or households to which those individuals belong;
 (c) the names, ages and sex of those individuals and the names of the heads of each of those families or households;
 (d) the rooms used by those individuals and families or households respectively.

(2) If the occupier makes default in complying with the requirements or furnishes a statement which to his knowledge is false in any material particular, he shall be guilty of an offence and shall be liable on summary convinction to a fine not exceeding level 2 on the standard scale. **[738]**

NOTES to section 168

Definitions: 'local authority', 'house': see s 338 below; 'family': see s 338 below and s 83 above; 'the standard scale': see the Criminal Procedure (Scotland) Act 1975 (c 21), s 289G and the Increase of Criminal Penalties Etc (Scotland) Order 1984, SI 1984/526. Level 2 is currently £100.

169. Revocation and variation.

(1) At any time after giving such a direction the local authority may on the application of any person having an estate or interest in the house—
 (a) revoke that direction, or
 (b) vary it so as to allow more people to be accommodated in the house.

(2) In exercising their powers under subsection (1) the local authority shall have regard to—
 (a) any works which have been executed in the house, or
 (b) any other change of circumstances. **[739]**

NOTES to section 169

Definitions: 'local authority', 'house': see s 338 below.

170. Appeal against refusal

(1) If the local authority refuse an application under section 169 or do not within 42 days from the making of such an application, or within such further period as the applicant may in writing allow, notify the applicant of their decision on the application, the applicant may appeal to the sheriff.

(2) The sheriff may revoke the direction or vary it in any manner in which it might have been varied by the authority. **[740]**

NOTES to section 170

Definition: 'local authority': see s 338 below.

Supplementary

171. Application of sections 156 to 161 to certain buildings comprising separate dwellings.

(1) Subject to the provisions of this section, sections 156 to 161 apply—
 (a) to a building which is not a house but comprises separate dwellings, two or more of which lack either or both of the following—
  (i) a sanitary convenience accessible only to those living in the dwelling, and
  (ii) personal washing facilities so accessible, and
 (b) to a building which is not a house but comprises separate dwellings, two or more of which are wholly or partly let in lodgings or occupied by members of more than one family,

being in either case a building all the dwellings in which are owned by the same person, as if references in those sections to a house which, or part of which, is let in lodgings or which is occupied by members of more than one family included references to any such building.

(2) A notice under section 161(3)(b) shall not by virtue of this section be served in respect of such a building.

(3) A direction under section 166 shall not by virtue of this section be given in relation to such a building.

(4) If a local authority make an order under section 157, as applied by subsection (1), in respect of any building at a time when another order under that section is in force as respects one of the dwellings in the building, they shall revoke that last-mentioned order.

(5) References to a house in sections 163, 164, 175 and 177 shall include references to a building to which this section applies. [741]

NOTES to section 171

Definitions: 'house': see s 338 below; 'family': see s 338 below and s 83 above.

172. Management code to be available for dwellings in certain tenements.

(1) If—
(a) all the dwellings in any tenement are owned by the same person, and
(b) all or any of those dwellings are without one or more of the standard amenities,
sections 156 to 160 shall apply to the tenement as if references in those sections to a house which, or a part of which, is let in lodgings, or which is occupied by members of more than one family included references to the tenement.

(2) If a local authority make an order under section 157, as applied by subsection (1), in respect of any tenement at a time when another order under that section is in force as respects one of the dwellings in the tenement, they shall revoke the last-mentioned order.

(3) References to a house in section 163 (so far as relating to appeals against notices under section 160) and in sections 164, 175 and 177 shall include references to a tenement to which this section applies.

(4) In this section—
'dwelling' means a building or part of a building occupied or intended to be occupied as a separate house;
'tenement' means a building which contains two or more flats. [742]

NOTES to section 172

Definitions: 'standard amenities': see ss 338 and 244 below; 'house', 'local authority': see s 338 below; 'family': see s 338 below and s 83 above.

173. Warrant to authorise entry.

(1) Where it is shown to the satisfaction of the sheriff, or of a justice of the peace or magistrate, on sworn information in writing, that admission to premises specified in the information is reasonably required by a person employed by, or acting on the instructions of, a local authority for the purpose—
(a) of survey and examination to determine whether any powers under the foregoing provisions of this Part should be exercised in respect of the premises, or
(b) of ascertaining whether there has been a contravention of any regulations or direction made or given under the foregoing provisions of this Part,
then, subject to this section, the sheriff, justice or magistrate may by warrant under his hand authorise that person to enter on the premises for the purposes mentioned in paragraphs (a) and (b), or for such of those purposes as may be specified in the warrant.

(2) A sheriff, justice or magistrate shall not grant a warrant under this section unless he is satisfied—

(a) that admission to the premises has been refused and, except where the purpose specified in the information—
   (i) is the survey and examination of premises to determine whether there has been a failure to comply with a notice under section 160 or section 161 or section 162, or
   (ii) is to ascertain whether there has been a contravention of any regulations or direction made or given under the foregoing provisions of this Part,
   that admission was sought after not less than 24 hours' notice of the intended entry had been given to the occupier; or
(b) that an application for admission to the premises would defeat the object of the entry.

(3) Every warrant granted under this section shall continue in force until the purpose for which the entry is required has been satisfied.

(4) Any person who, in the exercise of a right of entry under this section, enters any premises which are unoccupied, or any premises the occupier of which is temporarily absent, shall leave the premises as effectually secured against trespassers as he found them.

(5) Any power of entry conferred by this section—
(a) shall include power to [enter], if need be, by force, and
(b) may be exercised by the person on whom it is conferred either alone or together with any other persons. **[743]**

NOTES to section 173

Amendment: Sub-s (5) was amended by the Housing (Scotland) Act 1988 (c 43), s 72, Sch 7, para 7.
Definition: 'local authority': see s 338 below.

174. Application to sheriff where consent unreasonably withheld.

If on an application made by any person required by a notice under the foregoing provisions of this Part to execute any works it appears to the sheriff that any other person having an estate or interest in the premises has unreasonably refused to give any consent required to enable the works to be executed, the sheriff may give the necessary consent in place of that other person. **[744]**

175. Protection of superiors and owners.

(1) If the superior or owner of any lands and heritages gives notice to the local authority of his estate in those lands and heritages, the authority shall give to him notice of any proceedings taken by them in pursuance of the foregoing provisions of this Part in relation to those lands and heritages or any part thereof.

(2) Nothing in the foregoing provisions of this Part shall prejudice or interfere with the rights or remedies of any owner for the breach, non-observance or non-performance of any agreement or stipulation entered into by a lessee with reference to any house in respect of which a notice requiring the execution of works is served by a local authority under the foregoing provisions of this Part, or as respects which regulations made under section 156 are for the time being in force; and if any owner is obliged to take possession of a house in order to comply with any such notice the taking possession shall not affect his rights to avail himself of any such breach, non-observance or non-performance which has occurred before he so took possession. **[745]**

NOTES to section 175

Definitions: 'superior', 'land', 'local authority', 'owner', 'house': see s 338 below; 'lessee': see ss 177 and 190(1) below.

176. Identity and notice under Part VIII.

(1) A local authority shall take reasonable steps to identify the persons mentioned in subsection (2).

(2) Those persons are—
(a) the person having control of or managing premises;
(b) the person having an estate or interest in premises or any class of such persons,
upon whom the local authority require to serve a document under this Part.

(3) A person having an estate or interest in premises may for the purposes of this Part give notice to the local authority of his interest in the premises, and the authority shall enter the notice in their records. **[746]**

NOTES to section 176
Definition: 'local authority': see s 338 below.

177. Statutory tenant to be regarded as lessee, etc.

In this Part—
(a) references to a lessee of a house and to a person to whom a house is let include references to any person who retains possession of the house by virtue of the Rent (Scotland) Act 1984 [or Part II of the Housing (Scotland) Act 1988] and not as being entitled to any tenancy; and
(b) references to a person having an estate or interest in a house include references to any person who retains possession of the house as mentioned in paragraph (a). **[747]**

NOTES to section 177
Amendment: Section 177 was amended by the Housing (Scotland) Act 1988 (c 43), s 72, Sch 9, para 15.
Definitions: 'house', 'tenancy': see s 338 below; 'lessee': see ss 177 and 190(1) below;

Control orders

178. Making of control order.

(1) A local authority may make a control order in respect of a house in their district which, or a part of which, is let in lodgings, or which is occupied by members of more than one family if—
(a) a notice has been served in respect of the house under section 160 or 161 (notices requiring the execution of works),
(b) a direction has been given in respect of the house under section 166 (direction limiting number of occupants),
(c) an order under section 157 is in force in respect of the house (order applying management code), or
(d) it appears to the local authority that the state or condition of the house is such as to call for the taking of action under any of those sections,
and if it appears to the local authority that the living conditins in the house are such that it is necessary to make the control order in order to protect the safety, welfare or health of persons living in the house.

(2) A local authority may exclude from the provisions of a control order any part of the house which, when the control order comes into force, is occupied by a person who has an estate or interest in the whole of the house, and, except where the context otherwise requires, references in this Part to the house do not include references to any part of the house so excluded from the provisions of the control order.

(3) A control order shall come into force when it is made, and as soon as practicable after making a control order the local authority shall, in exercise of the power conferred in the following provisions of this Part and having regard to the duties imposed on them by the said provisions, enter on the premises and take all such immediate steps as appear to them to be required to protect the safety, welfare or health of persons living in the house.

(4) As soon as practicable after making a control order the local authority shall—
(a) post a copy of the control order, together with a notice as described in subsection (5), in some position in the house where it is accessible to those living in the house; and
(b) serve a copy of the control order, together with such a notice, on every person who, to the knowledge of the local authority—
   (i) was, immediately before the coming into force of the control order, a person managing the house or a person having control of the house, or
   (ii) is an owner or lessee of the house or a person holding a heritable security over the house.

(5) The notice referred to in subsection (4) shall set out the effect of the control order in general terms, referring to the rights of appeal against control orders conferred by this Part and stating the principal grounds on which the local authority consider it necessary to make a control order.

(6) As soon as practicable after making a control order the local authority shall cause the control order to be recorded in the General Register of Sasines or registered in the Land Register, as the case may be. **[748]**

NOTES to section 178

Definitions: 'local authority', 'house', 'owner': see s 338 below; 'family': see s 338 below and s 83 above; 'person managing the house': see s 190(1) below; 'lessee': see s 177 above and s 190(1) below.

179. General effect of control order.

(1) While a control order is in force the local authority—
(a) have the right to possession of the premises, and
(b) have the right to do, and to authorise others to do, in relation to the premises anything which any person having an estate or interest in the premises would, but for the making of the control order, be entitled to do, without incurring any liability to any such person except as expressly provided by this Part.

(2) Subject to subsection (3), the local authority may, notwithstanding that they do not, under this section, have an interest amounting to an estate in the premises, create an interest in the premises which, as near as may be, has the incidents of a lease and, subject to the provisions of section (4) and to any other express provision of this Part, any enactment or rule of law relating to landlords and tenants or leases shall apply in relation to any interest created under this section as if the local authority were the owner of the premises.

(3) Subject to the provisions of paragraphs 5(6) and 6(1) of Schedule 11, the local authority shall not, in exercise of the power conferred by this section, create any right in the nature of a lease or licence which is for a fixed term exceeding one month, [or] which is terminable by notice to quit (or an equivalent notice) of more than 4 weeks:

Provided that this subsection shall not apply to a right created with the consent in writing of the person or persons who would have power to create that right if the control order were not in force.

(4) On the coming into force of a control order any order under section 157, and any notice or direction under sections 160, 161, 162 or 166, shall cease to have effect as respects the house to which the control order applies, but without prejudice to any criminal liability incurred before the coming into force of the control order, or to the right of the local authority to recover any expenses incurred in carrying out any works.

(5) References in this Act or in any other enactment to housing accommodation provided or managed by a local authority shall not include references to any house which is subject to a control order, but this subsection shall not be taken as restricting the powers of acquiring land by agreement or compulsorily conferred on local authorities by Part I. **[749]**

Housing (Scotland) Act 1987 (c 26), s 180 [750]

NOTES to section 179
Amendment: Sub-s (3) was amended by the Housing (Scotland) Act 1988 (c 43), s 72, Sch 7, para 8.
Definitions: 'local authority', 'landlord', 'house': see s 338 below; 'lessee', 'licence': see s 190(1) below.

180. Effect of control order on persons occupying house.

(1) This section applies to a person who at the time a control order comes into force—
(a) is occupying any part of the house, and
(b) does not have an estate or interest in the whole of the house.

(2) Section 179 (general effect of control order) does not affect the rights or liabilities of such a person under any lease, licence or agreement, whether in writing or not, under which that person is occupying any part of the house at the time when the control order comes into force, and—
(a) any such lease, licence or agreement has effect, while the control order is in force, as if the local authority were substituted in it for any party to it who has an estate or interest in the house and who is not a person to whom this section applies; and
(b) any such lease continues to have effect as near as may be as a lease notwithstanding that the rights of the local authority, as substituted for the lessor, do not amount to an estate in the premises.

(3) Subject to the provisions of subsection (4) and to any other express provision to this Part, any enactment or rule of law relating to landlords and tenants or leases shall apply in relation to any lease to which the local authority become a party under this section as if the authority were the owner of the premises.

(4) Section 5 of the Rent (Scotland) Act 1984 (which excludes lettings by local authorities from being protected tenancies within the meaning of the Act) [and paragraph 11 of Schedule 4 to the Housing (Scotland) Act 1988 (which excludes letting by local authorities from being assured tenancies within the meaning of the Act)] shall not apply to any lease or agreement under which a person to whom this section applies is occupying any part of the house, and if immediately before the control order came into force any person to whom this section applies was occupying part of the house under a protected or statutory tenancy, within the meaning of the Rent (Scotland) Act 1984, [or an assured tenancy, within the meaning of the Housing (Scotland) Act 1988] nothing in this Part relating to control orders shall prevent the continuance of that protected, statutory [or assured] tenancy shall not affect the continued operation of [those Acts] in relation to that protected, statutory or assured tenancy after the coming into force of the control order.

(5) So much of the regulations made under section 156 as imposes duties on persons who live in a house to which the regulations apply (regulations prescribing management code) also applies to persons who live in a house as respects which a control order is in force.

(6) Without prejudice to the rights conferred on the local authority by section 179, the authority and any person authorised in writing by them, shall have right at all reasonable times, as against any person having an estate or interest in a house which is subject to a control order, to enter any part of the house for the purpose of—
(a) survey and examination, and
(b) carrying out any works.

(7) The rights conferred by subsection (6) shall, so far as reasonably required for the purpose of survey and examination of a part of a house subject to a control order, or for the purpose of carrying out any works in that part of a house, be exercisable as respects the part of the house which, by virtue of section 178(2), is not subject to the control order. [750]

NOTES to section 180

Amendment: Sub-s (4) was amended by the Housing (Scotland) Act 1988 (c 43), s 72, Sch 9, para 16.
Definitions: 'house', 'local authority': see s 338 below; 'lease', 'licence': see s 190(1) below.

181. Effect of control order in relation to furniture in furnished lettings.

(1) Subject to this section, if on the date on which a control order comes into force there is any furniture in the house which a resident in the house has the right to use in consideration of periodical payments to the dispossessed proprietor (whether included in the rent payable by the resident or not), the right to possession of the furniture shall, on that date and as against all persons other than the resident, vest in the local authority and remain vested in the authority while the control order remains in force.

(2) The local authority may, on the application in writing of the person owning any furniture to which subsection (1) applies, by notice served on that person not less than 2 weeks before the notice takes effect, renounce the right to possession of the furniture conferred by subsection (1).

(3) In respect of the period during which the local authority have the right to possession of any furniture in pursuance of subsection (1), the authority shall be liable to pay to the dispossessed proprietor compensation in respect of the use of any furniture the right to possession of which vests under that subsection at such rate as the parties may agree or as may be determined by the rent assessment committee constituted under section 44 of the Rent (Scotland) Act 1984 or under any corresponding enactment repealed by that Act for the area in which the house is situated.

(4) If the local authority's right to possession of any furniture conferred by subsection (1) is a right exercisable as against more than one person interested in the furniture, any such person may apply to the sheriff for an adjustment of the rights and liabilities of those persons as regards the furniture, and the sheriff may make an order for any such adjustment of rights and liabilities either unconditionally or subject to such terms and conditions (including terms or conditions with respect to the payment of money by any part to the proceedings to any other party to the proceedings by way of compensation, damages or otherwise) as he thinks just and equitable.

(5) Compensation due under this section—
(a) shall be payable by quarterly instalments, the first instalment being payable 3 months after the date when the control order comes into force;
(b) is to be considered as accruing due from day to day and shall be apportionable in respect of time accordingly.

(6) In this Part 'dispossessed proprietor' means the person by whom the rents or other periodical payments to which a local authority become entitled on the coming into force of a control order would have been receivable but for the making of the control order, and the successors in title of that person; and in this section 'furniture' includes fittings and other articles.

NOTES to section 181
Definitions: 'house', 'local authority': see s 338 below.

182. General duties of local authority when control order in force.

(1) The local authority shall—
(a) exercise the powers conferred on them by a control order so as to maintain proper standards of management in the house,
(b) take such action as is needed to remedy all the matters which they would have considered it necessary to remedy by the taking of action under any other provision of this Part if they had not made a control order.

(2) The local authority may fit out, furnish and supply any house subject to a control order with such furniture, fittings and conveniences as appear to them to be required.

(3) The local authority shall make reasonable provision for insurance of any premises subject to a control order, including any part of the premises which, by virtue of section 178(2), is excluded from the provisions of the control order, against destruction or damage by fire or other cause, and premiums paid for the insurance of the premises shall, for the purposes of the provisions of this Part, be treated as expenditure incurred by the local authority in respect of the premises.

(4) The local authority shall keep full accounts of their income and expenditure in respect of a house which is subject to a control order, and afford to the dispossessed proprietor, or any other person having an estate or interest in the house, all reasonable facilities for inspecting, taking copies of and verifying those accounts.

(5) While a control order is in force the local authority shall afford to the dispossessed proprietor, or any other person having an estate or interest in the house, any reasonable facilities requested by him for inspecting and examining the house. [752]

NOTES to section 182
Definitions: 'local authority', 'house': see s 338 below; 'expenditure incurred': see s 190(3) below; 'dispossessed proprietor': see s 190(1) below and s 181(6) above.

183. Compensation payable to dispossessed proprietor.

(1) The local authority shall be liable to pay the dispossessed proprietor compensation in respect of the period during which the control order is in force at an annual rate of an amount equal to one half of the gross annual value for rating purposes of the house as shown in the valuation roll on the date when the control order comes into force.

(2) Compensation due under this section—
(a) shall be payable by quarterly instalments, the first instalment being payable 3 months after the date when the control order comes into force;
(b) is to be considered as accruing due from day to day and shall be apportionable in respect of time accordingly.

(3) If at the time when compensation under this section accrues due the estate or interest of the dispossessed proprietor is subject to any heritable security or charge, the compensation shall be deemed to be comprised in that heritable security or charge.

(4) For the purposes of the references in this section to the gross annual value of a house—
(a) where after the date on which the control order comes into force the valuation roll is altered so as to vary the gross annual value of the house or of the lands and heritages of which house forms part, and the alteration has effect from a date not later than the date on which the control order comes into force, compensation shall be payable under this section as if the gross annual value of the house or lands and heritages shown in the valuation roll on the date when the control order came into force had been the amount of the value shown on the roll as altered; and
(b) if the house forms part only of any lands and heritages, such proportion of the gross annual value shown in the valuation roll for those lands and heritages as may be agreed in writing between the local authority and the person claiming the compensation shall be the gross annual value of the house;
and any dispute arising under paragraph (b) shall be determined by the sheriff on the application of either party.

(5) If different persons are the dispossessed proprietors of different parts of any house, compensation payable under this section shall be apportioned between them in such manner as they may agree (or as may, in default of agreement, be determined by the sheriff on the application of any such person) according to the proportions of the gross annual value of the house properly attributable to the parts of the house in which they are respectively interested.

(6) In the application of this section to any land and heritages whose net annual value is ascertained under subsection (8) of section 6 of the Valuation and Rating (Scotland) Act 1956 (and for which there is therefore no gross annual value shown in the valuation roll)—
  (a) in subsection (1), for the words 'one half of the gross' there shall be substituted the words '0.625 of the net', and
  (b) in each of subsections (4) and (5), for the word 'gross', whenever it occurs, there shall be substituted the word 'net'. [753]

NOTES to section 183
Definitions: 'local authority', 'house': see s 338 below; 'dispossessed proprietor': see s 190(1) below and s 181(6) above.

184. Duty to prepare management scheme.

(1) After a control order has been made, the local authority shall prepare a management scheme and shall, not later than 8 weeks after the date on which the control order comes into force, serve a copy of the scheme on—
  (a) every person who is to the knowledge of the authority—
    (i) a dispossessed proprietor, or
    (ii) an owner or lessee of the house, or
    a person holding a heritable security over the house, and
  (b) on any other person on whom the local authority served a copy of the control order.

(2) Part I of Schedule 11 has effect with respect to the matters to be provided for in a management scheme and for related matters.

(3) This section does not effect the powers conferred on a local authority by section 179 and, accordingly, a local authority may carry out any works in a house which is subject to a control order whether or not particulars of those works have been included in a management scheme. [754]

NOTES to section 184
Definitions: 'local authority', 'owner', 'house': see s 338 below; 'dispossessed proprietor': see s 190(1) below and s 181(6) above; 'lessee': see s 177 above and s 190(1) below.

185. Power of sheriff to modify or determine lease.

(1) Either the lessor or the lessee under any lease of premises which consist of or comprise a house which is subject to a control order, other than a lease to which section 180(2) applies, may apply to the sheriff for an order under this section.

(2) On any such application, the sheriff may make an order for the determination of the lease, or for its variation, and, in either case, either unconditionally or subject to such terms and conditions or subject to such terms and conditions (including terms or conditions with respect to the payment of money by any party to the proceedings to any other party to the proceedings by way of compensation, damages or otherwise) as the sheriff may think just and equitable to impose, regard being had to the respective rights, obligations and liabilities of the parties under the lease and to the other circumstances of the case.

(3) If on any such application the sheriff is satisfied that—
  (a) if the lease is determined and control order is revoked the lessor will be in a position, and intends, to take all such action to remedy the condition of the house as the local authority consider would have to be taken in pursuance of the powers conferred on them under this Part (other than those relating to control orders); and
  (b) the local authority intend, if the lease is determined, to revoke the control order,
the sheriff shall exercise the jurisdiction conferred by this section so as to determine the lease. [755]

NOTES to section 185

Definitions: 'lessor', 'lessee': see s 177 above and s 190(1) below; 'house', 'local authority': see s 338 below.

Appeals

186. Appeal against control order.

(1) Any person having an estate or interest in a house to which a control order relates, or, subject to subsection (2), any other person, may appeal to the sheriff against the control order at any time after the making of the control order, but not later than the expiry of a period of 6 weeks from the date on which a copy of the relevant scheme is served in accordance with section 184(1).

(2) The sheriff may, before entertaining an appeal by a person who had not, when he brought the appeal, an estate or interest in the house, require the appellant to satisfy the sheriff that he may be prejudiced by the making of the control order.

(3) The grounds of appeal are—
(a) that (whether or not the local authority have made an order or issued a notice or direction under sections 157, 160, 161 or 166) the state or condition of the house was not such as to call for the taking of action under any of those provisions;
(b) that it was not necessary to make the control order in order to protect the safety, welfare or health of persons living in the house;
(c) where part of the house was occupied by the dispossessed proprietor when the control order came into force, that it was practicable and reasonable for the local authority to exercise their powers under section 178(2) so as to exclude from the provisions of the control order a part of the house (or a greater part of the house than has been excluded);
(d) that the control order is invalid on the ground that any requirement of this Act has not been complied with or on the ground of some informality, defect or error in or in connection with the control order.

(4) In so far as an appeal under this section is based on the ground that the control order is invalid, the sheriff shall confirm the control order unless satisfied that interests of the appellant have been substantially prejudiced by the facts relied on by him.

(5) A control order shall, subject to the right of appeal conferred by this section, be final and conclusive as to any matter which could have been raised on any such appeal.

(6) Where a control order is revoked on an appeal under this section, the local authority shall as soon as practicable thereafter cause to be recorded in the General Register of Sasines or registered in the Land Register, as the case may be, a notice stating that the control order has been revoked as aforesaid. [756]

NOTES to section 186

Definitions: 'house', 'local authority': see s 338 below; 'dispossessed proprietor': see s 190(1) below and s 181(6) above.

187. Control order revoked on appeal.

(1) This section shall have effect if a control order is revoked by the sheriff on an appeal against the control order.

(2) If the local authority are in the course of carrying out any works in the house which, if a control order were not in force, the authority would have power to require some other person to carry out under the provisions of this Part or under any other enactment relating to housing or public health, and on the hearing of the appeal the sheriff is satisfied that the carrying out of the works could not be postponed until after the determination of the appeal because the works were urgently required for the sake of the safety, welfare or health of persons living in the house, or of other persons, the sheriff

may suspend the revocation of the control order until the works have been completed.

(3) Part II of Schedule 11 has effect in relation to matters arising on the revocation of a control order on appeal. **[757]**

NOTES to section 187
Definitions: 'local authority', 'house': see s 338 below.

Expiration and revocation of control order, etc

188. Expiration of control order, and earlier revocation by local authority or sheriff.

(1) A control order shall cease to have effect on the expiry of a period of 5 years beginning with the date on which it came into force.

(2) The local authority may at any earlier time, either on an application under this section or on their own initiative, by order revoke a control order.

(3) Not less than 21 days before the local authority revoke a control order they shall serve notice of their intention to revoke the control order on the persons occupying any part of the house, and on every person who is to the knowledge of the authority an owner or lessee of the house or a person holding a heritable security over the house.

(4) If any person applies to the local authority requesting the authority to revoke a control order, and giving the grounds on which the application is made, the authority shall, if they refuse the application, inform the applicant of their decision and of their reason for rejecting the grounds advanced by the applicant.

(5) Where the local authority propose to revoke a control order on their own initiative and apply to the sheriff under this subsection, the sheriff may take any of the following steps, to take effect on the revocation of the control order, that is—
  (a) approve the making of an order under section 157;
  (b) approve the giving of a notice under section 160 or section 161 or section 162; or
  (c) approve the giving of a direction under section 166;
and no appeal lies against any order or notice so approved. **[758]**

NOTES to section 188
Definitions: 'local authority', 'house': see s 338 below.

189. Effect of cessation of control order.

Part III of Schedule 11 (which sets out the consequences of a control order ceasing to have effect) shall have effect for the purposes of this Part. **[759]**

190. Interpretation of Part VIII.

(1) In this Part of this Act, unless the context otherwise requires—
'dispossessed proprietor' has the meaning given by section 181(6);
'establishment charges' means, in relation to any expenditure incurred by a local authority, the proper addition to be made to that expenditure to take account of overhead expenditure incurred by the authority, and to allow for a proper return of capital;
'lease' includes a sublease or any tenancy, and any agreement for a lease, sublease or tenancy, and references to a lessor or to a lessee or to a person to whom a house is let shall be construed accordingly;
'licence' means any right or permission relating to land but not amounting to an estate or interest therein;
'person managing a house' has the meaning given to it by section 156(5);
'surpluses on revenue account as settled by the scheme' has the meaning given by paragraph 1(3) of Schedule 11.

(2) References in this Part to the net amount of rents or other payments received by a local authority from persons occupying a house are references to the amount of the rent and other payments received by the authority from those persons under leases or licences, or in respect of furniture to which section 181(1) applies, after deducting income tax paid or borne by the authority in respect of those rents and other payments.

(3) References in this Part to expenditure incurred in respect of a house subject to a control order include, in a case where the local authority—
 (a) require persons living in a house to vacate the accommodation for any period while the local authority are carrying out works in the house, and
 (b) defray all or any part of the expenses incurred by or on behalf of those persons removing from and returning to the house, or provide housing accommodation for those persons for any part of that period,
references to the sums so defrayed by the local authority, and to the net cost to the authority of so providing housing accommodation.

(4) For the purposes of this Part the withdrawal of an appeal shall be deemed the final determination thereof having the like effect as a decision dismissing the appeal.   [760]

Part IX
GOVERNMENT GRANTS AND SUBSIDIES

Housing support grants to local authorities

191. Housing support grants: fixing of aggregate amount.

(1) For the purpose of assisting local authorities to meet reasonable housing needs in their areas, the Secretary of State shall make housing support grants in accordance with the provisions of this Part.

(2) Subject to subsection (5), for the purpose of fixing the aggregate amount of the housing support grants for any year, the Secretary of State shall, in respect of all local authorities, estimate the following amounts—
 (a) the aggregate amount of eligible expenditure which it is reasonable for local authorities to incur for that year; and
 (b) the aggregate amount of relevant income (other than housing support grants) which could reasonably be expected to be credited to the local authorities' housing revenue accounts for that year,
and the amount remaining after deducting the amount mentioned in paragraph (b) from the amount mentioned in paragraph (a) shall, subject to subsection (4) and section 193, be the aggregate amount of the housing support grants for that year.

(3) Before estimating the amount mentioned in paragraphs (a) and (b) of subsection (2) for any year, the Secretary of State shall consult with such associations of local authorities as appear to him to be concerned and shall take into consideration—
 (a) the latest information available to him as to the level of eligible expenditure and relevant income;
 (b) the level of interest rates, remuneration, costs and prices which, in his opinion, would affect the amount of eligible expenditure for that year; and
 (c) the latest information available to him as to changes in the general level of earnings which would affect the amount of relevant income which could reasonably be expected for that year.

(4) In fixing the aggregate amount of the housing support grants for any year, the Secretary of State may take into account the extent, if any, to which the aggregate amount of eligible expenditure which it was reasonable for local authorities to incur for any previous year differs or is likely to differ from the aggregate amount for that previous year which he estimated or re-estimated under this section or section 193 respectively.

(5) In estimating the amounts mentioned in paragraphs (a) and (b) of subsection (2) the

Secretary of State may leave out of account the eligible expenditure and relevant income of a local authority if (either or both)—
  (a) he estimates that the amount of that income will exceed the amount of that expenditure;
  (b) he determines, under section 192, that no proportion of the aggregate amount of the housing support grants is to be apportioned to that authority.

(6) In subsection (4), 'local authorities' does not include an authority whose eligible expenditure was, for the purpose of the estimate, left out of an account under subsection (5).

(7) The aggregate amount of the housing support grants, fixed in accordance with subsection (2) for any year, shall be set out in a housing support grant order made by the Secretary of State with the consent of the Treasury.

(8) A housing support grant order may be made in respect of any year before the beginning of that year.

(9) No housing support grant order shall be made until that order has been laid in draft before the Commons House of Parliament, together with a report of the considerations leading to the provisions of the order, and has been approved by a resolution of that House.

(10) In this Act—
'eligible expenditure', in relation to any year, means the expenditure which a local authority are required to debit to their housing revenue account for that year in pursuance of Schedule 15;
'relevant income', in relation to any year, means the income, payments, contributions (including any [contribution out of the general fund maintained under section 93 of the Local Government (Scotland) Act 1973]). and receipts which a local authority are required to credit to their housing revenue account for that year in pursuance of that Schedule. **[761]**

NOTES to section 191
Amendment: Sub-s (10) was amended by the Housing (Scotland) Act 1988 (c 43), s 72, Sch 8, para 4.
Definitions: 'local authorities'; see s 338 below.
Sub-ss (7)–(9): Housing support grant orders are made annually.

192. Apportionment of housing support grants.

(1) Subject to the provisions of this section, the proportion, if any, of the aggregate amount of the housing support grants payable for any year to a local authority shall be determined by the Secretary of State, after consulting with such associations of local authorities as appear to him to be concerned, by such method as may be prescribed.

(2) A prescribed portion of the aggregate amount may be apportioned to a particular local authority.

(3) The report accompanying a housing support grant order in accordance with section 191(9) shall contain a table showing in respect of each local authority, for the year in question—
  (a) the estimated amount of grant payable to that local authority; or
  (b) if no amount of grant is so payable, that fact.

(4) In prescribing the method of determining the proportion, if any, of the aggregate amount of the housing support grants payable to a local authority for any year, the Secretary of State may take into account any substantial difference in the actual amount of any element of their eligible expenditure as compared with any estimate of the amount of that element made by him in determining the proportion payable to them for a previous year.

(5) In prescribing the method of determining the proportion mentioned in subsection

(1) payable for any year to a local authority the Secretary of State shall have regard to any special needs affecting eligible expenditure.

(6) The Secretary of State may, for any year (in this subsection referred to as 'the current year'), prescribe such method of determining that proportion as to secure that no reduction in the amount of housing support grant payable to any local authority for the current year as compared with the amount of housing support grant so payable for the immediately preceding year is so great that there is an unreasonable increase for the current year over that preceding year in the amount of the authority's eligible expenditure which is required to be met by way of rent or [contributions out of the general fund maintained under section 93 of the Local Government (Scotland) Act 1973].

(7) In this section 'prescribed' means prescribed by a housing support grant order. [762]

NOTES to section 192

Amendment: Sub-s (6) was amended by the Housing (Scotland) Act 1988 (c 43), s 72, Sch 8, para 5.
Definitions: 'local authority': see s 338 below; 'housing support grant': see s 338 below and s 191 above; 'eligible expenditure': see s 191 above.

193. Variation of orders.

(1) Subject to the provisions of this section, the Secretary of State may re-estimate the aggregate amount of eligible expenditure estimated under section 191.

(2) He shall first consult such associations of local authorities as appear to him to be concerned.

(3) Then if it appears to him—
(a) that after that amount was estimated for any year, the eligible expenditure of local authorities for that year has been, or is likely to be, substantially increased or decreased by means of changes which have taken place or are likely to take place in the level of the matters specified in section 191(3)(b), and
(b) that inadequate account was taken of those changes when that amount was estimated,
he may re-estimate that amount.

(4) On such re-estimate he may, by an order made in the like manner and subject to the same provisions as a housing support grant order, increase or, as the case may be, decrease the amount fixed by the relevant housing support grant order as the aggregate amount of the housing support grants for that year.

(5) An order made under this section with respect to any year may, as respects that year, vary any matter prescribed by the relevant housing support grant order. [763]

NOTES to section 193

Definitions: 'eligible expenditure': see s 191 above; 'local authority': see s 338 below.
Sub-s (4): The power to make an order may be exercised at any time.

Grants to the Scottish Special Housing Association and other bodies

194. Grants payable to the Scottish Special Housing Association and development corporations.

(1) The Secretary of State may each year make grants, of such amount and subject to such conditions as he may determine, to . . . development corporations in accordance with the provisions of this section.

(2) Grants under this section shall be payable for any year to . . . development corporations in respect of the total net annual expenditure (as approved by the Secretary of State and calculated in accordance with rules made by him with the consent of the Treasury) necessarily incurred for that year by . . . any development corporation—

(a) in providing housing accommodation by—
  (i) erecting houses;
  (ii) converting any houses or other buildings into houses;
  (iii) acquiring houses;
(b) in improving housing accommodation so provided;
(c) in managing and maintaining any housing accommodation provided or improved;
(d) in improving the amenities of a predominantly residential area;
(e) in providing or converting buildings for use as hostels or as parts of hostels, and in improving, managing and maintaining buildings so provided or converted;
(f) in doing anything ancillary to any of the activities mentioned in paragraphs (a) to (e).

(3) In subsection (2) 'improving' includes altering, enlarging or repairing. **[764]**

NOTES to section 194

Amendment: Sub-ss (1) and (2) were amended by the Housing (Scotland) Act 1988 (c 43), s 3, Sch 2, para 10, Sch 10.

Definitions: 'development corporation', 'house': see s 338 below; 'hostel': see s 338 below and s 2(5) above.

195. Grants for affording tax relief to Scottish Homes.

(1) The Secretary of State may, on the application of [Scottish Homes], make grants to [Scottish Homes] for affording relief from—
(a) income tax (other than income tax which [Scottish Homes] is entitled to deduct on making any payment); and
(b) corporation tax.

(2) A grant under this section shall be of such amount, shall be made at such times and shall be subject to such conditions as the Secretary of State thinks fit.

(3) The conditions mentioned in subsection (2) may include conditions for securing the repayment in whole or in part of a grant made to [Scottish Homes] in the event of tax in respect of which the grant was made subsequently being found not to be chargeable or in such other events as the Secretary of State may determine.

(4) An application under this section shall be made in such manner and shall be supported by such evidence as the Secretary of State may direct.

(5) The Commissioners of Inland Revenue and their officers may disclose to the Secretary of State such particulars as he may reasonably require for determining whether a grant should be made under this section or whether a grant so made should be repaid or the amount of such grant or repayment. **[765]**

NOTES to section 195

Amendment: References to 'Scottish Homes' substituted by the Housing (Scotland) Act 1988 (c 43), s 3, Sch 2, para 1.

196. ...

NOTES to section 196

Amendment: Section 196 was repealed by the Housing (Scotland) Act 1988 (c 43), s 72, Sch 10.

197. Financial assistance to voluntary organisations concerned with housing.

(1) The Secretary of State may, with the consent of the Treasury and upon such terms and subject to such conditions as he may determine, give to a voluntary organisation assistance by way of grant or by way of loan, or partly in the one way and partly in the other, for the purpose of enabling or assisting the organisation to provide training or advice, or to undertake research, or for other similar purposes relating to housing.

(2) In this section 'voluntary organisation' means a body the activities of which are carried on otherwise than for profit, but does not include any public or local authority or a registered housing association. **[766]**

NOTES to section 197
Definitions: 'local authority', 'registered housing association': see s 338 below.

Payment of grants

198. Payment of grants and accounting provisions.

(1) Any grant to be paid by the Secretary of State under this Part shall be payable at such times and in such manner as he may determine and subject to such conditions as he may impose.

(2) Without prejudice to the generality of subsection (1), the making of any such payment shall be subject to the making of an application for the payment in such form, and containing such particulars, as the Secretary of State may from time to time determine. **[767]**

199. Termination of certain exchequer payments to housing authorities.

Schedule 12 shall have effect for the purpose of terminating certain exchequer payments to housing authorities. **[768]**

Slum clearance subsidy

200. . . .

NOTE to section 200
Amendment: Section 200 was repealed by the Housing (Scotland) Act 1988 (c 43), s 72, Sch 10.

Payment of subsidies

201. Payment of subsidies and accounting provisions.

(1) Any subsidy to be paid by the Secretary of State under this Part shall be payable at such times and in such manner as the Treasury may direct and subject to such conditions as to records, certificates, audit or otherwise, as the Secretary of State may, with the approval of the Treasury, impose.

(2) Without prejudice to the generality of subsection (1), the making of any such payment shall be subject to the making of a claim for the payment in such form, and containing such particulars, as the Secretary of State may from time to time determine.

(3) The aggregate amount of any one subsidy payable under this Part to a housing authority for any year shall be calculated to the nearest pound, by disregarding an odd amount of 50 pence, or less, and by treating an odd amount exceeding 50 pence as a whole pound.

(4) Subsection (1) applies to Exchequer contributions payable under the enactments specified in Schedule 13 as it applies to subsidies paid under this Part, and Schedule 13 shall have effect for the purposes of this subsection.

(5) Schedule 14 shall have effect for the purposes of specifying such Exchequer contributions as may be reduced, suspended or discontinued under section 202(3). **[769]**

Secretary of State's power to vary Exchequer contributions

202. Power of Secretary of State to reduce, suspend, discontinue or transfer particular Exchequer contributions.

(1) The Secretary of State may in the circumstances mentioned in subsection (2) reduce the amount of a subsidy to be paid under this Part or suspend or discontinue such payment or part of such payment.

(2) The circumstances are—
(a) where the Secretary of State is satisfied that the local authority have failed to discharge any of their functions;
(b) where the subsidy is payable subject to a condition, and the Secretary of State is satisfied that the condition has not been complied with.

(3) The Secretary of State may, in any of the circumstances mentioned in subsection (5), reduce the amount of any Exchequer contribution being an Exchequer contribution falling to be made under any of the enactments specified in Schedule 14 in respect of a particular subsidised unit, or suspend or discontinue the payment of such Exchequer contributions or part thereof, as he thinks just in those circumstances.

(4) Where an Exchequer contribution is made to a local authority in respect of a subsidised unit in relation to which an annual grant is payable by the authority to a development corporation or a housing association, then, if the amount of the Exchequer contribution is reduced or the payment of the Exchequer contribution or part of it is suspended or discontinued under this section, the authority may reduce the annual grant to a corresponding or any less extent or suspend the payment thereof, for a corresponding period or discontinue the payment, or of a corresponding part, as the case may be.

(5) The circumstances referred to in subsection (3) are—
(a) that the Exchequer contribution is to be made to a local authority and the Secretary of State is satisfied that the authority have failed to discharge any of their duties under this Act or that they have failed to exercise any power mentioned therein in any case where any such power ought to have been exercised;
(b) that the Exchequer contributions fall to be made or the subsidy falls to be paid subject to any conditions and the Secretary of State is satisfied that any of those conditions has not been complied with;
(c) that the subsidised unit has been converted, demolished or destroyed;
(d) that the subsidised unit is not fit to be used or has ceased to be used for the purpose for which it was intended;
(e) that the subsidised unit has been sold or has been leased for a stipulated duration exceeding 12 months;
(f) that the subsidised unit has been transferred, whether by sale or otherwise.

(6) Where the Secretary of State's power under this section to discontinue the payment of the whole or part of any Exchequer contributions to be made to a recipient authority in respect of a particular subsidised unit becomes exercisable in the circumstances mentioned in paragraph (e) or paragraph (f) of subsection (5) and the subsidised unit has become vested in or has been leased to another recipient authority, then, if the Secretary of State exercised that power he may make to that other authority Exchequer contributions of the like amount as he would otherwise have made to the first-mentioned authority if the conditions subject to which the first-mentioned Exchequer contributions fell to be made had been complied with.

(7) In this section—
'recipient authority' means a local authority, a development corporation, [or] a housing association . . .
'the subsidised unit' means the house, hostel or other land in respect of which Exchequer contributions fall to be made, whether they fall to be made in respect of it or its site or in respect of land comprising it or in respect of the cost of any houses, or the acquisition of any land, comprising it. **[770]**

NOTES to section 202

Amendment: Sub-s (7) was amended by the Housing (Scotland) Act 1988 (c 43), s 3, Sch 2, para 12.
Definitions: 'local authority', 'development corporation', 'housing association', 'house', 'land': see s 338 below; 'hostel': *Ibid* and s 2(5) above.

PART X
HOUSING ACCOUNTS OF LOCAL AUTHORITIES

203. The housing revenue account.

(1) A local authority shall keep a housing revenue account of the income and expenditure of the authority for each year in respect of the houses, buildings and land specified in Part I of Schedule 15, and Part I shall have effect for that purpose.

(2) A local authority may, with the consent of the Secretary of State, include in or exclude from the housing revenue account any individual house or other property or categories of houses or other properties.

(3) The Secretary of State may make a direction either generally or in relation to specified properties that any category of house or other properties shall be included in or excluded from the housing revenue account of a local authority.

(4) The land in respect of which the local authority are required by subsection (1) to keep a housing revenue account shall not include any land which the local authority have provided expressly for sale for development by another person.

(5) Part II of Schedule 15 shall have effect in relation to the operation of the housing revenue account.

(6) The Secretary of State may, as respects any year, after consultation with such associations of local authorities as appear to him to be concerned, by order amend Schedule 15.

(7) An order under subsection (6) shall be made by statutory instrument subject to annulment in pursuance of a resolution of either House of Parliament. [771]

NOTES to section 203

Definitions: 'local authority', 'house', 'land': see s 338 below.
Sub-s (6): The power to make an order has not been exercised.

204. Power of Secretary of State to limit estimated rate fund contributions to housing revenue account.

(1) The Secretary of State may by order impose, as respects a local authority or class thereof specified in the order, a limit to the amount of contribution out of their general fund which the authority or, as the case may be, an authority of the class may estimate that they will carry to the credit of their housing revenue account for the year specified in the order; and it shall be the duty of the local authority so to estimate that amount as not to exceed that limit.

(2) The limit referred to in subsection (1) may be expressed in whatever way the Secretary of State thinks fit.

(3) An order under this section shall be made by statutory instrument which shall be subject to annulment in pursuance of a resolution of either House of Parliament.

(4) Every local authority shall submit to the Secretary of State an estimate of the income and expenditure an account of which they are obliged, under section 203, to keep in their housing revenue account for the year next following.

(5) In subsection (1), 'general fund' means the fund maintained by a local authority under section 93 of the Local Government (Scotland) Act 1973. [772]

NOTES to section 204

Definition: 'local authority': see s 338 below.
Sub-s (1): Orders limiting general fund contributions have been made annually.

205. The rent rebate account.

(1) A local authority shall keep a rent rebate account for each year.

(2) The authority shall—
(a) credit that account with the amount of rent rebate subsidy payable to them under section 32 of the Social Security and Housing Benefits Act 1982;
(b) debit that account with—
 (i) the amount of the authority's rent rebates for the year, and
 (ii) the authority's costs of administering their rent rebates for the year.

(3) Where for any year a deficit is shown in the account, the local authority shall credit the account in respect of that year with an amount equal to the amount of the deficit. [773]

NOTE to section 205
Definition: 'local authority': see s 338 below.

206. The rent allowance account.

(1) A local authority shall keep a rent allowance account for each year.

(2) The authority shall—
(a) credit that account with the amount of rent allowance subsidy payable to them under section 32 of the Social Security and Housing Benefits Act 1982;
(b) debit that account with—
 (i) the amount of the authority's rent allowances for the year, and
 (ii) the authority's costs of administering their rent allowances for the year.

(3) Where for any year a deficit is shown in the account, the local authority shall credit the account in respect of that year with the amount of the deficit. [774]

NOTE to section 206
Definition: 'local authority': see s 338 below.

207. The slum clearance revenue account.

(1) A local authority shall keep a slum clearance revenue account for each year.

(2) That account shall include—
(a) the income and expenditure of the authority in respect of houses and other property acquired by them, or appropriated, for the purposes of Parts IV, V or VI other than houses acquired under Part IV for the purpose of bringing it or another house up to the tolerable standard; and
[(b) such of the expenditure of the authority in respect of houses and other property, being expenditure not included in paragraph (a), together with any income related to that expenditure as may be approved by the Secretary of State and falls within any of the following categories—
 (i) any payment under section 308 (payments to certain owner-occupiers and others in respect of houses not meeting tolerable standard which are purchased or demolished) other than any such payment in respect of an interest in a house which has been purchased by the local authority for the purpose of bringing that house or another house up to the tolerable standard;
 (ii) any payment under section 304 (payments in respect of well-maintained houses) other than any such payment in respect of an interest in a house which has been purchased by the local authority for the purpose of bringing that house or another house up to the tolerable standard;
 (iii) any payment under section 234(5) or (6) (payment of removal and other allowances to person displaced);
 (iv) such other expenditure as the Secretary of State may direct.]

(3) Schedule 16 shall have effect in relation to the slum clearance revenue account. [775]

NOTES to section 207

Amendment: In sub-s (2), para 6 was substituted by the Housing (Scotland) Act 1988 (c 43), s 72, Sch 9, para 17.

Definitions: 'local authority', 'house': see s 338 below; 'the tolerable standard': see s 338 below and s 86 above.

208. Application of receipts from disposal of certain land.

(1) Any money received by a local authority from the disposal of land to which this section applies shall be applied for a purpose for which the land which was the subject of the transaction was held.

(2) Subsection (1) shall not have effect if the Secretary of State approves the money being applied for another purpose [or has made directions under section 13(3)].

(3) Subsection (1) applies to land in respect of which income and expenditure is accounted for—
   (a) in the housing revenue account, or
   (b) in the slum clearance account. [776]

NOTES to section 208

Amendment: Sub-s (2) was amended by the Housing Act 1988 (c 50), s 132.
Definitions: 'local authority', 'land': see s 338 below.

209. Adjustment of accounts on appropriation of land.

(1) Where land is appropriated by a local authority for the purposes of Parts I or V or on the discontinuance of use for those purposes, such adjustment shall be made in the accounts of the local authority as the Secretary of State may direct.

(2) Any direction under this section may be either a general direction or a direction for any particular case.

(3) Where this section applies, section 25 of the Town and Country Planning (Scotland) Act 1959 (which also relates to the adjustment of accounts on appropriation of land) shall not apply. [777]

NOTES to section 209

Definitions: 'land', 'local authority': see s 338 below.

PART XI
RENTS AND SERVICE CHARGES

210. Rents for public sector housing.

(1) Subject to the provisions of this section, a local authority may charge such reasonable rents as they may determine for the tenancy or occupation of houses provided by them.

(2) A local authority shall from time to time review such rents and make such charges either of rents generally or of particular rents as circumstances may require.

(3) In determining standard rents to which their housing revenue account relates, a local authority shall take no account of the personal circumstances of the tenants. [778]

NOTES to section 210

Definitions: 'local authority', 'houses': see s 338 below; 'housing revenue account': see s 203 above.

211. Service charges.

(1) A local authority shall make a service charge for each year of such amount as they think reasonable in all the circumstances in respect of the following items to which the housing revenue account relates—
  (a) any garage, car-port or other car parking facilities provided by them in so far as not included within the terms of the tenancy of a house;
  (b) any service provided by them under the terms of the tenancy of a house;
  (c) any other item made available under section 3 or 5 or supplied under section 4 for which a charge was made in the financial year 1971–2 under sections 139 to 141 of the Act of 1966 and which has continued to be made available or supplied after that year.

(2) The Secretary of State may direct in relation to any service provided under paragraph (b) of subsection (1) either generally or in a particular case that no such service charge shall be made.

(3) Before making any such direction the Secretary of State shall consult—
  (a) such associations of local authorities as apear to him to be concerned;
  (b) any local authority with whom consultation appears to him to be desirable.

NOTES to section 211

Definitions: 'local authority', 'house': see s 338 below; 'housing revenue account': see s 203 above.

212. Rent increase notice.

(1) Where an authority lets a house held by it for housing purposes to a tenant it shall be an implied term of the tenancy that the rent or any other charge payable to the authority under the tenancy may be increased by notice ('rent increase notice') without the tenancy being terminated.

(2) A rent increase notice shall—
  (a) be in writing;
  (b) specify the increased rent and the date on which it has effect;
  (c) be given to the tenant at least 4 weeks before it has effect;
  (d) inform the tenant of his right to terminate the tenancy and of the steps to be taken if he wishes to do so;
  (e) inform him of the dates by which the notice of removal under section 213 must be received and the tenancy terminated if the increase is not to have effect.

(3) A rent increase notice given in accordance with this section shall have effect unless a removal notice is given in accordance with section 213.

(4) For the purposes of this section an authority is—
  (a) a regional, islands or district council;
  (b) a joint board or a joint committee;
  (c) a development corporation;
  (d) [Scottish Homes]
  (e) a water authority or a water development board.

(5) This section does not apply to a secure tenancy.

NOTES to section 212

Amendment: In sub-s (4) reference to Scottish Homes substituted by the Housing (Scotland) Act 1988 (c 43), s 3, Sch 2, para 1.
Definitions: 'house', 'development corporation', 'water authority', 'water development board': see s 338 below; 'secure tenancy': see s 338 below and s 44 above.

213. Removal notice.

(1) A tenant who has been given a rent increase notice may give the authority a removal notice terminating the tenancy.

(2) The removal notice shall have effect to terminate the tenancy if—
(a) it is given within 2 weeks of the date on which the rent increase notice was given, or such longer period as the notice may specify;
(b) it specifies a date for the termination of the tenancy within 4 weeks after the date on which it is given.

(3) Nothing in the terms of the tenancy (express or implied) shall prevent a tenant giving a removal notice that complies with subsection (2). [781]

PART XII
HOUSE LOANS AND OTHER FINANCIAL ASSISTANCE

House loans: general

214. Power of local authority to make advances for the purpose of increasing housing accommodation.

(1) A local authority may advance money to any person for the purpose of—
(a) acquiring a house;
(b) constructing a house;
(c) converting another building into a house or acquiring another building and converting it into a house; or
(d) altering, enlarging, repairing or improving a house; or
(e) subject to subsection (4), facilitating the repayment by means of the advance of the amount outstanding on a previous loan made for any of the purposes specified in paragraphs (a) to (d).

(2) The authority may make advances whether or not the houses or buildings are in the authority's area.

(3) In determining whether to advance money under subsection (1), the local authority shall have regard to any advice which may be given from time to time by the Secretary of State.

(4) An advance shall not be made for the purpose specified in paragraph (e) of subsection (1) unless the local authority satisfy themselves that the primary effect of the advance will be to meet the housing needs of the applicant by enabling him either to retain an interest in the house concerned or to carry out such works in relation to that house as would be eligible for an advance by virtue of paragraph (c) or (d) of that subsection.

(5) An advance under this section may be made in addition to assistance given by the local authority in respect of the same house under any other Act or any other provision of this Act.

(6) If it appears to a local authority that the principal effect of the making of an advance under subsection (1) in respect of any premises would be to meet the housing needs of the applicant, they may make the advance notwithstanding that it is intended that some part of the premises will be used or, as the case may be, will continue to be used, otherwise than as a house, and accordingly where, by virtue of this subsection, a local authority propose to make an advance in respect of any premises, the premises shall be treated for the purposes of subsections (1) to (4) as, or as a building to be converted into, a house.

(7) In this section any reference to a house includes a reference to any part share of it.

(8) Schedule 17 shall have effect in relation to the terms of an advance under this section. [782]

NOTES to section 214

Definitions: 'local authority', 'house': see s 338 below.

215. Requirements as to meeting tolerable standard.

(1) Before advancing money under section 214 for the purpose of acquiring a house, the local authority shall satisfy themselves that the house to be acquired will meet the tolerable standard.

(2) Before advancing money under this section for any of the purposes specified in paragraphs (b) to (d) of subsection (1), the authority shall satisfy themselves that the house to be constructed, altered, enlarged, repaired, improved or into which the building is to be converted, as the case may be, will, when the construction, alteration, enlargement, repair, improvement or conversion has been completed, meet that standard. [783]

NOTES to section 215

Definitions: 'house', 'local authority': see s 338 below; 'the tolerable standard': see s 338 below and s 86 above.

House loans: special cases

216. House loans to tenants exercising right to purchase.

(1) A tenant who seeks to exercise his right to purchase a house under Part III and who has received an offer to sell (or, as the case may be, an amended offer to sell) from the landlord shall be entitled, together with any joint purchaser under section 61(6) (and the said tenant and any joint purchaser are referred to in this section as 'the applicant') to apply—
  (a) in the case where the landlord is a development corporation (including an urban development corporation) or [Scottish Homes] to that body or
  [(b) in a case where the landlord is the Housing Corporation or a housing association registered in the register maintained by the Housing Corporation, to the Housing Corporation;
  (bi) in a case where the landlord is a housing association registered in the register maintained by Scottish Homes, to Scottish Homes;]
  (c) in any other case, to the local authority for the area in which the house is situated,
for a loan of an amount not exceeding the price fixed under section 62 to assist him to purchase the house.

(2) A loan application under subsection (1)—
  (a) must be served on the landlord or other body—
    (i) within one month after service on the tenant of the offer to sell (or, where there has been service of one or more amended offers to sell or there has been a determination by the Lands Tribunal under section 65(3) which does not require the issue of an amended offer to sell, of the latest of these); or
    (ii) within one year and 10 months after service of the application to purchase if the tenant has, in terms of section 67, a fixed price option as regards the house;
  (b) shall be in such form as the Secretary of State shall by order made by statutory instrument prescribe, and shall contain—
    (i) the amount of the loan which the applicant seeks;
    (ii) the applicant's annual gross income and his net income after payment of income tax and national insurance contributions;
    (iii) any liabilities in respect of credit sales or other fixed outgoings of the applicant; and
    (iv) a statement that the applicant has applied for and been unable to obtain a sufficient building society loan; and
  (c) shall be accompanied by evidence of the matters referred to in sub-paragraphs (ii) to (iv) of paragraph (b).

(3) Subject to such requirements as the Secretary of State may by order made by statutory instrument impose, a landlord or other body which receives an application under subsection (1) shall, where it is satisfied on reasonable inquiry (which shall include reasonable opportunity for the applicant to amend his application) that the information

contained in the loan application is correct, serve on the applicant an offer of loan, which shall specify a maximum amount of loan calculated in accordance with regulations made by statutory instrument by the Secretary of State.

(4) A landlord or other body to which application has been made under subsection (1) shall complete its inquiries and either—
(a) issue the offer of loan under subsection (3); or
(b) refuse the application on the ground that information contained in the loan application is incorrect in a material respect,
within 2 months of the date of service of the loan application.

(5) An applicant who wishes to accept an offer of loan shall do so along with his notice of acceptance under sections 66(1) or 67(1).

(6) An offer of loan under subsection (3) together with an acceptance under subsection (5) shall constitute an agreement by the landlord or other body, subject to such requirements as the Secretary of State may by order made by statutory instrument impose, to land to the applicant for the purpose of purchasing the house—
(a) the maximum amount of loan mentioned in subsection (3); or
(b) the amount of loan sought by the applicant,
whichever is the lesser, on the execution by the applicant of a standard security over the house.

(7) An applicant who is aggrieved by a refusal under subsection (4)(b), or by a failure to comply with the subsection, or by the calculation of maximum amount of loan mentioned in subsection (3) may, within 2 months of the date of the refusal or failure of the offer of loan, as the case may be, raise proceedings by way of summary application in the sheriff court for the district in which the house is situated for declarator that he is entitled to a loan in accordance with subsection (3).

(8) Where in proceedings under subsection (7) the sheriff grants declarator that the applicant is entitled to a loan, such declarator shall have effect as if it were an offer of loan of the amount specified in the declarator duly issued under this section by the landlord or other body.

(9) A statutory instrument made under subsection (3) or (6) shall be subject to annulment in pursuance of a resolution of either House of Parliament. [784]

NOTES to section 216

Amendments: In sub-s (1), paras (b), (bi) substituted by the Housing (Scotland) Act 1988 (c 43), s 3, Sch 2, para 13; reference to 'Scottish Homes' substituted by *Ibid*, para 1.
Definitions: 'tenant', 'tenancy', 'offer to sell', 'landlord': see s 82 above; 'development corporation', 'local authority', 'house', 'housing association', 'Lands Tribunal': see s 338 below.
Sub-s (2): See the Right to Purchase (Loan Application) (Scotland) Order 1980, SI 1980/1492, paras [1282] ff below.
Sub-ss (3), (6): See the Right to Purchase (Loans) (Scotland) Regulations 1980, SI 1980/1430, paras [1268] ff below.

217. Duty of local authorities to offer loans to meet expenses of improvement of houses in housing action areas.

(1) Where the owner or the lessee of a house situated in a housing action area is willing to carry out improvement works which are, in the opinion of the local authority, required in order to bring the house up to the standard specified under section 90(3) or by virtue of section 91(3), he may, not later than 9 months from the date of publication and service of a notice of a final resolution passed under Part I of Schedule 8, apply to the local authority for a loan.

(2) Subject to this section, if the local authority are satisfied that the applicant can reasonably be expected to meet obligations assumed by him in pursuance of this section in respect of a loan of the amount of the expenditure to which the application relates, the authority shall offer to make a loan of that amount to the applicant, the loan to be secured

to the authority by a standard security over the premises consisting of or comprising the house.

(3) Subject to this section, if the local authority are not so satisfied, but consider that the applicant can reasonably be expected to meet obligations assumed by him in pursuance of this section in respect of a loan of a smaller amount, the authority may, if they think fit, offer to make a loan of that smaller amount to the applicant, the loan to be secured as aforesaid.

(4) Any offer made by the local authority under this section shall contain a condition to the effect that, if an improvement grant or a repairs grant becomes payable under Part XIII in respect of the expenditure to which the application under this section relates, the authority shall not be required to lend a sum greater than the amount of the expenditure to which the application relates after deduction of the amount of the grant.

(5) The local authority shall not make an offer under the foregoing provisions of this section unless they are satisfied that—
(a) the applicant's estate or interest in the house amounts to ownership or a lease for a period which will not expire before the date for final repayment of the loan, and
(b) according to a valuation made on behalf of the local authority, the amount of the principal of the loan does not exceed the value which it is estimated the subjects comprised in the security will bear after improvement of the house or houses to the standard specified under section 90(3) or by virtue of section 91(3).

(6) The rate of interest payable on a loan under this section shall be a variable rate calculated under section 219.

(7) Subject to this section, the loan offered by the local authority under this section shall be subject to such reasonable terms as the authority may specify in their offer.

(8) The local authority's offfer may in particular include any such terms as are described in paragraphs 5 to 7 of Schedule 17 (repayment of principal and interest) and provision for the advance being made by instalments from time to time as the works of improvement progress.

(9) Where an improvement grant or repairs grant is payable partly in respect of expenditure to which the application under this section relates, and partly in respect of other expenditure, the reference in subsection (4) to an improvement grant or repairs grant shall be taken as a reference to the part of the grant which in the opinion of the local authority is attributable to the expenditure to which the application under this section relates. **[785]**

NOTES to section 217

Definitions: 'owner', 'house': see s 338 below; 'housing action area': see ss 89–91 above; 'improvement grant': see ss 338 and 236 below; 'repair grant': see ss 338 and 248 below.

---

218. Duty of local authority to offer loans to meet expenses of repairs.

(1) Where the person having control of a house is willing to carry out the works necessary to rectify the defects specified in the notice under section 108(2), he may, not later than 21 days from the date of service of the said notice, or from the date of determination of any appeal, apply to the local authority for a loan. **[786]**

NOTES to section 218

Definitions: 'house', 'local authorities': see s 338 below.

Rates of interest on home loans

219. Local authority home loan interest rates.

(1) Subject to subsections (2) and (3)—
(a) any advance of money under a power conferred by section 214 or under any other power to make loans for the like purposes; and

(b) any sum secured under any arrangement by which the price or part of the price of a house sold by a local authority is secured by a standard security; and
(c) any sum secured under any security which is taken over by a local authority under a power conferred by section 229 (local authority indemnities for building societies, etc),

is a variable interest home loan for the purposes of this section.

(2) This section does not apply to an advance made before 3rd October 1980 or to a sum secured in respect of the price of a house agreed to be sold before then or (where subsection 1(c) applies) to a security granted before then.

(3) This section shall not apply to an advance made in implement of a contract constituted by an offer of advance made before that date and an unqualified acceptance of that offer thereafter.

(4) Subject to section 220, a local authority shall, in respect of their variable interest home loans, charge a rate of interest which shall be equal to whichever is the higher of the following—
(a) the standard rate for the time being, as declared by the Secretary of State in accordance with subsection (5);
(b) the locally determined rate calculated in accordance with subsection (6).

(5) In considering what rate to declare as the standard rate for the purposes of subsection (4), the Secretary of State shall take into account interest rates charged by building societies in the United Kingdom and any movement in those rates.

(6) The locally determined rate for the purposes of this section shall be the rate which is necessary to service loan charges on money which is to be applied to making variable interest home loans during the relevant period of six months (referred to in subsection (7)), together with the addition of one quarter per cent to cover the administration cost of making and managing variable interest home loans.

(7) The locally determined rate, for the purposes of this section, shall be determined by each local authority for the period of 6 months not less than one month before the beginning of the relevant period.

(8) Nothing in this or the following two sections shall affect the operation of section 223(1)(b) (under which a part of certain loans may be free of interest for up to 5 years). [787]

NOTE to section 219

Definition: 'local authority': see s 338 below.

---

220. Variation of rate by local authority.

(1) Where the declaration of a new standard rate or, as the case may be, the determination of a new locally determined rate, affects the rate of interest chargeable under section 219 by a local authority the authority shall, as soon as practicable after such declaration or determination, serve in respect of each of its variable interest home loans a notice on the borrower which shall, as from the appropriate day—
(a) vary the rate of interest payable by him; and
(b) where, as the result of the variation, the amount outstanding under the advance or security would increase if the periodic repayments were not increased, increase the amount of the periodic repayments to such an amount as will ensure that the said outstanding amount will not increase.

(2) In subsection (1), 'the appropriate day' means such day as shall be specified in the notice, being—
(a) in the case of a new standard rate, a day not less than 2 weeks, nor more than 6 weeks, after service of the notice; and
(b) in the case of a new locally determined rate, the first day of the relevant period of 6 months. [788]

NOTES to section 220
Definition: 'local authority': see s 338 below.

221. Variation of rate by Secretary of State.

Notwithstanding anything contained in sections 219 and 220, but subject to section 230, the Secretary of State may, where he considers that the interest rate charged by a local authority does not satisfy the requirements of section 219(4), direct a local authority—
  (a) to charge an interest rate specified in the direction; and
  (b) to vary the rate in accordance with the provisions of section 220. **[789]**

NOTES to section 221
Definition: 'local authority': see s 338 below.

Assistance for first-time buyers

222. Advances to recognised lending institutions to assist first-time buyers.

(1) The Secretary of State may make advances to recognised lending institutions enabling them to provide assistance to first-time purchasers of house property in Great Britain where—
  (a) the purchaser intends to make his home in the property,
  (b) finance for the purchase of the property (and improvements, if any) is obtained by means of a secured loan from the lending institution, and
  (c) the purchase price is within the prescribed limits.

(2) In this section 'prescribed' means prescribed by order of the Secretary of State.

(3) An order—
  (a) may prescribe different limits from properties in different areas, and
  (b) shall be made by statutory instrument which shall be subject to annulment in pursuance of a resolution of the House of Commons. **[790]**

NOTES to section 222
Definitions: 'recognised lending institution': see s 224 below; 'house': see s 338 below.
Sub-ss (1), (2): See the Home Purchase Assistance (Price Limits) Order 1991, SI 1991/819, paras [1506c] ff below.

223. Forms of assistance and qualifying conditions.

(1) Assistance under section 222 (assistance for first-time buyers) may be given in the following ways—
  (a) the secured loan may be financed by the Secretary of State to the extent of £600 (that amount being normally additional to that which the institution would otherwise have lent, but not so that the total loan exceeds the loan value of the property);
  (b) £600 of the total loan may be made free of interest, and of any obligation to repay principal, for up to 5 years from the date of purchase; and
  (c) the institution may provide the purchaser with a bonus on his savings (which bonus shall be tax-exempt) up to a maximum of £110, payable towards the purchase or expenses arising in connection with it.

(2) The purchaser qualifies for assistance under subsection (1)(a) and (b) (interest-free loan) by satisfying the following conditions with respect to his own savings—
  (a) that he has been saving with a recognised savings institution for at least 2 years preceding the date of his application for assistance,
  (b) that throughout the 12 months preceding that date he had at least £300 of such savings, and

(c) that by that date he has accumulated at least £600 of such savings;
and he qualifies for assistance under subsection (1)(c) (bonus on savings) by satisfying the conditions specified in paragraphs (a) and (b) above.

(3) The Secretary of State may allow for the conditions to be relaxed or modified in particular classes of case.

(4) No assistance shall be given in any case unless the amount of the secured loan is at least £1,600 and amounts to not less than 25 per cent of the purchase price of the property.

(5) The Secretary of State may by order made with the consent of the Treasury—
(a) alter any of the money sums specified in this section;
(b) substitute a longer or shorter period for either or both of the periods mentioned in subsection (2)(a) and (b) (conditions as to savings);
(c) alter the condition in subsection (2)(c) so as to enable the purchaser to satisfy it with lesser amounts of savings and to enable assistance to be given in such a case according to reduced scales specified in the order;
(d) alter the percentage mentioned in subsection (4) (minimum secured loan).

(6) An order shall be made by statutory instrument which shall be subject to annulment in pursuance of a resolution of the House of Commons. [791]

NOTES to section 223

Definitions: 'recognised savings institutions': see s 225 below.
Sub-ss (5), (6): The power to make an order has not been exercised.

224. Recognised lending institutions.

(1) The lending institutions recognised for the purposes of section 222 (assistance for first-time buyers) are—
building societies,
local authorities,
development corporations,
[Scottish Homes]
banks,
insurance companies, and
friendly societies.

(2) The Secretary of State may by order made with the consent of the Treasury—
(a) add to the list in subsection (1), or
(b) direct that a named body shall no longer be a recognised lending institution;
but before making an order under paragraph (b) he shall give an opportunity for representations to be made on behalf of the body concerned.

(3) An order shall be made by statutory instrument. [792]

NOTES to section 224

Amendment: In sub-s (1) reference to Scottish Homes substituted by the Housing (Scotland) Act 1988 (c 43), s 3, Sch 2, para 1.
Definitions: 'building society', 'local authority', 'development corporation', 'bank', 'insurance company', 'friendly society': see s 338 below.
Sub-s (2): See the Home Purchase Assistance (Recognised Lending Institutions) Order 1982, SI 1982/976, paras [1324] ff below.

225. Recognised savings institutions.

(1) The savings institutions recognised for the purposes of section 223 (qualifying conditions as to savings) are—
building societies,
local authorities,
banks,
friendly societies,

the Director of Savings, and
the Post Office,
and savings institutions recognised for the purposes of the corresponding provisions in force in England or Wales or Northern Ireland.

In this section and in section 227 those corresponding provisions are—
(a) in relation to England and Wales, sections 445 to 449 of the Housing Act 1985;
(b) in relation to Northern Ireland, Part IX of the Housing (Northern Ireland) Order 1981.

(2) The Secretary of State may by order made with the consent of the Treasury—
(a) add to the list in subsection (1), or
(b) direct that a named body shall no longer be a recognised savings institution,
but before making an order under paragraph (b) he shall give an opportunity for representations to be made on behalf of the body concerned.

(3) An order shall be made by statutory instrument. [793]

NOTES to section 225

Definitions: 'building society', 'authority', 'bank', 'friendly society': see s 338 below.
Sub-s (2): See the Home Purchase Assistance (Recognised Savings Institutions) Order 1978, SI 1978/1785, paras [1261] ff below.

226. Terms of advances and administration.

(1) Advances to lending institutions under section 222 (assistance for first-time buyers) shall be on such terms as to repayment and otherwise as may be settled by the Secretary of State, with the consent of the Treasury, after consultation with lending and savings institutions or organisations representative of them; and the terms shall be embodied in directions issued by the Secretary of State.

(2) The following matters, among others, may be dealt with in directions issued by the Secretary of State—
(a) the cases in which assistance is to be provided;
(b) the method of determining the loan value of property for the purposes of section 223(1)(a) (limit on total loan);
(c) the method of quantifying bonus by reference to savings;
(d) the considerations by reference to which a person is or is not to be treated as a first-time purchaser of house property;
(e) the steps which must be taken with a view to satisfying the conditions in section 223(2) (conditions as to purchaser's own savings), and the circumstances in which those conditions are or are not to be treated as satisfied;
(f) the supporting evidence and declarations which must be furnished by a person applying for assistance, in order to establish his qualification for it, and the means of ensuring that restitution is made in the event of it being obtained by false representations;
(g) the way in which amounts paid over by way of assistance are to be repaid to the lending institutions and to the Secretary of State.

(3) The Secretary of State may, to the extent that he thinks proper for safeguarding the lending institutions, include in the terms an undertaking to indemnify the institutions in respect of loss suffered in cases where assistance has been given. [794]

NOTE to section 226

Definition: 'house': see s 338 below.

227. Modifications of building society law and disapplication of provisions of the Restrictive Trade Practices Act 1976 in relation to assistance for first-time buyers.

(1) So much of an advance by a building society which is partly financed under section

222 (assistance for first-time buyers) or the corresponding English or Northern Ireland provisions as is so financed shall be treated as not forming part of the advance for the purpose of determining—
 (a) whether the advance, or any further advance made within two years of the date of purchase, is beyond the powers of the society, and
 (b) the classification of the advance, or any such further advance, for the purposes of Part III of the Building Societies Act 1986.

(2) Section 16(3) and (5) of the Restrictive Trade Practices Act 1976 (recommendations by service supply associations to members) shall not apply to recommendations made to lending institutions and savings institutions about the manner of implementing sections 222 to 226 (assistance for first-time buyers) or the corresponding English or Northern Ireland provisions, provided that the recommendations are made with the approval of the Secretary of State, or as the case may be, the Department of Environment for Northern Ireland, which may be withdrawn at any time on one month's notice. **[795]**

NOTE to section 227
Definition: 'building society': see s 338 below.

228. Exclusion of Restrictive Trade Practices Act: agreements as to loans on security of new houses.

(1) In determining for the purposes of the Restrictive Trade Practices Act 1976 whether an agreement between building societies is one to which that Act applies by virtue of an order made, or having effect as if made, under section 11 of that Act (restrictive agreements as to services), no account shall be taken of any term (whether or not subject to exceptions) by which the parties or any of them agree not to grant loans on the security of new houses unless they have been built by or at the direction of a person who is registered with, or has agreed to comply with the standards of house building laid down or approved by, an appropriate body.

(2) In subsection (1)—
'appropriate body' means a body concerned with the specification and control of standards of house building which—
 (a) has its chairman, or the chairman of its board of directors or other governing body, appointed by the Secretary of State, and
 (b) promotes or administers a scheme conferring rights in respect of defects in the condition of houses on persons having or acquiring interest in them, and
'new house' means a building or part of a building intended for use as a private dwelling and not previously occupied as such.

(3) The reference in subsection (1) to a term agreed to by the parties or any of them includes a term to which the parties or any of them are deemed to have agreed by virtue of section 16 of the Restrictive Trade Practices Act 1976 (recommendations of services supply associations). **[796]**

NOTE to section 228
Definition: 'building society': see s 338 below.

Other assistance

229. Local authority indemnities for building societies, etc.

(1) A local authority may, with the approval of the Secretary of State, enter into an agreement with a building society or recognised body under which the authority binds itself to indemnify the building society or recognised body in respect of—
 (a) the whole or any part of any outstanding indebtedness of a borrower; and
 (b) loss or expense to the building society or recognised body resulting from the failure of the borrower duly to perform any obligation imposed on him by a heritable security.

(2) The agreement may also, where the borrower is made party to it, enable or require the authority in specified circumstances to take an assignation of the rights and liabilities of the building society or recognised body under the heritable security.

(3) Approval of the Secretary of State under subsection (1) may be given generally in relation to agreements which satisfy specified requirements, or in relation to individual agreements, and with or without conditions, as he thinks fit, and such approval may be withdrawn at any time on one month's notice.

(4) Before issuing any general approval under subsection (1) the Secretary of State shall consult with such bodies as appear to him to be representative of local authorities, and of building societies, and also with the Building Societies Commission.

(5) Section 16(3) and (5) of the Restrictive Trade Practices Ac 1976 (recommendations by services supply association to members) shall not apply to recommendations made to building societies or recognised bodies about the making of agreements under this section provided that the recommendations are made with the approval of the Secretary of State.

(6) In this section 'recognised body' means a body designated, or of a class or description designated, in an order under this subsection made by statutory instrument by the Secretary of State with the consent of the Treasury.

(7) Before making an order under subsection (6) varying or revoking an order previously so made, the Secretary of State shall give an opportunity for representations to be made on behalf of a recognised body which, if the order were made, would cease to be such a body. **[797]**

NOTES to section 229
Definitions: 'local authority' 'building society': see s 338 below.
Sub-ss (6), (7): See the Local Authorities (Recognised Bodies for Heritable Securities (Indemnities) Order 1987, SI 1987/1388, paras [1372] ff below.

230. Assistance by local authority for acquiring houses in need of repair and improvement.

(1) Notwithstanding any other provision of sections 219, 220 and 221, a local authority may, where the conditions set out in subsection (2) are satisfied, give assistance to a person acquiring a house in need of repair or improvement by making provision for waiving or reducing, for a period ending not later than 5 years after the date of an advance of money of the kind mentioned in section 219(1)(a) or of the granting of a security under an arrangement of the kind mentioned in section 219(1)(b), the interest payable on the sum advanced or remaining outstanding under the security, as the case may be.

(2) The conditions mentioned in subsection (1) are that—
(a) the assistance is given in accordance with a scheme which has been approved by the Secretary of State or which conforms with such requirements as may be specified by the Secretary of State by order made by statutory instrument with the consent of the Treasury; and
(b) the person acquiring the house has entered into an agreement with the local authority to carry out, within a period specified in the agreement, works of repair or improvement therein specified. **[798]**

NOTES to section 230
Definitions: 'local authority', 'building society': see s 338 below; 'improvement': see ss 338 and 236 below.
Sub-s (2): The power to make an order has not been exercised.

231. Loans by Public Works Loan Commissioners for provision or improvement of housing accommodation.

(1) The Public Works Loan Commissioners may, subject to the provisions of this section, lend money to any person entitled to any land either as owner or as lessee under a

lease of which a period of not less than 50 years remains unexpired at the date of the loan for the purpose of constructing or improving, or facilitating or encouraging the construction or improvement of, houses, and any such person may borrow from the Public Works Loan Commissioners such money as may be required for the purposes aforesaid.

(2) A loan for any of the purposes specified in subsection (1) shall be secured with interest by a heritable security over the land and houses in respect of which that purpose is to be carried out and over such other land and houses, if any, as may be offered as security for the loan.

(3) Any such loan may be made whether the person receving the loan has or has not power to borrow on bond and disposition in security or otherwise, independently of this Act, but nothing in this Act shall affect any regulation, statutory or otherwise, whereby any company may be restricted from borrowing until a definite portion of capital is subscribed for, taken or paid up.

(4) The following conditions shall apply in the case of any such loan—
(a) the period for repayment shall not exceed 40 years;
(b) no money shall be lent on the security of any land or houses unless the estate or interest therein proposed to be burdened is either ownership or a lease of which a period of not less than 50 years remains unexpired at the date of the loan;
(c) the money lent shall not exceed such proportion as is hereinafter authorised of the value, to be ascertained to the satisfaction of the Public Works Loan Commissioners, of the estate or interest in the land or houses proposed to be burdened in pursuance of subsection (2); but loans may be made by instalment from time to time as the building of houses or other work on the land so burdened progresses, so, however, that the total loans do not at any time exceed the amount aforesaid; and the heritable security may be granted accordingly to secure such loans so to be made from time to time.

(5) The proportion of such value as aforesaid authorised for the purpose of the loan shall be three-fourths but if the loan exceeds two-thirds of such value, the Public Works Loan Commissioners shall require, in addition to such heritable security as is mentioned in subsection (2), such further security as they may think fit. **[799]**

NOTES to section 231

Definitions: 'land', 'owner': see s 338 below; 'improvement': see ss 338 and 236 below; 'house': see s 338 below.

232. Power of court in cases relating to instalment purchase agreements.

(1) Where, under the terms of an instalment purchase agreement, a person has been let into possession of a house and, on the termination of the agreement or of his right to possession under it, proceedings are brought for possession of the house, the court may—
(a) adjourn the proceedings; or
(b) on making an order for possession of the house, supersede extract or postpone the date of possession;
for such period or periods as the court thinks fit.

(2) On any such adjournment, superseding of extract, or postponement, the court may impose such conditions with regard to the payment by the person in possession in respect of his continued occupation of the house and such other conditions as the court thinks fit.

(3) The court may revoke or from time to time vary any condition imposed by virtue of this section.

(4) In this section 'instalment purchase agreement' means an agreement for the purchase of a house under which the whole or part of the purchase price is to be paid in 3 or more instalments and the completion of the purchase is deferred until the whole or a specified part of the purchase price has been paid. **[800]**

NOTE to section 232
Definition: 'house': see s 338 below.

233. Power of local authority to assist in provision of separate service water pipes for houses.

(1) A local authority may if they think fit give assistance in respect of the provision of a separate service pipe for a house in their district which has a piped supply of water from a water main, but no separate service pipe.

(2) Subject to this section, the assistance shall be by way of making a grant in respect of all or any part of the expenses incurred in the provision of the separate service pipe.

(3) The reference to expenses in subsection (2) includes, in a case where all or any part of the works required for the provision of the separate service pipe are carried out by a water authority (whether in exercise of default powers or in any other case), a reference to sums payable by the owner of the house, or any other person, to the water authority for carrying out the works. **[801]**

NOTES to section 233
Definitions: 'local authorities', 'water authority': see s 338 below.

234. Financial assistance towards tenants' removal expenses.

(1) A local authority shall, in the performance of the functions of management of houses conferred on them by section 17, have power, subject to subsections (2) and (3), in every case where a tenant of a house held by it for housing purposes moves to another house, whether or not that other house is also owned by the local authority—
  (a) to pay any expenses of the removal;
  (b) where the tenant is purchasing the house, to pay any expenses incurred by him in connection with the purchase other than the purchase price.

(2) Paragraph (b) of subsection (1) shall only apply in a case where a tenant of a house moves to another house of the local authority if that house has never been let.

(3) A local authority may make their payment of expenses in connection with the purchase of a house subject to such conditions as they think fit.

(4) Nothing in this section shall affect the operation of section 34 of the Land Compensation (Scotland) Act 1973 (disturbance payments for persons without compensatable interests).

(5) The power conferred on a local authority by subsection (1) to make allowances towards the expenses incurred in removing by persons displaced in consequence of the exercise by the authority of their powers shall include power to make allowances to persons so displaced temporarily in respect of expenses incurred by them in storage of furniture.

(6) Where, as a result of action taken by a local authority under Part IV, the population of the locality is materially decreased, the authority may pay to any person carrying on a retail shop in the locality such reasonable allowance as they may think fit towards any loss which, in their opinion, he will thereby sustain, so, however, that in estimating any such loss they shall have regard to the probable future development of the locality. **[802]**

NOTES to section 234
Definitions: 'local authority', 'house': see s 338 below.

Contributions to assistance for elderly, etc

235. Contributions by other local authorities towards expenses of housing pensioners and disabled persons.

A regional or islands council may make any contribution they think fit towards expenditure incurred by a local authority in connection with—
   (a) the provision, maintenance and management, under this Act, of housing accommodation for disabled persons and persons of pensionable age; and
   (b) the exercise, in relation to housing accommodation so provided, or for the benefit of persons occupying such accommodation, of any of their functions under section 3, 4 or 5. [803]

NOTES to section 235
Definitions: 'local authority': see s 338 below; 'disabled person': *Ibid* and s 236 below.

PART XIII
LOCAL AUTHORITY GRANTS FOR IMPROVEMENT, REPAIR AND CONVERSION

Improvement grants

236. Power of local authorities to make improvement grants.

(1) Subject to the provisions of this Part, a local authority may give assistance by making an improvement grant in respect of—
   (a) works required for the provision of houses by the conversion of houses or other buildings;
   (b) works required for the improvement of houses.

(2) Subject to subsection (4), in this Part—
   (a) 'improvement', in relation to a house, includes—
      (i) alteration and enlargement, and
      (ii) in relation to a house for a disabled occupant, the doing of works required for making it suitable for his accommodation, welfare or employment;
   (b) any reference to works required for the provision or improvement of a house, whether generally or in any particular respect, includes a reference to any works of repair or replacement needed in the opinion of the local authority paying the grant for the purposes of enabling the house to which the improvement relates to attain a good state of repair,
and 'improved' shall be construed accordingly.

(3) In this section—
'disabled occupant' means a disabled person for whose benefit it is proposed to carry out works in respect of which an improvement grant is sought;
'disabled person' means a person who is substantially handicapped by illness, injury or congenital deformity;
'house for a disabled occupant' means a house which—
   (a) is a disabled occupant's only or main residence when an application for an improvement grant in respect of it is made; or
   (b) is likely in the opinion of the local authority to become a disabled occupant's only or main residence not later than the expiry of a reasonable period after the completion of the works in respect of which an improvement grant is sought.

(4) Any reference in this Part to works required for the improvement of a house does not include a reference to works specified in a notice under section 162 (which empowers a local authority to require the provision of means of escape in the case of fire in a house in multiple occupation) or to works required in connection with works so specified. [804]

[805]

NOTES to section 236
Definitions: 'local authority', 'house': see s 338 below.

237. Form of application.

An application for an improvement grant shall be in such form as may from time to time be prescribed and shall contain full particulars of—
  (a) the works which are proposed to be or are being carried out together with plans and specifications of the works;
  (b) the land on which those works are proposed to be or are being carried out; and
  (c) the expenses (including any professional fees) estimated to be incurred in executing the works, and where the application relates to the provision or improvement of more than one house, the estimate shall specify the proportion of the expenses attributable to each house proposed to be provided or improved.   [805]

NOTES to section 237
Definitions: 'improvement', 'improvement grant': see s 338 below and s 236(1) above; 'land', 'house': see s 338 below.

238. Power of local authority.

(1) Subject to this Part, a local authority may approve, or refuse to approve, such an application.

(2) If it approves the application, it shall make an improvement grant.   [806]

NOTES to section 238
Definitions: 'local authority': see s 338 below; 'improvement grant': *Ibid* and s 236(1) above.

239. Consent of Secretary of State.

(1) The Secretary of State may give directions to a local authority or to local authorities generally, requiring that an application for an improvement grant or all such applications of any class specified in the directions shall not be approved except with the consent of the Secretary of State and subject to any conditions which he may impose.

(2) It shall be the duty of any local authority to comply with any such directions.   [807]

NOTES to section 239
Definitions: 'local authority': see s 338 below; 'improvement grant': *Ibid* and s 236(1) above.

[239A. Power of Secretary of State to give direction to prevent duplications of grant.

(1) The Secretary of State may, so as to prevent the duplication of the making of grants under this Part in respect of the same works, give directions to—
  (a) a local authority;
  (b) local authorities generally; and
  (c) Scottish Homes;
as to the circumstances in which they, or any of them, may or may not exercise their powers under this Part [or are not to perform their duties under this Part.]

(2) It shall be the duty of Scottish Homes and of any local authority to whom directions have been given to comply with such direction.]   [808]

NOTES to section 239A
Section 239A was added by the Housing (Scotland) Act 1988 (c 43), s 2.
Amendment: Sub-s (1) was amended by the Local Government and Housing Act 1989 (c 42), s 195, Sch 11, para 95.

Definition: 'local authority': see s 338 below.

240. Conditions for approval of applications for improvement grant other than applications relating exclusively to the provision of standard amenities.

(1) A local authority shall not approve an application for an improvement grant—
(a) unless they are satisfied that the owner of every parcel of land on which the improvement works are to be or are being carried out (other than land proposed to be sold or leased under section [12(4)]), has consented in writing to the application and to being bound by any conditions imposed by or under section 246;
(b) if the improvement works specified in it have been begun, unless they are satisfied that there were good reasons for beginning the works before the application was approved.

(2) A local authority shall not approve any such application, other than an application to which section 244 (provision of standard amenities) applies—
(a) unless, subject to subsection (6), they are satisfied that—
 (i) the house or houses to which the application for an improvement grant relates will provide satisfactory housing accommodation for such period and conform with such requirements with respect to construction and physical condition and the provision of services and amenities as may be specified for the time being for the purposes of this section by the Secretary of State, and
 (ii) in a case where the house or houses to which the said application relates is or are comprised in a building containing more than one house, the works to be carried out on the house or houses will not prevent the improvement of any other house in that building;
(b) if the application is in respect of the improvement or conversion of a house provided after 15th June 1964, but the Secretary of State may give directions, either generally or with respect to any particular case, as to the waiving of this provision;
(c) if, subject to subsections (3) to (6), it is made by the owner of the house to which the application relates or by a member of his family and the house or any part thereof is to be occupied by that owner or by a member of his family after completion of the works and—
 (i) the rateable value of the occupied premises exceeds the prescribed limit; or
 (ii) if it is to be provided by the conversion of two or more houses, the aggregate of the rateable values of those houses exceeds the prescribed limit:
Provided that where sub-paragraph (i) applies, a local authority may approve such an application if it is made in relation to a part of the house which after completion of the works will be self-contained and is not to be occupied by the owner or by a member of his family.

(3) Paragraph (c) of subsection (2) shall not apply—
(a) where the house to which the application relates is in a housing action area for improvement declared under section 90 and is listed in the final resolution under section 92(4)(b) or (c) as requiring improvement or integration;
(b) where the house to which the application relates is subject to an improvement order made under section 88(1);
(c) in relation to an application for an improvement grant for the conversion of a building which does not at the date of the application consist of or include a house; or
(d) to a house which is to be occupied by a disabled person (as defined in section 236(3)) in so far as the application is in respect of works which his disability renders necessary if the house is to be suitable for his accommodation, welfare or employment.

(4) In paragraph (c) of subsection (2)—
'prescribed limit' means such limit of rateable value as the Secretary of State with the consent of the Treasury may prescribe; and different limits may be so prescribed for

different cases and for different classes of cases; and a limit so prescribed shall be prescribed by order of the Secretary of State made by statutory instrument which shall be subject to annulment by resolution of either House of Parliament; and 'rateable value' means the rateable value entered in the valuation roll and in force on the date of the application.

(5) The Secretary of State may by order made in a statutory instrument which shall be subject to annulment by resolution of either House of Parliament vary the provisions of paragraph (c) of subsection (2).

(6) The local authority may, with the approval of the Secretary of State, disregard any requirement specified by him under subsection (2)(a)(i) in any case where, in the opinion of the local authority, conformity with that requirement would not be practicable at a reasonable expense. **[809]**

NOTES to section 240

Amendment: Sub-s (1) was amended by the Housing (Scotland) Act 1988 (c 43), s 72, Sch 2, para 10.

Definitions: 'local authority', 'land', 'house': see s 338 below; 'improvement', 'improvement grant': *Ibid* and s 236(1) above; 'family': see s 338 below and s 83 above; 'disabled person': see s 338 below and s 236(3) above.

241. Approval of application for improvement grant.

(1) Where a local authority approve an application made under the provisions of this Part for an improvement grant, they shall notify the applicant and where appropriate, the owner, of the amount of the expense (as estimated in the application) approved by them as being attributable to each house proposed to be provided or improved (an amount hereinafter referred to in relation to improvement works as the 'approved expense' of executing those works), and of the amount payable, expressed as a percentage of the approved expense as a cash amount.

(2) In approving an application for an improvement grant a local authority may require as a condition of paying the grant that the improvement works are carried out within such period (which must not be less than a period of 12 months) as the local authority may specify or within such further period as the local authority may allow.

(3) Where a local authority—
(a) refuse an application, or
(b) approve an application but fix as the amount of an improvement grant an amount less than that which may be fixed by virtue of section 242 or 244,

they shall notify the applicant in writing of the grounds of their decision. **[810]**

NOTES to section 241

Definitions: 'local authority', 'owner', 'house': see s 338 below; 'improvement', 'improvement grant': *Ibid* and s 236(1) above.

242. Amount of improvement grant.

(1) Subject to the following provisions of this section, the amount of an improvement grant other than a grant paid under section 244 shall not exceed 50 per cent, or such other percentage as may be prescribed of the approved expense of executing the works, but the approved expense for an improvement grant including any amount allowed for the purposes of subsection (4) shall be subject to a maximum of [£12,600] or such other maximum as may be prescribed, in respect of each house to which the application relates.

(2) If, after an application for a grant has been approved by a local authority, the authority are satisfied that owing to circumstances beyond the control of the applicant the expense of the works will exceed the estimate contained in the application, they may, on receiving a further estimate, substitute a higher amount as the amount of the approved expense of executing the works, but that amount shall not exceed the maximum authorised by virtue of subsection (1).

(3) A local authority may allow for works for repair and replacement needed, in their opinion, for the purposes of enabling the house to attain a good state of repair—
   (a) where an application for an improvement grant relates wholly or partly to the provision of any or all of the standard amenities and—
      (i) on completion of the works the house is in the opinion of the local authority likely to be available for use as a house for a period of at least 10 years, a maximum approved expense not exceeding [£3,450] or such other amount as may be prescribed, or 50 per cent, or such other percentage as may be prescribed of the approved expense of executing the improvement works, whichever is the greater; or
      (ii) on completion of the works the house is in the opinion of the local authority likely to be available for use as a house for a period of less than 10 years, a maximum approved expense not exceeding [£345] (or such other amount as may be prescribed) for each standard amenity provided, but subject to a maximum of [£1,380] or such other amount as may be prescribed;
   (b) where an application does not so relate, a maximum approved expense not exceeding 50 per cent, or such other percentage as may be prescribed of the approved expense of executing the improvement works.

(4) If the local authority are satisfied that in any particular case—
   (a) there are good reasons for fixing a higher amount than that payable by virtue of subsection (1), that amount may be exceeded by such amount as the Secretary of State may approve; and the approval of the Secretary of State may be given either with respect to a particular case or with respect to a particular class of case;
   (b) the expense of executing the works was materially enhanced by measures taken to preserve the architectural or historic interest of the house or building to which the application relates, the amount payable by virtue of subsection (1) may be exceeded by such amount as the Secretary of State may approve.

(5) In any case where—
   (a) an improvement grant or repairs grant within the meaning of Part I of the Act of 1974, or
   (b) an improvement grant or repairs grant within the meaning of this Part, or
   (c) assistance under either of the following enactments—
      (i) section 1 of the Hill Farming Act 1946,
      (ii) section 22(2) of the Crofters (Scotland) Act 1955;
has been made or given in respect of a house and, within the period of 10 years beginning on the date on which the grant or assistance was paid or, if it was paid by instalments, the date on which the last instalment was paid, an improvement grant under this Part, other than a grant payable under section 244 or in respect of works for the benefit of a disabled occupant within the meaning of section 236, is made in respect of that house, the amount payable in relation to that improvement grant shall, when added to the unrepaid amount, if any, of that previous grant or assistance, not exceed 50 per cent, or such other percentage as may be prescribed in pursuance of subsection (1), of the maximum approved expense so prescribed.

(6) Where by virtue of the making on any occasion of an improvement grant in respect of the improvement of a house, the conditions specified in section [246] are required to be observed with respect to the house before the observance thereof by virtue of the making of an improvement grant on a previous occasion has ceased to be requisite, the provisions of sections 246, 247, 252(4) and Schedule 19 shall apply in relation to the house as regards each occasion on which an improvement grant is so made as if it were the only occasion on which it was so made.

(7) The percentage of the approved expense that may be prescribed under subsection (1) or (3) shall be prescribed by order of the Secretary of State made with the consent of the Treasury.

(8) An order made under subsection (7) shall be made by statutory instrument and shall not be made unless a draft has been laid before and approved by resolution of the House of Commons.

[811]

(9) The maximum approved expense that may be prescribed under subsection (1) or (3) shall be prescribed by order of the Secretary of State made by statutory instrument which shall be subject to annulment in pursuance of a resolution of either House of Parliament.

(10) An order under this section may make different provision with respect to different cases or descriptions of cases. [811]

NOTES to section 242

Amendment: Sub-s (1) and (3) were amended by the Housing (Improvement and Repairs Grants) (Approved Expenses Maxima) (Scotland) Order 1987, SI 1987/2269; sub-s (6) was amended by the Housing (Scotland) Act 1988 (c 43), s 72, Sch 7, para 11.

Definitions: 'improvement grant': see s 338 below and s 236(1) above; 'approved expenses': see s 241 above; 'house', 'local authority': see s 338 below; 'standard amenities': see ss 388 and s 244(6) below; 'repairs grant': see ss 338 and s 248 below; 'disabled occupant': see s 338 below and s 236(3) above.

Sub-ss (1), (3), (9) (10): See the Housing (Improvement and Repairs Grant) (Approved Expenses Maxima) (Scotland) Order 1987, SI 1987/2269, paras [1385] ff below.

243. Payment of improvement grant.

(1) An improvement grant in respect of the expenses incurred for the purposes of the execution of improvement works shall, subject to the following provisions of this section, be paid—
   (a) within one month of the date on which, in the opinion of the local authority, the house first becomes fit for occupation after the completion of the works; or
   (b) partly in instalments paid from time to time as the works progress and with a final settlement of the balance within one month of the completion of the works but the aggregate of the instalments paid shall not at any time before the completion of the improvement works exceed 50 per cent, or such other percentage fixed by virtue of section 242(1), or, as the case may be, section [244(7)] of the aggregate approved expense of the works executed up to that time.

(2) The payment of an improvement grant or of an instalment or the balance thereof shall be conditional on the improvement works, or, as the case may be, the part of the works which the local authority consider will entitle the applicant to payment of the instalment or of the balance of the grant, being executed to the satisfaction of the local authority.

(3) Where an instalment of an improvement grant is paid before the completion of the works, and the works are not completed within 12 months of the date of payment of the instalment, then that instalment and any further instalment paid by the local authority on account of the grant shall, on being demanded by the authority, forthwith become payable to them by the person to whom the instalments were paid, and the instalments shall carry interest at such reasonable rate as the local authority may determine from the date on which they were paid by the authority until repaid under this subsection. [812]

NOTES to section 243

Amendment: Sub-s (1) was amended by the Housing (Scotland) Act 1988 (c 43), s 72, Sch 7, para 12.

Definitions: 'improvement', 'improvement grant': see s 338 below and s 236(1) above; 'local authority', 'house': see s 338 below.

244. Duty of local authorities to make improvement grants where an application relates exclusively to the provision of standard amenities or to disabled occupant; and amount thereof.

(1) Subject to the provisions of this Part, a local authority shall, where an application in that behalf is made to the local authority, give assistance in respect of the improvement of any house by way of making an improvement grant in respect of the cost of executing works required for the house to be provided with one or more of the standard amenities

which it presently lacks, if on completion of the works the house will, in the opinion of the local authority—
(a) be provided with all of the standard amenities for the exclusive use of its occupants; and
(b) meet the tolerable standard.

(2) A local authority shall not make an improvement grant under this section in respect of a house comprised in a building containing more than one house, unless they are satisfied that the works carried out on the house will not prevent the improvement of any other house in the building.

(3) Where an application in that behalf is made to a local authority in relation to any house, an improvement grant shall be made under subsection (1) in respect of the cost of executing works required for the house to be provided with a standard amenity, notwithstanding that the house already has such a standard amenity, if in the opinion of the local authority the additional standard amenity to be provided is essential to the needs of a disabled occupant.

(4) Paragraph (a) of subsection (1) shall not apply where the house in respect of which application for a grant is made is not likely to be available for use as a house for a period of at least 10 years.

(5) Subsection (1) shall not apply in respect of a house which is or forms part of a house or building as regards which the local authority are satisfied that they have power to serve a notice under section 161 (power to require execution of works of descriptions other than work to make good neglect).

(6) Subject to subsection (8), the standard amenities for the purposes of this Part are the amenities which are described in the first column of Part I of Schedule 18 and which will be for the exclusive use of the occupants of the house to which the application relates.

(7) The amount of an improvement grant made under this section shall be 50 per cent or such other percentage as may be prescribed of the approved expense, which shall be subject to a limit determined in accordance with Part II of Schedule 18.

(8) The Secretary of State may by order vary the provisions of Schedule 18, and any such order may contain such transitional or other supplementary provisions as appear to the Secretary of State to be expedient.

(9) Section 86 shall have effect for determining whether a house meets the tolerable standard for the purposes of subsection (1) as it has effect for determining whether a house meets that standard for the purposes of Part IV.

(10) The Secretary of State may by order—
(a) vary the requirements of subsection (1)(a) and (b);
(b) vary the amount specified in subsection [(7)], so as to provide for different amounts of grant to apply for different classes of cases.

(11) Schedule 18 shall have effect for the purpose of specifying the standard amenities and the maximum eligible amount of improvement grant in respect thereof.

(12) The percentage of the approved expense that may be prescribed under subsection (7) or (10)(b) shall be prescribed by order of the Secretary of State made with the consent of the Treasury.

(13) An order made under subsection (8) or (10)(a) shall be made by statutory instrument which shall be subject to annulment in pursuance of a resolution of either House of Parliament.

(14) An order made under subsection (12) shall be made by statutory instrument and shall not be made unless a draft has been laid before and approved by resolution of the House of Commons. **[813]**

NOTES to section 244

Amendment: Sub-s (10) was amended by the Housing (Scotland) Act 1988 (c 43), s 72, Sch 7, para 13.

Definitions: 'improvement', 'improvement grant'; see ss 338 below and 236(1) above; 'local authority', 'house': see s 338 below; 'disabled occupier': see ss 238 and 236(3) above; 'the tolerable standard': see s 338 below and s 86 above.

Sub-ss (1)–(14): See the Housing (Improvement and Repairs Grant) (Approved Expenses Maxima) (Scotland) Order 1987, SI 1987/2269, paras [1385] ff below.

245. Grants restricted to applicant and his personal representatives.

In relation to a grant or an application for a grant, any reference in the preceding provisions of this Part to the applicant shall be construed, in relation to any time after his death, as a reference to his personal representatives. [814]

246. Conditions to be observed with respect to houses in respect of which an improvement grant has been made, and registration thereof.

(1) Where an application for an improvement grant has been approved by a local authority, the provisions of this section shall apply with respect to the house for a period of 5 years beginning with the date on which, in the opinion of the local authority, it first becomes fit for occupation after the completion of the improvement works, and shall, so long as those provisions are required to be so observed, be deemed to be part of the terms of any lease or tenancy of the house and shall be enforced accordingly.

(2) It shall be a condition of the grant that—
(a) the house shall not be used for the purposes other than those of a private dwelling-house, but a house shall not be deemed to be used for the purposes other than those of a private dwelling-house by reason only that part thereof is used as a shop or office, or for business, trade or professional purposes;
(b) the house shall not be occupied by the owner or a member of his family except as his only or main residence within the meaning of Part V of the Capital Gains Tax Act 1979;
(c) all such steps as are practicable shall be taken to secure the maintenance of the house in a good state of repair.

(3) The owner of the house shall, on being required to do so by the local authority, certify that the conditions specified in subsection (2) are being observed with respect to the house, and any tenant of the house shall, on being so required in writing by the owner, furnish to him such information as he may reasonably require for the purpose of enabling him to comply with the provisions of this subsection.

(4) A local authority shall not, as a prerequisite of approving a grant, require any conditions or obligations, other than the conditions mentioned in this Part or other statutory obligations to be observed with respect to a house in respect of which an improvement grant has been made under this Part.

(5) The provisions of Schedule 19 shall have effect in the event of a breach of any of the conditions mentioned in this section at a time when they are required to be observed with respect to a house.

(6) Where a local authority pay an improvement grant or, in a case where an improvement grant is payable partly in instalments as the improvement works progress and the balance after the completion of the works in respect of a house, they shall specify in the notice or record mentioned respectively in subsections (7) and (8) the matters specified in subsection (9).

(7) If subsection (6) applies, the local authority shall, where the applicant for the grant was not a tenant-at-will or was a tenant-at-will who since applying, has acquired his landlord's interest in the tenancy, cause to be recorded in the General Register of Sasines or registered in the Land Register, as the case may be, a notice in such form as may be prescribed.

(8) If subsection (6) applies, the local authority shall, where that applicant was and continues to be a tenant-at-will, keep a written record.

(9) The matters to be specified are—
(a) the conditions mentioned in this section which are required to be observed with respect to the house;
(b) the period for which the conditions are to be observed; and
(c) the provisions of Schedule 19 under which, on a breach of any of the said conditions at a time when they require to be observed, the owner of the house becomes liable to repay to the authority the amount repayable by virtue of that Schedule.

(10) Any expenses incurred under subsection (7) recording the notice in the Register of Sasines or registering it in the Land Register, as the case may be, shall be repaid to the local authority by the applicant. **[815]**

NOTES to section 246
Definitions: 'improvement', 'improvement grant': see s 338 below and s 236(1) above; 'local authority', 'tenant', 'tenancy', 'owner': see s 338 below; 'family': *Ibid* and s 83 above.

247. Voluntary repayment of improvement grants.

(1) The owner of a house in respect of the provision or improvement of which an improvement grant has been made or the holder of a heritable security over the house, being a heritable creditor entitled to exercise his power of sale, may, at any time when the conditions specified in section 246 are required to be observed with respect to the house, pay to the local authority the like amount as would become payable to them by virtue of Schedule 19 in the event of a breach of any of the conditions referred to in section 246(2), and on the making of the payment observance with respect to the house of those conditions shall cease to be requisite and the provisions of paragraph 7 of the said Schedule shall apply for the purposes of this subsection as they apply for the purposes of that Schedule.

(2) A sum paid under subsection (1) by a heritable creditor shall be treated as part of the sum secured by the heritable security. **[816]**

NOTES to section 247
Definitions: 'owner', 'house', 'local authority': see s 338 below; 'improvement', 'improvement grant': see s 338 below and s 236(1) above.

Repairs grants

248. Repairs grants.

(1) Subject to the provisions of this section, where an application for a repairs grant is duly made a local authority—
(a) shall approve the application in so far as it relates to the execution of works required by a notice under section 108(1) (repair notices); and
(b) in so far as it does not so relate, may approve the application in such circumstances as they think fit.

(2) A local authority shall not approve an application under this section unless they are satisfied that the house to which the application relates will provide satisfactory housing accommodation for such period as they consider reasonable.

(3) In considering whether or not to approve an application for a repairs grant, a local authority shall have regard to the question whether, in their opinion, the owner would, without undue hardship, be able to finance the expense of the relevant works without the assistance of a repairs grant;
Provided that this subsection shall not apply in any such case as may be prescribed.

(4) The amount of a repairs grant shall not exceed 50 per cent, or such other percentage as may be prescribed, of the approved expense of the works, but the approved expense

shall not exceed £5,500 or such other amount as may be prescribed in respect of each house to which the application relates.

(5) Sections 237 to 247 (other than sections [242(1), (3), (5) and (7) to (10) and 244]) shall apply in relation to an application for a repairs grant [or to a repairs grant] as they apply to an application for an improvement grant [or to an improvement grant] except that for the purposes of the application of section 243(1)(b), for the words 'section 242(1) or as the case may be section [244(7)]' are substituted the words 'section 248(4)':

Provided that section 240(2)(c) shall not apply in relation to an application for a repairs grant in respect of the replacement in a different material of such pipes, cisterns, tapes or other equipment used for the supply of water to a house as are wholly or partly made of lead.

(6) References in this section to a house shall, in relation to an application made under this section for a grant in respect of works which are to rectify defects specified in a notice under section 108(1), be construed as including references to premises other than a house; but where such application relates to such premises—
   (a) the local authority shall not, under subsection (2), approve the application unless they are satisifed that the premises form part of a building which contains a house or houses and that house or, as the case may be, all those houses will provide satisfactory housing accommodation as mentioned in that subsection;
   (b) subsection (4) shall be construed as if the reference in it to each house were a reference to each of the premises other than a house; and
   (c) subsection (5) shall be construed as if the enactments excepted by that subsection included sections 240(2) to (6), 246(1), (2), (3), and (5) to (10) and 247.

(7) A case that is prescribed under the proviso to subsection (3) shall be prescribed by order of the Secretary of State made by statutory instrument which shall be subject to annulment in pursuance of a resolution of either House of Parliament.

(8) The percentage of the approved expense that may be prescribed under subsection (4) shall be prescribed by order of the Secretary of State made with the consent of the Treasury.

(9) An order made under subsection (8) shall be made by statutory instrument and shall not be made unless a draft has been laid before and approved by resolution of the House of Commons.

(10) The maximum approved expense that may be prescribed under subsection (4) shall be prescribed by order of the Secretary of State made by statutory instrument which shall be subject to an annulment in pursuance of a resolution of either House of Parliament.

[(11) An order under this section may make different provision with respect to different cases or descriptions of cases.]

NOTES to section 248

Amendment: Sub-s (4) was amended by the Housing (Improvement and Repairs Grant) (Approved Expenses Maxima) (Scotland) Order 1987, SI 1987/2269, paras [1385] ff below; sub-s (5) was amended by the Housing (Scotland) Act 1988 (c 43), s 72, Sch 7, para 14, Sch 8, para 6; sub-s (6) was amended by *Ibid*, Sch 7, para 14; sub-s (11) was added by *Ibid*, Sch 8, para 6.

Definitions: 'local authority', 'house', 'owner': see s 338 below.

Sub-ss (4), (8)–(10): See the Housing (Improvement and Repairs Grant) (Approved Expenses Maxima) (Scotland) Order 1987, SI 1987/2269, paras [1385] ff below.

Grants for fire escapes

249. Grants for fire escapes for houses in multiple occupation.

(1) Subject to the provisions of this section, where an application for a grant for a fire escape in a house in multiple occupation is duly made, a local authority—
   (a) shall approve the application in so far as it relates to the execution of works specified in a notice served on any person, other than a public body, under section

162 (which empowers a local authority to require the provision of a means of escape from fire in a house in multiple occupation);
  (b) in so far as it is not so specified but is required in connection with works so specified, may approve the application.

(2) A local authority shall not approve an application under this section unless they are satisfied that at the time of completion of the works to which the application relates the house will be in reasonable repair (disregarding the state of internal decorative repair) having regard to its age, character and location.

(3) Where a local authority approve an application under this section they shall determine the maximum amount of expenses which they think proper to be incurred for the relevant works; but so much of such amount as relates to works referred to in—
  (a) paragraph (a) of subsection (1) shall not exceed [£9,315] or such other amount as may be prescribed under subsection (8);
  (b) paragraph (b) of that subsection shall not exceed [£3,340] or such other amount as may be prescribed under subsection (8).

(4) Subject to subsection (5), the amount of grant payable under subsection (1) above in relation to any application shall be 75 per cent of the maximum amount determined under subsection (3) above in relation thereto or such other percentage of that maximum amount as may be prescribed under subsection (9).

(5) If, in any case, it appears to the local authority by whom the application is approved that the applicant will not without undue hardship be able to finance the cost of so much of the work as is not met by the grant, they may, as regards that case, increase the percentage referred to in subsection (4) above to such percentage, not exceeding 90 per cent, as they think fit.

(6) Sections 236 to 239 and 241 to 247 (other than section [241(3)(b), section 242(1), (3) and (5) to (10)] and section 244) shall apply in relation to an application for a grant under subsection (1) [or to a grant under subsection (1)] as they apply in relation to an application for an improvement grant [or to an improvement grant] except that for the purposes of the application of section 243(1)(b), for the words 'section 242(1) or as the case may be section [244(7)]' are substituted the words 'section 248(4) or (5) as the case may be'.

(7) In subsection (1), 'public body' means a regional, island or district council or such other body as the Secretary of State may by order made by statutory instrument specify.

(8) The maximum amount of expenses prescribed under subsection (3)(a) or (b) shall be prescribed by order of the Secretary of State made by statutory instrument which shall be subject to annulment in pursuance of a resolution of either House of Parliament.

(9) The percentage of the maximum amount that may be prescribed under subsection (4) shall be prescribed by order of the Secretary of State made with the consent of the Treasury.

(10) An order made under subsection (9) shall be made by statutory instrument and shall not be made unless a draft has been laid before and approved by resolution of the House of Commons. [818]

NOTES to section 249

Amendments: Sub-s (3) was amended by the Housing (Improvement and Repairs Grant) (Approved Expenses Maxima) (Scotland) Order 1987, SI 1987/2269, paras [1385] ff below; sub-s (6) was amended by the Housing (Scotland) Act 1988 (c 43), s 72, Sch 7, para 15, Sch 8, para 7.

Definitions: 'local authority', 'house': see s 338 below; 'improvement grant': see s 338 below and s 236(1) above.

Sub-ss (3), (8)–(10): See the Housing (Improvement and Repairs Grant) (Approved Expenses Maxima) (Scotland) Order 1987, SI 1987/2269, paras [1385] ff below.

Sub-ss (4), (9): See the Housing (Grants for Fire Escapes in Houses in Multiple Occupation) (Prescribed Percentage) (Scotland) Order 1990, SI 1990/2242, paras [1504] ff below.

Grants for houses in housing action areas

250. Application of this Part to houses situated in a housing action area and power of local authority to give repairs grants in such areas and amount thereof.

(1) The provisions of this Part shall apply to houses which are to be brought up to the standard specified by a local authority under section 90 or 91 and which are situated in housing action areas for improvement or for demolition and improvement within the meaning of Part IV, but subject to the modifications contained in subsections (2) to (7) below.

(2) In section 242(1), for 'not exceed 50 per cent' there shall be substituted 'be 75 per cent'.

(3) In section 243(1), for '50 per cent' there shall be substituted '75 per cent'.

(4) In section 254(2), for '75 per cent' there shall be substituted '90 per cent'.

(5) If, in the case of a house which is in a housing action area on the date on which the application is approved for a grant under section 242(1) as read with subsection (2), it appears to the local authority by whom the application is approved that the applicant will not without undue hardship be able to finance the cost of so much of the improvement work as is not met by the grant, they may increase the percentage under the said subsection from 75 per cent to such percentage, not exceeding 90 per cent, as they think fit; but this subsection shall not apply where an applicant for an improvement grant is not the owner of the land to which the application relates.

(6) Section 238(1), in so far as it relates to refusal to approve an application, and s 244 shall not apply, but a local authority shall make an improvement grant to an owner of a house situated in a housing action area as aforesaid in respect of such improvement works as may, in their opinion, be required for the house to be brought up to the standard specified by the local authority in a resolution passed under section 90 or 91 in relation to that area:

Provided that an improvement grant shall not be made in pursuance of this subsection in respect of a house which is comprised in a building containing more than one house, if the local authority are of the opinion that the improvement works to be carried out on that house would prevent any other house in that building from being brought up to the standard specified as aforesaid.

(7) In section 248—
(a) for subsections (1) and (2) there shall be substituted the following subsections—
'(1) Subject to the following provisions of this section, where an application for a repairs grant is duly made, a local authority shall approve the application is so far as it relates to the execution of works to houses to which the provisions of this Part are applied by section 250(1).

(2) A local authority shall not approve an application under this section unless on completion of the works the house will attain the standard specified in the resolution passed under section 90 or 91.';
(b) in subsection (4), at the beginning there shall be inserted the words 'Subject to section [250(5)]' and for the words '50 per cent' there shall be substituted the words '75 per cent';
(c) in subsection (5), after the words 'section 244' there shall be inserted the words 'and subsections (3), (4) and (5) of section 249'. [819]

NOTES to section 250

Amendments: Sub-s (7) was amended by the Housing (Scotland) Act 1988 (c 43), s 72, Sch 7, para 16.

Definitions: 'house', 'local authority': see s 338 below; 'housing action area': see ss 89–91 above; 'improvement', 'improvement grant': see s 338 below and s 236(1) above.

Improvement of amenity grants

251. Powers of local authority for improvement of amenities.

(1) For the purposes of securing the improvement of the amenities of a predominantly residential area within their district, a local authority may—
- (a) carry out any works on land owned by them and assist (whether by grants or loans or otherwise) in the carrying out of any works on land not owned by them;
- (b) with the agreement of the owner of any land, carry out or arrange for the carrying out of works on that land at his expense, or at the expense of the local authority, or in part at the expense of both;
- (c) acquire any land by agreement;

and may be authorised by the Secretary of State to purchase any land compulsorily.

(2) The Acquisition of Land (Authorisation Procedure) (Scotland) Act 1947 shall apply to a compulsory purchase of land under subsection (1) as if that subsection had been in force immediately before the commencement of this Act. [820]

NOTES to section 251
Definitions: 'local authority', 'land': see s 338 below.

Grants for thermal insulation

252. Schemes for grants for thermal insulation.

(1) Local authorities shall make grants, in accordance with such schemes as may be prepared and published by the Secretary of State and laid by him before Parliament, towards the cost of works undertaken to improve the thermal insulation of dwellings in their district.

(2) Schemes under this section shall specify—
- (a) the descriptions of dwelling and the insulation works qualifying for grants, and
- (b) the persons from whom applications may be entertained in respect of different descriptions of dwelling.

(3) The grant shall be such percentage of the cost of the works qualifying for grant as may be prescribed, or such money sum as may be prescribed, whichever is the less.

(4) A scheme may provide for grants to be made only to those applying on grounds of special need or to be made in those cases on a prescribed higher scale; and for this purpose 'special need' shall be determined by reference to such matters personal to the applicant (such as age, disability, bad health and inability without undue hardship to finance the cost of the works) as may be specified in the scheme.

(5) In this section, 'prescribed' means prescribed by order of the Secretary of State made with the approval of the Treasury.

(6) An order shall be made by statutory instrument which shall be subject to annulment in pursuance of a resolution of the House of Commons. [821]

NOTES to section 252
Section 252 is prospectively repealed by the Social Security Act 1990 (c 27), s 15(11), but the repeal has not been brought into force. See note to Social Security Act 1990 (c 27), s 15.
Definition: 'local authority': see s 338 below.
Sub-ss (3), (5): See the Homes Insulation Grant Order 1987, SI 1987/2185, paras [1382] ff below and the Homes Insulation Grants Order 1988, SI 1988/1239, paras [1426] ff below.

253. Finance and administration of schemes under s 252.

(1) Finance for the making of grants under section 252 shall be provided to local authorities from time to time by the Secretary of State.

(2) A local authority is not required, nor has power, to make grants under section 252 in any year beyond those for which the Secretary of State has notified them that finance is committed for that year in respect of the authority's district.

(3) In the administration of grants under section 252 local authorities shall comply with any directions given to them by the Secretary of State after consultation with their representative organisations.

(4) The Secretary of State may, in particular, give directions as to—
(a) the way in which applications for grants are to be dealt with, and the priorities to be observed between applicants and different categories of applicant, and
(b) the means of authenticating applications, so that grants are only given in proper cases, and of ensuring that the works are carried out to any standard specified in the applicable scheme.

(5) The Secretary of State shall, with the approval of the Treasury, pay such sums as he thinks reasonable in respect of the administrative expenses incurred by local authorities in operating schemes under section 252. **[822]**

NOTES to section 253

Section 253 is prospectively repealed by the Social Security Act 1990 (c 27), s 15(11), but the repeal has not yet been brought into force. See note to Social Security Act 1990 (c 27), s 15.
Definition: 'local authority': see s 338 below.

Exchequer contributions

254. . . .

NOTE to section 254

Section 254 was repealed by the Housing (Scotland) Act 1988 (c 43), s 72, Sch 10.

255. . . .

NOTE to section 255

Section 255 was repealed by the Housing (Scotland) Act 1988 (c 43), s 72, Sch 10.

Agricultural tenants, etc

256. Application of this Part to agricultural tenants, etc.

(1) For the purposes of the provisions of this Part, a tenant, crofter, landholder or statutory small tenant shall be deemed to be the owner of any house, building or other land on his farm, croft or holding if in respect of the execution thereon of improvement works he would, on the termination of his tenancy, be entitled to compensation under the Agricultural Holdings (Scotland) Act 1949 or the Crofters (Scotland) Acts 1955 and 1961 or the Small Landholders (Scotland) Acts 1886 to 1931 (as the case may be) as for an improvement.

(2) Where by virtue of subsection (1) an improvement grant or a repairs grant is made to a crofter, a landholder or a statutory small tenant in respect of a house on his croft or holding, the local authority shall forthwith intimate to the landlord of the croft or holding that an improvement grant or a repairs grant has been so made, and shall inform him of the amount thereof.

(3) If at any time within the period during which conditions are required by section 246 to be observed with respect to a house provided on a farm, croft or holding otherwise than by the landlord thereof, compensation becomes payable in respect of the house, or of any improvement works executed in relation thereto, as for an improvement under the Agricultural Holdings (Scotland) Act 1949 or the Crofters (Scotland) Act 1955 and 1961 or the Small Landholders (Scotland) Acts 1886 to 1931 (as the case may be), so much of the value of the house or works as is attributable to the sum paid by way of improvement grant or repairs grant, shall be taken into account in assessing the compensation so payable and shall be deducted therefrom.

(4) The landlord of a farm, croft or holding on which there is a house with respect to which conditions are for the time being required to be observed by virtue of section 246,

shall not at any time within the period during which those conditions are so required to be observed be entitled to obtain any consideration by way of rent or otherwise in respect of so much of the value of the house, or of any improvement works executed in relation thereto, as is attributable to the sum paid by way of improvement grant or repairs grant. [823]

NOTES to section 256

Definitions: 'tenant', 'croft', 'crofter', 'landholder', 'owner', 'house', 'land', 'holding': see s 338 below; 'improvement', 'improvement grant': see s 338 below and s 236(1) above; 'repairs grant': see s 338 below and s 248 above.

[256A. Application of this Part to Scottish Homes.

This Part (except sections 253 to 255) shall apply to Scottish Homes as it applies to a local authority.] [824]

NOTE to section 256A

Section 256A was added by the Housing (Scotland) Act 1988 (c 43), s 2.
Definition: 'local authority': see s 338 below.

PART XIV
ASSISTANCE FOR OWNERS OF DEFECTIVE HOUSING

Eligibility for assistance

257. Designation of defective dwellings by Secretary of State.

(1) The Secretary of State may designate as a class any buildings each of which consists of or includes one or more dwellings if it appears to him that—
(a) buildings in the proposed class are defective by reason of their design or construction, and
(b) by virtue of the circumstances mentioned in paragraph (a) having become generally known, the value of some of or all of the dwellings concerned has been substantially reduced.

(2) A dwelling which is, or is included in a building in a class so designated is referred to in this Part as a 'defective dwelling'; and in this Part in relation to such a dwelling—
(a) 'the qualifying defect' means what, in the opinion of the Secretary of State, is wrong with the building in that class; and
(b) 'the cut-off date' means the date by which, in the opinion of the Secretary of State, the circumstances mentioned in subsection (1)(a) become generally known.

(3) A designation shall describe the qualifying defect and specify—
(a) the cut-off date,
(b) the date (being a date on or after the cut-off date) on which the designation is to come into operation,
(c) the period within which persons may seek assistance under this Part in respect of the defective dwellings concerned.

(4) A designated class shall not be described by reference to the area in which the buildings concerned are situated.

(5) Notice of a designation shall be published in the Edinburgh Gazette.

(6) Any question arising as to whether a building is or was at any time in a class designated under this section shall be determined by the Secretary of State. [825]

NOTES to section 257
Definition: 'dwelling': see s 302 below.

258. Variation or revocation of designation.

(1) The Secretary of State may—
(a) vary a designation under section 257, but not so as to vary the cut-off date, or
(b) revoke such a designation.

(2) The Secretary of State may by a variation of the designation extend the period referred to in section 257(3)(c) (period within which assistance must be applied for) whether or not it has expired.

(3) The variation or revocation of a designation does not affect the operation of the provisions of this Part in relation to a dwelling if, before the variation or revocation comes into operation, the dwelling is a defective dwelling by virtue of the designation in question and an application for assistance under this Part has been made.

(4) Notice of the variation or revocation of a designation shall be published in the Edinburgh Gazette. [826]

NOTES to section 258
Definitions: 'cut-off date': see ss 303 and 287 below and s 257 above; 'defective dwelling': *Ibid*.

259. Conditions of eligibility.

(1) Subject to the following provisions of this Part, a person to whom this section applies is eligible for assistance in respect of a defective dwelling for the purposes of this Part if—
(a) his interest in the dwelling is that of owner ('the owner's interest'), and
(b) one of the following sets of conditions is satisfied.

(2) This section applies to—
(a) an individual who is not a trustee,
(b) trustees, if all the beneficiaries are individuals, and
(c) personal representatives.

(3) The first set of conditions is that—
(a) there was a disposal by a public sector authority of the owner's interest in the dwelling before the cut-off date; and
(b) there has been no disposal for value by any person of the owner's interest in the dwelling on or after the cut-off date;

and for the purposes of this subsection where a public sector authority hold an interest in a dwelling a disposal of that interest by or under any enactment is to be treated as a disposal by the authority.

(4) The second set of conditions is that—
(a) a person to whom this section applies acquired the owner's interest in the dwelling on a disposal for value occurring within the period of 12 months beginning with the cut-off date;
(b) on the date of that disposal he was unaware of the association of the dwelling with the qualifying defect;
(c) the value by reference to which the price for the disposal was calculated did not take any, or any adequate, account of the qualifying defect; and
(d) if the cut-off date had fallen immediately after the date of the disposal, the first set of conditions would have been satisfied. [827]

NOTES to section 259
Definitions: 'defective dwelling', 'qualifying defect': see ss 303 and 287 below and s 257 above; 'dwelling', 'owner': see s 302 below; 'public sector authority': see ss 303 and 300 below.

260. Exceptions to eligibility.

A person is not eligible for assistance in respect of a defective dwelling if the local authority are of the opinion that—

(a) wo.k to the building that consists of or includes the dwelling has been carried out in order to deal with the qualifying defect, and

(b) on the completion of the work, no further work relating to the dwelling was required to be done to the building in order to deal satisfactorily with the qualifying defect. **[828]**

NOTES to section 260

Definitions: 'defective dwelling', 'qualifying defect': see ss 303 and 287 below and s 257 above; 'dwelling': see s 302 below; 'local authority': see s 338 below.

261. Construction of references to disposal, etc.

(1) References in this Part to a disposal include a part disposal; but for the purposes of this Part a disposal of an interest in a dwelling is a disposal of a relevant interest in the dwelling only if on the disposal the person to whom it is made acquires a relevant interest in the dwelling.

(2) Subject to subsection (3), where any interest in land is disposed of, the time at which the disposal is made is, for the purposes of this Part, the time the missives are concluded (and not, if different, the date of entry specified in the missives).

(3) If the missives contain a condition precedent (and in particular if they contain a condition relating to the exercise of an option) the time at which the disposal is made for those purposes is the time when the condition precedent is satisfied.

(4) References in this Part to a disposal of an interest for value are to a disposal for money or money's worth, whether or not representing full value for the interest disposed of.

(5) In relation to a person holding an interest in a dwelling formed by the conversion of another dwelling, references in this Part to a previous disposal of an interest in the dwelling include a previous disposal on which an interest in land which included that part of the original dwelling in which his interest subsists was acquired. **[829]**

NOTES to section 261

Definitions: 'dwelling': see s 302 below; 'relevant to interest': see s 303 below; 'land': see s 338 below.

Determination of entitlement

262. Application for assistance.

A person seeking assistance under this Part in respect of a defective dwelling shall make a written application to the local authority within the period specified in the relevant designation. **[830]**

NOTES to section 262

Definitions: 'dwelling': see s 302 below; 'defective dwelling': see ss 303 and 287 below and s 257 above; 'local authority': see s 338 below.

263. Application not to be entertained where grant application pending or approved.

(1) The local authority shall not entertain an application for assistance under this Part if—

(a) an application has been made in respect of the defective dwelling (whether before or after the relevant designation came into operation) for a grant under Part XIII, and

(b) the relevant works in relation to that grant include the whole or part of the work required to reinstate the dwelling, unless the grant application has been refused or has been withdrawn under subsection (2) or the relevant works have been completed.

(2) Where a person has applied for such a grant in respect of a dwelling and—
  (a) the dwelling is a defective dwelling, and
  (b) the relevant works include the whole or part of the work required to reinstate it,
he may withdraw his application, whether or not it has been approved, if the relevant works have not been begun.

(3) In this section 'relevant works', in relation to a grant, means works of improvement or repair within the meaning of Part XIII. [831]

NOTES to section 263

Definitions: 'local authority': see s 338 below; 'defective dwelling': see ss 303 and 287 below and s 257 above; 'dwelling': see s 302 below; 'work required to reinstate the dwelling': see ss 303 and 267 below.

264. Determination of eligibility.

(1) A local authority receiving an application for assistance under this Part shall as soon as reasonably practicable give notice in writing to the applicant stating whether in their opinion he is eligible for assistance in respect of the defective dwelling.

(2) If they are of opinion that he is not so eligible, the notice shall state the reasons for their view.

(3) If they are of opinion that he is so eligible, the notice shall inform him of his right to make such a claim as is mentioned in section 265(2) (claim that assistance by way of reinstatement grant is inappropriate in his case). [832]

NOTES to section 264

Definitions: 'local authority': see s 338 below; 'defective dwelling': see ss 303 and 287 below and s 257 above; 'dwelling': see s 302 below.

265. Determination of form of assistance to which applicant is entitled.

(1) A local authority receiving an application for assistance under this Part shall, if the applicant is eligible for assistance, determine [as soon as reasonably practicable] whether he is entitled to assistance by way of reinstatement grant or by way of repurchase.

(2) If the authority are satisfied, on a claim by the applicant to that effect, that it would be unreasonable to expect him to secure or await the carrying out of the work required to reinstate the defective dwelling, the applicant is entitled to assistance by way of repurchase.

(3) Subject to subsection (2), the applicant is entitled to assistance by way of reinstatement grant if the authority are satisfied that the conditions for such assistance set out in section 266 are met, and otherwise to assistance by way of repurchase. [833]

NOTES to section 265

Amendment: Sub-s (1) was amended by the Local Government and Housing Act 1989 (c 42), s 166.

Definitions: 'local authority': see s 338 below; 'defective dwelling': see ss 303 and 287 below and s 257 above; 'dwelling': see s 302 below.

266. Conditions for assistance by way of reinstatement grant.

(1) The conditions for assistance by way of reinstatement grant are, subject to any order under subsection (2)—
  (a) that the dwelling is a house (as defined in section 302);
  (b) that if the work required to reinstate the dwelling (together with any other work which the local authority are satisfied the applicant proposes to carry out) were carried out—

(i) the dwelling would be likely to provide satisfactory housing accommodation for a period of at least 30 years, and
(ii) an individual acquiring ownership of the dwelling with vacant possession would be likely to be able to obtain a loan on the security of it on satisfactory terms from a lending institution;
(c) that giving assistance by way of reinstatement grant is justified having regard, on the one hand, to the amount of reinstatement grant that would be payable in respect of the dwelling and, on the other hand, to the likely value of the dwelling with vacant possession after the work required to reinstate it has been carried out; and
(d) . . .

(2) The Secretary of State may by order amend the conditions set out in subsection (1) so as to modify or omit any of the conditions or to add or substitute for any of the conditions other conditions.

(3) An order—
(a) may make different provision for different classes of case,
(b) shall be made by statutory instrument, and
(c) shall not be made unless a draft of it has been laid before and approved by a resolution of each House of Parliament.

(4) An order does not affect an application for assistance made before the order comes into force. **[834]**

NOTES to section 266

Amendment: Sub-s (1)(d) was removed by the Housing Defects (Reinstatement Grant) (Amendment of Conditions for Assistance) (Scotland) Order 1988, SI 1988/987.
Definitions: 'dwelling': see s 302 below; 'work required to reinstate the dwelling': see ss 303 and 267 below.
Sub-ss (2), (3): See the Housing Defects (Reinstatement Grant) (Amendment of Conditions for Assistance) (Scotland) Order 1988, SI 1988/978.

267. Meaning of 'work required for reinstatement' and 'associated arrangement'.

(1) For the purposes of this Part the work required to reinstate a defective dwelling is the work relating to the dwelling that is required to be done to the building that consists of or includes the dwelling in order to deal satisfactorily with the qualifying defect, together with any further work—
(a) required to be done, in order to deal satisfactorily with the qualifying defect, to any garage or outhouse designed or constructed as that building is designed or constructed, being a garage or outhouse in which the interest of the person eligible for assistance subsists and which is occupied with and used for the purposes of the dwelling or any part of it, or
(b) reasonably required in connection with other work falling within this subsection.

[(1A) In any case where—
(a) the most satisfactory way of dealing with the qualifying defect is substantially to demolish the building that consists of or includes the defective dwelling or a part of that building, and
(b) it is practicable to rebuild the building or part concerned on, or substantially on, its existing foundations and reconstruct the dwelling to the same, or substantially the same, plan,
the work required to carry out those operations shall be regarded for the purposes of this Part as work required to reinstate the defective dwelling.] **[835]**

NOTES to section 267

Amendment: Sub-s (1A) was added by the Local Government and Housing Act 1988 (c 42), s 166.

Definitions: 'dwelling': see s 302 below; 'defective dwelling', 'qualifying defect': see ss 303 and 287 below and s 257 above; 'lending institution': see s 303 below.

268. Notice of determination.

(1) Where an applicant is eligible for assistance, the authority to whom the application was made shall as soon as reasonably practicable give him notice in writing (a 'notice of determination') stating the form of assistance to which he is entitled.

(2) If, on such a claim by the applicant as is mentioned in section 265(2) (claim that assistance by way of reinstatement grant is inappropriate in his case), the authority are not satisifed that it would be unreasonable to expect him to secure or await the carrying out of the work required to reinstate the defective dwelling, the notice shall state the reasons for their view.

(3) A notice stating that the applicant is entitled to assistance by way of reinstatement grant shall also state—
 (a) the grounds for the authority's determination;
 (b) the work which, in their opinion, is required to reinstate the defective dwelling;
 (c) the amount of expenditure which, in their opinion, may properly be incurred in executing the work;
 (d) the amount of expenditure which, in their opinion, may properly be incurred in entering into an associated arrangement;
 (e) the condition required by section 270 (execution of work to satisfaction of authority within specified period), including the period within which the work is to be carried out; and
 (f) their estimate of the amount of grant payable in respect of the dwelling in pursuance of this Part.

(4) A notice stating that the applicant is entitled to assistance by way of repurchase shall also state the grounds for the authority's determination and the effect of—
 (a) paragraphs [2, 3 and 7] of Schedule 20 (request for notice proposed terms of repurchase), and
 (b) sections [282, 284 and 285] (provisions for grant of tenancy to former owner-occupier of repurchased dwelling).

(5) References in the following provisions of this Part to a person entitled to assistance by way of reinstatement grant or, as the case may be, by way of repurchase are to a person who is eligible for assistance in respect of the dwelling and on whom a notice of determination has been served stating that he is entitled to that form of assistance. **[836]**

NOTES to section 268
Amendment: Sub-s (4) was amended by the Housing (Scotland) Act 1988 (c 43), s 72, Sch 7, para 19.
Definitions: 'work required to reinstate the defective dwelling': see s 303 below and s 267 above; 'defective dwelling': see ss 303 and 287 below and s 257 above; 'dwelling': see s 302 below.

Assistance by way of reinstatement grant

269. Reinstatement grant.

(1) Where a person is entitled to assistance by way of reinstatement grant, the local authority shall pay reinstatement grant to him in respect of—
 (a) the qualifying work, and
 (b) any associated arrangement,
subject to and in accordance with the following provisions of this Part.

(2) The 'qualifying work' means the work stated in the notice of determination, or in a notice under section 272 (notice of change of work required), to be the work which in the opinion of the local authority is required to reinstate the dwelling. **[837]**

NOTES to section 269

Definitions: 'person entitled to assistance': see s 303 below and s 268 above; 'local authority': see s 338 below; 'associated arrangement': see s 303 below and s 267 above; 'dwelling': see s 302 below.

270. Conditions of payment of reinstatement grant.

(1) It is a condition of payment of reinstatement grant that the qualifying work is carried out—
  (a) to the satisfaction of the local authority, and
  (b) within the period specified in the notice of determination, or that period as extended.

(2) The period so specified shall be such reasonable period (of at least 12 months), beginning with service of the notice, as the authority may determine.

(3) The authority shall, if there are reasonable grounds for doing so, by notice in writing served on the person entitled to assistance, extend or further extend the period for carrying out the qualifying work (whether or not the period has expired).

(4) Payment of reinstatement grant shall not be subject to any other condition, however expressed. **[838]**

NOTES to section 270

Definitions: 'local authority': see s 338 below; 'qualifying work': see s 269 above.

271. Amount of reinstatement grant.

(1) The amount of reinstatement grant payable is the appropriate percentage of whichever is the least of—
  (a) the amount stated in the notice of determination, or in a notice under section 272 (notice of change in work required or expenditure permitted), to be the amount of expenditure which, in the opinion of the local authority, may properly be incurred in executing the qualifying work and entering into any associated arrangement,
  (b) the expenditure actually incurred in executing the qualifying work and entering into any associated arrangement, and
  (c) the expenditure which is the maximum amount permitted to be taken into account for the purposes of this section.

(2) The appropriate percentage is 90 per cent or, in a case where the authority are satisfied that the person entitled to assistance would suffer financial hardship unless a higher percentage of the expenditure referred to in subsection (1) were paid to him, 100 per cent.

(3) The Secretary of State may by order vary either or both of the percentages mentioned in subsection (2).

(4) The maximum amount of expenditure permitted to be taken into account for the purposes of this section is the amount specified as the expenditure limit by order made by the Secretary of State, except in a case or description of a case in which the Secretary of State, on the application of a local authority, approves a higher amount.

(5) An order under subsection (4) may make different provision for different areas, different designated classes and different categories of dwelling.

(6) An order under this section shall be made by statutory instrument which shall be subject to annulment in pursuance of a resolution of the House of Commons. **[839]**

NOTES to section 271

Definitions: 'local authority': see s 338 below; 'qualifying work': see s 269 above.

[840]

Sub-s (3): The power has not been exercised.
Sub-s (4): See the Housing Defects (Expenditure Limit) Order 1984, SI 1984/1705. The maximum amount specified is £14,000.

272. Changes in work or expenditure.

Where the local authority are satisfied that—
(a) the work required to reinstate the defective dwelling is more extensive than that stated in the notice of determination or in a previous notice under this section, or
(b) the amount of the expenditure which may properly be incurred in executing that work is greater than that so stated, or
(c) there is an amount of expenditure which may properly be incurred in entering into an associated arrangement but no such amount is stated in the notice of determination or a previous notice under this section, or
(d) where such an amount is so stated, the amount of expenditure which may be properly so incurred is greater than that amount,

they shall by notice in writing served on the person entitled to assistance state their opinion as to that amount or, as the case may be, that work and that amount; and the amount of reinstatement grant shall be adjusted accordingly. **[840]**

NOTES to section 272

Definitions: 'local authority': see s 338 below; 'defective dwelling': see ss 303 and 287 below and s 257 above; 'dwelling': see s 302 below; 'work required to reinstate the defective dwelling': see s 303 below and s 267 above.

273. Payment of reinstatement grant.

(1) The local authority may pay reinstatement grant in respect of the qualifying work in a single sum on completion of the work or by instalments.

(2) No instalment shall be paid if the instalment, together with any amount previously paid, would exceed the appropriate percentage of the cost of so much of the qualifying work as has been executed at that time.

(3) The authority shall pay reinstatement grant in respect of an associated arrangement when payment in respect of the expenditure incurred in entering into the arrangement falls to be made. **[841]**

NOTES to section 273

Definitions: 'local authority': see s 338 below; 'qualifying work': see s 269 above; 'appropriate percentage': see s 271 above.

274. Repayment of grant for breach of condition.

(1) Where an amount of reinstatement grant has been paid in one or more instalments and the qualifying work is not completed within the period for carrying out the work, the local authority may, if they think fit, require the person who was entitled to assistance to repay that amount to them forthwith.

(2) The amount required to be repaid (or, if it was paid in more than one instalment, the amount of each instalment) shall carry interest, at such reasonable rate as the authority may determine, from the date on which it was paid until repayment. **[842]**

NOTES to section 274

Definitions: 'qualifying work': see s 269 above; 'local authority': see s 338 below.

Assistance by way of repurchase

275. Repurchase.

Schedule 20 shall have effect with respect to assistance by way of repurchase, as follows—

Part I—The agreement to repurchase.
Part II—Price payable and valuation. [843]

276. Repurchase by authority other than local authority.

Where the local authority give a notice of determination to a person stating that he is entitled to assistance by way of repurchase and they are of opinion that—
- (a) a relevant interest in the dwelling was disposed of by a public sector authority mentioned in column 1 of the following Table (or a predecessor mentioned there of such an authority),
- (b) there has been no disposal within paragraph (a) since the time of that disposal, and
- (c) any conditions mentioned in column 2 of the Table in relation to the authority are met,

they shall forthwith give that other authority a notice in writing, together with a copy of the notice of determination, stating that the authority may acquire, in accordance with this Part, the interest of the person entitled to assistance.

Table

Public sector authority	Conditions
1. A registered housing association (other than a co-operative housing association) or a predecessor housing association of that association.	None.
[2. Scottish Homes or the Scottish Special Housing Association.]	None.
3. A development corporation.	None.
4. Another local authority or a predecessor of that authority.	The local authority provide housing accommodation in the vicinity of the defective dwelling with which the dwelling may conveniently be managed.
5. Any other public sector authority prescribed by order of the Secretary of State, or a predecessor so prescribed.	Any conditions prescribed by the order.

(2) The other authority may, within the period of four weeks beginning with the service of the notice on them, give notice in writing to the local authority—
- (a) stating that they wish to acquire the interest, and
- (b) specifying the address of the principal office of the authority and any other address which may also be used as an address for service;

and the local authority shall forthwith give to the person entitled to assistance a transfer notice, that is, a notice in writing of the contents of the notice received by them and the effect of subsection (3).

(3) After a transfer notice has been given to the person entitled to assistance, the other authority shall be treated as the appropriate authority for the purposes of anything done or falling to be done under this Part, except that—
- (a) a request under paragraph 2 of Schedule [20] (request for notice of proposed terms of acquisition) may be made either to the local authority or to the other authority, and
- (b) any such request given to the local authority (whether before or after the notice) shall be forwarded by them to the other authority;

and references in this Part to 'the purchasing authority' shall be construed accordingly.

(4) An order under this section shall be made by statutory instrument. [844]

NOTES to section 276

Amendments: The Table was amended by the Housing (Scotland) Act 1988 (c 43), s 72, Sch 2, para 14; sub-s (3) was amended by *Ibid*, s 72, Sch 7, para 20.

Definitions: 'local authority', 'registered housing association', 'development corporation': see

s 338 below; 'relevant interest': see s 303 below; 'dwelling': see s 302 below; 'public sector authority': see ss 303 and 300 below; 'person entitled to assistance': see s 268 above.
Table: The power to make an order has not been exercised.

277. Interest subject to right of pre-emption, etc.

(1) This section applies where a person ('the owner') is entitled to assistance by way of repurchase in respect of a defective dwelling and there is a condition in the title relating to his interest in the dwelling whereby—
  (a) before disposing of the interest he must offer to dispose of it to a public sector authority, or
  (b) in the case of an interest under a lease, he may require a public sector authority who are his landlords to accept a surrender of the lease but is otherwise prohibited from disposing of it.

(2) If the public sector authority are the local authority in whose area the dwelling is situated, the condition in the title shall be disregarded for the purposes of Schedule 20 (repurchase).

(3) If the public sector authority are not the local authority, the provisions of this Part as to repurchase do not apply so long as there is such a condition in the title; but if—
  (a) the owner disposes of his interest to the public sector authority in pursuance of the condition in the title or lease, and
  (b) the interest acquired by that authority on the disposal subsists only in the land affected, that is to say, the defective dwelling and any garage, outhouse, garden, yard and pertinents belonging to or usually enjoyed with the dwelling or any part of it,
the owner is entitled to be paid by the local authority the amount (if any) by which 95 per cent of the defect-free value exceeds the consideration for the disposal.

(4) For the purposes of this section—
  (a) the 'consideration for the disposal' means the amount before any reduction required by section 72 (reduction corresponding to amount of discount repayable) or any provision to the like effect, and
  (b) the 'defect-free value' means the amount that would have been the consideration for the disposal if none of the defective dwellings to which the designation in question related had been affected by the qualifying defect. **[845]**

NOTES to section 277
Definitions: 'defective dwelling': see ss 303 and 287 below and s 257 above; 'dwelling': see s 302 below; 'public sector authority': see ss 303 and 300 below; 'local authority', 'owner': see s 338 below.

278. Compulsory purchase compensation to be made up to 95 per cent of defect-free value.

(1) Where a person ('the owner') has disposed of an interest in a defective dwelling, otherwise than in pursuance of Schedule 20 (repurchase), to an authority possessing compulsory purchase powers and—
  (a) immediately before the time of the disposal he was eligible for assistance under this Part in respect of the dwelling,
  (b) the amount paid as consideration for the disposal did not include any amount attributable to his right to apply for such assistance, and
  (c) on the disposal the authority acquired an interest in any of the affected land, that is to say, the defective dwelling and any garage, outhouse, garden, yard and pertinents belonging to or usually enjoyed with the dwelling or any part of it,
he is entitled, subject to the following provisions of this section, to be paid by the local authority the amount (if any) by which 95 per cent of the defect-free value exceeds the amount of the compensation for the disposal.

(2) For the purposes of this section—
(a) the 'amount of compensation for the disposal' means the amount that would have been the proper amount of compensation for the disposal (having regard to any relevant determination of the Lands Tribunal) or, if greater, the amount paid as the consideration for the disposal, and
(b) the 'defect-free' value means the amount that would have been the proper amount of compensation for the disposal if none of the defective dwellings to which the designation in question related had been affected by the qualifying defect;
but excluding, in either case, any amount payable for disturbance or for any other matter not directly based on the value of land.

(3) For the purposes of this section, it shall be assumed that the disposal occurred on a compulsory acquisition (in cases where it did not in fact do so).

(4) Where the compensation for the disposal fell to be assessed by reference to the value of the land as a site cleared of buildings and available for development, it shall be assumed for the purposes of determining the defect-free value that it did not fall to be so assessed.

(5) The amount payable by the local authority under this section shall be reduced by the amount of any payment made in respect of the defective dwelling under section 304 or 305 (payments for well-maintained houses).

(6) In this section 'authority possessing compulsory purchase powers' has the same meaning as in the Land Compensation (Scotland) Act 1963. **[846]**

NOTES to section 278

Definitions: 'defective dwelling': see ss 303 and 287 below and s 257 above; 'dwelling': see s 302 below; 'land', 'local authority': see s 338 below.

279. Supplementary provisions as to payments under s 277 or 278.

(1) The local authority are not required to make a payment to a person under—
(a) section 277 (making-up of consideration on disposal in pursuance of right of pre-emption, etc), or
(b) section 278 (making up of compulsory purchase compensation),
unless he makes a written application to them for payment before the end of the period of two years beginning with the time of the disposal.

(2) Where the authority—
(a) refuse an application for payment under section 277 on any grounds, or
(b) refuse an application for payment under section 278 on the grounds that the owner was not eligible for assistance in respect of the defective dwelling,
they shall give the applicant written notice of the reasons for their decision.

(3) Any question arising—
(a) under section 277 or 278 as to the defect-free value, or
(b) under section 278 as to the amount of compensation for the disposal,
shall be determined by the district valuer if the owner or the local authority so require by notice in writing served on the district valuer.

(4) A person serving a notice on the district valuer in pursuance of subsection (3) shall serve notice in writing of that fact on the other party.

(5) Before making a determination in pursuance of subsection (3), the district valuer shall consider any representation by the owner or the authority made to him within 4 weeks from the service of the notice under that subsection. **[847]**

NOTES to section 279

Definitions: 'local authority', 'owner': see s 338 below; 'defective dwelling': see ss 303 and 287 below and s 257 above; 'dwelling': see s 302 below; 'owner': see s 338 below.

280. Reimbursement of expenses incidental to repurchase.

(1) A person whose interest in a defective dwelling is acquired by the purchasing authority in pursuance of Schedule 20 (repurchase) is entitled to be reimbursed by the purchasing authority the proper amount of—
   (a) expenses in respect of legal services provided in connection with the authority's acquisition, and
   (b) other expenses in connection with negotiating the terms of that acquisition,
being in each case expenses which are reasonably incurred by him after receipt of a notice under paragraph 3 of that Schedule (authority's notice of proposed terms of acquisition).

(2) An agreement between a person and the purchasing authority is void in so far as it purports to oblige him to bear any part of the costs or expenses incurred by the authority in connection with the exercise by him of his rights under this Part. **[848]**

NOTES to section 280

Definitions: 'defective dwelling': see ss 303 and 287 below and s 257 above; 'dwelling': see s 302 below; 'purchasing authority: see s 276 above.

Effect of repurchase on occupier

281. Effect of repurchase on certain existing tenancies.

(1) Where an authority mentioned in section 44 (authorities satisfying the landlord's condition for secure tenancy) acquire an interest in a defective dwelling in pursuance of Schedule 20 (repurchase) and—
   (a) the land in which the interest subsists is or includes a house occupied as a separate dwelling, and
   (b) the interest of the person entitled to assistance by way of repurchase is, immediately before the completion of the authority's acquisition, subject to a tenancy of the house,
the tenancy shall not, on or after the acquisition, become a secure tenancy unless the conditions specified in subsection (2) are met.

(2) The conditions are—
   (a) that the tenancy was a protected tenancy throughout the period beginning with the making of an application for assistance under this Part in respect of the defective dwelling and ending immediately before the authority's acquisition; and
   (b) no notice was given in respect of the tenancy in accordance with any of Cases 11 to 14 and 16 to 21 in Schedule 2 to the Rent (Scotland) Act 1984 (notice that possession might be recovered under that Case) or under section [9(1)(d) of the Rent (Scotland) Act 1984] (notice that tenancy is to be a protected short tenancy). **[849]**

NOTES to section 281

Amendment: Sub-s (2) was amended by the Housing (Scotland) Act 1988 (c 43), s 72, Sch 7, para 21.

Definitions: 'secure tenancy': see s 338 below and s 44 above; 'defective dwelling': see ss 303 and 287 below and s 257 above; 'dwelling': see s 302 below; 'land': see s 338 below; 'house': see s 286 below; 'person entitled to assistance': see s 303 below and s 268 above.

282. Grant of tenancy to former owner-occupier.

(1) Where an authority acquire an interest in a defective dwelling in pursuance of Schedule 20 (repurchase), or in the circumstances described in section 277(3) (exercise of right of pre-emption, etc), and—
   (a) the land in which the interest subsists is or includes a house occupied as a separate dwelling, and
   (b) an individual is an occupier of the house throughout the period beginning with the making of an application for assistance under this Part in respect of the

dwelling and ending immediately before the completion of the authority's acquisition, and

(c) he is a person entitled to assistance by way of repurchase in respect of the defective dwelling, or the persons so entitled are in relation to the interest concerned his trustees,

the authority shall, in accordance with this section, either grant or arrange for him to be granted a tenancy of that house or another on the completion of their acquisition of the interest concerned.

(2) If the authority are among those mentioned in section [44(2)] (public sector authorities capable of granting secure tenancies) their obligation is to grant a secure tenancy.

(3) In any other case their obligation is to grant or arrange for the grant of either—
(a) a secured tenancy, or
(b) a protected tenancy other than one under which the landlord might recover possession under one of the cases in Part II of Schedule 2 to the Rent (Scotland) Act 1984 (cases in which the court must order possession).

(4) Where two or more persons qualify for the grant of a tenancy under this section in respect of the same house, the authority shall grant the tenancy, or arrange for it to be granted, to such one or more of them as they may agree among themselves or (if there is no such agreement) to all of them. **[850]**

NOTES to section 282

Amendment: In sub-s (2) reference to s 44(2) substituted by the Housing (Scotland) Act 1988 (c 43), s 72, Sch 7, para 22.

Definitions: 'defective dwelling': see ss 303 and 287 below and s 257 above; 'dwelling': see s 302 below; 'land': see s 338 below; 'house': see s 286 below; 'occupier': *Ibid*; 'person entitled to assistance': see s 303 below and s 268 above; 'secure tenancy': see s 338 below and s 44 above; 'grant of a secure tenancy': see s 286 below.

283. Grant of tenancy to former statutory tenant.

(1) Where an authority mentioned in section [44(2)] (public sector authorities capable of granting secure tenancies) acquire an interest in a defective dwelling in pursuance of Schedule 20 (repurchase), and—
(a) the land in which the interest subsists is or includes a house occupied as a separate dwelling, and
(b) an individual is an occupier of a house throughout the period beginning with the making of an application for assistance under this Part in respect of the dwelling and ending immediately before the completion of the authority's acquisition, and
(c) he is a statutory tenant of the house at the end of that period, and
(d) no notice was given in respect of the original tenancy in accordance with any of Cases 11 to 14 and 16 to 21 in Schedule 2 to the Rent (Scotland) Act 1984 (notice that possession might be recovered under that Case) or under section [9(1)(d) of the Rent (Scotland) Act 1984] (notice that tenancy is to be a [short tenancy]), and
(e) the interest of the person entitled to assistance would, if the statutory tenancy were a contractual tenancy, be subject to the tenancy at the end of the period mentioned in paragraph (b),

the authority shall grant him a secure tenancy (of that house or another) on the completion of their acquisition of the interest concerned.

(2) Where two or more persons qualify for the grant of a tenancy under this section in respect of the same house, the authority shall grant the tenancy to such one or more of them as they may agree among themselves or (if there is no such agreement) to all of them.

(3) If at any time after the service of a notice of determination it appears to the purchasing authority that a person may be entitled to request them to grant him a secure tenancy under this section, they shall forthwith give him notice in writing of that fact. **[851]**

NOTES to section 283

Amendment: Sub-s (1) was amended by the Housing (Scotland) Act 1988 (c 43), s 72, Sch 7, para 23.

Definitions: 'secure tenancy': see s 338 below and s 44 above; 'defective dwelling': see ss 303 and 287 below and s 257 above; 'dwelling': see s 302 below; 'land', 'statutory tenant': see s 338 below; 'house', 'occupier', 'grant of a secure tenancy': see s 286 below.

284. Alternative accommodation under s 282 or 283.

(1) The house to be let under the tenancy granted to a person—
- (a) under section 282 or 283 (grant of tenancy to former owner-occupier or statutory tenant of defective house acquired by authority), or
- (b) under arrangements made for the purposes of section 283,

shall be the house of which he is the occupier immediately before the completion of the authority's acquisition (the 'current house'), except in the following Cases—

Case 1

By reason of the condition of any building of which the current house consists or of which it forms part, the house may not safely be occupied for residential purposes.

Case 2

The authority intend, within a reasonable time of the completion of their acquisition of the interest concerned—
- (a) to demolish or reconstruct the building which consists of or includes the defective dwelling in question, or
- (b) to carry out work on any building or land in which the interest concerned subsists,

and cannot reasonably do so if the current house remains in residential occupation.

(2) In those Cases the house to be let shall be another house which, so far as is reasonably practicable in the case of that authority, affords accommodation which is—
- (a) similar as regards extent and character to the accommodation afforded by the current house,
- (b) reasonably suitable to the means of the prospective tenant and his family, and
- (c) reasonably suitable to the needs of the prospective tenant and his family as regards proximity to place of work and place of education. **[852]**

NOTES to section 284

Definitions: 'house': see s 286 below; 'statutory tenant', 'land': see s 338 below; 'defective dwelling': see ss 303 and 287 below and s 257 above; 'dwelling': see s 302 below.

285. Request for tenancy under s 282 or 283.

(1) An authority are not required to grant, or arrange for the grant of, a tenancy to a person under section 282 or 283 unless he requests them to do so in writing before—
- (a) in the case of an acquisition under Schedule 20 (repurchase), the service on the person entitled to assistance of an offer to purchase under paragraph [3] of that Schedule, or
- (b) in the case of an acquisition in the circumstances described in section 277(3) (acquisition in pursuance of right of pre-emption, etc), the time of the disposal.

(2) An authority receiving a request under subsection (1) shall, as soon as reasonably practicable, give notice in writing to the person making the request stating whether in their opinion either of the Cases in section 284(1) applies (cases in which tenancy may be of a house other than the current house).

(3) If their opinion is that either Case does apply, the notice shall also state which of the Cases is applicable and the effect of section 284. **[853]**

NOTES to section 285
Amendment: Sub-s (1) was amended by the Housing (Scotland) Act 1988 (c 43), s 72, Sch 7, para 24.
Definitions: 'person entitled to assistance': see s 303 below and s 268 above; 'house': see s 286 below.

286. Interpretation of ss 281 to 285.

In sections 281 to 285 (effect of repurchase on occupier)—
   (a) 'house' has the same meaning as in Part III (secure tenancies);
   (b) 'occupier', in relation to a house, means a person who occupies the house as his only or principal home or (in the case of a statutory tenant) as his residence;
   (c) references to the grant of a secure tenancy are to the grant of a tenancy which would be a secure tenancy assuming that the tenant under the tenancy occupies the house as his only or principal home. [854]

Local schemes

287. Designation of defective dwellings under local schemes.

(1) A local authority may by resolution designate as a class buildings in their area each of which consists of or includes one or more dwellings if it appears to them that—
   (a) buildings in the proposed class are defective by reason of their design or construction, and
   (b) by virtue of the circumstances mentioned in paragraph (a) having become generally known, the value of some or all of the dwellings concerned has been substantially reduced.

(2) Subsection (1) does not apply to a building in a class designated under section 257 (designation by the Secretary of State); but a building does not cease to be included in a class designated under this section by virtue of its inclusion in a class designated under that section.

(3) A dwelling which is, or is included in, a building in a class so designated is referred to in this Part as a 'defective dwelling'; and in this Part, in relation to such a dwelling—
   (a) 'the qualifying defect' means what, in the opinion of the authority, is wrong with the buildings in that class, and
   (b) 'the cut-off date' means the date by which, in the opinion of the authority, the circumstances mentioned in subsection (1)(a) became generally known.

(4) A designation shall describe the qualifying defect and specify—
   (a) the cut-off date,
   (b) the date (being a date falling on or after the cut-off date) on which the designation is to come into operation, and
   (c) the period within which persons may seek assistance under this Part in respect of the defective dwellings concerned.

(5) A designation may not describe a designated class by reference to the area (other than the authority's district) in which the buildings concerned are situated; but may be so described that within the authority's area there is only one building in the class.

(6) Any question arising as to whether a building is or was at any time in a class designated under this section shall be determined by the local authority concerned. [855]

NOTES to section 287
Definitions: 'local authority': see s 338 below; 'dwelling': see s 302 below.

288. Variation or revocation of designation under local schemes.

(1) The local authority may by resolution—
   (a) vary a designation under section 287, but not so as to vary the cut-off date, or

(b) revoke such a designation.

(2) The authority may by a variation of the designation extend the period referred to in section 287(4)(c) (period within which assistance must be applied for) whether or not it has expired.

(3) The variation or revocation of a designation does not affect the operation of the provisions of this Part in relation to a dwelling if, before the variation or revocation comes into operation, the dwelling is a defective dwelling by virtue of the designation in question and application for assistance under this Part has been made. **[856]**

NOTES to section 288

Definitions: 'local authority': see s 338 below; 'dwelling': see s 302 below.

289. Secretary of State's control over designation, variation or revocation.

(1) Where a local authority have passed a resolution under—
(a) section 287 (designation under local scheme), or
(b) section 288 (variation or revocation of designation under local scheme),
they shall give written notice to the Secretary of State of the resolution before the expiry of the period of 28 days beginning with the date on which it is passed.

(2) The designation, variation or revocation shall not come into operation before [the cut-off date or if it is later] the expiry of the period of 2 months [or such longer period as the Secretary of State may direct for the purposes of this subsection under subsection (2A) below] beginning with the receipt by the Secretary of State of the notice under subsection (1).

[(2A) If, within the period for the time being specified in or (by virtue of the previous operation of this subsection) for the purposes of subsection (2) above, the Secretary of State is satisfied that he does not have reasonably sufficient information to enable him to come to a decision with respect to the resolution concerned, he may direct for the purposes of that subsection that it shall have effect as if for the period so specified there were substituted such longer period as is specified in the direction.]

(3) If [before the cut-off date or, if it is later, the expiry of the period for the time being specified in or for the purposes of subsection (2) above] the Secretary of State serves notice in writing to that effect on the authority, the designation, revocation or variation shall not come into operation. **[857]**

NOTES to section 289

Amendments: Sub-ss (2) and (3) were amended by the Local Government and Housing Act 1989 (c 42), s 166; sub-s (2A) was added by *Ibid*.
Definition: 'local authority': see s 338 below.

Miscellaneous

290. Duty of local housing authority to publicise availability of assistance.

(1) A local authority shall, within the period of 3 months beginning with the coming into operation of—
(a) a designation under section 257 (designation of defective dwellings by the Secretary of State) or section 287 (designation of defective dwellings under local scheme), or
(b) a variation of such a designation,
publish in a newspaper circulating in their area a notice suitable for the purposes of bringing the effect of the designation or variation to the attention of persons who may be eligible for assistance in respect of such of the dwellings concerned as are situated within their area.

(2) No such notice need be published by a local housing authority who are of opinion—

(a) that none of the dwellings concerned are situated in their area, or
(b) that no-one is likely to be eligible for assistance in respect of the dwellings concerned which are situated in their area.

(3) If at any time it becomes apparent to a local authority that a person is likely to be eligible for assistance in respect of a defective dwelling within their area, they shall forthwith take such steps as are reasonably practicable to inform him of the fact that assistance is available. **[858]**

NOTES to section 290

Definitions: 'local authority': see s 338 below; 'defective dwelling': see s 303 below and ss 257 and 287 above; 'dwelling': see s 302 below.

291. Duties of public sector authority disposing of defective dwelling.

(1) A public sector authority shall, where a person is to acquire a relevant interest in a defective dwelling on a disposal by the authority, give him notice in writing before the time of the disposal—
(a) specifying the qualifying defect, and
(b) stating that he will not be eligible for assistance under this Part in respect of the dwelling.

(2) A public sector authority shall, before they convey a relevant interest in a defective dwelling in pursuance of completed missives to a person on whom a notice under subsection (1) has not been served, give him notice in writing—
(a) specifying the qualifying defect,
(b) stating, where the time of disposal of the interest falls after the cut-off date, that he will not be eligible for assistance under this Part, and
(c) stating the effect of subsection (3).

(3) A person on whom a notice under subsection (2) is served—
(a) is not obliged to complete the conveyance before the expiry of the period of 6 months beginning with the service of that notice on him, and
(b) may within that period withdraw from the transaction by notice in writing to the authority to that effect.

(4) Where a public sector authority are required to serve a notice under section 63(2), 68, 69 or 70 (landlord's response to notice claiming to exercise right to buy) in respect of a defective dwelling, the notice under subsection (1) shall be served with that notice.

(5) A notice under subsection (1) or (2) shall (except in the case of a notice under subsection (1) which is served in accordance with subsection (4)), be served at the earliest date at which it is reasonably practicable to do so. **[859]**

NOTES to section 291

Definitions: 'public sector authority': see ss 303 and 300 below; 'defective dwelling', 'qualifying defect': see s 303 below and ss 257 and 287 above; 'dwelling': see s 302 below; 'relevant interest': see s 303 below.

292. Reinstatement of defective dwelling by local authority.

(1) Where a relevant interest in a defective dwelling has been disposed of by a public sector authority, the local authority may, before the end of the period within which a person may seek assistance under this Part in respect of the dwelling, enter into an agreement with—
(a) any person holding an interest in the dwelling, or
(b) any person who is a statutory tenant of it,
to execute at his expense any of the work required to reinstate the dwelling.

(2) For the purposes of this section a disposal by or under an enactment of an interest in a dwelling held by a public sector authority shall be treated as a disposal of the interest by the authority. **[860]**

[861]

NOTES to section 292

Definitions: 'relevant interest': see s 303 below; 'defective dwelling': see s 303 below and ss 287 and 257 above; 'dwelling': see s 302 below; 'public sector authority': see ss 303 and 300 below; 'local authority' 'statutory tenant': see s 338 below; 'work required to reinstate the dwelling': see s 303 below and s 267 above.

293. Death of person eligible for assistance, etc.

(1) Where a person who is eligible for assistance in respect of a defective dwelling—
(a) dies, or
(b) disposes of his interest in the dwelling (otherwise than on a disposal for value) to such a person as is mentioned in section 259(2) (persons qualifying for assistance: individuals, trustees for individuals and personal representatives),
this Part applies as if anything done (or treated by virtue of this subsection as done) by or in relation to the person so eligible had been done by or in relation to his personal representatives or, as the case may be, the person acquiring his interest.

(2) In sections 277 to 279 (subsidiary forms of financial assistance) references to the owner of an interest in a defective dwelling include his personal representatives. [861]

NOTES to section 293

Definitions: 'defective dwelling': see s 303 below and ss 287 and 257 above; 'dwelling': see s 302 below; 'owner': see s 338 below.

294. Dwellings included in more than one designation.

The provisions of Schedule 21 have effect with respect to dwellings included in more than one designation. [862]

295. Application of Act in relation to lenders on security of defective dwelling.

(1) The Secretary of State may by regulations made by statutory instrument subject to annulment by either House of Parliament make provision for the purpose of conferring rights and obligations on any person who has granted a loan on the security of a defective dwelling where—
(a) a power of sale is exercisable by the lender, and
(b) the borrower is eligible for assistance in respect of the defective dwelling.

(2) The rights that may be conferred on a lender by regulations under this section are—
(a) rights corresponding to those conferred by this Part on a person holding a relevant interest in the defective dwelling, and
(b) the right to require the local authority to acquire in accordance with the regulations any interest in the defective dwelling to be disposed of in exercise of the power of sale,
and the rights that may be so conferred may be conferred in place of any rights conferred on any other person by this Part.

(3) Regulations under this section may provide that, where the conditions in subsection (1)(a) and (b) are or have been satisfied, this Part, the power of sale and any enactment relating to the power of sale in question shall have effect subject to such modifications as may be specified in the regulations.

(4) Regulations under this section—
(a) may make different provision for different cases, and
(b) may make incidental and consequential provision. [863]

NOTES to section 295

Definitions: 'defective dwelling': see s 303 below and ss 287 and 257 above; 'dwelling': see s 302 below; 'relevant interest': see s 303 below; 'local authority': see s 338 below.
Sub-s (1): See the Housing Defects (Application to Lenders) (Scotland) Regulations 1986, SI 1986/843, paras [1351] ff below.

296. . . .

NOTES to section 296

Section 296 was repealed by the Housing (Scotland) Act 1988 (c 43), s 72, Sch 10.

297. . . .

NOTES to section 297

Section 297 was repealed by the Housing (Scotland) Act 1988 (c 43), s 72, Sch 10.

Supplementary provisions

298. Service of notices.

(1) A notice or other document under this Part may be given to or served on a person, and an application or written request under this Part may be made to a person—
  (a) by delivering it to him or leaving it at his proper address, or
  (b) by sending it to him by post,
and also, where the person concerned is a body corporate, by giving or making it to or serving it on the secretary of that body.

(2) For the purposes of this section, and of section 7 of the Interpretation Act 1978 as it applies for the purposes of this section, the proper address of a person is—
  (a) in the case of a body corporate or its secretary, the address of the principal office of the body,
  (b) in any other case, his last known address
and also, where an additional address for service has been specified by that person in a notice under section 276(2) (notice of intention to assume responsibility for repurchase), that address. **[864]**

299. Jurisdiction of sheriff in Scotland.

(1) A sheriff of the sheriff court district within which the defective dwelling is situated has jurisdiction—
  (a) to determine any question arising under this Part; and
  (b) to entertain any proceedings brought in connection with the performance or discharge of any obligations so arising, including proceedings for the recovery of damages or compensation in the event of the obligations not being performed.

(2) Subsection (1) has effect subject to—
  (a) sections 257(6) and 287(6) (questions of designation to be decided by designating authority),
  (b) section 279(3) and paragraph [11(1) of Schedule 20] (questions of valuation to be determined by district valuer).

(3) Where an authority required by section 270(3) or paragraph 7 of Schedule 20 to extend or further extend any period fail to do so, the sheriff may extend or further extend that period until such date as he may specify. **[865]**

NOTE to section 299

Amendment: Sub-s (2) was amended by the Housing (Scotland) Act 1988 (c 43), s 72, Sch 7, para 26.

300. Meaning of 'public sector authority'.

(1) In this Part—
  (a) 'public sector authority' means—
    a regional, islands or district council (or a predecessor of such a council), a joint board and a joint committee of which every constituent member is, or is appointed by, such a council or predecessor of such a council,

a water authority,
the Housing Corporation,
[Scottish Homes],
a registered housing association other than a co-operative housing association (or a predecessor housing association of such an association),
a development corporation,
the National Coal Board, or
the United Kingdom Atomic Energy Authority,
or a body corporate or housing association specified by order of the Secretary of State in accordance with the following provisions;
(b) 'co-operative housing association' means a fully mutual housing association which is a society registered under the Industrial and Provident Societies Act 1965, and 'fully mutual', in relation to a housing association, means that the rules of the association—
  (i) restrict membership to persons who are tenants or prospective tenants of the association, and
  (ii) preclude the granting or assignation of tenancies to persons other than members.

(2) The Secretary of State may provide that a body corporate shall be treated as a public sector authority if he is satisfied—
(a) that the affairs of the body are managed by its members, and
(b) that its members hold office by virtue of appointment (to that or another office) by a Minister of the Crown under an enactment,
or if he is satisfied that it is a subsidiary of such a body.

(3) The Secretary of State may provide that a housing association shall be treated as a public sector authority if he is satisfied that the objects or powers of the association include the provision of housing accommodation for individuals employed at any time by a public sector authority or dependants of such individuals.

(4) Where the Secretary of State is satisfied that a body or association met the requirements of subsection (2) or (3) during any period, he may, whether or not he makes an order in respect of the body or association under that subsection, provide that it shall be treated as having been a public sector authority during that period.

(5) If the Secretary of State is satisfied that a body or association specified in an order under subsection (2) or (3) has ceased to meet the requirements of that subsection on any date, he may by order provide that it shall be treated as having ceased to be a public sector authority on that date.

(6) An order under this section shall be made by statutory instrument. **[866]**

NOTES to section 300
Amendment: In sub-s (1), reference to Scottish Homes substituted by the Housing (Scotland) Act 1988 (c 43), s 3, Sch 2, para 1.
Definitions: 'water authority', 'registered housing association', 'development corporation': see s 338 below.

---

301. Disposal of certain Crown interests in land treated as disposal by public sector authority.

References in this Part to a disposal of an interest in a dwelling by a public sector authority include a disposal of—
(a) an interest belonging to Her Majesty in right of the Crown,
(b) an interest belonging to, or held in trust for Her Majesty for the purposes of, a government department or Minister of the Crown. **[867]**

302. Meaning of 'dwelling' and 'house'.

(1) In this Part, 'dwelling' means any house, flat or other unit designed or adapted for living in.

(2) For the purposes of this Part a building so designed or adapted is a 'house' if it is a structure reasonably so called; so that where a building is divided into units so designed or adapted—
(a) if it is so divided horizontally, or a material part of a unit lies above or below another unit, the units are not houses (though the building as a whole may be), and
(b) if it is so divided vertically, the units may be houses.

(3) Where a house which is divided into flats or other units is a defective dwelling in respect of which a person is eligible for assistance, the fact that it is so divided shall be disregarded for the purposes of section 266(1)(a) (first condition for assistance by way of reinstatement: that the dwelling is a house). [868]

303. Interpretation.

In this Part—
'associated arrangement' has the meaning given by section 267(2);
'cut-off date' is to be construed in accordance with section 257(2) or, as the case may be, 287(3);
'defective dwelling' is to be construed in accordance with section 257(2) or, as the case may be, 287(3);
'interest in dwelling' includes an interest in land which is or includes the dwelling;
'lending institution' means a building society, a bank or an insurance company;
'person entitled to assistance' (by way of reinstatement grant or repurchase) is to be construed in accordance with section 268(5);
'public sector authority' has the meaning given by section 300;
'purchasing authority' is to be construed in accordance with section 276(3);
'qualifying defect' is to be construed in accordance with section 257(2) or, as the case may be, section 287(3);
'relevant interest' means the interest of the owner;
'work required to reinstate a defective dwelling' is to be construed in accordance with section 267(1). [869]

NOTES to section 303
Definitions: 'land', 'building society', 'bank', 'insurance company': see s 338 below; 'dwelling': see s 302 above.

Part XV
Compensation Payments

Payments for well-maintained houses

304. Payments in respect of well-maintained houses subject to closing orders etc.

(1) If—
(a) a house has been vacated in pursuance of a closing order or a demolition order, or purchased compulsorily under section 121 instead of the making of a closing order or a demolition order in respect of the building in which it is comprised; and
(b) any person has, within 3 months after the service of the closing order or demolition order, or of the notice of determination to purchase required by section 121(3), or after the confirmation of a compulsory purchase order, made a representation to the local authority that the house has been well maintained and that the good maintenance of the house is attributable wholly or partly to work carried out by him or at his expense; and
(c) leaving out of account any defects in the house in respect of any such matters as are mentioned in section 86, the representation is correct;
the local authority shall make to that person in respect of that house a payment calculated in accordance with section 306.

(2) If, on receiving a representation under subsection (1), the local authority consider that the condition specified in paragraph (c) of that subsection is not satisfied, they shall serve on the person by whom the representation was made notice that no payment falls to be made to him under that subsection.

(3) For the purposes of this section, a house comprised in a building which might have been the subject of a demolition order but which has, without the making of such an order, been vacated and demolished in pursuance of an undertaking for its demolition given to the local authority shall be deemed to have been vacated in pursuance of a demolition order made and served at the date when the undertaking was given.   **[870]**

NOTES to section 304

Definitions: 'house': see s 338 below; 'closing order': see s 338 below and ss 114 and 119 above; 'demolition order': see s 338 below and s 115 above; 'local authority': see s 338 below.

305. Payments in respect of well-maintained houses subject to compulsory purchase as not meeting the tolerable standard.

(1) Where as respects a house which is made the subject of a compulsory purchase order under Part IV as not meeting the tolerable standard, the local authority are satisfied that it has been well maintained, they shall make a payment calculated in accordance with section 306 in respect of the house.

(2) A payment under this section shall be made—
   (a)   if the house is occupied by an owner thereof, to him, or
   (b)   if the house is not so occupied, to the person or persons liable to maintain and repair the house, and, if more than one person is so liable, in such shares as the local authority think equitable in the circumstances:
Provided that, if any other person satisfied the local authority that the good maintenance of the house is attributable to a material extent to work carried out by him or at his expense, the authority may, if it appears to them to be equitable in the circumstances, make the payment, in whole or in part to him.

(3) The local authority shall, along with the notice which they serve on any person under paragraph 3(b) of Schedule 1 to the Acquisition of Land (Authorisation Procedure) (Scotland) Act 1947 in respect of the compulsory purchase of a house under Part IV, enclose a notice stating, subject to the calculation to be made under section 306, whether or not they intend to make a payment under this section in respect of the house.

(4) Any person aggrieved by a notice under subsection (3) which states that the local authority do not intend to make a payment under this section in respect of a house may, within 21 days of a service on him of that notice, refer the matter to the Secretary of State; and the Secretary of State may, if he thinks it appropriate to do so (after, if he considers it necessary, causing the house to be inspected by one of his officers), direct the local authority to make such a payment.   **[871]**

NOTES to section 305

Definitions: 'house', 'local authority', 'owner': see s 338 below; 'the tolerable standard': see s 338 below and s 86 above.

306. Calculation of amount payable for well-maintained houses.

(1) This section shall apply in relation to any payment in respect of a well-maintained house under section 304 or section 305.

(2) Subject to subsection (4), a payment to which this section applies shall be of an amount equal to the rateable value of the house multiplied by such multiplier as may from time to time be specified in an order made by the Secretary of State.

(3) An order made under subsection (2) shall be made by statutory instrument which shall be of no effect unless it is approved by a resolution of each House of Parliament.

(4) A payment to which this section applies shall not in any case exceed the amount (if any) by which the full compulsory purchase value of the house exceeds the restricted value thereof; and any question as to such value shall be determined, in default of agreement, as if it had been a question of disputed compensation arising on such a purchase.

(5) Where a payment falls to be made in respect of any interest in a house under section 308, no payment shall be made in respect of that house under section 304 or 305.

(6) In this section—
'full compulsory purchase value' has the same meaning as in section 311(2);
'rateable value' means the rateable value entered in the valuation roll last authenticated prior to the relevant date;
'restricted value' has the same meaning as in section 311(2); and
'the relevant date' in relation to any payment made with respect to any house means—
  (a) if the house was purchased compulsorily in pursuance of a notice served under section 121, the date when the notice was served;
  (b) if the house was vacated in pursuance of a demolition order or a closing order, or was declared not to meet the tolerable standard by an order under paragraph 2(1) of Schedule 2 to the Land Compensation (Scotland) Act 1963, the date when the order was made. [872]

NOTES to section 306

Definitions: 'house': see s 338 below; 'interest': see s 311 below.
Sub-s (2): The multiplier is currently 12.7. See the Housing (Payments for Well-Maintained Houses) (Scotland) Order 1983, SI 1983/1804.

Repayment of certain payments

307. Repayment of payments made in connection with closing or demolition order when revoked.

Where a payment in respect of a house has been made by a local authority under section 304, 305 or 308 in connection with a demolition order or a closing order and, the demolition order or the closing order is revoked by an order under section 116, then if at any time the person to whom the payment was made is entitled to an interest in the house (within the meaning of section 311(2)), he shall on demand repay the payment to the authority. [873]

NOTES to section 307

Definitions: 'house', 'local authority': see s 338 below; 'demolition order': see s 338 below and s 115 above; 'closing order': see s 338 below and ss 114 and 119 above.

Payments for houses not meeting tolerable standard

308. Right to and amount of payments for house not meeting tolerable standard.

(1) Where a house has been purchased at restricted value in pursuance of a compulsory purchase order made by virtue of sections 88 or 121 or paragraph 5 of Schedule 8, or in pursuance of an order under paragraph 2(1) of Schedule 2 to the Land Compensation (Scotland) Act 1963, or has been vacated in pursuance of a demolition order under section 115 or a closing order under section 114 or 119, then if—
  (a) on the relevant date and throughout the qualifying period the house was occupied as a private dwelling, and the person so occupying the house (or, if during that period it was so occupied by two or more persons in succession, each of those persons) was a person entitled to an interest in that house or a member of the family of a person so entitled, and
  (b) the full compulsory purchase value of the interest is greater than its restricted value,

the authority concerned shall make in respect of that interest a payment of an amount equal to the difference between the full compulsory purchase value and the restricted value.

(2) Any question as to the values referred to in subsection (1) shall be determined, in default of agreement, as if it had been a question of disputed compensation arising on such a purchase.

(3) Where an interest in a house purchased or vacated as described in subsection (1) was acquired by any person (in this subsection referred to as the first owner) on or after 1st August 1968 and less than 2 years before the relevant date, and a payment under the said subsection (1) in respect of that interest would have fallen to be made by the authority concerned had the qualifying period been a period beginning with the acquisition and ending with the relevant date, the authority concerned shall make to the person who was entitled to the interest at the date when the house was purchased or vacated a payment of the like amount, if—
  (a) the authority are satisfied that before acquiring the interest the first owner had made all reasonable inquiries to ascertain whether it was likely that the notice, resolution or order, by reference to which the relevant date is defined in section 311 would be served, passed or made within 2 years of the acquisition and that he had no reason to believe that it was likely; and
  (b) the person entitled to the interest at the date when the house was purchased or vacated was the first owner or a member of his family. **[874]**

NOTES to section 308

Definitions: 'house': see s 338 below; 'restricted value', 'relevant date', 'qualifying period', 'interest', 'full compulsory purchase value', 'the authority concerned': see s 311 below; 'family': see s 338 below and s 83 above; 'demolition order': see s 338 below and s 115 above.

309. Right of parties to certain agreements secured on, or related to, houses not meeting the tolerable standard to apply to sheriff for adjustment of the agreements.

(1) This section shall apply whether or not a payment falls to be made in respect of an interest in a house under section 308 where a house is purchased at restricted value in pursuance of a compulsory purchase order made by virtue of section 88, 120 or 121, or paragraph 5 of Schedule 8, or in pursuance of an order under paragraph 2(1) of Schedule 2 to the Land Compensation (Scotland) Act 1963, or has been vacated in pursuance of a demolition order or a closing order, and on the date of the making of the compulsory purchase or other order the house is occupied in whole or part as a private dwelling by a peson who throughout the relevant period—
  (a) holds an interest in the house, being an interest subject to a heritable security or charge, or
  (b) is a party to an agreement to purchase the house by instalments.

(2) Where the provisions of subsection (1) apply in the case of any house, any party to the heritable security, charge or agreement in question may apply to the sheriff who, after giving to other parties an opportunity of being heard, may, if he thinks fit, make an order—
  (a) in the case of a house which has been purchased compulsorily, discharging or modifying any outstanding liabilities of the person having an interest in the house, being liabilities arising by virtue of any bond or other obligation with respect to the debt secured by the heritable security or charge, or by virtue of the agreement, or
  (b) in the case of a house vacated in pursuance of a demolition order, or closing order, discharging or modifying the terms of the heritable security, charge or agreement,
and, in either case, either unconditionally or subject to such terms and conditions, including conditions with respect to the payment of money, as the sheriff may think just.

(3) In determining in any case what order, if any, to make under this section, the sheriff shall have regard to all the circumstances of the case, and in particular—
- (a) in the case of a heritable security or charge—
    - (i) to whether the heritable creditor or person entitled to the benefit of the charge acted reasonably in advancing the principal sum on the terms of the heritable security or charge; and in relation to this sub-paragraph he shall be deemed to have acted unreasonably if, at the time when the heritable security or charge was created, he knew or ought to have known that in all the circumstances of the case the terms of the heritable security or charge did not afford sufficient security for the principal sum advanced, and
    - (ii) where the heritable security or charge secures a sum which represents all or any part of the purchase price payable for the interest, to whether the purchase price was excessive, or
- (b) in the case of an agreement to purchase by instalments, to how far the amount already paid by way of principal, or, where the house has been purchased compulsorily, the aggregate of that amount and so much, if any, of the compensation in respect of compulsory purchase as falls to be paid to the seller, represents a fair price for the purchase.

(4) In this section 'the relevant period' means the period from the date of the making of the compulsory purchase or other order to—
- (a) in the case of a compulsory purchase order, the date of service or notice to treat (or deemed service of notice to treat) for purchase of the house or, if the purchase is effected without service of notice to treat, the date of completion of that purchase, and
- (b) in the case of any other order, the date of vacation of the house in pursuance of the order or of an order deemed to have been made and served in the terms of the next following subsection;

or, if the person referred to in subsection (1) dies before the date specified in paragraph (a) or (b), to the date of death.

(5) For the purposes of this section, a house which might have been the subject of a demolition order but which has, without the making of such an order, been vacated and demolished in pursuance of an undertaking for its demolition given to the local authority, shall be deemed to have been vacated in pursuance of a demolition order made and served at the date when the undertaking was given. **[875]**

NOTES to section 309

Definitions: 'house': see s 338 below; 'interest', 'restricted value': see s 338 below; 'demolition order': see s 338 below and s 115 above; 'closing order': see s 338 below and ss 114 and 119 above.

310. Provisions as to house subject to heritable security or purchased by instalments.

Section 309 (right of parties to certain agreements secured on, or related to, houses not meeting tolerable standard to apply to sheriff for adjustment of agreements) shall apply, whether or not a payment falls to be made in respect of an interest in a house under section 308, where the house not meeting the tolerable standard is purchased at restricted value in pursuance of a compulsory purchase order made by virtue of sections 88, 120 and 121 or paragraph 5 of Schedule 8, or in pursuance of an order under paragraph 2(1) of Schedule 2 to the Land Compensation (Scotland) Act 1963, or has been vacated in pursuance of a demolition order or a closing order as it applies where a house has been purchased or vacated before 25th August 1969 as described in section 309. **[876]**

NOTES to section 310

Definitions: 'house': see s 338 below; 'the tolerable standard': see s 338 below and s 86 above; 'interest', 'restricted value': see s 311 below; 'demolition order': see s 338 below and s 115 above; 'closing order': see s 338 below and ss 114 and 119 above.

311. Interpretation of sections 308 to 310

(1) In section 308, in relation to any house purchased or vacated, 'the relevant date' and 'the authority concerned' mean respectively—
 (a) if the house was purchased compulsorily in pursuance of a notice served under section 121, the date when and the authority by whom the notice was served;
 (b) if the house was comprised in an area declared by a final resolution passed under Part IV to be a housing action area, the date when notice of that resolution was published and served in accordance with the provisions of Part 1 of Schedule 8 and the authority by whom the resolution was passed;
 (c) if the house was declared not to meet the tolerable standard by an order under paragraph 2(1) of Schedule 2 to the Land Compensation (Scotland) Act 1963, the date when the order was made and the acquiring authority within the meaning of that Act;
 (d) if the house was vacated in pursuance of a demolition order or closing order, the date when and the authority by whom the order was made;
 (e) if the house was compulsorily purchased under section 88(4), the date when and the authority by whom the order was served;
and 'the qualifying period' means the period of 2 years ending with the relevant date, except that where that date is earlier than 31st July 1970, it means the period beginning with 1st August 1968 and ending with the relevant date.

(2) In sections 308 and 310—
'full compulsory purchase value', in relation to any interest in a house, means the compensation which would be payable in respect of the compulsory purchase of that interest if the house were not being dealt with under Part IV or Part VI as not meeting the tolerable standard, and, in the case of a house subject to a demolition order or closing order, the making of that order were a service of the notice to treat;
'interest' in a house does not include the interest of a tenant for a year or any less period or of a statutory tenant within the meaning of the Rent (Scotland) Act 1984; [or of a statutory assured tenant within the meaning of the Housing (Scotland) Act 1988;]
'restricted value': in relation to the compulsory purchase of a house, means compensation in respect thereof assessed under or by virtue of section 120 or 121 or Part III of Schedule 8.

(3) For the purposes of section 308, a house which might have been the subject of a demolition order but which has, without the making of such an order, been vacated and demolished in pursuance of an undertaking for its demolition given to the local authority having power to make the order shall be deemed to have been vacated in pursuance of a demolition order made and served by that authority at the date when the undertaking was given. **[877]**

NOTES to section 311
Amendment: Sub-s (2) was amended by the Housing (Scotland) Act 1988 (c 43), s 72, Sch 9, para 18.
Definitions: 'house': see s 338 below; 'demolition order': see s 338 below and s 115 above.

Payments to other local authorities

312. Payment of purchase money or compensation by one local authority to another.

(1) Any purchase money or compensation payable by a local authority under this Act in respect of any land, right or interest of another local authority which would but for this section be paid into a bank as provided by the Lands Clauses Acts may be otherwise paid and applied as the Secretary of State approves and determines.

(2) A determination of the Secretary of State under this section shall be final and conclusive. **[878]**

NOTES to section 312
Definitions: 'local authority': see s 338 below; 'bank': *Ibid.*

PART XVI
GENERAL AND MISCELLANEOUS

Byelaws

313. Byelaws with respect to houses in multiple occupation.

(1) The power of making and enforcing byelaws under section 72 of the Public Health (Scotland) Act 1897 with respect to houses or parts of houses which are let in lodgings or occupied by members of more than one family shall extend to the making and enforcing of byelaws imposing any duty (being a duty which may be imposed by the byelaws and which involves the execution of work) on the owner within the meaning of that Act of the said house, in addition to or in substitution for any other person having an interest in the premises, and prescribing the circumstances and conditions in and subject to which any such duty is to be discharged.

(2) For the purpose of discharging any duty so imposed, the owner or other person may at all reasonable times enter upon any part of the premises.

(3) Where an owner or other person has failed to carry out any work which he has been required to carry out under the byelaws, the local authority may, after giving to him not less than 21 days' notice in writing, themselves carry out the works and recover the costs and expenses.

(4) For the purpose of subsection (3), the provisions of Part V with respect to the enforcement of notices requiring the carrying out of work and the recovery of expenses by local authorities shall apply with such modifications as may be necessary.

(5) In this section 'owner', in relation to a house mentioned in subsection (1), means the person entitled to receive, or who would if the premises were let, be entitled to receive the rents of the premises, and includes a trustee, factor, tutor, or curator, and in the case of public or municipal property applies to the persons to whom the management is entrusted. **[879]**

NOTES to section 313
Definitions: 'house': see s 338 below; 'family': see s 338 below and s 83 above.

314. Byelaws with respect to accommodation for agricultural workers.

(1) A local authority shall make, with respect to bothies, chaumers and similar premises which are used for the accommodation of agricultural workers and are not part of a farmhouse, byelaws regarding any of the following matters—
  (a) the provision of a separate entrance in any case where the premises form part of other premises;
  (b) the provision of ventilation and floor area;
  (c) the provision of adequate heating and lighting;
  (d) the prevention of and safety from fire;
  (e) the provision of a ventilated larder and a fireplace or stove suitable for cooking food and sufficient cooking utensils;
  (f) the provision of furnishing, including the provision of a separate bed and bedding for each worker;
  (g) the provision of accommodation for personal clothing, and of facilities for personal ablution;
  (h) the painting, whitewashing or other cleansing of the premises at regular intervals;
  (i) intimation to the local authority by farmers of the number of workers employed by them who are accommodated in bothies or in chaumers or similar premises;

(j) such other matters as may from time to time be prescribed:
Provided that, if the local authority show to the satisfaction of the Secretary of State that it is unnecessary to make byelaws under this section, the Secretary of State may dispense with the making of such byelaws.

(2) Byelaws regarding the matters specified in paragraph (e) of subsection (1) shall apply only to premises in which the occupants cook their meals.

(3) Byelaws made by a local authority under this section may be limited to particular parts of the authority's area.

(4) Where a local authority fail, within such period as the Secretary of State may allow, to make with respect to any of the matters specified in subsection (1) byelaws which are in the opinion of the Secretary of State sufficient and satisfactory, the Secretary of State may himself make such byelaws which shall be of the like force and effect as if they had been made by the authority and confirmed. **[880]**

NOTES to section 314
Definitions: 'local authority', 'agricultural worker': see s 338 below.

315. Byelaws with respect to accommodation for seasonal workers.

(1) Subject to the provisions of this section, a local authority shall make byelaws for the whole or any part of their area with a view to providing proper accommodation for seasonal workers in respect of—
- (a) intimation to the local authority of the intention to employ seasonal workers;
- (b) the nature and extent of the accommodation to be provided for such workers, including due provision for—
    - (i) sleeping accommodation and separation of the sexes;
    - (ii) lighting, ventilation, cubic space, cleanliness and furnishing, including beds and bedding and cooking utensils;
    - (iii) storage of food, washing of clothes and drying of wet clothes;
    - (iv) water closets or privies for the separate use of the sexes; and
    - (v) a suitable supply of water;
- (c) determining the persons responsible for the provision of the accommodation required by the byelaws, taking into account the terms of current contracts;
- (d) inspection of the premises;
- (e) exhibition on the premises of the byclaws;
- (f) such other matters relating to the accommodation of seasonal workers (including determining the persons responsible for regulating the use by the workers of the accommodation) as may from time to time be prescribed.

(2) If the local authority show to the satisfaction of the Secretary of State that it is unnecessary to make byelaws under this section, the Secretary of State may dispense with the making of such byelaws.

(3) The Secretary of State may suspend, as respects the area of any local authority or any part of that area, the operation of any byelaw made under this section which affects agricultural interests in cases of emergency.

(4) If in consequence of any byelaws made under this section a farmer or a fruit grower is required to provide accommodation involving the erection of additional buildings, he may require the landlord to erect such buildings on terms and conditions to be determined, failing agreement, by the Secretary of State.

(5) In this section the expression 'seasonal workers' includes navvies, harvesters, potato-workers, fruit-pickers, herring-gutters, and such other workers engaged in work of a temporary nature as may from time to time be prescribed.

(6) Where a local authority fail, within such period as the Secretary of State may allow, to make in respect of any of the matters specified in subsection (1) byelaws which are in the opinion of the Secretary of State sufficient and satisfactory, the Secretary of State may

himself make such byelaws which shall have force and effect as if they had been made by the authority and confirmed. [881]

NOTE to section 315

Definition: 'local authority': see s 338 below.

316. Confirmation of byelaws.

For the purposes of section 202 of the Local Government (Scotland) Act 1973 (which relates to the procedure and other matters connected with the making of byelaws) the Secretary of State shall be the person by whom byelaws made under this Act are to be confirmed. [882]

Entry

317. Power of entry for survey, etc.

(1) Subject to the provisions of this section, any person authorised by a local authority or by the Secretary of State may at all reasonable times enter any house, premises or building—
   (a) for the purpose of survey and examination, where it appears to the local authority or the Secretary of State that survey or examination is necessary in order to determine whether any powers under this Act should be exercised in respect of any house, premises or building;
   (b) for the purpose of survey and examination, in the case of any house in respect of which a notice under this Act requiring the execution of works has been served or a closing order, or a demolition order has been made;
   (c) for the purpose of survey or valuation, in the case of houses, premises or buildings which the local authority are authorised to purchase compulsorily under this Act;
   (d) for the purpose of measuring the rooms of a house in order to ascertain for the purposes of Part VII the number of persons permitted to use the house for sleeping;
   (e) for the purpose of ascertaining whether there has been a contravention of any regulation or direction made or given under Part VIII;
   (f) for the purpose of ascertaining whether there has been an offence under section 165.

(2) Any person so authorised shall, except where entry is only for the purpose mentioned in paragraph (e) or paragraph (f) of subsection (1), give 24 hours' notice of his intention to enter any house, premises or building to the occupier thereof and to the owner, if the owner is known.

(3) An authorisation under this section shall be in writing and shall state the particular purpose or purposes for which the entry is authorised. [883]

NOTES to section 317

Definitions: 'local authority', 'house': see s 338 below.

Offences

318. Penalty for obstructing execution of Act.

If any person obstructs any officer of a local authority or any officer of the Secretary of State or any person authorised to enter houses, premises or buildings in pursuance of this Act in the performance of anything which such officer, authority or person is by this Act required or authorised to do, he shall be guilty of an offence and shall be liable on summary conviction to a fine not exceeding level 3 on the standard scale. [884]

NOTES to section 318

Definitions: 'local authority', 'house': see s 338 below; 'the standard scale': see the Criminal Procedure (Scotland) Act 1975 (c 21), s 289G and the Increase of Criminal Penalties Etc (Scotland) Order 1984, SI 1984/526. Level 3 is currently £400.

319. Penalty for preventing execution of works, etc.

(1) If any person, after receiving notice of the intended action—
(a) being the occupier of any premises, prevents the owner or other person having control of them, or his officers, agents, servants or workmen from carrying into effect with respect to those premises any of the provisions of Part VIII (other than section 173 and the provisions relating to control orders) or any of the provisions of Part V or any of the provisions of a byelaw made under section 313; or
(b) being the owner or occupier of any premises, or a person having control of any premises, prevents any officers, agents, servants or workmen of the local authority, from so doing; or
(c) being the occupier of any part of a house subject to a control order under Part VIII, prevents any officers, agents, servants or workmen of the local authority from carrying out any works in the house,

the sheriff or any two justices of the peace sitting in open court or any magistrate having jurisdiction in the place on proof thereof may order that person to permit to be done on the premises all things requisite for carrying into effect such provisions with respect to the premises or, in a case falling under paragraph (c), everything which the local authority consider necessary.

(2) If any such person fails to comply with such an order, he shall be guilty of an offence and shall be liable on summary conviction to a fine not exceeding level 3 on the standard scale. **[885]**

NOTES to section 319

Definitions: 'owner', 'local authority': see s 338 below; 'the standard scale': see the Criminal Procedure (Scotland) Act 1975 (c 21), s 289G and the Increase of Criminal Penalties Etc (Scotland) Order 1984, SI 1984/526. Level 3 is currently £400.

320. Penalty for damage to houses, etc.

Any person who wilfully or by culpable negligence damages or suffers to be damaged any house provided under this Act, or any of the fittings or appurtenances of any such house, including the drainage and water supply and any apparatus connected with the drainage or water supply, and the fence of any enclosure, shall be guilty of an offence and shall be liable on summary conviction to a fine not exceeding level 1 on the standard scale, without prejudice to any remedy for the recovery of the amount of the damage. **[886]**

NOTES to section 320

Definitions: 'house', 'apparatus': see s 338 below; 'the standard scale': see the Criminal Procedure (Scotland) Act 1975 (c 21), s 289G and the Increase of Criminal Penalties Etc (Scotland) Order 1984, SI 1984/526. Level 1 is currently £50.

321. Liability of directors, etc in case of offence by body corporate.

(1) Where an offence under this Act committed by a body corporate is proved to have been committed with the consent or connivance of, or to be attributable to any neglect on the part of, a director, manager, secretary or other similar officer of the body corporate, or a person purporting to act in any such capacity, he, as well as the body corporate, is guilty of an offence and liable to be proceeded against and punished accordingly.

(2) Subject to subsection (3) where a person is convicted of an offence under subsection (1) and the body corporate in question is liable under sections 152 to 177 to a higher penalty by reason of a previous conviction than it would have been if not so convicted,

that person shall be liable under those sections to the same penalties as the body corporate would be liable if a natural person, including imprisonment.

(3) The person mentioned in subsection (2) shall not be so liable if he shows—
(a) at the time of the offence he did not know of the previous conviction; and
(b) at the time of the previous conviction he was not acting, or purporting to act, as a director, manager, secretary, or other similar officer of the body corporate. [887]

Powers of sheriff for housing purposes

322. Sheriff may determine lease in certain cases.

(1) Where in respect of any premises that are leased—
(a) a closing order, a demolition order or a resolution passed under section 125 has become operative, and
(b) the lease is not determined,
the landlord, the tenant, or any other person deriving right under the lease may apply to the sheriff within whose jurisdiction the premises are situated for an order determining the lease.

(2) On any such application the sheriff, after giving to any subtenant or other person whom he considers to be interested in the matter an opportunity of being heard, may, if he thinks fit, order that the lease shall be determined, either unconditionally or subject to such terms and conditions (including conditions with respect to the payment of money by any party to the proceedings to any other party thereto by way of compensation or damages or otherwise) as he may think it just and equitable to impose.

(3) In making an order under subsection (2) the sheriff shall have regard to the respective rights, obligations and liabilities of the parties under the lease and to all the other circumstances of the case.

(4) The sheriff shall not be entitled to order any payment to be made by the landlord to the tenant in respect of the lease of a house.

(5) In this section the expression 'lease' includes a sublease and any tenancy or tacit relocation following on a lease. [888]

NOTES to section 322
Definitions: 'closing order': see s 338 below or ss 114 and 119 above; 'demolition order': see s 338 below and s 115 above; 'house': see s 338 below.

323. Sheriff may authorise superior to execute works, etc.

(1) Subject to the provisions of this section, the superior of any lands and heritages may apply to the sheriff for an order entitling him to enter on those lands and heritages to execute works (including demolition works) within such period as may be specified in the order.

(2) The sheriff may make such an order if—
(a) the following notices or orders under this Act in respect of those lands and heritages are not being complied with—
  (i) a notice requiring the execution of works, or
  (ii) a closing order, or
  (iii) a notice or resolution requiring the demolition of a building under Part VI, and
(b) the interests of the superior are thereby prejudiced, and
(c) the sheriff thinks it just to make the order.

(3) Before an order is made under this section notice of the application shall be given to the local authority. [889]

NOTES to section 323

Definitions: 'superior', 'land': see s 338 below.

324. Procedure on applications and appeals to sheriff.

(1) An application to the sheriff under paragraph 5 of Schedule 10 (restriction on contracting out) or section 110 (recovery of expenses by lessee) or Part VIII (houses in multiple occupation) shall be made by a summary application, and the sheriff's decision on any such application shall be final.

(2) The Court of Session may prescribe by rules of court the procedure on any appeal to the sheriff under this Act.

(3) The sheriff may, before considering an appeal which may be made to him under this Act, require the appellant to deposit such sum to cover the expenses of the appeal as may be prescribed by rules of court.

(4) The sheriff in deciding an appeal under this Act may make such order as he thinks just.

(5) Any such order shall be final.

(6) In the case of an appeal against a notice given or an order made by a local authority, the sheriff may either confirm, vary or quash the notice or order.

(7) The sheriff—
(a) may at any stage of the proceedings on an appeal under this Act, state a case to the Court of Session on any question of law that arises;
(b) shall do so if so directed by the Court of Session.

(8) A notice or order in respect of which an appeal lies to the sheriff under this Act (other than Part VIII) shall not have effect until either—
(a) the time for appealing has expired without an appeal being made, or
(b) in a case where an appeal is made, the appeal is determined or abandoned. **[890]**

Service

325. Occupier or tenant may be required to state interest.

(1) A local authority may, for the purpose of enabling them to serve—
(a) any order made by them under section 114 or section 115, or section 119; or
(b) any notice which they are by this Act authorised or required to serve,
require the occupier of any premises and any person who, either directly or indirectly, receives rent in respect of any premises to state in writing the nature of his own interest in the premises and the name and address of any other person known to him as having an interest in them whether as holder of a heritable security, lessee or otherwise.

(2) Any person who has been required by a local authority under subsection (1) to give them any information and either fails to do so or knowingly makes a false statement, shall be guilty of an offence and shall be liable on summary conviction to a fine not exceeding level 1 on the standard scale. **[891]**

NOTES to section 325

Definitions: 'local authority': see s 338 below; 'the standard scale': see the Criminal Procedure (Scotland) Act 1975 (c 21), s 289G and the Increase of Criminal Penalties Etc (Scotland) Order 1984, SI 1984/526. Level 1 is currently £50.

326. Service by description on certain persons whose identity is unknown and on a number of persons of one description.

(1) An order, notice or other document required or authorised to be served under this Act on any person as a person having control of premises may, if it is not practicable after

reasonable enquiry to ascertain the name or address of that person, be served by addressing it to him by the description of 'person having control of' the premises (naming them) to which it relates and by delivering it to some person on the premises or, if there is no person on the premises to whom it can be delivered, by affixing it, or a copy of it, to some conspicuous part of the premises.

(2) A document to be served on the person having control of premises, or on the person managing premises, or on the owner of premises under Parts IV, V, VI and VII may be served on more than one person who comes within those descriptions. **[892]**

Landlord's identity

327. Disclosure of landlord's identity.

(1) If the tenant of premises occupied as a house makes a written request for the landlord's name and address to any person who demands or to the last person who received rent payable under the tenancy or to any other person for the time being acting as agent for the landlord in relation to the tenancy, and that person fails without reasonable excuse to supply a written statement of the name and address within the period of 21 days beginning with the day on which he receives the tenant's request, that person shall be guilty of an offence and liable on summary conviction to a fine not exceeding level 4 on the standard scale.

(2) In any case where—
(a) in response to a request under subsection (1), a tenant is supplied with the name and address of the landlord of the premises concerned; and
(b) the landlord is a body corporate; and
(c) the tenant makes a further written request to the landlord for information under this subsection,
the landlord shall, within the period of 21 days beginning with the day on which he receives the request under this subsection, supply to the tenant a written statement of the name and address of every director and the secretary of the landlord.

(3) Any reference in subsection (1) or subsection (2) to a person's address is a reference to his place of abode or his place of business or, in the case of a company, its registered office.

(4) A request under subsection (2) shall be deemed to be duly made to the landlord if it is made to an agent of the landlord or to a person who demands the rent of the premises concerned, and any such agent or person to whom such a request is made shall as soon as may be forward it to the landlord.

(5) A landlord who fails without reasonable excuse to comply with a request under subsection (2) within the period mentioned in that subsection and a person who fails without reasonable excuse to comply with any requirement imposed on him by subsection (4) shall be guilty of an offence and liable on summary conviction to a fine not exceeding level 4 on the standard scale.

(6) In this section—
'landlord' means the immediate landlord and, in relation to premises occupied under a right conferred by an enactment, includes the person who, apart from that right, would be entitled to possession of the premises;
'tenant' includes a sub-tenant and a tenant under a right conferred by an enactment. **[893]**

NOTES to section 327

Definitions: 'house': see s 338 below; 'the standard scale': see the Criminal Procedure (Scotland) Act 1975 (c 21), s 289G and the Increase of Criminal Penalties Etc (Scotland) Order 1984, SI 1984/526. Level 4 is currently £1000.

328. Duty to inform tenant of assignation of landlord's interest.

(1) If the interest of the landlord under a tenancy of premises which consist of or include a house is assigned, the person to whom that interest is assigned (in this section referred to as 'the new landlord') shall, within the appropriate period, give notice in writing to the tenant of the assignation and of the name and address of the new landlord.

(2) In subsection (1), 'the appropriate period' means the period beginning on the date of the assignation in question and ending either two months after that date or, if it is later, on the first day after that date on which rent is payable under the tenancy.

(3) Subject to subsection (4), the reference in subsection (1) to the new landlord's address is a reference to his place of abode or his place of business or, if the new landlord is a company, its registered office.

(4) If trustees as such constitute the new landlord, it shall be a sufficient compliance with the obligation in subsection (1) to give the name of the new landlord, to give a collective description of the trustees as the trustees of the trust in question, and where such a collective description is given—
  (a) the address of the new landlord for the purpose of that subsection may be given as the address from which the affairs of the trust are conducted; and
  (b) a change in the persons who are for the time being the trustees of the trust shall not be treated as an assignation of the interest of the landlord.

(5) If any person who is the new landlord under a tenancy falling within subsection (91) fails, without reasonable excuse, to give the notice required by that subsection, he shall be guilty of an offence and liable on summary conviction to a fine not exceeding level 4 on the standard scale.

(6) In this section 'tenancy' includes a sub-tenancy and a statutory tenancy, within the meaning of the Rent (Scotland) Act 1984 [and a statutory assured tenancy within the meaning of the Housing (Scotland) Act 1988] and 'tenant' shall be construed accordingly.

(7) In this section 'assignation' means a conveyance or other transfer (other than in security), and any reference to the date of the assignation means the date on which the conveyance or other transfer was granted, delivered or otherwise made effective. **[894]**

NOTES to section 328

Amendment: Sub-s (6) was amended by the Housing (Scotland) Act 1988 (c 43), s 72, Sch 9, para 19.

Definitions: 'house': see s 338 below; 'the standard scale': see the Criminal Procedure (Scotland) Act 1975 (c 21), s 289G and the Increase of Criminal Penalties Etc (Scotland) Order 1984, SI 1984/526. Level 4 is currently £1000.

Powers of Secretary of State

329. Power of Secretary of State in event of failure of local authority to exercise powers.

(1) In any case where—
  (a) a complaint has been made to the Secretary of State as respects the district of any local authority, by any four or more local government electors of the area, that the local authority have failed to exercise any of their powers under this Act in any case where those powers ought to have been exercised; or
  (b) the Secretary of State is of opinion that an investigation should be made as to whether a local authority have so failed,
the Secretary of State may cause a public local inquiry to be held.

(2) If, after the inquiry has been held, the Secretary of State is satisfied that there has been such a failure on the part of the local authority, he may, after giving the authority an opportunity of making representations, make an order enabling him to exercise such of those powers as may be specified in the order.

(3) Any expenses incurred by the Secretary of State in exercising such powers shall be paid in the first instance out of moneys provided by Parliament, but the amount of those expenses as certified by the Secretary of State shall on demand by paid by the local authority to the Secretary of State and shall be recoverable as a debt due to the Crown.

(4) The payment of any such expenses shall, so far as the expenses are of a capital nature, be a purpose for which a local authority may borrow money.

(5) The Secretary of State may by order vest in and transfer to the local authority any property, debts or liabilities acquired or incurred by him in exercising the powers of the authority.

(6) If an order made under subsection (2) is revoked, the Secretary of State may, either by the revoking order or by a supplementary order, make such provision as appears to him desirable with respect to the transfer, vesting and discharge of any property, debts or liabilities acquired or incurred by the Secretary of State in exercising the powers and duties to which the order so revoked related. **[895]**

NOTE to section 329
Definition: 'local authority': see s 338 below.

330. Power of Secretary of State to prescribe forms, etc.

(1) Subject to the provisions of this Act, the Secretary of State may by statutory instrument make regulations prescribing—
 (a) the form of any notice, advertisement, statement or other document which is required or authorised to be used under, or for the purposes of, this Act;
 (b) any other thing required or authorised to be prescribed under this Act.

(2) The forms so prescribed or forms as near as may be to those forms shall be used in all cases to which those forms apply. **[896]**

NOTES to section 330
Sub-s (1): See the Housing Forms (Scotland) Regulations 1974, SI 1974/1982 as amended by SI 1975/1644 and the Housing Forms (Scotland) Regulations 1980, SI 1980/1647.

331. Regulations: procedure.

Subject to the provisions of this Act, regulations made by a statutory instrument under this Act shall be subject to annulment in pursuance of a resolution of either House of Parliament. **[897]**

332. Secretary of State's power to dispense with advertisements and notices.

(1) The Secretary of State may dispense with the publication of advertisements or the service of notices required to be published or served by a local authority under this Act, if he is satisfied that there is reasonable cause for dispensing with the publication or service.

(2) Any such dispensation may be given by the Secretary of State either before or after the time at which the advertisement is required to be published or the notice is required to be served, and either unconditionally or upon such conditions as to the publication of other advertisements or the service of other notices or otherwise as the Secretary of State thinks fit, due care being taken by the Secretary of State to prevent the interests of any person being prejudiced by the dispensation. **[898]**

NOTES to section 332
Definition: 'local authority': see s 338 below.

333. Local inquiries.

For the purposes of the execution of his powers and duties under this Act, the Secretary of State may cause such local inquiries to be held as he may think fit. **[899]**

Miscellaneous

334. Power of heir of entail to sell land for housing purposes.

Without prejudice to any powers, whether statutory or otherwise, already enjoyed by an heir of entail in possession of an entailed estate in Scotland to sell any part of such estate, any such heir in possession may, notwithstanding any prohibition or limitation in any deed of entail or in any Act of Parliament, sell any part or parts of such estate—
(a) to a local authority for any purpose for which a local authority may acquire land under this Act, or
(b) to a housing association for the purpose of the provision of houses,
without its being necessary to obtain the consent of the next heir, and without any restrictions as to the extented of ground to be sold, excepting however, from the provisions of this section the subjects excepted in section 4 of the Entail (Scotland) Act 1914:

Provided that the price of land so sold shall, in accordance with the provisions of the Entail Acts, be invested for behoof of the heir of entail in possession and succeeding heirs of entail. [900]

NOTES to section 334
Definitions: 'local authority', 'land', 'housing association': see s 338 below.

335. Crown rights.

Nothing in this Act shall affect prejudicially any estate, right, power, privilege or exemption of the Crown, or authorise the use of or interference with any land (including tidal lands below high-water mark of ordinary spring tides) belonging to Her Majesty in right of the Crown or to any government department, without the consent of Her Majesty or the government department, as the case may be. [901]

NOTES to section 335
Definition: 'land': see s 338 below.

336. Limitation on liability of trustee etc for expenses incurred by local authority.

(1) Where a local authority seek to recover expenses incurred by them under any enactment in respect of work done on a house from a person mentioned in subsection (2), that person's liability shall, if he proves the matters mentioned in subsection (3), be limited to the total amount of the funds, rents and other assets which he has, or has had, in his hands.

In this section 'house' includes a building which contains a house, or a part of such a building.

(2) The person mentioned in subsection (1) is a person who receives the rent of the house as trustee, tutor, curator, factor or agent for or of some other person or as the liquidator of a company.

(3) The matters that person requires to prove are—
(a) that he is a person mentioned in subsection (2); and
(b) that he has not, and since the date of service on him of a demand for payment of the expenses has not had, in his hands on behalf of that other person or, in the case of a liquidator of a company, on behalf of the creditors or members of the company, sufficient funds, rents and other assets to pay those expenses in full.

(4) Nothing in this section affects any right of a local authority to recover the whole or any part of those expenses from any other person. [902]

NOTE to section 336
Definition: 'local authority': see s 338 below.

337. ...

NOTES to section 337

Section 337 was repealed by the Local Government Act 1988 (c 9), s 41, Sch 7.

338. Interpretation.

(1) In this Act, unless the context otherwise requires—
'Act of 1966' means the Housing (Scotland) Act 1966;
'Act of 1968' means the Housing (Financial Provisions) (Scotland) Act 1968;
'Act of 1969' means the Housing (Scotland) Act 1969;
'Act of 1972' means the Housing (Financial Provisions) (Scotland) Act 1972;
'Act of 1974' means the Housing (Scotland) Act 1974;
'Act of 1978' means the Housing (Financial Provisions) (Scotland) Act 1978;
'Act of 1980' means the Tenants' Rights, Etc (Scotland) Act 1980;
'Act of 1985' means the Housing Act 1985;
'Act of 1986' means the Housing (Scotland) Act 1986;
'agricultural holding' means an agricultural holding within the meaning of the Agricultural Holdings (Scotland) Act 1949;
'agriculture' means the use of land for agricultural or pastoral purposes, or for the purpose of poultry farming or market gardening, or as an orchard or woodlands, or for the purpose of afforestation, and 'agricultural worker' shall be construed accordingly;
'apparatus' means sewers, drains, culverts, water-courses, mains, pipes, valves, tubes, cables, wires, transformers and other apparatus laid down or used for or in connection with the carrying, conveying or supplying to any premises of a supply of water, water for hydraulic power, gas or electricity, and standards and brackets carrying road lighting;
'bank' means—
(a) an institution authorised under the Banking Act 1987, or
(b) a company as to which the Secretary of State was satisfied immediately before the repeal of the Protection of Depositors Act 1963 that it ought to be treated as a banking company or discount company for the purposes of that Act;
'building regulations' means any statutory enactments, byelaws, rules and regulations or other provisions under whatever authority made, relating to the construction of new buildings and the laying out of and construction of new roads;
'building society' means a building society within the meaning of the Building Societies Act 1986;
'closing order' means a closing order made under sections 114 or 119;
'Corporation' means the Housing Corporation;
'croft' and 'crofter' have the like meanings respectively as in the Crofters (Scotland) Act 1955 and 1961;
'demolition order' has the meaning assigned to it by section 115;
'development corporation' means a development corporation established by an order made or having effect as if made under the New Towns (Scotland) Act 1968;
'disabled occupant' has the meaning assigned to it by section 236;
'disabled person' has the meaning assigned to it by section 236;
'Exchequer contribution' means a payment (other than a payment by way of advance or loan) which the Secretary of State is required or authorised by or under any Act relating to housing, to make for housing purposes;
'family' and any reference to membership thereof shall be construed in accordance with section 83;
'financial year', in relation to a local authority, has the same meaning as in section 96(5) of the Local Government (Scotland) Act 1973;
'flat' means a separate and self-contained set of premises, whether or not on the same floor and forming part of a building from some other part of which it is divided horizontally;

'friendly society' means a society registered under the Friendly Societies Act 1974 or earlier legislation;

'holding' has the like meaning as in the Small Landholders (Scotland) Acts 1886 to 1931;

'hostel' has the meaning assigned to it by section 2(5);

'house' (except in relation to Part XIV) includes any part of a building, being a part which is occupied or intended to be occupied as a separate dwelling, and, in particular, includes a flat, and includes also any yard, garden, out-houses and pertinents belonging to the house or usually enjoyed therewith and also includes any structure made available under section 1 of the Housing (Temporary Accommodation) Act 1944;

'housing action area' means a housing action area within the meaning of Part IV;

'housing association' has the same meaning as it has in the Housing Associations Act 1985;

'housing support grant' has the meaning assigned to it by section 191;

'improvement' has the meaning assigned to it by section 236(2);

'improvement grant' has the meaning assigned to it by section 236(1);

'insurance company' means an insurance company to which Part II of the Insurance Companies Act 1982 applies;

'land' includes any estate or interest in land;

'landholder' has the like meaning as in the Small Landholders (Scotland) Acts 1886 to 1931;

'Lands Tribunal' means the Lands Tribunal for Scotland;

'loan charges' means, in relation to any borrowed moneys, the sum required for the payment of interest on those moneys and for the repayment thereof either by instalments or by means of a sinking fund;

'local authority' means an islands council or a district council, and the district of a local authority means the islands areas or the district, as the case may be;

'official representation' means, in the case of a local authority, a representation made to the authority by the proper officer of the local authority;

'open space' means any land laid out as a public garden or used for the purposes of public recreation, and any disused burial ground;

'order for possession' has the meaning assigned to it by section 115(1) of the Rent (Scotland) Act 1984;

'overspill agreement' has the same meaning as in section 9(1) of the Housing and Town Development (Scotland) Act 1957;

'owner' includes any person who under the Lands Clauses Acts would be enabled to sell and convey land to the promoters of an undertaking, but in Part XIII and sections 99 to 104, in relation to a house, means the person who is for the time being entitled to receive the rent of the house or who, if the house were let, would be so entitled and a tenant-at-will;

'prescribed' means prescribed by regulations made by the Secretary of State by statutory instrument;

'proper officer', in relation to any purpose of a local authority, means an officer appointed for that purpose by that authority;

'public undertakers' means any corporation, company, body or person carrying on a railway, canal, inland navigation, dock, harbour, tramway, gas, electricity, water or other public undertaking;

'registered housing association' means a housing association registered under the Housing Associations Act 1985;

'regular armed forces of the Crown' means the Royal Navy, the regular forces as defined by section 225 of the Army Act 1955, the regular air force as defined by section 223 of the Air Force Act 1955, Queen Alexandra's Royal Naval Nursing Service and the Women's Royal Naval Service;

'repairs grant' has the meaning assigned to it by section 248;

'road' has the same meaning as it has in the Roads (Scotland) Act 1984;

'secure tenancy' has the meaning assigned to it by section 44;

'sell' and 'sale' include feu;

'a service charge' means any charge referred to in section 211;
'standard amenities' has the meaning assigned to it by section [244(6)];
'statutory small tenant' has the like meaning as in the Small Landholders (Scotland) Acts 1886 to 1931;
'statutory tenant' has the same meaning as it has in section 3 of the Rent (Scotland) Act 1984;
'superior' includes the creditor in a ground annual;
'tenancy' in Parts IV and XIII includes a sub-tenancy, a statutory tenancy within the meaning of section 115(1) of the Rent (Scotland) Act 1984 and a contract to which Part VII of that Act applies [and a statutory assured tenancy within the meaning of the Housing (Scotland) Act 1988] and 'tenant' shall be construed accordingly; and any reference to a tenancy of a house or to the tenant thereof shall be construed as including a reference to all the tenancies of that house or to all the tenants thereof as the case may be;
'tolerable standard' has the meaning assigned to it by section 86;
'water authority' has the meaning assigned to it by section 148 of the Local Government (Scotland) Act 1973;
'water development board' has the meaning assigned to it by section 109 of the Water (Scotland) Act 1980;
'year' means, in relation to a local authority, a financial year within the meaning of section 96(5) of the Local Government (Scotland) Act 1973 and, in relation to a development corportion, the Scottish Special Housing Association or a housing association, means a year ending on 31st March;
'the year 1986–87' means the year beginning in 1986 and ending in 1987, and so on.

(2) For the purposes of this Act—
(a) the person who for the time being is entitled to receive, or would, if the same were let, be entitled to receive, the rent of any premises, including a trustee, tutor, curator, factor or agent, shall be deemed to be the person having control of the premises; and
(b) a crofter or a landholder shall be deemed to be the person having control of any premises on his croft or holding in respect of which he would, on the termination of his tenancy, be entitled to compensation under the Crofters (Scotland) Acts 1955 and 1961 or, as the case may be, the Small Landholders (Scotland) Acts 1886 to 1931, as for an improvement.

(3) In this Act, any reference to the demolition of a building shall be deemed to include a reference to such reconstruction of the building as the local authority may approve; and where a building is so reconstructed any reference to selling, letting or appropriating the land, the building on which has been or will be demolished, shall, unless the context otherwise requires, be construed as a reference to selling, letting or appropriating the land and the reconstructed building. **[903]**

NOTES to section 338

Amendments: In sub-s (1) the definition of 'standard amenities' was amended by the Housing (Scotland) Act 1988 (c 43), s 72, Sch 7, para 27; the definition of tenancy was amended by *Ibid*, Sch 9, para 20.

339. Minor and consequential amendments, transitional provisions and repeals.

(1) This Act shall have effect subject to the transitional provisions and savings contained in Schedule 22.

(2) The enactments specified in Schedule 23 shall have effect subject to the amendments set out in that Schedule being minor amendments and amendments consequential on the provisions of this Act.

(3) The enactments specified in Schedule 24 are hereby repealed to the extent specified in the third column of that Schedule. **[904]**

340. Citation, commencement and extent.

(1) This Act may be cited as the Housing (Scotland) Act 1987.

(2) This Act shall come into force at the end of the period of 3 months beginning with the day on which it is passed.

(3) This Act extends to Scotland only. [905]

SCHEDULES

Section 10(4) SCHEDULE 1

RULES AS TO ASSESSMENT OF COMPENSATION WHERE LAND PURCHASED COMPULSORILY IN CERTAIN CIRCUMSTANCES

1.—If the Lands Tribunal are satisfied that the rent of any premises was enhanced by reason of their being used for illegal purposes, the compensation shall, so far as it is based on rental, be based on the rental which would have been obtainable if the premises were occupied for legal purposes. [906]

2.—If the Lands Tribunal are satisfied that the rent of any premises was higher than that generally obtained at the time for similar premises in the locality and that such enhanced rent was obtained by reason of the premises being overcrowded within the meaning of Part VII, the compensation shall, so far as it is based on rent, be based on the rent so generally obtained. [907]

3.—The local authority may tender evidence as to the matters mentioned in paragraphs 1 or 2 although they have not taken any steps to remedy them. [908]

4.—The Lands Tribunal shall (except as provided in section 15(1) of the Land Compensation (Scotland) Act 1963) have regard to, and make an allowance in respect of, any increased value which, in their opinion, will be given to other premises of the same owner by the demolition by the local authority of any buildings. [909]

5.—The Lands Tribunal shall embody in their award a statement showing separately whether compensation has been reduced by reference to the use of the premises for illegal purposes, to overcrowding, and to the considerations mentioned in paragraph 4 of this Schedule, and the amount (if any) by which compensation has been reduced by reference to each of those matters. [910]

NOTES to Schedule 1
Definitions: 'Lands Tribunal', 'local authority': see s 338 above.

Section 44(4), (5) SCHEDULE 2

TENANCIES WHICH ARE NOT SECURE TENANCIES

Premises occupied under contract of employment

1.—(1) A tenancy shall not be a secure tenancy if the tenant (or one of joint tenants) is an employee of the landlord or of any local authority or development corporation, and his contract of employment requires him to occupy the house for the better performance of his duties.

(2) In this paragraph 'contract of employment' means a contract of service or of

apprenticeship, whether express or implied, and (if it is express) whether it is oral or in writing. **[911]**

Temporary letting to person seeking accommodation

2.—A tenancy shall not be a secure tenancy if the house was let by the landlord expressly on a temporary basis to a person moving into an area in order to take up employment there, and for the purpose of enabling him to seek accommodation in the area. **[912]**

Temporary letting pending development

3.—A tenancy shall not be a secure tenancy if the house was let by the landlord to the tenant expressly on a temporary basis, pending development affecting the house.

In this paragraph 'development' has the meaning assigned to it by section 19 of the Town and Country Planning (Scotland) Act 1972. **[913]**

Temporary accommodation during works

4.—A tenancy shall not be a secure tenancy if the house is occupied by the tenant while works are being carried out on the house which he normally occupies as his home, and if he is entitled to return there after the works are completed—
(a) by agreement; or
(b) by virtue of an order of the sheriff under section 48(5). **[914]**

Accommodation for homeless persons

5.—A tenancy shall not be a secure tenancy if the house is being let to the tenant expressly on a temporary basis, in the fulfilment of a duty imposed on a local authority by Part II. **[915]**

Agricultural and business premises

6.—A tenancy shall not be a secure tenancy if the house—
(a) is let together with agricultural land exceeding two acres in extent;
(b) consists of or includes premises which are used as a shop or office for business, trade or professional purposes;
(c) consists of or includes premises licensed for the sale of excisable liquor, or
(d) is let in conjunction with any purpose mentioned in sub-paragraph (b) or (c). **[916]**

Police and fire authorities

7.—A tenancy shall not be a secure tenancy if the landlord is an authority or committee mentioned in—
(a) section 61(2)(a)(viii) and the tenant—
 (i) is a constable of a police force, within the meaning of the Police (Scotland) Act 1967, who in pursuance of regulations under section 26 of that Act occupies the house without obligation to pay rent or rates; or
 (ii) in a case where head (i) above does apply, is let the house expressly on a temporary basis pending its being required for the purposes of such a police force; or
(b) section 61(2)(a)(ix) and the tenant—
 (i) is a member of a fire brigade, maintained in pursuance of the Fire Services Act 1947, who occupies the house in consequence of a condition in his contract of employment that he live in close proximity to a particular fire station; or

(ii) in a case where head (i) above does not apply, is let the house expressly on a temporary basis pending its being required for the purposes of such a fire brigade. **[917]**

Houses part of, or within curtilage of, certain other buildings

8.—A tenancy shall not be a secure tenancy if the house forms part of, or is within the curtilage of, a building which mainly—
(a) is held by the landlord for purposes other than the provision of housing accommodation; and
(b) consists of accommodation other than housing accommodation. **[918]**

NOTES to Schedule 2
Definitions: 'tenant', 'tenancy': see s 82 above; 'secure tenancy', 'landlord': see ss 82 and 44 above; 'local authority', 'development corporation', 'house': see s 338 above.

Sections 48 and 51   SCHEDULE 3

GROUNDS FOR RECOVERY OF POSSESSION OF HOUSES LET UNDER SECURE TENANCIES

PART I
GROUNDS ON WHICH COURT MAY ORDER RECOVERY OF POSSESSION

1.—Rent lawfully due from the tenant has not been paid, or any other obligation of the tenancy has been broken. **[919]**

2.—The tenant (or any one of joint tenants) or any person residing or lodging with him or any sub-tenant of his has been convicted of using the house or allowing it to be used for immoral or illegal purposes. **[920]**

3.—The conditions of the house or of any of the common parts has deteriorated owing to acts of waste by, or the neglect or default of, the tenant (or any one of joint tenants) or any person residing or lodging with him or any sub-tenant of his; and in the case of acts of waste by, or the neglect or default of, a person lodging with a tenant or by a sub-tenant of his, the tenant has not, before the making of the order in question, taken such steps as he ought reasonably to have taken for the removal of the lodger or sub-tenant.
In this paragraph, 'the common parrts' means any part of a building containing the house and any other premises which the tenant is entitled under the terms of the tenancy to use in common with the occupiers of other houses. **[921]**

4.—The condition of any furniture provided for use under the tenancy, or for use in any of the common parts (within the meaning given in paragraph 3), has deteriorated owing to ill-treatment by the tenant (or any one of joint tenants) or any person residing or lodging with him or any sub-tenant of his; and in the case of ill-treatment by a person lodging with a tenant or a sub-tenant of his the tenant has not, before the making of the order in question, taken such steps as he ought reasonably to have taken for the removal of the lodger or sub-tenant. **[922]**

5.—The tenant and his spouse have been absent from the house without reasonable cause for a continuous period exceeding 6 months or have ceased to occupy the house as their principal home. **[923]**

6.—The tenant is the person, or one of the persons, to whom the tenancy was granted and the landlord was induced to grant the tenancy by a false statement made knowingly or recklessly by the tenant. **[924]**

7.—The tenant of the house (or any one of joint tenants) or any person residing or lodging with him or any sub-tenant of his has been guilty of conduct in or in the vicinity of the house which is a nuisance or annoyance and it is not reasonable in all the circumstances that the landlord should be required to make other accommodation available to him. [925]

8.—The tenant of the house (or any one of joint tenants) or any person residing or lodging with him or any sub-tenant of his has been guilty of conduct in or in the vicinity of the house which is a nuisance or annoyance and in the opinion of the landlord it is appropriate in the circumstances to require the tenant to move to other accommodation. [926]

9.—The house is overcrowded, within the meaning of section 135, in such circumstances as to render the occupier guilty of an offence. [927]

10.—It is intended within a reasonable period of time to demolish, or carry out substantial work on, the building or a part of the building which comprises or includes the house, and such demolition or work cannot reasonably take place without the landlord obtaining possession of the house. [928]

11.—The house has been designed or adapted for occupation by a person whose special needs require accommodation of the kind provided by the house and—
(a) there is no longer a person with such special needs occupying the house; and
(b) the landlord requires it for occupation (whether alone or with other members of his family) by a person who has such special needs. [929]

12.—The house forms part of a group of houses which has been designed, or which has been provided with or located near facilities, for persons in need of special social support, and—
(a) there is no longer a person with such a need occupying the house; and
(b) the landlord requires it for occupation (whether alone or with other members of his family) by a person who has such a need. [930]

13.—The landlord is a housing association which has as its object, or as one of its objects, the housing of persons who are in a special category by reason of age, infirmity, disability or social circumstances and the tenant (or one of joint tenants), having been granted a tenancy as a person falling into such a special category, has ceased to be in the special category, or for other reasons the accommodation in the house is no longer suitable for his needs, and the accommodation is required for someone who is in a special category. [931]

14.—The interest of the landlord in the house is that of a lessee under a lease and that lease either—
(a) has terminated, or
(b) will terminate within a period of 6 months from the date of raising of proceedings for recovery of possession. [932]

15.—(a) The landlord is an islands council; and
(b) the house is—
    (i) held by the council for the purposes of its functions as education authority; and
    (ii) required for the accommodation of a person who is or will be employed by the council for those purposes; and
(c) the council cannot reasonably provide a suitable alternative house for the accommodation referred to in sub-paragraph (b)(ii); and
(d) the tenant (or any one of joint tenants) is, or at any time during the tenancy has been or, where the tenancy passed to the existing tenant under section 52, the previous tenant at any time during the tenancy was, employed by the council for

the purposes of its functions as education authority and such employment has terminated or notice of termination has been given. **[933]**

16.—The landlord wishes to transfer the secure tenancy of the house to—
(a) the tenant's spouse (or former spouse); or
(b) a person with whom the tenant has been living as husband and wife,
who has applied to the landlord for such transfer; and either the tenant or (as the case may be) the spouse, former spouse or person, no longer wishes to live together with the other in the house. **[934]**

Part II
Suitability of Accommodation

1.—For the purposes of sections 48(3) and 51(3), accommodation is suitable if—
(a) it consists of premises which are to be let as a separate dwelling under a secure tenancy or under a protected tenancy within the meaning of the Rent (Scotland) Act 1984 [or under an assured tenancy within the meaning of the Housing (Scotland) Act 1988]; and
(b) it is reasonably suitable to the needs of the tenant and his family. **[935]**

2.—In determining whether accommodation is reasonably suitable to the needs of the tenant and his family, regard shall be had to—
(a) its proximity to the place of work (including attendance at an education institution) of the tenant and of other members of his family, compared with his existing house;
(b) the extent of the accommodation required by the tenant and his family;
(c) the character of the accommodation offered compared to his existing house;
(d) the terms on which the accommodation is offered to the tenant compared with the terms of his existing tenancy;
(e) if any furniture was provided by the landlord for use under the existing tenancy, whether furniture is to be provided for use under the new tenancy which is of a comparable nature in relation to the needs of the tenant and his family;
(f) any special needs of the tenant or his family. **[936]**

3.—If the landlord has made an offer in writing to the tenant of new accommodation which complies with paragraph 1(a) and which appears to it to be suitable, specifying the date when the accommodation will be available and the date (not being less than 14 days from the date of the offer) by which the offer must be accepted, the accommodation so offered shall be deemed to be suitable if—
(a) the landlord shows that the tenant accepted the offer within the time duly specified in the offer; or
(b) the landlord shows that the tenant did not so accept the offer, and the tenant does not satisfy the court that he acted reasonably in failing to accept the offer. **[937]**

NOTES to Schedule 3
Amendment: In Part II, para 1(a) was amended by the Housing (Scotland) Act 1988 (c 43), s 72, Sch 9, para 21.
Definitions: 'secure tenancy': see ss 82 and 44 above; 'tenant', 'tenancy', 'landlord': see s 82 above; 'house', 'housing association': see s 338 above; 'family': see s 83 above.

Section 55(6)   **SCHEDULE 4**

Terms of Secure Tenancy Relating to Subletting, etc

1. A secure tenant who wishes to assign, sublet or otherwise give up to another person possession of the house which is the subject of the secure tenancy or any part

thereof or take in a lodger shall serve on the landlord an application in writing for the landlord's consent, giving details of the proposed transaction, and in particular of any payment which has been or is to be received by the tenant in consideration of the transaction. [938]

2.—In relation to an application under paragraph 1, the landlord may consent, or may refuse consent, provided that it is not refused unreasonably. [939]

3.—(a) The landlord shall serve on the tenant notice in writing of consent or refusal, and in the case of refusal the reasons therefor, within one month of receipt of the application;
(b) where the landlord fails to serve a notice in accordance with paragraph (a) within the period therein mentioned, the landlord shall be deemed to have consented to the application. [940]

4.—A tenant who is aggrieved by a refusal (other than a refusal on the grounds provided for in section 55(2)) may raise proceedings by summary application in the sheriff court of the district in which the house is situated. [941]

5.—In proceedings under paragraph 4, the sheriff shall order the landlord to consent to the application unless it appears to him that the refusal is reasonable. [942]

6.—In deciding whether a refusal is reasonable the sheriff shall have regard in particular to—
(a) whether the consent would lead to overcrowding of the house in such circumstances as to render the occupier guilty of an offence under section 139; and
(b) whether the landlord proposes to carry out works on the house or on the building of which it forms part so that the proposed works will affect the accommodation likely to be used by the sub-tenant or lodger who would reside in the house as a result of the consent. [943]

NOTES to Schedule 4
Definitions: 'secure tenancy': see ss 82 and 44 above; 'tenant', 'tenancy', 'landlord': see s 82 above; 'house': see s 338 below; 'landlord': see s 82 above.

Section 57(3) SCHEDULE 5

Terms of Secure Tenancy Relating to Alterations, etc to House

1.—A secure tenant who wishes to carry out work shall serve on the landlord an application in writing for the landlord's consent, giving details of the work proposed to be carried out. [944]

2.—In relation to an application under paragraph 1, the landlord may—
(a) consent;
(b) refuse consent, provided that it is not refused unreasonably; or
(c) consent subject to such reasonable conditions as the landlord may impose. [945]

3.—The landlord shall intimate consent or refusal, and any conditions imposed, and in the case of refusal the reasons therefor, to the tenant in writing within one month of receipt of the application. [946]

4.—In the event that the landlord fails to make intimation in accordance with paragraph 3 within the period therein mentioned, the landlord shall be deemed to have consented to the application. [947]

5.—A tenant who is aggrieved by a refusal, or by any condition imposed under paragraph 2(c), may raise proceedings by summary application in the sheriff court of the district in which the house is situated. **[948]**

6.—In proceedings under paragraph 5, the sheriff shall order the landlord to consent to the application or, as the case may be, to withdraw the condition unless it appears to him that the refusal or condition is reasonable. **[949]**

7.—In deciding whether a refusal or a condition is reasonable the sheriff shall have regard in particular to—
(a) the safety of occupiers of the house or of any other premises;
(b) any expenditure which the landlord is likely to incur as a result of the work;
(c) whether the work is likely to reduce the value of the house or of any premises of which it forms part, or to make the house or such premises less suitable for letting or for sale; and
(d) any effect which the work is likely to have on the extent of the accommodation provided by the house. **[950]**

NOTES to Schedule 5
Definitions: 'secure tenancy': see ss 82 and 44 above; 'tenant', 'tenancy': see s 82 above; 'house': see s 338 above.

Section 77(3)   SCHEDULE 6

VESTING ORDER UNDER SECTION 77: MODIFICATION OF ENACTMENTS

The Town and Country Planning (Scotland) Act 1972 (c 52)

1.—Paragraphs 1(2), 6 to 13 and 16 to 39 of Schedule 24 only shall apply and in them any reference to a general vesting declaration shall be treated as a reference to an order under section 77. **[951]**

2.—The references in paragraphs 6, 7 and 37 of that Schedule to the end of the period specified in a general vesting declaration shall be treated as references to the date on which such an order comes into force and the reference in paragraph 9 thereof to the acquiring authority having made a general vesting declaration shall be treated as a reference to such order having come into force. **[952]**

3.—In paragraph 6 of that Schedule—
(a) the reference to every person on whom, under section 17 of the Lands Clauses Consolidation (Scotland) Act 1845, the acquiring authority could have served a notice to treat, shall be treated as a reference to every person whose interest in the land to which such order relates is vested by the order in the landlord; and
(b) sub-paragraph (a) shall be omitted. **[953]**

4.—The reference in paragraph 20(2) of that Schedule to the date on which the notice required by paragraph 4 thereof is served on any person shall be treated as a reference to the date on which such an order comes into force. **[954]**

5.—In paragraph 29 of that Schedule—
(a) sub-paragraph (1)(a) shall be omitted; and
(b) the reference in sub-paragraph (1)(b) to the date on which a person first had knowledge of the execution of the general vesting declaration shall be treated as a reference to the date on which such order came into force. **[955]**

The Land Compensation (Scotland) Act 1963 (c 51)

6.—Any reference to the date of service of a notice to treat shall be treated as a reference to the date on which an order under section 77 comes into force. **[956]**

7.—Section 25(2) shall be treated as if for the words 'the authority proposing to acquire it have served a notice to treat in respect thereof, or an agreement has been made for the sale thereof to that authority' there were substituted the words 'an order under section 77 of the Housing (Scotland) Act 1987 vesting the land in which the interest subsists in the landlord has come into force, or an agreement has been made for the sale of the interest to the landlord'. **[957]**

8.—In section 30—
(a) subsection (2) shall be treated as if at the end of paragraph (c) there were added the words—
'; or—
(d) where an order has been made under section 77 of the Housing (Scotland) Act 1987 vesting the land in which the interest subsists in the landlord.'; and
(b) subsection (3) shall be treated as if in paragraph (a) the words 'or (d)' were inserted after the words 'subsection (2)(b)'. **[958]**

9.—Any reference to a notice to treat in section 45(2) shall be treated as a reference to an order under the said section 77. **[959]**

10.—In Schedule 2, paragraph 2(1)(a) shall be treated as if the words 'or the coming into force of an order under section 77 of the Housing (Scotland) Act 1987 for the vesting of the land in the landlord' were inserted after the word 'land'. **[960]**

Section 81B [SCHEDULE 6A

CONSULTATION BEFORE DISPOSAL TO PRIVATE SECTOR LANDLORD

Disposals to which this Schedule applies

1.—(1) This Schedule applies to the disposal by a local authority of an interest in land as a result of which a secure tenant of the local authority will become the tenant of a private sector landlord.

(2) For the purposes of this Schedule the grant of an option which if exercised would result in a secure tenant of a local authority becoming the tenant of a private sector landlord shall be treated as a disposal of the interest which is the subject of the option.

(3) Where a disposal of land by a local authority is in part a disposal to which this Schedule applies, the provisions of this Schedule apply to that part as to a separate disposal.

(4) In this paragraph 'private sector landlord' means a person other than one of those set out in sub-paragraphs (i) to (iv) and (viii) and (ix) of paragraph (a) of subsection (2) of section 61. **[961]**

Application for Secretary of State's consent

2.—(1) The Secretary of State shall not entertain an application for his consent under section 12(7) to a disposal to which this Schedule applies unless the local authority certify either—
(a) that the requirements of paragraph 3 as to consultation have been complied with, or

(b) that the requirements of that paragraph as to consultation have been complied with except in relation to tenants expected to have vacated the house in question before the disposal;

and the certificate shall be accompanied by a copy of the notices given by the local authority in accordance with that paragraph.

(2) Where the certificate is in the latter form, the Secretary of State shall not determine the application until the local authority certify as regards the tenants not originally consulted—

(a) that they have vacated the house in question, or
(b) that the requirements of paragraph 3 as to consultation have been complied with;

and a certificate under sub-paragraph (b) shall be accompanied by a copy of the notices given by the local authority in accordance with paragraph 3. [962]

Requirements as to consultation

3.—(1) The requirements as to consultation referred to above are as follows.

(2) The local authority shall serve notice in writing on the tenant informing him of—
(a) such details of their proposal as the local authority consider appropriate, but including the identity of the person to whom the disposal is to be made,
(b) the likely consequences of the disposal for the tenant, and
(c) the effect of section 81A and the provision made under it (preservation of right to buy on disposal to private sector landlord) and of this Schedule,

and informing him that he may, within such reasonable period as may be specified in the notice, which must be at least 28 days after the service of the notice, make representations to the local authority.

(3) The local authority shall consider any representations made to them within that period and shall serve a further written notice on the tenant informing him—
(a) of any significant changes in their proposal, and
(b) that he may within such period as is specified (which must be at least 28 days after the service of the notice) communicate to the Secretary of State his objection to the proposal,

and informing him of the effect of paragraph 5 (consent to be withheld if majority of tenants are opposed). [963]

Power to require further consultation

4.—The Secretary of State may require the local authority to carry out such further consultation with their tenants, and to give him such information as to the results of that consultation, as he may direct. [964]

Consent to be withheld if majority of tenants are opposed

5.—(1) The Secretary of State shall not give his consent if it appears to him that a majority of the tenants of the houses to which the application relates do not wish the disposal to proceed; but this does not affect his general discretion to refuse consent on grounds relating to whether a disposal has the support of the tenants or on any other ground.

(2) In making his decision the Secretary of State may have regard to any information available to him; and the local authority shall give him such information as to the representations made to them by tenants and others, and other relevant matters, as he may require. [965]

Protection of purchasers

6.—The Secretary of State's consent to a disposal is not invalidated by a failure on his part or that of the local authority to comply with the requirements of this Schedule.' [966]

NOTES to Schedule 6A

Amendment: Schedule 6A was added by the Housing Act 1988 (c 50), s 135, Sch 16 with effect from 21 February 1992.

Definitions: 'local authority', 'house': see s 338 above; 'secure tenant', 'secure tenancy': see ss 82 and 44 above; 'tenant', 'tenancy': see s 82 above.

Section 93 SCHEDULE 7

PART I
CONSENT TO DEMOLITION OF LISTED BUILDINGS IN HOUSING ACTION AREAS, ETC

Buildings subject to compulsory purchase orders for demolition subsequently listed

1.—(1) In this paragraph, references to a compulsory purchase order are to a compulsory purchase order made under the provisions of Part IV in so far as the order relates to a building acquired for demolition under those provisions.

(2) Where a building to which a compulsory order applies (at any time after the making of the order) included in a list of buildings of special architectural or historic interest under section 52 of the Town and Country Planning (Scotland) Act 1972 or under any corresponding enactment repealed by that Act, the local authority making the order or its successor in the exercise of its functions relating to the order may, subject to sub-paragraph (3), apply to the Secretary of State (and only to him) under section 53 of the said Act of 1972 for consent to the demolition of the building.

(3) No such application may be made by virtue of sub-paragraph (2) after the expiry of the period of 3 months beginning with the date on which the building is included on the said list.

(4) The following provisions of this paragraph shall have effect where—
(a) an application for consent has been made under the said section 53, by virtue of sub-paragraph (2), and has been refused, or
(b) the period of 3 months mentioned in sub-paragraph (3) has expired without the authority having made such an application,
and in this paragraph 'relevant date' means the date of the refusal or, as the case may be, of the expiry of the period of 3 months.

(5) If, at the relevant date—
(a) the building has not vested in the authority, and
(b) no notice to treat has been served by the authority under section 17 of the Lands Clauses Consolidation (Scotland) Act 1845, in respect of any interest in the building,
the compulsory purchase order shall cease to have effect in relation to the building and, where applicable, the building shall cease to be comprised in a housing action area.

(6) Where a compulsory purchase order ceases to have effect, by virtue of sub-paragraph (5), in relation to a house which does not meet the tolerable standard, the authority concerned shall, in respect of the house, forthwith—
(a) serve a notice under section 108 (power of local authority to secure repair of house in state of serious disrepair), or
(b) make a closing order under Part VI,
whichever is appropriate.

(7) Where sub-paragraph (5) does not apply, the authority shall cease to be subject to the duty to demolish the building, and in relation to any interest in the building which at the relevant date has not vested in the authority the compulsory purchase order shall have effect as if—
(a) in the case of a house, it had been made and confirmed under Part I, and
(b) in any other case, it had been made and confirmed under Part VI of the Town and Country Planning (Scotland) Act 1972.

(8) If the building, or any interest in the building, was vested in the authority at the relevant date, it shall be treated—
(a) in the case of a house, as appropriated to the purposes of Part I, and
(b) in any other case, as appropriated to the purposes of Part VI of the said Act of 1972.

(9) As respects a building falling within sub-paragraph (2), where no notice to treat has, at the date on which the building is included in the list referred to in that sub-paragraph, been served under section 17 of the Lands Clauses Consolidation (Scotland) Act 1845, the authority shall not serve such a notice until after the relevant date. [967]

Buildings acquired by agreement for demolition subsequently listed

2.—(1) Where Part IV applies to a building purchased by a local authority by agreement, and at any time the building is included in a list of buildings of special architectural or historic interest under section 52 of the Town and Country Planning (Scotland) Act 1972 or under any corresponding enactment repealed by that Act, the authority or its successor in the exercise of the powers conferred by Part IV may, subject to sub-paragraph (2), apply to the Secretary of State (and only to him) under the said section 53 for consent to the demolition of the building.

(2) No such application may be made by virtue of sub-paragraph (1) after the expiry of the period of 3 months beginning with the date on which the building is included on the said list.

(3) Where—
(a) an application for consent has been made under the said section 53, by virtue of sub-paragraph (1), and has been refused, or
(b) the period of 3 months mentioned in sub-paragraph (2) has expired without the authority having made such an application,
the authority shall cease to be subject to the duty imposed by Part IV to demolish the building, which shall be treated—
(i) in the case of a house, as appropriated to the purposes of Part I of this Act, and
(ii) in any other case, as appropriated to the purposes of Part VI of the Town and Country Planning (Scotland) Act 1972. [968]

Part II
Rehabilitation Orders

Application and effect of rehabilitation orders

3.—(1) This Part of this Schedule applies to any house which—
(a) is included in a clearance area under Part III of the Act of 1966, or
(b) is included in a housing treatment area under Part I of the Act of 1969, where the resolution for the area provides for the demolition of the house,
being a house which—
(i) has been purchased by agreement or compulsorily at any time before 2nd December 1974 under section 38 of the Act of 1966 or section 7 of the Act of 1969 (provisions regarding acquisition of land in such areas), or
(ii) is subject to a compulsory purchase order which was made under the said section 38 or under the said section 7 (but not confirmed) before 2nd December 1974 and which, before 2nd March 1975, has been confirmed in accordance with Schedule 3 to the Act of 1966 or (as the case may be) in accordance with Schedule 1 to the Acquisition of Land (Authorisation Procedure) (Scotland) Act 1947 as applied by the said section 7, or
(iii) has been included in the area by virtue of section 41 of the Act of 1966 or section 9 of the Act of 1969 (land already belonging to the local authority).

(2) Where any house to which this Part of this Schedule applies in terms of sub-paragraph (1) does not comply with the full standard as defined in paragraph 12 and, in the opinion of the local authority, it is capable of being and ought to be improved to that standard, the authority may make and submit to the Secretary of State an order (in this Part of this Schedule referred to as a 'rehabilitation order') in relation to the house.

(3) In addition to applying to any house to which this Part of this Schedule applies in terms of sub-paragraph (1), a rehabilitation order may, if the local authority think fit, be made to apply to any other relevant land, as defined in paragraph 12.

(4) On the date on which a rehabilitation order becomes operative, the local authority shall cease to be subject to any duty to demolish or secure the demolition of buildings on any land included in the order, imposed by Part III of the Act of 1966 or Part I of the Act of 1969.

(5) Where by virtue of sub-paragraph (4) a local authority are freed from the duty to demolish or secure the demolition of a house which does not comply with the full standard, the authority shall take such steps as are necessary—
(a) to bring the house up to the full standard, or
(b) where it is not vested in the authority, to ensure that it is brought up to that standard.

(6) A local authority may accept undertakings for the purpose of sub-paragraph (5)(b) from the owner of a house, or any other person who has or will have an interest in a house, concerning works to be carried out to bring it up to the full standard and the time within which they are to be carried out.

(7) Any reference in sub-paragraph (2), (5) or (6) to a house being improved or brought up to the full standard shall be construed as including a reference to a house, after integration with any other house to which this Part of this Schedule applies and which does not comply with the full standard, being improved or brought up to the full standard. **[969]**

Miscellaneous provisions relative to rehabilitation orders

4.—Where the owner of a house to which this Part of this Schedule applies in terms of paragraph 3(1), and which does not comply with the full standard, requests the local authority to make a rehabilitation order in respect of the house, and the authority refuse to make the order, they shall give him in writing their reasons for so refusing. **[970]**

5.—Where a local authority have made a rehabilitation order they shall not, until after the date on which the order becomes operative or on which confirmation of the order is refused—
(a) serve notice to treat, under section 17 of the Lands Clauses Consolidation (Scotland) Act 1845, in respect of any land included in a compulsory purchase order made and confirmed by virtue of section 38 of the Act of 1966 or section 7 of the Act of 1969 which includes notice land as defined in paragraph 12; or
(b) demolish, without the consent of the Secretary of State, any building on notice land. **[971]**

6.—(1) Where—
(a) land included in a compulsory purchase order, made and confirmed by virtue of the said section 38 or the said section 7, is comprised in a rehabilitation order, and
(b) the rehabilitation order becomes operative in respect of that land, and
(c) no interest in the land has vested in the local authority before the date on which the rehabilitation order becomes operative, and
(d) neither the local authority nor a previous local authority entitled to serve a notice to treat in respect of any interest in the land under section 17 of the said Act of 1845 have done so before that date,
the compulsory purchase order shall cease to have effect in relation to that land on that

date, and if the land is included in a clearance area or housing treatment area, it shall cease to be so included.

(2) On and after the date on which a rehabilitation order becomes operative, in a case where sub-paragraph (1) does not apply in relation to an area of land comprised in that order, any compulsory purchase order relating to that land and confirmed by virtue of the said section 38 or the said section 7 shall have effect in relation to any interest in that land, which at the said date was not vested in the authority—
   (a) in so far as it relates to a house, as if it had been made and confirmed under Part I of this Act, and
   (b) in so far as it relates to land other than a house, as if it had been made and confirmed under Part VI of the Town and Country Planning (Scotland) Act 1972.

(3) Where a rehabilitation order becomes operative in respect of an area of land and any interest in that land is vested in the local authority at the date when the order becomes operative—
   (a) any such interest in a house shall be treated as appropriated to the purposes of Part I of this Act, and
   (b) any such interest in land other than a house shall be treated as appropriated to the purposes of Part VI of the said Act of 1972. **[972]**

7.—A rehabilitation order may be made and confirmed notwithstanding that the effect of the order in excluding any land from a clearance area or from a housing treatment area is to sever that area into two or more parts; and in any such case the provisions applicable to the area in Part III of the Act of 1966 or in Part I of the Act of 1969, relating to the effect of a compulsory purchase order when confirmed and to the proceedings to be taken after confirmation of such an order, shall apply as if those parts formed one clearance area or housing treatment area, as the case may be. **[973]**

Procedure for making and confirming rehabilitation orders

8.—A rehabilitation order shall be made in the prescribed form and shall describe, by reference to a map—
   (a) the house to which, in terms of paragraph 3(1), it applies and
   (b) the other land to which, in terms of paragraph 3(3), it applies. **[974]**

9.—(1) Before submitting a rehabilitation order to the Secretary of State for confirmation, the local authority, except in so far as the Secretary of State directs otherwise—
   (a) shall publish in one or more newspapers circulating within their district a notice in the prescribed form stating that such an order has been made and describing the land to which it applies, and naming a place where a copy of the order and its accompanying map may be seen at all reasonable hours, and
   (b) shall serve on any such person as is specified in sub-paragraph (2) a notice in the prescribed form stating—
      (i) the effect of the rehabilitation order,
      (ii) that it is about to be submitted to the Secretary of State for confirmation, and
      (iii) the time within which and the manner in which objections to the order can be made.

(2) The persons mentioned in sub-paragraph (1)(b) are—
(a) every person on whom notice was served of the making by virtue of section 38 of the Act of 1966 or section 7 of the Act of 1969 of any compulsory purchase order which, at the date of its confirmation, included any land subsequently comprised in the rehabilitation order;
(b) every successor in title of such a person;
(c) every owner, lessee and occupier of the relevant land other than a tenant for a month or a period less than a month;
(d) creditors in heritable securities over relevant land, so far as it is reasonably practicable to ascertain such persons; and

Housing (Scotland) Act 1987 (c 26), Sch 7 [977]

(e) every person on whom notice would have been required to be served under head (c) or (d) whose interest has been acquired under the said section 38 since the clearance area was declared to be such an area or (as the case may be) under the said section 7 since the housing treatment area was declared to be such an area.

(3) A notice under this paragraph shall be accompanied by a statement of the grounds on which the local authority are seeking confirmation of the rehabilitation order.

(4) A notice under this paragraph shall be served in accordance with section 5(3) of and paragraph 19 of Schedule I to the Acquisition of Land (Authorisation Procedure) (Scotland) Act 1947. [975]

10.—(1) If no objection is duly made by any of the persons on whom notices are to be served under paragraph 9, or if all objections so made are withdrawn, the Secretary of State may confirm the order with or without modifications.

(2) If any objection duly made is not withdrawn, the Secretary of State, before confirming the order, shall cause a public local inquiry to be held or afford to any person by whom an objection has been duly made and not withdrawn an opportunity of appearing before and being heard by a person appointed by the Secretary of State for the purpose.

(3) After considering any objections not withdrawn and the report of the person who held the inquiry or of the person appointed under sub-paragraph (2), the Secretary of State may confirm the order with or without modifications.

(4) The Secretary of State may require any person who has made an objection to state the grounds of the objection in writing, and may disregard the objection if he is satisfied that it relates exclusively to matters which can be dealt with by the tribunal by whom any compensation is to be assessed.

(5) The Secretary of State's power to modify a rehabilitation order includes power, subject to sub-paragraph (6), to extend it to any notice land.

(6) The Secretary of State shall not extend the application of a rehabilitation order to any land unless he has served on the following persons, namely—
- (a) the local authority who made the rehabilitation order,
- (b) every owner, lessee and occupier of that land, except a tenant for a month or a period less than a month, and
- (c) so far as it is reasonably practicable to ascertain such persons, on the creditor in every heritable security over any such land,

a notice stating the effect of his proposals, and has afforded them an opportunity to make their views known. [976]

11.—Paragraphs 6, 15 and 16 of Schedule 1 to the Acquisition of Land (Authorisation Procedure) (Scotland) Act 1947 (notification, challenge of validity and date of operation of orders) shall apply in relation to rehabilitation orders as if—
- (a) any reference to a compulsory purchase order were a reference to a rehabilitation order and any reference to compulsory purchase were a reference to rehabilitation under this Part of this Schedule;
- (b) any reference to the acquiring authority were a reference to the local authority;
- (c) the reference in the said paragraph 6 to paragraph 3 of that Schedule were a reference to paragraph 9 of this Schedule;
- (d) the reference in the said paragraph 15 to any such enactment as is mentioned in section 1(1) of that Act were a reference to this Part of this Schedule;
- (e) the references in the said paragraph 15 to any requirement of that Act and to any requirement of that Schedule thereof were references to any requirement of this Part of this Schedule and of any provision of that Act (or that Schedule, as the case may be) applicable to the rehabilitation order;
- (f) the references in the said paragraphs 15 and 16 to a certificate under Part III of that Schedule were deleted. [977]

Interpretation of this Part of this Schedule

12.—In this Part of this Schedule, unless the context otherwise requires—
'clearance area' means a clearance area under Part III of the Housing (Scotland) Act 1966;
'full standard', in relation to a house, means the standard of a house which—
    (a) meets the tolerable standard;
    (b) is in a good state of repair (disregarding the state of internal decorative repair) having regard to the age, character and locality of the house; and
    (c) is provided with all of the standard amenities;
'housing treatment area' means a housing treatment area under Part I of the Housing (Scotland) Act 1969;
'notice land' means land in relation to which a notice is to be served under paragraph 9;
'relevant land' means—
    (a) land in the clearance area or housing treatment area (as the case may be), including land which has been included in that area by virtue of section 41 of the Act of 1966 or section 9 of the Act of 1969 (land already belonging to the local authority); or
    (b) land surrounded by or adjoining that area, which the local authority or a previous local authority entitled to purchase the land under section 37 of the Act of 1966 or under section 6 of the Act of 1969 have determined to purchase (whether or not it has been so purchased).   [978]

PART III
APPLICATION OF ENACTMENTS RELATING TO COMPENSATION ON COMPULSORY PURCHASE, ETC, TO CASES UNDER PART I OR PART III OF THIS SCHEDULE

Compensation

13.—(1) Where, under Part I or II of this Schedule, a compulsory purchase order is to be treated as made under Part I of this Act or Part VI of the Town and Country Planning (Scotland) Act 1972, compensation for the compulsory acquisition of the land comprised in the compulsory purchase order is to be assessed in accordance with the provisions applying to a compulsory acquisition under Part I of this Act or, as the case may be, Part VI of the Act of 1972.

(2) Where, under Part I or II of this Schedule, land or any interest in land within any area is to be treated as appropriated by a local authority to the purposes of Part I of this Act, compensation for its compulsory acquisition shall (where it increases the amount) be assessed or re-assessed in accordance with the provisions applying to a compulsory acquisition under [Part I of this Act].

(3) Where, under paragraph 2 of Part I of this Schedule, or under Part II, any interest in land acquired by a local authority by agreement (after the declaration of a housing action area which relates to that land) is to be treated as appropriated for the purposes of Part I of this Act—
    (a) compensation shall (where sub-paragraph (2) would have increased the amount) be assessed and paid as if the acquisition were a compulsory acquisition, under . . . Part III of Schedule 8 . . . , to which the said sub-paragraph (2) applied; but
    (b) there shall be deducted from the amount of compensation so payable any amount previously paid in respect of the acquisition of that interest by the authority.

(4) Where sub-paragraph (2) or (3) applies, the local authority shall serve on the person entitled to the compensation a notice in the prescribed form giving particulars of the amount of compensation payable in accordance with the provisions applying to a compulsory acquisition under Part I of this Act, and if the person served does not, within 21 days from service of the notice, accept the particulars, or if he disputes the amount stated, the question of disputed compensation shall be referred to the Lands Tribunal.

(5) The notice shall be served not later than 6 months after—
(a) the relevant date, as defined in paragraph 1(4) of this Schedule, or
(b) the date on which the rehabilitation order becomes operative for the purposes of Part II of this Schedule,

(as the case may be), and paragraph 19 of Schedule 1 to the Acquisition of Land (Authorisation Procedure) (Scotland) Act 1947 (service of notices) shall apply to the notice.

(6) Sub-paragraph (2) shall be left out of account in considering whether, under sections 117 and 118 of the Lands Clauses Consolidation (Scotland) Act 1845, compensation has been properly paid for the land; and accordingly sub-paragraph (2) shall not prevent an acquiring authority from remaining in undisputed possession of the land.

(7) Where sub-paragraph (2) makes an increase in compensation to be assessed in accordance with sections 56 to 60 and 63 of the said Act of 1845 (absent and untraced owners)—
(a) a notarial instrument executed under section 76 of that Act before the latest date for service of a notice under sub-paragraph (4) shall not be invalid because the increase in compensation has not been paid, and
(b) it shall be the duty of the local authority, not later than 6 months after the said date, to proceed under the said sections and pay the proper additional amount into the bank.

(8) Any sum payable by virtue of this paragraph shall carry interest at the rate prescribed under section 40 of the Land Compensation (Scotland) Act 1963 from the time of entry by the local authority on the land, or from vesting of the land or interest, whichever is the earlier, until payment.

(9) In this paragraph, references to an increase in compensation shall be read as if any payments under—
(a) section 49 of the Act of 1966, section 11 of the Act of 1969 or section 30 of the Act of 1974 or section 305 of this Act (payments in respect of well-maintained houses and payments to owner-occupiers),
(b) section 160 of the Act of 1966 or section 38 of the Land Compensation (Scotland) Act 1963 (allowances to persons displaced),
(c) sections 18 to 20 of the Act of 1969 or sections 308 to 311 of this Act (payments to owner-occupiers and others in respect of houses not meeting the tolerable standard purchased or demolished), and
(d) section 34 of the Land Compensation (Scotland) Act 1973 (disturbance payments for persons without compensatable interests),

were, to the extent that they were made to the person in question, compensation in respect of the compulsory purchase. **[979]**

Extension of time limits for exercising powers under certain compulsory purchase orders

14.—In section 116 of the Lands Clauses Consolidation (Scotland) Act 1845 (time limits for exercising powers under compulsory purchase orders) there shall be added at the end the following paragraph—

'For the purposes of this section no account shall be taken of any period during which an authority are, by virtue of Schedule 7 to the Housing (Scotland) Act 1987 (which relates to buildings in housing action areas) prevented from serving notice to treat under section 17 of this Act.' **[980]**

NOTES to Schedule 7

Amendment: Para 13 was amended by the Housing (Scotland) Act 1988 (c 43), s 72, Sch 7, para 28.
Definitions: 'local authority', 'house': see s 338 above; 'the tolerable standard': see ss 338 and 86 above.

Section 95　　　　　　　　　SCHEDULE 8

PART I
HOUSING ACTION AREAS

Procedure after publication of draft resolution

1.—(1) The local authority shall have regard to any representations made to them by virtue of section 94 and, within a period of 2 months from the expiry of the period of 2 months mentioned in section 94(7), shall—
(a) subject to the provisions of sub-paragraph (2), pass a final resolution confirming the draft resolution, with or without modifications; or
(b) rescind the draft resolution.

(2) The power to make modifications by virtue of sub-paragraph (1)(a) shall not include power to extend the area defined in the draft resolution.

(3) The local authority shall, as soon as may be—
(a) send a copy of the final resolution and a copy of the map to the Secretary of State,
(b) publish in the manner required by section 94(5)(a) a notice that a final resolution has been made, or as the case may be, that the draft resolution has been rescinded and
(c) serve on such persons as were served with a notice in pursuance of section 94(5)(b), a notice stating the effect of any final resolution or, as the case may be, stating that the draft resolution has been rescinded,
and the provisions of section 94(6) shall apply to the publication and service of a notice under this paragraph as they apply to the publication and service of a notice under that section.

(4) The provisions of section 92 shall apply to a final resolution as they apply to a draft resolution.　　**[981]**

2.—Any notice authorised or required to be sent to any owner, lessee or occupier by virtue of section 94(5)(b) and paragraph 1(3)(c) may, if it is not practicable after reasonable inquiry to ascertain the name of such owner, lessee or occupier, be served by addressing it to him by the description of 'owner', 'lessee' or 'occupier', as the case may be, identifying the house to which it relates and by delivering it to some person in the house, or if there is no person in the house to whom it can be delivered, by affixing it, or a copy of it, to some conspicuous part of the house.　　　　　　　　　　　　　　　　　　**[982]**

PART II
POWERS OF LOCAL AUTHORITY IN RELATION TO ACQUISITION OF LAND FOR HOUSING ACTION AREAS

3.—(1) Subject to the provisions of sub-paragraph (2), where a local authority have published and served, in accordance with the provisions of section 94, a notice of the passing of a draft resolution made under section 89, 90 or 91 the local authority, from the date of the said publication and service, shall have power to purchase land by agreement in the area to which the said draft resolution relates, in order themselves to undertake, or otherwise secure, the demolition, or improvement to the standard specified under section 90(3) or by virtue of section 91(3) (as the case may be), of the houses or buildings.

(2) Where under sub-paragraph (1) the local authority purchase a house identified in accordance with section 92(4)(c), they may also purchase any other part of the building so identified if in their opinion it is necessary to purchase such other part in order to integrate it with that house.　　**[983]**

Land adjoining housing action area

4.—Where a local authority determining to acquire any land comprised in an area declared by them to be a housing action area, they may acquire also—
  (a) any land which is surrounded by the housing action area; and
  (b) any land adjoining the housing action area,
if the acquisition is reasonably necessary for the purpose of securing an area of convenient shape and dimensions or is reasonably necessary for the satisfactory development or use of the housing action area. **[984]**

Further provisions relating to acquisition of land

5.—(1) In so far as a resolution passed under section 89 or 91 provides that some or all of the buildings in a housing action area should be demolished, the powers of acquiring land comprised in or surrounded by or adjoining such an area conferred on a local authority by Part IV and this Schedule shall not be restricted by the fact that buildings within that area have been demolished since the area was declared to be a housing action area.

(2) Land for the purposes of Part IV and this Schedule may be acquired by a local authority by agreement under section 70 of the Local Government (Scotland) Act 1973 (acquisition of land by agreement).

(3) Subject to the provisions of sub-paragraph (4), a local authority may be authorised by the Secretary of State to purchase land compulsorily for the same purposes as they may acquire land by agreement under paragraphs 3 and 4, and the Acquisition of Land (Authorisation Procedure) (Scotland) Act 1947 shall apply in relation to any such compulsory purchase as if this Act had been in force immediately before the commencement of that Act, but subject to the following modifications—
  (a) the compulsory purchase order shall not be in the form prescribed under paragraph 2 of Schedule 1 to that Act, but shall be in a form prescribed under this paragraph;
  (b) the notices referred to in paragraphs 3 and 6 of the said Schedule 1 shall not be in the form prescribed under paragraphs, but shall be in a form prescribed under this paragraph;
  (c) the order shall show separately the houses in the housing action area which do not meet the tolerable standard and, as the case may be, that standard along with any other standard specified under section 90 or by virtue of section 91 and the land proposed to be purchased outside the area;
  (d) the order as confirmed by the Secretary of State shall not authorise the local authority to purchase any house on less favourable terms with respect to compensation than the terms on which the order would have authorised them to purchase the house if the order had been confirmed without modification;
  (e) if the Secretary of State is of opinion that any land included by a local authority in a housing action area ought not to have been so included, he shall on confirming the order so modify it as to exclude that land for all purposes from that area;
  (f) in section 1 of that Act, any reference to the said Schedule 1 shall be construed as a reference to that Schedule as modified by this sub-paragraph;
  (g) in Part IV of that Schedule any reference to that Act or that Schedule or any reference to any regulation made thereunder shall be construed respectively as a reference to that Act as modified by this sub-paragraph and as including a reference to any regulation made under this sub-paragraph;
  (h) section 3 of that Act (power to extinguish certain public rights of way over land acquired) shall be omitted.

(4) Where a local authority have published and served notice of a final resolution in accordance with the provisions of paragraph 1 declaring an area to be—
  (a) a housing action area for demolition, they shall submit any order authorising the compulsory purchase of land in the area to the Secretary of State within a period of 6 months from the date of the said publication and service,

(b) a housing action area for improvement or for demolition and improvement, any such order as aforesaid shall not be made by the local authority before the expiry of a period of 3 months and shall be submitted to the Secretary of State within a period of 9 months from the date of the said publication and service,

but the Secretary of State may in the circumstances of a particular case, allow such longer period for the periods of 6 months and 9 months mentioned respectively in paragraphs (a) and (b) as he thinks appropriate. **[985]**

Land belonging to local authority

6.—(1) A local authority may include in a housing action area any land belonging to them which they might have included in such an area if the land had not belonged to them.

(2) Where any land belonging to a local authority is included in a housing action area, or where any land belonging to a local authority is surrounded by or adjoins a housing action area and might have been purchased by the authority under paragraph 4 had it not been previously acquired by them, the provisions of Part IV and this Schedule shall apply in relation to any such land as if it had been purchased compulsorily by the authority as being land comprised in the housing action area or, as the case may be, as being land surrounded by or adjoining the housing action area. **[986]**

Local authority may take possession of land

7.—Section 11 (which provides that a local authority may take possession of land to be acquired by agreement or appropriated for the purposes of Part I) shall apply for the purposes of Part IV and this Schedule as it applies for the purposes of Part I. **[987]**

Local authority may sell or lease land

8.—A local authority who have under Part IV of this Schedule purchased any land comprised in or surrounded by or adjoining a housing action area, may—
   (a) where the land was purchased for the purpose of bringing the houses in the area up to the standard specified under section 90(3) or by virtue of section 91(3), sell or lease any such house to any person subject to the condition that that person will bring the house up to at least the appropriate standard and to any other restriction or condition that they may think fit; or
   (b) in any other case, sell or lease the land subject to such restrictions and conditions, if, any, as they think fit, or may, in accordance with section 73 of the Local Government (Scotland) Act 1973 (appropriation of land), appropriate the land for any purpose for which they are authorised to acquire land. **[988]**

Extinction of rights of way servitudes, etc

9.—(1) A local authority may, with the approval of the Secretary of State, by order extinguish any public right of way over any land purchased by them under Part IV of this Schedule or provide for the closing or diversion of any road in connection with the development of a housing action area.

(2) An order made by a local authority under sub-paragraph (1) shall be made in the prescribed form and be published in the prescribed manner, and, if any objection thereto is made to the Secretary of State before the expiry of 2 months from its publication, the Secretary of State shall not approve the order until he has caused a public local inquiry to be held into the matter.

(3) Where a local authority have resolved to purchase under Part IV of this Schedule land over which a public right of way exists, the authority may make and the Secretary of State may approve, in advance of the purchase, an order extinguishing that right as from the date on which the buildings on the land are vacated, or at the expiry of such period

after that date as may be specified in the order or as the Secretary of State in approving the order may direct.

(4) Upon the completion by a local authority of the purchase by them of any land under Part IV of this Schedule, all private rights of way and all rights of laying down, erecting, continuing or maintaining any apparatus on, under or over that land, and all other rights or servitudes in or relating to that land, shall be extinguished, and any such apparatus shall vest in the authority; and any person who suffers loss by the extinction or vesting of any such right or apparatus as aforesaid shall be entitled to be paid by the authority compensation to be determined by the Lands Tribunal in accordance with the Land Compensation (Scotland) Act 1963:

Provided that this sub-paragraph shall not apply to any right vested in public undertakers of laying down, erecting, continuing or maintaining any apparatus or to any apparatus belonging to public undertakers, and shall have effect as respects other matters subject to any agreement which may be made between the local authority and the person in or to whom the right or apparatus in question is vested or belongs. [989]

Provisions as to apparatus of public undertakers

10.—(1) Where the removal or alteration of apparatus belonging to public undertakers on, under or over land purchased by a local authority under Part IV of this Schedule or on, under or over a road running over or through or adjoining any such land is reasonably necessary for the purpose of enabling the authority to exercise any of the powers conferred upon them by that Part of this Schedule, the authority shall have power to execute works for the removal or alteration of the apparatus subject to and in accordance with the provisions of this paragraph.

(2) A local authority who intend to remove or alter any apparatus under the powers conferred by sub-paragraph (1) shall serve on the undertakers notice in writing of their intention, with particulars of the proposed works and of the manner in which they are to be executed and plans and sections thereof, and shall not commence any works until the expiry of a period of 28 days from the date of service of the notice, and the undertakers may within that period by notice in writing served on the authority—
- (a) object to the execution of the works or any of them on the ground that they are not necessary for the purpose aforesaid; or
- (b) state requirements to which in their opinion effect ought to be given as to the manner of, or the observance of conditions in, the execution of the works, as to the execution of other works for the protection of other apparatus belonging to the undertakers, or as to the execution of other works for the provision of substituted apparatus whether permanent or temporary;

and
- (i) if objection is so made to any works and not withdrawn, the local authority shall not execute the works unless they are determined by arbitration to be so necessary;
- (ii) if any such requirement as aforesaid is so made and not withdrawn, the local authority shall give effect thereto unless it is determined by arbitration to be unreasonable.

(3) A local authority shall make to public undertakers reasonable compensation for any damage which is sustained by them by reason of the execution by the authority of any works under sub-paragraph (1) and which is not made good by the provision of substituted apparatus.

Any question as to the right of undertakers to recover compensation under this sub-paragraph or as to the amount thereof shall be determined by arbitration.

(4) Where the removal or alteration of apparatus belonging to public undertakers or the execution of works for the provision of substituted apparatus whether permanent or temporary is reasonably necessary for the purposes of their undertaking by reason of the stopping up, diversion or alteration of the level or width of a road by a local authority under powers exercisable by virtue of Part IV of this Schedule, such undertakers may, by

notice in writing served on the authority, require them at the expense of the authority to remove or alter the apparatus or to execute the works, and, where any such requirement is so made and not withdrawn, the authority shall give effect thereto unless they serve notice in writing on the undertakers of their objection to the requirement within 28 days from the date of service of the notice upon them and the requirement is determined by arbitration to be unreasonable.

(5) At least 7 days before commencing any works which they are authorised or required under the provisions of this paragraph to execute, the local authority shall, except in case of emergency, serve on the undertakers notice in writing of their intention so to do, and the works shall be executed by the authority under the superintendence (at the expense of the authority) and to the reasonable satisfaction of the undertakers:

Provided that, if within 7 days from the date of service on them of notice under this sub-paragraph the undertakers so elect, they shall themselves execute the works in accordance with the reasonable directions and to the reasonable satisfaction of the local authority, and the reasonable costs thereof shall be repaid to the undertakers by the authority.

(6) Any difference arising between public undertakers and a local authority under sub-paragraph (5) and any matter which is by virtue of the provisions of this paragraph to be determined by arbitration shall—
   (a)   in the case of a question arising under sub-paragraph (3) be referred to and determined by the Lands Tribunal;
   (b)   in any other case be referred to and determined by an arbiter to be appointed, in default of agreement, by the Secretary of State.

(7) In this paragraph, references to the alteration of apparatus include references to diversion and to alterations of position or level. **[990]**

Savings for telecommunication apparatus, etc

11.—(1) Paragraph 23 of the telecommunications code (which provides a procedure for certain cases where works involve the alteration of telecommunication apparatus) shall apply to a local authority for the purposes of any works which they are authorised to execute under Part IV of this Schedule.

(2) Where in pursuance of an order under paragraph 9 a public right of way over land is extinguished or a road is closed or diverted, and, at the beginning of the day on which the order comes into operation, there is under, in, on, over, along or across the land or road any telecommunication apparatus kept installed for the purposes of a telecommunications code system, the operator of that system shall have the same powers in respect of that apparatus as if the order had not come into operation; but any person entitled to land over which the right of way subsisted shall be entitled to require the alteration of the apparatus.

(3) The proviso to sub-paragraph (4) of paragraph 9 shall have effect in relation to any right conferred by or in accordance with the telecommunications code on the operator of a telecommunications code system and to telecommunication apparatus kept installed for the purposes of any such system as it has effect in relation to rights vested in and apparatus belonging to statutory undertakers.

(4) Paragraph 1(2) of the telecommunications code (alteration of apparatus to include moving, removal or replacement of apparatus) shall apply for the purposes of the preceding provisions of this paragraph as it applies for the purposes of that code.

(5) Paragraph 21 of the telecommunications code (restriction on removal of telecommunication apparatus) shall apply in relation to any entitlement conferred by this paragraph to require the alteration, moving or replacement of any telecommunication apparatus as it applies in relation to an entitlement to require the removal of any such apparatus. **[991]**

PART III
COMPENSATION IN RESPECT OF LAND ACQUIRED COMPULSORILY

12.—(1) Where land is purchased compulsorily by a local authority under Part IV of this Schedule, the compensation payable in respect thereof shall, subject to the following provisions of this paragraph, be assessed by the Lands Tribunal in accordance with the Land Compensation (Scotland) Act 1963.

(2) In the case of the compulsory acquisition of a house which either is specified in the compulsory purchase order as not meeting the tolerable standard, or is specified in an improvement order under section 88, such compensation shall not (except by virtue of paragraph 3 of Schedule 2 to the said Act of 1963) exceed the value, at the time when the valuation is made, of the site of the house as a cleared site available for development in accordance with the requirements of the building regulations for the time being in force in the district.

(3) The reference in sub-paragraph (2) to compensation is a reference to the compensation payable in respect of the purchase exclusive of any compensation for disturbance or for severance or for injurious affection.

(4) Schedule 1 shall have effect in relation to the compulsory purchase of land under sub-paragraph (1), but shall not have effect in relation to a house to which sub-paragraph (2) applies. **[992]**

PART IV
ADJUSTMENT OF RELATIONS BETWEEN LESSORS AND LESSEES OF AGRICULTURAL HOLDINGS, ETC

13.—(1) Section 8 of the Agricultural Holdings (Scotland) Act 1949 (increases of rent for improvements carried out by landlord) shall apply as if references in subsection (1) of that section to improvements carried out at the request of the tenant included references to improvements carried out in compliance with a notice of a final resolution under Part I of this Schedule:
Provided that where the tenant has contributed to the cost incurred by the landlord in carrying out the improvement, the increase in rent provided for by the said section 8 shall be reduced proportionately.

(2) Any works carried out in compliance with a notice of a final resolution under Part I of this Schedule shall be included among the improvements specified in paragraph 18 of Schedule 1 to the said Act of 1949 (tenant's right to compensation for erection, alteration or enlargement of buildings), but subject to the power conferred by section 79 of that Act to vary the said Schedule 1; and sections 51 and 52 of that Act (which make that right to compensation subject to certain conditions) shall not apply to any works carried out in compliance with such a notice:
Provided that where a person other than the tenant claiming compensation has contributed to the cost of carrying out the works in compliance with any such notice, compensation in respect of the works, as assessed under section 49 of the said Act of 1949, shall be reduced proportionately.

(3) Any works carried out in compliance with a notice of a final resolution under Part I of this Schedule shall—
  (a) if carried out on a croft, be permanent improvements on that croft and be deemed to be suitable to the croft for the purposes of section 14(1)(a) of the Crofters (Scotland) Act 1955 (crofter's right to compensation for improvements);
  (b) if carried out on a holding, be permanent improvements on that holding and be deemed to be suitable to the holding for the purposes of section 8(a) of the Crofters Holdings (Scotland) Act 1886 (landholder's right to compensation for improvements).

(4) In this paragraph, unless the context otherwise requires—

'dwelling' means a building or part of a building occupied or intended to be occupied as a separate house;
'tenant'—
(a) has the same meaning as in section 115(1) of the Rent (Scotland) Act 1984 but does not include a tenant holding under a lease granted for a period of more than 21 years at a rent of less than two-thirds of the net annual value for rating purposes of the leased premises, or a heritable creditor in possession; and
(b) includes, in relation to a dwelling, a person employed in agriculture (as defined in section 17 of the Agricultural Wages (Scotland) Act 1949) who occupies or resides in the dwelling as part of the terms of his employment,
and 'tenancy' shall be construed accordingly.
References in this paragraph to a tenant occupying a dwelling include, in the case of a tenant within head (b) of this definition, a tenant residing in the dwelling, and 'occupation' and 'occupied' and related expression shall be construed accordingly; and in relation to a dwelling occupied by such a tenant 'the person having control' of the dwelling means, in this paragraph, the employer or other person by whose authority the tenant occupies the dwelling. **[993]**

NOTES to Schedule 8
Definition: 'local authority', 'owner', 'house', 'land', 'apparatus', 'public undertaker': see s 338 above.

Sections 109(5), 131(2), 164(4)

SCHEDULE 9

Recovery of Expenses by Charging Order

1.—Where under sections 108(3), 131(2) and 164(4) a local authority have themselves incurred expenses in relation to a house or building, they may make in favour of themselves an order (in this Schedule referred to as a 'charging order') providing and declaring that the house or building is thereby charged and burdened with an annuity to pay the amount of the expenses. **[994]**

2.—The annuity charged shall be such sum not exceeding such sum as may be prescribed, as the local authority may determine for every £100 of the said amount and so in proportion for any less sum, and shall commence from the date of the order and be payable for a term of 30 years to the local authority. **[995]**

3.—A charging order shall be in such form as may be prescribed and shall be recorded in the General Register of Sasines, or registered in the Land Register, as the case may be. **[996]**

4.—Every annuity constituting a charge by a charging order duly recorded in the General Register of Sasines or registered in the Land Register, as the case may be, shall be a charge on the premises specified in the order and shall have priority over—
(a) all future burdens and incumbrances on the same premises, and
(b) all existing burdens and incumbrances thereon except—
(i) feuduties, teinds, ground annuals, stipends and standard charges in lieu of stipends;
(ii) any charges created or arising under any provision of the Public Health (Scotland) Act 1897 or any Act amending that Act, or any local Act authorising a charge for recovery of expenses incurred by a local authority, or under this Schedule; and
(iii) any charge created under any Act authorising advances of public money. **[997]**

5.—A charging order duly recorded in the General Register of Sasines or registered in the Land Register, as the case may be, shall be conclusive evidence that the charge specified therein has been duly created in respect of the premises specified in the order. **[998]**

6.—Every annuity charged by a charging order may be recovered by the person for the time being entitled to it by the same means and in the like manner in all respects as if it were a feuduty. **[999]**

7.—A charging order and all sums payable thereunder may be from time to time transferred in like manner as a bond and disposition in security and sums payable thereunder. **[1000]**

8.—Any owner of, or other person interested in, premises on which an annuity has been charged by any such charging order shall at any time be at liberty to redeem the annuity on payment to the local authority or other person entitled thereto of such sum as may be agreed upon or, in default of agreement, determined by the Secretary of State. **[1001]**

NOTES to Schedule 9
Definitions: 'local authority', 'house': see s 338 above.

Section 113   SCHEDULE 10

Landlord's Repairing Obligations

Obligations to repair

[(1) This paragraph applies to any contract (whether entered into before or after the coming into force of Schedule 8 to the Housing (Scotland) Act 1988) for letting a house for human habitation under which no rent is payable or the rent payable is less than that specified by order made by the Secretary of State.

(1A) In determining whether this paragraph applies to any contract, there shall be disregarded such part (if any) of the sums payable by the tenant as is expressed (in whatever terms) to be payable in respect of services, repairs, maintenance or insurance unless it could not have been regarded by the parties to the tenancy as a part so payable.

(1B) An order under sub-paragraph (1) above may specify different rents in relation to—
(a)   different kinds of houses;
(b)   different areas.

(1C) An order under sub-paragraph (1) above may specify rent by reference to such periods or such different periods or such other factors or such combinations thereof as may be specified in the order.

(1D) An order under sub-paragraph (1) above shall be made by statutory instrument subject to annulment in pursuance of a resolution of either House of Parliament.

(1E) This paragraph does not apply to a contract for the letting by a local authority of any house purchased or retained by the authority under section 121 or paragraph 5 of Schedule 8 for use for housing purposes.]

(2) In any contract to which this paragraph applies there shall, notwithstanding any stipulation to the contrary, be implied a condition that the house is at the commencement of the tenancy, and an undertaking that the house will be kept by the landlord during the tenancy, in all respects reasonably fit for human habitation:
Provided that that condition and the undertaking shall not be implied when a house is let for a period of not less than 3 years upon the terms that it will be put by the lessee into a condition in all respects reasonably fit for human habitation, and the lease is not determinable at the option of either party before the expiration of 3 years.

(3) The landlord, or any person authorised by him in writing, may at reasonable times

of the day, on giving 24 hours' notice in writing to the tenant or occupier, enter any premises in respect of which this paragraph applies for the purpose of viewing their state and condition.

(4) In determining for the purposes of this paragraph whether a house is fit for human habitation, regard shall be had to the extent, if any, to which by reason of disrepair or sanitary defects the house falls short of the provisions of any building regulations in operation in the district.

(5) In this paragraph—
(a) the expression 'landlord' means any person who lets to a tenant for human habitation any house under any contract to which this paragraph applies, and includes his successors in title; and
(b) the expression 'house' includes part of a house; and
(c) the expression 'sanitary defects' includes lack of air space or of ventilation, darkness, dampness, absence of adequate and readily accessible water supply or of sanitary arrangements or of other conveniences, and inadequate paving or drainage of courts, yards or passages. **[1002]**

Application of paragraph 1 to houses occupied by agricultural workers otherwise than as tenants

2.—Notwithstanding any agreement to the contrary, where under any contract of employment of a workman employed in agriculture the provision of a house or part of a house for the occupation of the workman forms part of the remuneration of the workman, and the provisions of paragraph 1 are inapplicable by reason only of the house not being let to the workman, there shall be implied as part of the contract of employment the like condition and undertaking as would be implied under those provisions if the house or part of the house were so let, and those provisions shall apply accordingly as if incorporated in this paragraph, with the substitution of 'employer' for 'landlord' and such other modifications as may be necessary:

Provided that this paragraph shall not affect the obligation of any person other than the employer to repair a house to which this section applies or any remedy for enforcing any such obligation. **[1003]**

Repairing obligations in short leases of houses

3.—(1) In any lease of a house, being a lease to which this paragraph applies, there shall be implied a provision that the lessor will—
(a) keep in repair the structure and exterior of the house (including drains, gutters and external pipes); and
(b) keep in repair and proper working order the installations in the house—
  (i) for the supply of water, gas and electricity, and for sanitation (including basins, sinks, baths and sanitary conveniences but not, except as aforesaid, fixtures, fittings and appliances for making use of the supply of water, gas or electricity), and
  (ii) for space heating or heating water;

and any provision that the lessee will repair the premises (including any that he will put in repair or deliver up in repair, or will paint, point or render the premises, or pay money in lieu of repairs by the lessee or on account of repairs by the lessor) shall be of no effect so far as it relates to any of the matters mentioned in paragraphs (a) and (b) of this paragraph.

[(1A) If a lease to which this paragraph applies is a lease of a house which forms part only of a building, then, subject to sub-paragraph (1B) of this paragraph, the provision implied by this paragraph (hereinafter referred to as 'the implied repairs provision') shall have effect as if—
(a) the reference in paragraph (a) of sub-paragraph (1) of this paragraph to the house included a reference to any part of the building in which the lessor has an interest; and

(b) any reference in paragraph (b) of sub-paragraph (1) of this paragraph to installations in the house included a reference to installations which, directly or indirectly, serve the house and in which the lessor has an interest.

(1B) Nothing in sub-paragraph (1A) of this paragraph shall be construed as requiring the lessor to carry out any works or repairs unless the disrepair (or failure to maintain in working order) is such as to affect the lessee's enjoyment of the house or of any common parts.

(1C) In sub-paragraph (1B) of this paragraph 'common parts' in relation to any building or part of a building includes the structure and exterior of that building or part and any common facilities within it.]

. . .

(2) [The implied repairs provision] shall not be construed as requiring the lessor—
(a) to carry out any works or repairs for which the lessee is liable by virtue of his duty to use the premises in a proper manner, or would be so liable apart from any express undertaking on his part;
(b) to rebuild or reinstate the premises in the case of destruction or damage by fire, or by tempest, flood or other inevitable accident; or
(c) to keep in repair or maintain anything which the lessee is entitled to remove from the house;

and sub-paragraph (1) of this paragraph shall not avoid so much of any provision as imposes on the lessee any of the requirements mentioned in head (a) or head (c) of this sub-paragraph.

(3) In determining the standard of repair required by the implied repairs provision in relation to any house, regard shall be had to the age, character and prospective life of the house and the locality in which it is situated.

[(3A In any case where—
(a) the implied repairs provision has effect as mentioned in sub-paragraph (1A) of this paragraph; and
(b) in order to comply with the provision the lessor needs to carry out works or repairs otherwise than in, or to an installation in, the house; and
(c) the lessor does not have sufficient right in the part of the building or the installation concerned to enable him to carry out the required works or repairs,

then, in any proceedings relating to a failure to comply with the implied repairs provision, so far as it requires the lessor to carry out the works or repairs in question, it shall be a defence for the lessor to prove that he used all reasonable efforts to obtain, but was unable to obtain, such rights as would be adequate to enable him to carry out the works or repairs].

(4) In any lease in which the implied repairs provision is implied there shall also be implied a provision that the lessor, or any person authorised by him in writing, may at reasonable times of the day, on giving 24 hours' notice in writing to the occupier, enter the premises comprised in the lease for the purpose of viewing their condition and state of repair.

(5) In this paragraph and in paragraphs 4 and 5, unless the context otherwise requires, the following expressions have the meaning hereby assigned to them respectively, that is to say—
(a) 'lease' includes a sublease, and 'lessor', in relation to a lease, include respectively any person for the time being holding the interest of lessor, and any person for the time being holding the interest of lessee, under the lease, and
(b) 'lease of a house' means a lease whereby a building or part of a building is let wholly or mainly as a private dwelling and 'house', in relation to such a lease, means that building or part of a building. **[1004]**

Application of paragraph 3

4.—(1) Subject to the provisions of this paragraph, paragraph 3 applies to any lease of a house granted on or after 3rd July 1962 being a lease for a period of less than 7 years.

(2) For the purpose of this paragraph a lease—
(a) shall be treated as a lease for a period of less than 7 years if it is determinable at the option of the lessor before the expiration of 7 years from the commencement of the period of the lease, and
(b) shall be treated as a lease for a period of 7 years or more if it confers on the lessee an option for renewal for a period which, together with the original period, amounts to 7 years or more, and it is not determinable as mentioned in head (a) of this sub-paragraph.

(3) Where a lease (hereinafter referred to as 'the new lease') of a house is granted—
(a) to a person who, when or immediately before the new lease is granted, is or was the lessee of the house under another lease, or
(b) to a person who was the lessee of the house under another lease which terminated at some time before the new lease is granted and who, between the termination of that other lease and the grant of the new lease, was continuously in possession of the house or entitled to the rents or profits thereof,
paragraph 3 shall not apply to the new lease unless the other lease, if granted on or after 3rd July 1962, was a lease to which that paragraph applies, or, if granted before the said date, would have been such a lease if it had been granted on or after that date.

(4) Paragraph 3 shall not apply to any lease of a house which is a tenancy of an agricultural holding.

(5) In the application of this paragraph to a lease for a period part of which falls before the date of the granting of the lease, that part shall be left out of account and the lease shall be treated as a lease for a period commencing with the date of the granting.

Restriction on contracting out

5.—(1) The sheriff may, on the application of either party to a lease, by order made with the consent of the other party concerned, authorise the inclusion in the lease, or in any agreement collateral to the lease, of provisions excluding or modifying in relation to the lease the provisions of paragraph 3 with respect to the repairing obligations of the parties if it appears to him, having regard to the other terms and conditions of the lease and to all the circumstances of the case, that it is reasonable to do so, and any provision so authorised shall have effect accordingly.

(2) Subject to sub-paragraph (1) any provision, whether contained in a lease to which paragraph 3 applies or in any agreement collateral to such a lease, shall be void so far as it purports to exclude or limit the obligations of the lessor or the immunities of the lessee under that section, or to provide for an irritancy of the lease or impose on the lessee any penalty, disability or obligation, in the event of his enforcing or relying upon those obligations or immunities.

NOTES to Schedule 10
Amendments: Para 1(1) to 1(1E), para 3(1A) to 3(1C), and para 3(3A) were inserted by the Housing (Scotland) Act 1988 (c 43) s 72, Sch 8, para 9. Para 3(2) was amended by *Ibid*. The amendments do not affect leases entered before 2 January 1989 or leases entered into pursuant to a contract made before 2 January 1989.
Definitions: 'local authority', 'agricultural worker': see s 338 above.
Para 1: See the Landlords' Repairing Obligation (Specified Rent) (Scotland) No 9 Order 1988, SI 1988/2155. The rent specified is £300 per week.

Sections 164(4), 184(2), 187(3), 189

SCHEDULE 11

Houses in Multiple Occupation: Control Orders

Part I
Management Schemes

1.—(1) A management scheme shall give particulars of all works which in the opinion of the local authority—
   (a) the local authority would have required to be carried out under the provisions of Part VIII (other than those relating to control orders), or under any other enactment relating to housing or public health, and
   (b) constitutes work involving capital expenditure.

(2) A management scheme shall also—
   (a) include an estimate of the cost of carrying out the works of which particulars are given in the scheme; and
   (b) specify what is in the opinion of the local authority the highest number of individuals or households who should, having regard to the considerations set out in subsections (1) to (3) of section 161, live in the house having regard to its existing condition and to its future condition as the works progress which the authority carry out in the house; and
   (c) include an estimate of the balances which will from time to time accrue to the local authority out of the net amount of the rent and other payments received by the authority from persons occupying the house after deducting—
      (i) compensation payable by the authority under section 181 and section 183, and
      (ii) all expenditure, other than expenditure of which particulars are given under subsection (2), incurred by the authority in respect of the house while the control order is in force, together with the appropriate establishment charges.

(3) In this Schedule, references to surpluses on revenue account as settled by the scheme are references to the amount included in the scheme by way of an estimate under sub-paragraph (2)(c), subject to any variation of the scheme made by the local authority under sub-paragraph (4), or made by the sheriff on an appeal or an application under the following provisions of this Schedule.

(4) The local authority may at any time vary the scheme in such a way as to increase the amount of the surpluses on revenue account as settled by the scheme for all or any periods (including past periods).

Recovery by local authority of capital expenditure

2.—(1) Account shall be kept by the local authority for the period during which a control order is in force showing—
   (a) the surpluses on revenue account as settled by the management scheme, and
   (b) the expenditure incurred by the authority in carrying out works of which particulars were given in the scheme.

(2) Balances shall be struck in the account at half-yearly intervals so as to ascertain the amount of expenditure under sub-paragraph (1)(b) which cannot be set off against the said surpluses on revenue account, and (except where the control order is revoked by the sheriff on an appeal against the control order and the account under this section is no longer needed) the final balance shall be struck at the date when the control order ceases to have effect.

(3) So far as, at the end of any half-yearly period, expenditure is not set off against the said surpluses on revenue account, the expenditure shall, for the purposes of this paragraph, carry interest at such reasonable rate as the local authority may determine until it is to set off or until a demand for such expenditure is served by local authority under section 109(1), as applied by sub-paragraph (6).

(4) So far as there is any sum out of the said surpluses on revenue account not required to meet any expenditure incurred by the local authority, it shall go to meet interest under sub-paragraph (3).

(5) Except where the control is revoked by the sheriff on an appeal against the control order under the following provisions of this Schedule, on and after the time when the control order ceases to have effect the expenditure reasonably incurred by the local authority in carrying out works of which particulars were given in the scheme, together with interest as provided in this paragraph, shall, so far as not set off in accordance with this paragraph against the surpluses on revenue account as settled by the scheme, be recoverable from the dispossessed proprietor.

(6) Sections 108(6) (exercise of power of local authority to secure repair of house in state of serious disrepair without prejudice to other powers) and 109 (recovery by local authority of expenses) shall, subject to any necessary modifications, apply for the purpose of enabling the local authority to recover from the dispossessed proprietor any expenditure which, by virtue of sub-paragraph (5), is recoverable from him as they apply for the purpose of enabling a local authority to recover expenses incurred by them in executing works under sections 108(3) to (5) and 109(1).

(7) Sections 111 (appeals) and 112 (date of operation of notices, etc) shall apply in relation to a demand by the local authority for the recovery of any such expenditure and to an order made by the local authority with respect to any such expenditure as they apply in relation to a demand for the recovery of expenses incurred by a local authority in executing works under section 108(3) to (5) and to an order made by a local authority with respect to an order made by a local authority with respect to any such expenses.

(8) The local authority may make a charging order in favour of themselves in respect of any such expenditure, and Schedule 9 shall, with any necessary modifications, apply to a charging order so made in like manner as it applies to a charging order made under that Schedule.

(9) Section 178(2) shall not apply so as to restrict the effect of any charging order made by virtue of sub-paragraph (8) to the part of the house to which a control order is applied.

(10) For the purposes of this paragraph, references to the provisions of a scheme include references to those provisions as varied under the Schedule and if when the control order ceases to have effect, proceedings under the following provisions of this Schedule are pending which may result in a variation of the scheme, those proceedings may be continued until finally determined; and if any expenditure which, by virtue of sub-paragraph (5), is recoverable from the dispossessed proprietor is recovered from him before the final determination of those proceedings, the local authority shall be liable to account for any money so recovered which, having regard to the decision in the proceedings as finally determined, they ought not to have recovered.

Part II
Appeal and Review

3.—(1) Within 6 weeks from the date on which a copy of the relevant scheme is served in accordance with section 184(1), any person having an estate or interest in the house may appeal to the sheriff against the scheme on all or any of the following grounds, that is to say—
- (a) that having regard to the condition of the house and to the other circumstances, any of the works of which particulars are given in the scheme (whether already carried out or not) are unreasonable in character or extent, or are unnecessary;
- (b) that any of the works do not involve expenditure which ought to be regarded as capital expenditure;
- (c) that the number of individuals or households living in the house, as specified by the local authority in the scheme, is unreasonably low;
- (d) that the estimate of the surpluses on revenue account in the scheme is unduly low on account of some assumptions, whether as to rents charged by the local authority or otherwise, made by the authority in arriving at the estimate as to matters, which are within the control of the authority.

(2) On an appeal under this paragraph the sheriff may, as he thinks fit, confirm or vary the scheme.

(3) If an appeal has been brought against the control order and the sheriff decides on the appeal to revoke the control order, the sheriff shall not proceed with any appeal against the scheme relating to that control order.

(4) Proceedings on an appeal against a scheme shall, so far as practicable, be combined with proceedings on any appeal against the control order to which the scheme relates. [1009]

4.—(1) Without prejudice to the right of appeal against a scheme conferred by paragraph 3, either the local authority or any person having an estate or interest in the house to which the scheme relates may at any time apply to the sheriff for a review of the estimate of the surpluses on revenue account in the scheme.

(2) On an application under this paragraph, the sheriff may, as he thinks fit, confirm or vary the scheme, but the sheriff shall not on such an application vary the scheme so as to affect the provisions thereof relating to the works.

(3) On an application under this paragraph the surpluses on revenue account as settled by the scheme may be varied for all or any periods including past periods, and the sheriff shall take into consideration whether in the period since the control order came into force the actual balances mentioned in paragraph 1(2)(c) have exceeded, or been less than, the surpluses on revenue account as settled by the scheme as for the time being in force, and shall also take into consideration whether there has been any change in circumstances such that the number of persons or households who should live in the house, or the net amount of the rents and other payments receivable by the local authority from persons occupying the house, ought to be greater or less than was originally estimated.

5.—(1) If a local authority refuse an application to revoke a control order under section 188(4) or do not within 42 days from the making of the application or within such further period as the applicant may in writing allow, inform the applicant of their decision on the application, the applicant may appeal to the sheriff, and the sheriff may revoke the control order:
Provided that, if an appeal has been brought under this paragraph then, except with the leave of the sheriff, another appeal shall not be so brought, whether by the same or a different appellant, in respect of the same control order until the expiry of a period of 6 months beginning with the final determination of the first-mentioned appeal.

(2) If on an appeal under this paragraph the local authority represent to the sheriff that revocation of the control order would unreasonably delay completion of any works of which particulars were given in the relevant scheme under Part VIII and which the authority have begun to carry out, the sheriff shall take the representations into account and may, if he thinks fit, revoke the control order as from the time when the works are completed.

(3) If an appellant under this paragraph has an estate or interest in the house which, apart from the rights conferred on the local authority by the provisions of Part VIII relating to control orders, and apart from the rights of persons occupying any part of the house, would give him the right to possession of the house, and that estate or interest was, when the control order came into force, subject to a lease for a term of years which has subsequently expired, then, if that person sastisfies the sheriff that he is in a position and intends, if the control order is revoked, to demolish or reconstruct the house or to carry out substantial work of construction on the site of the house, the sheriff shall revoke the control order.

(4) Where in a case falling under sub-paragraph (3), the sheriff is not satisfied as therein mentioned, but would be so satisfied if the date of revocation of the control order were a date later than the date of the hearing of the appeal, the sheriff shall, if the appellant so requires, make an order for the revocation of the control order on that later date.

(5) Where the sheriff on an appeal under sub-paragraph (1) decides to revoke a control order in respect of a house from the dispossessed proprietor of which any amount will be

recoverable by virtue of Part VIII, the sheriff may make it a condition of the revocation of the control order that the appellant first pays off to the local authority that amount, or such part of that amount, as the sheriff may specify.

(6) Where the sheriff on an appeal under sub-paragraph (1) revokes a control order, he may authorise the local authority to create under section 179(2) interests which expire, or which the dispossessed proprietor can terminate, within 6 months from the time when the control order ceases to have effect being interests which, notwithstanding subsection (3) of that section, are for a fixed term exceeding one month, or are terminable by notice to quit (or an equivalent notice) of more than 4 weeks.

(7) Where a control order is revoked by the local authority under section 188(2), or by the sheriff on an appeal under sub-paragraph (1), the local authority shall as soon as practicable thereafter cause to be recorded in the General Register of Sasines or registered in the Land Register, as the case may be, the revocation order made by them or, as the case may be, a notice stating that the control has been revoked by the sheriff as aforesaid. **[1010]**

6.—(1) A sheriff who revokes a control order on appeal may authorise the local authority to create under section 179(2) interests which expire, or which the dispossessed proprietor can terminate, within 6 months from the time when the control order ceases to have effect, being interests which, notwithstanding subsection (3) of section 179, are for a fixed term exceeding one month, or are terminable by notice to quit (or an equivalent notice) of more than 4 weeks.

(2) The sheriff shall take into consideration whether the state or condition of the house is such that any action ought to be taken by the local authority under the provisions of Part VIII (other than those relating to control orders) and shall take all or any of the following steps accordingly, that is to say—
  (a) approve the making of an order under section 157;
  (b) approve the giving of a notice under section 160 or section 161 or section 162; or
  (c) approve the giving of a direction under section 166;
and no appeal against any order or notice so approved shall lie under section 158 or section 163.

(3) In respect of the period from the coming into force of the control order until its revocation by the sheriff, the local authority shall, subject to this paragraph, be liable to pay to the dispossessed proprietor the balances which from time to time accrued to the authority out of the net amount of the rent and other payments received by the authority while the control order was in force from persons occupying the house after deducting—
  (a) compensation payable by the local authority under section 181 and section 183, and
  (b) all expenditure, other than capital expenditure, incurred by the local authority in respect of the house while the control order was in force, together with the appropriate establishment charges.

(4) If the sheriff is satisfied that the balances which the local authority are, under sub-paragraph (3), liable to pay to the dispossessed proprietor are unduly low for any reason within the control of the authority, having regard to the desirability of observing the standards of management contained in regulations made under section 156 and to the other standards which the authority ought to observe as to the number of persons living in the house and the rents which they ought to charge, the sheriff shall direct that, for the purposes of the authority's liability to the dispossessed proprietor under this paragraph, the balances under sub-paragraph (3) shall be deemed to be such greater sums as the sheriff may direct:
Provided that the sheriff shall not under this sub-paragraph give a direction which will afford to the dispossessed proprietor a sum greater than what he may, in the opinion of the sheriff, have lost by the making of the control order.

(5) If different persons are dispossessed proprietors in relation to different parts of the

house, sums payable under this paragraph by the local authority shall be apportioned between them in the manner provided by section 183(5).

(6) For the purpose of enabling the local authority to recover capital expenditure incurred by them in carrying out works in the house in the period before the control order is revoked, the authority may on the hearing of the appeal apply to the sheriff for approval of those works on the ground that they were works which, if a control order had not been in force, the authority could have required some other person to carry out under the foregoing provisions of Part VIII (other than those relating to control orders), or under any other enactment relating to housing or public health, and that the carrying out of the works could not be postponed until after the determination of the appeal because the works were urgently required for the sake of the safety, welfare or health of the persons living in the house, or other persons.

(7) Any expenditure reasonably incurred by the local authority in carrying out works approved under sub-paragraph (6)—
  (a) may be deducted by the local authority out of the balances which the authority are, under sub-paragraph (3), liable to pay to the dispossessed proprietor;
  (b) so far as not so deducted, shall be recoverable from the dispossessed proprietor.

(8) Any expenditure recoverable by the local authority from the dispossessed proprietor by virtue of sub-paragraph (7)(b) shall carry interest at such reasonable rate as the local authority may determine from the date when the control order is revoked; and sub-paragraph (6) to (8) of paragraph 2 shall, with any necessary modifications, apply for the purpose of enabling the authority to recover any such expenditure. **[1011]**

Powers of court to restrict recovery of possession

7.—(1) The provisions of this paragraph apply where—
  (a) a local authority have made an order under Part I of Schedule 1 to the Acquisition of Land (Authorisation Procedure) (Scotland) Act 1947, as applied to the acquisition of land under this Act (other than section 121) authorising the compulsory acquisition of a house which is let in lodgings or which is occupied by members of more than one family; and
  (b) any premises forming part of that house are at a time in the relevant period occupied by a person (in this paragraph referred to as 'the former lessee') who was the lessee of those premises when the order was made or became the lessee thereof after the order was made, but who is no longer the lessee thereof.

(2) In this paragraph 'the relevant period' means the period beginning with the making of that order and ending on the third anniversary of the date on which the order becomes operative or, if at a time before the expiration of the said period, the Secretary of State notifies the local authority that he declines to confirm the order, or the order is quashed by a court, the period beginning with the making of the order and ending with that time.

(3) Subject to the provisions of this paragraph, in proceedings in any court of competent jurisdiction instituted during the relevant period to enforce against the former lessee the right to recover possession of the premises the court may if it thinks fit—
  (a) suspend the execution of any decree of removing or warrant of ejection or other like order made in the proceedings for such period, not extending beyond the end of the period of three years beginning on the relevant date and subject to such conditions, if any, as the court thinks fit; and
  (b) from time to time vary the period of suspension (but not so as to enlarge that period beyond the end of the said period of 3 years, or terminate it), and vary the terms of the said decree, warrant or other like order in other respects.

(4) For the purposes of sub-paragraph (3), 'the relevant date' means—
  (a) if the compulsory purchase order concerned has become operative before the date on which the court exercises its powers under that sub-paragraph, the date on which the order became operative; and

(b) in any other case the date on which the court exercises or, as the case may be, exercised its power and paragraph (a) of that sub-paragraph in relation to the decree of removing or warrant of ejection or other like order in question.

(5) If at any time the Secretary of State notifies the local authority that he declines to confirm the compulsory purchase order, or that order is quashed by a court, or, whether before or after that order has been submitted to the Secretary of State for confirmation, the authority decide not to proceed with it, it shall be the duty of the authority to notify the person entitled to the benefit of the decree of removing or warrant of ejection or other like order, and that person shall be entitled, on applying to the court, to obtain an order terminating the period of suspension, but subject to the exercise of such discretion in fixing the date on which possession is to be given as the court might exercise apart from this sub-paragraph if it were then making such a decree, warrant or other like order for the first time.

(6) Sub-paragraphs (3) to (5) shall not apply where the person entitled to possession of the premises is the local authority. **[1012]**

Part III
Consequences of Cessation of Control Order

Transfer of landlord's interest in tenancies and agreements

8.—(1) On and after the date on which the control order ceases to have effect any lease, licence or agreement in which the local authority were substituted for any other party by virtue of section 180 shall have effect as if for the authority there were substituted in the lease, licence or agreement the original party or his successor in title.

(2) On and after the date on which the control order ceases to have effect any agreement in the nature of a lease or licence created by the local authority shall have effect as if the dispossessed proprietor were substituted in the agreement for the authority.

(3) If the dispossessed proprietor is a lessee, nothing in any superior lease shall impose any liability on the dispossessed proprietor or any superior lessee in respect of anything done in pursuance of the terms of an agreement in which the dispossessed proprietor is substituted for the local authority by virtue of this paragraph. **[1013]**

Cases where leases have been modified while control order was in force

9.—If under section 185 the sheriff modifies or determines a lease, the sheriff may include in the order modifying or determining the lease provisions for modifying the effect of paragraph 8 in relation to the lease. **[1014]**

Interpretation

10.—References in this Part of this Schedule to the control order ceasing to have effect are references to its ceasing to have effect whether on revocation or in any other circumstances. **[1015]**

Part IV
Recovery of Expenses by Local Authority Executing Works under Section 164

11.—(1) Sections 108(6) (exercise of power of local authority to secure repair of house in state of serious disrepair without prejudice to other powers) and 109 (recovery by local authority of expenses) shall, subject to any necessary modifications, apply for the purpose of enabling a local authority to recover any expenses reasonably incurred by them in carrying out works under section 164 as they apply for the purpose of enabling a

local authority to recover expenses incurred by them in executing works under section 108(3), but—
  (a) the person from whom such expenses may be recovered shall be the person on whom the notice was served, and
  (b) if that person was only properly served with the notice as trustee, tutor, curator, factor or agent for or of some other person, then the expenses may be recovered either from him or from that other person, or in part from him and in part from that other person.

(2) Sections 111 (Appeals) and 112 (Date of operation of notices etc) shall apply in relation to a demand by a local authority for the recovery of such expenses and to an order made by a local authority with respect to any such expenses as they apply in relation to a demand for the recovery of expenses incurred by a local authority in executing works under section 108(3) and to an order made by a local authority with respect to any such expenses.

(3) Where a local authority have incurred such expenses, it shall be competent for them to make a charging order in favour of themselves in respect of such expenses; and Schedule 9 shall, with any necessary modifications, apply to a charging order so made in like manner as it applies to a charging order made under that Schedule.

(4) If a local authority apply to the sheriff and satisfy him—
  (a) that any such expenses reasonably incurred by them (with the interest accrued due thereon) have not been, and are unlikely to be, recovered, and
  (b) that some person is profiting by the execution of the works in respect of which the expenses were incurred to obtain rents or other payments which would not have been obtainable if those works had not been executed,
the sheriff, if satisfied that that person has had proper notice of the application, may order him to make such payment or payments to the local authority as may appear to the sheriff to be just. [1016]

NOTES to Schedule 11
Definitions: 'local authority', 'house': see s 338 above; 'lease', 'lessee', 'licence': see s 190 above.

Section 199   SCHEDULE 12

TERMINATION OF EXCHEQUER PAYMENTS TO LOCAL AUTHORITIES AND CERTAIN PERIODICAL PAYMENTS TO OTHER PERSONS

1.—(1) No payment shall be made—
  (a) for the year 1979–80 or any subsequent year to a local authority under any of the enactments specified in Part I of the Table in paragraph 2;
  (b) for the year 1978–79 or any subsequent year to—
    (i) the Scottish Special Housing Association under any of the enactments specified in Parts II or III of that Table;
    (ii) a development corporation under any of the enactments specified in Part II of that Table.

(2) The right of a local authority to receive any payment under any of the enactments specified in Part I of that Table or section 105 of the Housing (Scotland) Act 1950 shall be extinguished unless an application has been made for the payment before 31st March 1980 or such later date as the Secretary of State may in exceptional circumstances allow.

(3) Subject to the following provisions of this paragraph, where—
  (a) information given to the Secretary of State on any such application as is mentioned in sub-paragraph (2) for a payment includes any particulars which are, and are stated to be, based on an estimate; and
  (b) it appears to the Secretary of State—
    (i) that the estimate is reasonable, and

(ii) that, assuming the estimate were correct, the information and other particulars given on the application are sufficient to enable him to determine the amount of the payment;

the Secretary of State may accept the estimate and make a payment accordingly.

(4) Any payment made in pursuance of sub-paragraph (3) so far as it is based on an estimate of the cost of land may be adjusted when the final cost of the land is ascertained.

(5) Where any payment is made in pursuance of sub-paragraph (3), the recipient shall not be entitled to question the amount of the payment on a ground which means that the estimate was incorrect.

(6) Where the Secretary of State is not satisfied that the estimate is reasonable, he may, if he thinks fit, accept the application and make a payment of such amount as appears to him reasonable.

(7) No housing association grant under Part II of the Housing Association Act 1985 shall be paid to a local authority, the Association or a development corporation in respect of any project completed after 31st March 1979.

(8) No payment shall be made for the year 1979–80 or any subsequent year under—
(a) section 27(1) of the Housing (Scotland) Act 1949, section 89(1) of the Housing (Scotland) Act 1950 or section 21(1) of the 1968 Act (exchequer contributions for hostels); or
(b) section 33 of the Housing Act 1974 or section 55 of the Housing Associations Act 1985 (hostel deficit grants),

to a local authority, the Association or a development corporation.

TABLE

PART I

Payments to local authorities

Chapter	Act	Section
1968 c 31	The Housing (Financial Provisions) (Scotland) Act 1968.	Section 13.
1969 c 34	The Housing (Scotland) Act 1969.	Section 59(1) so far as the payments thereunder relate to land to which the housing revenue account relates.
1972 c 46	The Housing (Financial Provisions) (Scotland) Act 1972.	Sections 2, 3 and 4.

PART II

Payments to Scottish Special Housing Association and development corporations

Chapter	Act	Section
1968 c 31	The Housing (Financial Provisions) (Scotland) Act 1968.	Section 13.
1969 c 34	The Housing (Scotland) Act 1969.	Section 59(1).
1972 c 46	The Housing (Financial Provisions) (Scotland) Act 1972.	Sections 8, 9 and 10.

* * *

Housing (Scotland) Act 1987 (c 26), Sch 15 [1021]

NOTES to Schedule 12
Amendment: In paragraph 2, Part III was repealed by the Housing (Scotland) Act 1988 (c 43), s 3, Sch 2, para 15.
Definitions: 'local authority', 'development corporation', 'land': see s 338 above; 'hostel': *Ibid* and s 2(5) above.

Section 201(4)   SCHEDULE 13

ENACTMENTS SPECIFYING EXCHEQUER CONTRIBUTIONS

The Housing (Scotland) Act 1950.

The Housing (Scotland) Act 1962, Part I.

The Housing (Financial Provisions) (Scotland) Act 1968.

★ ★ ★   [1019]

NOTES to Schedule 13
Amendment: Schedule 13 was repealed in part by the Housing (Scotland) Act 1988 (c 43), s 72, Sch 10.

Section 201(5)   SCHEDULE 14

ENACTMENTS SPECIFYING EXCHEQUER CONTRIBUTIONS THAT MAY BE REDUCED, SUSPENDED OR DISCONTINUED

The Housing (Scotland) Act 1950, sections 105, 110 and 121.

The Housing (Scotland) Act 1962, sections 12(3) and 14.

The Housing (Financial Provisions) (Scotland) Act 1978, Part I, Part II (except sections 26 and 50) and section 58(4).

. . .

The Housing (Financial Provisions) (Scotland) Act 1972, Part 1.

. . .

★ ★ ★   [1020]

NOTES to Schedule 14
Amendment: Schedule 14 was repealed in part by the Housing (Scotland) Act 1988 (c 43), s 72, Sch 10.

Section 203   SCHEDULE 15

THE HOUSING REVENUE ACCOUNT

PART I
APPLICATION OF ACCOUNT

1.—(1) The houses, buildings and land specified for the purposes of section 203(1) (the housing revenue account) are—
(a) all houses and other buildings which have been provided after 12th February 1919 for the purpose of—
    (i) Part III of the Housing (Scotland) Act 1925, or
    (ii) any enactment relating to the provision of housing accommodation for the working classes repealed by that Act, or
    (iii) Part V of the Housing (Scotland) Act 1950, or
    (iv) Part VII of the Act of 1966, or

(v) Part I of this Act;
(b) all land which after that date has been acquired or appropriated for the purposes of any of the enactments mentioned or referred to in paragraph (a) including—
  (i) all land which is deemed to have been acquired under Part III of the said Act of 1925 by virtue of section 15(4) of the Housing (Scotland) Act 1935, and
  (ii) any structures on such land which were made available to a local authority under section 1 of the Housing (Temporary Accommodation) Act 1944;
(c) all dwellings provided or improved by the local authority in accordance with improvement proposals approved by the Secretary of State under—
  (i) section 2 of the Housing (Scotland) Act 1949, or
  (ii) section 105 of the said Act of 1950, or
  (iii) section 13 of the Act of 1968,
  and all land acquired or appropriated by the authority for the purpose of carrying out such proposals;
(d) all houses in housing action areas within the meaning of Part II of the Housing (Scotland) Act 1974 or Part IV of this Act which have been purchased by the local authority under Part II of the said Act of 1974 or Part IV of this Act for the purpose of bringing them or another house up to the standard specifed under section 16(3) or by virtue of section 17(3) of the Housing (Scotland) Act 1974 or section 90(3) or 91(3) of this Act;
(e) all buildings provided or converted for use as lodging houses (that is to say houses not occupied as separate dwellings) or hostels as defined in section 138(4) of the Act of 1966 and section 2(5) of this Act or as parts of lodging houses or hostels.

(2) Where a house is for the time being vested in a local authority by reason of the default of any person in carrying out the terms of any arrangements under which assistance in respect of the provision, reconstruction or improvement of the house has been given under any enactment relating to housing, the house shall be deemed for the purposes of sub-paragraph (1) to be a house which has been provided by the authority under Part VII of the Act of 1966 or Part I of this Act.

(3) The houses and other property to which a local authority's housing revenue account relates shall include any property brought within the account before 27th August 1972—
(a) with the consent of the Secretary of State given under section 60(1)(f) of the Act of 1968, or
(b) by virtue of subsection (2) of the said section (house vesting in local authority on default of another person). **[1021]**

PART II
OPERATION OF ACCOUNT

Credits

2.—(1) For each year a local authority shall carry to the credit of the housing revenue account amounts equal to—
(a) the income receivable by the local authority from standard rents;
(b) any income receivable by the local authority for that year in respect of service charges, supplementary charges, feuduties and any other charges in respect of houses and other property to which the account relates;
(c) the housing support grant payable to the local authority for that year;
(d) any income receivable by the local authority for that year in respect of all such buildings as are referred to in paragraph 1(1)(e);
(e) any payments received by the local authority from another local authority in pursuance of any overspill agreement, being payments such as are mentioned in paragraph 3(f) of this Schedule;
(f) any contributions received by the local authority under section 101(1) of the Housing Act 1964 or section 235, in so far as amounts equal to the expenditure towards which those contributions are made fall to be debited to the account;

(g) income, and receipts in the nature of income, being income or receipts arising for that year from the investment or other use of money carried to the account;
(h) any other income of any description, except a contribution out of the general fund kept under section 93 of the Local Government (Scotland) Act 1973, receivable by the local authority for that year, being income relating to expenditure falling to be debited to the account for that year;
(i) such other income of the local authority as the Secretary of State may direct.

(2) Subject to sub-paragraph (3), where any house or other property to which the account relates has been sold or otherwise disposed of, an amount equal to any income of the local authority arising from the investment or other use of capital money received by the authority in respect of the transaction shall be carried to the credit of the account.

(3) Sub-paragraph (2) shall not apply—
(a) where the Secretary of State otherwise directs as respects the whole or any part of such income, or
(b) as respects income from capital money carried to a capital fund under paragraph 23 of Schedule 3 to the Local Government (Scotland) Act 1975.

(4) An amount equal to any income of the local authority arising from an investment or other use of borrowed moneys in respect of which the authority are required under paragraph 3 below to debit loan charges to the account shall be carried to the credit of the account.

(5) For any year, the local authority may, with the consent of the Secretary of State, carry to the credit of the account, in addition to the amounts required by the foregoing provisions of this Schedule, such further amounts, if any, as they think fit. **[1022]**

Debits

3.—Subject to paragraph 4 of this Schedule, for each year a local authority shall debit to the housing revenue account amounts equal to—
(a) the loan charges which the local authority are liable to pay for that year in respect of money borrowed by a local authority for the purpose of—
   (i) the provision by them after 12th February 1919 of housing accommodation under the enactments referred to in paragraph 1(1)(a),
   (ii) the provision or improvement by them of dwellings in accordance with improvement proposals approved by the Secretary of State under section 2 of the Housing (Scotland) Act 1949 or under section 105 of the Housing (Scotland) Act 1950 or under section 13 of the Act of 1968,
   (iii) meeting expenditure on the repair of houses and other property to which the account relates,
   (iv) the improvement of amenities of residential areas under section 251 on land to which the account relates,
   (v) the alteration, enlargement or improvement under section 2(3) of any house:
Provided that a local authority may, with the approval of the Secretary of State, debit to the account any payments, of which the amount and period over which they are payable have been approved by him, to meet outstanding capital debt in respect of any house which, being a house to which the account related—
   (a) was demolished after 27th July 1972; or
   (b) was disposed of after 25th May 1978;
(b) the taxes, feuduties, rents and other charges which the local authority are liable to pay for that year in respect of houses and other property to which the account relates;
(c) the expenditure incurred by the local authority for that year in respect of the repair, maintenance, supervision and management of houses and other property to which the account relates, other than the expenditure incurred by them in the administration of a rent rebate scheme;
(d) the expenditure incurred by the local authority for that year in respect of all such buildings as are referred to in paragraph 1(1)(e);

(e) the arrears of rent which have been written off in that year as irrecoverable, and the income receivable from any houses to which the account relates during any period in that year when they were not let;
(f) any payments made by the local authority to another local authority or a development corporation in pursuance of any overspill agreement, being payments towards expenditure which, if it had been incurred by the first-mentioned authority, would have been debited by them to their housing revenue account in pursuance of this paragraph;
(g) such other expenditure incurred by the local authority as the Secretary of State directs shall be debited to the housing revenue account. **[1023]**

4.—A local authority shall not debit to the housing revenue account amounts equal to—
(a) expenditure on the provision of anything under section 3 or 5 (which relate respectively to the powers of a local authority to provide shops, etc, and laundry facilities) or the supply of anything under section 4 (which relates to the power of a local authority to provide furniture, etc), or
(b) any part of expenditure attributable to site works and services of a house or houses or other property to which the housing revenue account relates which exceeds the expenditure required for the provision of the house or houses or other property:
Provided that nothing in sub-paragraph (a) shall apply to expenditure on the provision of—
(i) anything referred to in paragraphs (a) and (b) of section 211(1) in respect of which the local authority are required to make a service charge;
(ii) any garage, car-port or other car-parking facilities provided by the local authority under the terms of the tenancy of a house,
and the exclusion from the housing revenue account of expenditure on the supply or provision of anything under sections 4 or 5 shall not extend to such expenditure when incurred in relation to a hostel or a lodging-house. **[1024]**

Supplemental

5.—Any requirement of this Schedule as respects any amount to be debited or credited to the account may be met by taking in the first instance an estimate of the amount, and by making adjustments in the account for a later year when the amount is more accurately known or is finally ascertained. **[1025]**

6.—A local authority may, with the consent of the Secretary of State, exclude from the housing revenue account any of the items of income or expenditure mentioned in the foregoing provisions of this Schedule, or may with such consent include any items of income or expenditure not mentioned in those foregoing provisions. **[1026]**

7.—Where it appears to the Secretary of State that amounts in respect of any items of income or expenditure other than those mentioned in the foregoing provisions of this Schedule ought properly to be credited or debited to a housing revenue account, or that amounts in respect of any of the items of income and expenditure mentioned in the foregoing provisions of this Schedule which ought properly to have been credited or debited to the account have not been so credited or debited, or that any amounts have been improperly credited or debited to the account, he may, after consultation with the local authority, give directions for the appropriate credits or debits to be made or for the rectification of the account, as the case may require. **[1027]**

8.—The Secretary of State may direct that items of income or expenditure, either generally or of a specific category, shall be included in or excluded from the account. **[1028]**

9.—(1) If at any time a credit balance is shown in the housing revenue account, the whole or part of it may be made available for any purpose for which the general fund of the local authority maintained under section 93 of the Local Government (Scotland) Act 1973 may lawfully be applied.

(2) If for any year a deficit is shown in the said account, the local authority shall carry to the credit of the account a . . . contribution [out of the said general fund] of an amount equal to the deficit. **[1028A]**

10.—References in this Schedule to houses and other property to which the housing revenue account of a local authority relates shall be construed as references to houses, buildings, land and dwellings in repect of which the authority are required by section 203 and Part I of this Schedule to keep the account. **[1029]**

NOTES to Schedule 15
Amendment: Para 9(2) was amended by the Housing (Scotland) Act 1988 (c 43), s 72, Sch 8, para 10.
Definitions: 'house', 'land', 'overspill agreement', 'local authority': see s 338 above; 'housing action area': see ss 89–91 above; 'hostel': see ss 338 and 2(5) above; 'housing support grant': see ss 338 and 191 above.

Section 207(3) SCHEDULE 16

The Slum Clearance Revenue Account

Credits

1.—For each year a local authority shall carry to the credit of the slum clearance revenue account amount equal to—
(a) the income from the rents, feuduties and other charges in respect of houses and other property to which the account relates;
. . .
(c) any income from the investment or other use of capital obtained from the disposal of houses and other property to which the account relates;
(d) any expenses incurred by the local authority in the demolition of a building to which the account relates which they have recovered from the owner of the building;
(e) such other income of the local authority as the Secretary of State may direct. **[1030]**

2.—Where for any year a deficit is shown in the account, the local authority shall carry to the credit of the account in respect of that year an amount equal to the amount of the deficit. **[1031]**

Debits

3.—For each year a local authority shall debit to the slum clearance revenue account amounts equal to—
(a) the loan charges which the local authority are liable to pay for that year referable to the amount of expenditure incurred by the local authority which falls within section 207(2);
(b) the taxes, feuduties, rents and other charges which the local authority are liable to pay for that year in respect of houses and other property to which the account relates;
(c) the expenditure incurred by the local authority for that year in respect of the repair, maintenance, supervision and management of houses and other property to which the account relates;
(d) the expenditure incurred by the local authority for that year in respect of the purchase, demolition, and clearance of sites of houses and other property to which the account relates where that expenditure is not met from capital;

(e) the arrears of rent which have been written off in that year as irrecoverable and the income receivable from any houses to which the account relates during any period in that year when they were not let;
(f) such other expenditure incurred by the local authority as the Secretary of State directs. **[1032]**

Supplemental

4.—Any surplus shown in a slum clearance revenue account at the end of a year shall be credited to the general fund kept under section 93 of the Local Government (Scotland) Act 1973. **[1033]**

5.—A local authority may, with the consent of the Secretary of State, exclude from the slum clearance revenue account any of the items of income or expenditure mentioned in the foregoing provisions of this Schedule, or may with such consent include any items of income or expenditure not mentioned in those foregoing provisions. **[1034]**

6.—The Secretary of State may direct that items of income or expenditure either generally or of a specific category, shall be included in or excluded from the slum clearance revenue account. **[1035]**

NOTES to Schedule 16
Amendment: Sub-s 1(b) was repealed by the Housing (Scotland) Act 1988 (c 43), s 57, Sch 10.
Definitions: 'local authority', 'house': see s 338 above.

Section 214(8) SCHEDULE 17

CONDITIONS RELATING TO HOUSE LOANS

1.—The provisions of this Schedule shall have effect with respect to an advance under section 214. **[1036]**

2.—The advance, together with interest thereon, shall be secured by a heritable security. **[1037]**

3.—The amount of the principal of the advance shall not exceed the value of the subjects disponed or assigned in security, or as the case may be, the value which it is estimated the subjects disponed or assigned in security will bear when the construction, conversion, alteration, enlargement, repair or improvement has been carried out. **[1038]**

4.—The heritable security shall provide for repayment of the principal—
(a) by instalments (of equal or unequal amounts) beginning either on the date of the advance or at a later date, or
(b) at the end of a fixed period (with or without a provision allowing the local authority to extend that period) or on the happening of a specified event before the end of that period. **[1039]**

5.—It shall also provide for the payment of instalments of interest throughout the period beginning on the date of the advance and ending when the whole of the principal is repaid. **[1040A]**

6.—In the event of any of the conditions subject to which the advance is made not being complied with, the balance for the time being unpaid shall become repayable on demand by the local authority. **[1040B]**

7.—That balance may in any event be repaid at any term of Whitsunday or Martinmas by the debtor after one month's written notice of intention to repay has been given to the authority. **[1041]**

8.—Where the advance is for any of the purposes specified in paragraphs (b) to (d) of section 214(1) it may be made by instalments from time to time as the works of construction, conversion, alteration, enlargement, repair or improvement progress. **[1042]**

9.—The advance shall not be made except after a valuation duly made on behalf of the local authority. **[1043]**

10.—No advance shall be made unless the estate or interest in the lands proposed to be disponed or assigned in security is either ownership or a lease of which a period of not less than 10 years in excess of the period fixed for the repayment of the advance remains unexpired on the date on which the security is granted. **[1044]**

11.—In this Schedule, any reference, in relation to an advance, to a heritable security shall include a reference to such heritable security as may be agreed between the parties making and receiving the advance. **[1045]**

NOTE to Schedule 17
Definition: 'local authority': see s 338 above.

SCHEDULE 18

Standard Amenities

[Part I
List of Amenities and Maximum Eligible Amounts

Description of amenity	Maximum Eligible Amount
Fixed bath or shower	£450
Hot and cold water supply at a fixed bath or shower	£570
Wash-hand basin	£170
Hot and cold water supply at a wash-hand basin	£305
Sink	£450
Hot and cold water supply at a sink	£385
Water closet	£680]

[1045A]

Part II
Limit on Amount of Approved Expenses for Standard Amenities

1.—Subject to paragraph 3, the total amount of approved expense for the provision of standard amenities in respect of any one application shall not exceed the sum of the amounts allowable under the following provisions of this Part of this Schedule. **[1046]**

2.—Subject to paragraph 4, for each of the standard amenities provided there shall be allowed an amount of approved expense not exceeding the maximum eligible amount specified for an amenity of that description in the second column of Part I of this Schedule or the amount substituted therefor under the following provisions of this Part of this Schedule. **[1047]**

3.—Subject to the provisions of section 242, the maximum eligible amount specified in the second column of Part I of this Schedule may be exceeded by such amount as the local authority approved if the local authority are satisfied in any particular case that an increased estimate for the works is justifiable. **[1048]**

4.—An amount shall not be allowed for more than one amenity of the same description; and no amount shall be allowed for an amenity of any description if at the time the works were begun the house was provided with an amenity of that description, except where the works involved interference with or replacement of that amenity and the local authority are satisfied that it would not have been reasonably practicable to avoid the interference or replacement. **[1049]**

NOTES to Schedule 18
Amendment: Schedule 18 was amended by the Housing (Improvement and Repairs Grant) (Approved Expenses Maxima) (Scotland) Order 1987, SI 1987/2269, paras [1385] ff below.
Definition: 'local authority': see s 338 above.

Section 246(5)   SCHEDULE 19

CONSEQUENCES OF BREACH OF CONDITIONS OF IMPROVEMENT GRANT

1.—Subject to paragraphs 4 and 5, the local authority shall forthwith demand the repayment to them by the owner for the time being of the house of the whole amount of any sums paid by the authority by way of improvement grant in respect of the expenses incurred for the purpose of the execution of those works together with interest thereon for the period from the date of payment of the grant, or where the grant was paid in instalments, from the date of payment of the final settlement of the balance by the authority to the date of repayment to the authority. **[1050]**

2.—If the local authority are satisified that the breach of any condition is capable of being remedied, they may, with the consent of the Secretary of State and subject to such conditions (if any) as he may approve, direct that the operation of section 246 shall in relation to the breach be suspended for such period as appears to them to be necessary for enabling the breach to be remedied and if the breach is remedied within that period may direct that the said provisions shall not have effect in relation to the breach. **[1051]**

3.—If the local authority are satisfied that the breach although not capable of being remedied was not due to the act, default or connivance of the owner for the time being of the house, they may, with the like consent and subject to such conditions as mentioned in paragraph 2, direct that the said provisions shall not have effect in relation to the breach. **[1052]**

4.—Upon the satisfaction of a liability of an owner of a house to make payment under paragraph 1 above to a local authority observance with respect to the house of the conditions specified in section 246 shall cease to be required. **[1053]**

5.—On the application of the local authority, the sheriff within whose jurisdiction is situated any house with respect to which the conditions specified in section 246 are for the time being required to be observed may, whether or not any other relief is claimed, grant an interdict restraining a breach or apprehended breach in relation to the house of any of those conditions. **[1054]**

6.—(1) In any case where in pursuance of paragraph 4, observance of any conditions specified in section 246 ceases to be required with respect to a house the local authority shall so state in the notice mentioned in sub-paragraph (2) or the record mentioned in sub-paragraph (3).

(2) Where the applicant for the grant was not a tenant-at-will, or was a tenant-at-will who, since applying, has acquired his landlord's interest in the tenancy the local authority shall cause to be recorded in the General Register of Sasines or registered in the Land Register, as the case may be, a notice in the prescribed form.

(3) Where that applicant was, and continues to be, a tenant-at-will, the local authority shall keep a written record of the fact.

(4) The cost of such recording in the Register of Sasines or such registration in the Land Register shall be repaid to the authority by the owner of the house. **[1055]**

7.—In the event of a breach of any of the conditions specified in section 246 at a time when they are required to be observed with respect to a house it shall be competent for the local authority to make a charging order in favour of themselves for the amount that becomes payable to them by virtue of that Schedule in consequence of such a breach, and the provisions of Schedule 9 shall, subject to any necessary modifications, apply to a charging order so made in the manner as they apply to a charging order made under that Schedule. **[1056]**

8.—In this Schedule, 'interest' means compound interest calculated at such reasonable rate as the local authority may determine and with yearly rests. **[1057]**

NOTES to Schedule 19
Definitions: 'local authority', 'house', 'owner': see s 338 above; 'improvement grant': *Ibid* and s 236(1) above.

Section 275　　　　　　　　SCHEDULE 20

Assistance by way of Repurchase

Part I
The Agreement to Repurchase

The interest to be acquired

1.—In this Schedule, 'the interest to be acquired' means the interest of the person entitled to assistance by way of repurchase, so far as subsisting in—
(a)　the defective dwelling, and
(b)　any garage, outhouse, garden, yard and pertinents belonging to or usually enjoyed with the dwelling or a part of it. **[1058]**

Request for notice of proposed terms of acquisition

2.—A person who is entitled to assistance by way of repurchase may, within the period of three months beginning with the service of the notice of determination, or that period as extended, request the purchasing authority in writing to notify him of the proposed terms and conditions for their acquisition of the interest to be acquired. **[1059]**

Authority's notice of proposed terms

3.—The purchasing authority shall, within the period of three months beginning with the making of a request under paragraph 2, serve on the person so entitled [an offer to purchase] in writing specifying the proposed terms and conditions including those that are reasonably necessary to enable the authority to receive a good and marketable title and stating their opinion as to the value of the interest to be acquired. **[1060]**

Unreasonable terms

4.—Where an offer to purchase is served on the person so entitled and he wishes to sell but he considers that a term or condition contained in the offer to purchase is unreasonable, he may request the authority to strike out or vary the term or condition by serving on the authority, within one month after service of the offer to purchase, a notice in writing setting out his request; and if the authority agree they shall accordingly serve an amended offer to purchase within one month of service of the said notice setting out the request. **[1061]**

Appeal

5.—A person so entitled who is aggrieved by the refusal of an authority to agree to strike out or vary a term or condition or by their failure timeously to serve an amended offer to purchase may within one month of the refusal or failure apply by way of summary application to the sheriff for determination of the matter; and the sheriff may, as he thinks fit, uphold the term or condition or strike it out or vary it and where his determination results in a variation of the terms or conditions of the offer to purchase he shall order the authority to serve on the person entitled an amended offer to purchase within one month thereafter. **[1062]**

Notice of acceptance

6.—The person so entitled may at any time within the period of six months beginning with—
  (a) the service of the offer to purchase by the authority; or
  (b) the service of an amended offer to purchase under paragraph 4; or
  (c) the date of the determination of the sheriff;
serve a notice of acceptance on the authority. **[1063]**

Extensions

7.—The authority shall, if there are reasonable grounds for doing so, by notice in writing served on the person so entitled, extend (or further extend) the period within which—
  (a) under paragraph 2, he may request them to notify him of the terms and conditions proposed for their acquisition of the interest to be acquired;
  (b) under paragraph 4, he may request them to strike out or vary the term or condition;
  (c) under paragraph 5, he may apply to the sheriff for determination of a matter; or
  (d) under paragraph 6, he may serve a notice of acceptance on them;
whether or not the period has expired. **[1064]**

Interest acquired to be treated as if acquired under Part I

8.—An interest acquired by a local authority under this Part of this Schedule shall be treated as acquired under section 9. **[1065]**

Part II
Price Payable and Valuation

The price

9.—(1) The price payable for the acquisition of an interest in pursuance of this Part is 95 per cent of the value of the interest at the relevant time.

(2) In this Schedule, 'the relevant time' means the time at which the notice under

paragraph 3 (authority's notice of proposed terms of acquisition) is served on the person entitled to assistance. **[1066]**

The value

10.—(1) For the purposes of this Schedule, the value of an interest at the relevant time is the amount which, at that time, would be realised by a disposal of the interest on the open market by a willing seller to a person other than the purchasing authority on the following assumptions—
  (a) that none of the defective dwellings to which the designation in question relates is affected by the qualifying defect;
  (b) that no liability has arisen under the provisions in section 72;
  (c) that no obligation to acquire the interest arises under this Part; and
  (d) that (subject to the preceding paragraphs) the seller is selling with and subject to the rights and burdens with and subject to which the disposal is to be made.

(2) Where the value of an interest falls to be considered at a time later than the relevant time and there has been since the relevant time a material change in the circumstances affecting the value of the interest, the value at the relevant time shall be determined on the further assumption that the change had occurred before the relevant time.

(3) In determining the value of an interest no account shall be taken of any right to the grant of a tenancy under section 282 (former owner-occupier) or section 283 (former statutory tenant). **[1067]**

Determination of value

11.—(1) Any question arising under this Schedule as to the value of an interest in a defective dwelling shall be determined by the district valuer in accordance with this paragraph.

(2) The person entitled to assistance or the purchasing authority may require that value to be determined or redetermined by notice in writing served on the district valuer—
  (a) within the period beginning with the service on the person entitled to assistance of an offer to purchase under paragraph 3 (authority's notice of proposed terms of acquisition) and ending with the conclusion of missives; or
  (b) after the end of that period but before the parties enter into an agreement for the acquisition of the interest of the person so entitled, if there is a material change in the circumstances affecting the value of the interest.

(3) A person serving notice on the district valuer under this paragraph shall serve notice in writing of that fact on the other party.

(4) Before making a determination in pursuance of this paragraph, the district valuer shall consider any representation made to him, within four weeks of the service of the notice under this paragraph, by the person entitled to assistance or the purchasing authority. **[1068]**

Certain grant conditions cease to have effect

12.—Where the interest to be acquired is or includes a house in relation to which a grant has been made under Part XIII—
  (a) observance with respect to the house of any of the conditions specified in section 246 (conditions to be observed with respect to a house in respect of which a grant has been made) shall cease to be required with effect from the time of disposal of the interest and paragraph 6 of Schedule 19 (requirements as to records when observance of conditions ceases to be required) shall apply as it applies in the case there mentioned; and

(b) the owner for the time being of the house shall not be liable to make in relation to the grant any payment under Schedule 19 (consequences of breach of conditions) unless the liability to do so arises from a demand made before the time of disposal of the interest. **[1069]**

NOTES to Schedule 20
Amendment: Para 3 was amended by the Housing (Scotland) Act 1988 (c 43), s 72, Sch 7, para 29.
Definitions: 'defective dwelling': see ss 303, 257 and 287 above; 'dwelling': see s 302 above; 'person entitled to assistance': see ss 303 and 268 above; 'purchasing authority': see ss 303 and 276 above; 'local authority': see s 338 above; 'house': see s 302 above.

Section 294   SCHEDULE 21

DWELLINGS INCLUDED IN MORE THAN ONE DESIGNATION

Introductory

1.—This Schedule applies in relation to a defective dwelling where the building that the dwelling consists of or includes falls within two or more designations under section 257 (designation by Secretary of State) or 287 (designation under local scheme). **[1070]**

Cases in which later designation to be disregarded

2.—Where a person is already eligible for assistance in respect of a defective dwelling at a time when another designation comes into operation, the later designation shall be disregarded if—
(a) he would not be eligible for assistance in respect of the dwelling by virtue of that designation, or
(b) he is by virtue of an earlier designation entitled to assistance by way of repurchase in respect of the dwelling. **[1071]**

In other cases any applicable designation may be relied on

3.—Where a person is eligible for assistance in respect of a defective dwelling and there are two or more applicable designations, this part has effect in relation to the dwelling as if—
(a) references to the designation were to any applicable designation;
(b) references to the provision by virtue of which it is a defective dwelling were to any provision under which an applicable designation was made;
(c) references to the qualifying defect were to any qualifying defect described in an applicable designation;
(d) references to the period within which persons may seek assistance under this Part were to any period specified for that purpose in any applicable designation; and
(e) the reference in section 271(1)(c) (amount of reinstatement grant) to the maximum amount permitted to be taken into account for the purposes of that section were to the aggregate of the maximum amounts for each applicable designation. **[1072]**

Procedure to be followed where later designation comes into operation

4.—The following provisions of this Schedule apply where—
(a) notice has been given to a person under section 264 (determination of eligibility) stating that he is in the opinion of the local authority eligible for assistance in respect of defective dwelling, and
(b) after the notice has been given another designation comes into operation designating a class within which the building that consists of or includes the dwelling falls. **[1073]**

5.—(1) The local authority shall, as soon as reasonably practicable, give him notice in writing stating whether in their opinion the new designation falls to be disregarded in accordance with paragraph 2.

(2) If in their opinion it is to be disregarded the notice shall state the reasons for their view. **[1074]**

6.—(1) This paragraph applies where it appears to the authority that the new designation does not fall to be disregarded.

(2) They shall forthwith give him notice in writing—
(a) stating the effect of the new designation and of paragraph 3 (new designation may be relied on) and sub-paragraph (3) below (entitlement to be redetermined), and
(b) informing him that he has the right to make a claim under section 265(2) (claim that assistance by way of reinstatement grant is inappropriate in his case).

(3) They shall as soon as reasonably practicable—
(a) make a further determination under section 265(1) (determination of form of assistance to which person is entitled), taking account of the new designation, and
(b) give a further notice of determination in place of the previous notice;
and where the determination is that he is entitled to assistance by way of repurchase, the notice shall state the effect of paragraph 7 (cases where reinstatement work already begun or contracted for). **[1075]**

7.—(1) This paragraph applies where a person entitled to assistance by way of reinstatement grant is given a further notice of entitlement under paragraph 6 stating that he is entitled to assistance by way of repurchase; and 'the reinstatement work' means the work stated in the previous notice or in a notice under section 272 (change of work required).

(2) Where in such a case—
(a) he satisfies the authority that he has, before the further notice was received, entered into a contract for the provision of services or materials for any of the reinstatement work, or
(b) any such work has been carried out before the further notice was received, and has been carried out to the satisfaction of the appropriate authority,
the previous notice (and any notice under section 272 (change of work required)) continues to have effect for the purposes of reinstatement grant in relation to the reinstatement work or, in a case within paragraph (b), such of that work as has been carried out as mentioned in that paragraph, and the authority shall pay reinstatement grant accordingly.

(3) Where in a case within sub-paragraph (2) the reinstatement work is not completed but part of the work is carried out to the satisfaction of the appropriate authority within the period stated in the notice in question—
(a) the amount of reinstatement grant payable in respect of that part of the work shall be an amount equal to the maximum instalment of grant payable under section 273(2) (instalments not to exceed appropriate percentage of cost of work completed), and
(b) section 274 (repayment of grant in event of failure to complete work) does not apply in relation to reinstatement grant paid in respect of that part of the work. **[1076]**

NOTES to Schedule 21

Definitions: 'defective dwelling': see ss 303, 257 and 287 above; 'dwelling': see s 302 above; 'qualifying defect': see ss 303, 257 and 287 above; 'local authority': see s 338 above; 'person entitled to assistance': see ss 303 and 268 above.

Section 339　　　　　　　　SCHEDULE 22

TRANSITIONAL PROVISIONS AND SAVINGS

PART I
TRANSITIONAL PROVISIONS

General

1.—The re-enactment of provisions in, and the consequent repeal of those provisions by this Act, does not affect the continuity of those provisions.

2.—In so far as—
(a) any requirement, prohibition, determination, order or regulation made by virtue of an enactment repealed by this Act, or
(b) any direction or notice given by virtue of such an enactment, or
(c) any proceedings begun by virtue of such an enactment, or
(d) anything done or having effect as if done,

could, if a corresponding enactment in this Act were in force at the relevant time, have been made, given, begun or done by virtue of the corresponding enactment, it shall, if effective immediately before the corresponding enactment comes into force, continue to have effect thereafter as if made, given, begun or done by virtue of that corresponding enactment.

3.—Where any enactment passed before this Act, or any instrument or document refers either expressly or by implication to an enactment repealed by this Act the reference shall (subject to its context) be construed as or as including a reference to the corresponding provision of this Act.

4.—Where any period of time specified in any enactment repealed by this Act is current at the commencement of this Act, this Act has effect as if its corresponding provision had been in force when that period began to run.

5.—(1) The general rule is that the provisions of this Act apply, in accordance with the foregoing paragraphs, to matters arising before the commencement of this Act as to matters arising after that commencement.

(2) The general rule has effect subject to any express provision to the contrary, either in this Schedule or in connection with the substantive provision in question.

(3) The general rule does not mean that the provisions of this Act apply to cases to which the corresponding repealed provisions did not apply by virtue of transitional provision made in conection with the commencement of the repealed provisions (such transitional provisions, if not specifically reproduced, are saved by paragraph 8).

(4) The general rule does not apply so far as a provision of this Act gives effect to an amendment made in pursuance of a recommendation of the Scottish Law Commission.

Persons holding office

6.—Any person who at the commencement of this Act is holding office or acting or serving under or by virtue of any enactment repealed by this Act or by the Act of 1966 shall continue to hold his office or to act or serve as if he had been appointed under this Act.

Security of tenure of tenants of regional councils, etc

7.—Notwithstanding the repeal by this Act of section 16(2) and (3)(b) of the Tenants' Rights, Etc (Scotland) Act 1980, those provisions shall continue to have effect for the purposes of paragraph 4 of the Housing (Scotland) Act 1986 (Consequential, Transitional and Supplementary Provisions) Order 1986 (application of transitional provisions relating to secure tenant's right to written lease to tenants of regional councils, police authorities and fire authorities). **[1084]**

Part II
Savings

General saving for old transitional provisions

8.—The repeal by this Act of a provision relating to the coming into force of a provision it reproduces does not affect the operation of that provision, in so far as it is not specifically reproduced but remains capable of having effect, in relation to the corresponding provision of this Act. **[1085]**

General saving for old savings

9.—(1) The repeal by this Act of an enactment previously repealed subject to savings does not affect the continued operation of those savings.

(2) The repeal by this Act of a saving made on the previous repeal of an enactment does not affect the operation of the saving in so far as it is not specifically reproduced but remains capable of having effect. **[1086]**

Transfers under section 14 of the Housing (Homeless Persons) Act 1977

10.—(1) The repeal by this Act of section 14 of the Housing (Homeless Persons) Act 1977 (transfers of property and staff) does not affect the operation of any order previously made under that section.

(2) The transfer of an employee in pursuance of such an order shall be treated—
(a) for the purposes of section 94 of the Employment Protection (Consolidation) Act 1978 (redundancy payments) as occurring on a change in the ownership of a business;
(b) for the purposes of Schedule 13 to that Act (continuity of employment) as occurring on the transfer of an undertaking. **[1087]**

Use of existing forms, etc

11.—Any document made, served or issued on or after this Act comes into force which contains a reference to an enactment repealed by this Act shall be construed, except so far as a contrary intention appears, as referring or, as the context may require, including a reference to the corresponding provision of this Act. **[1088]**

Secure tenant: reimbursement of cost of work done before 3rd October 1980

12.—The repeal of section 24(1) of the Tenants' Rights, Etc (Scotland) Act 1980 does not affect the operation of that section in relation to works carried out before 3rd October 1980. **[1089]**

Contributions under sections 106 and 121 of the Housing (Scotland) Act 1950 (c 34) and section 14 of the Housing (Scotland) Act 1962 (c 28)

13.—Contributions remain payable by the Secretary of State under sections 106 and 121 of the Housing (Scotland) Act 1950 and section 14 of the Housing (Scotland) Act 1962 (contributions payable annually for periods of between 20 and 60 years). **[1090]**

★ ★ ★

NOTES to Schedule 23
Schedule 23 amends other enactments.

* * *

NOTES to Schedule 24
Schedule 24 repeals other enactments.

TABLE OF DERIVATIONS

1. The following abbreviations are used in this Table:

Acts of Parliament

1897	=	The Public Health (Scotland) Act 1897 c 38.
1914	=	The Housing Act 1914 c 31.
1950	=	The Housing (Scotland) Act 1950 c 34.
1954	=	The Housing (Repairs and Rents) (Scotland) Act 1954 c 50.
1959	=	The Housing Purchase and Housing Act 1959 c 33.
1962	=	The Housing (Scotland) Act 1962 c 28.
1964	=	The Housing Act 1964 c 56.
1966	=	The Housing (Scotland) Act 1966 c 49.
1967	=	The Housing (Financial Provisions, Etc) (Scotland) Act 1967 c 20.
1968	=	The Housing (Financial Provisions) (Scotland) Act 1968 c 31.
1969	=	The Housing (Scotland) Act 1969 c 34.
1970	=	The Housing (Amendment) (Scotland) Act 1970 c 5.
1971 (c 28)	=	The Rent (Scotland) Act 1971 c 28.
1971 (c 58)	=	The Sheriff Courts (Scotland) Act 1971 c 58.
1971	=	The Housing Act 1971 c 76.
1972	=	The Housing (Financial Provisions) (Scotland) Act 1972 c 46.
1972 (c 52)	=	The Town and County Planning (Scotland) Act 1972 c 52.
1973	=	The Housing (Amendment) Act 1973 c 5.
1973 (c 56)	=	The Land Compensation (Scotland) Act 1973 c 56.
1973 (c 65)	=	The Local Goverment (Scotland) Act 1973 c 65.
1974 (c 39)	=	The Consumer Credit Act 1974 c 39.
1974 (c 44)	=	The Housing Act 1974 c 44.
1974	=	The Housing (Scotland) Act 1974 c 45.
1975 (c 21)	=	The Criminal Procedure (Scotland) Act 1975 c 21.
1975	=	The Housing Rents and Subsidies (Scotland) Act 1975 c 28.
1977	=	The Housing (Homeless Persons) Act 1977 c 48.
1978	=	The Housing (Financial Provisions) (Scotland) Act 1978 c 14.
1978 (c 27)	=	The Home Purchase Assistance and Housing Corporation Guarantee Act 1978 c 27.
1978 (c 48)	=	The Homes Insulation Act 1978 c 48.
1980 (c 51)	=	The Housing Act 1980 c 51.
1980	=	The Tenants' Rights, Etc (Scotland) Act 1980 c 52.
1980 (c 61)	=	The Tenants' Rights, Etc (Scotland) Amendment Act 1980 c 61.
1981 (c 23)	=	The Local Government (Miscellaneous Provisions) (Scotland) Act 1981 c 23.
1981	=	The Housing (Amendment) (Scotland) Act 1981 c 72.
1982 (c 24)	=	The Social Security and Housing Benefits Act 1982 c 24.
1982	=	The Local Government and Planning (Scotland) Act 1982 c 43.
1982 (c 45)	=	The Civic Government (Scotland) Act 1982 c 45.
1982 (c 48)	=	The Criminal Justice Act 1982 c 48.
1984 (c 12)	=	The Telecommunications Act 1984 c 12.
1984 (c 18)	=	The Tenants' Rights, Etc (Scotland) Amendment Act 1984 c 18.
1984 (c 31)	=	The Rating and Valuation Amendment (Scotland) Act 1984 c 31.
1984	=	The Housing Defects Act 1984 c 50.
1984 (c 58)	=	The Rent (Scotland) Act 1984 c 58.
1985 (c 69)	=	The Housing Associations Act 1985 c 69.
1985	=	The Housing (Consequential Provisions) Act 1985 c 71.
1986 (c 53)	=	The Building Societies Act 1986 c 53.

| 1986 (c 63) | = | The Housing and Planning Act 1986 c 63. |
| 1986 | = | The Housing (Scotland) Act 1986 c 65. |

Subordinate Legislation

SI 1983/271	=	The Housing (Improvement of Amenities of Residential Areas) (Scotland) Order 1983.
SI 1983/492	=	The Housing (Standard Amenities Approved Expense) (Scotland) Order 1983.
SI 1983/493	=	The Housing (Improvements or Repair Grants) (Approved Expenses Maxima) (Scotland) Regulations 1983.
SI 1983/1804	=	The Housing (Payments for Well-maintained Houses) (Scotland) Order 1983.

2. The Table does not show the effect of Transfer of Functions Orders.

3. The letter R followed by a number indicates that the provision gives effect to the Recommendation bearing that number in the Scottish Law Commission's Report on the Consolidation of the Housing Acts for Scotland (Cmnd 104).

4. The entry 'drafting' indicates a provision of a mechanical or editorial nature affecting the arrangement of the consolidation; for instance a provision introducing a Schedule.

Provision	Derivations
1(1)	1966 s 137; 1974 s 50(1), Sch 3 para 9; 1974 s 27(3)
(2)	1966 s 137; 1969 s 69(2), Sch 6 para 18; 1974 s 50(1), Sch 3 para 9
(3)	1966 s 137; 1969 s 69(2), (3), Sch 6 para 18, Sch 7, 5
(4)	1970 (c 44) ss 3(1), (2)
2(1)	1966 s 138
(2)	1966 s 138(1)
(3)	1966 s 138(2)
(4)	1966 s 138(3); 1978 s 16(1), Sch 2 Pt I para 1
(5)	1966 s 138(4); 1978 s 16(1), Sch 2 Pt I para 1
3(1)–(3)	1966 s 139(1)
(4)	1966 s 139(2)
4(1)	1966 s 140(1)
(2)	1966 s 140(2); 1984 (c 39) s 192, Sch 4 Pt I para 27
5(1)	1966 s 141(1)
(2)	1966 s 141(2)
(3)	1966 s 141(3); 1976 (c 66) Sch 8
6(1)	1966 s 177(1), Sch 5; 1981 (c 23) s 40, Sch 3 para 10; R 1
(2)	1966 s 177(2); 1980 Sch 5
7	1966 s 147
8	1966 s 148
9(1)	1966 s 142
(2)	1966 s 142 proviso
10(1)	1966 s 143(1); 1974 s 50(1), Sch 3 para 10, Sch 5
(2)	1966 s 143(2)
(3)	1966 s 143(3)
(4)	1966 s 143(4)
11	1966 s 144
12(1)	1966 s 145(1); 1978 s 16(1), Sch 2 Pt I para 2(a); 1980 ss 8(3)(a), 8(4)
(2)	1966 s 145(2)
(3)	1966 s 145(3)
(4)	1966 s 145(4)
(5)	1966 s 145(5); 1980 Sch 5
(6)	1966 s 145(8)
(7)	1966 s 145(6); 1972 s 79(1), Sch 9 para 7; 1978 s 16(1), Sch 2 Pt I para 2
(8)	1966 s 145(6A), 1973 (c 65) s 237(2); 1980 ss 8(3)(c), 8(4)
(9)	1966 s 145(7); 1980 s 76(b)
(10)	1966 s 145(7) proviso; 1980 s 76(b)

545

Provision	Derivations
12(11)	1945 s 145(9)
13	1966 s 146; 1972 s 79(1), Sch 9 para 8
14(1)	1980 s 8(1); 1986 Sch 1 para 9
(2)	1980 s 8(1), (2)
15(1)	1966 s 178; R 1
(2)	1966 s 178 proviso
16	1966 s 179
17(1)	1966 s 149(1); 1972 Sch 11, Pt V; R 2
(2)	1966 s 149(2)
18	1966 s 150(1); R 2
19(1)	1980 s 26(1); 1986 Sch 1 para 13
(2)	1980 s 26(2); 1986 Sch 1 para 13
(3)	1980 s 26(3); 1986 Sch 1 para 13
(4)	1980 s 26(4)
20(1)	1966 s 151(1), (2); 1969 s 69(2), Sch 6 para 19; 1977 s 6(2)
(2)	1980 s 26A; 1986 Sch 1 para 13; R 2
21(1)	1980 s 27(1); 1981 Sch 3 para 45
(2)	1980 s 27(1A); 1986 s 8
(3)	1980 s 27(1B); 1986 s 8
(4)	1980 s 27(2); 1981 (c 23) Sch 3 para 45
(5)	1980 s 27(2A); 1981 (c 23) Sch 3 para 45
(6)	1980 s 27(3); 1981 (c 23) Sch 3 para 45
22(1)	1975 s 5(1)
(2)	1975 s 5(2); 1980 s 81(a)
(3)	1975 s 5(3); 1980 s 81(b)
(4)	1975 s 5(4); 1985 Sch 2 para 27
(5)	1975 s 5(5)
23(1)	1966 s 175(1); 1972 Sch 9 para 10
(2)	1966 s 175(2); 1974 (c 44) Sch 13 para 14; 1985 Sch 2 para 10(2)
(3)	1966 s 175(3); 1974 (c 44) Sch 13 para 14
(4)	1966 s 175(4)
(5)	1966 s 175(5)
(6)	1969 s 59A; 1974 s 50(1), Sch 3 para 32; 1978 s 16(2), Sch 3
Part II	
24(1)	1977 s 1(1); 1985 Sch 2 para 37
(2)	1977 s 1(1)
(3)	1977 s 1(2); 1986 s 21(2)
(4)	1977 s 1(3)
25(1)	1977 s 2(1)(2)
(2)	1977 s 2(3)
(3)	1977 ss 2(3), 19(1)
(4)	1977 s 2(4)
26	1977 s 17(1)–(4)
27(1)–(3)	1977 s 18(1)–(3)
(4)	1975 s 15
28(1)	1977 s 3(1), (2)
(2)	1977 s 3(2), (3)
29	1977 s 3(4)
30(1)–(4)	1977 s 8(1)–(4)
(5)	1977 s 8(8), (9); R 3
31(1)	1977 s 4(1)
(2)	1977 s 4(5)
(3)	1977 s 4(2), (3)
(4)	1977 s 4(2)
32(1)	1977 s 4(1)
(2)	1977 s 4(4)
(3)	1977 s 4(2)
(4)	1977 s 4(6)
(5)	1977 s 4(7); 1986 s 21(3)
33(1)	1977 s 5(1); 1985 Sch 2 para 37
(2)	1977 s 5(1)
(3)	1977 s 5(11)

Housing (Scotland) Act 1987 (c 26), Sch 24 [1091]

Provision	Derivations
33(4)	1977 s 5(7), (8)
(5)	1977 s 5(9)
(6)	1977 s 5(10)
34(1)	1977 s 5(6)
(2)	1977 s 5(3), (4), (5)
(3)	1977 s 8(5)
(4)	1977 s 8(8), (9); R 3
35(1)	1977 s 6(1)
(2)	1977 s 10
36(1)	1977 s 7(1), (2)
(2)	1977 s 7(1), (3)
(3)	1977 s 7(4), (5)
(4)	1977 s 7(6), (7)
(5)	1977 s 7(8), (9), (10)
(6)	1977 s 8(6), (7)
(7)	1977 s 8(10), (11)
(8)	1977 s 7(1), (3) drafting
37	1977 s 12
38	1977 s 9(1)
39(1)	1977 s 13(1)
(2)	1977 s 13(2), (3)
(3)	1977 s 13(4)
(4)	1977 s 13(7)
(5)	1977 s 13(5), (6)
40(1)	1977 s 11(1)
(2)	1977 s 11(2), (3)
(3)	1977 s 11(4)
(4)	1977 s 11(5); 1975 (c 21) s 289F, s 289G, 457A
41	1977 s 16
42	1977 s 18A; 1985 Sch 2 para 37
43	1977 s 19(1); 1985 Sch 2 para 37
Part III	
44(1)	1980 s 10(1), (2)
(2)	1980 s 10(3)
(3)	1980 s 10(4)(a)
(4)	1980 s 10(4)(b); 1984 (c 18) s 5; 1986 Sch 1 para 10
(5)	1980 s 10(5)
(6)	1980 s 10(6)
45	1980 s 11(1)–(5); 1985 Sch 2 para 45(4); R 4
46(1)	1980 s 12(1)
(2)	1980 s 12(2)
47(1)	1980 s 14(1)
(2)	1980 s 14(2); 1981 (c 23) Sch 3 para 43
(3)	1980 s 14(3)
(4)	1980 s 14(4)
48(1)	1980 s 15(1); 1981 Sch 3 para 44; Sch 1 para 12(a)
(2)	1980 s 15(2); 1986 Sch 1 para 12(b)
(3)	1980 s 15(3); 1986 Sch 1 para 12(c)
(4)	1980 s 15(4)
(5)	1980 s 15(5); 1984 s 6
49(1)	1980 s 18(1)
(2)	1980 s 18(2)
(3)	1980 s 18(3)
(4)	1980 s 18(4)
50(1)	1980 s 19(1)
(2)	1980 s 19(2)
(3)	1980 s 19(3)
(4)	1980 s 19(4)
51(1)	1980 s 20(1)
(2)	1980 s 20(2)
(3)	1980 s 20(3)
52(1)	1980 s 13(1)

Provision	Derivations
52(2)	1980 s 13(2); 1986 Sch 1 para 11
(3)	1980 s 13(3)
(4)	1980 s 13(4)
(5)	1980 s 13(5)
(6)	1980 s 13(6)
(7)	1980 s 13(7)
53(1)	1980 s 16(1)
(2)	1980 s 16(3)
(3)	1980 s 16(6)
54(1)	1980 s 17(1)
(2)	1980 s 17(2); 1984 (c 58) s 117(1), Sch 8
(3)	1980 s 17(3)
(4)	1980 s 17(4)
(5)	1980 s 17(5)
(6)	1980 s 16(6)
55(1)	1980 s 21(1)
(2)	1980 s 21(2)
(3)	1980 s 21(3)
(4)	1980 s 21(4); 1984 (c 58) s 117(1), Sch 8
(5)	1980 s 21(6)
(6)	1980 s 21(7)
56	1980 s 22(1), (2)
57	1980 s 23(1)–(3)
58	1980 s 24(1)–(3)
59	1980 s 25
60	1980 s 17A(1)–(4); 1984 s 7
61(1)	1980 s 1(1); 1982 (c 43) Sch 4
(2)	1980 s 1(3), 10(2), (11), (12); 1986 s 1(2), Sch 1 para 1(h)(iii) and (iv)
(3)	1980 s 9A; 1984 s 20
(4)	1980 s 1(11); 1986 Sch 1 para 1(f)
(5)	1980 s 1(2)
(6)	1980 s 1(4); 1986 Sch 1 para 1(b)
(7)	1986 Sch 1, para 1(g)
(8)	1980 s 1(11B); 1986 Sch 1 para 1(g)
(9)	1980 s 1(11C); 1986 Sch 1 para 1(g)
(10)	1980 s 1(12); 1984 ss 1, 2; 1986 Sch 1 para 1(h)
(11)	1980 s 1(10); 1984 (c 18) ss 2, 8; 1984 (c 36) Sch 3 para 47; 1986 Sch 1 para 1(e)
62(1)	1980 s 1(5); 1986 Sch 1 para 1(c)
(2)	1980 s 1(5), (6)
(3)	1980 ss 1(5), 9A; 1984 s 1; 1984 (c 50), s 20; 1986 s 2(1)(a) to (c); Sch 1 para 1(c); 1986 (c 63) s 3
(4)	1980 s 1(5A); 1986 Sch 1 para 1(d); 1986 s 2(1)(d)
(5)	1980 s 1(5B); 1986 (c 63) s 3
(6)	1980 s 1(5C); 1986 (c 63) s 3
(7)	1980 s 1(7); 1986 s 3
(8)	1980 s 1(7A); 1986 s 3
(9)	1980 s 1(8); 1986 s 3(2)
(10)	1980 s 1(9)
(11)	1986 s 3(4)
(12)	1986 s 3(4)
(13)	1986 s 3(5)
63(1)	1980 s 2(1)
(2)	1980 s 2(2); 1984 (c 18) ss 4(2), 8(1)
64(1)	1980 s 4(1); 1982 s 53(2)(a)
(2)	1980 s 4(2)
(3)	1980 s 4(3); 1982 s 53(2)(b), Sch 4
(4)	1980 s 4(4); 1980 (c 61) s 2(a)
(5)	1980 s 4(5)
(6)	1980 s 4(6)
(7)	1980 s 4(7); 1986 Sch 1 para 5(a)

Provision	Derivations
64(8)	1980 s 4(7A); 1986 Sch 1 para 5(b)
(9)	1980 s 4(8); 1980 (c 61) s 2(a)
65(1)	1980 s 2(3)
(2)	1980 s 2(4)
(3)	1980 s 2(5)
66(1)	1980 s 2(6); 1982 Sch 3 para 39; 1986 Sch 1 para 4
(2)	1980 s 2(7)
67(1)	1980 s 2(8), (11); 1981 (c 23) Sch 3 para 40; 1982 Sch 3 para 39; 1984 ss 3, 4(2)
(2)	1980 s 2(9)
(3)	1980 s 2(11)
68	1980 s 3(1)–(4)
69(1)	1980 s 3A(1), (7); 1980 (c 61) s 1(2)
(2)–(6)	1980 s 3A(2)–(6)
70	1980 s 3B(1)–(2); 1984 (c 18) s 4
71(1)	1980 s 7(2); 1982 s 55, Sch 3 para 40
(2)	1980 s 7(3) s 55(1)(b)
(3)	1980 s 7(4)
72(1)–(3)	1980 s 6(1)–(3); 1986 Sch 1 para 7
(4)	1981 Sch 3 para 42
(5)	1980 s 6(5); 1982 s 54
(6)	1980 s 6(5); 1986 Sch 1 para 7(c)
(7)	1980 s 6; 1986 Sch 1 para 7(d)
73	1980 s 6A; 1986 Sch 1 para (8)
74	1980 s 7(1)
75	1980 s 1(1A); 1982 s 53(1); 1986 Sch 1 para 1(a)
76	1980 s 1B; 1986 Sch 1 para 3
77(1)	1980 s 1A; 1981 (c 23) s 35(1)
(2)	1980 s 1A(2); 1981 (c 23) s 35(2); 1986 Sch 1 para 2
(3)	1980 s 1A(3); 1981 (c 23) s 35(3)
(4)	1980 s 1A(4); 1981 (c 23) s 35(4)
(5)	1980 s 1A(5); 1981 (c 23) s 35(5)
(6)	1980 s 1A(6); 1981 (c 23) s 35(6)
(7)	1980 s 1A(7); 1981 (c 23) s 35(7)
78	1980 s 4A; 1986 s 4
79	1980 s 9B; 1986 s 5
80	1980 s 25A; 1986 s 7
81	1980 s 9C; 1986 s 6
82	1980 s 82; 1982 (c 61) s 2(f); 1982 Sch 2 para 39(b); 1986 Sch 1 para 16
83	1980 s 82A; 1986 Sch 1 para 17
84	1980 s 83
Part IV	
85	1974 s 13(1)–(3)
86	1974 s 14(1)–(3)
87(1)	1966 s 180(1), (2); 1969 Sch 6 para 23; 1973 (c 65) Sch 27 Part I para 2
(2)	1966 s 180(5)
(3)	1966 s 180(6)
88(1)	1974 s 14A(1); 1978 s 10
(2)	1974 s 14A(1A); 1980 s 71
(3)	1974 s 14A(3); 1978 s 10
(4)	1974 s 14A(4); 1978 s 10
(5)	1974 s 14A(5); 1978 s 10
(6)	1974 s 14A(6); 1978 s 10
(7)	1974 s 14A(7); 1978 s 10
(8)	1974 s 14A(8); 1978 s 10
89(1)	1974 s 15(1)
(2)	1974 s 15(2); 1978 Sch 2 para 22
(3)	1974 s 15(3); 1978 Sch 2 para 22
90(1)	1974 s 16(1)
(2)	1974 s 16(2)
(3)	1974 s 16(3)
(4)	1974 s 16(4); 1978 Sch 2 para 23

[1091]   Housing (Scotland) Act 1987 (c 26), Sch 24

Provision	Derivations
91(1)	1974 s 17(1)
(2)	1974 s 17(2)
(3)	1974 s 17(3)
(4)	1974 s 17(4); 1978 Sch 2 para 24(a)
(5)	1975 s 17(5); 1978 Sch 2 para 24(b)
92	1974 s 18(1)–(4)
93	1974 (c 44) s 116A; 1975 Sch 3 para 16
94	1974 s 19(1)–(7)
95(1)	1974 ss 20, 21
(2)	1974 ss 22, 23, 26, 28, 31–34, 36A
(3)	1974 s 29
(4)	1974 s 25; 1966 ss 80, 87
96	1974 s 27(1)–(3)
97(1)	1974 s 35(1)
(2)	1974 s 35(2)
(3)	1974 s 35(3)
(4)	1974 s 35(4); 1975 (c 21) ss 289E, 289G; 1982 (c 48) s 54
(5)	1974 s 35(5)
(6)	1974 s 35(6)
(7)	1974 s 35(7)
98	1974 s 36
99	1974 s 37(1)–(3)
100	1974 s 38(1), (2)
101	1974 s 39(1), (2)
102	1974 s 40; 1984 (c 58) Sch 8 Pt II
103	1974 s 41
104	1974 s 42
105(1)	1974 s 43(1); 1978 Sch 2 para 43
(2)	1974 s 43(2)
(3)	1974 s 43(3)
106	1974 s 44(1); 1978 Sch 2 para 26
107	1974 s 44A; 1978 Sch 2 para 27
Part V	
108(1)	1969 s 24(1)
(2)	1969 s 24(1); 1978 Sch 2 para 6(a), (b)
(3)	1969 s 24(2); 1978 Sch 2 para 6(c)
(4)	1969 s 24(2)
(5)	1969 s 24(2)
(6)	1969 s 24(3)
(7)	1969 s 24(4)
(8)	1969 s 24(6); 1978 Sch 2 para 6(d)
109(1)	1969 s 25(1)
(2)	1969 s 25(1A); 1978 Sch 2 para 7
(3)	1969 s 25(2)
(4)	1969 s 25(3); 1973 (c 65) s 121; 1981 (c 23) Sch 2 para 15
(5)	1969 s 25(4)
110(1)	1969 s 26(1)
(2)	1969 s 26(1)
(3)	1969 s 26(2)
(4)	1969 s 26(3)
111(1)	1969 s 27(1)
(2)	1969 s 27(2)
112	1969 s 28
113	1966 ss 6–11
Part VI	
114(1)–(2)	1966 s 15(1); 1969 Sch 6 para 4(a); 1973 (c 65) Sch 27 para 2(1)
(3)	1966 s 17(1), (2); 1969 Sch 6 para 5
(4)	1966 s 17(2); 1969 Sch 6 para 5; 1980 s 84, Sch 5
(5)	1966 s 17(3); 1980 s 84, Sch 5
115	1966 s 15(2); 1969 Sch 6 para 4(b), (c); 1973 (c 65) Sch 27 Pt I para 2(1)
116	1966 s 15(3); 1969 Sch 6 para 4(d)

Provision	Derivations
117(1)–(3)	1966 s 15(4); 1969 Sch 6 para 4(d)
(4)	1966 s 15(5)
(5)	1966 s 15(6)
118(1)	1966 s 15(7)
(2)	1966 s 15(8)
119(1)	1966 s 18(1); 1969 Sch 6 para 6(a); 1972 (c 52) Sch 21 Pt II
(2)	1966 s 18(2); 1969 Sch 6 para 6(b); 1972 (c 52) Sch 21 Pt II
(3)	1966 s 18(3)
120(1)	1966 s 19(1); 1969 Sch 6 para 7(a)
(2)	1966 s 19(1A); 1969 Sch 6 para 7(b)
(3)	1966 s 19(2); 1969 Sch 6 para 7(c)
(4)	1966 s 19(3); 1969 Sch 6 para 7(d)
(5)	1966 s 19(4); 1969 Sch 6 para 7(d)
(6)	1966 s 19(6); 1969 Sch 6 para 7(e); 1974 Sch 3 para 5
121(1)–(2)	1966 s 20(1); 1969 Sch 6 para 8(a), Sch 7
(3)	1966 s 20(2); 1969 Sch 7
(4)	1966 s 20(3)
(5)	1966 s 20(4); 1969 Sch 6 para 8(b)
(6)	1966 s 20(5); 1969 Sch 6 para 8(c)
(7)	1966 s 20(6); 1969 Sch 6 para 8(c)
(8)	1966 s 20(8)
(9)	1966 s 20(9)
122(1)–(2)	1966 s 21; 1974 Sch 3 para 6; 1975 (c 21) s 289E; 1982 (c 48) s 54
123	1966 s 22(1)–(3)
124(1)	1966 s 23(1)
(2)	1966 s 23(2)
(3)	1966 s 23(3)
(4)	1966 s 23(4); 1974 Sch 3 para 7
125(1)	1966 s 56(1)
(2)	1966 s 56(2)
(3)	1966 s 56(3)
(4)	1966 s 56(4)
(5)	1966 s 56(5); 1975 (c 21) s 289G; 1982 (c 48) s 54
(6)	1966 s 56(6)
(7)	1966 s 56(7)
126(1)	1966 s 57(1)
(2)	1966 s 57(1)
(3)–(4)	1966 s 57(1)
(5)	1966 s 57(2)
(6)	1966 s 57(3)
127(1)	1966 s 181(1)
(2)–(3)	1966 s 181(2)
(4)–(5)	1966 s 181(3)
(6)	1966 s 181(4); 1975 (c 21) s 289E; 1982 (c 48) s 54
128	1966 s 182; 1969 Sch 6 para 24
129(1)	1966 ss 26(1), 57(4); 1969 Sch 7
(2)	1966 s 26(1)
(3)	1966 s 26(4)
130	1966 s 27; 1969 Sch 7
131(1)–(2)	1966 s 30; 1969 Sch 6 para 12
(3)	1966 s 30(2); 1969 Sch 7
132(1)	1966 s 31(1)
(2)	1966 s 31(2); 1969 Sch 7
133	1966 s 33(1), (2)
134	1984 (c 12) Sch 4 para 45; 1986 (c 44) Sch 7 para 2(7)
Part VII	
135	1966 s 89(1); drafting
136(1)	1966 s 89(1)(a)
(2)	1966 ss 89(1)(a), 99
137(1)	1966 s 89(1)(b)
(2)	1966 ss 89(2), 99
(3)	1966 Sch 5

Provision	Derivations
137(4)	1966 s 94(4)
(5)	1966 s 198
(6)	1966 s 94(5)
138(1)	1966 s 91(1)
(2)	1966 s 91(1)
(3)	1966 s 91(1); 1980 Sch 5
(4)	1966 s 91(1)
(5)	1966 s 91(1)
(6)	1966 s 91(2); 1980 Sch 5
(7)	1966 s 91(3)
139(1)	1966 s 90(1)
(2)	1966 ss 90(2), (3), 92(5), and 93(3)
(3)	1966 s 90(1); 1975 (c 21) ss 289c, 289g; 1982 (c 48) s 54
140(1)	1966 s 90(2)
(2)	1966 s 90(2)(b)
141	1966 s 90(3)
142(1)	1966 s 92(1)
(2)	1966 s 92(1)
(3)	1966 s 92(2)
(4)	1966 s 92(3)
(5)	1966 s 92(3)
(6)	1966 s 92(4)
143(1)	1966 s 93(1)
(2)	1966 s 93(1), (2)
144(1)	1966 s 94(1)
(2)	1966 s 94(1); 1975 (c 21) ss 289c, 289g; 1982 (c 48) s 54
(3)	1966 s 94(3)
145	1966 s 95(1)
146(1)	1966 s 88(1)
(2)	1966 s 88(1)
(3)	1966 s 88(1), (3)
(4)	1966 s 88(1)
(5)	1966 s 88(1)
(6)	1966 s 88(2)
147(1)	1966 s 96(2)
(2)	1966 s 96(2); 1975 (c 21) ss 289c, 289g; 1982 (c 48) s 54
148(1)	1966 s 94(2)
(2)	1966 s 94(2)
149	1966 s 97
150	1966 s 96(1)
151	1966 s 99
Part VIII	
152(1)	1966 s 100(1)
(2)	1966 s 100(2)
(3)	1966 s 100(2); 1966 s 100(3)
(4)	1966 s 100(4)
(5)	1966 s 100(5)
153	1966 s 101(1)–(4); 1969 (c 19) s 10(1)
154	1966 s 101(4)
155(1)	1966 s 102(1)
(2)	1966 s 102(2); 1975 (c 21) ss 289c, 289g; 1982 (c 48) s 54
156(1)	1966 s 103(1)
(2)	1966 s 103(2)
(3)	1966 s 103(3)
(4)	1966 s 103(4); 1975 (c 21) ss 289c, 289g; 1982 (c 48) s 54
(5)	1966 s 103(5)
(6)	1966 s 103(5)
157(1)	1966 s 104(1)
(2)	1966 s 104(2)
(3)	1966 s 104(3)
(4)	1966 s 104(3)
(5)	1966 s 104(6)

Provision	Derivations
158(1)	1966 s 104(4)
(2)	1966 s 104(5)
(3)	1966 s 104(5)
(4)	1966 s 104(6)
159(1)	1966 s 104(7)
(2)	1966 s 104(7)
160(1)	1966 s 105(1)
(2)	1966 s 105(2)
(3)–(4)	1966 s 105(3)
(5)	1966 s 105(4)
161(1)	1966 s 106(1)
(2)	1966 s 106(2)
(3)	1966 s 106(1), (3)
(4)	1966 s 106(3)
(5)–(6)	1966 s 106(1), (5)
(7)	1966 s 106(4)
(8)	1966 s 106(6)
162(1)	1966 s 107(1)
(2)	1966 s 107(1); 1982 s 52(2)
(3)	1966 s 107(2); 1973 (c 65) Sch 12 para 8
(4)	1966 s 107(3)
(5)	1966 s 107(4)
(6)	1966 s 107(5)
163(1)	1966 s 108(1)
(2)	1966 s 108(1)
(3)	1966 s 108(2)
(4)	1966 s 108(3)
(5)	1966 s 108(4)
164(1)	1966 s 109(1)
(2)	1966 s 109(1)
(3)	1966 s 109(2)
(4)	drafting, 1966 s 109(3)–(6)
165(1)	1966 s 110(1), (1A); 1975 (c 21) ss 289C, 289G; 1982 (c 48) s 54
(2)	1966 s 110(1)
(3)	1966 s 110(2)
(4)	1966 s 110(3)
(5)	1966 s 110(4)
166(1)	1966 s 111(1)
(2)	1966 s 111(2)
(3)	1966 s 111(3)
(4)	1966 s 111(4); 1980 s 65(1)(e); SI 1980/1387
(5)	1966 s 111(5); 1980 s 65(1)(e); 1975 (c 21) ss 289C, 289G; 1982 (c 48) s 54
167(1)	1966 s 112(1)
(2)	1966 s 112(2)
168	1966 s 112(5); 1980 s 65(1)(f); 1975 (c 21) ss 289C, 289G; 1982 (c 48) s 54
169(1)	1966 s 112(3)
(2)	1966 s 112(3)
170	1966 s 112(4)
171(1)	1966 s 113(1)
(2)	1966 s 113(1), proviso (i)
(3)	1966 s 113(1), proviso (ii)
(4)	1966 s 113(2)
(5)	1966 s 113(3)
172(1)	1966 s 114(1)
(2)	1966 s 114(2)
(3)	1966 s 114(3)
(4)	1966 s 114(4); 1969 s 5; Sch 6 para 15; R 5
173	1966 s 115
174	1966 s 116
175	1966 s 117
176(1)–(2)	1966 s 192(2)
(3)	1966 s 192(3)

Provision	Derivations
177	1966 s 119
178	1966 s 120(1)–(6)
179(1)	1966 s 121(1)
(2)	1966 s 121(2)
(3)	1966 s 121(3)
(4)	1966 s 121(4)
(5)	1966 s 121(5)
180(1)	1966 s 122(1)
(2)	1966 s 122(2)
(3)	1966 s 122(3)
(4)	1966 s 122(4); 1971 (c 28) Sch 18 Pt II; 1984 (c 58) Sch 8 Pt II
(5)	1966 s 122(5)
(6)	1966 s 122(6)
(7)	1966 s 122(7)
181(1)	1966 s 123(1)
(2)	1966 s 123(2)
(3)	1966 s 123(3); 1971 (c 28) Sch 18 Pt II; 1984 (c 58) Sch 8 Pt II
(4)	1966 s 123(4)
(5)	1966 s 123(5)
(6)	1966 s 123(6)
182(1)	1966 s 124(1)
(2)	1966 s 124(2)
(3)	1966 s 124(3)
(4)	1966 s 124(4)
(5)	1966 s 124(5)
183(1)	1966 s 125(1)
(2)	1966 s 125(2)
(3)	1966 s 125(3)
(4)	1966 s 125(4)
(5)	1966 s 125(5)
(6)	1966 s 125(6); 1981 (c 23) s 40, Sch 3 para 8
184(1)	1966 s 126(1)
(2)	Drafting
(3)	1966 s 126(6)
185(1)	1966 s 128(1)
(2)	1966 s 128(2)
(3)	1966 s 128(3)
186(1)	1966 s 129(1)
(2)	1966 s 129(2)
(3)	1966 s 129(3)
(4)	1966 s 129(4)
(5)	1966 s 129(5)
(6)	1966 s 129(6)
187(1)	1966 s 130(1)
(2)	1966 s 130(2)
(3)	Drafting
188(1)	1966 s 133(1)
(2)	1966 s 133(2)
(3)	1966 s 133(3)
(4)	1966 s 133(4)
(5)	1966 s 133(10)
189	Drafting
190	1966 s 136(1)–(4)
Part IX	
191(1)	1978 s 1(1)
(2)	1978 s 1(2); 1981 (c 23) s 21(1)(a)(ii), (2)
(3)	1978 s 1(3)
(4)	1978 s 1(4)
(5)	1978 s 1(4A); 1981 (c 23) s 21(1)(b)
(6)	1978 s 1(4B); 1981 (c 23) s 21(1)(b)
(7)	1978 s 1(5)
(9)	1978 s 1(6)

Provision	Derivations
191(10)	1978 s 1(7); 1981 (c 23) s 21(1)(c)
192(1)	1978 s 2(1); 1981 (c 23) s 22
(2)	1978 s 2(1)
(3)	1978 s 2(2); 1981 (c 23) s 22
(4)	1978 s 2(3); 1981 (c 23) s 22
(5)	1978 s 2(4)
(6)	1978 s 2(5)
(7)	1978 s 2(7)
193	1978 s 3
194(1)	1978 s 4(1); 1986 s 18(1)
(2)	1978 s 4(2), (4); 1986 s 18(1)
(3)	1978 s 4(3)
195(1)–(5)	1978 s 4A(1)–(5); 1986 s 18(2)
196(1)	1968 s 25(1)
(1)(c)	1970 (c 5) s 1
(1)(f)	1978 Sch 2 Pt I para 4
(1)(g)	1978 Sch 2 Pt I para 4
(1)(g)(i)	1981 s 1(1)
(1)(g)(ii)	1968 s 25(1); 1970 (c 5) s 1; 1978 Sch 2 para 4; 1976 (c 11) s 1(1); 1981 s 1(1)
(2)	1968 s 25(2)
(3)	1968 s 25(3)
(4)	1985 (c 69) Sch 2 para 16(3)
(5)	1985 (c 69) Sch 2 para 16(3)
(6)	1968 s 25(5)
(7)	1968 s 25(6); 1972 Sch 9 para 16
197	1978 s 5; 1985 Sch 2 para 39(2)
198(1)	1978 s 6(1)
(2)	1978 s 6(2)
199	drafting; 1978 s 7; 1968 s 59; 1985 Sch 2 para 39(3)
200(1)	1972 s 7(2)
(2)	1972 s 7(4)
(3)	1972 s 7(5)
201(1)	1972 s 13(1)
(2)	1972 s 13(2)
(3)	1972 s 13(3)
(4)	1968 s 57(1)
(5)	1968 s 58(1)
202(1)	1968 s 58(1); 1972 s 73(a)
(2)	1968 s 58(1), (3)(aa)
(3)	1968 s 58(1)
(4)	1968 s 58(2)
(5)	1968 s 58(3); 1969 Sch 6 para 40; 1974 Sch 3 para 21; 1972 s 73(a); 1975 Sch 3 para 2
(6)	1968 s 58(4)
(7)	1968 s 58(5); 1972 Sch 9 para 20(a)(i)
Part X	
203(1)	1972 s 23(1); 1947 Sch 3 para 42; 1978 s 11(1)(a)
(2)	1972 s 23(4)
(3)	1972 s 23(5)
(4)	1972 s 23(3); 1978 s 11(1)(b)
(5)	1972 s 23(7)
(6)	1978 s 11(3)
(7)	1978 s 11(4); Interpretation Act 1978 s 14
204	1972 s 23A; 1984 (c 31) s 8
205	1972 s 24
206	1972 s 25
207	1972 s 26
208	1972 s 74
209	1972 s 75
Part XI	
210	1975 s 1(2)–(4)

[1091]   *Housing (Scotland) Act 1987 (c 26), Sch 24*

Provision	Derivations
211	1972 s 32(1), (2), (3)
212(1)	1969 s 62(1); 1975 Sch 3 para 3(1); R 2
(2)–(3)	1969 s 62(1), (3)
(4)	1969 s 62(5), (6); 1973 (c 54) Sch 12 para 22(a), (b); 1975 Sch 1 para 3(2)
(5)	1969 s 62(8); 1980 s 17(7)(c)
213	1969 s 62(3); 1975 (c 28) Sch 3 para 3(1)
Part XII	
214(1)–(2)	1968 s 49(1); 1974 s 45(2); 1980 ss 29, 84 Sch 5
(3)	1968 s 49(1A); 1980 s 29
(4)	1968 s 49(2A); 1974 s 45(3)
(5)	1968 s 49(4)
(6)	1968 s 49(5); 1974 s 45(5)
(7)	1968 s 49(5); 1978 Sch 2 Pt I para 5
(8)	drafting
215	1968 s 49(2); 1969 Sch 6 para 39
216(1)–(9)	1980 s 5(1)–(9); 1981 Sch 3 para 41; 1986 Sch 1 para 6
217(1)	1974 s 24(1)
(2)	1974 s 24(2)
(3)	1974 s 24(3)
(4)	1974 s 24(4)
(5)	1974 s 24(5)
(6)	1974 s 24(6); 1980 s 29(2)
(7)	1974 s 24(7)
(8)	1974 s 24(8)
(9)	1974 s 24(9)
218	1969 s 24A; 1978 s 9
219(1)	1980 s 30(1)
(2)	1980 s 30(2)
(3)	1980 s 30(3)
(4)	1980 s 30(4)
(5)	1980 s 30(5); 1986 Sch 3
(6)	1980 s 30(6)
(7)	1980 s 30(7)
(8)	1980 s 30(10)
220	1980 s 30(8); 1986 Sch 1 para 15(b)
221	1980 s 30(9)
222(1)	1978 (c 27) s 1(1)
(2)	1978 (c 27) s 1(2)
(3)	1978 (c 27) s 1(2)
223(1)	1978 (c 27) s 1(4)
(2)	1978 (c 27) s 1(3), (5)
(3)	1978 (c 27) s 1(3)
(4)	1978 (c 27) s 1(5)
(5)	1978 (c 27) s 1(6)
(6)	1978 (c 27) s 2(7)
224(1)	1978 (c 27) Sch 1 Pt I; 1986 (c 53) Sch 18
(2)	1978 (c 27) s 2(1)
(3)	1978 (c 27) s 2(7)
225(1)	1978 (c 27) Sch 1 Pt II
(2)	1978 (c 27) s 2(1)
(3)	1978 (c 27) s 2(7)
226(1)	1978 (c 27) s 2(2)
(2)	1978 (c 27) s 2(3)
(3)	1978 (c 27) s 2(4)
227(1)	1978 (c 27) ss 3(1), (3), (4), 4(2); 1986 (c 53) Sch 18 para 18
(2)	1978 s 2(5); 1985 (c 71) Sch 2 para 40(2)
228(1)–(3)	1984 s 28(1)–(3)
229(1)	1980 s 31(1); 1986 s 9
(2)	1980 s 31(2)
(3)	1980 s 31(3)
(4)	1980 s 31(4)
(5)	1980 s 31(5)

556

Provision	Derivations
229(6)	1980 s 31(5A); 1986 s 9
(7)	1980 s 31(5B); 1986 s 9
230(1)	1980 s 30(11)
(2)	1980 s 30(12)
231	1968 s 52
232	1980 s 74
233(1)	1968 s 51(1)
(2)	1968 s 51(2)
(3)	1968 s 51(4)
234(1)–(3)	1972 s 71(1)–(3); R 2
(4)	1972 s 71; 1973 (c 56) s 34(7)
(5)	1966 s 160(3)
(6)	1966 s 160(4)
235	1964 s 101; 1966 s 212(5); 1973 (c 65) Sch 12 para 5
Part XIII	
236(1)	1974 s 1(1)
(2)	1974 s 1(3); 1978 Sch 2 para 16(a)
(3)	1974 s 1(4); 1978 Sch 2 para 16(b)
(4)	1974 s 1(3A); 1982 Sch 3 para 29
237	1974 s 2(2)
238	1974 ss 2(1), 3(1)
239	1974 s 2(4)
240(1)	1974 s 2(3)(a); 1980 s 66(1); 1974 s 2(3)(b); 1980 s 66(1)
(2)	1974 s 3(2)(a); 1978 Sch 2 Pt I para 17; 1974 s 3(2)(b); 1978 Sch 2 Pt I para 17; 1974 s 3(2); 1978 Sch 2 para 17; 1980 s 67
(3)	1974 s 3(3), (5); 1980 s 67
(4)	1974 s 3(3A); 1980 s 67
(5)	1974 s 3(3B); 1980 s 67
(6)	1974 s 3(4); 1978 Sch 2 Pt I para 17
241	1974 s 4; 1980 s 66(4)(a)
242(1)	1974 s 5(1); SI 1983/493
(2)	1974 s 5(2)
(3)	1974 s 5(3); 1980 s 68; SI 1983/493
(4)	1974 s 5(4)
(5)	1974 s 5(5); 1978 Sch 2 para 18(b); 1982 s 51
(6)	1974 s 5(6)
(7)	1974 s 48(3), 49(3); 1978 Sch 2 para 28; R 6(1)
(8)	1974 ss 48(3), 49(3); 1978 Sch 2 para 28; R 6(1)
(9)	1974 ss 48(3)
(10)	1974 s 5(1A), (3A)
243(1)	1974 s 6(1); Sch 2 para 40; 1982 Sch 3
(2)	1974 s 6(2)
(3)	1974 s 6(3); 1981 Sch 2 para 35
244(1)	
(2)	1974 s 7(1A); Sch 2 para 19
(3)	1974 s 7(1AA); 1982 s 51
(4)	1974 s 7(1B); 1980 s 69
(5)	1974 s 7(2)
(6)	1974 s 7(3)
(7)	1974 s 7(4)
(8)	1974 s 7(5)
(9)	1974 s 7(6)
(10)	1974 s 7(7); 1980 s 66(2)
(11)	drafting
(12)	1974 ss 48(3), 49(3); 1978 Sch 2 para 28
(13)	1974 s 48(3)
(14)	1974 ss 48(3), 49(3)
245	1974 s 8(1); 1980 s 66(4)(c)
246(1)	1974 s 9(1)
(2)	1974 s 9(2)
(3)	1974 s 9(6); 1981 Sch 3 para 29
(4)	1974 s 9(7)

Provision	Derivations
(5)	1974 s 9(8)
(6)	1974 s 9(9); 1978 Sch 2 para 20; 1979 (c 33) Sch 2 para 5; 1980 s 66(4)(d)(ii)
247	1974 s 10
248(1)	1974 s 10A(1); 1978 s 8
(2)	1974 s 10A(2); 1980 s 70; 1981 Sch 3 para 30
(3)	1974 s 10A; 1980 s 66(4)(e); 1982 Sch 3
(4)	1974 s 10A(4); SI 1983/493
(5)	1974 s 10A(5); 1982 Sch 3 para 31
(6)	1974 s 10A(6); 1982 (c 45) Sch 3 para 4
(7)–(9)	1974 s 49(3); 1978 Sch 2 para 28
(10)	1974 s 48(3)
249	1974 s 10B; 1982 (c 43) s 52; R 6(2)
250(1)–(4)	1974 s 11(1)–(4); 1978 Sch 2 para 41(a)
(5)	1974 s 2(3A); 1974 s 11(5); 1980 s 66(1)
(6)	1974 s 11(6); 1978 Sch 2 para 21(a), (b)
(7)	1974 s 11(7); 1980 Sch 2 para 41(b)
251(1)	1969 s 58(1); 1974 s 44(2)
(2)	1969 s 58(2)
252	1978 (c 48) s 1
253	1978 (c 48) s 1
254	1974 s 12; 1982 Sch 2 para 32
255(1)	1969 s 59(1); 1974 Sch 3 para 31(a)
(2)	1978 Sch 3
(3)	1969 s 59(1A); 1974 Sch 3 para 31(b)
(4)	1969 s 59(2); 1974 Sch 3 para 31(c)
(5)	1969 s 59(3); 1980 s 32
(6)	1969 s 59(4); SI 1983/271
(7)	1969 s 59(5); SI 1983/271
(8)	1969 s 59(5A); 1974 (c 85) Sch 3 para 31(d); SI 1983/271
(9)	1969 s 59(6); 1974 Sch 3 para 31(e)
(10)	1969 s 59(7)
256	1968 s 53; 1974 Sch 3 para 20
Part XIV	
257(1)	1984 s 1(1)
(2)	1984 s 1(2)
(3)	1984 s 1(3)
(4)	1984 s 1(7)
(5)	1984 s 1(5)
(6)	1984 s 1(6)
258(1)	1984 s 1(4), (5)
(4)	1984 s 1(4), (5)
259(1)	1984 s 2(1)
(2)	1984 s 2(7)
(3)	1984 s 2(2)
(4)	1984 s 2(3)
260	1984 s 2(5)
261	1984 ss 2(6), (8), 27(7)
262	1984 s 3(1)
263(1)	1984 s 3(8)
(2)	1984 s 3(9)
(3)	1984 s 3(9)
264(1)	1984 s 4(1)
(2)	1984 s 4(1)(a)
(3)	1984 s 4(1)(b)
265(1)	1984 s 3(2)
(2)	1984 s 3(3), (5)
(3)	1984 s 3(3)
266(1)	1984 s 3(4), (11)
(2)	1984 s 3(6)
(3)	1984 s 3(6)
(4)	1984 s 3(6)
267(1)	1984 s 3(7)

Provision	Derivations
267(2)	1984 s 4(6)
268(1)	1984 s 4(2)
(2)	1984 s 4(2)
(3)	1984 s 4(3)
(4)	1984 s 4(4)
(5)	1984 s 4(5)
269(1)	1984 s 5(1)
(2)	1984 s 5(2)
270(1)	1984 s 5(3)
(2)	1984 s 5(4)
(3)	1984 s 5(5)
(4)	1984 s 5(3)
271(1)	1984 Sch 1 para 1(1)
(2)	1984 Sch 1 para 1(2)
(3)	1984 Sch 1 para 1(3)
(4)	1984 Sch 1 para 2(1)
(5)	1984 Sch 1 para 2(2)
(6)	1984 s 24(1), (5)
272	1984 Sch 1 para 3
273(1)	1984 Sch 1 para 4(1)
(2)	1984 Sch 1 para 4(2)
(3)	1984 Sch 1 para 4(3)
274(1)	1984 Sch 1 para 5(1), (2)
(2)	1984 Sch 1 para 5(2)
275	1984 s 7; drafting
276(1)	1984 s 26(2)
(2)	1984 s 26(3), (4)
(3)	1984 s 26(5), (6)
(4)	1984 s 24(1)
277(1)	1984 s 9(1), (12)
(2)	1984 s 9(2)
(3)	1984 s 9(3)
(4)	1984 s 9(4)
278(1)	1984 s 8(1)
(2)	1984 s 8(2)
(3)	1984 s 8(3)(a)
(4)	1984 s 8(3)(b)
(5)	1984 s 8(3)(c)
(6)	1984 s 8(9)
279(1)	1984 ss 8(4), 9(6)
(2)	1984 ss 8(5), 9(7)
(3)	1984 ss 8(6), 9(8)
(4)	1984 ss 8(8), 9(10)
(5)	1984 ss 8(7), 9(9)
280(1)	1984 s 11(1)
(2)	1984 s 11(2)
281(1)	1984 ss 9(5), 10(1), 26(7), (8)
(2)	1984 s 10(10), (11)
282(1)	1984 ss 9(5), 10(1), (3), 26(7), (8)(a)
(2)	1984 s 9(5), 10(3)
(3)	1984 ss 10(3), 26(7), (8)(b)
(4)	1984 ss 10(5), 26(8)(d)
283(1)	1984 ss 9(5), 10(1), (4), (11), 26(7)(b)
(2)	1984 s 10(5)
(3)	1984 s 10(9)
284(1)	1984 ss 10(1), (6), 26(8)(e), Sch 3 paras 1, 2
(2)	1984 s 10(6), Sch 3 para 3
285(1)	1984 ss 9(5)(b), 9(12)(d), 10(7), (12)(d), 26(8)(c), (f)
(2)	1984 s 10(8)
(3)	1984 s 10(8)
286	1984 s 10(1)(b), (2), Sch 3 para 1
287(1)	1984 s 12(1), (5)

Provision	Derivations
287(2)	1984 s 12(2)
(3)	1984 s 12(3)
(4)	1984 s 12(4)
(5)	1984 s 12(9)
(6)	1984 s 12(8)
288(1)	1984 s 12(5)
(2)	1984 s 12(5)
(3)	1984 s 12(5)
289(1)	1984 s 12(6)(a)
(2)	1984 s 12(6)(b)
(3)	1984 s 12(7)
290(1)	1984 s 14(1)
(2)	1984 s 14(1)
(3)	1984 s 14(2)
291(1)	1984 s 14(3)
(2)	1984 s 14(4), (8)
(3)	1984 s 14(5), (8)
(4)	1984 s 14(6)
(5)	1984 s 14(7)
292(1)	1984 s 16(1)
(2)	1984 s 16(2)
293(1)	1984 s 3(10)
(2)	1984 ss 8(10)(a), 9(11)
294	Drafting
295	1984 s 23
296(1)	1984 s 19(1)
(2)	1984 s 19(2)
(3)	1984 s 19(3)
(4)	1984 s 19(5)
(5)	1984 s 19(6)
(6)	1984 s 19(7), (8)
297(1)	1984 s 19(3)
(2)	1984 s 19(4), 24(1)
(3)	1984 s 19(3), (4)(c)
298(1)	1984 s 15(1)
(2)	1984 s 15(2)
299	1984 s 18
300(1)	1984 Sch 1 para 1
(2)	1984 Sch 1 para 2(1)(a), (3)
(3)	1984 Sch 1 para 3(1)(a), (3)
(4)	1984 Sch 1 paras 2(1)(b), 3(1)(b)
(5)	1984 Sch 1 paras 2(2), 3(2)
(6)	1984 s 24(1)
301	1984 s 27(4)
302(1)	1984 s 27(2)
(2)	1984 s 27(2)
(3)	1984 s 27(3)
303	Drafting
Part XV	
304(1)	1966 s 25(1); 1969 Sch 6 para 11, Sch 7; 1974 Sch 2 para 8
(2)	1966 s 25(2)
(3)	1966 s 25(3)
305(1)	1974 s 30(1); 1978 Sch 2 para 25(a)
(2)	1974 s 30(2)
(3)	1974 s 30(3); 1978 Sch 2 para 25(b)
(4)	1974 s 30(4); 1978 Sch 2 para 25(b)
306(1)	1969 s 21(1); 1974 Sch 3 para 30
(2)	1969 s 21(2); SI 1983/1804
(3)	1969 s 21(5)
(4)	1969 s 21(3)
(4)	1969 s 21(4); 1974 Sch 3 para 30
(6)	1969 s 21(5)

Housing (Scotland) Act 1987 (c 26), Sch 24 [1091]

Provision	Derivations
307	1969 s 23; R 7
308(1)	1969 s 18(1); 1974 Sch 3 para 26; 1978 Sch 2 para 30
(2)	1969 s 18(2)
(3)	1969 s 18(3)
309(1)	1967 s 18(1); 1969 Sch 6 para 32; 1974 Sch 3 para 15; 1978 Sch 2 para 30
(2)	1967 s 18(2); 1969 Sch 6 para 32
(3)	1967 s 18(3)
(4)	1967 s 18(5)
(5)	1967 s 18(6)
310	1969 s 19; 1974 Sch 3 para 27; 1978 Sch 2 para 31
311(1)	1969 s 20(1); 1974 Sch 3 para 28; 1978 Sch 2 para 32
(2)	1969 s 20(2); 1974 Sch 3 para 29
(3)	1969 s 20(3)
312	1966 s 161
Part XVI	
313(1)	1966 s 169(1)
(2)	1966 s 169(2)
(3)	1966 s 169(3)
(4)	1966 s 169(3)
(5)	1966 s 169(2); 1969 Sch 6 para 22
314	1966 s 170
315(1)	1966 s 171(1)
(2)	1966 s 171(1) proviso
(3)	1966 s 171(2)
(4)	1966 s 171(3)
(5)	1966 s 171(4)
(6)	1966 s 171(5)
316	1966 s 172; 1973 (c 65) s 237(2)
317(1)	1966 s 183; 1968 s 66; 1969 s 66; 1974 s 49(1)
(2)	1966 s 183(2)
(3)	1966 s 183(3)
318	1966 s 184; 1982 (c 48) s 54, Sch 6 para 22
319(1)	1966 ss 169(2), 185(1); 1969 Sch 6 para 26, Sch 7
(2)	1966 s 185(2); 1980 s 65(1)(g); 1982 (c 48) s 54, Sch 6 para 23
320	1966 s 186; 1969 (c 19) s 10(1); 1982 (c 48) s 54
321(1)	1966 s 118(1); R 8
(2)	R 8
(3)	1966 s 118(2)
(4)	1966 s 118(2) proviso
322	1966 s 187
323	1966 s 188
324	1966 s 190(2)–(5); 1969 Sch 6 para 27; 1971 (c 58) s 35
325(1)	1966 s 192(4); 1969 Sch 6 para 28(1); 1974 Sch 3 para 13
(2)	1966 s 192(5); 1982 (c 48) s 54
326(1)	1966 s 192(6); 1969 Sch 6 para 28(b); 1974 Sch 3 para 13
(2)	1966 s 192(7); 1969 Sch 6 para 28(c); 1974 Sch 3 para 13
327	1974 (c 44) s 121
328	1974 (c 44) s 122
329(1)	1966 s 193(1)
(2)	1966 s 194(1)
(3)	1966 s 194(2)
(4)	1966 s 194(3)
(5)	1966 s 194(4)
(6)	1966 s 196(3)
330	1966 s 197; R 1
331	1966 s 198; 1974 s 48(4)
332	1966 s 199; R 1
333	1966 s 200; R 1
334	1966 s 203
335	1966 s 205
336(1)	1954 s 14(1)
(2)	1954 s 14(1)

Provision	Derivations
336(3)	1954 s 14(1)
(4)	1954 s 14(1)
337	1966 s 204
338(1)	1966 ss 1, 208(1); 1973 Sch 12 para 6; 1974 Sch 13 para 15
'development corporation'	1968 s 67(2)
'Exchequer contribution'	1968 s 67(2)
'financial year'	1968 s 67(2)
'house'	1966 s 208(1); 1972 s 78(1); R 9
'housing action area'	1974 s 49
'housing association'	1974 s 49
'improvement'	1974 s 49
'improvement grant'	1974 s 49
'land'	1972 s 78(1)
'loan charges'	1968 s 67(2)
'local authority'	1966 s 1; 1973 Sch 12 para 6
'official representation'	1966 s 180(1); 1973 (c 65) Sch 27 Part I para 2
'order for possession'	1974 s 49
'overspill agreement'	1972 s 78(1)
'owner'	1966 s 208(1); 1974 s 49
'prescribed'	1966 s 208(1); 1974 s 49; 1980 s 73; 1982 (c 43) Sch 3 para 33
'proper officer'	drafting
'public undertakers'	1973 (c 65) s 235(2)
'repair grants'	1974 s 49
'a service charge'	1972 s 78(1)
'standard amenities'	1974 s 49
'superior'	1966 s 208(1); 1974 Sch 13 para 15
'tenancy'	1974 s 49
'tolerable standard'	1974 s 49
'year'	1972 s 78(1)
'the year 1986–87'	1972 s 78(1)
(2)	1966 s 208(2)
(3)	1966 s 208(3)
339	Drafting
340	Drafting
	SCHEDULES
Sch 1	1966 Sch 4
Sch 2	1980 Sch 1; 1986 s 10, Sch 1 para 18
Sch 3	
Part I	1980 Sch 2 Pt I
para 6	1986 Sch 1 para 19(b)
para 10	1986 Sch 1 para 19(a)
para 15	1984 (c 18) s 6
para 16	1986 s 11
Part II	1980 Sch 2 Pt II
Sch 4	1980 s 21(7), Sch 3
Sch 5	1980 s 23(3), Sch 4
Sch 6	1980 s 1A(3), Sch A1; 1981 s 35(3)
Sch 7	
Part I	
para 1	1974 (c 44) Sch 10A para 1; 1975 (c 28) Sch 3 para 18; 1978 (c 14) Sch 2 para 15
(1)–(9)	para 1(1)–(9)
para 2	para 2(1)–(3)
Part II	
para 3	para 4; 1978 (c 14) Sch 2 para 15
(1)–(6)	para 4(1)–(6)
(7)	para 4(7); 1978 Sch 2 para 15
para 4	para 5
para 5	para 6
para 6	para 7(1)–(3)

Provision	Derivations
para 7	para 8
para 8	para 9
para 9	para 10(1)–(4)
para 10	para 11(1)–(6)
para 11	para 12
para 12	para 13
Part III	
para 13	para 14(1)–(9)
para 14	para 15
Sch 8	
Part I	
para 1	1974 s 20(1)–(4)
para 2	1974 s 21
Pt II	
para 3	1974 s 22(1), (2)
para 4	1974 s 23
para 5	1974 s 26(1)–(4)
para 6	1974 s 28
para 7	1974 s 31
para 8	1974 s 32
para 9	1974 s 33
para 10	1974 s 34(1)–(7)
para 11	1974 s 36A; 1984 (c 12) Sch 4 para 61
Pt III	
para 12(1), (3), (4)	1974 s 29(1), (3), (4)
(2)	1974 s 29(2); 1978 Sch 2 para 42(a), (b)
Pt IV	
para 13(1)–(3)	1966 s 80; 1974 s 25
(4)	1966 s 87(1), (2); 1974 s 25(1)
Sch 9	1966 Sch 2
Sch 10	
para 1(1)	1966 s 6(1); 1969 Sch 6 para 3(a); 1974 Sch 3 para 4
(2)	1966 s 6(2)
(3)	1966 s 6(3)
(4)	1966 s 6(3A); 1969 Sch 6 para 3(b)
(5)	1966 s 6(4); 1969 Sch 6 para 3(c)
para 2	1966 s 7(1)
para 3	1966 s 8(1)–(5)
para 4	1966 s 9(1)–(5)
para 5	1966 s 10(1), (2)
Sch 11	
Pt I	
para 1	1966 s 126(2)–(5)
para 2	1966 s 127(1)–(8)
Pt II	
para 3	1966 s 131(1)–(4)
para 4	1966 s 132(1)–(3)
para 5(1)–(6)	1966 s 133(4)–(9)
(7)	1966 s 133(11)
para 6(1)–(7)	1966 s 130(3)–(9)
(8)	1966 s 130(10); 1981 (c 23) Sch 2 para 11
para 7(1)	1966 s 135(1)
(2)	1966 s 135(1); 1974 (c 44) Sch 13 para 12
(3)	1966 s 135(2); 1974 (c 44) Sch 13 para 12
(4)	1966 s 135(2A); 1974 (c 44) Sch 13 para 12
(5)	1966 s 135(3)
(6)	1966 s 135(4)
Pt III	
para 8	1966 Sch 6 para 1
para 9	1966 Sch 6 para 3
para 10	1966 Sch 6 para 4

Provision	Derivations
Pt IV	
para 11	1966 s 109(3)–(6); 1969 Sch 6 para 14
Sch 12	1978 s 7, Sch 1
Sch 13	1968 Sch 5; 1969 Sch 6 para 45; 1974 Sch 3 para 24
Sch 14	1968 Sch 6; 1969 Sch 6 para 46; 1974 Sch 3 para 25
Sch 15	
Pt I	
para 1(1)	1972 s 23(1)
(2)	1972 s 23(2)
(3)	1972 s 23(6)
Pt II	
para 2	1972 Sch 4 para 1; 1978 Sch 2 Pt II para 37
para 3	1972 Sch 4 para 2; 1978 Sch 2 Pt II para 38; 1986 Sch 2 para 2
para 4	1972 Sch 4 para 3
para 5	1972 Sch 4 para 7
para 6	1972 Sch 4 para 8
para 7	1972 Sch 4 para 9
para 8	1972 Sch 4 para 10
para 9	1972 Sch 4 para 11; 1975 (c 28) Sch 1 Pt I para 1(4); 1980 s 28(2)
para 10	1972 Sch 4 para 12
Sch 16	1972 Sch 5
Sch 17	1968 s 49(3); 1974 (c 45) s 45(4)
para 3	R 10
Sch 18	
Pt I	1974 Sch 1 Pt I; SI 1983/492
Pt II	1974 Sch 1 Pt II
Sch 19	
para 1	1974 Sch 2 para 1; 1981 (c 23) Sch 3 para 31(a)
para 2	1974 Sch 2 para 2
para 3	1974 Sch 2 para 4
para 4	1974 Sch 2 para 5
para 5	1974 Sch 2 para 6
para 6	1974 Sch 2 para 7; 1978 Sch 2 para 29; 1981 Sch 2 para 31(b); SI 1980/1412
para 7	1974 Sch 2 para 8
para 8	1974 Sch 2 para 9; 1981 Sch 2 para 36
Sch 20	
Pt I	
para 1	1984 s 7(1)
para 2	1984 s 7(1)
para 3	1984 s 7(2), (3)
para 4	1984 s 7(4)
para 5	1984 s 7(5)
para 6	1984 s 7(6)
para 7	1984 s 7(7)
para 8	1984 s 7(8)
Pt II	
para 9	1984 Sch 2 para 1(1), (2)
para 10(1)	1984 Sch 2 para 2(1), (2)(a)–(c), (e), (3)
(2)	1984 Sch 2 para 2(2)(d)
(3)	1984 Sch 2 para 2(1)
para 11(1)	1984 Sch 2 para 3(1)
(2)	1984 Sch 2 para (8)
(3)	1984 Sch 2 para 3(6)
(4)	1984 Sch 2 para 3(5)
para 12	1984 Sch 2 para 5
Sch 21	
para 1	1984 s 13(1)–(4)
para 2	1984 s 13(1)
para 3	1984 s 13(2)
para 4	1984 s 13(3), (4)(a)
para 5	1984 s 13(3)

Provision	Derivations
para 6	1984 s 13(4)(b), (5), (6)
para 7	1984 s 13(7), (8)
Sch 22	
Pt I	Drafting
para 6	1966 s 212(3)
para 7	SI 1986/2139
Pt II	Drafting
Sch 23	Drafting
para 1	1974 Sch 3 paras 1, 2
para 4	1974 Sch 13 para 1
para 10	1969 Sch 9; 1974 Sch 3 para 3; 1966 Sch 9
para 15	1974 Sch 3 para 33
para 18	1974 Sch 3 para 47
Sch 24	Drafting

[1091]

Housing (Scotland) Act 1988
(c 43)

ARRANGEMENT OF SECTIONS

Part I
Scottish Homes

Establishment and functions

1	Scottish Homes	[1092]
2	General functions of Scottish Homes	[1093]
3	Dissolution of SSHA and transfer of its property, rights, liabilities and obligations to Scottish Homes	[1094]
4	Regulation of housing associations in Scotland and transfer to Scottish Homes of certain property, rights, liabilities and obligations of Housing Corporation	[1095]

Finance and administration

5	Determination of financial duties of Scottish Homes	[1096]
6	Government grants to Scottish Homes	[1097]
7	Borrowing by and government loans to Scottish Homes . . .	[1098]
8	Guarantees	[1099]
9	Limit on borrowing etc	[1100]
10	Miscellaneous financial directions	[1101]
11	Accounts, annual report of Scottish Homes, etc	[1102]

Part II
Rented Accommodation

Assured tenancies

12	Assured tenancies	[1103]
13	Letting of a house together with other land	[1104]
14	Tenant sharing accommodation with person other than landlord . .	[1105]
15	Certain sublettings not to exclude any part of sublessor's premises from assured tenancy	[1106]

Assured tenancies—security of tenure

16	Security of tenure	[1107]
17	Fixing of terms of statutory assured tenancy	[1108]
18	Orders for possession	[1109]
19	Notice of proceedings for possession	[1110]
20	Extended discretion of court in possession claims	[1111]
21	Special provisions applicable to shared accommodation	[1112]
22	Payment of removal expenses in certain cases	[1113]

Assured tenancies—rents and other terms

23	Limited prohibition on assignation etc without consent	[1114]
24	Increases of rent under assured tenancies	[1115]
25	Determination of rent by rent assessment committee	[1116]
26	Access for repairs	[1117]

Assured tenancies—miscellaneous

27	Prohibition of premiums etc on assured tenancies	[1118]
28	Effect of termination of tenancy on sub-tenancies which are or are under assured tenancies	[1119]
29	Restriction on diligence	[1120]
30	Duty of landlord under assured tenancy to provide written tenancy document and weekly rent book	[1121]
31	Right of succession of spouse	[1122]

Short assured tenancies

32	Short assured tenancies	[1123]
33	Recovery of possession on termination of a short assured tenancy	[1124]
34	Reference of rents under short assured tenancies to rent assessment committee	[1125]
35	Disapplication of rent assessment committee's functions under section 34	[1126]

Protection from eviction

36	Damages for unlawful eviction	[1127]
37	The measure of damages	[1128]

★ ★ ★

Power to repeal sections 33 and 58 of Rent (Scotland) Act 1984

41	Power of Secretary of State to repeal sections 33 and 58 of Rent (Scotland) Act 1984 and to reduce phasing progressively.	[1129]

Phasing out of Rent (Scotland) Act 1984 and other transitional provisions

42	New protected tenancies restricted to special cases.	[1130]
43	Removal of special regimes for tenancies of housing associations etc	[1131]
44	New 'Part VII' contracts limited to transitional cases	[1132]
45	Transfer of existing tenancies	[1133]
46	Statutory tenants: succession	[1134]

General provisions

* * *

48	Rent assessment committees: procedure and information powers	[1136]
49	Information as to determination of rents	[1137]
50	Powers of local authorities for the purposes of giving information	[1138]
51	Application to Crown	[1139]
52	Saving for common law as to effect of notice of termination upon tacit relocation	[1140]
53	Orders and regulations	[1141]
54	Notice under Part II	[1142]
55	Interpretation of Part II	[1143]

PART III

CHANGE OF LANDLORD: SECURE TENANTS

56	Right conferred by Part III	[1144]
57	Persons by whom right may be exercised	[1145]
58	Application to exercise rights conferred by this Part and offer to sell	[1146]
59	Variation of conditions	[1147]
60	Notice of acceptance	[1148]
61	Refusal of applications	[1149]
62	Reference of Lands Tribunal	[1150]
63	Consent for subsequent disposals	[1151]
64	Extension etc of relevant periods	[1152]

PART IV

MISCELLANEOUS AND GENERAL

65	'Cost floor' limit on discount on price of house purchased by secure tenant	[1153]
66	Schemes for payments to assist local authority tenants to obtain other accommodation	[1154]
67	Abolition and capitalisation of certain subsidies and contributions	[1155]

* * *

70	Rent officers: additional functions relating to housing benefit etc	[1156]

* * *

73	Finance	[1157]
74	Short title, commencement and extent	[1158]

SCHEDULES:

Schedule 1—Scottish Homes	[1159–1177]
Schedule 2—Amendments consequential on establishing of Scottish Homes and abolition of SSHA	[1178]

* * *

Schedule 4—Tenancies which cannot be assured tenancies	[1179–1191]
Schedule 5—Grounds for possession of houses let on assured tenancies	[1192–1218]
Part I—Grounds on which sheriff must order possession	[1192–1199]
Part II—Grounds on which sheriff may order possession	[1200–1208]
Part III—Suitable alternative accommodation	[1209–1215]
Part IV—Notices relating to recovery of possession	[1216–1218]

Schedule 6—Statutory or statutory assured tenants by succession . **[1219–1220]**

* * *

Part II—Statutory assured tenants by succession—modification of enactments . . . . **[1219–1220]**

* * *

An Act to establish a body having functions relating to housing; and, as respects Scotland, to make further provision with respect to houses let on tenancies; to confer on that body and on persons approved for the purpose the right to acquire from public sector landlords certain houses occupied by secure tenants; to make new provision as to the limit on discount on the price of houses purchased by secure tenants; to provide for the making of local authority grants to assist local authority tenants to obtain accommodation otherwise than as such tenants; to abolish, and make interim provision for the capitalisation of, certain subsidies and contributions relating to housing; to make further provision about rent officers and the administration of housing benefit and rent allowance subsidy; to make provision for the disposal of housing land by development corporations; and for connected purposes. [2nd November 1988]

Be it enacted by the Queen's most Excellent Majesty, by and with the advice and consent of the Lords Spiritual and Temporal, and Commons, in this present Parliament assembled, and by the authority of the same, as follows:—

PART I
SCOTTISH HOMES

Establishment and functions

1. Scottish Homes.

(1) There shall be a body to be known as Scottish Homes.

(2) Schedule 1 to this Act shall have effect with respect to the constitution and proceedings of and other matters relating to Scottish Homes.

(3) Scottish Homes shall have the general functions of—
(a) providing, and assisting in the provision of, finance to persons or bodies intending to provide, improve, repair, maintain or manage housing;
(b) providing, improving, repairing, maintaining and managing housing (whether solely or in conjunction with any other person or body);
(c) promoting owner-occupation (especially by those seeking to purchase for the first time), the wider ownership of housing by its occupants and a greater choice of tenancy arrangements;
(d) promoting the provision and improvement of housing and the improvement of management of housing (whether by its occupants or otherwise);
(e) promoting and assisting the development of housing associations, maintaining a register of housing associations and exercising supervision and control over registered housing associations;
(f) undertaking, and assisting the undertaking of, the development, redevelopment and improvement of the physical, social, economic and recreational environment related to housing;
(g) such other general functions as are conferred upon Scottish Homes by or under this Act or any other enactment. **[1092]**

2. General functions of Scottish Homes.

(1) Scottish Homes may do anything, whether in Scotland or elsewhere, which is calculated to facilitate or is incidental or conducive to the discharge of its general functions.

Housing (Scotland) Act 1988 (c 43), s 2 [1093]

(2) Without prejudice to the generality of subsection (1) above and subject to subsection (3) [and 3A)] below Scottish Homes may—
(a) make grants;
(b) make loans;
(c) acquire, hold and dispose of securities;
(d) guarantee obligations (arising out of loans or otherwise) incurred by other persons, or grant indemnities;
(e) provide or assist in the provision of advisory or other services or facilities for any person;
(f) acquire land by agreement or gift;
(g) acquire land (including servitudes or other rights in or over land by the creation of new rights) compulsorily;
(h) hold and manage land and dispose of, or otherwise deal with, land held by it;
(j) acquire and dispose of plant, machinery, equipment and other property;
(k) develop land or carry out works on land, and maintain or assist in the maintenance of any such works;
(l) make land, plant, machinery, equipment and other property available for use by other persons;
(m) appoint other persons to act as its agents;
(n) act as agent for other persons;
(o) form companies within the meaning of the Companies Act 1985;
(p) form partnerships with other persons;
(q) promote, provide or assist in the provision of, training in matters relating to housing;
(r) carry out, commission or assist in the provision of, research and development;
(s) promote, or assist in the promotion of publicity relating to its general functions and powers and to matters relating to housing;
(t) make such charge as it thinks fit for any of its services;
(u) accept any gift or grant made to it for the purposes of any of its general functions and powers and, subject to the terms of the gift or grant and to the provisions of this Act, apply it for those purposes;
(v) turn its resources to account so far as they are not required for the exercise of any of its general functions and powers.

(3) The powers of Scottish Homes mentioned—
(a) in subsection (2)(a) to (d), (m) and (o) above may be exercised only with the approval of the Secretary of State given with the consent of the Treasury or in accordance with a general authority given by him with such consent;
(b) in subsection (2)(e) to (l) above [other than the power under paragraph (h) to dispose of land], may be exercised only in accordance with arrangements made [between it and] the Secretary of State.

[(3A) The power conferred by subsection (2)(h) above upon Scottish Homes to dispose of land may be exercised only with the consent of the Secretary of State (which consent may be given in relation to particular cases or classes of case and may be made subject to conditions).]

(4) For the purpose of the acquisition of land by Scottish Homes by agreement—
(a) the Lands Clauses Acts (except so much of them as relates to the acquisition of land otherwise than by agreement, the provisions relating to access to the special Act and sections 120 to 125 of the Lands Clauses Consolidation (Scotland) Act 1845); and
(b) sections 6 and 70 to 78 of the Railway Clauses Consolidation (Scotland) Act 1845 (as originally enacted and not as amended by section 15 of the Mines (Working Facilities and Support) Act 1923),
shall be incorporated with this section and in construing those Acts for the purposes of this section this section shall be deemed to be the special Act and Scottish Homes to be the promoters of the undertaking or company, as the case may require.

(5) For the purpose of the acquisition of land by Scottish Homes compulsorily the

Housing (Scotland) Act 1988 (c 43), s 2

Acquisition of Land (Authorisation Procedure) (Scotland) Act 1947 shall apply as if Scottish Homes were a local authority and as if this section were contained in an Act in force immediately before the commencement of that Act.

(6) * * *

(7) For the purposes of section 278 of the Town and Country Planning (Scotland) Act 1972 (general vesting declarations) Scottish Homes shall be deemed to be a public authority to which that section applies.

(8) * * *

(9) * * *

(10) The Secretary of State may give Scottish Homes directions of a general or specific character as to the exercise of its general functions and powers and it shall be the duty of Scottish Homes to comply with any such directions.

(11) Section 71 of the Race Relations Act 1976 (local authorities: general statutory duty) shall apply to Scottish Homes as it applies to a local authority. **[1093]**

NOTES to section 2
Amendments: Sub-ss (2) and (3) amended by the Local Government and Housing Act 1989 (c 42), s 179; sub-s (3A) added by *Ibid.*; sub-s 6 repealed by *Ibid.*
Sub-s (8): Sub-s (8) amends the Housing (Scotland) Act 1987 (c 26).
Sub-s (9): Sub-s (9) amends the Housing (Scotland) Act 1987 (c 26).

3. Dissolution of the SSHA and transfer of its property, rights, liabilities and obligations to Scottish Homes.

(1) The Scottish Special Housing Association shall be dissolved on such date as the Secretary of State may by order specify (the 'specified date') and all heritable or moveable property wherever situated held by the Scottish Special Housing Association immediately before the specified date shall, on that date, be transferred to and vest in Scottish Homes and all rights, liabilities and obligations of the Scottish Special Housing Association to which it was entitled or subject immediately before the specified date shall, on that date, be transferred to Scottish Homes.

(2) * * *

(3) Schedule 2 to this Act has effect for the purpose of making other amendments to the enactments specified in that Schedule consequential upon the abolition of the Scottish Special Housing Association and the establishment of Scottish Homes and for connected purposes.

(4) An order under this section shall be made by statutory instrument subject to annulment in pursuance of a resolution of either House of Parliament. **[1094]**

NOTES to section 3
Sub-s (1): See the Housing (Scotland) Act 1988 (Specified Date) Order 1988, SI 1988/2192. The specified date was 1 April 1989.
Sub-s (2): Sub-s (2) amends the Housing (Scotland) Act 1987 (c 26).

4. Regulation of housing associations in Scotland and transfer to Scottish Homes of certain property, rights, liabilities and obligations of Housing Corporation.

(1) Every housing association to which this subsection applies, that is to say, every housing association which immediately before the specified date—
  (a) was registered in the register maintained under section 3(1) of the Housing Associations Act 1985 by the Housing Corporation; and
  (b) was a society registered under the Industrial and Provident Societies Act 1965, and had its registered office for the purposes of that Act in Scotland,

Housing (Scotland) Act 1988 (c 43), s 7 [1098]

shall on the specified date, cease to be registered in the register so maintained by the Housing Corporation and shall, as from that date, be registered by virtue of this subsection in the register maintained under section 3(1) of the Housing Associations Act 1985 by Scottish Homes.

(2) The Secretary of State shall, not later than one month before the specified date, notify every housing association which appears to him to be one to which, on that date, subsection (1) above will apply of that fact and of the effect of that subsection.

(3) As soon as may be after the specified date, Scottish Homes shall notify the assistant registrar of friendly societies for Scotland of every registration which has taken place by virtue of subsection (1) above.

(4) . . .

(5) All heritable or moveable property held in Scotland by the Housing Corporation immediately before the specified date shall, on that date, be transferred to and vest in Scottish Homes and all rights, liabilities and obligations relating to or arising in connection with—
(a) the housing associations to which subsection (1) above applies, and
(b) land in Scotland held by unregistered housing associations,
being rights, liabilities and obligations to which the Housing Corporation was entitled or subject immediately before the specified date shall, on that date, be transferred to Scottish Homes.

(6) Any question as to whether any property, right, liability or obligation has been transferred to Scottish Homes under subsection (5) above shall be determined by the Secretary of State.

(7) In this section, 'specified date' has the same meaning as in section 3 above. [1095]

NOTES to section 4
Amendment: Sub-s (4) was repealed by the Housing Act 1988 (c 50), s 140, Sch 18.

Finance and administration

5. Determination of financial duties of Scottish Homes.

(1) The Secretary of State may, with the approval of the Treasury, determine the financial duties of Scottish Homes, and different determinations may be made in relation to different general functions, powers and activities of Scottish Homes.

(2) The Secretary of State shall give Scottish Homes notice of every determination, and a determination may—
(a) relate to a period beginning before the date on which it is made;
(b) contain incidental or supplemental provisions; and
(c) be varied by a subsequent determination. [1096]

6. Government grants to Scottish Homes.

(1) The Secretary of State may, with the consent of the Treasury, make such grants to Scottish Homes as appear to him to be required to enable Scottish Homes to meet the expenses it incurs in the exercise of its general functions and powers.

(2) A grant under subsection (1) above may be subject to such conditions as the Secretary of State may determine. [1097]

7. Borrowing by and government loans to Scottish Homes.

(1) For the purposes of the exercise of any of its general functions or powers Scottish Homes may borrow money from the Secretary of State and may, with the consent of the Secretary of State given with the approval of the Treasury, borrow money, whether in sterling or otherwise, from any other persons or body, whether in the United Kingdom or elsewhere.

(2) Scottish Homes may borrow money from any of its wholly owned subsidiaries without obtaining the consent of the Secretary of State.

(3) It shall be the duty of Scottish Homes to secure that none of its wholly owned subsidiaries borrows money otherwise than from Scottish Homes or from another wholly owned subsidiary of Scottish Homes, except with the consent of the Secretary of State and the approval of the Treasury.

(4) The Secretary of State may lend to Scottish Homes any sums which Scottish Homes has power to borrow from him under subsection (1) above, for such purposes as the Secretary of State may specify and the Treasury may issue to the Secretary of State out of the National Loans Fund any sums necessary to enable the Secretary of State to make loans in pursuance of this subsection.

(5) Any loans made in pursuance of subsection (4) above shall be repaid to the Secretary of State at such times and by such methods, and interest on the loans shall be paid to him at such times and at such rates, as he may from time to time direct; and all sums received by the Secretary of State in pursuance of this subsection shall be paid into the National Loans Fund.

(6) The Secretary of State shall prepare in respect of each financial year an account of the sums issued to him in pursuance of subsection (4) above and the sums received by him in pursuance of subsection (5) above and of the disposal by him of those sums, and shall send the account to the Comptroller and Auditor General before the end of the month of November next following the end of that year; and the Comptroller and Auditor General shall examine, certify and report on the account and lay copies of it and of his report before each House of Parliament.

(7) The Secretary of State shall not make a loan or give a direction in pursuance of this section except with the approval of the Treasury; and the form of the account prepared in pursuance of subsection (6) above and the manner of preparing it shall be such as the Treasury may direct.

(8) In this section and in sections 8, 10 and 11 below, 'financial year' means the period beginning with the commencement of this section and ending with 31st March of the calendar year next following such commencement and each subsequent period of 12 months ending with 31st March.

8. Guarantees.

(1) The Treasury may guarantee, in such manner and on such conditions as they think fit, the repayment of the principal of and the payment of interest on any sums which Scottish Homes borrows from a person other than the Secretary of State.

(2) Immediately after a guarantee is given under this section, the Treasury shall lay a statement of the guarantee before each House of Parliament, and where any sum is issued for fulfilling a guarantee so given, the Treasury shall lay before each House of Parliament a statement relating to that sum, as soon as possible after the end of each financial year, beginning with that in which the sum is issued and ending with that in which all liability in respect of the principal of the sum and in respect of interest on it is finally discharged.

(3) Any sums required by the Treasury for fulfilling a guarantee under this section shall be charged on and issued out of the Consolidated Fund.

(4) If any sums are issued in fulfilment of a guarantee given under this section, Scottish Homes shall make to the Treasury, at such time and in such manner as the Treasury from time to time direct, payments of such amounts as the Treasury so direct in or towards repayment of the sums so issued and payments of interest, at such rate as the Treasury so direct, on what is outstanding for the time being in respect of sums so issued.

(5) Any sums received by the Treasury in pursuance of subsection (4) above shall be paid into the Consolidated Fund.

9. Limit on borrowing etc.

(1) The aggregate amount outstanding by way of principal of—
(a) money borrowed by Scottish Homes under section 7(1) above;

(b) money borrowed by wholly owned subsidiaries of Scottish Homes with the consent of the Secretary of State and approval of the Treasury under section 7(3) above;
(c) money borrowed by the Scottish Special Housing Association or the Housing Corporation the repayment of which is a liability or obligation transferred to Scottish Homes under section 3(1) or 4(5) above;
(d) sums issued by the Treasury in fulfilment of guarantees under section 8 above,

shall not exceed £1,000 million or such greater sum not exceeding £1,500 million as the Secretary of State may specify by order made with the consent of the Treasury.

(2) An order under subsection (1) above shall be made by statutory instrument and no such order shall be made unless a draft of it has been laid before and approved by the House of Commons.

(3) In ascertaining the time limit imposed by subsection (1) above, interest payable on a loan made by the Secretary of State to Scottish Homes which, with the approval of the Treasury, is deferred and treated as part of the loan shall, so far as outstanding, be treated as outstanding by way of principal. **[1100]**

NOTES to section 9

Sub-ss (1), (2): The power to make an order has not been exercised.

10. Miscellaneous financial directions.

(1) If for a financial year the revenues of Scottish Homes exceed the total sums properly chargeable to revenue account, it shall apply the excess in such manner as the Secretary of State may, after consultation with Scottish Homes direct; and the Secretary of State may direct that the whole or part of the excess be paid to him.

(2) The Secretary of State may give directions to Scottish Homes as to matters relating to—
(a) the establishment or management of reserves;
(b) the carrying of sums to the credit of reserves; or
(c) the application of reserves for the purposes of the functions of Scottish Homes.

(3) The Secretary of State may direct Scottish Homes to pay to him the whole or part of any sums for the time being standing to the credit of its reserves or being of a capital nature and not required for the exercise of its functions.

(4) The Secretary of State may act under this section only with the approval of the Treasury.

(5) It shall be the duty of Scottish Homes to comply with directions under this section. **[1101]**

11. Accounts, annual report of Scottish Homes, etc.

(1) Scottish Homes shall keep proper accounts and other records in relation to the accounts and shall prepare in respect of each of its financial years a statement of account in such form as the Secretary of State may, with the approval of the Treasury, determine.

(2) The statement of account prepared by Scottish Homes for each financial year shall be submitted to the Secretary of State at such time as he may direct.

(3) The Secretary of State shall, on or before the end of the month of August in any year, transmit to the Comptroller and Auditor General the statement of account prepared by Scottish Homes under this section for the financial year last ended.

(4) The Comptroller and Auditor General shall examine and certify the statement of account transmitted to him under this section and lay before Parliament copies of the statement of account together with his report thereon.

(5) Scottish Homes shall provide the Secretary of State with such information relating to its general functions, powers, activities and proposed activities as he may from time to

time require, and for that purpose shall permit any person authorised in that behalf by the Secretary of State or the Comptroller and Auditor General to inspect and make copies of its accounts, books, documents or papers, and shall afford to that person such explanation thereof as he may reasonably require.

(6) It shall be the duty of Scottish Homes to make to the Secretary of State, as soon as possible after the end of each financial year, a report dealing with the activities of Scottish Homes during that year.

(7) It shall be the duty of the Secretary of State to lay before each House of Parliament a copy of each report received by him under subsection (6) above. **[1102]**

PART II
RENTED ACCOMMODATION

Assured tenancies

12. Assured tenancies.

(1) A tenancy under which a house is let as a separate dwelling is for the purposes of this Act an assured tenancy if and so long as—
  (a) the tenant or, as the case may be, at least one of the joint tenants is an individual; and
  (b) the tenant or, as the case may be, at least one of the joint tenants occupies the house as his only or principal home; and
  (c) the tenancy is not one which, by virtue of subsection (2) below, cannot be an assured tenancy.

(2) If and so long as a tenancy falls within any paragraph of Schedule 4 to this Act, it cannot be an assured tenancy; and in that Schedule 'tenancy' means a tenancy under which a house is let as a separate dwelling. **[1103]**

NOTES to section 12
Definitions: 'tenancy', 'house', 'let', 'tenant': see s 55 below.

13. Letting of a house together with other land.

(1) If, under a tenancy, a house is let together with other land, then, for the purposes of this Act—
  (a) if and so long as the main purposes of the letting is the provision of a home for the tenant or, as the case may be, at least one of the joint tenants, the other land shall be treated as part of the house; and
  (b) if and so long as the main purpose of the letting is not as mentioned in paragraph (a) above, the tenancy shall be treated as not being one under which a house is let as a separate dwelling.

(2) Nothing in subsection (1) above affects any question whether a tenancy is precluded from being an assured tenancy by virtue of any provision of Schedule 4 to this Act. **[1104]**

NOTES to section 13
Definitions: 'tenancy', 'house', 'let', 'tenant': see s 55 below.

14. Tenant sharing accommodation with person other than landlord.

(1) Where a tenant has the exclusive occupation of any accommodation (in this section referred to as 'the separate accommodation')—
  (a) the terms as between the tenant and his landlord on which he holds the separate accommodation include the use of other accommodation ('the shared

accommodation') in common with another person or other persons, not being or including the landlord, and
   (b) by reason only of the circumstances mentioned in paragraph (a) above, the separate accommodation would not, apart from this section, be a house let on an assured tenancy,
the separate accommodation shall be deemed to be a house let on an assured tenancy and the following provisions of this section shall have effect.

(2) While the tenant is in possession of the separate accommodation, any term of the tenancy terminating or modifying, or providing for the termination or modification of, his right to the use of any of the shared accommodation which is living accommodation shall be of no effect.

(3) Where the terms of the tenancy are such that, at any time during the tenancy, the persons in common with whom the tenant is entitled to the use of the shared accommodation could be varied or their number could be increased, nothing in subsection (2) above shall prevent those terms from having effect so far as they relate to any such variation or increase.

(4) In this section 'living accommodation' means accommodation of such a nature that the fact that it constitutes or is included in the shared accommodation is sufficient, apart from this section, to prevent the tenancy from constituting an assured tenancy of a house. **[1105]**

NOTES to section 14

Definitions: 'tenant', 'tenancy', 'landlord', 'house', 'let': see s 55 below; 'assured tenancy': see s 12 above.

15. Certain sublettings not to exclude any part of sublessor's premises from assured tenancy.

(1) Where the tenant of a house has sublet a part but not the whole of the house, then, as against his landlord or any superior landlord, no part of the house shall be treated as excluded from being a house let on an assured tenancy by reason only that the terms on which any person claiming under the tenant holds any part of the house includes the use of accommodation in common with other persons.

(2) Nothing in this section affects the rights against, and liabilities to, each other of the tenant and any person claiming under him, or of any two such persons. **[1106]**

NOTES to section 15

Definitions: 'tenant', 'house', 'landlord', 'let': see s 55 below; 'assured tenancy': see s 12 above.

Assured tenancies—security of tenure

16. Security of tenure.

(1) After the termination of a contractual tenancy which was an assured tenancy the person who, immediately before that termination, was the tenant, so long as he retains possession of the house without being entitled to do so under a contractual tenancy shall, subject to section 12 above and sections 18 and 32 to 35 below—
   (a) continue to have the assured tenancy of the house; and
   (b) observe and be entitled to the benefits of all the terms and conditions of the original contract of tenancy so far as they are consistent with this Act but excluding any—
      (i) which makes provision for the termination of the tenancy by the landlord or the tenant; or
      (ii) which makes provision for an increase in rent (including provision whereby the rent for a particular period will or may be greater than that for an earlier period) otherwise than by an amount specified in [or fixed by reference to

factors specified in] that contract or by a percentage there specified [or fixed by reference to factors there specified] of an amount of rent payable under the tenancy.

[(1A) The factors referred to in subsection (1)(b)(ii) above must be—
(a) factors which, once specified, are not wholly within the control of the landlord; and
(b) such as will enable the tenant at all material times to ascertain without undue difficulty any amount or percentage falling to be fixed by reference to them.]

and references in this part of this Act to a 'statutory assured tenancy' are references to an assured tenancy which a person is continuing to have by virtue of this subsection, subsection (1) of section 31 below, or section 3A of the Rent (Scotland) Act 1984.

(2) A statutory assured tenancy cannot be brought to an end by the landlord except by obtaining an order of the sheriff in accordance with the following provisions of this Part of this Act.

(3) Notwithstanding anything in the terms and conditions of tenancy of a house being a statutory assured tenancy, a landlord who obtains an order for possession of the house as against the tenant shall not be required to give him any notice to quit.   [1107]

NOTES to section 16
Amendments: Sub-s (1) amended by the Local Government and Housing Act 1989 (c 42), s 195, Sch 11, para 99; sub-s (1A) added by *Ibid*.
Definitions: 'tenancy', 'tenant', 'house', 'landlord', 'order for possession': see s 55 below; 'assured tenancy': see s 12 above.

17. Fixing of terms of statutory assured tenancy.

(1) In this section, in relation to a statutory assured tenancy 'the former tenancy' means the tenancy on the termination of which the statutory assured tenancy arises.

(2) Not later than the first anniversary of the termination of the former tenancy, the landlord may serve on the tenant, or the tenant may serve on the landlord, a notice in the prescribed form—
(a) proposing terms of the statutory assured tenancy other than as to the amount of the rent different from those which have effect by virtue of section 16(1)(b) above; and
(b) proposing, if appropriate, an adjustment of the rent to take account of the proposed terms.

(3) Where a notice has been served under subsection (2) above—
(a) within the period of three months beginning on the date on which the notice was served on him, the landlord or the tenant, as the case may be, may refer the notice to a rent assessment committee under subsection (4) below in the prescribed form; and
(b) if the notice is not so referred, then, with effect from such date, not falling within the period of three months referred to in paragraph (a) above, as may be specified in the notice, the terms proposed in the notice shall become terms of the tenancy in substitution for any other terms dealing with the same subject matter and the amount of the rent shall be varied in accordance with any adjustment so proposed.

(4) Where a notice under subsection (2) above is referred to a rent assessment committee, the committee shall consider the terms proposed in the notice and shall determine whether those terms, or some other terms (dealing with the same subject matter as the proposed terms), are such as, in the committee's opinion, might reasonably be expected to be found in a contractual assured tenancy of the house concerned, being a tenancy—
(a) which begins at the termination of the former tenancy; and

(b) which is granted by a willing landlord on terms which, except in so far as they relate to the subject matter of the proposed terms, are those of the statutory assured tenancy at the time of the committee's consideration.

(5) Whether or not a notice under subsection (2) above proposes an adjustment of the amount of the rent under the statutory assured tenancy, where a rent assessment committee determine any terms under subsection (4) above, they shall, if they consider it appropriate, specify such an adjustment to take account of the terms so determined.

(6) In making a determination under subsection (4) above, or specifying an adjustment of an amount of rent under subsection (5) above, there shall be disregarded any effect on the terms or the amount of the rent attributable to the granting of a tenancy to a sitting tenant.

(7) Where a notice under subsection (2) above is referred to a rent assessment committee, then, unless the landlord and the tenant otherwise agree, with effect from such date as the committee may direct—
(a) the terms determined by the committee shall become terms of the statutory assured tenancy in substitution for any other terms dealing with the same subject matter; and
(b) the amount of the rent under the statutory assured tenancy shall be altered to accord with any adjustment specified by the committee,

but for the purposes of paragraph (b) above, the committee shall not direct a date earlier than the date on which the notice in question was referred to them.

(8) Nothing in this section requires a rent assessment committee to continue with a determination under subsection (4) above if the tenancy has been brought to an end by order of the sheriff under this Part of this Act or if the landlord and tenant give notice in writing that they no longer require such a determination. [1108]

NOTES to section 17

Sub-s (2): The prescribed forms are contained in the Assured Tenancies (Forms) (Scotland) Regulations 1988, SI 1988/2109, paras [1440] ff below.

Sub-ss (2)–(8): The constitution of rent assessment committees is described in the Rent (Scotland) Act 1984 (c 58), s 44, Sch 4.

Definitions: 'statutory assured tenancy', 'tenancy', 'landlord', 'tenant', 'prescribed', 'house': see s 55 below.

18. Orders for possession.

(1) The sheriff shall not make an order for possession of a house let on an assured tenancy except on one or more of the grounds set out in Schedule 5 of this Act.

(2) The following provisions of this section have effect, subject to section 19 below, in relation to proceedings for the recovery of possession of a house let on an assured tenancy.

(3) If the sheriff is satisfied that any of the grounds in Part I of Schedule 5 to this Act is established then, subject to subsection (6) below, he shall make an order for possession.

(4) If the sheriff is satisfied that any of the grounds in Part II of Schedule 5 to this Act is established, he shall not make an order for possession unless he considers it reasonable to do so.

(5) Part III of Schedule 5 to this Act shall have effect for supplementing Ground 9 in that Schedule and Part IV of that Schedule shall have effect in relation to notices given as mentioned in Grounds 1 to 5 of that Schedule.

(6) The sheriff shall not make an order for possession of a house which is for the time being let on an assured tenancy, not being a statutory assured tenancy, unless—
(a) the ground for possession is Ground 2 or Ground 8 in Part I of Schedule 5 to this Act or any of the grounds in Part II of that Schedule, other than Ground 9 or Ground 10 or Ground 17; and

(b) the terms of the tenancy make provision for it to be brought to an end on the ground in question.

(7) Subject to the preceding provisions of this section, the sheriff may make an order for possession of a house on grounds relating to a contractual tenancy which has been terminated; and where an order is made in such circumstances, any statutory assured tenancy which has arisen on that termination shall, without any notice, end on the day on which the order takes effect. **[1109]**

NOTES to section 18

Definitions: 'order for possession', 'tenancy', 'let': see s 55 below; 'assured tenancy': see s 12 above; 'statutory assured tenancy': see s 16 above.

19. Notice of proceedings for possession.

(1) The sheriff shall not entertain proceedings for possession of a house let on an assured tenancy unless—
   (a) the landlord (or, where there are joint landlords, any of them) has served on the tenant a notice in accordance with this section; or
   (b) he considers it reasonable to dispense with the requirement of such a notice.

(2) The sheriff shall not make an order for possession on any of the grounds in Schedule 5 to this Act unless that ground [and particulars of it are] specified in the notice under this section; but the grounds specified in such a notice may be altered or added to with the leave of the sheriff.

(3) A notice under this section is one [in the prescribed form] informing the tenant that—
   (a) the landlord intends to raise proceedings for possession of the house on one or more of the grounds specified in the notice; and
   (b) those proceedings will not be raised earlier than the expiry of the period of two weeks or two months (whichever is appropriate under subsection (4) below) from the date of service of the notice.

(4) The minimum period to be specified in a notice as mentioned in subsection (3)(b) above is—
   (a) two months if the notice specifies any of Grounds 1, 2, 5, 6, 7, 9 and 17 in Schedule 5 to this Act (whether with or without other grounds); and
   (b) in any other case, two weeks.

(5) The sheriff may not exercise the power conferred by subsection (1)(b) above if the landlord seeks to recover possession on Ground 8 in Schedule 5 to this Act.

(6) Where a notice under this section relating to a contractual tenancy—
   (a) is served during the tenancy; or
   (b) is served after the tenancy has been terminated but relates (in whole or in part) to events occurring during the tenancy,
the notice shall have effect notwithstanding that the tenant becomes or has become tenant under a statutory assured tenancy arising on the termination of the contractual tenancy.

(7) A notice under this section shall cease to have effect 6 months after the date on or after which the proceedings for possession to which it relates could have been raised. **[1110]**

NOTES to section 19

Amendments: Sub-s (2) and (3) were amended by the Housing Act 1988 (c 50), s 140, Sch 17, para 85.

Sub-s (3): The prescribed forms are contained in the Assured Tenancies (Forms) (Scotland) Regulations 1988, SI 1988/2109, paras [1440] ff below.

Definitions: 'proceedings for possession', 'house', 'tenancy', 'landlord', 'tenant', 'order for possession', 'prescribed': see s 55 below; 'assured tenancy'; see s 12 above; 'statutory assured tenancy': see s 16 above.

20. Extended discretion of court in possession claims.

(1) Subject to subsection (6) below, the sheriff may adjourn for such period or periods as he thinks fit, proceedings for possession of a house let on an assured tenancy.

(2) On the making of an order for possession of a house let on an assured tenancy or at any time before the execution of such an order, the sheriff, subject to subsection (6) below, may—
   (a) sist or suspend execution of the order; or
   (b) postpone the date of possession,
for such period or periods as he thinks fit.

(3) On any such adjournment as is referred to in subsection (1) above or on any such sist, suspension or postponement as is referred to in subsection (2) above, the sheriff, unless he considers that to do so would cause exceptional hardship to the tenant or would otherwise be unreasonable, shall impose conditions with regard to payment by the tenant of arrears of rent (if any) and rent or payments in respect of occupation after the termination of the tenancy and may impose such other conditions as he thinks fit.

(4) If any such conditions as are referred to in subsection (3) above are complied with, the sheriff may, if he thinks fit, recall any such order as is referred to in subsection (2) above.

(5) In any case where—
   (a) at a time when proceedings are brought for possession of a house let on an assured tenancy, any person having occupancy rights under section 1 or 18 of the Matrimonial Homes (Family Protection) (Scotland) Act 1981 is in occupation of the house; and
   (b) the assured tenancy is terminated as a result of those proceedings,
that person, so long as he or she remains in occupation, shall have the same rights in relation to, or in connection with, any such adjournment as is referred to in subsection (1) above or any such sist, suspension or postponement as is referred to in subsection (2) above, as he or she would have if those occupancy rights were not affected by the termination of the tenancy.

(6) This section does not apply if the sheriff is satisfied that the landlord is entitled to possession of the house on the ground specified in section 33(1) of this Act or on any of the grounds in Part I of Schedule 5 to this Act.   **[1111]**

NOTES to section 20
Definitions: 'proceedings for possession', 'house', 'let', 'tenancy', 'order for possession', 'tenant', 'landlord': see s 55 below; 'assured tenancy': see s 12 above.

21. Special provisions applicable to shared accommodation.

(1) This section applies in a case falling within subsection (1) of section 14 above and expressions used in this section have the same meaning as in that section.

(2) Without prejudice to the enforcement of any order made under subsection (3) below, while the tenant is in possession of the separate accommodation, no order shall be made for possession of any of the shared accommodation, whether on the application of the immediate landlord of the tenant or on the application of any person from whom that landlord derives title, unless a like order has been made, or is made at the same time, in respect of the separate accommodation; and the provisions of section 17 above shall have effect accordingly.

(3) On the application of the landlord, the sheriff may make such order as he thinks just either—
   (a) terminating the right of the tenant to use the whole or any part of the shared accommodation other than living accommodation; or
   (b) modifying his right to use the whole or any part of the shared accommodation, whether by varying the persons or increasing the number of persons entitled to the use of that accommodation, or otherwise.

(4) No order shall be made under subsection (3) above so as to effect any termination or modification of the rights of the tenant which, apart from section 14(2) above, could not be effected by or under the terms of the tenancy. **[1112]**

NOTES to section 21

Definitions: 'tenant', 'landlord', 'order for possession', 'tenancy': see s 55 below; 'separate accommodation', 'shared accommodation': see s 14 above.

22. Payment of removal expenses in certain cases.

(1) Where the sheriff makes an order for possession of a house let on an assured tenancy on Ground 6 or Ground 9 in Schedule 5 to this Act (but not on any other ground), the landlord shall pay to the tenant a sum equal to the reasonable expenses likely to be incurred by the tenant in removing from the house.

(2) Any question as to the amount payable by the landlord to a tenant by virtue of subsection (1) above shall be determined by agreement between the landlord and the tenant or, in default of agreement, by the sheriff. **[1113]**

NOTES to section 22

Definitions: 'order for possession', 'house', 'tenancy', 'landlord', 'tenant': see s 55 below; 'assured tenancy': see s 12 above.

Assured tenancies—rents and other terms

23. Limited prohibition on assignation etc without consent.

(1) Subject to subsection (2) below, it shall be an implied term of every assured tenancy that, except with the consent of the landlord, the tenant shall not—
(a) assign the tenancy (in whole or in part); or
(b) sublet or part with possession of the whole or any part of the house let on the tenancy.

(2) Subsection (1) above does not apply if, under the terms of the tenancy, there is provision prohibiting or permitting (whether absolutely or conditionally) assignation, subletting or parting with possession by the tenant. **[1114]**

NOTES to section 23

Definitions: 'assured tenancy': see s 12 above; 'tenancy', 'landlord', 'tenant', 'house': see s 55 below.

24. Increases of rent under assured tenancies.

(1) For the purpose of securing an increase in the rent under [a statutory] assured tenancy, the landlord may serve on the tenant a notice in the prescribed form proposing a new rent to take effect—
(a) if the tenancy was [at the time of service of the notice] a contractual tenancy (whether or not renewed by operation of tacit relocation), immediately after its termination; or
(b) if the tenancy was [at the time of service of the notice] not such a contractual tenancy, at any time during the tenancy,
but not earlier than the expiry of the minimum period after the date of service of the notice.

(2) The minimum period referred to in subsection (1) above is—
(a) if the assured tenancy is for 6 months or more, 6 months;
(b) if the assured tenancy is less than 6 months, the duration of the tenancy or one month (whichever is the longer).

(3) Where a notice is served under subsection (1) above, a new rent specified in the

notice shall take effect as mentioned in the notice unless, before the beginning of the period to which the new rent relates—
  (a) the tenant refers the notice to a rent assessment committee in the prescribed form; or
  (b) the landlord and the tenant agree on a variation of the rent which is different from that proposed in the notice or agree that the rent should not be varied.

(4) Where a notice is served under subsection (1) above but the rent under the tenancy has previously been increased (whether by agreement or by virtue of a notice under subsection (1) above or a determination under section 25 below) the new rent shall take effect not earlier than the first anniversary of the date on which that increase took effect.

(5) Nothing in this section
[(a) extends to a statutory assured tenancy of which there is a term] which makes provision for an increase in rent (including provision whereby the rent for a particular period will or may be greater than that for an earlier period) by an amount specified in [or fixed by reference to factors specified in] the tenancy contract or by a percentage there specified [or fixed by reference to factors there specified] of an amount of rent payable under the tenancy, [or
  (b) affects the operation of any term of a contractual tenancy which makes provision for an increase in rent (including provision whereby the rent for a particular period will or may be greater than that for an earlier period).]

[(6) The factors referred to in subsection (5) above must be—
  (a) factors which, once specified, are not wholly within the control of the landlord; and
  (b) such as will enable the tenant at all material times to ascertain without undue difficulty any amount or percentage falling to be fixed by reference to them.] [1115]

NOTES to section 24

Amendments: Sub-ss (1), (5) amended by the Local Government and Housing Act 1989 (c 42), s 195, Sch 11, para 99; sub-s (6) added by *Ibid*.
Sub-s (1): The prescribed forms are contained in the Assured Tenancies (Forms) (Scotland) Regulations 1988, SI 1988/2109, paras [1440] ff below.
Definitions: 'statutory assured tenancy': see s 16 above; 'tenancy', 'landlord', 'tenant', 'prescribed': see s 55 below; 'assured tenancy': see s 12 above.

25. Determination of rent by rent assessment committee.

(1) Where, under subsection (3)(a) of section 24 above, a tenant refers to a rent assessment committee a notice under subsection (1) of that section, the committee shall determine the rent at which, subject to subsections (2) and (3) below, the committee consider that the house might reasonably be expected to be let in the open market by a willing landlord under an assured tenancy—
  (a) which begins at the beginning of the period to which the new rent specified in the notice relates;
  (b) the terms of which (other than those relating to rent) are the same as those of the tenancy to which the notice relates; and
  (c) in respect of which the same notices, if any, have been given under any of Grounds 1 to 5 of Schedule 5 to this Act, as have been given (or have effect as if given) in relation to the tenancy to which the notice relates.

(2) In making a determination under this section, there shall be disregarded any effect on the rent attributable to—
  (a) the granting of a tenancy to a sitting tenant;
  (b) an improvement carried out by the tenant or a predecessor in title of his unless the improvement was carried out in pursuance of the terms of the tenancy; and
  (c) a failure by the tenant to comply with any terms of the tenancy.

(3) In this section 'rent' includes any sums payable by the tenant to the landlord on

[1116]

account of the use of furniture or for services, whether or not those sums are separate from the sums payable for the occupation of the house concerned or are payable under separate agreements.

(4) Where any rates in respect of the house concerned are borne by the landlord or a superior landlord, the rent assessment committee shall make their determination under this section as if the rates were not so borne.

(5) In any case where—
  (a) a rent assessment committee have before them at the same time the reference of a notice under section 17(2) above relating to a tenancy (in this subsection referred to as 'the section 17 reference') and the reference of a notice under section 24(1) above relating to the same tenancy (in this subsection referred to as 'the section 24 reference'); and
  (b) the date specified in the notice under section 17(2) above is not later than the first day of the new period specified in the notice under section 24(1) above; and
  (c) the committee propose to hear the two references together,
the committee shall make a determination in relation to the section 17 reference before making their determination in relation to the section 24 reference and, accordingly, in such a case the reference in subsection (1)(b) above to the terms of the tenancy to which the notice relates shall be construed as a reference to those terms as varied by virtue of the determination made in relation to the section 17 reference.

(6) Where a notice under section 24(1) above has been referred to a rent assessment committee, then, unless the landlord and the tenant otherwise agree, the rent determined by the committee (together with, in a case where subsection (4) above applies, the appropriate amount in respect of rates) shall be the rent under the tenancy with effect from the beginning of the period to which the new rent specified in the notice relates or, if it appears to the rent assessment committee that that would cause undue hardship to the tenant, with effect from such date as the committee may direct (being a date after the beginning of that period but not after the date when the committee determined the rent).

(7) Nothing in this section requires a rent assessment committee to continue with their determination of a rent for a house if the tenancy has been brought to an end by order of the sheriff under this Part of this Act or if the landlord and tenant give notice in writing that they no longer require such a determination.

(8) Nothing in this section or section 24 above affects the right of the landlord and the tenant under an assured tenancy to vary by agreement any term of the tenancy (including a term relating to rent). **[1116]**

NOTES to section 25

Definitions: 'tenant', 'house', 'landlord', 'tenancy': see s 55 below; 'assured tenancy': see s 12 above.

26. Access for repairs.

It shall be an implied term of every assured tenancy that the tenant shall afford to the landlord reasonable access to the house let on the tenancy and all reasonable facilities for executing therein any repairs which the landlord is entitled to execute. **[1117]**

NOTES to section 26

Definitions: 'assured tenancy': see s 12 above; 'tenancy', 'tenant', 'landlord', 'house': see s 55 below.

Assured tenancies—miscellaneous

27. Prohibition of premiums etc on assured tenancies.

Sections 82, 83 and 86 to 90 of the Rent (Scotland) Act 1984 (which make it an offence to require premiums and advance payment of rent in respect of protected tenancies and

make related provision) shall apply in relation to assured tenancies as they apply in relation to protected tenancies (including protected tenancies which are regulated tenancies), but with the following modifications—
 (a) section 83(5) shall not apply; and
 (b) section 88(1) shall apply as if for the references to 12th August 1971 there were substituted references to the date of commencement of this section. [1118]

NOTES to section 27
Protected tenancies and regulated tenancies are defined by the Rent (Scotland) Act 1984 (c 58), Part I, paras [249] ff above.
Amendments: 'assured tenancies;: see s 12 above; 'tenancy': see s 55 below.

28. Effect of termination of tenancy on subtenancies which are or are under assured tenancies.

(1) If the sheriff makes an order for possession of a house from a tenant nothing in the order shall affect the right of any sub-tenant to whom the house or any part of it has been lawfully sublet on an assured tenancy before the commencement of the proceedings to retain possession by virtue of this Part of this Act, nor shall the order operate to give a right to possession as against any such sub-let.

(2) Where an assured tenancy of a house is terminated, either as a result of an order for possession or for any other reason, any sub-tenant to whom the house or any part of it has been lawfully sublet shall, subject to the provisions of this Act, be deemed to become the tenant of the landlord on the same terms as he would have held from the tenant if the tenant's assured tenancy had continued.

(3) A tenancy which, but for paragraph 2 of Schedule 4 to this Act, would have been an assured tenancy shall be treated for the purposes of subsection (2) above as an assured tenancy. [1119]

NOTES to section 28
Definitions: 'order for possession', 'tenant', 'tenancy', 'landlord': see s 55 below; 'assured tenancy': see s 12 above.

29. Restriction on diligence.

No diligence shall be done in respect of the rent of any house let on an assured tenancy except with the leave of the sheriff; and the sheriff shall, with respect to any application for such leave, have the same powers with respect to adjournment, sist, suspension, postponement and otherwise as are conferred by section 20 above in relation to proceedings for possession of such a house. [1120]

NOTES to section 29
Definitions: 'house', 'let', 'tenancy': see s 55 below; 'assured tenancy': see s 12 above.

30. Duty of landlord under assured tenancy to provide written tenancy document and weekly rent book.

(1) It shall be the duty of the landlord under an assured tenancy (of whatever duration)—
 (a) to draw up a document stating (whether expressly or by reference) the terms of the tenancy;
 (b) to ensure that it is so drawn up and executed that it is probative or holograph of the parties; and
 (c) to give a copy of it to the tenant.

(2) On summary application by a tenant under an assured tenancy, the sheriff shall by order—
 (a) where it appears to him that the landlord has failed to draw up a document which

fairly reflects the existing terms of the tenancy, draw up such a document or, as the case may be, adjust accordingly the terms of such document as there is; and
(b) in any case, declare that the document (as originally drawn up or, where he has drawn it up or adjusted it, as so drawn up or adjusted) fairly reflects the terms of the assured tenancy;

and, where the sheriff has made such a declaration in relation to a document which he has drawn up or adjusted, it shall be deemed to have been duly executed by the parties as so drawn up or adjusted.

(3) A tenant shall not be required to make payment in respect of anything done under subsection (1) above.

(4) Where, under an assured tenancy, rent is payable weekly, it shall be the duty of the landlord to provide a rent book.

(5) A rent book shall contain such notices which shall be in such form and shall relate to such matters as may be prescribed and otherwise shall comply with such requirements as may be prescribed.

(6) If, at any time, the landlord fails to comply with any requirement imposed by or under subsection (4) or (5) above he and any person who on his behalf demands or receives rent in respect of the tenancy shall be liable, on summary conviction, to a fine not exceeding level 4 on the standard scale.

(7) Where an offence under subsection (6) above committed by a body corporate is proved to have been committed with the consent or connivance of, or to be attributable to any neglect on the part of, a director, manager, secretary or other similar officer of the body corporate, or a person purporting to act in any such capacity, he, as well as the body corporate, is guilty of an offence and liable to be proceeded against and punished accordingly. **[1121]**

NOTES to section 30

Sub-s (5): See the Assured Tenancies (Rent Book) (Scotland) Regulations 1988, SI 1988/2085, paras [1437] ff below.

Definitions: 'landlord', 'tenancy', 'tenant', 'prescribed: see s 55 below; 'assured tenancy': see s 12 above; 'the standard scale': level 4 is currently £1,000. See the Increase of Criminal Penalties Etc (Scotland) Order 1984, SI 1984/526.

31. Right of succession of spouse.

(1) In any case where—
(a) the sole tenant under an assured tenancy dies; and
(b) immediately before the death the tenant's spouse was occupying the house as his or her only or principal home; and
(c) the tenant was not himself a successor as explained in subsection (2) or (3) below,

the tenant's spouse shall, as from the death and for so long as he or she retains possession of the house without being entitled to do so under a contractual tenancy, be entitled to a statutory assured tenancy of the house.

(2) For the purposes of this section, a tenant was a successor in relation to a tenancy—
(a) if the tenancy had become vested in him either by virtue of this section or under the will or intestacy of a previous tenant; or
(b) if he was a statutory assured tenant by virtue of section 3A of the Rent (Scotland) Act 1984; or
(c) if at some time before the tenant's death the tenancy was a joint tenancy held by him and one or more other persons and, prior to his death, he had become the sole tenant by survivorship; or
(d) in the case of a tenancy (hereinafter referred to as 'the new tenancy') which was granted to him (alone or jointly with others) if—
(i) at some time before the grant of the new tenancy he was, by virtue of paragraph (a), (b) or (c) above, a successor to an earlier tenancy of the same or substantially the same house as is let under the new tenancy; and

Housing (Scotland) Act 1988 (c 43), s 33 [1124]

    (ii) at all times since he became such a successor he has been a tenant (alone or jointly with others) of the house which is let under the new tenancy or of a house which is substantially the same as that house.

(3) No order for possession under Ground 7 of Schedule 5 to this Act shall be made—
(a) in relation to a case to which this section relates by virtue of subsection (1) above; or
(b) where the tenant's spouse succeeds to the tenancy under the will or intestacy of the tenant.

(4) For the purposes of this section a person who was living with the tenant at the time of the tenant's death as his or her wife or husband shall be treated as the tenant's spouse. [1122]

NOTES to section 31

Definitions: 'tenant', 'tenancy', 'house', 'order for possession': see s 55 below; 'statutory assured tenancy': see s 16 above; 'assured tenancy': see s 12 above.

Short assured tenancies

32. Short assured tenancies.

(1) A short assured tenancy is an assured tenancy—
(a) which is for a term of not less than six months; and
(b) in respect of which a notice is served as mentioned in subsection (2) below.

(2) The notice referred to in subsection (1)(b) above is one which—
(a) is in such form as may be prescribed;
(b) is served before the creation of the assured tenancy;
(c) is served by the person who is to be the landlord under the assured tenancy (or, where there are to be joint landlords under the tenancy, is served by a person who is to be one of them) on the person who is to be the tenant under that tenancy; and
(d) states that the assured tenancy to which it relates is to be a short assured tenancy.

(3) Subject to subsection (4) below, if, at the ish of a short assured tenancy—
(a) it continues by tacit relocation; or
(b) a new contractual tenancy of the same or substantially the same premises comes into being under which the landlord and the tenant are the same as at that ish, the continued tenancy or, as the case may be, the new contractual tenancy shall be a short assured tenancy, whether or not it fulfils the conditions in paragraphs (a) and (b) of subsection (1) above.

(4) Subsection (3) above does not apply if, before the beginning of the continuation of the tenancy or, as the case may be, before the beginning of the new tenancy, the landlord or, where there are joint landlords, any of them serves written notice in such form as may be prescribed on the tenant that the continued or new tenancy is not to be a short assured tenancy.

(5) Section 25 above shall apply in relation to a short assured tenancy as if in subsection (1) of that section the reference to an assured tenancy were a reference to a short assured tenancy. [1123]

NOTES to section 32

Sub-s (2): See the Assured Tenancies (Forms) (Scotland) Regulations 1988, SI 1988/2109, paras [1440] ff below.
Definitions: 'assured tenancy': see s 12 above; 'tenancy', 'prescribed, 'landlord', 'tenant': see s 55 below.

33. Recovery of possession on termination of a short assured tenancy.

(1) Without prejudice to any right of the landlord under a short assured tenancy to recover possession of the house let on the tenancy in accordance with sections 12 to 31 of this Act, the sheriff shall make an order for possession of the house if he is satisfied—

(a) that the short assured tenancy has reached its ish;
(b) that tacit relocation is not operating;
(c) that no further contractual tenancy (whether a short assured tenancy or not) is for the time being in existence; and
(d) that the landlord (or, where there are joint landlords, any of them) has given to the tenant notice stating that he requires possession of the house.

(2) The period of notice to be given under subsection (1)(d) above shall be—
  (i) if the terms of the tenancy provide, in relation to such notice, for a period of more than two months, that period;
  (ii) in any other case, two months.

(3) A notice under paragraph (d) of subsection (1) above may be served before, at or after the termination of the tenancy to which it relates.

(4) Where the sheriff makes an order for possession of a house by virtue of subsection (1) above, any statutory assured tenancy which has arisen as at that ish shall end (without further notice) on the day on which the order takes effect. **[1124]**

NOTES to section 33
Definitions: 'landlord', 'tenancy', 'house', 'let', 'tenant', 'order for possession': see s 55 below; 'short assured tenancy': see s 32 above.

34. Reference of rents under short assured tenancies to rent assessment committee.

(1) Subject to subsection (2) and section 35 below, the tenant under a short assured tenancy may make an application in the prescribed form to a rent assessment committee for a determination of the rent which, in the committee's opinion, the landlord might reasonably be expected to obtain under the short assured tenancy.

(2) No application may be made under this section if the rent payable under the tenancy is a rent previously determined under this section of section 25 above.

(3) Where an application is made to a rent assessment committee under subsection (1) above with respect to the rent under a short assured tenancy, the committee shall not make such a determination as is referred to in that subsection unless they consider—
(a) that there is a sufficient number of similar houses in the locality let on assured tenancies (whether short assured tenancies or not); and
(b) that the rent payable under the short assured tenancy in question is significantly higher than the rent which the landlord might reasonably be expected to be able to obtain under the tenancy, having regard to the level of rents payable under the tenancies referred to in paragraph (a) above.

(4) Where, on an application under this section, a rent assessment committee make a determination of a rent for a short assured tenancy—
(a) the determination shall have effect from such date as the committee may direct, not being earlier than the date of the application;
(b) if at or after the time when the determination takes effect, the rent which, apart from this paragraph, would be payable under the tenancy exceeds the rent so determined, the excess shall be irrecoverable from the tenant; and
(c) no further new rent for a tenancy of the house shall take effect under section 24(3) or 25 above until after the first anniversary of the date on which the determination takes effect.

(5) Subsections (3), (4) and (7) of section 25 above apply in relation to a determination of rent under this section as they apply in relation to a determination under that section. **[1125]**

NOTES to section 34
Sub-s (1): See the Assured Tenancies (Forms) (Scotland) Regulations 1988, SI 1988/2109, paras [1440] below, and the Rent Assessment Committee (Assured Tenancies) (Scotland) Regulations 1989, SI 1989/81, paras [1454] ff below.

Housing (Scotland) Act 1988 (c 43), s 36 [1127]

Definitions: 'tenant', 'tenancy', 'prescribed', 'landlord', 'house', 'let': see s 55 below; 'short assured tenancy': see s 32 above.

35. Disapplication of rent assessment committee's functions under section 34.

(1) If the Secretary of State by order so provides, section 34 above shall not apply in such cases or to tenancies of houses in such areas or in such other circumstances as may be specified in the order.

(2) No order shall be made under this section unless a draft of the order has been laid before, and approved by a resolution of, each House of Parliament. [1126]

NOTES to section 35
The power to make an order has not been exercised.
Definitions: 'tenancy', 'house': see s 55 below.

Protection from eviction

36. Damages for unlawful eviction.

(1) This section applies if, at any time after 3 December 1987, a landlord or any person acting on his behalf unlawfully deprives the residential occupier of any premises of his occupation of the whole or part of the premises.

(2) This section also applies if, at any time after 6 July 1988, a landlord or any person acting on his behalf—
(a) attempts unlawfully to deprive the residential occupier of any premises of his occupation of the whole or part of the premises; or
(b) knowingly or having reasonable cause to believe that the conduct is likely to cause the residential occupier of any premises—
  (i) to give up his occupation of the premises or any part thereof; or
  (ii) to refrain from exercising any right or pursuing any remedy in respect of the premises or part thereof,
  does acts [likely] to interfere with the peace or comfort of the residential occupier of members of his household, or persistently withdraws or withholds services reasonably required for the occupation of the premises as a residence,
and, as a result, the residential occupier gives up his occupation of the premises as a residence.

(3) Subject to the following provisions of this section, where this section applies, the landlord shall, by virtue of this section, be liable to pay to the former residential occupier, in respect of his loss of the right to occupy the premises in question as his residence, damages assessed on the basis set out in section 37 below.

(4) Any liability arising by virtue of subsection (3) above—
(a) shall be in the nature of a liability in delict; and
(b) subject to subsection (5) below, shall be in addition to any liability arising apart from this section (whether in delict, contract, or otherwise.)

(5) Nothing in this section affects the right of a residential occupier to enforce any liability which arises apart from this section in respect of his loss of the right to occupy premises as his residence; but damages shall not be awarded both in respect of such a liability and in respect of a liability arising by virtue of this section on account of the same loss.

(6) No liability shall arise by virtue of subsection (3) above if—
(a) before [the date on which the proceedings to enforce the liability are finally decided], the former residential occupier is reinstated in the premises in question in such circumstances that he becomes again the residential occupier of them; or
(b) at the request of the former residential occupier, the sheriff makes an order as a result of which he is reinstated as mentioned in paragraph (a) above.

[(6A) For the purposes of subsection (6)(a) above, proceedings to enforce a liability are finally decided—
(a) if no appeal may be made against the decision in these proceedings;
(b) if an appeal may be made against the decision with leave and the time limit for applications for leave expires and either no application has been made or leave has been refused;
(c) if leave to appeal against the decision is granted or is not required and no appeal is made within the time limit for appeals; or
(d) if an appeal is made but is abandoned before it is determined.

[(6B) If, in proceedings to enforce a liability arising by virtue of subsection (3) above, it appears to the court—
(a) that, prior to the event which gave rise to the liability, the conduct of the former residential occupier or any person living with him in the premises concerned was such that it is reasonable to mitigate the damages for which the landlord would otherwise be liable, or
(b) that, before the proceedings were begun, the landlord offered to reinstate the former residential occupier in the premises in question and either it was unreasonable of the former residential occupier to refuse that offer, or, if he had obtained alternative accommodation before the offer was made, it would have been unreasonable of him to refuse that offer if he had not obtained that accommodation,
the court may reduce the amount of damages which would otherwise be payable by such an amount as it thinks appropriate.]

(7) In proceedings to enforce a liability arising by virtue of subsection (3) above, it shall be a defence for the defender to prove that he believed, and had reasonable cause to believe—
(a) that the residential occupier had ceased to reside in the premises in question at the time when he was deprived of occupation as mentioned in subsection (1) above, or, as the case may be, when the attempt was made or the acts were done as a result of which he gave up his occupation of those premises; or
(b) that, where the liability would otherwise arise by virtue only of [the doing of acts or] the withdrawal or withholding of services, he had reasonable grounds for [doing the acts or] withdrawing or withholding the services in question.

(8) In this section—
(a) 'residential occupier,' in relation to any premises, means a person occupying the premises as a residence whether under a contract or by virtue of any enactment or rule of law giving him the right to remain in occupation or restricting the right of any other person to recover possession of the premises;
(b) 'the right to occupy,' in relation to a residential occupier, includes any restriction on the right of another person to recover possession of the premises in question;
(c) 'former residential occupier,' in relation to any premises, means the person who was the residential occupier until he was deprived of or gave up his occupation as mentioned in subsection (1) or subsection (2) above (and, in relation to a former residential occupier, 'the right to occupy' and 'landlord' shall be construed accordingly). **[1127]**

NOTES to section 36
Amendments: Sub-ss (2), (6) and (7) were amended by the Housing Act 1988 (c 50), s 140, Sch 17, paras 86, 88; sub-ss (6A) and (6B) were added by *Ibid*, para 88.
Definition: 'landlord': see s 55 below.

37. The measure of damages.

(1) The basis for the assessment of damages referred to in section 36(3) above is the difference in value, determined as at the time immediately before the residential occupier ceased to occupy the premises in question as his residence, between—

(a) the value of the landlord's interest determined on the assumption that the residential occupier continues to have the same right to occupy the premises as before that time; and
(b) the value of the landlord's interest determined on the assumption that the residential occupier has ceased to have that right.

(2) For the purposes of the valuations referred to in subsection (1) above, it shall be assumed—
(a) that the landlord is selling his interest in the premises on the open market to a willing buyer;
(b) that neither the residential occupier nor any member of his family wishes to buy; and
(c) that it is unlawful to carry out any substantial development of any of the land in which the landlord's interest subsists or to demolish the whole or part of any building on that land.

(3) Subsection (8) of section 36 above applies in relation to this section as it applies in relation to that.

(4) Section 83 of the Housing (Scotland) Act 1987 (meaning of 'members of a person's family') applies for the purposes of subsection (2)(b) above.

(5) The reference in subsection (2)(c) above to substantial development of any of the land in which the landlord's interest subsists is a reference to any development other than—
(a) development for which planning permission is granted by a general development order for the time being in force and which is carried out so as to comply with any condition or limitation subject to which planning permission is so granted; or
(b) a change of use resulting in a building on the land or any part of such a building being used as, or as part of, one or more dwelling-houses;
and in this subsection 'general development order' has the same meaning as in section 40(3) of the Town and Country Planning (Scotland) Act 1972 and other expressions have the same meaning as in that Act. [1128]

NOTES to section 37
Definition: 'landlord': see s 55 below.

* * *

NOTES to sections 38–40
Sections 38–40 amend the Rent (Scotland) Act 1984 (c 58).

Power to repeal sections 33 and 58 of Rent (Scotland) Act 1984

41. Power of Secretary of State to repeal sections 33 and 58 of Rent (Scotland) Act 1984 and to reduce phasing progressively.

(1) The Secretary of State may by order repeal sections 33 (phasing of rent increases) and 58 (phasing of progression to registered rent) of the Rent (Scotland) Act 1984.

(2) An order under subsection (1) above may amend any enactment (including this Act).

(3) No order under subsection (1) above shall be made unless a draft of it has been laid before and approved by a resolution of each House of Parliament.

* * *

NOTES to section 41
The power to make an order has not been exercised.
Sub-ss (4), (5): Sub-ss (4) and (5) amend the Rent (Scotland) Act 1984 (c 58).

Phasing out of Rent (Scotland) Act 1984 and other transitional provisions

42. New protected tenancies restricted to special cases.

(1) A tenancy which begins on or after the commencement of this section cannot be a protected tenancy, unless—
- (a) it is entered into in pursuance of a contract made before the commencement of this section; or
- (b) it is granted to a person (alone or jointly with others) who, immediately before the tenancy was granted, was the protected tenant (or one of the protected tenants) or a statutory tenant of the same landlord; or
- (c) it is granted to a person (alone or jointly with others) in the following circumstances—
  - (i) prior to the grant of the tenancy, an order for possession of a dwelling-house was made against him (alone or jointly with others) on the court being satisfied as mentioned in section 11(1)(a) of the Rent (Scotland) Act 1984 (suitable alternative accommodation available) or on it appearing to the court, under section 48(2)(b) or (c) of the Housing (Scotland) Act 1987, that other suitable accommodation was available; and
  - (ii) the tenancy is of the premises which constitute the suitable alternative accommodation as to which the court was so satisfied or, as the case may be, the other suitable accommodation which appeared to the court to be available; and
  - (iii) in the proceedings for possession the court directed that the tenancy would be a protected tenancy; or
- (d) it is granted in compliance with a direction under section 51(2)(ii) of the Housing (Scotland) Act 1987 (power of sheriff to direct that tenant of wrongfully repossessed house be given suitable alternative accommodation) or in pursuance of section 282(3)(b) of that Act (grant of tenancy upon acquisition by public sector authority of defective dwelling).

(2) In subsection (1)(b) above 'protected tenant' and 'statutory tenant' do not include—
- (a) a tenant under a short tenancy;
- (b) a protected or statutory tenant of a dwelling-house which was let under a short tenancy which has ended and in respect of which either there has been no grant of a further tenancy or any grant of a further tenancy has been to the person who, immediately before the grant, was in possession of the dwelling-house as a protected or statutory tenant,

and in this subsection 'short tenancy' includes a tenancy which, in proceedings for possession under Case 15 in Schedule 2 to the Rent (Scotland) Act 1984, is treated as a short tenancy.

(3) Expressions used in this section have the same meaning as in the Rent (Scotland) Act 1984.

NOTES to section 42

Definitions: The expressions 'tenancy', 'protected tenancy', 'tenant', 'statutory tenant', 'landlord', and 'short tenancy', are all defined in the Rent (Scotland) Act 1984 (c 58), paras [248] ff above.

---

43. Removal of special regimes for tenancies of housing associations etc.

(1) In this section—
- (a) 'housing association tenancy' means a tenancy to which Part VI of the Rent (Scotland) Act 1984 applies;
- (b) 'secure tenancy' has the same meaning as in Part III of the Housing (Scotland) Act 1987.

(2) A tenancy which is entered into on or after the commencement of this section cannot be a housing association tenancy unless—

(a) it is entered into in pursuance of a contract made before the commencement of this section; or
(b) it is granted to a person (alone or jointly with others) who, immediately before the tenancy was granted, was the tenant (or one of the tenants) under a housing association tenancy of the same landlord; or
(c) it is granted to a person (alone or jointly with others) in the following circumstances—
   (i) prior to the grant of the tenancy, an order for possession of a dwelling-house was made against him (alone or jointly with others) on the court being satisfied as mentioned in paragraph (b) or paragraph (c) of subsection (2) of section 48 of the Housing (Scotland) Act 1987; and
   (ii) the tenancy is of the premises which constitute the suitable accommodation as to which the court was so satisfied; and
   (iii) in the proceedings for possession the court directed that it would be a housing association tenancy.

(3) A tenancy which is entered into on or after the commencement of this section cannot be a secure tenancy unless—
(a) the interest of the landlord belongs to—
   (i) an islands or district council, or a joint board or joint committee of an islands or district council or the common good of an islands or district council, or any trust under the control of an islands or district council; or
   (ii) a regional council, or a joint board or joint committee of 2 or more regional councils, or any trust under the control of a regional council; or
   (iii) a development corporation within the meaning of the New Towns (Scotland) Act 1968 (including an urban development corporation within the meaning of Part XVI of the Local Government, Planning and Land Act 1980); or
   (iv) the Scottish Special Housing Association; or
   (v) Scottish Homes; or
   (vi) a police authority in Scotland; or
   (vii) a fire authority in Scotland; or
(b) it is entered into in pursuance of a contract made before the commencement of this section; or
(c) it is granted to a person (alone or jointly with others) who, immediately before it was entered into, was the secure tenant (or any one of the secure tenants) of the same landlord; or
(d) it is granted to a person (alone or jointly with others) in the following circumstances—
   (i) prior to the grant of the tenancy, an order for possession of a house was made against him (alone or jointly with others) on the court being satisfied as mentioned in paragraph (b) or paragraph (c) of subsection (2) of section 48 of the Housing (Scotland) Act 1987; and
   (ii) the tenancy is of premises which constitute the suitable accommodation as to which the court was so satisfied; and
   (iii) in the proceedings for possession referred to in sub-paragraph (i) above the court directed that it would be a secure tenancy. **[1131]**

44. New 'Part VII' contracts limited to transitional cases.

(1) No contract entered into after the commencement of this section shall be a Part VII contract for the purposes of the Rent (Scotland) Act 1984 unless it is entered into in pursuance of a contract made before the commencement of this section.

(2) If the terms of a Part VII contract are varied after the commencement of this section then, subject to subsection (3) below—
(a) if the variation affects the amount of the rent which, under the contract, is payable for the dwelling in question, the contract shall be treated as a new contract entered into at the time of the variation (and subsection (1) above shall have effect accordingly); and

(b) if the variation does not affect the amount of the rent which, under the contract, is so payable, nothing in this section shall affect the determination of the question whether the variation is such as to give rise to a new contract.

(3) Any reference in subsection (2) above to a variation affecting the amount of the rent which, under a contract, is payable for a dwelling does not include a reference to—
(a) a reduction or increase effected under section 66 of the Rent (Scotland) Act 1984 (power of rent assessment committees); or
(b) a variation which is made by the parties and has the effect of making the rent expressed to be payable under the contract the same as the rent for the dwelling which is entered in the register under section 67 of the Rent (Scotland) Act 1984.

(4) Section 70(2) of the Rent (Scotland) Act 1984 (no cancellation of registration of rent until after 3 years) shall cease to have effect.

(5) In this section 'rent' has the same meaning as in Part VII of the Rent (Scotland) Act 1984. **[1132]**

45. Transfer of existing tenancies.

(1) The provisions of subsection (3) below apply in relation to a tenancy which was entered into before, or pursuant to a contract made before, the commencement of this section if—
(a) at that commencement or, if it is later, at the time it is entered into, the interest of the landlord is held by a public body (within the meaning of subsection (4) below); and
(b) at some time after that commencement the interest of the landlord ceases to be so held.

(2) The provisions of subsection (3) below also apply in relation to a tenancy which was entered into before, or pursuant to a contract made before, the commencement of this section if—
(a) at that commencement or, if it is later, at the time it is entered into, it is a housing association tenancy; and
(b) at some time after that commencement, it ceases to be such a tenancy.

(3) On and after the time referred to in subsection (1)(b) or, as the case may be, subsection (2)(b) above—
(a) the tenancy shall not be capable of being a protected tenancy or a housing association tenancy;
(b) the tenancy shall not be capable of being a secure tenancy unless (and only at a time when) the interest of the landlord under the tenancy is (or is again) held by a public body; and
(c) paragraph 1 of Schedule 4 to this Act shall not apply in relation to it, and the question whether at any time thereafter it becomes (or remains) an assured tenancy shall be determined accordingly.

(4) For the purposes of this section, the interest of a landlord under a tenancy is held by a public body at a time when—
(a) it belongs to an islands or district council, or a joint board or joint committee of an islands or district council or the common good of an islands or district council, or any trust under the control of an islands or district council; or
(b) it belongs to a regional council, or a joint board or joint committee of 2 or more regional councils, or any trust under the control of a regional council; or
(c) it belongs to a development corporation within the meaning of the New Towns (Scotland) Act 1968 (including an urban development corporation within the meaning of Part XVI of the Local Government, Planning and Land Act 1980); or
(d) it belongs to the Scottish Special Housing Association; or
(e) it belongs to Scottish Homes; or
(f) it belongs to a police authority in Scotland; or
(g) it belongs to a fire authority in Scotland; or

(h) it belongs to Her Majesty in right of the Crown or to a government department or is held in trust for Her Majesty for the purposes of a government department.

(5) In this section—
(a) 'housing association tenancy' means a tenancy to which Part VI of the Rent (Scotland) Act 1984 applies; and
(b) 'protected tenancy' has the same meaning as in that Act. [1133]

46. Statutory tenants: succession.

* * *

(4) If and so long as a house is subject to an assured tenancy to which a person has become entitled by succession, section 18 of and Schedule 5 to this Act shall have effect subject to the modifications in Part II of Schedule 6 to this Act. [1134]

NOTES to section 46
Sub-ss (1)–(3) amend the Rent (Scotland) Act 1984 (c 58).
Definitions: 'house', 'tenancy': see s 55 below; 'assured tenancy': see s 12 above.

General provisions

* * * [1135]

NOTES to section 47
Section 47 amends the Rent (Scotland) Act 1984 (c 58).

48. Rent assessment committees: procedure and information powers.

(1) * * *

(2) The rent assessment committee to whom a matter is referred under this Part of this Act may by notice in the prescribed form served on the landlord or the tenant require him to give to the committee, within such period of not less than fourteen days from the service of the notice as may be specified in the notice, such information as they may reasonably require for the purposes of their functions.

(3) If any person fails without reasonable excuse to comply with a notice served on him under subsection (2) above, he shall be liable on summary conviction to a fine not exceeding level 3 on the standard scale.

(4) Where an offence under subsection (3) above committed by a body corporate is proved to have been committed with the consent or connivance of, or to be attributable to any neglect on the part of, any director, manager or secretary or other similar officer of the body corporate or any person who was purporting to act in any such capacity, he as well as the body corporate shall be guilty of that offence and shall be liable to be proceeded against and punished accordingly. [1136]

NOTES to section 48
Sub-s (1) amends the Rent (Scotland) 1984 (c 58).
Sub-s (2): For the prescribed form see the Assured Tenancies (Forms) (Scotland) Regulations 1989, SI 1989/2109, paras [1440] ff below.
Definitions: 'prescribed', 'landlord', 'tenant': see s 55 below; 'the standard scale': level 3 is currently £400. See the Increase of Criminal Penalties Etc (Scotland) Order 1984, SI 1984/526.

49. Information as to determination of rents.

(1) The rent assessment panel shall keep and make publicly available, in such manner as is specified in an order made by the Secretary of State, such information as may be so specified with respect to rents under assured tenancies which have been the subject of, or taken into account on, references or applications to, or determinations by, rent assessment committees.

[1137] *Housing (Scotland) Act 1988 (c 43), s 49*

(2) A copy of any information kept under subsection (1) above, purporting to be certified under the hand of an authorised officer of the rent assessment panel shall, unless the contrary is shown, be deemed to have been signed by such officer and be sufficient evidence of that information.

(3) An order under subsection (1) above—
(a) may prescribe the fees to be charged for the supply of a copy, including a certified copy, of any of the information kept by virtue of that subsection; and
(b) may make different provision with respect to different cases or description of case, including different provision for different areas. **[1137]**

NOTES to section 49
Sub-s 3: See the Assured Tenancies (Rent Information) (Scotland) Order 1989, SI 1989/685, paras [1467] ff below.
Definitions: 'assured tenancy': see s 12 above; 'tenancy': see s 55 below.

50. Powers of local authorities for the purposes of giving information.

(1) Any local authority shall have power to publish information, for the assistance of landlords and tenants, as to their rights and duties under the provisions of this Part of this Act and as to the procedure for enforcing those rights or securing the performance of those duties. **[1138]**

NOTES to section 50
Definitions: 'landlord', 'tenant': see s 55 below.

51. Application to Crown.

(1) Subject to subsection (2) below and paragraph 10 of Schedule 4 to this Act, this Part of this Act applies in relation to premises in which there subsists, or at any material time subsisted, a Crown interest as it applies in relation to premises in relation to which no such interest subsists or ever subsisted.

(2) Sections 36 and 37 of this Act do not bind the Crown but sections 38 to 40 of this Act bind the Crown to the extent provided for in section 26 of the Rent (Scotland) Act 1984.

(3) In this section 'Crown interest' means an interest which belongs to Her Majesty in right of the Crown or to a government department, or which is held in trust for Her Majesty for the purposes of a government department. **[1139]**

52. Saving for common law as to effect of notice of termination upon tacit relocation.

Nothing in this Part of this Act prejudices any rule of law relating to the effect of the giving of notice of termination of a lease upon the operation of tacit relocation. **[1140]**

53. Orders and regulations.

(1) Any power of the Secretary of State to make orders or regulations under this Part of this Act shall be exercised by statutory instrument.

(2) A statutory instrument containing any order or regulation under this Part, other than an order under section 35 or 41 above, shall be subject to annulment in pursuance of a resolution of either House of Parliament.

(3) Orders or regulations under this Part may make different provision for different cases or circumstances or different areas and may contain such incidental, supplemental or transitional provisions as the Secretary of State thinks fit. **[1141]**

54. Notice under Part II.

A notice served under this Part of this Act on a person or notice so given to him may be served or given—
(a) by delivering it to him;
(b) by leaving it at his last known address; or
(c) by sending it by recorded delivery letter to him at that address. [1142]

55. Interpretation of Part II.

(1) In this Part of this Act, except where the context otherwise requires—
'house' includes a part of a house;
'landlord' includes any person from time to time deriving title from the original landlord and also includes, in relation to a house, any person other than a tenant who is, or but for the existence of an assured tenancy would be, entitled to possession of the house;
'let' includes 'sub-let';
'order for possession' means decree of removing or warrant of ejection or other like order; and 'proceedings for possession' shall be construed accordingly;
'prescribed' means prescribed by regulations made by the Secretary of State;
'statutory assured tenancy' shall be construed in accordance with section 16(1) of this Act;
'tenancy' includes 'sub-tenancy' and an agreement for a tenancy or sub-tenancy; and
'tenant' includes a sub-tenant and any person deriving title from the original tenant or sub-tenant.

(2) Any reference in this Part of this Act to the beginning of a tenancy is a reference to the day when the lease of the house let on the tenancy commences.

(3) Where two or more persons jointly constitute either the landlord or the tenant in relation to a tenancy, then, except where otherwise provided, any reference in this Part of this Act to the landlord or to the tenant is a reference to all the persons who jointly constitute the landlord or the tenant, as the case may require. [1143]

PART III
CHANGE OF LANDLORD: SECURE TENANTS

56. Right conferred by Part III.

(1) This Part of this Act has effect for the purpose of conferring on any person who has been approved under section 57 below or Scottish Homes the right to acquire from a public sector landlord any house—
(a) which, on the relevant date, is occupied by a qualifying tenant; and
(b) of which, on that date, the landlord is heritable proprietor,
and any other heritable property of which, on that date, the landlord is heritable proprietor and which will reasonably serve a beneficial purpose in connection with the occupation of the house; and, in this Part of this Act 'house' includes any such property.

(2) In subsection (1) above, 'heritable proprietor' includes any person entitled under section 3 of the Conveyancing (Scotland) Act 1924 (disposition by uninfeft person) to grant a disposition.

(3) The following are public sector landlords for the purposes of this Part of this Act, namely—
(a) an islands or district council, or a joint board or joint committee of an islands or district council or the common good of an islands or district council, or any trust under the control of an islands or district council;
(b) a development corporation within the meaning of the New Towns (Scotland) Act 1968 (including an urban development corporation within the meaning of Part XVI of the Local Government Planning and Land Act 1980);

(c) the Scottish Special Housing Association;
(d) the Housing Corporation;
(e) Scottish Homes.

(4) A secure tenant is a qualifying tenant for the purposes of this Part unless he is obliged to give up possession of the house in pursuance of an order of the court or will be so obliged at a date specified in such an order.

(5) The right conferred by this Part of this Act does not extend to a house—
(a) which is one of a group which has been provided with facilities (including a call system and the services of a warden) specially designed or adapted for the needs of persons of pensionable age or disabled persons;
(b) which has facilities which are substantially different from those of an ordinary house and has been designed or adapted for occupation by—
  (i) a person of pensionable age; or
  (ii) a disabled person,
whose special needs require accommodation of the kind provided by the house; or
(c) which is in an area which is, by order made by the Secretary of State on the application of the islands or district council in whose area it is situated, designated a rural area.

(6) The right conferred by this Part of this Act does not arise in relation to a house if—
(a) it is held by an islands council for the purposes of its functions as an education authority and is required for the accommodation of a person who is or will be employed by the council for those purposes; and
(b) the council is not likely to be able reasonably to provide other suitable accommodation for that person.

(7) An order under subsection (5)(c) above may be made only if within the designated rural area more than one-third of all relevant houses have been acquired under this Part of this Act or purchased, whether under Part III of the Housing (Scotland) Act 1987 (which confers the right to buy upon certain public sector tenants) or otherwise, and the Secretary of State is satisfied that an unreasonable proportion of the houses so acquired or purchased consists of houses which have been resold and are not—
(a) being used as the only or principal homes of the owners; or
(b) subject to regulated tenancies within the meaning of section 8 of the Rent (Scotland) Act 1984, or assured tenancies for the purpose of Part II of this Act.

(8) An order under subsection (5)(c) above shall be made by statutory instrument which shall be subject to annulment in pursuance of a resolution of either House of Parliament.

(9) For the purposes of subsection (7) above a 'relevant house' is one of which—
(a) at 3rd October 1980, the islands or district council in whose area it was situated;
(b) at 7th January 1987, a registered housing association (within the meaning of the Housing Associations Act 1985)
was landlord.

(10) In this Part of this Act 'the relevant date', in relation to an acquisition or proposed acquisition under this Part, means the date on which is made the application under section 58 below seeking to exercise the right conferred by this Part.

(11) In section 14(2) of the Housing (Scotland) Act 1987 (houses which may be sold by local authorities without consent of Secretary of State) in paragraph (a) there shall be added at the end the words 'or, in pursuance of Part III of the Housing (Scotland) Act 1988 (change of landlord)'. **[1144]**

NOTES to section 56
Sub-ss (5), (7), (8): The power to make an order has not been exercised.

57. Persons by whom right may be exercised.

(1) The right conferred by this Part shall not be exercisable except by a person who has been approved by Scottish Homes under this section (in this Part of this Act referred to as an 'approved person') or by Scottish Homes; and neither a public sector landlord (other than Scottish Homes), nor a regional council, or a joint board or joint committee of two or more regional councils or any trust under the control of a regional council, may be so approved.

(2) An approval under this section—
  (a) may be given to a particular person or to persons of a particular description;
  (b) may apply either generally or in relation to particular acquisitions or acquisitions made in a particular area or within a particular period;
  (c) may, in relation to a particular person, specify the maximum number to which the approval extends of houses to be acquired by him under this Part of this Act;
  (d) may be given subject to conditions.

(3) An approval under this section may be revoked by Scottish Homes, but without prejudice to any transaction previously completed. **[1145]**

NOTES to section 57
Definitions: 'Scottish Homes': see s 1 above; 'public sector landlord': see s 56(3) above.

58. Application to exercise rights conferred by this Part and offer to sell.

(1) For the purposes of exercising the right conferred by this Part of this Act, the applicant (that is to say, the approved person or, as the case may be, Scottish Homes) shall serve on the landlord a notice in such form as may be prescribed (in this Part of this Act referred to as an 'application')—
  (a) containing a statement that the applicant seeks to exercise the right conferred by this Part of this Act; and
  (b) accompanied by the consent in writing of the qualifying tenant to an approach being made to their existing landlord.

In this subsection, 'prescribed' means prescribed by regulations made by the Secretary of State by statutory instrument subject to annulment in pursuance of a resolution of either House of Parliament.

(2) In subsection (1) above the reference to the qualifying tenant includes any spouse of his or hers who occupies the house as his or her only or principal home and, where there is a joint tenancy, each joint tenant's spouse who so occupies the house, and in this subsection the reference to a tenant's or joint tenant's spouse includes a person of the opposite sex who is living with the tenant or joint tenant as if he or she were the tenant's or joint tenant's husband or wife.

(3) The applicant shall, at the same time as he serves an application, serve a copy of it on the qualifying tenant and on Scottish Homes (where the applicant is not Scottish Homes).

(4) An application shall cease to have effect—
  (a) if the applicant withdraws it; or
  (b) if the qualifying tenant withdraws his consent,
by notice thereof served upon the landlord.

(5) Where an application is served under this section and the landlord does not serve notice of refusal under section 61 below, it shall within 2 months after service of the application serve on the applicant a notice (in this Part referred to as an 'offer to sell notice') stating—
  (a) the market value of the house on the date of service of the application;
  (b) any conditions which the landlord intends to impose under subsection (9) below
and containing an offer to sell the house to the applicant at a price equal to that value and under those conditions.

(6) For the purposes of subsection (5) above, the market value of a house shall be determined by either—
(a) a qualified valuer nominated by the landlord and accepted by the applicant; or
(b) the district valuer,
as the landlord thinks fit.

(7) In determining the market value of a house for the purposes of subsection (5) above, regard shall be had to the price which, on the relevant date, it would realise if sold on the open market by a willing seller on the following assumptions, namely—
(a) that it was sold subject to the tenancy held by the qualifying tenant but otherwise with vacant possession;
(b) that it was to be conveyed with the same rights and subject to the same burdens as it would be in pursuance of the right of acquisition under this Part of this Act;
(c) that the only prospective purchasers were Scottish Homes or the persons who, on that date, were approved under section 57 above; and
(d) that the applicant would, within a reasonable period carry out such works as are reasonably necessary to put the house into the state of repair required by the landlord's repairing obligations.

(8) Where the circumstances are such that, on the relevant date, a house, if offered for sale in accordance with subsection (7) above, would not realise any price then—
(a) for the purposes of that subsection, the price shall be taken to be—
 (i) such amount as would require to be paid to Scottish Homes or a person who, on the relevant date, was approved under section 57 above in order that it or he would willingly so acquire the house, expressed as a negative; or
 (ii) where Scottish Homes or that person would willingly so acquire it for no consideration, nil;
(b) the market value of the house may be determined under that subsection to be a negative value or nil;
(c) where the market value is so determined, the reference in subsection (5) above to a price equal to the market value shall be construed accordingly and references in this section to selling a house and the purchaser of it shall be construed respectively as references to disposing of it and the acquirer of it; and
(d) where, by virtue of paragraph (c) above, the price of the house is in the negative, the obligation to pay shall be upon the landlord.

(9) The landlord shall, at the same time as it serves an offer to sell notice serve a copy of the notice upon the qualifying tenant.

(10) An offer to sell under this section may be under such conditions as are reasonable, provided that—
(a) they shall not reduce the tenant's enjoyment and use of the house as tenant of the applicant from that which he had as tenant of the landlord; and
(b) they shall include such terms as are necessary to entitle the applicant to receive a good and marketable title to the house.

(11) A condition which imposes a new charge or an increase of an existing charge for the provision of a service in relation to the house shall provide for the charge to be in reasonable proportion to the cost to the landlord of providing the service.

(12) No condition shall be imposed under this section which has the effect of requiring the applicant or the tenant to pay any expenses of the landlord.   [1146]

NOTES to section 58
Sub-s (1): See the Right to Purchase from a Public Sector Landlord (Scotland) Regulations 1989, SI 1989/423, paras [1463] ff below.
Definitions: 'approved person': see s 57 above; 'Scottish Homes': see s 1 above; 'qualifying tenant': see s 56 above.

59. Variation of conditions.

(1) Where an offer to sell notice is served on an applicant and he wishes to exercise the right conferred by this Part of this Act, but—
 (a) he considers that a condition contained in the offer to sell is unreasonable; or
 (b) he wishes to have a new condition included in it,
he may request the landlord to strike out or vary the condition, or to include the new condition as the case may be, by serving on the landlord within one month after service of the offer to sell notice a notice in writing setting out his request; and if the landlord agrees, it shall accordingly serve an amended offer to sell on the applicant within one month of service of the notice setting out the request.

(2) An applicant who is aggrieved by the refusal of the landlord to agree to strike out or vary a condition, or to include a new condition, or by his failure timeously to serve an amended offer to sell, may, within one month or, with the consent of the landlord given in writing before the expiry of the said period of one month, within 2 months of the refusal or failure, refer the matter to the Lands Tribunal for Scotland (hereinafter in this Part of this Act referred to as the Lands Tribunal) for determination.

(3) In proceedings under subsection (2), the Lands Tribunal may, as it thinks fit, uphold the condition or strike it out or vary it, or insert the new condition, and where its determination results in a variation of the terms of the offer to sell, it shall order the landlord to serve on the applicant an amended offer to sell accordingly within 2 months thereafter. **[1147]**

60. Notice of acceptance.

(1) Where an offer to sell notice is served upon an applicant and he wishes to exercise the right conferred by this Part of this Act and—
 (a) he does not dispute the offer to sell by timeously serving a notice setting out a request under section 59(1) above or by referring the matter to the Lands Tribunal under section 62(1) below; or
 (b) any such dispute has been resolved,
the applicant shall serve a notice of acceptance on the landlord within 2 months or whichever is the latest of—
 (i) the service upon the applicant of the offer to sell;
 (ii) the service on him of an amended offer to sell (or if there are more than one, of the latest amended offer to sell);
 (iii) a determination by the Lands Tribunal under section 59(3) above which does not require service of an amended offer to sell;
 (iv) a finding or determination of the Lands Tribunal in a matter referred to it under subsection (1) of section 62 below,
or within such longer period as may be agreed between the applicant and the landlord.

(2) A notice of acceptance under subsection (1) above is of no effect unless the qualifying tenant and the applicant have concluded a lease of the house for a period immediately subsequent to the sale of the house in pursuance of this Part of this Act, being a lease which is conditional upon that sale proceeding.

(3) If a notice of acceptance under subsection (1) above is not served within the period specified in or, as the case may be, agreed under that subsection, the application to which the notice relates shall lapse.

(4) Where an offer to sell (or an amended offer to sell) has been served on the applicant and a relative notice of acceptance has been duly served on the landlord, a contract of sale of the house shall be constituted between the landlord and the applicant on the terms contained in the offer (or amended offer) to sell. **[1148]**

NOTE to section 60

Definition: 'qualifying tenant': see s 56 above.

61. Refusal of applications.

(1) Where a landlord on which an application has been served—
(a) disputes the applicant's right under this Part of this Act it shall, by notice (in this Part of this Act referred to as a 'notice of refusal') served within one month after service of the application, refuse the application;
(b) after reasonable inquiry (which shall include reasonable opportunity for the applicant to amend the application), considers that any of the information contained in the application is incorrect in a material particular, it shall, by notice of refusal served within 2 months after the application, refuse the application.

(2) A notice of refusal shall specify the grounds on which the landlord disputes the applicant's right under this Part of this Act or, as the case may be, the correctness of the information.

(3) Where a landlord serves a notice of refusal on an applicant, the applicant may, within one month thereafter apply to the Lands Tribunal for a finding that the applicant is entitled to exercise the right conferred by this Part on such terms as it may determine. **[1149]**

62. Reference to Lands Tribunal.

(1) Where—
(a) a landlord which has been duly served with an application fails to issue timeously either an offer to sell or a notice of refusal;
(b) the Lands Tribunal has made a determination under section 59(3) above and the landlord has failed to issue an amended offer to sell within 2 months thereafter;
(c) the Lands Tribunal has made a finding under section 61(3) above and the landlord has not, within 2 months, duly progressed the application in accordance with that finding;
(d) a landlord has served an offer to sell which does not comply with a requirement of this Part of this Act,

the applicant may refer the matter to the Lands Tribunal by serving on its clerk a copy of any notice served and of any finding or determination made under this Part of this Act together with a statement of his grievance.

(2) On a reference to the Lands Tribunal under subsection (1) above, it shall consider whether any of paragraphs (a) to (d) thereof apply and, if it so finds, it may serve an offer to sell notice and do otherwise as the landlord might do in pursuance of such notice; and anything done by it under this subsection shall have effect as if done by the landlord.

(3) Nothing in this section shall affect the provisions of any other enactment relating to the enforcement of a statutory duty whether under that enactment or otherwise. **[1150]**

63. Consent for subsequent disposals.

(1) A person other than Scottish Homes who acquires any property under this Part of this Act shall not dispose of it except with the consent in writing of Scottish Homes.

(2) Any consent for the purposes of subsection (1) above may be given either in respect of a particular disposal or in respect of disposals of any class or description (including disposals in particular areas) and either unconditionally or subject to conditions.

((2A) Before giving any consent for the purposes of subsection (1) above, Scottish Homes—
(a) shall satisfy itself that the person who is seeking the consent has taken appropriate steps to consult the tenant of the house (or, as the case may be, each house) of which the property proposed to be disposed of consists of and

(b) shall have regard to the response of such tenant to that consultation.]

(3) The consent of Scottish Homes under section 9 of the Housing Associations Act 1985 (control of dispositions) is not required for any disposal, or disposals of any class or description, in respect of which consent is given under subsection (1) above.

(4) In this section references to disposing of property include references to—
(a) granting or disposing of any interest in property;
(b) entering into a contract to dispose of property or to grant or dispose of any such interest; and
(c) granting an option to acquire property or any such interest. [1151]

NOTES to section 63
Amendment: Sub-s (2A) added by the Housing Act 1988 (c 50), s 140, Sch 17, para 89.
Definition: 'Scottish Homes': see s 1 above.

64. Extension etc of relevant periods.

(1) In this section 'relevant period' means any period within which anything is required by this Part to be done by either of the parties, that is to say, the applicant and the landlord.

(2) At any time before the end of any relevant period, or any such period as previously extended under this subsection, the other party may, by a written notice served on the party to whom the requirement relates, extend or further extend that period.

(3) Where—
(a) the applicant is the party to whom the requirement relates; and
(b) the relevant period, or that period as extended under subsection (2) above, expires without his doing what he is required by this Part to do within that period,
his application claiming to exercise the right conferred by this Part shall be deemed to be withdrawn, but without prejudice to his making a further such application. [1152–1153]

PART IV
MISCELLANEOUS AND GENERAL

* * *

NOTE to section 65
Section 65 amends the Housing (Scotland) Act 1987 (c 26), ss 62 and 76.

66. Schemes for payments to assist local authority tenants to obtain other accommodation.

(1) In accordance with a scheme made by a local authority and approved by the Secretary of State under this section, the authority may make grants to or for the benefit of qualifying tenants of the authority with a view to assisting each person to whom or for whose benefit a grant is made to obtain accommodation otherwise than as a tenant of the authority either—
(a) by acquiring an interest in a house, or
(b) by carrying out works to a house to provide additional accommodation; or
(c) by both of those means.

(2) A scheme under this section shall contain such provisions as the local authority

considers appropriate together with any which the Secretary of State may require as a condition of his approval and, without prejudice to the generality, a scheme may include provisions specifying, or providing for the determination of—
(a) the persons who are qualifying tenants for the purposes of the scheme;
(b) the interests which qualifying tenants may be assisted to acquire;
(c) the works for the carrying out of which grants may be made;
(d) the circumstances in which a grant may be made for the benefit of a qualifying tenant;
(e) the amount of the grant which may be made in any particular case and the terms on which it may be made;
(f) the limits on the total number and amount of grants which may be made; and
(g) the period within which the scheme is to apply.

(3) The Secretary of State may approve a scheme made by a local authority under this section with or without conditions and, where a scheme has been approved, the authority shall take such steps as it considers appropriate to bring the scheme to the attention of persons likely to be able to benefit from it and shall take such other steps (if any) as the Secretary of State may direct in any particular case to secure publicity for the scheme.

(4) The Secretary of State may revoke an approval of a scheme under this section by a notice given to the local authority concerned; and where such a notice is given, the revocation shall not affect the operation of the scheme in relation to any grants made or agreed before the date of the notice.

(5) Where a scheme made by a local authority under this section has been approved, a person dealing with the authority shall not be concerned to see or enquire whether the terms of the scheme have been or are being complied with; and any failure to comply with the terms of a scheme shall not invalidate any grant purporting to be made in accordance with the scheme unless the person to whom the grant is made has actual notice of the failure.

(6) In this section, 'local authority' and 'house' have respectively the meanings assigned to those expressions by section 338(1) of the Housing (Scotland) Act 1987. **[1154]**

67. Abolition and capitalisation of certain subsidies and contributions.

(1) No subsidy or contribution shall be made under the following provisions of the Housing (Scotland) Act 1987 (the 'superseded provisions')—
(a) section 200 (slum clearance subsidy);
(b) section 254 (contributions towards improvement grants, repairs grants and grants for fire escapes);
(c) section 255 (contributions for improvement of amenities);
(d) section 296 (contributions towards certain other expenses)

in respect of any expense or expenditure incurred by a local authority on or after 1st April 1989.

(2) No claim for subsidy or contribution under any superseded provision in respect of or towards any expense or expenditure incurred by a local authority before 1st April 1989 shall be entertained by the Secretary of State unless—
(a) it is received by him before 1st October 1989; and
(b) any information reasonably required by him in relation to any such claim is received by him within two months after the receipt by him of the claim.

(3) Where two or more periodic payments of a subsidy or contribution under a superseded provision would, apart from this subsection, fall to be made on or after 1st April 1989, these payments shall be capitalised and made as follows—
(a) if one or more earlier such payments have been made before that date, the Secretary of State shall, instead of making the remaining payments, pay an amount equal to the appropriate percentage of the relevant capital amount;
(b) if no earlier such payment has been made before that date, the Secretary of State

shall, instead of making any such payments, pay such amount as appears to him to be equal to the appropriate percentage of the relevant expenditure.

(4) In subsection (3) above—
'the appropriate percentage, in relation to a relevant capital amount, means the percentage specified in or under the superseded provision in relation to the subsidy or contribution to which the capital amount relates and, in relation to a subsidy or contribution, means the percentage specified in or under the superseded provision in relation to that subsidy or contribution;
'the relevant capital amount', in relation to a subsidy or contribution, means the sum of—
(a) such amount as the Secretary of State considers would, on the date of his payment under subsection (3)(a) above, be payable by the local authority were they then to repay a loan, repayable over twenty years, taken out by them from the Public Works Loan Commissioners to meet their expense or, as the case may be, expenditure in respect of or towards which the subsidy or contribution was made; and
(b) any other amount which he considers would be then payable on such repayment of that loan;
'relevant expenditure', in relation to a subsidy or contribution, means the expense or expenditure in respect of which the subsidy or contribution was made.

(5) Payment made under subsection (3) above shall be—
(a) applied in reduction or extinguishment of such debt (whether then payable or not) of the local authority as the Secretary of State thinks fit; or
(b) made to the local authority; or
(c) partly so applied and partly so made.

(6) Payments made to a local authority under subsection (5) above shall be applied by them in the repayment of such debt and in such manner as the Secretary of State directs.

(7) Notwithstanding the repeal by this Act of section 254 of the Housing (Scotland) Act 1987, subsection (4) of that section (obligation upon local authority to pay to Secretary of State sums recovered by them in consequence of breach of conditions of improvement grant or by way of voluntary repayment of such grant) shall continue to have effect in relation to expense incurred under that section by a local authority prior to 1st April 1989, being expense in respect of which contributions were made under that section.

(8) Paragraph 1(b) of Schedule 16 to the Housing (Scotland) Act 1987 (duty of local authority to credit slum clearance subsidy to slum clearance revenue account) shall cease to have effect on 1st April 1989. **[1155]**

★ ★ ★

NOTES to sections 68 and 69
These sections amend the Rent (Scotland) Act 1984 (c 58).

70. Rent officers: additional functions relating to housing benefit etc.

(1) The Secretary of State may by order require rent officers to carry out such functions as may be specified in the order in connection with housing benefit and rent allowance subsidy.

(2) An order under this section—
(a) shall be made by statutory instrument which, except in the case of the first order to be made, shall be subject to annulment in pursuance of a resolution of either House of Parliament;
(b) may make different provision for different cases or classes of case and for different areas; and

(c) may contain such transitional, incidental and supplementary provisions as appear to the Secretary of State to be desirable;

and the first order under this section shall not be made unless a draft of it has been laid before, and approved by a resolution of, each House of Parliament.

* * *

(6) In this section 'housing benefit' and 'rent allowance subsidy' have the same meaning as in Part II of that Act. **[1156]**

NOTES to section 70

Sub-ss (1), (2): See the Rent Officers (Additional Functions) (Scotland) Order 1990, SI 1990/396 as amended by SI 1991/533, paras [1487A] ff below.

Sub-ss (3)–(5): Sub-ss (3) to (5) amend the Social Security Act 1986 (c 50).

Sub-ss (6): 'that Act' refers to the Social Security Act 1986 (c 50).

* * *

NOTE to section 71

Section 71 amends the New Towns (Scotland) Act 1968 (c 16).

* * *

NOTES to section 72

Section 72 amends the Housing (Scotland) Act 1987 (c 26) and other enactments.

73. Finance

There shall be defrayed out of money provided by Parliament—
(a) any expenses of the Secretary of State incurred under this Act;
(b) any increase attributable to this Act in the sums so payable under any other enactment. **[1157]**

74. Short title, commencement and extent.

(1) This Act may be cited as the Housing (Scotland) Act 1988.

(2) This Act shall come into force as follows—
(a) section 69 and section 72 (so far as relating to Schedule 7) and this section and that Schedule, shall come into force on the day this Act is passed;
(b) sections 36 to 40, 65, 67 and 71; and
section 72 (so far as relating to Schedule 8 and to the entries in Schedule 10 in respect of sections 62(11) to (13) and 151 of the Housing (Scotland) Act 1987); and Schedule 8; and
in Schedule 10, those entries;

shall come into force at the end of the period of two months beginning with the day on which this Act is passed;

(c) section 72 (so far as relating to the entry in Schedule 10 relating to paragraph (1)(b) of Schedule 16 to the Housing (Scotland) Act 1987) and that entry shall come into force on 1st April 1989;
(d) the remaining provisions shall come into force on such days as the Secretary of State may, by order made by statutory instrument, appoint and different days may be so appointed for different provisions or for different purposes.

(3) An order under subsection (2) above may make such transitional provision as appears to the Secretary of State necessary or expedient in connection with the provisions brought into force by the order.

(4) Subject to subsection (5) below, this Act extends to Scotland only.

(5) So much of sections 3 and 72 and Schedules 2, 9 and 10 as relates to enactments extending to England and Wales, section 4 and Schedule 3 extend also to England and Wales. **[1158]**

NOTES to section 74

Sub-s (1): The Act was passed on 2 November 1988, so ss 69 and 72 (so far as relating to Sch 7), and 74, Sch 7 came into force on that day, and ss 36 to 40, 65, 67 and 71, s 72 (in part), Sch 8 and Sch 10 (in part) came into force on 2 January 1989.

Sub-s (2): See the Housing (Scotland) Act 1988 (Commencement) Order, SI 1988/2038 which brought into force the following provisions on the following days: on 1 December 1988—ss 1, 2, 3(1), (3) and (4), 4–11, 73, Sch 1, Sch 2, para 3(a); on 2 January 1989—ss 12–35, 41–55, 66, 68, 70, 72 (remainder), Sch 4, 5, 6, 9 (except paras 7 and 17); on 1 April 1989, the remaining sections.

SCHEDULES

Section 1   SCHEDULE 1

SCOTTISH HOMES

Incorporation

1.—Scottish Homes shall be a body corporate and shall have a common seal. **[1159]**

Status

2.—Scottish Homes shall be a public body for the purposes of the Prevention of Corruption Acts 1889 to 1916. **[1160]**

3.—It shall not—
(a) be regarded as a servant or agent of the Crown;
(b) have any status, immunity or privilege of the Crown;
(c) be exempt from any tax, duty, rate, levy or other charge whatsoever, whether general or local,
and its property shall not be regarded as property of, or held on behalf of, the Crown. **[1161]**

Membership

4.—(1) The members of Scottish Homes shall be—
(a) not more than 9 persons appointed by the Secretary of State; and
(b) its chief executive (whose membership shall be ex officio).

(2) The Secretary of State shall—
(a) satisfy himself, before he appoints a person to be a member, that that person will have no such financial or other interest as is likely to affect prejudicially the performance of his functions as a member; and
(b) satisfy himself from time to time with respect to each member that he has no such interest,
and a person who is a member or whom the Secretary of State proposes to appoint as a member shall, whenever requested by the Secretary of State to do so, furnish the Secretary of State with such information as he may consider necessary for the purpose of carrying out his duty under this paragraph. **[1162]**

5.—(1) The members of Scottish Homes (other than the chief executive) shall, subject to the following provisions, hold and vacate office in accordance with the terms of their appointment.

(2) A member may resign his membership by written notice to the Secretary of State.

(3) The Secretary of State may remove a member from office if he is satisfied that that member—
  (a) has been adjudged bankrupt, or made an arrangement with his creditors, or had his estate sequestrated, or granted a trust deed for his creditors or a composition contract;
  (b) is incapacitated by physical or mental illness;
  (c) has been absent from meetings of Scottish Homes for a period longer than 3 consecutive months without the permission of Scottish Homes;
  (d) is otherwise unable or unfit to discharge the functions of a member, or is unsuitable to continue as a member. **[1163]**

Chairman and deputy chairmen

6.—(1) The Secretary of State shall appoint one of the members of Scottish Homes to be chairman and may appoint one or more to be deputy chairman or deputy chairmen; and the chairman and deputy chairmen shall, subject to the following provisions, hold and vacate those offices in accordance with the terms of their appointment.

(2) The chairman or a deputy chairman may resign his office by written notice to the Secretary of State.

(3) If the chairman or a deputy chairman ceases to be a member of Scottish Homes, he also ceases to be chairman or a deputy chairman. **[1164]**

Remuneration, allowances and pensions

7.—(1) The Secretary of State may pay the chairman, a deputy chairman and members (other than the chief executive) of Scottish Homes such remuneration as he may, with the approval of the Treasury, determine.

(2) Scottish Homes may pay them such reasonable allowances as may be so determined in respect of expenses properly incurred by them in the performance of their duties.

(3) Where a person (other than the chief executive) ceases to be a member of Scottish Homes otherwise than on the expiry of his term of office, and it appears to the Secretary of State that there are special circumstances which might make it right for that person to receive compensation, the Secretary of State may, with the approval of the Treasury, direct Scottish Homes to make that person a payment of such amount as the Secretary of State may, with the approval of the Treasury, determine. **[1165]**

8.—The Secretary of State may, with the consent of the Treasury, determine to pay in respect of a person's office as chairman, deputy chairman or member (other than the chief executive) of Scottish Homes—
  (a) such pension, allowance or gratuity to, or in respect of, that person on his retirement or death as may be so determined; or
  (b) such contribution or other payments towards provision for such pension, allowance or gratuity as may be so determined. **[1166]**

Staff

9.—The Secretary of State shall, after consultation with the chairman or person designated to be chairman, make the first appointment of the chief executive of Scottish Homes on such terms and conditions as he may, with the consent of the Treasury, determine; and thereafter Scottish Homes may, with the approval of the Secretary of State, make subsequent appointments to that office on such terms and conditions as it may, with the approval of the Secretary of State given with the consent of the Treasury, determine. **[1167]**

10.—(1) Subject to paragraph 11 below, Scottish Homes may appoint on such terms and conditions as it may, with the approval of the Secretary of State given with the consent of the Treasury, determine, such other employees as it thinks fit.

(2) Scottish Homes shall, in respect of such of its employees as it may determine, with the approval of the Secretary of State given with the consent of the Treasury, make such arrangements for providing pensions, allowances or gratuities as it may determine; and such arrangements may include the establishment and administration, by Scottish Homes or otherwise, of one or more pension schemes.

(3) The reference in sub-paragraph (2) above to pensions, allowances or gratuities in respect of employees of Scottish Homes includes a reference to pensions, allowances or gratuities by way of compensation to or in respect of any such employee who suffers loss of office or employment or loss or diminution of emoluments.

(4) The Secretary of State with the consent of the Treasury may, by statutory instrument subject to annulment in pursuance of a resolution of either House of Parliament, make regulations providing for—
  (a) the transfer to, and administration by, Scottish Homes of any superannuation fund maintained by the Scottish Special Housing Association in terms of the provisions of any scheme made under section 7 of the Superannuation Act 1972;
  (b) the modification, for the purposes of the regulations, of the said section 7 or any scheme thereunder.

(5) If an employee of Scottish Homes becomes a member of Scottish Homes and was by reference to his employment by Scottish Homes a participant in a pension scheme administered by it for the benefit of its employees—
  (a) Scottish Homes may determine that his service as a member shall be treated for the purposes of the scheme as service as an employee of Scottish Homes whether or not any benefits are to be payable to or in respect of him by virtue of paragraph 8 above; but
  (b) if Scottish Homes determines as aforesaid, any discretion as to the benefits payable to or in respect of him which the scheme confers on Scottish Homes shall be exercised only with the consent of the Secretary of State given with the approval of the Treasury. **[1168]**

11.—(1) Scottish Homes shall, not later than such date as the Secretary of State may determine, make an offer of employment by it to each person employed immediately before that date by—
  (a) the Scottish Special Housing Association;
  (b) the Housing Corporation, in connection with its functions in Scotland,
and any question as to the persons to whom an offer of employment is to be made under this paragraph shall be determined by the Secretary of State.

(2) The terms of the offer shall be such that they are, taken as a whole, not less favourable to the person to whom the offer is made than the terms on which he is employed on the date on which the offer is made.

(3) An offer made in pursuance of this paragraph shall not be revocable during the period of 3 months commencing with the date on which it is made. **[1169]**

12.—(1) Where a person becomes an employee of Scottish Homes in consequence of an offer made under paragraph 11 above, then, for the purposes of the Employment Protection (Consolidation) Act 1978, his period of employment with the Scottish Special Housing Association or, as the case may be the Housing Corporation, shall count as a period of employment by Scottish Homes, and the change of employment shall not break the continuity of the period of employment.

(2) Where an offer is made in pursuance of paragraph 11(1) above to any person employed as is mentioned in that paragraph, none of the agreed redundancy procedures applicable to such a person shall apply to him and where that person ceases to be so employed—

(a) on becoming a member of the staff of Scottish Homes in consequence of that paragraph; or
(b) having unreasonably refused the offer,

Part VI of the Employment Protection (Consolidation) Act 1978 shall not apply to him and he shall not be treated for the purposes of any scheme under section 24 of the Superannuation Act 1972 or any other scheme as having been retired on redundancy.

(3) Without prejudice to sub-paragraph (2) above, where a person has unreasonably refused an offer made to him in pursuance of paragraph 11(1)(b) above the Housing Corporation shall not terminate that person's employment unless it has first had regard to the feasibility of employing him in a suitable alternative position with it.

(4) Where a person continues in employment in the Scottish Special Housing Association or, as the case may be, the Housing Corporation either—
(a) not having unreasonably refused an offer made to him in pursuance of this paragraph; or
(b) not having been placed in a suitable alternative position as mentioned in sub-paragraph (3) above,

he shall be treated for all purposes as if the offer mentioned in paragraph 11(1) above had not been made. **[1170]**

13.—(1) Any dispute as to whether an offer under sub-paragraph (1) of paragraph 11 above complies with sub-paragraph (2) of that paragraph shall be referred to and be determined by an industrial tribunal.

(2) An industrial tribunal shall not consider a complaint referred to it under sub-paragraph (1) above unless the complaint is presented to the tribunal before the end of the period of 3 months beginning with the date of the offer of employment or within such further period as the tribunal considers reasonable in a case where it is satisfied that it was not reasonably practicable for the complaint to be presented before the end of the period of 3 months.

(3) Subject to sub-paragraph (4) below there shall be no appeal from the decision of an industrial tribunal under this paragraph.

(4) An appeal to the Employment Appeal Tribunal may be made only on a question of law arising from the decision of, or in proceedings before, an industrial tribunal under this paragraph. **[1171]**

Proceedings

14.—The quorum of Scottish Homes and the arrangements for its meetings shall be such as it may determine, subject to any directions given by the Secretary of State. **[1172]**

15.—(1) A member who is directly or indirectly interested in a contract made or proposed to be made by Scottish Homes, or in any other matter whatsoever which falls to be considered by Scottish Homes, shall disclose the nature of his interest at a meeting of Scottish Homes, and the disclosure shall be recorded in the minutes of the meeting.

(2) Such a member shall not—
(a) in the case of any such contract, take part in any deliberation or decision of Scottish Homes with respect to the contract; and
(b) in the case of any other matter, take part in any deliberation or decision of Scottish Homes with respect to it if Scottish Homes decides that the interest in question might prejudicially affect the member's consideration of the matter.

(3) For the purposes of this paragraph, a notice given by a member at a meeting of Scottish Homes to the effect that he is a member of a specified body corporate or firm and is to be regarded as interested in any contract which is made with the body corporate or firm after the date of the notice, and in any other matter whatsoever concerning the body

corporate or firm which falls to be considered by Scottish Homes after that date, shall be a sufficient disclosure of his interest.

(4) A member need not attend in person a meeting of Scottish Homes in order to make a disclosure which he is required to make under this paragraph, if he takes reasonable steps to secure that the disclosure is made by a notice which is taken into consideration at such a meeting. [1173]

16.—The validity of any proceedings of Scottish Homes shall not be affected by any vacancy among its members or by any defect in the appointment of a member or by any failure to comply with any requirement of paragraph 15 above. [1174]

Committees

17.—(1) For and in connection with the discharge of its general functions or powers Scottish Homes may establish such committees (whose members need not be members of Scottish Homes) as appear to it to be appropriate, and the composition and remit of such committees and the terms on which their members hold office shall be determined by Scottish Homes.

(2) Scottish Homes shall pay to members of any committee established under sub-paragraph (1) above who are not members of Scottish Homes travelling and other allowances, including compensation for loss of remunerative time, in accordance with arrangements to be determined by the Secretary of State with the approval of the Treasury. [1175]

Execution of documents

18.—A document is validly executed by Scottish Homes if it is subscribed on its behalf by one of its members or by any other person duly authorised in that behalf. [1176]

19.—A document shall be presumed, unless the contrary is shown, to have been validly executed by Scottish Homes if it bears to have been subscribed on its behalf by one of its members or by any other person duly authorised in that behalf and to have been sealed with its common seal (whether attested by witnesses or not). [1177]

NOTES to Schedule 1
Para 10: See the Housing (Scotland) (Superannuation Fund) Regulations 1989, SI 1989/422.
Definition: 'Scottish Homes': see s 1 above.

SCHEDULE 2

Amendments Consequential on Establishing of Scottish Homes and Abolition of SSHA

General

1.—Subject to the following provisions of this Schedule, for any reference in any enactment, or in any instrument made under any enactment, to the Scottish Special Housing Association there shall be substituted a reference to Scottish Homes.

★ ★ ★ [1178]

NOTES to Schedule 2
Paras 2–17 amend various enactments.

★ ★ ★

NOTES to Schedule 3
Schedule 3 was repealed by the Housing Act 1988 (c 50), s 140, Sch 18.

SCHEDULE 4

Tenancies which cannot be Assured Tenancies

Tenancies entered into before commencement

1.—A tenancy which is entered into before, or pursuant to a contract made before, this Schedule comes into force. **[1179]**

Tenancies at a low rent

2.—(1) A tenancy under which, at any time after this Schedule comes into force, either no rent is payable or the rent payable is less than that specified by order made by the Secretary of State, but no tenancy which is or, at any time, was an assured tenancy shall cease to be an assured tenancy by virtue only of this paragraph of this Schedule.

(2) In determining whether the rent under a tenancy falls within sub-paragraph (1) above, there shall be disregarded such part (if any) of the sums payable by the tenant as is or was expressed (in whatever terms) to be payable in respect of services, repairs, maintenance or insurance, unless it could not have been regarded by the parties to the tenancy as a part so payable.

(3) An order under sub-paragraph (1) above may specify different rents in relation to—
(a) different kinds of houses;
(b) different areas.

(4) An order under sub-paragraph (1) above may specify rent by reference to such periods or times or such other factors or such combinations thereof as may be specified in the order. **[1180]**

Tenancies of shops

3.—A tenancy to which the Tenancy of Shops (Scotland) Act 1949 applies. **[1181]**

Licensed premises

4.—A tenancy under which the house consists of or comprises premises licensed for the sale of alcoholic liquor for consumption on the premises. **[1182]**

Tenancies of agricultural land

5.—(1) A tenancy under which agricultural land, exceeding two acres, is let together with the house.

(2) In this paragraph 'agricultural land' has the same meaning as in section 115(1) of the Rent (Scotland) Act 1984. **[1183]**

Tenancies of agricultural holdings

6.—A tenancy under which the house—
(a) is comprised in an agricultural holding (within the meaning of the Agricultural Holdings (Scotland) Act 1949); and
(b) is occupied by the person responsible for the control (whether as tenant or as servant or agent of the tenant) of the farming of the holding. **[1184]**

Lettings to students

7.—(1) A tenancy which is granted to a person who is pursuing, or intends to pursue, a course of study provided by a specified educational institution and is so granted either by that institution or by another specified institution or body of persons.

(2) In sub-paragraph (1) above 'specified' means specified, or of a class specified, for the purposes of this paragraph by regulations made by the Secretary of State. **[1185]**

Holiday lettings

8.—A tenancy the purpose of which is to confer on the tenant the right to occupy the house for a holiday. **[1186]**

Resident landlords

9.—(1) A tenancy in respect of which the following conditions are fulfilled—
(a) that the house forms part only of a building;
(b) subject to sub-paragraph (2) below, that the tenancy was granted by a person who, at the time when he granted it, occupied as his only or principal home another house which also forms part of the building;
(c) that, at the time when the tenancy was granted, there was an ordinary means of access—
  (i) to or from the house by way of that other house; or
  (ii) to or from that other house by way of the house
  (whether or not that access was available to the tenant as of right); and
(d) subject to sub-paragraph (3) below, at all times since the tenancy was granted the interest of the landlord under the tenancy has belonged to a person who, at the time he owned that interest, occupied as his only or principal home another house which also formed part of the building.

(2) The condition in sub-paragraph (1)(b) above shall be deemed to be fulfilled if the tenancy was granted by trustees and, at the time when the tenancy was granted, the interest of the landlord under the tenancy thereby created was held on trust for a person who was entitled to the liferent or to the fee or a share of the fee of that interest and who occupied as his only or principal home a house which forms part of the building referred to in sub-paragraph (1)(a) above.

(3) In determining whether the condition in sub-paragraph (1)(d) above is at any time fulfilled with respect to a tenancy, there shall be disregarded—
(a) any period of not more than 28 days beginning with the date of the conveyance of the interest of the landlord under the tenancy to an individual who, during that period, does not occupy as his only or principal home another house which forms part of the building concerned;
(b) if, within a period falling within paragraph (a) above, the individual concerned notifies the tenant in writing of his intention to occupy as his only or principal home another such house as is referred to in that paragraph, the period beginning with the date of the conveyance mentioned in that paragraph and ending—
  (i) at the expiry of the period of 6 months beginning on that date; or
  (ii) on the date on which the interest of the landlord under the tenancy ceases to be held by that individual; or
  (iii) on the date on which the condition in sub-paragraph (1)(c) above again applies,
  whichever is the earliest; and
(c) any period of not more than 24 months beginning with the date of death of the landlord under the tenancy during which the interest of the landlord under the tenancy is vested in his executor.

(4) Throughout any period which, by virtue of sub-paragraph (3)(a) or (b) above, falls to be disregarded for the purpose of determining whether the condition in sub-paragraph

(1)(d) above is fulfilled with respect to a tenancy, no order for possession of the house subject to that tenancy shall be made, other than an order which might be made if that tenancy were or, as the case may be, had been an assured tenancy.

(5) During any period—
(a) when—
  (i) the interest of the landlord under the tenancy referred to in sub-paragraph (1) above is vested in trustees; and
  (ii) that interest is held on trust for a person who is entitled to the liferent or to the fee or a share of the fee of that interest and who occupies as his residence a house which forms part of the building referred to in sub-paragraph (1)(a) above;
(b) of not more than 24 months beginning with the date of death of the occupier referred to in sub-paragraph (a)(ii) above and ending with the date of occupation of the house by any other person who is entitled to the liferent or to the fee or to a share of the fee of that interest,

the condition in sub-paragraph (1)(d) above shall be deemed to be fulfilled and, accordingly, no part of that period shall be disregarded by virtue of sub-paragraph (3) above.

(6) This paragraph does not apply to a tenancy of a house which forms part of a building if the tenancy is granted to a person who, immediately before it was granted, was an assured tenant of that house or of any other house in that building.

(7) For the purposes of this paragraph—
(a) 'conveyance' includes the grant of a tenancy and any other conveyance or transfer other than upon death;
(b) 'the date of the conveyance' means the date on which the conveyance was granted, delivered or otherwise made effective. **[1187]**

Crown tenancies

10.—A tenancy under which the interest of the landlord belongs to Her Majesty in right of the Crown or to a government department or is held in trust for Her Majesty for the purposes of a government department but not including such a tenancy if it is under the management of the Crown Estate Commissioners. **[1188]**

Local authority and other tenancies

11.—A tenancy under which the interest of the landlord belongs to—
(a) a regional, islands or district council, or a joint board or joint committee as respectively defined by the Local Government (Scotland) Act 1973, or the common good of an islands or district council or any trust under the control of a regional, islands or district council;
(b) a development corporation within the meaning of the New Towns (Scotland) Act 1968;
(c) the Scottish Special Housing Association;
(d) Scottish Homes;
(e) a co-operative housing association within the meaning of section 1 of the Housing Associations Act 1985; and
(f) an urban development corporation within the meaning of Part XVI of the Local Government, Planning and Land Act 1980.

Accommodation for homeless persons

11A.—A tenancy granted expressly on a temporary basis in the fulfilment of a duty imposed on a local authority by Part II of the Housing (Scotland) Act 1987. **[1189]**

Shared ownership agreements

12.—A tenancy under a shared ownership agreement within the meaning of the Housing Associations Act 1985. **[1190]**

Transitional cases

13.—(1) A protected tenancy within the meaning of the Rent (Scotland) Act 1984.

(2) A housing association tenancy, being a tenancy to which Part VI of that Act applies.

(3) A secure tenancy within the meaning of Part III of the Housing (Scotland) Act 1987. **[1191]**

NOTES to Schedule 4
Amendment: Para 11A added by the Housing Act 1988 (c 50), s 140, Sch 17, para 90.
Para 2: The amount specified is £6. See the Assured Tenancies (Tenancies at a Low Rent) (Scotland) Order 1988, SI 1988/2069, paras [1435] ff below.
Para 7: See the Assured Tenancies (Exceptions) (Scotland) Regulations 1988, SI 1988/2068.
Definitions: 'tenancy', 'house', 'tenant', 'landlord': see s 55 above; 'assured tenancy': see s 12 above.

SCHEDULE 5

GROUNDS FOR POSSESSION OF HOUSES LET ON ASSURED TENANCIES
PART I
GROUNDS ON WHICH SHERIFF MUST ORDER POSSESSION

Ground 1

Not later than the beginning of the tenancy the landlord (or, where there are joint landlords, any of them) gave notice in writing to the tenant that possession might be recovered on this Ground or the sheriff is of the opinion that it is reasonable to dispense with the requirement of notice and (in either case)—
(a) at any time before the beginning of the tenancy, the landlord who is seeking possession or, in the case of joint landlords seeking possession, at least one of them occupied the house as his only or principal home; or
(b) the landlord who is seeking possession or, in the case of joint landlords seeking possession, at least one of them requires the house as his or his spouse's only or principal home, and neither the landlord (or, in the case of joint landlords, any one of them) nor any other person who, as landlord, derived title from the landlord who gave the notice mentioned above acquired the landlord's interest in the tenancy for value. **[1192]**

Ground 2

The house is subject to a heritable security granted before the creation of the tenancy and—
(a) as a result of a default by the debtor the creditor is entitled to sell the house and requires it for the purpose of disposing of it with vacant possession in exercise of that entitlement; and
(b) either notice was given in writing to the tenant not later than the date of commencement of the tenancy that possession might be recovered on this Ground or the sheriff is satisfied that it is reasonable to dispense with the requirement of notice. **[1193]**

Ground 3

The house is let under a tenancy for a specified period not exceeding eight months and—
(a) not later than the date of commencement of the tenancy the landlord (or, where there are joint landlords, any of them) gave notice in writing to the tenant that possession might be recovered under this Ground; and

(b) the house was, at some time within the period of 12 months ending on that date, occupied under a right to occupy it for a holiday;

and for the purposes of this Ground a tenancy shall be treated as being for a specified period—
  (i) not exceeding eight months, if it is determinable at the option of the landlord (other than in the event of an irritancy being incurred) before the expiration of eight months from the commencement of the period of the tenancy; and
  (iii) exceeding eight months, if it confers on the tenant an option for renewal of the tenancy for a period which, together with the original period, exceeds eight months, and it is not determinable as mentioned in paragraph (i) above. **[1194]**

Ground 4

Where the house is let under a tenancy for a specified period not exceeding 12 months and—
  (a) not later than the date of commencement of the tenancy the landlord (or, where there are joint landlords, any of them) gave notice in writing to the tenant that possession might be recovered on this Ground; and
  (b) at some time within the period of 12 months ending on that date the house was subject to such a tenancy as is referred to in paragraph 7(1) of Schedule 4 to this Act;

and for the purposes of this Ground a tenancy shall be treated as being for a specified period—
  (i) not exceeding 12 months, if it is determinable at the option of the landlord (other than in the event of an irritancy being incurred) before the expiration of 12 months from the commencement of the period of the tenancy; and
  (ii) exceeding 12 months, if it confers on the tenant an option for renewal of the tenancy for a period which, together with the original period, exceeds 12 months, and it is not determinable as mentioned in paragraph (i) above. **[1195]**

Ground 5

The house is held for the purpose of being available for occupation by a minister or a full-time lay missionary of any religious denomination as a residence from which to perform the duties of his office and—
  (a) not later than the beginning of the tenancy the landlord (or, where there are joint landlords, any of them) gave notice in writing to the tenant that possession might be recovered on this ground; and
  (b) the sheriff is satisfied that the house is required for occupation by such a minister or missionary as such a residence. **[1196]**

Ground 6

The landlord who is seeking possession or, where the immediate landlord is a registered housing association within the meaning of the Housing Associations Act 1985, a superior landlord intends to demolish or reconstruct the whole or a substantial part of the house or to carry out substantial works on the house or any part thereof or any building of which it forms part and the following conditions are fulfilled (and in those conditions the landlord who is intending to carry out the demolition, reconstruction or substantial works is referred to as 'the relevant landlord')—
  (a) either—
    (i) the relevant landlord (or, in the case of joint relevant landlords, any one of them) acquired his interest in the house before the creation of the tenancy; or
    (ii) none of the following persons acquired his interest in the house for value—
      (A) the relevant landlord (or, in the case of joint relevant landlords, any one of them);

(B) the immediate landlord (or, in the case of joint immediate landlords, any one of them), where he acquired his interest after the creation of the tenancy;

(C) any person from whom the relevant landlord (or any one of joint relevant landlords) derives title and who acquired his interest in the house after the creation of the tenancy; and

(b) the relevant landlord cannot reasonably carry out the intended work without the tenant giving up possession of the house because—
   (i) the work can otherwise be carried out only if the tenant accepts a variation in the terms of the tenancy and the tenant refuses to do so;
   (ii) the work can otherwise be carried out only if the tenant accepts an assured tenancy of part of the house and the tenant refuses to do so; or
   (iii) the work can otherwise be carried out only if the tenant accepts either a variation in the terms of the tenancy or an assured tenancy of part of the house or both, and the tenant refuses to do so; or
   (iv) the work cannot otherwise be carried out even if the tenant accepts a variation in the terms of the tenancy or an assured tenancy of only part of the house or both. [1197]

Ground 7

The tenancy has devolved under the will or intestacy of the former tenant and the proceedings for the recovery of possession are begun not later than twelve months after the death of the former tenant or, if the sheriff so directs, after the date on which, in his opinion, the landlord (or, where there are joint landlords, any of them) became aware of the former tenant's death.

For the purposes of this Ground, the acceptance by the landlord of rent from a new tenant after the death of the former tenant shall not be regarded as creating a new tenancy, unless the landlord agrees in writing to a change (as compared with the tenancy before the death) in the amount of the rent, the period of the tenancy, the premises which are let or any other term of the tenancy. [1198]

Ground 8

Both at the date of the service of the notice under section 19 of this Act relating to the proceedings for possession and at the date of the hearing, at least three months' rent lawfully due from the tenant is in arrears. [1199]

Part II
Grounds on which Sheriff may order Possession

Ground 9

Suitable alternative accommodation is available for the tenant or will be available for him when the order for possession takes effect. [1200]

Ground 10

The following conditions are fulfilled—
(a) the tenant has given a notice to quit which has expired; and
(b) the tenant has remained in possession of the whole or any part of the house; and
(c) proceedings for the recovery of possession have been begun not more than six months after the expiry of the notice to quit; and
(d) the tenant is not entitled to possession of the house by virtue of a new tenancy. [1201]

Ground 11

Whether or not any rent is in arrears on the date on which proceedings for possession are begun, the tenant has persistently delayed paying rent which has become lawfully due.

Ground 12

Some rent lawfully due from the tenant—
(a) is unpaid on the date on which the proceedings for possession are begun; and
(b) except where subsection (1)(b) of section 19 of this Act applies, was in arrears at the date of the service of the notice under that section relating to those proceedings.

Ground 13

Any obligation of the tenancy (other than one related to the payment of rent) has been broken or not performed.

Ground 14

The condition of the house or of any of the common parts has deteriorated owing to acts of waste by, or the neglect or default of, the tenant or any one of joint tenants or any person residing or lodging with him or any sub-tenant of his; and, in the case of acts of waste by, or the neglect or default of, a person lodging with a tenant or a sub-tenant of his, the tenant has not, before the making of the order in question, taken such steps as he ought reasonably to have taken for the removal of the lodger or sub-tenant.

In this Ground, 'the common parts' means any part of a building containing the house and any other premises which the tenant is entitled under the terms of the tenancy to use in common with the occupiers of other houses.

Ground 15

The tenant or any other person residing or lodging with him in the house has been guilty of conduct in or in the vicinity of the house which is a nuisance or annoyance, or has been convicted of using the house or allowing the house to be used for immoral or illegal purposes.

Ground 16

The condition of any furniture provided for use under the tenancy has deteriorated owing to ill-treatment by the tenant or any other person residing or lodging with him in the house and, in the case of ill-treatment by a person lodging with the tenant or by a sub-tenant of his, the tenant has not taken such steps as he ought reasonably to have taken for the removal of the lodger or sub-tenant.

Ground 17

The house was let to the tenant in consequence of his employment by the landlord seeking possession or a previous landlord under the tenancy and the tenant has ceased to be in that employment.

PART III
SUITABLE ALTERNATIVE ACCOMMODATION

1.—For the purposes of Ground 9 above, a certificate of the local authority for the area in which the house in question is situated, or, where the house in question is in a new town, of the development corporation established for its purposes under the New Towns (Scotland) Act 1968 or, in any case, of Scottish Homes, certifying that the authority, the Corporation or, as the case may be, Scottish Homes, will provide suitable alternative accommodation for the tenant by a date specified in the certificate, shall be conclusive evidence that suitable alternative accommodation will be available for him by that date. **[1209]**

2.—Where no such certificate as is mentioned in paragraph 1 above is produced to the sheriff, accommodation shall be deemed to be suitable for the purposes of Ground 9 above if it consists of either—
  (a) premises which are to be let as a separate dwelling such that they will then be let on an assured tenancy, other than—
    (i) a tenancy in respect of which notice is served not later than the beginning of the tenancy that possession might be recovered on any of Grounds 1 to 5 above; or
    (ii) a short assured tenancy, within the meaning of Part II of this Act; or
  (b) premises to be let as a separate dwelling on terms which will, in the opinion of the sheriff, afford to the tenant security of tenure reasonably equivalent to the security afforded by Part II of this Act in the case of an assured tenancy of a kind mentioned in paragraph (a) above,
and, in the opinion of the sheriff, the accommodation fulfils the relevant conditions as defined in paragraph 3 below. **[1210]**

3.—(1) For the purposes of paragraph 2 above, the relevant conditions are that the accommodation is reasonably suitable to the needs of the tenant and his family as regards proximity to place of work, and either—
  (a) similar as regards rental and extent to the accommodation afforded by houses provided in the neighbourhood by any local authority or development corporation or by Scottish Homes for persons whose needs as regards extent are, in the opinion of the sheriff, similar to those of the tenant and of his family; or
  (b) reasonbly suitable to the means of the tenant and to the needs of the tenant and his family as regards extent and character; and
that, if any furniture was provided for use under the assured tenancy in question, furniture is provided for use in the accommodation which is either similar to that so provided or is reasonably suitable to the needs of the tenant and his family.

(2) For the purposes of sub-paragraph (1)(a) above, a certificate of a local authority or development corporation or of Scottish Homes stating—
  (a) the extent of the accommodation afforded by houses provided by that body to meet the needs of tenants with families of such number as may be specified in the certificate; and
  (b) the amount of the rent charged by that body for houses affording accommodation of that extent,
shall be conclusive evidence of the facts so stated. **[1211]**

4.—Accommodation shall not be deemed to be suitable to the needs of the tenant and his family if the result of their occupation of the accommodation would be that it would be an overcrowded house for the purposes of Part VII of the Housing (Scotland) Act 1987. **[1212]**

5.—Any document purporting to be a certificate of a local authority or development corporation named therein or of Scottish Homes issued for the purposes of this Part of this Schedule and to be signed by the proper officer of that body shall be received in evidence and, unless the contrary is shown, shall be deemed to be such a certificate without further proof. **[1213]**

6.—Local authorities, development corporations and Scottish Homes may, for the purposes of this Part of this Schedule, furnish particulars as to the availability, extent and character of alternative accommodation. **[1214]**

7.—In this Part of this Schedule 'local authority' means an islands or district council. **[1215]**

Part IV
Notices relating to recovery of Possession

8.—(1) If, not later than the beginning of a tenancy (in this paragraph referred to as 'the earlier tenancy'), the landlord gives such a notice in writing to the tenant as is mentioned in any of Grounds 1 to 5 in Part I of this Schedule, then, for the purposes of the Ground in question and any further application of this paragraph, that notice shall also have effect as if it had been given immediately before the beginning of any later tenancy falling within sub-paragraph (2) below.

(2) Subject to sub-paragraph (3) below, sub-paragraph (1) above applies to a later tenancy—
 (a) which takes effect immediately on termination of the earlier tenancy; and
 (b) which is granted (or deemed to be granted) to the person who was the tenant under the earlier tenancy immediately before it was terminated; and
 (c) which is of substantially the same house as the earlier tenancy.

(3) Sub-paragraph (1) above does not apply in relation to a later tenancy if, not later than the beginning of the tenancy, the landlord gave notice in writing to the tenant that the tenancy is not one in respect of which possession can be recovered on the ground in question. **[1216]**

9.—Where paragraph 8(1) above has effect in relation to a notice given as mentioned in Ground 1 in Part I of this Schedule, the reference in paragraph (b) of that ground to the landlord's interest in the tenancy is a reference to such an interest in the earlier tenancy and in any later tenancy falling within paragraph 8(2) above. **[1217]**

10.—Where paragraph 8(1) above has effect in relation to a notice given as mentioned in Ground 3 or Ground 4 in Part I of this Schedule, any second or subsequent tenancy in relation to which the notice has effect shall be treated for the purpose of that Ground as beginning at the beginning of the tenancy in respect of which the notice was actually given. **[1218]**

NOTES to Schedule 5
Definitions: 'assured tenancy': see s 12 above; 'tenancy', 'landlord', 'tenant', 'house', 'let': see s 55 above'; 'short assured tenancy': see s 32 above.

Section 46   SCHEDULE 6

Statutory or Statutory Assured Tenants by Succession

* * *

Part II
Statutory Assured Tenants by Succession—Modification of Enactments

2.—In relation to the assured tenancy to which the person becomes entitled by succession, section 18 of this Act shall have effect as if in subsection (3) after the word 'established' there were inserted the words 'or that the circumstances are as specified in any of Cases 11, 12, 17, 18, 19, and 21 in Schedule 2 to the Rent (Scotland) Act 1984'. **[1219]**

3.—(1) In relation to the assured tenancy to which the person becomes entitled by succession, any notice given for the purpose of Case 13, Case 14 or Case 16 of Schedule 2 to the Rent (Scotland) Act 1984 to the original tenant (within the meaning of Schedule I to the Rent (Scotland) Act 1984) shall be treated as having been given for the purposes of whichever of Grounds 4 to 6 in Schedule 5 to this Act corresponds to the Case in question.

(2) Where sub-paragraph (1) above applies, the regulated tenancy of the said original tenant shall be treated, in relation to the assured tenancy of the person so entitled, as the 'earlier tenancy' for the purposes of Part IV of Schedule 5 to this Act. **[1220]**

NOTES to Schedule 6
Part I: Part I of Schedule 6 amends the Rent (Scotland) Act 1984 (c 58).
Definitions: 'assured tenancy': see s 12 above; 'tenancy', 'tenant': see s 55 above; 'regulated tenancy': see the Rent (Scotland) Act 1984 (c 58), ss 8, 115.

* * *

NOTES to Schedule 7
Schedule 7 amends the Housing (Scotland) Act 1987 (c 26).

* * *

NOTES to Schedule 8
Schedule 8 amends the Housing (Scotland) Act 1987 (c 26).

* * *

NOTES to Schedule 9
Schedule 7 amends various enactments.

* * *

NOTES to Schedule 10
Schedule 10 amends various enactments.

Local Government and Housing Act 1989
(c 42)

* * *

168. Contributions towards costs of housing mobility arrangements.

(1) The Secretary of State may with the consent of the Treasury make grants or loans towards the cost of arrangements for enabling or assisting persons to move and become,—
(a) in England and Wales, tenants or licensees of dwellings; and
(b) in Scotland, tenants of houses.

(2) The grants or loans may be made subject to such conditions as the Secretary of State may determine and may be made so as to be repayable or, as the case may be, repayable earlier if there is a breach of such a condition.

(3) In this section—
'dwelling' means a building or a part of a building occupied or intended to be occupied as a separate dwelling;

'house' has the same meaning as in the Housing (Scotland) Act 1987; and
'tenant' does not include a tenant under a long lease within the meaning of the Landlord and Tenant Act 1987 or, as respects Scotland, under a lease for a period exceeding 20 years.

(4) * * * [1221]

NOTES to section 168
Sub-s (4): Sub-s (4) repeals s 80 of the Housing Act (Scotland) 1987 (c 26).

* * *

170. Powers of local authorities and Secretary of State as respects services, etc, for owners and occupiers of houses for work on them: Scotland.

(1) A relevant authority shall have power to provide professional, technical and administrative services for owners or occupiers of houses in connection with their arranging or carrying out relevant works or to encourage or facilitate the carrying out of such works, whether or not on payment of such charges as the authority may determine.

(2) Relevant works are such works as may be specified in regulations made by the Secretary of State and such works may be so specified by reference to such factors (including factors relating to persons of such descriptions as may be so specified) as the Secretary of State thinks fit.

(3) It shall be the duty of a relevant authority exercising any power conferred by subsection (1) above—
(a) to consider whether or not to make a charge for exercising it; and
(b) to take such measures as are reasonably available to them to secure contributions from other persons towards the cost of exercising it.

(4) A relevant authority shall have power to give financial assistance in any form to—
(a) any housing association,
(b) any charity, or
(c) any body, or body of any description, approved by the Secretary of State,
towards the cost of the provision by that association, charity or body of services of any description for owners or occupiers of houses in arranging works of maintenance, repair or improvement or the encouraging or facilitating the carrying out of such works.

(5) It shall be the duty of a relevant authority—
(a) in deciding whether to exercise any power conferred by subsection (4) above in relation to any association, charity or body, to have regard to the existence and extent of any financial assistance available from other persons to that association, charity or body; and
(b) in exercising any power conferred by subsection (4) above in relation to any association, charity or body—
   (i) to have regard to whether that association, charity or body has made or will make charges and their amount; and
   (ii) to encourage the association, charity or body to take such measures as are reasonably available to them to secure contributions from other persons.

(6) The Secretary of State may, with the consent of the Treasury, give financial assistance in any form to any person in respect of expenditure incurred or to be incurred by that person in connection with the provision, whether or not by that person, of services of any description for owners or occupiers of houses in arranging or carrying out works of maintenance, repair or improvement, or in connection with the encouraging or facilitating, whether or not by that person, the carrying out of such works.

(7) The giving of financial assistance under subsection (6) above shall be on such terms (which may include terms as to repayment) as the Secretaray of State, with the consent of the Treasury, considers appropriate.

(8) The person receiving assistance shall comply with the terms on which it is given and compliance may be enforced by the Secretary of State.

(9) In this section—
'charity' means any body, corporate or not, established for charitable purposes;
'charitable purposes' shall be construed in the same way as if it were contained in the Income Tax Acts;
'house' has the meaning given by section 338 of the Housing (Scotland) Act 1987;
'housing association' means a housing association within the meaning of section 1(1) of the Housing Association Act 1985, or a body established by such a housing association for the purpose of, or having among its purposes or objects, those mentioned in section 4(3)(e) of that Act (providing services of any description for owners or occupiers of houses in arranging or carrying out works of maintenance, repair or improvement, or encouraging or facilitating the carrying out of such works);
'relevant authority' means a regional, islands or district council. [1222]

NOTES to section 170

Sub-s (2): The power to make regulations has not yet been exercised.

171. Winding up of home purchase assistance scheme.

(1) The Secretary of State may by order make provision for the purpose of bringing to an end the scheme for assistance for first-time buyers which—
- (a) as respects England and Wales, is contained in sections 445 to 450 of the Housing Act 1985, and
- (b) as respects Scotland, is contained in sections 222 to 227 of the Housing (Scotland) Act 1987,

and in the following provisions of this section, the enactments specified in paragraphs (a) and (b) above together with any orders and directions made under those enactments are referred to as 'the assistance legislation'.

(2) Without prejudice to the generality of the power conferred by subsection (1) above, an order under that subsection—
- (a) may specify a date or dates with effect from which account will no longer be taken under the assistance legislation of matters specified in the order;
- (b) may vary the terms of advances to lending institutions so as to commute what would otherwise be a number of payments or repayments to or by such an institution into a single payment or a smaller number of payments of such amount and payable at such time or times as may be determined in accordance with the order; and
- (c) may provide for the amendment or repeal, in whole or in part, of the assistance legislation with effect from such date or dates and subject to such transitional provisions as may be specified in the order.

(3) The following powers, namely,—
- (a) the powers conferred on the Secretary of State by subsection (3) of section 446 of the Housing Act 1985 and subsection (3) of section 223 of the Housing (Scotland) Act 1987 to relax or modify the conditions in subsection (2) of each of those sections respectively (conditions qualifying a purchaser for assistance), and
- (b) any power to make an order under any provision of the assistance legislation,

may be so exercised as to make provision for the purpose referred to in subsection (1) above.

(4) The power to make an order under subsection (1) above shall be exercisable by statutory instrument which shall be subject to annulment in pursuance of a resolution of either House of Parliament. [1223]

NOTES to section 171

Sub-s (1): See the Home Purchase Assistance (Winding Up of Scheme) Order 1990, SI 1990/374, paras [1485] ff below.

★ ★ ★

Social Security Act 1990
(c 27)

* * *

Energy efficiency in certain dwellings etc

Grants for the improvement of energy efficiency in certain dwellings etc.

15.—(1) The Secretary of State may make or arrange for the making of grants—
(a) towards the cost of carrying out work—
 (i) for the purpose of improving the thermal insulation of dwellings, or
 (ii) otherwise for the purpose of reducing or preventing the wastage of energy in connection with space or water heating in dwellings; and
(b) where any such work is, or is to be, carried out, towards the cost of providing persons with advice relating to thermal insulation or to the economic and efficient use of domestic appliances or of facilities for lighting, or for space or water heating, in dwellings;

but no grants shall be made under this section except in accordance with regulations made by the Secretary of State.

(2) The regulations may make provision with respect to—
(a) the descriptions of dwelling and work in respect of which a grant under subsection (1)(a) above may be made;
(b) the nature and extent of the advice with respect to the provision of which grants under subsection (1)(b) above may be made;
(c) the descriptions of person from whom an application for a grant under subsection (1)(a) or (b) above may be entertained;
(d) the persons to whom such an application is to be made;
(e) the payment of such grants to persons other than the applicant;
(f) the conditions on which such a grant may be made.

(3) The regulations—
(a) may specify or make provision for determining the amount or maximum amount of any grant under this section; and
(b) may include provision requiring work to comply with standards of materials and workmanship (whether prescribed standards, or standards otherwise laid down from time to time by a prescribed person) if it is to be eligible for a grant under subsection (1)(a) above.

(4) Subsections (1) to (3) above shall apply in relation to any building in multiple occupation as they apply in relation to a dwelling; and for this purpose 'building in multiple occupation' means a building which is occupied by persons who do not form a single household, exclusive of any part of the building which is occupied as a separate dwelling by persons who form a single household.

(5) The Secretary of State may delegate any of his functions in relation to grants under this section to such persons or bodies of persons as he may determine, and may pay to any person or body of persons to whom functions are so delegated, or upon whom functions are otherwise conferred under or by virtue of this section, such fees as may be agreed.

(6) Without prejudice to the generality of the powers conferred by this section, the regulation may make provision for any of the following matters, that is to say—
(a) for appointing for any particular area a person or body of persons (an 'administering agency') to perform in that area such functions as the Secretary of State may confer upon that person or body for the purposes of, or otherwise in connection with, this section (whether those functions are prescribed, or specified otherwise than in regulations);
(b) for the administering agency for any area to select, in accordance with criteria (whether prescribed criteria, or criteria otherwise laid down from time to time by

a prescribed person), and register as the network installer for any particular locality within their area, a person or body of persons capable of carrying out, or arranging for the carrying out of, work in respect of which grants under subsection (1)(a) above may be made, to perform in that locality such functions as the Secretary of State or that agency may confer upon that person or body for the purposes of, or otherwise in connection with, this section (whether those functions are prescribed, or specified otherwise than in regulations);
(c) for the allocation by the Secretary of State to an administering agency of the sums which are to be available to that agency in any period for the purpose of making grants under this section in that period, and for the re-allocation of any sums so allocated;
(d) for the allocation by an administering agency to a network installer of an amount which represents the total amount of grant under this section which the agency determines is, or is to be, available for any period in respect of work carried out, and advice given, by that installer and any sub-contractors of his in that period, and for the re-allocation of any amount so allocated.

(7) The provision that may be made in regulations by virtue of subsection (6) above includes provision—
(a) for the making of appointments, or the conferring of functions, under that subsection to be effected in whole or in part by or under a contract made between prescribed persons and for requiring any such contract to contain prescribed terms and conditions or terms and conditions with respect to prescribed matters;
(b) for terminating any appointment as an administering agency or any registration as a network installer;
(c) for conferring upon network installers the exclusive right to apply for grants by virtue of subsection (4) above;
(d) for conferring upon administering agencies functions relating to the general oversight of network installers and the verification of claims made, and information supplied, by them.

(8) The power to make regulations under this section shall be exercisable by statutory instrument made with the consent of the Treasury; and any statutory instrument containing regulations under this section shall be subject to annulment in pursuance of a resolution of the House of Commons.

(9) Regulations under this section—
(a) may make different provision with respect to any labour involved, materials used or other items comprised in the carrying out of work; and
(b) may make different provision for different cases and different areas.

(10) In this section—
'functions' means powers and duties and includes the exercise of a discretion with respect to any matter;
'prescribed' means specified in, or determined in accordance with, regulations under this section.

(11) Sections 252 and 253 of the Housing (Scotland) Act 1987 (grants for thermal insulation) shall cease to have effect. **[1223A]**

NOTES to section 15

Sub-ss (1)–(3) and (6)–(9): See the Home Energy Efficiency Regulations 1990, SI 1990/1791 and paras [1487R] ff below.
Subs (11): The scheme of home energy efficiency grants is intended to replace the scheme of home insulation grants operated under the Housing (Scotland) Act 1987 (c 26), s 252 and SI 1987/2185, but sub-s (11) has not yet been brought into force.

---

* * *

2. STATUTORY INSTRUMENTS

The Housing (Computation of Floor Area) Regulations (Scotland) 1935
SI 1935/912

(These regulations were made by the Department of Health for Scotland under the Housing (Scotland) Act 1930, s 44, and the Housing (Scotland) Act 1935, s 7, and came into operation on 18 September 1935)

1. (*Citation*)

2. The Interpretation Act, 1889, applies to the interpretation of these Regulations as it applies to an Act of Parliament.

3. For the purposes of the First Schedule to the Housing (Scotland) Act, 1935, the floor area of a room shall be ascertained in the following manner:—
  (1) Subject to the provisions of paragraph (2) of this Article the floor area shall be computed on measurements made within the finished walls, and any floor area formed by a bay or oriel window or a window bossing shall be included; and
  (2) There shall be excluded from the computation of the floor area:—
     (a) any part of the floor over which the vertical height of the room is less than five feet, and
     (b) any part of the floor which is occupied by a chimney breast or by a fixed bed, fixed press or other fixture, or is immediately under a sink, and
     (c) any part of the floor which is contained in or forms part of a wall press
     so, however, that the provisions of sub-paragraph (b) and (c) shall apply only as respects floor area not excluded by virtue of the provisions of sub-paragraph (a).

Given under the Official Seal of the Department of Health for Scotland, this 18th day of September, in the year One thousand nine hundred and thirty-five.

NOTES to SI 1935/912

Reg 2: The Interpretation Act 1889 (c 63) has been replaced by the Interpretation Act 1978 (c 30).

SI 1964/1371 [1226]

The Housing (Management of Houses and Buildings in Multiple Occupation) (Scotland) Regulations 1964

SI 1964/1371

(These regulations were made by the Secretary of State for Scotland under s 13 of the Housing Act 1961 (c 65) as applied to Scotland by s 71 of the Housing Act 1964 (c 56) and came into operation on 10 September 1964)

ARRANGEMENT OF REGULATIONS
(This list is not printed in the Regulations)

PART I
PRELIMINARY

1	Application, citation and commencement	[1226]
2	Interpretation	[1227]

PART II
DUTIES OF MANAGEMENT

3	General	[1228]
4	Water supply and drainage	[1229]
5	Supply of gas and electricity and installation for lighting and heating	[1230]
6	Rooms and installations used in common by persons living in the same house	[1231]
7	Other parts of the house used in common by persons living in the house	[1232]
8	Accommodation let to tenants or lodgers	[1233]
9	Roof, windows and ventilation	[1234]
10	Means of escape from fire	[1235]
11	Miscellaneous parts of the premises	[1236]
12	Disposal of refuse and litter	[1237]
13	General safety of occupants	[1238]

PART III
ANCILLARY PROVISIONS

14	Manager's duty to display certain documents for information	[1239]
15	Manager's duty to inform local authority about occupancy of the house	[1240]
16	Duties of occupants	[1241]
17	Register of managers	[1242]
18	Provision of information by persons with an estate or interest in a house	[1243]

Part I
Preliminary

1. *(Citation and commencement)*

2. Interpretation.

(1) In these regulations the following expressions have the meanings hereinafter assigned to them, namely—

'the Act of 1961' means, subject to paragraph (4) of this regulation, the Housing Act 1961;

'the Act of 1964' means the Housing Act 1964;

'flat' means a separate set of premises, whether or not on the same floor, constructed for use for the purposes of a dwelling and forming part of a building from some other part of which it is divided horizontally;

'manager order' means an order under section 12 of the Act of 1961 applying the regulations to a house and 'the relevant management order', in a reference to a house or part of a house, means the management order in force with respect to that house;

'manager', in relation to a house, means the person who is an owner or a lessee of the house and who, directly or through an agent or trustee receives or is entitled to receive rent or other payments from persons who are tenants of parts of the house, or who are lodgers; and, where those rents or other payments are received through another person as his agent or trustee, includes that other person;

'the Rent Acts' means the Rent and Mortgage Interest Restriction Acts 1920 to 1939;

'rents' means rents or other payments from tenants of parts of a house, or from lodgers therein, and 'the rents', in relation to a person who is an owner or lessee of a house or an agent or trustee through whom rents are received, means such rents or other payments as are received by, or through that person;

'staircase' includes a landing;

'standard amenities' has the like meaning as in section 43(1) of the Act of 1964;

'tenement' means a building which as constructed contained, and which contains, two or more flats.

(2) In these regulations—
(a) references to a house include references to—
　(i) a building which is not a house but comprises separate dwellings, two or more of which do not have a sanitary convenience and personal washing facilities accessible only to those living in the dwelling,
　(ii) a building which is not a house but comprises separate dwellings, two or more of which are wholly or partly let in lodgings or occupied by members of more than one family, and
　(iii) a building comprising a tenement, all or any of the dwellings in which were, on 13th November 1963, without one or more of the standard amenities,
　(being in any case a building all the dwellings in which are owned by the same person);
(b) references to a lessee of a house include references to—
　(i) a tenant or sub-tenant of the house,
　(ii) any person holding the interest of lessee under a sub-lease of the house, and
　(iii) any person who retains possession of the house by virtue of the Rent Acts and not as being entitled to any tenancy;
(c) references to a person having an estate or interest in a house include references to a person who retains possession of the house by virtue of the Rent Acts as aforesaid; and
(d) references to an agent or trustee shall include a reference to a tutor, curator or factor.

(3) Any requirement of these regulations (however expressed) with respect to repair shall be construed as requiring a standard of repair that is reasonable in all the circumstances, and in determining the appropriate standard of repair for a room in, or

for any part of, a house regard shall be had to the age, character and prospective life of the house.

(4) Any reference in these regulations to a provision of the Act of 1961 shall be construed as a reference to that provision as applied to Scotland in section 71 of the Act of 1964 subject to the adaptations set out in Parts I and II of Schedule 3 to that Act and as so applied set out in Part III of the said Schedule 3.

(5) The Interpretation Act 1889 shall apply for the interpretation of these regulations as it applies for the interpretation of an Act of Parliament. [1227]

PART II
DUTIES OF MANAGEMENT

3. General.

(1) When a management order is made as respects any house it shall be the duty of a person who is manager of the house by virtue of being an owner or lessee thereof who receives the rents—
- (a) if he does not live in the house, to make such arrangements (including arrangements for adequate supervision of the house) as may be necessary to enable him, directly or through an agent authorised in that behalf, to discharge effectively his obligations under the following regulations;
- (b) in any case, to inform any person who is his agent or trustee, and through whom he receives the rents, that the order has been made and that these regulations accordingly apply to the house and impose obligations on that person.

(2) Where a person who is manager of a house by virtue of being an agent or trustee through whom rents are received is aware that some action is required to discharge an obligation of the manager under the following regulations, he shall, unless he discharges that obligation himself, take such steps as may be necessary to bring the need for action promptly to the attention of the owner or lessee of the house who receives the rents through him; and where he receives from the local authority a material complaint with respect to management of the house of which he is manager as aforesaid, such a person shall, if required by the authority so to do,—
- (a) transmit that complaint to the said owner or lessee, and
- (b) provide the local authority with the name and address of the person to whom the complaint is accordingly transmitted;

but this paragraph shall not be taken as exempting a person who is a manager of a house by virtue of being an agent or trustee through whom rents are received from the obligations imposed on managers by the following regulations or from liability for failure without reasonable excuse to comply with them.

(3) Nothing in the following regulations shall be taken to require or authorise anything to be done in connection with water supply, drainage, or the supply of gas or electricity otherwise than in accordance with any enactment relating thereto, or to oblige the manager of a house to take, in a matter connected therewith, any action which is the responsibility of a local authority or statutory undertaker, other than such action as may be necessary to bring the matter promptly to the attention of the local authority or statutory undertaker concerned.

(4) In this regulation—
- (a) 'enactment' includes an enactment in any local act and an order, rule, regulation, byelaw or scheme made under or by virtue of any Act, including any order or scheme confirmed by Parliament;
- (b) 'statutory undertaker' means any person authorised by an enactment to construct, work or carry on any undertaking for the supply of gas, electricity or water or other public undertaking. [1228]

4. Water supply and drainage.

(1) The manager shall ensure that all means of water supply and drainage in the house (including the curtilage, if any) are in and are maintained in a proper state of repair, a clean condition and good order, and shall, in particular, ensure—
- (a) that any tank, cistern or similar receptacle, provided for the storage of water for drinking or other domestic purposes is effectively covered, and that all such receptacles and the water stored in them are kept in a clean and proper condition;
- (b) that any water fitting which is so placed, whether inside or outside the house, as to render it liable to damage by frost shall (unless it is an overflow pipe) be reasonably protected against such damage.

For this purpose 'water fitting' includes any pipe (other than a main), tap, cock, valve, ferrule, meter, cistern, bath, water closet, soil pan or other similar apparatus used in connection with the supply or use of water.

(2) The manager shall not unreasonably cause a supply of water to any tenant or lodger in the house to be interrupted. **[1229]**

5. Supply of gas and electricity and installation for lighting and heating.

(1) The manager shall ensure that the installations in the house—
- (a) for the supply of gas and electricity,
- (b) for lighting, and
- (c) for space heating or heating water,

serving any part of the house used in common by persons living in the house, are in and are maintained in repair and proper working order, and that installations for lighting in places to which this regulation applies are readily available for use by tenants and lodgers to such extent and at such times as those persons may reasonably require.

(2) The last foregoing paragraph shall extend to installations for lighting on staircases and at entrances to the house which are used by tenants or lodgers, whether in common or otherwise, except any staircase which is comprised in a part of the house let to a tenant or lodger as his living accommodation and which either does not open directly on to a part of the house used in common or is separated from such part by a door.

(3) The manager shall not unreasonably cause a supply of gas or electricity to any tenant or lodger in the house to be interrupted. **[1230]**

6. Rooms and installations used in common by persons living in the same house.

(1) The manager shall ensure that the following rooms and installations in the house (including the curtilage, if any) are in and are maintained in a proper state of repair (including, where appropriate, reasonable decorative repair), a clean condition and good order:—
- (a) all rooms used in common by persons living in the house, not being parts of the house to which the next following regulation relates;
- (b) such of the following installations as are used in common by persons living in the house, namely, sanitary conveniences, baths, sinks, wash-basins, and installations for cooking or for storing food;
- (c) in the case of any room used in common by persons living in the house, being a kitchen, bathroom, water closet, lavatory or washhouse, such installations therein (if any) as are not subject to any of the foregoing provisions of these regulations.

(2) Nothing in this regulation shall oblige the manager to repair, keep in repair or maintain anything which a tenant or lodger is entitled to remove from the house. **[1231]**

7. Other parts of the house used in common by persons living in the house.

(1) The manager shall ensure that such of the following parts of the house as are used in common by persons living in the house are in and are maintained in a proper state of

repair (including reasonable decorative repair), a clean condition and good order and are kept reasonably free from obstruction:—
  (a) staircases, passageways and corridors;
  (b) halls and lobbies;
  (c) entrances to the house, including entrance doors, porches and entrance steps;
  (d) balconies.

(2) The last foregoing paragraph shall extend to any staircase, passageway, or corridor which gives access to the living accommodation of a tenant or lodger in the house and which, though not itself used in common, opens directly on to a part of the house so used from which it is not separated by a door.

(3) The manager's duties under this regulation shall, without prejudice to the generality thereof, include duties to ensure (in places to which this regulation applies) that all handrails, railings, balustrades, and banisters are kept in good order and repair, that any missing handrails, railings, balustrades, and banisters are replaced, and that such additional handrails, railings, balustrades, and banisters as are necessary for the safety of tenants or lodgers living in the house are provided. [1232]

8. Accommodation let to tenants or lodgers.

(1) The following provisions of this regulation shall have effect with respect to the repair and maintenance of premises (being a room or set of rooms in a part of any house to which the regulations apply) which are let to a tenant or lodger as his living accommodation, and to the repair and maintenance of the installations therein, but shall be without prejudice to other provisions of these regulations insofar as they may extend to such premises or installations.

(2) It shall be the duty of the manager, when he lets any premises as aforesaid, to ensure at the commencement of the letting—
  (a) that the premises are, internally, in a reasonable state of structural repair, and in a clean condition; and
  (b) that the installations therein for the supply, and for making use of the supply, of water, gas and electricity, and for sanitation (including installations therein for space heating or heating water) are in a reasonable state of repair and proper working order.

(3) With respect to premises which on the date of the making of the relevant management order are let to a tenant or lodger as his living accommodation, it shall be the duty of the manager, subject to the provisions of paragraph (5) of this regulation, to take within a reasonable time thereafter such steps (if any) as may be necessary—
  (a) to put the premises, internally, in a reasonable state of structural repair; and
  (b) to put in a reasonable state of repair and proper working order the installations in the premises—
    (i) for the supply of water, gas and electricity, and for sanitation (including basins, sinks, baths and sanitary conveniences but not except as aforesaid, fixtures, fittings and appliances for making use of the supply of water, gas or electricity), and
    (ii) for space heating or heating water.

(4) While premises to which this regulation applies are occupied by a tenant or lodger as his living accommodation it shall be the duty of the manager, subject to the provisions of the next following paragraph, to ensure that the installations falling within subparagraph (b) of the last foregoing paragraph are kept in repair and proper working order:

Provided that the manager shall not be required by this paragraph to carry out any repair the need for which arises in consequence of use of the premises otherwise than in a tenant-like manner by the person to whom they are let.

(5) Nothing in this regulation shall oblige the manager to repair, keep in repair or maintain anything which a tenant or lodger is entitled to remove from the premises. [1233]

9. Roof, windows and ventilation.

(1) The manager shall ensure that all windows and other means of ventilation in any part of the house occupied or used (whether in common or otherwise) by tenants or lodgers, are in and are maintained in good order and repair:

Provided that, save insofar as may be necessary for the proper discharge of any other of his duties under these regulations, the manager shall not be required to carry out, in a part of the house which is for the time being let to a tenant or lodger as his living accommodation, any repair to a window or other means of ventilation the need for which arises after the date of the relevant management order in consequence of use of that part otherwise than in a tenant-like manner by the person to whom it is let.

(2) The manager shall ensure that the roof of the building comprising the house or, so far as under his control, the roof of the building of which the house forms part, is in and is maintained in good order and repair. **[1234]**

10. Means of escape from fire.

(1) The manager shall ensure that all means of escape from fire in the house (including any escape apparatus) are in and are maintained in proper repair and good order and are kept free from obstruction, and that there are displayed in the house with respect to such means of escape as aforesaid (other than any exit in ordinary use) such notice as the local authority, after consultation with the fire authority for the area in which the house is situated, may, if they think fit, reasonably require.

(2) In this regulation, the expression 'fire authority' means in relation to any area, the authority for the time being constituted the fire authority for that area under the Fire Service Act 1947, except that in relation to an area the fire brigade for which is administered by such a joint committee as is mentioned in section 36(4)(b) of that Act, it means that joint committee. **[1235]**

11. Miscellaneous parts of the premises.

(1) The manager shall ensure that every outbuilding, yard, area and forecourt, which belongs to the house and is used in common by persons living in the house, is in and is maintained in a proper state of repair, a clean condition and good order, and that any garden so used belonging to the house is kept in a tidy condition.

(2) The manager shall ensure that boundary walls, fences and railings (including basement areas railings), insofar as they belong to the house, are kept and maintained in reasonable repair so as not to constitute a danger to persons living on the premises.

(3) If any part of the house is subject to a closing order, or not in use, the manager shall ensure that such part, including any passage and staircase directly giving access to it, is kept reasonably clean and free from refuse and litter.

(4) In this regulation 'closing order' means an order made by a local authority under section 9(1) of the Housing (Scotland) Act 1950. **[1236]**

12. Disposal of refuse and litter.

The manager shall ensure that refuse and litter are not allowed to accumulate in, or in the curtilage of, the house save where properly stored pending disposal, and to that end he shall, in particular,—
 (a) provide, and maintain the provision of, suitable refuse and litter bins or other suitable receptacles on a scale adequate to the requirements of tenants and lodgers in the house except insofar as such provision is made by the local authority, and
 (b) make such supplementary arrangements for the disposal of refuse and litter from the house as may be necessary having regard to any existing service provided by the local authority. **[1237]**

SI 1964/1371 [1241]

13. **General safety of occupants.**

The manager shall ensure that such precautions are taken as are reasonably required, having regard to structural conditions in the house and to the number of persons living there, to protect tenants and lodgers and members of their households from injury as the result of those conditions; and in particular he shall (without prejudice to any of his foregoing obligations) ensure as respects any roof or balcony which is not in all respects safe, either that reasonable measures are taken to prevent access thereto or that it is made safe, and that such safeguards as may be necessary are provided against the danger of accidents resulting from the presence on staircases and landings of windows, the sills of which are at or near floor level. [1238]

Part III
Ancillary Provisions

14. **Manager's duty to display certain documents for information.**

(1) The manager of a house to which these regulations apply shall cause to be displayed in a suitable position in the house so as to be readily accessible to the occupants—
  (a) a notice containing the name and address of the person (or of each person) who is a manager of the house, describing him as manager and, where appropriate as agent or trustee for the receipt of rents;
  (b) a copy of the relevant management order and a copy of these regulations; and
  (c) if the local authority so require, such notice as the authority may provide for indicating briefly the main provisions of these regulations relating to management of the house and the provisions of the Act of 1961 as respects failure to comply with them;
and he shall take all reasonable steps to ensure that the documents which are displayed in accordance with this regulation remain so displayed (with only requisite amendments) while the relevant management order is in force.

(2) The manager shall make such amendments to the foregoing documents as may from time to time be required, and, in the case of amendments of these regulations and to the notice referred to in sub-paragraph (c) of the last foregoing paragraph, as are brought to his attention by the local authority. [1239]

15. **Manager's duty to inform local authority about occupancy of the house.**

The manager of a house to which these regulations apply shall, when required by the local authority so to do, provide the authority with such of the following particulars as they may require (and in such time and manner as they may reasonably specify) with respect to occupancy of the house, or, where part only of the house is occupied by tenants or lodgers, with respect to occupancy of that part:—
  (a) the number of individuals and households accommodated;
  (b) the number of individuals in household;
  (c) the ages and sex of those individuals;
  (d) the purpose for which each room in the house, or in the relevant part of the house is being used. [1240]

16. **Duties of occupants.**

With a view to ensuring that the manager can effectively carry out the duties with which he is charged by these regulations, it shall be a general obligation of tenants and lodgers and members of their households, accommodated in the house, to take reasonable care not to hinder or frustrate the due performance of those duties, and in particular, every such person, insofar as he is able, shall—
  (a) allow the manager, at all reasonable times, to enter any room or other place comprised in that person's tenancy or lodging, for purposes connected with the carrying out by the manager of his duties;

(b) provide the manager, at his request, with all such information as he may reasonably require for the purpose of his duties;
(c) comply with any reasonable arrangements made by the manager for the storage and disposal of refuse and litter; and
(d) take reasonable care to avoid causing damage to anything which the manager is obliged by these regulations to keep in repair. **[1241]**

17. Register of managers.

(1) The local authority shall maintain a register of the names and addresses of persons who are for the time being managers of houses to which these regulations apply, and shall include therein such particulars as they reasonably believe to be correct relating to the capacity in which such persons are managers, that is to say whether as owners or lessees receiving rents, or as agents or trustees through whom rents are received.

(2) As soon as may be after making or amending an entry in the register in reliance on information obtained otherwise than from the person to whom such entry relates the local authority shall take reasonable steps to bring the entry or amendment to the notice of the said person.

(3) The local authority shall, at the request of a person who appears to them to have an interest or prospective interest in a house, to be resident therein, or to be otherwise sufficiently concerned therewith, disclose to him the contents of any entry in the register relating to that house. **[1242]**

18. Provision of information by persons with an estate or interest in a house.

(1) When a management order is made in respect of a house, an owner or lessee of the house who receives or is entitled to receive the rents shall, on being served with a copy of the order and warned in writing (whether by means of a note appended to the copy of the order or otherwise) of the requirements of this paragraph, provide the local authority with the following information—
(a) his name and address,
(b) particulars of his estate or interest in the house,
(c) particulars sufficient to show what parts of the house are let to tenants, or lodgers, from whom he is in receipt of rents, and
(d) the name and address of any agent or trustee through whom he receives such rents.

(2) Without prejudice to any other requirement of this regulation, a person who has an estate or interest in a house or any part of a house to which these regulations apply shall, at the request of the local authority, provide the authority with such of the following items of information as they may require, namely—
(a) any of those mentioned in the last foregoing paragraph;
(b) the name and address of any other person known to him to be manager of the house, with particulars showing how he knows that such person is manager;
(c) if he is a person who receives the rents through another person as his agent or trustee, whether, and in what respects, such other person is authorised to act in matters connected with the management of the house apart from the receipt of rents.

(3) An owner or lessee of a house to which these regulations apply shall, if at any time he appoints a person to receive the rents as his agent or trustee, forthwith give the local authority notice of the fact together with the name and address of the person appointed.

(4) A person who acquires or ceases to hold an estate or interest in a house to which these regulations apply shall, if he thereby becomes or ceases to be manager of the house, forthwith give the local authority notice of the fact together with particulars of the estate or interest which he has acquired or ceased to hold, and, where he has sold or transferred the estate or interest to some other person, the name and address of that person.

(5) The information called for by or under this regulation shall, except insofar as the

local authority may in any particular case otherwise allow, be provided to the authority in writing; and any information requested by the local authority under paragraph (2) of this regulation shall be given to them within such time, if any, as they may reasonably specify. [1243]

NOTES to SI 1964/1371

Reg 1: The Interpretation Act 1889 (c 63) has been replaced by the Interpretation Act 1978 (c 30).
Reg 2: The Housing Act 1961 (c 65) and the Housing Act 1964 (c 56) have both been repealed. Houses in multiple occupation are now regulated under the Housing (Scotland) Act 1987 (c 26), Part VIII, paras [722] ff above.

The Protected Tenancies (Exceptions) (Scotland) Regulations 1974
SI 1974/1374

(*These regulations were made by the Secretary of State for Scotland under the Rent (Scotland) Act 1971 (c 20), s 2(4) as added by the Rent Act 1974 (c 51), s 2(2), and came into operation on 14 August 1974*)

1. Citation, commencement and interpretation.

(1) (*Citation and Commencement*)

(2) The Interpretation Act 1889 shall apply for the interpretation of these regulations as it applies for the interpretation of an Act of Parliament. [1244]

2. Specified institutions.

There are hereby specified for the purposes of section 2(1)(bb) of the Rent (Scotland) Act 1971 as inserted by section 2(1) of the Rent Act 1974 (tenancies excepted from definition of 'protected tenancy') the educational institutions set out in the Schedule annexed hereto and any other institution or body of persons by which any of the said educational institutions is provided. [1245]

SCHEDULE

Educational institutions specified for the purposes of section 2(1)(bb) of the Rent (Scotland) Act 1971

(a) Any university, university college and any constituent college, school or hall of a university.
(b) Any Central Institution within the meaning of section 145(10) of the Education (Scotland) Act 1962 and recognised by the Central Institutions (Recognition) (Scotland) Regulations 1973.
(c) Any College of Education within the meaning of section 145(14) of the Education (Scotland) Act 1962 as amended.
(d) Any establishment of Further Education financed and controlled by an Education Authority within the meaning of sections 4 and 145(21) of the Education (Scotland) Act 1962 as amended.
(e) Any approved Association approved by the Secretary of State under Regulation 8 of the Further Education (Scotland) Regulations 1959. [1246]

NOTES to SI 1974/1374

Reg 1(2): The Interpretation Act 1889 (c 63) has been replaced by the Interpretation Act 1978 (c 30).

The Housing (Homeless Persons) (Appropriate Arrangements) (No 2) Order 1978

SI 1978/661

(*This order was made by the Secretary of State for Scotland under the Housing (Homeless Persons) Act 1978 (c 48), ss (8)–(10), and came into operation on 28 April 1978*)

1. (*Citation and commencement*)

2. Interpretation.

(1) The Interpretation Act 1889 shall apply for the interpretation of this order as it applies for the interpretation of an Act of Parliament.

(2) In this order 'the Act' means the Housing (Homeless Persons) Act 1978.

(3) In this order references to any enactment shall be construed as references to that enactment as amended, extended or applied by or under any other enactment.

3. Appropriate arrangements.

Where both the notifying authority and the notified authority are housing authorities in Scotland, the appropriate arrangements for the purpose of section 5 of the Act, shall be the arrangements set out in Part I of the Schedule to this order, which are the arrangements agreed by the Convention of Scottish Local Authorities.

4.—(1) Where either the notifying authority or the notified authority is a housing authority in England or Wales and the other of those authorities is a housing authority in Scotland, the appropriate arrangements for the purposes of section 5 of the Act shall be the arrangements set out in Part I of the Schedule to this order as modified by Part II of that Schedule, which are arrangements agreed by the associations of relevant authorities specified in paragraph (2) below.

(2) The associations of relevant authorities mentioned in paragraph (1) above are:—
(a) The Association of District Councils,
(b) The Association of Metropolitan Authorities,
(c) The London Boroughs Association, and
(d) The Convention of Scottish Local Authorities.

Articles 3 and 4   SCHEDULE

APPROPRIATE ARRANGEMENTS
PART I

1. Panel of persons who may be appointed.

The Convention of Scottish Local Authorities shall draw up and from time to time revise a panel of persons who may be appointed under paragraph 5 below to determine questions falling to be determined under section 5 of the Act.

2. Proper officers.

(1) The proper officer for the purposes of paragraphs 4 and 5 below shall be the President of the Convention of Scottish Local Authorities.

(2) In the case of the absence or incapacity of the President mentioned in sub-paragraph (1) above his functions under paragraph 5 below shall be exercised by, and any report under paragraph 4 below may be made to the Vice President of the Convention of Scottish Local Authorities. [1252]

3. Determination by person agreed upon by authorities.

(1) If—
(a) before the end of the period of 21 days following—
  (i) the day on which a notification under section 5(1) of the Act is received by the notified authority, or
  (ii) the day on which the Housing (Homeless Persons) (Appropriate Arrangements) (No. 2) Order 1978 came into operation,
  whichever is the later, or
(b) after the end of that period but before a person has been appointed under paragraph 5 below to determine the question,
any question which falls to be determined under section 5 of the Act in relation to that notification has not been determined by agreement between the notifying authority and the notified authority, and those authorities have made arrangements for that question to be determined by a person agreed upon by them, the question may be determined by that person.

(2) Where the notifying authority and the notified authority have made arrangements under sub-paragraph (1) above—
(a) they shall jointly submit a report to the person agreed upon by them;
(b) paragraph 4(2) and (3) below shall apply to that report as they apply to a report made under paragraph 4(1) below;
(c) paragraphs 6 to 9 below shall, with any necessary modifications, apply to the determination of any question by that person as they apply to the determination of a question by a person appointed under paragraph 5 below; and
(d) if either of those authorities have made a report under paragraph 4 below they shall forthwith inform the person to whom they made the report that the arrangements have been made. [1253]

4. Report to proper officer.

(1) If—
(a) at the end of the period of 21 days mentioned in sub-paragraph (1) of paragraph 3 above—
  (i) any such question as is mentioned in that sub-paragraph has not been determined by agreement between the notifying authority and the notified authority, and
  (ii) those authorities have not made arrangements for that question to be determined as provided in paragraph 3 above; or
(b) before the end of that period both those authorities have agreed that they will be unable either—
  (i) to determine that question by agreement, or
  (ii) to make arrangements for that question to be determined as provided in that paragraph
  before the end of that period,
the notifying authority shall, and the notified authority may, report that fact in writing to the person who is, under paragraph 2 above, the proper officer for the purposes of this paragraph in relation to the authority making the report.

(2) A report under sub-paragraph (1) above—
(a) shall identify the notifying authority, the notified authority, and the person to whom the notification under section 5(1) of the Act relates, and
(b) subject to sub-paragraph (3) below, shall contain either—
  (i) a statement, agreed by both those authorities, that the question which they have not determined by agreement is the question whether subsection (3) or (5) of section 5 of the Act applies to that person, or
  (ii) a statement, agreed by both those authorities, setting out the particular question or questions falling to be determined under that section which they have not determined by agreement.

(3) If a report under sub-paragraph (1) above does not contain a statement falling within sub-paragraph (2)(b) above, it shall be deemed to contain a statement falling within sub-paragraph (2)(b)(i) above. **[1254]**

5. Appointment of person to determine question.

(1) Subject to sub-paragraph (3) below, the person who receives a report or reports under paragraph 4 above shall appoint a person who is for the time being a member of the panel drawn up under paragraph 1 above to determine the question.

(2) When an appointment is made under sub-paragraph (1) above, the person who is the proper officer—
(a) shall inform the notifying authority and the notified authority in writing of the appointment; and
(b) shall transmit to the appointed person a copy of the report, or as the case may be, copies of the reports, made under paragraph 4 above.

(3) No appointment shall be made under sub-paragraph (1) above after the proper officer has been informed under sub-paragraph (2)(d) of paragraph 3 above that arrangements have been made under that paragraph, and an appointment made after any such arrangements have been made shall be of no effect. **[1255]**

6. Determination of question.

(1) Where a report under paragraph 4 above contains a statement falling within sub-paragraph (2)(b)(ii) of that paragraph, the appointed person shall not determine any question that is not set out in the statement.

(2) Except as otherwise provided in this paragraph, the procedure for the determination of any question to which a statement contained or deemed to be contained in a report under paragraph 4 above relates shall be such as the appointed person may in his discretion determine.

(3) For the purpose of determining any such question the appointed person, in so far as such information and representations appear to him to be proper and relevant to the matters in issue—
(a) shall take into account—
  (i) any representations made orally or in writing by the notifying authority and the notified authority, and
  (ii) any information provided in response to an invitation under (b) below;
(b) shall invite the person to whom the notification under section 5(1) of the Act relates to provide him with information; and
(c) may take into account information obtained from, and representations made by, any person orally or in writing.

(4) An invitation under sub-paragraph (3)(b) above—
(a) may be given orally or in writing;
(b) may specify the matters concerning which information may be provided; and
(c) shall specify whether the information may be provided—
  (i) orally,
  (ii) in writing, or
  (iii) either orally or in writing. **[1256]**

7. Notification of determination.

(1) The appointed person shall notify his determination, and his reasons for it, in writing to the notifying authority and the notified authority.

(2) A determination notified by the appointed person in accordance with sub-paragraph (1) above shall, notwithstanding that any requirement in this Schedule has not been complied with in relation to his appointment or in relation to the procedure adopted by him for the determination of the question, be final and binding on both authorities.

(3) The appointed person shall have power to correct any clerical mistake or error arising from any accidental slip or omission in his notification of a determination. **[1257]**

8. Costs.

(1) Subject to sub-paragraphs (2) and (3) below, the notifying authority and the notified authority shall each pay their own costs of the determination.

(2) The appointed person—
(a) may give directions as to the payment of the costs of the determination, and
(b) shall, where information has been provided orally, in response to an invitation under paragraph 6(3)(b) above, by the person to whom the notification under section 5(1) of the Act relates, give directions as to the payment by the notifying authority or the notified authority or by both of those authorities of any travelling expenses reasonably incurred by that person.

(3) Without prejudice to the generality of sub-paragraph (2)(a) above, the directions that may be given thereunder include directions as to—
(a) any costs of the notifying authority and the notified authority, and
(b) any costs incurred by any person from whom the appointed person has obtained information, or who has made representations, orally or in writing. **[1258]**

9. Determination of question by agreement.

(1) At any time before a determination has been notified under paragraph 7 above the notifying authority and the notified authority may jointly report to the appointed person that they have determined a question by agreement.

(2) Where a report under sub-paragraph (1) above is made, the appointed person shall not determine, but paragraph 8 above shall apply as if he had determined, any question to which that report relates. **[1259]**

Part II

10. Part I of this Schedule shall have effect with the substitution for paragraphs 1, 2 and 5 of the following paragraphs:

'1. Panel of persons who may be appointed.

The Association of District Councils, the Association of Metropolitan Authorities, the London Boroughs Association and the Convention of Scottish Local Authorities shall draw up and from time to time revise a panel of persons who may be appointed under paragraph 5 below to determine questions falling to be determined under section 5 of the Act.

2. Proper officers.

(1) The proper officer for the purposes of paragraphs 4 and 5 below shall be—
(a) in relation to the council of a non-metropolitan district in England and Wales, the Chairman of the Association of District Councils;
(b) in relation to any other housing authority in England and Wales except the council of a London borough and the Common Council of the City of London,

the Chairman of the Association of Metropolitan Authorities, and in relation to the council of a London borough and to the Common Council of the City of London, the Chairman of the London Boroughs Association; and
(c) in relation to a district or islands council in Scotland, the President of the Convention of Scottish Local Authorities.

(2) In the case of the absence or incapacity of the Chairman or President of any body mentioned in sub-paragraph (1) above his functions under paragraph 5 below shall be exercised by, and any report under paragraph 4 below may be made to, a person nominated in that behalf by that body, or in the case of the Convention of Scottish Local Authorities the Vice President.

5. Appointment of person to determine question.

(1) Subject to sub-paragraph (4) below, a person who receives from an authority a report under paragraph 4 above shall transmit a copy of the report to the person who is the proper officer in relation to the other authority identified in the report and jointly with him appoint a person who is for the time being a member of the panel drawn up under paragraph 1 above to determine the question.

(2) Subject to sub-paragraph (4) below, where two proper officers have failed to agree on a person to appoint under sub-paragraph (1) above—
  (a) each of them shall nominate a person who is for the time being a member of the panel drawn up under paragraph 1 above, and
  (b) the person who is the proper officer in relation to the notifying authority shall—
    (i) decide by lot between the persons so nominated, and
    (ii) appoint the person on whom the lot falls to determine the question.

(3) When an appointment is made under sub-paragraph (1) or (2) above, the person who is the proper officer in relation to the notifying authority—
  (a) shall inform the notifying authority and the notified authority in writing of the appointment; and
  (b) shall transmit to the appointed person a copy of the report, or as the case may be, copies of the reports, made under paragraph 4 above.

(4) No appointment shall be made under sub-paragraph (1) or (2) above after a proper officer has been informed under sub-paragraph (2)(d) of paragraph 3 above that arrangements have been made under that paragraph, and an appointment made after any such arrangements have been made shall be of no effect.' **[1260]**

NOTES to SI 1978/661

Reg 2: The Interpretation Act 1889 (c 63) has been replaced by the Interpretation Act 1978 (c 30). The references to the Housing (Homeless Persons) Act 1978 (c 48) should now be construed as references to the corresponding provisions of the Housing (Scotland) Act 1987 (c 26).

SI 1978/1785 [1264]

The Home Purchase Assistance (Recognised Savings Institutions) Order 1978

SI 1978/1785

(This order was made by the Secretary of State for Scotland and other Ministers under the Home Purchase Assistance and Housing Corporation Guarantee Act 1978 (c 27), s 2(1) and (7), and came into operation on 5 December 1978)

1. *(Citation and commencement)* [1261]

2. The Interpretation Act 1889 shall apply for the interpretation of this order as it applies for the interpretation of an Act of Parliament. [1262]

3. The savings institutions specified in the Schedule to this order are added to Part II of the Schedule to the Home Purchase Assistance and Housing Corporations Guarantee Act 1978. [1263]

SCHEDULE

The Clydebank Municipal Bank Limited
Cumnock Municipal Bank Limited
Cunninghame District Municipal Bank Limited
Kilsyth and Cumbernauld District Municipal Bank Limited
Motherwell District Municipal Bank Limited
The Stockton-on-Tees Municipal Savings Bank Limited
Strathkelvin District Municipal Bank Limited
West Lothian District Municipal Bank Limited. [1264]

NOTES to SI 1978/1785

Reg 2: The Interpretation Act 1889 (c 63) has been replaced by the Interpretation Act 1978 (c 30).
Reg 3: The reference to the Home Purchase Assistance and Housing Corporation Guarantee Act 1978 (c 27), should now be construed as a reference to the Housing (Scotland) Act 1987 (c 26), s 225.

[1265]	SI 1980/1389

The Secure Tenancies (Proceedings for Possession) (Scotland) Order 1980

SI 1980/1389

(This order was made by the Secretary of State for Scotland under the Tenants' Rights, Etc (Scotland) Act 1980 (c 52), s 14(3), and came into operation on 3 October 1980)

1. *(Citation and commencement)* [1265]

2. Any notice served under section 14 of the Tenants' Rights, Etc (Scotland) Act 1980 on a tenant under a secure tenancy, within the meaning of Part II of that Act, shall be in the form set out in the Schedule to this order. [1266]

SCHEDULE

NOTICE OF PROCEEDINGS FOR RECOVERY OF POSSESSION

This notice is to inform you,   (name(s) of secure tenant(s)) that   , being the landlord of the dwellinghouse at

may, at any time during the period of 6 months beginning on
(see Note 2), raise proceedings for possession of that dwellinghouse on the following grounds:

which is/are deemed to fall within the terms of paragraph(s)   (see Note 3) of Part I of Schedule 2 to the Tenants' Rights, Etc (Scotland) Act 1980.

Signed ....

Date ....

Notes for the guidance of tenants

1. This notice is a warning that your landlord may be going to raise proceedings against you in the sheriff court to gain possession of your house. It is not a notice to quit and it does not affect your right to continue living in the house or your obligation to pay rent. You cannot be evicted from your house unless the sheriff court grants your landlord a possession order. You should read the rest of the notes carefully to find out what might happen if your landlord does start possession proceedings against you.

2. Now that this notice has been served on you there is no other preliminary step which your landlord need take before starting court action against you for possession of the house referred to in the notice. The date given in the notice is the earliest date on which your landlord can take court action. After that date the landlord is allowed to start possession proceedings against you at any time during the following 6 months. If that 6 month period passes without possession proceedings being started, your landlord would have to serve another one of these notices on you before it could start court action for possession and that notice would, like this one, have to give you at least 4 weeks warning before court action could be started.

3. Your landlord has explained in the notice the reason or reasons why it is considering taking possession proceedings against you. In order to help you understand your legal position if proceedings are taken, the paragraph number (referring to Part I of Schedule 2 of the Tenants' Rights, Etc (Scotland) Act 1980) which applies to your landlord's reason for considering possession proceedings is given near the end of the notice. (If, for example, your landlord's reason for considering possession proceedings is rent arrears, the paragraph number given will be 1.) If the number is between 1 and 7, read note 4 below; if the number is between 8 and 14, read note 5 below. If the number is 10, read paragraph 6 below as well as paragraph 5.

4. If the paragraph number given near the end of the notice is between 1 and 7, and your landlord does take court action for possession against you, the sheriff court will be concerned with whether the facts on which your landlord is founding are correct (for example, whether you are in rent arrears if that is the reason which your landlord has given) and, if it decides that the facts are correct, whether it is reasonable that you should be evicted, which will depend on the circumstances of your case. The court can postpone a decision on the case and impose conditions on you, for example about paying off rent arrears, if it wishes; if you obey the conditions the court would not normally grant your landlord a possession order afterwards. If a possession order is granted against you your landlord will have to evict you once the date given in the order is passed, unless it decides to grant you a new tenancy of your house. If it evicts you it will not be under any obligation to rehouse you. Any action which might be taken by a local authority under its powers and duties in relation to some categories of homeless people is a separate matter and you should not assume that you will be entitled to rehousing.

5. If the paragraph number given near the end of the notice is between 8 and 14, the court must grant a possession order against you provided the landlord can show that it (the landlord) has arranged for suitable alternative accommodation to be available to you. In considering whether alternative accommodation offered to you is suitable the court has to take account of the following points:—
   (a) how near it is to the place where you or any of your family work or go to school, college, etc, compared to the house which you live in now;
   (b) how *large* a house you and your family need;
   (c) its *character* compared to the house which you live in now;
   (d) the *terms* on which it is offered to you compared to the terms of the tenancy of the house which you live in now;
   (e) if the landlord provides any furniture in the house you live in now, whether the house offered will be provided with furniture which is as useful to you;
   (f) any special needs of you and your family.
Your landlord must make you an offer of alternative accommodation in writing, and must give you at least 14 days to make up your mind about the offer. Until your landlord has done this the court will not grant a possession order. Once it has been done the court will grant a possession order unless you tell the court that you do not consider the offer suitable and explain why.

6. If the paragraph number given near the end of the notice is 10, and your landlord only wants to move you out of your house temporarily while works are carried out, the court will make an order entitling you to return to your house once the works are

completed. This will not affect your right to suitable alternative accommodation but you will not become the secure tenant of the house that you are moved to, so that you will have no right to stay there once the house which you live in now is ready for you to move back to.

7. If you are at all uncertain about what this notice means or of your rights you should obain advice as quickly as possible. You may be able to get this from your landlord, from a number of sources of free and independent advice such as your local Citizens' Advice Bureau or Housing Advice Centre or from a solicitor. If you need to employ a solicitor, legal aid may be available, depending on your income.

8. These Notes are intended for the guidance of tenants and are not to be regarded as an authoritative interpretation of the law. **[1267]**

NOTES to SI 1980/1389

General: References to the Tenants' Rights, Etc (Scotland) Act 1980 (c 52) should now be read as references to the corresponding provisions of the Housing (Scotland) Act 1987 (c 26).

The Right to Purchase (Loans) (Scotland) Regulations 1980

SI 1980/1430

(*These regulations were made by the Secretary of State for Scotland under the Tenants' Rights, Etc (Scotland) Act 1980 (c 52), s 5(3), and came into operation on 17 October 1980*)

ARRANGEMENT OF REGULATIONS
(*This list is not printed in the Regulations*)

1	Citation and commencement	**[1268]**
2	Maximum amount of loan	**[1269]**
3	Available annual income	**[1270]**
4	Income from employment	**[1271]**
5	Income from a business	**[1272]**
6	Other income	**[1273]**
7	Adjustment for temporary reduction in income	**[1274]**
8	Income from more than one source	**[1275]**
9	Deductions for commitments	**[1276]**
10	Estimates	**[1277]**
11	Applicants comprising more than one person	**[1278]**
12	Appropriate factors	**[1279]**
13	Terms of loan	**[1280]**
14	Information to be contained in the offer of loan	**[1281]**

1.—(1) (*Citation and commencement*)

(2) In these regulations, unless the context otherwise requires—
'admissible source' means a source of income of the applicant which is to be taken into account for the purposes of these regulations;
'assessment date' means the date of the applicant's loan application under section 5 of the Tenants' Rights, Etc (Scotland) Act 1980;
'applicant' has the meaning given to it by section 5(1) of the Tenants' Rights, Etc (Scotland) Act 1980. **[1268]**

SI 1980/1430 [1272]

2. **Maximum amount of loan.**

The maximum amount of loan to be specified in an offer of loan served under section 5(3) of the Tenants' Rights, Etc (Scotland) Act 1980 shall be the amount to be taken into account as the applicant's available annual income multiplied by the appropriate factor. [1269]

3. **Available annual income.**

An applicant's available annual income is to be calculated by taking the amount which in accordance with regulations 4 to 8 is to be taken into account as his annual income and deducting from it in accordance with regulation 9 sums related to his commitments. [1270]

4. **Income from employment.**

(1) This regulation applies to income from an employment which the applicant has at the assessment date.

(2) No acount shall be taken of income from a casual or temporary employment.

(3) The amount to be taken into account as the applicant's annual income from an employment to which this regulation applies, which is not excluded from account by paragraph (2), ia an amount calculated—
  (a) if his pay does not normally vary from one pay period to another, by multiplying the amount of his pay for his last pay period before the assessment date by the number of his pay periods in a year; or
  (b) if his pay normally varies from one pay period to another, by multiplying his average pay for a pay period, calculated in accordance with paragraph (4), by the number of his pay periods in a year.

(4) For the purposes of paragraph (3)(b), the applicant's average pay for a pay period shall be calculated by taking his pay for the period of 13 weeks ending on his last pay day before the assessment date and dividing it by the number of his pay periods in that period.

(5) An adjustment shall be made in calculating the applicant's annual income from an employment if, as a result of a pay settlement reached before the assessment date, his pay has changed and the change affects his pay for a period to be taken into account in calculating his annual income from the employment or a subsequent period ending on or before the assessment date.

(6) The adjustment shall secure that the calculation is based on the applicant's rate of pay after the change occurs.

(7) In this regulation—
'employment' includes office; and
'pay' means gross pay before any statutory or other deduction and includes any commission, bonus, allowance (other than an expense allowance), tip, gratuity or other payment made to an applicant in connection with his employment, but does not include any benefit in kind. [1271]

5. **Income from a business.**

(1) This regulation applies to income from a business carried on by the applicant (whether or not with any other person) at the assessment date.

(2) The amount to be taken into account as the applicant's annual income from the business is an amount equal to the net profit of the business for the basis year or, if he shares the net profit with any other person, his share of the net profit for that year.

(3) Subject to paragraph (4), the basis year is a period of 12 months ending on any date in the month preceding the assessment date.

(4) If—
(a) on the assessment date figures for the period of 12 months mentioned in paragraph (3) are not readily available to the applicant but figures for an earlier period of 12 months ending in that period are; and
(b) the applicant requires the landlord or, if the landlord is a housing co-operative, the district or islands council to take the figures for the earlier period of 12 months into account,
the basis year shall be the earlier period of 12 months.

(5) In this regulation 'business' includes any trade, profession or vocation. **[1272]**

6. Other income.

(1) This regulation applies to income, which the applicant has at the assessment date, from a source to which regulations 4 and 5 do not apply.

(2) No account shall be taken of state benefits other than benefits under—
(a) sections 35 and 36 of the National Insurance Act 1965 (graduated retirement benefits);
(b) sections 8, 15 and 16 of the Social Security Pensions Act 1975 (widower's retirement pensions, widow's and widower's invalidity pensions); and
(c) the following provisions of the Social Security Act 1975—
sections 15, 16 and 36 (invalidity benefits);
sections 25 and 26 (widow's benefits);
sections 28, 29, 39 and 40 (retirement pensions);
sections 57(1) and (6) (disability benefits);
sections 67(1) and (2)(a), 69, 70, 71(1) and (2), and 72(1) and (2) (industrial death benefits); and
section 76 (industrial disease benefits) to the extent that it relates to any benefit by way of pension or other periodical payments.

(3) The amount to be taken into account as the applicant's annual income from a source to which this regulation applies, which is not excluded from account by paragraph (2), is the gross amount of that income, before any statutory or other deduction, for the period of 12 months ending on the assessment date.

(4) In this regulation 'state benefits' means any benefits under the Family Income Supplements Act 1970, the Social Security Acts 1975 to 1980, the Child Benefit Act 1975 and the Supplementary Benefits Act 1976. **[1273]**

7. Adjustment for temporary reduction in income.

(1) If the applicant's income from an admissible source is temporarily reduced below its normal level for any period taken into account in determining his annual income from that source but has been restored to its normal level by the assessment date, the amount taken into account as his annual income from that source shall be adjusted.

(2) The adjustment shall secure that the amount taken into account as his annual income from that source is what it would have been if the reduction had not occurred. **[1274]**

8. Income from more than one source.

If the applicant has income from more than one admissible source, the amount to be taken into account as his annual income shall be the total amount of his annual income from all admissible sources determined in accordance with the provisions of these regulations. **[1275]**

9. Deductions for commitments.

(1) Sums related to the applicant's commitments are to be deducted from the amount to be taken into account as his annual income if at the assessment date he is liable to make—

(a) any maintenance payments; or
(b) any payments under a credit agreement; or
(c) any payments under a court order;
and the payments are likely to continue for more than 18 months after the assessment date.

(2) The sums which are to deducted are sums equal in total to the total of the payments, for which the conditions in paragraph (1) are satisfied, for the period of 12 months beginning with the assessment date.

(3) In this regulation—
'credit agreement' means a loan agreement, hire purchase agreement or other agreement for credit; and
'maintenance payment' means any payment by the applicant for the maintenance of a dependent child under the age of 16 or for the maintenance of his spouse or former spouse. [1276]

10. Estimates.

The landlord or, if the landlord is a housing co-operative, the district or islands council may accept any estimate made for the purposes of any of the preceding provisions of these regulations. [1277]

11. Applicants comprising more than one person.

Where the applicant comprises more than one person, the preceding provisions of these regulations are to be applied separately to detemine the amount of each person's available annual income. [1278]

12. Appropriate factors.

(1) This regulation specifies the appropriate factor to be applied as a multiplier of the applicant's available annual income to arrive at the limit imposed by regulation 2.

(2) Where the applicant comprises only one person the appropriate factor is 2.5 unless he is aged 60 or over, in which case it is either 2, if he is aged 60–64, or 1, if he is aged 65 or above. The age of the applicant is to be taken as his age on the date on which an application to purchase was served under section 2(1) of the Tenants' Rights, Etc (Scotland) Act 1980 in respect of the house which the applicant has applied for a loan to assist him to purchase (or, where there has been more than one such application, the last of them).

(3) Where the applicant comprises more than one person, the appropriate factor is 1, subject to paragraph (4).

(4) Where the applicant comprises more than one person but the available annual income of one of those persons is such that the maximum amount of loan which would be derived from treating that person as if he were the only person comprising the applicant would be greater than the maximum amount of loan which would be derived from the application of paragraph (3) that person shall be deemed to be the only person comprising the applicant and the appropriate factor shall be as provided in paragraph (2). [1279]

13. Terms of loan.

(1) Any offer of loan served by a landlord or, where the landlord is a housing co-operative, by an islands or district council shall contain an undertaking by the landlord to make available a loan on the terms specified in paragraphs (2) and (3) or on such other terms as may be agreed by the applicant prior to service of a notice of acceptance under section 5(5) of the Tenants' Rights, Etc (Scotland) Act 1980.

(2) Repayment of the loan shall be in equal instalments of principal and interest combined.

(3) The period over which repayment is to be made shall be 25 years but shall be capable of being extended by the lender. **[1280]**

14. Information to be contained in the offer of loan.

Any offer of loan served by a landlord or, where the landlord is a housing co-operative, by an islands or district council shall be accompanied by a statement of the amount of the monthly repayment, gross and net of tax relief calculated at the standard rate of income tax on the full amount of the interest which the applicant would be required to pay on a loan of the amount requested in his loan application or the maximum amount of loan specified in the offer of loan, whichever is the lesser, on the terms specified in regulation 13 (or such other terms as the applicant has agreed to) and at the interest rate which would be charged if the loan were commencing on the date of service of the offer of loan. **[1281]**

NOTES to SI 1980/1430

General: References to the Tenants' Rights, Etc (Scotland) Act (c 52) should now be read as references to the corresponding provisions of the Housing (Scotland) Act 1987 (c 26).

The Right to Purchase (Loan Application) (Scotland) Order 1980

SI 1980/1492

(This order was made by the Secretary of State for Scotland under the Tenants' Rights, Etc (Scotland) Act 1980 (c 52), s 5(2)(b), and came into operation on 15 October 1980)

1. *(Citation and commencement)* [1282]

2. Any loan application served under section 5(1) of the Tenants' Rights, Etc (Scotland) Act 1980 shall be in the form set out in the Schedule to this order. [1283–1284]

SCHEDULE

Tenants' Rights, Etc (Scotland) Act 1980
Application for Loan

This form is for use in making an application for a loan from an islands or district council, new town development corporation or the Scottish Special Housing Association where an application to purchase under the *right to buy* provisions of the Tenants' Rights, Etc (Scotland) Act 1980 has been made and an offer to sell has been received. No other form can be used for this purpose.

Every person *named in an offer to sell* should fill in a separate form but they *must* all be sent together.

This form MUST be sent within ONE MONTH of the date of an offer to sell (or if you have asked for changes to the offer to sell, either the date of any amended offer to sell or of a decision by the Lands Tribunal that the offer to sell should not be amended).

When you send this form you will need to send evidence of your income and evidence that you have been unable to obtain a *sufficient* loan from a building society; this is explained further in the notes accompanying this form (see Note 10) but you should make sure that you allow yourself time to obtain this evidence.

The authority's ability to deal quickly with loan applications is likely to depend to a large extent on the information provided in this form. It is for that reason to the advantage of applicants to ensure that the questions that relate to them are carefully and accurately answered. Please read the notes accompanying the form with care: they will help you to understand why the questions are asked. If, when you have studied the form and read the notes, you still feel that you do not fully understand how you should complete it, you may be able to get help from an official of your authority's housing department, or from a solicitor.

Please write clearly and complete the form in ink.

IMPORTANT: ANYONE WHO DELIBERATELY GIVES FALSE INFORMATION ON THIS FORM IS COMMITTING A SERIOUS OFFENCE WHICH MAY LEAD TO PROSECUTION.

SI 1980/1492 [1285]

APPLICATION FOR LOAN

SECTION 1

TO BE COMPLETED BY ALL APPLICANTS

1. Address of House:
2. Full Name (use block capitals):
3. Your age *on the date of your application to purchase:*
4. Date of offer to sell (see Note 1):
5. Name of your landlord (if different from the authority applied to for a loan (see Note 2)):
6. Selling price stated in the offer to sell: £........
7. Amount of loan for which you are applying (see Note 3): £........

SECTION 2

FOR APPLICANTS IN REGULAR EMPLOYMENT (see Note 4)

The loan authority will need full and accurate details of your pay in order to decide the amount of loan to which you—and any joint purchasers—are entitled. Please fill in this section carefully: if you cannot recall all the details, your employer's pay section should be able to provide them.

1. Are you in regular employment?   YES ☐   NO ☐
   (Tick the appropriate box)

   If your answer is NO, this section does not concern you; move on to section 3.

2. Name and address of your employer:

3. Do you normally receive about the same amount of pay each pay period? (see Note 5)

      YES ☐   NO ☐

4. If your answer to question 3 above is YES, state the amount of *gross* pay you received for your last pay period, and state whether you are paid weekly, monthly or in any other way.

   Amount of pay: £........

   How paid:

5. If your answer to question 3 is NO, state your total *gross* pay (see Note 6) for the last 13 weeks, ending with the last week in which you were paid before you send off this form, and the number of pay periods (eg 13 if you are paid weekly, three if you are paid monthly).

   Amount of pay: £........

   Number of pay periods:

6. If you receive any tips or gratuities, any commission, bonus, allowance (other than an expense allowance), or other payment in connection with your work and you have not included such payments as part of your pay in answer to questions 4 or 5 above, state the amount of such payments over the last 13 weeks (ending with the last week before you send off this form).

   Amount of payments: £........

7. If a pay settlement has been *agreed* which will affect your pay for the pay periods of which you have given details, please give details below:

THE INFORMATION GIVEN IN THIS SECTION MUST BE SUPPORTED BY EVIDENCE.

Your pay slips or a letter from your employer confirming the accuracy of the statements you have made will be acceptable for this purpose. Evidence should be sent with this form.

SI 1980/1492 [1285]

SECTION 3

FOR APPLICANTS WITH A BUSINESS INTEREST (see Note 7)

The loan authority will need full and accurate details of any income you have from your business in order to decide the amount of loan to which you—and any joint applicants—are entitled. Please fill in this section carefully.

1. Do you receive income from any business interest? YES ☐ NO ☐

   If your answer is NO, this section does not concern you; move on to section 4.

2. What net profit did the business or businesses achieve within the period of 12 months ending with any convenient date in the month before you send off this form?

   Net profit for the 12 months period ending on :£........

   Note: If the information requested above is not readily available you may require that figures for any earlier period of 12 months are taken into account. If you wish to do so give details of the amount of profit and the dates of the earlier period:

   Profit: £........

   Dates:

3. Was this profit shared with any other person? YES ☐ NO ☐

4. If your answer to question 3 is YES, what was *your* share of the profit? £........

THE INFORMATION GIVEN IN THIS SECTION MUST BE SUPPORTED BY EVIDENCE. A letter from your accountant confirming the accuracy of the statements you have made will be acceptable for this purpose. Evidence should be sent with this form.

[1285]

SI 1980/1492

SECTION 4

FOR APPLICANTS WITH OTHER SOURCES OF INCOME

The loan authority may be able to take other sources of income into account when calculating the amount of loan to which you—and any joint applicants—are entitled. It is therefore in your own interest to give details of any income you may have from any source not included in sections 2 and 3 (see Note 8).

1. Do you receive income from any other source (except state benefits)?

   YES ☐   NO ☐

   If your answer is NO, move on to section 5.

2. If your answer to question 1 is YES, describe these sources of income below:

3. Over the period of 12 months ending with the date on which this form is sent off, what was your income before tax from these sources (if more than one, please list separately)?

THE INFORMATION GIVEN IN THIS SECTION MUST BE SUPPORTED BY EVIDENCE. Any statement of the income which you have (or a letter) from your accountant or bank manager will be acceptable for this purpose. Evidence should be sent with this form.

SI 1980/1492 [1285]

SECTION 5

FOR APPLICANTS RECEIVING STATE BENEFITS

Most state benefits will *not* be taken into account as sources of income when calculating the amount of loan to which you—and any joint applicants—are entitled. However, the following state benefits (see Note 9) will be counted: if you receive any of them please enter the amount you have received from each in the period of 12 months ending with the date on which this form is sent off.

state retirement pension (including graduated retirement benefit):	£
disability pension:	£
invalidity pension:	£
widow's pension:	£
industrial death benefit:	£
industrial disease benefit:	£
war pension:	£
war widow's pension:	£

THE INFORMATION GIVEN IN THIS SECTION MUST BE SUPPORTED BY EVIDENCE, which must be sent with this form.

SECTION 6

FOR APPLICANTS WHOSE INCOME FROM ANY SOURCE HAS BEEN TEMPORARILY REDUCED

If any income of which you have given details in sections 2–5 was temporarily reduced during the period for which you have given information, please give details below so that an adjustment can be made. (Details should include the reason for reduction, dates, amounts, type of income, normal level of income etc.)

SI 1980/1492 [1285]

SECTION 7

FOR ALL APPLICANTS

The loan authority will base your loan entitlement not only on your income, but also on any firm financial commitments you may have. *All* applicants should check whether they have commitments of this type and should complete this section.

Are you liable to make and to continue to make for the next 18 months any of the following payments—

	Write YES or NO	Amount you will pay in the 12 months beginning with the date on which you send off this form	Likely duration of payments
a. a maintenance payment to your husband or wife, or former husband or wife?			
b. a maintenance payment to a dependent child under the age of 16?			
c. payment under a court order?			
d. payments under a loan agreement?			
e. payments under a hire purchase agreement?			
f. payments under any other credit agreement?			

THE INFORMATION GIVEN IN THIS SECTION MUST BE SUPPORTED BY EVIDENCE. Copies of maintenance or court orders, or of credit agreements, will be acceptable for this purpose. They should be sent with this form.

SECTION 8

FOR ALL APPLICANTS

All applicants must complete this declaration:

> The information given by me on this form is, to the best of my knowledge, correct. I hereby give notice that I seek to exercise my right under section 5 of the Tenants' Rights, Etc (Scotland) Act 1980 to apply for a loan to assist me to purchase under section 1 of that Act the house in which I live, and declare that I have been unable to obtain a sufficient loan for that purpose from a building society (see Note 10).

Signed:

Date:

IMPORTANT: ANYONE WHO DELIBERATELY GIVES FALSE INFORMATION ON THIS FORM IS COMMITTING A SERIOUS OFFENCE WHICH MAY LEAD TO PROSECUTION.

MAKE SURE YOU HAVE ATTACHED ALL THE NECESSARY EVIDENCE OF YOUR STATEMENTS BEFORE YOU RETURN THIS FORM. [1285]

NOTES to SI 1980/1492

General: References to the Tenants' Rights, Etc (Scotland) Act 1980 (c 52) should now be read as references to the corresponding provisions of the Housing (Scotland) Act 1987 (c 26).

The Housing (Forms) (Scotland) Regulations 1980
SI 1980/1647

(These regulations were made by the Secretary of State for Scotland under the Housing (Scotland) Act 1966 (c 49), s 197(1), and came into operation on 3 December 1980)

1. *(Citation and commencement)* [1286]

2. Revocation.

The Housing (Forms) (Scotland) Regulations 1978 are hereby revoked except in so far as the forms prescribed are required to be used in connection with proceedings after the date on which these regulations come into operation and consequent upon action taken before that date. [1287]

3. The forms set out in the Schedule hereto, or forms as near thereto as circumstances permit, shall be the forms to be used for the purposes of the Housing (Scotland) Act 1969 and the Housing (Scotland) Act 1974 in the cases to which those forms are applicable. [1288]

SCHEDULE

List of Forms

Form	Purpose	Reference to section of the Act
	Housing (Scotland) Act 1969	
1	Notice requiring the person having control of a house to execute works to remedy repair defects	24
	Housing (Scotland) Act 1974	
2	Application for improvement grant	2(2)
3	Application for repairs grant	2(2) and 10A
4	Order requiring the owner of the house to execute works of improvement	14A
5	Notice of payment of improvement grant or repairs grant	9(9), 10A(5), 11(7)
6	Notice of cessor or partial cessor of conditions of improvement grant or repairs grant	9(9), 10(1), 10A(5) 11(7) and paragraph 7 of Schedule 2
7	Notice about a well maintained payment	30(1)

Form 1

Form of notice to person having control of a house in serious disrepair

WARNING: IF IN DOUBT ABOUT THE EFFECT OF THIS NOTICE CONSULT YOUR LOCAL AUTHORITY OR A SOLICITOR

THE HOUSING (SCOTLAND) ACT 1969

To[1] .... the person having control of the house[2] ....

Take notice that—

(1) the[3] .... the local authority under the Housing (Scotland) Act 1969 (hereinafter referred to respectively as 'the local authority' and 'the Act'), are satisfied that the above-mentioned house is in a state of serious disrepair; and

(2) in exercise of the powers conferred upon them by section 24(1) of the Act the local authority require you within a period of[4] .... days, ending on .... 19........., to execute the works necessary to rectify the following defects:—

[5]

In the opinion of the local authority the rectification of these defects will bring the house up to such a standard of repair as is reasonable having regard to the age, character and location, and disregarding the internal decorative repair, of the house.

Dated .... 19.........

[6] ....

NOTES FOR YOUR INFORMATION

(To be incorporated in the notice and any copies thereof)

1. The person having control of a house is defined in section 208(2) of the Housing (Scotland) Act 1966 as a person who for the time being is entitled to receive, or would, if the house were let, be entitled to receive, the rent of the house, including a trustee, tutor, curator, factor or agent.

2. Section 24(4) of the House (Scotland) Act 1969 provides that where a local authority are of the opinion that a house in their district is in need of repair although not in a state of serious disrepair and that it is likely to deteriorate rapidly, or to cause material damage to another house, if nothing is done to repair it, they may deem it to be in a state of serious disrepair for the purposes of section 24.

3. Any person aggrieved by this notice may, in accordance with the provisions of section 27 of the Act, appeal to the Sheriff against the notice, and may also appeal to the Sheriff against any demand for the recovery from him of expenses incurred by the local

authority in executing works, or against an order made by the local authority under section 25(2) of the Act with respect to any such expenses, or against a charging order with respect to any such expenses made by the local authority in accordance with the provisions of Schedule 2 to the Act. The appeal must be brought WITHIN 21 DAYS AFTER THE DATE OF THE SERVICE OF THE NOTICE, DEMAND OR ORDER, and no proceedings may be taken by the local authority to enforce any notice, demand or order whilst an appeal against it is pending. On appeal against a demand for the recovery of expenses incurred by a local authority in executing works or against an order under section 25(2) or a charging order made by a local authority with respect of any such expenses, no question can be raised which might have been raised on an appeal against the original notice requiring the execution of the works (ie this notice).

4. Provided certain statutory conditions are met the Council are required to offer a repair grant to assist with the cost of the work. They can also be required to offer a loan to cover the balance of the cost. Further information can be obtained from the local authority.

5. Sub-section (6) of section 24 of the Housing (Scotland) Act 1969 defines 'house'—
'Any reference in this Part of this Act to a house shall be construed as including a reference to a building which comprises or includes (a) a house or houses; or (b) a house or houses and other premises.'
The effect of this wide definition is that in tenements or in other buildings which comprise a mixture of houses and non-housing premises, all owners of premises may be within the scope of repairs notices. That is, the owners of non-residential premises may have a responsibility for repairs to the building in which their premises are located.

6. Under section 25(1A) of the Housing (Scotland) Act 1969, local authorities can recover their expenses in carrying out repairs undertaken when owners do not themselves comply with a repairs notice under section 24 of that Act. Local authorities can apportion these expenses amongst different owners of different parts of a building, whether houses or other premises.

7. Sub-sections (2) and (3) of section 24 and sub-section (1), (2) and (3) of section 25 provide as follows:
(here quote sub-sections (2) and (3) of section 24 and sub-sections (1), (2) and (3) of section 25).

8. Sub-sections (1) and (2) of section 14 of the Housing (Repairs and Rents) (Scotland) Act 1954 relating to the limitation of liability of trustees, etc, for expenses of local authorities, provide as follows—
(here quote sub-section (1) and (2) of section 14).

9. Section 26 of the Act, which relates to the recovery by lessees of a proportion of expenses incurred in repairing a house, provides as follows:
(here quote the whole of section 26).

Notes for Guidance in Completing this Form

1. Insert name and address of the person having control of the house.
2. Insert such description of the house as may be sufficient for identification.
3. Insert name of local authority.
4. Insert a reasonabale time, not being less than 21 days.
5. Insert the defects.
6. Insert name and designation of authorised officer.

Form 2

Form of application to local authority for improvement grant

READ THE NOTES ATTACHED BEFORE COMPLETING THIS FORM

This form should be completed and sent to the District or Islands Council in whose area the house is situated. A separate application must be made for each separate building to be improved. (One building may of course contain a number of separate houses.)

THE IMPROVEMENT WORK SHOULD NOT BE STARTED BEFORE THE COUNCIL HAVE GIVEN APPROVAL <u>IN WRITING</u> TO THE APPLICATION FOR GRANT. <u>IF YOU START WORK BEFORE THE APPLICATION IS APPROVED THE COUNCIL MAY NOT BE ABLE TO GIVE GRANT.</u> YOU SHOULD, THEREFORE, ENSURE THAT ANY PERSON ACTING FOR YOU IN THESE MATTERS DOES NOT START WORK BEFORE YOU HAVE THE APPROVAL OF THE COUNCIL IN WRITING.

A CONSENT GIVEN FOR PLANNING OR BUILDING REGULATIONS PURPOSES WHICH MAY ALSO BE REQUIRED IS NOT SUFFICIENT.

THE HOUSING (SCOTLAND) ACT 1974

APPLICATION FOR IMPROVEMENT GRANT

I/We hereby make application to the Council for improvement grant in respect of the works proposed to be carried out on the under-mentioned property in accordance with the particulars given below and with the plans of the house (or buildings) before and after improvement and the specifications which accompany this application.

*(I/We desire payment by instalments as the work proceeds.)

Date .... Signature of [Applicant] [Agent] ....

Address ....
*Delete if not applicable

DECLARATION BY OWNER

I   being the owner for the time being of the house referred to in this application hereby consent to making application for improvement grant toward the cost of works which he is to carry out as shown below. I give this consent in the full knowledge that I and my successor shall be bound for a period of 5 years by any conditions of grant imposed under section 9 of the Housing (Scotland) Act 1979. I understand that any breach of the conditions is likely to lead to a demand for repayment of the grant together with interest. (See Note 4.)

1. Address of property to be improved   ....
   or converted.   ....

2. (a) Full name and address of   ....
   applicant.   ....
                                                                     ....

SI 1980/1647 [1290]

    (b) Name and address of agent (if applicable)

    (c) Name and address of owner (if not the applicant)

3. Was the house built or provided by conversion after 15th June 1964? (See Note 1.)

4. Has the occupier, if other than the applicant agreed to the works being done?

5. (See Notes 2 and 10.)
    (a) Is the house security for a loan?
    (b) If so, give name and address of lender.
    (c) Has the lender given any necessary consent to the making of this application?

6. (See Notes 5 and 10.)
    (a) Has grant or assistance from public funds ever been given in respect of the property?
    (b) If so, say when.
    (c) Is an application for such assistance pending?

7. (See Note 3.)
    (1) Does the application for improvement grant provide for the adaptation of a house to make it suitable for the accommodation, welfare or employment of a disabled occupant? If 'Yes', 7(2)(a) and (b) do not apply.
    (2) If the application for improvement grant relates to a building which at the date of the application already consists of or includes a house, please state:
        (a) Whether on completion of the works the house, or any part thereof, is to be occupied by the owner or a member of his family?
        (b) The rateable value of the house at the date of this application.

8. If on completion of the works the house is to be occupied by the owner, or a member of his family, will the house be his only or main residence?

9. Give a short description of the existing accommodation.

　　　..
　　　..
　　　..
　　　..

10. Is the property situated in a Housing Action Area? (See Note 11.)　..

　　If it is,
　　(a) Are the improvement works for which grant is sought necessary to bring the house up to the standard specified for the area?　..
　　(b) Will the house satisfy the standard specified for the area when the proposed improvement and repair works are completed?　..

　　If it is not,
　　(c) Is it the subject of an improvement order? (See Note 12.)　..
　　(d) Will the house satisfy the standard specified in the order when the proposed improvement and repair works are completed?　..

11. The standard amenities existing or to be provided for the first time for the exclusive use of the occupants are listed at (a) to (g) below. Enter a tick against each of the standard amenities in column A or B as appropriate. (See Notes 6 to 10.)

	A Amenity already available	B Amenity to be provided for the first time
(a) A fixed bath or shower. If reasonably practicable the fixed bath must be in a bathroom.	....	....
(b) A hot and cold water supply at a fixed bath or shower.	....	....
(c) A wash hand-basin	....	....
(d) A hot and cold water supply at a wash hand-basin.	....	....
(e) A sink.	....	....
(f) A hot and cold water supply at a sink.	....	....
(g) A water closet.	....	....

12. Do you claim that it is not practicable at reasonable expense to provide the house with all the standard amenities? (If so say why.) (See Note 6.) ....

13. (See Notes 7–9.)
    Summarise works proposed and give their cost.
    (i) Specify works to provide standard amenities.

    ....
    ....
    ....
    ....

    Cost £ ....
    (ii) Specify other improvement works.

    ....
    ....
    ....

    Cost £ ....
    (iii) Specify other works of repairs or replacement for which grant is sought.

    ....
    ....

    Cost £ ....
    (iv) Professional fees £ ....
    (v) VAT £ ....

14. Name and address of person who prepared the plans and specifications.

    ....
    ....
    ....

15. When is it intended the works should:
    (a) Start? ....
    (b) Finish? ....

Notes

Further details of the grants available may be obtained at the offices of the Council.

Depending on the nature of the work to be done, planning permission may have to be obtained from the local planning authority. It may also be necessary to obtain warrant from the building authority. Advice should be sought at the offices of the local authority. Approval for building regulation purposes or approval for planning purposes is not the same as grant approval.

Any grant-aided works must be carried out to the satisfaction of the Council. Inspection by officials of the Council will therefore normally be necessary.

If the local authority do not approve the application or if they fix as the amount of grant an amount less than that which may be fixed under the Statute they must notify the applicant in writing of the grounds on which they have decided so to do.

THE FOLLOWING NOTES ARE INTENDED TO ASSIST YOU IN COMPLETING THE FORM

1. Houses built or provided by conversion after 15th June 1964 will not qualify for grant except by direction of the Secretary of State. If you believe that you should receive grant your Council will advise you how to proceed.

2. The applicant must be the owner of the house or have both the owner's consent to the application being made and his agreement to abide by the conditions of grant. If the

applicant is not the occupier of the house, the occupier's consent to the proposed improvements should be obtained before making the application. (In general a landlord may not carry out improvements without the consent of the tenant but see Note 11(d) below.) If the house is security for a loan, the building society or other lender should be notified of the application for grant. A copy of the necessary letter of consent from lender or tenant should be attached to this application.

3. Where a house is to be occupied by the owner, it must generally have a rateable value below a prescribed limit. Exceptions to this rule are houses in Housing Action Areas, houses subject to improvement order, houses which are to be adapted to meet the needs of a disabled occupant and certain works of conversion. Further particulars may be obtained from the Council.

4. If granted, the payment of grant will be subject to the following conditions which will apply to the house for a period of 5 years from the date of the payment of grant:
   (a) the house shall not be used for purposes other than those of a private dwelling house;
   (b) the house shall not be occupied by the owner or a member of his family except as his only or main residence within the meaning of section 29 of the Finance Act 1965;
   (c) all steps as are practicable shall be taken to secure the maintenance of the house in a good state of repair.
In addition the Council may impose the following condition:
   (d) the house at all times which is it not occupied by the applicant or by a member of his family will be let or kept available for letting.
If any of these conditions are breached, the Council may demand the repayment of the grant either in part or in full together with compound interest at a statutorily fixed rate for the period the grant has been in the hands of the applicant. In signing the declaration on this form, the owner acknowledges his liability under these provisions.

5. If grant has been paid on this house from other sources of public funds eg agricultural, crofting or housing grants then any grant paid under the application may be reduced proportionately.

6. To qualify for a grant the house, after improvement, must normally be provided with all the standard amenities listed in Question 11 for the exclusive use of the occupants. If the Council consider in circumstances of any application that all of the amenities cannot or should not reasonably be provided, they may still pay a grant provided that at least the amenities referred to at (e), (f) and (g) are provided but in such case applicants must give their reasons for not providing all of the amenities.

7. (a) The improvement works can include alteration and enlargement and such repairs and replacements as are needed, in the opinion of the local authority, for the purpose of enabling the house to attain a good state of repair.
   (b) The cost of repairs and replacements in the approved expense determined by the local authority in approving an application for improvement grant cannot exceed 50 per cent of the total approved expense.

8. The giving of an improvement grant is generally at the discretion of the Council. However, the Council cannot refuse a valid application for a grant for the provision of one or more of the standard amenities as listed in Question 11 of this form provided they are satisfied that after the works specified in the application are carried out, the house will meet the tolerable standard. If the Council are satisfied that the house will have a useful life of at least 10 years, they can insist that the house be provided with all the standard amenities. Works of repair and replacement can be included in applications for standard amenities up to a maximum of £2,000 for houses which have a future life expectancy of 10 years or more or £200 per amenity being installed up to a maximum of £800 for those houses whose life expectancy is less than 10 years.

9. If after the application is approved, the Council are satisfied that owing to circumstances beyond the control of the applicant the expense of the works will exceed the

estimate contained in the application, they may on production of a further estimate substitute a higher amount as the amount of the approved expense.

10. Some questions on this application may require information available to the owner who, where he is not the applicant, should be asked to complete them when he signs the declaration.

Housing action areas
11. The owner, lessee and/or occupier will already have been informed by the Council if the house is situated in an area for which the Council have made a final resolution declaring it to be a housing action area for improvement, or for demolition and improvement. The following conditions apply in such a housing action area:
- (a) The Council are empowered to secure that all houses in the area (other than any to be demolished in a housing action area for demolition and improvement) are brought up to the standard which they have specified for the area. The specified standard is that houses must meet the tolerable standard and must be in a good state of repair having regard to their age, character and locality. (The state of internal decorative repair is disregarded for this purpose.) If the Council are satisfied that the houses in the area have a future life of at least 10 years, they may also specify that all the houses must be provided with all of the standard amenities.
- (b) The Council must give grant for improvement works which in their opinion are required to bring a house up to the standard specified.
- (c) Grant will be payable on approved improvement work at the rate of 75 per cent of the approved expense (or up to 90 per cent if the Council considers that the owner cannot without undue hardship finance his share of the cost).
- (d) The owner of a house can require a tenant to vacate it if it is required for integration with other property in terms of the resolution, or to allow access or temporarily to vacate the house for such time as is needed to carry out necessary improvements or repairs. If the tenant refuses to allow access or to vacate the house the owner can apply to the Sheriff for an order requiring him to do so.

Improvement orders
12. (a) The Council may serve an order on the owner of a sub-tolerable standard house requiring the owner to improve the house within 180 days of the making of the order—for this purpose 'sub-tolerable' includes the lack of fixed bath or shower. This period may be extended if the Council are satisfied that steps are being taken to carry out the works required for the house to be improved and put into a good state of repair. Furthermore, if the house has a future life of at least 10 years, they may also require the house to be provided with all the standard amenities.
- (b) The Council must give a grant for improvement works which in their opinion are required to bring the house up to the standard specified in the improvement order.
- (c) Grant will be payable on approved improvement works at the rate of 75 per cent of the approved expense, or at 90 per cent in cases where the owner is able to satisfy the local authority that he would not be able without undue hardship, to finance the expense of the works without the assistance of this higher rate of grant. This rate is available only to the person served with the improvement order ie the owner.
- (d) The Council may also be obliged to offer a loan towards the cost of works not met by grant.
- (e) Failure to carry out the necessary works within 180 days, or such longer period as the Council may approve, may lead to your house being acquired by the Council, with your agreement, or by compulsory purchase. **[1290]**

Form 3

Form of application to local authority for repairs grant

READ THE NOTES ATTACHED BEFORE COMPLETING THIS FORM

This form should be completed and sent to the District or Islands Council in whose area the house is situated. A separate application must be made for each separate house to be repaired.

THE REPAIR WORK SHOULD NOT BE STARTED BEFORE THE COUNCIL HAVE GIVEN APPROVAL IN WRITING TO THE APPLICATION FOR GRANT. IF YOU START WORK BEFORE THE APPLICATION IS APPROVED THE COUNCIL MAY NOT BE ABLE TO GIVE GRANT. YOU SHOULD, THEREFORE, ENSURE THAT ANY PERSON ACTING FOR YOU IN THESE MATTERS DOES NOT START WORK BEFORE YOU HAVE THE APPROVAL OF THE COUNCIL IN WRITING.

A CONSENT GIVEN FOR PLANNING OR BUILDING REGULATIONS PURPOSES WHICH MAY ALSO BE REQUIRED IS NOT SUFFICIENT.

THE HOUSING (SCOTLAND) ACT 1974

Application for Repairs Grant

I/We hereby make an application to the Council for repairs grant in respect of the works proposed to be carried out on the under-mentioned property in accordance with the particulars given below and with the plans of the house before and after repair and the specifications which accompany this application.

*(I/We desire payment by instalments as the work proceeds.)

Date .... Signature of [Applicant] [Agent] ....

....

Address ....

*Delete if not applicable.

Declaration by Owner

I .... being the owner for the time being of the house referred to in the application hereby consent to .... making application for improvement grant towards the cost of works which he is to carry out as shown below. I give this consent in the full knowledge that I and my successors shall be bound for a period of 5 years by any conditions of grant imposed under section 9 of the Housing (Scotland) Act 1974. I understand that any breach of the conditions is likely to lead to a demand for repayment of the grant together with interest.

1. Address of property to be repaired. ....

2. (a) Full name and address of applicant. ....

   (b) Name and address of agent (if applicable). ....

(c) Name and address of owner (if not the applicant). ....

3. Was the house built or provided by conversion after 15th June 1964? (See Note 2.) ....

4. (See Note 3.)
Has the occupier, if other than the applicant, agreed to the work being done? ....

5. (See Note 3.)
(a) Is the house security for a loan? ....
(b) If so, give name and address of lender.
....
....
....

(c) Has the lender given any necessary consent to the making of this application? ....

6. (See Note 4.)
Please state:
(a) Whether on completion of the works the house or any part thereof is to be occupied by the owner? ....
(b) The rateable value of the house at the date of this application. ....

7. If on completion of the works the house is to be occupied by the owner, or a member of his family, will the house be his only or main residence? (See Note 5.)
....
....

8. Give a short description of the existing accommodation.
....
....
....

9. Is the house the subject of a repairs notice under section 24(1) of the Housing (Scotland) Act 1969? (See Note 6.) ....
If it is will the repair works proposed remedy the defects specified in the repairs notice? ....

10. Is the property situated in a Housing Action area (See Note 8.) ....
If it is will the house satisfy the standard specified for the area when the proposed repair works are completed? ....

11. (See Note 7.)
    Summarise works proposed and give their cost. (Complete (a) or (b) or (c).)
    (a) If the house is in a housing action area specify repair work needed to bring the house up to the standard specified for the area.
        Cost   £ ....
    (b) If the house is the subject of a repairs notice specify repair work needed to rectify defects specified in repairs notice. (See Note 5.)
        Cost   £ ....
    (c) For houses not in a housing action area and not the subject of a repairs notice, specify repair work needed to enable the house to attain a good state of repair.
        Cost   £ ....
    (d) Professional fees.   £ ....
    (e) VAT   £ ....

12. Name and address of person who prepared the plans and specifications.

13. When it is intended the works should
    (a) Start?
    (b) Finish?

14. Is the property a listed building within the meaning of Part IV of the Town and Country Planning (Scotland) Act 1972, or is it subject to a building preservation notice under section 56 of that Act?

Notes

This grant is available only where the owner is able to satisfy the local authority that he would not be able, without undue hardship, to finance the expense of the works without the assistance of grant.

Further details of the grants available may be obtained at the offices of the local authority.

Depending on the nature of the work to be done, planning permission may have to be obtained from the local planning authority. It may also be necessary to obtain warrant from the building authority. Advice should be sought at the offices of the local authority. Approval for building regulation purposes or approval for planning purposes is not the same as grant approval.

Any grant-aided works must be carried out to the satisfaction of the Council. Inspection by officials of the Council will therefore normally be necessary.

If the local authority do not approve the application or if they fix as the amount of grant an amount less than that which may be fixed under the Statute they must notify the applicant in writing of the grounds on which they have decided to do so.

THE FOLLOWING NOTES ARE INTENDED TO ASSIST YOU IN COMPLETING THE FORM

1. Houses built or provided by conversion after 15th June 1964 will not qualify for grant except by direction of the Secretary of State. If you believe you should receive grant your Council will advise you how to proceed.

2. The applicant must be the owner of the house or have the owner's consent to the application being made and his agreement to abide by the conditions of grant. If the applicant is not the occupier of the house, the occupier's consent to the proposed repairs should be obtained before making the application. (In general a landlord may not carry out repairs without the consent of the tenant but see Note 8(e) below.) If the house is security for a loan, the building society or other lender should be notified of the application for grant. A copy of any necessary letter of consent from lender or tenant should be attached to this application.

3. Houses with a rateable value above a prescribed limit, and which on completion of the works are to be occupied by the owner, may be excluded from grant. Further particulars may be obtained from the local authority.

4. If granted, the payment of grant will be subject to the following conditions which will apply to the house for a period of 5 years from the date of the payment of grant:
 (a) the house shall not be used for purposes other than those of a private dwelling house;
 (b) the house shall not be occupied by the owner or a member of his family except as his only or main residence within the meaning of section 29 of the Finance Act 1965;
 (c) all steps as are practicable shall be taken to secure the maintenance of the house in a good state of repair.
In addition the Council may impose the following conditions:
 (d) the house at all times which it is not occupied by the applicant or by a member of his family will be let or kept available for letting;
If any of these conditions are breached, the Council may demand the repayment of the grant either in part or in full together with compound interest at a statutorily fixed rate for the period the grant has been in the hands of the applicant. In signing the declaration on this form, the owner acknowledges his liability under these provisions.

5. Under section 24(1) of the Housing (Scotland) Act 1969, as amended by paragraph 5 of Schedule 2 to the Housing (Financial Provisions) (Scotland) Act 1978, a local authority may serve on the person having control of the house a notice requiring him to execute, within a reasonable period (not less than 21 days), works which will rectify the repair defects specified in the repairs notice. Failing compliance with such a notice the local authority may carry out the works themselves and retrieve the costs.

6. If after the application is approved, the Council are satisfied that owing to circumstances beyond the control of the applicant the expense of the work will exceed the estimate contained in the application, they may on production of a further estimate substitute a higher amount as the amount of the approved expense.

Housing action areas

7. The owner, lessee and/or occupier will already have been informed by the Council if the house is situated in an area for which the Council have made a final resolution declaring it to be a housing action area for improvement, or for demolition and improvement. The following conditions apply in such a housing action area:—
 (a) The Council are empowered to secure that all houses in the area (other than any to be demolished in a housing action area for demolition and improvement) are brought up to the standard which they have specified for the area. The specified standard is that houses must meet the tolerable standard and must be in a good state of repair having regard to their age, character and locality. (The state of internal decorative repair is disregarded for this purpose.) If the Council are

satisfied that the houses in the area have a future life of at least 10 years they may also specify that all the houses must be provided with all of the standard amenities.
(b) The Council must give grant for repair works which in their opinion are required to bring a house up to the standard specified.
(c) Grant will be payable on approved repair work at the rate of 75 per cent of the approved expense (or up to 90 per cent if the Council considers that the applicant cannot without undue hardship finance his share of the cost).
(d) In considering whether to approve an application for a repairs grant the Council have to decide whether an applicant could pay the whole cost of the repairs without hardship. Any person applying for this grant will therefore be asked to provide details of income and other assets and commitments.
(e) The owner of a house can require a tenant to vacate it if it is required for integration with other property in terms of the resolution, or to allow access or temporarily to vacate the house for such time as is needed to carry out necessary improvements or repairs. If the tenant refuses to allow access or to vacate the house the owner can apply to the Sheriff for an order requiring him to do so. **[1291]**

FORM 4

Form of order requiring the owner of a house to execute works of improvement

WARNING

If you are in doubt about the effect of this notice you should ask for guidance at your Council Offices at [Quote address] ....
..., or consult a Solicitor

THE HOUSING (SCOTLAND) ACT 1974

To[1] .... the owner of the house[2] ....

Take notice that—

1. the[3] ....Council, the local authority for the purposes of the Housing (Scotland) Act 1974 as amended by the Housing (Financial Provisions) (Scotland) Act 1978 and the Tenants' Rights, Etc (Scotland) Act 1980 hereinafter referred to respectively as 'the local authority' and 'the Act') are satisfied that the above-mentioned house, which is not situated in a housing action area. [fails to meet the tolerable standard in the following respects—][4] [and] [lacks a fixed bath or shower].

2. in exercise of the powers conferred on them by section 14A(1) of the Act, the local authority order you within a period of 180 days, ending on[5] ....
........................19......... to improve the house by the execution of works:
(a) to bring it up to the tolerable standard;
(b) to put it into a good state of repair;[6] [and, in consideration of the local authority being satisfied that the house has a future life of not less than 10 years,
(c) to provide it with all the standard amenities which it presently lacks]*,
(d) to provide a fixed bath or shower with suitable supplies of hot and cold water]*.

DATED .... 19.........

[7] ....

Delete if not applicable.

Notes for your Information

(To be incorporated in the Order and any copies thereof)

1. Section 14A(1) of the Housing (Scotland) Act 1974 provides that where a local authority are satisfied that a house which is not in a housing action area fails to meet the tolerable standard they may serve an Order on the owner requiring him to execute work within a period of 180 days in order to:
    (a) bring the house up to the tolerable standard;
    (b) put it into a good state of repair; and
    (c) provide a fixed bath or shower.
In addition, if the local authority are satisfied that the house has a future life of not less than 10 years, they may at their discretion, require that the house is provided with all the standard amenities.

2. A house shall meet the tolerable standard if it:
[Insert here sub-sections (a) to (i) of section 14(1) of the 1974 Act as amended].

3. It is for the local authority to decide what constitutes 'a good state of repair'. The state of internal decorative repair will be disregarded for this purpose, but the age, character and locality of the house will be taken into account.

4. The standard amenities are:
[Insert here list of standard amenities as in Part I of Schedule 1 to the 1974 Act].

5. Any person aggrieved by this Order may in accordance with the provisions of section 26 of the Housing (Scotland) Act 1966, appeal to the Sheriff against the Order. The appeal must be brought within 21 days after the date of the service of the Order and no proceedings may be taken by the local authority to enforce the Order whilst an appeal against it is pending.

6. Under subsections (7) and (8) of section 14A of the Housing (Scotland) Act 1974 the local authority may be obliged to make an improvement grant and/or a loan towards the cost of the improvement works. Further advice should be sought from the local authority about grant and loan assistance.

7. Failure to execute the necessary improvement works within 180 days, or such period as may be determined on appeal, may lead to the local authority acquiring the house, by agreement or by compulsory purchase, in order that the necessary works may be carried out.

Notes for Guidance in Completing this Form

1. Insert the name and residence or place of business of the owner of the house.

2. Insert such description of the house as may be sufficient for identification.

3. Insert the name of the local authority.

4. Insert the items on which the house fails to meet the tolerable standard.

5. Insert the date of expiry of the 180 day period for execution of the works.

6. Delete in so far as not applicable.

7. Insert name and designation of authorised officer.

[1292]

FORM 5

Form of notice of payment of improvement grant or repairs grant

THE HOUSING (SCOTLAND) ACT 1974

NOTICE OF PAYMENT OF IMPROVEMENT GRANT OR REPAIRS GRANT

[1][Whereas the[2] .... Council, the Local authority under the Housing (Scotland) Act 1974 (hereinafter referred to respectively as 'the local authority' and 'the Act') have, in accordance with the provisions of the Act, paid to[3] .... an improvement grant of £[4] .... in respect of improvement works relating to the house described in the schedule hereto. Now therefore notice is hereby given, in accordance with the provision of section 9(9) of the Act, that:—]

[1][Whereas the[2] .... Council the local authority under the Housing (Scotland) Act 1974 (hereinafter referred to respectively as 'the local authority' and 'the Act') have, in accordance with the provisions of the Act, paid to[3] .... a repairs grant of £[4] .... in respect of the works of repair to the house described in the schedule hereto.

Now therefore notice is hereby given in accordance with the provisions of section 9(9) as read with section 10A(5) of the Act, that:—]

1. For the period of 5 years commencing on[5] .... 19.........
the following conditions shall be observed with respect to the said house:—
   (a) the house shall not be used for purposes other than those of a private dwelling house;
   (b) the house shall not be occupied by the owner or a member of his family except as his only or main residence within the meaning of section 29 of the Finance Act 1965;
   (c) all steps as are practicable shall be taken to secure the maintenance of the house in a good state of repair;
   [(d) [5]the house at all times at which it is not occupied by the applicant or by a member of his family will be let or kept available for letting].

2. [1][(a) In the event of a breach of any of the conditions specified at (a), (b) and (c) in paragraph 1 above at a time when they are required as aforesaid to be observed with respect to the said house, there shall on being demanded by the local authority, forthwith become payable to them by the owner for the time being of the said house the whole amount of any sums paid by the local authority by way of improvement grant or repairs grant in respect of the expenses incurred for the purpose of executing the said improvement works or works of repair together in the case of each such sum, with interest thereon (as defined in paragraph 9 of Schedule 2 to the Act) for the period from the date of payment of the [1][final instalment of the] grant by the local authority to the date of repayment of the grant to the local authority].

[1][(b) In the event of a breach of the condition specified at (d) in paragraph 1 above at a time when it is required as aforesaid to be observed with respect to the said house, the local authority may if they consider it reasonable for them to do so decide not to recover the sums paid by them by way of improvement grant or repairs grant or where they do not so consider, recover from the owner for the time being of the said house the whole amount of any sums paid by them by way of improvement grant or repairs grant or the appropriate amount (as defined in paragraph 9 of Schedule 2 to the Act) of the grant which may be outstanding together with compound interest (as so defined) for the period from the date of payment of the

¹[final instalment of the] grant by the local authority to the date of repayment of the whole amount or appropriate amount of the grant to the local authority as the case may be].

Dated .... 19.........

⁶ ....

SCHEDULE

All and Whole .... (in the County of ....) (in the District of .... and the County of ....) being (part of) the subjects described in (Disposition etc) by .... in favour of .... dated .... and recorded in the Division of the General Register of Sasines applicable to the County of ....
on .... 19.........
A separate notice should be used for each resultant house.

NOTES FOR GUIDANCE IN COMPLETING THIS FORM

1. Delete in so far as not applicable.

2. Insert the name of the local authority.

3. Insert the name, designation and address of the recipient of the grant.

4. Insert, in words, the appropriate amount.

5. Insert the date from which the period begins in accordance with section 9(1) of the Act.

6. Insert name and designation of authorised officer.

7. A copy of this notice should be sent to the owner in those cases where he is not the applicant.

FORM 6

Form of notice of cessor or partial cessor of conditions of improvement grant or repairs grant

THE HOUSING (SCOTLAND) ACT 1974

Notice of ¹[Partial] Cessor of Conditions of Improvement Grant or Repairs Grant

Whereas by Notice of Payment of Improvement Grant or Repairs Grant amounting to £² .... paid to³ .... dated .... 19.........
and recorded in the Division of the General Register of Sasines applicable to the County of .... on .... 19........., it is provided that there shall with respect to the house described in the schedule hereto be observed certain conditions specified in the said Notice;

And Whereas, in accordance with the provisions of ¹[section 10 of] [paragraph [3] [5] of Schedule 2 to] the Housing (Scotland) Act 1974 (hereinafter referred to as 'the Act') [as read with section 10A(5) of the Act] observance of [all the conditions in] [condition (d) in paragraph 1 of] the said Notice of Payment has ceased to be requisite with respect to the said house;

Now therefore, the⁴ .... as the local authority under the Act, hereby give notice, in accordance with the provisions of paragraph 7 of Schedule 2 to the Act, that, as from⁵ .... 19......... ¹[all the conditions in] [condition (d) in paragraph 1 of] the said Notice of Payment of Improvement Grant or Repairs Grants no longer[1] [apply] [applies] to the said house.

Dated .... 19.........

..........6..

SCHEDULE

Description of the house to which the foregoing notice relates[7]—

1. Delete in so far as not applicable.

2. Insert in words the amount of the sum as in the notice of payment of grant.

3. Insert name designation and address of the recipient of the grant.

4. Insert the name of the local authority.

5. Insert the appropriate date of cessation of the conditions in accordance with paragraph 3 or 5 of Schedule 2 to the Act.

6. Insert name and designation of authorised officer.

7. Repeat the description contained in the schedule in the relevant recorded notice of payment of grant. A separate notice should be used for each house. **[1294]**

FORM 7

Form of notice about a well maintained payment

WARNING: IF IN DOUBT ABOUT THE EFFECT OF THIS NOTICE CONSULT YOUR LOCAL AUTHORITY OR A SOLICITOR

THE HOUSING (SCOTLAND) ACT 1974

To[1] ....
[2][owner] [lessee] [occupier] of the house at[3] ....

Take notice that[4] ....
the local authority under the Housing (Scotland) Act 1974 in exercise of the powers conferred upon them by section 30(1) of the said Act

[5][are satisfied that the above mentioned house has been well maintained and intend to make a payment in accordance with and subject to the calculation to be made under section 21 of the Housing (Scotland) Act 1979]

[5][are not satisfied that the above mentioned house has been well maintained and do not intend to make a payment under section 21 of the Housing (Scotland) Act 1969. You have a right to make representations to the Secretary of State about this matter, and any such representations should be made in writing to the Secretary, Scottish Development Department[6]........................ by[7] .... 19.........]

Dated .... 19.........

..........8..

SI 1980/1665 [1297]

Notes for Guidance in Completing this Form

1. Insert name and address of the person to whom this notice is addressed.
2. Delete in so far as inappropriate to the particular notice.
3. Insert such description of the house as may be sufficient for identification.
4. Insert name of local authority.
5. Delete whichever is inapplicable.
6. Insert address.
7. Insert date 21 days from service of this notice.
8. Insert name and designation of authorised officer.   [1295]

NOTES to SI 1980/1647

General: References to the Housing (Scotland) Act 1966 should now be read as references to the corresponding provisions of the Housing (Scotland) Act 1987 (c 26).

The Rent Assessment Committees (Scotland) Regulations 1980
SI 1980/1665

(These regulations were made by the Secretary of State for Scotland under the Rent (Scotland) Act 1971 (c 28), ss 46(1)(b) and 99(1)(b), and the Tenants' Rights, Etc (Scotland) Act 1980 (c 52), s 52(2), and came into operation on 1 December 1980)

ARRANGEMENT OF REGULATIONS
(This list is not printed in the Regulations)

1	Citation and commencement	[1296]
2	Interpretation	[1297]
3	Revocation	[1298]
4	Hearings	[1299]
5	Documents	[1300]
6	Inspection of Dwelling house	[1301]
7	Decisions	[1302]
7A		[1303]
8	Giving of Notices, etc	[1304]

1. *(Citation and commencement)*   [1296]

2. **Interpretation.**

(1) In these regulations unless the context otherwise requires,
'the Act' means the Rent (Scotland) Act 1971;
'chairman' means the chairman of a committee;
'committee' means a rent assessment committee, to which a reference is made and which is constituted in accordance with the provisions of Schedule 5 to the Act;
'hearing' means the meetings or meetings of a committee to hear oral representations made in relation to a reference;
'Part VII contract' means a contract to which section 85(1) of the Act applies which is

673

referred by a party to a committee under sections 87 or 90 of the Act as amended by section 9(4) of the Rent Act 1974 and section 52 of the Tenants' Rights, Etc (Scotland) Act 1980;

'party' means, in the case where a reference is subject to a hearing, any person who is entitled under regulation 4(2) of these regulations to receive notice of the date, time and place of the hearing and, in the case where a reference is not to be subject to a hearing, any person who is entitled to make representations in writing to the committee;

'reference' means a matter which is referred by a rent officer to a committee under paragraphs 6 or 11 or Schedule 6 to the Act, or an application for a certificate of fair rent which is referred by a rent officer to a committee under paragraphs 2 or 6 of Schedule 7 to the Act or a Part VII contract.

(2) For the purpose of any of these regulations relating to procedure at a hearing, any reference to a party shall be construed as including a reference to a person authorised by that party to be heard on his behalf whether or not that person is an advocate or a solicitor.

[1297]

3. Revocation.

The Rent of Furnished Houses Control (Scotland) Regulations 1943, the Landlord and Tenant (Rent Control) (Scotland) Regulations 1949, and the Rent Assessment Committees (Scotland) Regulations 1971 are hereby revoked. **[1298]**

4. Hearings.

(1) Where a reference is to be subject to a hearing, the committee shall appoint a date, time and place for a hearing.

(2) A committee shall give not less than ten days' notice in writing of the date, time and place so appointed for a hearing—
  (a) to the landlord and the tenant where the reference is a matter referred to the committee under paragraph 6 of Schedule 6 to the Act; or
  (b) to the applicant where the reference is a matter relating to an application for the registration of a rent for a dwellinghouse in accordance with a certificate of fair rent referred to the committee under paragraph 9 of Schedule 6 to the Act; or
  (c) to the applicant where the reference in an application for a certificate of fair rent referred to the committee under paragraphs 2 or 6 of Schedule 7 to the Act and, in a case to which paragraph 9 of that Schedule applies, to the tenant; or
  (d) to the lessor and the lessee where the reference is a Part VII contract referred to the committee by either the lessor or the lessee; or
  (e) to the lessor and the lessee and the local authority where the reference is a Part VII contract referred to the committee by the local authority.

(3) A hearing shall be in public unless for special reasons the committee otherwise decide, but nothing in these regulations shall prevent a member of the Council on Tribunals or of its Scottish Committee in that capacity from attending any hearing.

(4) At a hearing—
  (a) the parties shall be heard in such order and, subject to the provisions of these regulations, the procedure shall be such as the committee shall detemine; and
  (b) a party may call witnesses, give evidence on his own behalf and cross-examine any witnesses called by the other party.

(5) The committee at their discretion may on their own motion, or at the request of the parties or one of them, at any time and from time to time postpone or adjourn a hearing; but they shall not do so at the request of one party only unless, having regard to the grounds upon which and the time at which such request is made and to the convenience of the parties, they deem it reasonable to do so. The committee shall give to the parties such notice of any postponed or adjourned hearing as they deem to be reasonable in the circumstances.

(6) If a party does not appear at a hearing, the committee, on being satisfied that the

requirements of this regulation regarding the giving of notice of a hearing have been duly complied with, may proceed to deal with the reference upon the representations of any party present and upon the documents and information which they may properly consider. **[1299]**

5. Documents.

(1) Where the reference is to be subject to a hearing, the committee shall take all reasonable steps to ensure that there is supplied to each of the parties before the date of the hearing—
- (a) a copy of, or sufficient extracts from, or particulars of, any document relevant to the reference which has been received from the rent officer or from a party (other than a document which is in the possession of such party or of which that party has previously been supplied with a copy by the rent officer); and
- (b) a copy of any document which embodies results of any enquiries made by or for the committee for the purposes of that reference, or which contains relevant information in relation to fair rents previously determined for other dwelling houses and which has been prepared for the committee for the purposes of that reference.

(2) At any hearing where—
- (i) any document relevant to the reference is not in the posession of a party present at such hearing; and
- (ii) such party has not been supplied with a copy of, or relevant extracts from, or particulars of, such document by the rent officer or by the committee in accordance with the provisions of paragraph (1) of this regulation,

then unless—
- (a) such party consents to the continuation of the hearing; or
- (b) the committee consider that such party has a sufficient opportunity of dealing with such document without an adjournment of the hearing,

the committee shall not consider such document until after they have adjourned the hearing for a period which they consider will afford such party a sufficient opportunity of dealing with such document.

(3) Where a reference is not to be subject to a hearing the committee shall supply to each of the parties a copy of, or sufficient extracts from, or particulars of, any such document as is mentioned in paragraph (1)(a) of this regulation (other than a document excepted from that paragraph) and a copy of any such document as is mentioned in paragraph (1)(b) of this regulation, and they shall not reach their decision until they are satisfied that each party has been given a sufficient opportunity of commenting upon any document of which a copy or from which extracts or of which particulars has or have been so supplied, and upon the other party's case. **[1300]**

6. Inspection of dwellinghouse.

(1) The committee may on their own motion and shall at the request of one of the parties (subject in either case to any necessary consent being obtained) inspect the dwellinghouse which is the subject of the reference.

(2) An inspection may be made before, during or after the close of the hearing, or at such stage in relation to the consideration of the representations in writing as the committee shall determine.

(3) The committee shall give such notice in writing as they deem sufficient of an inspection to the party or parties and shall allow each party and his representative to attend any such inspection.

(4) Where an inspection is made after the close of a hearing the committee may, if they consider that it is expedient to do so on account of any matter arising from the inspection, re-open the hearing; and if the hearing is to be re-opened paragraph (2) of regulation 4 of these regulations shall apply as it applied to the original hearing, save in so far as its requirements may be dispensed with or relaxed with the consent of the parties. **[1301]**

7. Decisions.

(1) The decision of the committee upon a reference shall be recorded in a document signed by the chairman (or in the event of his absence or incapacity, by another member of the committee) which . . . shall contain no reference to the decision being a majority (if that be the case) or to any opinion of a minority.

(2) The chairman (or in the event of his absence or incapacity, another member of the committee) shall have power, by a certificate under his hand, to correct any clerical or accidental error or omission in the said document.

(3) A copy of the said document and of any such correction shall be sent by the committee to the party or parties and, where the reference was made by the Rent Officer, to the Rent Officer. **[1302]**

7A.—(1) Where the committee are requested, on or before the giving or notification of the decision, to state the reasons for the decision, those reasons shall be recorded in a document.

(2) Regulation 7 above shall apply to the document recording the reasons as it applies to the document recording the decision.' **[1303]**

8. Giving of notices, etc.

Where any notice or other written matter is required under the provisions of these regulations to be given or supplied by the committee to a party or parties, it shall be sufficient compliance with the regulations if such notice or matter is sent by post to the party for whom it is intended at his usual or last known address or if that party has appointed an agent to act on his behalf in relation to the reference, to that agent at the address of the agent supplied to the Committee. **[1304]**

NOTES to SI 1980/1665

Amendments: Reg 7(1) was amended by the Rent Assessment Committees (Scotland) Regulations 1982, SI 1982/259; reg 7A was added by *Ibid*.

Reg 2(1): The Rent (Scotland) Act 1971 (c 20) was repealed by the Rent (Scotland) Act 1984 (c 58): references to the 1971 Act should be construed as references to the corresponding provisions of the 1984 Act.

For the definition of 'rent assessement committee' now see the Rent (Scotland) Act 1984 (c 58), s 44 & Sch 4; for the meaning of 'Part VII Contract' now see *Ibid* ss 63(7) & 115; for the meaning of 'reference' now see *Ibid*, Schs 5 and 6.

SI 1980/1666 **[1307]**

The Short Tenancies (Prescribed Information) (Scotland) Order 1980

SI 1980/1666

(*These regulations were made by the Secretary of State for Scotland under the Tenants' Rights, Etc (Scotland) Act 1980 (c 52), s 34(4), and came into operation on 1 December 1980*)

1.—(1) (*Citation and commencement*) **[1305]**

2. Prescription of notice.

Where a landlord intends to grant a short tenancy within the meaning of section [9 of the Rent (Scotland) Act 1984] he shall, before the tenancy is created, serve on the person to whom the tenancy is to be granted a notice in writing in the form, or in a form substantially to the like effect, prescribed in the Schedule to this order. **[1306]**

SCHEDULE

Specimen of the form of notice that a person proposing to accept a short tenancy must receive from the landlord before the tenancy is created.

To ....
 (Name of proposed tenant)

IMPORTANT—PLEASE READ THIS NOTICE CAREFULLY.
IF THERE IS ANYTHING YOU DO NOT UNDERSTAND YOU
SHOULD GET ADVICE (FOR EXAMPLE, FROM A
SOLICITOR OR A CITIZENS' ADVICE BUREAU) BEFORE
YOU AGREE TO TAKE A SHORT TENANCY.

NB This document is important; keep it in a safe place.

1. You are proposing to take a tenancy of the dwelling-house at

....

from .... 19 ... to .... 19 ...
 (day) (month) (year) (day) (month) (year)

2. Before you take the tenancy I am required by law to tell you that your tenancy is to be a *protected short tenancy*. Under a short tenancy provided you adhere to the conditions of the tenancy, you are entitled to remain in the dwelling-house for the period specified in paragraph 1. At the end of this period, however, unlike normal Rent Act tenancies, the landlord has an absolute right to repossession if he wants. Full details about short tenancies are given in the Scottish Development Department booklet 'Short Tenancies' obtainable free from rent officers, council offices, housing aid centres and citizens' advice bureaux. You are strongly advised to read this booklet before you agree to take a short tenancy.

*3. A fair rent of   per   is already registered for the dwelling-house under the Rent (Scotland) Act 1971.

This is the most you can be required to pay as rent until such time as a higher rent is registered. If I apply for a higher rent to be registered you will be told about my application and you will have the opportunity of a consultation with the rent officer if you disagree with the rent I propose. Unless there has been a change of circumstances I cannot apply until three years after the effective date of the existing registration.

*3. A fair rent has not yet been registered for the dwelling under the Rent (Scotland) Act 1971. However, a certificate of fair rent under the Rent (Scotland) Act 1971 has been issued in respect of the dwelling-house. The rent specified in the Certificate is   per   and I am required by law to apply for this rent to be registered within 14 days of the start of the tenancy.

This is the most you can be required to pay as rent until such time as a higher rent is registered. If I apply for a higher rent to be registered you will be told about my application and you will have the opportunity of a consultation with the rent officer if you disagree with the amount I propose. Unless there has been a change of circumstances I cannot apply until three years after the effective date of the existing registration.

4. This notice (which does not commit you to taking the tenancy) is given to you on .... 19......

Signed ....

(on behalf of) ....

....

....

(Name and address of landlord)

SPECIAL NOTE FOR EXISTING TENANTS.
IF YOU ARE ALREADY A PROTECTED OR STATUTORY TENANT UNDER THE RENT (SCOTLAND) ACT 1971 YOUR PRESENT TENANCY CANNOT BY LAW BE CONVERTED INTO A SHORT TENANCY BUT IF YOU GIVE IT UP AND TAKE A SHORT TENANCY IN SOME OTHER ACCOMMODATION YOU WILL ALMOST CERTAINLY HAVE LESS SECURITY THAN UNDER YOUR EXISTING TENANCY WHEN THE SHORT TENANCY COMES TO AN END.

NOTES to SI 1980/1666

Reg 2: The reference to the Rent (Scotland) Act 1984 (c 50) was substituted by virtue of that Act, s 117, Sch 9.

Schedule: The references to the Rent (Scotland) Act 1984 were substituted by virtue of that Act, s 117, Sch 9.

---

*The landlord must delete whichever does not apply.

SI 1980/1670 [1313]

The Cancellation of Registration (Procedure) (Scotland) Regulations 1980

SI 1980/1670

(*These regulations were made by the Secretary of State for Scotland under the Rent (Scotland) Act 1971 (c 28), ss 46, 44A(4) and 44B, and came into operation on 1 December 1980*)

1. (*Citation and commencement*) [1308]

2. In these regulations—
'the Act' means the Rent (Scotland) Act 1971;
'application' means an application for the cancellation of a registration which is made to the rent officer under section 44A or, as the case may require, under section 44B of the Act;
'rent agreement' means a rent agreement within the meaning of section 44A of the Act, of which a copy accompanies an application made under that section; and
'registration' means the rent registered for the dwellinghouse under Part IV of the Act which it is sought to cancel by the application. [1309]

3. On receiving an application made under either section 44A or section 44B of the Act, the rent officer may, as the case may require, by notice in writing served on the landlord or the tenant or on both the landlord and the tenant require him or them to give to the rent officer, within such period of not less than 14 days from the service of the notice as may be specified in the notice, such information as he may reasonably require regarding such of the particulars contained in the application or such of the terms of the rent agreement as may be specified in the notice. [1310]

4. Where it appears to the rent officer, after making such inquiry, if any, as he thinks fit, and considering any information supplied to him in pursuance of regulation 3 above that in the case of an application made under section 44A of the Act the rent payable under the rent agreement does not exceed a fair rent for the dwellinghouse, or that, in the case of an application made under section 44B of the Act, the dwellinghouse is not let on or subject to a regulated tenancy, he shall, subject in the case of an application made under section 44A of the Act, to sub-section (6) of that section, cancel the registration without further proceedings. [1311]

5. Where the rent officer, in carrying out his functions under these regulations in respect of an application made under section 44A of the Act, inspects a dwellinghouse, he shall explain to the tenant or to his spouse, if either is present at the inspection, the procedure governing an application. [1312]

6.—(1) Where the rent officer does not cancel the registration in pursuance of regulation 4 above, he shall serve a notice under this regulation.

(2) Where the application was made under section 44A of the Act, a notice under this regulation shall be served on the landlord and the tenant informing them that the rent officer proposes, at a time (which shall be not earlier than 7 days after the service of the notice) and place specified in the notice to consider, in consultation with the landlord and tenant, or such of them as may appear at that time and place, whether the registration ought to be cancelled.

(3) At any such consultation, the landlord and the tenant may each be represented by a

person authorised by him in that behalf, whether or not that person is an advocate or solicitor.

(4) Where the application was made under section 44B of the Act, a notice under this regulation shall be served on the landlord informing him of the reasons why the rent officer cannot cancel the registration. **[1313]**

7. Any notice to be served under these regulations and any notification required to be given under section 44A(8) of the Act (notification of rent officer's decision) may be sent by post or delivered—
 (a) to the landlord and, where there is one, to the tenant at their respective addresses given in the application; or
 (b) where the application is made by an agent on behalf of the landlord or, where there is one, the tenant to that agent at the address of the agent given in the application. **[1314]**

8. The Cancellation of Registration (Procedure) (Scotland) Regulations 1972 are hereby revoked but the revocation shall not affect the validity of any application made or notice given under these regulations before the commencement of these regulations. **[1315]**

NOTES to SI 1980/1670

Reg 2: The Rent (Scotland) Act 1971 (c 28) has been repealed. The references to ss 44A and 44B should now be read as references to the Rent (Scotland) Act 1984 (c 58), ss 51 and 52 respectively.

The Housing (Percentage of Approved Expense for Improvement Grants) (Scotland) Order 1980

SI 1980/2029

(*This order was made by the Secretary of State for Scotland under the Housing (Scotland) Act 1974 (c 45), ss 5(1), (1A) and 49(3), and came into operation on 20 December 1980*)

1. (*Citation, commencement and interpretation*) **[1316]**

2. Revocation.

The Housing (Percentage of Approved Expense for Improvement Grants) (Scotland) Order 1978 is hereby revoked. **[1317]**

3. Percentage of approved expense.

In respect (a) of that class of houses which:
 (i) are not houses in a housing action area, and
 (ii) fail to meet the tolerable standard, and
 (b) of that class of houses which:
 (i) are not houses in a housing action area, and
 (ii) lack a fixed bath or shower provided with an adequate supply of both hot and cold water within the house,

there shall be substituted in section 5(1) of the Housing (Scotland) Act 1974 for the figure '50', the figure '75'. **[1318]**

4. In respect of that class of houses for which improvement orders have been made in terms of section 14A(1) of the said Act, there shall be substituted in the said section 5(1) for the words 'not exceed 50' the words 'be 75'. **[1319]**

5. In respect of that class of houses where the applicant is the owner and application for grant has been approved under the said section 5(1) as read with Article 4 of this order and the applicant will not without undue hardship be able to finance the cost of so much of the improvement work as is not met by the grant said percentage may be increased from 75 per cent to a higher percentage not exceeding 90 per cent. **[1320]**

6. The provisions of this order shall not apply to an application for house improvement grant approved prior to the date on which the order comes into operation. **[1321]**

NOTES to SI 1980/2029

Reg 3: The Housing (Scotland) Act 1974 (c 45) has been repealed. The reference to s 5(1) of that Act should now be read as a reference to the Housing (Scotland) Act 1987 (c 26), s 242(1).

The Protected Tenancies (Further Exception) (Scotland) Regulations 1982

SI 1982/702

(These regulations were made by the Secretary of State for Scotland under the Rent (Scotland) Act 1971 (c 28), s 2(4), and came into operation on 21 June 1982)

1. *(Citation and commencement)* **[1322]**

2. **Specified body.**

The Royal College of Surgeons of Edinburgh is specified for the purposes of paragraph (bb) of section 2(1) of the said Act of 1971 (tenancies excepted from definition of 'protected tenancy'). **[1323]**

NOTES to SI 1982/702

Reg 2: The Rent (Scotland) Act 1971 (c 28) has been repealed. The reference to s 2(1)(bb) of that Act should now be read as a reference to the Rent (Scotland) Act 1984 (c 58), s 2(1)(c).

The Matrimonial Homes (Forms of Consent) (Scotland) Regulations 1982

SI 1982/971

(*This order was made by the Secretary of State for Scotland under the Matrimonial Homes (Family Protection) (Scotland) Act 1981 (c 59), s 6(3) as applied by s 9(2), and came into operation on 1 September 1982*)

1.—(1) These regulations may be cited as the Matrimonial Homes (Form of Consent) (Scotland) Regulations 1982 and shall come into operation on 1st September 1982.

(2) In these regulatrions—
'the Act' means the Matrimonial Homes (Family Protection) (Scotland) Act 1981 and, in a case where section 9(1) of the Act applies, any reference in these regulations to the entitled spouse and to the non-entitled spouse shall be construed in accordance with section 9(2)(a) of the Act. **[1323A]**

2. The consent of the non-entitled spouse to any dealing of the entitled spouse relating to a matrimonial home shall be—
   (a) where the consent is given in a deed effecting the dealing, in or as nearly as may be in the form set out in Schedule 1 to these regulations; or
   (b) where the consent is given in a separate document, in or as nearly as may be in the form set out in Schedule 2 to these regulations. **[1323B]**

SCHEDULE 1

Consent to be Inserted in the Deed Effecting the Dealing

(The following words should be inserted where appropriate in the deed. The consenter should sign as a party to the deed.)

... with the consent of AB *(designation)*, the spouse of the said CD, for the purposes of the Matrimonial Homes (Family Protection) (Scotland) Act 1981...
[To be attested] **[1323C]**

SCHEDULE 2

Consent in a Separate Document

I, AB *(designation)*, spouse of CD *(designation)*, hereby consent, for the purposes of the Matrimonial Homes (Family Protection) (Scotland) Act 1981, to the undernoted dealing of the said CD relating to *(here describe the matrimonial home or the part of it to which the dealer relates: see Note 1)*.

Dealing referred to:—
(Here describe the dealing: see Note 2.)
[To be attested].

Note 1
The expression 'matrimonial home' is defined in section 22 of the Matrimonial Homes (Family Protection) (Scotland) Act 1981 as follows:—

' "matrimonial home" means any house, caravan, houseboat or other structure which has been provided or has been made available by one or both of the spouses as, or has become, a family residence and includes any garden or other ground or building attached to, and usually occupied with, or otherwise required for the amenity or convenience of, the house, caravan, houseboat or other structure.'

Note 2

The expression 'dealing' is defined in section 6(2) of the Matrimonial Homes (Family Protection) (Scotland) Act 1981 as follows:—

' "dealing" includes the grant of a heritable security and the creation of a trust but does not include a conveyance under section 80 of the Lands Clauses Consolidation (Scotland) Act 1845.' **[1323D]**

The Home Purchase Assistance (Recognised Lending Institutions) Order 1982

SI 1982/976

(*This order was made by the Secretary of State for the Environment under the Home Purchase Assistance and Housing Corporation Guarantee Act 1978, s 2(1) and (7) and came into operation on 18 August 1982*)

1. (*Citation and commencement*)

2. National Westminster Home Loans Limited is added to Part I of the Schedule to the Home Purchase Assistance and Housing Corporation Guarantee Act 1978.

NOTES to SI 1982/976

The Home Purchase Assistance and Housing Corporation Guarantee Act 1978 (c 27) has been repealed. For recognised lending institutions, now see the Housing (Scotland) Act 1987 (c 26), ss 222–227.

The Secure Tenancies (Abandoned Property) (Scotland) Order 1982

SI 1982/981

(*This order was made by the Secretary of State for Scotland under the Tenants' Rights Etc (Scotland) Act 1980 (c 52), s 19(4), and came into operation on 2 August 1982*)

ARRANGEMENT OF ORDER
(*This list is not printed in the order*)

1	Citation and commencement	[1326]
2	Procedure	[1327]
3–7		[1328]
8	Register of abandoned property	[1333]

1. (*Citation and commencement*)

(1) . . .

(2) In this Order—
'the Act' means the Tenants' Rights, Etc (Scotland) Act 1980.

2. **Procedure.**

(1) Where property is found in a house to which section 19(1) of the Act applies the landlord shall immediately serve notice on the tenant that the property is available for delivery into his or his agents hands at a place specified in the notice on payment of any sum payable in terms of Article 5(1) of this Order and that if the property is not collected by the tenant from the specified place on or before the date specified in the notice (being a

date not less than 28 days from the date of service of the notice and not earlier than the date on which the landlord repossesses the house) it may be disposed of in accordance with the other provisions of this Order.

(2) The notice provided for in Paragraph (1) of this Article shall be served by posting it to the tenant in a recorded delivery letter addressed to him at his last known address or by leaving the notice for him at that address. [1327]

3.—(1) Where property is respect of which a notice under Article 2 of this Order has been served on the tenant has not been collected by the date specified in the notice the property shall, subject to Paragraph (2) of this Article, be stored by the landlord for a period of 6 months from the date on which the landlord took possession of the dwelling-house and after expiry of the said period the landlord may sell any item remaining in its custody.

(2) Paragraph (1) of this Article shall not apply to any property the value of which would not, in the opinion of the landlord, exceed the amount which the landlord would be entitled to deduct under Article 7 of this Order from the proceeds of any sale of such item. [1328]

4. Where property to which Paragraph (1) of Article 3 does not apply and in respect of which a notice under Article 2 has been served on the tenant has not been collected by the date specified in the notice the landlord may sell or otherwise dispose of it in the manner which in its opinion is most expedient. [1329]

5.—(1) Subject to Paragraph (2) of this Article, where at any time prior to the sale or disposal of property under this Order the tenant, or any other person who appears to the landlord to have a right of ownership or of possession in the property, arranges for delivery to himself of any item the landlord shall relinquish custody of that item upon receipt of a payment equal to the amount of any expense incurred by the landlord in complying with this Order in relation to that item or such lesser amount (including a nil amount) as the landlord may think fit.

(2) Nothing in this Article shall affect the landlord's exercise of its right of hypothec. [1330]

6. Nothing in Articles 2 to 5 of this Order shall prevent the exercise by any person or authority of any power under any enactment relating to public health or public safety. [1331]

7. Where a landlord sells property under Article 3 of this Order it may deduct from the proceeds of sale the amount of any expense incurred by it in complying with this Order in relation to that property and, if there is any remainder after deduction of such amount, the amount of any arrears of rent. [1332]

8. Register of abandoned property.

(1) Landlords shall maintain a register of houses in which property has been found on the exercise of their powers under section 19 of the Act.

(2) A house shall remain on the register until after the expiry of a period of 5 years from the date on which the landlord took possession of the house.

(3) The landlord shall make the register available for inspection by members of the public at all reasonable times. [1333]

NOTES to SI 1982/981

General: The Tenants' Rights, Etc (Scotland) Act 1980 (c 52) has been repealed. References to s 19 of that Act should now be read as references to the Housing (Scotland) Act 1987 (c 26), s 30.

The Housing (Disapplication of Financial Hardship Provision for Repairs Grant) (Scotland) Order 1982

SI 1982/1154

(This order was made by the Secretary of State for Scotland under the Housing (Scotland) Act 1974 (c 45), ss 10A(3) and 49(3), and came into operation on 10 September 1982)

1. *(Citation and commencement)*

2. **Disapplication of provisions of section 10A(3) of the Housing (Scotland) Act 1974.**

    Article 3 of this order applies to applications for repairs grants (under section 10A of the said Act of 1974) approved by local authorities on or after 10th September 1982.

3. The provisions of section 10A(3) of the said Act of 1974 shall not apply to applications where the relevant works are in respect of:—
    - (i) works exclusively to replace in a different material such pipes, tanks, cisterns, taps or other equipment used for a supply of water to a house as are wholly or partly made of lead; and
    - (ii) works which in the opinion of the local authority are of a substantial and structural character.

NOTES to SI 1982/1154

General: The Housing (Scotland) Act 1974 (c 45) has been repealed. References to s 10A(3) of that Act should now be read as references to the Housing (Scotland) Act 1978 (c 26), s 248(3).

The Housing (Percentage of Approved Expense for Improvement Grants) (Disabled Occupants) (Scotland) Order 1982
SI 1982/1809

(This order was made by the Secretary of State for Scotland, under the Housing (Scotland) Act 1974 (c 45), ss 5(1), (1A), and 49(3), and came into operation on 9 December 1982)

1. *(Citation and commencement)* [1337]

2. Percentage of approved expense.

In relation to an improvement grant in respect of the improvement of a house for a disabled occupant where the improvement works consist of or include works needed to meet a requirement arising from the particular disability from which the occupant suffers the percentage prescribed for the purposes of section 5(1) of the Housing (Scotland) Act 1974 is, subject to Article 3 of this order, 75 per cent. [1338]

3. The provisions of Article 2 of this order shall apply to an application for house improvement grant under section 5(1) of the Housing (Scotland) Act 1974, approved by the local authority on or after the date on which this Order comes into operation. [1339]

NOTES to SI 1982/1809

General: The Housing (Scotland) Act 1974 (c 45) has been repealed. The amount of an improvement grant is now governed by the Housing (Scotland) Act 1987 (c 26), s 242.

[1340] SI 1984/514

The Housing (Percentage of Approved Expense for Repairs Grants) (Lead Plumbing Works) (Scotland) Order 1984

SI 1984/514

(This order was made by the Secretary of State for Scotland under the Housing (Scotland) Act 1974 (c 45), ss 10A(4), (5), 5(A), and came into operation on 1 April 1984)

1. *(Citation and commencement)* [1340]

2. Percentage of approved expense.

Subject to article 3 of this order, where an application for a repairs grant relates to works exclusively to replace in a different material such pipes, tanks, cisterns, taps or other equipment used for the supply of water to a house as are wholly or partly made of lead, the percentage prescribed under section 10A(4) of the Housing (Scotland) Act 1974 shall be 75 per cent, instead of 50 per cent. [1341]

3. The provisions of article 2 of this order shall apply to an application for a repairs grant under section 10A(4) of the Housing (Scotland) Act 1974, made to the local authority on or after 1st April 1984. [1342]

NOTES to SI 1984/514

General: The Housing (Scotland) Act 1974 (c 45) has been repealed. On the amount of repairs grants, now see the Housing (Scotland) Act 1987, s 248(4), (5).

SI 1985/297 [1346]

The Housing (Limits of Rateable Value for Improvement Grants and Repairs Grants) (Scotland) Order 1985

SI 1985/297

(This order was made by the Secretary of State for Scotland under the Housing (Scotland) Act 1974 (c 45), ss 3(2)(c), (3A) and 48(2) and came into operation on 1 April 1985)

1. *(Citation and commencement)* [1343]

2. Revocation.

The Housing (Limits of Rateable Value for Improvement Grants) (Scotland) Order 1978 and the Housing (Limits of Rateable Value for Repairs Grants) (Scotland) Order 1978 are hereby revoked. [1344]

3. Limits of rateable value.

In respect of any application made on or after 1st April 1985 for an improvement grant or repairs grant, for a house to be occupied by the owner or by a member of his family after completion of the works, the limit of rateable value beyond which a local authority shall not approve the application shall be:—
 (a) in the case of an improvement grant that set out in Column A or Column B of the Schedule hereto; and
 (b) in the case of a repairs grant that set out in Column A of the Schedule hereto,
in relation to each of the authorities listed in the Schedule. [1345]

Article 3	SCHEDULE

LIMITS OF RATEABLE VALUE

The limit of rateable value in respect of each house before improvement or conversion shall be:—
 (a) where a single house is to be improved, or where a number of houses are to be converted into a lesser number of houses, the appropriate figure in Column A of the Table;
 (b) where a single house is to be converted into two or more houses, the appropriate figure in Column B of the Table.
The limit of rateable value in respect of each house before repair shall be the appropriate figure in Column A of the Table.

TABLE

Local Authority	£ Column A	£ Column B
Islands Councils		
Orkney	585	1,170
Shetland	825	1,650
Western Isles	585	1,170
District Councils		
Berwickshire	1,000	2,000
Ettrick and Lauderdale	850	1,700
Roxburgh	910	1,820
Tweeddale	865	1,730
Clackmannan	805	1,610
Falkirk	890	1,780
Stirling	940	1,880
Annandale and Eskdale	890	1,780
Nithsdale	880	1,760
Stewartry	890	1,780
Wigtown	940	1,880
Dunfermline	950	1,900
Kirkcaldy	940	1,880
North East Fife	925	1,850
City of Aberdeen	1,065	2,130
Banff and Buchan	840	1,680
Gordon	880	1,760
Kincardine and Deeside	870	1,740
Moray	805	1,610
Badenoch and Strathspey	890	1,780
Caithness	675	1,350
Inverness	910	1,820
Lochaber	845	1,690
Nairn	890	1,780
Ross and Cromarty	890	1,780
Skye and Lochalsh	715	1,430
Sutherland	690	1,380
East Lothian	1,040	2,080
City of Edinburgh	1,135	2,270
Midlothian	1,000	2,000
West Lothian	1,015	2,030
Argyll and Bute	875	1,750
Bearsden and Milngavie	1,255	2,510
Clydebank	970	1,940
Clydesdale	995	1,990
Cumbernauld and Kilsyth	990	1,800
Cumnock and Doon Valley	870	1,740
Cunninghame	935	1,870
Dumbarton	1,040	2,080
East Kilbride	1,065	2,130
Eastwood	1,090	2,180
City of Glasgow	940	1,880
Hamilton	1,055	2,110
Inverclyde	1,015	2,030
Kilmarnock and Loudoun	925	1,850

Local Authority	£ Column A	£ Column B
Kyle and Carrick	965	1,930
Monklands	1,040	2,080
Motherwell	1,080	2,160
Renfrew	1,025	2,050
Strathkelvin	1,025	2,050
Angus	940	1,880
City of Dundee	970	1,940
Perth and Kinross	1,090	2,180

[1346]

NOTES to SI 1985/297

General: The Housing (Scotland) Act 1974 (c 45) has been repealed. The power to prescribe limits of rateable values for repairs grants is now contained in the Housing (Scotland) Act 1987 (c 26), s 240(2), (4); however, domestic rates were abolished by the Abolition of Domestic Rates Etc (Scotland) Act 1987 (c 47). Statutory references to rateable values are to be construed in accordance with s 5 of that Act which preserves the use of rateable values for certain purposes. The reference to rateable value will be taken to be a reference to the rateable value which appears in relation to that property in the valuation roll in force immediately before 1 April 1989.

The Protected Tenancies and Part VII Contracts (Rateable Value Limits) (Scotland) Order 1985
SI 1985/314

(This order was made by the Secretary of State for Scotland under the Rent (Scotland) Act 1984, ss 1(2) and 64(2), and came into operation on 1 April 1985)

1. *(Citation and commencement)* [1347]

2. Interpretation.

In this order—
'the Act' means the Rent (Scotland) Act 1984. [1348]

3. Increase in rateable value limits.

In relation to dwellinghouses comprising or forming part of lands and heritages for which a rateable value is first shown on the valuation roll on or after 1st April 1985, the sum of £600 specified in sections 1(1)(a) and 64(1) of the Act shall be increased to £1,600 in each case. **[1349]**

4. Revocation.

The Protected Tenancies and Part VII Contracts (Rateable Value Limits) (Scotland) Order 1985 is hereby revoked. **[1350]**

NOTES to SI 1985/314

General: Domestic rates were abolished by the Abolition of Domestic Rates Etc (Scotland) Act 1987 (c 47). Statutory references to rateable values are to be construed in accordance with s 5 of that Act which preserves the use of rateable values for certain purposes. The reference to rateable value will be taken to be a reference to the rateable value which appears in relation to that property in the valuation roll in force immediately before 1 April 1989.

The Housing Defects (Application to Lenders) (Scotland) Regulations 1986

SI 1986/843

(*These regulations were made by the Secretary of State for Scotland under the Housing Defects Act 1984 (c 50), s 23, and came into operation on 12 June 1986*)

ARRANGEMENT OF REGULATIONS
(*This list is not printed in the Regulations*)

1	Citation and commencement	**[1351]**
2	Application of regulations	**[1352]**
3	Modification of the Act	**[1353]**
4–13		**[1354]**
14	Modification of power of sale	**[1364]**

1. (*Citation and commencement*)

(1) . . .

(2) In these regulations, 'the Act' means the Housing Defects Act 1984 and references to sections and to Schedules (without more) and to the sections of and Schedules to the Act.

(3) In these regulations 'lender' means the creditor and 'borrower' means the debtor under a heritable security constituted over a defective dwelling and the expressions 'heritable security', 'creditor' and 'debtor' shall have the same meanings as in section 9 of the Conveyancing and Feudal Reform (Scotland) Act 1970. **[1351]**

2. Application of regulations.

(1) These regulations apply where—
(a) a borrower who has obtained a loan on the security of a defective dwelling is eligible for assistance under the Act in respect of the dwelling, and
(b) a power of sale has become exercisable by the lender, and
(c) the lender has obtained vacant possession of the defective dwelling.

(2) Where vacant possession of a defective dwelling has already been obtained by a lender on the date on which these regulations come into operation, it shall for the purpose of these regulations be treated as if it was obtained on that date.

(3) Where the lender is also the appropriate authority, these regulations shall apply for the purpose of the acquisition of the defective dwelling by the appropriate authority as they apply where the lender and the appropriate authority are not the same. **[1352]**

3. Modification of the Act.

Where these regulations apply, the Act shall have effect subject to the modifications specified below being modifications to confer on the lender rights corresponding to those conferred by the Act on the borrower and in place of those rights. **[1353]**

4.—(1) In section 2(3)(a) for 'applies' substitute 'applied at the time of the acquisition,'.

(2) At the beginning of section 2(5) for 'No person' substitute 'No lender'. [1354]

5.—(1) At the beginning of section 3(1) for 'Any person' substitute 'Any lender'.

(2) For section 3(3) to (7) substitute—
'(3) If the applicant is a lender, the applicant is entitled to assistance by way of repurchase.'.

(3) In section 3(9) before 'A person' insert 'A lender to' and for 'his' substitute 'the'.

(4) After section 3(10) insert—
'(10A) Where a lender becomes eligible for assistance in respect of a defective dwelling, this Act applies as if anything done (or treated by virtue of subsection (10) as done) by or in relation to the person who was previously so eligible had been done by or in relation to the lender; but if a notice under section 4 (Notice of determination) had been served stating that the applicant was entitled to assistance by way of reinstatement grant then—
(a) if the qualifying work had not been commenced before the lender became eligible for assistance, that notice shall be regarded as not having been served and the authority shall comply again with sections 3 and 4, and
(b) if the qualifying work had been commenced before the lender became eligible for assistance that notice shall continue in force (notwithstanding section 3(3)) but paragraph 5 of Schedule 1 (Repayment of grant for breach of condition) shall apply to the lender only in respect of instalments paid to the lender.'. [1355]

6. Omit section 4(1)(b). [1356]

7. In section 7 for 'person' (wherever that word occurs) substitute 'lender'. [1357]

8.—(1) In section 8 for 'person' and 'owner' (wherever the words occur) substitute 'lender'.

(2) In section 8(1) for paragraph (a) substitute—
'(a) there was, in pursuance of the power of sale, a disposal of the interest of the borrower in a defective dwelling by a lender who immediately before the time of disposal was eligible for assistance in respect of the dwelling,'.

(3) For section 8(8), substitute—
'(8) A lender or the housing authority serving a notice on the district valuer under subsection (6) above shall serve notice in writing of that fact on the other party.'

(4) In section 8, at the end add—
'(11) Any amount paid by the housing authority under this section to a lender shall be treated as money received by the lender arising from the sale.' [1358]

9.—(1) For section 9(1) substitute—
'(1) This section applies where a lender is entitled to assistance by way of repurchase in respect of a defective dwelling and there is a condition in the title to the dwelling whereby, before the lender disposes of the interest, the lender must offer to dispose of it to a public sector authority.'

(2) In section 9(2) and (7) to (11) for 'owner' substitute 'lender'.

(3) For section 9(3) substitute—
'(3) If the public sector authority concerned are not the appropriate authority, then—
(a) so long as the condition mentioned in subsection (1) above applies, the lender is not to be treated for the purposes of section 7 of this Act as entitled to assistance by way of repurchase, and

(b) if the lender disposes of the interest to the public sector authority in pursuance of the power of sale and the interest acquired by that authority on the disposal subsists only in the defective dwelling and any garage, outhouse, garden, yard and pertinents belonging to or usually enjoyed with the dwelling or any part of it, the lender is entitled to be paid by the housing authority the amount (if any) by which 95% of the defect-free value exceeds the consideration for the disposal, and the amount so paid shall be treated as money received by the lender arising from the sale.' **[1359]**

10. In section 10(4)(c) for 'person' substitute 'lender'. **[1360]**

11. In section 11 for 'person' (wherever that word occurs) there shall be substituted 'lender'. **[1361]**

12. In section 26(2) for 'any person' substitute 'a lender'. **[1362]**

13. In Schedule 2, Part I in paragraphs 1(2), 3(5), 3(6) (where occurring for the second time) and 3(8) for 'person' there shall be substituted 'lender'. **[1363]**

14. Modification of power of sale.

(1) Where these regulations apply, the power of sale in question and any enactment relating to the power of sale shall have effect subject to such modifications (if any) as are necessary to enable full effect to be given to these regulations and to the Act as modified by these regulations.

(2) Without prejudice to the foregoing generality—
(a) the exercise by a lender of the rights conferred by these regulations in relation to a defective dwelling shall be deemed to be sufficient compliance with the requirements of section 25 of the Conveyancing and Feudal Reform (Scotland) Act 1970 (Exercise of power of sale), and
(b) section 27 of that Act (Application of proceeds of sale) shall apply for the purposes of the disposal by the lender of the price determined under Schedule 2 for the defective dwelling as it applies for the disposal of the proceeds of sale by a creditor in a heritable security who has effected a sale of the security subjects under that Act. **[1364]**

NOTES to SI 1986/843

Reg 1(2): The Housing Defects Act 1984 (c 50) has been repealed. Assistance for owners of defective housing is now governed by the Housing (Scotland) Act 1987 (c 26), ss 257–303.

Reg 4: For s 2(3)(a) of the 1984 Act see the Housing (Scotland) Act 1987 (c 26), s 259(4). For s 2(5) of the 1984 Act now see the Housing (Scotland) Act 1987 (c 26), s 260.

Reg 5: For ss 3(1), 3(3) to (7) and 3(9) of the 1984 Act now see the Housing (Scotland) Act 1987 (c 26), ss 262, 265–267, 263 respectively. For paragraph 5 of Schedule 1 of the 1984 Act, now see *Ibid*, s 274.

Reg 6: For s 4(1)(b) of the 1984 Act, now see the Housing (Scotland) Act 1987 (c 26), s 264(3).

Reg 7: For s 7 of the 1984 Act now see the Housing (Scotland) Act 1987 (c 26), s 275, Sch 20, Part I.

Reg 8: For s 8 of the 1984 Act, now see the Housing (Scotland) Act 1987 (c 26), ss 278, 279. For s 8(1) of the 1984 Act, now see *Ibid*, s 278(1). For s 8(8) of the 1984 Act, now see *Ibid*, s 279(4).

Reg 9: For s 9(1) to (3) and 9(7) to (11) of the 1984 Act, now see the Housing (Scotland) Act 1987 (c 26), ss 277(1) to (3) and 279(2) to (3) respectively.

Reg 10: For s 10(4)(c) of the 1984 Act, now see the Housing (Scotland) Act 1987 (c 26), s 283(1).

Reg 11: For s 11 of the 1984 Act, now see the Housing (Scotland) Act 1987 (c 26), s 280.

Reg 12: For s 26(2) of the 1984 Act, now see the Housing (Scotland) Act 1987 (c 26), s 276(1).

Reg 13: For Sch 2, paras 1(2), 3(5), (6), and (8) of the 1984 Act, now see the Housing (Scotland) Act (c 26), Sch 20, paras 9, 11(4), (3) and (2) respectively.

SI 1986/2138 [1368]

The Right to Purchase (Application Form) (Scotland) Order 1986

SI 1986/2138

(This order was made by the Secretary of State for Scotland under the Tenants' Rights, Etc (Scotland) Act 1980 (c 52), s 2(1) and came into operation on 7 January 1987)

1. *(Citation and commencement)* [1365]

2. Any tenant under a secure tenancy, within the meaning of Section 10 of the Tenants' Rights, Etc (Scotland) Act 1980, wishing to exercise his right to purchase under section 1 of that Act shall, as required by section 2 of that Act, do so by serving on the landlord a notice in the form specified in the Schedule to this order. [1366]

3. The Right to Purchase (Application Form) (Scotland) Order 1984 is hereby revoked. [1367]

Article 2   SCHEDULE

[HOUSING (SCOTLAND) ACT 1987]

APPLICATION TO PURCHASE

This form is divided into several sections. Section 1 must be completed by sole tenants and Section 2 by joint tenants; the other sections are for use by both sole tenants and joint tenants, although not all of them will need to be completed in every case.

Please write clearly and complete the form in ball point pen or ink. Where a YES or NO answer is required, tick the approprite box.

SECTION 1

TO BE COMPLETED BY SOLE TENANTS ONLY

Address of house:
Telephone no:

Surname:
First names:
Do you have a husband/wife who lives with you?

YES ☐   NO ☐

If you have answered YES to the above question, please ask your husband/wife to sign this declaration:

   I understand that my husband/wife, who is the sole tenant of the house named on this form, is applying to buy the house at the above address, and that my consent to the purchase is necessary. I hereby declare that I consent to the proposed purchase.

Signed:
Date:

Now turn to section 3

SECTION 2

To be Completed by Joint Tenants Only

Address of house:
Telephone no:

All joint tenants should insert their names below and indicate, by ticking the appropriate boxes, whether they wish to be joint purchasers, and whether they have a husband/wife who lives with them. (Details of persons who wish to be joint purchasers but who are *not* joint tenants should be given in section 5.)

1.   Surname:

   First names:

   Are you applying to be a joint purchaser?   YES ☐   NO ☐

   Do you have a husband/wife who lives with you?   YES ☐   NO ☐

2.   Surname:

   First names:

   Are you applying to be a joint purchaser?   YES ☐   NO ☐

   Do you have a husband/wife who lives with you?   YES ☐   NO ☐

3.   Surname:

   First names:

   Are you applying to be a joint purchaser?   YES ☐   NO ☐

   Do you have a husband/wife who lives with you?   YES ☐   NO ☐

4.   Surname:

   First names:

   Are you applying to be a joint purchaser?   YES ☐   NO ☐

   Do you have a husband/wife who lives with you?   YES ☐   NO ☐

If any joint tenant is not applying to be a joint purchaser, he/she should be asked to sign this declaration:

> I understand that my joint tenant(s) is/are applying to buy the house at the above address. I do not wish to become a joint purchaser but I understand that my consent to the purchase is necessary, I hereby declare that I consent to the proposed purchase.

Signed: Signed:
Date: Date:
Signed: Signed:
Date: Date:

If any of the joint tenants listed above, whether or not they wish to be joint purchasers, are married and their husband/wife lives in the house with them but is not also a joint tenant, their husband/wife should be asked to sign this declaration:

I understand that those joint tenants who have indicated above their wish to be joint purchasers are applying to buy the house at the above address and that my consent to the purchase is necessary. I hereby declare that I consent to the proposed purchase.

Signed: Signed:
Date: Date:
Signed: Signed:
Date: Date:

Now turn to section 3

SECTION 3

To be Completed by Sole and Joint Tenants

Please give complete details of your present tenancy and any previous periods of occupation of publicly provided housing. In the case of joint tenants, if the details are the same for all or some of those tenants, they need only be given once. Please also give details of any breaks of *less than 12 months* between periods of tenancy. Once you have given details of 30 years of occupation (or 15 years if you live in a flat) not counting breaks, there is no need to give further details. You should also stop if you reach a break of more than 12 months.

Please now fill in the following sheet(s) using a separate page for each person.

If you have stopped before you have given details of 30 years of occupation (or 15 years if you live in a flat) because you have reached a break of more than 12 months, turn now to *section 4*. Otherwise turn now to *section 5*.

Surname:
First names:

Date residence began (see footnote)	Date residence finished	Name of landlord	Address of house	Status (tenant, husband/wife of tenant, child of tenant)

Note: Please give details of your present tenancy first, and then details of previous tenancies, working backwards.

SECTION 4

To be Completed by Sole and Joint Tenants

IF YOU HAVE HAD A BREAK IN OCCUPATION OF *between 12 and 24 months* turn back to the page which you have filled out in section 3, draw a line across the page, give details of the break and then add details of any earlier periods of occupation and breaks of up to 12 months. If you reach another break of between 12 and 24 months before you have listed 30 years occupation (or 15 years if you live in a flat) simply draw another line across the page and follow these instructions again.

Now turn to section 5

SECTION 5

To be Completed by Sole and Joint Tenants

(a) Do you wish at this stage to include any joint purchaser *other than a joint tenant* in your application?

YES ☐   NO ☐

If your answer is no, turn now to section 6

(b) If so, please name joint purchaser(s)

	Surname	First names
1		
2		
3		
4		

(c) What relation is/are the named joint purchaser(s) to you?

1	
2	
3	
4	

If any of the joint purchasers named above is the husband or wife of the tenant (or of one of the joint tenants), and that joint purchaser's past tenancy or occupation of publicly provided accommodation is longer than that of the tenant (or of any of the joint tenants) that joint purchaser should turn back to section 3 and fill in a new page, not forgetting to look also at section 4.

(d) Is/are the joint purchaser(s) at least 18 years of age?

1	YES ☐	NO ☐
2	YES ☐	NO ☐
3	YES ☐	NO ☐
4	YES ☐	NO ☐

(e) Has each of the named joint purchasers lived with you for the last 6 months as their only or principal home?

1	YES ☐	NO ☐
2	YES ☐	NO ☐
3	YES ☐	NO ☐
4	YES ☐	NO ☐

(f) If your answer to either of the above questions for *any* of the proposed joint purchasers is NO, it may help if you provide additional information. If you wish to provide additional information, please do so below:

(g) Please ask any joint purchasers to sign the declaration below:

I certify that the information given in this form concerning me is to the best of my knowledge correct. I hereby give notice that I wish to be considered as a joint purchaser.

Signed:
Date:
Signed:
Date:
Signed:
Date:
Signed:
Date:

Now turn to section 6

SECTION 6

To be Completed by Sole and Joint Tenants

In deciding the purchase price of your house the Valuer will need to be aware of any improvements which you have made to the house yourself. Please enter details below.

Now turn to section 7

SECTION 7

To be Completed by all Tenants who wish to apply to Purchase (Joint Purchasers who are not Tenants should not Complete this Declaration)

Sole tenants and joint tenants (provided that they have indicated in section 2 that they are applying to be joint purchasers) should complete this declaration:

The information given by me on this form is, to the best of my knowledge, correct. I hereby give notice that I seek to exercise my right under section [61 of the Housing (Scotland) Act 1987] to buy the house of which I am tenant.

Signed:
Date:
Signed:
Date:
Signed:
Date:
Signed:
Date:

NOTES to SI 1986/2138

Reg 2: The Tenants' Rights, Etc (Scotland) Act 1980 (c 52) has been repealed. The references to ss 1, 2 and 10 of that Act should now be read as references to the Housing (Scotland) Act 1987 (c 26), ss 61, 62 and 44 respectively.

Schedule: The references to the Housing (Scotland) Act 1987 (c 26) are substituted by virtue of Schedule 22, para 3 of that Act.

The Right to Purchase (Prescribed Persons) (Scotland) Order 1986

SI 1986/2140

(This order was made by the Secretary of State for Scotland, under the Tenants' Rights, Etc (Scotland) Act 1980 (c 52), s 1(10)(u) and came into operation on 7 January 1987)

1. Citation and commencement.

This order shall be cited as the Right to Purchase (Prescribed Persons) (Scotland) Order 1986 and shall come into operation on 7th January 1987.

2. Prescribed persons.

The persons listed in the Schedule to this order and any predecessor of any of those persons are hereby prescribed under section 1(10)(u) of the Tenants' Rights, Etc (Scotland) Act 1980.

Article 2   SCHEDULE

A Minister of the Crown, other than a Minister specified in paragraph (k), (m), (n), (o), (r) or (t) of section 1(10) of the Tenants' Rights, Etc (Scotland) Act 1980 in relation to a dwelling-house used for the purpose set out in that paragraph.
A Government Department
The Agricultural and Food Research Council
The British Airports Authority
The British Gas Corporation
The British Railways Board
The British Steel Corporation
The British Waterways Board
The Central Electricity Generating Board
The Civil Aviation Authority
The Countryside Commission for Scotland
The Electricity Council
The Highlands and Islands Development Board
The Medical Research Council
The National Bus Company
The National Coal Board
The Natural Environment Research Council
The Nature Conservancy Council
The North of Scotland Hydro Electric Board
The Post Office
The Science and Engineering Research Council
The Scottish Transport Group
The Scottish Sports Council
The South of Scotland Electricity Board
The Sports Council
The Sports Council for Wales

NOTES to SI 1986/2140

This order was made by the Secretary of State for Scotland, under the Tenants' Rights, Etc (Scotland) Act 1980 (c 52), s 1(10)(u) and came into operation on 7 January 1987.

The Tenants' Rights, Etc (Scotland) Act 1980 (c 52) has been repealed. The reference to sections 1(10)(u) of that Act should now be read as a reference to the Housing (Scotland) Act 1987 (c 26), s 61(11)(w).

Schedule: The Tenants' Rights, Etc (Scotland) Act 1980 (c 52) has been repealed. The references to paragraphs (k), (m), (n), (o), (r), and (t) of section 10(1) of that Act should now be read as references to the Housing (Scotland) Act 1987 (c 26), s 61, paras (m), (o), (p), (q), (t) and (v) respectively.

The Local Authorities (Recognised Bodies for Heritable Securities Indemnities) (Scotland) Order 1987

SI 1987/1388

(This order was made by the Secretary of State for Scotland under the Tenants' Rights, Etc (Scotland) Act 1980 (c 52), s 31(5A), and came into force on 13 August 1987)

1. *(Citation and commencement)* [1372]

2. The bodies set out in Schedule 1 to this Order are hereby designated for the purposes of section 31 of the Tenants' Rights, Etc (Scotland) Act 1980. [1373]

3. The classes or descriptions of bodies set out in Schedule 2 to this Order are hereby designated for the purposes of section 31 of the Tenants' Rights, Etc (Scotland) Act 1980. [1374]

Article 2   SCHEDULE 1

BODIES DESIGNATED FOR THE PURPOSES OF SECTION 31 OF THE TENANTS' RIGHTS, ETC (SCOTLAND) ACT 1980

1. The Bank of England.
2. The Post Office. [1375]

Article 3   SCHEDULE 2

CLASSES OR DESCRIPTIONS OF BODIES DESIGNATED FOR THE PURPOSES OF SECTION 31 OF THE TENANTS' RIGHTS, ETC (SCOTLAND) ACT 1980

1. Insurance companies to which Part II of the Insurance Companies Act 1982 applies.
2. Recognised banks and licensed institutions within the meaning of the Banking Act 1979 or authorised institutions under the Banking Act 1987.
3. Friendly societies and branches thereof which are registered within the meaning of the Friendly Societies Act 1974. [1376]

NOTES to SI 1987/1388

Regs 2, 3: The Tenants' Rights, Etc (Scotland) Act 1980 (c 52) has been repealed. References to s 31 of that Act should now be read as references to the Housing (Scotland) Act 1987 (c 26), s 229. Designations of bodies or classes or descriptions of bodies are now made under s 229(6).

The Housing Corporation (Recognised Bodies for Heritable Securities Indemnities) (Scotland) Order 1987

SI 1987/1389

(This order was made by the Secretary of State for Scotland under the Housing Associations Act 1985 (c 69), s 86(6), and came into force on 13 August 1987)

1. *(Citation and commencement)*

2. The bodies set out in Schedule 1 to this Order are hereby designated for the purposes of section 86 of the Housing Associations Act 1985.

3. The classes or descriptions of bodies set out in Schedule 2 to this Order are hereby designated for the purposes of section 86 of the Housing Associations Act 1985.

Article 2   SCHEDULE 1

BODIES DESIGNATED FOR THE PURPOSES OF SECTION 86 OF THE HOUSING ASSOCIATIONS ACT 1985

1. The Bank of England.
2. The Post Office.

Article 3   SCHEDULE 2

CLASSES OR DESCRIPTIONS OF BODIES DESIGNATED FOR THE PURPOSES OF SECTION 86 OF THE HOUSING ASSOCIATIONS ACT 1985

1. Insurance companies to which Part II of the Insurance Companies Act 1982 applies.
2. Recognised banks and licensed institutions within the meaning of the Banking Act 1979 or authorised institutions under the Banking Act 1987.
3. Friendly societies and branches thereof which are registered within the meaning of the Friendly Societies Act 1974.

The Homes Insulation Grants Order 1987

SI 1987/2185

(*This order was made as respects Scotland by the Secretary of State for Scotland under the Housing (Scotland) Act 1987 (c 26), s 252(3), (5) and came into force on 1 February 1988*)

1. (*Citation and commencement*) **[1382]**

2. Prescribed percentage and amount

For the purposes of the Homes Insulation Scheme 1987, there is hereby prescribed:
(a) as the percentage of the cost of the works qualifying for grant 90 per cent.; and
(b) (superceded by SI 1988/1239, para [1426] below) **[1383]**

NOTES to SI 1987/2185
The Homes Insulation Scheme 1987 is laid before Parliament and published in a circular from the Scottish Development Department (SDD Circular 25/87 as amended by Circulars Nos 15/1988 and 18/1989).

The Housing (Improvement and Repairs Grants) (Approved Expenses Maxima) (Scotland) Order 1987

SI 1987/2269

(*This order was made by the Secretary of State for Scotland under the Housing (Scotland) Act 1987 (c 26), ss 242(1), (3), (9) and (10), 244(8), 248(4) and (10), and 249(3) and (8), and came into force on 5 February 1988*)

1. (*Citation and commencement*)

(1) . . .

(2) In this Order—
'the Act' means the Housing (Scotland) Act 1987; and
'housing association' means a registered housing association within the meaning of the Housing Associations Act 1985. **[1385]**

2. Application

The provisions of this Order shall apply in relation to any application for an improvement grant or repairs grant, or for a grant for a fire escape under section 249 of the Act, which is approved by the local authority on or after the date of coming into force of this Order. **[1386]**

3. Maximum amounts of approved expenses

In each of the provisions of the Act specified in column 1 of the Schedule to this Order, there are prescribed, in place of the amounts specified opposite thereto in column 2 thereof, the amounts specified in column 3 in respect of the cases described in column 4 of that Schedule. **[1387]**

4. List of standard amenities and maximum of approved expenses

Schedule 18 to the Act (standard amenities) is hereby varied by substituting for Part I thereof the following:— **[1388]**

PART I
LIST OF AMENITIES AND MAXIMUM ELIGIBLE AMOUNTS

Description of amenity	Maximum eligible amount
A fixed bath or shower	£450
A hot and cold water supply at a fixed bath or shower	£570
A wash-hand basin	£170
A hot and cold water supply at a wash-hand basin	£305
A sink	£450
A hot and cold water supply at a sink	£385
A water closet	£680

5. Revocations

The Housing (Standard Amenities Approved Expense) (Scotland) Order 1983 and the Housing (Improvement and Repair Grants) (Approved Expenses Maxima) (Scotland) Regulations 1983 are hereby revoked. **[1389]**

Article 3

SCHEDULE

MAXIMUM AMOUNTS OF APPROVED EXPENSES

Column 1 Provisions of Act	Column 2 Existing amount	Column 3 New amounts	Column 4 Cases applicable
Section 242(1) (Maximum amount of approved expenses for the purposes of improvement grants in respect of each house to which the application relates)	£10,200	£12,600 £17,100 £19,700	(i) All cases other than cases (ii) and (iii) (ii) Rehabilitation of pre-1914 tenements in housing action areas other than those to which case (iii) applies (iii) Rehabilitation of pre-1914 tenements in housing action areas carried out by housing associations
Section 242(3)(a)(i) (Maximum amount of approved expenses for works of improvement and repair where the application for improvement grant relates to the provision of standard amenities and the house is likely to be available for use for a period of at least 10 years)	£ 3,000	£ 3,450	All cases

Column 1 *Provisions of Act*	Column 2 *Existing amount*	Column 3 *New amounts*	Column 4 *Cases applicable*
Section 242(3)(a)(ii) (Maximum amount of approved expenses for each standard amenity provided in any house, where the house is likely to be available for use for a period of less than 10 years)	£ 300	£ 345	All cases
Section 242(3)(a)(ii) (Maximum aggregate amount of approved expenses for standard amenities in respect of any house to which an application for an improvement grant relates, where the house is likely to be available for use for a period of less than 10 years)	£ 1,200	£ 1,380	All cases
Section 248(4) (Maximum amount of approved expenses for the purposes of repairs grants in respect of each house to which the application relates)	£ 4,800	£ 5,500	All cases
Section 249(3)(a) (Maximum amount of approved expenses for the purposes of grants for a fire escape for certain works)	£ 8,100	£ 9,315	All cases
Section 249(3)(b) (Maximum amount of approved expenses for the purposes of grants for a fire escape for certain works)	£ 3,000	£ 3,340	All cases

[TEXT CONTINUES ON PAGE 705]

SI 1988/395 [1395]

The Registered Housing Associations (Accounting Requirements) Order 1988
SI 1988/395

(This order was made, as respects Scotland, by the Secretary of State for Scotland, under the Housing Associations Act 1985 (c 69), s 24(1), (2), and (5) and came into force on 1 April 1988)

ARRANGEMENT OF ARTICLES
(This list is not printed in the order)

1	Citation, commencement and revocation	[1395]
2	Interpretation	[1396]
3	Application	[1397]
4	General accounting requirements	[1398]
5	Balance sheet and notes to the accounts	[1399]
6	Income and expenditure account	[1400]
7	Preparation of statement of source and application of funds	[1401]
8	Preparation of additional financial statements	[1402]
9	Method of distinguishing housing activities in the accounts	[1403]
10	Constitution of Grant Redemption Fund	[1404]
Schedule 1	Balance sheet and notes to the accounts	[1405–1419]
Schedule 2	Income and Expenditure account of an association which is not a co-ownership society	[1420]
Schedule 3	Income and Expenditure account of a co-ownership society	[1421]
Schedule 4	Property revenue account of an association which is not a co-ownership society	[1422]
Schedule 5	Statement of housing administration costs of an association which is not a co-ownership society	[1423]
Schedule 6	Housing cost and finance statement of a co-ownership society	[1424]
Schedule 7	Modified accounting requirements for application to small associations in accordance with article 4(2)	[1425]

1. (*Citation, commencement and revocation*)

2. **Interpretation**

In this Order, unless the context otherwise requires—

'the 1965 Act' means the Industrial and Provident Societies Act 1965;

'the 1968 Act' means the Friendly and Industrial and Provident Societies Act 1968;

'the 1985 Act' means the Housing Associations Act 1985;

'accounts' means the balance sheet, the income and expenditure account, the statement of source and application of funds and additional financial statements required by this Order, and notes to the accounts;

'almshouse' means a corporation or body of persons which is a charity and which is prevented by its rules or constituent instrument from granting tenancies of dwellings occupied for the purposes of the charity;

'association' means a registered housing association within the meaning of the 1985 Act;

'1965 Act society' means an association which is registered under the 1965 Act;

'balance sheet' means the balance sheet required for the purposes of section 39(1) of the 1965 Act or, as the case may be, paragraph 2(1) of Schedule 3 to the 1985 Act;

'balance sheet date' means the date on which the period of account ends;

'co-ownership society' means a 1965 Act society in the case of which—
  (i) the rules of the society restrict membership to persons who are tenants or prospective tenants of the association and preclude the granting or assignment (or, in Scotland, assignation) of tenancies to persons other than members, and
  (ii) each tenant (or his personal representatives) will, under the terms of the tenancy agreement or of the agreement under which he became a member of the society, be entitled, on his ceasing to be a member and subject to any conditions stated in either agreement, to a sum calculated by reference directly or indirectly to the value of his housing accommodation;

'grant for rent phasing' means as much of the housing association grant for a project as does not exceed the amount, taken into account in the calculation of that grant, which relates to the inability of the association to recover the full amount of the fair rent registered under Part VI of the Rent Act 1977 or, in Scotland, Part VI of the Rent (Scotland) Act 1984 by reason of the provisions thereof;

'housing cost and finance statement' means the statement required by article 8(c) of this Order;

'housing land' means land and buildings held by an association for the purpose of providing housing accommodation (including accommodation to be provided by disposal on sale or on lease);

'income and expenditure account' means the revenue account required for the purposes of section 3(2) of the 1968 Act or, as the case may be, paragraph 2(1) of Schedule 3 to the 1985 Act;

'large association' means, in relation to a period of account, an association which on the day when that period begins, is providing more than 250 units of accommodation;

'long lease' means a lease the unexpired term of which at the balance sheet date is not less than 50 years and, in Scotland, includes a lease which is the subject of a decree under Section 9(4) of the Land Tenure Reform (Scotland) Act 1974;

'managing body' means—
  (a) in relation to a 1965 Act society, the committe of management or other directing body of the society;
  (b) in relation to a charity which is a company within the meaning of the Companies Act 1985, the board of directors of the company;
  (c) in relation to any other charity, the trustees of the charity;

'notes to the accounts' means notes to the balance sheet, the income and expenditure account, the statement of source and application of funds and the additional financial statements required by this Order;

SI 1988/395 [1399]

'period of account' means the period to which the income and expenditure account relates;
'property equity account' means an account showing the extent to which the association's capital expenditure on its property has been financed from its own resources;
'property revenue account' means the account required by article 8(a) of this Order;
'public authority' means any body of persons authorised by or under any Act to carry on a railway, dock, water or other public undertaking;
'rent', in relation to housing accommodation, includes any sum payable for or in consideration of the use or occupation of that accommodation;
'small association' means, in relation to a period of account, an association which, on the day when that period begins, is providing 250 or less units of accommodation;
'unit of accommodation' means, in the case of a hostel, the accommodation provided for one individual, and in any other case, a dwelling; and
'vacant accommodation' means housing accommodation available for occupation which has been vacant at any time during the period of account. [1396]

3. Application

This Order applies in relation to the accounts of every association in respect of any period of account commencing on or after the date when this Order comes into force; and in respect of any earlier period of account, the Orders revoked by this Order shall apply as if those Orders had not been revoked. [1397]

4. General accounting requirements

(1) The accounts of every large association and every co-ownership sociey shall comply—
(a) if the association is not an almshouse, with the requirements contained in this Order except Schedule 7 hereto;
(b) if the association is an almshouse, with the requirements contained in this Order except articles 6, 7 and 8 and Schedules 2 to 7 hereto.

(2) The accounts of every small association which is not a co-ownership society shall comply either with the requirements specified in paragraph (1)(a) or (b) of this article (as appropriate) or with those requirements amended by Schedule 7 to this Order.

(3) Nothing in this Order shall prejudice or affect the duties imposed by section 3(1) of the 1968 Act or, as the case may be, paragraph 2 of Schedule 3 to the 1985 Act insofar as they require a true and fair view to be given of the state of affairs of an association and of its income and expenditure; and accordingly where it is necessary to depart from the requirements of this Order so as to give such a true and fair view—
(a) nothing in this Order shall prevent such a departure from those requirements, but
(b) the fact of any such departure, the reasons for it and its effect shall be recorded in the notes to the accounts of the association.

(4) Nothing in this Order shall prevent the accounts of an association from giving more information than is required by this Order.

(5) Save for the information required to be shown in accordance with Part I of Schedule 1 to this Order, paragraph 12 of Part II of Schedule 1 to this Order and paragraph 14(f) to (i) of Part III of Schedule 1 to this Order, amounts which in the particular context of any provision of this Order are not material may be disregarded for the purposes of that provision.

(6) Any requirement in this Order to prepare information in a specified form shall be satisfied if it is prepared in a form substantially to the like effect. [1398]

5. Balance sheet and notes to the accounts

(1) The information referred to in Part I of Schedule 1 to this Order shall be shown, in the manner thereby required, in the balance sheet.

(2) The information referred to in Part II of Schedule 1 to this Order shall be shown, in the manner thereby required, in the balance sheet or in notes to the accounts.

(3) The information referred to in Part III of Schedule 1 to this Order shall be shown, in the manner thereby required, in notes to the accounts. **[1399]**

6. Income and expenditure account

The income and expenditure account of an association—
(a) which is not a co-ownership society, shall be in the form set out in Schedule 2 to this Order;
(b) which is a co-ownership society, shall be in the form set out in Schedule 3 to this Order. **[1400]**

7. Preparation of statement of source and application of funds

An association shall prepare a statement of source and application of funds which shall show the disposition during the period of account and the previous period of account of all funds received or receivable by the association in each period, and the sources thereof. **[1401]**

8. Preparation of additional financial statements

In addition to the balance sheet, income and expenditure account, statement of source and application of funds, notes to the accounts and any other accounts which it is required to prepare apart from this Order, an association shall prepare the following additional financial statements—
(a) unless it is a co-ownership society, a property revenue account in the form set out in schedule 4 to this Order;
(b) unless it is a co-ownership society, a statement of housing administration costs in the form set out in Schedule 5 to this Order; and
(c) if it is a co-ownership society, a statement showing the cost of the housing accommodation of the society and the finance thereof ('the housing cost and finance statement') in the form set out in Schedule 6 to this Order. **[1402]**

9. Method of distinguishing housing activities in the accounts

(1) Where an association undertakes any activities which are not housing activities the method by which that association shall distinguish in its accounts between its housing activities and other activities shall be as set out in paragraph (2) of this article.

(2) The method shall be—
(a) to identify those items which relate solely to housing activities; and
(b) to apportion those items which relate to housing and other activities. **[1403]**

10. Constitution of the Grant Redemption Fund

(1) The Grant Redemption Fund of an association shall be constituted and shown in the accounts according to the method set out in this article, and in this article 'Fund' means Grant Redemption Fund.

(2) The surpluses calculated in the manner determined by the Secretary of State under section 53(3) of the 1985 Act shall be shown as such in the property revenue account or, in the case of a co-ownership society or almshouse, in the income and expenditure account of the association.

(3) The Fund shall be shown in the balance sheet, and the sums shown under paragraph (2) of this article shall be transferred to that Fund.

(4) Where sums stand in the Fund in respect of previous periods, they shall be accumulated with any sums transferred to the Fund in respect of the period of account. **[1404]**

SI 1988/395 [1412]

Article 5   SCHEDULE 1

BALANCE SHEET AND NOTES TO THE ACCOUNTS

PART I
INFORMATION TO BE SHOWN IN THE BALANCE SHEET

1. All amounts shown in the balance sheet for the balance sheet date shall be accompanied by the corresponding amounts for the preceding balance sheet date (if any). [1405]

2. The various items shown in the balance sheet shall be sufficiently particularised to disclose their nature and the distinction where applicable between different activities of the association. [1406]

3. Housing land shall be distinguished from other assets. [1407]

4.—(1) Fixed assets shall be entered in the balance sheet at their net book value, calculated in accordance with this paragraph.

(2) The net book value of the fixed assets which comprise housing land of an association which is not a co-ownership society shall be accompanied in the balance sheet by the elements in that calculation.

(3) The net book value of any fixed asset other than housing land is the difference between the cost of that asset and the amount provided for depreciation thereof.

(4) The net book value of any housing land belonging to a co-ownership society shall be calculated in accordance with the housing cost and finance statement of that society.

(5) The net book value of any other housing land shall be calculated according to the difference between its cost and the sum of—
(a) the total amount provided for depreciation;
(b) all housing association grant received in respect thereof; and
(c) the total amount transferred to the property equity account (if any) in respect of that land.

(6) The cost to be entered under this paragraph for any asset is the cost of its acquisition and the cost of any works carried out thereupon. [1408]

5. There shall be itemised the aggregate amount (where applicable) for each of the following—
(a) reserves;
(b) provision for future cyclical repairs and maintenance to housing accommodation;
(c) any other provision (not being in respect of depreciation of assets or bad debts);
(d) the Grant Redemption Fund; and
(e) investments. [1409]

6. The balance sheet shall distinguish between loans to the association which—
(a) were incurred for the purposes of the acquisition of, or works upon, housing land; or
(b) were incurred for other purposes. [1410]

7. The balance sheet shall show the amount included with current assets in respect of revenue deficit grant and hostel deficit grant receivable. [1411]

PART II
INFORMATION TO BE SHOWN IN THE BALANCE SHEET OR IN NOTES TO THE ACCOUNTS

8.—(1) Where during the period of account any of the following events have occurred—

(a) fixed assets have been acquired or disposed of;
(b) amounts provided for depreciation have been increased or adjusted;
(c) housing association grant has been received in relation to fixed assets; or
(d) amounts have been transferred to or from the property equity account (if any) of the association,

the resulting variations in the cost, the total amount provided for depreciation, the total housing association grant received, the balance on the property equity account, and the net book value of or in relation to the fixed assets of the association shall be stated in accordance with this paragraph.

(2) The variations referred to above shall be set out in sufficient detail to show their nature and cause, together with the relevant opening and closing amounts.

(3) Where the amount of the reserves or the provisions for the balance sheet date differs from the corresponding amount for the previous balance sheet date, or where amounts have been transferred to or from the reserves or the provisions during the period of account the following shall be stated—
(a) the amounts transferred to or from the reserves or the provisions as the case may require;
(b) the source of all amounts transferred to the reserves or, as the case may be, provisions; and
(c) in the case of a transfer occasioned otherwise than by applying a provision to the purpose for which it was established, how the amounts transferred have been applied. **[1412]**

9. Housing land belonging to the association shall be itemised according to the amounts attributable to—
(a) land held by it under a long lease;
(b) land held by it under other leases;
(c) all other land held by it. **[1413]**

10. The method used to arrive at the provision for future cyclical repairs and maintenance to housing accommodation shall be stated. **[1414]**

11.—(1) There shall be itemised the total amounts of all loans advanced to the association by each of the following—
(a) the Public Works Loan Commissioners;
(b) local authorities;
(c) the Housing Corporation;
(d) building societies (within the meaning of the Building Societies Act 1986) and banks;
(e) present or former members of the association; and
(f) any other persons.

(2) In relation to each loan referred to in this paragraph the names of the guarantors (if any) shall be stated.

(3) In relation to secured loans, there shall be itemised the total amounts of—
(a) all loans secured by a charge on the assets of the association;
(b) all loans secured by a charge on the assets of other persons, together with the names of such persons. **[1415]**

12.—(1) Where a 1965 Act society has made a loan to a member of its managing body or to an officer of the society, there shall be stated—
(a) the date on which the loan was made;
(b) the name of the borrower;
(c) whether the loan, if made to an officer, was made under his contract of employment with the association (if any);
(d) the total amount outstanding in respect of the loan; and

(e) the terms; including the rate of interest, on which the loan is, or purports to be, repayable.

(2) Where a 1965 Act society has made a loan to an employee other than an officer of the society, there shall be stated—
(a) the aggregate number of loans to such employees;
(b) the aggregate amount of such loans outstanding;
(c) the purposes of the loans; and
(d) the terms, including the rates of interest, on which the loans are, or purport to be, repayable. [1416]

13. The following items shall be stated where applicable, namely—
(a) the amount included with current assets in respect of arrears of rent, together with the amount deducted therefrom for bad or doubtful debts;
(b) so much of any grant for rent phasing received as is not shown in the property revenue account (if any);
(c) particulars of any charge on the assets of the association to secure the liabilities of another person;
(d) the basis on which the amount set aside for tax is calculated;
(e) the total amount or estimated amount of any material capital expenditure not provided for, distinguishing the amount contracted for and the amount not contracted for but decided upon by the association;
(f) the means by which and the persons by whom the expenditure referred to in the foregoing sub-paragraph is intended to be financed;
(g) the general nature and the total estimated amount of any other material contingent liabilities not provided for. [1417]

PART III

INFORMATION TO BE SHOWN IN NOTES TO THE ACCOUNTS

14. There shall be stated—
(a) the average number of employees of the association, as ascertained from the average number of persons employed in each week of the period of account;
(b) the total remuneration of the employees of the association in the period of account;
(c) the total of the social security costs incurred by the association on behalf of such employees;
(d) the total of other pension costs so incurred;
(e) the total remuneration, including expenses, of the auditors of the association;
(f) any payments by way of fees or other remuneration or by way of expenses to a member of the association, being neither a member of the managing body nor an officer nor an employee thereof;
(g) any payments by way of fees or other remuneration or by way of expenses to a member of the managing body, being neither an officer nor an employee of the association;
(h) any payments by way of fees or other remuneration or by way of expenses to an officer of the association, not being an employee;
(i) any other payments or benefits granted, to the persons referred to in section 15(1)(a) to (d) of the 1985 Act. [1418]

15. Any material amount withdrawn from a provision otherwise than for the purpose for which that provision was established shall be stated. [1419]

Article 6(a)   SCHEDULE 2

INCOME AND EXPENDITURE ACCOUNT OF AN ASSOCIATION WHICH IS NOT A CO-OWNERSHIP SOCIETY

INCOME AND EXPENDITURE ACCOUNT OF (NAME OF ASSOCIATION) FOR THE PERIOD ENDED

	£	£	*Preceding period* £	£

Property revenue account summary
    Total income
    less
    Expenditure before transfer to Grant Redemption Fund
    Transfer to Grant Redemption Fund

Surplus/(deficit) for the period

Development administration
    Grant receivable for acquisition and development (Note 1)
    Grant receivable for projects where completion has become impossible
    less
    Management expenses
    Abortive development costs (Note 2)

Surplus/(deficit) for the period

Fees for architects' and surveyors' services (Note 3)
    Fees receivable
    less
    Management expenses

Surplus/(deficit) for the period

Managed associations (Note 4)
    Fees and recoveries
    less
    Management expenses

Surplus/(deficit) for the period

Sales of housing accommodation (Note 5)
    Proceeds of sale
    less
    Net book value of accommodation sold
    representing—
        Loan debt repayable
        Housing association grant repayable to the Secretary of State
        Other
    Management expenses

Surplus/(deficit) for the period

SI 1988/395 [1420]

| | £ | £ | £ | £ |

Housing accommodation held for disposal (Note 6)
    Proceeds of sales
    Housing association grant receivable
    (other than grant for acquisition and
    development)
    (Note 1)
    Grant receivable for acquisition and
    development
    less
    Management expenses
    Cost of sales

Surplus/(deficit) for the period

Other income and expenditure (housing activities)
    Income
    Gross investment income
    Donations
    Other
    less Expenditure
    Interest not attributable to housing
    accommodation
    Interest on Grant Redemption Fund
    Other—specify

Surplus/(deficit) for the period

Other income and expenditure (non-housing activities)
    Income
    less
    Expenditure

Surplus/(deficit) for the period

Total surplus/(deficit) for the period before taxation and deficit grant

Taxation
less
Grant receivable from the Secretary of State under section 62 of the 1985 Act

add
Revenue deficit grant receivable
Hostel deficit grant receivable

Total surplus/(deficit) for the period after taxation and deficit grants

Surplus/(deficit) at beginning of period

Prior period adjustments

Transfers to/from reserves

Surplus/(deficit) at end of period [1420]

Notes

1. *Grant receivable for acquisition and development* means so much of the housing association grant payable as relates to the administrative cost of acquiring and developing housing accommodation.

2. *Abortive development costs* means costs incurred on projects abandoned prior to completion.

3. *Fees for architects' and surveyors' services* means fees payable by the association in respect of the services of architects and surveyors employed by the association.

4. *Managed associations* means associations whose affairs are managed by the association to which the account relates in consideration of a fee.

5. *Sales of housing accommodation* includes leases granted in consideration of a premium.

6. *Houses held for disposal* means houses disposed of by the association after it has exercised the powers referred to in section 4(3)(c), (d) and, in Scotland, (h) of the 1985 Act.

Article 6(b)   SCHEDULE 3

INCOME AND EXPENDITURE ACCOUNT OF A CO-OWNERSHIP SOCIETY

INCOME AND EXPENDITURE ACCOUNT OF (NAME OF ASSOCIATION) FOR THE PERIOD ENDED

	£	£	Preceding period £	£

Income
Rents
less Losses arising from vacant
accommodation and bad debts

Interest and dividends receivable
Other

Total income
less Expenditure
    Expenses of management
    Repairs and maintenance—
        Current repairs and maintenance
        (Note 1)
        Cyclical repairs and maintenance
        (including provision for future repairs
        and maintenance) (Note 2)
    Service costs
    Interest payable on loans by Housing
    Corporation
    Interest payable on loans by a building
    society
    Other interest payable
    Depreciation
        (a)   equal to repayment of loan
              principal
        (b)   other

less transfer to Grant Redemption Fund

SI 1988/395 [1421]

	£	£	£	£

Gross surplus/(deficit) for the period before taxation
less Taxation
Surplus/(deficit) for the period after taxation

Surplus/(deficit) at beginning of period

Prior period adjustments

Transfers to/from reserves

Surplus/(deficit) at end of period [1421]

Notes

1. *Current repairs and maintenance* means works of repair or maintenance undertaken from time to time as the occasion requires.

2. *Cyclical repairs and maintenance* means works of repair or maintenance undertaken at intervals in accordance with a programme of works.

Article 8(a)

SCHEDULE 4

PROPERTY REVENUE ACCOUNT OF AN ASSOCIATION WHICH IS NOT A CO-OWNERSHIP SOCIETY

PROPERTY REVENUE ACCOUNT OF (NAME OF ASSOCIATION) FOR THE PERIOD ENDED

	Housing accommo-dation (excluding hostels and shared ownership schemes) (Note 3)	Hostels	Shared ownership schemes (Note 3)	Total	Preceding period
	£	£	£	£	£

INCOME
Rents (excluding service charges) receivable
Service charges receivable
less Rates (including domestic water rates) recoverable from tenants
    Losses arising from vacant accommodation and bad debts
Payments from central and local government
Grant for rent phasing
Other

Total income

EXPENDITURE
Management expenses
Repairs and maintenance—
    Current repairs and maintenance (Note 1)
    Cyclical repairs and maintenance (including provision for future repairs and maintenance) (Note 2)

Service costs
Interest (attributable to housing accommodation) payable on loans from—
  (a) the Public Works Loan Commissioners, local authorities and the Housing Corporation;
  (b) present or past members of the association;
  (c) a bank;
  (d) other persons
Depreciation—
  (a) equal to repayment of loan principal
  (b) other
Other

Total expenditure

Surplus/(deficit) for the period before transfer to Grant Redemption Fund
Transfer to Grant Redemption Fund

Surplus/(deficit) for the period transferred to general income and expenditure account

Notes

1. *Current repairs and maintenance* means works of repair or maintenance undertaken from time to time as the occasion requires.
2. *Cyclical repairs and maintenance* means works of repair or maintenance undertaken at intervals in accordance with a programme of works.
3. *Shared ownership schemes* means housing accommodation the subject of a shared ownership lease or, in Scotland, a shared ownership agreement.

[1422]

Article 8(b)

SCHEDULE 5

STATEMENT OF HOUSING ADMINISTRATION COSTS OF AN ASSOCIATION WHICH IS NOT A CO-OWNERSHIP SOCIETY

Notes

1. *Management costs* means management expenses taken from the property revenue account and *maintenance costs* means the repairs and maintenance costs from the same account.

2. *Maintenance allowances* and *management allowances* are the allowances determined by the Secretary of State for the purposes of calculating expenditure under sections 54(3) and 55(3) of the 1985 Act.

3. *Averages* in Part A are calculated by dividing the total by—
   (i) for Table 1, the number of units of accommodation occupied or available for occupation excluding any unit occupied by a warden or caretaker;
   (ii) for Table 2, the number of such units so occupied or available but including any unit occupied by a warden or caretaker, where the number of units is the arithmetical average of those at the beginning and end of the period of account.

PART A—Housing accommodation (excluding hostels)

	Total £	Average per unit £
Table 1 Management		
Management costs		
Maximum management allowances		
Cost over/(under) maximum allowances		

	Total £
Table 3 Total maintenance	
Current maintenance costs	
Cyclical maintenance costs	
Total maintenance costs	

Table 1 Management
Management costs
Maximum management allowances

Cost over/(under) maximum allowances

Table 2 Current maintenance
Current maintenance costs
Maximum current maintenance allowances

Cost over/(under) maximum allowances

Table 2 Current maintenance
Current maintenance costs
Maximum current maintenance allowances
Maximum cyclical maintenance allowances

Total maximum maintenance allowances

Total costs over/(under) total maximum allowances

PART B—Hostels

Total
£

Table 1 Management
Management costs
Maximum management allowances

Cost over/(under) maximum allowances

Table 2 Current maintenance
Current maintenance costs
Maximum current maintenance allowances

Cost over/(under) maximum allowances

Table 3 Total maintenance
Current maintenance costs
Cyclical maintenance costs

Total maintenance costs

Maximum current maintenance allowances
Maximum cyclical maintenance allowances

Total maximum maintenance allowances

Total costs over/(under) total maximum allowances

Total
£

Article 8(c)   SCHEDULE 6

HOUSING COST AND FINANCE STATEMENT OF A CO-OWNERSHIP SOCIETY

PART A—COST OF HOUSING LAND AND ACCOMMODATION FOR THE PERIOD ENDED

	£	*Preceding period* £
COST		
At beginning of period		
Additions during period		
Sales during period (Note 1)	( )	( )
At end of period		
HOUSING ASSOCIATION GRANT		
At beginning of period		
Additions during period		
Repayments made to the Secretary of State	( )	( )
At end of period		
REVALUATION ON RE-LETTINGS (Note 2)		
At beginning of period		
Movement during period attributable to re-lettings		
Movement during period attributable to sales (Note 1)	( )	( )
At end of period		
DEPRECIATION		
At beginning of period		
Charge during period		
Attributable to sales (Note 1)	( )	( )
At end of period		
NET BOOK VALUE OF LAND AND HOUSING ACCOMMODATION AT END OF PERIOD		
CAPITALISED UNPAID INTEREST ON LOANS TO THE ASSOCIATION		
At beginning of period		
Capitalised during period		
At end of period		

PART B—FINANCE OF HOUSING ACCOMMODATION FOR THE PERIOD ENDED

	£	Preceding period £
LOANS AND ACCRUED INTEREST ON LOANS BY THE HOUSING CORPORATION		
At beginning of period		
Advanced during period		
Interest accrued during period		
Interest accrued and capitalised during period		
Repaid during period	( )	( )
At end of period		
LOANS AND ACCRUED INTEREST ON LOANS BY A BUILDING SOCIETY		
At beginning of period		
Advanced during period		
Interest accrued during period		
Interest accrued and capitalised during period		
Repaid during period	( )	( )
At end of period		
REVALUATION RESERVE		
At beginning of period		
Addition to reserve on re-lettings during period		
Amount distributed to past members during period	( )	( )
Transfer from general reserve during period		
Reduction attributable to sales (Note 1)	( )	( )
At end of period		

Notes

1. *Sales*, in relation to housing accommodation, includes leases granted in consideration of a premium.

2. *Revaluation on re-lettings* means the valuation made when vacant housing accommodation is re-let.

Article 4(2)　　　　　　　　SCHEDULE 7

MODIFIED ACCOUNTING REQUIREMENTS FOR APPLICATION TO SMALL ASSOCIATIONS IN ACCORDANCE WITH ARTICLE 4(2)

1. In article 2 (interpretation), there shall be substituted for the definition of 'accounts' and 'notes to the accounts' the following—

"accounts" means the balance sheet, income and expenditure account, and notes to the accounts;

"notes to the accounts" means notes to the balance sheet, income and expenditure account and the additional financial statement required by this Order;'.

2. For article 6 (income and expenditure account), there shall be substituted—

Income and expenditure account.

6.—(1) The income and expenditure account shall show the following information—
   (a) as income—
      (i) rents (excluding service charges) receivable after deducting rates (including domestic water rates) recoverable from tenants and losses arising from vacant accommodation and bad debts;
      (ii) service charges receivable;
      (iii) grants and subsidies receivable from the Secretary of State or a public authority (distinguishing between payments for acquisition and development of housing accommodation and those for projects where completion has become impossible but excluding grant receivable under section 62 of the 1985 Act);
      (iv) interest and dividends from investments;
      (v) net surpluses from sales of property (including leases granted at a premium);
      (vi) all other income;
   (b) as expenditure—
      (i) management expenses;
      (ii) the costs of repairs and maintenance, including provision for future works;
      (iii) service costs, showing separately those relating to hostels and those relating to other housing accommodation;
      (iv) interest on loans attributable to housing land;
      (v) depreciation equal to repayment of loan principal;
      (vi) other depreciation;
      (vii) amounts transferred to the Grant Redemption Fund;
      (viii) administrative costs of acquiring and developing housing accommodation;
      (ix) cost of housing projects where completion has become impossible;
      (x) all other expenditure.

(2) The income and expenditure account shall also show—
   (a) the gross surplus or deficit for the period of account, ascertained by deducting expenditure from income, but before deducting the tax or crediting the grant referred to below;
   (b) the amount charged to revenue for corporation tax and income tax, together with grant receivable under section 62 of the 1985 Act;
   (c) the overall surplus or deficit for the period of account, after deducting the tax and crediting the grant referred to in (b) above;
   (d) amounts transferred to or withdrawn from reserves.

(3) All amounts shown in the income and expenditure account for the period of account shall be accompanied by the corresponding amounts for the preceding period (if any).'

3. Article 7 (statement of source and application of funds) shall be omitted.

4. For article 8 (preparation of additional financial statements) there shall be substituted—

Preparation of additional financial statement.

8. In addition to any other accounts which it is required to prepare apart from those required by virtue of this Order, the association shall prepare a statement of housing administration costs which shall be in the form set out in Schedule 5 to this Order.'

5. For article 10(2) there shall be substituted—

'(2) The surpluses calculated in the manner determined by the Secretary of State under section 53(3) of the 1985 Act shall be shown as such in the income and expenditure account.'.

6. In paragraph 4 of Part I of Schedule 1 (value of fixed assets in the balance sheet), the words 'which is not a co-ownership society' in sub-paragraph (2), and sub-paragraph (4), shall be omitted.

7. Schedules 2, 3, 4 and 6 shall be omitted. [1425]

The Homes Insulation Grants Order 1988
SI 1988/1239

(*This order was made, as respects Scotland, by the Secretary of State for Scotland, under the Housing (Scotland) Act 1987 (c 26), s 252(3) and (5), and came into force on 15 August 1988*)

1. (*Citation and commencement*) [1426]

2. Prescribed amount.

For the purposes of the Homes Insulation Scheme 1987 as amended, £144 is prescribed as the money sum payable as grant. [1427]

The Assured Tenancies (Notices to Quit (Prescribed Information) (Scotland) Regulations 1988
SI 1988/2067

(*These regulations were made by the Secretary of State for Scotland under the Rent (Scotland) Act 1984 (c 58), s 112 and came into force on 2 January 1989*)

1. (*Citation and commencement*) [1428]

2. Where a notice to quit is given by a landlord to terminate an assured tenancy under the Housing (Scotland) Act 1988 that notice shall contain the information set out in the Schedule to these Regulations. [1429]

Regulation 2   SCHEDULE

INFORMATION TO BE CONTAINED IN THE NOTICE TO QUIT

1. Even after the Notice to Quit has run out, before the tenant can lawfully be evicted, the landlord must get an order for possession from the court. [1430]

2. If a landlord issues a Notice to Quit but does not seek to gain possession of the house in question the contractual assured tenancy which has been terminated will be replaced by a statutory assured tenancy. In such circumstances the landlord may propose new terms for the tenancy and may seek an adjustment in rent at annual intervals thereafter. **[1431]**

3. If a tenant does not know what kind of tenancy he has or is otherwise unsure of his rights he can obtain advice from a solicitor. Help with all or part of the cost of legal advice and assistance may be available under the Legal Aid legislation. A tenant can also seek help from a Citizens Advice Bureau or Housing Advisory Centre. **[1432]**

The Assured Tenancies (Exceptions) (Scotland) Regulations 1988

SI 1988/2068

(*These regulations were made by the Secretary of State for Scotland under the Housing (Scotland) Act 1988 (c 43), s 53(3) and Schedule 4, para 7, and came into force on 2 January 1989*)

1. (*Citation and commencement*) **[1433]**

2. For the purposes of paragraph 7 of Schedule 4 to the Housing (Scotland) Act 1988 (tenancies granted to a person who is pursuing or intends to pursue a course of study which cannot be assured tenancies), there are specified the following educational institutions and bodies of persons or classes thereof—
 (a) any university, university college and any constituent college, school or hall of a university;
 (b) any central institution within the meaning of section 135(1) of the Education (Scotland) Act 1980;
 (c) any college of education within the meaning of that section;
 (d) any institution for the provision of further education within the meaning of that section which is administered by an education authority;
 (e) any association approved by the Secretary of State under regulation 8 of the Further Education (Scotland) Regulations 1959; and
 (f) The Royal College of Surgeons of Edinburgh. **[1434]**

SI 1988/2085 [1439]

The Assured Tenancies (Tenancies at a Low Rent) (Scotland) Order 1988

SI 1988/2069

(*This order was made by the Secretary of State for Scotland under the Housing (Scotland) Act 1988 (c 43), s 53(3) and Schedule 4, para 2, and came into force on 2 January 1989*)

1. (*Citation and commencement*) [1435]

2. For the purposes of paragraph 2 of Schedule 4 to the Housing (Scotland) Act 1988 (tenancies at a low rent), there is specified—
  (a) in the case of a tenancy where the rent is payable weekly, a rent of £6 per week; and
  (b) in the case of a tenancy where the rent is payable for any other period, a rent calculated for that period at the rate of £6 per week. [1436]

The Assured Tenancies (Rent Book) (Scotland) Regulations 1988

SI 1988/2085

(*These regulations were made by the Secretary of State for Scotland under the Housing (Scotland) Act 1988 (c 43), ss 30(5), 53(3) and 55(1), and came into force on 2 January 1989*)

1. (*Citation and commencement*) [1437]

2. For the purposes of section 30(5) of the Housing (Scotland) Act 1988 (matters relating to which it is the duty of a landlord to provide under an assured tenancy where the rent is payable weekly), every rent book shall contain a notice to the tenant which shall be in the form and relate to such matters as are set out in the Schedule to these Regulations. [1438]

Regulation 2   SCHEDULE

Form of notice to be inserted in every rent book used in the case of an assured tenancy
where the rent is payable weekly

INFORMATION FOR TENANT

NOTE 1 Rents for assured and short assured tenancies are freely negotiable between landlord and tenant. In certain circumstances you may, however, have a right to apply to a rent assessment committee for a determination of a market rent.

725

NOTE 2 Landlords must keep the amounts for rent, furniture and services up to date.

1. Address of the house ....
   ....
   ....

2. Name, address and telephone number of landlord (and agent if any)
   ....
   ....
   ....

3. **Rent to be recovered.**

   (1) If a market rent has been agreed between landlord and tenant (including a case where a market rent for a statutory assured tenancy has been determined by a rent assessment committee but has been varied by agreement between tenant and landlord)—
   - (a) the rent payable under the tenancy is £   per week; the date from which the rent applies is   ;
   - (b) if furniture or services are provided the amount which is apportioned to them under the tenancy is—
     Furniture £...............   Services £...............

   (2) If a market rent has been determined by a Rent Assessment Committee—
   - (a) the rent payable under the tenancy as determined by the rent assessment committee is £   per week; the date from which the rent applies is   ;
   - (b) if furniture or services are provided the amount to be apportioned to them under the tenancy agreement as determined by the rent assessment committee is—
     Furniture £...............   Services £...............
     The date from which these payments apply is   .

4. **Type of assured tenancy.**

   There are different types of assured tenancy and your rights as tenant in relation to such matters as rent adjustments and security of tenure will depend on the type you have. Your tenancy will be one of three kinds—

   An assured tenancy: that is an assured tenancy which is contractual because a tenancy agreement or contract of tenancy is still in force; or

   A statutory assured tenancy: that is a tenancy which arises after the termination of a contractual assured tenancy but where the tenant continues to retain possession of the house without a new contractual tenancy agreement being created; or

   A short assured tenancy: that is a special type of assured tenancy in existence for a set period under which the landlord has served on the tenant a notice under section 32 of the Housing (Scotland) Act 1988 informing him that the tenancy is a short assured tenancy. Like a normal assured tenancy a short assured tenancy can either be contractual or statutory. A short assured tenancy gives special rights to a landlord in relation to repossession of the house and special rights to a tenant in relation to applications to a rent assessment committee for a rent determination.

5. **Rent adjustment.**

   Rent for most assured and short assured tenancies will be freely negotiated between landlord and tenant. In most cases both parties will also agree on a formal mechanism to allow adjustment to be made on a periodic basis, for example, to allow an annual increase by a certain agreed figure. Such agreements should be clearly set out in the written document which a landlord is obliged to supply to a tenant under an assured or short assured tenancy. Rent adjustment can in certain circumstances be sought other than through a mechanism built into a tenancy agreement. You should note that—
   - (a) if yours is a contractual assured tenancy, not later than 12 months after its termination either you or your landlord may, by serving a notice AT1 on the

other, propose new terms for the statutory assured tenancy which arises, and, if appropriate, an adjustment to the rent to take account of the new terms. Both landlords and tenant have a right to refer such new proposals to a rent assessment committee for a determination on the proposed terms and any proposed rent adjustment, but must do so within 3 months of the notice AT1 being served;

(b) if yours is a statutory assured tenancy, your landlord may serve a notice AT2 proposing a new rent at any time (but not more often than once a year). He must give you appropriate notice. If your tenancy is for 6 months or more, he must give 6 months notice. If your tenancy is for less than 6 months, he must give you one month's notice or the same length of time as the duration of the tenancy, whichever is longer. If a notice is served on you there is a right to apply to a rent assessment committee for a determination of a market rent although you must do so before the day on which the new rent proposed by the landlord would take effect;

(c) if yours is a short assured tenancy, paragraphs (a) and (b) will also apply as appropriate. However, if you are a tenant under a short assured tenancy and you believe your rent is excessive you may at any time apply to a rent assessment committee for a rent determination. The Committee will make a determination unless it has previously already done so for the tenancy or unless it has difficulty establishing a market rent for the tenancy because there are insufficient similar tenancies in the locality for comparison purposes.

6. Determination by a rent assessment committee (RAC).

(1) Once a rent determination has been made by the RAC no further increase in rent may be made within 12 months unless the landlord and tenant agree otherwise.

(2) Except in the case of a determination made for a short assured tenancy, it is open to a landlord and tenant to agree to vary the terms of the determination made by the RAC if they so wish

7. Security of tenure.

(1) The landlord can recover possession of a house under an assured tenancy only by obtaining an order for possession from the sheriff. This means that if he serves a notice to quit on you, you do not need to leave by the date stated on the notice. Before you can be evicted the landlord must first get an order for possession from the sheriff. In certain circumstances the sheriff must order possession, for example, if a short assured tenancy has reached its expiry date, or if the landlord requires the premises for his own home, or if a full 3 months rent is in arrears. In other circumstances the sheriff may only grant possession if he considers it reasonable to do so, for example, if the tenant is alleged to have broken or not performed an obligation of the tenancy, or has been guilty of conduct in or in the vicinity of the house which is a nuisance or annoyance.

(2) It is a criminal offence for the landlord or for anyone else to try to make you leave your home by using force, by harassing you or your family, by withdrawing services or by interfering with your home or your possessions. If anyone does this you should contact the police immediately.

8. Housing benefit.

If you consider that you cannot afford the rent which is charged you should apply to your local authority for housing benefit. You may obtain further information on housing benefit and on other matters concerning your assured tenancy from your local authority or citizens' advice bureau.

The Assured Tenancies (Forms) (Scotland) Regulations 1988
SI 1988/2109

(These regulations were made by the Secretary of State for Scotland under the Housing (Scotland) Act 1988 (c 43), ss 17(2) and (3), 19(3), 24(1) and (3), 32(2) and (4), 34(1), 48(2), 53(3) and 55(1), and came into force on 2 January 1989)

1. (*Citation and commencement*) **[1440]**

2. In these Regulations, 'the Act' means the Housing (Scotland) Act 1988. **[1441]**

3. The forms set out in the Schedule to these Regulations shall be the forms to be used for the purposes of the Act in the cases to which those forms are applicable. **[1442]**

Regulation 3

SCHEDULE

LIST OF FORMS

Form No	Purpose	Statutory references to the Act
AT1(L)	Notice by landlord proposing terms of a statutory assured tenancy different from the terms of the former tenancy	Section 17(2)
AT1(T)	Notice by tenant proposing terms of a statutory assured tenancy different from the terms of the former tenancy	Section 17(2)
AT2	Notice of an increase of rent under an assured tenancy	Section 24(1)
AT3(L)	Application by a landlord to a rent assessment committee for a determination of the terms of a statutory assured tenancy	Section 17(3)
AT3(T)	Application by a tenant to a rent assessment committee for a determination of the terms of a statutory assured tenancy	Section 17(3)
AT4	Application by a tenant to a rent assessment committee for determination of rent for a statutory assured tenancy or short assured tenancy	Sections 24(3) and 34(1)
AT5	Notice by landlord that tenancy is a short assured tenancy	Section 32(2)
AT6	Notice by landlord of intention to raise proceedings for possession of a house let on an assured tenancy	Section 19(3) as amended by paragraph 85 of Schedule 17 to the Housing Act 1988
AT7	Notice by landlord that the continued or new tenancy is not to be a short assured tenancy	Section 32(4)

SI 1988/2109 [1444]

Form No	Purpose	Statutory references to the Act
AT8	Notice by rent assessment committee served on the landlord or the tenant requiring such information as the committee may reasonably require for the purposes of their functions	Section 48(2)

[1443]

FORM AT1(L): FOR USE ONLY BY A LANDLORD

ASSURED TENANCIES AT1(L)

HOUSING (SCOTLAND) ACT 1988

NOTICE UNDER SECTION 17(2) PROPOSING TERMS OF A STATUTORY ASSURED TENANCY DIFFERENT FROM THE TERMS OF THE FORMER TENANCY

IMPORTANT: INFORMATION FOR TENANT(S)

This notice proposes a change in the terms of your tenancy (and possibly an adjustment to the rent to reflect the change) for the house at the address in part 2. The new terms (and rent, if appropriate) will take effect from the date specified unless you and your landlord negotiate different terms or you refer this notice to a Rent Assessment Committee within three months of the date of service of this notice using a special form AT3(T). The Rent Assessment Committee will determine whether the proposed terms are reasonable and can specify adjustments to the terms and to the rent. You should give your response to the proposed changes by returning part 7 of this notice to your landlord.

Please read this notice carefully before responding.

Part 1. This notice is served on .... (tenant's name) as tenant by .... (landlord's name) as landlord under section 17(2) of the Housing Scotland) Act 1988.

NOTE 1 TO TENANT.
YOUR LANDLORD MAY PROPOSE A CHANGE OF TENANCY TERMS BY THIS MEANS ONLY IF THE TENANCY IS A STATUTORY ASSURED TENANCY. IF YOU ARE IN DOUBT ABOUT WHAT KIND OF TENANCY YOU HAVE YOU SHOULD CONSULT A SOLICITOR OR AN ORGANISATION WHICH GIVES ADVICE ON HOUSING MATTERS.

[1444]   SI 1988/2109

Part 2. Address of house to which this notice relates:-

....
....
....
....

(Please be as specific as possible. For example, if the tenancy is of a flat give the location in stair, eg 1F1).

Part 3. Name, address and telephone number of landlord, and of agent (if any):-

.... landlord(s)   .... agent
....
....
....

NOTE 2 TO TENANT.
THIS NOTICE PROPOSES CHANGES TO THE TERMS OF THE TENANCY FOR THE HOUSE TO WHICH THE NOTICE RELATES. YOUR LANDLORD MUST GIVE YOU AT LEAST THREE MONTHS NOTICE OF THE CHANGES. THEY WILL TAKE EFFECT FROM THE DATE SPECIFIED IF YOU DO NOT ACT WITHIN THREE MONTHS OF THE DATE OF SERVICE OF THE NOTICE. READ THE NOTICE CAREFULLY. IF YOU ARE IN DOUBT ABOUT WHAT ACTION YOU SHOULD TAKE, GET ADVICE IMMEDIATELY FROM A SOLICITOR OR AN ORGANISATION WHICH GIVES ADVICE ON HOUSING MATTERS.

Part 4. I your landlord(s)/I your landlord's agent* give you notice of proposed changes in the terms of your tenancy for the house at the address in part 2. The proposed changes are shown in paragraph (c) of part 6 of this notice and are to come into effect on .... (date).

Signed ....
Landlord/Landlord's agent

Date ....

NOTE 3 TO TENANT.
YOUR LANDLORD MAY ALSO PROPOSE THAT YOUR RENT IS TO BE ADJUSTED TO TAKE ACCOUNT OF THE PROPOSED NEW TENANCY TERMS. IF SO THE LANDLORD MUST ALSO COMPLETE PART 5 OF THE NOTICE.

---

* delete as appropriate

SI 1988/2109 [1444]

Part 5. I your landlord(s)/I your landlord's agent* give you notice of an adjustment of rent shown in paragraph (d) of part 6 of this notice to take account of the tenancy terms. I am proposing that the adjustment is to come into effect on .... date).

                                        Signed ....
                                        Landlord/Landlord's Agent
                                        Date ....

* delete as appropriate

NOTE 4 TO TENANT.
IF YOU DO NOT WISH TO ACCEPT THE TERMS PROPOSED OR WISH TO REFER THE PROPOSALS TO A RENT ASSESSMENT COMMITTEE THEN A MEETING WITH YOUR LANDLORD TO DISCUSS THE PROPOSALS MIGHT BE HELPFUL. YOU SHOULD, HOWEVER, KEEP IN MIND THE THREE MONTH TIME-LIMIT FOR REFERRING THE PROPOSALS TO A RENT ASSESSMENT COMMITTEE.

Part 6.

    a. Date(s) on which the assured tenancy agreement or contract of tenancy began.

    b. Date when the notice to quit terminating the assured tenancy expired or, if your tenant succeeded to a tenancy, the date on which he succeeded.

    c. The proposed changes to the terms of the tenancy are:
       (**Note to the Landlord.**
       The exact nature of the changes should be specified. Attach a copy of the written document setting out the terms of the tenancy agreement. Continue on additional sheets of paper if necessary).

    d. Existing rent for the house   £ ..... (per/week*/month*/year*)
       Proposed adjustment plus/minus   £ ..... (per/week*/month*/year*)
       Proposed new rent   £ ..... (per/week*/month*/year*)

* delete as appropriate

> **NOTE 5 TO TENANT.**
> TO REFER YOUR LANDLORD'S PROPOSALS TO A RENT ASSESSMENT COMMITTEE YOU MUST USE FORM AT3(T) (OBTAINABLE FROM THE CLERK TO THE RENT ASSESSMENT COMMITTEE, THE RENT REGISTRATION SERVICE, CITIZENS ADVICE BUREAU OR HOUSING ADVISORY CENTRE) THE APPLICATION SHOULD BE SENT TO THE CLERK TO THE LOCAL RENT ASSESSMENT COMMITTEE (SEE TELEPHONE BOOK FOR ADDRESS). THE RENT ASSESSMENT COMMITTEE IS AN INDEPENDENT BODY WHICH CHARGES NO FEE.
>
> **NOTE 6 TO TENANT.**
> DETACH PART 7 AND RETURN IT TO THE SENDER OF THE NOTICE AS SOON AS POSSIBLE. HOWEVER IF YOU DECIDE TO DISCUSS THE PROPOSAL(S) WITH YOUR LANDLORD *DO NOT COMPLETE PART 7 NOW*, BUT REMEMBER THERE IS A THREE MONTH TIME-LIMIT FOR REFERRING THE PROPOSALS TO A RENT ASSESSMENT COMMITTEE.
>
> **NOTE 7 TO TENANT.**
> THIS IS AN IMPORTANT DOCUMENT AND YOU SHOULD KEEP IT IN A SAFE PLACE.

Part 7. (This part of the notice is for the use of the tenant.)

To .... (name)
(Landlord*/Landlord's Agent*)

I acknowledge receipt of notice AT1(L) dated .... 19 ...... (date of notice) and give you notice that:- (*delete as appropriate)

* I accept the proposed terms of the statutory tenancy [and the proposed adjustment to the rent*.]

* I do not accept the proposed terms of the statutory assured tenancy and/or the proposed adjustment to the rent, and intend to refer this notice to a Rent Assessment Committee.

Signed ....

....
(Tenant/Tenant's Agent)

Date ....
(If tenancy is a joint tenancy all tenants or their agents should sign).

SI 1988/2109 [1445]

FORM AT1(T): FOR USE ONLY BY A TENANT

ASSURED TENANCIES   AT1(T)

HOUSING (SCOTLAND) ACT 1988

NOTICE UNDER SECTION 17(2) PROPOSING TERMS OF A STATUTORY ASSURED TENANCY DIFFERENT FROM THE TERMS OF THE FORMER TENANCY

IMPORTANT: INFORMATION FOR LANDLORDS(S)

This notice proposes a change in the terms of the tenancy (and possibly an adjustment to the rent to reflect the change) for the house at the address in part 2. The new terms (and rent, if appropriate) will take effect from the date specified unless you and the tenant negotiate different terms or you refer this notice to a Rent Assessment Committee using a special form AT3(L) within three months of the date of service of this notice. The Rent Assessment Committee will determine whether the proposed terms are reasonable and can specify adjustments to the terms and the rent. You should give your response to the proposed changes by returning part 6 of this notice to your tenant.

Please read this notice carefully before responding.

Part 1. This notice is served on .... (landlord's name) as landlord by .... (tenant's name) as tenant under section 17(2) of the Housing (Scotland) Act 1988.

NOTE 1 TO LANDLORD.
YOUR TENANT MAY PROPOSE A CHANGE OF TENANCY TERMS BY THIS MEANS ONLY IF THE TENANCY IS A STATUTORY ASSURED TENANCY. IF YOU ARE IN DOUBT WHAT KIND OF TENANCY YOU HAVE YOU SHOULD CONSULT A SOLICITOR OR AN ORGANISATION WHICH GIVES ADVICE ON HOUSING MATTERS.

Part 2. Address of house to which this notice relates:-

....
....
....
....

(Please be as specific as possible. For example, if the tenancy is of a flat give the location in stair, eg 1F1).

> **NOTE 2 TO LANDLORD**
> THIS NOTICE PROPOSES CHANGES TO THE TERMS OF THE TENANCY FOR THE HOUSE TO WHICH THE NOTICE RELATES. YOUR TENANT MUST GIVE YOU AT LEAST THREE MONTHS NOTICE OF THE CHANGES. THEY WILL TAKE EFFECT FROM THE DATE SPECIFIED IF YOU DO NOT ACT WITHIN THREE MONTHS OF THE DATE OF SERVICE OF THIS NOTICE. READ THE NOTICE CAREFULLY. IF YOU ARE IN DOUBT WHAT ACTION YOU SHOULD TAKE, GET ADVICE IMMEDIATELY FROM A SOLICITOR OR AN ORGANISATION WHICH GIVES ADVICE ON HOUSING MATTERS.

Part 3. I your tenant(s)/I your tenant's agent* give notice of proposed changes in the terms of the tenancy for the house at the address in part 2. The proposed changes are shown in paragraph (c) of part 5 of this notice and are to come into effect on .... (date).

Signed ....
(In a joint tenancy all tenants should sign)

Date ....

> **NOTE 3 TO LANDLORD.**
> IF YOUR TENANT PROPOSES THAT THE RENT IS TO BE ADJUSTED TO TAKE ACCOUNT OF THE PROPOSED NEW TENANCY TERMS, PART 4 MUST ALSO BE COMPLETED.

Part 4. I your tenant(s)/I your tenant's agent* give notice of an adjustment of rent as shown in paragraph (d) of part 5 of this notice to take account of the proposed terms.
The adjustment is to come into effect on .... (date).

Signed ....
(In a joint tenancy all tenants should sign)

Date ....

* delete as appropriate

> **NOTE 4 TO LANDLORD.**
> IF YOU DO NOT WISH TO ACCEPT THE TERMS PROPOSED OR WISH TO REFER THE PROPOSALS TO A RENT ASSESSMENT COMMITTEE THEN A MEETING WITH THE TENANT TO DISCUSS THE PROPOSALS MIGHT BE HELPFUL. YOU SHOULD, HOWEVER, KEEP IN MIND THE THREE MONTH TIME-LIMIT FOR REFERRING THE PROPOSALS TO A RENT ASSESSMENT COMMITTEE.

Part 5.
    a. Date(s) on which your assured tenancy agreement or contract of tenancy began.   ....
    b. Date when the notice to quit terminating the assured tenancy expired or, if you succeeded to the tenancy, the date on which you succeeded.   ....
    c. The proposed changes to the terms of the tenancy are:
    (Note to the Tenant.
    The exact nature of the changes should be specified. Attach a copy of the written document setting out the terms of the tenancy agreement. Continue on additional sheets of paper if necessary).   ....
    d. Existing rent for the house   £ ..... (per/week*/month*/year*)
    Proposed adjustment plus/minus   £ ..... (per/week*/month*/year*)
    Proposed new rent   £ ..... (per/week*/month*/year*)

* **delete as appropriate**

NOTE 5 TO LANDLORD.
TO REFER YOUR TENANT'S PROPOSALS TO A RENT ASSESSMENT COMMITTEE YOU MUST USE FORM AT3(L) (OBTAINABLE FROM THE CLERK OF THE RENT ASSESSMENT COMMITTEE, THE RENT REGISTRATION SERVICE, CITIZENS ADVICE BUREAU OR HOUSING ADVISORY CENTRE). THE APPLICATION SHOULD BE SENT TO THE CLERK OF THE LOCAL RENT ASSESSMENT COMMITTEE (SEE TELEPHONE BOOK FOR ADDRESS). THE RENT ASSESSMENT COMMITTEE IS AN INDEPENDENT BODY WHICH CHARGES NO FEE.

NOTE 6 TO LANDLORD.
DETACH PART 6 AND RETURN IT TO THE SENDER OF THE NOTICE AS SOON AS POSSIBLE. HOWEVER IF YOU DECIDE TO DISCUSS THE PROPOSAL(S) WITH YOUR TENANT *DO NOT* COMPLETE PART 6 NOW, BUT REMEMBER THAT THERE IS A THREE MONTH TIME-LIMIT FOR REFERRING THE PROPOSALS TO THE RENT ASSESSMENT COMMITTEE.

NOTE 7 TO LANDLORD.
THIS IS AN IMPORTANT DOCUMENT AND YOU SHOULD KEEP IT IN A SAFE PLACE.

Part 6. (This part of the notice is for the use of the landlord)

    To .... (name)
    (tenant*/tenants' agent*)

I acknowledge receipt of notice AT1(T) dated .... 19 ...... (date of notice)

[1445]   SI 1988/2109

and give you notice that:- (*delete as appropriate)
* I accept the proposed terms of the statutory tenancy [and the proposed adjustment to the rent.]*
* I do not accept the proposed terms of the statutory assured tenancy and/or the proposed adjustment to the rent, and intend to refer this notice to a Rent Assessment Committee.*

Signed ....
....
(landlord/landlord's agent)
Date ....

* delete as appropriate.

[1445]

FORM AT2: FOR USE ONLY BY A LANDLORD

ASSURED TENANCIES   **AT2**

HOUSING (SCOTLAND) ACT 1988

NOTICE UNDER SECTION 24(1) OF AN INCREASE OF RENT UNDER AN ASSURED TENANCY

IMPORTANT: INFORMATION FOR TENANT(S)

This notice informs you as tenant(s) that your landlord(s) wish(es) to increase the rent for your assured tenancy. The new rent will take effect unless you reach an agreement with your landlord that the rent should be a different amount or unless you refer this notice to a Rent Assessment Committee for a rent determination using a special form AT4. If you do apply to the Committee you must do so **before the date on which the new rent is due to take effect**. You should give your landlord your response to the proposed new rent by returning to him part 3 of this notice.

Please read this notice carefully before responding.

Part 1.   To ....
(name of tenant(s))
of ....
....
....
(address of tenant(s))

SI 1988/2109 [1446]

> NOTE 1 TO TENANT.
> YOUR LANDLORD MUST GIVE YOU AT LEAST THE FOLLOWING AMOUNT OF NOTICE OF A RENT INCREASE. IF THE ASSURED TENANCY IS FOR 6 MONTHS OR MORE, 6 MONTHS NOTICE MUST BE GIVEN. IF THE TENANCY IS FOR LESS THAN 6 MONTHS, THE NOTICE GIVEN MUST BE THE SAME LENGTH AS THE ORIGINAL TENANCY BUT CANNOT BE LESS THAN ONE MONTH.

Part 2. This gives you notice that ....
(name of landlord)
of ....
....
....
(address of landlord)

proposes to charge a new rent of £ ....
        [per year]*   [per month]*   [per week]*
for your tenancy of the house at the address in part 1.

The new rent is to take effect from .... (date)

    Signed .... (Landlord(s)/Landlord's Agent)

    Date ....

Address of Agent (if appropriate)
....
....

> IMPORTANT: FOR THE ATTENTION OF TENANT(S) NOTES 2 TO 4
>
> 2. A LANDLORD MAY PROPOSE A NEW RENT BY THIS MEANS ONLY IF THE TENANCY IS A STATUTORY ASSURED TENANCY. IF YOU ARE IN DOUBT ABOUT WHAT KIND OF TENANCY YOU HAVE YOU SHOULD CONSULT A SOLICITOR OR AN ORGANISATION WHICH GIVES ADVICE ON HOUSING MATTERS.
>
> 3. THE PROPOSED NEW RENT WILL TAKE EFFECT ON THE DATE SPECIFIED UNLESS YOU REACH SOME OTHER AGREEMENT WITH YOUR LANDLORD OR UNLESS YOU REFER THE NOTICE TO A RENT ASSESSMENT COMMITTEE FOR A RENT DETERMINATION BEFORE THE DATE ON WHICH THE NEW RENT TAKES EFFECT.
>
> 4. IF YOU DECIDE TO REFER THIS NOTICE TO THE RENT ASSESSMENT COMMITTEE YOU MUST DO SO USING FORM AT4 (OBTAINABLE FROM THE CLERK TO THE RENT ASSESSMENT COMMITTEE, THE RENT REGISTRATION SERVICE, CITIZENS ADVICE BUREAU OR HOUSING ADVISORY CENTRE). THE APPLICATION SHOULD BE MADE TO THE LOCAL RENT ASSESSMENT COMMITTEE (SEE TELEPHONE BOOK FOR ADDRESS). THE RENT ASSESSMENT COMMITTEE IS AN INDEPENDENT BODY WHICH CHARGES NO FEE.

* delete as appropriate.

[1446]   SI 1988/2109

IMPORTANT: FOR THE ATTENTION OF TENANT(S) NOTES 5 TO 7

5. YOUR LANDLORD CANNOT INCREASE YOUR RENT BY THIS METHOD MORE OFTEN THAN ONCE EVERY 12 MONTHS.

6. DETACH PART 3 AND RETURN IT TO YOUR LANDLORD AS SOON AS POSSIBLE. HOWEVER IF YOU WISH TO DISCUSS THE PROPOSED NEW RENT WITH YOUR LANDLORD *DO NOT* COMPLETE PART 3 NOW. *BUT REMEMBER* IF YOU DECIDE TO REFER THE NEW RENT TO THE RENT ASSESSMENT COMMITTEE YOU MUST DO SO BEFORE THE DATE ON WHICH THE NEW RENT IS DUE TO TAKE EFFECT.

7. THIS IS AN IMPORTANT DOCUMENT AND IT SHOULD BE KEPT IN A SAFE PLACE.

Part 3. (This part is for the use of the tenant).

To ....
(Landlord*/Landlord's Agent)

*I/We acknowledge receipt of the notice AT2 dated .... 19.... and give you notice that

*I/We accept the new rent to apply from
.... 19....

*I/We do not accept the new rent to apply from

.... 19.... and

propose to refer the matter to a Rent Assessment Committee for a rent determination.

Signed .... (Tenant*/Tenant's agent)

(If the tenancy is a joint tenancy all tenants or their agents should sign)

Date ....
Address of tenant's agent(s) (if appropriate)

....
....

* delete as appropriate.
                                                                    [1446]

SI 1988/2109 [1447]

FORM AT3(L): FOR USE ONLY BY A LANDLORD

ASSURED TENANCIES   AT3(L)

HOUSING (SCOTLAND) ACT 1988

Application by a landlord to a Rent Assessment Committee for a determination of the terms of a statutory assured tenancy and, if appropriate, rent for that tenancy under Section 17(3) of the Housing (Scotland) Act 1988.

IMPORTANT: INFORMATION FOR LANDLORD(S)

This form should be used by a landlord who wishes to refer to a Rent Assessment Committee a Notice AT1(T) served on him by his tenant to propose a change in the terms of a tenancy agreement for the house at the address in part 1. You should read this application form carefully. Complete the form as fully as you can. Insert 'NOT KNOWN' where the information is not available. Where boxes are shown tick only one. It would be helpful if you would type your answers or use BLOCK LETTERS in BLACK INK and send 2 copies of the form if possible, to the Clerk to the Rent Assessment Committee.

This form must be with the Clerk to the Committee within 3 months of the date on which your tenant served on you Notice AT1(T).

Part 1. Address of House being let.

....

....

Part 2. Name, address and telephone number of landlord.

....

....

Name, address and telephone number of landlord's agent (if any).

....

....

Part 3. Name and telephone number of tenant(s)

....

....

Name, address and telephone number of tenant's agent (if any).

....

....

Part 4. Details of House.

Say what kind of house it is, such as a detached or terraced house or flat or part of a house. (If a flat give location in stair eg 1F1.)

....

Give number and type of rooms (eg bedroom, living room).

....

Is there any accommodation or facilities shared with another tenant? If yes, give details. ☐ No ☐ Yes

....
....

Is there any accommodation or facilities shared between tenant and landlord? If yes, give details. ☐ No ☐ Yes

....
....

Does the tenancy include a garage, garden, yard or any other separate building or land? If yes, give details. ☐ No ☐ Yes

....
....

Part 5. Services

Are services provided under the tenancy (such as cleaning, heating or hot water supply)? If yes, give details. ☐ No ☐ Yes

....
....

What charge is made for these services at present?

....

Part 6. Furniture

Is furniture provided under the tenancy? If yes, please attach a list of the furniture provided. If you do not have one prepare one and attach it to this form. ☐ No ☐ Yes

....
....
....

Part 7. Improvements

During the present or any former tenancy has the tenant or any previous tenant carried out any improvement or replaced fixtures, fittings or furniture for which he is (or he was) **not** responsible under the terms of the tenancy? If yes, give details including the cost (actual or estimated) and the approximate date on which the work was carried out. ☐ No ☐ Yes

....
....

SI 1988/2109 [1447]

....
....
....

Part 8. Disrepair

Is there any disrepair or other defect to the house or to any fixtures, fittings or furniture due to a failure to comply with the terms of the present or any former tenancy? If yes, give details. ☐ No ☐ Yes

....
....
....
....
....

Part 9. I apply for the proposed terms of the statutory assured tenancy [and the proposed adjustment to the rent]* to be determined by a Rent Assessment Committee.

Signed ....

[Landlord(s)]   [Landlord's Agent]*

In the case of joint landlords all landlords should sign.

.... (date)

* delete as appropriate

Part 10. In submitting your application you should attach copies of certain documents which will be required by the Rent Assessment Committee to help it make a determination. You should attach the following:-

    a. A copy of the existing tenancy agreement or written document setting out the terms of the tenancy. ☐

    b. A copy of Notice AT1(T) served on you by your tenant (including any attachments to that form). ☐

    c. If you provide furniture, a list of the furniture. ☐

    d. If the tenancy is a short assured tenancy a copy of Notice AT5 which you served on the tenant. ☐

Any documents which you send with this application will be returned to you as soon as possible.

Tick each box to indicate that you have attached the relevant form.

Please send this application form to the Clerk to the Rent Assessment Committee for your area (see telephone book for the address).

[1447]

[1448] SI 1988/2109

FORM AT3(T): FOR USE ONLY BY A TENANT

ASSURED TENANCIES   **AT3(T)**

HOUSING (SCOTLAND) ACT 1988

Application by a tenant to a Rent Assessment Committee for a determination of the terms of a statutory assured tenancy and, if appropriate, rent for that tenancy under Section 17(3) of the Housing (Scotland) Act 1988.

IMPORTANT: INFORMATION FOR TENANT(S)

This form should be used by a tenant who wishes to refer to a Rent Assessment Committee a Notice AT1(L) served on him by his landlord to propose a change in the terms of a tenancy agreement for the house at the address in part 1. You should read this application form carefully. Complete the form as fully as you can. Insert 'NOT KNOWN' where the information is not available. Where boxes are shown tick only one. It would be helpful if you would type your answers or use BLOCK LETTERS in BLACK INK and send 2 copies of the form if possible, to the Clerk to the Rent Assessment Committee.

This form must be with the Clerk to the Committee within 3 months of the date on which your landlord served on you Notice AT1(L).

Part 1. Address of House being let.

....

....

Part 2. Name, address and telephone number of landlord.

....

....

Name, address and telephone number of landlord's agent (if any).

....

....

Part 3. Name and telephone number of tenant(s)

....

....

Name, address and telephone number of tenant's agent (if any).

....

....

Part 4. **Details of House.**

Say what kind of house it is, such as a detached or terraced house or flat or part of a house. (If a flat give location in stair eg 1F1.)

....

Give number and type of rooms (eg bedroom, living room).

....
....

Is there any accommodation or facilities shared with another tenant? If yes, give details. ☐ No ☐ Yes

....
....

Is there any accommodation or facilities shared between tenant and landlord? If yes, give details. ☐ No ☐ Yes

....
....

Does the tenancy include a garage, garden, yard or any other separate building or land? If yes, give details. ☐ No ☐ Yes

....
....

Part 5. Services

Are services provided under the tenancy (such as cleaning, heating or hot water supply)? If yes, give details. ☐ No ☐ Yes

....
....

What charge is made for these services at present?

....

Part 6. Furniture

Is furniture provided under the tenancy? If yes, please attach a list of the furniture provided. If you do not have one prepare one and attach it to this form. ☐ No ☐ Yes

....
....
....

Part 7. Improvements

During the present or any former tenancy have you or has any previous tenant carried out any improvement or replaced fixtures, fittings or furniture for which you are (or he was) **not** responsible under the terms of the tenancy? If yes, give details including the cost (actual or estimated) and the approximate date on which the work was carried out. ☐ No ☐ Yes

....
....

....
....
....

Part 8.   Disrepair

Is there any disrepair or other defect to the house or to any fixtures, fittings or furniture due to a failure to comply with the terms of the present or any former tenancy? If yes, give details.   ☐ No ☐ Yes

....
....
....
....
....

Part 9.   I apply for the proposed terms of the statutory assured tenancy [and the proposed adjustment to the rent]* to be determined by a Rent Assessment Committee.

Signed ....

[tenant(s)]   [tenant's agent]*

In the case of joint tenants all tenants should sign.

.... (date)

* delete as appropriate

Part 10.   In submitting your application you should attach copies of certain documents which will be required by the Rent Assessment Committee to help it make a determination. You should attach the following:-

   a. A copy of your existing tenancy agreement or written document setting out the terms of the tenancy.   ☐

   b. A copy of Notice AT1(L) served on you by your landlord (including any attachments to that form).   ☐

   c. If your landlord provides furniture, a list of the furniture.   ☐

   d. If your tenancy is a short assured tenancy a copy of Notice AT5 served on you by the landlord.   ☐

Any documents which you send with this application will be returned to you as soon as possible.

Tick each box to indicate that you have attached the relevant form. If you do not have a copy of any of these forms, consult your Solicitor, local Citizens Advice Bureau or Housing Advisory Centre.

Please send this application form to the Clerk to the Rent Assessment Committee for your area (see telephone book for the address).

SI 1988/2109 [1449]

FORM AT4: FOR USE ONLY BY A TENANT

ASSURED TENANCIES AT4

HOUSING (SCOTLAND) ACT 1988

Application by a tenant to a rent assessment committee for a determination of rent under sections 24(3) and 34(1) of the Housing (Scotland) Act 1988.

IMPORTANT: INFORMATION FOR TENANT(S)

This form should be used if you as tenant are seeking a determination of rent from the Rent Assessment Committee for your assured or short assured tenancy. This might be as a result of a Notice AT2 having been served on you by your landlord (a Notice AT2 proposes an increase in rent for an assured tenancy), or, if you are a tenant of a short assured tenancy, because you would like the Committee to look at the rent you are being charged. Please note that tenants of short assured tenancies have different rights to apply to Rent Assessment Committees from other assured tenants. You are therefore advised to read this application form carefully. Complete the form as fully as you can. Insert 'NOT KNOWN' where the information is not available. Where boxes are shown tick only one. It would be helpful if you would type your answers or use BLOCK LETTERS in BLACK INK and send 2 copies of the form, if possible, to the Clerk of the Rent Assessment Committee.

Part 1. Address of House being let.

....
....

Part 2. Name, address and telephone number of landlord.

....
....

Name, address and telephone number of landlord's agent (if any).

....
....

Part 3. Name and telephone number of tenant(s)

....
....

Name, address and telephone number of tenant's agent (if any).

....
....

Part 4. Details of House.

Say what kind of house it is, such as a detached or terraced house or flat or part of a house. (If a flat give location in stair eg 1F1.)

....

Give number and type of rooms (eg bedroom, living room).

....
....

Is there any accommodation or facilities shared with another tenant? If yes, give details. ☐ No ☐ Yes

....
....

Is there any accommodation or facilities shared with the landlord? If yes, give details. ☐ No ☐ Yes

....
....

Does the tenancy include a garage, garden, yard or any other separate building or land? If yes, give details. ☐ No ☐ Yes

....
....

Part 5. Services

Does the landlord provide any services (such as cleaning, heating or hot water supply)? If yes, give details. ☐ No ☐ Yes

....
....

What charge is made for these services at present?

....

Part 6. Furniture

Does the landlord provide any furniture? If yes, please attach a list of the furniture provided. If you do not have one prepare one and attach it to this form. ☐ No ☐ Yes

....
....
....

Part 7. Improvements

During the present or any former tenancy have you or has any previous tenant carried out any improvement or replaced fixtures, fittings or furniture for which you are (or he was) **not** responsible under the terms of the tenancy? If yes, give details including the cost (actual or estimated) and the approximate date on which the work was carried out. ☐ No ☐ Yes

....
....

SI 1988/2109 [1449]

....
....
....

Part 8. Disrepair

Is there any disrepair or other defect to the house or to any fixtures, fittings or furniture due to a failure to comply with the terms of the present or any former tenancy? If yes, give details. ☐ No ☐ Yes

....
....
....
....
....

Part 9. What rent are you paying now?

£ .... [per week*] [per month*] [per year*]
If you are responding to a rent increase proposed by your landlord please attach a copy of Notice AT2 which gave notice of the proposed new rent.

* delete as appropriate

Part 10. I apply to the Rent Assessment Committee for a rent determination for the house at the address in part 1 above.

Signed .... (tenant or tenant's agent)

Date ....

(In the case of joint tenants all tenants should sign.)

Part 11. In submitting your application you should attach copies of certain documents which will be required by the Rent Assessment Committee to help it make a determination. You should attach the following:-

    a. A copy of your existing tenancy agreement or written document setting out the terms of the tenancy. ☐

    b. A copy of Notice AT2 if one has been served on you by your landlord (including any attachments to that form). ☐

    c. If your landlord provides furniture, a list of the furniture; and ☐

    d. If your tenancy is a short assured tenancy a copy of Notice AT5 served on you by the landlord. ☐

Any documents which you send with this application will be returned to you as soon as possible.

Tick each box to indicate that you have attached the relevant form.

[1449] SI 1988/2109

Please send this application form to the Clerk to the Rent Assessment Committee for your area (see telephone book for the address).

[1449]

FORM AT5: FOR USE ONLY BY A LANDLORD

ASSURED TENANCIES AT5

HOUSING (SCOTLAND) ACT 1988

NOTICE UNDER SECTION 32 TO BE SERVED ON A PROSPECTIVE TENANT OF A SHORT ASSURED TENANCY

IMPORTANT: INFORMATION FOR PROSPECTIVE TENANT(S)

This notice informs you as prospective tenant(s) that the tenancy being offered by the prospective landlord(s) is a short assured tenancy under Section 32 of the Housing (Scotland) Act 1988.

Please read this notice carefully.

Part 1. To ....

(name of prospective tenant(s))

NOTE 1 TO PROSPECTIVE TENANT.
TO BE VALID THIS NOTICE MUST BE SERVED BEFORE THE CREATION OF A TENANCY AGREEMENT. A SHORT ASSURED TENANCY WILL NOT EXIST IF A VALID NOTICE HAS NOT BEEN SERVED.

Part 2. I your prospective landlord(s)/I your prospective landlord's agent*

....

(name of landlord(s))

of ....

....

....

(address and telephone number of landlord(s))

give notice that the tenancy being offered to you of the

house at ....

....

....

(address of house)

* **delete as appropriate**

748

to which this notice relates is to be a short assured tenancy in terms of Section 32 of the Housing (Scotland) Act 1988.

Signed ....
(landlord(s) or landlords' agent)

Date ....

NOTE 2 TO PROSPECTIVE TENANT.
A SHORT ASSURED TENANCY IS A SPECIAL FORM OF TENANCY. UNLESS IT FOLLOWS IMMEDIATELY AFTER ANOTHER SHORT ASSURED TENANCY OF THE SAME HOUSE, (WITH THE SAME TENANT) IT MUST BE FOR NOT LESS THAN 6 MONTHS.

NOTE 3 TO PROSPECTIVE TENANT.
A LANDLORD OF A SHORT ASSURED TENANCY HAS SPECIAL RIGHTS TO REPOSSESS THE HOUSE. IF THE LANDLORD TERMINATES THE TENANCY BY ISSUING A VALID NOTICE TO QUIT AND GIVES THE TENANT AT LEAST 2 MONTHS NOTICE (OR A LONGER PERIOD IF THE TENANCY AGREEMENT PROVIDES) OF HIS INTENTION TO REPOSSESS THE HOUSE THE COURT MUST GRANT THE LANDLORD AN ORDER ALLOWING HIM TO EVICT THE TENANT IF HE APPLIES FOR ONE AT THE END OF THE TENANCY PERIOD SET OUT IN THE TENANCY AGREEMENT.

Part 3. Address and telephone number of agents if appropriate

of landlord(s) agent   **of Tenant(s) agent**

....
....
....
....

NOTE 4 TO PROSPECTIVE TENANT.
A TENANT OF A SHORT ASSURED TENANCY HAS A SPECIAL RIGHT TO APPLY TO A RENT ASSESSMENT COMMITTEE FOR A RENT DETERMINATION FOR THE TENANCY.

NOTE 5 TO PROSPECTIVE TENANT.
IF YOU AGREE TO TAKE UP THE TENANCY AFTER YOUR LANDLORD HAS SERVED THIS NOTICE ON YOU YOUR TENANCY WILL BE A SHORT ASSURED TENANCY. YOU SHOULD KEEP THIS NOTICE IN A SAFE PLACE ALONG WITH THE WRITTEN DOCUMENT SETTING OUT THE TERMS OF TENANCY WHICH YOUR LANDLORD MUST PROVIDE UNDER SECTION 30 OF THE HOUSING (SCOTLAND) ACT 1988 ONCE THE TERMS ARE AGREED.

NOTE 6 TO PROSPECTIVE TENANT.
IF YOU REQUIRE FURTHER GUIDANCE ON ASSURED AND SHORT ASSURED TENANCIES, CONSULT A SOLICITOR OR ANY ORGANISATION WHICH GIVES ADVICE ON HOUSING MATTERS.

[1450]   SI 1988/2109

SPECIAL NOTES FOR EXISTING TENANTS

1. If you already have a regulated tenancy, other than a short tenancy, should you give it up and take a new tenancy in the same house or another house owned by the same landlord, that tenancy **cannot** be an assured tenancy or a short assured tenancy. Your tenancy will continue to be a regulated tenancy.

2. If you have a short tenancy under the Tenant's Rights, Etc (Scotland) Act 1980 or the Rent (Scotland) Act 1984 your landlord **can** offer you an assured tenancy or short assured tenancy of the same or another house on the expiry of your existing tenancy.

3. If you are an existing tenant and are uncertain about accepting the proposed short assured tenancy you are strongly advised to consult a solicitor or any organisation which gives advice on housing matters.   [1450]

FORM AT6: FOR USE ONLY BY A LANDLORD

ASSURED TENANCIES   AT6

**HOUSING (SCOTLAND) ACT 1988
AS AMENDED BY PARAGRAPH 85 OF SCHEDULE 17
TO THE HOUSING ACT 1988**

**NOTICE UNDER SECTION 19 OF INTENTION
TO RAISE PROCEEDINGS FOR POSSESSION**

IMPORTANT: INFORMATION FOR TENANT(S)

This notice informs you as tenant that your landlord intends to apply to the Sheriff for an Order for possession of the house at the address in Part 1, which is currently occupied by you.

Part 1. To ....
                                                    (name of tenant(s))
         of ....
         ....
         ....
         ....
                                                    (address of house)

NOTE 1 TO TENANT.
IF YOU ARE UNCERTAIN ABOUT WHAT THIS NOTICE MEANS, OR IF YOU ARE IN DOUBT ABOUT ANYTHING IN IT, OR ABOUT ITS VALIDITY OR WHETHER IT IS FILLED IN PROPERLY YOU SHOULD IMMEDIATELY CONSULT A SOLICITOR OR AN ORGANISATION WHICH GIVES ADVICE ON HOUSING MATTERS. YOU MAY ALSO FIND IT HELPFUL TO DISCUSS THIS NOTICE WITH YOUR LANDLORD.

SI 1988/2109 [1451]

Part 2. I/we [on behalf of]* your landlord(s)

....
.... (name(s) of landlord(s))
of ....
....
....
.... (address and telephone number of landlord(s))

inform you that I/we* intend to raise proceedings for possession of the house at the address in Part 1 above on the following ground/grounds* being a ground/grounds* for possession as set out in Schedule 5 to the Housing (Scotland) Act 1988.

....
....
....
(give the ground number(s) and fully state ground(s)
as set out in Schedule 5 to the Housing (Scotland) Act 1988:
continue on additional sheets of paper if required)

NOTE 2 TO TENANT.
A FULL LIST OF THE 17 GROUNDS FOR POSSESSION IN SCHEDULE 5 TO THE HOUSING (SCOTLAND) ACT 1988 TOGETHER WITH INFORMATION ON YOUR RIGHTS AS TENANT IS GIVEN IN THE BOOKLET 'ASSURED TENANCIES IN SCOTLAND. A GUIDE FOR LANDLORDS AND TENANTS'. IT IS AVAILABLE FROM ANY OFFICE OF THE RENT ASSESSMENT COMMITTEE, CITIZENS ADVICE BUREAU, HOUSING ADVISORY CENTRE OR FROM THE RENT REGISTRATION SERVICE.

Part 3. I/we also inform you that I/we are seeking possession under the above ground/grounds* for the following reasons:

....
....
....
....
(state particulars of how you believe the ground(s) have
arisen: continue on additional sheets of paper if required)

* **delete as appropriate**

NOTE 3 TO TENANT.
YOUR LANDLORD MUST GIVE YOU PROPER NOTICE BETWEEN SERVING THIS NOTICE AND RAISING COURT PROCEEDINGS. IF <u>ANY</u> OF GROUNDS, 1, 2, 5, 6, 7, 9 AND 17 APPLY, WITH OR WITHOUT OTHER GROUNDS, 2 MONTHS NOTICE MUST BE GIVEN. YOUR LANDLORD MUST ALSO GIVE YOU 2 MONTHS NOTICE IF YOUR TENANCY IS A SHORT ASSURED TENANCY AND YOUR LANDLORD IS SEEKING REPOSSESSION ON THE GROUND THAT THE TENANCY PERIOD HAS EXPIRED. IF <u>ONLY</u> OTHER GROUNDS APPLY, ONLY 2 WEEKS NOTICE NEED BE GIVEN.

Part 4. Proceedings will not be raised before .... (date) (which is the earliest date at which proceedings can be raised under Section 19 of the Housing (Scotland) Act 1988).

Signed .... (Landlord(s) or Landlord's agent)

Date ....

* delete as appropriate

NOTE 4 TO TENANT.
IF YOUR LANDLORD DOES NOT RAISE COURT PROCEEDINGS THIS NOTICE AT6 WILL CEASE TO HAVE EFFECT 6 MONTHS AFTER THE EARLIEST DATE ON WHICH COURT PROCEEDINGS COULD HAVE BEEN RAISED (SEE PART 4 OF THE NOTICE).

NOTE 5 TO TENANT.
IF YOU WANT TO CONTEST YOUR LANDLORD'S INTENTION TO REPOSSESS YOUR HOME, YOU ARE STRONGLY ADVISED TO TAKE LEGAL ADVICE WITHOUT DELAY AND BEFORE THE EXPIRY OF THE TIME LIMIT GIVEN BY THE NOTICE. HELP WITH ALL OR PART OF THE COST OF LEGAL ADVICE MAY BE AVAILABLE UNDER THE LEGAL AID LEGISLATION.

NOTE 6 TO TENANT.
REMEMBER BEFORE YOU MUST LEAVE YOUR HOME, YOUR LANDLORD MUST HAVE DONE 3 THINGS:

1. SERVED ON YOU A NOTICE TO QUIT (NOTE CAREFULLY THAT THIS MAY HAVE BEEN SERVED AT AN EARLIER STAGE IN THE TENANCY TO CHANGE THE TENANCY FROM A CONTRACTUAL TO A STATUTORY ASSURED TENANCY); AND
2. SERVED ON YOU AN AT6 (THIS NOTICE); AND
3. OBTAINED A COURT ORDER.

NOTE 7 TO TENANT.
THIS IS AN IMPORTANT DOCUMENT AND YOU SHOULD KEEP IT IN A SAFE PLACE.

SI 1988/2109 [1452]

FORM AT7: FOR USE ONLY BY A LANDLORD

ASSURED TENANCIES   AT7

HOUSING (SCOTLAND) ACT 1988

NOTICE UNDER SECTION 32(4) THAT A NEW OR CONTINUING TENANCY IS NOT TO BE A SHORT ASSURED TENANCY

IMPORTANT: INFORMATION FOR TENANT(S)

This notice informs you as tenant that your landlord is proposing to offer you a new tenancy which is not a short assured tenancy, or to continue your existing tenancy, as an assured tenancy, not as a short assured tenancy. Please read this notice carefully.

Part 1. To ....
                                                              (name of tenant(s))
of ....
....
....
....
                                                              (address of tenant(s))

NOTE 1 TO TENANT.
YOU SHOULD NOTE THAT THIS NOTICE SERVED BY YOUR LANDLORD CHANGES YOUR TENANCY FROM A SHORT ASSURED TENANCY TO AN ASSURED TENANCY. PLEASE READ THIS NOTICE CAREFULLY. IF YOU ARE IN DOUBT ABOUT WHAT IT MEANS, YOU MAY WISH TO DISCUSS THE NOTICE WITH YOUR LANDLORD OR CONSULT A SOLICITOR OR AN ORGANISATION WHICH GIVES ADVICE ON HOUSING MATTERS.

Part 2.   I/We* [on behalf of]* your landlord(s)
....
                                                              (name(s) of landlord(s))
of ....
....
....
                                                              (address and telephone number of landlord(s))

Give notice that:

*[Your tenancy of the house at the address in Part 1 is to continue with its current terms and conditions but that as from .... (date) it will no longer be a short assured tenancy.]

*[Your new tenancy of the house at the address in Part 1 which takes effect from .... (date) will not be a short assured tenancy.]

Notice AT5 which informed you that your original tenancy was a short assured tenancy, and which was served on you on .... (date of service of notice AT5) no longer applies.

   Signed .... (Landlord(s) or Landlord's agent)

   Date ....

* delete as appropriate

NOTE 2 TO TENANT.
YOUR LANDLORD MUST SERVE THIS NOTICE ON YOU BEFORE THE BEGINNING OF THE NEW TENANCY OR BEFORE THE EXISTING TENANCY'S EXPIRY DATE IF IT IS TO CONTINUE. IF HE DOES NOT, THE NOTICE HAS NO EFFECT.

NOTE 3 TO TENANT.
AS A TENANT OF AN ASSURED TENANCY (RATHER THAN OF A SHORT ASSURED TENANCY) YOUR RIGHTS TO MAKE AN APPLICATION TO A RENT ASSESSMENT COMMITTEE FOR A DETERMINATION OF YOUR RENT WILL CHANGE. A TENANT OF AN ASSURED TENANCY CAN REFER TO THE RENT ASSESSMENT COMMITTEE A RENT INCREASE PROPOSED BY THE LANDLORD ONLY IN CERTAIN CIRCUMSTANCES. FURTHER INFORMATION ABOUT THIS IS AVAILABLE IN 'ASSURED TENANCIES IN SCOTLAND—A GUIDE FOR LANDLORDS AND TENANTS'.

NOTE 4 TO TENANT.
IN AN ASSURED TENANCY YOUR LANDLORD CANNOT REPOSSESS YOUR HOME SOLELY BECAUSE THE EXPIRY DATE IN THE TENANCY AGREEMENT HAS BEEN REACHED BUT OTHERWISE THE SECURITY OF TENURE OF AN ASSURED TENANT IS THE SAME AS THAT OF A TENANT WITH A SHORT ASSURED TENANCY.

NOTE 5 TO TENANT.
YOU SHOULD RETAIN THIS NOTICE AND KEEP IT IN A SAFE PLACE ALONG WITH THE WRITTEN DOCUMENT PROVIDED BY YOUR LANDLORD SETTING OUT THE TERMS OF YOUR TENANCY.

SI 1988/2109 [1453]

ASSURED TENANCIES　　　　　　　　　　　　　　　　　　　　AT8

HOUSING (SCOTLAND) ACT 1988

NOTICE UNDER SECTION 48(2) REQUIRING THAT A LANDLORD OR TENANT SUPPLY THE RENT ASSESSMENT COMMITTEE WITH INFORMATION

IMPORTANT:

This Notice is served on you by the Rent Assessment Committee. It requires you to supply the Committee with the information detailed in Part 3 below. This information is needed to allow the Committee to make a determination of rent or terms of the tenancy as provided for by the Housing (Scotland) Act 1988. You should provide the information by the date in Part 4. Failure to provide the information may make you liable to summary conviction and a fine.

Please read this Notice carefully before responding

Part 1. To .... landlord/tenant*

Part 2. An application has been made to the Rent Assessment Committee for consideration of:

* the terms of the statutory assured tenancy

* the terms of the statutory assured tenancy and a consequent adjustment in rent to reflect those terms

* an increase in rent for the statutory assured tenancy

* the rent under the short assured tenancy

for the house at:

....
....
....
....
(address of house let under the tenancy)

* delete as appropriate

Part 3. To help the Committee consider this application further information is needed from you.
The further information required is:

....
....
....
....
....

755

[1453] SI 1988/2109

....
....
....
....
....
....
....

Part 4. You should send this information to the address given in Part 5 of this Notice by .... (date). **NOTE**: The date must be not less than 14 days after the date on which this notice is served. If you do not comply with this Notice without reasonable excuse you will be liable on summary conviction to a fine not exceeding level 3 on the standard scale. If you are not clear exactly what information you are to provide to the Committee, please contact me immediately.

Part 5. Signed ....

for the Rent Assessment Committee

....
....
....
....

(address and telephone number of Committee)

Date................

[1453]

SI 1989/81 [1455]

The Rent Assessment Committee (Assured Tenancies) (Scotland) Regulations 1989
SI 1989/81

(*These regulations were made by the Secretary of State for Scotland under the Rent (Scotland) Act 1984 (c 58), s 53(1) (6), and came into force on 20 February 1989*)

ARRANGEMENT OF REGULATIONS
(*This list is not printed in the Regulations*)

1	Citation and commencement	[1454]
2	Interpretation	[1455]
3	Application	[1456]
4	Committee response to a reference	[1457]
5	Hearings	[1458]
6	Documents	[1459]
7	Inspection of house	[1460]
8	Decisions	[1461]
9	Giving of notices, etc	[1462]

1. (*Citation and commencement*) [1454]

2. Interpretation.

(1) In these Regulations, unless the context otherwise requires—
'the 1984 Act' means the Rent (Scotland) Act 1984;
'the 1988 Act' means the Housing (Scotland) Act 1988;
'assured tenancy' and 'short assured tenancy' have the meanings assigned to them respectively by sections 12 and 32 of the 1988 Act and 'statutory assured tenancy' has the meaning assigned to it by section 16 of the 1988 Act;
'chairman' means the chairman of a committee;
'committee' means a rent assessment committee, to which a reference is made and which is constituted in accordance with the provisions of Schedule 4 to the 1984 Act;
'hearing' means the meeting or meetings of a committee to hear oral representations made in relation to a reference;
'party' means, in the case where a reference is subject to a hearing, any peson who is entitled under regulation 5(2) of these Regulations to receive notice of the date, time and place of the hearing and, in the case where a reference is not to be subject to a hearing, any person who is entitled to make representations in writing to the committee;
'reference' means a matter which is referred to a committee by a landlord or a tenant under regulation 3 of these Regulations.

(2) For the purpose of any of these regulations relating to procedure at a hearing, any reference to a party shall be construed as including a reference to a person authorised by that party to be heard on his behalf, whether or not that person is an advocate or a solicitor. [1455]

NOTES to regulation 2

Reg 2(1): For ss 12, 16, and 32 of the 1988 Act see paras [1103], [1107] and [1123] above; for Sch 4 to the 1984 Act see paras [401–412] above.

3. Application.

These Regulations apply to any of the following references to the committee—
(a) a reference by a landlord or by a tenant under section 17(3) of the 1988 Act of a notice which has been served under section 17(2) of that Act (a notice proposing terms of a statutory assured tenancy and, if appropriate, an adjustment of the rent to take account of the proposed terms);
(b) a reference by a tenant under section 24(3) of the 1988 Act of a notice which has been served under section 24(1) of that Act (notice proposing an increase in rent under an assured tenancy);
(c) an application by a tenant under section 34(1) of the 1988 Act (application for a determination of the rent which the landlord might reasonably be expected to obtain under a short assured tenancy). **[1456]**

NOTES to regulation 3
Reg 3: For ss 17, 24, and 31 of the 1988 Act see paras [1108], [1115], and [1122] above.
Definitions: 'reference', 'committee' 'assured tenancy', 'short assured tenancy', '1988 Act': see reg 2(1).

4. Committee response to a reference.

(1) When a reference is made to a committee, the committee shall as soon as practicable thereafter serve on the landlord and on the tenant a notice specifying a period of not less than 14 days from the service of the notice during which either representations in writing or a request to make oral representations may be made to the committee by either party.

(2) Where within the period specified in paragraph (1) of this regulation, or such further period as the committee may allow, the landlord or the tenant requests to make oral representations, the committee shall give him an opportunity of being heard at a hearing in accordance with regulation 5 below.

(3) The committee may make such inquiries, if any, as they think fit and consider any information supplied or representations made to them relevant to the matters to be determined by them, but shall give the parties adequate opportunity for considering such information and representations and may hold a hearing whether or not the parties have requested one. **[1457]**

NOTES to regulation 4
Definitions: 'reference', 'committee' 'party' and 'leasing': see reg 2(1).

5. Hearings.

(1) Where a reference is to be subject to a hearing, the committee shall appoint a date, time and place for a hearing.

(2) A committee shall give not less than 10 days' notice in writing to the landlord and the tenant of the date, time and place so appointed to a hearing.

(3) A hearing shall be in public unless for special reasons the committee otherwise decide, but nothing in these Regulations shall prevent a member of the Council on Tribunals or of its Scottish Committee in that capacity from attending any hearing.

(4) At a hearing—
(a) a party may be heard either in person or by a person authorised by him in that behalf, whether or not that person is an advocate or a solicitor;
(b) the parties shall be heard in such order and, subject to the provision of these Regulations, the procedure shall be such as the committee shall determine; and
(c) a party may call witnesses, give evidence on his own behalf and cross-examine any witnesses called by the other party.

(5) The committee at their discretion may on their own motion, or at the request of the

parties or one of them, at any time and from time to time postpone or adjourn a hearing; but they shall not do so at the request of one part only unless, having regard to the grounds upon which and the time at which such request is made and to the convenience of the parties, they deem it reasonable to do so. The committee shall give to the parties such notice of any postponed or adjourned hearing as they deem to be reasonable in the circumstances.

(6) If a party does not appear at a hearing, the committee, on being satisfied that the requirements of this regulation regarding the giving of notice of a hearing have been duly complied with, may proceed to deal with the reference upon the representations of any party present and upon the documents and information which they may properly consider. **[1458]**

NOTES to regulation 5
Definitions: 'reference', 'hearing', 'committee' and 'party': see reg 2(1).

6. Documents.

(1) Where the reference is to be subject to a hearing, the committee shall take all reasonable steps to ensure that there is supplied to each of the parties before the date of the hearing—
- (a) a copy of, or sufficient extracts from, or particulars of, any document relevant to the reference which has been received from a party (other than a document which is in the possession of such party or of which that party has previously been supplied with a copy); and
- (b) a copy of any document which embodies results of any enquiries made by or for the committee for the purposes of that reference, or which contains relevant information in relation to rents or other tenancy terms previously determined for other houses and which has been prepared for the committee for the purposes of that reference.

(2) At any hearing where—
- (a) any document relevant to the reference is not in the possession of a party present at such hearing; and
- (b) such party has not been supplied with a copy of, or relevant extracts from, or particulars of, such document by the committee in accordance with the provisions of paragraph (1) of this regulation,

then unless—
- (i) such party consents to the continuation of the hearing; or
- (ii) the committee consider that such party has a sufficient opportunity of dealing with such document without an adjournment of the hearing,

the committee shall not consider such document until after they have adjourned the hearing for a period which they consider will afford such a party a sufficient opportunity of dealing with such document.

(3) Where a reference is not to be subject to a hearing, the committee shall supply to each of the parties a copy of, or sufficient extracts from, or particulars of, any such document as is mentioned in paragraph (1)(a) of this regulation (other than a document excepted from that paragraph) and a copy of any such document as is mentioned in paragraph (1)(b) of this regulation, and they shall not reach their decision until they are satisfied that each party has been given a sufficient opportunity of commenting upon any document of which a copy or from which extracts or of which particulars has or have been so supplied, and upon the other party's case. **[1459]**

NOTES to regulation 6
Definitions: 'reference', 'hearing', 'committee' and 'party': see reg 2(1).

7. Inspection of house.

(1) The committee may on their own motion and shall at the request of one of the

parties (subject in either case to any necessary consent being obtained) inspect the house which is the subject of the reference.

(2) An inspection may be made before, during or after the close of the hearing, or at such stage in relation to the consideration of the representations in writing as the committee shall determine.

(3) The committee shall give such notice in writing as they deem sufficient on an inspection to the party or parties and shall allow each party and his representative to attend any such inspection.

(4) Where an inspection is made after the close of a hearing, the committee may, if they consider that it is expedient to do so on account of any matter arising from the inspection, re-open the hearing; and if the hearing is to be re-opened, paragraph (2) of regulation 5 of these Regulations shall apply as it applied to the original hearing, save in so far as its requirements may be dispensed with or relaxed with the consent of the parties. **[1460]**

NOTES to regulation 7
Definitions: 'committee', 'party', 'reference', and 'hearing': see reg 2(1).

8. Decisions.

(1) The decision of the committee upon a reference shall be recorded in a document signed by the chairman (or, in the event of his absence or incapacity, by another member of the committee) which shall contain no reference to the decision being a majority (if that be the case) or to any opinion of a minority.

(2) Where the committee are requested, on or before the giving or notification of the decision, to state the reasons for the decision, those reasons shall be recorded in the said document.

(3) The chairman (or, in the event of his absence or incapacity, another member of the committee) shall have power, by a certificate under his hand, to correct any clerical or accidental error or omission in the document.

(4) A copy of the document and of any such correction shall be sent by the committee to the party or parties. **[1461]**

NOTES to regulation 8
Definitions: 'committee', 'reference'; 'chairman', and 'party': see reg 2(1).

9. Giving of notices, etc.

Where any notice or other written matter is required under the provisions of these Regulations to be served, given or supplied by the committee to a party or parties, it shall be sufficient compliance with the Regulations if such notice or matter is served, given or supplied—
  (a) by delivering it to him or to his agent where a party has appointed an agent to act on his behalf;
  (b) by leaving it at his or his agent's last known address; or
  (c) by sending it by recorded delivery letter to him or his agent at that address. **[1462]**

NOTES to regulation 9
Definitions: 'committee' and 'party': see reg 2(1).

SI 1989/423 [1466]

The Right To Purchase From A Public Sector Landlord (Application Form) (Scotland) Regulations 1989
SI 1989/423

(These regulations were made by the Secretary of State for Scotland under the Housing (Scotland) Act 1988 (c 43), s 58(1), and came into force on 3 April 1989)

1. *(Citation and commencement)* [1463]

2. **Interpretation.**

   In these Regulations:
   'the Act' means the Housing (Scotland) Act 1988;
   'applicant' means a person who has been approved by Scottish Homes under section 57 of the Act or, as the case may be, Scottish Homes; and
   'public sector landlord' has the same meaning as in section 56(3) of the Act. [1464]

3. **Form of Notice.**

   For the purposes of section 58(1) of the Act (which requires an applicant wishing to exercise the right conferred by Part III of the Act to acquire a house from a public sector landlord to serve a notice on that landlord), there is prescribed the notice in the form set out in the Schedule hereto or in a form substantially to the like effect. [1465]

Regulation 3　　　　　　　　　SCHEDULE

FORM OF NOTICE

HOUSING (SCOTLAND) ACT 1988
NOTICE OF APPLICATION TO PURCHASE UNDER SECTION 58

I, [inset name and address of applicant], hereby give notice that I seek to exercise the right conferred by Part III of the Housing (Scotland) Act 1988 ('the Act') to acquire the house specified in Part I of this Notice from you, [insert name and address of public sector landlord].

As required by section 58(1)(b) of the Act, this Notice is accompanied by the consent in writing of the qualifying tenant or tenants (including the persons mentioned in section 58(2) of the Act) to this approach being made to you. Information about the qualifying tenant(s) and those other persons is given in Part II of this Notice.

[Where the applicant is not Scottish Homes] I am approved by Scottish Homes under section 57 of the Act. I attach a copy of the document issued by Scottish Homes in terms of which I am approved.

　　　　　　　　　　　　　　　　　Signed: ....

　　　　　　　　　　　　　　　　　Date: ....

PART I
HOUSE TO BE ACQUIRED

Address of the house
to be acquired:

Any other heritable property which will reasonably serve a beneficial purpose in connection with the house which it is proposed to acquire:

PART II
INFORMATION ABOUT QUALIFYING TENANT(S) AND OTHER PERSONS

Name of tenant or,
in the case of joint tenants,
the name of each joint tenant:

Name of spouse of each tenant
(including any person living with
tenant as a spouse);

Date Tenancy Commenced:

SI 1989/423 [1471]

NOTES to SI 1989/423

Reg 2: For ss 56 and 57 of the Housing (Scotland) Act 1988 (c 43) see paras [1144] and [1145] above.

Reg 3: For s 58 of the Housing (Scotland) Act 1988 (c 43), see para [1146] above. Part III of that Act comprises ss 56–64. See paras [1144] to [1152] above.

The Assured Tenancies (Rent Information) (Scotland) Order 1989

SI 1989/685

(*This order was made by the Secretary of State for Scotland under the Housing (Scotland) Act 1988 (c 43), s 49, and came into force on 17 May 1989*)

1. (*Citation and commencement*) **[1467]**

2. The information with respect to rents under assured tenancies to be kept by the rent assessment panel (whether it is kept in documentary form or otherwise) shall be kept in such manner—
(a) that the entry in respect of each tenancy shows, or
(b) if kept otherwise than in documentary form that each entry when displayed or printed shows,
the information specified in the Schedule to this Order. **[1468]**

3. The rent assessment panel shall keep the specified information available for public inspection without charge during usual office hours at the office of the panel. **[1469]**

4. A person requiring a copy of any specified information certified under the hand of an authorised officer of the rent assessment panel shall be entitled to obtain it on payment of a fee of £1.50 for the specified information relating to each entry. **[1470]**

Article 2 SCHEDULE

Information with respect to rents under assured tenancies to be kept by rent assessment panel:

1. Address and description of subjects of let.

2. Details of any accommodation which is shared including whether it is shared with the landlord or somebody else.

3. Names and addresses of landlord and tenant.

4. Duration of tenancy if short assured tenancy.

5. Rent applying before application is made.

6. Details of any furniture and services provided by the landlord and the amount of the rent which is attributable to the use of furniture or for services.

[1471]

7. Kind of application, for example, whether (a) proposing new terms and rent, (b) proposing new rent or (c) determination of rent for short assured tenancy.

8. Date and details of determination including revised rent and whether or not linked with change in the terms of the tenancy.

9. Reasons for a refusal to make a determination of the kind mentioned in 7(c) above.

10. Any other factor taken into consideration by the rent assessment committee in making a determination. [1471]

The Limits on Rent Increases (Scotland) Order 1989

SI 1989/2469

(*This order was made by the Secretary of State for Scotland under the Rent (Scotland) Act 1984 (c 58), s 33(1) and (2), and came into force on 5 February 1990*)

ARRANGEMENT OF REGULATIONS
(*This list is not printed in the Regulations*)

1	Citation and commencement	[1472]
2	Interpretation	[1473]
3	Calculation of previous rent limit	[1474]
4	Effect of notice of increase	[1475]
5	Permitted increase	[1476]
6	Restriction on rent increases in cases of further registration	[1477]
7	Successive tenancies	[1478]
8	New tenancies	[1479]
9	Transitional	[1480]
10		[1481]
11		[1482]
12	Supplemental	[1483]
13	Revocation	[1484]

1. (*Citation and commencement*) [1472]

2. **Interpretation.**

In this Order—
'the 1984 Act' means the Rent (Scotland) Act 1984;
'first period' means the period of 12 months beginning with the date of registration;
'noted amount' means the amount of the registered rent noted as fairly attributable to the provision of services under section 49(2)(b) of the 1984 Act;
'permitted increase' means the amount by which the rent for any first period or subsequent period may be increased calculated in accordance with article 5(2) or (3) of this Order as the case may be;
'previous rent limit' means, as the case may require and subject to article 3 of this Order, either—
   (a) where the increase is the first to be made since the date of registration of the rent, the amount payable by way of rent on that date; or
   (b) in all other cases, the amount payable by way of rent on the most recent anniversary of that date;

'registered' in relation to rent means registered under Part V of the 1984 Act and 'registration' shall be construed accordingly; and

'subsequent period' means the period of 12 months beginning on the date of the first anniversary of the date of registration. **[1473]**

NOTES to Article 2
For s 49 of the 1984 Act see para [297] above.
Part V of the 1984 Act comprises ss 43–54. See paras [291] to [302] above.

3. Calculation of previous rent limit.

Where the previous rent limit included a noted amount as defined in article 2 of this Order the previous rent limit shall, for the purposes of article 5 of this Order, be reduced by the amount or amounts so payable. **[1474]**

NOTES to Article 3
Definitions: 'previous rent limit', and 'noted amount': see Article 2.

4. Effect of notice of increase.

(1) Where a rent for a dwellinghouse under a regulated tenancy is registered on or after the date of commencement of this Order and the rent payable under the tenancy for any statutory period (or part thereof) is less than the amount so registered, it shall not be increased by a notice of increase under section 29(2)(b) of the 1984 Act except to the extent permitted by article 5 of this Order, and any such notice which purports to increase it further shall have effect to increase it to the extent so permitted but no further.

(2) Paragraph (1) of this article shall not affect any increase in respect of a noted amount within the meaning of article 2 of this Order. **[1475]**

NOTES to Article 4
Reg 4(1): For s 29 of the 1984 Act see para [277] above.
Definitions: '1984 Act' and 'noted amount': see Article 2.

5. Permitted increase.

(1) Subject to paragraph (4) of this article, the rent may be increased in any first period or subsequent period to the aggregate of the following:—
  (a) the amount of the previous rent limit, calculated in accordance with article 3 of this Order; and
  (b) the noted amount (if any) as defined in article 2 of this Order; and
  (c) the permitted increase, calculated in accordance with paragraph (2) or (3) of this article, as the case may be.

(2) The permitted increase in respect of the first period shall be the greatest of the following amounts:—
  (a) £104; or
  (b) one quarter of the previous rent limit, ascertained in accordance with article 3 of this Order; or
  (c) one half of the difference between the previous rent limit ascertained in accordance with article 3 of this Order and the registered rent.

(3) The permitted increase in respect of the subsequent period shall be such amount as is required to increase the previous rent limit calculated in accordance with article 3 of this Order to the registered rent.

(4) Nothing in this article—
  (a) shall permit the rent to be increased above the amount of the registered rent;
  (b) shall prevent or limit an increase in any sums in a rent which are variable by virtue of section 49(6) of the 1984 Act. **[1476]**

NOTES to Article 5

Reg 5(4): For s 49 of the 1984 Act, see para [297] above.
Definitions: 'first period', 'subsequent period', 'previous rent limit', 'noted amount', 'permitted increase', 'registered' and '1984 Act': see Article 2.

6. Restriction on rent increases in cases of further registration.

(1) Where, on or after the commencement of this Order—
(a) a registration is superseded by another registration,
(b) the new registration permits the rent to be increased above the amount payable under the former registration,
(c) the new registration takes effect within 12 months of an increase in rent recoverable in respect of the former registration, and
(d) the increase mentioned in sub-paragraph (c) above is less than the increase (in consequence of the new registration) permitted by virtue of article 5(4)(a) of this Order,

the total additional rental income in the period of 12 months (beginning with an anniversary of the date of the former registration) in which the new registration occurs shall not, by virtue of a permitted increase taking effect within 12 months of an increase which falls within sub-paragraph (d) of this paragraph, be increased above the permitted increase which, but for article 5(4)(a) of this Order, would have been recoverable in respect of that period.

(2) Where the circumstances specified in paragraph (1)(a) to (c) above apply and the date of registration of the former registration occurred before the commencement of this Order, the total additional rental income in the period of twelve months in which the new registration occurs shall not exceed the increase, calculated in accordance with article 5(2) or (3) of this Order, which would, but for this paragraph, be permitted. **[1477]**

NOTES to Article 6
Definitions: 'registration' and 'permitted increase': see Article 2.

7. Successive tenancies.

Where—
(a) a rent for a dwellinghouse which is subject to a regulated tenancy is registered; and
(b) at a time when the rent payable under the tenancy is less than the registered rent the tenant, or any person who might succeed him as statutory tenant, becomes the tenant under a new regulated tenancy of the dwellinghouse,

the rent limit for any contractual period of the new regulated tenancy beginning before the registered rent becomes payable shall be the amount to which, if the first mentioned tenancy had continued, the rent payable thereunder could have increased in accordance with the provisions of this Order for a statutory period beginning at the same time. **[1478]**

NOTES to Article 7
Definition: 'registered': see Article 2.

8. New tenancies.

This Order shall not apply to the rent under any regulated tenancy of a dwellinghouse which was granted after the date of registration of the rent if the person to whom it was granted was neither the tenant under any previous regulated tenancy of that dwellinghouse nor any person who might have succeeded such a tenant as a statutory tenant of the dwellinghouse. **[1479]**

SI 1989/2469 [1484]

NOTES to Article 8
Definition: 'registered': see Article 2.

9. Transitional.

Where a rent has been registered before the date this Order comes into force but the full amount of the registered rent has not become payable by that date, the provisions of this Order shall apply to the next permitted increase which would have become due under the Increase of Rent Restriction (Scotland) Order 1980 as if it were a permitted increase due at the beginning of a first period under this Order. [1480]

NOTES to Article 9
Definitions: 'registration' and 'permitted increase': see Article 2.

10. Where a rent is registered before this Order comes into force in the circumstances specified in section 50(2) of the 1984 Act the date of registration shall be deemed to be the date of the first day after expiry of the period of three years mentioned in section 46(3) of the 1984 Act. [1481]

NOTES to Article 10
Definitions: 'registered' and 'registration': see Article 2.

11. Where a rent has been registered by the rent officer before the commencement of this Order and a rent determined by a rent assessment committee is registered after the commencement of this Order in substitution for that rent, the provisions of section 33 of the 1984 Act shall have effect as if only the rent determined by the rent assessment committee had been registered; but the date of registration shall be deemed for the purposes of that section (but not for the purposes of section 29(3) of the 1984 Act) to be the date on which the rent determined by the rent officer was registered. [1482]

NOTES to Article 11
For ss 29 and 33 of the 1984 Act see paras [277], [281] above.
Definitions: 'registered', 'registration', and '1984 Act': see Article 2.

12. Supplemental.

In ascertaining for the purpose of this Order whether there is any difference between amounts or what that difference is, such adjustments shall be made as may be necessary to take account of periods of different lengths; and for that purpose a month shall be treated as one twelfth and a week as one fifty-second of a year. [1483]

13. Revocation.

The Increase of Rent Restriction (Scotland) Order 1980 is hereby revoked. [1484]

The Home Purchase Assistance (Winding Up of Scheme) Order 1990

SI 1990/374

(This order was made, as respects Scotland, by the Secretary of State for Scotland under the Local Government and Housing Act 1989 (c 42), ss 171(1) and (2)(a), and came into force on 31 March 1990)

1. *(Citation and commencement)* **[1485]**

2. **Winding Up Provisions.**

1st April 1990 is specified as the date from which account will no longer be taken under the assistance legislation of—
   (a) any notice given on or after that date under paragraph 34(5) of the Home Purchase Assistance Directions 1978, or
   (b) any period of two years as described in paragraph 34(8) of those Directions which starts to run on or after that date. **[1486]**

3. 1st April 1993 is specified as the date from which account will no longer be taken under the assistance legislation of the making of any application for assistance. **[1487]**

The Rent Officers (Additional Functions) (Scotland) Order 1990

SI 1990/396

(This order was made by the Secretary of State for Scotland under the Housing (Scotland) Act 1988 (c 43), s 70, and came into force on 2 April 1990)

1. *(Citation and commencement)* **[1487A]**

2. **Interpretation.**

(1) In this Order, unless the context otherwise requires—
'child' means a person under the age of 16;
'determination' means a determination (including an interim and further determination) made in accordance with Schedule 1 to this Order;
'dwelling' has the same meaning as in the Social Security Act 1986;
'local authority' has the same meaning as it has in the Social Security Act 1986 in relation to Scotland;
'occupier' means a person (whether or not identified by name) who is stated, in the application for a determination, to occupy the dwelling;
'relevant time' means the time the application for the determination is made or, if earlier, the tenancy ends;
'rent' has the same meaning as in section 25 of the Housing (Scotland) Act 1988, except that the reference to the house in subsection (3) shall be construed as a reference to the dwelling;

'size criteria' means the standards relating to bedrooms and rooms suitable for living in specified in Schedule 2 to this Order; and
'tenancy' includes any other right of occupancy and references to a tenant, a landlord or any other expression appropriate to a tenancy shall be construed accordingly.

(2) In this Order any reference to a notice or application is to a notice or application in writing, and any notice by a rent officer may be sent by post. **[1487B]**

3. Additional Functions.

(1) Where in connection with housing benefit and rent allowance subsidy, a local authority applies to a rent officer for determinations relating to a tenancy of a dwelling (and is required by regulations made under section 30(2B)(a) or (2C) of the Social Security Act 1986 to make that application), the rent officer shall (subject to article 5) make the determinations and give notice in accordance with Schedule 1 to this Order.

(2) If a rent officer needs further information in order to make determination, he shall serve notice on the local authority requesting that information and until he receives it paragraph (1) shall not apply to the making of that determination. **[1487C]**

4. If, within the period of 10 weeks beginning with the date on which the local authority was given notice of a determination, the local authority applies (in connection with housing benefit and rent allowance subsidy) to a rent officer for a re-determination, a rent officer (subject to article 5) shall make the re-determination and give notice in accordance with Schedule 3 to this Order and a rent officer whose advice is sought as provided for in that Schedule shall give that advice. **[1487D]**

5.—(1) No determination or re-determination shall be made if the application for it is withdrawn.

(2) No determination or re-determination shall be made under paragraph 1 of Schedule 1 to this Order (or that paragraph as applied by Schedule 3 to this Order) if the tenancy is an assured tenancy and—
- [(a) (i) a determination under section 34 of the Housing (Scotland) Act 1988 has taken effect in relation to the tenancy; or
  - (ii) within the period of 12 months ending with the date on which the application for a determination (or, as the case may be a re-determination) was received, a determination under section 25 or 34 of that Act took effect (or would have taken effect but for the agreement of the landlord and tenant) in relation to the tenancy or a tenancy of the same dwelling on terms which were substantially the same (disregarding the terms relating to the amount of rent) as the terms of tenancy were on that date; or
  - (iii) within the period mentioned in sub-paragraph (ii) an application was made under section 34 of that Act in relation to such a tenancy as is referred to in that sub-paragraph and a determination was precluded by sub-section (3)(b) of that section; and
- (b) in respect of the circumstances described in sub-paragraphs (a)(ii) and (iii) there has been no substantial change in the condition of the dwelling (including the making of improvements) or in the terms of the tenancy, other than relating to the amount of the rent, within the period mentioned in sub-paragraph (a)(ii).] **[1487E]**

6. Revocation.

The Rent Officers (Additional Functions) (Scotland) Order 1989 and the Rent Officers (Additional Functions) (Scotland) Amendment Order 1989 are hereby revoked. **[1487F]**

Articles 2(1) and 3(1) SCHEDULE 1

DETERMINATIONS

1. **Rent determinations.**

(1) The rent officer shall determine whether, in his opinion, the rent payable under the tenancy of the dwelling at the relevant time is significantly higher than the rent which the landlord might reasonably be expected to obtain under the tenancy at that time, having regard to the level of rent under similar tenancies of similar dwellings in the locality (or as similar as regards tenancy, dwelling and locality as is reasonably practicable), but on the assumption that no one who would have been entitled to housing benefit has sought or is seeking the tenancy.

(2) If the rent officer determines under sub-paragraph (1) that the rent is significantly higher, the rent officer shall also determine the rent which the landlord might reasonably be expected to obtain under the tenancy at the relevant time, having regard to the same matter and on the same assumption as in sub-paragraph (1). **[1487G]**

2. **Size and rent determinations.**

(1) The rent officer shall determine whether the dwelling, at the relevant time, exceeds the size criteria for its occupiers.

(2) If the rent officer determines that the dwelling exceeds the size criteria, the rent officer shall also determine the rent which a landlord might reasonably be expected to obtain at the relevant time for a tenancy which is similar to the tenancy of the dwelling, on the same terms (other than the term relating to the amount of rent) and of a dwelling which is in the same locality as the dwelling, but which—
   (a) accords with the size criteria for its occupiers;
   (b) is in a reasonable state of repair; and
   (c) corresponds in other respects, in the rent officer's opinion, as closely as is reasonably practicable to the dwelling.

(3) When making a determination under paragraph 2(2), the rent officer shall have regard to the same matter and make the same assumption as in paragraph 1(1), except that in judging the similarity of other tenancies and dwellings the comparison shall be with the tenancy of the second dwelling referred to in paragraph 2(2) and the assumption shall be made in relation to that tenancy. **[1487H]**

3. **Services determinations.**

(1) Where the rent officer makes a determination under paragraph 1(2), 2(2) or (where no determination is to be made under paragraph 1(2)) paragraph 1(1) and the dwelling is not in a hostel (within the meaning of regulation 12A of the Housing Benefit (General) Regulations 1987, he shall also determine whether, in his opinion, any of the rent at the relevant time is fairly attributable to the provision of services which are ineligible to be met by housing benefit and, if so, the amount which in his opinion is so attributable (except where he considers the amount is negligible).

(2) In sub-paragraph (1) 'rent' in relation to a determination under paragraph 1(2) or 2(2) means the rent determined under paragraph 1(2) or 2(2) and, in relation to a determination under paragraph 1(1), means the rent payable under the tenancy at the relevant time; and 'services' means services performed or facilities (including the use of furniture) provided for, or rights made available to, the tenant, but not the provision of meals (including the preparation of meals or provision of unprepared food), [or the provision of services to which any service charge for fuel relates.] **[1487I]**

4. **Medical, nursing and other care services.**

Where the rent includes any of the charges specified in sub-paragraph (d), (e) or (f) of paragraph 1 of Part I of Schedule 1 to the Housing Benefit (General) Regulations 1987, the rent officer, when making a determination, shall assume that—

SI 1990/396 [1487O]

(a) the items to which the charges relate were not to be provided or made available; and
(b) the rent payable under the tenancy at the relevant time is such amount as is specified in the application as the rent which would have been payable under the tenancy at that time if those items were not to be provided or made available. [1487J]

5. Interim and further determinations.

If notice of a determination under paragraph 1 or 3 is not given to the local authority within the 5 day period mentioned in paragraph 6(a) solely because the rent officer intends to arrange an inspection of the dwelling before making such a determination, the rent officer shall make both an interim determination and a further determination. [1487K]

6. Notifications.

The rent officer shall give notice to the local authority of a determination—
(a) except in the case of a further determination, within the period of 5 working days beginning with the date on which the rent officer received the application or, where the rent officer requests further information under article 3(2), with the date on which he received the information, or as soon as practicable after that period; and
(b) in the case of a further determination, within the period of 20 working days beginning with the date on which notice of the interim determination was given to the local authority, or as soon as practicable after that period. [1487L]

7.—(1) If the rent officer becomes aware that the application is not one to which article 3(1) applies, the rent officer shall give the local authority notice to that effect.

(2) If the rent officer is precluded by article 5(2) from making a determination or a re-determination under paragraph 1 (or that paragraph as applied by Schedule 3), the rent officer shall give the local authority notice of the rent determined by the rent assessment committee [or, where the rent assessment committee has not made a determination, the rent payable under the tenancy when the application to the rent assessment committee was made.] [1487M]

Article 2(1)　　　　　　　　SCHEDULE 2

Size Criteria

1. One bedroom shall be allowed for each of the following categories of occupier (and each occupier shall come within only the first category for which he is eligible)—
(a) a married couple or an unmarried couple (within the meaning of Part II of the Social Security Act 1986);
(b) a person who is not a child;
(c) two children of the same sex;
(d) two children who are less than ten years old;
(e) a child. [1487N]

2. The number of rooms (excluding any allowed as a bedroom under paragraph 1) suitable for living in allowed are—
(a) if there are fewer than four occupiers, one;
(b) if there are more than three and fewer than seven occupiers, two;
(c) in any other case, three. [1487O]

Article 4 SCHEDULE 3

RE-DETERMINATIONS

1. Schedules 1 and 2 (except paragraph 5 of Schedule 1) shall apply in relation to a re-determination as they apply to a determination, subject to the following:—
(a) references in Schedule 1 to the relevant time shall be references to the time the original application for the determination is made or, if earlier, the tenancy ends; and
(b) for sub-paragraphs (a) and (b) of paragraph 6 of Schedule 1 there shall be substituted 'within the period of 20 working days beginning with the date of receipt of the application for a re-determination, or as soon as is reasonably practicable after that period'. **[1487P]**

2. The rent officer making the re-determination shall seek and have regard to the advice of one or two rent officers in relation to the re-determination. **[1487Q]**

NOTES to SI 1990/396
Amendments: Sub-paras (a) and (b) of Article 5(2) substituted by the Rent Officers (Additional Functions) (Scotland) Order 1991, SI 1991/533; paras 3(2) and 7(2) of Schedule 1 amended by *Ibid*. The amendments came into force on 1 April 1991 and do not have effect in a case where an application is made for redetermination in relation to a determination made before the amendments came into force.

The Home Energy Efficiency Grants Regulations 1990
SI 1990/1791

(*This order was made by the Secretary of State for Energy under the Social Security Act 1990 (c 27), s 15, and came into force on 1st October 1990*)

1. (*Citation and commencement*) **[1487R]**

2. **Interpretation.**
(1) In these Regulations, unless the context otherwise requires—
'the Act' means the Social Security Act 1990;
'administering agency' means a person or body of persons for the time being appointed under regulation 16;
'applicant' means a person who has made an application under regulation 4;
'building in multiple occupation' has the meaning given to it by section 15(4) of the Act;
'communal area' means a building in multiple occupation, and 'communal area grant' shall be construed accordingly;
'energy advice' means advice relating to thermal insulation or to the economic and efficient use of domestic appliances or of facilities for lighting, or for space or water heating, in dwellings where work as specified in sub-paragraphs (a), (b) or (c) of paragraph (1) of regulation 6 is, or is to be, carried out;
'draughtproofing' means the draughtproofing of external and internal doors including any door or hatch to any roof space and windows excluding kitchen and bathroom windows;
'grant' means a grant made in accordance with these Regulations but shall exclude a communal area grant;
'insulated additional roof space' means roof space which has been added to the

dwelling and in all or any part of which there is insulation material of a thickness of 50 millimetres or more;

'network installer' means a person or body of persons for the time being registered for a locality under regulation 14;

'roof space' means space between the roof of a dwelling and the ceiling of any room which is used or available for use for the purposes of living accommodation and which is not wholly separated from the roof by any other room; and

'works' means the work specified in paragraph (1) of regulation 6.

(2) Unless the context otherwise requires, any reference in these Regulations to a numbered regulation is a reference to the regulation in these Regulations bearing that number; and any reference in a regulation to a numbered paragraph is a reference to the paragraph of that regulation bearing that number.

(3) Words and expressions to which meanings are assigned by these Regulations shall (unless the contrary intention appears) have the same respective meanings in any document issued by or on behalf of the Secretary of State under these Regulations. **[1488]**

3. Persons who may apply for a grant.

(1) An application for a grant may be entertained from a person—
(a) who is the householder of and is resident in the dwelling in respect of which the application is made; and
(b) who at the time of making the application is, or whose spouse with whom he or she is living is, in receipt of any income support, housing benefit, family credit or community charge benefit (within the meaning of section 20 of the Social Security Act 1986).

(2) For the purpose of this regulation—
(a) 'householder' means a person, who alone or jointly with others, is—
   (i) in England and Wales, a freeholder, lessee or tenant (and 'lessee' shall include a sub-lessee and 'tenant' shall include a sub-tenant and, without prejudice to the generality of the term, include a person who has an assured tenancy, a protected tenancy, a secure tenancy or a statutory tenancy);
   (ii) in Scotland, an owner or tenant; and 'owner' includes any person who under the Lands Clauses Acts would be enabled to sell and convey land to the promoters of an undertaking, and 'tenant' includes sub-tenant and any person who has a statutory tenancy under section 3(1) of the Rent (Scotland) Act 1984, or who has entered into a contract to which Part VIII of that Act applies, or who has a statutory assured tenancy within the meaning of section 16(1) of the Housing (Scotland) Act 1988;
(b) 'spouse' includes a person with whom the applicant is living as husband or wife; and
(c) a person shall not be treated as resident in a dwelling unless he is residing there as his only or main residence. **[1489]**

4. Application for a grant.

(1) An application for a grant shall be made to the administering agency for the area, save that where the applicant intends that the works are to be undertaken by the network installer for the locality the application shall be made to that network installer.

(2) An application shall be in writing, signed by the applicant and in such form, subject to regulation 5, as is laid down by the administering agency. **[1490]**

5. The form of application shall state that—

(a) any necessary permission for the works has been obtained;
(b) reasonable access to the dwelling in respect of which the application is made will be given to a representative of the administering agency to inspect the dwelling and the works;

(c) no payment in respect of the works which are the subject of the application is being applied for or has been made under the Homes Insulation Act 1978 or section 521 of the Housing Act 1985 or section 252 of the Housing (Scotland) Act 1987 or Part VIII of the Local Government and Housing Act 1989.

6. Work for which a grant may be made.

(1) A grant may be made in respect of work which provides—
- (a) (i) insulation in any roof space, other than insulated additional roof space, including the insulation of any cold water tank and any water supply, overflow and expansion pipes; and
  - (ii) where there is no means of access to any roof space for the purpose of carrying out the work, such a means of access, including a permanent means of access, such provision being made at the same time as the provision of insulation in any roof space in accordance with sub-paragraph (a)(i); or
- (b) draughtproofing and insulation of any hot water tank or cylinder which is not already insulated by any means; or
- (c) insulation and draughtproofing as specified in sub-paragraphs (a) and (b); and
- (d) energy advice.

(2) The work shall comply with such standards, including standards of materials and workmanship, as are laid down from time to time by the administering agency with the approval of the Secretary of State.

7. By whom the works may be done.

Subject to paragraph (2) of regulation 6, works may be carried out by any person including, except in relation to energy advice, the applicant.

8. Dwellings eligible for a grant.

(1) Any dwelling is eligible for a grant except, in respect of work specified in sub-paragraphs (a) and (c) of paragraph (1) of regulation 6, a dwelling in which there is or has been at any time, during the period when the applicant has been resident in the dwelling, insulation material of a thickness of 50 millimetres or more in all or any part of any roof space.

(2) A dwelling which is within the exception in paragraph (1) shall nonetheless be eligible for a grant if all the insulation material of a thickness of 50 millimetres or more in the roof space—
- (a) is insulating a water tank, cylinder, water supply pipe, or overflow or expansion pipe; or
- (b) is in insulated additional roof space.

9. Procedure after application to the network installer.

(1) Where an application has been made to the network installer for the locality, he shall consider whether there appears to be eligibility for grant.

(2) If the network installer is not satisfied that there is eligibility for grant, he shall so notify the applicant in writing, return the application to the applicant and inform him that he may send the application to the administering agency for the area for determination.

(3) If the network installer is satisfied that there is eligibility for grant, he shall—
- (a) send the application to the administering agency for the area for determination, and at the same time certify to the administering agency in writing that he has carried out such verification as to the eligibility for grant as may be laid down from time to time by the administering agency; and
- (b) decide whether, pending determination of the application by the administering agency, he is prepared to carry out the work on the basis that, subject to the liability of the applicant as described in (i) below, he will, in the event that the administering agency should not approve the grant, bear the cost of the work; and

(i) if he is so prepared, notify the applicant in writing that he is prepared to carry out the work on the basis that, unless the application for grant is not approved or the claim not paid by the administering agency on grounds of a material misrepresentation, the applicant shall be liable to pay in respect of the work only the contribution as specified in column 2 of the Table in regulation 11 together with such amount as has been agreed in writing between the applicant and the network installer before the making of the application as representing the amount by which the full cost of the works exceeds the sum of the grant and the contribution; or

(ii) if he is not so prepared, notify the applicant in writing that he is awaiting determination of the application by the administering agency.

(4) For the purpose of this regulation 'material misrepresentation' means any representation by or on behalf of the applicant in respect of any of the matters relating to eligibility for grant which is false in a material particular. [1495]

10. Procedure after application to the administering agency.

(1) On receipt of an application, the administering agency for the area, in considering whether to approve a grant, shall determine whether there is eligibility for grant and, if there is, whether there are sufficient funds to make payment of the grant having regard to any amounts otherwise allocated or to be allocated in accordance with these Regulations.

(2) Subject to paragraph (3), the administering agency shall send written notification of whether grant has been approved to the applicant and to any person or body of persons nominated by the applicant to carry out the works.

(3) Where the application has been sent by a network installer under paragraph (3) of regulation 9, the administering agency shall send written notification of whether grant has been approved to the network installer and, save where the work has been done by the network installer by virtue of sub-paragraph (b)(i) of paragraph (3) of regulation 9 and the grant has been approved by the administering agency, to the applicant.

(4) When notifying the applicant that grant has not been approved, the administering agency shall inform the applicant as to the reasons. [1496]

11. Calculation of the size of grant.

(1) The amount of any grant shall be determined in accordance with the following Table and paragraphs (2), (3) and (4)—

TABLE

(1)	(2)	(3)	(4)	(5)
Work under regulation	Applicant's contribution	Work carried out by applicant	Trainee labour	Non-trainee labour
6(1)(a)	£10	£140	£155	£175
6(1)(b)	£7	£78	£93	£113
6(1)(c)	£15	£220	£240	£270
6(1)(d)	Nil	No grant available	£10	£10

(2) Where the work is carried out by the applicant, the grant for the work specified in column 1 of the Table shall be the lesser of—

(a) the sum calculated by deducting from the cost of materials used, the contribution shown in column 2 of the Table; and
(b) the figure shown in column 3 of the Table.

(3) Where the work is carried out by a person other than the applicant, the grant for the work specified in column 1 of the Table shall be the lesser or—
(a) the sum calculated by deducting from the amount properly charged for the work, the contribution shown in column 2 of the Table; and
(b) the figure shown in column 4 or column 5 of the Table, as applicable.

(4) Column 4 of the Table shall apply where the work is carried out wholly or mainly by persons receiving training under arrangements by virtue of section 2(1) of the Employment and Training Act 1973; otherwise column 5 shall apply.   **[1497]**

12. Claim for and payment of grant.

(1) The conditions for payment of grant are that—
(a) the work in respect of which a grant was approved has been completed;
(b) a claim in respect of that work has been made to the administering agency for the area by the applicant or, where the work has been carried out by a network installer, by that network installer;
(c) the claim is in such form as is required by the administering agency and contains—
  (i) a declaration signed by the applicant that the work has been carried out;
  (ii) a declaration signed by the person responsible for carrying out the work (and in this regulation such expression shall include the applicant where he has carried out the work) that the work had not been started nor, where the applicant did the work himself, the materials purchased before notice was received in accordance with sub-paragraph (b)(i) of paragraph (3) of regulation 9 or paragraph (2) or regulation 10 as appropriate;
  (iii) a declaration signed by the person responsible for carrying out the work that the work complies with the standards provided for in paragraph (2) of regulation 6; and
  (iv) where energy advice has been given, a declaration signed by the person responsible for the giving or the supervision of the giving of that advice that it has been given or supervised as appropriate by such person possessing such qualifications as may have been laid down from time to time by the administering agency with the approval of the Secretary of State;
(d) in any case where the administering agency has inspected the dwelling, it is satisfied that the work complies with the standards provided for in paragraph (2) of regulation 6.

(2) Where the conditions for payment are satisfied, the administering agency shall pay the grant—
(a) to the claimant; or
(b) at the request of the claimant in writing, to a person authorised by him to receive the payment.   **[1498]**

13. Communal area grant.

(1) An administering agency may make communal area grants in respect of works, except energy advice, in communal areas.

(2) A person whose dwelling is in a building, another part of which is a building in multiple occupation, may when applying for a grant for works to his dwelling indicate in his application that he believes that the building is a building suitable for a communal area grant and on receipt of the application the administering agency shall deal with the indication in accordance with the following provisions of this regulation.

(3) The administering agency shall make such enquiries as it sees fit as to the proportion of the dwellings in the building which are dwellings ('relevant dwellings') resided in

by a person from whom an application for a grant may be entertained under paragraph (1) of regulation 3.

(4) If the administering agency determines that—
(a) at least half of the dwellings in the building are relevant dwellings; and
(b) the building is one where work in respect of the communal areas would be justified on the grounds of reducing or preventing the wastage of energy,
the administering agency may appoint a person or body of persons to carry out work of the nature, to the extent and subject to such of the provisions of these Regulations as apply to works, all as may be laid down by the administering agency, and may, on completion of the work, pay to that person or body such sum as may have been agreed as the communal area grant in respect of that work. [1499]

14. Network installers.

(1) The administering agency for any area shall, in accordance with criteria laid down from time to time by the Secretary of State—
(a) invite applications for registration as a network installer;
(b) determine the particular locality for which each network installer within its area is to be registered;
(c) select and register as a network installer, for any particular locality within its area, a person or body of persons capable of carrying out, or arranging for the carrying out of, the work specified in sub-paragraphs (a), (b) and (c) of paragraph (1) of regulation 6.

(2) The administering agency shall establish procedures for the general oversight of the network installer and the verification of claims made, and information supplied, by him.

(3) Any registration may be terminated by the administering agency with the approval of the Secretary of State for reasonable cause. [1500]

15. Allocation of amounts to network installers.

(1) A network installer shall at the request of an administering agency submit a written estimate of the works which he considers he is likely to carry out during any future period.

(2) An administering agency may, in respect of a future period specified by it, allocate and notify in writing to a network installer an amount which is to be the total sum available for grants in respect of works to be carried out by the network installer and any sub-contractor of his during that period. [1501]

16. Administering agencies.

(1) The Secretary of State may in accordance with the following paragraphs appoint a person or body of persons to perform in any particular area such functions as he may confer upon that person or body, being functions specified by the Secretary of State for the purposes of, or otherwise in connection with, the making of grants and communal area grants.

(2) The Secretary of State may allocate to an administering agency sums which are to be available to that agency in any period for the purpose of making grants and communal area grants in that period, and may re-allocate any sums so allocated.

(3) The appointment of, or the conferring of functions in addition to those contained in these Regulations upon, an administering agency may be effected in whole or in part by or under a written contract entered into between the Secretary of State and that administering agency.

(4) The Secretary of State may include such terms and conditions in any contract under paragraph (3) as he may consider appropriate, and may include terms and conditions relating to all or any of the items specified in the Schedule.

(5) Nothing in these Regulations shall require the Secretary of State to allocate any sums to any administering agency and no administering agency shall allocate amounts or approve grants unless money for the purpose has been made available to it by the Secretary of State. **[1502]**

Regulation 16(4)   SCHEDULE

CONTRACTUAL ITEMS

A written contract between the Secretary of State and an administering agency may include provision for all or any of the following—
- (a) the services to be provided by the administering agency;
- (b) the appointment and registration of network installers;
- (c) procedures for the general oversight of, and the verification of claims made, and information supplied, by persons carrying out work;
- (d) the design, production and dissemination of forms of application and claim for grant;
- (e) the setting of standards, including standards of materials and workmanship;
- (f) the specifying of the qualifications to be possessed, and the persons who are to possess them and the circumstances in which they are to be possessed, in respect of the giving of energy advice;
- (g) the allocation and payment of grants;
- (h) consultation and liaison with the Secretary of State and other persons or bodies of persons;
- (i) duration of the contract;
- (j) the payment of fees to the administering agency;
- (k) the accounting for grants and remuneration;
- (l) the collection, handling, storage and protection of data;
- (m) the recovery of sums due from the administering agency;
- (n) the liabilities of the parties under the contract;
- (o) assignment of obligations;
- (p) termination of—
  - (i) the contract with the administering agency; and
  - (ii) registration by the administering agency of a network installer;
- (q) arbitration;
- (r) notices under the contract. **[1503]**

NOTES to SI 1990/1791

General: The scheme of energy efficiency grants is intended to replace the scheme of home insulation grants operated under the Housing (Scotland) Act 1987 (c 26), s 252 and SI 1987/2185. Section 252 of the 1987 Act is prospectively repealed by the Social Security Act 1990, s 15, but the repeal has not yet been brought into force.

SI 1991/227 [1506B]

The Housing (Grants for Fire Escapes in Houses in Multiple Occupation) (Prescribed Percentage) (Scotland) Order 1990

SI 1990/2242

(*This order was made by the Secretary of State for Scotland under the Housing (Scotland) Act 1987 (c 26), s 249(4) and (9), and came into force on 21 November 1990*)

1. (*Citation, commencement and interpretation*)

(2) In this Order—
'the Act' means the Housing (Scotland) Act 1987. [1504]

2. Application.

This Order shall apply in relation to any application for a grant for a fire escape under section 249 of the Act duly made on or after the date of coming into force of this Order. [1505]

3. Percentage of grant.

In section 249(4) of the Act there is prescribed in place of the percentage there specified a percentage of 20 per cent. [1506]

The Race Relations Code of Practice (Rented Housing) Order 1991

SI 1991/227

(*This order was made, as respects Scotland, by the Secretary of State for Scotland under the Race Relations Act 1976 (c 74), s 47, and came into force on 30 April 1991*)

1. (*Citation and commencement*) [1506A]

2. Code of Practice.

The day appointed for the coming into effect of the Code of Practice in Rented Housing for the elimination of racial discrimination and the promotion of equal opportunities (ISBN 1-85442-034-8), issued by the Commission for Racial Equality under section 47(7) of the Race Relations Act 1976 is 1st May 1991. [1506B]

[1506C]

The Home Purchase Assistance (Price-limits) Order 1991
SI 1991/819

(This order was made, as respects Scotland, by the Secretary of State for Scotland under section 222 of the Housing (Scotland) Act 1987 (c 26) and came into force on 1 May 1991)

1. *(Citation and commencement)* [1506C]

2. **Prescribed price-limits.**

The amounts mentioned in the Schedule to this Order are prescribed as the price-limits for the purposes of section 445 of the Housing Act 1985 or section 222 of the Housing (Scotland) Act 1987 (as the case may be) in respect of house property situated in the areas mentioned in relation thereto in that Schedule. [1506D]

3. **Revocation.**

The Home Purchase Assistance (Price-limits) Order 1989 is hereby revoked. [1506E]

SCHEDULE

Area	Price-limit
The counties of Cleveland, Durham, Northumberland and Tyne and Wear	£38,500
The counties of Humberside, North Yorkshire, South Yorkshire and West Yorkshire	£44,200
The counties of Derbyshire, Leicestershire, Lincolnshire, Northamptonshire and Nottinghamshire	£45,700
The counties of Cambridgeshire, Norfolk and Suffolk	£57,400
Greater London	£83,600
The counties of Bedfordshire, Berkshire, Buckinghamshire, East Sussex, Essex, Hampshire, Hertfordshire, Isle of Wight, Kent, Oxfordshire, Surrey and West Sussex	£69,900
The counties of Avon, Cornwall, Devon, Dorset, Gloucestershire, Somerset and Wiltshire and the Isles of Scilly	£54,900
The counties of Hereford and Worcester, Shropshire, Staffordshire, Warwickshire and West Midlands	£46,000
The counties of Cheshire, Cumbria, Greater Manchester, Lancashire and Merseyside	£45,500
Wales	£40,800
Scotland	£38,100

[1506F]

Notes to SI 1991/819

The Home Purchase Assistance Scheme will be wound up with effect from 1 April 1993. See paras [1223] and [1485] ff above.

The Civic Government (Scotland) Act 1982 (Licensing of Houses in Multiple Occupation) Order 1991

SI 1991/1253

(*This order was made by the Secretary of State for Scotland under the Civic Government (Scotland) Act 1982 (c 45), s 44, and came into force on 3 June 1991*)

1. (*Citation and commencement*)

2. Interpretation.

(1) In this Order, unless the context otherwise requires—

'the Act' means the Civic Government (Scotland) Act 1982;

'family' and the reference to membership thereof shall be construed in accordance with section 83 of the Housing (Scotland) Act 1987;

'house' includes any part of a building, being a part which is occupied as a separate dwelling and, in particular, includes a flat;

'house in multiple occupation' means a house (other than a house in respect of which a control order under section 178 of the Housing (Scotland) Act 1987 is in force) which is the only or principal residence of more than 4 persons, being persons who are not all members either of the same family or of one or other of 2 families.

(2) For purposes of the definition of 'house in multiple occupation' in paragraph (1) above, a house in which a person undertaking a full time course of education resides during term time shall, during the period of that person's residence, be regarded as being his only or principal residence.

(3) For purposes of this Order, dwellings comprised within a building which, although otherwise separate, share use of a sanitary convenience or of personal washing facilities shall be taken to form part of a single house.

3. Licensing of houses in multiple occupation.

(1) Use of premises as a house in multiple occupation is hereby designated as an activity for which, subject to a resolution of the licensing authority in relation to it in accordance with section 9 of the Act, a licence shall be required.

(2) Part I of the Act shall have effect, subject to the modification specified in the Schedule to this Order, for the purposes of the licensing of the use of premises as a house in multiple occupation.

Article 3(2)

SCHEDULE

Modification of Part I of the Act

In paragraph 5(2) of Schedule 1 to the Act (to which effect is given for purposes of the licensing of the use of premises as a house in multiple occupation by article 3(2) of this Order) there shall be added after the words 'such reasonable conditions' the words '(other than conditions relating to the amount of rent or other charges which may be imposed upon occupiers of the house)'.

The Rent Regulation (Forms and Information etc) (Scotland) Regulations 1991

SI 1991/1521

(This order was made by the Secretary of State for Scotland under the Rent (Scotland) Act 1984 (c 58), ss 41(1), and 53(1) as applied by ss 56(2), 80(1) and 112, and came into force on 5 August 1991)

ARRANGEMENT OF REGULATIONS
(This list is not printed in the regulations)

1	Citation and commencement	[1510]
2	Interpretation	[1511]
3	Register of rents	[1512]
4	Notices to quit	[1513]
5	Form and content of rent books	[1514]
6	Forms	[1515]
7	Fee for certified copy	[1516]
8	Revocations and transitional provisions	[1517]
	Schedule 1—Particulars with regard to the tenancy which the register of rents is required to contain	[1518]
	Schedule 2—Information to be contained in a notice to quit	[1519]
	Schedule 3—Form of notice to be inserted in every rent book	[1520]
	Schedule 4—The form of, and information to be contained in, every rent book	[1521]
	Schedule 5—List of forms	[1522]

SI 1991/1521 [1517]

1. (*Citation and commencement*) [1510]

2. **Interpretation.**

In these Regulations—
(a) 'the Act' means the Rent (Scotland) Act 1984; and
(b) a reference to a numbered Schedule is a reference to the Schedule to these Regulations bearing that number. [1511]

3. **Register of rents.**

The particulars prescribed in Schedule 1 shall be the particulars with regard to the tenancy which the register of rents is required to contain in pursuance of section 45(2)(a) or of that section as applied by section 56(2) of the Act. [1512]

4. **Notices to quit.**

Where a notice to quit is given by a landlord on or after the coming into force of these Regulations to determine—
(a) a protected tenancy; or
(b) a Part VII contract,
the notice shall contain, in such form as may be, the information set out in Schedule 2. [1513]

5. **Form and content of rent books.**

(1) Every rent book or similar document provided by a landlord for use in respect of a dwellinghouse, which is let on or subject to a regulated tenancy, shall contain a notice to the tenant in the form set out in Schedule 3, or in a form substantially to the same effect, of all the matters referred to in the said form.

(2) Every rent book or similar document, required by section 79(1) of the Act (rent books under Part VII contracts) shall be in the form set out in Schedule 4, or in a form substantially to the same effect, and shall contain the information referred to in the said form. [1514]

6. **Forms.**

The forms set out in Schedule 5, or forms substantially to the same effect, shall be the forms to be used for the purposes of the Act in the cases to which those forms are applicable. [1515]

7. **Fee for certified copy.**

For the purposes of section 45(4) of the Act (register of rents) the fee to be paid for a certified copy of any entry in the register of rents shall be £1.50. [1516]

8. **Revocations and transitional provision.**

The Regulations specified in Schedule 6 are hereby revoked except insofar as the forms, notices and information so prescribed are required to be used in connection with proceedings after the date on which these Regulations come into force and consequent upon action taken before that date. [1517]

Regulation 3   SCHEDULE 1

Particulars with regard to the tenancy which the register of rents is required to contain.

1. The name and address of both the landlord and the tenant.

2. The name and address of the landlord's agent (if any).

3. Whether Part VI of the Rent (Scotland) Act 1984 (rent limit for dwellinghouses let by housing associations and the Housing Corporation) applies to the tenancy.

4. Whether furniture is provided by the landlord.

5. The services provided by the landlord.

6. The respective liability of the landlord and the tenant for the maintenance and repair of the dwellinghouse.

7. Any other terms of the tenancy taken into consideration in determining a fair rent for the dwellinghouse.   **[1518]**

Regulation 4   SCHEDULE 2

Information to be contained in a notice to quit

1. Even after the notice to quit has run out, before the tenant can lawfully be evicted, the landlord must get an order for possession from the court.

2. A tenant who does not know if he or she has any right to remain in possession after a notice to quit runs out or is otherwise unsure of his or her rights should obtain advice without delay and before the notice to quit expires. Advice can be obtained from a solicitor, a Citizens' Advice Bureau, a Housing Aid Centre, a Rent Officer or the office of the Rent Assessment Committee. Some solicitors give a free first interview and help with all or part of the cost of legal advice may be available.   **[1519]**

Regulation 5(1)   SCHEDULE 3

Form of notice to be inserted in every rent book or similar document used in respect of a dwelling let on or subject to a regulated tenancy

INFORMATION FOR TENANT

NOTE: YOUR TENANCY IS A REGULATED TENANCY. THIS AFFECTS THE RENT WHICH MAY BE LAWFULLY RECOVERED FOR THE DWELLING AND IMPOSES RESTRICTIONS ON THE LANDLORD'S RIGHT TO RECOVER POSSESSION OF IT. THE LANDLORD MUST KEEP THE ENTRIES UP TO DATE.

1. Address of the dwelling ....
....

2. Name, address and telephone number of the landlord and his agent (if any) ......
....

3. RENT LAWFULLY RECOVERABLE
    (a) If no rent is registered—
        (i) the rent payable as from [date] under the tenancy is £   per
        (ii) if furniture or services are provided the amount (if any) which is apportioned to them under the tenancy agreement is—
        Furniture £................ Services £................
    (b) If a fair rent has been registered—
        (i) the registered rent is £   per   including £   for furniture and services.

        (The word 'variable' should be added after the amount of the registered rent if the entry in the register permits the landlord to vary the rent to take account of changes in the cost of providing services or maintaining or repairing the dwelling in accordance with the terms shown in the register, without having to have a new rent registered.)

        *(ii) The landlord may increase the rent up to the registered rent only by the following annual amount prescribed by order made under section 33 of the Rent (Scotland) Act 1984
        From (date)   by (amount of the increase) £   per   to £   per
        From (date)   by (amount of the increase) £   per   to £   per
    * Delete if inapplicable.

4. ALTERATIONS IN RENT WHERE NO RENT REGISTERED
    (a) Where no rent has been registered then, unless you enter a rent agreement (see paragraph (c) below) the rent can only be increased for one or more of a limited number of reasons, for example increases in the cost of services provided.
    (b) You or your landlord or both of you acting together may apply at any time to the rent officer to have a fair rent registered.
    (c) As an alternative to having a fair rent registered you and your landlord may agree to increase the rent under the existing tenancy or to enter into a new tenancy agreement for the same house at an increased rent. The agreement must be in writing and contain a conspicuous statement at the top that (1) your security of tenure will not be affected if you refuse to agree; (2) the agreement will not deprive you or the landlord of the right to apply at any time to the rent officer for registration of a fair rent; and (3) if a rent is registered any increase in rent will be subject to a maximum annual limit.

5. ALTERATIONS IN RENT WHERE FAIR RENT REGISTERED
    (a) The landlord may not charge more than the registered rent, or, if the increase of rent is subject to a maximum annual limit (see paragraph 3(b)(ii) above), more than is permitted under the relevant provisions. In certain cases the registered rent may vary to take account of changes in the cost of providing services or of maintaining or repairing the dwelling, but only if there is a note on the register to this effect.
    (b) The registered rent normally lasts for 3 years and cannot be changed without applying to the Rent Officer.
        The only circumstances where a Rent Officer will accept an application for re-registration within 3 years are:—
        (i) Where the application is made by you and the landlord acting together; or
        (ii) where there has been a change in the circumstances which were taken into account when the rent was registered; or
        (iii) where the application is made by the landlord alone within 3 months of the expiry of the 3 year period (but the new registration cannot take effect until the expiry of the 3 year period).

At the expiry of that 3 year period, if you and the landlord have entered into a rent agreement, you may both apply to the Rent Officer for the cancellation of the registration, but the Rent Officer will only cancel it if he is satisfied that the agreed rent does not exceed a fair rent.

(c) Further information on rents of regulated tenancies is set out in a Scottish Office Environment Department booklet available free of charge from Rent Officers, Housing Aid Centres, Citizens' Advice Bureaux and local Council Offices.

6. SUB-LETTING

(a) If you sub-let the dwelling and you are not permitted to do this under your tenancy agreement, your landlord may apply to the sheriff for an order for possession to get the dwelling back (see paragraph 7).

(b) If you sub-let any part of the dwelling on a regulated tenancy—

(i) you must give the landlord, within 14 days, a statement in writing of the sub-letting, giving particulars of occupancy, including the rent charged. The penalty for failing to do this without reasonable excuse, or for giving false particulars, is a fine not exceeding level 1 on the standard scale of fines set out in section 298G of the Criminal Procedure (Scotland) Act 1975. When you have once given the landlord the particulars, you need not do so again if the only change is a change of sub-tenant; and

(ii) if you overcharge your sub-tenant, the landlord may apply to the sheriff for an order for possession.

7. SECURITY OF TENURE

(a) The landlord can recover possession of a dwellinghouse subject to a regulated tenancy only by obtaining an order for possession from the sheriff. This means that if he serves a notice to quit on you, you do not have to leave by the date stated in the notice. If you feel you cannot move out at that time, before you can be evicted the landlord must first get an order for possession from the sheriff. The sheriff, except in certain cases, will only grant an order for possession if he thinks it reasonable to do so and either there is suitable accommodation available for you to go to or one of a limited number of conditions is satisfied (for example you have failed to pay the rent lawfully due, or you or your family have been a nuisance or annoyance to neighbours).

(b) A tenancy cannot be terminated until a valid notice is served. To be valid, a notice to quit must be in proper form and in writing and give the appropriate period of notice which must always be at least four weeks before the date on which it is to take effect.

In the case of a short tenancy as defined in section 9 of the Rent (Scotland) Act 1984, the landlord must also serve a notice on the tenant of his intention to apply for an order for possession.

(c) It is a criminal offence for the landlord or for anyone else to try to make you leave by using force, by threatening you or your family, by withdrawing services, or by interfering with your home or your possessions. If anyone does this, you should contact the police immediately.

8. HOUSING BENEFIT

If you have difficulty in paying your rent you should apply to your District or Islands Council for Housing Benefit. You may obtain further information about Housing Benefit from your local Council Offices, or Citizens' Advice Bureau. **[1520]**

Regulation 5(2) SCHEDULE 4

The form of, and the information to be contained in, every rent book or similar document required by section 79(1) of the Rent (Scotland) Act 1984 to be provided for use in respect of a dwellinghouse under a contract to which Part VII of the Act applies.

INFORMATION FOR TENANTS

NOTE: YOU OCCUPY THIS DWELLINGHOUSE UNDER A CONTRACT TO WHICH PART VII OF THE RENT (SCOTLAND) ACT 1984 APPLIES. THIS AFFECTS THE RENT WHICH YOUR LANDLORD MAY LAWFULLY RECOVER AND CONFERS A DEGREE OF SECURITY OF TENURE. YOUR LANDLORD MUST KEEP THE ENTRIES UP TO DATE.

1. Address of the dwellinghouse and description of the premises to which the contract relates ....

2. Name, address and telephone number of the landlord and of his agent (if any)
   ....

3. RENT LAWFULLY RECOVERABLE
   (a) If no rent is registered
       (i) The rent payable as from [date] under the contract is £   per week,
       (ii) if furniture or services are provided the amount (if any) which is apportioned to them under the contract is

       Furniture £............ Services £............
   (b) If a reasonable rent has been registered following determination by the rent assessment committee
       (i) *A rent of £............ per week for the dwellinghouse comprised in the contract was approved by the rent assessment committee on ....
       (ii) *The rent for the dwellinghouse comprised in the contract was *reduced/increased* by the rent assessment committee to £............ on ....

       * Delete if inapplicable

4. ALTERATIONS IN RENT
   (a) Either you or the landlord may refer the contract to the rent assessment committee to fix a reasonable rent. On such a reference, the rent assessment committee may approve the rent payable under the contract or may reduce or increase the rent to such sum as they consider reasonable or may, if they think fit in all the circumstances dismiss the reference. Any approval, reduction or increase may be limited to the rent payable in respect of a particular period.
   (b) The rent determined by the rent assessment committee is registered and it then becomes a criminal offence for any person to require or receive, on account of rent for that dwelling under any contract, more than the registered rent. Any overpayment of rent may be recovered by you.
   (c) Once a rent has been registered, then for three years after the rent was last considered by the rent assessment committee no new application for the registration of a different rent can be made, except by you and the landlord acting together, or where there has been a change in the circumstances taken into account when the rent was last considered—for example a change in the terms of the tenancy or in the furniture supplied, or in the condition of the dwellinghouse.
   (d) If you agree to a change in rent or any other terms of the contract without reference to the rent assessment committee you will no longer have a Part VII contract.

5. SECURITY OF TENURE

(a) The landlord can recover possession of a dwellinghouse subject to a Part VII contract only by obtaining an order for possession from the sheriff. This means that if he serves a notice to quit on you, you do not have to leave by the date stated in the notice. If you feel you cannot leave at that time, before you can be evicted the landlord must first get an order for possession from the sheriff.

(b) A tenancy cannot be terminated until a valid notice is served. To be valid a notice to quit must be in proper form and in writing and give at least four weeks' notice.

(c) When the notice to quit takes effect the landlord is entitled, if you do not leave voluntarily, to obtain an order for possession of the dwelling from the sheriff. The landlord cannot evict you from the dwelling without such an order from the sheriff and it is a criminal offence for him or for anyone to try to make you leave by using force, by threatening you or your family, by withdrawing services or by interfering with your home or your possessions. If anyone does this, you should contact the police immediately.

6. HOUSING BENEFIT

If you have difficulty in paying your rent, you should apply to your District or Islands Council for Housing Benefit. You may obtain further information about Housing Benefit from your local Council Offices or Citizens' Advice Bureau.

Regulation 6

SCHEDULE 5

List of forms

Form No	Purpose	Statutory References to the Act
1	Notice of increase of rent under a regulated tenancy where a rent has been registered under section 49 of the Act.	Sections 29(2), 32 and 33
2	Application for the registration of a rent, unsupported by a certificate of fair rent where the dwellinghouse is or is to be let under a regulated tenancy or where the interest of the landlord belongs to a housing association	Sections 46 and 56
3	Application for a certificate of fair rent where the dwellinghouse is or is to be let under a regulated tenancy or where the interest of the landlord belongs to a housing association	Sections 47 and 56 and Schedule 6
4	Application for the registration of a rent, supported by a certificate of fair rent, where the dwellinghouse is or is to be let under a regulated tenancy or where the interest of the landlord belongs to a housing association	Sections 47 and 56
5	Application by joint applicants or by a landlord alone for the cancellation of a registration of rent	Sections 51 and 52
6	Notice requiring further information to be given to a rent assessment committee	Section 56 and paragraph 8 of Schedule 5

SI 1991/1521 [1523]

FORM NO 1

RENT (SCOTLAND) ACT 1984

NOTICE OF INCREASE OF RENT UNDER A REGULATED TENANCY WHERE A RENT HAS BEEN REGISTERED UNDER SECTION 49 OF THE RENT (SCOTLAND) ACT 1984 (NOTE 1)

Date ....

To ....

1. A rent of £ ...... per ...... was registered on .... *(Note 2)* as the fair rent for the dwellinghouse situated at .... of which you are the tenant.

[2. In the register it is noted that the fair rent includes an amount in respect of the provision of services, provided by the landlord—'the noted amount'—and that the noted amount recorded by the Rent Officer is £ ......]
Delete words in square brackets if they do not apply.

3. Accordingly, I hereby give you notice that your rent will be increased from your present rent of £ ...... per ...... to a new rent of £ ...... per ...... and the date from which the new rent is to take effect is .... *(Note 3)*.
    Your new rent is made up of the following elements—
    (a) the amount of the previous rent limit *(Note 4)*   £ .... per annum
ADD
    (b) permitted increase *(Note 5)*   £ .... per annum
PLUS
    (c) the noted amount (if any)   £ .... per annum
Total of the above, being the rent lawfully recoverable from   £ .... per annum
you as tenant of the dwellinghouse
Deduct the amount of the rent which at present is lawfully   £ .... per annum
payable by you as tenant of the dwellinghouse
The amount of the increase is   £ .... per annum

....
(Signature of landlord or agent)

....
(Address of landlord or agent)

NOTES

(To be incorporated in the notice)

1. This notice of increase is required if:
    (a) The tenancy is a regulated tenancy as defined in the Rent (Scotland) Act 1984 ('the Act'); *and*
    (b) the tenancy is a statutory tenancy, or will become one as a result of the operation of this notice (see section 32(3) of the Act); *and*
    (c) a rent has been registered for the house which is higher than the rent payable at present.
The maximum amount by which a rent may be increased may be limited by the phasing arrangements set out in the Limits on Rent Increases (Scotland) Order 1989 (S.I. 1989/2469). The limits cannot be evaded by a landlord granting to the tenant a new tenancy of the house. The limits are described in Note 5.

2. Insert the date upon which the rent determined by the Rent Officer or by the Rent

Assessment Committee was registered for the dwellinghouse. The rent register may be inspected at the office of the Rent Officer.

3. The date from which the new rent takes effect must not be earlier than:
   (a) the date of registration in paragraph 1 of the notice; *and*
   (b) four weeks before the date of service of the notice; *and*
   (c) where an application for a fair rent (other than a joint application or following a change of circumstances) is made within the last 3 months of the period of 3 years commencing when the registration of a fair rent took effect, the first day after the expiry of that period of 3 years; *and*
   (d) if the tenancy is contractual, the date on which the tenancy could be terminated by a notice to quit served by the landlord at the same time as this notice.

4. The previous rent limit is the amount, excluding the 'noted amount' (if any) which was payable for the last rental period beginning—
   (a) before the date of registration; *or*
   (b) as the case may require, before each subsequent anniversary of that date.

5. The permitted increase is set by the Limits on Rents Increases (Scotland) Order 1989. This provides that for the first annual stage (which is the period of 12 months beginning with the date of registration) the rent can be increased by the greatest of:
   £104 a year; *or*
   one quarter of the previous rent limit; *or*
   one half of the total increase required to take the rent payable to the registered rent: Provided that the rent payable can never be increased above the registered rent. For the second stage (which starts on the first anniversary of the date of registration) the rent payable can be increased to the registered rent. **[1523]**

FORM NO 2

RENT (SCOTLAND) ACT 1984

APPLICATION FOR REGISTRATION OF A RENT

Use this form when applying for the registration of a rent (UNSUPPORTED BY A CERTIFICATE OF FAIR RENT) where the dwellinghouse is at present let on a regulated tenancy or on a secure tenancy from a registered housing association	All sections MUST be completed. Insert 'NOT KNOWN' where the information requested is not available. Where boxes are shown, please tick. Please send the form to the Rent Registration Office for the area in which the dwellinghouse is situated.
1. Address of dwellinghouse	
2. a. Name, address and telephone number of landlord:	And of agent (if any):
b. If landlord is a registered housing association	Please tick ☐
3. Name and telephone number of tenant:	And of agent (if any) (include address):

SI 1991/1521 [1524]

RENT
4. Please state the rent which you want registered as a fair rent
£...... per week/month/quarter/year
Include the amount of rent to be charged for any services or furniture provided by the landlord

PREVIOUS REGISTRATION
5. Has a rent already been registered for the dwellinghouse?   YES ☐   NO ☐
IF YES
  a. please state: the registration number   ....
  the effective date of registration   ....

(These details are shown on the Notification of Registration sent to the landlord and tenant at the time of the last registration).

  b. Have there been any substantial changes (including any improvements or alterations) in the condition of the dwellinghouse since the previous registration?   YES ☐   NO ☐
  If YES, please give details

  c. If this application is being made within 2 years and 9 months of the date of the previous registration, and it is not a joint application, please state why you are applying again: ....

DETAILS OF DWELLINGHOUSE
6. a. State what kind of dwellinghouse it is, such as a detached or terraced house, a flat, or room(s). (If a flat, give location in block eg 1 up Right; if room(s) give location or room number.)

  b. Give number and types of rooms (such as kitchen, livingroom);

  c. Is any accommodation/facility (such as bathroom or kitchen) shared with others?   YES ☐   NO ☐
  If YES, please give details

  d. Does the tenancy include a garage, garden, yard or any other separate building or land?   YES ☐   NO ☐
  If YES, please give details

SERVICES
7. a. Does the landlord provide any services such as cleaning, heating or hot water supply?   YES ☐   NO ☐
  If YES, please give details or attach a separate list if necessary

  b. If YES, what do you think is a fair charge for services, to be included in the rent?   £...... per week/month/quarter/year

FURNITURE

8. a. Does the landlord provide any furniture?

    YES ☐   NO ☐

    If YES, please attach a copy of the inventory of furniture or, if you do not have a copy, please make up your own list and attach it.

  b. If YES, what do you think is a fair charge for furniture, to be included in the rent?

    £...... per week/month/quarter/year

BUSINESS USE

9. a. Is any part of the dwellinghouse used for conducting any type of business such as a shop, office, surgery etc?

    YES ☐   NO ☐

    If YES, please give details

  b. If YES, please state what you consider to be a fair rent for the parts of the dwellinghouse used for business purposes:

    £...... per week/month/quarter/year

DETAILS OF TENANCY

10. a. Do you have a copy of the tenancy agreement?

    YES ☐   NO ☐

    (The Rent Officer may wish to see it later)

  b. When did the tenancy begin? ....

  c. What is the present rent? £ ....

  d. How often is rent payable?

    Weekly ☐   Monthly ☐

    Quarterly ☐   Yearly ☐

  e. Under the terms of the tenancy, what repairs are the landlord's responsibility?

  f. Under the terms of the tenancy, what repairs are the tenant's responsibility?

  g. Is the tenancy a short tenancy?

    YES ☐   NO ☐

IMPROVEMENTS AND DISREPAIR

11. a. Has the tenant improved or replaced anything (including furniture if it is provided) which he is not required to do so under the tenancy agreement?

    YES ☐   NO ☐

    If YES, please give details

  b. Has the tenant caused any disrepair or other defect to the dwellinghouse (or furniture if it is provided) because he has not complied with the tenancy agreement?

    YES ☐   NO ☐

    If YES, please give details

SI 1991/1521 [1525]

I/WE APPLY FOR REGISTRATION OF A RENT

Signature of Landlord/Agent   (Signature of Tenant/Agent)

Date ....   Date ....

Where there are joint landlords or joint tenants they should each sign unless one acts as an agent for the rest. In such a case he should state that he is acting as agent. In the case of a landlord and tenant applying together, both must sign. [1524]

FORM NO 3

RENT (SCOTLAND) ACT 1984

APPLICATION FOR FOR CERTIFICATE OF FAIR RENT

Use this form if you are the owner or the landlord intending:

a. to provide a dwellinghouse by erection or conversion of premises; or
b. to make improvements in a dwellinghouse; or
c. to let a dwellinghouse which is not already let

and the tenancy will be a regulated tenancy or a secure tenancy by a registered housing association.

All sections MUST be completed. Insert 'NOT KNOWN' where the information requested is not available.

Where boxes are shown, please tick.

Please send the form to the Rent Registration Office for the area in which the dwellinghouse is situated.

1. Address of dwellinghouse	
2. a. Name, address and telephone number of landlord:	And of agent (if any):
b. If landlord is a registered housing association	Please tick ☐
3. a. Is the dwellinghouse vacant?	YES ☐ NO ☐
b. if YES, who should the Rent Officer contact about access for inspection?	
4. Name and telephone number of tenant (if any): (include address if tenant is currently residing elsewhere)	And of agent (if any) (include address):

791

RENT

5. Please state the rent which you want shown on the Certificate of Fair Rent

£...... per week/month/quarter/year

Include the amount of rent to be charged for any services or furniture which you provide.

GROUNDS OF APPLICATION (cross out whichever does not apply)
6. a. Erection/conversion

   b. Improvements to dwellinghouse

   c. Proposal to let dwellinghouse

Give a brief description (including the estimated cost) of any proposed works or improvements and attach a copy of any relevant plans and specifications.

PREVIOUS REGISTRATION
7. a. Has a rent already been registered for the dwellinghouse?   YES ☐   NO ☐

   b. If YES, please state: the registration number
   ....
   the effective date of registration
   ....

   (These details are shown on the Notification of Registration sent to the landlord and tenant at the time of the last registration.)

DETAILS OF HOUSE
8. a. State what kind of dwellinghouse it is, such as a detached or terraced house or a flat, or room(s). If a flat, give location in block eg 1 up Right; if room(s) give location or room number.

   b. Give number and type of rooms (such as kitchen, living room):

   c. Does the tenancy include a garage, garden, yard or any other separate building or land?   YES ☐   NO ☐
   If YES, please give details

DETAILS OF TENANCY
9A. If the dwellinghouse is ALREADY LET

   a. What is the present rent?   £ ....

   b. How often is the rent payable?   Weekly ☐   Monthly ☐   Quarterly ☐   Yearly ☐

   c. Under the terms of the tenancy what repairs are the landlord's responsibility?

SI 1991/1521 [1525]

   d. Under the terms of the tenancy what repairs are the tenant's responsibility?

   e. Has the tenant improved or replaced anything (including furniture if it is provided) which he is not required to do under the tenancy agreement?   YES ☐   NO ☐
If YES, please give details

   f. Has the tenant caused any disrepair or other defect to the dwellinghouse (or furniture if it is provided) because he has not complied with the tenancy?   YES ☐   NO ☐
If YES, please give details

9B. If the dwellinghouse is NOT ALREADY LET and it is proposed to grant a tenancy, please state:

   a. The proposed duration of the tenancy   ....

   b. How often will the rent be payable   Weekly ☐   Monthly ☐
Quarterly ☐   Yearly ☐

   c. What repairs will be the landlord's responsibility?

   d. What repairs will be the tenant's responsibility?

SERVICES

10. a. Will the landlord provide any services? eg cleaning, heating, hot water supply etc?   YES ☐   NO ☐
If YES, please give details or attach a separate list if necessary

    b. If YES, what do you think is a fair charge for services, to be included in the rent?   £...... per week/month/quarter/year

FURNITURE

11. a. Will the landlord provide any furniture?   YES ☐   NO ☐
If YES, please give details or provide a copy of the inventory.

    b. If YES, what do you think is a fair charge for furniture to be included in the rent?   £...... per week/month/quarter/year

BUSINESS USE

12. a. Is any part of the dwellinghouse to be used for conducting any type of business such as a shop, office, surgery etc?   YES ☐   NO ☐
If YES, please give details

    b. If YES, please state what you think would be a fair rent for the part of the dwellinghouse used for business purposes: £...... per week/month/quarter/year

[1525]

I/WE APPLY FOR A CERTIFICATE OF FAIR RENT FOR THE PREMISES NAMED IN QUESTION 1 ABOVE

Signed .... (Landlord/Agent) Date ....
If there are joint landlords each should sign unless one acts as an agent for the rest. In such a case he should state that he is acting as agent. **[1525]**

FORM NO 4

RENT (SCOTLAND) ACT 1984

APPLICATION FOR REGISTRATION OF A RENT

Use this form when applying for the registration of a rent where SUPPORTED BY A CERTIFICATE OF FAIR RENT and the tenancy is a regulated tenancy or a secure tenancy granted by a registered housing association

All sections MUST be completed. Insert 'NOT KNOWN' where the information requested is not available.

Where boxes are shown please tick the correct one.

Please send the form to the Rent Registration Service Office for the area in which the dwellinghouse is situated.

1. Address of dwellinghouse	
2. Name, address and telephone number of landlord:	And of agent (if any):
3. Details of certificate of fair rent:	i. Number ...... ii. When dated ......
4. a. If the dwellinghouse was not subject to a tenancy when the certificate of fair rent was issued, has a regulated tenancy or a secure tenancy from a registered housing association now been granted? b. If YES, please state: 　i Name of tenant 　ii Date tenancy commenced 　iii Duration of tenancy and rental period 　vi Whether the terms of the tenancy are as shown in the certificate of fair rent.	YES ☐　NO ☐
5. Where proposed works are specified in the certificate of fair rent have these works been carried out in accordance with the plans and specifications sent with the application for the certificate of fair rent?	YES ☐　NO ☐ If YES, please give details
6. If no alterations were mentioned in the certificate of fair rent, is the condition of the dwellinghouse still the same?	YES ☐　NO ☐

SI 1991/1521 [1526]

7. If the certificate of fair rent stated an amount for services and/or furniture, are these services and/or furniture being provided? YES ☐ NO ☐

I/WE APPLY FOR THE REGISTRATION OF A RENT IN ACCORDANCE WITH THE CERTIFICATE OF FAIR RENT

Signed .... (Landlord/Agent) Date ....
If there are joint landlords each should sign unless one acts as an agent for the rest. In such a case he should state that he is acting as agent. [1526]

FORM NO 5

RENT (SCOTLAND) ACT 1984

APPLICATION FOR THE CANCELLATION OF A REGISTRATION OF RENT

IMPORTANT: AN APPLICATION TO CANCEL THE REGISTRATION OF A RENT CANNOT BE ENTERTAINED UNTIL 3 YEARS AFTER THE DATE ON WHICH THE REGISTERED RENT TOOK EFFECT OR WAS CONFIRMED BY THE RENT OFFICER

Use Part A if you are applying under section 51 of the Act which enables a landlord and tenant who have entered into a rent agreement to apply jointly to the rent officer for the registration of a rent to be cancelled. Before the rent officer will agree to such a cancellation he must be satisfied that the rent payable under the agreement does not exceed a fair rent.

Use Part B if you are applying under section 52 of the Act which enables a registration of rent to be cancelled if a landlord applies because the dwellinghouse is no longer let on a regulated tenancy.

PART A

To the Rent Officer   Date ....

We jointly apply, under section 51 of the Rent (Scotland) Act 1984, for the cancellation of the registration of rent for the dwellinghouse situated at ....

We have entered into a rent agreement a copy of which is enclosed. NOTE. YOU **MUST** SEND A COPY OF YOUR RENT AGREEMENT WITH THIS APPLICATION

Date last registration took effect

Name, address and telephone number of   ....
the landlord

Name, address and telephone number of   ....
the landlord's agent (if any)

Name and address of tenant   ....

Name, address and telephone number of   ....
the tenant's agent (if any)

Has there been any change in the condition of the dwellinghouse since the date of last registration?	YES ☐	NO ☐

If YES, is the change due to

(i) any disrepair or other defect attributable to a failure by the tenant (including a former tenant) to comply with the terms of the tenancy, or	YES ☐	NO ☐
(ii) any improvement (including the replacement of any fixture or fitting) carried out by the tenant (including a former tenant) other than under the terms of the tenancy	YES ☐	NO ☐

Signed ....
Landlord/agent

....
Tenant/agent

PART B

To the Rent Officer   Date ....

I apply under section 52 of the Rent (Scotland) Act 1984 for the cancellation of the registration of rent for the dwellinghouse situated at ....

The dwellinghouse is not currently let on a regulated tenancy.

Date last registration took effect	....
Name, address and telephone number of the landlord	....
Name, address and telephone number of the landlord's agent (if any)	....
Date on which the dwellinghouse ceased to be let on a regulated tenancy	....

Signed ....
Landlord/agent

SI 1991/1521 [1528]

FORM NO. 6

RENT (SCOTLAND) ACT 1984

NOTICE REQUIRING A LANDLORD OR TENANT TO SUPPLY THE RENT ASSESSMENT COMMITTEE WITH INFORMATION

IMPORTANT: This Notice is served on you by the Rent Assessment Committee. It requires you to supply the Committee with the information detailed in Part 3 below. This information is needed to allow the Committee to make a determination of rent as provided for by the Rent (Scotland) Act 1984. You should provide the information by the date in Part 4. Failure to provide the information may make you liable to summary conviction and a fine.

Please read this Notice carefully before responding

Part 1. To .... landlord/tenant*

Part 2. The Rent Officer has referred to the Rent Assessment Committee the application for the registration of rent for the house at:

....

....

(address of house let under the tenancy)

*delete as appropriate

Part 3. To help the Committee consider this application further information is needed from you. The further information required is:—

....

....

....

....

....

....

....

....

....

....

....

....

....

Part 4. You should send this information to the address given in Part 5 of this Notice by .... (date) **NOTE:** The date must be not less than 14 days after the date on which this Notice is served. If you do not comply with this Notice without reasonable excuse you will be liable on summary conviction to a fine not exceeding level 3 on the standard scale. If you are not clear exactly what information you are to provide to the Committee, please contact me immediately.

Part 5. Signed ....
for the Rent Assessment Committee

....
....
....
....
(address and telephone number of Committee)
Date ....
[1528]

Regulation 8 　　　　　SCHEDULE 6　　　　　**[1529]**

* 　 * 　 *

The Housing (Preservation of Right to Buy) (Scotland) Regulations 1992
SI 1992/325

(*This order was made by the Secretary of State for Scotland under sections 81A and 338(1) of the Housing (Scotland) Act 1987 (c 26) and came into force on 13 March 1992*)

1. (*Citation and commencement*) **[1530]**

2. **Interpretation.**

In these Regulations unless the context otherwise requires—
'the Act' means the Housing (Scotland) Act 1987;
'co-operative housing association' has the same meaning as in section 300(1)(b) of the Act;
'qualifying person' means a person occupying a house as his only or principal home and who—
(a) was the former secure tenant or former joint secure tenant of a house and whose former secure tenancy ceased to be such on the disposal by the landlord of the house to his current private sector landlord;
(b) became entitled to succeed on the death of the former secure tenant to a statutory assured tenancy under section 31 of the Housing (Scotland) Act 1998; or
(c) as the spouse of a former secure tenant became a tenant of a house by virtue of an order of the court under section 13 of the Matrimonial Homes (Family Protection) (Scotland) Act 1981;
'qualifying house' means the house referred to in the chapeau to paragraphs (a), (b) and (c) of the definition of 'qualifying person'. **[1531]**

3. **Preserved right to buy.**

Where a landlord disposes of an interest in a house to a private sector landlord the continued application under section 81A(1) of the Act of the right to buy provisions shall be subject to regulation 5 and to the additions, exceptions, adaptations and modifications specified in Schedule 1 to these Regulations. **[1532]**

798

4. The right to buy provisions as they continue to apply in accordance with regulation 3 are set out in Schedule 2 to these Regulations. [1533]

5. The right to buy provisions shall not continue to apply where—
(a) the disposal of a house is in exercise of the right conferred by Part III of the Housing (Scotland) Act 1988; or
(b) the disposal of a house is to a co-operative housing association. [1534]

6. Where the right to buy provisions continue to apply, the private sector landlord shall not dispose of less than his whole interest in a qualifying house without the consent in writing of the Secretary of State. [1535]

7. In any case where the sheriff makes an order for possession of a qualifying house under ground 9 in Schedule 5 to the Housing (Scotland) Act 1988 (suitable alternative accommodation) the right to buy provisions and these Regulations shall apply to the house which is or will be available by way of alternative accommodation as they apply to the qualifying house. [1536]

Regulation 3 SCHEDULE 1

MODIFICATIONS OF THE RIGHT TO BUY PROVISIONS OF THE ACT

1. In section 61 (secure tenant's right to purchase)—
(a) in subsection (1) for the words from 'a tenant of a house' to 'applies' substitute 'a qualifying person', for the words 'joint tenants' substitute 'qualifying persons' and for the word 'house' substitute 'qualifying house';
(b) in subsection (2)—
  (i) for the words from 'This section' to 'tenancy' substitute 'This section applies to every qualifying house';
  (ii) omit paragraph (a);
  (iii) in paragraph (b) omit the words from 'house' to the end and substitute 'qualifying house'; and
  (iv) in paragraph (c) for the word 'tenant' substitute 'qualifying person' and at the end add 'or of the qualifying house or any other house provided by the landlord which was a qualifying house';
(c) in subsection (2A) after the word 'house' where it occurs for the first time add 'or qualifying house' and for the words 'the house' where they occur for the second and third times substitute 'that house';
(d) in subsection (3) for the words from 'house' to 'tenant' substitute 'qualifying house let to the qualifying person following acquisition by the landlord of a defective dwelling previously purchased by the qualifying person if the qualifying person';
(e) in subsection (4)—
  (i) in paragraphs (a) and (f) for the word 'house' substitute 'qualifying house'; and
  (ii) omit paragraphs (d) and (e);
(f) in subsection (5)—
  (i) for the words from 'tenant' to 'joint tenant,' where it occurs for the first time substitute 'qualifying person';
  (ii) for the words 'house' substitute 'qualifying house'; and
  (iii) for the words 'joint tenant' where they occur for the second time substitute 'qualifying person';
(g) in subsection (6) for the word 'tenant' substitute 'qualifying person' and for the word 'house' substitute 'qualifying house'; and
(h) omit subsection (8) and (9); and
(i) in subsection (10)—
  (i) in paragraph (a) for the words 'joint tenants' in sub-paragraph (i) substitute 'more than one qualifying person' and in sub-paragraph (iii) for the words 'tenant, joint tenant' substitute 'qualifying person';

[1537]

(ii) in paragraph (a) omit sub-paragraphs (iv) and (v); and
(iii) in paragraph (b) for the word 'house' where it occurs in sub-paragraph (iii) for the first and second time substitute 'qualifying house', for the words 'joint tenant' substitute 'qualifying person' and after the words 'the tenant' add 'or of a qualifying person'. [1537]

2. In section 62 (the price)—
(a) in subsections (1) and (2) for the word 'tenant' substitute 'qualifying person' and for the word 'house' substitute 'qualifying house';
(b) in subsection (3)—
   (i) for the words 'the house' substitute 'the qualifying house';
   (ii) in paragraph (b) after the words 'a house' insert 'or of a qualifying house';
(c) in subsection (4)—
   (i) for the word 'tenant' substitute 'qualifying person';
   (ii) for the words 'joint tenants' substitute 'more than one qualifying person'; and
   (iii) after the word 'house' insert 'or qualifying house'; and
(d) in subsection (6A) for the word 'house' substitute 'qualifying house'.

3. In section 63 (application to purchase etc.)—
(a) in subsection (1)—
   (i) for the word 'tenant' substitute 'qualifying person';
   (ii) for the word 'house' where it occurs for the first time substitute 'qualifying house'; and
   (iii) in paragraph (b) after the word 'house' add 'including the qualifying house'; and
(b) in subsection (2)—
   (i) for the words 'sections 68 to 70' substitute 'section 68 or 69';
   (ii) for the word 'tenant' substitute 'qualifying person'; and
   (iii) for the word 'house' substitute 'qualifying house'. [1539]

4. In section 64 (conditions of sale)—
(a) for the word 'tenant', except where it occurs for the second time in subsection (1)(a), substitute 'qualifying person';
(b) for the word 'house' except where it occurs for the third time in subsection (4) substitute 'qualifying house';
(c) in subsection (4) omit the words 'Subject to subsection (6)'; and
(d) omit subsections (6) to (9). [1540]

5. In section 65 (variation of conditions) for the word 'tenant' substitute 'qualifying person'. [1541]

6. In section 66 (notice of acceptance)—
(a) for the word 'tenant' substitute 'qualifying person' and for the word 'house' substitute 'qualifying house'; and
(b) in paragraph (vi) of subsection (1) for the words 'on the landlord' substitute 'in accordance with that section'. [1542]

7. In section 67 (fixed price option) for the word 'tenant' substitute 'qualifying person' and for the word 'house' substitute 'qualifying house'. [1543]

8. In section 68 (refusal of applications)—
(a) for the word 'tenant's' substitute 'qualifying person's';
(b) for the word 'house' substitute 'qualifying house';
(c) in subsection (1) omit the words from 'or' where it first occurs to the end; and
(d) for the word 'tenant' substitute the words 'qualifying person'. [1544]

9. In section 69 (Secretary of State's power to authorise refusal to sell)—
(a) for the word 'house' except where it occurs for the second time in subsection (1), substitute 'qualifying house';

SI 1992/325 [1557]

(b) in subsection (1A) for the word 'houses' substitute 'qualifying houses'; and
(c) for the word 'tenant' substitute 'qualifying person'. [1545]

10. Omit section 70 (power to refuse to sell certain houses required for educational purposes). [1546]

11. In section 71 (reference to Lands Tribunal) for the word 'tenant' substitute 'qualifying person'. [1547]

12. In section 72 (recovery of discount on early re-sale)—
(a) for the words 'person' and 'tenant' respectively substitute 'qualifying person' and for the word 'house' substitute 'qualifying house'; and
(b) in subsection (1) after the word 'shall' insert the words 'on the request of the landlord.' [1548]

13. In section 73 (cases where discount etc. is not recoverable) for the word 'house' substitute 'qualifying house'. [1549]

14. In section 74 (duties of landlords) for the word 'house' substitute 'qualifying house' and for the word 'tenant' substitute 'qualifying person'. [1550]

15. In section 75 (agreements affecting right to purchase)—
(a) for the word 'person' substitute 'qualifying person' and
(b) in subsection (1)(b) omit the words 'mentioned in section 61(2)(a)(i) or (ii)'. [1551]

16. Omit sections 76 and 77. [1552]

17. In section 78 (Secretary of State may give directions to modify conditions of sale)—
(a) in subsection (2)(b) for the word 'tenant' substitute 'qualifying person'; and
(b) omit subsection (4). [1553]

18. In section 79(1) (financial or other assistance for persons involved in proceedings) for the words 'tenant or purchaser' substitute 'qualifying person'. [1554]

19. Omit sections 81, 81A and 81B. [1555]

20. In section 84A (application of right to buy to cases where landlord is lessee)—
(a) in subsection (1)—
 (i) omit the words '(but not 76 or 77)';
 (ii) in paragraph (a) for the words 'tenant of a house let on a secure tenancy' substitute 'qualifying person';
(b) for the word 'tenant' substitute 'qualifying person' and for the word 'house' substitute 'qualifying house';
(c) in subsection (5) for the word 'tenant' substitute 'qualifying person's';
(d) in subsection (6) for the words 'subsection (5) and (9)' substitute 'subsection (5)'. [1556]

21. In section 216 (loans)—
(a) for the word 'tenant' substitute 'qualifying person' and for the word 'house' substitute 'qualifying house'; and
(b) for the word 'landlord' except where it occurs for the first time, substitute 'former landlord'. [1557]

Regulation 4   SCHEDULE 2

The Right to Buy Provisions as they Apply in Cases where the Right to Buy is Preserved

61. Right to buy.

(1) Notwithstanding anything contained in any agreement, a qualifying person (or such one or more of qualifying persons as may be agreed between them) shall, subject to this Part, have the right to purchase the qualifying house at a price fixed under section 62.

(2) This section applies to every qualifying house where—
- (b) the landlord is the heritable proprietor of the qualifying house; and
- (c) immediately prior to the date of service of an application to purchase, the qualifying person has been for not less than 2 years in occupation of a house (including accommodation provided as mentioned in subsection (11)(n)) or of a succession of houses provided by any persons mentioned in subsection (11) or of the qualifying house or any other house provided by the landlord which was a qualifying house.

(2A) For the purposes of subsection (2)(c), where the house or qualifying house was provided by a housing association which, at any time while that house was so provided, was not a registered housing association, the association shall, if it became a registered housing association at any later time, be deemed to have been a registered association at all times since it first provided that house.

(3) This section also applies to a qualifying house let to the qualifying person following acquisition by the landlord of a defective dwelling previously purchased by the qualifying person if the qualifying person would not otherwise have the right to purchase under this Part; and where it so applies—
- (a) paragraph (c) of subsection (2) shall not have effect;
- (b) the words 'beyond 2' in section 62(3)(b) shall not have effect.

(4) This section does not apply—
- (a) to a qualifying house that is one of a group which has been provided with facilities (including a call system and the services of a warden) specially designed or adapted for the needs of persons of pensionable age or disabled persons; or
- (b) where a landlord which is a registered housing association has at no time received a grant under—
  - (i) any enactment mentioned in paragraph 2 of Schedule I to the Housing Associations Act 1985 grants under enactments superseded by the Housing Act 1974
  - (ii) section 31 of the Housing Act 1974 (management grants);
  - (iii) section 41 of the Housing Associations Act 1985 (housing association grants);
  - (iv) section 54 of that Act (revenue deficit grants);
  - (v) section 55 of that Act (hostel deficit grants);
  - (vi) section 59(2) of that Act (grants by local authorities);
  - (vii) section 50 of the Housing Act 1988 (housing association grants); or
  - (viii) section 51 of that Act (revenue deficit grants); or
- (c) where such a landlord has at no time let (or had available for letting) more than 100 dwellings; or
- (f) where, within a neigbourhood, the qualifying house is one of a number (not exceeding 14) of houses with a common landlord, being a landlord which is a registered housing association, and it is the practice of that landlord to let at least one half of those houses for occupation by any or all of the following—
  - (i) persons who have suffered from, or are suffering from, mental disorder (as defined in the Mental Health (Scotland) Act 1984, physical handicap or addiction to alcohol or other drugs;
  - (ii) persons who have been released from prison or other institutions;
  - (iii) young persons who have left the care of a local authority,

and a social service is, or special facilities are, provided wholly or partly for the purpose of assisting those persons.

(5) Where the spouse of a qualifying person occupies the qualifying house as his only or principal home but is not himself a qualifying person, the right to purchase the qualifying house under subsection (1) shall not be exercised without the consent of such spouse.

(6) A qualifying person may exercise his right to purchase, if he so wishes, together with one or more members of his family acting as joint purchasers, provided—
   (a) that such members are at least 18 years of age, that they have, during the period of 6 months ending with the date of service of the application to purchase, had their only or principal home with the qualifying person and that their residence in the qualifying house is not a breach of any obligation of the tenancy; or
   (b) where the requirements of paragraph (a) are not satisfied, the landlord has consented.

(7) The Secretary of State may by order made by statutory instrument amend, or add to, the descriptions of persons set out in sub-paragraph (i) to (iii) of paragraph (f) of subsection (4).

(10) In this section and the following section—
   (a) references to occupation of a house include occupation—
      (i) in the case of more than one qualifying person, by any one of them;
      (ii) by any person occupying the house rent-free;
      (iii) as the spouse of the qualifying person or of any such person;
   (b) for the purpose of determining the period of occupation—
      (i) any interruption in occupation of 12 months or less shall be regarded as not affecting continuity; and
      (ii) any interruption in occupation of more than 12 months and less than 24 months may at the discretion of the landlord be regarded as not affecting continuity; and
      (iii) there shall be added to the period of occupation of a qualifying house by a qualifying person any earlier period during which he was at least 16 years of age and occupied the qualifying house as a member of the family of the tenant or of a qualifying person or of one or more of the joint tenants of the house.

(11) The persons providing houses referred to in subsection (2)(c) (occupation requirement for exercise of right to purchase) and in section 62(3)(b) (calculation of the discount from the market value) are—
   (a) a regional, islands or district council in Scotland; any local authority in England and Wales or in Northern Ireland; and the statutory predecessors of any such council or authority, or the common good of any such council, or any trust under the control of any such council;
   (b) the Commission for the New Towns;
   (c) a development corporation, an urban development corporation; and any development corporation established under corresponding legislation in England and Wales or in Northern Ireland; and the statutory predecessors of any such authority;
   (d) Scottish Homes and the Scottish Special Housing Association;
   (e) a registered housing association;
   (f) the Housing Corporation;
   (g) a housing co-operative within the meaning of section 22 or a housing co-operative within the meaning of section 27B of the Housing Act 1985;
   (h) the Development Board for Rural Walks;
   (i) the Northern Ireland Housing Executive or any statutory predecessor;
   (j) a police authority or the statutory predecessors of any such authority;
   (k) a fire authority or the statutory predecessors of any such authority;
   (l) a water authority in Scotland; any water authority constituted under corresponding legislation in England and Wales or in Northern Ireland; and the statutory predecessors of any such authority;

(m) the Secretary of State, where the house was at the material time used for the purposes of the Scottish Prison Service or of a prison service for which the Home Office or the Northern Ireland Office have responsibility;
(n) the Crown, in relation to accommodation provided in connection with the service whether by the tenant or his spouse as a member of the regular armed forces of the Crown;
(o) the Secretary of State, where the house was at the material time used for the purposes of a health board constituted under section 2 of the National Health Services (Scotland) Act 1978 or for the purposes of a corresponding board in England and Wales, or for the purposes of the statutory predecessors of any such board; or the Department of Health and Social Services for Northern Ireland, where the house was at the material time used for the purposes of a Health and Personal Services Board in Northern Ireland, or for the purposes of the statutory predecessors of any such board;
(p) the Secretary of State, or the Minister of Agriculture, Fisheries and Food, where the house was at the material time used for purposes of the Forestry Commission;
(q) the Secretary of State, where the house was at the material time used for purposes of a State Hospital provided by him under section 90 of the Mental Health (Scotland) Act 1984 or for the purposes of any hospital provided under corresponding legislation in England and Wales;
(r) the Commissioners of Northern Lighthouses;
(s) the Trinity House;
(t) the Secretary of State, where the house was at the material time used for the purposes of Her Majesty's Coastguard;
(u) the United Kingdom Atomic Energy Authority;
(v) the Secretary of State, where the house was at the material time used for the purposes of any function transferred to him under section 1(2) of the Defence (Transfer of Functions) Act 1964 or any function relating to defence conferred on him by or under any subsequent enactment;
(w) such other person as the Secretary of State may by order made by statutory instrument subject to annulment in pursuance of a resolution of either House of Parliament prescribe. **[1558]**

62. The price.

(1) Subject to subsection (6A), the price at which a qualifying person shall be entitled to purchase a qualifying house under this Part shall be fixed as at the date of service of the application to purchase by subtracting a discount from the market value of the qualifying house.

(2) The market value for the purposes of this section shall be determined by either—
(a) a qualified valuer nominated by the landlord and accepted by the qualifying person; or
(b) the district valuer

as the landlord thinks fit as if the qualifying house were available for sale on the open market with vacant possession at the date of service of the application to purchase.

For the purposes of this subsection, no account shall be taken of any element in the market value of the qualifying house which reflects an increase in value as a result of work the cost of which would qualify for a reimbursement under section 58.

(3) Subject to subsection (5), the discount for the purposes of subsection (1) shall be—
(a) 32 per cent. of the market value of the qualifying house except—
  (i) where the qualifying house is a flat, it shall be 44 per cent. of the market value;
  (ii) where the qualifying house is one to which section 61(3) applies, it shall be 30 per cent. or, where it is a flat, 40 per cent. of the market value;
together with
(b) an additional one per cent. or, where the qualifying house is a flat, two per cent., of the market value for every year beyond 2 of continuous occupation by the

appropriate person, immediately preceding the date of service of the application to purchase, of a house or of a qualifying house (including accommodation provided as mentioned in section 61(11)(n)) or of a succession of houses provided by any persons mentioned in section 61(11),

up to a maximum discount of 60 per cent., or where the qualifying house is a flat, 70 per cent. of the market value.

(4) For the purposes of subsection (3)—
(a) the 'appropriate person' is the qualifying person, or if it would result in a higher discount and if she is cohabiting with him at the date of service of the application to purchase, his spouse; and where more than one qualifying person are joint purchasers the 'appropriate person' shall be whichever qualifying person (or, as the case may be, spouse) has the longer or longest such occupation; and
(b) where the house or qualifying house was provided by a housing association which, at any time while the house or qualifying house was so provided was not a registered housing association, the association shall, if it became a registered housing association at any later time, be deemed to have been a registered housing association at all times since it first provided the house or qualifying house.

(5) The Secretary of State may by order made with the consent of the Treasury provide that, in such cases as may be specified in the order—
(a) the minimum percentage discount,
(b) the percentage increase for each complete year of the qualifying period after the first two, or
(c) the maximum percentage discount,

shall be such percentage higher than that specified in subsection (3), as may be specified in the order.

(6) An order under subsection (5)—
(a) may make different provision with respect to different cases or descriptions of case,
(b) may contain such incidental, supplementary or transitional provisions as appear to the Secretary of State to be necessary or expedient, and
(c) shall be made by statutory instrument and shall not be made unless a draft of it has been laid before and approved by resolution of each House of Parliament.

(6A) Except where the Secretary of State so determines, the discount for the purpose of subsection (1) shall not reduce the price below the amount which, in accordance with a determination made by him, is to be taken as representing so much of the costs incurred in respect of the qualifying house as, in accordance with the determination, is to be treated as—
(a) incurred in the period commencing with the beginning of the financial year of the landlord which was current 5 years prior to the date of service of the application to purchase the qualifying house or such other period as the Secretary of State may by order provide; and
(b) relevant for the purposes of this subsection,

and if the price before discount is below that amount, there shall be no discount.

(6B) An order under subsection (6A) shall be made by statutory instrument subject to annulment in pursuance of a resolution of either House of Parliament and may make different provision in relation to different cases or circumstances or different areas.

(10) Where at the date of service of an offer to sell under section 63 any of the costs referred to in subsection (6A) are not known, the landlord shall make an estimate of such unknown costs for the purposes of that subsection. **[1559]**

PROCEDURE

63. Application to purchase and offer to sell.

(1) A qualifying person who seeks to exercise a right to purchase a qualifying house under section 61 shall serve on the landlord a notice (referred to in this Part as an

'application to purchase') which shall be in such form as the Secretary of State shall by order made by statutory instrument prescribe, and shall contain—
   (a)   notice that the qualifying person seeks to exercise the right to purchase;
   (b)   a statement of any period of occupancy of a house including the qualifying house on which the qualifying person intends to rely for the purposes of section 61 and 62; and
   (c)   the name of any joint purchaser within the meaning of section 61(6).

(2) Where an application to purchase is served on a landlord, and the landlord does not serve a notice of refusal under section 68 or 69 it shall, within 2 months after service of the application to purchase, serve on the qualifying person a notice (referred to in this Part as an 'offer to sell') containing—
   (a)   the market value of the qualifying house determined under section 62(2);
   (b)   the discount calculated under section 62(3);
   (c)   the price fixed under section 62(1);
   (d)   any conditions which the landlord intends to impose under section 64; and
   (e)   an offer to sell the qualifying house to the qualifying person and any joint purchaser named in the application to purchase at the price referred to in paragraph (c) and under the conditions referred to in paragraph (d).

64. Conditions of sale.

(1) Subject to section 75, an offer to sell under section 63(2) shall contain such conditions as are reasonable, provided that—
   (a)   the conditions shall have the effect of ensuring that the qualifying person has as full enjoyment and use of the qualifying house as owner as he has had as tenant;
   (b)   the conditions shall secure to the qualifying person such additional rights as are necessary for his reasonable enjoyment and use of the qualifying house as owner (including, without prejudice to the foregoing generality, common rights in any part of the building of which the qualifying house forms part) and shall impose on the qualifying person any necessary duties relative to rights so secured; and
   (c)   the conditions shall include such terms as are necessary to entitle the qualifying person to receive a good and marketable title to the qualifying house.

(2) A condition which imposes a new charge or an increase of an existing charge for the provision of a service in relation to the qualifying house shall provide for the charge to be in reasonable proportion to the cost to the landlord of providing the service.

(3) No condition shall be imposed under this section which has the effect of requiring the qualifying person to pay any expenses of the landlord.

(4) No condition shall be imposed under this section which has the effect of requiring the qualifying person or any of his successors in title to offer to the landlord, or to any other person, an option to purchase the qualifying house in advance of its sale to a third party, except in the case of a qualifying house which has facilities which are substantially different from those of an ordinary house and which has been designed or adapted for occupation by a person of pensionable age or disabled person whose special needs require accommodation of the kind provided by the qualifying house.

(5) Where an option to purchase permitted under subsection (4) is exercised, the price to be paid for the qualifying house shall be determined by the district valuer who shall have regard to the market value of the qualifying house at the time of the purchase and to any amount due to the landlord under section 72 (recovery of discount on early re-sale).

65. Variation of conditions.

(1) Where an offer to sell is served on a qualifying person and he wishes to exercise his right to purchase, but—
   (a)   he considers that a condition contained in the offer to sell is unreasonable; or
   (b)   he wishes to have a new condition included in it; or
   (c)   he has not previously notified the landlord of his intention to exercise that right together with a joint purchaser, but now wishes to do so; or

(d) he has previously notified the landlord of his intention to exercise that right together with any joint purchaser but now wishes to exercise the right without that joint purchaser,

he may request the landlord to strike out or vary the condition, or to include the new condition, or to make the offer to sell to the qualifying person and the joint purchaser, or to withdraw the offer to sell in respect of the joint purchaser, as the case may be, by serving on the landlord within one month after service of the offer to sell a notice in writing setting out his request; and if the landlord agrees, it shall accordingly serve an amended offer to sell on the qualifying person within one month of service of the notice setting out the request.

(2) A qualifying person who is aggrieved by the refusal of the landlord to agree to strike out or vary a condition, or to include a new condition, or to make the offer to sell to the qualifying person and the joint purchaser, or to withdraw the offer to sell in respect of any joint purchaser under subsection (1), or by his failure timeously to serve an amended offer to sell under the said subsection, may, within one month or, with the consent of the landlord given in writing before the expiry of the said period of one month, within two months of the refusal or failure, refer the matter to the Lands Tribunal for determination.

(3) In proceedings under subsection (2), the Lands Tribunal may, as it thinks fit, uphold the condition or strike it out or vary it, or insert the new condition or order that the offer to sell be made to the qualifying person and the joint purchaser, or order that the offer to sell be withdrawn in respect of any joint purchaser, and where its determination results in a variation of the terms of the offer to sell, it shall order the landlord to serve on the qualifying person an amended offer to sell accordingly within 2 months thereafter. **[1562]**

66. Notice of acceptance.

(1) Where an offer to sell is served on a qualifying person and he wishes to exercise his right to purchase and—
  (a) he does not dispute the terms of the offer to sell by timeously serving a notice setting out a request under section 65(1) or by referring the matter to the Lands Tribunal under subsection (1)(d) of section 71; or
  (b) any such dispute has been resolved;

the qualifying person shall, subject to section 67(1), serve a notice of acceptance on the landlord within 2 months of whichever is the latest of—
  (i) the service on him of the offer to sell;
  (ii) the service on him of an amended offer to sell (or if there is more than one, of the latest amended offer to sell);
  (iii) a determination by the Lands Tribunal under section 65(3) which does not require service of an amended offer to sell;
  (iv) a finding of determination of the Lands Tribunal in a matter referred to it under section 71(1)(d) where no order is made under section 71(2)(b);
  (v) the service of an offer to sell on him by virtue of subsection (2)(b) of section 71;
  (vi) where a loan application under subsection (2)(a)(i) of section 216 (loans) has been served in accordance with that section, the service of a relative offer or refusal of loan; or
  (vii) where section 216(7) (loans) is invoked, the decision of the court.

(2) Where an offer to sell (or an amended offer to sell) has been served on the qualifying person and a relative notice of acceptance has been duly served on the landlord, a contract of sale of the qualifying house shall be constituted between the landlord and the qualifying person on the terms contained in the offer (or amended offer) to sell. **[1563]**

67. Fixed price option.

(1) Where an offer to sell (or an amended offer to sell) is served on a qualifying person, but he is unable by reason of the application of regulations made under section 216(3) (loans) to obtain a loan of the amount for which he has applied, he may, within 2 months of service on him of an offer of loan, or (as the case may be) of the date of a declarator by

the sheriff under section 216(7) (loans), whichever is the later, serve on the landlord a notice to the effect that he wishes to have a fixed price option, which notice shall be accompanied by a payment to the landlord of £100, and in that event he shall be entitled to serve a notice of acceptance on the landlord at any time within 2 years of the service of the application to purchase:

Provided that where, as regards the qualifying house, the qualifying person has served a loan application in accordance with subsection (2)(a)(ii) of section 216 (loans), he shall be entitled (even if the said period of 2 years has expired) to serve an notice of acceptance on the landlord within 2 months of whichever is the later of—

(a) the service of a relative offer, or refusal, of loan; or
(b) where section 216(7) is invoked, the decision of the court.

(2) The payment of £100 mentioned in subsection (1) shall be recoverable—
(a) by the qualifying person, when he purchases the qualifying house in accordance with that subsection or, if he does not, at the expiry of the period of 2 years mentioned therein;
(b) by the qualifying person, when the landlord recovers possession of the qualifying house under subsection (3); or
(c) by his personal representatives, if he dies without purchasing the qualifying house in accordance with that subsection.

(3) The existence of a fixed price option under subsection (1) shall not prevent the landlord from recovering possession of the property in any manner which may be lawful, and in that event the option shall be terminated. **[1564]**

68. Refusal of applications.

(1) Where a landlord on which an application to purchase has been served disputes the qualifying person's right to purchase a qualifying house under section 61, it shall by notice (referred to in this Part as a 'notice of refusal') served within one month after service of the application to purchase, refuse the application.

(2) Where a landlord on which an application to purchase has been served, after reasonable enquiry (which shall include reasonable opportunity for the qualifying person to amend his application), is of the opinion that information contained in the application is incorrect in a material respect it shall issue a notice of refusal within 2 months of the application to purchase.

(3) A notice of refusal shall specify the grounds on which the landlord disputes the qualifying person's right to purchase or, as the case may be, the accuracy of the information.

(4) Where a landlord serves a notice of refusal on a qualifying person under this section, the qualifying person may within one month thereafter apply to the Lands Tribunal for a finding that he has a right to purchase the qualifying house under section 61 on such terms as it may determine. **[1565]**

HOUSES PROVIDED FOR SPECIAL PURPOSES

69. Secretary of State's power to authorise refusal to sell certain houses provided for persons of pensionable age.

(1) This section applies to a qualifying house which has facilities which are substantially different from those of an ordinary house and which has been designed or adapted for occupation by a person of pensionable age whose special needs require accommodation of the kind provided by the qualifying house.

(1A) This section applies only to qualifying houses first let on a secure tenancy before 1st January 1990.

(2) Where an application to purchase a qualifying house is served on a landlord and it appears to the landlord that—

(a) the qualifying house is one to which this section applies; and
(b) the qualifying person would, apart from this section, have a right under section 61 to purchase the qualifying house.

the landlord may, within one month after service of the application to purchase, instead of serving an offer to sell on the qualifying person, make an application to the Secretary of State under this section.

(3) An application under subsection (2) shall specify the facilities and features of design or adaptation which in the view of the landlord cause the qualifying house to be a qualifying house to which this section applies.

(4) Where the Secretary of State has received an application under this section and it appears to him that the qualifying house concerned is one to which this section applies, he shall authorise the landlord to serve on the qualifying person a notice of refusal under this section, which shall be served as soon as is practicable after the authority is given and in any event within one month thereafter.

(5) A notice of refusal served under subsection (4) shall specify the facilities and features specified for the purposes of subsection (3) and that the Secretary of State's authority for service of the said notice has been given.

(6) Where the Secretary of State refuses an application made under subsection (2), the landlord shall serve on the qualifying person an offer to sell under section 63(2)—
(a) within the period mentioned in that section; or
(b) where the unexpired portion of that period is less than one month or there is not an unexpired portion of that period, within one month of the Secretary of State's refusal. **[1566]**

★ ★ ★

LANDS TRIBUNAL

71. Reference to Lands Tribunal.

(1) Where—
(a) a landlord who has been duly served with an application to purchase fails to issue timeously either an offer to sell (even if only such offer to sell as is mentioned in paragraph (d)) or a notice of refusal; or
(b) the Lands Tribunal has made a determination under section 65(3) (variation of terms of offer to sell) and the landlord has failed to issue an amended offer to sell within 2 months thereafter; or
(c) the Lands Tribunal has made a finding under section 68(4) (refusal of right to purchase) or has made an order under subsection (2)(b) of this section and the landlord has not duly progressed the application to purchase in accordance with that finding or, as the case may be, order, within 2 months thereafter; or
(d) a landlord has served an offer to sell whose contents do not conform with the requirements of paragraphs (a) to (e) of section 63(2) (or where such contents were not obtained in accordance with the provisions specified in those paragraphs),

the qualifying person (together with any joint purchaser) may refer the matter to the Lands Tribunal by serving on the clerk to that body a copy of any notice served and of any findings or determination made under this Part, together with a statement of his grievance.

(2) Where a matter has been referred to the Lands Tribunal under subsection (1), the Tribunal shall consider whether in its opinion—
(a) any of paragraphs (a) to (c) of that subsection apply, and if it so finds it may—
 (i) give any consent, exercise any discretion, or do anything which the landlord may give, exercise or do under or for the purposes of sections 61 to 84; and
 (ii) issue such notices and undertake such other steps as may be required to complete the procedure provided for in sections 63 and 65 to 67;

and any consent given, any discretion exercised, or anything done, under the foregoing provisions of this subsection shall have effect as if it had been duly given, exercised or done by the landlord; or
  (b) paragraph (d) of that subsection applies, and if it so finds it may order the landlord to serve on the qualifying person an offer to sell, in proper form, under section 63(2) within such time (not exceeding 2 months) as it may specify.

(3) Nothing in this section shall affect the operation of the provisions of any other enactment relating to the enforcement of a statutory duty whether under that enactment or otherwise. **[1567]**

RECOVERABILITY OF DISCOUNT

72. Recovery of discount on early re-sale.

(1) A qualifying person who has purchased a qualifying house in exercise of a right to purchase under section 61, or any of his successors in title, who sells or otherwise disposes of the qualifying house (except as provided for in section 73) before the expiry of 3 years from the date of service of a notice of acceptance by the qualifying person under section 66, shall on the request of the landlord be liable to repay to the landlord, in accordance with subsection (3), a proportion of the difference between the market value determined, in respect of the qualifying house, under section 62(2) and the price at which the qualifying house was so purchased.

(2) Subsection (1) applies to the disposal of part of a qualifying house except in a case where—
  (a) it is a disposal by one of the parties to the original sale to one of the other parties; or
  (b) the remainder of the qualifying house continues to be the only or principal home of the person disposing of the part.

(3) The proportion of the difference which shall be paid to the landlord shall be—
  (a) 100 per cent. where the disposal occurs within the first year after the date of service of notice,
  (b) 66 per cent. where it occurs in the second such year, and
  (c) 33 per cent. where it occurs in the third such year.

(4) Where as regards a qualifying house or part of a qualifying house there is, within the period mentioned in subsection (1), more than one disposal to which that subsection would (apart from the provisions of this subsection) apply, that subsection shall apply only in relation to the first such disposal of the qualifying house, or part of the qualifying house.

(5) Where a landlord secures the liability to make a repayment under subsection (1) the security shall, notwithstanding section 13 of the Conveyancing and Feudal Reform (Scotland) Act 1970, have priority immediately after—
  (a) any standard security granted in security of a loan either—
    (i) for the purchase of the qualifying house, or
    (ii) for the improvement of the qualifying house,
    and any interest present or future due thereon (including any such interest which has accrued or may accrue) and any expenses or outlays (including interest thereon) which may be, or may have been, reasonably incurred in the exercise of any power conferred on the lender by the deed expressing the said standard security; and
  (b) if the landlord consents, a standard security over the qualifying house granted in security of any other loan, and in relation thereto any such interest, expenses or outlays as aforesaid.

(6) For the avoidance of doubt, paragraph (a) of subsection (5) applies to a standard security granted in security both for the purpose mentioned in sub-paragraph (i) and for

SI 1992/325 [1572]

that mentioned in sub-paragraph (ii) as it applies to a standard security so granted for only one of those purposes.

(7) The liability to make a repayment under subsection (1) shall not be imposed as a real burden in a disposition of any interest in the qualifying house. **[1568]**

73. Cases where discount etc. is not recoverable.

(1) There shall be no liability to make a repayment under section 72(1) where the disposal is made—
(a) by the executor of the deceased owner acting in that capacity; or
(b) as a result of a compulsory purchase order; or
(c) in the circumstances specified in subsection (2).

(2) The circumstances mentioned in subsection (1)(c) are that the disposal—
(a) is to a member of the owner's family who has lived with him for a period of 12 months before the disposal; and
(b) is for no consideration:
Provided that, if the disponee disposes of the qualifying house before the expiry of the 3 year period mentioned in section 72(1), the provisions of that section will apply to him as if this was the first disposal and he was the original purchaser. **[1569]**

DUTIES OF LANDLORDS

74. Duties of landlords.

It shall be the duty of every landlord of a qualifying house to which sections 61 to 84 and section 216 apply to make provision for the progression of applications under those sections in such manner as may be necessary to enable any qualifying person who wishes to exercise his rights under this Part to do so, and to comply with any regulations which may be made by statutory instrument by the Secretary of State in that regard. **[1570]**

75. Agreements affecting right to purchase.

(1) Subject to sections 61(1), 67(1) and 72(1)—
(a) no qualifying person exercising or seeking to exercise a right to purchase under section 61(1) shall be obliged, notwithstanding any agreement to the contrary, to make any payment or to lodge any deposit with the landlord which he would not have been obliged to make, or as the case may be lodged, had he not exercised (or sought to exercise) the right to purchase;
(b) a landlord is required neither to enter into, nor to induce (or seek to induce) any qualifying person to enter into, such agreement as is mentioned in paragraph (a), or into any agreement which purports to restrict that qualifying person's rights under this Part.

(2) Paragraph (a) of subsection (1) does not apply to the expenses in any court proceedings. **[1571]**

★ ★ ★

POWERS OF SECRETARY OF STATE

78. Secretary of State may give directions to modify conditions of sale.

(1) Where it appears to the Secretary of State that the inclusion of conditions of a particular kind in offers to sell would be unreasonable he may by direction require landlords generally, landlords of a particular description, or particular landlords not to include conditions of that kind (or not to include conditions of that kind unless modified in such manner as may be specified in the direction) in offers to sell served on or after a date so specified.

(2) Where a condition's inclusion in an offer to sell—
(a) is in contravention of a direction under subsection (1); or
(b) in a case where the qualifying person has not by the date specified in such a direction served a relative notice of acceptance on the landlord, would have been in such contravention had the offer to sell been served on or after that date,
the condition shall have no effect as regards the offer to sell.

(3) A direction under subsection (1) may—
(a) make different provision in relation to different areas, cases or classes of case and may exclude certain areas, cases or classes of case; and
(b) be varied or withdrawn by a subsequent direction so given. **[1572]**

79. Secretary of State may give financial and other assistance for tenants involved in proceedings.

(1) Where, in relation to any proceedings, or prospective proceedings, to which this section applies, a qualifying person is an actual or prospective party, the Secretary of State may on written application to him by the qualifying person give financial or other assistance to the applicant, if the Secretary of State thinks fit to do so:
Provided that assistance under this section shall be given only where the Secretary of State considers—
(a) that the case raises a question of principle and that it is in the public interest to give the applicant such assistance; or
(b) that there is some other special consideration.

(2) This section applies to—
(a) any proceedings under sections 61 to 84 and section 216; and
(b) any proceedings to determine any question arising under or in connection with those sections other than a question as to market value for the purposes of section 62.

(3) Assistance by the Secretary of State under this section may include—
(a) giving advice;
(b) procuring or attempting to procure the settlement of the matter in dispute;
(c) arranging for the giving of advice or assistance by a solicitor or counsel;
(d) arranging for representation by a solicitor or counsel;
(e) any other form of assistance which the Secretary of State may consider appropriate.

(4) In so far as expenses are incurred by the Secretary of State in providing the applicant with assistance under this section, any sums recovered by virtue of an award of expenses, or of an agreement as to expenses, in the applicant's favour with respect to the matter in connection with which the assistance is given shall, subject to any charge or obligation for payment in priority to other debts under the Legal Aid (Scotland) Act 1986 and to any provision of that Act for payment of any sum into the Scottish Legal Aid Fund, be paid to the Secretary of State in priority to any other debts.

(5) Any expenses incurred by the Secretary of State in providing assistance under this section shall be paid out of money provided by Parliament; and any sums received by the Secretary of State under subsection (4) shall be paid into the Consolidated Fund. **[1573]**

* * *

GENERAL

82. Interpretation of this Part.

In this Part and in sections 14, 19, 20 and 216, except where provision is made to the contrary,
'application to purchase' has the meaning assigned to it by section 63;
'family' and any reference to membership thereof shall be construed in accordance with section 83;

'fire authority' means a fire authority for the purposes of the Fire Services Acts 1947 to 1959 or a joint committee constituted by virtue of section 36(4)(b) of the Fire Services Act 1947;

'heritable proprietor' in relation to a house, includes any landlord entitled under section 3 of the Conveyancing (Scotland) Act 1924 (disposition of the dwelling-house etc. by persons uninfeft) to grant a disposition of the house;

'housing co-operative' has meaning assigned to it by section 22;

'landlord' means a person who lets a house to a tenant for human habitation, and includes his successors in title;

'offer to sell' has the meaning assigned to it by section 63(2) and includes such offer to sell as is mentioned in section 71(1)(d);

'police authority' means a police authority in Scotland within the meaning of section 2(1) or 19(9)(b) of the Police (Scotland) Act 1967 or a joint police committee constituted by virtue of subsection (2)(b) of the said section 19 and any police authority constituted in England and Wales or Northern Ireland under corresponding legislation;

'secure tenancy' means a secure tenancy within the meaning of section 44;

'tenancy' means any agreement under which a house is made available for occupation for human habitation, and 'leases', 'let' and 'lets' shall be construed accordingly;

'tenant' means a person who leases a house from a landlord and who derives his right therein directly from the landlord, and in the case of joint tenancies means all the tenants. **[1574]**

83. Members of a person's family.

(1) A person is a member of another's family for the purposes of this Act if—
(a) he is the spouse of that person or he and that person live together as husband and wife; or
(b) he is that person's parent, grandparent, child, grandchild, brother, sister, uncle, aunt, nephew or niece.

(2) For the purposes of subsection (1)(b)—
(a) a relationship by marriage shall be treated as a relationship by blood;
(b) a relationship of the half-blood shall be treated as a relationship of the whole blood;
(c) the stepchild of a person shall be treated as his child; and
(d) a child shall be treated as such whether or not his parents are married. **[1575]**

84. Service of notices.

(1) A notice or other document which requires to be served on a person under any provision of this Part or of section 216 may be given to him—
(a) by delivering it to him;
(b) by leaving it at his proper address; or
(c) by sending it by recorded delivery post to him at that address.

(2) For the purposes of this section and of section 7 of the Interpretation Act 1978 (references to service by post) in its application to this section, a person's proper address shall be his last known address. **[1576]**

84A. Application of right to buy to cases where landlord is lessee.

(1) Sections 61 to 84 and 216 (the 'right to buy' provisions) shall, with the modifications set out in this section, apply so as to provide for—
(a) the acquisition by the qualifying person of the landlord's interest in the qualifying house as lessee under a registered lease of the qualifying house or of land which includes it or as assignee of that interest; and
(b) the obtaining of a loan by the qualifying person in that connection,

as these sections apply for the purposes of the purchase of a qualifying house by the qualifying person from the landlord as heritable proprietor of it and the obtaining by the qualifying person of a loan in that connection.

(2) References in the right to buy provisions to the purchase or sale of a qualifying house shall be construed respectively as references to the acquisition or disposal of the landlord's interest in the qualifying house by way of a registered assignation of that interest and cognate expressions shall be construed accordingly.

(3) The reference in section 6(2)(b) to the landlord's being the heritable proprietor of the qualifying house shall be construed as a reference to the landlord's being the holder of the interest of the lessee under a registered lease of the qualifying house or of land which includes it.

(4) References in the right to buy provisions to the market value of or price to be paid for a qualifying house shall be construed respectively as references to the market value of the landlord's interest in the qualifying house and to the price to be paid for acquiring that interest.

(5) References in section 64(1) to the qualifying person's enjoyment and use of a qualifying house as owner shall be construed as references to his enjoyment and use of it as assignee of the landlord's interest in the qualifying house.

(6) The reference in subsection (4) of section 64 to an option being offered to the landlord or to any other person to purchase the qualifying house in advance of its sale to a third party shall be construed as a reference to an option being offered to have the interest acquired by the qualifying person reassigned to the landlord or assigned to the other person in advance of its being disposed of to a third party; and the references in subsection (5) of that section to an option to purchase shall be construed accordingly.

(7) In this section and section 76—
'registered lease' means a lease—
(a) which is recorded in the general register of sasines; or
(b) in respect of which the interest of the lessee is registered in the Land Register of Scotland,
under the Registration of Leases (Scotland) Act 1857; and
'registered assignation' means, in relation to such a lease, an assignation thereof which is so recorded or in respect of which the interest of the assignee has been so registered. **[1577]**

* * *

QUALIFYING HOUSE LOANS: SPECIAL CASES

216. Qualifying house loans to qualifying persons exercising right to purchase.

(1) A qualifying person who seeks to exercise his right to purchase a qualifying house under Part III and who has received an offer to sell (or, as the case may be, an amended offer to sell) from the landlord shall be entitled, together with any joint purchaser under section 61(6) (and the said qualifying person and any joint purchaser are referred to in this section as 'the applicant') to apply—
(a) in the case where the former landlord is a development corporation (including an urban development corporation) or Scottish Homes, to that body; or
(b) in a case where the former landlord is the Housing Corporation or a housing association registered in the register maintained by the Housing Corporation, to the Housing Corporation;
(bi) in a case where the former landlord is a housing association registered in the register maintained by Scottish Homes, to Scottish Homes;
(c) in any other case, to the local authority for the area in which the qualifying house is situated,
for a loan of an amount not exceeding the price fixed under section 62 to assist him to purchase the qualifying house.

(2) A loan application under subsection (1)—
(a) must be served on the former landlord or other body—

(i) within one month after service on the qualifying person of the offer to sell (or, where there has been service of one or more amended offers to sell or there has been a determination by the Lands Tribunal under section 65(3) which does not require the issue of an amended offer to sell, of the latest of these); or
(ii) within one year and 10 months after service of the application to purchase if the qualifying person has, in terms of section 67, a fixed price option as regards the qualifying house;
(b) shall be in such form as the Secretary of State shall by order made by statutory instrument prescribe, and shall contain—
 (i) the amount of the loan which the applicant seeks;
 (ii) the applicant's annual gross income and his net income after payment of income tax and national insurance contributions;
 (iii) any liabilities in respect of credit sales or other fixed outgoings of the applicant; and
 (iv) a statement that the applicant has applied for and been unable to obtain a sufficient building society loan; and
(c) shall be accompanied by evidence of the matters referred to in sub-paragraphs (ii) to (iv) of paragraph (b).

(3) Subject to such requirements as the Secretary of State may by order made by statutory instrument impose, a former landlord or other body which receives an application under subsection (1) shall, where it is satisfied on reasonable inquiry (which shall include reasonable opportunity for the applicant to amend his application) that the information contained in the loan application is correct, serve on the applicant an offer of loan, which shall specify a maximum amount of loan calculated in accordance with regulations made by statutory instrument by the Secretary of State.

(4) a former landlord or other body to which application has been made under subsection (1) shall complete its inquiries and either—
(a) issue the offer of loan under subsection (3); or
(b) refuse the application on the ground that information contained in the loan application is incorrect in a material respect,
within 2 months of the date of service of the loan application.

(5) An applicant who wishes to accept an offer of loan shall do so along with his notice of acceptance under sections 66(1) or 67(1).

(6) An offer of loan under subsection (3) together with an acceptance under subsection (5) shall constitute an agreement by the former landlord or other body, subject to such requirements as the Secretary of State may by order made by statutory instrument impose, to lend to the applicant for the purpose of purchasing the qualifying house—
(a) the maximum amount of loan mentioned in subsection (3); or
(b) the amount of loan sought by the applicant,
whichever is the lesser, on the execution by the applicant of a standard security over the qualifying house.

(7) An applicant who is aggrieved by a refusal under subsection (4)(b), or by a failure to comply with the said subsection, or by the calculation of maximum amount of loan mentioned in subsection (3) may, within 2 months of the date of the refusal or failure or of the offer of loan, as the case may be, raise proceedings by way of summary application in the sheriff court for the district in which the qualifying house is situated for declarator that he is entitled to a loan in accordance with subsection (3).

(8) Where in proceedings under subsection (7) the sheriff grants declarator that the applicant is entitled to a loan, such declarator shall have effect as if it were an offer of loan of the amount specified in the declarator duly issued under this section by the former landlord or other body.

(9) A statutory instrument made under subsection (3) or (6) shall be subject to annulment in pursuance of a resolution of either House of Parliament. **[1578]**

[1579] SI 1992/619

The Race Relations Code of Practice (Non-Rented Housing) Order 1992

SI 1992/619

(This order was made by the Secretary of State under s 47(7) of the Race Relations Act 1976 (c 74), and came into force on 1 April 1992)

1. *(Citation and commencement)* [1579]

2. Code of Practice.

The day appointed for the coming into effect of the Code of Practice in Non-Rented Housing for the elimination of racial discrimination and the promotion of equal opportunities (ISBN 1-85442-073-9) issued by the Commission for Racial Equality under section 47(7) of the Race Relations Act 1976 is 18th June 1992. [1580]

Note to SI 1992/619
The Code of Practice itself is not included in this volume.

Index

accommodation—
  agricultural workers, for, making of byelaws [880]
  seasonal workers, for, making of byelaws [881]
agricultural employees [273]
agricultural holding [1184]
agricultural land [248], [916], [1183]
agricultural tenants, improvement and repairs grants payable to [823]
assured tenancies—
  assignation, limited prohibition on [114]
  contractual tenancy [1103], [1107]
  definition [1103], [1105]
  diligence, restriction on [1120]
  exclusions [1179–1191]
  landlords' duties—
    weekly rent book, provision of [1121]
    written tenancy document, provision of [1121]
  premiums, prohibition of [1118]
  recovery of possession [1107], [1109–1113], [1192–1218]
  rent assessment committee, determination of rent by [1116]
  rent increases [1115]
  repairs, access for [1117]
  security of tenure [1107]
  shared accommodation [1105]
  short assured tenancy. *See* SHORT ASSURED TENANCY
  statutory assured tenancy—
    definition [1107]
    fixing terms of [1108]
    recovery of possession [1109–1113], [1192–1218]
  succession to tenancy, rights of spouse [1122]
  subletting, limited prohibition on [1114]
  sub-tenancies, effect of termination of assured tenancy on [1119]

byelaws—
  agricultural workers' accommodation [880]
  local authority housing, regulation of [586]
  multiple occupation, houses in [879]
  seasonal workers' accommodation [881]

caravan dwellers—
  home loss payments, to [165]
  rehousing, of [167]
caution, ejection actions, in [2]
change of landlord. *See* LANDLORD, CHANGE OF
closing and demolition orders—
  appeals, against [699]
  building subject to preservation notice [689]
  charging order [701]
  closing order, definition of [684]
  demolition order, definition of [685]
  expenses of demolition [694–701]
  listed buildings [689]

closing and demolition orders—*contd*
  obstructive building, demolition of [695], [696]
  offences [692]
  powers of local authority—
    acquisition and repair of building [691]
    compulsory purchase [690], [694]
  recovery of possession [697], [698]
  revocation [686]
  service [688]
  superiors and owners, protection of [702]
  suspension order [687]
common stairs—
  cleaning and painting, of [216]
  fire precautions, in [217]
  lighting, of [214]
compensation payments—
  houses below tolerable standard, payment for [871], [874–876]
  well maintained houses, payments for [870], [872]
  See also HOME LOSS PAYMENTS
Crown, rights of [179], [252], [275], [364], [901], [1188]

defective housing—
  assistance to owners—
    application for assistance [830–831]
    conditions of eligibility [827]
    death of person eligible [861]
    determination of eligibility [832]
    determination of form of assistance [833]
    exceptions to eligibility [828]
  designation of defective dwellings—
    local schemes of designation [855–857]
    national scheme of designation [825], [826]
  disposal of dwelling, public authority duties [859]
  lenders on security, application of Act to [863]
  publicising availability of assistance, local authority duty [858]
  reinstatement, of dwelling, by local authority [860]
  reinstatement grant—
    amount [839]
    conditions for assistance [834]
    conditions of payment [838]
    changes in work or expenditure [840]
    definition [837]
    payment [841]
    repayment [842]
  repurchase, assistance by way of—
    compulsory purchase compensation [846]
    effect on existing tenancies [849]
    grant of tenancy—
      alternative accommodation [852]
      former owner, to [850]
      former statutory tenant, to [851]

References are to paragraphs

defective housing—*contd*
  repurchase, assistance by way of—*contd*
    incidental expenses, reimbursement of [848]
    pre-emption, interest subject to right of [845]
  demolition. *See* CLOSING AND DEMOLITION ORDER, HOUSING ACTION AREAS
disabled persons—
  contributions towards local authority housing costs by regional and islands councils [803]
  improvement grants [809], [813]
development corporations [589], [591], [764], [770], [1189]

ejection caution [2]
eviction. *See* ILLEGAL EVICTION, RECOVERY OF POSSESSION

fair rent. *See* RENT AND PROTECTED TENANCY

government grants and subsidies—
  development corporations, grants to—
    payment of grant [764]
  housing support grant—
    aggregate amount [761]
    apportionment of grant [762]
    variation of grant [763]
  housing associations, grants to—
    See HOUSING ASSOCIATIONS
  payment of grants [769]
  Scottish Homes—
    general grants, to [1097]
    tax relief [765]
  voluntary associations, grants to [766]
grants—
  amenity improvement grant [820]
  conversion, for [804]
  fire escape, provision [818]
  government grants. *See* GOVERNMENT GRANTS AND SUBSIDIES
  housing support grant. *See* GOVERNMENT GRANTS AND SUBSIDIES
  improvement grants—
    agricultural tenants [823]
    amount [811]
    application [805], [809]
    approval [810]
    conditions [809]
    disabled occupants [813]
    housing action areas, in [819]
    local authorities' powers [804]
    payment [812]
    Secretary of State's powers [807], [808]
    standard amenities [813]
    voluntary repayment [816]
  local authorities, to. *See* GOVERNMENT GRANTS AND SUBSIDIES
  repairs grants—
    agricultural tenants [823]
    amount [817]
    application [805], [809], [817]
    approval [810], [817]

grants—*contd*
  repairs grants—*contd*
    conditions [809], [817]
    housing action areas [809], [819]
    payment [809], [812]
    Secretary of State's powers [807], [808], [817]
    voluntary repayment [816], [817]
  Scottish Homes, administration of improvement and repairs grants, etc, by [824]
  thermal insulation grants [821], [822], [1223A]

harassment [270]
homeless persons—
  accommodation—
    available for occupation [609]
    charges for [603]
    meaning of [592]
  application for accommodation or assistance [596]
  code of guidance [605]
  co-operation between authorities [606]
  duties of local authority—
    advice and assistance, provision of [599], [600]
    inquiry into application for accommodation or assistance [596]
    interim duty to provide accommodation [597]
    notification of decision and reasons [598]
    permanent accommodation, provision of [599], [603]
    temporary accommodation, provision of [599]
    protection of moveable property of homeless persons [604]
  false statements in connection with application [608]
  financial assistance to voluntary organisations [607]
  guidance to local authorities [605]
  homelessness [592]
  intentional homelessness [594]
  local connection [595]
  offences [608]
  priority need for accommodation [593]
  referral of application to other local authority [601], [602]
  threatened with homelessness [592]
  voluntary organisations, assistance to [607]
home loss payments—
  amount [163]
  application for [164]
  caravan dwellers, to [165]
  conditions [161]
  discretionary payments [161], [164], [165]
  rehousing displaced occupants [166], [167]
home loans. *See* HOUSE LOANS
house loans—
  first time buyers, assistance for—
    forms of assistance [791]
    generally [790]
    recognised lending institutions [792]

References are to paragraphs

house loans—*contd*
  first time buyers, assistance for—*contd*
    recognised savings institutions [793]
    terms of advances [794]
  improvement of houses in housing action areas, for [785]
  interest rates [787–789]
  indemnities for building societies [797]
  public works loan commissioners, loans by [799]
  repairs, to meet expenses of [786]
  right to purchase, loans for exercise of [784]
  tolerable standard, requirements as to [783]
houses in multiple occupation. *See* MULTIPLE OCCUPATION
housing accounts, local authorities of—
  housing revenue account—
    duty to keep housing revenue account [771]
    rate fund contribution, Secretary of State's power to limit [772]
  rent allowance account [774]
  rent rebate account [773]
  slum clearance revenue account [775]
housing action areas—
  application for possession of house [669–671]
  demolition, for [659]
  demolition and improvement, for [660]
  improvement, for [661]
  local authority powers [665–667], [676]
  procedure [665], [981–993]
  rehousing of displaced persons [668]
housing associations. *See also*, INDUSTRIAL AND PROVIDENT SOCIETIES
  accounts [447], [479], [480]
  amalgamations [474]
  audit [477], [478]
  committee [489]
  committee members—
    appointment of [472]
    payments to [469–470]
    removal of [471]
  constitution. *See* RULES
  definition [457]
  disposal of land [464–466]
  dissolution [474]
  grants, to [491], [492], [512], [1093]
  guidance, to [488]
  housing corporation [458]
  inquiry into affairs of [482–485]
  landlords, as. *See* ASSURED TENANCIES, HOUSING ASSOCIATION TENANCIES, HOUSING CO-OPERATIVES, SECURE TENANCIES
  local authorities, arrangements with [492–494]
  members—
    advances to [97]
    benefits to [467], [468]
    conditions for membership [96]
    corporate bodies, as [95]
    payments to [467], [469], [470]
  loans—
    public works loan commissioners [495]
    Scottish Homes officers [507–511]

housing associations—*contd*
  registration [461]
    appeals, removal against [463]
    eligibility for registration [460]
    removal [462]
  rules [85–91], [473]
  Scottish Homes—
    grants to housing associations [512], [1093]
    loans to housing associations [507–511]
    powers [475], [482–485], [507–516]
  tenants of. *See* ASSURED TENANCIES, HOUSING ASSOCIATION TENANCIES, HOUSING CO-OPERATIVES, SECURE TENANCIES
  winding up [474–475]
housing association tenancies—
  definition [1131]
  rent limit [305]
  rent phasing [306]
  rent registration [304]
  restriction, on creation of [1131]
housing authorities. *See* LOCAL AUTHORITIES
housing co-operatives—
  co-operative housing association [457], [613], [866]
  local authority housing functions, exercise by [590]
  secure tenancies [613]
housing management. *See* LOCAL AUTHORITIES

illegal eviction—
  agricultural employees [273]
  civil remedies [1127], [1128]
  exclusions [272]
  offences [270]
  residential occupiers [270]
industrial and provident societies—
  accounts [113], [114]
  amalgamation [124]
  banking, societies not to engage in [83]
  books [118–121]
  contracts, property, etc [104–112]
  disputes [134]
  dissolution [129–133]
  members—
    advances to [97]
    corporate bodies, as [95]
    liability in dissolution, of [131]
    payments, to [102], [103]
    offences, by [135], [136]
  offences [135–142]
  officers [115], [116], [135], [136]
  register of members and officers [118]
  registration—
    appeals, against cancellation, refusal, supension [94]
    cancellation, of [92]
    effect, of [79]
    eligibility for registration [77], [78]
    registrar [147]
    suspension, of [93]
  rules—
    amendment [86]
    conditions, regarding [87–90]
    registration [85]

References are to paragraphs

landlord—
change, of: secure tenants—
- application to acquire house [1146]
- approval of prospective landlords [1145]
- lands tribunal, reference to [1150]
- procedure [1146–1149]
- qualifying tenants [1144]
- subsequent disposals, consent required [1151]
- *See also* LOCAL AUTHORITIES—SALE OF HOUSES

duties, of. *See* ASSURED TENANCIES, PROTECTED TENANCIES, SECURE TENANCIES *and*—
- assignation of interest, duty to inform tenant [894]
- identity, duty to disclose [893]
- rent book, duty to provide [361], [1121]
- repairs [683], [1002–1006]

housing association, as. *See* ASSURED TENANCIES, HOUSING ASSOCIATION TENANCIES, SECURE TENANCIES

local authority, as. *See* SECURE TENANCIES

offences, by [270], [361], [714], [893], [1121]

private sector. *See* ASSURED TENANCIES, PROTECTED TENANCIES

repairs, landlord's obligations [683], [1002–1006]

resident [254], [1187]

leases—
assignation, of [3], [5], [10], [13], [16], [17], [623], [894], [1114]
- assignations in security [6–17]
- cost, of [74–76]
- determination of, Sheriff, by [755], [888]
- long lease, dwellinghouse, of, [68–73], [175–181]
- modification, of [755]
- real right, acquisition of by tenant [1], [4]
- registration, of [3–31]
- termination, of. *See* NOTICE TO QUIT, RECOVERY OF POSSESSION
- written lease, tenant's right to—
  - assured tenancy, in [1121]
  - secure tenancy, in [621]

local authorities—
accounts. *See* HOUSING ACCOUNTS

allocation of housing—
- admission to housing list [587]
- priority on housing list [588]
- publication of rules [589]

amenities of locality, duty to have regard to [573]

board and laundry facilities, power to provide [572]

furniture, power to provide [571]

housing accommodation, power to provide [569]

housing co-operatives, exercise of functions by [590]

housing needs, duty to consider [568]

land—
- acquisition for housing purposes [576]
- disposal and dealings [579], [580]
- procedure for acquisition [577]

local authorities—*contd*
landlord, as. *See* SECURE TENANCIES

management of housing [585]

race relations [182]

sale of houses—
- consent required [581]
- consent not required [582]
- consultation of tenants [650]
- power of sale [579], [961–966]
- preservation of right to buy [649]
- resale, consent required [580]

local authority functions. *See* LOCAL AUTHORITY *and*—
- byelaws [586], [879–881]
- closing and demolition orders [684–704]
- common stairs [214], [216], [217]
- compensation payments [161–165], [870–878]
- defective housing [825–869]
- grants [804–824]
- homeless persons [592–611]
- housing accounts [771–777]
- housing action areas [659–677]
- home loans [782–803]
- multiple occupation [722–760]
- overcrowding [705–721]
- repairs [678–683]

matrimonial home—
definition [202]

dealing—
- effect of [188]
- heritable creditors, interests of [190]

division and sale, of [200]

exclusion order [186], [187]

matrimonial interdict [187]

occupancy rights—
- cohabiting couples [199]
- spouse, of [183], [184]

transfer of tenancy [194]

multiple occupation—
buildings comprising separate dwellings [741]

control order—
- appeal, against [756]
- compensation [753]
- effect—
  - furniture [751]
  - general [749]
  - persons occupying house [750]
- expiry, of [758]
- lease, modification of [755]
- local authority duties [754]
- making, of [748]
- management scheme [754]
- revocation, of [757], [758]

compliance with standards, notice requiring [731]

definition [722]

execution of works—
- appeals, against [733]
- local authority, carrying out works [734]
- notices requiring [731]
- penalties [735]

References are to paragraphs

Index

multiple occupation—*contd*
  fire escape, provision of—
    appeal, against [733]
    notice requiring [732]
  houses in multiple occupation [722]
  licensing, of [204–211B], [1507–1509]
  management code—
    application to house, by order [727]
    appeals, against [728]
    registration, of [729]
    Secretary of State's power to provide [726]
  overcrowding [736]
  owner, protection of interests [745]
  statutory tenant [747]
  superior, protection of interests [745]

notice to quit—
  assured tenancies, and [1428–1432]
  form, of [50–51], [55–64]
  length, of [35], [49], [360]
  Part VII Contract, and [319–324]
  protected tenancies, and [1513], [1519]
  removings, generally [32–42], [360]
  See also RECOVERY OF POSSESSION
notice of removal. *See* NOTICE TO QUIT

overcrowding—
  definition [705]
  exceptions [710], [711], [713]
  landlord—
    offence [714]
    recovery of possession [715]
  licence [712]
  local authority powers and duties—
    enforcement [720]
    information—
      giving [718]
      requiring [717]
      publishing [719]
    inspection [715]
    reports and proposals [715]
  penalties [709]
  permitted numbers, increase of [708]
  room standard [706]
  space standard [707]

Part VII Contract—
  definition [311], [312]
  notice to quit [319–324]
  register of rents [315]
  registration of rent [315–318]
  rent assessment committee—
    powers of [314]
    reference to [313]
  rent book, duty to provide [327]
  restriction on creation, of [1132]
  premiums—
    assured tenancies, in [1118]
    protected tenancies, in [330–336]
protected tenancies—
  assured tenancies, distinguished from [1191]
  definition [248]
  diligence, restriction on [358]

protected tenancies—*contd*
  exceptions [249], [252], [253], [254]
  offences [330–336], [355], [361]
  premiums [330–336]
  recovery of possession [259–262], [391–400]
  rent book, duty to provide [361]
  restriction on creation, of [1130]
  sharing accommodation—
    landlord, with [344]
    other persons, with [345]
  short tenancy. *See* SHORT TENANCY
  statutory tenancy—
    change of tenant [265]
    definition [250]
    recovery of possession [259–260], [262], [391–400]
    terms and conditions [263]
  sub-letting [347], [348]
  sub-tenancy [267]
  succession [250], [251], [367–390]

race relations—
  housing code of practice [182]
recovery of possession—
  assured tenancies, in—
    grounds [1192–1208]
    notice of intention to raise proceedings [1110]
    order for possession [1109]
    power to adjourn proceedings [1111]
    shared accommodation [1112]
    suitable alternative accommodation [1209–1215]
  notice to quit—
    assured tenancies, and [1428–1432]
    form, of [50–51], [55–64]
    length, of [35], [49], [360]
    Part VII Contract, and [319–324]
    protected tenancies, and [1513], [1519]
    removings, generally [32–42], [360]
  protected tenancies, in—
    grounds [259], [391], [392]
    order for possession [259]
    power to adjourn proceedings [260]
    suitable alternative accommodation [395–400]
  secure tenancies, in—
    grounds [615], [919–934]
    notice of intention to raise proceedings [615]
    order for recovery of possession [616]
    power to adjourn proceedings [616]
    other suitable accommodation [616], [935–937]
  short tenancies, in [261], [262], [392]
  short assured tenancies, in [1122]
  statutory tenancies, in [259], [260], [391–400]
  statutory assured tenancies, in [1109–1112], [1192–1208]
  tenancies, generally [37–64], [360]
regulated heritable security [339–342]
regulated tenancies—
  assured tenancies, distinguished from [1191]
  definition [256]

References are to paragraphs

regulated tenancies—*contd*
  rent, in [277–302]
  restriction on creation, of [1130]
removings. *See* NOTICE TO QUIT, RECOVERY OF POSSESSION
rent—
  assured tenancies, in—
    adjustment, of [1108]
    increases [1115]
    recovery of possession [1109], [1199], [1202], [1203]
    rent assessment committee [1116]
  fair rent. *See* REGULATED TENANCIES, IN
  housing association tenancies, in—
    rent increases [307]
    rent limit [305]
    rent phasing [306]
    rent registration [304]
  protected tenancies, in. *See* REGULATED TENANCIES, IN
  public sector tenancies, in—
    generally [778]
    removal notice [781]
    rent increase notice [780]
    secure tenancy [622]
    service charges [779]
  regulated tenancies, in—
    excess payments, recovery of [284], [285]
    fair rent—
      certificate of [295], [429–438]
      determination, of [296]
    rent agreements [282–284]
    rent increases [280], [281]
    rent limits [277], [278]
    rent registration—
      amount [297]
      application, for [294], [413–428]
      cancellation, of [299], [300]
      effect, of [298]
      register of rents [293]
      registration areas [291]
      rent officers [291]
  secure tenancies, in. *See* PUBLIC SECTOR TENANCIES, IN
  short assured tenancies, in [1125]
rent assessment committee—
  assured tenancies [1116]
  constitution [292], [401–402]
  regulated tenancies [296]
  short assured tenancies [1125]
repairs—
  building in need of [212], [1002–1006]
  landlord's obligations [678–683]
  loans, for [782]
  local authority powers. *See* REPAIRS NOTICE
  secure tenants' right to repair [628]
repairs notice—
  appeals, against [681]
  execution of works [678]
  power to serve [678]
  recovery of expenses—
    local authority, by [679]
    tenant, by [680]
  serious disrepair [678]

right to buy, secure tenants'—
  agreements affecting [643]
  application to buy [631]
  conditions of sale—
    generally [632]
    variation of [633]
  discount—
    amount [630]
    irrecoverable [641]
    recovery, of [640]
  excluded tenancies [629]
  disposal to private sector landlord—
    consultation [650]
    preservation of right to buy [649]
  fixed price option [635]
  joint tenants [629]
  landlords duties [642], [644]
  lands tribunal, references to [639]
  local authority loans [782–803]
  member of a person's family [652]
  notice of acceptance [634]
  notice of refusal [636]
  offer to sell [631]
  price [630]
  qualifying tenants [629]
  refusal of application [636]
  resale, recovery of discount [640]
  Secretary of State's powers—
    assistance to purchasers [647]
    authorisation of refusal to sell [637], [638]
    modification of conditions of sale [646]
    requiring information [648]
    vesting order [645]

Scottish Homes—
  accounts [1102]
  annual report [1102]
  borrowing—
    powers [1099]
    limit [1110]
  constitution and proceedings [1092], [1159–1177]
  directions, given by Secretary of State—
    duplication of grants [808]
    financial [1101]
    general and specific [1093]
  financial duties [1096]
  functions [1093]
  government grants [1097]
  guarantees [1099]
  housing associations, regulation of [1095]
  landlord, as—
    housing list, publication of rules [589]
    Scottish Special Housing Association, transfer of assets [1094]
  landlord, change of—
    approval of prospective landlords [1145]
    subsequent disposals, consent required [1151]
  powers [1093]
  tax relief [765]
secure tenancies—
  abandonment [617–618]
  assignation [623]

References are to paragraphs

Index

secure tenancies—*contd*
  co-operative housing association, as landlord [613]
  definition [612]
  excluded tenancies [612], [911–918]
  possession, recovery of possession. *See* RECOVERY OF POSSESSION
  qualifying landlords [612], [629]
  repairs and improvements—
    compensation, for [626]
    effect on rent [627]
    landlord's consent [625]
    tenants right to carry out [628]
  rent [622]
  right to buy. *See* RIGHT TO BUY, SECURE TENANTS'
  subletting [623], [938–943]
  succession [620]
  termination [614]
  terms, variation of [622]
  written lease, tenants' right to [621]
security of tenure. *See* ASSURED TENANCIES, PROTECTED TENANCIES, SECURE TENANCIES
short assured tenancies—
  definition [1123]
  recovery of possession [1124]
  rent, reference to rent assessment committee [1125]
  rent assessment committee, disapplication of functions [1126]
short tenancies—
  definition [257]
  effect [261]
  recovery of possession [262]
statutory tenancies—
  change of tenant [265]
  definition [250]
  recovery of possession [259], [260], [391–400]
  terms and conditions [263]
statutory assured tenancies—
  definition [1107]
  fixing terms of [1108]
  recovery of possession [1109–1111], [1192–1208]
  succession to assured tenancy [584]

statutory assured tenancies—*contd*
  succession to protected tenancy [251], [376–390]
subletting—
  assured tenancies, in [1114], [1119]
  protected tenancies, in [267], [347], [348]
  recovery of possession, effect on [267], [1119]
  rent rules [624]
  secure tenancies, in [623], [938–943]
sub-tenancies. *See* SUBLETTING
succession—
  assured tenancies, to [584]
  protected tenancies, to [250], [251], [376–390]
  secure tenancies, to [620]

tenant, tenancy—
  agricultural holdings, of [1184]
  agricultural land, of [248], [916], [1183]
  business premises [916]
  crown tenancies [252], [1188]
  educational institution, of [249], [1185]
  employment contracts, and [391], [911]
  holiday lettings [249], [1186]
  licensed premises, of [1182]
  police and fire authorities, of [917]
  shared ownership agreement [1190]
  shops, of [65–67], [1181]
  temporary—
    development, pending [913]
    homeless persons accommodation [915], [1189]
    persons moving to take up employment [912]
    works, during [914]
  See also ASSURED TENANCIES, HOUSING ASSOCIATION TENANCIES, PROTECTED TENANCIES, SECURE TENANCIES
tenants' choice. *See* LANDLORDS, CHANGE OF
tolerable standard—
  definition [656]
  improvement of houses [658]
  local authority duty [655]
  official representation [657]

voluntary transfer. *See* LOCAL AUTHORITIES—SALE OF HOUSES